The FBI's
RACON

The FBI's

RACON

RACIAL CONDITIONS IN THE UNITED STATES DURING WORLD WAR II

Compiled and
Edited by

Robert A. Hill

Northeastern University Press
BOSTON

NORTHEASTERN UNIVERSITY PRESS

Library of Congress Cataloging-in-Publication Data

The FBI's RACON: racial conditions in the United States during World War II / compiled and edited by Robert A. Hill.
p. cm.
Includes bibliographical references and index.
ISBN 1-55553-227-6 (acid-free paper)
1. Internal security—United States—History—20th century—Sources. 2. Afro-Americans—History—1877–1964—Sources. 3. World War, 1939–1945—United States—Sources. 4. United States. Federal Bureau of Investigation—Archives. 5. United States—Race relations—Sources. I. Hill, Robert A.
E743.5.F35 1995
973′.0496—dc20 95-5661

Designed by Books By Design, Inc.

Composed in Cheltenham by Coghill Composition, Richmond, Virginia. Printed and bound by The Maple Press, York, Pennsylvania. The paper is Classic Book, an acid-free stock.

MANUFACTURED IN THE UNITED STATES OF AMERICA

99 98 97 96 95 5 4 3 2 1

It's so high you can't get over it
So low, you can't get under it,
And so wide, you can't get round it
You must come through the living gate . . .

TRADITIONAL

CONTENTS

EDITORIAL NOTE

The present edition of the FBI's *Survey of Racial Conditions in the United States* was collated using parallel copies of the original monograph. The principal copy-text was the declassified copy of the FBI's original two-volume monograph, released to me by the FBI in 1980 under provisions of the Freedom of Information–Privacy Act (FOIPA).

The original survey forms a part of FBI file 100-135, entitled "Foreign-Inspired Agitation Among the American Negroes." This investigation first came to my notice in 1979 while I was researching the FBI's coverage during the 1940s of Marcus Garvey's Universal Negro Improvement Association (UNIA). Information contained in FBI file 100-88143 included an extensive excerpt from a September 1942 report on "Agitation Among Negroes in New York Field Division" (New York file number 100-33761). The excerpt detailed what it referred to as "Alleged Pro-Japanese Activities" of the UNIA and the Ethiopian Pacific Movement. The report also disclosed that the information had been requested by the FBI in a letter dated August 28, 1942, and that the New York field office had been conducting "a survey of apparent causes or reasons for agitation among negro[e]s in the New York City area." Armed with this information, I submitted a follow-up FOIPA request for release of the file authorizing the investigation. It was in this manner that I learned that the FBI had conducted an extensive wartime internal security investigation of African Americans.

Release of material from file 100-135 began in April 1980. Declassification of the *Survey of Racial Conditions in the United States* took place later that year. The photocopy arrived with numerous deleted passages, however, consisting of information that the FBI considered to be exempt from public disclosure, under Section 552 and 552a of the FOIPA. Other material was also withheld by the FBI for referral to the Departments of the Army and Navy for a determination as to its releasability. In all, there were a total of 112 pages affected by official censorship.

The present work represents, in effect, parallel texts of the original FBI survey, collated from the FBI's copy and from two unsanitized carbon copies among the presidential collections of the Franklin D. Roosevelt Library, Hyde Park, New York, and the Harry S. Truman Library, Independence, Missouri. All three sources have been used to produce both a redacted as well as an integrated text. Restored passages are clearly distinguishable through the use of bold, gray type as well as black bars to accentuate the deletions made by the FBI. By making explicit the censored material, the present work hopes to fulfill a public function by allowing the reader to have a clear picture of how the FBI interprets and applies the legal provisions of the FOIPA.

In compiling the present text, then, approximately 150 restorations of deleted passages have been made. By far the largest group (78) consists of passages that the FBI deleted under (b) (7) (C)—"investigatory records compiled for law enforcement purposes, the disclosure of which would constitute an unwarranted invasion of the personal privacy of another person." (An example of how this exemption was applied was the deletion of the entire personal name index that formed part of the larger index of the survey.) The second largest group of deletions (43) was material denied under (b) (7) (D), disclosure of which would, it was claimed, "reveal the identity of a confidential source or reveal confidential information furnished only by the confidential source." Far fewer in number (10) were the deletions made under (b) (1), explained as "information which is currently and properly classified pursuant to Executive Order 12065 in the interest of national defense or foreign policy, for example, information involving intelligence sources or methods." The remaining group of restorations consists of material that the FBI withheld for referral to the Departments of the Army (9) and Navy (6).[1]

The FBI's original copy contains a large number of handwritten file references and various published sources of information. The actual references are set in italics in the text. They were most likely instituted by the FBI internal security division as a means of annotating the report. They now also serve a valuable function for the reader insofar as they provide an inventory and guide to the array of the FBI's investigative sources used in preparing the survey.

Among the changes made to the original, the present work furnishes five pages deleted from the Detroit section of the original report. These pages were contained in the FBI's report to the White House following the cataclysmic Detroit race riot of June 1943. The restored pages deal with "collateral matters," such as the attempt by the Special Committee to Investigate Un–American Activities of the House of Representatives to involve itself in investigating the Detroit riot. For reasons that are still unclear, the FBI removed these pages from its report on wartime racial conditions, perhaps because of what they revealed about the placement and operation of FBI informants within the federal government, in particular the FBI's infiltration of Congressman Martin Dies's Special Committee to Investigate Un–American Activities, the result of FBI director J. Edgar Hoover's determined effort to retain effective control of the anti-radical wartime crusade.[2]

As well as restoring the full text of the original survey, the present work also includes a number of pertinent FBI documents that are critical to an understanding of the overall investigation upon which the survey was based. These documents relate to the instructions commissioning the survey in the first place and how the final report was received. Not only do they enable the reader to comprehend the objectives that drove the preparation of the FBI survey and that governed the entire investigation, through-

---

[1]A critical account of the FBI's implementation of the FOIPA's provisions is contained in "Understanding Deletions in FBI Documents," in Ward Churchill and Jim Vander Wall, *The COINTELPRO Papers: Documents from the FBI's Secret Wars Against Domestic Dissent* (Boston, MA: South End Press, 1990), pp. 23–32.

[2]Kenneth O'Reilly, "The Roosevelt Administration and Legislative-Executive Conflict: The FBI vs. the Dies Committee," *Congress and the Presidency*, Vol. 10 (Spring 1983): 79–93, and *Hoover and the Un–Americans: The FBI, HUAC, and the Red Menace* (Philadelphia: Temple University Press, 1983); cf. Walter Goodman, *The Committee: The Extraordinary Career of the House Committee on Un–American Activities* (New York: Farrar, Straus, 1968).

out, they also clarify how the FBI used and evaluated the information once it was obtained and how, most importantly, it helped to lay the groundwork for the rise and fall of the FBI's entire counterintelligence program directed against African Americans and political dissidents.

In establishing the text, I have silently corrected obvious typographical errors: for example, transposed characters or simple misspellings. All errors of punctuation and grammar, however, have been retained as they are in the original. The original report included two separate indexes, namely, a subject index of organizations and an index of individual names. These have now been collapsed into a single all-inclusive index, which has been expanded to include additional entries based on a more comprehensive vetting of references in the text.

An extensive chronology of events for the period has also been included to aid the reader in following the evolution of the FBI's intelligence-gathering role and black responses to wartime racism. Finally, a selected bibliography of primary and secondary sources has been provided to facilitate further investigation of the subject.

A NOTE ON SOURCES

Survey of Racial Conditions in the United States was commissioned by FBI Director J. Edgar Hoover on 22 June 1942. The final report was prepared on 15 August 1943 and presented to the FBI director on 10 September 1943. Classified as "Secret," it was assembled and produced by the FBI's Security Division (later renamed the Internal Security Division, and, still later, the Domestic Intelligence Division). Only six copies are known to have been disseminated.

The survey itself forms a bulky enclosure to FBI headquarters file 100-135, serial 191, section 8, captioned "Foreign-Inspired Agitation Among American Negroes—Internal Security" (the "100" classification designates the character of the investigation, i.e., internal security). The complete file consists of approximately 77,000 pages. By way of making comparison, it should be pointed out that the Martin Luther King, Jr., FBI investigative file consists of 17,000 pages of released material.

"Foreign-Inspired Agitation Among American Negroes" consists of 385 volumes of investigative reports and correspondence. The years 1942–45 comprise thirteen volumes, including sixteen sub-sections made up of newspaper clippings and sub-files of FBI field divisions. For the period after 1945, there are a total of 291 volumes of various sub-files, encompassing all of the FBI's field divisions. Further sub-sections of these sub-files comprise a total of sixty-five volumes. There are also eighty-one volumes of newspaper clippings.

FBI headquarters maintained separate files for each field division, e.g., the headquarters' file for the New York field division in the extant case was numbered 100-HQ-135-34, the final two digits corresponding to the number of the New York field division. In addition to these headquarters sub-files, field divisions also maintained their own investigative files, e.g., New York (100-28627), Detroit (100-6781), Cincinnati (100-3607), Norfolk (100-1691).

Two extant copies of the original report are to be found outside FBI headquarters in Washington, D.C. One is located at the Franklin D. Roosevelt Library, Hyde Park, New York, in the Franklin D. Roosevelt Papers, Official File 10B, FBI Reports, No. 2420. The second carbon copy is located at the Harry S. Truman Library, Independence, Missouri, in the Papers of Harry S. Truman, White House Central Files (Confidential), Justice Department, Box 21, Folder No. 5 of 10 and Folder No. 6 of 10.

The copy that is located in the Truman Library was declassified by the Department of Justice on 21 September 1972, though the final unsanitized copy was not made available until 17 January 1979. Use of the Roosevelt Library's copy was likewise restricted as late as October 1980, after which an uncensored copy became available, but the exact date is not recorded in the file.

ACKNOWLEDGMENTS

I should like to thank the several individuals and institutions without whose support this work would have been impossible. I am particularly mindful of the assistance and unfailing courtesies of the archivists upon whom I have depended: Nancy Snedeker and Robert Parkes, Franklin D. Roosevelt Library, Hyde Park, New York; Raymond D. Geselbracht and Randy Sowell, Harry S. Truman Library, Independence, Missouri; Timothy Connelly, Research Archivist, National Historical Publications and Records Commission, Washington, D.C.; John K. Vandereedt, Civil Reference Branch, National Archives, Washington, D.C.; Philip M. Runkel, Marquette University Library, Milwaukee, Wisconsin; and Lynn Conway, Department of Archives and Manuscripts, The Catholic University of America, Washington, D.C.

As all who have faced the peculiar challenges of investigating political surveillance and penetrating the veil that protects it will attest, the search is one that is full of pitfalls. The secrecy that surrounds the gathering and processing of intelligence informs as well as derives its special force from the closed world of bureaucratic hierarchy. The task of research necessitates not only an understanding by civil servants of scholarly needs, but it also demands a tolerance on the part of scholars for the uncertainty of shifting administrative procedures. For facilitating the declassification and release of official documents, and for their many courtesies in responding to numerous inquiries over the years, I wish to acknowledge and extend my gratitude to the staffs of the Freedom of Information–Privacy Acts Section, Information Resources Division, Federal Bureau of Investigation, Washington, D.C.; the Records Management Division, Justice Management Division, and Office of Information and Privacy in the Office of Legal Policy, U.S. Department of Justice, Washington, D.C.; the Naval Criminal Investigative Service, Department of the Navy, Washington Navy Yard, Washington, D.C.; and the Freedom of Information/Privacy Office, U.S. Army Intelligence and Security Command, Department of the Army, Fort George G. Meade, Maryland. I should also like to acknowledge and thank the knowledgeable staff of the FOIA/PA Reading Room of the FBI in the J. Edgar Hoover Building, Washington, D.C., for its efficient service and prompt response to inquiries associated with the present work.

Uncovering new historical materials represents only the first but necessary step in a lengthy and seemingly never ending process of interpretation and articulation. This is where the perspective of one's peers makes such a world of difference. I am thus indebted for their advice and assistance to Richard Cuoto, Martin Glaberman, Vincent Harding, Maurice Isserman, Kenneth O'Reilly, Harvard Sitkoff, Marshall F. Stevenson, Jr., William Strickland, Athan Theoharis, Joe Trotter, Patrick S. Washburn, and Robert H. Zieger. I should also like to thank my editors at Northeastern University Press, particularly William Frohlich, for their support of the project and for their patience in allowing me the necessary time to complete it. Without the assistance and expertise of Nancy Benjamin of Books By Design, Inc., Somerville, Massachusetts, the task of turning a multi-tiered manuscript into a publishable book would have been far more difficult than it proved to be. Her unflagging spirit and assistance throughout all phases of the lengthy production process were of inestimable value. I wish to express my deep appreciation for her dedication, advice, and high standards of professionalism.

For helping with the research process, and especially for wrestling so efficiently with the amazing proliferation of paper that intelligence dossiers generate, I should like to acknowledge my research assistant, Joshua Friedland. In addition, I would like to express my gratitude to Erika Blum for her keen editorial eye and for her characteristic efficiency in conducting computer-based searches of the scholarly literature. I would like also to acknowledge and express deep appreciation to my colleague, Chin C. "Kelvin" Kao, for preparing an electronic concordance file of the manuscript, by means of which entries were generated for preparation of the index. He assisted further by creating an electronic search file of the entire manuscript and generating the final index. Erika Blum also edited and checked the index, for which I wish once again to thank her. As always, I owe a special debt of gratitude to my wife, Diane, for her never-failing support and understanding.

Finally, it gives me great pleasure to acknowledge the research support of UCLA's International Studies and Overseas Programs (ISOP) and the Ford Foundation that underwrote the cost of photo duplicating the FBI and other intelligence records upon which the present work is based. For his encouragement and support over the years, I should also like to acknowledge the exemplary leadership provided by ISOP's founding director, the late James S. Coleman.

The FBI's

RACON

It may seem strange that there were some in the 1940s who were seeking to give our country every opportunity to distance itself from the barbarism of Adolph Hitler and to adhere to the principles of egalitarianism with which it had long flirted but had never really embraced. I was among those who sought to give my country such an opportunity. There is, however, a point beyond which the most patient, long-suffering loyalist will not go.

John Hope Franklin
"Their War and Mine"
Journal of American History
September 1990

INTRODUCTION

"Listen to the way Negroes are talking these days!"
Roi Ottley, *New World A-coming*, 1943

In his autobiography Malcolm X describes his reaction upon hearing from the draft board in New York in 1943. Right away Malcolm had put the word out on the street that he "was frantic to join . . . the Japanese Army," because the notion of serving in America's Jim Crow army was so anathema to him. When "Detroit Red," as Malcolm was known during his incarnation as Harlem drug pusher, pimp, and all around hustler, presented himself for induction, he was promptly shown to the army psychiatrist on account of his provocative behavior. Feigning a mixture of trust and paranoia, Malcolm informed the army shrink about his secret plan—

> Daddy-o, now you and me, we're from up North here, so don't tell nobody . . . I want to get sent down South. Organize them nigger soldiers, you dig? Steal us some guns, and kill up crackers![1]

Malcolm was undoubtedly putting on an act in order to get himself disqualified for military service, which is exactly what happened.[2] But if his histrionic behavior was calculated to deceive, it does not necessarily follow that Malcolm was disguising his true feelings about fighting for America or towards white America. Many other young African-American males held similar feelings and views at the time. "By [the] time you read this," a young Harlemite informed an interviewer during World War II, "I will be fighting for Uncle Sam, the bitches, and I do not like it worth a damn. I'm not a spy or a saboteur, but I don't like goin' over there fightin' for the white man—so be it."[3]

This feeling that the real conflict was not "over there" but "over *here*" was widespread enough among African Americans for the federal government to take it seriously. An African American signing himself "Prince Rano" and writing from the Bronx in September 1942 informed President Roosevelt of his aggrieved feelings. The letter was emblematic of how many African Americans viewed the issue of the war and patriotism at this critical juncture in the nation's mobilization effort:

> 9/3/42
>
> Mr. President
>
> Let me start this way. I am a American of African desent. Which you and the rest called Nergo Nigger Colored and many more names which is and insult to me and my race[.]

And Irish is called Irish-American and so forth. Why in the world cant we be called Africans-American. Which all of my race will except with a clear mind.

My ancestors lived in New England for the pass three hundred years. They fought in all the wars from 1775 to the present war. And they were gunner with Decatur when he were clearing the pirates out of North Africa.

My twin brother is in the Army of all the places, they sent him were down south. And that were the frist he ever been south. And he is not afriad of them dam Fascist that runs the south.

The African Americans are not protected down south or any where. Every time I pick up the paper Some poor African American soldiers are getting shot lynch or hung. and framed up. We black men are getting tired. There is a limit to everything. Our day is coming.

There is so much to say. We will never forget. And I will be darned if you get me in your forces.

/s/ Prince Rano[4]

The hostility embodied in these examples signified more than the withholding of African-American allegiance or a rebuke to an America that defined patriotism in terms of the white majority. While these elements are certainly present, the examples contain a positive aspect as well. The powerful feelings that World War II unleashed among African Americans went beyond revenge to encompass the revolutionary goal of toppling one of the pillars of the American state: the system of racial discrimination and segregation known as Jim Crow.

The readiness of blacks to embark upon a popular struggle to end American racism was expressed, for example, by Clifford Townsend, an African-American labor activist, in a speech he gave at a special "Conference on Racial Problems," at Chicago's city hall, on June 5, 1943. According to the report of his remarks, Townsend announced to the gathering that "Negro soldiers were ready to take up their guns and 'clean up' the South" and that "98 per cent of the Negroes are ready to die for freedom."[5] The New Orleans police department reported evidence of mounting black resistance to segregation in the latter part of May 1943, stating that, whereas in 1940 a total of 300 screens used to segregate blacks and whites on streetcars and buses in the city of New Orleans were removed and thrown out of the cars unlawfully, the figure for 1941 jumped to 455 and in 1942 "841 were jerked from their places." For the first three months of 1943 alone, 330 screens had been removed. Such actions were considered, according to the source of the report, "indicative of the growing general state of unrest among the Negroes in the New Orleans area."[6] In Tupelo, Mississippi, for example, U.S. military intelligence considered it significant enough to report: "Negroes are stated to be getting 'uppity'. Recently two Negro women pushed two white girls off a path in this town."[7]

During World War II, American officials conceived of black rebelliousness as a problem of "Negro morale."[8] For African Americans, the problem of morale was reducible to the simple proposition—fighting for white America. "White folks talking about the Four Freedoms and we ain't got none" was the cynical view of many blacks.[9]

Although supposedly fought in the name of the celebrated Four Freedoms, World War II actually served not only to strengthen but also to extend outside of the South the system of racial segregation—segregation in the armed forces, segregation of black blood by the Red Cross in its blood banks, discrimination in hiring African Americans in defense industries, the harassment and shooting by white military and civilian police of black soldiers in uniform, all of which contributed to the disaffection of African Americans toward the war effort. The resultant feeling of resentment was not confined to any particular group but was widespread among all classes of the black community.

> As a matter of fact, in many regions the more frequently the slogans of democracy are raised for the general population the lower Negro morale. The general bitterness was summed up by a young Negro who, on being inducted into the army, said, "Just carve on my tombstone, 'Here lies a black man killed fighting a yellow man for the protection of a white man.' "[10]

With the federal government adopting the position that any relaxation of the rigid system of segregation would negatively affect the morale of the white majority as well as offend the sentiment and support of a Southern-dominated Congress—"The Army did not create the [race] problem . . . The Army is not a sociological laboratory; to be effective it must be organized and trained according to the principles which will assure success" was how an Army spokesman attempted to justify discrimination in the armed forces in 1941 to a group of black newspaper reporters[11]—meant that nothing effectively could be done about the problem of "Negro morale" without it being perceived as destroying the racial status quo. Horace Cayton accurately summed up the dilemma:

> A large group of white persons in America do not wish to change the position of the Negro. Just as there is a feeling in the non-white world that things are changing, that this is the time to press for gains, so there is a feeling among whites that their position of dominance is being challenged and that they must resist any encroachment on their prerogatives. The problem of building Negro morale, therefore, is one of maintaining the color line—which is considered necessary for the morale of white soldiers, workers, and civilians—while appeasing the rising Negro public opinion with verbal and token gains whenever the tension becomes too great. This difficult task is complicated by the conflict between those who wish to stimulate Negroes from coast to coast to demand complete equality now and those who suggest the organization of a League to Maintain White Supremacy.[12]

After examining the feasibility of official responses, in the form of either repression or concession, that might be employed to meet "the Negroes' insistence on equal participation," Cayton attempted to spell out the social implications of America's wartime racial crisis. Pointing clearly to the struggle that would emerge after World War II as blacks continued to challenge the racial status quo, Cayton offered this conclusion:

> Any real change in the morale of Negroes will come only with a real change in the position of the Negro in the social structure of the country. Such a change

> will involve, especially in the South, a complete revamping of the social relations between the races. That is something which this country will not voluntarily undertake.[13]

By destroying "whatever illusion American Negroes may have had remaining about white sincerity, about white Americans' willingness to grant them equality," World War II brought about, as Charles Silberman was later to remark, a crucial alteration in American race relations. "World War Two not only shattered Negroes' illusions about white sincerity, it destroyed their fear of white authority as well." Abandoning their fear of speaking out and embracing the tactics of militant protest on an unprecedented scale, African Americans made two important discoveries during World War II, namely, that the system of white supremacy was not impregnable and that mass militancy, such as the March on Washington Movement of 1940–42 led by A. Philip Randolph, president of the Brotherhood of Sleeping Car Porters, could effectively challenge the system and produce results. Randolph's call for African Americans to march on Washington "evoked considerable interest among the colored people," according to the FBI, and forced President Roosevelt to issue his famous Executive Order 8802 banning discrimination in defense industries and establishing the Fair Employment Practices Committee (FEPC). "The seeds of the protest movements of the 1950s and 1960s," Charles Silberman accurately observes, "were sown by the March on Washington."[14]

The movements of the 1950s and 1960s were also foreshadowed when the FBI embarked, in June 1942, on an all-embracing and continuing internal security investigation into "Foreign-Inspired Agitation Among the American Negroes." The aim of the investigation was to uncover the source(s) of the rising tide of black resistance to the wave of racial discrimination unleashed by the national defense program. The FBI investigation of blacks did not terminate at the end of World War II, however. It would continue for the next decade and a half, forming the intelligence substrate of subsequent FBI counter-intelligence operations against African Americans. The initial findings of the investigation form the basis of the Bureau's comprehensive *Survey of Racial Conditions in the United States.*

The name given to the FBI's wartime investigation—"Foreign-Inspired Agitation Among the American Negroes"—linked African Americans with the triple specter of spies, sabotage, and subversives used by FBI director J. Edgar Hoover following the outbreak of the European war in 1939 to fan public hysteria in the U.S.[15] Speaking to an American Legion conference in September 1940, for example, Hoover warned that a "fifth column of destruction" was on the march in America. "Scheming peddlers of foreign 'isms'," he called them, declaring that foreign powers had been sending agents to America to carry on a campaign to recruit as allies "the disloyal and malcontent."[16]

Commissioned in June 1942 and completed in August 1943, the FBI investigation was, in September 1944, code-named RACON—acronym for "racial conditions"—a hotly contested area that Hoover and the FBI would continuously monitor and intervene in over the next several decades.[17] *Survey of Racial Conditions in the United States* was the title chosen for the extraordinary study resulting from the wartime investigation. Published here for the first time, it constitutes a document of considerable historical importance that will necessitate a reassessment of the extant scholarly literature on the various aspects of African-American participation in World War II.[18] Focusing upon the pivotal year of the war, 1942–43, the study supplies a significant body of new data for what is still an otherwise sparsely documented area of African-American history. The report also fills a critical gap in studies of federal political surveillance and the evolution of the FBI away from a purely investigative into a counterintelligence agency.

The report was produced from digests of information specially prepared by all fifty-six field divisions of the FBI. Compiled by the FBI's vaunted internal security division, the data contained in the *Survey of Racial Conditions in the United States* spans the entire range of World War II black protest. The survey illustrates in unprecedented detail the depth and breadth of the white backlash against the demands of the African-American community. Encompassing a wide diversity of topics, the survey describes the complex and multifaceted struggles of African Americans—black workers in defense industries; racial conflicts in the military; the influence of the outspoken wartime black press; Japanese influences on the antiwar sentiment among blacks; Communist Party organizing and membership in the black community; African-American Islamic movements; and the upsurge of independent black organizations, including in-depth analyses of the mobilization surrounding the March on Washington Movement and the greatly expanded National Association for the Advancement of Colored People (NAACP). The overriding goal of the survey was to monitor and find ways to stem the rising tide of wartime racial protest and racial disorder that swept the country from 1940 on and that reached a crescendo of violence in the summer of 1943.

After the devastating Japanese attack on Pearl Harbor, Hoover was suddenly vulnerable to criticism that he had failed in his job of protecting the country. An anonymous memo making the rounds of government at the time called for the presidential commission investigating the circumstances of the Japanese attack to examine "the adequacy of the FBI, the agency directed by the President and supposed by the public and Congress to deal with the fifth column in our territory."[19] It was one of the most difficult moments in his career and Hoover had to scramble to save his job. Determined to deflect all blame away from the Bureau, Hoover sent a memo to the president, on December 12, 1941, in which he attempted to pin the blame for the disaster on the alleged failures of naval intelligence officers and the military authorities in Hawaii. Shortly afterward, however, the joint congressional commission appointed to investigate the circumstances surrounding attack revealed the misleading nature of Hoover's charge.[20]

Amidst the panic unleashed by the Japanese attack on Pearl Harbor, Hoover and the FBI faced a public relations disaster, a concern that was doubly critical since public relations was the first priority of the Bureau's work in law enforcement and intelligence surveillance. Faced with the problem of repairing the tarnished image of the FBI, Hoover moved with the desperation of a man aware that his political survival depended upon it. Possessing a monopoly vis-á-vis other federal intelligence agencies such as the army's Military Intelligence Division (MID) and the navy's Office of Naval Intelligence (ONI)—a position required through a succession of presidential directives between 1939 and 1942—Hoover ordered the FBI into action to find evidence of Japanese "fifth-column" activity in the U.S. Thus, on December 9, 1941, one day after congress declared a state of war with Japan, the FBI's New York field division was ordered by Hoover to inform him of the status of what, until that point in time, had been a desultory probe of pro-Japanese propaganda.

The source for this investigation did not originate with the FBI, however; it was brought to its attention by a "confidential" exposé published in the *Hour*, a "confidential bulletin" edited by Albert E. Kahn and published privately. Entitled "Pro-Axis Propaganda in Harlem," the report appeared in the August 23, 1941, issue; it revealed that pro-Japanese agents were engaged in a conspiracy to spread pro-Axis propaganda among the black population in Harlem, although, it was careful to point out, these efforts were making little headway. "The purpose of such fifth column activity, which seeks unscrupulously to capitalize upon legitimate grievances of the Negroes," the report explained, "is to split Americans into opposing camps, white against black, and thus to weaken the country as a whole and hamper the defense effort." Among the black collaborators whom it named as being involved in pro-Axis propaganda effort was Robert Jordan, described as the head of the "Ethiopian Pacific League, Inc. . . . a nationalist (fascist) organization."[21]

Hoover learned of the report on September 13, 1941, after it was brought to his attention by the FBI's Washington, D.C., field office. A transcript of the report was forwarded by Hoover to the attention of special agent E. J. Connelley of the FBI's New York field office on September 18, accompanied with nothing more than a routine instruction that cases should be opened on the individuals specifically mentioned in the article, namely, Arthur Reid, Robert Jordan, and "Ras de Killer." There was no hint of any urgency in Hoover's letter of instruction.

In the meantime, the staff of the FBI internal security division in Washington, D.C., set about conducting a review of its files for any information that it could find on the subject of pro-Axis organizations among blacks. The review turned up negligible information, the summary of which amounted to a mere two paragraphs which were forwarded, on November 19, to the New York field office, along with the request that it should seek to make contact with "sources" in Harlem to determine "whether in fact they [Negroes] are being used for the distribution of pro-Axis propaganda." The investigation, Hoover directed, "should be in the nature of a preliminary inquiry for the initial purpose of determining whether these groups are in fact subversive in the sense that they are under foreign control."[22]

The preliminary reports of the New York investigation were received at FBI headquarters on December 30, 1941. When Hoover responded, on January 13, 1942, he was of the view that "a successful prosecution under the Sedition Act might be had against subject [Robert] Jordan and possibly others," in accordance with the urgent guidelines that the FBI issued to all special agents in charge of field offices on December 31, 1941. "It is the Bureau's desire that this case receive immediate and vigorous attention," the FBI director declared. In addition, he pointed out that the investigation of the "Harlem Negro Pro-Japanese Group" should search for "any connection between Japanese and negroes and what influence, if any, the Japanese Institute of New York City has over the Ethiopian Pacifist League, Inc."[23]

At the same time that Hoover was preparing to respond to the New York field office's preliminary investigation, a conference of African-American leaders was also meeting in New York to consider the problems that faced "Negro citizens in a world at war" as well as the wartime role of blacks. Called by Judge William Hastie, the recently appointed civilian aide to the secretary of war, and sponsored by the National Urban League, the conference, which met on January 10, 1942, soon created a nationwide controversy after it was announced that the black leaders present, representing seventeen leading national organizations, had adopted a resolution 36–5, with 15 abstentions, declaring that the black community was not "whole-heartedly, unselfishly, all-out in support of the present war effort."[24]

The dissemination of news of the meeting led immediately to charges of disloyalty on the part of African Americans. The *Pittsburgh Courier* felt obliged to try to counter the charges with the statement that "the Japanese, Germans, Italians and their Axis stooges know that it is futile to seek spies, saboteurs or Fifth Columnists among American Negroes. . . . Every attempt in that direction has been a miserable failure."[25]

Feeling confident that he was now about to score a major public relations coup, Hoover sent an urgent telex to the Bureau's New York office, on January 20, 1942: "Bureau authority granted to present case to United States Attorney for prosecution under Sedition Act." Hoover also submitted an extensive report to Attorney General Francis Biddle regarding the activities of the black pro-Axis organizations in Harlem. He provided the attorney general with a sample of the sort of statements that the Ethiopian Pacific Movement's president, Leonard Robert Jordan, had been making before audiences in Harlem.[26] It was reported that Jordan made the following statement in a speech on January 18, 1942:

> The black man is not a citizen of any country. Before the negro agrees to fight he should get a guarantee as to just what he is going to get out of it and should refuse to fight until guaranteed equal representation. England is a two-headed snake and America is a five-headed snake. You should not believe the false propaganda of the Allies but should be guided by the reports from Japan. America is rotten. The United States Navy is knocked out of the Pacific. Japan is not interested in Japan alone but is interested in the 150,000,000 darker races of the world and they all should wake up and start fighting for her.
>
> In a few days Japan will have China allied with the Axis, Haile Selassie has commended me for this work and the black man won't stand by and see Japan whipped like Ethiopia. The black race would be suckers to go into the United States Navy because he could not progress any further than a cook but in Japan he is ranked according to ability and those that have [the] interest of the black man at heart should make every effort to give Japan protection.
>
> Japan is out to liberate all the darker races so that they can have their own country and have the black man rule the black man. There is no reason why [the] dark man should help the white man. I do not believe in killing unless a man is guilty but I see no way out of it. The negroes' attention and good will should go to none other than the Rising Sun. Japan is going to win the war. The next leading power will be the Rising Sun. They will establish a new League of

> Nations and give Africa freedom. A dark man in South Africa is not allowed on the street car with the white man. Japan is going to South Africa to liberate them. Those people are praying for the Rising Sun.
>
> This is going to be a race war and you must be ready. When you are drafted start a whispering campaign among your comrades. Remind them of the wrongs perpetrated on them by the whites. Tell them not to remember Pearl Harbor but to remember Africa . . .[27]

Named by President Roosevelt to the post of attorney general in August 1941, a position that he would retain throughout the duration of World War II, Francis Biddle, a wealthy Philadelphia lawyer, came to the Justice Department with the reputation of being a convinced civil libertarian. Shortly after taking office as attorney general, Biddle told an interviewer for *The New York Times Magazine* that "the most important job an Attorney General can do in a time of emergency is to protect civil liberties."[28] Biddle's civil libertarian philosophy had been profoundly shaped in the course of his year's service as secretary to Supreme Court Justice Oliver Wendell Holmes. It was an experience that, in the words of the *New York Times*, was "the dominant one in Francis Biddle's life. It gave point and direction to all subsequent mental growth."[29] Biddle believed, for example, that the sedition statutes were, in his words, "harmful."[30]

Such strong libertarian views did not endear the new head of the Department of Justice to Hoover who had pushed hard but unsuccessfully after World War I for congressional passage of a peacetime sedition act. Prior to Biddle's appointment, moreover, Roosevelt had asked Robert Jackson, Biddle's predecessor, "How does Francis get along with Hoover?" Hoover for his part expressed the concern that Biddle's liberal views would make him "soft" on Communists. Conversely, among the strongest supporters of Biddle's appointment were African Americans who professed to see in the new attorney general "a friend of the colored people of America."[31] After he was confirmed, Biddle looked back over his performance as Solicitor General and determined that one of the things that he felt proudest of was "our campaign for the Negroes, the long fight which was beginning to tell. . ."[32]

Hoover's ideological distrust of Biddle was the exact opposite of the political confidence that Biddle inspired in many African Americans. "I had come into office with the stamp of a 'liberal,'" Biddle noted, "and Hoover must have suspected that I would be too soft, particularly now that a war was on."[33] The contrast between the two men could not have been more marked and nowhere did they diverge more than in relation to African Americans.

Their opposing views were thrown into sharp focus shortly after America's entry into World War II. On January 25, 1942, Cleo Wright was lynched in Sikeston, Missouri—the first lynching of an African American following Pearl Harbor. Arrested for allegedly assaulting a white woman, Wright was shot and severely injured during his initial apprehension. The following day Wright was forcibly removed from his jail cell by a white lynch mob and dragged in a dying condition through the streets of Sikeston behind an automobile. He was finally set on fire and burned to death in front of the church in the black section of Sikeston. The murder of Wright, for which no indictment was returned, incensed the patriotic feelings of blacks nationwide, resulting in the NAACP's adoption of the slogan—"Remember Pearl Harbor . . . and Sikeston, Mo."[34]

The lynching of Cleo Wright immediately drew the Department of Justice into the arena of federal support for the enforcement of black civil rights for the first time, through the equal protection clause of the Fourteenth Amendment and Reconstruction statutes. Whereas the federal government had not previously supported battles for the protection of the civil rights of African Americans, Wright's lynching, coming as it did as the nation was being mobilized to fight a war for democracy, seemed to raise "the possibility of broadening the executive branch's commitment to civil rights and, consequently, the Supreme Court's interpretation of the equal protection clause."[35]

On February 10, 1942, Biddle ordered the Justice Department into the case. Simultaneously, he ordered Hoover to investigate the incident on behalf of the Civil Liberties Unit of the Justice Department's Criminal Division. Created by New Deal Attorney General Frank Murphy in 1939, the establishment of the Civil Liberties Unit (later renamed the Civil Liberties Section and subsequently elevated to the status of the Civil Rights Division) represented "a turning point in official thinking," since the Justice Department was now required to investigate and prosecute violations of civil rights, thus setting the stage for subsequent federal intervention in the field of civil rights enforcement.[36]

The political embarrassment arising from Wright's lynching was compounded the following month by a racial clash in Detroit when whites sought to obstruct blacks taking occupancy of the Sojourner Truth housing project that was built with federal money for black defense workers.[37] Acutely sensitive to the low state of black morale and the use of both incidents by Japanese propaganda, Biddle continually pressed both the FBI and the Civil Liberties section to intensify their investigations. Federal prosecutors failed in their efforts during hearings of the grand jury in May and June 1942, however, to come up with an indictment against Wright's lynchers and local police officials. Although jurors agreed that Wright had been denied due process, they issued a report on July 30 that found that the lynchers had nonetheless committed no federal offense.[38]

Following the negative report of the federal grand jury looking into Cleo Wright's lynching, Biddle had no choice except to close the case. In the meantime, the FBI had done its best to deflect responsibility for the lynching of Cleo Wright away from local whites. Instead, it sought to somehow link the lynching to the agitation of "Japanese elements [that] are attempting to incite riots" on the part of blacks. This was the same view offered by a Civil Liberties section attorney. Based on FBI investigative reports, he proposed that a grand jury investigate the Pacific Movement of the Eastern World for allegedly recruiting blacks in the area of St. Louis, Mo. "It is to be noted that in several instances the Sikeston lynching is prominently mentioned as being one of the talking points by the organization," the attorney claimed.[39] Following World War II, President Truman's Committee on Civil Rights would criticize the efforts of both the Civil Liberties section and the FBI in protecting the civil rights of blacks during World War II, going so far as to accuse the FBI of "superficial and unintelligent work."[40] As later events would amply confirm, Hoover was resistant to the idea of using the FBI to investigate violations of civil rights.[41]

During the time that the FBI was drawn into investigating the lynching of Cleo Wright, Hoover was also engaged in trying, though without much success, to secure approval from Biddle and his assistant attorney general to proceed with the prosecution of Leonard Robert Jordan and other leaders of the Ethiopian Pacific Movement on charges of sedition. However, the FBI found itself constrained by the guidelines imposed by the Criminal Division of the Justice Department on December 16, 1941, that imposed strict limits on the methods and procedures that the FBI could employ to obtain the records of "organizations believed to be inimical to the internal security of the United States."[42]

Between January and July 1942—the same period during which the FBI was involved in the Sikeston, Mo., lynching investigation—Hoover addressed no less than thirteen separate memoranda to both Attorney General Biddle and Assistant Attorney General Berge, seeking their approval to obtain the records of the Ethiopian Pacific Movement as well as their permission to present the case to the U.S. Attorney in New York for prosecution under the Espionage Act. It was the first sedition indictment that Hoover would seek following America's entry into World War II. Hoover was to follow it up shortly afterward by attempting to secure an indictment of the *Baltimore Afro-American* newspaper, stemming from an article that appeared in the December 20, 1941, issue which discussed what Japan's attitude toward blacks would be if it won the war. "The colored races as a whole would benefit . . . this would be the first step in the darker races coming back into their own" was the view expressed by a Richmond, Va., printer, an opinion with which two other black respondents concurred. On January 30, Hoover requested that Berge advise as to whether a violation of the sedition statutes had been committed.[43]

Hoover presented the initial summary of developments in the New York investigation of Jordan and the Ethiopian Pacific Movement to the attorney general on January 21, 1942. For the next six months he was in continuous communication with his superiors in the Justice Department, with each memorandum and report ending with a plea to the attorney general to allow the prosecution of Jordan and his associates to proceed. In a memorandum to Assistant Attorney General Wendell Berge on July 27, 1942, Hoover decided to increase the pressure still further. "It will be noted that from the above statements made by Jordan and other speakers appearing before the meetings of the Ethiopian Pacific Movement, Inc.," Hoover declared, "that their statements are growing more vicious and that they boast of the fact that the Federal Government will not interfere with their activities. I should appreciate being advised if you contemplate prosecuting the individuals connected with this movement or if you desire additional investigation in this regard.[44]

The attorney general finally granted authorization, on August 3, 1942, for the case to be presented to a federal grand jury in New York, but even then he refrained from specifying what possible charges would be brought or against which individuals other than Jordan they would be directed. Indeed, the exact nature of the indictment was kept a tightly guarded secret until September 14, 1942, at which date the U.S. Attorney released a 3,000-word story to the press disclosing that Jordan and three of his associates were being indicted for sedition. Although the FBI's New York field office had participated in the grand jury proceedings, it would learn of the indictment through the New York newspapers. Nowhere in the published news report, moreover, was any mention made of the FBI.[45]

As FBI publicity chief Louis Nichols was quick to note, "a very studious effort was being made, not only to circumvent but to circumscribe the Bureau."[46] The FBI had been cheated out of its public relations victory, moreover, by an attorney general who, ironically, prided himself on his reputted defense of civil liberties. Undoubtedly, Hoover would have been angered by Biddle's maneuvering. Unsparing as he was in his efforts to insure that "his wartime activities got all the publicity possible," Hoover made public relations the overriding goal of everything that the FBI did, on the ground that it was essential to the proper carrying out of the bureau's mission.[47] Like his gossip-columnist friend Walter Winchell, Hoover would seek to manipulate public opinion as the self-appointed arbiter of political loyalty in a nation reeling from wartime hysteria that he had helped to foster.[48]

In what was an obvious effort to settle political scores, Hoover communicated to President Roosevelt that Biddle was frustrating the Bureau's efforts to deal with the seditious threat to the national defense program. This information was relayed via presidential aide Stephen Early, on the very same day, March 20, 1942, that the attorney general came under attack by the president. During a cabinet meeting held that day, Roosevelt declared that something had to be done to put an end to publication of "subversive sheets" and demanding that Biddle take "vigorous action" against seditionists.[49] Whether Roosevelt saw Early's confidential memorandum before the cabinet meeting, and if he had seen it, whether it contributed to the stern rebuke delivered by him to the attorney general, is not known. Nevertheless, the hand of Hoover in stoking Roosevelt's anger toward Biddle is easily detectable. Biddle was certainly aware of Hoover's malicious streak, for, as he was warned about it by no less a figure than "Chief Justice Stone [who] had appointed him [Hoover] when Stone was Attorney General; and Stone gave me a key to Hoover's complex character: if Hoover trusted you he would be absolutely loyal; if he did not, you had better look out."[50] Stephen Early's report to the president amply confirms the soundness of this judgment:

> I saw J. Edgar Hoover this morning and told him that you wanted action taken against publishers of seditious matter. Hoover agreed that much seditious writing and publishing is going on in the country.
>
> But, Hoover told me his hands were tied by the Attorney General and until some of the Attorney General's instructions had been changed his agents could not operate.
>
> Under a direction by the Attorney General, Hoover said his agents could not apply for warrants of arrests to any United States Attorneys. His men must, in all cases where sedition is charged, apply to the Department of Justice in Washington for warrants.
>
> Hoover further stated that the Attorney General has publicly stated that he will not have any men arrested for sedition unless he, as Attorney General, personally approves the case in advance of the arrest.
>
> The warrant for the arrest must be obtained from the Department of Justice—not from the United States Attorneys . . .

> Hoover said that he and his men have been blocked by the Attorney General time and time again in case after case.
>
> I told Mr. Hoover that you nevertheless wanted action on sedition cases and that he should advise the Attorney General of your desires as I outlined them to him. He said he would do this immediately. He felt, however, that it would be necessary for the President in person to talk to the Attorney General before he [Hoover] would be permitted to act in these cases.[51]

The political pressure upon Biddle at this time was enormous. On March 25, 1942, he was forced to convene a press conference to announce that he would be filing sedition charges shortly. He attempted to explain that he had moved slowly in the investigation of sedition because he believed that "we would get stronger cases—and we have." With indictments prepared, events now moved rapidly behind the scenes. The federal government's crackdown against seditionists began in earnest on March 27, 1942, with the arrest of groups of right-wing fascists in Chattanooga, Los Angeles, and Noblesville, Ind. With the exception of one acquittal, all those indicted were found guilty.[52]

The reality was that both Hoover and Biddle were engaged in circumventing the other. Biddle tried his best to circumscribe Hoover's authority. In this game of bureaucratic cat and mouse, Hoover enjoyed the real advantage of being able to claim that he was carrying out the president's wishes, whereas the attorney general was continually on the defensive for having to frustrate the president's wishes. The two men could not have been more different politically. "It was suggested in a column," Biddle noted in his autobiography, "that Edgar Hoover had little sympathy with his chief's view that there should be no prosecution unless the speech or writing directly affected the war effort." As for his relationship with the president, Biddle acknowledged resignedly: "He was not much interested in the theory of sedition, or in the constitutional right to criticize the government in wartime. He wanted this anti-war talk stopped."[53]

The president would eventually criticize Hoover's investigative zeal for "spending too much time investigating suspected Communists in the Government and out, but particularly in the Government, and ignoring the Fascist minded groups both in the Government and out," but it seems to have been motivated largely by Roosevelt's wish to placate the liberal feelings of the First Lady.[54] The figure of Eleanor Roosevelt casts a long shadow over the FBI's wartime investigation of racial agitation due to the ubiquitous rumor regarding the formation of so-called "Eleanor Clubs" among African-American female domestics.[55] In September 1942, an unsigned report on the subject was sent to Hoover. Although the original is damaged, thus making it difficult to decipher the text, the following reconstruction shows that the objective of the report was to link the First Lady with racial unrest. Captioned "Eleanor Clubs," the report confided to Hoover:

> These clubs are an actual fact. They have been started at Washington [and have?] spread out like a fan to other sectors. It seems as though some pressure [has been brought?] upon the F. B. I. not to dig into these very deep because

> Mrs. F. D. R. issue[d?] . . . that the F. B. I. had investigated them and there was nothing to it.
>
> Eleanor has been playing ball with that group of negroes that Cong[ress] accuses of being Communists. We mean Mary Bethune, William Pickens, Ben Dav[is] [and a] few others hanging around Washington.[56]

The First Lady's significance for African Americans would move Walter White to remember how "especially stirring was the moral leadership of Mrs. Eleanor Roosevelt on human rights." Noting that "her enemies and critics used every device of criticism and slander to stop her," White remarks on her undaunted courage: "[S]he continued to speak and act as her conscience dictated. She gave to many Americans, particularly Negroes, hope and faith which enabled them to continue the struggle for full citizenship."[57]

The effect of Hoover's deliberate attempts to circumvent the attorney general's authority and consequent censure he received merely increased the need that Hoover felt to keep the Justice Department in the dark in order to pursue his own independent political agenda. Moreover, the level of Hoover's annoyance would have increased when he learned, on February 16, 1942, that although the U.S. Attorney in New York was interested in prosecution of Jordan and the Ethiopian Pacific Movement, since he believed that the "elements of sedition violation exist," no authorization for Jordan's arrest or indictment would be forthcoming, as Hoover was informed by teletype from the FBI's New York field office, "for reason of policy on racial angles . . . to preclude any possibility of criticism of the Dept[.] of Justice on [grounds of] racial discrimination which has been played up considerably by [the] colored element in this area."[58]

Such coddling of blacks Hoover must have found repugnant, since it offended his Jim Crow morality to the point where he was capable of evincing "racial hostility so strong that it could overwhelm any sense of fairness or justice."[59] Hoover's racial ire was further aroused the following month after *Atlanta Daily World* columnist Cliff MacKay ("The Globe Trotter") published a column criticizing Hoover for his alleged refusal to appoint blacks as FBI agents. As soon as Hoover learned of the column, he immediately wrote to *Birmingham World* editor Emory O. Jackson, who had reprinted the column in its issue of March 27, 1942, declaring it to be a "grossly" inaccurate statement and "a slander in my opinion upon the many loyal, patriotic Negro members of this Bureau."[60]

At a subsequent meeting at FBI headquarters in Washington, D.C., FBI publicity chief Louis B. Nichols cowed Jackson with a warning to him that "certain subversive forces were seeking to use the Negro press to stir up disunity."[61] Hoover's agitated state during the troubled spring of 1942 would only have compounded his already well-known hypersensitivity to criticism. Criticism by blacks, however, was something that Hoover never countenanced. MacKay's column attacking the discriminatory hiring practices of the Bureau might thus have acted as a goad to Hoover, all the more because the criticism was true.[62] The same distemper was later to cause Martin Luther King, Jr., to be targeted due to his criticism of the complicity of FBI agents in Albany,

Georgia. "From this point on," according to Powers, "Hoover treated King as a personal enemy as well as a Communist."[63] Still infuriated by King's attack, Hoover would use King's criticism as the basis for labeling the civil rights leader two years later as the "most notorious liar" in America.[64]

While awaiting the decision of the attorney general, it was obviously to Hoover's advantage to give the impression that he was adhering to the investigative procedures laid down by the Justice Department in its December 16, 1941, memorandum, since he was even then circumventing the authority of the attorney general by preparing to launch a preemptive counter-intelligence program against the black community. "Hoover was no fool," notes Kenneth O'Reilly. "He kept most of the FBI's quite extensive record of insubordination and unilateralism safely out of sight."[65]

This was certainly the case with Hoover's circumvention of the attorney general's order regarding termination of the FBI's Custodial Detention Program that Hoover had established in June 1940 "to select 'dangerous' individuals for arrest in time of emergency."[66] Hoover sought to implement the detention program when he informed Berge that "many of the subjects [in the investigation of the Ethiopian Pacific Movement] are aliens and are subject to custodial detention as well as prosecution under the Sedition laws."[67] The roots of the program went back to the list that the FBI began preparing in November 1939 of individuals "on whom information is available indicating strongly that [their] presence at liberty in this country in time of war or national emergency would constitute a menace to the public peace and safety of the United States Government."

Made up of individuals "with strong Nazi tendencies" and "with strong Communist tendencies," the list was expanded in 1940–41 to include "Communistic, Fascist, Nazi or other nationalistic background" as well as persons described as "pronouncedly pro-Japanese."[68] Since the Custodial Detention Program was made subject to supervision by the Justice Department's Special War Policies Unit, although Hoover had strongly resisted any idea of supervision when the program was established, and since all wartime detention warrants had to be authorized and issued by the attorney general, the machinery did exist for oversight by the Justice Department of this aspect of FBI domestic intelligence. However, when Biddle decided, in July 1943, to order the scrapping of the Custodial Detention List, Hoover, instead of abolishing the list, simply directed that its name be changed from Custodial Detention List to Security Index and carried on as before. It would be revised periodically as additional names were added, resulting in the spawning of such other later intelligence lists as the Reserve (or Communist) Index, the Agitator Index, and the Rabble Rouser Index.[69]

On July 11, 1942, Hoover again wrote to Berge, but this time he went beyond his usual closing. "It is desired that you advise me as soon as possible whether or not in your opinion the subjects may be prosecuted under any Federal statute," Hoover explained, "inasmuch as they are becoming more radical at each meeting and because of the fact that there is a widespread action among negroes in all sections of the country which indicates that several sources are purposely creating unrest among the negro element which is believed to be against the best interests of this country."[70]

Although it was buried in the dense thicket of FBI summaries, Hoover's statement signaled that a new phase of the investigation had been reached. The FBI was now operating with an expanded definition of its coordinates, one that reflected a change in the overall official estimate of the problem. It was shown in the extensive evaluation of "Japanese Racial Agitation Among American Negroes" prepared by MID on April 15, 1942. After giving a detailed description of Japanese propaganda strategy, MID concluded that "Japanese-sponsored agents and organizations are active among the Negroes of the United States, successfully promoting sedition and espionage." Among the report's list of recommendations, it was suggested that "agents of the Counterintelligence Group, including Negro agents, should undertake an investigation of the Negro situation as it affects the Army."[71]

The change in the official estimate of the problem was also expressed at a cabinet meeting held on May 22, 1942, at which "there was a discussion of the Negro situation which everybody seemed to think was rather acute."[72] Encouraged by this shift in official thinking at this juncture, Hoover determined that he would intervene to deal with the problem. Indeed, Hoover's memorandum of July 11, 1942, contained the basic rationale for what he was himself attempting. Neither the attorney general nor his deputy were privy to what was certainly one of the most ambitious internal security programs ever attempted by the FBI.[73]

Officially launched in June 1942, the FBI's investigation into "Foreign-Inspired Agitation Among the American Negroes" was clearly modeled on the counterintelligence program described in the MID evaluation report on "Japanese Racial Agitation Among American Negroes." Similarly, the stated aim of the FBI program was to prepare a survey "to ascertain the extent of agitation among the American negroes in the United States."[74] The official Bureau letter inaugurating the program was sent to the special agents in charge of the 56 FBI field divisions ordered to participate in the preparation of the survey. It began by alluding to the penetration of Japanese propaganda among American Negroes. "Since the declaration of war by the United States against the Axis powers," the letter mandating the investigation opened, "the Bureau has received complaints and information from all sections of the country that it is believed the Axis Powers have endeavored to create racial agitation among American negroes which would cause disunity and would serve as a powerful weapon for adverse propaganda."

The second major source of disaffection identified in the letter was the Communist Party. This was followed by a third category made up of "certain influential and prominent negroes with apparently no present subversive affiliations [who] have been conducting similar campaigns of agitation to those related above." The fourth target of the FBI investigation was "the colored newspapers or publications," for the reason that the black press reflected "the true feelings of many of the colored communities."[75] The FBI was deliberately casting its intelligence net as wide as possible in order "to ascertain the extent of agitation among the negroes." The principal objective behind the investigation of "Communist-inspired racial agitation," listed second in the hierarchy of topics to be investigated, was Hoover's search for evidence showing "Communist exploitation of racial matters involving civil rights cases"—the domestic area in which Hoover was vulnerable to pressure from the attorney general.[76]

Such was the emphasis placed on "the activity of the Communist Party among the Negro race" that Special Agents had to be cautioned that it was "not meant to de-emphasize in any way the significance of full and complete coverage of all racial matters by this Bureau." By linking the cause of civil rights with Communist subversion, it would appear that Hoover hoped to undermine and discredit both simultaneously by smearing one with the other and vice versa. An example of Communist Party "exploitation" of civil rights causes was *Daily Worker* editorial (August 3, 1942) on the government's handling of the grand jury investigation into the lynching of Cleo Wright. Entitled "Prosecution, Not Whitewashing," the editorial declared:

> It is high time that the prosecution of the [Cleo] Wright, [Willie] Vinson and [Private Jessie] Smith lynchers be taken up vigorously and that the Constitutional rights of Negro citizens be unconditionally upheld. Failure of the Department of Justice to do so only plays into the hands of the defeatists and Fifth Columnists, and hampers the anti-jim crow policies laid down by President Roosevelt and the Fair Employment Practice Committee. Labor and other patriotic Americans are doing a major service to national unity and to the war effort by insisting that the Department of Justice apprehend and punish the lynchers and violators of Negro Rights.

Hoover submitted the editorial to Assistant Attorney General Wendell Berge with a request that it be examined for "violation of the Sedition or related statutes."[77]

In the case of investigating those "groups and individuals with apparently no present subversive affiliations [that] are also conducting similar programs of agitation," it would appear that the intelligence thus collected was intended to be used to discredit them. This was to be achieved by establishing a link between the said individuals and groups with racial disturbances or demonstrations. At the very top of the FBI's list of concerns, special agents were instructed to be on the lookout for "racial disturbances or potential racial outbreaks which may have an effect upon the national security" and "racial disturbances which may receive national notoriety."[78]

Among some of the more notable individuals and groups fitting Hoover's description would have been Walter White, executive secretary of the NAACP; Thurgood Marshall, NAACP special counsel; T. Arnold Hill, director of the National Urban League; and Judge William Hastie, appointed by Roosevelt one week before the election of 1940 to serve as a civilian aide to the Secretary of War (1940–43).[79] Hoover had met with Walter White, in November 1941, at the request of the attorney general, ostensibly to discuss a couple of civil rights cases in Texas, but in reality to have "a long talk" with White about "Nazi, Communist, and Fascist agitators."

Hoover emerged from the meeting confident that he had White's assurance that he would report any information that he might obtain concerning "subversive activities." In order to facilitate the process, Hoover made a point of giving the NAACP secretary the home telephone number of every FBI Special Agent along with the request that he have the local NAACP branches communicate with the Bureau's field offices. "I told Mr. White," Hoover noted after the meeting, "that I feel it is important that reputable Negro organizations be diligently alert to keep Nazism, Communism, and Fascism from attaching themselves to Negro movements."[80]

The black elite was not immune, however, to the wave of militancy that swept the black community during 1941–42. Hoover's injunction to have the political activities of its members investigated testified to the significant level of intraracial unity that had been attained. The aim was not merely to silence the voice of pro-Axis propagandists and Communists. Ultimately, the investigation's purpose as well as the goal of the survey were "to make it possible for the Bureau to keep currently abreast with such agitation and to be cognizant of the identities of groups and individuals responsible for the same."

The aspirations of the black community, whether emanating from "certain influential and prominent negroes with apparently no present subversive affiliations" or from "colored newspapers . . . which appear to be pro-Axis or pro-Communist in nature," were now held to be suspect and had to be monitored. All sections of the African-American community were thus tainted with the brush of political subversion. Hoover chose to end his instructions with the invidious disclaimer, however, that they were not "to be interpreted [to mean] that the American negroes are a subversive group."[81] A similar disavowal was subsequently included in the introduction to the *Survey of Racial Conditions in the United States*—

> The information contained in the ensuing pages of this study does not, nor is it meant to, give rise to an inference that Negroes as a whole or the Negro people in a particular area are subversive or are influenced by anti-American forces. At the same time, it must be pointed out that a number of Negroes and Negro groups have been the subjects of concentrated investigation made on the basis that they have reportedly acted or have exhibited sentiments in a manner inimical to the Nation's war effort.[82]

The statement contains a not too subtle hint that the FBI might have been contemplating using the Custodial Detention Program as a means of suppressing racial agitation among African Americans. At the time that the investigation was launched, Hoover had instructed the agents in charge of FBI field that "in the event any individual or organization is discovered disseminating propaganda to the American negroes which tends to create unrest or dissatisfaction in the American form of Government, individual cases [should] be opened and . . . these cases [should] be vigorously followed for possible prosecution under the Sedition statutes, Selective Service Act, Registration Act or Voorhis Act." In a follow-up letter dated October 3, 1942, Hoover again emphasized that prosecution was a priority, upbraiding Special Agents for submitting reports that contained "many instances wherein information is set forth which would justify the opening of separate cases. However, there is no mention made that separate investigations are being instituted in those instances."[83]

In all, a total of eighteen African Americans during World War II would eventually be convicted for sedition and/or conspiracy to commit sedition under the Espionage Act (50 USCS § 33 and 18 USCS § 2388), with a much larger number, approximately two hundred, convicted for selective service violations under the Selective Training and Service Act of 1940.[84]

Unable and unwilling to meet or grant the demands underlying what the survey described as "the agitation among and by members of the Negro race in this country to remove alleged discrimination against them,"[85] Hoover was embarked on a strategy of repression in 1942–43 against African Americans and their supporters that would in time cause incalculable damage to American society. Ignoring the conclusions put forward by the resultant *Survey of Racial Conditions in the United States* regarding the economic, social, and political causes of racial unrest, Hoover choose instead to focus attention and resources toward removing the supported shortcomings of FBI informant coverage of blacks. The seeds that would lead Hoover to employ the resources of the FBI against later civil rights activists were being planted in 1943, giving him 20 years to prepare for the rise of the black freedom movement of the 1960s.[86]

From this perspective, the FBI's 1943 *Survey of Racial Conditions in the United States* is a significant benchmark by which to measure the evolution and development of FBI counterintelligence against African Americans. In early August 1943, just a couple of days after the outbreak of rioting in Harlem and one week before the final draft of the survey was completed, Hoover issued the following directive to all FBI field offices:

> You are undoubtedly aware of the current widespread racial unrest in the country. In connection with this situation, I desire to be furnished with the extent of informant coverage through which accurate and immediate information can be obtained and which will reflect the true conditions existing in those Field Divisions where the most trouble exists.
>
> In view of the reported unrest and tense race relationship in your Field Division as evidenced by information you have supplied, you are instructed to immediately make a survey of the informant coverage in this matter.[87]

What Hoover's instruction reveals is that there was in actuality two separate, though related, surveys simultaneously proceeding: a survey of racial conditions and a survey of racial informants. The result of this combined undertaking was to be the organization and implementation of an extensive system of FBI informant coverage of the African-American community that was to last well beyond the exigencies of World War II. The program guiding its development would eventually reach its apogee in the 1970s, when, according to Kenneth O'Reilly, the FBI "operated an army of some 7,500" informants, with field offices required, in the words of the FBI, " 'to thoroughly saturate every level of activity in the ghetto.' "[88]

In addition to the enormous amount of data compiled by FBI informant coverage of racial unrest during World War II, the double-pronged survey of racial conditions also paved the way for the development of later FBI programs that were to be employed against blacks. But whereas Hoover always felt the need to assure himself and the FBI of some cover of legality for most intelligence operations, it does not appear that he felt any such compunction where the surveillance of African Americans was concerned. This would not only accustom Hoover and the FBI to a pattern of abuse regarding black rights; it also contributed to the series of COINTELPRO (counterintelligence) programs that the Bureau would employ against the entire spectrum of American political dissent. Hoover's racial arrogance played no small part in cultivating that hubris of power which would be in time his and the Bureau's undoing.

The prince of darkness is a gentleman.
—*King Lear* 3.4.143

World War II marked Hoover's second tour of duty in terms of the political surveillance of African-American political unrest or what was called Negro subversion during World War I. Hoover began his career in political intelligence during the Red Scare that enveloped America at the conclusion of World War I. One year after initially joining the Department of Justice, Hoover was appointed in July 1917 to head the General Intelligence Division (GID). He quickly won a name for himself and what would become known as the "Radical Division," for its role in tracking the identities and activities of a wide assortment of radicals. The zealous Hoover and his staff of clerks compiled the dossiers that formed the basis for the brutal postwar suppression of radicals that climaxed with the infamous Palmer raids of 1919–20. Hoover's GID was also responsible for generating files on the individual black radicals making up the "New Negro" movement which created a sort of parallel Black Scare after World War I.[89]

The anti-radical fury of the Palmer raids and Red Scare hysteria ran out of steam by the early twenties, however. It gave away to the crusade known as prohibition that was to engulf the Bureau of Investigation (the name was changed in 1935 to the Federal Bureau of Investigation) in a web by which corruption spread among the entire organization. When Harlan Fiske Stone succeeded the discredited Harry M. Daugherty as attorney general in March 1924, he came to office with a mandate to reform the Bureau. He tapped J. Edgar Hoover, then aged 29 and already known for his zeal and dedication, to take over the scandal-ridden Bureau. Hoover became permanent director on December 10, 1924, and remained as head of the Bureau until his death in 1972—a tenure of 48 years.

At the time that Hoover assumed leadership, the Bureau was in a shambles and thoroughly demoralized. Official concern with radicals, on the wane amid the post-war stabilization of social and economic conditions, was replaced with a more conscientious effort at professional law enforcement, as Attorney General Stone attempted to raise public confidence in the agency by redirecting the Bureau's attention to dealing with organized crime and the gangsterism brought on by prohibition and the Great Depression. Charged with the major task of cleaning up the rampant corruption, Hoover set about his mission of reforming the Bureau with a zeal and an efficiency that would quickly win for him the plaudits of his superiors and the gratitude of the nation.

Hoover was appointed with the written understanding that the Bureau would cease to be involved in the sort of political investigations that had helped to bring it into national disrepute during the Red Scare. "The Activities of the Bureau are to be limited strictly to investigations of violation of law, under my direction or under the direction of an Assistant Attorney General regularly conducting the work of the Department of Justice," declared Stone in a statement of the guidelines that were to serve as a constitution for the reorganized Bureau.[90] Under the new dispensation, the Bureau's General Intelligence Division, which Hoover had led from its inception, was mothballed:

> A strict limitation of the Bureau's activities to investigations of "violations of law" meant an end to the General Intelligence Division and to the investigation of political beliefs and associations. To ensure that there was no misunderstanding, Stone repeatedly stated that "the Bureau of Investigation is not concerned with political or other opinions of individuals. It is concerned only with their conduct and then only with such conduct as is forbidden by the laws of the United States." Hoover announced a new hands-off policy toward radicalism. "Our bureau carries on no investigations of matters that are not contrary to federal statutes. There is no federal statute against entertaining radical ideas, and we are wasting no time collecting information that we cannot use." Hoover even said he was refraining from speaking out against communism because if he were "to start making speeches enlarging on the 'red menace' the agents of the Bureau naturally would take the cue and begin looking for radicals all over the place."[91]

More than a decade would elapse before Hoover would once again re-engage in political intelligence-gathering. During this twelve-year hiatus, Hoover and the FBI's G-Men arose to become celebrities and icons of American popular culture, as the mass media lavished extensive coverage on their successfully waged war against a host of Depression-era criminals and kidnappers. The result, as one of Hoover's biographers has noted, was that the director and his G-Men became American legends during the thirties—the adventures of the G-Man forming a sort of national cult.[92]

The FBI's political intelligence activities remained suspended until 1934, when Roosevelt ordered an investigation of "the Nazi movement in this country," specifically the "anti-racial" and "anti-American" activities of native American fascists, for "any special connection with official representatives of the German government in the United States." The FBI conducted a one-time investigation that Hoover described as "a so-called intelligence investigation." Two years later, in 1936, Roosevelt again called upon Hoover but this time he was asked to look into "the traffickings of Fascists and Communists in the country." The president wanted to secure, according to a memorandum by Hoover, "a broad picture of the general movement and its activities as [they] may affect the economic and political life of the country as a whole." By October 1938, Hoover informed President Roosevelt that the "present purposes and scope" of FBI political surveillance activities included the collection of "information dealing with various forms of activities of either a subversive or so-called intelligence type."[93]

Thus began a new chapter in the history of systematic domestic surveillance activities as Hoover set about re-building the FBI's intelligence capability on the basis of a series of presidential directives issued by Roosevelt between 1936 and 1943.[94] The result was the establishment of a permanent domestic intelligence structure based upon several vaguely defined presidential directives to collect intelligence about "subversive activities" that were unrelated to law enforcement.

"When Roosevelt was first elected, the Bureau had only 266 investigators, 66 accountants, a budget of less than $3 million, and no formal intelligence responsibilities," notes Kenneth O'Reilly. "By the time Roosevelt died in 1945," the institutional reality was that "the FBI had become, in one way, what the New Deal president intended it to be—a thriving bureaucracy with clearly defined missions in the areas of crime control and national security."[95] With the outbreak of World War II in 1939, the importance of the FBI's political intelligence role escalated rapidly, as the demand for intelligence expanded at an almost exponential rate. It was "wartime exigencies [that] encouraged the unregulated use of intrusive intelligence techniques" and that also saw "the FBI [begin] to resist supervision by the Attorney General."[96]

Through a succession of presidential directives intended to strengthen America's preparedness for war, Hoover had emerged as the clearly dominant figure within the intelligence establishment. By December 1941 when America was thrust into World War II, Hoover and the FBI had achieved an almost complete ascendancy in the field of domestic political intelligence. Moreover, Roosevelt placed the FBI in charge of intelligence operations in the Western Hemisphere with the exception of the Panama Canal Zone. The result was that by 1941–42 Hoover had been catapulted into the position of one of the most powerful figures in the entire federal government.

Hoover's position as the chief official voice on domestic security matters was ratified by the intelligence delimitation agreement and approved by President Roosevelt in June 1940. It placed the FBI in charge of coordinating all federal intelligence services as well as preventing enemy spying and acts of sabotage within the U.S. and throughout the Western Hemisphere. According to Richard Gid Power, "This put Hoover in the public eye as the man in charge of the war against the Axis on the home front (or the 'F. B. I. Front,' as he called it) and gave him a popular status only a little lower than Roosevelt and the military's top brass."[97] In February 1942, Hoover negotiated a revision of the delimitation agreement that reconfirmed the FBI's monopoly in internal security matters by limiting the sphere of domestic surveillance in which military intelligence could operate. The revised agreement also gave to the FBI responsibility for conducting all investigations "involving civilians in the United States," though the agreement called for the Bureau to keep military and naval intelligence branches informed of "important developments . . . including the names of individuals definitely known to be connected with subversive activities."[98]

The FBI's ascendancy was hardly related to its investigative competence in 1940–42. The fact is that the FBI's monopoly rested more upon Hoover's strong political ties to Roosevelt than it did to any proven record of investigative achievement. For practical as well as political reasons, Roosevelt came to rely increasingly on Hoover's usefulness in intelligence matters. As a trusted confidant of the president, Hoover grew increasingly accustomed, with Roosevelt's approval, to acting independently of the Department of Justice, particularly where the investigation of sedition and subversion was concerned. "Not infrequently," observed Biddle, the president "would call Edgar Hoover about something that he wanted done quietly, usually in a hurry; and Hoover would promptly report it to me, knowing the President's habit of sometimes saying afterward, 'By the way, Francis, not wishing to disturb you, I called Edgar Hoover the other day about. . . .' "[99]

Although Hoover's victory over the other intelligence agencies achieved for the FBI a monopoly in the sphere of internal security, as far as the surveillance of African Americans was concerned the quality of the intelligence gathered by MID and ONI, with the exception of civil rights investigations, was superior to the FBI's meager efforts up until 1941–42. In fact, the FBI's initial investigation of the black press during

World War II resulted from a complaint received in 1940 from the Military Intelligence Division that the *Chicago Defender* contained "propaganda which might hinder the Government in securing registrations from negroes who come within the draft age."[100] Again, in 1941, the FBI investigated the *Pittsburgh Courier* at the request of the War Department which complained that the newspaper was engaged "in questionable activities with reference to the national defense program."[101]

In reality, when Hoover called for the FBI to investigate the sources of agitation among African Americans in 1942, it was obliged to go outside by turning to MID and ONI for their assistance. At a meeting three months after the FBI commenced its "contemplated study . . . concerning the Negro situation," FBI supervisor F. W. Winterrowd of the internal security division contacted officials of MID and ONI to inform them that "the Bureau would like to have a study made by them of information concerning trouble with the Negro situation" in areas under their respective investigative jurisdictions. These officials were told that "if they had information concerning possible radical or subversive influences in surrounding territories of the areas in which trouble occurred and its relation to that trouble, the same would also be appreciated." MID officials informed Winterrowd that "a study was contemplated by them prior to the writer's [Winterrowd's] visit and that the same would include a digest of information concerning trouble in various areas over which G-2 has investigative jurisdiction, the relation of the surrounding area to the same, as well as an estimate of enemy potentiality."

Adopting a deceptively deferential pose, Winterrowd sought to allay any suspicion of FBI poaching. "The Bureau, of course, was not attempting to force itself into matters of primary concern to the Office of Military Intelligence." Winterrowd reported to his superiors what he had said, though he had been quick to add that "the results of such a study made by that Service would be fitted into the general study to be made by the Bureau." Officials of ONI were likewise "informed that the Bureau had no intention of inserting itself into matters over which that Office has jurisdiction but that it was desired to fit the results of any compilation of information in this matter made by them in [connection] with the study made by the Bureau."[102]

Forced to make a credible case for continued FBI dominance over domestic intelligence, Hoover would fall back on the subject of racial unrest, an area in which his "rigid Jim Crow mores" could be expected to trigger his "instinctive antagonism toward black protest."[103] Prior to the Japanese attack at Pearl Harbor, however, the subject of blacks did not seem to have elicited the same repressive response from Hoover, perhaps because the public relations value to be derived was not as great as it was coming after Pearl Harbor. Kenneth O'Reilly finds a similar shift in Hoover's shifting relationship with African Americans during the modern civil rights movement:

> Prudence told Hoover to keep a distance from the risky and unpleasant challenges posed by the Negro Question, to avoid the sort of engagement that might push his Bureau towards an open and inextirpable conflict with black America—or, for that matter, his own states' rights constituents. And that is exactly what he did over the course of the four decades since 1919. But he never stopped spying and he never stopped plotting how to avoid civil rights work . . . He never stopped

preparing for that day when his Bureau would no longer be able to dodge the Negro Question.[104]

What the evidence suggests is that, at least in the case of racial tension, the FBI's dominance over domestic intelligence was not so much warranted by its previous record as by the power of presidential patronage and the politics of bureaucratic rivalry. The FBI had been inactive in the field of political intelligence after Stone and Hoover set about reforming the bureau in 1924. It was not until 1936 that the FBI had once again become involved, at Roosevelt's request, in collecting political intelligence on radical opponents of his administration, including communists, fascists, and German sympathizers. The lag in intelligence was most pronounced where African Americans were concerned. There was considerable disarray, moreover, in the absence of any central coordinating body. This was pointed out in October 1933 by a military intelligence official attached to Army Corps Area VII in Kansas City. In a "Special Report on [the] 'Pacific Movement' (Jap-Negro)," Major J. M. Moore observed:

> The "Pacific Movement" has almost as many investigators as it has members: Immigration Service, Secret Service, Dept[.] of Justice, and Kansas City Detective Squad, while the Navy is in full cry. . . . It is recommended that in such cases, when first reports reach Washington, one agency of the Government be designated to conduct whatever investigation is desired, and that field agencies of other bureaux or branches be told to keep out unless called on for help. There has been so much uncoordinated, and largely ill-advised activity in this present matter, that, if it were serious, the valuable chance of quiet investigation would have been lost.[105]

The lacuna in FBI surveillance of blacks preceding the outbreak of World War II was first noticed in 1983 by the historian Nancy J. Weiss. "Even the watchdogs of the federal establishment, J. Edgar Hoover and the Federal Bureau of Investigation, who later fastened intently on the struggle for racial equality as a vehicle of communist subversion," she observed, "virtually ignored racial matters before 1941."[106] Weiss based this assessment on a careful inventory of the FBI files that she had received, under the Freedom of Information Act, relating to "the three principal organizations concerned with racial advancement in this period," namely the National Association for the Advancement of Colored People (NAACP), the National Urban League, and the National Negro Congress. What she discovered, and what many additional FBI files that have been now released confirm, was the almost complete absence of reports *before* 1941:

> Of 895 pages of material released to me from the FBI's main file on the NAACP (file number 61-3176) for the period 1933–1945, only 6 pages dealt with the years before 1941. In the case of the National Urban League, 12 of 125 pages in the FBI file captioned "National Urban League" for the years 1933–1945 dealt with the years before 1941; this percentage is considerably higher, but the subjects were completely innocuous. Even the National Negro Congress, which

was widely acknowledged to be "radical," if not under communist influence, seemed not to attract any serious attention from Hoover and his colleagues. Of 2,974 pages of material released to me from the FBI's files on the National Negro Congress, 55 concern the period before 1941.[107]

In the aftermath of Japan's attack on Pearl Harbor and the consequent threat that it posed to the FBI's continued monopoly of domestic intelligence, Hoover rushed to demonstrate that the FBI was competent to exercise its domestic intelligence responsibility. He attempted to do so partly by attributing the growth of wartime racial tensions in America to foreign inspiration. The opening statement of the FBI's *Survey of Racial Conditions in the United States*, presented to Hoover in August 1943, refers to "a period in excess of two years [during which] the Federal Bureau of Investigation has received reports and allegations of forces with foreign influence with anti-American ideology working among the Negro people of this country as well as exploiting them. . . . Upon receipt of such complaints and allegations, investigation and inquiries were promptly instituted."[108]

The first document in the FBI file on Foreign-Inspired Agitation Among American Negroes is dated March 25, 1942. The documents in the file dated from March through June 1942 consist mainly of intelligence reports referred by other investigative agencies to the FBI. After reactivating the General Intelligence Division to investigate communist subversion at the request of Roosevelt following the signing of the Nazi-Soviet non-aggression pact in August 1939, the FBI's surveillance machinery moved into high gear in 1940, during which began what Maurice Isserman has referred to as "the most ferocious and concerted anti-radical campaign since the Palmer raids of 1920." The creation of what Isserman calls the "Red Scare of 1940" was attributable not only to Roosevelt's authorization of the previous year, but also the work of Congress which, according to Isserman, "in an election year, needed little persuasion to solve the nation's security problems in a time of international menace at the expense of the traditional scapegoats, aliens and radicals." It was what accounted for the passage in June 1940 of the Alien Registration Act, better known as the Smith Act ("the first peacetime federal sedition law passed since the Alien and Sedition Acts of 1798"), followed in October 1940 by passage of the Registration of Certain Organizations Act ("Voorhis Act"), designed to combat internal threats to national security by prohibiting "subversive activities."[109]

Following the fall of France in June 1940, the FBI had unleashed a nationwide propaganda campaign against "fifth columnists," with Hoover delivering numerous ominous public warnings against them, at the same time denouncing the communists for their "parrot-like followers in classrooms, in pulpits, in the press and in high places of government." He went so far as to declare, in a speech to the New York State Police Chiefs Association, in July 1940, that "fascism and Nazism did not come into being until the wickedly winding way was paved by communism."[110] As part of the intensified investigation of "fifth column" suspects, Hoover also announced at a federal anti-"fifth-column" conference that all FBI field offices had been placed on a 24-hour schedule.[111] The president also sent a message to the two-day federal-state conference on law enforcement problems and national defense, in which he called upon Congress and state legislatures to enact additional laws to deal with "subversive activities, seditious acts and those things which might slow up or break down our common defense program."[112]

Addressing an American Legion conference in September 1940, Hoover announced that a "fifth column of destruction" was on the march in America. He called upon the Legion to work with FBI investigators in combating "the scheming peddlers of foreign 'isms' " and asked for its members' aid in keeping the FBI informed of suspicious activities. He asserted that foreign powers had been sending agents to America to carry on a campaign to recruit as allies "the disloyal and malcontent."[113]

"It is a new kind of militancy."
Federal Bureau of Investigation
Survey of Racial Conditions in the United States
(August 1943)

The FBI's awareness of African Americans emerged as part of this wider campaign directed against communists and "fifth columnists." Like these other groups, blacks fell under official suspicion as a potential threat to the national defense buildup that was in progress throughout the country. The organizational takeover of the National Negro Congress by Communist adherents was confirmed in April 1940 by the resignation of A. Philip Randolph as president, after it voted at its third annual meeting for a resolution of non-intervention in the European war.[114] At around the same time, the Committee on Participation of Negroes in the National Defense Program was organized under the aegis of the *Pittsburgh Courier,* to give African Americans a political voice in implementation of the national defense effort. Launched in May 1940 and headed by Dr. Rayford W. Logan of Howard University, the group represented the first national committee organized to press for equal participation of blacks in civilian and military aspects of the defense program.[115]

The turning of the FBI's attention to African Americans can be traced in the steady stream of almost daily intelligence reports that Hoover supplied to the Roosevelt White House, starting in November 1939 and continuing right up until Roosevelt's death in April 1945.[116] The earliest report regarding racial unrest came in a brief memorandum dated May 31, 1941, followed by an expanded report on June 19, 1941, regarding the "Negro March on Washington."[117] The initial report erroneously attributed authorship of the plans for the march to the moribund National Negro Congress (NNC), the body from which A. Philip Randolph had split in April 1940 because of his belief that it had been taken over by the Communist Party.[118]

The report was forwarded to the White House after a lapse of four months from the date of Randolph's meeting with former NNC members to discuss his proposal that 10,000 African Americans should march on Washington, D.C. (the slogan that Randolph put forward for the march was "We loyal Negro-American citizens demand the right to work and fight for our country"). The first report was issued, moreover, a month and a half after Randolph's announcement, on April 12, 1941, that "plans for an all-out march of ten thousand Negroes on Washington are in the making and a call will be issued in the next few weeks to keep in their minds night and day the idea that all roads lead to Washington, D.C."[119]

On May 1, the March on Washington Committee finally issued its "Call to Negro America to March on Washington for Jobs and Equal Participation in National Defense on July 1, 1941" (Hoover's May 31 memorandum gave the date for the march as *June 1*). Immediately following the official announcement, mass support for the movement spread rapidly throughout the national African-American community, vastly exceeding the projected goal of the march organizers—in all, it was estimated that some 100,000 African Americans stood ready and were mobilized to march on Washington by the proposed date.[120]

Hoover's second memorandum to the White House on the subject of Randolph and the proposed march on Washington dated June 18, 1941, was accompanied by a two-page report lacking in any substantive information on the movement, particularly the tremendous flurry of organizational activity and propaganda that issued from the movement's official call to march. It concentrated instead on the reaction of the Communist Party, which served the FBI at this point as its principal source of intelligence on African-American developments.

After noting that Randolph "in April 1940 [had] severed his connection with the National Negro Congress because of its alleged control and domination by the Communist Party," the report focused on the latter's reaction. "Of particular significance is the attitude of the Communist Party concerning the proposed March," the report declared, adding: "It appears that the Communist Party has not been invited to participate in this March. The Party, however, has expressed a very real interest in the proposed undertaking. James W. Ford, leading Negro member of the Communist Party and three times its candidate for Vice President of the United States, has issued numerous statements in support of the said March." The report provided extensive excerpts from Ford's statements, in which he tried to show the connection between black support for the march and "the trends of militancy to be observed at the present moment." The report advised that "there is some indication that the Communist Party will endeavor to convert the March into a Communist demonstration." The report concluded by quoting Ford's proposal to the effect that "The Negro people, together with their white friends and allies, should use the occasion of the March on Washington to make a tremendous demonstration against jim-crowism and the imperialist war."[121]

Whatever their limitations, these early FBI reports made up for their fumbling quality by the sheer amount of voluminous detail on the actual organizing of the March on Washington Movement contained in the synoptic *Survey of Racial Conditions in the United States* in 1943. The information presented in the report remains after 50 years still the most detailed chronicle that exists on not only the structure of the movement; most importantly, it also identifies and describes the roles of the various individuals and groups who participated in the movement's meetings and assisted in extending the outreach of the movement throughout all sections of the African-American community.

The appendix in section 2 of the survey covers in considerable detail the movement's origin, organization, official leadership, membership, planning meetings, conferences, propaganda, and the reception that the movement received from different organizations within the black community. Particularly valuable from an historical perspective is the section dealing with the movement's commitment to "Non-Violent Good Will Direct Action." It reveals far more about the formulation of the strategy within the March on Washington Movement in 1942–43 than any other published source to date. It also discloses extremely valuable information regarding the critically important role that was played in the articulation of its philosophy by leaders of the pacifist Fellowship of Reconciliation and the nascent Committee of Racial Equality (later renamed Congress of Racial Equality [CORE]). The survey demonstrates in concrete detail the remarkable significance of the March on Washington Movement and the significance of its pioneering role in shaping the direction of the post-war civil rights struggle and its strategy of nonviolent direct action.[122]

The initial FBI report on the March on Washington Movement was submitted to the White House only four days before Germany's invasion of the Soviet Union, whereupon the position of the Communist Party changed drastically from attacking the war as an "imperialist war" to calling for all-out support for Roosevelt's war program, support for which Ford had only just criticized Randolph, declaring that Randolph's aim was "without a doubt to head off any real struggle of the Negro people against this war program."[123] The Communist Party's radical switch from its previous position that "This is not the Negro's war" to that of "All Out for the War of National Liberation" had profound repercussions on its attitude toward the struggle of African Americans against discrimination. "By the fall of 1941," notes Maurice Isserman, "the Communists were arguing that a too militant defense of black rights at home would interfere with the war effort."[124]

With this change of position, the Communist Party witnessed a steep decline in support among African Americans. During the six months between the reversal of the Communist Party's position on the war and the Japanese attack on Pearl Harbor in December 1941, there was also a marked decrease in FBI surveillance of African Americans. Whether this was due to the Communist Party's fundamental change of attitude toward President Roosevelt and the war program still remains to be investigated. In any event, after June 18–19, 1941, Hoover's intelligence reports to the White House bearing on racial tensions remained in abeyance until after the Japanese struck at Pearl Harbor.[125] By March 1942, the FBI was so intent on pursuing every potential piece of evidence that would support its theory of Communist subversion that it called for "technical surveillance" (the term used to describe electronic surveillance) to be instituted against the moribund National Negro Congress.[126] The following month Hoover informed the White House that the Communist Party was planning to intensify its organizational drive among blacks by telling them that the party's program was their only hope of equality, at the same time as it claimed credit for "eliminating discrimination against Negroes in defense plants and for racial equality in the U.S. navy."[127] Hoover had been informed by the Office of Naval Intelligence in January 1942 that whereas "no indication of Japanese penetration or infiltration" of mainstream black organizations had been reported, "many instances of Communist Party penetration and infiltration of these groups have been reported."[128]

Sparked by racism in the national defense buildup and by the aggressive racism they encountered in the military, African Americans were inspired to press their own demands in giant protest meetings during World War II. The example of the successful organizing efforts of militant industrial unions beginning in the mid-1930s was an important source of inspiration for these protests. The success achieved by the formation of the Committee for Industrial Organization (CIO) in November 1935, inaugurating nationwide mass organizing to establish industrial unionism, set the stage for the new era of African-American militancy symbolized by the widespread support that greeted A. Philip Randolph's proposal for a March on Washington in July 1941 and the broad appeal of the *Pittsburgh Courier's* Double V campaign in February 1942, calling for victory abroad over fascism and victory at home over racial discrimination.[129]

Another important stimulus was the African-American sense of solidarity with other non-white people. "The growing identification of the American Negro with non-white people all over the world is no figment of Nazi propaganda," declared Horace Cayton, adding: "Whereas for years Negroes have felt that their position was isolated and unalterable, some of them are now beginning to feel that dark people throughout the world will soon be on the march."[130] The achievement of non-white solidarity was a constant theme affirmed by African-American leaders during World War II. "The American Negro has such an outlook," allowed Paul Robeson. "It dates from the Fascist invasion of Ethiopia in 1935. Since then, the parallel between his own interests and those of oppressed peoples abroad has been impressed upon him daily as he struggles against the forces which bar him from full citizenship, from full participation in American life."[131] Adam Clayton Powell, Jr., the militant New York black leader, went even further. "We must be sure", Powell declared, "that out of this war must come freedom for all countries with colored peoples in them."[132]

Randolph's proposal itself, the shock of the broad response to his summons to march, and the breadth of the Double V campaign caught the government totally by surprise. President Roosevelt was obliged to offer, in return for Randolph's agreeing to "cancel" the march, his now famous Executive Order 8802 prohibiting racial discrimination in defense industries and establishing the President's Committee on Fair Employment Practices (FEPC). The success of the Double V campaign, coming after the debacle of Pearl Harbor, was the occasion for Hoover to unleash the full force of the FBI against the black community.

It was in many ways a replay of the situation that America had witnessed during and immediately following World War I in the case of the "New Negro" radical movement. In 1941–42, however, the stakes were much higher. The militancy and rebellious spirit of African Americans were far more encompassing than in 1917–21. As architect of the Bureau's GID in 1917–21, moreover, Hoover was already familiar with some of the antecedent elements that bridged the two eras and that went into the making of the new wartime black movement. Nevertheless, he, too, had been caught unaware by the intensity of black militancy both before and after the United States entered World War II.

Hoover took a strong interest in the findings of the FBI's nationwide investigation into "Foreign-Inspired Agitation Among American Negroes." How much of this was simply the political reflex of his deep-seated Negrophobia[133] and how much was his scrambling to stay abreast of the nation's mounting racial crisis is difficult to determine. As the investigation developed, however, Hoover concentrated the Bureau's efforts on a number of key cities. When the results were not received as fast as he wished, special agents in charge [SAC] of FBI field offices were threatened. "I pointed out to SAC Donegan [in New York]," FBI supervisor J. K. Mumford informed the head of the Bureau's internal security division, D. M. Ladd, who was charged by Hoover with overall responsibility for the investigation, "that this is a special project which has been assigned to some five or six key offices, that it must be handled as a special assignment with necessary priority over other matters, that it cannot wait, and must be given immediate attention."[134] The following month Hoover increased the pressure still further, sending out a bulletin to all special agents in charge of FBI field offices. After reviewing the state of the investigation, and complaining that it was not aggressive enough in coming up with criminal prosecutions, Hoover warned:

> "The important nature of the survey being made by the Field concerning the captioned matter [Foreign-Inspired Agitation Among the American Negroes; Internal Security] cannot be over-emphasized and I am holding you strictly responsible for handling it in a logical, careful and exhaustive manner."[135]

The resulting survey was completed in just a little over a year. On September 10, 1943, FBI internal security head D. M. Ladd presented Hoover with a draft copy of *Survey of Racial Conditions in the United States*—all 730 pages of it. The investigation on which it was based had been in operation for 14 months, but the investigation would continue over the next 18 years. It forms the basis of all that the FBI would later embark upon in its epic struggle against the black and radical movements that were to re-emerge in the 1950s and 1960s. While it evokes all the feeling and flavor of American wartime racism toward African Americans, it shows, more importantly, how the movement to fight discrimination was forged during World War II and how the resolute stance of African Americans in facing the entrenched power of Jim Crow helped to advance the cause of black freedom and pave the way for the civil rights and other social movements of the postwar years.

Viewed from this perspective, the FBI study of the World War II black movement achieves a level of historical significance, 50 years after it was produced, that few if any original documents from this period still possess.

> "Now, in the year 1942, is the time; here, in the United States of America, is the place for 13,000,000 Negro Americans to make their fight for freedom, in the land in which they were born and where they will die."
>
> —Chester B. Himes, "Now Is the Time! Here Is the Place!" (September 1942)

White Americans found the mood of African Americans during World War II to be menacing. "Segregation, the word and all it stands for, has become anathema to the Negro, so far as he is represented by his more vocal leaders of today," reported a *New York Times* journalist in August 1943, writing the week after New York was shaken by extensive rioting in Harlem.[136] Although a majority of white Americans found the indomitable attitude of blacks threatening, that fact merely confirmed what the experience of war had always been for American society. Given its racial bifurcation, America's conflicts inevitably and rapidly degenerated into domestic conflicts. As Ralph Ellison has explained, "historically most of this nation's conflicts of arms have been—at least for Afro-Americans—wars-within-wars. Such was true of the Civil War, the last of the Indian Wars, of the Spanish American War, and of World Wars I and II."[137]

James Baldwin was 19 in 1943, the summer that Harlem erupted in racial violence. He has stated that he could sense a "directionless, hopeless bitterness" that summer. The Harlem riot was sparked when a white police officer attempted to arrest a black woman for disorderly conduct at the Braddock Hotel.[138] The fact that the riot was started by a rumor of a black soldier being shot after he had supposedly come to the assistance of the black woman being arrested merely proved, as Baldwin himself noted, that the mass of African Americans "preferred the invention because this invention expressed and corroborated their hates and fears so perfectly."[139] Five people were killed during the Harlem riot and scores were injured before order was finally restored. Harlem was never the same again, though it was only one among several cities where interracial clashes erupted during 1943, with the bloodiest of the entire war having occurred in Detroit in June 1943.

The Harlem conflagration occurred, coincidentally, as Baldwin's father lay dying. It provided an eerie sort of backdrop, he tells us, to his mourning. As Baldwin recounts it, he and his family found themselves, on the morning of August 3, driving their father "to the graveyard through a wilderness of smashed plate glass" in Harlem. "It frightened me, as we drove him to the graveyard through those unquiet, ruined streets," Baldwin recalls, "to see how powerful and overflowing this bitterness could be and to realize that this bitterness now was mine."[140]

To help support his family, Baldwin worked during 1943 on the construction of the Army Quartermaster depot in Belle Mead, New Jersey. "Working in defense plants, working and living among southerners, white and black," Baldwin found himself traumatized by the experience. "That year in New Jersey," he recalled, "lives in my mind as though it were the year during which, having an unsuspected predilection for it, I first contracted some dread, chronic disease, the unfailing symptom of which is a kind of blind fever, a pounding in the skull and fire in the bowels."[141] Baldwin has commented elsewhere on the effect upon him of the mounting racial tensions of the war, which, according to his testimony, marked a decisive moment in his life and in the lives of African Americans generally. "What happened in defense plants and army camps had repercussions, naturally, in every Negro ghetto," he remembers. "The treatment accorded the Negro during the Second World War, marks, for me, a turning point in the Negro's relation to America. To put it briefly, and somewhat too simply, a certain hope died, a certain respect for white Americans faded."[142]

For African Americans, World War II was like the proverbial best of times and worst of times. "What a grand time was the war!" declared Langston Hughes in his poem "World War II" included in *Montage of a Dream Deferred*. He recalls the period with a sense of nostalgia, but it is accompanied by a tone of subtle irony in the response:

What a grand time was the war!
    My, my, my!
In wartime we had fun,
Sorry that old war is done!
What a grand time was the war,
    My, my![143]

At the time, fighting in a Jim Crow army for America and for freedom abroad brought home to African Americans the painful anomaly of America's political hypocrisy. In "How About It, Dixie," which appeared in a collection with the significant title *Jim Crow's Last Stand,* Hughes reflects on the situation—

Freedom's not just
To be won Over There.
It means Freedom at home, too—
Now—*right here!*[144]

The July 1942 beating of Roland Hayes, the acclaimed black tenor, by Southern policemen in his hometown of Rome, Georgia, following a brief argument between his wife and a shoestore clerk, caused Hughes to warn—

Negroes
Sweet and docile,
Meek, humble, and kind.
Beware the day
They change their minds![145]

In "Southern Negro Speaks," Hughes challenged the definition of patriotic loyalty that allowed the propagandists of the racial status quo to charge African Americans with disloyalty for claiming their freedom—

Funny thing about white folks
Wanting to go and fight
Way over in Europe
For freedom and light
When right here in Alabama—
Lord have mercy on me!—
They declare I'm a Fifth Columnist
If I say the word, *Free.*[146]

"WE HAVE A STAKE IN THIS FIGHT . . . WE ARE AMERICANS, TOO!" was the militant cry with which the *Pittsburgh Courier* gave voice to its extraordinarily popular Double V campaign, signifying "Victory at home; victory abroad."[147] It seems that there had never been a more opportune time for African Americans to assail the ears of the nation with their claims for equality. "What an opportunity the crisis has been . . . for one to persuade, embarrass, compel and shame our government and our nation . . . into a more enlightened attitude toward a tenth of its people!" proclaimed the *Courier.*[148] The statement that best sums up the prevailing mood of racial optimism that buoyed black hopes during the national emergency came from *Courier* columnist Joseph D. Bibb. "When the war ends the colored American will be better off financially, spiritually and economically," Bibb wrote. "War may be hell for some, but it bids fair to open up the portals of heaven for us."[149]

Ralph Ellison, prior to his leaving the United States to serve as a cook in the merchant marine during World War II, took a somewhat similar, if more mundane, view. Reporting on an interview with an African-American woman regarding her family's trials and tribulations during the war, Ellison found the African-American community searching for the "gate of freedom," while at the same time struggling with "confusion, war-made confusion." Sensing the possibilities of a "democratized" America opened up by the war, Ellison perceived that the imperative for the black community in the midst of such powerful contradictory impulses was to steady itself. "The problem is go get around, over, under and through this confusion," Ellison counseled.[150]

One powerful pole of this "confusion" was immortalized by Ellison in *Invisible Man*, embodied in the figure of "Ras the Destroyer . . . calling for the destruction of everything white in Harlem."[151] The story of Ellison's street orator which forms the subplot of the novel—"Ras the Exhorter become Ras the Destroyer upon a great black horse"[152]— was not based upon some wild imaginary character. The story was told from the perspective of the real life Randolph Wilson, alias "Ras de Killer," one of the band of nationalist ultra-black orators who re-emerged on the streets of Harlem in 1939–40.

Such was the impression that the diversity of wartime black activism made on Ellison's imagination that his classic novel could be said to represent a kind of literary offering to a singular moment in black history. Only a brief mention of "Ras de Killer" appears in the FBI's *Survey of Racial Conditions in the United States* (p. 191), in the context of "individuals who agitate in Harlem" (pp. 190–94), but his identity can be reconstructed from the records of the FBI's investigation of the Ethiopian Pacific Movement with which he was affiliated and whose activities provided the initial impetus behind the far larger FBI investigation into "Foreign-Inspired Agitation Among American Negroes." Arrested on October 13, 1941, "while making speeches on the streets of Harlem and agitating among the colored race," "Ras de Killer" was originally featured in the exposé that appeared in *The Hour* in August 1941:

> A third outstanding Negro Fifth Columnist, who specializes in betraying the interests of his people, is Ras de Killer. De Killer advocates Japanese control of the whole of Asia. Like [Robert] Jordan, he is in favor of transplanting all American Negroes to Africa. He tells his followers that the Jews are responsible for all their hardships and he does whatever he can to prevent Negroes from joining labor unions and other progressive organizations.[153]

At the time this report was published and after the FBI was informed about it, Hoover admitted that "No record whatsoever is contained in the files of this Bureau regarding Ras de Killer."[154] The information from his Selective Service Board records filed March 25, 1941, however, revealed that he was born Randolph Wilson on September 10, 1910, in Prince Anne County, Maryland. He gave as his alias "Ras de Killer" and claimed that his occupational experience was "organizing black people for our return to Africa," and "lecturer," which he had done for eleven years as "an independent worker." He followed no other occupation, he claimed, though he had done some work in 1930 and 1931 in "electric wiring." He gave as his place of employment 169 West 133rd Street in Harlem, which was the address also of the Harlem headquarters of Marcus Garvey's Universal Negro Improvement Association (UNIA), of which he was a member. In the statement regarding his classification, Wilson declared: "As a leader and organizer of the negro people I feel that my presence among them would be more advantageous towards the National Defense than my presence in the armed forces would be."[155]

One of the most notable features of the FBI's *Survey of Racial Conditions in the United States* is the valuable light that it sheds on the resurgent but still too little known black nationalism of World War II. One Cleveland source of information, in the words of the report, attested that "there is now existing more of a nationalistic tendency than heretofore ever existed and the reason for this is that the Negro is becoming interested in the 'plight' of his race as a whole."[156] The survey's coverage of the various strands of wartime black nationalism still surpasses in depth and breadth anything that has been published to date. It provides an extraordinarily full synopsis of data that can be used to broaden the snippets of African-American racial consciousness that are contained in studies of wartime race relations, such as Carey McWilliams, *Brothers Under the Skin* (1943), Howard O. Odum, *Race and Rumors of Race* (1943), Charles S. Johnson, *To Stem This Tide: A Survey of Racial Tension Areas in the United States* (1943), and Gunnar Myrdal, *An American Dilemma* (1944).

What the FBI study shows is the central significance of Garvey's UNIA as the progenitor as well as incubator of the welter of new nationalist formations that sprang up in the U.S. in the 1930s, all of which absorbed and adapted UNIA principles of racial independence, African redemption and colonization, and Afro-Asiatic racial solidarity. The various divisive tendencies into which the original Garvey movement broke up, following the deportation of Garvey from the U.S. in 1927, formed the basis of a large number of off-shoots from the parent UNIA, with each group reflecting a close relationship in terms of officers, membership, speakers, organizational ritual, and political tenets. But so strong did the tide of black nationalist feeling become during World War II that it temporarily revived even the fortunes of the otherwise moribund UNIA, leading Horace Cayton to go so far as to predict that "black America is ready for a nationalistic movement such as Garvey's when the right demogogic leadership presents itself." The basis for the predicted revival was the heightened racial consciousness spawned by the war and the "feeling that a change in status for the Negro is imminent."[157]

Despite its decline, the UNIA thus managed to spawn a proliferation of new groups, producing an outpouring of black nationalism in the ten-year period between

1933 and 1943. Among the babel of contending voices were such groups as the Addeynue Allahe Universal Arabic Association, African Moslem Welfare Society of America, African Nationalist Pioneering Movement, Afro-American National Infantry, Afro-American Benevolent Improvement Association, Colored American National Organization, Development of Our Own, Ethiopian Pacific Movement, Ethiopian World Federation, House of Israel, Industrial and Clerical Alliance, International Reassemble of the Church of Freedom League, Liberian American League, March Toward Liberty of the Black Man in America, Moorish Science Temple of America, Nation of Islam, National Congress of Afro-American People, Pacific Movement of the Eastern World, Peace Movement of Ethiopia, and Universal Temple of Tranquility. The wealth of data collected by the FBI on these groups and described in the *Survey of Racial Conditions in the United States* underscore the crucial importance of the FBI's study for an understanding of black nationalism in America both before and during World War II.

> A new spirit has grown among American Negroes.
> —Office of Facts and Figures, *Negroes in a Democracy at War* (May 1942)

From this volatile combination of racial militancy and misery, an uneasy mixture of hope and dread, rejection and participation, repression and a burgeoning sense of freedom, a new African-American consciousness began to take shape. Submerged for the most part beneath the war propaganda of the day, it was not always visible. "Although few people recognized it," noted one scholar, "the war was working a revolution in American race relations."[158] In view of the profound transformation that the war wrought in the political consciousness of African Americans, notes another scholar, "the importance of World War II is hard to deny."[159]

The war released all the pent-up racial tensions that the exigencies of defense mobilization forced upon American society, particularly in the areas of migration, employment, and military service. Each of these factors, separately and together, had a transforming effect upon the 13,000,000 African Americans who made up America's largest minority group.

During the decade spanning World War II, a major shift of the black population occurred: more than 3,000,000 moved north and west from the Southern states. That decade also witnessed an extraordinarily rapid urbanization of African Americans, which took place at twice the rate of the general population, resulting in a population of more than 6,500,000 blacks living in urban communities at the time of World War II. At the peak of wartime production, the government's War Manpower Commission estimated that 1,250,000 blacks were employed in semiskilled and skilled jobs in industry, constituting 7.2 percent of total war industry employment with 15 percent in skilled categories.

Federal employment of blacks rose from 8.4 percent to 12.5 percent during these years, with an estimated 50 percent occupying upgraded jobs. Another significant development of the war was the widespread entry of African Americans into the ranks of organized labor, bringing the total number of unionized black workers to approximately 1,500,000. Black enrollment in the military also equalled their ratio in the population, with more than 700,000 blacks serving in the army, with 5,000 officers, and 74,000 men in the navy.[160]

Far more than any other single event of the twentieth century, World War II reshaped the social and demographic contours of the African-American community. Equally as profound, however, was the effect that the experience of the war had on the African-American people's consciousness of themselves. "Gone are the Negroes of the old banjo and singin' roun' the cabin doors," announced Roi Ottley in 1943. "Old Man Mose is dead! Instead, black men have become noisy, aggressive, and sometimes defiant."[161] Replying to criticism published in the white press of the *Courier*'s Double V campaign, columnist George S. Schuyler observed, in June 1942, that "the old days of scared, timid, ignorant Negroes are gone forever."[162] Expanding on its Double V campaign, the *Courier* declared that blacks "would be less than men if, while we are giving up our property and sacrificing our lives, we do not agitate, contend, and demand those rights guaranteed to all free men . . . this would be neither patriotism nor common sense."[163]

The fact is that the national mobilization surrounding World War II presented to American society an unprecedented opportunity to attack the national cancer of segregation. Although a few feeble steps in this direction were undertaken by the federal government—Executive Order 8802, which sought to ban discrimination in defense industries, and the appointment of the president's Fair Employment Practice Committee—these and other measures were always in response to the political pressure of African Americans. Furthermore, these interventions were never sustained. An important opportunity was thus allowed to slip. Neither wartime black militancy nor the national rhetoric of unity and sacrifice in the face of world war proved sufficient to bend America's will toward correcting its racial distortions. What was a singular opportunity for action became instead a reason for its postponement.

The war crisis served, ironically, to strengthen the institutional grip of Jim Crow and the powerful political forces supporting it, making all the more necessary the modern civil rights revolution that was given the task of completing a process begun during World War II. In actuality, the war did little to alter the climate of white opinion in the South or, for that matter, in the nation as a whole: 92 percent of the public during the war years reported favoring continued racial segregation.[164] "If anything, racial intolerance in that region [the South]," it has been noted, "seemed to increase during the 1940s." Immediately following the end of World War II, at least nine blacks were lynched within a period of two months. There were also reported numerous instances of mob action against blacks.[165]

The ascendancy of the Southern states and their representatives was already a major factor in national politics after the election of 1936, when the Roosevelt administration became ever more dependent upon Southern support. The political power of the South expanded even further during the war emergency and paved the way for the massive resistance that greeted the challenge of civil rights and black equality during World War II and after.[166] The political foundation underpinning this resistance was laid during World War II, as Neil Wynn has pointed out:

> In the face of violent and sudden criticism from the North, the threats of bodies such as the March on Washington Movement, and the outbreak of riots in 1943, the liberals tended to side with their more extreme brethren rather than the blacks. The same was also true in Congress where the issue of race generally united Southerners in opposition to the rest of the country. . . . This opposition could not be ignored nor overruled because the South was vital to the Democratic party and to the President, both in getting reform and then war measures passed in Congress and in securing victory in presidential elections. . . . [A]fter the defeat of many Democrats in the North and mid-West in the elections of 1942, the Dixiecrats formed the backbone of the [Democratic] party in Congress.[167]

As to how World War II redistributed political power, the modern civil rights movement might best be interpreted as the interrupted or delayed response of African Americans to the consolidation of power and influence by the Democratic Party in the South during the New Deal and World War II. In this context, the FBI was a key bulwark defending the ascendancy of Southern Jim Crow power in national politics. The FBI thus expressed, particularly where African Americans were concerned, all the values of the resurgent South in opposing the struggle to put an end to racial discrimination both during and after World War II.

Showing just how difficult and protracted this struggle for the future would be becomes the main value of the FBI's secret *Survey of Racial Conditions in the United States*. In the process, the report documents several important developments in African Americans' wartime experience. It confirms, for example, the key role played by the black press during World War II in championing and communicating the insurgent demands of the African-American community. The survey frankly admits that "one of the most effective and important forces attracting the attention of the colored race and swaying their opinion is the Negro press." This view is amply confirmed in the main body of the report, which contains a multitude of references to the editorial personnel and opinions of 80 black newspapers (53 percent of the 155 black newspapers published in the U.S. during World War II), viewed as "sources of unrest or discontent among the Negro race in the area in question." The strategic position occupied by the black press in the estimation of the FBI was also shown in the special appendix devoted to the subject in the *Survey of Racial Conditions in the United States*, including an in-depth survey of "those Negro newspapers which have the largest circulation in this country."[168]

World War II marked the high point of achievement for the black press. Circulation increased 40 percent through the war years, during which it functioned "primarily to foster race solidarity and prod increasing militancy, [and] campaigned to embarrass America's war for democracy by publicizing America's jim-crow policies and practices."[169] Its achievement was all the more significant for its having been accomplished in the face of official intimidation, with repeated threats made from the president on down.[170] The main official complaint was the deleterious effect that black newspapers, and the outspokenness of their columns in exposing racial atrocities, were believed to have on the state of Negro morale.[171]

The radical tenor of the black press was especially marked during the spring of

1942, as may be gauged from a *Courier* editorial that informed its readers of the wish of government officials to suppress "all critical comment. . . . [T]o the Negro press and public this trend cannot be viewed with complacency."[172] *Courier* writer George S. Schuyler for his part mocked the "Hysteria over Negroes," musing:

> The hysteria of Washington officialdom over Negro morale is at once an astonishing, amusing and shameful spectacle. . . . It is shameful that the only "remedy" they are now able to put forward is jim crowism on a larger scale and suppression of the Negro newspapers, i.e., further departure from the principles of democracy.[173]

The high point of the black press's resolute stance in the face of threats of government repression came in June 1942, when the publisher of the *Chicago Defender*, John Sengstacke, confronted Attorney General Francis Biddle, in a face-to-face meeting at the Department of Justice in Washington, D.C., and bluntly informed him, "You have the power to close us down, so if you want to close us, go ahead and attempt it!"[174]

From the perspective of the black press's achievement during World War II, it might be useful to compare its relationship to the black movement of World War II to its later relationship with the civil rights movement of the 1950s and 1960s. Whereas the black press formed a key component of the black movement during World War II, the civil rights movement of the 1950s and 1960s evolved largely without the help of a vibrant black media. This made the modern civil rights struggle far more dependent upon the white media for articulating its aims and objectives as well as for mobilizing nationwide support than was the earlier wartime movement. What is remarkable about the success of the wartime black press is that it mobilized such overwhelming black support with a total circulation of a mere 1,276,600.[175]

The key importance of World War II black newspapers is linked with yet another feature that the *Survey of Racial Conditions in the United States* underscores, namely, the high level of solidarity that the wartime crisis evoked, bringing together individuals and groups from all strata of the African-American community in an unsurpassed show of racial unity. It was symbolized by the instantaneous success and breadth of the Double V campaign, around which the African-American community rallied with a sense of common purpose that it has rarely ever again achieved.

The resolute temper and easy mixing of the classes that gave to the period its amazing cultural fluidity are poignantly captured by James Baldwin. In describing the atmosphere in Harlem in the summer of 1943, Baldwin recalled: "I had never before been so aware of policemen, on foot, on horseback, on corners, everywhere, always two by two. Nor had I ever been so aware of small knots of people. They were on stoops and on corners and in doorways, and what was striking about them, I think, was that they did not seem to be talking. Never, when I passed these groups, did the usual sound of a curse or a laugh ring out and neither did there seem to be any hum of gossip. There was certainly, on the other hand, occurring between them communication extraordinarily intense." Baldwin then goes on make the following significant social observation:

> Another thing that was striking was the unexpected diversity of the people who made up these groups. Usually, for example, one would see a group of sharpies standing on the street corner, jiving the passing chicks; or a group of older men, usually, for some reason, in the vicinity of a barber shop, discussing baseball scores, or the numbers, or making rather chilling observations about women they had known. Women, in a general way, tended to be seen less often together—unless they were church women, or very young girls, or prostitutes met together for an unprofessional instant. But that summer I saw the strangest combinations: large, respectable, churchly matrons standing on the stoops or the corners with their hair tied up, together with a girl in sleazy satin whose face bore the marks of gin and the razor, or heavy-set, abrupt, no-nonsense older men, in company with the most disreputable and fanatical "race" men, or these same "race" men with the sharpies, or these sharpies with the churchly women. Seventh Day Adventists and Methodists and Spiritualists seemed to be hobnobbing with Holyrollers and they were all, alike, entangled with the most flagrant disbelievers; something heavy in their stance seemed to indicate that they had all, incredibly, seen a common vision, and on each face there seemed to be the same strange, bitter shadow.[176]

Baldwin captures in prose the powerful ethos of solidarity and reality of association that characterized relations between the different classes of African Americans in this era. What must also be emphasized is the broadly proletarian character of the renewal that Baldwin's valuable reminiscence describes. Such veteran observers of race relations as Will Alexander, Edwin Embree, and Charles S. Johnson, observed in 1942 that "the characteristic movements among Negroes are now for the first time becoming proletarian, as contrasted to upper class or intellectual influence that was typical of previous movements. The present proletarian direction grows out of the increasing general feelings of protest against discrimination, especially in the armed forces and in our war activities generally."[177]

This was the background to the letter written to the *Pittsburgh Courier* in January 1942, by the 26-year-old cafeteria worker at the Cessna Aircraft Corporation in Wichita, James G. Thompson, that sparked the idea of the Double V campaign. The response to the campaign quickly took on the character of a social movement. The same general impetus also underlay the wartime expansion of the NAACP, which saw its membership swell nearly ten times and the number of its chapters triple: from 355 branches and a membership of 50,556 in 1940, the NAACP increased to a total of 1,073 branches with a membership of nearly 450,000 in 1946.[178] The same was true for the remarkable increase in circulation of black newspapers during World War II. "My observation has been that the Negro newspapers are largely following, not leading, the colored people," affirmed *Courier* columnist George Schuyler.[179]

With the profusion of information describing the multifaceted struggle against racial discrimination, the FBI survey underscores the dominant proletarian character of the World War II black movement. It was a time when African-American expression in history, literature, drama, and social analysis reflected the distinct imprint of proletarian values more strongly than at any other period in American history.[180] The annunciation of the movement was the publication W. E. B. Du Bois's *Black Reconstruction* (1935). As the titles of some of the chapters indicate ("Black Worker," "The General Strike," "The Black Proletariat in South Carolina," and "The Black Proletariat in Mississippi and Louisiana") Du Bois's thesis was that the "black worker" was the "underlying cause" of the political conflict that toppled Reconstruction governments. In this connection, the book sought to vindicate the widespread cessation of work by the former slaves of the South which Du Bois depicted as a tantamount to a "general strike" and which the author went so far as to claim was partially responsible for the North's victory in the Civil War. Du Bois's celebration of the freedmen was also emblematic of black labor as the cornerstone "not only of the Southern social structure, but of Northern and English manufacturing and of European and world-wide commerce."[181]

African-American intellectuals and activists, led by such as Abram Harris, John Davis, E. Franklin Frazier, Robert C. Weaver, and Ralph Bunche, would come together during the thirties around a program for organizing black workers into industrial unions that they saw as the means of overcoming the weight of economic oppression that rested on blacks. Recent scholarship shows that it was these African-American intellectuals, rather than organized labor, who were primarily responsible for initiating the alliance of black and white labor during the thirties, as had previously been thought.[182] The importance and value of the FBI's *Survey of Racial Conditions in the United States* to the study of the African-American working class during the era of Jim Crow and World War II can hardly be exaggerated.

The labor program espoused by these African-American intellectuals parallels the proletarian ethos and gritty naturalism of black writing made famous by Richard Wright in *Uncle Tom's Children* (1938) and *Native Son* (1940), as well as his ideologically charged *Twelve Million Black Voices: A Folk History of the Negro in the United States* (1941). The same emphasis informs Chester Himes's first two novels, *If He Hollers Let Him Go* (1945) and *Lonely Crusade* (1947), both of which are set in wartime Los Angeles.[183] Their protagonists are black workers involved in fighting discrimination on the job as well as organizing black workers into industrial unions. Their stories are told in the hard, brutal language of ordinary black folk, reflecting the contemporary struggles of black workers in the national defense program.

Not surprisingly, Himes became the subject of FBI surveillance after his essay "Negro Martyrs Are Needed" appeared in the May 1944 issue of *The Crisis*. Himes propounded the need for a "Negro revolution" to secure equality and freedom by enforcing the rights guaranteed to all citizens by the Constitution. The FBI's New York field division remarked with alarm at its appearance: "Heretofore the NAACP has been a relatively moderate Negro organization, but this [Himes's article] may be the start of a campaign of extreme radicalism. . . . The article in question regarding the Negro Plan of Revolution has the approval of the NAACP for in an editorial note preceding the article it is stated that the author argues brilliantly for revolution and leaders in the tradition of Gabriel and Nat Turner." After receiving this memo from New York, J. Edgar Hoover promptly forwarded a photostatic copy of Himes's article to Assistant Attorney General Tom C. Clark, calling attention to the article's summons to revolutionary action. Clark, who would later be appointed attorney general, responded to Hoover with the view that "further investigation is warranted and the Criminal Division would appreciate being furnished with the information that you secure." Hoover then notified the New York field office that the Justice Department was requesting an investigation of the publication, but with the added caution:

> Additionally, the Bureau desires that this inquiry, which has been requested, be conducted as discreetly as possible, particularly any phases thereof which might or might seem to concern "The Crisis." As indicated, the Department has requested an investigation of [Himes] individually. However, you should, of course, continue whatever examinations you have made of "The Crisis" in connection with your general coverage of Negro activities.[184]

The same proletarian commitment can be seen in the work of Ralph Ellison, who, incidentally, reported on the 1943 Harlem race riot for the *New York Post,* the surrealistic reenactment of which concludes the narrative of his novel *Invisible Man* (1952). Ellison's own choice of wartime service reflects his proletarian sensibility:

> I myself had chosen the merchant marine as a more democratic mode of service (as had a former colleague, a poet, who was lost off Murmansk on his first trip to sea), and as a seaman ashore in Europe I had been encountering numerous Negro soldiers who gave me vivid accounts of the less-than-democratic conditions under which they fought and labored. But having had a father who fought on San Juan Hill, in the Philippines and in China, I knew that such complaints grew out of what was by then an archetypical American dilemma: How could you treat a Negro as equal in war and then deny him equality during times of peace? I also knew of the trials of Negro airmen, who after being trained in segregated units and undergoing the abuse of white officers and civilians alike were prevented from flying combat missions.[185]

The same proletarian bent would inform the great African-American war novel *And Then We Heard the Thunder* (1963) by John Oliver Killens, which tells the story of a segregated World War II amphibious unit; the novel culminates in a racial battle between black and white soldiers that was based on an actual racial explosion that occurred in Brisbane, Australia, in 1943. "You ain't even a second-class citizen any more," one of the black characters in the novel observes to another, "you're a second-class soldier."[186] Employed with the New Deal's National Labor Relations Board in Washington, D.C., from 1936 until 1942, Killens left to serve in the U.S. Amphibian Forces in the South Pacific until 1945. Both his civilian and wartime experiences influence the ethos of his remarkable novel. Following the war, Killens returned to working with the National Labor Relations Board, where he spent the next two years as a CIO organizer of black and white workers before he gave up, finally, in frustration.[187]

The cultural movement of World War II that most strongly expressed proletarian overtones was the "zoot-suit" phenomenon that was identified with Mexican-American and African-American youths. It was "pegged pants, a root [zoot] suit with a reet pleat, and a stuffed cuff [that] started the shit off," acknowledged one of the participants in the August 1943 Harlem riot in giving a description of the dress code of the 1940s hipster.[188] The zoot suit become not only a badge of social defiance; it was construed into an alternative aesthetic signifying the kind of "cool" rebellion that carried enormous personal as well as symbolic meaning for young African-American and Mexican-American males during World War II.

The subject receives special treatment in the FBI's coverage of wartime conditions in Los Angeles, where riots resulted in June 1943. Its manifestation elsewhere, in cities such as Detroit (" 'zoot suit' colored boys") and Philadelphia ("young Negroes—the 'zoot suit' type"), was also remarked on by FBI investigators. In the black community of Roxbury, Boston, the zoot suit likewise became the dress code of the black hipster, as described in Malcolm X's autobiography. He would later be disabused of the notion that it concealed some liberating or positive meaning. But this was only after his conversion to and assimilation of the culturally conservative precepts of the teachings of the Nation of Islam and its leader, Elijah Mohammed.

In reality, the zoot suit was emblematic of the generational and cultural shift that surfaced in the U.S. during World War II among rebellious youth; for African Americans and Mexican Americans it expressed a new-found ethnic identity and provided a badge of undaunted masculinity. Malcolm acquired his first zoot suit after he moved to Boston from Lansing, Michigan, in February 1941. "Like hundreds of thousands of country-bred Negroes who had come to the Northern black ghetto before me, and have come since," he subsequently recalled, "I'd also acquired all the other fashionable ghetto adornments—the zoot suits and conk [straightened hair] that I have described, liquor, cigarettes, then reefers—all to erase my embarrassing background."[189] His obvious pride in the new fashion revealed itself in the affecting account that he gives:

> When I modeled the zoot for Ella, she took a long look and said, "Well, I guess it had to happen." I took three of those twenty-five-cent sepia-toned, while-you-wait pictures of myself, posed the way "hipsters" wearing their zoots would "cool it"—hat angled, knees drawn close together, feet wide apart, both index fingers jabbed toward the floor. The long coat and swinging chain and the Punjab pants were much more dramatic if you stood that way. One picture, I autographed and airmailed to my brothers and sisters in Lansing, to let them see how well I was doing. I gave another one to Ella, and the third to Shorty, who was really moved: I could tell by the way he said, "Thanks, homeboy." It was part of our "hip" code not to show that kind of affection.[190]

The zoot suit was to achieve its greatest notoriety as a result of the first six days of June 1943, when a series of bloody "zoot suit" race riots occurred in Los Angeles. The riots were, in actuality, a series of premeditated assaults upon members of Mexican youth gangs by white servicemen who were on leave in Los Angeles. Their reign of terror had been preceded during May by the circulation of rumors claiming that the wives of navy men in Los Angeles had been robbed and raped by "zoot suiters." It was said that lone servicemen had been attacked by Mexican gangs and that several servicemen had been hospitalized. As a result, white servicemen organized themselves into large vigilante groups and set out to find Mexican gangs. They attacked Mexican "zoot-suiters" with weighted ropes and clubs, tearing and cutting their suits off after they were apprehended. (A ten-page report on the Los Angeles rioting reveals that there were two instances in which blacks who were not wearing zoot suits were also attacked by white servicemen.) During the six days of clashes, 112 people were reported to have been hospitalized, with 150 others hurt, and 114 arrested. Other so-called "zoot-suit" clashes were reported in Philadelphia, Pittsburgh, Baltimore, and other large cities, though they were not on the scale of the riots in Los Angeles, where the city council resorted to banning the wearing of "zoot suits."[191]

In these and other ways, the FBI survey assists in clarifying the crucial relationship subsisting between the beliefs and institutions of the African-American community and the social agendas of young black workers during World War II.[192] At the same time, the survey describes the conditions of black industrial workers and their links with the movement of organized labor. Approximately 60 AFL and CIO unions and union locals are mentioned in the report, reflecting the support for black demands that left-led CIO unions and union organizers generated. It also illustrates the intense resistance that was mounted by certain white unions, mainly AFL, against the black drive to desegregate production.

The question of support or nonsupport for civil rights by the new industrial unions in the late thirties and forties and the impact of industrial unionism on the state of race relations generally have been major issues in the historiography of the American labor movement since the 1980s. The role of blacks in the growth of the CIO and the question of whether this role paved the way for racial integration are also themes that have been hotly debated by scholars.[193] How these issues played themselves out in the context of wartime production and how local differences affected the content of the relationship that arose from one area to another between unions and the black community are matters of the greatest importance for labor historians, as they struggle to get closer to the daily experience of workers as well as try to understand the phenomenon in larger, more theoretical terms. The salience of local struggles within the broad movement toward industrial unionism is amply illustrated by the comment of the FBI's Birmingham field division regarding labor unions. "A source of information has volunteered the opinion," the report states, "that labor unions are perhaps [one] of the most important phases in connection with any discussion of the racial conditions existing at the present time in the South." The FBI report goes on to state:

> [I]t is stated that in view of the large number of Negroes employed in the various mines and mills in the vicinity of the Alabama industrial area, many union organizers and representatives are naturally attracted with the prospect of increasing membership through the securing of Negro members. They are stated to openly advocate better positions or better work for the Negro and insist in some instances upon their being placed in certain elevated positions.
>
> It is further stated that during the meetings of labor unions no rules or regulations governing the seating of those in attendance exists, thus resulting in social intercourse between white and Negro people. It is further pointed out that the

> majority of the members of various unions address one another with the prefix of "Brother." It is concluded that the Negroes receiving this treatment, which is a different social feeling extended to them, naturally expect the same treatment at other times.[194]

At the same time that there has been a new and salutary emphasis on the importance of local struggles, there has also been a growing interest in the "search for new areas of African-American initiative during this phase of 20th century industrial unionism."[195] The FBI's survey will contribute to this search by making better known the existence of a number of such initiatives. For example, the survey reported that in Atlanta "several Negroes known to have Communist connections have created an organization known as the Atlanta Workers Council which meets at the headquarters of the National Urban League in Atlanta. This organization is said to be presently attempting to organize Negro domestic workers."[196]

The report sheds new light on the changing relationship between mainstream organizations, such as the Urban League, and organized labor at the local level. For example, the FBI's Baltimore field office reported that the Baltimore Urban League "[c]ooperates with Local CIO Union No. 43 IUMSWA [International Union of Marine and Shipbuilding Workers of America], Communist dominated." Similarly, the report found that the Urban League branch in Milwaukee collaborated with local unions to advance the interest of black workers. "Early in May 1943," according to the FBI's survey, "the Executive Secretary of the Urban League in Milwaukee informed that during the previous month, the Urban League had planned to cooperate with the Congress of Industrial Organizations to encourage Negroes to join labor unions in war plants and to become active members so that they would have the protection of the union in the postwar period. He informed that no specific unions were designated which the Negroes should join."[197]

The FBI survey discloses, moreover, the identities of various local black activists, providing crucial information that can be used not only to recover the story of black labor, but also to reconstruct the relationship between black activism and local black communities. To cite just one example, the survey includes the following from Baltimore:

> According to information received, the principal agitator at the shipyards [Bethlehem Steel Shipyards] was John Albert Jacobs, who is colored and twenty-seven years of age. He was born in Georgia and has been in the company employ since 1937. William R. Sandlin and George B. Boulding, both colored, were also reportedly active agitators. Jacobs was described as an eloquent mob leader.[198]

The survey reveals the identity of another important black labor organizer in the San Francisco area for whom the struggle between black autonomy and the demands of Communist Party overlords became a central issue. It disclosed the following information:

> The Communist Party in the San Francisco area has exhibited considerable interest in the Shipyard Workers Committee Against Discrimination. This organiza-

> tion was formed in 1942 and has been under the recognized leadership of one Roy Thompson. The purpose of the organization is to combat "Jim Crow" local labor unions. Recently Thompson appeared to direct his activities at breaking up these local unions and in turn setting up a separate Negro union. Thompson has been criticized by Communist Party leaders in the area, although he is sympathetic with the Party he is not a member of it, for his actions in this matter[,] their claim being that Thompson does not know what he is doing and has not been fully integrated into the Party to the extent that he can understand and dictate Party policies. According to the latest reports, this committee has approximately 160 members, both white and Negroes, who represent the various Bay area shipyards. The committee is said to have furnished the Communist Party in the area with twenty Negro recruits. More recent information which has been reported reflects that the Party contemplates deposing Thompson in view of what they term his "nationalistic attitude."[199]

Elsewhere in the survey, the FBI San Francisco office reports that "Thompson is stated to have been militantly opposed to the white leadership of the union having the bargaining rights in this area for shipyard workers." This was a reference to the International Brotherhood of Boilermakers, Ironworkers, Shipbuilders, Welders and Helpers of America, AFL, which organized several Jim Crow locals that Thompson set out to challenge and overturn. The report goes on to reveal that "Thompson's actions opposed the Party's plan of infiltrating the 'Jim Crow' union locals with the view of thereafter obtaining control of them and the Party for this reason opposed Thompson's tactics."[200]

With so much of the wartime struggle of African Americans centered on conditions in the defense program, a great deal of scholarly attention has been focused on an examination of industrial unions in opposing discrimination in jobs and segregation in the workplace. Here, again, researchers have felt the same need to get closer to the actual experience of workers at the plant level. A valuable illustration is contained in the survey's Detroit section:

> In April 1943, it was reported that there was considerable agitation and tension among employees of the Plymouth Motor Car Company, especially in Department 81 which is said to employ quite a few Negroes. A source of information has informed that it is very apparent that resentment of Negroes being employed there exists among the white employees. In this connection, a pamphlet was made available as distributed by C. George "Pop" Edelen, President of Local 51, UAW-CIO (an alleged member of the Communist Party), entitled "Plymouth Management Intimidates Workers." This pamphlet stated, among other things, "We call upon all stewards on every shift to be on the lookout for these elements in the supervision and the 'company stooges' who are intimidating the Negro women in the plants. They should be reported to the local union office and they will be properly investigated by the Government."[201]

The Detroit section of the survey contains a great deal of primary data on the Detroit black community and the role of black workers in the automobile industry and the UAW. It also documents the wartime fight waged by workers and radical organizations against job and housing discrimination, while at the same time showing the cleavages and fissures that the racial strife engendered by the war produced in white UAW responses. This is illustrated, for example, in the observation made in the survey that "in the Packard Motor Car Company strike, during the first part of June 1943, R. J. Thomas, President of the United Automobile Workers of America, CIO, publicly blamed the Klan under conditions where it was distinctly to his advantage to cover lack of union discipline inasmuch as many of the minor union officials and union members actively participated."[202]

The importance that the FBI gave to labor issues in investigating wartime racial conditions was directly linked to the role that Communist Party organizers played in the formation and functioning of industrial unions. Writing in 1949, the black communist organizer Abner Berry recalled how "millions of black workers looked to the CIO as their salvation in the early days of that organization," at the same time claiming that, with the progressive role played by the CIO during this formative period, the black worker was given "equality, freedom, dignity, and decent working conditions."[203] The question of the relationship between the CIO and black workers is deeply intertwined with another issue, namely, the relationship of the Communist Party to the African-American movement during World War II.[204]

"It has become a truism of writing on the CP [Communist Party] in World War Two that the Communists 'abandoned' all efforts on behalf of blacks after June 22, 1941," remarks Maurice Isserman, referring to the impact of Hitler's attack upon the Soviet Union in making the Communist Party abruptly reverse its previous political position opposing the war as "imperialist" to supporting it as a "people's war." "Between 1939 and 1941 the American Communists had attacked the war against nazism as 'phony' and 'imperialist'," recalled Walter White. "In the process they had played up the Negro question to the hilt in the *Daily Worker*, enumerable pamphlets, and countless meetings." The abruptness of the party's policy reversal was stunning. The change caused a sizeable defection of black members and sympathizers from the party's fold:

> On no issue [of Communist-Party policy and strategy] was the reversal so noticeable as the Negro question. While on the day before the attack, denial of justice and opportunity to the American Negro had been almost the number-one item on the agenda of the American Communist party, on the day after, the issue had been dropped completely, in subordination to the new party line that nothing, absolutely nothing, must be allowed to interfere with the new "holy war" against the nazis.[205]

Isserman makes a valiant effort to revise this view of Communist abandonment with a more nuanced interpretation. "The Communists did not abandon the struggle for black rights during the war, but rather forced that struggle into narrow channels," he maintains. He explains the change this way: "The CP limited its struggle for black rights to those areas that it believed benefited the war effort. The policy proved an inadequate response to the black community's demands for redress of long-standing grievances, but it was not the 'abandonment' so often alleged."[206]

With an abundance of data not readily obtainable from other sources, the FBI's *Survey of Racial Conditions in the United States* provides a significant amount of new empirical data for testing the tenability of the two opposing views of Communist Party involvement and/or abandonment. What the survey points to, however, is the party's ambivalence. The FBI's New York special agent alluded to this fact in a report in January 1943. "It is apparent," he observed, "that, although the Communists are loyal to the Allied cause in an effort to obtain a victory for Russia, they are quick to attack any person or group of persons criticizing the Negroes, an action which is in furtherance of their attempt to gain a large membership among the Negro population in the Communist Party."[207] Any reexamination of the Communist Party's role in the anti-racist struggle of World War II will definitely have to consult the FBI's 1943 survey.[208]

> Speak tenderly to Jerusalem, and cry to her that she has served her term,
> that her penalty is paid, that she has received from the Lord's hand
> double for all her sins.
> —*The Book of the Prophet Isaiah* 40:2

"For a long time," Richard Wright acknowledged, "I toyed with the idea of writing a novel in which a Negro Bigger Thomas would loom as a symbolic figure of American life, a figure who would hold within himself the prophecy of our future." Wright spoke these words in March 1940, in a lecture at Columbia University immediately after *Native Son* was published, explaining "How 'Bigger' Was Born." The lecture was delivered at a time when, in his words, "the whole world is caught in the pangs of war and change."[209] At the end of World War II, speaking on a New York radio forum, Wright claimed to find fulfillment of his prophetic Bigger Thomas in the wartime struggles of the African-American community. "But listen," he urged his radio audience, referring to America's race problem, "here is something of great and decisive importance that is overlooked." According to Wright, "Twenty-five years ago there were only a few thousand Negroes clamoring for justice. But today there are 13 million, and they resent the degradation of their second-class citizenship. Gradual solutions are out of date. They [the white establishment] hide the present gravity of this problem which confronts the Nation for the first time in all of its tragic fullness."[210]

To understand how America reached this crisis point, I can think of no better account than the FBI's wartime *Survey of Racial Conditions in the United States*. The figure of Wright's rebellious Bigger Thomas looms over its pages and the extraordinary story that they tell. Confronting him is the intrepid J. Edgar Hoover whose presence is to be felt throughout the report. Symbolizing the forces of rebellion and reaction, they would continue to confront each other in the postwar civil rights struggle that, ultimately, would transform America. What the FBI's World War II investigation of blacks shows is that it was designed and executed from its inception as a measure aimed at halting the African-American challenge to Jim Crow.

Studies of domestic spying against African Americans have tended with few exceptions to focus either on the period of repression following World War I or the sixties' backlash against the black freedom struggle. The importance of the present work is that it will now enable researchers to fill a significant gap in tracing the expansion of political surveillance as planned and directed by Hoover and the FBI during World War II. For this and other reasons, the *Survey of Racial Conditions in the United States* represents a landmark document, both for its coverage of the racial turmoil occasioned by World War II and for what it reveals about the transformation of the FBI into a political counterintelligence agency.

"If President Roosevelt's original purpose in expanding FBI monitoring of dissent derived from a concern about foreign-directed activities—to confirm whether or not American fascists and communists were agents of foreign powers—he had unwittingly opened a Pandora's box," observes Athan Theoharis. Within a span of only five years, the FBI underwent a fivefold expansion in its personnel—from an organization of approximately 900 agents in 1940 to approximately 5,000 by 1945.[211]

After Pearl Harbor, official concern with the subversive potential of foreign-inspired agitation was directed against the African-American community and the racial tensions attendant upon its subjugation. Official concern with African Americans would become a key factor in the FBI's transition from law enforcement to intelligence to domestic counterintelligence. This was the import of the FBI internal security division memorandum that was sent out in August 1942 to the Birmingham, Chicago, Detroit, Miami, New Orleans, and New York field divisions. "The purpose of these letters," it declared, "is to instruct the above-named Offices to conduct additional surveys in their Field Divisions to ascertain information reflecting the reasons or causes of unrest and agitation among the Negroes in those areas." In his letter to the selected field offices, Hoover explained why this special project had been assigned to this select group of key field offices and why the project had to be handled with special priority over other matters:

> I want to ascertain through highly discreet inquiries what preventive steps are being taken within the area in question to alleviate or to cope with such situation [pertaining to economic, social or political circumstances which possibly add to the unrest or dissatisfaction among the Negroes in this area.] I must insist upon the utmost discretion in this particular phase of your survey so that absolutely no impression may be given or inference taken that the Bureau is inquiring into matters of local concern. . . .
>
> I want this survey assigned to at least one experienced Agent in your Office who is entirely familiar with local conditions as they exist in this matter. I expect that you will afford this project your most expeditious attention and careful supervision. I cannot overemphasize the highly important nature of it.[212]

The FBI's wartime investigation of "Foreign-Inspired Agitation Among the American Negroes" and the resulting *Survey of Racial Conditions in the United States* formed the basis after World War II of the FBI's expanded counterintelligence operations against African Americans. These COINTELPRO operations would continue unabated until the denouement of Watergate, followed by the public revelations of the

1975 Senate Committee's investigation into intelligence abuses that brought demands for curtailment of the FBI as well as an increase in its political accountability. The loss of public support was dramatic. According to Richard Gid Powers, "In 1937 it would have been hard to find a man in America more universally admired than J. Edgar Hoover; forty years later his reputation had totally collapsed." When Hoover died in 1972, "the bureau's reputation, a reputation that Hoover had built and guarded with fanatical vigilance during his forty-eight-year tenure, was in shambles."[213]

World War II provided Hoover with "a patriotic consensus supporting his counterintelligence work" that solidified the FBI's overwhelmingly favorable public image. Its ascendancy accelerated even further with the bureau's expanded political role during the years of the Cold War. However, the civil rights movement gradually inaugurated a new national consensus in the 1950s and 1960s, with the result that Hoover was forced increasingly onto the defensive. "Hoover's public stand against King for the first time pitted the FBI director not just against outcasts from the American consensus," observes Powers, "but against the millions of mainstream Americans who regarded the civil rights movement as a moral crusade and Martin Luther King as the keeper of the American conscience."[214]

Challenged from within by the struggle for civil rights, the American "patriotic consensus" finally collapsed under the tremendous weight and political strain of the Vietnam war. Hoover's counterattacks against both the civil rights and antiwar movements, accompanied by the erosion of constitutional guarantees that FBI's tactics entailed, would have disastrous results. According to Power, FBI counterintelligence operations eventually led to the "total rejection by the public of Hoover's carefully nurtured FBI legend. To put it bluntly, the G-Man was defunct." And with the collapse of popular support, the reputation of the FBI "was buried and all but forgotten. The FBI's pop culture image was now that of the phone tapper, the bedroom bugger, the blackmailer; the scandal monger, the racist, the character assassin; the poisoner of the well of intellectual and political freedom."[215]

The FBI's 1942–43 investigation into "Foreign-Inspired Agitation Among the American Negroes" would survive the wartime emergency and continue in force over the next 16 years, all the while acquiring different labels, renamed "Racial Matters" in September 1947, and "Racial Situation" in July 1956. This latter title was retained until November 1958, when the investigation again became known as "Racial Matters."[216] After World War II the underlying objective of preventing "communist subversion" was upgraded and redirected into broader intelligence undertakings. It was integrated into revamped programs such as COMINFIL (Communist Infiltration), a part of which was devoted specifically to communist influence in relation to the "Negro question." In 1964, the COMINFIL program was expanded to include a concurrent program code-named CIRM (Communist Influence in Racial Matters), which was "designed to precisely spell out the full extent of the communist influence in racial matters."

In 1965–66 the FBI launched a still broader investigation into "General Racial Matters," with the aim of collecting "racial intelligence." This was expanded, in turn, into a series of surveys covering demonstrations, racial violence, and riots under the rubrics of "Racial Conditions Reporting" and "Civil Disturbance Investigations."[217] This sequence of investigations of the political activities of African Americans, and racial conditions generally, reached its climax during the turbulent years 1966–68. In 1966, the FBI launched its notorious COINTELPRO program aimed at "Black Hate Groups," with the intention of disrupting not only radical black organizations, but also mainstream civil rights groups and their leaders.

This was followed, in August 1967, by an extensive series of black community surveillance programs that were carried out under such names as "Ghetto Informant Program" and "Black Nationalist TOPLEV Informant Program," both of which were designed to penetrate black nationalist and community-based organizations. There were, in addition, numerous other programs that the FBI formulated and put into operation throughout this period, including the 1968 "Black Nationalist Organizations Investigation," which was related to student protests at Columbia University and other college campuses; the 1970 investigation of black student unions to identify their goals and leaders; the 1970 Key Black Extremist Program, aimed at investigating key black activists who were allegedly violence-prone; and, finally, the Black Panther COINTELPRO, the purpose of which was to disrupt and destroy the Black Panther Party.[218]

These programs reveal a variety of FBI activities that encompassed a wide spectrum of investigatory functions, from intelligence concerning race riots and racial unrest to collecting information on Communist infiltration, from informant penetration of black nationalist and civil rights organizations to full-fledged disruption or neutralization of individuals and organizations. What the FBI's 1943 *Survey of Racial Conditions in the United States* confirms is the basic interconnection of each of these different categories and activities so far as the network of surveillance is concerned. It thus helps to explain how the FBI could slip so easily from intelligence undertakings and enter into the realm of counterintelligence.

Scholarly research and knowledge of FBI political surveillance and methods have grown enormously within recent years. At the same time, the history of African Americans in the era of Jim Crow is continuing its remarkable renascence. The FBI's *Survey of Racial Conditions in the United States* makes clear how closely these two fields are related. In addition to describing their topical connection, it also explains in greater detail than other hitherto available published accounts *why* the fate of Hoover's FBI and African Americans became so inextricably bound together in the last days of Jim Crow. In the final analysis, African Americans played a decisive role in liberating America from the combined thralldom of Jim Crow and J. Edgar Hoover.

Martin Luther King, Jr. Day
January 16, 1995

NOTES

1. *The Autobiography of Malcolm X* (New York: Grove Press, 1965), 106–8.
2. The Army disqualified Malcolm X for service on grounds of "psychopathic personality inadequate, sexual perversion, psychiatric rejection" (Clayborne Carson, *Malcolm X: The FBI File,* edited by David Gallen [New York: Carroll & Graf, 1991], 58–59). Malcolm's exercise in "talking crazy" represents what the anthropologist James C. Scott describes as "strange theater," namely, behavior that reduces the risk of reprisal even while it expresses an act of calculated resistance (James C. Scott, *Domination and the Arts of Resistance: Hidden Transcripts* [New Haven, Conn.: Yale University Press, 1990], 21, 93).
3. Kenneth B. Clark and James Barker, "The Zoot Effect in Personality: A Race Riot Participant," *Journal of Abnormal and Social Psychology,* 40 (April 1945): 145.
4. Enclosure in memo, J. Edgar Hoover, director, FBI, to SAC (special-agent-in-charge), New York, 11/18/42, FOREIGN-INSPIRED AGITATION AMONG THE AMERICAN NEGROES IN THE NEW YORK FIELD DIVISION; INTERNAL SECURITY, Bureau Files 100-HQ-135-34-68 and 100-141449-1.
5. Federal Bureau of Investigation, *Survey of Racial Conditions in the United States,* Secret, 8/15/43, FOREIGN-INSPIRED AGITATION AMONG THE AMERICAN NEGROES; INTERNAL SECURITY, Bureau File 100-135-191.
6. *Survey of Racial Conditions in the United States,* Section 1, 332. An eloquent analysis of "unorganized, day-to-day resistance to segregated public space" in the area of public transportation in Birmingham, Alabama, during World War II is provided in Robin D. G. Kelley, " 'We Are Not What We Seem': Rethinking Black Working-Class Opposition in the Jim Crow South." *Journal of American History,* 80 (June 1993): 102–10. Kelley states that "in the twelve months beginning September 1941, there were at least 88 cases of blacks occupying 'white' space on public transportation, 55 of which were open acts of defiance in which African-American passengers either refused to give up their seats or sat in the white section," adding that "this is only part of the story; reported incidents and complaints of racial conflict totaled 176," 104.
7. U.S. War Department, Military Intelligence Division, MID 291.2 Negroes, "Racial Conflict in the South," July 2, 1942.
8. Arnold M. Rose, *The Negro's Morale: Group Identification and Protest* (Minneapolis: University of Minnesota Press, 1949); Ulysses Lee, *The Employment of Negro Troops,* Special Studies, United States Army in World War II (Washington, D.C.: Office of the Chief of Military History, U.S. Army, 1966), 300–347; Richard M. Dalfiume, *Desegregation of the U.S. Armed Forces: Fighting on Two Fronts, 1939–1953* (Columbia: University of Missouri Press, 1969), 105–47.
9. Quoted in Charles E. Silberman, *Crisis in Black and White* (New York: Random House, 1964), 61.
10. Horace R. Cayton, "Fighting for White Folks?," *Nation,* September 26, 1942, 267.
11. Cited in Silberman, *Crisis in Black and White,* 60.
12. Cayton, "Fighting for White Folks?," 269.

13. Ibid., 270.

14. Franklin D. Roosevelt Library, Hyde Park, New York (hereafter FDRL), OF [Official Collection] 10-B, no. 2194, box 16, J. Edgar Hoover, Federal Bureau of Investigation, Washington, D.C., to Major General Edwin M. Watson, Secretary to the President, The White House, June 26, 1942; Silberman, *Crisis in Black and White,* 61–65; cf. Herbert Garfinkel, *When Negroes March: The March on Washington Movement in the Organizational Politics for FEPC* (New York: Free Press, 1959); Malcolm Ross, *All Manner of Men* (New York: Reynal & Hitchcock, 1948); Thomas E. Blantz, *A Priest in Public Service: Francis J. Haas and the New Deal* (Notre Dame: University of Notre Dame Press, 1982). Scholars such as Richard Dalfiume, Ulysses Lee, Harvard Sitkoff, Lee Finkle, Neil Wynn, August Meier, Elliot Rudwick, and A. Russell Buchanan, have added greatly to the appreciation of the World War II black movement and its significance in the formation of the post-World War II civil rights struggle (see also Richard Kluger, *Simple Justice: The History of Brown v. Board of Education and Black America's Struggle for Equality* [New York: Knopf, 1976]; Doug McAdam, *Political Process and the Development of Black Insurgency, 1930–1970* [Chicago: University of Chicago Press, 1982]; Aldon D. Morris, *The Origins of the Civil Rights Movement: Black Communities Organizing for Change* [New York: Free Press, 1984]; and Richard A. Couto, *Lifting the Veil: A Political History of Struggles for Emancipation* [Knoxville: University of Tennessee Press, 1993]).

15. "Hoover had played a major role in the administration's strategy of responding to the public hysteria over spies and sabotage; instead of giving the public a reasonable appraisal of the extremely small danger of sabotage, the government magnified the problem so as to magnify the government's success in coping with it. For two years, the public had been hearing that sabotage was as dangerous a threat to the country as the possibility of direct enemy attack" (Richard Gid Powers, *Secrecy and Power: The Life of J. Edgar Hoover* [New York: Free Press, 1987], 246).

16. "President Calls American Legion to Fight War Threat to Freedom," *The New York Times,* September 24, 1940.

17. Bureau Bulletin, No. 51, 9/13/44, Bureau File 100-135, stated: "(D) FOREIGN-INSPIRED AGITATION AMONG THE AMERICAN NEGROES; INTERNAL SECURITY. It has been noted that a number of the Field Divisions have been using varying captions for teletype communications and letters which concern the instant matter. In order to conserve time and to create a more uniform way of captioning teletype communications and letters which concern the captioned matter, you are instructed in the future to use the code word RACON followed by the name of the Field Division and the character Internal Security or 'IS' in the case of teletype communications. This word will signify 'racial conditions.' This caption is only to be used with respect to teletype communications and letters. The captioning which has been used in the past, namely, 'Foreign-Inspired Agitation Among the Negroes in the . . . . . . Field Division; Internal Security' will be used for all reports submitted in this matter."

18. References to the FBI monograph are cited in Kenneth O'Reilly, *"Racial Matters": The FBI's Secret File on Black America, 1960–1972* (New York: The Free Press, 1989), 19; and Patrick S. Washburn, *A Question of Sedition: The Federal Government's Investigation of the Black Press During World War II* (New York: Oxford University Press, 1986), viii, 179–86, 260 n.; and "J. Edgar Hoover and the Black Press in World War II," *Journalism History,* 13 (Spring 1986): 29–30. Two more scholars, Athan G. Theoharis and John Stuart Cox, in their book, *The Boss: J. Edgar Hoover and the Great*

American Inquisition (Philadelphia: Temple University Press, 1988), 191–92, together allude to the Savannah and Birmingham field office investigations that contributed to the preparation of the FBI study, but they do not refer to the monograph directly.

19. Don Whitehead, *The F.B.I. Story* (New York: Random House, 1956), 186.
20. Powers, *Secrecy and Power*, 239–48. Powers characterizes Hoover's report to the president as "a reckless performance, especially since Hoover's report to Roosevelt was so obviously motivated by his vested interest in deflecting blame away from the Bureau and, incidentally, settling some old scores with bureaucratic rivals" (242).
21. "Pro-Axis Propaganda in Harlem," *The Hour*, 111 (August 23, 1941): 1.
22. Letter, J. Edgar Hoover, FBI, Washington, D.C., to SAC, New York, 12/9/41, Re: Arthur Reid, Robert Jordan, Ras de Killer; memo, H. E. White, SAC, Washington, D.C., to R. Kramer, FBI, Washington, D.C., 9/13/41; Hoover to E. J. Connelley, assistant director, FBI, SAC, New York, 9/18/41, Re: Arthur Reid, Robert Jordan, Ras de Killer; Hoover to SAC, New York, 11/19/41, Re: African Patriotic League, Ethiopian Pacifist League, Inc.; Ethiopian Pacific Movement, Inc., et al.; Internal Security-J; Selective Service; Sedition, Bureau File 100-56894.
23. Letter, P. E. Foxworth, assistant director, FBI, SAC, New York, to the director, Washington, D.C., Re: Robert Jordan alias Robert Gordon, Ethiopian Pacifist League, Inc., Sedition-Internal Security, 12/30/41; Hoover to SAC New York, 1/13/42, Bureau File 100-56894; "G-Men to Investigate Report of Japanese Bribe to Leaders," *Amsterdam Star News*, January 3, 1942. At this stage of its investigation, the New York FBI field office was confused about the principal pro-Axis organization, namely, the Ethiopian Pacific Movement, which it erroneously identified as being the same as the African Patriotic League.
24. Florence Murray, comp., *The Negro Handbook 1944* (New York: Current Reference Publications, 1944), 1; "Negro Groups Find An Apathy To War," *The New York Times*, January 11, 1942. Hastie was appointed to his position on October 27, 1940. He submitted his resignation on January 5, 1943, in protest against the official failure to redress the problem of racial discrimination in the military (Gilbert Ware and Robert Jerome Glennon, *William Hastie: Grace under Pressure* [New York: Oxford University Press, 1984]; Phillip McGuire, "Judge Hastie, World War II, and Army Racism," *Journal of Negro History*, 62 (1977): 351–62; Walter White, *How Far the Promised Land?* [New York: Viking Press, 1955], 89–93).
25. *Pittsburgh Courier*, January 17, 1942. In a confidential memorandum addressed to the secretary of state, following the Japanese attack on Pearl Harbor, Dr. Joseph L. Johnson, formerly U.S. Minister to Liberia in the 1920s, asserted: "I do know that certain Negro leaders in this country are pro-Japanese and have been for a long time. Robert S. Abbott, for many years editor of the Chicago *Defender* was pro-Japanese. So also was Robert L. Vann, Editor of the *Pittsburgh Courier* and at one time Assistant Attorney General of the United States" (Joseph L. Johnson, M.D., Columbus, Ohio, to the Honorable Secretary of State, Washington, D.C., Subject: Japanese Diplomacy and Sentiments, December 12, 1941, enclosed copy in Bureau File 100-135-X).
26. Teletype, Hoover to SAC, New York, 1/20/42, Re: Ethiopian Pacific Movement, Internal Security-J; memo, Hoover to Attorney General Francis Biddle, Washington, D.C., 1/21/42, Bureau File 100-56894.
27. Memo, Hoover, FBI, to Assistant Attorney General Wendell Berge, Department of Justice, Washington, D.C., 1/22/42, Bureau File 100-56894.

28. Cabell Phillips, " 'No Witch Hunts'," *The New York Times Magazine*, September 21, 1941, 8, quoted in Washburn, *A Question of Sedition*, 67.

29. Phillips, "No Witch Hunts," 8, quoted in Patrick S. Washburn, "FDR Versus His Own Attorney General: The Struggle Over Sedition, 1941–42," *Journalism Quarterly*, 62 (Winter 1985): 717; cf. Francis Biddle, *A Casual Past* (Garden City, N.Y.: Doubleday, 1961), 261ff.

30. Francis Biddle, *In Brief Authority* (Garden City, N.Y.: Doubleday, 1962), 151, 226, quoted in Washburn, "FDR Versus His Own Attorney General," 717.

31. Biddle, *In Brief Authority*, 164, 166; Washburn, *A Question of Sedition*, 50. Biddle recalled that "At about the same time, there were suggestions by a columnist of a row between Hoover and me. A New York *Herald-Tribune* reporter was sent to ask me whether if I were made Attorney General I would fire the director of the Federal Bureau of Investigation. My denial was not published" (165).

32. Biddle, *In Brief Authority*, 169. Washburn quotes Herbert Wechsler, a special assistant to Biddle from 1941 to 1944, as stating in an interview that Biddle was "an almost passionate" supporter of blacks (*A Question of Sedition*, 185).

33. *In Brief Authority*, 258.

34. Dominic J. Capeci, Jr., "The Lynching of Cleo Wright: Federal Protection of Constitutional Rights during World War II," *Journal of American History*, 72 (March 1986): 867; cf. Louis Cantor, *A Prologue to the Protest Movement: The Missouri Sharecropper Roadside Demonstrations of 1939* (Durham, N.C.: Duke University Press, 1969): 3–17.

35. Capeci, Jr., "The Lynching of Cleo Wright," 859–60.

36. Ibid., 871–72; cf. Sidney Fine, *Frank Murphy: The Washington Years* (Ann Arbor: University of Michigan Press, 1984), 76–96; Robert K. Carr, *Federal Protection of Civil Rights: Quest for a Sword* (Ithaca, N.Y.: Cornell University Press, 1947), 169; John T. Elliff, "Aspects of Federal Civil Rights Enforcement: The Justice Department and the FBI, 1939–1964," *Perspectives in American History*, 5 (1971): 605–07; Robert Zangrando, *The NAACP Crusade Against Lynching, 1909–1950* (Philadelphia: Temple University Press, 1980), 154–55; O'Reilly, *"Racial Matters,"* 22–24.

37. "Asks Inquiry on Negroes; Biddle Wants Civil Rights Data on Detroit Housing Project," *The New York Times*, March 10, 1942; cf. Dominic J. Capeci, Jr., *Race Relations in Wartime Detroit: The Sojourner Truth Housing Controversy of 1942* (Philadelphia: Temple University Press, 1984).

38. Capeci, Jr., "The Lynching of Cleo Wright," 877–84.

39. Memo, Sylvester Myers, Civil Rights Section, Department of Justice, Washington, D.C., to Victor Rotnem, Criminal Division, Department of Justice, 6/24/42, File 146-10-2; Assistant Attorney General Wendell Berge to the director, FBI, Re: Pacific Movement of the Eastern World, Inc., et al., 7/2/42, 7/13/42, 7/15/42, Bureau File 65-40879. The attorney general gave his approval, on July 14, 1942, for a grand jury investigation of the "activities of Japanese agents with Negroes" (Assistant Attorney General Wendell Berge to Harry C. Blanton, U.S. Attorney, St. Louis, Missouri, 7/15/42, Department of Justice File 146–10–2). The linkage between the Sikeston lynching and the FBI's investigation is explicit in Berge's instructions to U.S. Attorney Harry C. Blanton: "The Federal Bureau of Investigation has been instructed to furnish you with complete copies of any pertinent investigative reports of this matter, as well as the Sikeston lynching investi-

gation. The Federal Bureau of Investigation has also been informed as to the authorization of this Grand Jury investigation and instructed to render such additional investigative service as may be ordered by your office in connection with this matter or any tag ends which may yet remain relative to the Sikeston lynching case. In the event that there appears to be a correlation between the Sikeston lynching case and this matter, Mr. Rotnem will explain this phase of the matter to you when you talk to him."

40. President's Committee on Civil Rights, *To Secure These Rights: The Report of the President's Committee on Civil Rights* (Washington, D.C.: U.S. Government Printing Office, 1947), 114, quoted in Capeci, Jr., "The Lynching of Cleo Wright," 884, n. 66.

41. Elliff, "Aspects of Federal Civil Rights Enforcement," 630, 640, 652; Richard Kluger, *Simple Justice: The History of Brown v. Board of Education and Black America's Struggle for Equality* (New York: 1975), 700–47; O'Reilly, *"Racial Matters,"* 27–29, 61–63, *passim*; Powers, *Secrecy and Power*, 323–32, 367–69, 407–12. The dubious attitude shown by the FBI in civil rights cases was earlier displayed in its investigation of the June 1940 lynching of Elisha Davis in Brownsville, Haywood County, Tenn. (Richard A. Couto, *Lifting the Veil: A Political History of Struggles for Emancipation* [Knoxville: University of Tennessee Press, 1993], 158–65).

42. Memo, D. M. Ladd, FBI, to Hoover, 1/21/42; Hoover to the attorney general, 1/21/42; Hoover to Assistant Attorney General Wendell Berge, 1/22/42, Bureau File 100–56894; cf. "Francis Biddle and decision regarding supervision of FBI by Assistant Attorney General," *The Official and Confidential File of FBI Director J. Edgar Hoover* (Wilmington, Delaware: Scholarly Resources, 1988), microfilm edition, Roll 3-0284, Folder 23.

43. "The Inquiring Reporter," *Baltimore Afro-American*, December 20, 1941; memo, J. Edgar Hoover to Wendell Berge, Department of Justice, Washington, D.C., January 30, 1942, Bureau File 100–63963. Berge replied that the article was within the law, since the statements were "mere expressions of individual opinion as to the possible course of future events" and that they were not "false statements" that would have made them liable to the federal statutes. In addition, there was no evidence that the statements were intended to harm the armed forces or interfere with recruiting or enlistment in the military (Berge to Hoover, February 5, 1942, cited in Washburn, *A Question of Sedition*, 62, 224 n. 76).

44. Memo, D. M. Ladd, FBI, to the director, 1/21/42; Hoover to the attorney general, 1/21/42; Hoover to Berge, 1/22/42; Ladd to the director, 1/31/42; Hoover to the attorney general, 2/19/42; Hoover to Berge, 2/19/42; Hoover to the attorney general, 4/2/42; Hoover to Berge, 4/29/42; Hoover to the attorney general, 6/18/42; Hoover to Berge, 6/13/42; Hoover to Berge, 6/16/42; Hoover to Berge, 6/18/42; Hoover to Berge, 7/11/42; Hoover to Berge, 7/27/42, Bureau File 100-56894. While waiting upon Justice Department approval, Hoover had to make do with a complaint filed against Jordan alleging violation of the Alien Registration Act on account of his failure to notify immigration officials of a change of address. He was apprehended on February 18, 1942, and tried on March 9, 1942. Jordan was found guilty on three counts charging violation of the Alien Registration Act, with a recommendation of clemency from the jury. He was given a concurrent sentence of ten days on each of the three counts (memo, Duane L. Traynor to D. M. Ladd, FBI, 2/17/42; J. K. Mumford to Ladd, 3/4/42; Ladd to the director, 3/10/42).

45. Memo, D. M. Ladd, FBI, to the director, 8/4/42; Ladd to E. A. Tamm, FBI, 8/25/42; Ladd to Tamm, 9/14/42; Ladd to the director, 9/14/42, Bureau File 100-56894.
46. Memo, L. B. Nichols, FBI, to Clyde A. Tolson, assistant director, FBI, 9/28/42, Bureau File 100–56894. Nichols protested to his counterpart in the Justice Department that "the Bureau had received instructions from the Department that there was to be no publicity on this matter, that we had not been told it was going before a Grand Jury, although we knew this to be a fact, that we had abided by the Department's instructions only to learn that the United States Attorney in New York, who had very little to do with the case, had given out a 3,000 word story."
47. Richard Gid Powers, *G-Men: Hoover's FBI in American Popular Culture* (Carbondale and Edwardsville: Southern Illinois University Press, 1983), 217.
48. There was a racial aspect to the relationship forged between the FBI and Winchell, as shown in the following March 1944 FBI memo: "In your column of February 7, 1944, you reported as follows—'Warning: some pressure outfits are plotting to foment race disturbances by causing a series of inflammatory incidents in nearly all the prominent New York hotels . . . The program may even be extended to a nation-wide basis. Certain persons are being coached on what to say and do in lobbies and cafes.' Walter, this item is of real interest to us, and I would like, very much, to get more details. Could you give me a lead,—the source, or something to help me follow through?" (memo, A. F., FBI, New York, to W. W., 3/6/44, Bureau File 100-135-34-275; cf. O'Reilly, *"Racial Matters": The FBI's Secret File on Black America, 1960–1972*, 22, 209, 288). The important reciprocal role of Hoover and Winchell in the political and social life of each other is extensively described and analyzed in Curt Gentry, *J. Edgar Hoover: The Man and the Secrets* (New York: W. W. Norton, 1991), 219–20, passim, and Neal Gabler, *Winchell: Gossip, Power and the Culture of Celebrity* (New York: Alfred A. Knopf, 1994), 197–202, passim. Gabler asserts: "Perhaps the greatest affinity between them [Hoover and Winchell] was that they both traded in secrets: Hoover with his thick investigative files, Winchell with his gossip. Their lives were predicated on the clandestine, and perhaps no two men so fully appreciated the value of secrets—of finding them, deploying them, protecting oneself from them. No two men so *believed* in secrets," 202. It was customary for Hoover and the FBI to feed Winchell with gossip and political items for publication in his gossip column and for his radio program: "Winchell was probably the first nationally known radio commentator developed by the FBI. We sent Winchell information regularly. He was our mouthpiece" (William C. Sullivan, *The Bureau: My Thirty Years in Hoover's FBI* [New York: W. W. Norton, 1979], 94).
49. FDRL, Francis Biddle Papers, Cabinet Meetings, January-June 1942 folder, private typewritten notes, March 20, 1942, cited in Washburn, "FDR Versus His Own Attorney General," 720.
50. Biddle, *In Brief Authority*, 258.
51. FDRL, President's Secretary's File, box 56, PSF: Justice [Department] folder, Stephen T. Early to the President, March 20, 1942; Washburn, *A Question of Sedition*, 68–69. Biddle's reluctance to launch wartime sedition prosecutions in the face of presidential pressure as well as pressure from Hoover forms the basis of Washburn's *A Question of Sedition*. According to Washburn, "Biddle was the key individual" (8).
52. Washburn, *A Question of Sedition*, 76–77; "FDR Versus His Own Attorney General," 722.

53. Biddle, *In Brief Authority*, 236–37.
54. Memo, Francis Biddle, attorney general, Washington, D.C., to J. Edgar Hoover, FBI, May 29, 1942, Bureau File 66-6201-15-1-332, in Official and Confidential Files of J. Edgar Hoover, no. 1, folder 136. In his attempt at rebuttal, Hoover declared: "I regret that the President has reached this conclusion for he must have been misinformed as to the facts and record. . . . I am definitely of the opinion that the relative danger to this country of pro-Axis and pro-Communist activities has been properly evaluated and that the effort expended in investigation of the organizations and individuals affiliated with these ideologically opposed groups has been proper" (ibid., memo, Hoover, FBI, to the attorney general, June 1, 1942, marked Exhibit 2). The suspicion that Roosevelt's criticism of the Bureau was largely motivated by his wife's concern is based on the "memorandum for Mrs. Roosevelt" from the president, transmitting Hoover's memorandum "re the investigation of suspected Communists in and out of the govt. service" (FDRL, PSF [President's Secretary's File], Justice [Department], June 17, 1942).
55. Memo, F. L. Welch to J. K. Mumford, supervisor, internal security division, FBI, Washington, D.C., Re: Eleanor Clubs, 9/15/42, Bureau File 100–135–42. "It appears to be a common rumor and topic of conversation throughout the South that there are such clubs and that they are being organized by the female negro household servants to foster demands for shorter hours and better working conditions," Hoover wrote to inform the First Lady. "In fact, several allegations have been received that individually identified negro servant girls have demanded shorter hours or better pay with the statement that they were members of an 'Eleanor Club,' but in each instance when checked out, the employer has denied that any such demand was made and the employee has denied any such affiliation" (memo, J. Edgar Hoover to Malvina C. Thompson, secretary to Mrs. Roosevelt, The White House, September 18, 1942, Bureau File 100-135-Section 2; see also Do Not File Memo, Ladd to the director, 9/11/42, and Do Not File Memo, Ladd to Tamm, 10/21/42, Bureau File 62-116758). For a succinct descriptive summary of FBI surveillance of the First Lady, see Athan Theoharis, *The Boss: J. Edgar Hoover and the Great American Inquisition* (Philadelphia: Temple University Press, 1988), 191–93 n.
56. Letter, J. Edgar Hoover, FBI, to [SAC?], Pittsburgh, personal, 11/3/42, enclosing a copy of original, in Bureau File 100-135-74.
57. White, *How Far the Promised Land?*, 73.
58. Teletype, P. E. Foxworth, SAC, New York, to Hoover, Washington, D.C., 2/16/42, Bureau File 100-56894.
59. Powers, *Secrecy and Power*, 128. In reviewing a memorandum from American Civil Liberties Union (ACLU) official Morris L. Ernst, a longtime Hoover ally and personal attorney, on the subject of "the four freedoms," FBI assistant directors Edward A. Tamm and Clyde Tolson advised Hoover: "You cannot subscribe to some of the statements that are contained in this memorandum. For example, Mr. Ernst advocates continued action on the part of the Civil Liberties Union in seeking the admission of negroes to restaurants in New York. . . ." (memo, E. A. Tamm and Clyde Tolson, FBI, to the director, Washington, D.C., 12/12/41, Bureau File 100-135). A thorough account of the Hoover-Ernest relationship is provided by Gentry, *J. Edgar Hoover: The Man and the Secrets*, 233–37 ff.
60. Cliff MacKay, "A Note to Mr. Hoover," *Birmingham World*, March 27, 1942; SAC, Birmingham, Alabama, to J. Edgar Hoover, FBI, April 4, 1942; Hoover to Emory O. Jackson, April 10, 1942, Bureau file 94-8-1399; quoted in Washburn, *A Question of*

Sedition, 230, n. 59. MacKay's response to Hoover appeared in "Now Just Who is Subversive?" *Birmingham World*, July 10, 1942, quoted in Washburn, ibid., 83; cf. "Washington Gestapo," *The Nation*, July 24, 1943: "J. Edgar Hoover, who has steadfastly refused to include Negroes among his 4,800 special agents, has a long record of hostility to Negroes" (94–95), cited in Washburn, ibid., 171.

61. Memo, L. B. Nichols to Clyde M. Tolson, FBI, 4/24/42, Re: The Birmingham World, Bureau File 100-6582-9X.

62. During his meeting with Jackson, Nichols sought to defend "the Director's views—that the Director made no distinction between race, color, or creed; that it was a well established fact that we have literally scores of colored people working in the Bureau in every position from messenger to Special Agent" (ibid). While the statement was technically correct, it was negated by the reality of the FBI's discriminatory hiring practices. One recent biographer has summed up their effect thus: "For decades J. Edgar Hoover had resisted hiring blacks for anything except the most menial jobs in the FBI. Under pressure from the NAACP, and to keep them from being drafted during World War II, Crawford and a few others, all chauffeurs or office help, had been made special agents, though their duties remained much the same. . . . When appointed director in 1924, he had inherited one black special agent, James Amos, who had served as Theodore Roosevelt's bodyguard, valet, and friend (Roosevelt died in Amos's arms) and whose main job, under Hoover, was cleaning the weapons on the firing range. In addition to Amos, the FBI's other black SAs [Special Agents] included the director's three chauffeurs (James Crawford, in Washington, D.C.; Harold Carr, in New York City; and Jesse Strider, in Los Angeles; and two SOG [seat of government, also known as FBI headquarters] employees, Worthington Smith and Sam Noisette. . . . 'Mister Sam' had the most conspicuous job, serving as majordomo of Hoover's office. His duties, not necessarily in the order of their importance, were to usher in visitors, hand the director a fresh towel when he emerged from his private bathroom, help him into his coat, and wield the flyswatter" (Gentry, *J. Edgar Hoover: The Man and the Secrets*, 39, 280; cf. William Sullivan, *The Bureau: My Thirty Years in Hoover's FBI*, 121–26).

63. Powers, *Secrecy and Power*, 372–73; David J. Garrow, *Bearing the Cross: Martin Luther King, Jr., and the Southern Christian Leadership Conference* (New York: Vintage Books, 1986), 667 n. 53; O'Reilly, "*Racial Matters*," 120–21.

64. Garrow, *Bearing the Cross*, 360.

65. Kenneth O'Reilly, "The Roosevelt Administration and Black America: Federal Surveillance Policy and Civil Rights during the New Deal and World War II Years," *Phylon*, 48 (1987): 20.

66. Powers, *Secrecy and Power*, 233. By December 1940, the FBI had assembled a "custodial detention index" of 6,000 names based on "a list of persons whose activities were considered so dangerous as to justify consideration of their detention in the event of a national emergency" (Senate Select Committee to Study Governmental Operations with Respect to Intelligence Activities, *Supplementary Detailed Staff Reports on Intelligence Activities and the Rights of Americans. Final Report*, Book III, 94th Congress, 2d session, "The Development of FBI Domestic Intelligence Investigations," 417–22).

67. Memo, J. Edgar Hoover to Assistant Attorney General Wendell Berge, Department of Justice, Washington, D.C., Re: Robert O. Jordan et al., 4/29/42, Bureau File 100-56894.

68. *Supplementary Detailed Staff Reports on Intelligence Activities and the Rights of Americans. Final Report*, Book III, "The Development of FBI Domestic Intelligence Investigations," 413–17.

69. Ibid., 420–21; Athan Theoharis, *Spying on Americans: Political Surveillance from Hoover to the Huston Plan* (Philadelphia: Temple University Press, 1978), 157, 255 n. 6, 262 n. 22; Gentry, *J. Edgar Hoover*, 213, 229–30, 244.

70. Memo, J. Edgar Hoover to Assistant Attorney General Wendell Berge, Department of Justice, Washington, D.C., Re: Robert O. Jordan et al., 4/29/42; Hoover to Berge, 6/13/42; Hoover to Berge, 7/11/42, Bureau File 100-56894.

71. Memo, Col. J. T. Bissell, assistant executive officer, Military Intelligence Service, G-2, War Department General Staff, Washington, D.C., to J. Edgar Hoover, FBI, 4/22/42, enclosing copy of "Japanese Racial Agitation Among American Negroes," prepared by Evaluation Section, MID 291.2, Japanese, 4/15/42, Bureau File 100-135-XI.

72. FDRL, Papers of Francis Biddle, Cabinet meetings, Container 1, January-June 1942 folder, May 22, 1942, cited in Washburn, *A Question of Sedition*, 80–81; "J. Edgar Hoover and the Black Press in World War II," 28. The meeting also explored ways of dealing with the black press, including a suggestion by the president that Attorney General Biddle and Postmaster General Frank Walker "talk to some of the editors of the Negro Press to see what could be done to prevent their subversive language."

73. Biddle was not originally provided with a copy of *Survey of Racial Conditions in the United States*: "It will be noticed that no copy of the memorandum [covering the survey] is contemplated for transmission to the Attorney General" (memo, Edward A. Tamm, FBI, to the director, 9/11/43, Bureau File 100-135-161). At the foot of Tamm's memorandum the following handwritten comments appear: "Tolson: What do you think?;" "I agree with Mr. Tamm. OK. H[oover]". A copy of the original was sent to Biddle only after his office telephoned the Bureau and formally requested a copy (memo, John Edgar Hoover, FBI, to the attorney general, 10/12/43, Bureau File 100-135-165). There is no evidence of Biddle's opinion regarding either the investigation or the survey. Washburn is of the opinion that his silence "would not have been surprising in view of his well-known sympathy for blacks" (*A Question of Sedition*, 185). It is also not clear how Biddle learned of the survey. In addition to the copy sent to the White House, only two other copies were originally sent out from the FBI, namely, to the directors of MID and ONI.

74. Memo, J. K. Mumford to D. M. Ladd, FBI, and head, Internal Security Division, Re: FOREIGN-INSPIRED AGITATION AMONG THE AMERICAN NEGROES; INTERNAL SECURITY, 12/6/42, Bureau File 100-135-1. It is also possible that the idea for the FBI survey of racial conditions might have originated with the FBI's confidential monograph series, *General Intelligence Survey in the United States*, begun in early 1942 (J. Edgar Hoover, director, FBI, to the secretary of state, Washington, D.C., May 5, 1942, Record Group 59, confidential, 800.2021/851, National Archives, Washington, D.C.). The April 1942 issue of the FBI's *General Intelligence Survey in the United States* included a section on the dissemination of "Japanese propaganda to American negroes in connection with racial agitation," viz., "This propaganda holds that the negroes entering the Armed Forces are being discriminated against. It is reported that much of this propaganda is being disseminated by the lower class negro preachers and in some instances has been traced back to negro intellectuals, who base their agitation on racial equality."

75. "After receiving [in 1980] the section about black publications that had been ignored by historians using the Roosevelt Library for over seven years," notes Washburn, "I suddenly

was on my way to a dissertation and now this book" (Washburn, *A Question of Sedition,* viii). Washburn views the FBI wartime survey as Hoover's "major attack against the black press" which, according to him, represented "the last serious threat during the war. . . . It was his [Hoover's] chief wartime thunderbolt against the black press" (165, 167).

76. In his autobiography Biddle offered this interpretation of the reasons for Hoover's reluctance to become involved in the prosecution of civil rights cases: "Hoover prided himself on working co-operatively with the local police, and it must have been peculiarly distasteful to him to develop, in the deep South, evidence of the maltreatment of Negroes on which to bring prosecutions, in many cases against local police who had joined in violating some constitutional rights. Yet when I discussed these cases with him, suggesting that he might add to his reputation by thus espousing the liberal cause, he raised no objection to making test cases, although we both knew that his success might be at the price of intense resentment [in the deep South] of such 'Yankee interference.' Without his co-operation the test cases would have never been put together" (*In Brief Authority,* 260).

77. Memo, J. Edgar Hoover, FBI, to Assistant Attorney General Wendell Berge, Washington, D.C., August 7, 1942, Bureau File 100-135-19.

78. FDRL, Roosevelt Papers (hereafter FDR Papers), OF 4952, Southern Conference for Human Welfare, J. Edgar Hoover to Marvin H. McIntyre, Secretary to the President, May 7, 1942; OF 10-B, box 16, no. 2194, Hoover to Major General Edwin M. Watson, Secretary to the President, June 26, 1942; FBI Bulletin, August 1942, Sec. (G) FOREIGN-INSPIRED AGITATION AMONG THE AMERICAN NEGROES; INTERNAL SECURITY-X, 2–3, Bureau File 100-135-2.

79. Cf. Walter White, *A Man Called White: The Autobiography of Walter White* (New York: Viking Press, 1948); Carl T. Rowan, *Dream Makers, Dream Breakers: The World of Justice Thurgood Marshall* (Boston: Little, Brown, 1993); Mark V. Tushnet, *Making Civil Rights Law: Thurgood Marshall and the Supreme Court, 1936–1961* (New York: Oxford University Press, 1994); Gilbert Ware and Robert Jerome Glennon, *William Hastie: Grace under Pressure* (New York: Oxford University Press, 1984); Jesse Thomas Moore, Jr., *A Search for Equality: The National Urban League, 1910–1961* (University Park: Pennsylvania State University Press, 1981); Gloster B. Current, "Walter White and the Fight for Freedom." *Crisis,* 76 (1969): 113–19, 134–35; Phillip McGuire, "Judge Hastie, World War II, and Army Racism." *Journal of Negro History,* 62 (1977): 351–62; cf. John B. Kirby, *Black Americans in the Roosevelt Era: Liberalism and Race* (Knoxville: University of Tennessee Press, 1980).

80. Letter, J. Edgar Hoover to Walter White, 11/12/41, Bureau File 61–3176–18X9; memo, Hoover to Clyde Tolson and E. A. Tamm, FBI, 11/14/41, Bureau File 61-3176-18X11, quoted in Kenneth O'Reilly, "Hoover's FBI and Black America," in David Gallen, ed., *Black Americans: The FBI Files* (New York: Carroll & Graf, 1994), 19.

81. Confidential letter, J. Edgar Hoover, FBI, to SAC Albany, Atlanta, Baltimore, Birmingham, Boston, Buffalo, Butte, Charlotte, Chicago, Cincinnati, Cleveland, Dallas, Denver, Des Moines, Detroit, El Paso, Grand Rapids, Honolulu, Houston, Huntington, Indianapolis, Jackson, Juneau, Kansas City, Knoxville, Little Rock, Los Angeles, Louisville, Memphis, Miami, Milwaukee, Newark, New Haven, New Orleans, New York, Norfolk, Oklahoma City, Omaha, Philadelphia, Phoenix, Pittsburgh, Portland, Providence, Richmond, St. Louis, St. Paul, Salt Lake City, San Antonio, San Diego, San Francisco, San Juan, Savannah, Seattle, Sioux Falls, Springfield, Washington, D.C.,

Quantico, Re: Foreign-Inspired Agitation Among the American Negroes; Internal Security, 6/22/42, Bureau File 100-135-1. The full text of the letter and other relevant FBI documents are reprinted in the addendum to the present volume.

82. *Survey of Racial Conditions in the United States*, 75.

83. Letter, J. Edgar Hoover, FBI, to SAC Albany, etc., Re: Foreign-Inspired Agitation Among the American Negroes; Internal Security, 3/10/42, no. 108, series 142, Bureau File 100-135-57.

84. These figures were compiled from FBI files and court records of the various sedition trials. They reflect a much greater number of prosecutions and convictions of African Americans than those reported in Florence Murray, "The Negro and Civil Liberties during World War II," *Social Forces*, 24 (December 1945); American Civil Liberties Union, *Liberty on the Home Front* (New York: American Civil Liberties Union, 1945), 33–34; Neil A. Wynn, *The Afro-American and The Second World War* (New York: Holmes & Meier, 1975), 103–5. The progression of the various prosecutions are described in the Chronology of Events accompanying the present volume.

85. Memo, J. Edgar Hoover, FBI, to the attorney general, Washington, D.C., 1/26/43, Bureau File 100-135-102.

86. Cf. "The Use of Informants in FBI Domestic Intelligence Investigations," 227–55, passim, in Senate Select Committee to Study Governmental Operations with Respect to Intelligence Activities, *Supplementary Detailed Staff Reports on Intelligence Activities and the Rights of Americans. Final Report of the Select Committee to Study Governmental Operations with Respect to Intelligence Activities*, Book III, 94th Congress, 2d session; memo, "Confidential Informants," 8/29/46, Bureau File 66-2554-5407.

87. Letter, J. Edgar Hoover, FBI, to SAC, New York, personal attention, Re: Informant Coverage of Racial Conditions in the New York Field Division, 8/5/1943.

88. Kenneth O'Reilly, "Hoover's FBI and Black America," 51, in David Gallen, ed., *Black Americans: The FBI Files* (New York: Carroll & Graf, 1994); see also O'Reilly, *"Racial Matters": The FBI's Secret File on Black America, 1960–1972*, 261–92, passim. FBI Assistant Director D. M. Ladd, head of the Bureau's internal security division, submitted his review and evaluation of the surveys resulting from Hoover's instruction regarding "informant coverage of racial conditions," on September 14, 1943; it is reprinted and included with other pertinent FBI documents in the Addendum.

89. Powers, *Secrecy and Power*, 56–129; Robert K. Murray, *Red Scare: A Study in National Hysteria, 1919–1920* (Minneapolis: University of Minnesota Press, 1955); Michael R. Belknap, "The Mechanics of Repression: J. Edgar Hoover, the Bureau of Investigation, and the Radicals, 1917–1925," *Crime and Social Justice*, 7 (Spring-Summer 1977): 49–58; Mark Ellis, "Federal Surveillance of Black Americans during the First World War," *Immigrants and Minorities*, 12 (1993): 1–20; Robert A. Hill, " 'The Foremost Radical Among His Race': Marcus Garvey and the Black Scare, 1918–1921," *Prologue: Journal of the National Archives*, 16 (Winter 1984): 215–31; Theodore Kornweibel, Jr., "Apathy and Dissent: Black America's Negative Responses to World War I," *South Atlantic Quarterly*, 80 (Summer 1981): 322–338; and "Black on Black: The FBI's First Negro Informants and Agents and the Investigation of Black Radicalism during the Red Scare," *Criminal Justice History*, 8 (1987): 121–36; David Williams, "The Bureau of Investigation and Its Critics, 1919–1921: The Origins of Federal Political Surveillance," *Journal of American History*, 68 (December 1981):

560–579; and " 'They Never Stopped Watching Us': FBI Political Surveillance, 1924–1936," *UCLA Historical Journal*, 2 (1981): 5–28.

90. Alpheus Thomas Mason, *Harlan Fiske Stone: Pillar of the Law* (New York: Viking Press, 1956), 151.

91. Powers, *Secrecy and Power*, 147.

92. Powers, *G-Men: Hoover's FBI in American Popular Culture*, xi.

93. Senate Select Committee to Study Governmental Operations with Respect to Intelligence Activities, *Intelligence Activities and the Rights of Americans. Final Report*, Book II, 94th Congress, 2d session, 25–26; *Final Report. Supplemental Reports on Intelligence Activities*, Book VI, 94th Congress, 2d session, 133; cf. Whitehead, *The FBI Story*, 188.

94. *Intelligence Activities and the Rights of Americans. Final Report*, Book II, 26–28.

95. O'Reilly, "The Roosevelt Administration and Black America," 12; "A New Deal for the FBI: The Roosevelt Administration, Crime Control, and National Security," *Journal of American History*, 69 (December 1982): 638–58; *"Racial Matters,"* 18–22.

96. *Intelligence Activities and the Rights of Americans. Final Report*, Book II, 22.

97. Powers, *G-Men: Hoover's FBI in American Popular Culture*, 217.

98. FDRL, FDR Papers, OF 10-B, FBI Folder 1168, box 15, "Delimitation of Investigative Duties of the Federal Bureau of Investigation, the Office of Naval Intelligence and the Military Intelligence Division/Agreement for Coordination . . . ," 2/9/42, enclosed in J. Edgar Hoover, FBI, Washington, D.C., to Major General Edwin M. Watson, Secretary to the President, 2/18/42; J. Edgar Hoover to Hon. Harry L. Hopkins, The White House, 12/7/43, enclosing memorandum, 11/11/43, OF 10-B, FBI folder 2452F, box 19. For an analysis of the 1940 and 1942 delimitation agreements, see Theoharis, *Spying on Americans*, 76, and Frank Donner, *The Age of Surveillance: The Aims and Methods of America's Political Intelligence System* (New York: Alfred A. Knopf, 1980), 289, 319.

99. Biddle, *In Brief Authority*, 182–83. According to Washburn, "documents show that in the war's first three months Roosevelt continually sought out Hoover, not Biddle, when he was angered at the press overstepping what he felt were its wartime boundaries" (*A Question of Sedition*, 49).

100. Memo, J. E. Clegg to the director, FBI, 9/30/40; John Edgar Hoover to Lawrence M. C. Smith, 10/10/40; Hugh A. Fisher to Hoover, 11/7/40, Bureau File 100-122319, quoted in Washburn, "J. Edgar Hoover and the Black Press in World War II," 27.

101. Special Agent Report, Federal Bureau of Investigation, 10/21/41; Hoover to Assistant Chief of Staff, War Department, G-2, 11/29/41, Bureau File 100-31159, quoted in Washburn, "J. Edgar Hoover and the Black Press in World War II," 27.

102. Memo, E. H. Winterrowd for Mr. Mumford, RE: AGITATION AMONG THE NEGROES; INTERNAL SECURITY, 9/8/42, Bureau File 100-135-33). At the Washington National Records Center, the Records of the War Department General and Special Staffs, Record Group 165, and the Records of the Army Staff, Record Group 319, contain the Security Classified Intelligence Reference Publications ("P" File), 1940–45; the Intelligence (G-2) Library Publications ("P" File), 1946–51; the Army Intelligence Decimal File, 1941–46; and the G-1 Cross Reference Sheets to G-1 Security Classified General Correspondence, 1941–48. The files of the Army Service Forces, Record Group 319, con-

tain mimeographed reports on the racial situation within regional units throughout the U.S. The Records of the Office of the Chief of Naval Operations, Record Group 38, at the National Archives, Washington, D.C., contain the investigative files of the Office of Naval Intelligence.

103. Powers, *Secrecy and Power*, 127–28.

104. O'Reilly, *"Racial Matters,"* 47.

105. J. M. Moore, Special Report on "Pacific Movement (Jap-Negro)," secret, October 25, 1933, Records of the War Department, General and Special Staffs, Office of the Chief of Staff, Military Intelligence Division, Record Group 165, 10218–261/85, National Archives, Washington, D.C.

106. Nancy J. Weiss, *Farewell to the Party of Lincoln: Black Politics in the Age of FDR* (Princeton, N.J.: Princeton University Press, 1983), 36. According to O'Reilly, "By 1938 the FBI had a special 'Negroes' category as part of its domestic communist and native fascist infiltration investigations" ("The Roosevelt Administration and Black America," 20), but he does not specify the intelligence data on African Americans that was gathered or developed as a result of these investigations (cf. Washburn, *A Question of Sedition*, 29, 33–34, 39–40).

107. Weiss, *Farewell to the Party of Lincoln*, 36 n. 4.

108. *Survey of Racial Conditions in the United States*, 75. The file number of the investigation—100–135—represents an unusually low number (Linda Kloss, Freedom of Information-Privacy Acts Section, Information Resources Division, Federal Bureau of Investigation, U.S. Department of Justice, Washington, D.C., telephone communication, with author, July 12, 1994). For sake of comparison, it should be pointed out that the file number of the Bureau's investigation of the "Communist Party, USA, Counterintelligence Program, Internal Security-C" was 100–3. The main file numbers of the Bureau's investigations of Allah Temple of Islam, A. Philip Randolph, and the March on Washington Movement were, respectively, 100-6582, 100-55616, and 100-95014. A list of pertinent FBI files and their respective file numbers is contained in the bibliography accompanying the present volume.

109. Maurice Isserman, *Which Side Were You On? The American Communist Party during the Second World War* (Urbana: University of Illinois Press, 1982, 1993), 67–68.

110. *The New York Times*, July 24, 1940, 13; see also Hoover's statement, ibid., July 7, 1940, 7.

111. Ibid., August 6, 1940, 1; August 7, 1940, 2.

112. Ibid., August 6, 1940, 1.

113. Ibid., September 24, 1940, 1; see also report of Hoover's speech on the anti-"fifth column" drive to the National Police Academy, October 1, 1940, 14.

114. Jervis Anderson, *A. Philip Randolph: A Biographical Portrait* (Berkeley: University of California Press, 1973, 1986), 234, 237.

115. Office of the Director, Intelligence Division, Army Service Forces, Headquarters First Service Command, War Department, "Recent Trends in Negro Leadership," April 23, 1943, 1, enclosure in FBI File 100–135–125; cf. Kenneth Robert Janken, *Rayford W. Logan and the Dilemma of the African-American Intellectual* (Amherst: University of Massachusetts Press, 1993).

116. FDRL, OF 10-B, Numbered FBI Reports, box 20, Calendar and Index of Numbered FBI Reports. Of the total of 2,991 FBI intelligence reports submitted by Hoover to the

White House, 40 deal specifically with various aspects of racial unrest (nos. 835, 1147, 1157, 1160, 2007a, 2083, 2093, 2182, 2297, 2303b, 2304a, 2322b, 2351, 2353, 2354a, 2355a, 2355b, 2355c, 2356a, 2356b, 2357a, 2373, 2375, 2377, 2378, 2379, 2403a, 2412, 2416a, 2420, 2431a, 2437a, 2443, 2461b, 2493, 2495a, 2505, 2524, 2525, 2527).

117. FDRL, OF 10-B, Numbered FBI Reports, box 13, no. 794, J. E. Hoover to Major General Edwin M. Watson, Secretary to the President, The White House, Washington, D.C., May 31, 1941; box 14, no. 835, Hoover to Watson, June 19, 1941.

118. Anderson, *A. Philip Randolph*, 234–40; Record, *The Negro and the Communist Party*, 195–98.

119. Quoted in Garfinkel, *When Negroes March*, 56; cf. Anderson, *A. Philip Randolph;* Paula F. Pfeffer, *A. Philip Randolph: Pioneer of the Civil Rights Movement* (Baton Rouge: Louisiana State University Press, 1990); Daryl Pinckney, "Keeping the Faith," *New York Review of Books*, November 22, 1990, 29–34.

120. *New York Amsterdam News*, May 31, 1941; War Department, Military Intelligence Service, Washington, D.C., to J. Edgar Hoover, FBI, May 7, 1943, enclosing Army Service Forces, Headquarters First Service Command, Boston, Mass., "Fellowship of Reconciliation," April 23, 1943, Bureau File 100-135-125.

121. FDRL, OF 10-B, Numbered FBI Reports, box 14, no. 835, "Memorandum Re: March on Washington Movement," enclosure to J. E. Hoover to Major General Edwin M. Watson, Secretary to the President, The White House, Washington, D.C., June 19, 1941.

122. Cf. August Meier and Elliott Rudwick, *CORE: A Study in the Civil Rights Movement 1942–1968* (New York: Oxford University Press, 1973), 11, 14–15, 21. The total number of entries for A. Philip Randolph and the March on Washington in the FBI survey represents the largest of any individual and/or group.

123. "Memorandum Re: March on Washington Movement," 2.

124. Record, *The Negro and the Communist Party*, 184ff.; Isserman, *Which Side Were You On?*, 119.

125. Hoover's second report on the March on Washington Movement was dated June 12, 1942. Even at this late date, Hoover felt constrained to point out that "the information contained in this memorandum was received by the Federal Bureau of Investigation from outside confidential sources" (FDRL, OF 10-B, box 14, no. 835, J. E. Hoover to Major General Edwin M. Watson, Secretary to the President, The White House, Washington, D.C., June 19, 1941). Coincidentally, the report was forwarded on the same day that the FBI's internal security division presented for approval "the form letter to all Special Agents in Charge, requesting that a survey be made to ascertain the extent of agitation among the American negroes in the United States" (memo, J. K. Mumford to D. M. Ladd, FBI, 6/12/42, Re: FOREIGN-INSPIRED AGITATION AMONG THE AMERICAN NEGROES; Internal Security, Bureau File 100-135-24[?]).

126. Memo, E. G. Fitch, FBI, to D. M. Ladd, Re: National Negro Congress, Chicago, Illinois, 3/11/42, Bureau File 61–6728–220. The classification number 61 refers to the investigation of "treason".

127. FDRL, OF 10-B, Numbered FBI Reports, no. 2093, J. E. Hoover to The White House, Washington, D.C., April 17, 1942.

128. Memo for Lawrence M. C. Smith, chief, Special War Policies Unit, War Division, Re: Negro Press, 1/30/42, with reference to ONI 61-10556-375, 639, in Bureau File 100-135-15.

129. Washburn, "The *Pittsburgh Courier's* Double V Campaign," 73–86; cf. also Beth Bailey and David Farber, "The 'Double V' Campaign in World War II Hawaii: African Americans, Racial Ideology, and Federal Power," *Journal of Social History*, 26 (Summer 1993): 817–43.

130. Cayton, "Fighting for White Folks?," 268.

131. Paul Robeson, "American Negroes in the War," address delivered at the New York Herald Tribune Forum on Current Problems, November 16, 1943, New York, distributed by the Anti-Discrimination Committee of the Indiana State CIO, 1. Martin Duberman, *Paul Robeson* (New York: Alfred A. Knopf, 1988), makes no mention of this particular address by Robeson. The extraordinary political effect upon African Americans created by the Italo-Ethiopian War is described in George S. Schuyler, *Ethiopian Stories*, ed. and comp. Robert A. Hill (Boston: Northeastern University Press, 1994); William R. Scott, *The Sons of Sheba's Race: African Americans and the Italo-Ethiopian War, 1935–1941* (Bloomington: Indiana University Press, 1993), Joseph E. Harris, *African-American Reactions to War in Ethiopia, 1936–1941* (Baton Rouge: Louisiana State University Press, 1994), and Robin D. G. Kelley, " 'This Ain't Ethiopia, But It'll Do'," in Danny Duncan Collum, ed., *African Americans in the Spanish Civil War: "This Ain't Ethiopia, But It'll Do"* (New York: G. K. Hall, 1992), 5–57. For a description of the strongly held anti-colonial views of African American activists during World War II, see Hollis R. Lynch, *Black American Radicals and the Liberation of Africa: The Council on African Affairs, 1937–1955* (Ithaca: Africana Studies and Research Center, Cornell University, 1978); "Pan-African Responses in the United States to British Colonial Rule in Africa in the 1940s," in Prosser Gifford and Wm. Roger Louis, eds., *The Transfer of Power in Africa: Decolonization, 1940–1960* (New Haven: Yale University Press, 1982), 57–86.

132. Quoted in Office of Facts and Figures, Bureau of Intelligence, "Negroes in a Democracy at War," Survey of Intelligence Materials, no. 25, May 27, 1942, enclosed in Bureau File 100–135. After learning of its existence at a White House meeting in August 1942, Hoover expressed his interest "in the opinion analysis on the Negro problem" and was immediately forwarded a copy of the report (memo, Oscar Cox, Department of Justice, Washington, D.C., to J. Edgar Hoover, FBI, Subject: Negro Problem, 8/15/42, Bureau File 100-135-34-41). Arguing strongly in favor of the protection of Negro rights, the report concluded: "So long as inequities exist for Negroes in American life, the Axis propaganda machine possesses a powerful fulcrum upon which to rest the lever of domestic division. This fulcrum must be removed—not only for the sake of the Negroes, but also for the sake of assuring mankind everywhere of whatever race or color, that we are engaged in a people's war for freedom, justice and social security," 29.

133. Hoover's racial attitudes towards African Americans are well documented (see Powers, *Secrecy and Power*, 127–28, 324, 461; William C. Sullivan, *The Bureau: My Thirty Years in Hoover's FBI*, 121–26, 268–69, 273; Gentry, *J. Edgar Hoover: The Man and the Secrets*, 500 n.; Donner, *The Age of Surveillance*, 121, 214 fn).

134. Memo, J. K. Mumford, FBI, Washington, D.C., to Mr. Ladd, 9/11/42, RE: AGITATION AMONG NEGROES IN THE NEW YORK FIELD DIVISION; INTERNAL SECURITY, Bureau File 100-HQ-135-34-37.

135. Letter, J. Edgar Hoover, FBI, Washington, D.C., to SACs, 10/3/42, FOREIGN-INSPIRED AGITATION AMONG THE AMERICAN NEGROES; INTERNAL SECURITY, Bulletin 108, Series 1942, Bureau File 100-135-57.

136. Turner Catledge, "Behind Our Menacing Race Problem," *New York Times Magazine*, August 8, 1943, 7, 15.

137. Ralph Ellison, *Invisible Man* (New York: Vintage Books, 1952, 1989), xii.

138. Malcolm X was a participant-observer in the Harlem riot in August 1943. He describes its background and the actual eruption thus: "All through the war, the Harlem racial picture never was too bright. Tension built to a pretty high pitch. . . . Finally, rumor flashed that in the Braddock Hotel, white cops had shot a Negro soldier. I was walking down St. Nicholas Avenue; I saw all of these Negroes hollering and running north from 125th Street. Some of them were loaded down with armfuls of stuff. I remember it was the bandleader Fletcher Henderson's nephew 'Shorty' Henderson who told me what had happened. Negroes were smashing store windows, and taking everything they could grab and carry—furniture, food, jewelry, clothes, whiskey. Within an hour, every New York City cop seemed to be in Harlem. Mayor LaGuardia and the NAACP's then Secretary, the famed Walter White, were in a red firecar, riding around pleading over a loudspeaker to all of those shouting, milling, angry Negroes to please go home and stay inside" (*The Autobiography of Malcolm X*, 114; cf. Dominic J. Capeci, Jr., "The Harlem Riot of 1943," Ph.D. diss., University of California, Riverside, 1970, 188–205).

139. James Baldwin, *Notes of a Native Son* (Boston: Beacon Press, 1955, 1983), 109–10.

140. Ibid., 85, 88; cf. David Leeming, *James Baldwin: A Biography* (New York: Alfred A. Knopf, 1994), 38–42.

141. Baldwin, *Notes of a Native Son*, 92, 94.

142. Ibid., 99; quoted in J. Milton Yinger, *A Minority Group in American Society* (New York: McGraw-Hill, 1965), 52.

143. Langston Hughes, "World War II," *Harlem Quarterly* (Winter 1949–50), 9, reprinted in Arnold Rampersad and David Roessel, eds., *The Collected Poems of Langston Hughes* (New York: Alfred A. Knopf, 1994), 415.

144. Langston Hughes, "How About It, Dixie," *Jim Crow's Last Stand* (Atlanta: Negro Publication Society of America, 1943), reprinted in Rampersad and Roessel, *The Collected Poems of Langston Hughes*, 291.

145. Langston Hughes, "Roland Hayes Beaten," in *One Way Ticket* (New York: Alfred A. Knopf, 1949), 86, quoted in Wynn, *The Afro-American and the Second World War*, 97.

146. Langston Hughes, "Southern Negro Speaks," *Opportunity* (October 1941), 308, reprinted in Rampersad and Roessel, eds., *The Collected Poems of Langston Hughes*, 238.

147. "The Courier's Double 'V' for a Double Victory Campaign Gets Country-Wide Support," *Pittsburgh Courier*, February 14, 1942. The phrase, "We Are Americans, Too," which became popular in black communities during World War II, was the title of a patriotic song written by Andy Razaf and Eubie Blake (Roi Ottley, *'New World A-coming': Inside Black America* [Boston: Houghton Mifflin, 1943], 321).

148. *Pittsburgh Courier*, January 10 and August 8, 1942.

149. Joseph D. Bibb, "We Gain by War," *Pittsburgh Courier*, October 10, 1942.

150. Ralph Ellison, "The Way It Is," *New Masses*, October 22, 1942, reprinted in *Shadow and Act* (New York: Random House, 1964), 291; editorial comment, *Negro Quarterly*,

vol. 1 (Winter 1943): 295–302. After Ellison returned to the United States at the end of World War II, and while he was recuperating on a farm in Waitsfield, Vermont, the idea for *Invisible Man* came to him. This occurred at the same time that an "abortive short novel about World War II—to which he [Ellison] had devoted a year—was jettisoned" (Leonard J. Deutsch, "Ralph Ellison," in Trudier Harris and Thadious M. Davis, eds., *Dictionary of Literary Biography, 76: Afro-American Writers, 1940–1955* (Detroit: Gale Research, 1988), 41.

151. Ellison, *Invisible Man*, 485; cf. Robert A. Hill, introduction, in Schuyler, *Ethiopian Stories*, 15.

152. Ibid., 556.

153. "Pro-Axis Propaganda in Harlem," *The Hour*, 111 (August 23, 1941), 2.

154. Letter, J. Edgar Hoover, FBI, to SAC, New York, Re: African Patriotic League; Ethiopian Pacifist League, Inc.; Internal Security-G-J, 11/19/41, Bureau File 100-56894-X.

155. Report, New York Field Division, Federal Bureau of Investigation, Custodial Detention-J, "Randolph Wilson (colored) alias, Ras de Killer," 6/17/43, New York File 100-15432, in Bureau Main File 100-56894-30. In his Selective Service occupational questionnaire filed July 22, 1942, Wilson gave as his present job that of "writer" and claimed that his duties involved those of a teacher and writer of "Negro philosophy." It was believed that "subsequent to Wilson's arrest by the New York Police in October of 1941 he has not engaged in any street speaking or made any statements that might cause his arrest" (ibid).

156. *Survey of Racial Conditions in the United States*, 106.

157. Cayton, "Fighting for White Folks?," 268–69. As the basis for his impression, Cayton offered the following evidence: "There has been a revival of the Universal Negro Improvement Association, the old Garvey movement, which focused the attention of several million Negroes on a program glorifying the colored races. Its recent national convention, the first for several years, held in Cleveland in August [1942], was attended by more than 400 delegates. This was the largest convention since the peak of the movement. Considerable attention was given to the application of the Atlantic Charter to Africa" (269, fn.).

158. Richard M. Dalfiume, "The 'Forgotten Years' of the Negro Revolution," *Journal of American History*, 55 (June 1968): 103; cf. Harvard Sitkoff, "Racial Militancy and Interracial Violence in the Second World War," *Journal of American History*, 58 (December 1971): 661–681, and *A New Deal for Blacks: The Emergence of Civil Rights as a National Issue–The Depression Decade* (New York: Oxford University Press, 1978); Lee Finkle, "The Conservative Aims of Militant Rhetoric: Black Protest During World War II," *Journal of American History*, 60 (December 1973): 692–713.

159. Wynn, *The Afro-American and the Second World War*, 128.

160. Walter Yust, ed., *10 Eventful Years; a Record of Events of the Years Preceding, Including and Following World War II, 1937 through 1946* (Chicago: Encyclopedia Britannica, 1947), 281–82, 284.

161. Ottley, *'New World A-coming,'* 306. At the time that Ottley's book was published, Hoover requested that the New York field office secure and forward a copy to FBI headquarters: "For your information reviews of this book reflect information concerning conditions, individuals and possibly organizations in which the Bureau is interested with respect to the captioned matter" (memo, J. Edgar Hoover, FBI, to SAC, New York, 8/27/43, RE: FOREIGN-INSPIRED AGITATION AMONG THE AMERICAN NEGROES; INTERNAL

SECURITY, Bureau File 100-HQ-135–34–146). A copy of Ottley's book was obtained and forwarded to FBI headquarters on September 25, 1943 (memo, SAC New York, E. E. Conroy, to the director, Bureau File 100-HQ-135–34–159).

162. George S. Schuyler, "News and Reviews," May 27, 1942, quoted in Washburn, "The *Pittsburgh Courier's* Double V Campaign," 81.

163. *Pittsburgh Courier,* August 8, 1942.

164. Clayton R. Koppes and Gregory D. Black, "Blacks, Loyalty, and Motion-Picture Propaganda in World War II," *Journal of American History,* 73 (September 1986): 387.

165. J. Wayne Dudley, " 'Hate' Organizations of the 1940s: The Columbians, Inc.," *Phylon,* 42 (Fall 1981), viz., "One of the first race riots to occur in the South started in Columbia, Tennessee, on February 14, 1946. On August 10, 1946, racial riots occurred in Athens, Alabama, injuring between fifty and one hundred people. Other violence occurred at Magee, Mississippi, on August 20; at Crowley, Louisiana, on August 26; and at Florence, South Carolina, on September 19. In addition, mob violence occurred in Carrollton, Georgia; Hurtsboro, Alabama; and Mount Pleasant, Tennessee," 262–63.

166. Wynn, *The Afro-American and the Second World War,* 109; cf. Morton Sosna, *In Search of the Silent South: Southern Liberals and the Race Issue* (New York: Columbia University Press, 1977, 204–8; Numan V. Bartley, *The Rise of Massive Resistance: Race and Politics in the South During the 1950's* (Baton Rouge: Louisiana State University Press, 1969).

167. Wynn, *The Afro-American and the Second World War,* p.111.

168. *Survey of Racial Conditions in the United States,* Section 2, Appendix, "The Negro Press," 421. The survey selected for analysis seven of the black newspapers with the largest circulation in the country: *Baltimore Afro-American, New York Amsterdam Star News, People's Voice, Black Dispatch, Chicago Defender, Michigan Chronicle,* and *Pittsburgh Courier.* For a discussion of the FBI's findings, see Washburn, *A Question of Sedition,* 179–85.

169. Sitkoff, "Racial Militancy and Interracial Violence in the Second World War," 662; cf. Ralph N. Davis, "The Negro Newspapers and the War," *Sociology and Social Research,* 27 (May–June 1943): 373–80.

170. "As I was leaving his office one day in December of 1942 President Roosevelt called me back to say that pressure was being brought to bear on him and the Department of Justice to indict the editors of some of the more flamboyant Negro newspapers for 'sedition' and 'interference with the war effort.' The idea to me was fantastic and absurd. I asked the President what evidence, if any, there was that any of the editors he mentioned were guilty of relations with any foreign power, or of any act which could be interpreted as treasonable, under the wise and tolerant provisions of the Constitution. The President told me he had seen no evidence which would stand up in court, but that the stories which had been published in a few of the papers were so clearly biased and inaccurate that some of the men high in government believed that convictions could be secured" (Walter White, *A Man Called White: The Autobiography of Walter White* [New York: Viking Press, 1948], 207; and Washburn, *A Question of Sedition,* 6, 8).

171. "By the time of the Japanese attack on Pearl Harbor, many in America, both inside and outside of the government were worried over the state of Negro morale. There was fear that the Negro would be disloyal. The depth of white ignorance about the causes for the Negro's cynicism and low morale is obvious from the fact that the black press was blamed

for the widespread discontent" (Dalfiume, "The 'Forgotten Years' of the Negro Revolution," 100).

172. "Is Criticism to be Suppressed?" *Pittsburgh Courier,* May 16, 1942.

173. George S. Schuyler, "Hysteria Over Negroes," *Pittsburgh Courier,* May 2, 1942.

174. Interview, John Sengstacke (Washburn, *A Question of Sedition,* 90).

175. Murray, ed., *The Negro Handbook,* I, 201; *Survey of Racial Conditions in the United States,* 419.

176. Baldwin, *Notes of a Native Son,* 99–100.

177. "Memorandum of conferences of Alexander, Johnson, and Embree on the Rosenwald Fund's Program in Race Relations, June 27, 1942," Fisk University, Special Collections, Rosenwald Fund Papers, Race Relations Folder, quoted in Dalfiume, "The 'Forgotten Years' of the Negro Revolution," 100, n. 47.

178. Sitkoff, "Racial Militancy and Interracial Violence in the Second World War," 662–63; Dalfiume, "The 'Forgotten Years' of the Negro Revolution," 99–100; Charles R. Lawrence, "Negro Organizations in Crisis: Depression, New Deal, World War II," Ph.D. diss., Columbia University, 1953, 103.

179. George S. Schuyler, "Views and Reviews," *Pittsburgh Courier,* April 11, 1942.

180. The black actor Canada Lee, who played in the starring role of Bigger Thomas in the stage adaptation of Richard Wright's *Native Son,* makes a brief walk-on appearance in the FBI monograph (*Survey of Racial Conditions in the United States,* 617); cf. Glenda E. Gill, "Careerist and Casualty: The Rise and Fall of Canada Lee," *Freedomways,* 21 (1981): 15–27). Addison C. Gayle Sr. (337), father of the literary scholar of the same name, is referred to in the report as the organizer of the True Democratic League in Newport News, Virginia, in 1941. The survey also includes references to the activities of the Chicago-based Carl Hansberry (100, 475), father of playwright Lorraine Hansberry.

181. W. E. B. Du Bois, *Black Reconstruction in America: An Essay Toward a History of the Part Which Black Folk Played in the Attempt to Reconstruct Democracy in America, 1860–1880* (New York: Harcourt, Brace, 1935), 3–16, 55–84; Francis L. Broderick, *W. E. B. Du Bois: Negro Leader in a Time of Crisis* (Stanford: Stanford University Press, 1959), 183. According to Arnold Rampersad, "The black worker is the hero in this canvas [*Black Reconstruction*], as he is the hero of the struggle of workers everywhere against capitalist exploitation" (*The Art and Imagination of W. E. B. Du Bois* [New York: Schocken Books, 1976, 1990], 237). Du Bois's progressive engagement with the ideologies of labor and the radical left would eventually lead to his becoming one of the most outspoken post-World War II critics of American capitalism and imperialism (cf. Manning Marable, *W. E. B. Du Bois: Black Radical Democrat* [Boston: Twayne, 1986] and Gerald Horne, *Black & Red: W. E. B. Du Bois and the Afro-American Response to the Cold War, 1944–1963* [Albany: State University of New York Press], 1986).

182. Keith Griffler, "The Black Radical Intellectual and the Black Worker: The Emergence of a Program for Black Labor, 1918–1938," Ph.D. dissertation, Ohio State University, 1993; cf. Robert C. Weaver, *Negro Labor: A National Problem* (New York: Harcourt, Brace, 1946).

183. Harris and Davis, eds., *Afro-American Writers, 1940–1955;* Mark Naison, "Richard Wright and the Communist Party," *Radical America,* 13 (1979): 60–63; Martin Kilson, "Politics and Identity among Black Intellectuals," *Dissent,* 28 (1981): 339–349;

Chester Himes, *If He Hollers Let Him Go* (Garden City, N.Y.: Doubleday, Doran, 1945); *Lonely Crusade* (New York: Alfred A. Knopf, 1947); Sam Gon Kim, "Black Americans' Commitment to Communism: A Case Study Based on Fiction and Autobiographies by Black Americans," Ph.D. dissertation, University of Kansas, 1986; Richard Wright, *Native Son and How "Bigger" Was Born*, introduction by Arnold Rampersad (New York: HarperPerennial, 1993), and *Uncle Tom's Children*, introduction by Richard Yarborough (New York: HarperPerennial, 1938; 1993).

184. Memo, SAC, New York, E.E. Conroy, to the director, FBI, 5/26/44, RE: NEGRO PLAN OF REVOLUTION, INTERNAL SECURITY-C, Bureau File 100-HQ-135-34-306; memo, Tom C. Clark, assistant attorney general, Washington, D.C., to the director, 6/29/44, INTERNAL SECURITY; SEDITION, Bureau File 100-HQ-135-34-352; memo, J. Edgar Hoover, FBI, to SAC, New York, 7/10/44, Bureau File 100-HQ-135-34-352. For the first interview granted by Clark to a black newspaper, see A.M. Wendell Malliet, "Tom Clark, New Attorney General, Has Good Record with Negro," *New York Amsterdam News*, June 23, 1945.

185. Ellison, *Invisible Man*, xiii; cf. Jerry Gafio Watts, *Heroism and the Black Intellectual: Ralph Ellison, Politics, and Afro-American Intellectual Life* (Chapel Hill: University of North Carolina Press, 1994) and Eric J. Sundquist, ed., *Cultural Contexts for Ralph Ellison's* Invisible Man (Boston: Bedford Books, 1995).

186. John Oliver Killens, *And Then We Heard the Thunder* (New York: Alfred A. Knopf, 1963), quoted in Silberman, *Crisis in Black and White*, 61.

187. Thadious M. Davis and Trudier Harris, *Dictionary of Literary Biography, 33: Afro-American Fiction Writers After 1955* (Detroit: Gale Research, 1984), 146.

188. Clark and Barker, "The Zoot Effect in Personality," 144.

189. *The Autobiography of Malcolm X*, 57. For an insightful discussion of the zoot phenomenon, see Robin D. G. Kelley, "The Riddle of the Zoot: Malcolm Little and Black Cultural Politics During World War II," in Joe Wood, ed., *Malcolm X: In Our Own Image* (New York: St. Martin's Press, 1992), 155–182; cf. also Clark and Barker, "The Zoot Effect in Personality," 143–148; Steve Chibnall, "Whistle and Zoot: The Changing Meaning of a Suit of Clothes," *History Workshop Journal*, 20 (Autumn 1985): 56–81; Stuart Cosgrove, "The Zoot-Suit and Style Warfare," *History Workshop Journal*, 18 (Autumn 1984): 77–91; and R. L. Fregoso, "The Representation of Cultural-Identity in Zoot Suit," *Theory and Society*, 22 (October 1993): 659–74.

190. *The Autobiography of Malcolm X*, 53.

191. "Mexican Youth Gangs ('Zoot Suiters')," *Survey of Racial Conditions in the United States*, 376–82; cf. Mauricio Mazon, *The Zoot-Suit Riots: The Psychology of Symbolic Annihilation* (Austin: University of Texas Press, 1984); Chester Himes, "Zoot Riots Are Race Riots," *Crisis*, 50 (July 1943): 200–201, 222.

192. Cf. Robin D. G. Kelley, *Hammer and Hoe: Alabama Communists during the Great Depression* (Chapel Hill: University of North Carolina Press, 1990); Earl Lewis, *In Their Own Interests: Race, Class, and Power in Twentieth-Century Norfolk, Virginia* (Berkeley: University of California Press, 1991); Neil R. McMillen, *Dark Journey: Black Mississippians in the Age of Jim Crow* (Urbana: University of Illinois Press, 1990); Joe William Trotter, Jr., *Coal, Class, and Color: Blacks in Southern West Virginia, 1915–1932* (Urbana: University of Illinois Press, 1990); Eric Arnesen, "The African-American Working Class in the Jim Crow Era," *International Labor and Working-Class History*, 41 (Spring 1992): 58–75.

193. Marshall F. Stevenson, Jr., "Challenging the Roadblocks to Equality: Race Relations and Civil Rights in the CIO, 1935–1955," Center for Labor Research Working Paper, Ohio State University, 1992; see also the special thematic issue, "Race and the CIO," *International Labor and Working-Class History,* 44 (Fall 1993): 1–63.

194. *Survey of Racial Conditions in the United States,* 269.

195. Stevenson, "Challenging the Roadblocks to Equality," 4.

196. *Survey of Racial Conditions in the United States,* 256.

197. Ibid., 13, 108; cf. Jesse Thomas Moore, Jr., *A Search for Equality,* 81; Dona Cooper Hamilton, "The National Urban League during the Depression, 1930–1939: The Quest for Jobs for Black Workers," Ph.D. dissertation, Columbia University, 1982.

198. *Survey of Racial Conditions in the United States,* ibid., 84.

199. Ibid., 391.

200. Ibid., 578.

201. Ibid., 69. Meier and Rudwick conclude that "the important job advances that blacks made in the auto industry during World War II were the product of a complicated interaction involving not only blacks and union leaders but the crucial intervention of the federal bureaucracies as well" (ix). Stevenson asserts that this book is "still the single best history of black participation in a single CIO union" ("Challenging the Roadblocks to Equality," 49, n. 3). For an appraisal critical of Meier and Rudwick's book, see Martin Glaberman, "Black Workers in the Labor Movement," *New Politics,* 1 (Winter 1988): 115–23.

202. *Survey of Racial Conditions in the United States,* ibid., 134.

203. *Daily Worker,* November 20, 1949.

204. Cf. Donald T. Critchlow, "Communist Unions and Racism: A Comparative Study of the Response of the United Electrical Workers and the National Maritime Union to the Black Question During World War Two," *Labor History,* 17 (Spring 1976): 237–44; August Meier and Elliott Rudwick, "Communist Unions and the Black Community: The Case of the Transport Workers Union, 1934–1944," *Labor History,* 23 (Spring 1982): 165–97; Michael Goldfield, "Race and the CIO: The Possibilities for Racial Egalitarianism During the 1930s and 1940s," *International Labor and Working-Class History,* 44 (Fall 1993): 1–32.

205. White, *How Far the Promised Land?*, 221.

206. Isserman, *Which Side Were You On?*, 141–43. Irving Howe and Lewis Coser maintain that "the CP believed the struggle for Negro rights should be suspended entirely during the war" (*The American Communist Party: A Critical History 1919–1957* [Boston: Beacon Press, 1957], 416). Sumner Rosen criticizes the Communist Party for "abandoning its commitment to Negro equality" during World War II. "The CIO, in contrast," he maintains, "continued its pressure to improve the economic status of Negro workers . . . When the Communists downgraded the issue of Negro rights, the first meaningful differences between the two groups began to become clear" (Sumner Rosen, "The CIO Era, 1935–55," in Julius Jacobson, ed., *The Negro and the American Labor Movement* [Garden City, NY: Anchor/Doubleday, 1968], 197).

207. Memo, P. E. Foxworth, SAC, New York, to the director, 1/12/43, FOREIGN-INSPIRED AGITATION AMONG AMERICAN NEGROES IN NEW YORK FIELD DIVISION; INTERNAL SECURITY, Bureau File 100-HQ-135-34-79. In July 1945, when assaults upon the leadership of Communist Party leader Earl Browder caused Communist spokesmen to

criticize the party's wartime performance, Benjamin J. Davis, Jr., the black councilman in Harlem, attacked Browder for allegedly weakening the policy of the party in combating racial discrimination ("Cause for Examination of Negro Work," *Daily Worker*, July 22, 1945; Gerald Horne, *Black Liberation/Red Scare: Ben Davis and the Communist Party* [Newark: University of Delaware Press, 1994], 137–45, passim). Browder was stripped of party leadership in July 1945 by a 93–0 vote and a few months later, in February 1946, was expelled from the reconstituted Communist Party. The reconversion of the Communist Party following the repudiation of Browder's leadership is described in Record, *The Negro and the Communist Party*, 226–35; Isserman, *Which Side Were You On?*, 216–32; Edward Johanningsmeier, *Forging American Communism: The Life of William Z. Foster* (Princeton: Princeton University Press, 1994), 293–313; Michele Fraser Ottanelli, " 'What the Hell Is These Reds Anyways?' The Americanization of the Communist Party of the United States, 1930–1945," Ph.D. dissertation, Syracuse University, 1987; and Roger Elliot Rosenberg, "Guardian of the Fortress: A Biography of Earl Russell Browder, U.S. Communist Party General-Secretary from 1930–1944," Ph.D. dissertation, University of California, Santa Barbara, 1982. Communist Party advocacy of black rights during 1942–43 is described in FBI confidential monograph, *The Communist Party and the Negro* [1919–1952], 2/20/53, and *The Communist Party and the Negro, 1953–1956*, 10/23/56, SAC Letter, no. 56–55.

208. Morris Childs, one of the two brothers who allegedly implicated Martin Luther King, Jr. as the subject of Communist Party influence, shows up in the 1943 FBI report in his position as chairman of the Communist Party's District 8 (Chicago). Childs reportedly "extended money for the down payment of the Coliseum rental" for the Chicago unit of the March on Washington Movement, as part of the party's design to influence and gain leadership of the movement (515). Childs' recruitment as a key informant for the FBI code-named "Solo" forms the cornerstone of David J. Garrow's exposé of the FBI's surveillance of King (*The FBI and Martin Luther King, Jr.: From "Solo" to Memphis* [New York: W. W. Norton, 1981], 35–40, 86, 239–40, n. 47). Garrow maintains that " 'Solo' was the best 'confidential' source the FBI has ever had" (86).

209. "How 'Bigger' Was Born," in Richard Wright, *Early Works* (New York: Library of America, 1991), 867.

210. Kenneth Kinnamon and Michel Fabre, eds., *Conversations with Richard Wright* (Jackson: University Press of Mississippi, 1993), p.75. Wright drew attention to the Harlem's wartime riot: "In August 1943, a racial outbreak swept that unhappy ghetto. Why? They had jobs, but they did not have respect, justice, freedom of living space. They had jobs, but their sons and daughters were being kicked and hounded in the Army and the Navy and they resented it" (74–75).

211. Athan G. Theoharis, "Dissent and the State: Unleashing the FBI, 1917–1985," 43–44, in *History Teacher*, 24 (November 1990): 41–52; "The FBI and Dissent in the United States," 86–110, in C. E. S. Franks, ed., *Dissent and the State* (Toronto: Oxford University Press, 1989).

212. Letter, J. Edgar Hoover, FBI, to SAC, New York, INTERNAL SECURITY, 8/27/42, Bureau file 100-HQ-135-34; memo, J. K. Mumford to Ladd, RE: AGITATION AMONG NEGROES IN NEW YORK FIELD DIVISION, 9/11/42, Bureau File 100-135-34-37.

213. Powers, *G-Men*, 262, 264.

214. Ibid., 265.

215. Ibid., 255.

216. Memo, J. Edgar Hoover, FBI, to the attorney general, 9/22/47, RACIAL MATTERS, Bureau File 100-HQ-135–34–564; memo, Hoover to Assistant Attorney General William F. Tompkins, 7/20/56, RACIAL SITUATION INFORMATION CONCERNING (INTERNAL SECURITY), Bureau File 100-HQ-135-34-596; airtel, SAC, New York, to the director, 1/24/57, "Racial Situation, N. Y.," Bureau File 100-128214; teletype, SAC, New York, to the director, 12/6/58, BOMBINGS AND ATTEMPTED BOMBINGS: RACIAL MATTERS, Bureau File 100-HQ-135-34-614.

217. *Intelligence Activities and the Rights of Americans. Final Report*, Book II, 71–72; *Supplementary Detailed Staff Reports on Intelligence Activities and the Rights of Americans. Final Report,* Book III, 475–83; *Hearings. Federal Bureau of Investigation,* 6, 609; O'Reilly, *"Racial Matters,"* 128, 140; and *Black Americans*, 18. For a useful table tracing the evolution of the various post-World War II FBI investigations, see William W. Keller, *The Liberals and J. Edgar Hoover: Rise and Fall of a Domestic Intelligence State* (Princeton: Princeton University Press, 1989), 166–74.

218. *Supplementary Detailed Staff Reports on Intelligence Activities and the Rights of Americans. Final Report,* Book III, "The Development of FBI Domestic Intelligence Operations," 373–558; O'Reilly, *"Racial Matters,"* 261–324; Keller, *The Liberals and J. Edgar Hoover*, 167, 180–84. During the 1960s the FBI also carried out special intelligence assignments for the President, conducting a special investigation of "Urban Ghetto Riots" for President Johnson in 1964 and providing coverage of the black demonstrations during the Democratic National Convention the same year (Keller, 175).

SECTION 1

Survey of Racial Conditions in the United States

(SECRET)

Federal Bureau of Investigation
United States Department of Justice
J. Edgar Hoover, Director

I

INTRODUCTION

August 15, 1942

For a period in excess of two years the Federal Bureau of Investigation has received reports and allegations of forces with foreign influence and with anti-American ideology working among the Negro people of this country as well as exploiting them. Based thereon, inquiries and investigations have been undertaken to determine why particular Negroes or groups of Negroes or Negro organizations have evidenced sentiments for other "dark races" (mainly Japanese) or by what forces they were influenced to adopt in certain instances un-American ideologies. Observations and inquiries have been made into the maneuverings on the part of subversive groups to exploit members of the Negro race in this country.

From the data which have been developed through the investigative jurisdiction of the Federal Bureau of Investigation, as well as from information voluntarily supplied by various sources, this survey has been prepared. It portrays the existing picture in this matter as based upon these data and this information, broken down hereinafter according to the areas enveloped by the fifty-six Field Divisions of this Bureau. To supplement this section, there has been prepared a compilation of information in the form of an appendix which forms the second section. The appendix deals with organizational activity and is meant to elaborate on references to various organizations and groups throughout the body of this survey.

It is pointed out that the myriad factors to be considered in racial conditions in this country, including, broadly, economic, political and social aspects, have presented themselves in practically all of the areas included in this survey. They necessarily have had to be considered inasmuch as these factors have been outlined and described by sources of information in their opinions or conclusions based upon their reasoning as to the causes of racial unrest or dissatisfaction. It might be noted these aspects have also been referred to by various sources in an attempt to controvert some of the allegations that there is un-American–inspired agitation among colored people in certain areas.

The information contained in the ensuing pages of this study does not, nor is it meant to, give rise to an inference that Negroes as a whole or the Negro people in a particular area are subversive or are influenced by anti-American forces. At the same time, it must be pointed out that a number of Negroes and Negro groups have been the subjects of concentrated investigation made on the basis that they have reportedly acted or have exhibited sentiments in a manner inimical to the Nation's war effort.

It has been stated previously that reports and allegations have been received by the Federal Bureau of Investigation concerning the reasons for racial conditions as they exist in certain areas. They have been numerous and have been augmented by innumerable complaints received from the public in a majority of the Field Divisions of this

Bureau. The complaints have related to unrest, discontent and disaffection among members of the Negro race. They have included allegations of statements or utterances by members of the colored race which on the surface appear to be definitely in opposition to the war effort. At the same time, there have been instances of subversive activities alleged to exist among certain Negroes.

Upon receipt of such complaints and allegations, investigations and inquiries were promptly instituted. The results thereof, along with additional information reported to the Federal Bureau of Investigation, are set out immediately hereinafter in the form of digests, grouped in geographical areas of the United States. Preceding each geographical area is an introduction summarizing the important factors and forces considered responsible for racial unrest and discontent in the area involved. Following the digests is set forth the conclusion. Thereafter, forming Section Two of this survey, is the appendix which includes information concerning organizational activity among the Negroes of this country.

II

NORTHERN SECTION OF THE UNITED STATES

There are set forth in the following pages that data received by those Field Divisions of the Federal Bureau of Investigation which are grouped alphabetically in this section devoted to the industrial North. Briefly, it includes those areas East of the Mississippi River, beginning with Milwaukee, Wisconsin, in the North and ending in Springfield, Illinois, at the Southwestern border and stretching East along the Ohio River to include at the Southeastern portion the cities of Washington, D.C., and Baltimore, Maryland.

To summarize, the information reflects there are myriad factors to be considered in the racial situation in this area. In industrial centers and particularly in the larger cities there has been a tremendous increase in immigrants coming from other States, especially the South and rural areas. This migration has included both white and Negro people. As a result, increased housing shortages, crowded transportation facilities and an overcrowding of amusement and recreational facilities have become decidedly more acute. This, coupled with the increased tempo of living since the country's national defense effort was begun, has added to the complexity of conditions. There has also been an increase in returns from employment as well as added chances for employment. Persons never before accustomed to the increased tempo and complex nature of living have experienced them, perhaps for the first time.

A new militancy or aggressiveness has been reported to be existent among the Negro population throughout this particular section of the country. Old boundaries are crossed by the lifting of many restrictions to which these people have heretofore been subjected in other sections.

One of the primary results of all this has been a demand by Negroes, both individually and collectively, for increased and better employment, the erasure of alleged discrimination in industry, better housing and more and diversified recreation. Added with these are those political and economic demands which are made for the Negro population not only in this section but in other sections of the country, particularly the South, where there naturally exist long-established customs, habits and methods not pertinent to the North. The abolition of the poll tax, the breaking down of "Jim Crow" laws and the cry for doing away with alleged discrimination in the Armed Forces have been tossed into the way of living of these Negroes. Yet, in many instances they do not appear to be directly or even remotely affected; however, the adoption of these demands by respective Negro groups and organizations in this Northern section establishes the idea of the new militancy or aggressiveness.

Numerous spontaneous riots, clashes and fights involving the two races have occurred in varying degrees. No plan for organized effort in these has been reported or brought to light, yet their occurrence reflects a tenseness heretofore not prevalent. Increase in crime and juvenile delinquency has been apparent.

It will be noted from the ensuing pages there are numerous forces, social, political and economic in origin, which break into the picture of racial conditions and relations in this section of the country. Of subversive forces, the most outstanding is the Communist Party, which, it will be noted, is active in every Field Division, influencing the Negro population. This, of course, includes various arms of the Party such as groups and organizations it influences or controls.

There are also to be considered the number of cults, groups and organizations which are reported in many instances to have decidedly anti-white sympathies. Usually their size is small; however, the influence which they have cannot be estimated by the amount of membership in view of the wide possibilities of individual members spreading their sentiments. While there has been no apparent connection between numerous reports of expressions or activities anti-white in character on the part of individual Negroes, their existence and prevalency should be considered in relation to the anti-white groups.

There are in varying degrees of militancy a number of Negro organizations which can be classified as unaffiliated or independent in nature. These groups, while with different leadership and in many instances entirely different membership, have, almost as a whole, championed the advancement of the Negro race in an aggressive manner.

An important factor to be considered in this section of the country is the Negro press and the effect it has, as well as the make-up and character of its content.

There will be noted hereinafter, especially in the information appearing in the digests concerning industrial Northern cities, several instances of walkouts and refusals to work with Negroes on the part of white people. An example of this is evidence[d] in the Packard Motor Car Company strike in the early part of June 1943 when approximately 25,000 white workers went out on an unauthorized strike in protest of the upgrading of Negro workers in one of the departments in the plant. Refusals to work, however, have not been solely confined to members of the white race. It will be noted that there are several instances appearing hereinafter reflecting protest demonstrations by Negro workers in condemnation of alleged failure on the part of various industries to place them in skilled or better-paying jobs. It is believed that consideration should be given to both white and Negro activity along these lines, especially inasmuch as such activity and the attitude it infers have a definite bearing on race relationship and racial conditions in this country.

Having a definite bearing in the field of labor, as far as they affect race relationship, are the varying policies of different unions and locals thereof in the acceptance of Negroes into their ranks in an unqualified manner. This has been said to lead to consternation and confusion in the minds of Negroes.

Among the social and economic factors which are apparent are the inadequate housing and recreational facilities, alleged instances of discrimination against Negroes in employment and in other phases of everyday life, and the reported shortage of educational facilities.

Reports have been received in a number of areas in this section that a degree of unrest and dissatisfaction among the Negro people in this portion of the United States possibly results from what is described as a lack of good Negro leadership. There is an apparent lack of coordination and many times a lack of cooperation among this leadership. This situation has been pointed to by both Negro and white sources of information as a matter that should be remedied. These sources have, on several occasions, expressed their opinion that the present-day Negro leadership is selfish, chauvinistic and centered in its own self-advancement.

In examining the situation in this area, it is believed significant to note that preventive or alleviating measures for bettering racial conditions and race relationship are said to be generally absent. There have been, however, reports of recent attempts on the part of local governmental authorities establishing racial commissions and making attempts to establish better race relationship.

Immediately following are digests of information received by the Field Divisions of the Federal Bureau of Investigation which are to be considered in connection with this section of the country. [*100-135-191*]

Albany Field Division

It was reported during the latter part of July, 1942, that no foreign inspired agitation existed among the American negroes in the territory covered by the Albany Field Division. The approximate negro population in Albany, New York is reported to be 3,000. In Schenectady, New York, the negro population is reported to be 1,100 and in Syracuse, New York, 2,082.

Throughout the entire Albany area alleged discrimination with regard to employment and housing conditions is said to be the main cause for discontent among the Negroes. Furthermore, there has been an influx of Negro families in this area which is said to be a possible source of trouble. Large increases are expected in the population of Negroes in this area in view of the fact national defense industries are employing skilled Negro employees.

The Albany Inter-racial Council, Inc., and the Booker T. Washington Community Center are reportedly the most active organizations. It is stated these organizations are interested primarily in the welfare of the colored people. It is reported the Albany Inter-racial Council, Inc., operates the Booker T. Washington Community Center.

In the area of Syracuse, New York, there have been rumors to the effect that the negro soldier is being discriminated against in the South. These rumors seem to have resulted from newspaper stories appearing in the Afro-American, the Pittsburgh Courier and the Chicago Defender. It is reported there also have been rumors concerning discrimination against negro persons relative to rental of housing facilities and eating places which appear to be based on a local social problem. The negro housing problem in the vicinity of Syracuse appears to be serious as large increases are expected among the negroes as the result of employment by national defense plants of skilled negro employees.

It is reported that a group of alleged Communists held a meeting at Syracuse, New York, on August 9, 1942, and laid emphasis on "Jim Crowism" in the United States Army.

In the vicinity of Utica, New York, where it is said there are some eight hundred

Negroes residing, unemployment and housing conditions are said to be the most prevalent causes for discontent and unrest. Reports have been received to the effect that there is unrest among the Negroes in this area although no indications have been reported reflecting un-American or un-patriotic sentiments. Many of the Negroes are said to be employed on bean farms in neighboring communities.

Sources of information who have been interviewed in this city and in its vicinity state that although the bean farms help the unemployment situation to some extent that is still one of the main factors in the discontent among the Negroes there. No indications of Communist Party activity or activity of pro-Axis organizations have been reported.

In the areas including the cities of Albany, Syracuse, Rochester and Utica, such Negro newspapers as the Chicago Defender, the Pittsburgh Courier and the Afro-American are circulated and contain many statements relative to the mistreatment of the Negroes in the Armed Forces, defense industries and in other walks of civilian life. It is said that these newspapers tend to further the unrest or dissatisfaction which is caused by economic, social or political matters. One local Negro newspaper is published here, the Progressive Herald, published in Syracuse, New York. This newspaper is said to be a staunch supporter of the Republican Party and has never contained writings or articles of a radical nature. [*100-135-2-3*]

During the latter part of October, 1942, Ben Davis, Jr., negro Communist and candidate during the 1942 elections for congressman at large on the Communist Party ticket in New York State, made a speech in Syracuse, New York, seeking votes there. During his visit, he is reported as having obtained the help of the mayor of that city to obtain lodging at a hotel, restricted for white people. He also reportedly obtained the support of a number of the local negro citizens who formed the Non-Partisan Committee for Ben Davis. [*100-135-2*]

An isolated complaint was received in January, 1943 that a colored maid of a white family in Albany made the statement, "If the Japs win maybe the colored people will have a better chance in this country." The employer was astonished at this remark and could recall no similar statements made by the maid. The inquiries conducted in this regard fail to reflect that the maid making these statements had any connections with any subversive or un-American group or organization, on the contrary it was ascertained she belonged to two well established negro social organizations. This maid who made the statement expressed her ignorance of the Japanese Race being colored and informed she had never seen a member of the Japanese Race and expressed having difficulty understanding how a person could be a member of the colored race without looking like a Negro.

This incident has been cited as an example of a Negro, according to the employer, repeating a statement she had heard someone else make. [*100-135-2-6*]

Baltimore Field Division

Numerous complaints have been received that the American Negroes favor a Japanese victory in the present war. Investigations have been made concerning these complaints to ascertain if the complaints were foreign-inspired, but the investigations were made with negative results.

An outside source advises that the pro-Japanese propaganda among the colored people does not originate from Japanese sources but starts within the colored people themselves.

The Baltimore edition of the colored newspaper "Afro-American" tends to agitate racial feelings by stressing race discriminations within and outside the Armed Forces.

Investigation has revealed that the Japanese and German propaganda among the Negroes in the vicinity of Baltimore, Maryland, affects only the "fanatical fringe" of the colored population.

It has been reported with regard to the State of Maryland, especially in and around Bethesda, Maryland, allegations have been made to the effect that large groups of Negroes have been purchasing knives and other dangerous weapons. Sources of information interviewed with regard to this advised that there has been no out of the ordinary purchasing of such items by Negroes although one store is alleged to have had approximately one hundred Negro men purchase knives from it. This information was subsequently looked into and it was found that a contingent of Negro soldiers had stopped at a hardware store and that some twelve to eighteen of the individuals bought hunting knives there.

The main offices of the "Afro-American," a Negro newspaper with national circulation, are in Baltimore, Maryland. It has constantly published articles of a militant nature demanding extended rights and privileges for Negroes and, in some instances, carried on active campaigns with regard to local Negro matters.

Allegations of the existence of "Eleanor Clubs" among Negro domestics in this area have been reported; yet, inquiries based on the allegations that the "Eleanor Clubs" are foreign-inspired, have failed to reflect anything pointing to their actual existence.

It has been reported that in the Snow Hill, Maryland, area, there are farms on which reportedly a large number of Negroes work in growing fruits and vegetables for nearby canning plants. It is said that recently these Negroes have become very independent and unsatisfactory as workers, although, they are earning more than ever before. Some of the Negroes, allegedly, have been heard to make such remarks as "when the Japs come over they won't bother us; they are only after the white people," and "after the war, the whites will be working for the colored people." No indications, however, have been reported to the effect that any foreign forces are at work inspiring such sentiments.

In such areas as Salisbury, Pocomoke City, and in Princess Anne, Maryland, isolated reports have been received alleging that individual Negroes have made anti-American statements which allegedly contained sympathy for the Axis powers. Inquiries and investigation relative to these allegations failed to reflect any organized un-Americanism among the Negroes in the areas mentioned.

It was reported that in the City of Baltimore there has been a Moorish Movement for at least eighteen or nineteen years. It was said that there are separate groups in the Movement. One of the groups, which is said to exist in the vicinity of Freemont Avenue and Lead Street in Baltimore, has been described as being composed of a "low type" of individual. Recently a selective service board in the area has come in contact with several members of one of the groups of the Movement, and they have been described as being highly incensed when they are labeled as Negroes, feeling rather that they are "Moors." It should be stated that in connection with these groups a confidential source of information has advised that during his long residence in the City of Baltimore and because of its popularity among Negro inhabitants, he could with reason say that no Japanese inspired activity among the Negroes in Baltimore has come to his attention. He went on to say, however, that the only agitation presently influencing the Negroes of that city is that of the Communist Party and its various fronts.

The Communist Party in this area, mainly through Dr. Albert Blumberg, his wife Dorothy Blumberg, Selma and Sinch O'Har, Young Communist League leaders, have been agitating considerably among Negroes, endeavoring to obtain them jobs with the Telephone Company in Baltimore and with the Baltimore Transit Company. In this activity, reports indicate the Party has worked in cooperation with certain writers of the Baltimore "Afro-American." In this connection the following information reported concerning a state meeting, sponsored by the Communist Party on September 2, 1942, is believed to be significant:

The meeting was held on the corner of Arlington and Mosher Streets, and the main speaker was William C. Taylor, then Chairman of the Baltimore, Maryland Communist Party, who began by stating that the attention of the colored people should be focused on the impending political election. He stated that the people such as Governor Dickson of Alabama and Governor Talmadge of Georgia ought to be defeated. He continued, saying that individuals who believed in equal opportunities for all and who fight for the Negroes' freedom ought to be elected. He pointed out that Negroes ought not to sell their votes to crusader white politicians for $2.00 or a glass of beer, or according to Talmadge, Negroes should continue to accept the $2.00 or a glass of beer but ought to cast his vote for the Negro candidate. He warned the Negroes present not to listen to the members of their own race who were merely tools in the hands of white politicians, who advocated that Negroes seek no change in their conditions and said that Negroes controlled by white politicians are "Uncle Toms."

On April 16, 1943, a mass meeting was sponsored by the Total War Employment Committee at the Enon Baptist Church in Baltimore. There were approximately 17,000 people present, seven or eight being white. The principal speaker at this meeting was Reverend Adam Clayton Powell, Jr., of New York City, a Negro councilman and preacher there. Powell labeled Baltimore as the worst city in America for discrimination and race hatred. He said Negroes everywhere were showing dissatisfaction but that with the proper organization and direction Negroes should be able to sway certain important elections. He praised the Total Employment Committee for its connections with the Chesapeake and Potomac Power Company and the Baltimore Transit Company of that city.

Recently the informants have advised that the Communist Party is actively engaged in attempting to organize Negro workers at the Bethlehem Shipyards.

A source of information who is in a position to observe activities among Negroes in the Baltimore area, especially has expressed the opinion that potential racial trouble is the most outstanding item in the present picture of the geographic area which includes Baltimore. He said the consensus of opinion of local reliable contacts continue in the belief that Southern Negroes will not plan any violence, but being emotionally controlled, they may be led into violence and disorder by a "spark" that ignites the resentment kept smouldering in them by the constant inflammatory propaganda of the Negro press, the Communist leaders and other outside influence being brought to bear on them.

On July 28, 1943 at 7:00 A.M. a strike occurred at the Bethlehem Steel Shipyards, Sparrows Point, Maryland. Involved in this strike were eight hundred Negroes, workers of the shipyards. It is stated that these workers ceased work in protest of the company's excluding Negroes from the company-conducted riveting school. The actual outbreak developed when, on July 26, 1943, colored employees were allowed to enter the school. The white members of the school immediately raised the issue and to appease them, it is stated, the management excluded the Negroes, whereupon the eight hundred Negroes ceased work.

It appears that constant efforts at conciliation on the part of the management resulted in the majority of the strikers returning to work on July 29, and on that day approximately two hundred colored workers were discharged for refusal to resume work. It is also reported that the white workers refused to work on any job with colored workers and on July 29 threatened to drive them from the yards. The management, to avert violence, ordered all employees out of the yards until Monday, August 2, 1943. The total number of workers involved is stated to be five thousand white and fifteen hundred colored.

As of August 3, 1943 the situation had quieted, and practically all of the workers reported for work, returning to their jobs without any incidents occurring. At that time, however, a small faction of the workers did fail to report for work, held meetings attended by approximately forty men and protested the agreement with the workers to return to their jobs. The meetings are said to have lacked organization and leadership. Seven men were suspended from their work and subsequently discharged for their agitational efforts during the trouble. Police agencies which had been stationed at the yard withdrew during the afternoon of August 3, 1943. The United States Army, however, retained a force at Logan Field, which is near the yard, although it did not station men on the shipyard's property.

It is reported that the shipyard is under contract with the United States Maritime Commission and ninety per cent of its output is for that agency. No portion of the plant is government owned, although a small percentage of the facilities is being rented from the United States Maritime Commission. The work stoppage resulted in complete cessation of production from Friday morning, July 30, 1943, through Saturday, July 31, 1943.

The Bethlehem Steel Shipyards had a contract with the Industrial Union Marine and Shipbuilding Workers of America, CIO, Local No. 33. The Union was represented by Phillip Van Gelder, National Secretary and Treasurer; Edward Denhard, Executive Secretary; and Louis Dane, President of Local No. 33. Management representatives advised that employees had for all practical purposes repudiated the Union and advised that this was not a Union affair and that they would not be influenced by the Union. Reportedly, members of the United States Conciliation Service, War Production Board, President's Committee on Fair Employment and other organizations conferred with management and Union officials; however, all efforts at conciliation to date have failed.

According to the information received, the principal agitator at the shipyards was John Albert Jacobs, who is colored and twenty-seven years of age. He was born in Georgia and has been in the company employ since 1937. William R. Sandlin and George E. Boulding, both colored, were also reportedly active agitators. Jacobs was described as an eloquent mob leader. It was stated that the attitude of the white workers at that time was absolute refusal to return to jobs with colored workers and colored workers were demanding equal opportunity with whites in all respects.

During several weeks prior to that time rumors were received which indicated a state of extreme tension between the white and colored residents of Baltimore, Maryland, and it was reported that any serious incidents occurring at the proper time to engage the attention of large numbers of white and colored persons might then have precipitated a serious race riot in Baltimore. This, it was stated, was particularly true in view of the fact that this city has a large, unassimilated, migratory white and Negro population.

On Saturday, July 10, 1943, the interracial friction at the Bethlehem Fairfield Shipyards resulted in a fight among several white and Negro employees in the plant cafeteria. This fight resulted in several individuals, white and black, being arrested and fined by the local police. Reportedly, the colored workers initiated the fight due to their insistence that they should be allowed equal rights. Following the fight, plant police were holding four colored workers for the local police, and it is reported that four shop stewards caused considerable difficulty by insisting that the plant police give them a complete report of the incident. These shop stewards were white employees.

One of the white employees involved in this affair stated that a race riot in Baltimore, Maryland was imminent. He advised that in almost every section of the city there was talk among the whites of a coming riot and that there were four to five fights during each shift between white and colored workers at the Bethlehem Fairfield Shipyards. He also stated that the Negroes were being urged to "start something" by members of the Communist Party at the yard. He also advised that he knew the inside workings of the Communist Party inasmuch as he had formerly been a Communist. According to this informant, Milton Moskowitz, one of the four shop stewards referred to herein, was one of the principal agitators in the yard who was making an effort to create racial hatred and prejudice. Moskowitz along with Bernie Silezson and Martin Garfinkel, two other reported agitators in the yard, were, reportedly, members of the Communist Party and active in labor affairs of Local Union No. 43 of the Industrial Union Marine and Shipbuilding Workers of America, CIO.

The following elements were reportedly believed to be contributing factors to the racial tension existing in the Baltimore area:

1. Afro-American Negro newspaper publishes editions which constantly agitate the colored population by means of inflammatory articles.
2. The CIO labor newspapers, which stress racial, job and social equality.
3. Communist agitation over a period of months.
   a. Preaches doctrines of racial equality.
   b. Fosters interracial groups and dances.
   c. Agitates for equal rights and job opportunities.
   d. Urges Negroes to support CIO labor candidates to prevent Negro segregation and inequality in job opportunities.
   e. Street meetings in Negro districts for recruiting of members.
4. Scheduled labor union elections at Glenn L. Martin and Bethlehem Fairfield.
   a. CIO group in control at Bethlehem believed to be Communist dominated and pro-Negro.
   b. Anti-Communist group in Fairfield is attempting to oust Communists from control.
   c. Electioneering at Glenn L. Martin's by independent union features anti-Negro bias.
5. Over-crowded housing conditions together with the inability to settle the housing project dispute.
6. Over-crowded transportation facilities and street car incidents.
7. Present picketing of the Chesapeake and Potomac Telephone Company by Negroes because of their refusal to hire Negro operators.
   a. Sponsored by the Total War Employment Commission (Communist dominated).
   b. Young Communist League activity in utilities dispute.
8. Existing feeling and tension in Baltimore resulting from the recent Detroit and Beaumont race riots.
   a. Informant advises Negroes expect and wait for a riot in Baltimore.
9. National Association for Advancement of Colored People continues to agitate against Jim Crow segregation, and for equal rights.
10. Baltimore Urban League (colored) urges the elimination of racial barriers; expanding of job opportunities. Cooperates with Local CIO Union No. 43 IUMSWA, Communist dominated.
11. Miscellaneous. On July 3, 1943, Negro alleged to have roughly handled white woman in Bethlehem Fairfield Shipyards.

    Unconfirmed rumors of a race riot in Baltimore scheduled for July 4, 1943.

    July 4, 1943, a Negro's hand was cut by a bayonet of a Coast Guardsman during an incident at the Bethlehem Fairfield Shipyards.

12. Unconfirmed rumor that local Negroes planned action July 8, 1943 designed to remove segregation barriers by attempting to gain admittance to restaurants, theaters and other facilities restricted to whites.

    Collection of numerous knives, clubs and some guns taken from the workers at the Bethlehem Fairfield Yards during the past weeks.

    A fight between approximately thirty whites and Negroes several weeks ago in section of Baltimore where white and colored neighborhoods meet.

Boston Field Division

A survey in this area fails to show information reflecting any pro-Axis inspired agitation among the Negroes. In the State of Massachusetts there are said to be approximately 55,000 Negroes, of whom 47,000 are native born, while 8,000 are foreign born.

Reported to be active in this area are branches of the National Association for the Advancement of Colored People and the National Negro Congress, a Communist front organization. The causes being furthered by both of these organizations are the establishment of separate units for colored and white soldiers in the Army and sailors in the Navy and agitation by these groups for increased employment of Negroes in defense industries and Governmental agencies.

At the present time no indications have been received evidencing influence of the Communist Party in these particular policies. Rather they are said to be the result of the decisions of the leaders of these groups, decided independently of Communist influence. It is noted, however, that the National Negro Congress activity forms potential grounds for agitation for the Communist Party.

A prominent Negro source of information who is said to be well known in the Boston area has been contacted for information in his possession indicating possible pro-German or pro-Japanese activity among the Negroes. This source of information has advised that he knows of no attempts to agitate among members of his race by members of pro-Axis organizations or individuals favoring ultimate pro-Axis domination of the United States.

With regard to Communist activity among the Negro population in the Boston area, the source of information has advised that it is possible Communists may infiltrate legitimate Negro organizations existing in this area inasmuch as these organizations are composed of people from many walks of life. The informant advised, however, that the more important Negro organizations in this area have for their purpose propagandizing for better conditions for Negroes.

Two Negro newspapers are published in this area, namely, "The Boston Chronicle" and "The Boston Guardian." No information as yet has been received reflecting articles or editorials printed in these newspapers which are of an un-American tenor.

A prominent Negro **publisher** in the Boston area has advised that for the past ten years he has observed no agitation among Negro groups in this vicinity. He advised, however, that approximately ten years ago an unknown Japanese held meetings in Boston, the exact purpose of which never was clear to him. It was his opinion, however, that this Japanese was interested primarily in the collections he obtained rather than any movement involving the colored races of the world. It was his recollection that this individual left Boston for New York where he continued his activities and was subsequently arrested. He could furnish, however, no specific details.

On April 27, 1943 the Boston branch of the National Association for the Advancement of Colored People sponsored a mass meeting at the People's Baptist Church in Boston which was attended by approximately two hundred twenty Negroes. The purpose was a membership drive to obtain three thousand additional members. At the meeting Julian B. Steele, president of the local branch, urged all to participate in the membership drive so that a united fight could be made to combat the growing wave of "reactionary southernism." He referred to a housing project in Boston called Old Orchard Park, a wing of which was set aside for Negroes in a segregated partition. Steele also mentioned, according to reports, several Negro soldiers stationed in the South who forwarded their membership fees, and how one soldier in Georgia had written that the Army was fighting not only on the two battle fronts but in the South on a third front—namely, fighting the Negro. [*135-6-12*]

Several other speeches were made mainly dealing with matters of discrimination and with organizational details. It was announced that the Boston branch intended in no way to lessen its pressure to have Negroes admitted to other housing projects, as well as to the Old Orchard Park project, without segregation.

Buffalo Field Division

It is reported the Communist Party in this area at the present time is centering most of its activity among the Negro population and is using "Jim Crowism" as the main talking point.

On July 19, 1942, the Communist Party in the Buffalo area sponsored a "Conference for full use of Negro labor power to produce for Victory". There were many prominent individuals from Buffalo who were in no way connected with the Communist Party listed among the sponsors. One of the main speakers at this meeting was Ferdinand Smith, National Secretary of the National Maritime Union, a reported Negro Communist Party member. Alleged instances of discrimination in employment and other phases of Negro life were dealt with.

Relative to the Communist Party in and around the Buffalo area, it is reported that at all of the large Party meetings, the question of racial discrimination has been discussed and various defense plants in and around Buffalo have been condemned for failing to hire Negro labor. It has also been reported with regard to the Communist

Party Negro members who at one time dropped out, that they have rejoined the Party because of the activities by the Party in allegedly attempting to obtain employment for Negroes in industry in this section.

In and around Rochester, New York, it has been reported that the Communist Party has been exceedingly active among the Negro population of that City, but that it has been unsuccessful in recruiting many members from this source.

Also active in the Rochester area is the National Association for the Advancement of Colored People Chapter. It is reported that in one of the meetings of this Chapter, in March 1942, two members of the Communist Party who stood on their feet and announced their affiliation with the Communist Party urged members of the Chapter to combine with the Party in order to "Effectively fight against the discrimination shown to the Negroes."

In and around the vicinity of Elmira, New York, it is reported that the head of the local chapter of the National Association for the Advancement of Colored People, Miss Philippa Stowe, an assistant to Bernard Burton, secretary of the Communist Party there, is reportedly able to effectively spread Communist propaganda among the Negroes in that City through her position with this organization. It is reported that with the exception of the Communist agitation in and around this City, there has been no subversive propaganda spread among the Negro people.

With regard to Japanese agitation among the Negroes in and around Rochester, New York, it has been reported that a small meeting of Negro people was held in the summer of 1941 which was addressed by a Japanese student. It is alleged that at the meeting the Japanese speaker talked concerning discrimination shown to the Negroes in the United States and hinted that in a conflict to come, Japanese and Negro people should combine to overcome the white race against which they would be pitted. The source of information supplying the same was unable to furnish further identifying or substantiating information.

The Hamitic Mohammedan Club is said to have a building at Central Avenue and Leopold Street in Rochester, New York. Members of the club have stated that Mohammedans have always been friendly with the Fascist Powers and gave an illustration in the fact that the Moors led Franco's Army in the Spanish Revolution. Several members are also alleged to have talked about Japanese military might and how that is the only country in all history that has never lost a war. Investigation of this group is continuing.

A Mohammedan group reportedly active in this area has styled itself the Addeynue Allahe Universal Arabic Association Incorporated. It is said the group originated in Buffalo in 1938 and at the present time has approximately 250 members in Buffalo, New York and 75 active members in Rochester, New York. Members have been described as believing they are of Arabic or African descent and have for a number of years been living under a slave name. It is said that their belief is that their American name was given them by slave masters who took them captive and brought them to the United States. Because of this, it is reported they feel they must change their names and adopt those which their forefathers bore. It is reported that the Moslem belief is followed by them. The allegation has been received that this particular group has caused some unrest among the Negro community in Buffalo because of their difference in religious views and their beliefs that they are not really Negroes.

A source of information has advised that several years prior to the interview he had been told by an unknown member of the organization that the organization has a deep hatred for all Jewish people; although no further specific information has been received relative to such allegations.

It has been reported that all of the members of this organization, who are eligible to be inducted into the armed forces under the Selective Training and Service Act have registered as conscientious objectors and were so classified. In this connection several of the known members of the organization made claims for exceptions on the grounds that they are unable to eat food other than that prepared by members of their own faith. And because of this, they could consequently not eat the food served them in the armed forces. One of these known members in his form No. 97 (conscientious objector form) stated "I believe in peace at all times and that there should never be *no* war. *Do not* believe in fighting but in case of war __ must help in some way to defend the country in which I live". The individual making this claim is known now as **Arresa Rukabun** and formerly known as **Troy Vaughn.** In this same form **Rukabun** gave his religious sect as being "Moslem Believers in the religion of Islam, its governments and Mecca which is in Arabia". **Rukabun** also stated in a letter written to his Selective Service Board under date of **January 21, 1942,** that he could take no active part in the military service and added "I am of the Mohamm*a*d faith and __ is known to the world over as Moslem which the Japs *or* in the *menority* of . . . since the Japs *or* of Dark Race I regard them and *respeck* them as my people." [*100-135-7*]

In the Rochester area the Addeyune Allahe Universal Arabic Association, Inc., has conducted classes in a school at its headquarters at 473 Central Avenue, Rochester, New York. The alleged professor in charge of these classes was one **Mohammed Ez Al Deen.** A confidential informant has reported the professor's talks were much in favor of Japan winning the present war and that he was bitter against the white race. Another teacher at the school, one **Mobarrak Hasson** is said to have expressed similar beliefs and the hope that the white race will be conquered in the war. [*100-135-7-14*]

During the period of February through May 1943 the Communist Party in Rochester, Buffalo and Niag[a]ra Falls pointed much of its efforts toward recruiting new members from the Negro population in these cities. In connection with its recruiting activities, the Party has distributed numerous pamphlets, a large number of which concerned the history of the Negro. It attempts to obtain support of Negroes by pointing to its own efforts in allegedly removing discrimination and segregation barriers existing against the Negroes. A representative of the Negro race has referred to the Communist Party's activities among the Negroes and has expressed the opinion that it should be kept in mind that with the problems of racial discrimination continually confronting the Negro people, they present a fertile field for the activities of a group which on the surface appeared to be fighting in their behalf.

Another representative of a well organized Negro organization has said that to the best of his knowledge there is no deliberate agitation among the Negroes in this city;

rather, it is his opinion the problem of racial discrimination is of sufficient import in itself that no deliberate agitation is needed to supplement it.

Chicago Field Division

Social and Economic Conditions

According to the 1940 census, the Negro population in the City of Chicago and its environs totals approximately 300,000 persons. It is stated that this number has remained almost constant during the past thirty years. Recently, however, there has been an influx of Negroes from the South, said to be coming to the Chicago area primarily to seek employment in Defense industries.

The vast majority of this population lives on the South Side of Chicago, between 14th Street on the North and 70th Street on the South, Cottage Grove Avenue on the East and Halstead Street on the West. The area is densely populated; in many instances several families live together in two rooms or in small apartments. The Negro section is located in what was formerly a white residential section. The residential buildings were originally attractive and well constructed but have since been allowed to deteriorate and become run down. Many of them do not have adequate toilet facilities and there is improper lighting in a vast majority of the residences. Sanitation in this area, however, is considered good, the proper disposal of waste being effective.

It is said that the crime rate for this area has always been very high and that there has been on an average of two and three murders a week which seldom are publicized in any of the newspapers.

It is said that in this area, although there are quite a few Negroes earning salaries in connection with defense work far above those to which they are accustomed, the vast majority of them are in a very poor economic condition. One of the larger Negro associations in this area is a taxicab association involving several thousand owners and drivers of Negro jitney buses. This is a close-knit association and hundreds are said to receive good wages.

There are several thousand small Negro churches scattered throughout the Negro area which provide the focal point for most of the social activities of these people. Each of the churches has a few members from the immediate neighborhood and in many instances there is a formal dress ritual or mysticism which retains the interest of the group. In recent years athletic contests among Negroes have increased to the point that there recently were observed several softball and baseball teams playing in games which had attracted thousands of spectators.

There is one major high school in this area, the Du Sable High School, which provides a frequent meeting place for various Negro organizations. In this regard a teacher of history in this school has advised that during the past twenty years in the Chicago area he has observed very little gain in the average Negro's education or his feeling of social responsibility. This lack of gain is attributed to the inability of the average Negro to obtain responsible employment. Furthermore, the uneducated Negro is stated to be deeply interested in fanatical or mystical organizations, of which there are many in Chicago, because of the fact that it gives the individual Negro some feeling of importance to be associated with a secret organization of this type. In this connection, this same source of information has advised that the attraction for the mystical or fanatical has existed for over a period of years and that very little of it, in his estimation, comes from actual foreign-inspired propaganda and agitation.

Attitude of the Negro Toward the War

Several sources of information have advised that there is a great deal of lack of interest, if not opposition, to the war effort at the present time. The Negroes in this area of Chicago are said to be poorly organized and uncooperative in Civilian Defense activity, in their purchase of war bonds and stamps and in enlistment in the Armed Forces. With regard to Civilian Defense activity, an informant who is active in Civilian Defense work in the South Side of Chicago advises that members of the Chicago Office of Civilian Defense have conducted lectures and have been active in publicizing the value of thorough organization in the Civilian Defense program. The general response to this has been "Why should we cooperate with Civilian Defense? This is the white man's war. Let him take care of us."

In the sale of war bonds and stamps, this same informant also advises of endeavoring to sell the same to persons residing in his residential block and informs that his attempts were met with opposition, although those same individuals have money for nonessential and luxury items.

Another source of information, a Negro, who is highly educated and who is employed in a Governmental capacity, advises that he has discovered that the attitude among the colored population in the Chicago area toward the war effort has been uncooperative and that there is a great deal of unrest with an undercurrent of dissatisfaction throughout the area. This source of information advises that much of the unrest and dissatisfaction can be traced to the age-old question of the Negro and the white man as a result of centuries of discrimination and class separation. He has stated that in discussions with hundreds of colored people in this area, many have expressed the general theme that the present conflict does not concern the Negro. He advises, however, that the Negroes are quite concerned over discrimination being showed them with respect to defense industry employment.

A well educated and intelligent colored professional man in the South Side of Chicago has been interviewed with respect to the Negro situation there and he advises that the average Negro feels very keenly his inability to obtain a position with many of the Government agencies and his additional inability to obtain employment in defense industries on a comparative basis with the white man. The opinion has been expressed by this source of information that the reason Negroes are not more educated than they are at present is because there are many college graduates among the Negro people who cannot obtain a position commensurate with their training. He believes the Negro in general is patriotic although his class consciousness has developed to the point where the Negro regards the war effort with but a lukewarm interest. This source of information states he is aware of the undercurrent of dissatisfaction but advises that more of this can be traced to the feeling of class consciousness and a lack of proper education of the Negroes by responsible authorities. He advises that among the intelligent colored people there is no doubt that an American victory will be beneficial to the Negro race but that the majority of the colored people in this area have not had this brought to their attention forcibly enough or often enough. He has further stated that he believes the situation is improving among the majority of Negro people with respect to cooperation in the war effort because of the fact that a considerable number of colored youths have been called into the Armed Forces.

Organizations Active Among the Negroes in This Area

Investigation and inquiries made with respect to foreign-inspired agitation among the Negroes in this area have failed to reveal pro-German and pro-Nazi activities among the Negroes in this area. However, several individuals, Negroes, have been reported as having alleged German sympathies but investigations of these individuals have failed to reveal there is any organized appeal made in the colored area by pro-German forces. An anonymous complaint has been received to the effect that Negro preachers of two different colored churches on the South Side of Chicago have made remarks to the effect that when defeat comes to the United States the Negroes will make slaves of the white race. Investigation of this matter has not shown any connection with any outside source.

Many reports have been received indicating that pro-Japanese forces have conducted some work among the Negro race in an effort to win their sympathy to the Japanese Government. The line of attack is stated to be that the colored population comprises about 85 per cent of the total population of the world and that inasmuch as the Japanese are also of the colored race all such people should band together to defeat the white people. An investigation of these reports has revealed several extremely radical groups believing in the Islamic religion or following mystical teachings and preachings that Allah is the living god who is to set them all free.

Moorish Science Temple of America

This group is active in the Negro area in Chicago and is said to be the largest preaching the belief of Allah and the Islamic religion. The Koran is their bible and a five-point star on a red flag constitutes the Moorish flag. The organization in Newark, New Jersey, was allegedly founded in approximately 1913. In 1928 the Moorish Science Temple produced an offspring in Pittsburgh and Detroit and a National Convention was held in Chicago at which time there were estimated to be seventeen temples with more than 15,000 members. Several flare-ups within the ranks causing dissension therein have resulted in several independent branches. In Chicago there are six individuals claiming to be the true successors of the prophet Noble Drew Ali, the founder of the original group.

A confidential source of information has advised that some of the officers of the group appear to be making a racket of their organization in that none of them have gainful employment and are allegedly living on the dues collected from their members. All of the groups are extremely secretive and ritualistic and meetings are generally held in the homes of the leaders, the members being taught in these meetings consistently that the black man is superior to the white man. The membership of the various groups following the various leaders is said to vary from 50 to 200 persons.

Investigations of each of these groups bearing the name Moorish Science Temple of America are being conducted.

Allah Temple of Islam

Another of the groups teaching belief in the Islam religion is the Allah Temple of Islam, the main chapter of which is located at 104 East 51st Street, Chicago, Illinois. It is estimated that from 200 to 300 Negroes in the City of Chicago are members of this Temple. Investigation of this group reveals that the members are for the most part from the lower class of Negroes and are strong believers in mysticism. One of the leaders of this group, Gulam Bogens, who has also been known as Elijah Mohammed and Elijah Muck Wuck, is presently under $5,000 bond for failure to register under the Selective Training and Service Act. A Federal Grand Jury sitting in Chicago returned an indictment on October 23, 1942, against Elijah Mohammed in eight counts, charging sedition. An indictment was also returned at this time against Linn Karriem and Pauline Baher, as well as Sultan Mohammed of Milwaukee, Wisconsin, and David Jones of Washington, charging them with conspiracy to commit sedition.

It was reported that various leaders of the Japanese people believed the Government was justified in arresting the leader of this cult. These Japanese were said to have stated there was no Japanese activity within the organization in recent years and if there had been any Japanese individual active in the organization he must have returned to Japan long ago.

In December, 1942, Elijah Mohammed was sentenced in Washington on a violation of the Selective Service Act for a term of from one to five years. The United States Attorney in Chicago advised on May 27, 1943, he was considering dismissing the indictment on the sedition charges against this individual and presenting the facts to the Department for an opinion.

The Peace Movement of Ethiopia

This organization, said to be large and independent, has headquarters at 3144 South State Street, Chicago, Illinois, and sponsors meetings at this address and business sessions on Wednesday evenings. The general sessions of the group, open to the public, are held at the Boulevard Hall, 366 East 47th Street, on Sunday evenings and attract an average crowd of from 200 to 350 persons. The organization was founded by Madam Mittie Maud Lena Gordon, a large mulatto, born in Webster Parish,

Louisiana. She is stated to have been active in colored movements of a radical nature for a great number of years, having lost a son in a race riot near Springfield, Illinois, in 1928 or 1929. The alleged objectives of the organization are the return of Negroes to Ethiopia or Liberia. Madam Gordon was arrested on September 20, 1942, on charges of violation of the Sedition Statutes and sentenced [to] two years and placed on probation three years after the termination of her sentence.

The Colored American National Organization (The Washington Park Forum)

This organization meets in Washington Park, 53rd and South Park Avenue, Chicago, on Sunday afternoons in open forum. The organization has been meeting for a considerable period of time and its leader, a college graduate, one Stokely Delmar Hart, is stated to have made many seditious remarks indicating his intense displeasure of any activity of the white man and reflecting his sympathies with Japan and his wish for a Japanese victory. This individual was arrested on September 20, 1942, on charges of violation of the Sedition Statutes. Hart was found guilty May 27, 1943, and was sentenced to three years in the custody of the Attorney General on June 11, 1943. Motion for a new trial, probation and arrest of judgment were overruled.

Universal Negro Improvement Association

This organization is comparatively inactive in the Chicago area at the present time and the membership of it is presently small in number. It is reported, however, that members of this group are expanding their activities among former members of the Peace Movement of Ethiopia. It is said that the members of the organization are critical of the white race but there is no indication that members of this organization are encouraged to violate the Selective Training and Service Act or to be non-cooperative with the war effort.

This organization traces back to the Marcus Garvey Movement among the Negroes subsequent to the last war in which the program for the return to Africa was promoted.

Just subsequent to the National Conference of the March on Washington Movement it was reported that [A. Philip] Randolph and James R. Stewart, national head of this organization, conferred relative to the merging of their forces in a common objective. One Toliber, a leader of a unit of the Universal Negro Improvement Association at 3636 South Cottage Grove, Chicago, Illinois, is said to have been asked by the March on Washington Movement to unite with it. The total number of members of the March on Washington Movement in Chicago is approximately 5700 members, while the strength of the Universal Negro Improvement Association in Chicago is not known, although it is believed to be small.

The arrest of the leaders of the Washington Park Forum, the Peace Movement of Ethiopia, and the Allah Temple of Islam, and 70 members of the latter group by agents of the Federal Bureau of Investigation on September 20, 1942, is said to have had a desirable effect in the area, and the reaction among the vast majority of the colored population as reported by sources of information and its publication, is said to have been good. However, reports concerning individual Negroes have been received subsequently to the effect that pro-Japanese or pro-German statements were made by them. These, of course, are all subject matters of investigation and inquiries are being continued.

Communist Party Influence Among the Negroes in Chicago

The Communist Party since the invasion of Russia by Germany has agitated on behalf of the Negro, urging that additional rights be granted him in economic, political and cultural matters. At the same time, however, it urged the Negro population to support the national war effort completely. However, in its work among the Negroes, the Party has combined its agitation on their behalf with the remainder of the Communist Party line.

The following statements made by John Williamson, National Committee member of the Communist Party, at the Midwest Conference of Communist Party leaders held at the Sherman Hotel, Chicago, Illinois, on March 18 and 19, 1943, reflect the attitude of the Party toward Negroes:

> "We must see ourselves as a force for unity of all the Negro people. The war is changing the thinking and actions of the Negroes, a change of attitude under the pressure of the March on Washington Movement. The fact that while previously it was anti-war in its main outlook, today it has changed so that it now has incorporated the war as one of its issues.
>
> "Under our leadership, labor unions must be in the forefront of the anti-poll tax drive. Later we must exhibit activity to abolish all Jim Crow practices with special attention to the various aspects of this problem as affects the Army. The special question of transportation in the South, in the Air Corps and the danger of the War Department calling solely on Negro troops to be dispatched to the farms, all of these things we must learn to prevent, to solve them and to overcome them. We must fight for the re-establishment of the Fair Employment Practices Committee.
>
> "In this connection, we should strive to strengthen the existing labor victory committees, to establish them whenever possible to further activize and extend the National Negro Congress which is reviving its activities, exp[a]nding it as a real factor towards the Unity Movement of the Negroes and in the course of all this, to conduct ourselves to make our own contributions and our own position clear so that we will be able to recruit even larger numbers of Negro workers into the Party."

A speech was made at this same Conference by Phillip Bart, Organizational Secretary of the Communist Party for District 8, including the Indiana-Illinois area, in which he reported on the membership recruiting drive. He referred to the figure of 39 per cent as being the proportion of Negroes who had been recruited into the Party since the beginning of the membership drive on January 1, 1943. The total number was set by him at 137 new members of the Negro race. This figure, of course, represents an out of proportion number of Negro recruits as compared with the number of white recruits.

In the Chicago area the Communist Party has been working for and among Negroes there through mainly its influence in labor unions and the International Workers Order, especially in promoting its program as to the manner in which Negroes should be treated. This is in addition to its recruiting campaign. The actual effect on the Negroes as a result of the Communist Party's activities is more a result of the Party's agitational campaign for Negro rights rather than its attempt to recruit them.

The following details are set forth concerning a Conference on Racial Problems, held on June 5, 1943 in the aldermanic chambers of the City Hall in Chicago, Illinois which are believed to exemplify the Communist Party's exploitation of the Negroes—in this case using the Detroit riots of June 20–22, 1943 as a means to its end:

This conference is reported to have been called by Fullerton Fulton of the Chicago Industrial Union Council, CIO. Confidential informants of this Bureau have advised that Communist Party leaders in the Chicago area also had a definite part in the arrangements for the meeting. Approximately 175 people, the majority of whom were white, attended.

According to Fullerton Fulton, the purpose of the meeting was to guard against the danger of race riots in the Chicago area and to reiterate that the Congress of Industrial Organizations will not tolerate racial discrimination in Chicago.

Mayor Edward J. Kelly of Chicago appeared by invitation and spoke briefly advising of the dangers of unnecessary stimulation in interracial problems. He left the meeting early subsequent to informing that he had given a statement to the press relative to a committee he would appoint to study these problems.

The following individuals were the principal speakers at the meeting: A. L. Foster, Executive Secretary of the Chicago Urban League; Samuel Levin, President of the Illinois State Industrial Union Council, CIO; Oscar Brown, President of the Chicago Chapter of the National Association for the Advancement of Colored People; Edward A. Strong, National Secretary of the National Negro Congress, a Communist front organization; Earl B. Dickerson, reported Communist sympathizer, who represented the Chicago Civil Liberties Committee; Michael Mann, Secretary of the Chicago Industrial Union Council, CIO; Robert Travis, Vice President of the Illinois State Industrial Union Council, CIO, and member of the Executive Committee of District 8 of the Communist Party; William L. Patterson, Director of the Abraham Lincoln School and member of District 8 of the Communist Party; Clifford Townsend, a labor union representative; Louise Thompson, Midwest Director of the International Workers Order and member of the Executive Committee of District 8 of the Communist Party; and Frank McCullough, reported Communist sympathizer and representative from the Mullenbach Institute.

In substance, Foster is reported to have stated that interracial understanding is contingent upon better housing conditions and elimination of discrimination in the Armed Forces and industry. He is said to have blamed neighborhood Negro newspapers for fomenting hatred and prejudices.

Oscar Brown in his talk reportedly stated that there are approximately 250 major defense industries in Chicago which refuse employment to Negroes and by so doing act in a subversive manner. He blamed the present situation on discrimination in the administration of the Selective Training and Service Act and on segregation in the Armed Forces.

Edward Strong, reported Communist, declared the outbreak in Detroit was not a race riot but an organized insurrection against the United States. He claimed that of the 28 Negroes killed, almost all were killed by policemen and that of 1,300 persons in jail in Detroit, 1200 were Negroes.

Earl B. Dickerson stated the Negro people should join forces with the Congress of Industrial Organizations as the best way to obtain their desires. He claimed there is a "second front" in the United States and that Negroes are not content to sit back as they did in the first World War but rather were demanding full equality at the present time.

Robert Travis, previously identified, demanded that school text books be revised to delete anti-Negro statements and reportedly called for a drastic reorganization of the Chicago Police Department.

William L. Patterson attributed the Detroit race riots to Fascists, the Ku Klux Klan, German-American Bund elements, and industrial manufacturers who refused to adhere to the President's order concerning discrimination.

Clifford Townsend in his turn stated Negro soldiers were ready to take up their guns and "clean up" the South. He reportedly said that 98 per cent of the Negroes are ready to die for freedom.

Louise Thompson is said to have concurred with the comments of the previous speakers.

At the end of the meeting a 12-point program, with certain amendments, was unanimously adopted. This program included the formation of a continuation committee to work with the one to be appointed by Mayor Kelly. It also urged sending a telegram to the President urging him to address the people of this country and ask them to avoid actions leading to mob violence.

In summarizing the effect of the Communist Party on the Negroes in this area, it is believed that although the Party is soliciting all-out cooperation on the part of Negroes in the war effort, it is constantly through its various forces, bringing to the attention of the Negroes alleged instances of discrimination, segregation and denial of equal rights, the effect of which only serves to further agitate the Negroes residing there.

The Chicago Defender

The Chicago Defender was started as a private enterprise by Robert S. Abbott, one of the leading colored men of his day. Abbott died in 1940 and left his estate, including the Robert S. Abbott Publishing Company, in the form of a trust. At the present, James B. Cashin, Negro attorney, is chairman of the Trustee Board. It should be stated that Cashin is reported to be one of the wealthiest Negroes of the United States and bears an excellent reputation.

John Sengstacke, a nephew of Robert S. Abbott, is presently the active manager of the publication. Sengstacke is a young college graduate and is highly thought of. The widow of Robert S. Abbott, Mrs. Edna Abbott, is the present Vice President.

Metz T. P. Lochard is the Secretary-Treasurer. Lochard has been with the publication for approximately twenty-five years, having worked his way from the position of an office boy to that of Secretary-Treasurer. Lucius Harper is the editorial manager and is in a large part responsible for the policy of the Chicago Defender.

Considerable information has been reported concerning Metz Lochard and Lucius Harper. Confidential sources of information have reported that these two individuals have been present at many meetings of the Communist Party District No. 8 in Chicago, Illinois, and that at several meetings held since July 1942 both Harper and Lochard have been seated on the speakers' platform and have made addresses at meetings of the Communist Party. With regard to Harper, it has been stated that he takes advantage of every opportunity to appear at the Communist Party affairs and that his political party work has always been the Communist Party's work.

A review of the editorials appearing in the Chicago Defender reveals that the publication is strongly behind the war effort and that it is most active in calling for a second front. A review of the issues of the paper also reveals that a considerable number of news items dealing with alleged discrimination against the Negro in army camps and alleged acts of brutality against Negro soldiers appear in its issues. Numerous sources of information interviewed in this area state that the newspaper is one of the leading exponents of a program for unification of the Negroes. Likewise the recent lynchings in Mississippi have brought headlines in the Chicago Defender and occasioned a great deal of unrest among the Negroes in this area. Confidential sources of information reported that the attitude among the general Negro classes following the lynchings has not been good.

The Pittsburgh Courier, the Chicago edition of it, is the only other Negro newspaper with an office in Chicago. A. N. Fields, an attorney and a former assistant Illinois State attorney, is the head of the Chicago branch of the Pittsburgh Courier. A confidential source of information has advised that Fields is a very responsible Negro who bears an excellent reputation. Informant has further advised that the quality of this paper is determined in Pittsburgh and not in Chicago and that A. N. Fields has therefore very little to do with the editorial policy or management of the paper.

March on Washington Movement

On June 30, 1943, the National Conference of the March on Washington Movement convened in Chicago, Illinois and it has been scheduled to continue through July 4, 1943, culminating in a demonstration in the form of a parade on Sunday, July 4, 1943. The first session of the Conference took place on the evening of June 30, 1943, and was attended by approximately 500 persons. A. Philip Randolph, National

Leader of this organization, presided, and he is related to have said that the March on Washington Movement was founded to express condemnation of those Governmental policies which permit racial discrimination and segregation. He is said to have announced that the Convention would consider the development of what he described [as] a powerful non-partisan political bloc to bring pressure on Congress for the enactment of the anti-poll tax and anti-lynching bills. This political bloc, according to Randolph, will ask that Negroes be given "first-class citizenship status."

Randolph is reported to have also stated the President would be requested to form a national race commission for the purpose of achieving a Congressional investigation of race riots.

Dr. Lawrence Ervin, who is the Eastern Regional Director of the organization, also spoke at the opening meeting and stated the "Negro must fight for his rights" and "who in hell is going to tell the Negro how he should go about getting his rights."

At 12:00 noon, July 1, 1943, a business session of the Convention was held and in attendance were approximately 110 people. The Credentials Committee at this meeting made various reports. The Convention's program was outlined and permanent national committees previously appointed by the Executive Board of this organization were announced.

An afternoon session was held on July 1 which was attended by approximately 270 delegates and members of the public. A discussion on "The Outlook and Future of the Fair Employment Practices Committee" was engaged in by Earl B. Dickerson and Milton P. Webster, both of Chicago, who were former members of this Committee, and Harold Stevens and Thurman Dodson, delegates to the Convention from Washington, D.C. A dispute arose between the Protestants and Catholics when Dodson is said to have attacked the President for appointing Monsignor Haas as head of the Fair Employment Practice[s] Committee on the ground that Monsignor Haas was not suitable because of his training as a Catholic priest. Stevens, a Washington delegate, led the dispute against Dodson.

There were two resolutions adopted at the afternoon meeting of July 1, one condemning the action of Monsignor Haas for his decision in the Alabama Dry Dock and Shipbuilding Corporation case in Mobile, Alabama, which permitted Negroes to work on only four of the ways in the shipyards. This action was labelled as discrimination against Negroes. The second resolution was an appeal to have Dickerson and Webster reappointed to the new committee of the Fair Employment Practice[s] Committee.

It is said that both of the resolutions were sent to the President by telegram. In this connection, Randolph is reported to have read a resolution in the form of a telegram to the minority and majority leaders of both Houses of Congress, to the Vice President, and to Congressman Fish of New York in which an appeal was made that legislation be passed to create a "Commission on Race in America." It is allegedly desired that this commission rule on all racial questions arising in the United States. The last resolution was unanimously adopted.

A confidential informant has also advised that a decision on an actual march on the City of Washington will not be reached or discussed in open meetings at the Convention until an answer has been received to the three previously mentioned resolutions.

The evening session of July 1, 1943, was held at the Metropolitan Community Church, and approximately 600 persons attended. The speakers included Layle Lane, New York Unit Secretary of the organization; Carl Hansberry, wealthy Negro Chicago real estate owner; Cordelia Green Johnson, President of the Beauty Culturists League of America; Henry Johnson, United Mine Worker Union representative; Bayard Rustin, Fellowship of Reconciliation; Dr. George Edward Haynes of the Federal Council of Churches in America, all of whom are Negroes. All of the speakers criticized the discrimination against the segregation of the Negroes in labor and in the armed forces. Among other things urged were that Negroes secure political, social, and economic freedom by the use of purchasing power and the right to vote, to be found in the total Negro population. Hansberry advised Negroes to take advantage of all legal means to secure freedom from racial discrimination. Bayard Rustin of the Fellowship of Reconciliation, which organization has been cooperating with the March on Washington Movement in the "direct action non-violence program" to secure Negroes' rights, urged that the March on Washington Movement follow this program. This program includes Negroes testing "Jim Crow" laws and customs through the use of non-violence. Rustin said that violence would be suicidal and that no results would come from the use of force.

It should be noted that the Fellowship of Reconciliation, a militant pacifist organization, has provided some of its membership to assist in such a program which is copied after the technique used by Mohandas Gandhi of India.

E. Pauline Myers, National Executive Secretary of the March on Washington Movement, in a meeting on the morning of [July] 2, as well as other speakers, stressed the importance of members not responding to violence on the part of white agitators and policemen. At this meeting a program was suggested whereby Negroes would be educated by this organization for teaching non-violence technique to include approaching white proprietors of restaurants, bus companies, and theaters to secure services for both Negroes and whites. It should be noted this program was outlined largely by members of the Fellowship of Reconciliation.

A committee on this program decided on the morning of July 2 that experiments would be made with the non-violence technique in the cities of New York, Washington, Richmond, Chicago, and Los Angeles. The committee also recommended that the organization establish an institute to teach this technique with headquarters at New York City.

The conference continued through July 4, 1943, and ended with a mass meeting at the Du Sable High School in Chicago. In attendance were approximately 2200 Negroes. Among the speakers were Dr. Charles Wesley Burton, President of the Chicago Unit; Dr. William Stuart Nelson, Director of the "Action Program" of the March on Washington Movement; Dr. E. Stanley Jones, white, a missionary to India who has been described as an aide to Mohandas Gandhi; A. Philip Randolph; Dr. James Horace, Negro preacher at the Monumental Baptist Church; and Rev. T. B. Chapman, Shilo Baptist Church, Englewood, Illinois.

The rallying power of the Chicago Unit of the March on Washington Movement cannot be definitely established although as will be noted from above approximately 2200 Negroes were in attendance at the last session of the National Conference. At a meeting held by the organization in the summer of 1942, approximately 8200 persons attended. Thus it can be seen a degree of support is had among the 300,000 Negroes in Chicago. There is, of course, to be considered, influence through the activities and utterances of the members in Chicago.

Cincinnati Field Division

Concerning the general situation among the Negro inhabitants of this area, it has been reported that there appeared to be dissatisfaction and anger because of discrimination against them as well as an apathy towards the war effort. A number of reports have been received to the effect that Negro inhabitants of the area have made such remarks as "why should I fight for this so-called democracy when my people have no equal opportunity with the whites and when by fighting we would merely be killed by the Japanese instead of lynched by Southern whites." There have also been allegations received that some of the inhabitants have become arrogant and unamenable to law and order. Two incidents have been pointed out wherein Negroes have thrown rocks at police cars and where the police officers involved did not dare to do anything about it. It is further alleged that this attitude on the part of the Negroes in the area has become increasingly noticeable. It has been the subject of many reports to the Cincinnati Office of the Federal Bureau of Investigation. The general feeling in the area was described as being in danger and that someone is apparently scaring the Negroes to an anti-white hatred. It is also alleged that the publicity organization which is responsible for a part of the attitude is the Pittsburgh Courier.

There are seven Negro newspapers published in the territory covered by the Cincinnati Field Division. The editorial policy of all these newspapers follows the national war effort and advocates better conditions for the Negroes.

The editor of "Union" published at Cincinnati, Ohio, wrote a front page editorial on December 18, 1941, containing statements that Japan merits credit and appreciation. The editor asked why some colored people call the Japanese names, and wanted to know if it was to curry favor with the whites. The organizations active in the vicinity of the Cincinnati Field Division are as follows:

The Universal Negro Improvement Association is active in Cincinnati, Ohio, and James R. Stewart, the president of this organization, made a speech at Cincinnati on February 22, 1942, in which he stated, "We will remember Missouri and then Pearl Harbor"—"To hell with Pearl Harbor." Stewart also made a speech in Cincinnati on May 17, 1942, in which he allegedly made pro-Japanese statements.

It is reported the original purpose of the Universal Negro Improvement Association was the redemption of Africa, transporting all Negroes there, and setting up an independent government controlled and operated by Negroes. It is said the organization has approximately two hundred members.

The March on Washington organization has had some activity in Columbus, Ohio, even though a definite organization has not been formed. It is reported that colored people at Dayton, Ohio, have not supported the movement very strongly but there has been discussion of the movement in the local colored papers.

An organization known as the March on Tokyo is reportedly active in the vicinity of Columbus, Ohio, but an outside source reports that the primary interest of the colored people connected with this movement was to win the war and to make the winning of equal rights for the colored, a secondary cause.

The Double V Program has been quite active in the vicinity of Cincinnati. It should be noted this organization was started by a colored person from Kansas, and was adopted by the Pittsburgh Courier newspaper which conducted a campaign to organize chapters throughout the United States. This organization is also active in the vicinity of Dayton and Columbus, Ohio.

In this area local chapters of the National Association for the Advancement of Colored People are in existence and are continuing their campaign against discrimination and denial of equal rights to Negroes. The organization is active in Cincinnati, Columbus, Dayton, Hamilton, Hillsboro, Lockland, Newark, Portsmouth, Steubenville, Urbana and Zanesville, Ohio.

In the vicinity of Columbus, Ohio, the Communist Party has also been active in agitating and propagandizing among the Negroes for their support. As indicative of this it was reported that on August 26, 1942, a Communist Party meeting was held in the Negro Masonic Hall in Columbus, Ohio, at which Ruth Ferloss, organizational secretary of the Columbus Communist Party urged everyone to write the President protesting the sentence of the three Negro soldiers in Louisiana to death on [a] rape charge. It was further reported that it was announced on August 31, 1942, at a Communist Party meeting in Columbus, Ohio, that the Party was having some success in recruiting Negro professors at Wilberforce University, a Negro educational college at Dayton, Ohio.

Another organization in the Columbus, Ohio, area, reported to be formed and sponsored by Negroes is the Vanguard League which is active in agitating for Negro rights. It is stated that its president, Frank Snearer is reportedly a Communist Party member. [*100-135-11-6*]

In the Dayton, Ohio area an organization known as the Swastika Club is said to have been active. Actually the organization had no Axis leanings. It is said to be composed of young, married Negro couples and is thoroughly patriotic. Recently the name of the organization was changed to the Eight Twenty-Five Club to remove all doubt.

Among the Negro newspapers in this area are the Dayton Forum, published at Dayton, Ohio, the Butler County American, published at Hamilton, Ohio, and the Ohio State News, published at Columbus, Ohio. These newspapers have a patriotic appeal and urge full participation by the Negroes in the war effort. [*100-135-11-6.7*]

An incident occurring in Xenia, Ohio, during the last part of January and early in February 1943 has been reported in which near riots resulted between white and Negro people in that city because of the refusal by motion picture theater operators to admit Negroes to afternoon and evening performances. This trouble is said to have been instigated by student representatives of Wilberforce University and Antioch College. It was also reported that some of the professors at these two colleges were in the matter. In this connection, a letter has been furnished by a confidential and reliable source written by one of the white students instigating Negroes to test segregation measures in the theaters. This letter is set forth in part to exemplify the type of agitation conducted by such white forces:

"The action we took Tuesday night was very successful. The Negro students got here at five. We ate, had a meeting and then started out. It was very carefully planned. The object was to diffuse the Negro students throughout the theatre after the movie had started. Small groups started out for the movie, getting there before time at set intervals. The Negroes, of course, were separated. The Wilberforce students sat in the Jim Crow section. I and John Deihl timed it so that we were the last pair of white students to get there. We were followed by a Negro couple. We got to the theatre a couple of minutes late and gave the sign to the couple behind to go in as the picture had started. They walked in, after buying their tickets, and went all the way down the aisle past the Jim Crow section which is in the very back. The owner followed them right down to tell them to go back. As he went down, all the Wilberforce students got up and quietly diffused throughout the theatre, seating themselves by the Antiochians who were by the aisle. Dennis, the owner, then, had to lean over 2 people to tell the Negroes to go back and was completely ignored by all. There wasn't a thing he could do and he knew it. We really broke a precedent. We had a meeting upon returning after the show. A Negro student and I had formed a proposition which I presented at the meeting. I pointed out that this wouldn't be enough, that we would have to approach the Negroes in town and get them to cooperate in similar manner in the future. Though legally within our rights, the very fact that there are "Jim Crow" sections in Springfield and Dayton makes it clear that it is tremendously difficult to get a suit filed, without continual postponement, etc. I proposed an action committee to deal with problems of discrimination here and in Xenia. The committee would be composed of our and Wilberforce's students and would meet as frequently as possible. Any idea for action would be taken to the respective COC committees and we would thus get mass action. The motion was passed and I was elected one of the 4 members—which made me a bit embarrassed as I had suggested the creation of the sub-committee."

At Columbus, Ohio, a prominent Negro has offered his opinions and information relative to the restless attitude on the part of Negroes there. He has pointed to the Curtiss-Wright Corporation in that city where he alleged there is an extremely tense atmosphere. He has referred to several fights involving only two people, usually a white and a Negro employee. With reference to these fights, he has alleged that a foreman in one of the departments at Curtiss-Wright had called Negro employees together and told them he hoped they could band together for self-protection in leaving the plant and returning to their homes which, according to the source of information, inferred it would be perfectly all right for Negroes to start fights with white workers. He has cited another instance in which he alleged a shop steward of a union at this plant had advised

Negroes in the union to fight back and to resist slurs on their race. The source of information stated such instances only serve to incite Negroes and to encourage them to commit acts of violence.

The source of information continued in referring to the Curtiss-Wright Plant situation, saying that it was aggravated by the fact that for the first time Negroes have been obtaining positions of good pay and responsibility. Then, he has added, many of the workers are whites from Kentucky and other southern States who resent working side by side in comparable positions with Negroes. He furnished the opinion that over and above the antipathy between the southern whites and the Negroes there is possibly outside influence being asserted which is purposely inciting Negroes and helping them form the attitude they are beginning to take in this area.

[*"Ohio State News," Columbus, Ohio*]

There are a large number of Negro organizations in this area, the leaders of which express sentiments varying from a militant nature in demanding equal rights to an anti-white feeling bordering on a pro-Japanese sentiment. In this connection, a white confidential source of information has advised of being in touch with Negro leaders of the various organizations in Cincinnati for a number of years. He stated that during the last two or three years it has become plain that a large percentage of Negroes in the poorer class in Cincinnati were pro-Japanese in their sentiments. He related one cannot approach any Negro, with the exception of some of the better educated and more wealthy individuals, without hearing at one time or another praise for the Japanese or statements by the maker that he would prefer Japan to win the war. He gave as an explanation for this the teachings of such men as Mimo De Guzman which fell on the receptive ears of Negroes in the early 1930's and the repetition of them by Negroes who accepted the teachings of De Guzman.

This source continued, stating that spreading pro-Japanese sentiment has been easy in that Negroes had already been filled with the idea they were unjustly dealt with by the white people in this country and were willing to accept any other "master" in preference. He has also offered the opinion that allegiance to a foreign power and talk of rebellion, along with the use of titles and uniforms, have been appealing to many Negroes' minds.

Among the more militant Negro groups in the Cincinnati, Dayton, Columbus and Springfield areas, at meetings of which pro-Japanese or at least anti-white sentiments have been expressed, are the Universal Negro Improvement Association, the Future Outlook League, the Good Samaritan Negro Improvement Association, and the Moslem Sect. There are also such militant organizations which confine themselves to strong anti-discrimination and segregation views as the Urban League, the March on Washington Movement, the Double V Clubs and the Vanguard League. There is, of course, the continued agitation in these areas by the Communist Party working through its fronts, urging Negroes to engage in the war effort wholeheartedly but at the same time playing upon alleged instances of discrimination and the denial of equal rights, thus exploiting the Negro and causing added unrest.

The full import of the influence of the above-mentioned anti-white and in some instances pro-Japanese groups cannot be evaluated inasmuch as while the attendance at the meetings rarely exceeds 250 or 300 persons, the extent of spreading and teaching by members of the principles dealt with is not known. However, the number of complaints received of individual Negroes expressing pro-Japanese sentiments have increased and are not confined merely to one particular area. In all instances, however, those organizations expressing an anti-American or pro-Japanese attitude are under investigation and are receiving constant attention. [*100-135-11*]

Cleveland Field Division

General

A source of information who is believed to be in close contact with the Negro population in the Cleveland area has been contacted for his views regarding the racial situation there. He has stated that from his experience and observations there are two distressing things among the Negro population of Cleveland at the present time. One is the inability to obtain employment for which they are qualified and the other is the alleged mistreatment accorded Negro soldiers in Army encampments in Southern States. He has advised that he has heard of no Negro openly expressing any desire of an alliance with a foreign power and that he has never heard one suggest such crimes as espionage or sabotage. He added, however, that he believes there is a strong feeling among Negroes that they should use every law, device, and measure of pressure available, in fact, anything short of subversive activity itself, to obtain for themselves rights and privileges which they have never before been accorded. It was his further opinion that the Northern Negro is becoming more interested in his situation than ever before.

This same source of information has advised that he believes there is a great amount of discontent among Negro boys between 18 and 25 years of age. He pointed out that such Negroes have finished high school and feel that they are as well equipped to assume positions in certain industries or at least as well equipped to receive training in preparation for these positions as are any white people. He continued stating that these individuals have been denied opportunities and for that reason they are disgruntled at the white people because they are in control of defense plants. As a result, he stated Negroes in this age bracket "carry a chip on their shoulders" and as a further result rowdyism, purse snatching and petty crimes among Negroes are increasing. In summation he stated that he believed most of the trouble or the unrest and agitation among the Negroes is a result of discrimination against them by white people.

Another source of information, a Negro, who has been interviewed has advised that the attitude of Negroes generally in the Cleveland area with reference to the present war effort is that they are discontented because they cannot obtain defense employment. He added that he felt the Negroes are not enthusiastic over entering into the Army inasmuch as they feel the United States Army is the only organization which has use for Negroes. As a consequence, he concludes that he is being denied equal rights and opportunities. This same source of information has related that he has obtained no indications reflecting any indication that the Negro's attitude is influenced by foreign-inspired agitation. He has stated that Negroes are interested in no other country and feel the United States is their home. He added that in his opinion Negroes feel their problem is one to be solved at the home front. He said that he believed the consensus of opinion among the Negroes in this area relative to the international situation is that although they are not satisfied with their treatment in this country, they, as a whole, do not believe they would receive better treatment under any other government or any other form of government.

Another source of information who is in a position to know and understand the Negro situation in this area, has been interviewed and has advised that he believes there is no disloyalty among the Negroes and that there is the feeling that they do not want the United States or the United Nations to be defeated but at the same time the Negroes do want some of the hardships and limitations which they suffer lifted. Continuing, he advised that among the more intelligent Negroes there is no attempt to use the present situation as a lever for bargaining power to gain the ends that the Negro race has, as a whole, been seeking. He said, however, that there is considerable effort among the unlettered class to accomplish this. He believes that there is now existing more of a nationalistic tendency than heretofore ever existed and the reason for this is that the Negro is becoming interested in the "plight" of his race as a whole. He said there is a considerable amount of discrimination against Negroes especially by defense industries and that in his opinion the way to overcome these discriminations is to place qualified Negroes in positions and let them prove that they, even though they are Negroes, could do the same job as the white man.

With regard to the Negroes' entrance into the armed forces, he advised that a considerable portion of the Negroes had resigned themselves to the inevitable and reasoned that they might as well join the Army. The same source pointed out although a considerable number of Negroes wanted the war to last some period of time they felt the Negro race as a whole would accomplish more in an international crisis toward having the limitations and discriminations against them removed than in ordinary times. He said that they did not wish to see the United Nations lose the present war but they would like to see the United States and England get shocked very hard before victory, hoping that it would make them realize that discriminations practiced against the Negroes were wrong. He believed that there was no actual subversive element among them. It should be pointed out at this time that the opinion expressed by this source of information with regard to the Negroes, desiring England and the United States to be shocked, has not been supported by other sources of information interviewed.

Organizations in Cleveland Area

The Unity for Victory Conference

The Unity for Victory Conference was held September 19–20, 1942, at the Cedar Y.M.C.A. It was a two-day affair which was broken down into various discussion groups with each group reporting to the General Assembly at the close of the Conference. It was attended by white people from various defense plants and a representative of the Fair Employment Practices Committee in Cleveland, Ohio. No information has been received reflecting any subversive activities as far as the group is concerned. However, the issues which were agreed upon by various panels, reportedly were comparable to those usually adopted in Communist Party or Communist delegated meetings. They were the urging of the immediate opening of a second front, the urging of the formation of volunteer mixed regiments, the urging that Negroes insist that the Secretary of War request citizens in the South to protect Negro soldiers through the creation of more Negro Military Police, the agreeing that Red Cross discrimination against the Negroes must be eliminated, and the urging that discrimination against Negroes be eliminated in connection with defense employment and training.

The Grant Lodge of the Fraternal Order of Vulcan

This organization which has offices in the Woodland Market Building, Cleveland, Ohio, recently held a mass meeting in Youngstown, Ohio, on September 15, 1942. The meeting dealt with various alleged discriminatory practices against and denial of, equal rights to Negroes.

The organization is a fraternal order organized for the purpose of uniting Negroes to pool their resources for economic independence and to provide jobs in various types of business for its members. It also has the purpose of breaking down prejudice against the Negroes.

The Future Outlook League, Incorporated

This organization has its headquarters in Cleveland, Ohio, and has also been in existence in the Alliance, Ohio, area. Its President is John O. Holly, a Negro, who makes militant speeches at Negro gatherings, reportedly following the line of fighting racial discrimination against the Negroes in war plants, as well as seeking employment for them in industry. There have been reports that some of the speeches assume the aspect of "anti-white." It has held meetings in various cities of Ohio, including Alliance, Youngstown, Cleveland, Columbus and Toledo. It is reported to have some affiliation with the Vanguard League, and at one time it is reported to have offered its support to the March on Washington Movement.

Recently Holly contacted officials of the Ohio Bell Telephone Company at Cleveland, Ohio, demanding that Negro girls be employed as telephone operators and threatening in effect that if such action was not taken by the company, a mass meeting would be held in front of the telephone building in Cleveland. Holly is reported to have warned that when a group of people gather in such a manner, anything might happen. The outcome of Holly's conference with the Telephone Company officials has not been reported. However, it is known that no meeting such as threatened by Holly took place before the telephone building in Cleveland.

It is further reported that this organization succeeded in changing the policy of the Palmer Machine Company in Akron, Ohio, with regard to the hiring of Negro women. This was also the case with the Globe Crayon Company.

This organization is said to employ an individual by the name of Dewey M. Young, who is said to be the legal advisor and special investigator of the organization. Young is reported to have advised that his work is to investigate the circumstances surrounding reported acts of discrimination against Negroes and to proffer charges against those discriminating.

The Universal Negro Improvement Association

This organization, which has its national headquarters at 2200 East 40th Street, Cleveland, Ohio, has for its national president, James R. Stewart, subject of an active investigation being conducted by the Federal Bureau of Investigation. It publishes a monthly magazine entitled "The New Negro World." Investigation of the organization to date reveals that it caters to the more ignorant class of Negroes and has for its purpose the redemption of Africa and the transporting of all Negroes who are interested in going there from this country to ultimately establish a free and independent government controlled and operated by Negroes only.

It is pointed out that in the February issue of "The New Negro World," which is edited by Stewart, an editorial written by Stewart was to the effect that if Negroes were to be discriminated against as they have been in the past, then he would say "to Hell with Pearl Harbor" rather than "Remember Pearl Harbor."

The Negro Press

In the Cleveland area there are two publications published by Negroes which are the "Call and Post," a weekly newspaper with offices at 2319 East 55th Street, and the "Cleveland Herald," a weekly newspaper published at 2290 East 71st Street. It is reported these two newspapers have consistently for over a year, dealt in a militant fashion with matters affecting Negroes. There are being set out hereinafter various types of articles appearing these papers since August 1941.

In August and September 1941, there were articles complaining about "Jim Crowism" in the armed forces and the treatment afforded Negroes in the armed forces in Southern States. Other articles, however, during these two months were matters of general interest containing very little agitation against discrimination.

During the period September 20 to October 19, 1941, there were articles first referring to alleged mistreatment of Negroes in the South and its potential effect on the war effort and an accompanying demand for fair treatment for the Negroes there. Another article alleged that there was discrimination against Jews and Negroes in the Air Forces of both the Army and the Navy. Another article, however, at this time reflected that the Negroes were better off under the United States Government than under Axis Domination. Still another article reflected that Negroes were buying Defense Bonds and that if Hitler was counting on race prejudice as a disrupting factor in the United States he was "counting his chickens before they hatched."

During the period of October 20 to November 19, 1941, an article reflected that the Negro has no pride in the way he is treated in the United States but that under Axis domination he would be thrown into barbarism. Another article pointed out that labor unions were discriminating against Negroes in employment in United States defense industries.

During the period November 20, through December 19, 1941, articles entitled "Comments on Current Events" reflected that the policy of the Negro is to fight for the defeat of Hitler but at the same time to extend democratic rights to all people. There was also an article during this period depicting the great disadvantages the Negro would suffer under Axis domination. Another article during this period discussed the attack on Pearl Harbor as a "stab in the back" and went on to state that in spite of mistreatment of the Negro in this country he was ready to serve in the armed forces.

During the period from December 20, 1941, to January 19, 1942, it was said that Negroes were expecting better and more generous treatment from his fellow citizens.

During the period January 20 to February 19, 1942, considerable space was devoted to the lynching and burning of a Negro in Sikeston, Missouri, it being pointed out that such instances did not make the Negro happy, however, he was still loyal.

During the period February 20 through March 19, 1942, an editorial appeared expressing the hope for more employment for Negro women. Another article during this period reflected that "white supremacy" in the Orient was taking a "beating." During this period it was also pointed out that a great tragedy existed in the wasted labor caused by discrimination against the Negroes.

During the period of March 20 through April 19, 1942, editorials appeared complaining about the alleged mistreatment and discrimination practiced in the armed forces against the Negroes.

During the period April 20 to May 19, 1942, articles appeared stating that the continued enlistment of Negroes in that area as messmen in the United States Navy, the only capacity in which they were able to serve, was an indication of the unquestioned loyalty of the Negro. Another article during this period pointed out that of all the discriminations practiced against the American Negro in the Northern States the Polish people seemed to have the biggest part. Another article appeared defending the Negro press stating that it was not subversive and opposed to the war effort but opposed rather to the way Negroes were being treated in the present war effort.

Youngstown, Ohio

In this area sources of information interviewed advise they believe there is no foreign-inspired agitation among the Negroes there but stated rather it is the general and widespread belief that there is discrimination existing against the Negroes. One source of information has cited the fact that there are many Negroes in the Army and that as a consequence their relatives in civilian life would not oppose the war effort.

One source of information was interviewed who is reportedly "extremely liberal if not radical" in many of his views, has advised that the proper way to solve the Negro problems is by one of three methods:

1. Through interracial committees with no publicity or fanfare.
2. Mass meetings.
3. Agitation against racial discrimination.

He stated that as far as the average Negro was concerned he believed that he is making money, having a good time, and not doing much thinking. He related, however, that on the other hand, thinking Negroes believe the final outcome of the Indian situation will be an indication possibly of what will happen to the Negroes in the United States.

A Negro member of the Veterans of Foreign Wars who has been contacted with regard to the Negro situation in and around Youngstown, Ohio, has advised that the only information he has received with regard to un-American activities among Negroes are those of the Jehovah's Witnesses sect.

With regard to the popularity and the effectiveness of Negro organizations in and around Youngstown, it was reported that inasmuch as there is no Negro District in that area, for that reason it is difficult for organizations to operate and maintain strength.

Future Outlook League

Until recently the Future Outlook League existed in Youngstown, Ohio, and had for its president a Negro by the name of Bertram Carlson. Carlson is said to have been close to the Communist Party, if not a member of it and at one time solicited membership into the Party. He was arrested in Cleveland, Ohio, in October 1941 for carrying a dangerous weapon on the night of a dinner given in honor of the Communist Party Secretary for Cuyahoga County. The organization had for its purpose the agitation for anti-discrimination moves.

National Association for the Advancement of Colored People

This organization is active in the Youngstown, Ohio, area and is headed by Reverend H. B. Gibson who is said to have caused considerable agitation relative to the mistreatment of Negroes by white people in this area.

Communist Party

Although it has a general interest in obtaining cooperation of Negroes in the war effort, the Communist Party still is active in the Cleveland and Youngstown area in agitating for and among the Negroes. There are various indications that the purpose for such agitation is to gain the support of Negroes rather than to aid them in their alleged plight. [*100-135-12*]

Detroit Field Division

In the Detroit area, where there are well over 100,000 Negroes, there are all of the settings for a boom city. In all phases of the economic and social life in this city and its environs there is an electrified air. Much of this has been the result of an abnormal increase in the population during the past three years of both whites and Negroes. This increase can be set forth as follows:

White people: Totalling 450,000 persons

Negroes: Totalling approximately 35,000 persons

The general increase in the population has added to the congestion in the Detroit area, especially in regard to amusement facilities, eating places, public transportation and traffic. It has also created a great and deplorable congestion and shortage of housing facilities both for Negroes and whites.

These factors, taken into consideration with the increased tempo of life brought about by the war and the preparation for it, are supplemented by reported social and economic inequalities between whites and Negroes in the area, as well as by subversive and allegedly un-American forces exploiting the Negro population. All of these forces, each with its proportionate share, contribute to make the general Negro population in Detroit antagonistic, unsatisfied and unsympathetic in many instances with the war effort.

Set forth hereinafter is that information broken down into its various phases which has been received, along with the confidential opinions and conclusions of confidential sources of information, which reflects these various forces among the Negro population in Detroit:

Pro-Japanese and Anti-White Influence

The records of an investigation by this Bureau reflect that in 1933 and 1934 a Japanese propagandist, Naka Nakane, an alien was very active and to some extent, not measurable at this time, effective among the Negroes in Detroit. He originated in 1933 what was then termed a secret organization for Negroes,

the Development of Our Own, by representing himself as Satakata Takahashi, a Major in the Japanese army, and stating he was the representative in the United States of the Japanese Black Dragon Society, an ultra-nationalistic patriotic group. The Development of Our Own was incor-porated in Lansing, Michigan, as a patriotic brotherhood. Through this organization Nakane was said to have promised assistance, arms and money to the Negroes in a war against the white race, claiming that Japanese agents were all over the United States in the interests of his organization working through the Universal Negro Improvement Association.

Nakane was deported to Japan on April 20, 1934, but reappeared on August 29 of the same year at Vancouver in possession of $2,000, although he was without funds when deported four months earlier. He illegally re-entered the United States at Buffalo, New York, on January 11, 1939, and again became active in the organization. He was arrested on June 22, 1939, for this illegal entry and the attempted bribery of an immigration inspector. He was sentenced to a term of three years' imprisonment and a fine of $4,500 on September 28, 1939. He was subsequently transferred to the Medical Center for Federal Prisoners at Springfield, Missouri, where he was to be released February 27, 1942. Prior to his release, however, a Presidential Warrant was issued for him and he was again turned over to the Immigration and Naturalization Service in whose custody he remained constantly until April 2, 1942, when the Attorney General of the United States affirmed the order of internment recommended by the Enemy Alien Hearing Board. Nakane has since been interned as a dangerous alien enemy.

Because of the colorful character of Nakane's propaganda, his effects in Detroit have been magnified clear out of proportion to his actual ability. Occasionally there crops up, usually in an individual Negro, a pro-Japanese sentiment. This is not prevalent and there is no evidence indicating Japanese propaganda planned, participated in, or set off the riots.

Nakane was to some extent successful in fomenting anti-white sentiment, and it is probable that some of the anti-white sentiment stems back to his influence many years ago.

Investigations have been made of the Moorish Science Temple of America and the Allah Temple of Islam in Detroit, primarily along Selective Service lines. There have been revealed forms of this cultism existing in spots throughout the Negro population in Detroit as units of these two organizations. In membership and influence among Negroes generally, these organizations are minor. Their inception and activities are primarily a result of Negro cognizance of inferiority rather than anything foreign inspired.

Five members of the Allah Temple of Islam in Detroit have been questioned regarding their failure to register under the Selective Training and Service Act of 1940 as amended. Three of the five have been released at the direction of the United States Attorney upon their agreeing to register. Two, however, were held and pleaded guilty for failure to register. In the interviews with these individuals all refused to admit any person had counseled them to evade the provisions of this Act. They all did advise they refused to register because they were registered with the Holy City of Mecca and, therefore, should not be registered again.

There is a branch of the Universal Negro Improvement Association in Detroit which meets at 1516 Russell Street. A Reverend Wheat, said to be formerly of Chicago, Illinois, is described as the Detroit leader, while one William Sherril has been organization head in the Detroit area. In this connection, it should be pointed out that Sherril in 1939 as a candidate for the Common Council of Detroit polled more than 15,000 votes. The extent of membership in this organization is not presently known. However, it is known that in July 1942 a meeting was held at the headquarters of the organization and approximately 300 attended. Reverend Wheat spoke at this meeting and reportedly admonished Negroes to reject the white man's ideas and to think independently and said that white men have suppressed defenseless Negroes. He is said to have urged that Negroes take advantage of the war situation to secure their rights.

William L. Sherril is the author of a regular column published in the Negro newspaper, "The Michigan Chronicle." In October 1942, in one of his articles in his column entitled "Listen, America," he expressed himself as follows:

> ". . . . We cannot defeat Japan—we cannot destroy Hitlerism until we have honestly set forth to defeat and destroy the enemies of tolerance, fair play, justice and interracial good will within our own borders. . . . We can't expect 100 per cent of our population to stand wholeheartedly behind the Cause for which we say we fight when only the 90 per cent is permitted the right to work anywhere, the right to live anywhere, the right to vote anywhere, and the right to be protected by the law, anywhere."

Pro-German or Fascist Influence

It is said that the better class of Negroes in the Detroit area is definitely opposed to the Axis beliefs and they will do anything in their power to assist the United States in defeating its enemies. With regard to German or Italian inspired agitation, trouble and unrest, no information has been received to the effect that such forces are at work among the Negroes in this area.

Communist Exploitation of the Negroes

Outside of economic and social forces and influence, the Communist Party and its various elements are believed to be by far the most responsible of all subversive groups. While the exploitation of the Negro population in Detroit has been one of its foremost activities since 1931, the Party's campaign in Negro agitation has been accelerated during the past three years.

There has been an intensified drive for membership among the Negroes in this area by the Communist Party and special efforts have been made to recruit Negroes, especially, according to confidential informants, those who are skilled workers or who have recently completed their trade training. The approach made by the Communist Party is that the Negroes should support the war effort in an all-out manner; yet, at the same time the Party decries alleged abuses or of discrimination against them. It not only pertains to the denial of equal rights and instances of discrimination, but supports social intercourse and the abolition of separation of races. In this connection, a confidential informant who has been in the Party and is well schooled in its techniques **and who presently serves as a private intelligence gatherer** has advised the consensus of opinion among Party members is that no trouble will result from their disruptive efforts until after the war when Negro labor and employees hired during the war will be replaced by men returning from the Armed Forces. The opinion was offered that the Communist Party believes that after the war is over there will be at least a short period of unemployment, after which men returning from the Armed Services will replace the newly trained skilled workers including the Negroes who will be forced out and onto a waiting list. Discontent will be the result and according to the source of information the Party believes the Negroes who will be replaced will then become good Party members.

This same source of information has also advised of knowing of instances where well-trained and educated Negroes in Detroit have been discriminated against as far as obtaining employment is concerned. This in turn causes discontent and a cynicism which fertilizes the Negro's mind to a point where he is receptive to Communism.

The Communist Party in the Detroit area has, besides adopting an intensive recruiting campaign among Negroes, extended its efforts through both white and Negro Communist Party members to control or influence Negro organizations. These organizations, in their order of importance, are the National Association for the Advancement of Colored People Detroit Branch, the Citizens Committee for Jobs in War Industries, the Metropolitan Detroit Council for Fair Employment Practices, the Negro Youth Council for Victory and Democracy, the National Negro Congress, and "The Michigan Chronicle."

The Civil Rights Federation, which is guided by Jack Raskin, has been exceedingly active in agitating for and among Negroes in the Detroit area. The Civil Rights Federation is described as a Communist front organization and Raskin, its Executive Secretary, is stated to be extremely close to the Communist Party, and Pat Toohey, State Secretary of the Communist Party for the State of Michigan. In its attempt to influence and agitate among Negro organizations, the organization is reported to have received through Jack Raskin from John Dancy, Negro director of the Detroit Urban League, the mailing list of some 750 names which is said to reach practically every Negro organization in Detroit.

The organization has been extremely active in making plans to circulate a petition among prominent people to be sent to the Fair Employment Practice[s] Committee with regard to the alleged discrimination in Detroit against Negroes. It has also been actve in circulating petitions urging the recipient thereof to write his Senator and Congressman to support the Geyer anti-poll tax bill.

Mention should be made generally of Jack Raskin and his activities with regard to the Negro situation in this area. Raskin, who is reported to be a member of the Communist Party and organizer of Section 9 of the Communist Party in Michigan, is in frequent contact with Pat Toohey, Secretary of the Communist Party of Michigan, with reference to meetings, maneuvers and other activities directly connected with the Negro situation. He is often in contact, giving instructions or suggestions, with Negro leaders who are either sympathetic to the Communist cause or are closely affiliated with the Communist Party. He has also worked, according to a confidential informant, with Governmental representatives concerned with the Negro problem in Detroit, offering suggestions and support. In one instance, he planned with a Governmental representative to secure skilled Negro women workers for the purpose of directing them to various industries in Detroit where they were to apply for jobs. The purpose of this was to obtain cases of alleged discrimination so that certain employers could be cited.

Following is a list of leading Detroit Negro Communists and sympathizers who are reportedly active in the Party's work among their race. It is believed significant to set these names out along with their respective capacities:

Christopher Columbus Alston—Executive Secretary of the National Negro Congress: member and organizer of Communist Party.

James Anderson—Member of Section 1, Communist Party in Detroit since 1931; has been assigned to aid in building Communist Section in Ford Local 600, United Automobile Workers of America, CIO.

Ernest Austin, alias James Austin—Reported to have been a member of the James Ashford Branch of the Young Communist League in 1939.

William V. Banks—Reported to have been a member of the Communist Party from 1931 to 1933.

Joseph Harris Billups, alias Joe Hill—Candidate for Congress on the Communist Party ticket in 1932.

Alex Black, alias Robert Black—Has been a member of the James Ashford Branch of the Young Communist League and is employed by the Department of Public Works in Detroit.

Mamie Geraldine Bledsoe—Michigan sponsor of National Free Browder Congress; member Sojourner Truth Citizens Committee, Metropolitan Detroit Fair Employment Council; active in affairs of Civil Rights Federation.

Rose Blount—Worker and organizer in the Communist Party; prominent in Nathaniel Turner Club and International Negro Congress.

Jane Brown—Member in 1939 of Young Communist League; reported at present time to be Communist sympathizer.

William Brown—Has been interested in Detroit Workers School organized by Communist Party.

Eddie Butler—Member of Unit No. 2, Communist Party, since 1935, has been a member of International Labor Defense.

Anne Cash—Distributed and circulated Party literature and petitions in year 1935, 1936, and 1940.

Don Antonia Clarke—Former Financial Secretary of the James Ashford Branch of the Young Communist League.

Veal Clough, alias Veal Clouth—Employee Ford Motor Company; reported Communist Party member and organizer.

John Conyers—Sponsor second Michigan conference of National Negro Congress; alleged Communist Party member.

Gloster Current—Executive Secretary of the National Association for the Advancement of Colored People; member of Sponsorship Committee of the Free Browder Congress; reported to be constantly in contact with the offices of the Civil Rights Federation, a "Communist front," and the Communist Party.

Leon F. Curtiss—Militant member of the Communist Party and Young Communist League.

John Dancy—Director Detroit Urban League; sponsor Michigan Free Browder Congress.

Curtis Davis, alias Clifford Hill—Has been President of James Ashford Branch of Young Communist League; active in the Communist Party sub-organizing committee; was on Negro committee of the Communist Party.

Tom Dennis, Jr.—Employee Willow Run Bomber Factory; reported member of the Young Communist League.

Otis Eaton—Employee Ford Motor Company; active in affairs of Civil Rights Federation.

Robert Evans—Detroit attorney; appeared at a Negro mass meeting on July 24, 1942, sponsored by the Communist Party, at which time he exhibited a ticket for the Ella Reeve Bloor birthday party.

Charles C. Diggs—Michigan State Senator; Communist sympathizer; spoke with James Ford, National Committeeman of the Party, at a Negro mass meeting on July 24, 1942.

Luke Fennell—Reported Communist Party member.

Mrs. Margaret Ferguson—In 1940 signed petition to place Communist Party on Michigan ballot; was Recording Secretary of the State Committee, International Workers Order in 1941; is said to be active in the Civil Rights Federation.

Mrs. Rosa Gragg—President of the Detroit Association of Women's Clubs; is said to have cooperated closely with Jack Raskin, Executive Secretary of Civil Rights Federation, and Pat Toohey, Michigan State Secretary of the Communist Party.

Walter Hardin, also known as Walter Harding—Member of Michigan Sponsoring Committee, National Free Browder Committee; alleged Communist.

Mattie Henderson—Former leader in Section 1 of the Communist Party; said to have been active in Communist Party as late as 1940.

Ben Hicks—Reported Communist sympathizer.

Reverend Charles C. Hill—Active in Civil Rights Federation and cooperates closely with it.

Joe B. Hill—Member of the James Ashford Unit, Young Communist League.

Henrietta Jackson—Member James W. Ford Unit of the Communist Party, Detroit.

Paul Kirk—Active in Communist Party affairs; said to have attended National Training School of Communist Party in New York City in 1935.

William Latimore—Has been a member of the Young Communist League in Detroit.

Felix B. Maise—Active since 1923 in the Communist Party; has been an organizer in District 7; now a member of the Organizing Committee, Ford Local 600, United Automobile Workers of America, CIO.

Louis Martin—Editor of the Michigan Chronicle; sponsor of the Committee to Free Earl Browder; presently active in Party affairs.

Hedges Mason—Reported Communist Party member; former member of the National Executive Board of the National Negro Congress, a Communist front.

David Mates—Member of the Communist Party Michigan State Committee.

Doctor James J. McClendon—Sponsor of the National Free Browder Congress; said to associate with Communist Party members.

Frank McDonald—Member of the Communist Party.

Reverend John Miles—Active member District 7, Communist Party; active in Civil Rights Federation; member of the National Negro Congress and the National Association for the Advancement of Colored People.

C. Heyward Naben, also known as Hayward C. Naben—Alleged section organizer of the Communist Party.

Leslie Powell—Member of Section 1, Communist Party.

Ivory Scott—Recently was active member in James Ashford Branch, Young Communist League.

John Simmons—(brother of LeBron Simmons)—Associate of Communist Party members and attendant of Communist Party affairs.

LeBron Simmons—President of the National Negro Communist Unit in Detroit and member of Negro Committee, District 7, Communist Party.

Ellsworth Steen—Said to be an active organizer of Communist Party in Flint, Michigan.

Frank Sykes—Has been active in Communist Party since 1934; spoke at a meeting on July 24, 1940, where candidacy of James W. Ford for the Vice Presidency of the United States was promoted.

Shelton Tappes—Associate of Communist Party members and affiliated with Civil Rights Federation; President of Ford Local 600, United Automobile Workers of America, CIO.

Thomas Edward Tolan—Supported Citizens Committee to Free Earl Browder; Chairman of Greater Detroit Unit; close associate of Communist Party members and affiliated with the Civil Rights Federation.

Herb Walker—Alleged President of Bomber Branch of the Young Communist League.

William Paul Wells, alias Paul Wills—Janitor, Chrysler Corporation; alleged advocate of Communism.

Beulah Whitby—Close associate of Communist Party members; a supporter of National Free Browder Congress; National President of the Alpha Kappa Alpha Society.

Reverend Horace A. White—Sponsor of Citizens Committee to Free Earl Browder; said to be an active supporter of Communist Party.

John White—Communist Party sympathizer.

Ed Williams—Reported active figure in Communist Party channels since 1931.

Lonnie Williams—Active in Communist Party since 1934; candidate for Attorney General of State of Michigan on Communist Party ticket in 1934; is said to have attended Lenin University in Moscow in 1935.

Merrill C. Work—One time member of the Negro Committee of the Communist Party; former Communist candidate for Lieutenant Governor of the State of Michigan.

Paul Wykoff—Chairman of the Sponsorship Committee of Negro Youth Win the War Conference; associate of Communist Party members and affiliated with Civil Rights Federation.

J. N. Young—Associate of Communist Party members.

James Banks—Member of West Side Branch of the Young Communist League.

Elmer Barnes—Member of Roy Hudson-Wonders Branch of the Young Communist League.

William Bartley—Alleged Communist, Jackson, Michigan.

Frank Berry—Member of the West Side Branch of the Young Communist League.

Reverend William Bowman—Reportedly active in affairs of the Communist Party, Pontiac, Michigan; reportedly in employ of the Ford Motor Car Company.

John Crump—Reported to have signed Communist Party petition, 1940.

Carl Hubbard—A reported Communist, Jackson, Michigan.

Marshal Jones—A reported Communist, Jackson, Michigan.

Alfonse Lee—Reported member, Unit 5, Section 2, District 7, Communist Party.

Mable Lee-Smith—Alleged President of Young Communist League.

Charles Tyson—Reportedly active in affairs of Young Communist League.

Edy Wilson—President, Ford-Roy Hudson Branch, Young Communist League.

With regard to the Negro membership in the Communist Party in the Detroit area, the following information has been reported with respect to the recent recruiting campaign of both the Party and the Young Communist League:

The Party expected to recruit 500 new members from February 1 to May 1, 1943, in Detroit. Of the 120 new members first recruited, 54 were Negroes which represented a percentage of well over 45 per cent. On April 13, 1943, it was reported at a Young Communist League meeting that 60 per cent of the 291 new recruits were Negroes. This figure was compared with a total of only 6 per cent of Negro members in the Young Communist League one and one-half years previous.

[*100-135-16-82 pa 6; 100-135-16-88 pa 6.*]

Subsequent reports as to the recruiting campaign were received that 885 new recruits were obtained. Approximately 50 per cent of the new recruits were Negroes. This figure brought the total of the Communist Party membership in District No. 7 to approximately 1,800. [*100-3-12-716*]

The following information is set forth to reflect an example of Communist maneuvering with regard to the Negroes in the Detroit area. On December 24, 1942, Gloster B. Current, Negro, Executive Secretary of the National Association for the Advancement of Colored People in Detroit, held a lengthy conference with Pat Toohey, Secretary of District 7 of the Communist Party for the State of Michigan. This conference was called by Toohey, a white man, who reportedly desired to acquaint Current with regard to the housing and dormitory situation at Willow Run. (The FHA has erected dormitories near the Willow Run Plant of the Ford Motor Car Company for the occupancy of employees of the Willow Run Plant.) Current is said to have informed Toohey he had visited the Willow Run bomber plant the previous week with other reported Communists. Toohey in turn is said to have told Current the members of the Federal Housing Administration were willing and agreeable to mix occupancy of the project if the United Automobile, Aircraft and Agricultural Implement Workers of America, CIO, would make a decision. Toohey reportedly stated the Union leaders refused to take a firm stand because of the great excess of Southerners in Detroit, while other Union leaders were frightened. Toohey was said to have asserted there had been a meeting of top union officials a short time previous at which time they said they wanted the FHA to make a decision and they did not care which way it went. Toohey stated to Current if he and any others were approached on the matter they should take a firm stand inasmuch as the point brought up by the Union leaders was not actually the feeling of the automobile workers but was merely the fear expressed by some of their leaders as a result of recent disturbances in some of the plants. Toohey is said to have then warned [that] Current had been approached by prominent leaders, including Union leaders who had persuaded him to accept an incorrect position. Toohey then explained there was a coming election in the various locals of the UAW and that there had been a decided change

in the membership with 400,000 new members coming in with "different ideas" and 1,000,000 members having gone into the Army. Toohey is further related to have remarked some of the Union leaders would raise the point that it was not the prerogative of the Union but of the FHA to decide on the mixed occupancy.

Toohey is further said to have explained the answer in avoiding trouble of bi-racial occupied homes was in the securing of a reasonable selection of tenants and not permitting undesirables to move in. He then is said to have referred to building up community spirit.

Other Radical Groups

In the Detroit area there are several Communistic and radical groups, in many of which membership is comparatively small, which agitate for added rights for the Negro. These groups are the Socialist Workers Party, the Proletarian Party and the Socialist Labor Party. These groups, while not large in membership, are extremely active in distributing pamphlets and other literature pertaining to the Negro situation. Their demands are militant and all vie among themselves for Negro support.

Negro Organizations

There are a number of Negro organizations in the Detroit area, the largest of which is the Detroit branch of the National Association for the Advancement of Colored People. A large majority of these organizations are reported to have Communist influence in them in varying degrees. All are militant in their programs to obtain equal rights for Negroes, to abolish discrimination and segregation, and to generally urge the betterment of Negroes.

The National Association for the Advancement of Colored People

The Detroit branch of the National Association for the Advancement of Colored People, located at 446 East Warren Avenue, is led by Dr. James J. McClendon, President, and Gloster Current, Executive Secretary. This organization is said to have a membership of from 15,000 to 20,000. It stages large meetings in addition to holding regular business meetings. Its objectives are similar to those of the national organization. They are:

1. Educate America with regard to the Negroes.
2. Fight against racial prejudice.
3. End lynching.
4. Improve cultural conditions among the Negroes.
5. Secure votes for the Negro and educate the Negro in voting.

The Communist influence in this organization in Detroit is reported to consist of Dr. McClendon who is said to have constantly engaged in activities which follow the Communist Party line and, further, Gloster Current who is said to be an active Communist Party member.

On April 11, 1943, this organization sponsored, along with the Interracial Committee of the United Automobile, Aircraft and Agricultural Implement Workers of America, CIO, an anti-discrimination parade and rally in Detroit in which approximately 2,000 Negroes took part. Participants included such organizations as the Socialist Party, the Workers Party, the Communist Party, the Citizens Committee for Jobs in War Industries, the National Negro Congress, various unions, Negro churches and miscellaneous civic groups. The general theme of the meeting was to demand the United States to cease discrimination. No violence took place during the parade. An exceedingly active part was taken in the parade and rally by members of the Communist Party and by Communist Party sympathizers. Among the speakers were Dr. James McClendon, Walter Harden of the Interracial Committee of the Union, Gloster Current, Reverend Charles A. Hill, reported Communist, Walter Reuther, Leonard D. V. Smith, and Michigan State Senator Charles C. Diggs.

A resolution called "The Cadillac Charter" requested the abolition of discrimination, segregation in housing and in the Army, the poll tax, and lynching.

[*100-135-16-83*]

National Negro Congress

The Detroit Council of this organization has its headquarters at 585 Gratiot Avenue, Detroit, Michigan. Its officers are as follows:

LeBron Simmons, President

Coleman Young, Executive Secretary

Hodges Mason)
Jennetta Welch)
John Conyers)
Nathaniel Smith)
Samuel Fanroy)
Reverend Charles Hill) Executive Board
Luke Fennell)
Robert Evans)
Arthur Perry)
Walter Carey)
Quill Petway)

Its program has been made up of the following matters:

1. Rent control.
2. Fair employment project council.

3. Participation in the fall elections of 1942.
4. Participation in and contributions to various "Win the War Conferences."

A confidential source of information has advised with regard to this organization that it is one of the contact fronts through which a great deal of the work of the Communist Party and the Civil Rights Federation is conducted. LeBron Simmons, Gloster Current and Coleman Young are said to be often in contact with Pat Toohey, Michigan State Secretary of the Communist Party, and with Jack Raskin, Executive Secretary of the Civil Rights Federation.

The West Side Industrial Neighborhood Committee

This organization sponsored a meeting held on August 27, 1942, at Milford and Vinewood Avenues, Detroit. The circular advertising this meeting stated: "We, men workers, are fighting to secure jobs in industry for you." Approximately 200 people are said to have attended the meeting and several individuals alleged to have connections in the Detroit area spoke. Among them were Charles C. Diggs, State Senator Stanley Nowak, LeBron Simmons, Charles A. Hill. The speakers dealt generally with alleged discriminations in defense industries and referred to the President's Fair Employment Practice[s] Committee and his executive order creating it.

Metropolitan Detroit Council for Fair Employment Practices

This organization, which has been organized in the City of Detroit, is headed by Edward W. McFarland and Miss Zaio Woodford, white attorney who is Chairman of the Grievances Committee. The organization has been active and working on the matter of alleged discrimination against Negro women at the Ford Bomber Plant at Willow Run, Michigan. It should be stated that Miss Woodford was a member of the original organizing committee of the Council at its inception in January 1942. She was also a sponsor of the Michigan Free Browder organization, a Communist front organization, and at present she is active in the affairs of the Civil Rights Federation, another Communist front.

On August 20, 1942, the Council held a meeting at the Lucy Thurman branch of the YWCA in Detroit, the purpose of which specifically was to discuss the subject of alleged discrimination against Negro women at the Ford Bomber Plant. The meeting is stated to have served as a climax to the picketing of the Ford River Rouge Plant (Gate No. 2) from 1:00 P.M. to 4:30 P.M. on that day. At the meeting Miss Woodford related that on May 29, 1942, a committee called on Harry Bennett of the Ford Motor Car Company who she said promised the committee that there would be no discrimination in the employment of women at the Bomber Plant. She continued, saying that since the visit there more than 1,000 women had been employed but not a single Negro woman. She alleged that complaints of this discrimination had been increasing so rapidly that the committee had drafted a telegram setting forth the facts of the case and sent it to Dr. McLane, Chairman of the President's Committee on

Fair Employment Practice, urging the Committee to hold a hearing with regard to the matter. At the time, Miss Woodford said no reply had been received from either Dr. McLane or from Mr. Ford who had been forwarded a copy.

It was said at the meeting that a general discussion then took place as to what part the United Automobile Workers of America Local should have in the case. It was decided that the Union could be of no help until Negro women were employed, at which time they should exert all efforts to maintain peace and harmony. It was then proposed that a questionnaire be drawn up and mailed to candidates for the State Legislature to determine their position on proposed fair employment legislation for the State of Michigan to be drawn up by a committee to which were named Miss Woodford, LeBron Simmons, who is a reported Communist, and others. Miss Woodford then stated that the "Daily Press" had failed to give any publicity to the alleged discriminatory practices and it was then decided that a report of the committee would necessarily have to talk to the various editors in an attempt to "straighten" them out in this difficulty.

The meeting was attended by approximately 50 persons representing various civil organizations in Detroit such as the Urban League, the National Association for the Advancement of Colored People, and the Civil Rights Federation.

More recent activities reportedly engaged in by this organization are the cooperating with the Civil Rights Federation and other groups in attempting to procure biracial occupancy of the Willow Run housing project and the planning of an interracial youth committee of the organization as a contemplated step to bring about the eventual and permanent integration of Negroes and whites.

The Afro-American Benevolent Employment Association

In August 1942 it was reported that the Briggs Manufacturing Plant had been approached by groups and urged to employ Negro women in their plants. It is stated that there was considerable pressure placed on the company but that the company absolutely refused to deal with or make negotiations with individuals who approached it. In this connection, it has been confidentially reported that the company deems itself quite liberal regarding the employment of Negro men but that it absolutely drew the line when colored women were involved.

At the same time the Ford Motor Car Company had been picketed near its personnel offices, circulars were distributed advertising a meeting held on August 23, 1942, at the Ebeneezer A.M.E. Church under the auspices of the Afro-American Benevolent Employment Association. On the circular it was stated "IF WE MUST FIGHT FOR VICTORY, WE MUST WORK AT ALL JOBS AND SERVE IN ALL MILITARY BRANCHES OF OUR GOVERNMENT, WITHOUT BEING JIM CROWED." Advertised as speakers were Reverend Charles A. Hill, William L. Sherril and Charles C. Diggs, Michigan State Senator. These individuals have previously been referred to as reported Communist sympathizers.

The meeting was held and was attended by approximately 200, the purpose of which, as presented by L. D. Smith, the principal speaker, was to "stir the people" and to let them know what is happening with respect to their "democratic rights." The meeting on August 23, 1942, was described by a source of information as one not having the purpose of good Americanism but the sole purpose was stirring Negroes into racial resentment.

Again, on October 3, 1942, a meeting was held under the auspices of this organization. It was attended by approximately 20 Negro men and women. Leonard D. Smith was again the main speaker. He is said to have consumed the entire time of the meeting in his speech which is said to have lacked unison and coherence but was forcible in effect. The topic of his speech was alleged to have been the effect of alleged injustices and inequalities said to have been forced on the Negroes in this country.

March on Washington Movement

On September 26 and 27, 1942, a national policy conference of the March on Washington Movement was held in Detroit, Michigan. Approximately 35 Negro delegates were in attendance from various large cities, including New York, Washington, St. Louis, Chicago, Detroit, and Tampa, Florida. At the conference the organization's principles were formulated and the United States was divided into five regions which were in turn subdivided into lesser units. The purpose of the meeting was to institute a membership campaign to muster enough members for any concerted mass action. The question as to whether or not a march on the City of Washington would be made was postponed for discussion until the national convention could be held in Chicago sometime in May 1943. This organization in Detroit is alleged to have Communist influence in it, however, the National Committee of the organization has continuously opposed the Communist Party.

Negro Youth Council for Victory and Democracy

This organization was originally led by Edward Tolan, Negro athlete and reported member of the Communist Party, and Harper Poulson, active member of the Young Communist League. The reported purpose of the organization was to bring about interracial understanding between white and Negro youth. It has also devoted its program to such matters as anti-poll tax bill and employment of Negroes in defense industries. In all of its activities it is reported that Communist Party members and sympathizers take an active interest. The attendance at its meetings varies at 20 and over. In April 1943 its leader, Edward Tolan, was inducted into the United States Army and the leadership was given to a youthful Negro, one Arthur Bowman, who has in the past worked with the Republican Party. Bowman is said to oppose Communist influence in the group. However, Harper Poulson and other reported Communists interested in the organization are said to have inaugurated a campaign to discredit Bowman.

Negro Publications

The following Negro publications are printed in the Detroit area:

The "Michigan Chronicle"—Louis Martin, Editor, Detroit; the "Detroit Tribune"—J. Edward McCall, Editor; the "Detroit World Echo", Detroit; "Hamtramck News"; "Detroit Echo"; "Pittsburgh Courier", Detroit edition, John R. Williams, Editor; "Flint News", Flint, Michigan; the "Lansing Echo", Lansing, Michigan; the "Lansing State Echo"; the "Macomb County Echo", Mt. Clemens, Michigan; and the "Pontiac Echo", Pontiac, Michigan.

With regard to the "Michigan Chronicle", said to have the largest distribution, it has been reported that because of strong Communist tendencies of its editor, Louis Martin, and by virtue of its printing news concerning the activities of Negroes in the Communist Party, it is believed to be to some extent influenced by the Communist Party. However, from general and outward appearances it deals with matters of interest to the Negro race in general.

The "Michigan Chronicle" is owned by the same company that owns the "Chicago Defender". The majority of its general news comes through the Associated Negro Press. Its editorial policy and local news apparently is directed by Martin and follows the Communist Party line. In this regard, a confidential informant has advised that James W. Ford on February 7, 1942, in speaking at the Fort Wayne Hotel in Detroit, stated Louis Martin told him he wrote no editorials or invaded no issues which did not take the same side as the Communist Party. It might be noted that Ford is a member of the National Committee of the Communist Party.

An examination made of the issues of the "Michigan Chronicle" over a period of several years has revealed the editorials written by Louis Martin have always been in accord with the current policy and program of the Party at that particular time. The paper has publicized to the fullest extent the activities of local organizations, several of which are reportedly Communist inspired and infiltrated which have as their objective the elimination of discrimination against the Negro. Local instances of alleged discrimination are given prominent attention and those in which some form of violence has been displayed have always been attributed to the Ku Klux Klan. Scandals, shootings, murders, divorces, lawsuits, family trouble—all are given front-page attention by the newspaper. [*100-1223-19-27*]

The "Racial Digest", a magazine which is styled similarly to that of the "Reader's Digest", is published in the Detroit area. The exact circulation of the magazine is not known; however, it is a Negro publication and contains many articles pointing out alleged racial prejudices and discriminations. It has contained articles by Reverend Charles A. Hill and L[oui]s Martin, both reported to have close Communist connections. It has printed condensations from such publications as the "New Masses" and the newspaper "PM", the former of which is said to be closely allied with the Communist Party.

The Sojourner Truth Housing Project

This housing project was erected by the Federal Defense Housing Administration with Federal funds with the original purpose of providing adequate housing facilities for Negro workers and their families engaged in national defense work. The project is located at Nevada and Fenlon Streets, a site which was recommended by the Detroit Housing Commission. It is named after a colored woman missionary, now deceased, who went by the name Sojourner Truth, and who is reported to have been active in the State of Michigan in the interest of the advancement of Negroes.

Because this project was located in a white neighborhood a violent storm of opposition arose to the Negro occupancy of the project and it is said to have caused the Federal Defense Housing Administration to change its regulations with respect to the occupancy so that only white persons were to take up residence there. This change resulted in a concerted effort on the part of the Michigan branch of the Communist Party and its front organizations, including the Civil Rights Federation, in an attempt to have the original regulations as to the occupancy placed in effect again. Delegates were sent to Washington, D.C., and in February 1942 the regulations were changed and the project was designated exclusively for Negroes. On February 28, 1942, the Negroes attempted to move in. White residents of the community and anti-Negro agitators of the National Workers League attacked them and a minor riot occurred. Almost one hundred Negroes and several white persons were arrested.

The riot caused a delay in the occupancy of the premises for approximately two months. However, in the month of April 1942 Negro families moved quietly into the project. The Communist Party, which was evidently active in agitation for Negro occupancy of the project, considered it a great victory and is presently attempting to apply its activities to other Government housing projects which are now being erected in the Detroit area.

The Colonel Hamtramck Housing Project

As an aftermath of the "Sojourner Truth victory" of the Party, members are reported to have immediately begun agitation for Negro occupancy of the captioned housing project. This project was being built in the City of Hamtramck with Federal funds for the purpose of housing war workers. No regulations have been formulated as to whether the project is for the use of Negro or white workers or both. Nevertheless the Communist Party and its fronts, except the Civil Rights Federation, have been constantly agitating and demanding that Negro workers be given their full share in the occupancy. Recently, under the direction of the Negro attorney and reported Communist leader, LeBron Simmons, a temporary injunction was applied for and secured restraining the City of Hamtramck and its housing commission in designating the project for white workers only.

According to a confidential source of information, the injunction was to the effect that the Hamtramck Housing Authority could grant no more than 93 per cent of the project to white people and that there must be at least 7 per cent Negroes mixed in with them. It is said that segregation is not desired and rather interracial mixing in various units of the project is being sought after by the Communist Party.

Racial Trouble in Detroit Schools

Negroes in the Detroit area attend the same schools as do white people and from information received there has apparently been no agitation or trouble in the schools other than minor arguments among Negro and white pupils. However, on September 23, 24 and 25, 1942, at Lincoln High School in Detroit there occurred a race riot. The school has an attendance of approximately 600 out of which there are between 75 and 80 Negro students. In 1941 there had also been a race riot there.

On September 23, 1942, the Police Department of Detroit received a call from the High School to the effect that a riot had started after a Negro student had accidentally bumped into a white boy in a locker room. Three white boys were arrested and later released. Several Negroes were also arrested because of the participation. According to information received, the white boys were the cause of the trouble.

The "Detroit News" under date of January 14, 1943, stated 150 Negroes calling themselves "the Brewster Street gang" entered the Norvell School, 2963 Arndt Street, Detroit, at 3:50 P.M., on January 13 to beat up a certain Negro girl who allegedly was not a member of the gang. According to the article, when their entrance was opposed by a white teacher, the white schoolteacher was struck on the face and suffered a minor injury. Lieutenant Charles D'hondt of the Hunt Station, who, according to the paper, conducted an investigation, was quoted as saying the gang was led by a 15-year-old Negro girl. In addition to striking the white schoolteacher, it was said that the girls attacked three Negro teachers and a janitor who had been called to lock the door. [*100-135-16-68*]

On April 5, 1943, a fight broke out between Negro and white children of the Lowell Junior High School in Flint, Michigan, resulting in a general melee after school had been dismissed. On April 6 and 7, 1943, older boys from other schools, both Negro and white, gathered at the Lewis Street Bridge in Flint and a general riot ensued. Rocks were thrown, fist fighting was prevalent and according to reports some of the youths, particularly the Negroes, were carrying knives. An estimate was made that 1,000 persons of both the white and Negro races participated, requiring a large number of uniformed police to disperse them. After two hours the police were finally able to disband the group. It is related that after city officials addressed the public schools the children agreed to stop fighting on both sides.

Racial Controversies in National Defense Plants

In recent months considerable activity has been entered into by the Party in agitation among the Negroes because of three so-called "wildcat strikes" occurring early in the Summer of 1942 at the Dodge, Packard and Hudson Defense Plants in Detroit. The reported cause of all three of these strikes was the refusal of white employees to work side by side with Negroes who had been promoted to positions equal with theirs.

The Party, through Jack Raskin, Executive Secretary of the Civil Rights Federation, has insisted that this trouble was instigated by the Ku Klux Klan and Raskin is said to have originated the plan to have the Department of Justice investigate the "fifth column" activities in the above referred to plants.

Publicity is said to have been given to the strikes by all Communist organizations in the Detroit area. The "Michigan Chronicle," a Negro newspaper, under date of June 27, 1942, under the editorship of Louis Martin, referred to previously as a reported Communist leader, issued an editorial under the caption "Klan Plot Race War in Factories, U.S. May Act." Martin charged that the racial discrimination in Detroit, including the Sojourner Truth Housing Project, the Packard, Dodge and Hudson Defense Plant strikes and the trouble of the Hamtramck Housing Project, is a part of a pattern set out by the Ku Klux Klan and "their fifth column allies." He referred to a protest conference immediately following the strike at the Hudson Naval Ordnance Plant which was sponsored by the National Association for the Advancement of Colored People, the National Negro Congress, the Civil Rights Federation, the Detroit Irwin [Urban?] League and International Committee of the United Automobile Workers of America, CIO. This meeting, it should be stated, was conceived and planned by Jack Raskin, Executive Secretary of the Civil Rights Federation.

Subsequently, at the convention of the United Automobile Workers of America, CIO, Raskin's plan of having the Department of Justice investigate the alleged fifth column activities in Detroit was introduced and was voted down immediately inasmuch as the United Automobile Workers of America considered it an attempt by the Civil Rights Federation to have an investigation made of the Union. It is said as a consequence relations between the Civil Rights Federation and the Union are presently strained.

In other sections of this summary references have been made to agitational moves for the employment of Negro women, especially at the Ford Motor Car Company. It is believed that the circumstances surrounding this should be set out.

On August 20, 1942, approximately 800 marchers formed a picket line around Gate No. 2 of the Ford Plant in Detroit. The picket line marched around this gate for approximately three and one-half hours. There was no disorder during the entire period of picketing.

Regarding the situation at the Ford Motor Car Company in the employment of Negroes, it is reported that arrangements were being made as rapidly as possible to hire Negro women in the Bomber Plant and in the Ypsilanti Plant, but the company needed to be very careful in placing Negro women among many white Southerners who had been hired in the plant inasmuch as careless placing would be likely to cause disturbances. For that reason the company had been very slow to hire Negro women.

In November 1942 a confidential informant advised of a rather acute racial situation in existence at the Foundry of the Ford Motor Car Company. The Foundry employees were said to be equally divided as to white and colored persons. During October and November 1942, according to the informant, numerous small instances of walkouts and slowdowns caused by the racial animosity occurred. [redacted]

It was reported in November 1942 a white employee at the Ford Island Park Plant in Detroit was attacked by two Negroes because of a remark made by him to one of them. The two Negroes, as well as the white employee, were discharged because of their participation in the fracas. It is alleged that officials of the Union, contrary to contract provisions of the company, pulled a Negro worker off the production line to get a statement relative to the dispute. A deduction was thereafter made in the pay of the Negro worker for the time lost conferring with the Union officials. The Negro worker verbally abused the foreman and disciplinary action was taken by the company. A two-hour work stoppage on Army tank production reportedly took place caused by the Union officials protesting disciplinary action taken against the last-named Negro worker. In this connection, newspaper accounts were to the effect the Union was dissatisfied because the discharged men were fired without their grievances being properly handled.

It was also reported in November 1942 by a confidential informant that the 400 white and 300 Negro employees of the Detroit Steel Castings Company maintained tense feelings. It was said that some of the Negroes were of a low character, having poor morals, drinking excessively and remaining absent from the plant. It was said that there were approximately 25 or 30 Negroes who caused the trouble and threatened fellow employees, both white and Negro.

It was confidentially reported that on or about January 11, 1943, at the Hudson Plant on Jefferson Avenue in Detroit, a white foreman attempted to have a Negro loafing on the job return to work. An argument ensued and the Negro reportedly attacked the foreman and was joined by another Negro standing nearby. A white plant protection official is said to have attempted unsuccessfully to separate the combatants after which he shot each Negro in the leg.

On January 12, 1943, George Clarence Myers, a Negro, age 19, was indicted for sabotage in connection with his activities at the Chrysler Plant, East Jefferson Avenue, Detroit, where he was employed as a janitor. Myers had written obscene and unpatriotic statements across the face of patriotic posters in the Plant, one of which was "Your son should have died long go. The Japs are going to win anyway." Another was "Americans are our enemies in the United States; they are rotten ——." Further, Myers kicked off gauges from a machine at the Plant causing about $50 worth of damage and delay in the production of tank motors. Upon questioning, he stated his reason for committing the acts was that he wanted to quit the Chrysler Plant and take a better job at the Ford Plant, and there was some delay about his release. He denied any affiliations with any un-American organizations and his mother and sister advised they knew of no pro-Japanese organization with which he was connected. Plant protection officials at the Chrysler Plant said they observed other Negro employees were quite incensed over Myers' activities and some had offered to do him bodily harm.

In April 1943 it was reported that there was considerable agitation and tension among employees of the Plymouth Motor Car Company, especially in Department 81 which is said to employ quite a few Negroes. A source of information has informed that it is very apparent that resentment of Negroes being employed there exists among the white employees. In this connection, a pamphlet was made available as distributed by C. George "Pop" Edelen, President of Local 51, UAW-CIO (an alleged member of the Communist Party), entitled "Plymouth Management Intimidates Workers." This pamphlet stated, among other things, "We call upon all stewards on every shift to be on the lookout for these elements in the supervision and the 'company stooges' who are intimidating the Negro women in the plant. They should be reported to the local union office and they will be properly investigated by the Government."

It was reported on March 6, 1943, by a confidential source of information that for the previous three or four days there had been a great deal of Negro agitation at the Packard Plant in Detroit where an attempt had been made to employ Negro girls which, in turn, aroused many protests from white female employees. It was alleged that a former president of the Packard Local 190, UAW-CIO, one Kurt Murdock, had attempted to keep Negroes out of the Packard Plant. It was also reported in March that there had been numerous racial incidents in Department FF of the Packard Plant, including a two-hour walkout, when a Negro was put on the assembly line and when union stewards favored Negroes and made derogatory remarks to white workers. It is related that on March 18, 1943, 2,300 whites walked out of the Packard Plant in protest of the company hiring Negro women. It is said that approximately 1,000 man-hours were lost in this particular strike.

Another strike occurred at this Plant on March 20, 1943, when 250 white employees of the Gear Division stopped work in protest against the employment of four Negro women as machine operators. The white workers are said to have refused to resume work until the four Negro women were fired. The strike was unauthorized and the Union officials attempted to make the strikers resume work.

On April 12, 1943, an additional strike reportedly occurred at the Packard Plant when 100 Negro men remained away from work for one day in a dispute with the management over seniority rights. Christopher Alston, member of the Communist Party and Chairman of the Interracial Committee of Local 190, UAW-CIO, at the Packard Plant stated his Committee was in no way responsible for the strike but alleged something would have to be done for the workers and the matter would be taken up with the management.

On March 18, 1943, at the Aluminum Company of America in Detroit a tense racial situation reportedly developed over the hiring of Negro employees. A few whites and Negroes are said to have alternately walked out of the plant all during the day and in the afternoon 400 Negroes are related to have congregated in one part of the plant and refused to work.

On March 19, 1943, 160 white persons are said to have walked out of the United States Rubber Company in Detroit because of Negro women being employed. Some of the trouble was laid to Union organizers creating racial disturbances for a political front. No confirmation of this was received, however. It was also said that the white workers disliked the Negroes using the same locker rooms. It was further alleged that several Southern people in the plant refused to take any supervision from Negroes.

On March 19, 1943, an undetermined number of men are alleged to have walked out of the Wilson Foundry and Machine Company because of the racial issue.

It is related that on March 17, 1943, one Negro walked out of the Chrysler Highland Park Plant because his demand for higher wages did not go through regular channels. On the following morning eight Negroes in the Janitor and Shipping Department allegedly walked out in protest of this man being fired. During the day of March 18, 180 employees also reportedly walked out of the Plant because of the racial question. On March 19, 1943, it was reported that at a meeting of Negro members of Local 490, UAW-CIO, at this Plant, who were on strike, the following grievances were stated as being the reasons for their strike:

Failure to remove Negro women from heavy jobs and use them in semiskilled work for which they were allegedly trained.

Failure to upgrade Negro men.

On March 26, 1943, two Negro employees hired by the Vickers, Incorporated, Plant were said to have been the reason for 200 white persons leaving their work. Later additional white people quit, demanding segregation of the Negroes and separate rest room facilities.

It was reported that on March 23, 1943, a number of Negro men went on strike at the Chrysler Lynch Road Plant in Detroit, protesting the hiring of Negro women to mop floors. It is said that the women refused to mop the floors, stating the mops and the buckets were too heavy. The company in turn was reported to have provided lighter mops and buckets with rollers. However, the women are said to have still refused to work. The Negro men then joined them in the strike which was settled on March 25, 1943.

On April 13, 1943, 200 Negroes in the Dodge Division (Foundry) of the Chrysler Motor Car Company reportedly refused to work from 12:00 noon to 4:00 P.M. because one Negro woman had been demoted in her job which allegedly it was later shown she was not able to perform.

On the night of April 8, 1943, at the Ford River Rouge Plant, one Glen Wagner, a white foreman, in the course of an argument with a Negro, Paul Jackson, called Jackson a "Nigger." Jackson hit Wagner who later died as a result of a fractured skull. Jackson was indicted for manslaughter.

At this same plant, on the night of April 9, 1943, two Negroes reportedly attacked a truck driver inside the plant after "catching" a ride on his truck and seriously injuring him. The driver, not sure of their identity, believed they were workers in the Foundry. On the night of April 10, 1943, two keymen of Local 600, UAW, reportedly smuggled a Negro into the plant who had no reason to be there. The officials took action against the keymen and the entire steel foundry, about 1,000 men, is said to have gone on strike for one hour.

At the Willow Run Plant on April 9, 1943, a Negro woman reportedly fomented an unauthorized strike by 15 white women, after which she was transferred to the River Rouge Plant.

Allegations were received in March 1943 that the Detroit Street Railway was having an unusual amount of difficulty as a result of having hired many Negro employees during the previous months. At the time, approximately one-third of the bus drivers were said to be Negroes. According to unconfirmed reports since these Negroes were employees there had been an abnormal amount of service delays. It was said that the Negroes, almost to a man, were imbued with a rebellious attitude and were sullen and surly in their work. An unknown Negro of the Detroit Street Railway is alleged to have remarked that when the Japs take over the United States the Negroes will have their place in the Senate. It was also said that many white Southerners had taken positions as drivers and conductors on the vehicles and it was expected that serious racial trouble might result.

It was alleged in April 1943 by a confidential source that an informant advised the chief aim of a number of Negroes in both the Steel and Aluminum Foundries of the Ford River Rouge Plant seemed to be to make life miserable for white people by making an issue of almost anything that might arise. Another informant of this source has reportedly advised that the Negro committeemen in the Aluminum Foundry of this Plant argue almost constantly and incite other workers by their arguments with the foreman. Allegedly these Negro committeemen attempt to slow up production by talking to the workmen when they are attempting to do their jobs. Remarks are said to be constantly made against the white people employed there. This particular informant has related that since the death of the foreman who was killed by the Negro worker in the Foundry the Negroes have not created as much disturbances.

It has been further alleged that the main cause of the strikes which occurred in the Foundries of the River Rouge Plant was the constant bickering between the United Automobile, Aircraft and Agricultural Implement Workers of America, CIO, and the Ford Motor Car Company. Each little grievance is allegedly magnified into a large issue which will determine whether the Company or the Union has the upper hand with the employees.

On March 28, 1943, 32 out of 64 employees, all Negroes, in the "Chip Pulling" and Janitor Departments of the Plymouth Motor Car Company went on strike in protest against the Government's order freezing jobs. These men demanded either releases from their jobs or additional pay. The Union was not behind the strike, according to information received.

It was reported that on May 15, 1943, the Hudson Naval Arsenal hired its first Negro toolmaker who went to work in the toolroom on May 14, 1943. All of the white employees there left the room refusing to work with him. The strike spread to the second shift which came on in the morning and 600 workers in all are reported to have refused to work. The strike was unauthorized by Local 150 of the UAW-CIO, which Union, through its officials, attempted to persuade the workers to return to their jobs without success. After a one-day layoff the men returned to their work and apparently continued as in normal times, working with the Negro employee.

The following information is set forth relative to the strike at the Packard Motor Car Company plant June 3, 1943:

Sometime prior to the strike Carl Purcell, Chief Steward of Department K. D. Packard Local No. 190190, United Automobile, Aircraft and Agricultural Implement Workers of America, CIO, was asked by the management of the Packard Motor Car Company if there would be objection to the upgrading of three Negro semiskilled employees in the Tear Down and Reassemble Department of the Aircraft Division at that plant. Purcell is said to have stated there would be no objection. During the last week of May 1943 three Negroes were placed in this department. Subsequently white employees there walked out on strike. The Negroes are said to have then been removed and negotiations were reportedly made with union officials who assured that further interruption would not be caused.

On June 2, 1943, two Negroes were returned to this particular department and on the following day, June 3, all white employees of the department walked out followed by all other employees of the Packard Motor Car Company. Approximately 25,000 employees were involved and the particular plant manufacturing airplane and marine engines was shut down.

The strike was declared an outlaw wildcat affair and on June 6, 1943, R. J. Thomas, President of the United Automobile, Aircraft and Agricultural Implement Workers of America, CIO, made a public speech at the Convention of the National Association for the Advancement of Colored People in Detroit, stating he had absolute evidence the strike was promoted by the Ku Klux Klan and its reported successor organization in Detroit, the United Sons of America, and that he was turning over evidence to the Federal Bureau of Investigation and would demand a Congressional investigation. He added that transcripts giving names and other evidence had been turned over to the FBI in Detroit. At the same time allegations were received that the Union made feeble and superficial attempts to have the men return to work.

With reference to the allegations that the Ku Klux Klan had instigated the strike, the following information reported by a highly confidential and reliable informant is set forth:

According to the confidential and reliable informant, Jack Raskin conversed under pretext on June 4, 1943, with one J. L. Charles, an alleged member of the United Sons of America. Raskin is said to have stated in his call to Charles that he was "one of the boys" in the organization. According to the confidential informant, this conversation was witnessed by Albert Deutsch, a reporter for "PM". Raskin allegedly said, "We really got them guessing, haven't we?" and Charles is said to have replied in the affirmative. According to the informant, when Raskin asked when the strikers would return to work, Charles said, "Well, I don't know, don't know—it shouldn't have been, you know, my goodness, it shouldn't have been. They shouldn't have let them black alligator baits in there". The informant stated Charles indicated that "our boys" were going to continue the fight, apparently meaning the strike, although there is no indication he referred to members of the United Sons of America. Charles allegedly did say the Packard Plant is a "white man's plant," and allegedly indicated members of the United Sons of America were in the strike. The confidential informant further reported he heard Charles say in answer to

a leading question from Raskin that it would be good for members of the United Sons of America to get together and plan the strike further, "Yes, work it out and have a, have a real showdown".

This entire affair was reportedly presented to the Wayne County Michigan, Prosecutor, William B. Dowling, who indicated that no investigation would be undertaken by his office because of there being no basis for local prosecution. The information claimed to have been presented to this Bureau has not been received from Raskin or other Communists but only from a confidential informant in the Civil Rights Federation. The substance of this conversation was printed in the newspaper "PM" and also in the "Detroit News". The "Detroit News" indicated that the information had come from R. J. Thomas, as did "PM". Raskin was not identified in either of the articles.

Later in the day of June 4, 1943, after Raskin had his pretext conversation, he is said to have talked with Goodman who discouraged him from contacting the FBI, expressing the opinion that he, Goodman, did not believe it could be actually proven the Ku Klux Klan was behind the Packard strike.

It is to be noted that no data of any sort along these lines were turned over to the Federal Bureau of Investigation either by R. J. Thomas or by Jack Raskin, Executive Secretary of the Civil Rights Federation in Detroit and organizer for Section 9 of the Communist Party for the State of Michigan. In this connection, a confidential opinion has been offered to the effect that blame placed by R. J. Thomas on the Ku Klux Klan was distinctly to his advantage as a means of covering the lack of union discipline in the strike, it being alleged there were many of the minor union officials and union members who participated in the strike.

On June 7, 1943, it was reported publicly by the Packard Motor Car management that the striking employees were returning to work and the three Negroes whose upgrading was the reported cause of the original controversy maintained their status. One foreman and twenty-six other workers were discharged by the War Department for their activities in connection with the strike.

During the entire affair and subsequent thereto no information or indications were reported to the Federal Bureau of Investigation that subversive elements among the employees or activities of the Ku Klux Klan or any similar allegedly anti-Negro organization were responsible for the strike.

In connection with this particular section dealing with racial disturbances in plants, it is believed significant that the following information be set forth:

It is reported confidentially that on March 25, 1943, a Government field representative of an agency handling matters of Negro discrimination contacted another Governmental representative connected with the Hudson Naval Arsenal in Detroit, at which time the former advised of a Negress having come to his office who complained that she had been discharged as a result of discrimination at the Hudson Naval Arsenal. The latter Governmental representative in checking into the matter found that the department in which the Negress had worked ran out of work and that she had been transferred to another department where she complained the objects were too heavy for her to move. Employment officials told her that inasmuch as no other work was available she must necessarily be released but would be recalled when work was available.

These circumstances were explained to the first Governmental official who told the latter, however, that the case must necessarily be turned over to Reverend Hill. This is Reverend Charles A. Hill, Chairman of the Citizens Committee for Jobs in War Industries, an organization which has considerable Communist influence in it. On the same day Hill is reported to have contacted the official at the Hudson Naval Arsenal and directed him to re-employ the Negress "or else". He refused to listen to the facts which the Governmental official had secured and insisted that racial discrimination was the reason for the Negress being discharged.

On March 31, 1943, a delegation consisting of Reverend Charles Hill, Negro; Forrest Sheffield, Negro, affiliated with several Communist influenced groups; and Gloster Current, Negro, affiliated with several reportedly Communist influenced groups, visited the offices of the Federal Bureau of Investigation in Detroit to urge an investigation of alleged subversive forces causing anti-Negro demonstrations in Detroit war plants. It was pointed out by the delegation that plants had failed to utilize trained and skilled Negro employees. The jurisdiction of the Federal Bureau of Investigation was pointed out to him and upon leaving, Hill, who acted as principal spokesman, conceded he had no evidence of fifth column or subversive activity at work in the Detroit plants. [*100-135-16-8*]

It was reported in May 1943 that a representative of a Governmental agency interested in Negro discrimination had been in contact with Jack Raskin, who has been previously referred to herein as Executive Secretary of the Civil Rights Federation and reportedly an organizer for Section 9 of the Communist Party, State of Michigan, relative to obtaining cases on Negro discrimination. It is reported that this Governmental representative was advised by Raskin how to obtain cases of discrimination as well as complaints. This same individual who is said to have been in contact with Raskin is reported to have been in the past very close to Raskin, seeking Raskin's judgment as well as supplying Raskin with plans of the Governmental agency he represented. [*100-211520*]

Riots

Set forth hereinafter is information relative to recent racial disturbances and riots occurring in Detroit and its environs. It is supplemental to that data concerning racial friction and trouble reported under previous handings, including "Racial Controversies in National Defense Plants" and "Racial Trouble in Detroit Schools".

Eight-Mile Road Affair

It was reported that on March 24, 1943, subsequent to a fight between Negro and white students at Lincoln High School in the Ferndale area, a group of white hoodlums allegedly instituted a reign of terror among Negro residents of the Eight-Mile Road Community which did not subside until March 26, 1943, when State and city police covered the area. It is said that hoodlums rode through the district in automobiles firing shots. Windows were smashed in four business establishments. A continued animosity was reported between youths at Lincoln High School. Three buildings containing four bullet holes were reported and on Friday, March 26, 1943, Negroes were alleged to have sat in the windows of their homes with firearms waiting for further violence. In this connection, it was said that the "zoot suit" colored boys from another section who constantly fight with Negro youths of the Eight-Mile Road area joined with the latter. By the next day, however, the situation had become quiet. The Eight-Mile Road section is described as a poor slum area. Subsequent to this situation a student council was formed at the Lincoln High School to formulate a program so as to prevent the occurrence of a similar situation.

The "Michigan Chronicle" of April 10, 1943, carried an article alleging that on the night of April 5, 1943, a "Klan inspired mob" of approximately 100 white members terrorized the Central Avenue section of Detroit's west side, smashing windows of the homes of seven Negro residents. It was said that the mob paraded the avenue from Tireman to Warren Avenue unchallenged by the police. The article continued, saying that feeling was running high in this community and that most of the men had been absent from their jobs apparently well armed anticipating the return of the mob. No confirmation of this information has been reported.

Detroit Riots—June 20–22, 1943

Origin of Trouble

Sunday night, June 20, 1943, was an exceptionally hot and sultry night and the amusement parks and recreational facilities in the Detroit area were jammed. Belle Isle, an amusement resort on the Detroit River, was exceedingly crowded and there was an unusual proportion of Negroes there according to the reports. Belle Isle is one of the chief recreational centers for the Detroit area. Until several years ago it was practically exclusively a playground for white people, although no color restrictions were in effect. Recently, however, the opposite situation has been true.

The Detroit police have advised that on Sunday, June 20, 1943, when the riot started, at the peak of the day approximately 100,000 people were on Belle Isle and estimates have been made that 60 to 90 per cent of those there were Negroes. This, along with Negroes crowding other places heretofore usually attended by white persons, caused a growing resentment among white people who object to close association with Negroes.

As nearly as can be determined, the riot started as a result of an altercation on the north end of the bridge leading from Detroit proper to Belle Isle, the north end being the part that is on the Detroit mainland side. The altercation was either between a single white and several Negroes or between a single Negro and several whites. The exact identity of those taking part is not known. It appears that immediately after the argument began, white people, including sailors, came to the rescue of those whites already engaged, while Negroes assisted their brethren.

The police were called and attempted to establish order with some degree of success. However, in the meantime the word spread like wildfire across the bridge to Belle Isle and many incidents occurred there of a riotous nature. At this point, it should be brought out that reports were received of a group of Negroes on June 20, 1943, snatching lunches from white women and knocking them down. White persons who allegedly attempted to assist these women are said to have been deliberately attacked by other Negroes. It was originally suggested that this was possibly the origin of the trouble.

Belle Isle was emptied as rapidly as possible from the time the riot began at approximately 11:35 P.M. on June 20, the Negroes returning to their sections of town and the whites spreading to their homes. The riots spread as the Negroes returned to their homes in their areas, primarily the Hastings Street section which is known as Paradise Valley.

Incidents During Riot

At 1:00 A.M. Monday, June 21, 1943, the fighting and rioting had spread to the principal Negro sections in Detroit, particularly in the Hastings Street and Forest Street section. At that time, approximately 100 arrests had been made by the Detroit Police Department. Casualties were inflicted mainly as a result of beatings. There were incidents reported in which Negroes dragged white people from their automobiles and beat them.

Stores in the Negro section were looted and this continued on during the morning of June 21. There was a great amount of property damage and destruction done in the Negro areas. On the morning of June 21, 1943, rioting broke out near the Hotel Detroiter, located just outside the main downtown business section of Detroit. This particular trouble involved several hundred people. There were also on this same morning several sporadic outbreaks in the congested Negro areas. Many automobiles had been overturned and a number of groups of Negroes were milling around in the Negro sections, especially in the vicinity of Hastings Street, carrying bricks and other missiles.

Until approximately 10:30 P.M., June 21, 1943, there were sporadic outbursts of trouble which included such activities as the beating of Negroes by white people in white areas of Detroit and the looting and destruction of property by Negroes in the Negro sections of this city. Much of the rioting after noon of June 21, 1943, was instigated, according to the reports received, by gatherings and groups of white persons in the white districts which are adjacent to colored areas in Detroit. These persons stopped street cars, automobiles and busses and dragged Negroes from them, mauling and beating them and chasing them on their way. According to the information received, this activity resulted in at least one death. Many of the white persons were teen-age youths with a sprinkling of girls. One such incident occurred on Fort Street adjacent to the Federal Building at about 5:30 P.M., June 21. This was witnessed by Agents of the Federal Bureau of Investigation and they observed approximately 200 youths stopping several street cars and busses from which they dragged

Negroes whom they severely beat. These persons were dispersed by Detroit police and police auxiliaries.

Prior to the quelling of the disturbances white people were in complete charge of the white districts and just before the declaration of martial law these individuals roamed the streets in large numbers and disturbances were caused whenever a Negro was seen in these areas. Several pitched battles occurred on the border of Hastings Street in the Negro district which is located just outside of the downtown area. It was necessary for the police to use forceful measures on several occasions.

In connection with the looting of stores, it was said that this was done presumably by Negroes in the Negro area. It was further reported that these stores and businesses which were looted were, in the main, operated by Jewish business people.

No accurate figures as to the actual injury to production in the Detroit area resulting from the riots have been reported. Examples have been cited, however, one of which is to the effect that only three persons reported for work at the Bohn Aluminum Plant No. 3 which is a large foundry employing exclusively Negro personnel. It was alleged that 60 per cent of the Negro employees at the Ford Motor Car Company failed to report for duty on June 21, 1943. In addition, a large number of white persons are believed to have absented themselves from their employment since it was necessary for them to travel through the Negro district to reach their places of employment. Allegations were also received that a number of smaller plants necessarily had to decrease production because of employees being absent from work. It was also said that practically all of the scrap yards which employed large numbers of Negroes were shut down completely.

It was reported on June 23, 1943, that production in the Detroit area was not affected as much as might be supposed as a result of the riots. The Fisher Body Company Plant No. 21 operated at 60 per cent capacity, while Plants 37 and 40 operated at 65 per cent capacity. The various ord[n]ance plants in the Detroit area according to the Military Intelligence Service lost 15 per cent in their production.

Negroes at the following plants did not appear for work on the first shift of June 22, 1943, although they were gradually returning at the later shift:

Michigan Steel Castings Corporation
Detroit Steel Castings Corporation
L. A. Young Company
Boxing Department, Dodge Motor Car Company
The Garwood Plant
The Budd Wheel Company
The Budd Manufacturing Company

A state of martial law, pursuant to orders issued by the President, was declared in Detroit, Michigan, and troops moved into the city at 10:20 P.M. This was subsequent to the request of Governor Kelly made at 6:00 P.M., June 21, 1943, that Federal troops be dispatched to Detroit to be placed under State control. It was also said that at 9:05 P.M., June 21, 1943, the Governor of Michigan admitted that the situation in Detroit was out of control and requested assistance.

At approximately 11:00 P.M., June 21, 1943, the situation had definitely improved after troops had been in the city for approximately thirty minutes. The rioters broke up their groups.

Several military police battalions had been bivouacked at Fort Wayne, Michigan. These, along with two battalions from the Office of the Provost Marshal, were sent to Detroit, in all totalling 2,500 men. The situation was brought under control by 3:00 A.M., June 22, 1943, and since that time no violence has occurred.

At Hamtramck, Michigan

The Police Department of Hamtramck, Michigan, suburb of Detroit, advised on June 23, 1943, that feelings were running high among the Negroes and white people in that area. Fifty-three persons, including fifteen Negroes, had been arrested for rioting and fighting. The prisoners were questioned by the Police Department for evidence of subversive inspiration in the rioting with negative results.

At Fort Custer, Michigan

A development collateral to the Detroit situation has been reported as taking place at Fort Custer, Michigan, where on June 21, 1943, at approximately 11:30 P.M., 280 Negro soldiers, members of the 543rd Quartermaster's Negro Battalion, broke into the Quartermaster's warehouse at Fort Custer. There they secured 178 rifles and a large quantity of ammunition which they loaded into several Army trucks. These trucks are said to have proceeded down a road at Fort Custer in the general direction of Detroit. The assumption was they were on their way to Detroit. Later investigation made by military authorities disclosed the Negroes, approximately 70 per cent of whom were from Detroit, Michigan, were stopped by a sentry at Fort Custer. They abandoned the truck[s] and threw away a quantity of the ammunition and guns. It is said that they apparently intended to proceed to Detroit to assist other Negroes there. Ten of them have been taken into custody by commanding officers at Fort Custer and are awaiting court martial for mutiny. No one was injured during this particular incident.

Arrests, Injuries and Deaths

According to the latest reports, 34 persons met their death, and out of the first 31 deaths reported, 3 were white persons, while 28 were Negroes. About 700 persons were injured and there were approximately 900 arrests. While no police officers were killed, in excess of 50 were said to have been injured in various degrees, one having been seriously hurt as a result of being shot by a Negro. Approximately 650 persons were hospitalized, a considerable number of whom were injured seriously. Of 54 persons who were given 90-day jail sentences in the Recorder's Court in Detroit on June 23, 1943, 22 were white, while 32 were Negroes. Four persons, including three Negroes, were found not guilty.

Reports of Negroes Being Well Armed

According to a report received in Washington, Negroes were said to have been well armed with firearms during the trouble. The Detroit Office of the Federal Bureau of Investigation in checking with the Police Department, whose statistics were by no means accurate or complete, indicated that out of 900 arrests there were 93 cases in which individuals carried concealed weapons. The exact number of guns found on persons was not revealed. However, there were persons arrested who carried other concealed weapons such as razors, knives and bayonets. The persons arrested carrying concealed weapons were not broken down into white and black categories.

The individual who was believed to be the original source of this report that Negroes were well armed with firearms was contacted and he advised he procured his information from an unknown informant whom he believed to be reliable and who allegedly knows considerable relative to the Negro situation in Detroit. His information was that Negroes have been purchasing guns from pawnshops, secondhand stores and similar sources for some time. However, the purchases and possession of firearms by Negroes, according to the informant, was not due to a planned attempt to arm Negroes in Detroit, but rather due to individual desires of Negroes to protect themselves as a result of the increasing interracial feelings. The original source stated that he believed a representative cross-section survey of white persons in Detroit would probably reveal a like proportion possessing guns.

The Detroit Police Department reported to the Detroit Office of the Federal Bureau of Investigation that there had been an increase in the number of guns found on Negro arrestees. Their opinion was that this increase was a result of the feeling between whites and Negroes having been intensified. The Police Department also reported in October 1942 that for the previous four months permits for Negroes to purchase firearms had tripled. At that time the local officials said they did not know the reason for this other than they believed the Negroes were preparing for any trouble which might arise with white people.

Re Ku Klux Klan

In every racial disturbance of any magnitude, including strikes which have occurred recently, there have been public charges that the Ku Klux Klan or its successor organization in Michigan, the United Sons of America, fitted into the picture as being largely or primarily and even sometimes exclusively responsible. Information received concerning the Ku Klux Klan or its successor organization in Detroit, the United Sons of America, reflects that most of the members unquestionably dislike Negroes and, probably, privately many of them are in sympathy with any racial activity wherein Negroes receive harsh treatment. The opinion has been offered that if the circumstances were right, members of this organization would probably assist in any anti-Negro activity they possibly could.

No tangible evidence has been developed indicating the organization either planned or perpetrated the instant riots or had advance knowledge of them. As an example, the United Sons of America group had a meeting scheduled for Sunday night, June 20, 1943, the evening the riots began. Only six or eight members attended this meeting. Included in the group was a confidential informant. The informant has stated the proceedings were desultory. No mention whatsoever was made of the impending riot and the members, after having a few drinks, went to their homes, according to the informant, at 10:00. The riot broke out at 11:35 P.M. on June 20, 1943.

The opinion has been offered to representatives of this Bureau that neither the Klan nor the United Sons of America is big enough or important enough to be responsible for a riot of this sort even though they possibly would confidentially like to take credit for it if they could.

The Ku Klux Klan has been blamed publicly by someone for almost every important racial difficulty in the Detroit area in recent months. In every instance it was to the advantage of the accusers to place the blame elsewhere than among themselves. For example, in the Packard Motor Car Company strike, during the first part of June 1943, R. J. Thomas, President of the United Automobile Workers of America, CIO, publicly blamed the Klan under conditions where it was distinctly to his advantage to cover lack of union discipline inasmuch as many of the minor union officials and union members actively participated. The Communist Party and its forces, especially the Detroit Civil Rights Federation, it has been alleged, found it to their advantage to blame the Ku Klux Klan and the fifth column so that attention may be diverted from its own inflammatory agitation among the exploitation of the Negroes.

As an example for the lack of any bases for these accusations against the Klan by the Communist Party, it is reported by a highly confidential and reliable informant that Jack Raskin, Secretary of the Civil Rights Federation and reportedly an organizer for the Communist Party, in a conference on the morning of June 25, 1943, told Ernest Goodman, attorney and counsel for the Civil Rights Federation who has also been active in defending Communists, "We have nothing definite to substantiate the allegations that the Klan or fifth column was back of the race riot." This statement occurred after several days of loud and vehement allegations by the Party that these forces started the race riot. The allegations have been included in statements to this effect to the newspapers by various persons.

Fact Finding Board

On June 24, 1943, Governor Harry J. Kelly of Michigan appointed what he called a Fact Finding Board to inquire into the racial disturbances and determine particularly whether these disturbances were planned. This Board is composed of Herbert Rushton, Attorney General for the State of Michigan; William Dowling, Prosecuting Attorney of Wayne County; Oscar Olander, Commissioner of the Michigan State Police; and John Witherspoon, Commissioner of the Detroit Police Department.

This Board apparently immediately convened and after reviewing the facts presented, as well as the information previously available, reported to the Governor that as a result of its study there is no evidence at this time indicating that the riots were planned or inspired. The facilities of each of the members of this Board are presently being used intensively in the making of additional inquiries to ascertain whether or not the disturbances were, in fact, planned. The Detroit Police Department is extending every effort in this investigation and has assigned a large number of detectives to work on this problem. In addition, the Michigan State Police are also conducting inquiries, and the Attorney General of the State of Michigan and the Wayne County Prosecutor's Office have added their staffs to assist in bringing to light any information that would be of assistance in determining the facts in this matter. It is incumbent upon this Board, of course, to report immediately to the Governor any facts brought to its attention indicating that riots were other than of a spontaneous character.

The Board, it is understood, recommended against a grand jury proceeding at this time on the theory that there are no facts presently available to justify the calling of a body of this type and, consequently, no reason for its existence. The Board has also publicly invited all persons who have any information indicating that the disturbances were planned or inspired to furnish this information so that it may be considered and investigated completely.

Interracial Committee

In addition to the above-mentioned Fact Finding Board, Mayor Edward Jeffries of Detroit on June 25, 1943, appointed what he has termed an Interracial Committee to study the general problem in Detroit and to endeavor to ascertain the real causes, effects and solutions to the problems which have been precipitated by the recent riots. The Committee appointed by Mayor Jeffries is as follows:

Chairman, William J. Norton, Executive Vice President and Executive Secretary of the Children's Fund of Michigan; Committee members: Reverend Charles A. Hill, Negro, Chairman of the Interracial Citizens Committee and Pastor of the Hartford Avenue Baptist Church; Louis E. Martin, Negro, editor of the "Michigan Chronicle," a Negro newspaper; Mrs. Beulah Whitby, Negro, Executive Secretary of the Emergency Welfare Evacuation Service, Detroit Office of Civilian Defense; Walter Harding, Director of the Interracial Division of the United Automobile Workers of America, CIO; Charles H. Mahoney, Negro, of the State Department of Labor; Reverend George W. Saber, Negro; Eugene Schaeffer, Chairman of the Board of the Urban League; Fred N. Butzel, Attorney; Reverend Benjamin Jay Bush, D.D., Westminster Presbyterian Church; Mrs. Adelia Starrett, member of the Public Welfare Commission; and John F. Ballenger, Superintendent of Public Welfare.

The following information has been reported concerning the individuals designated:

Walter Harding, also known as Walter Hardin, has been reported to have been a member of the Michigan Sponsoring Committee of the Citizens Committee to Free Earl Browder. He has been alleged to be a Communist.

Reverend Charles C. Hill has been active in the Civil Rights Federation and has cooperated closely with it. This organization is a Communist front, reportedly.

Louis E. Martin was a sponsor of the Citizens Committee to Free Earl Browder. He is said to have been at times active in Communist Party affairs.

Beulah Whitby is reported to be closely associated with Communist Party members. She was a supporter of the National Free Browder Congress. She is also said to be President of the Alpha Kappa Alpha Society.

Contributing Factors in Riots

Confidential sources have supplied their opinions and certain conclusions relative to the riots. They have advised that thinking people in the Detroit area, although shocked by the riots, were not surprised. It has been a topic of general conversation in the Detroit area for the past two or three years and remarks have been heard that "sooner or later there is going to be a blow-up." In this connection, representatives of this Bureau in Detroit have informed that they have heard varying versions of this theme on innumerable instances during the past two years.

These sources have pointed to the abnormal increase in the population of Detroit which, they informed, has added to the congestion in Detroit, especially as it concerns amusement facilities, restaurants, public transportation and traffic. There has also been a deplorable congestion and a shortage of housing facilities, both for Negroes and whites. These are confronted with many white persons' antipathy toward close and intimate association with Negroes (this, according to the sources, being particularly true with many of the southern white people who have come to Detroit during the past few years) and the Negro's natural desire to receive complete equality with white people. These sources have cited the Sojourner Truth Housing dispute which has previously been referred to as well as the work stoppages and strikes, a number of which have been set forth hereinbefore.

The following statistics with regard to the population and the recent influx of people in Detroit who have come for employment are set forth:

As of April 1940 the population of Detroit proper was 1,623,452 of which number 149,119 represented the nonwhite population. This provided a ratio of nonwhite to the total population of 9.2 per cent. Figures in 1942, based upon sugar rationing, reflected the total population of Detroit to be 1,910,000 this being an increase over 1940 of 17.6 per cent. No figures are available, however, as to the increase in the Negro population. Since 1940, according to the records of the United States Employment Service, approximately 292,000 workers have come to the City of Detroit, of which total 101,000 were from southern States. Of the 101,000 approximately 50 per cent came from the States of Tennessee, Kentucky and Arkansas.

It is also reported that during the week of June 14–22, 1943, 3,438 persons migrating from outside the State of Michigan had registered with the United States Employment Service, of which number there were 653 nonwhites, or approximately 19 per cent.

In connection with these statistics, the following are set out to reflect the employment of Negroes in industry in the Detroit area:

In May 1940 22,000 Negroes were employed in 185 major industrial plants, constituting 5.6 per cent of the total employees. In December 1942 this number rose to 35,000, or 6.7 per cent of the total, and in May 1943 the total had reached the figure of 55,000 Negro employees in these plants, or 8.2 per cent. An estimate has been made that approximately 3,500 additional employees can be added to the figure of 55,000 to make up for small industrial plants which have not been reported. There are also figures available reflecting that 20 per cent of all employees are in a skilled labor classification, of which total 6.7 per cent are Negroes.

The following figures and accompanying information are set forth to reflect the wage increases in the Detroit area as they pertain to industrial employment:

Since 1941 wage increases, according to the War Manpower Commission, had been in excess of 20 per cent, which figure is based upon the 15 per cent permitted by the Little Steel Formula as well as on the applications for wage increases which have passed through the War Manpower Commission. It has been pointed out that as a natural and logical conclusion this figure is much higher for Negro employees than the average white employees because of the large influx of Negro workers into war industries who had formerly been employed in lower-paying occupations or who had been unemployed. According to the Detroit Board of Commerce, the average weekly wage of factory workers in 1940 was $35.80 whereas at the present time the figure has increased to $58.50 representing a 39 per cent raise.

Communist Party Influence and Other Radical Groups

For the past several years the Communist Party and its front groups particularly have followed a well defined line of blatantly, emphatically and many times in an inflammatory manner backing Negroes and Negro groups in every issue. (This has been evidenced during the situation in Detroit, as will be set forth hereinafter.)

Groups such as the Socialist Workers Party, the Socialist Labor Party, the Workers Party and the Socialist Party have been vying with each other and with the Communist Party for the favor and the political support of the Negroes. Their memberships have attended various Negro meetings, distributed pamphlets, solicited members and made superlative promises and assurances, all of which is believed to be conducive to consternation and confusion among the Negroes themselves.

Negro Press and Leadership

There appears to be no strong, generally respected and accepted Negro leader among the Negroes in Detroit. There are many leaders among the Negroes, none of whom seems to have a majority of the following but practically all of whom are influenced to varying degrees by the inflammatory Communist Party line.

The Negro press, principally the "Michigan Chronicle," which is probably the most widely read Negro newspaper in the Detroit area, is also subject to this inflammatory influence, and the articles appearing therein vividly reflect this. These articles in their general tone result in continually keeping a racial problem boiling and discouraging reasonable approaches to the problem.

Influx of White Southerners

Although statistics on the number of white southerners who have come to the Detroit area in recent months or years are not available, it is definitely established that there has been a substantial number in the Detroit area. Along with some ignorant and class-conscious white persons who have come from the South have been the aggravated feelings against the Negro and objections to close association with Negroes, both socially and at work.

Juvenile Delinquency and Hoodlumism

In recent months the Police Department and the Detroit Office of this Bureau have encountered an increasing tendency of teen-age whites and Negroes to roam and engage in activities in gangs or packs. Hoodlumism has been definitely on the increase in this area. As an example, several months ago the Detroit Office of this Bureau investigated the theft of two machine guns from a State troop armory, in which one of the gangs of hoodlum whites had planned and perpetrated the robbery. One of the subjects of the case, Andrew Tarovetta, was placed on probation. This individual was arrested during the riots as one of the rioting hoodlums.

From the personal observation of representatives of the FBI in Detroit it is known that after the first six or eight hours of rioting, most of the principal trouble outside the Negro section was spearheaded by gangs of sometimes several hundred teen-age whites who had the appearance of high school students recently let out for the summer vacation.

The following information concerning juvenile delinquency is being set forth as an indication of this particular problem:

	January to May 1942	January to May 1943
Murder*	1	12
Assault	40	85
Malicious destruction of property	27	64
Carrying concealed weapons	14	37
Escape	74	72
Armed robbery	3	13
Breaking and entering	156	273
Disturbing the peace	77	91
Indecent liberties	5	14
Investigation	166	256
Out-of-city truants	142	319
Robbery	27	30
Auto theft	157	177
Drunkenness	—	13
Larceny	316	366
Forgery	1	4
Truants from home	126	148

	January to May 1942	January to May 1943
Violation of parole	96	109
Incorrigible	43	46
Truants from school	61	80
Attempted rape	1	3
Lodgers	37	38
Gross indecency	1	6
Vicious violation of traffic	22	29

*The twelve arrests of juveniles for the crime of murder were the result of murders committed by gang activity.

A juvenile is defined in the State of Michigan as any person who has not reached his seventeenth birthday.

Records of the Detroit Juvenile Detail reflect that 1,685 juveniles were taken into custody during the first five months of 1942. In the first five months of 1943, 2,435 juveniles were arrested. In analyzing the increase of juvenile committed crimes, the records of the Juvenile Detail indicate a rather stable juvenile problem prior to 1940. In 1940, 1941 and 1942 the records reflect a slow, steady increase in the latter type of crime activity. From information available for the first five months of 1943 the increase in juvenile crimes has been startling. It has been observed that the crimes committed in the last five months have been of a more vicious nature than those committed in the past. It was also pointed out that June of 1943 would see the greatest number of juveniles committed to the Juvenile Detention Home in the City of Detroit since that home was established. From the records it has been ascertained that forty per cent of the youngsters arrested for the commission of crimes lack proper parental supervision in that both parents are employed.

The opinion has been expressed that the percentage of Negro juvenile offenders has increased a considerable amount in the first five months of 1943. It is stated that the police had been bothered particularly by gangs of young Negroes, usually numbering five to ten members, attacking both colored and white. There is no apparent purpose for the attacks other than the fact that the victim receives a severe beating. It has been observed that these gangs will attack both colored and white people; however, it is estimated that the attacks on white people number approximately two-thirds of all assaults. It was also stated that there had been few instances of white gangs attacking Negroes brought to his attention.

With reference to the race riot of June 21, 1943, it has been observed that the bulk of the juvenile crimes in the City of Detroit for the past two and one-half years have been committed by juveniles who have resided for many years in Detroit. However, in the case of the above-referred-to riot the records reflect that the juveniles arrested have resided for a comparatively short time in the City of Detroit. It was further noted that many juveniles arrested have come to Detroit from the southern part of the United States.

With reference to the situation that existed in the Detroit schools during the riot, it is advised that the intermediary schools in the riot section of the city were practically deserted during the time the riot was in progress. Many of the students came to school on the morning of June 21 and left school when word of the riot had spread through the school. Many of the students were taken out of the schools by their parents.

It is said that no actual trouble in the schools occurred during the riots and, further, there has been little trouble in the schools during the past several years. However, in some of the schools where both Negro and white students are in attendance trouble has occurred, usually starting with a fight between a white and a Negro boy, thereafter each race taking respective sides in the argument. It was indicated, however, that no trouble of any serious proportion has occurred in the Detroit schools.

However, as an example of youth delinquency, there occurred on Sunday, June 13, 1943, a riot at Eastwood Park, a large amusement place in East Detroit, where approximately seventy teen-age white hoodlums entered the park en masse and ejected all of the Negroes there. At the same time some stationed themselves outside the park and kept other Negroes from entering. The police finally quelled the riot, and the Chief of Police in East Detroit assigned as the basic reason for this riot the increasing numbers of Negroes who have gone to Eastwood Park during the past few months, where they have at times virtually taken over the park, their attitude and actions being arrogant, belligerent and insulting, particularly to white women.

With reference to the general crime situation in the City of Detroit with a view in mind of its general effect on the tense situation that has existed in Detroit for the past several years the following figures are presented. Crime figures in general show an increase in crime since 1940 of 1.2 per cent. It is here noted that although the colored population of Detroit is only approximately 9 per cent of the total population, 37 per cent of the crimes in 1942 were committed by colored persons. In some specific cases, namely, crimes against persons, 40 per cent were committed by colored persons. In crimes against property 51 per cent were committed by colored persons, and in the specific crime of carrying concealed weapons and possessing weapons colored persons have committed 74 per cent of this crime.

Racial Policy of the City Administration

The Negro vote in Detroit is valuable and much sought after. At times it constitutes a balance of electoral power. According to the best sources of information, there is consequently a definite tendency in the city administration, principally on the part of elected officials making policy, to cater to the Negro element.

In this connection, the Police Department for some time in the past has been operating under the "kid gloves" policy with respect to Negro lawbreakers and those accused of breaking the law. As an example, two months ago in an interview with the press, Commissioner John Witherspoon made the statement which was widely quoted that the Police Department had adopted the "kid gloves" policy. This seems to have had the effect of dissipating respect for the power and authority of the Detroit Police Department among the Negroes so that at the time the rioting broke out police officers were under a distinct disadvantage from the outset.

Negro Pressure Groups

There are active in Detroit and the surrounding area a number of Negro organizations, principal among which is the Detroit branch of the National Association for the Advancement of Colored People which is composed of between 15,000 and 20,000 members. The policies of this and other Negro groups without exception are claimed to be strongly influenced by the Communist Party and as a result reasonable action is not a keynote in their activities.

The method of operation of these groups seems to make for widespread publicity and agitation upon every incident in which discrimination is involved or alleged. Instances are known to have been created. A typical example has been cited by a confidential informant in which during a recent conference between Jack Raskin, who has been referred to hereinbefore, and one Jack Burke, described as a field representative of the Fair Employment Practice[s] Committee, Burke urged Raskin to find Negro women who were to go to war plants and seek jobs on the possibility that discrimination might be developed and an issue raised.

High Wages and Employment Rate Among Negroes

The wages in Detroit are extremely high. Many Negroes are employed in war industries and it is a matter of general knowledge that they are receiving as a class a higher re[m]u[n]eration at the present time than ever before in their history. They have consequently money to spend as well as the urge to spend it at the same places where white people find their amusement and do their business. This draws white people and Negroes into close association, much more so than in normal times. This was the situation at Belle Isle on Sunday, June 20, 1943, where the rioting began.

Communist Party Exploitation of the Situation

Shortly after the outbreak of trouble the Communist Party was reported to take the stand that it would do everything possible to abate the riot and contemplated holding meetings to this end. The Committee for Jobs in War Industries, a reported Communist front group, took the same stand and intended to operate through its structure to carry out this policy of the Party. Patrick Toohey, National Committee member and Michigan State Secretary of the Party, conferred with Gene Dennis, a member of the National Committee of the Communist Party, relative to the riot and made claims that the situation was Axis inspired. He informed at that time of contemplated delegations to visit Washington for the purpose of meeting with the Attorney General and other Governmental officials and making demands for an investigation. In New York City Israel Amter discussed with Gene Dennis a delegation to be sent to Detroit so that a report on the situation could be made to the Communist Party. In this connection, Sam Don, a member of the editorial staff of the "Daily Worker," was to leave New York City on June 21, 1943, for Detroit, where he was scheduled to assist Patrick Toohey.

The Party line, which was adopted relative to the riots in Detroit, was expressed by Patrick Toohey at a meeting of Communist Party organizers on the night of June 22, 1943. He stated, "The brunt of the attack has been against the Negroes. Hundreds of unsuspecting Negroes have been led into murderous bloodshed. I mustn't use the word race riot—it is Hitler's Fifth Column. The Negroes are not responsible. We exonerate them. We must punish the hoodlums and protect the Negroes. This is Axis inspired."

Committee for Jobs in War Industries

On June 21, 1943, a meeting was held under the sponsorship of this Committee at the Lucy Thurman Y.W.C.A. in Detroit. Approximately 200 persons, mostly Negroes, were present. However, there were also in attendance Harper Poulson, white, Young Communist League member; Patrick Toohey, white, Secretary of the Michigan State Communist Party; Adeline Kohl, white, Secretary of the Michigan Young Communist League; Christopher Alston, Negro, reported member of the Communist Party; Michigan State Senator Stanley Nowak, white, reported member of the Communist Party; and Jack Raskin, white, reportedly an organizer for Section 9 of the Communist Party in Michigan and Executive Secretary of the Civil Rights Federation.

The meeting was chaotic and all Negroes present seemed thoroughly aroused. The chairman had difficulty in maintaining order and those in attendance, according to the informant, seemed interested in airing their grievances against white persons instead of discussing a possible solution. Mayor Jeffries, Police Commissioner Witherspoon, Mr. R. J. Thomas, President of the United Automobile Workers of America, CIO, and others became so disgusted with the proceedings they left before the meeting was over.

Harper Poulson made a speech in a highly emotional manner that Negroes throughout the entire affair behaved like gentlemen and patriotic Americans and, further, that the riot was a result only of the work of the Ku Klux Klan and the fifth column in Detroit. According to informants, the remarks of Poulson appeared to be in adherence to the policy the Communist Party will follow in connection with its stand on the riots. Poulson is also said to have demanded an investigation by Mayor Jeffries of the fifth column in Detroit.

Charges Made by Communist Forces

Patrick Toohey at a meeting of Communist Party Section Organizers on June 22, 1943, in Detroit, stated that the brunt of the attack in the recent rioting had been directed against the Negroes and "the action of the Police Department was miserable." Toohey further stated, "The soul of the Mayor is blacked with these killings. There were leaders and professional troublemakers." He advised of touring the scenes with Stanley Nowak and witnessing the alleged fact that police were not impartial but rather against Negroes. Toohey further stated that Negroes were not responsible in any degree for the rioting and they did not start the riots but rather that subversive forces and a fifth column conspiracy designed to upset and shake the people on the eve of "the second front" were alone responsible. He claimed that the disturbance was national in scope.

At this meeting Toohey is said to have further advised that the Attorney General must be compelled to instigate an investigation based upon information by Communist Party members. James W. Ford, Negro member of the National Committee of the Communist Party, spoke at this meeting and affirmed what Toohey had said and advised that Toohey's remarks were in line with the general policy of the Party. Toohey thereupon requested affidavits be obtained showing who incited the riots and these affidavits be turned over to Jack Raskin of the Civil Rights Federation to be placed at the disposal of a grand jury. It should be noted that the "Detroit Free Press" for June 23, 1943, contained a long statement issued by the Communist Party captioned "Units for Freedom—Smash the Fifth Column." This statement followed generally Toohey's remarks and mentions that "the anti-Negro riots" were an Axis-inspired effort to wreck the unity of the American people. It stated that the Negro people must be exonerated from any responsibility for these riots. It urged that Detroit citizens demand that the Director of the Federal Bureau of Investigation and the City Prosecutor in Detroit, Mr. Dowling, act upon "the great amount of information given them in the past year as to the work and activities of Detroit's fifth column, especially the Ku Klux Klan." Police officers were accused of delivering the brunt of their attack against the Negro people.

Delegations to Washington

A number of delegations visited Washington on the morning of June 23, 1943, to make protests and demands concerning the Detroit situation. All of these groups are believed to have been Communist inspired. Moran Weston of the Negro Labor Victory Committee in New York City, said to be a Communist controlled Negro organization, dealt with Bjorne Halling, Executive Secretary of the C.I.O. Maritime Committee, in endeavoring to make appointments with various Governmental officials. Arrangements were made also through Sadie Sokolove, a reported Communist Party member in

Washington, for the delegation's use of a meeting room at the Cafeteria Workers Union, C.I.O. building in Washington.

A confidential informant has advised that Hoyt Haddock of the C.I.O. Maritime Committee also endeavored to make appointments for the delegations. He is alleged to have contacted Mr. Marvin McIntyre and a confidential informant has advised that Haddock was informed by Mr. McIntyre that a delegation would be received only on the condition that it had a petition to present, but that he, Mr. McIntyre, would not discuss the Detroit situation. It is also reported that Haddock made arrangements for a delegation to see Mr. Victor Rotnem of the Department of Justice. Like arrangements were also reportedly made to see Mr. McGrady, Special Assistant to the Secretary of War handling labor matters, and Rear Admiral Charles W. Fisher, Director of Shore Establishments, United States Navy.

A confidential informant of this Bureau succeeded in joining the delegations and was with the one having an interview with Mr. Rotnem. According to the informant, the delegation sought action by the Department of Justice against the people instigating the riot. Mr. Rotnem did not seem particularly concerned with the matter, according to the informant who also advised that the discussion was most unsatisfactory. Charges were made by the delegation that the Ku Klux Klan had incited the strike in the Packard Motor Car Company and had also been the instigator of the Detroit riots. Mr. Rotnem, according to the informant, told the group that an act of Congress would be required to prosecute the Ku Klux Klan, inasmuch as it was reportedly made up of loyal Americans and was without foreign domination.

The informant's group was then sent to interview Rear Admiral Fisher, who expressed the concern of the Navy Department over recent racial violence but said that his Department could do nothing and told them to press for action from the Department of Justice.

Other groups from the delegations visiting Washington contacted the Office of War Information, the American Federation of Labor, the Congress of Industrial Organizations and the White House. Following the various visits the entire membership of the delegations met in the office of Vito Marcantonio where they reported on their interviews. Charles A. Collins, Negro, Executive Secretary of the Negro Labor Victory Committee and reported Communist, according to the informant, related the results of his group's interview with Mr. McIntyre, Presidential Secretary. Collins said Mr. McIntyre was of the opinion that the rioting was sporadic and just a reaction to racial difficulties without any subversive influences.

The informant advised that among those present in the delegations there were individuals from Detroit, New York, Baltimore and Philadelphia. The following known or reported Communists took part: Ben Davis, Jr., National Committee member of the Party; Moran A. Weston, reported Communist and Charles A. Collins of New York City; Shelton Tapps, Detroit Negro and associate of Communists; and Jewell Mazique, Washington, D.C. [Communist] Party organizer.

At Chicago, Illinois

In connection with the racial disturbances at Detroit, Communist Party leaders in Chicago called a mass meeting on June 22, 1943, to have been held June 25, 1943, in the aldermanic chambers of the City Council. Communist Party leaders, according to the informants of the Chicago Office, stressed the fact that the Detroit situation must not happen in Chicago.

At New York City

It was reported in New York that a group of individuals believed to have been connected with the New York State Committee of the Communist Party met on June 25, 1943, for the purpose of discussing "the race riot situation." These persons, the identities of whom are not known, agreed upon a proposal for mass demonstrations for Negroes and whites for the purpose of fostering the solidarity in uniting the Negro and the labor movement. It was determined that the Party would distribute leaflets throughout Greater New York advocating that steps be taken to prevent "Hitler's hand from striking in New York." It was decided that meetings should be held in the heart of Harlem as well as in various white neighborhoods in New York City. These meetings and demonstrations will not be held under the name of the Party but rather under the name of Communist influenced and dominated groups.

With reference to the distribution of leaflets, the New York Office was supplied one which was distributed by the Upper West Side Section of the Communist Party, entitled "The Enemy Within." Briefly this leaflet states that every Negro in America must wonder whether his countrymen are making war against the Nazis and the Japanese or against him. It inquires concerning the individuals who make Americans fight among themselves and asks whether the Jews or Catholics will have to lock themselves in their homes to prevent a similar fate. It urges that everyone write or telegraph the President concerning this positive evidence of Fascism.

Collateral Matters

Possible Dies Investigation of Detroit Situation

It was publicly announced on June 24, 1943, that Representative Martin Dies disclosed that the Detroit race riots have been traced to racial animosities stirred up by Japanese agents. He is quoted as having stated that he is in possession of reports submitted before the rioting started which revealed underground promoting of Japanese agents to incite Negroes against the whites in Detroit. Dies referred to Major Takahashi as the chief Japanese agent now in an internment camp and as being active in organizing the National Workers League. Takahashi, or Naka Nakane, has been dealt with hereinbefore.

It is noted that Congressman Dies is alleged to have charged that the Ku Klux Klan is also responsible for fomenting the race riots in Detroit. The information contained in this Bureau's files reflects that the only organization in the Detroit area that can be connected with the Ku Klux Klan is the United Sons of America; that the United Sons of America is composed of former members of the Detroit Chapter of the Ku Klux Klan; and that although this particular society is admittedly "anti-negro" in nature, an extensive investigation has been conducted and to date no information has been secured which would indicate that the officers or members of the United Sons of America are in any way responsible for the instigation of these racial outbursts.

The National Workers' League in Detroit, Michigan, was founded in 1938 by Parker Sage. Most of those who were in the League during its inception dropped out of active membership soon after its founding with the exception of Sage, W. R. Lyman, Jr., and Garland L. Alderman. Lyman was strongly anti-Semitic, and Garland L. Alderman was once chairman of the Pontiac Chapter of the America First Committee. It was also charged that the National Workers' League cooperated with the America First Committee and the German-American Bund but no specific facts were established with respect to these allegations.

In the spring of 1942 investigation was conducted to determine the activities of the National Workers' League in connection with the race riot that occurred in the Sojourner Truth Housing Project at Detroit, Michigan. As a result, on April 16, 1942, a Federal Grand Jury at Detroit, Michigan, returned an indictment against Parker Sage, head of the National Workers' League; Garland L. Alderman, Secretary of the National Workers' League, and Virgil Chandler, Executive Vice President, 7-Mile Fenelon Improvement Association, Detroit, Michigan, charging them with violation of Section 51, Title 18, U.S. Code, which is a civil rights statute, and Section 6, Title 18, U.S. Code, which relates to seditious conspiracy and among other things also makes it unlawful to delay the execution of any law of the United States. In January, 1943, the Department of Justice brought this case before a special grand jury in Detroit with the view to indicting six members of the National Workers' League for sedition; however, the case was no billed by the grand jury.

The investigation in this case did not disclose that Takahashi or any Japanese was active in or interested in the National Workers' League of Detroit, and the investigation indicated that the National Workers' League is a Fascist inclined rather than a Communist Front organization.

As a matter of interest the Detroit newspaper entitled "Free Speech" on the night of June 24, 1943, contained an editorial which was very scathing in nature and which invited Martin Dies to stay away from Detroit. It is also reported that the Mayor of Detroit in a public statement made on June 25, 1943, suggested that Dies stay away from that city and further an editorial in the Detroit News of June 25, 1943, also takes the same line.

A highly confidential and reliable informant has reported to this Bureau of being advised of a contact on June 25, 1943, between Gerald L. K. Smith and United States Senator Robert Reynolds of North Carolina. The informant has reported that Smith suggested that Congressman Dies have an investigation conducted of the Detroit affair. Smith is said to have specifically requested that Dies be contacted and told that Communists in Detroit were "scared to death" for fear Dies would proceed to Detroit for an investigation of the riot. Smith allegedly said that "Reds" in Detroit were trying to blame the riot on good people such as Henry Ford and himself.

Smith allegedly mentioned he did not want his name revealed to Dies, but that Dies should be encouraged to proceed to Detroit because investigating this matter would be the most sensational thing Dies has ever done. The informant advised that Smith commented that Communists in Detroit have been promoting intermarriages and intermingling of whites and blacks and he had in his possession an affidavit executed by a Negro which set forth that if a colored Communist Party member asked for a date with a white female member and was turned down, the female member of the Party would be immediately suspended from the organization.

Inflammatory Pictures in "PM" June 23, 1943

Since the occurrence of the disturbances in Detroit, "PM" newspaper has labeled the situation as a planned attack on the Negro race instigated by Fascists. The following is a paragraph taken from an article written by Albert Deutsch, entitled "Whose Riots?", and contained in the June 25, 1943, issue, typifying its stand:

> "We have tended to think of sabotage too much in terms of strictly enemy aliens. It is time to strike hard and swiftly against the native pro-fascist elements in such war areas as Detroit. Native Americans of Japanese ancestry have been thrown into concentration camps on mere suspicion that they might be disloyal. Why tolerate the known pro-fascist natives, who are consciously or unconsciously doing a major job for the Axis?"

The June 23, 1943, issue devoted pages ten to nineteen inclusive to pictures of the riot with highly descriptive captionings. While there are a few photographs in this section showing white people having received injuries, the large majority of the pictures involve Negroes being beaten or chased.

A confidential informant of the New York Office who has been long acquainted with Harlem and who has served as a reliable informant on Negro matters in the New York Office, has advised of contacts made by him in the Harlem district since the disturbances in Detroit. He has advised of seeing soldiers on leave gathered in groups with their civilian friends looking at the riot pictures in the newspaper "PM" and expressing their disgust and resentment. This informant has also reported of conversations with various inhabitants in whom this issue of "PM" has caused considerable resentment, especially against the white race.

Summation

From the information submitted concerning the Negro situation in Detroit prior to the rioting, as well as that supplied concerning the recent disturbances, it is strongly apparent that the trouble was of a spontaneous nature and not planned or organized. While there have been numerous complaints that there was subversive activity or pro-Axis instigation connected with the riots, they have all been uniformly in the nature of allegations and not factual statements.

Grand Rapids Field Division

In the area covered by Southwestern Michigan, including such cities as South Haven and Benton Harbor and Cass County, Michigan, no indications have been reported reflecting un-Americanism or subversive activities among the Negroes. Inquiries have also been conducted in Kalamazoo and Ionia Counties, Michigan, with negative results. This is true in Lake, Newaygo and Muskegon Counties. There have been however few complaints received in the City of Grand Rapids concerning individual Negroes making remarks reflecting possibly a pro-Japanese sympathy. These reports have been isolated, however, and mainly reflect remarks by individuals who made them when they were intoxicated or who did not realize their full import.

Unconfirmed reports are that approximately ten years ago, between 1930 and 1935, there was an attempt by an individual believed to have been Japanese to form a chapter of the Pacific Movement of the Eastern World. No specific information in this connection was furnished. Contacts made among Negro sources of information in this area brought out the opinion that such a movement had little effect on the 4,000 Negroes in the City of Grand Rapids.

There have also been reports that at least two individuals allegedly possessing a Communistic view have attempted to assert themselves in the activities of the National Association for the Advancement of Colored People branch of Grand Rapids. Their efforts, according to sources of information, have been fruitless. These individuals are said to be white people. With regard to the National Association for the Advancement of Colored People branch, no indications have been reported that this organization is engaged in subversive activities or is endeavoring to create unrest among Negroes there.

After the recent Detroit race riot many complaints were received regarding negro activities. Most of these complaints arose in Muskegon, Michigan, where the greater portion of the Negroes in the Grand Rapids Field Division reside. Rumors at that time were that a riot would break out at almost any time. The Negroes were alleged to be holding secret meetings in anticipation of any trouble. No reports were received indicating any subversive influence.

The Michigan State Police in this territory and the Muskegon Police Department have been active in investigating many rumors regarding Negro activity since the riot in Detroit and practically all of these have been unfounded.

Reports received reflect that there is much feeling of mutual distrust between the whites and colored in Muskegon due to a number of causes. Muskegon is strictly an industrial center. Three large foundries are located in that area and the greater portion of the Negroes are employed in these plants. Due to the man power shortage, it has been necessary to import a large number of Negroes from the South to work in the plants. As a result, an acute housing shortage has arisen, thereby causing overcrowding and discontent among the Negroes. Many of these Negroes from the South come and work for only a short period of time and then return there. However, this is not always the case. This importation has caused resentment among the white workers, who state that after the war is over, many of the Negro laborers will remain and will have to be taken care of by private relief agencies in the event of another depression.

Further reports indicate that at the present time there is nearing completion a housing project in Muskegon Heights, Michigan, which consists of 176 units. This project was originally intended as a white housing project but was subsequently changed by Government order. The units are constructed near the adjoining residences occupied by the whites and, therefore, there has arisen some discussion which indicates that the white residents bitterly oppose the location of Negroes in that area.

In one instance a white resident, adjoining the project, is alleged to have stated that she could start a race riot in five minutes in Muskegon, Michigan. Information reported reflects that the person making this statement was **Anna Van Tubergen, 817 Hinman Street, an employee at the Norge Corporation.** She denied making the statement but stated that she was very bitter because the project was being located next to her home and because she had had to give up 180 feet of her lot in order that the project could be completed. She said that it was understood that when the project was located in Muskegon, it was to be a white housing project. She related that there was a great deal of feeling between the whites and colored working in the various plants in Muskegon and that this was due to a general dislike between the two races. She said she did not anticipate any trouble with her new negro neighbors but that she certainly wanted them to keep their distance and to keep off her property or otherwise trouble would start.

With reference to the secret meetings alleged to have been held by the Negroes, it was ascertained that the meeting referred to was a meeting held by the Negro Elks Club in Muskegon, which has been organized recently. This meeting was held in the C. I. O. Hall in Muskegon and was a regular meeting of that organization. At the present time the membership is reportedly composed of 63 members, including many of the Negro leaders in Muskegon and Muskegon Heights, Michigan. Jim Austin, 618 Ottawa Street, Muskegon, a recognized Negro leader in the community, is the Exalted Ruler. Meetings are held on the first and third Sunday of each month.

The lodge is said to have no permanent meeting place at the present time and the first rumor was that the meeting of some organization was being held in the basement of 813 Pine Street and that plans were formulated at that meeting by the Negroes to protect themselves in the event any trouble arose. It was reported that one of the first meetings held by the Elks Lodge was held at 813 Pine Street, but the rumors regarding the activity at that meeting were ascertained to be unfounded and there was no indication reported of any activity by the members in anticipation of any trouble. There is no indication that the present Negro Elks Club is subversive in any way and, on the contrary, information reported indicates it is a legitimate organization.

It was reported that on July 3, 1943, three Negroes were attempting to buy guns and ammunition at Fremont, Michigan, from three hardware stores. The tag number of the car occupied by the Negroes was secured and it was ascertained that it was the property of one **Willie McGrue, 6032 Beechwood Street**, Detroit, Michigan. A subsequent check by the Michigan State Police disclosed that **McGrue was a foreman at the** Ford Motor Company in Detroit and that he was highly regarded and considered a reputable citizen. The attempted purchase of the shotgun and ammunition was made by **McGrue**, according to his story, for the purpose of hunting on his trip to visit a friend named **George Foster, near Hesperia.**

A confidential informant who is an employee at the Campbell, Wyant & Cannon Foundry in Muskegon advised that he has been making observation of the situation in Muskegon and at no point has he been able to ascertain that any radical group or foreign element was attempting to stir up any trouble, but he attributed the entire situation to the fact that there was a general feeling of racial hatred among the whites and colored.

He said that in the foundries the whites resented the use of the same bath facilities by the Negroes. The whites resent the fact that in one of the foundries a Negro is the head of the union; namely, Lakely Foundry, Muskegon, Michigan. He reported that only a few white men would attend meetings of the local union because there were so many Negroes at the meetings and as a result the Negroes in that local had gained control of the union. He was positive in his belief that no subversive elements were at work to create any discord among the races.

Recently many complaints have been received from various plants in the Muskegon territory that there was a large absenteeism among the Negro workers in the plant. These absenteeisms usually result over the week-end and the Negroes do not show up for work until around the middle of the week. The personnel manager in the various plants advise that many of these Negroes are shakeout men in the foundry and are very necessary in the war effort and when there is absenteeism among that group it causes dislocations throughout the entire plant.

The Factory Manager of the Campbell, Wyant & Cannon Foundry, Plant No. 3 has expressed the opinion that something was back of the absenteeism of the workers. However, he was unable to indicate any particular group or individuals who were trying to get the Negro workers to stay away from their jobs. When questioned about this situation, a confidential informant has advised that many of the Negroes were receiving high salaries and that they spend their week-ends in gambling and drinking and are unable to return to their jobs at the first of the week.

The Campbell, Wyant and Cannon Plant at Muskegon, a foundry manufacturing material in connection with the war effort and having a third class priority is said to have experienced a "walk out" on July 19, 1943. It is alleged that eighty-five Negroes employed at the plant on July 19, 1943, refused to continue work under a white steward at the plant. Thereafter the tension is said to have risen to the point where the plant had to close down. Thereupon officials of the plant reportedly requested State Police protection as a precautionary measure, and leaders of the local of the United Automobile, Aircraft and Agricultural Implement Workers of America, CIO, at the plant were endeavoring to arrange a "back to work" settlement.

No indications have been received of any organized subversive activity in connection with this situation.

Indianapolis Field Division

In the northern part of the State of Indiana in the City of Gary, an organization known as the "Development of our Own" is reported to be active. It is stated that this organization, although having relatively few active members in that city, preaches racial equality and ultimate domination by the colored people. It is also stated to be pro-Japanese and has held meetings to that effect. In the same city, information has been reported to the effect that a Moorish Cult was at one time existent, and it is believed to have been broken up a few years ago, leading to the organization of the "Development of our Own." This latter group, reportedly pro-Japanese, has recently gone underground.

In connection with the "Development of our Own," the section concerning the Chicago Field Division should be reviewed. Several members in the Gary, Indiana, section have advised that there was a pro-Japanese sentiment among the members, and Emmanual Pharr has been listed as a leader. The Gary unit has been led by one Gentral Pope, the president of the organization.

It is also reported that a unit of the Peace Movement of Ethiopia has had a unit in Gary, Indiana, which has been led by one Harry Collins. This organization in Gary is said to have collected money for Mrs. Gordon, the president of the organization, who was arrested and convicted in Chicago, Illinois. An informant, who has attended meetings of this unit in Gary and the surrounding area, particularly at Indiana Harbor, has advised that there was a small attendance, not exceeding twenty-four adults.

In the City of Indianapolis there is a unit of the Universal Negro Improvement Association which is said to be extremely small in size, its meetings being attended by approximately eight to twelve individuals. Informants who have attended meetings have advised that the agenda dealt with the return of Negroes to Africa. No indications have been received that pro-Axis or pro-Japanese sympathies are prevalent among the members. There is also active in this city unit No. 15 of the Moorish Science Temple of America, which is said to meet every Friday and Sunday evenings. Its meetings are reportedly attended by approximately twenty-five persons. To date no indications have been reported that there is any un-American or pro-Axis activity connected with the group.

At one time there existed in the City of Indianapolis an organization described as the Black, Brown and Yellow Society of America, the purpose of which was alleged to be the obtaining of representation of its members in the League of Nations. An additional aim of the organization was to assist Negroes to obtain their rights. The leader of this organization in 1942 stated his group had nothing to do with Japanese or Chinese nationals and that the organization had no affiliations of any sort. No recent indications of this organization's being active have been reported.

Another organization said to be active in the Indianapolis area during the latter part of 1942 was a group known as "Jobs and Justices for Negroes," which was described as extremely race conscious. It was reportedly organized in 1942 to allegedly cooperate with the National Association for the Advancement of Colored People, the Urban League and Negro churches. The organization, according to reports, has since been inactive. It should be noted, however, that at one time the Communist Party in Indianapolis appointed various members for the purpose of cooperating with this group.

Throughout the State of Indiana it has been ascertained that the Communist Party has been agitating among the Negroes in an attempt to make them conscious of racial discrimination. The Party is also stated to be very much interested in recruiting Negroes into the Party. In the Calumet area of Indiana, including Gary, Hammond and East Chicago, the Communist front organization, the International Workers Order, has organized a colored lodge, which, however, is stated to have but a few members. It has been reported that the Communist Party, especially in Indianapolis, considered the possibility of opening at least one Party center in the Negro district, which was considered an implement in the Party campaign to recruit Negro members. In this connection it should be noted that Party functionaries are making every effort to recruit Negroes in the Indiana area, stating they are the only group truly advocating the elimination of discrimination. Much of their work centers on the manufacturing concerns, where it is said some degree of success has been attained.

Subsequent information has been received that the Negro center planned by the Party in Indianapolis was established at 1208 North Senate Avenue in that city. As of June 20, 1942, when the formal opening took place, local functionaries of the Party were disappointed at the sparse turnout at the dedication.

In the latter part of May, 1943, the Communist Party in Indiana, especially in Indianapolis, was concentrating on sending the proper delegates to the conference of the National Association for the Advancement of Colored People. Suggestions were made that several known Negro Communists be sent. In this connection, Elmer Johnson, the Executive Secretary of the Indianapolis section of the Communist Party, instructed one of the proposed delegates that he should attempt to have a resolution adopted at the conference setting out details of alleged discrimination at various industrial plants and have it sent to the Fair Employment Practice Committee for investigation.

On June 23, 1943, a meeting was held at Communist Party headquarters in Indianapolis and, according to a confidential informant, Party functionaries were greatly concerned over the riots in Detroit during June 20–22, 1943. The Party officials are said to have contacted several local Negro leaders, at which time they placed blame for the Detroit riots on the Ku Klux Klan, Father Coughlin, Henry Ford and Gerald L. K. Smith. They also reportedly claimed that the riots were a part of the national conspiracy against the war effort. Plans were made to hold a meeting in this regard.

On June 11, 12 and 13, 1943, "The Indianapolis Institute on Race Relations and the Non-Violence Solutions" were sponsored by the Fellowship of Reconciliation at the Negro YMCA. At the meeting on June 12 approximately sixty persons attended, forty being white and the remainder colored. Bayard Rustin, Negro, youth secretary of the organization, explained the "action project," whereby members both Negro and white would enter a restaurant not catering to Negroes and request service in a group. Any discrimination or refusal to serve the Negroes would result in formal protests. At the June 13, 1943, meeting, James Farmer, race relations secretary of the Fellowship of Reconciliation, spoke on the topic "spiritual basis for non-violence." Approximately seventy people attended, the figure being divided equally as to race. At this time he explained non-violence direct action technique and advised that Negroes should not put up with racial discrimination and segregation. *[100-135-22-47]*

It is reported that various civic leaders in the city of Indianapolis have been concerned over the Negro situation in that city. It is further reported confidentially that local law enforcement authorities have in the past exhibited some laxity in coping with the situation; furthermore, scattered complaints have been received reflecting that there is a strong feeling against the white people on the part of the Negroes. On the night of August 15, 1942, a riot took place at one of the Negro night clubs in Indianapolis. This riot was started after two white policemen arrested a prostitute outside the establishment. The policemen were severely beaten and mauled by a mob which was estimated to range from one hundred to two hundred colored men. No information, however, has been received in regard to this riot reflecting possible pro-Axis agitation as the cause thereof.

In the City of Evansville, Indiana, there are approximately 8,000 Negroes. Active there are the National Association for the Advancement of Colored People, the Negro Ministerial Alliance and the Council of Clubs. No information has been reported by confidential sources in this area reflecting organized agitation among the Negroes there.

Several instances reported to have taken place at the Chrysler Evansville Ordnance Plant, Evansville, Indiana, are said to reflect the attitude of at least some Negroes living in this area. It is said that a number of the members of this race, working at this plant, are engaging in practices bordering on the obnoxious, mainly that of pushing themselves into lines at lunch wagons and taking other advantages on every possible occasion. The general report is that the white employees as a whole have been considerate with the Negro employees there.

Milwaukee Field Division

Informants in this area advise that the 12,000 Milwaukee Negroes are loyal and behind the war effort. A small group of Negroes, however, calling themselves Moslems, refused to register under the Selective Training and Service Act or take part in the "white man's war." The leader of this group has been indicted for violation of the Selective Training and Service Act and the members identified. The leader of the group has denied any Japanese connection on the part of this group but admitted that since the Japanese are a colored race, there is close connection with the Negro race. The activities of the group are, of course, being closely followed.

The Universal Negro Improvement Association, led by James K. Stewart, Cleveland, Ohio, sponsored a meeting on June 7, 1942, in Milwaukee, which was attended by approximately 250 Negroes. Stewart was the main speaker and his theme was "why fight for the white men when the white men never fight for them. . . ." This organization and its leader are receiving close attention.

The Communist Party in and around Milwaukee, Wisconsin, is reported to be actively engaged in agitating to end alleged discrimination in the Armed Forces and the national defense effort against the Negroes. In this connection, several mass meetings have been sponsored by the Party in the Negro section, at which time protests against the lynching of Negroes were made and Martin Dies was attacked. Such other measures as the establishment of a mixed army ending segregation of Negroes and full enforcement of the Thirteenth, Fourteenth and Fifteenth Amendments were demanded.

It was reported that there are approximately 42 Negro Communists in the State of Wisconsin, with approximately 36 of the total in Milwaukee. In this connection, a branch organizer is stated to have informed a Negro that the Negroes can only reach their true and due position under the Russian type of government and for that reason the Negro should work hard to bring Communism and the Russian government to the United States.

An organization, not subversive in nature, known as the Milwaukee Urban League, is stated to have been active during the past ten years in that city. This organization is reported to be chiefly interested in securing employment for Negro men and women in defense factories. The organization is supported by the Community Fund in Milwaukee. No reports have been received that this organization is agitating among the Negroes.

Recently the "Wisconsin Enterprise Blade," a weekly Negro newspaper, has been revived in the Milwaukee area. Its last publication was in the Fall of 1940 when it was discontinued because of financial difficulties. Its ex-publisher, J. Anthony Josey, is attempting to secure financial support to republish the publication so that a number of the large industrial plants in Milwaukee may be circulated. It is thought the support from the Republican Party and industrial plants in and around Milwaukee is sought by the publisher.

Other newspapers which are distributed in this area are the Pittsburgh Courier, which is said to have a circulation of approximately 650 copies in the City of Milwaukee, the Chicago Defender with approximately 155, and the Chicago Bee with approximately a 50-copy circulation.

A confidential source of information has advised that the Communist Party activity among the Negroes in this area has little effect in that it is believed former Negro Communists have lost interest in the Party. This is laid to the fact that Negroes have secured jobs and do not feel that the Party has anything to offer them. In this regard it is said the Communist Party officials have been complaining about the lack of Negro attendance at their meetings and stated that the membership dues and subscriptions to the Daily Worker have dropped off considerably.

At one time in 1941, the March on Washington Movement organization was active in the City of Milwaukee, however, since that time it was discontinued. At present, however, it is believed that the Committee will be revived in the very near future. It is reported that in the past there were no indications of any subversive activity on the part of the members of the movement when it existed in the City of Milwaukee, but it was said by a Negro source of information that if the group would fall into the hands of a wrong group, it could definitely become subversive.

On December 8, 1942, a meeting was held in Walker Hall of the Milwaukee Auditorium, Milwaukee, Wisconsin, at which Dr. Max Yergan, reported Communist and member of the Council on African Affairs, was the principal speaker. It is reported that there were approximately 150 people present, most of whom were Negroes. The invocation was said to have been delivered by Reverend I. M. Coggs, who was followed by Dr. Frank E. Baker of the Milwaukee State Teacher's College who acted as chairman of the meeting. Congressman elect Howard J. McMurray addressed the meeting. He spoke on "Freedom of Fear," linking this subject with that of "What Causes War?", according to reports.

Dr. Baker is reported to have introduced Dr. Max Yergan, Executive Director of the Council on African Affairs, an individual who has been reported to be a Communist and who has in fact been affiliated with many Communist front organizations. Dr. Yergan is said to have condemned the action in the Senate which blocked the passage of the anti-poll tax bill. He is then said to have called for greater democracy for the American Negro, for China, India and Africa. He reportedly warned the negro people of Fascism, pointing out the results of "Rule of Minority" in the conquered countries. He then is said to have urged that the Negro people of Africa be given arms so that they might join the Allies in fighting the Axis. He also is said to have urged this discrimination against the Negro in the armed forces, industry and in society be stopped. He also is said to have urged that a second front on the continent of Europe be opened. This last statement of Yergan's is, of course, in direct harmony with the Communist Party line.

Prosecution has recently been authorized against five individuals, members of a Moslem group in Milwaukee, for violation of the Selective Training and Service Act. The information developed concerning them reflects that they have counselled evasion of this law.

A complaint has been received relative to a former minister of a church known as the Church of Christ in God whose name is Clarence F. Dickerson. This individual, a Negro, is alleged to be making pro-Japanese statements and extolling the Moslem faith in connection with his alleged pro-Japanese statements; it is noted, however, that he is reported to have made highly exaggerated utterances and to have given the impression that he is highly important in the Moslem faith.

Relative to the activities of members of the Moslem group in the Milwaukee area, a confidential source of information has advised that there were perhaps two or three hundred Moslem members in the city, but as of 1941 the only active members were a group of men and women totaling approximately twenty-five. It was said that at that time they had no recognized leader. Inquiries are, of course, being continued relative to this sect, and their advocacy of non-participation in war for Negroes.

In September, 1942 an organization known as the "National Progressive Negroes of America, Incorporated" was incorporated in the State of Wisconsin, the purpose of which was allegedly to further the service of Negroes to God, country and Negro race. The promoter of this organization was Moses Joseph Albany, who allegedly at one time was head of the Pacific Movement of the Eastern World in Kansas City, Missouri.

The membership of this organization did not reach large proportions and it is said to have consisted of sixty-seven members. On February 9, 1943, Albany was arrested by the police in Milwaukee on a vagrancy charge. On the same date, the vice president of the group, one Meshack Jones, was arrested on a bigamy charge. Albany had a considerable criminal background, having served several sentences for housebreaking, assault with intent to kill, carrying concealed weapons, robbery, grand larceny and other crimes. While in Wisconsin, Albany made a living telling fortunes and blessing homes to make them lucky. He also dealt in prostitution. On February 16, 1943, he was sentenced to ninety days in the house of correction, and upon the completion of his sentence he was immediately to leave Milwaukee. The organization which was begun by Albany was thereafter disbanded.

It was reported in February, 1943 that Ned Sparks, Secretary of the Communist Party for the State of Wisconsin, after ascertaining that "rank and file" Negroes had been recruited into the Party became angry with another Party functionary who had done the recruiting and stated that the Party desired only quality and not quantity in its Negro recruiting. He ordered that only outstanding Negroes should be recruited, saying that ordinary Negroes were not an asset to the Party because they would not work. He pointed out that they are active as members for a short time and then drop out.

The above incident can be cited as an example of how the Party is willing to exploit Negroes, yet cannot successfully use them as working members. It also reflects the lack of sincerity in the Party's program, especially with respect to Negroes. It is to be noted that these remarks by Sparks were directed to Katherine Hartmann, an organizer for the International Fur and Leather Workers Union of the United States and Canada, CIO, and an active Communist Party member. [*100-135-31-12*]

In connection with the Party's activities in recruiting Negroes, a confidential informant has advised that the Party's activity in Milwaukee in March, 1943, did not amount to much for several reasons. He also pointed out that former active Negro members in the Milwaukee area do not even admit their former connections any more. He informed that in his opinion the only reason Communists ever gained any sort of a foothold in the Negro district was because in the early years of the Party's recruiting, Negroes were furnished a chance to socialize with white girls. He claimed that the novelty of this soon wore off, and that the vast majority of the Negroes became employed and do not have time to engage in Communism. Subsequent to March, 1943, however, in April and in May, the Party in the Milwaukee area is said to have renewed its activity in attempting to obtain Negro recruits. New organizers were appointed for the Negro section, and it was planned that prominent Communist speakers would appear at membership meetings to discuss some topic of vital interest to the Negro people. The Party also took an active part in a drive for better Negro housing.

There has been established in the City of Milwaukee an Interracial Labor Relations Committee, which has representatives from the National Association for the Advancement of Colored People and various CIO industrial unions. The Communist Party has taken an active part in this council and has supplied speakers for it. On June 13, 1943, Meyer Adelman, an active member of the Communist Party, spoke in place of Harold Christoffel, President of the Milwaukee County Industrial Union Council, CIO. An informant has advised that Adelman delivered a very radical speech in which he said that he was going to obtain a group of Negro girls and take them to the Wisconsin Telephone Company with the demand that they be hired. He informed that he was sure the telephone company would not hire them but that it would start a fight. He also stated that he intended to get a group of Negro soldiers and take them to two prominent hotels where a demand would be made that they supply lodging for them at $1 per night. He added according to the informant, that he was also sure these hotels would not agree and that he, Adelman, would thereupon start "raising hell." He is said to have also remarked that the profits of all retail stores in the City of Milwaukee be distributed equally among the population. The source of information has advised that after Adelman's speech he had heard considerable comment on the part of Negroes that they were disgusted with Adelman and his remarks.

In April, 1943 it was reported that a strained relationship existed between Negro students at the University of Wisconsin in Madison and Navy men assigned to the Naval Radio Training School in Madison. It is said that several fist fights have occurred between southern Navy men and the Negroes, and as a result thereof there has been considerable activity on the part of Negro students in an attempt to abolish discrimination. Some time previously, in November, 1942, an organization known as the Negro Cultural Foundation was organized at the University of Wisconsin and its constitution was approved. The membership of this organization is approximately thirty. Its president, Argyle Stoute, is said to have been the organizer of the Negro Cultural Foundation. He is reported to have been expelled from New York University because of his agitational activity.

In February, 1943 a group known as the "Vanguard" was organized by Dr. Frederick Burkhardt, a professor of philosophy at the University of Wisconsin. In April, 1943 the organization took up the question of Negro discrimination and segregation. Professor Burkhardt at the meeting spoke of the problem of Negro troops stationed at Truax Field and mentioned the policy of the United Service Organization in the City of Madison, especially with regard to Negro discrimination and segregation. In June, 1943 it was reported that the "Vanguard" had discontinued its activity for the summer months.

Early in May, 1943 the Executive Secretary of the Urban League in Milwaukee informed that during the previous month, the Urban League had planned to cooperate with the Congress of Industrial Organizations to encourage Negroes to join labor unions in war plants and to become active members so that they would have the protection of the union in the postwar period. He informed that no specific unions were designated which the Negroes should join. However, he did point out that certain craft unions affiliated with the American Federation of Labor prohibited Negroes from joining. He further advised that his organization was attempting to campaign throughout the country to persuade A F of L craft unions to lift their ban against Negroes. He pointed out that in the past whenever Negroes have secured good jobs in factories they have done poor work and, consequently, lost the opportunity to become permanent employees. He stated that in this connection, education should be given to Negroes so that this situation could be remedied and they could find their places in industry.

Shortly after the riots in Detroit, a meeting was held in the offices of the Urban League in Milwaukee to form an Interracial War Council, reportedly done in accordance with instructions issued by the national headquarters of the Urban League for the purpose of continuing friendly relations between Negro and white inhabitants of this country. There were present at this meeting besides well-known Negro leaders, two members of the Communist Party, one a Negro and the other Josephine Nordstrand, Executive Secretary of the Wisconsin State Conference on Social Legislation, a Communist front. At this meeting Nordstrand proposed a mass rally. However, it was objected to because of the Communist connections, and the resolution was subsequently withdrawn. However, Josephine Nordstrand went ahead and made plans for a rally, calling on a number of prominent Negro leaders for their support. This rally was subsequently held on June 29, 1943 at which there were one hundred twenty persons present, thirty-two being white and the balance Negroes. A number of known Communists were recognized by informants. Edward Strong of the National Negro Congress, a Communist Party member, was the first speaker, who spoke not only on the Negro situation but reviewed the present war. He then referred to the Detroit riots, attacking the way the police handled the situation, and accused the fifth column as being responsible for them. The next speaker was James Dorsey, President of the National Association for the Advancement of Colored People in Milwaukee, who urged that Negroes in the area not engage in trouble with white people, saying that the odds were decidedly against them. He then referred to a large number of youthful Negroes who have engaged in vandalism and hoodlumism in the Milwaukee area. He also stated that Negroes who have been clamoring for employment in defense industries have utterly failed to perform their duties satisfactorily once they are so employed. He urged that if the Negro does his part in the war effort and shows white people he is capable of doing comparable work to them, his employment will be on a much higher level at the completion of the war. With regard to the speech made by Dorsey, it is reported that the Communist Party decided to prepare a Negro statement to be signed by trade unionists in the Milwaukee area condemning Dorsey for his statements and his failure to completely endorse the Negroes' side of the riots in Detroit.

With regard to the general situation among the Negro population in the Milwaukee area, after the Detroit riots it is reported that Negroes were more or less stirred up over the incident, although no indications were received of any organized movement or Negro agitation.

A number of incidents have occurred in the Sixth Ward of Milwaukee, a Negro section, mainly involving youthful Negroes who are said frequently band together in a crowd of from three hundred to four hundred, especially on weekends, and cause considerable commotion by yelling and shouting and forcing people off of the sidewalks. According to informants, the Milwaukee Police Department so far has effectively broken up such gatherings and serious trouble has not been caused. An informant has stated, however, that if these individuals decided to roam the streets in the white residential areas, trouble might ensue.

Another source of information has advised of hearing anti-Semitic talk in the Sixth Ward area but has added that this has been going on for a number of years, and in his opinion, it is meaningless. He has also informed of hearing considerable talk about the

Detroit riots, and some by Negroes who stated that more white people were killed in these riots than were reported by the newspapers. He said further, it appeared to him that Negroes were glad the papers did not print the true facts, inasmuch as this would have led to more trouble. This same informant, a Negro, who is cognizant of the situation in the Milwaukee area, has informed that Negroes as a whole feel they are getting along well at the present time and have no desire to cause trouble. ▬▬▬

Newark Field Division

According to the 1940 census, there are approximately 250,000 Negroes in the State of New Jersey, with the heaviest Negro population centered in Essex, Hudson, Mercer, Monmouth, Union, Atlantic, Bergen and Camden Counties. The City of Newark leads the cities in New Jersey with a population of approximately 45,000 Negroes, followed by Atlantic City with approximately 16,000, Jersey City 13,000 and Camden 12,000.

The following Negro publications are the most widely distributed in the State of New Jersey:

The New Jersey Guardian, published in Newark, with an approximated circulation of 32,000.

The New Jersey Herald News, published in Newark, with a reported circulation of 22,000.

The Echo, published in Red Bank, New Jersey, circulation unknown.

The Afro-American, although not published in New Jersey, is said to have a comparatively wide circulation.

All of the foregoing publications are published weekly.

In the New Jersey metropolitan area, centered in and around Newark, New Jersey, sources of information advise there is no foreign-inspired agitation among the Negroes in that area although there are frequent voicings of dissatisfaction and unrest. The unrest, or dissatisfaction, is said to be a result of domestic, social and economic problems, and it has been further claimed that utterances condemning the national defense program usually result from the refusal of employers to employ qualified colored labor in the face of existing vacancies in industries manufacturing national defense material.

With regard to these expressions of dissatisfaction, it is stated that they do not mean the Negroes are disloyal to the United States, but rather are expressions of appreciation of knowledge of the anti-Negro tendencies in the United States. The opinion was also expressed concerning Negroes in this area that a false conception is obtained when Negroes voice dissatisfaction, especially as to the scarcity of opportunities for advancement during the present national emergency, in that certain groups tend to say such unrest is foreign-inspired. This source of information advised that the real cause, in his opinion, is the existence of actual discrimination and that the situation could become more serious even without foreign inspiration. Another phase of the situation, as expressed by this source of information, is to the effect that the Negro population is increasing its efforts to be of assistance to the gaining momentum of the national defense program; yet this effort on the part of the Negroes will be met by some factions with the rising tide of antagonism "that the Negroes must be kept in their place."

Sources of information contacted in the City of Newark advise of no reports or indications that pro-Japanese or pro-German forces are at work among the Negroes. However, it is stated that much of the "propaganda" urging Negroes to strive for equal rights and the abolishment of "Jim Crowism" is furthered by Communist Party agitation, although the original movement toward such betterment for the Negro actually sprung from the ranks of the Negroes prior to Communist infiltration. Certain nonspecific reports of alleged Japanese speaking to and mingling with Negroes several years ago were received, but no such influence is reportedly active at the present time.

In the cities of Kearny and Jersey City, inquiries as to the possible existence of pro-Axis activity among the Negroes fails to reflect such activity at the present time. In Jersey City, however, it was reported that the Communist Party had attempted to agitate among the colored population but had never met with success because of the attitude of the administration in that city toward the Communists.

Among the various organizations composed of members of the Negro race in the State of New Jersey are the National Association for the Advancement of Colored People, the Urban League, the Moorish Science Temple of America, and the House of Israel. With regard to the first two of these organizations, no indications have been received of any pro-Axis influence in them. The Moorish Science Temple of America is said to be active in the cities of Newark, Camden, Glassboro and Montclair. In Newark there are two branches, one of which believes in the reincarnation of Noble Drew Ali, the founder of the Temple, while the other follows the dictates of C. Kirkman Bey, Chicago, Illinois. The exact extent of membership in this State is not known; however, the larger group in Newark is said to have a membership of approximately 300, while the smaller group has an active membership of approximately 55. Both of the groups have expressed definite anti-white sentiments. Investigations are being continued relative to the various temples throughout the State. Numerous reports have been received indicating pro-Japanese sentiments on the part of individual members of the sect.

With regard to the organization known as the House of Israel, a group claiming to be Jewish, although actually cultists who are pro-Japanese, has been broken up through the arrest of seven of its members for violations of the Selective Training and Service Act. The original group was composed of approximately twelve adults. The leader, whose real name is believed to be Rubin Thomas, used the name Rubin Israel and collected two dollars a week per family from his members to support a school in which he taught alleged doctrines.

At one time in the State of New Jersey there were active groups of the Universal Negro Improvement Association as well as the Pacific Movement of the Eastern World.

With regard to Communist Party activities in the State of New Jersey, the general Communist Party line prevails, urging assistance and an all-out effort in the war program. There are a number of Negroes who have been active in running for offices on the Communist Party ticket as well as several who are organizers for various industrial unions. Confidential sources indicate there are approximately 370 Negro Party members out of a total Negro population of 250,000. Of this number 118 were Party members as of January 1943, while the other 252 are new recruits secured during the membership campaign beginning in February 1943 and ending in May 1943. According to informants, this increase is not believed to indicate any real change in the general Negro attitude toward the Party which, they claim, remains skeptical.

The Negro sources of information and confidential informants who have been contacted for information in their possession relative to reported instances of foreign-inspired agitation among the members of their race have convincingly stated that they know of no current foreign-inspired causes of Negro unrest, although they do feel that the Negro is not getting a fair type of treatment in the current war effort and that this coupled with the fact that this designation generally is still re[g]arded leads him to feel that he has a questionable stake in the war. *[100-135-32]*

During the early part of June 1943 there were several disturbances among Negro and Italian high school youths in Newark resulting in the fatal shooting of a Negro boy by an Italian youth. In connection with these disturbances rumors of pending race riots began to circulate and reached a climax the week end of June 26, 1943, as adults throughout the city, according to reports, Negroes particularly, became increasingly incensed over the interracial aspects of the fatal shooting. Negro citizens are said to have complained vehemently that the Newark Police Department had not given them proper treatment and protection from Italian hoodlums. There were charges that an improper investigation had been made of the incidents and several Negro organizations called on or petitioned Newark city officials for a better coverage in Newark's race danger zones, particularly the 1st and 3rd Wards.

According to sources of information, tension among the Negro citizens in Newark has increased since these incidents. These informants have pointed out that since the beginning of the war both Negro and white people have filtered into Newark to seek better jobs. This has resulted in increased friction between the races, according to the informants, and Negroes are said to feel the pressure also of letters they receive from their relatives in the Armed Forces containing incidents of alleged racial discrimination in the Armed Forces. A source of information has further advised that although there was a peaceful settlement in the Italian-Negro difficulties, there is still a tension and a considerable amount of this exists among Negro youths. This same informant has added that pictures in the local newspapers of the victims of the Detroit race riots incited the Negro youth and pointed out that the average Negro can only see the pictures and cannot read the captions and he, therefore, personally resents the beatings of Negroes portrayed in the pictures without attempting to analyze the background circumstances.

New Haven Field Division

For the purpose of convenience the summary of information regarding this area concerning agitation among the Negroes, will be broken down according to the larger cities:

In the vicinity of Ansonia, Connecticut, it is reported that the Negro population of this area has been rapidly increasing, there now being approximately 3500 Negroes, most of whom have come from the Southern States and the Harlem Section of New York City. Contacts made with sources of information in this area reveal that there are no indications of any foreign inspired agitation among the Negroes here, and that a majority of trouble experienced is with lowering the number of violations of the law on the part of Negroes.

In the vicinity of Bridgeport, Connecticut, it is reported that the Negro population has been increasing because of prospective employment in defense industries there. No indications, however, have been reported reflecting unrest or dissatisfaction caused by un-American elements. In this area there has recently been issued a small newspaper or magazine entitled "Modern People", published in the Y.M.C.A. building, 1146 Barnham Avenue, Bridgeport, Connecticut. This magazine is stated to contain articles concerning discrimination against Negroes by local industries and, all in all, demands more rights and privileges for Negroes. The Bridgeport Herald, published in Bridgeport, Connecticut, is also stated to be active in its criticism of discrimination against the Negroes and alleged "Jim Crow" practices in the army camps. In the issue of this paper dated July 19, 1942, an article appeared concerning "Jim Crow" practices in army camps and the following was included in the article: "These things of which I have spoken happen each and every day in the camps that I have been in, and I think it is time somebody took time to see why the racial hatreds of the prejudiced South have to penetrate into the United States Army Camps. What kind of morale will Jim Crow practices bring to negro troops? After all, we are Americans too." The above statement was said to have been contained in a letter written by a Sergeant located at Fort Benning, Georgia. Numerous other articles have appeared in this paper concerning Negroes, including one which was dated August 2, 1942, and entitled "New Negro now Fights for Complete Equality", and another in the issue dated August 2, 1942, entitled, "Racial Discrimination Charged in War Plants." It should be noted that no indications have been received reflecting un-Americanism inspiring these articles.

In and around Greenwich, Connecticut, it is stated, there is but a small Negro population, the larger part of which work as servants in private homes. The only active organizations in this area are said to be the Committee for Jobs for Negroes and the Colored Republican Club. The former club is said to be active also in Stamford and Fort Chester, New York. It has its headquarters at 20 Oakridge Street, Greenwich, Connecticut, and its avowed purpose is to combat racial discrimination in defense plants in southwestern Connecticut.

At the present time, in and around Hartford, Connecticut, it is reported, there are approximately 10,000 Negroes. Among the Negro organizations in Hartford are the

National Association for the Advancement of Colored People, the North End Federated Club and the Moorish Science Temple of America.

Investigation is being conducted as a result of the report of an unidentified Japanese individual visiting in Hartford on the night of December 9, 1942, and speaking to the congregation of the Holy Ghost Church in this city. This individual is reported to have stated that Japanese were friends of the colored race and that it was best for the Negroes to join with Japan because it was to their best interests to do so. He is reported to have called the people there his brothers and sisters. Investigation into this matter has failed to reveal this individual's identity but the indications are that his efforts did not make much impression on the colored people in this area.

In this region it is stated that the editor of the Hartford Times, has criticized the failure of the community to take steps toward furnishing recreational facilities for Negroes in the 77th Coast Artillery stationed in Hartford, Connecticut. It is stated however, that in the Spring of 1942 a great deal was done to furnish facilities for the colored troops through the efforts of both colored and white organizations such as the Community Church, City of Hartford, Negro Citizens Community Council and the Independent Social Circle. With regard to the activity of the Social Circle, it is reported that this organization has subscribed to the Philadelphia Afro-American and the Pittsburgh Courier, both Negro newspapers, for the benefit of the men in the 77th Coast Artillery. An opinion has been expressed that such publications are not inducive to peaceable relations as both have been described as extremely radical in their opinions. It is also reported that the Chicago Defender, Negro newspaper, is distributed in the City of Hartford.

Information has been received reflecting that the Negro population in the vicinity of New Haven, Connecticut, is rapidly increasing. The majority of the Negroes are stated to be coming from the Southern States and from the Harlem Section of New York City. The Negro population in this area, at the present time, is estimated at from ten to twelve thousand; and it is stated that it has been growing to such an extent that it has been necessary for the local police department to employ three Negroes as policemen in the Negro district.

Among the Negro organizations reported to be active in the City of New Haven, are the Negro Community Council, The National Association for the Advancement of Colored People, the Webster Institute, the Dixwell Community House, the Tents of America, and the Sons and Daughters of the South. It is also reported that the Negro churches in this area wield a heavy influence among the Negroes. A Reverend Richard A. G. Foster, Pastor of the Varick Memorial Zion Church is said to be very prominent among the Negroes in this area. Numerous newspaper articles have carried stories of sermons and speeches made by Reverend Foster. On August 9, 1942, Reverend Foster reportedly spoke at a large gathering at which he requested the Negroes to unite in obtaining their rights. He is quoted as having said, "If we want segregation against us to cease, then we must stand together so that the powers that be, will recognize and see us as a powerful force. If we want job discrimination discontinued in New Haven and in the State, then we must not take no for an answer when we are prepared to have better jobs." It is reported with respect to Reverend Foster that he at one time was affiliated with a Communist front organization, the American Peace Mobilization, and that on March 20, 1941, he signed a round robin letter which opposed America's participation in war as a violation of constitutional rights.

In the vicinity of New Haven, Connecticut, it has also been reported that the Connecticut Conference of Social and Labor Legislation is active among the Negro population. This organization has been reported to have close Communist connections.

Information received concerning the area including Stamford, Connecticut, does not indicate that there is any foreign inspired or un-American activity, or agitation among the four thousand Negroes in this area. It is reported that Negroes in this area are quiet as a whole and that the only organizations active there are the Stamford Branch of the National Association for the Advancement of Colored People and the organization known as the Committee for Jobs for Negroes.

It is reported that in and around Waterbury, Connecticut, there has been a rapid increase in the Negro population as a result of the demand for labor. No information, however, has been received reflecting un-American activity among or by the Negroes in this area. [*100-135-33*]

There has been in existence in the City of Hartford a branch of the Moorish Science Temple of America, which is said to have a charter, duly granted by the national organization. As to the membership of this organization, it is said that there are approximately one hundred fifty. A regional convention of this organization was held in Hartford in September, 1942, when approximately two hundred officers and delegates met. The general underlying philosophy in the speeches made at this convention was that of the religion involving the worship of Allah. It is alleged that the agitation which this organization causes is among the less educated and less wealthy class of Negroes in Hartford.

In the cities of New London, Torrington, Wallingford, Danbury, Norwich, Naugatuck, West Hartford, Plainville, Shelton, Wethersfield, East Hartford, Middletown, Groton, Westbrook, Old Lyme, Essex, Saybrook, Chester, Haddam, Durham, North Branford, East Haven, Guilford, Madison, Clinton and Killingly, inquiries have been made for evidences of organized subversive activity among the Negroes, and these have met with negative results. It is to be noted that in most of these communities the Negro population is small.

On October 24, 1942 a Conference to End Discrimination in New Haven was held in that city and adopted general resolutions for the doing away with discrimination and segregation and denial of equal rights to Negroes.

In the Stamford area an organization known as the Committee to Promote Fair Employment Practice has been organized, the purposes of which are to provide full and equal opportunities for Negroes in employment in war industries as well as in training opportunities. This organization is said to have the support of various Negro pastors in that city as well as professional men.

Reports from the Bridgeport area indicate, especially with regard to industrial plants, that individuals alleged to have Communist sympathies have been agitating, particularly among the Negro employees. The industrial plants alleged to have been involved in this situation are the Stamford Rolling Mills, the Stewart Die Casting Company, the Jenkins Brothers Plant, the Bell Map Company, the Bridgeport Brass Company, and the Aluminum Corporation of America, Bridgeport. The individuals involved in the agitating, according to the reports, are Irving Dichter and Sam Gruber, the former reportedly being a member of the Communist Party in Bridgeport, while the latter has reportedly attended Communist Party functions. It is said that their activities center on the Negro employees in the foundries of the plants.

[*100-135-33-18*]

During the night of June 30–July 1, 1943, rioting broke out in the vicinity of Hallen and Main Streets in New London, Connecticut. It took place between Negro members of the United States Maritime Training School at Fort Trumbull, New London, and white naval enlisted men reportedly stationed at the State Pier, New London. According to reports, Negro seamen of the Maritime School and the white naval seamen engaged in throwing rocks at one another. The trouble was broken up by police, who used their night sticks, and the Negro seamen left the scene of the rioting and walked in the direction of the Maritime Training School. At approximately 12:30 A.M. on July 1, the Negro seamen again reportedly got out of control and police were again called to break up the disturbance. The identities of the white seamen were not reported, however, the Maritime Training School identified thirty of the Negro seamen and confined them during an investigation. No indications were received that outside forces had attempted to stir up racial difficulties among the Maritime seamen.

New York Field Division

Geographical Distribution of Negroes in New York City

The Negro population of New York City as shown in the 1940 census was estimated at approximately 458,444 and it has been further estimated that this figure constitutes approximately 95 per cent of the New York State urban Negro population. The Negro population in New York City is concentrated mainly in Harlem and in the Columbus Hill district in Manhattan, while in Brooklyn it is mainly in the Bedford-Stuyvesant area.

The precincts of New York City having the largest Negro populations are described hereinafter:

Seventh Precinct: Takes in Rivington Street from Allen Street to East River to Pike Street to East Broadway to the West side of Allen Street, and back to Rivington Street.

Colored population approximately 2,500 out of total population of 180,000.

Nineteenth Precinct: Is made up of Spanish-Negro population of approximately 500, located on 75th Street from Third Avenue to Second Avenue.

Twenty-fourth Precinct: Running from 86th Street north to 125th Street Central Park West, Manhattan Avenue West to the Hudson River.

Negro population of approximately 11,000 being centered in the vicinity of Manhattan Avenue and Morningside Avenue, and from Cathedral Parkway to 125th Street. There is also a mixed colored and Puerto Rican population located on 98th or 99th Streets from Columbus Avenue to Central Park West.

Thirtieth Precinct: Takes in the district of 125th to 165th Streets and from St. Nicholas Avenue and Edgecomb Avenue west to the Hudson River. This is a residential section of approximately 140,000. This entire section is practically all colored.

Twenty-third Precinct: Has about 5,000 Negroes who reside between 97th and 102nd Streets and First and Third Avenues.

Twenty-fifth Precinct: Has a colored population of approximately 7,000 residing from 117th Street and East River to Pleasant Avenue and from 129th Street to the Harlem River and from Lexington Avenue to Fifth Avenue.

Twenty-eighth Precinct: Has a Negro population of 100,000 out of a total population of 125,000. The Negroes are residing between 110th and 116th Streets from Eighth Avenue to Manhattan Avenue, and between 116th and 130th Streets, between Lenox Avenue and St. Nicholas Avenue.

Thirty-second Precinct: Has a total population of 180,000 practically all of which are Negroes; takes in territory from 130th Street, Harlem River, from Fifth Avenue to St. Nicholas and Bradhurst Avenues.

Fortieth Precinct: Negro population approximately 2,000; takes in all territory south of 149th Street in the Bronx.

Forty-first Precinct: Running from Boston Road south from Bronx River to 169th Street; Prospect Avenue south from 169th Street to 149th Street and 149th Street south to East River.

Has a total population of 250,000 of which 4,000 are Negroes. No information is available as to the exact location of the colored population.

Forty-second Precinct: From 149th Street to 169th Street; from Grand Concourse to Prospect Avenue.

Has a Negro population of 2,500 out of a total population of 192,500.

Forty-fourth Precinct: Runs from 149th Street [to] 182nd Street and from Grand Concourse to Harlem River. Has a Negro population of 500.

Forty-eighth Precinct: From 169th Street to 180th Street and Bronx Park south from Grand Concourse to Boston Road and Bronx River. Has a Negro population of 2,000.

Forty-seventh Precinct: From 219th Street to 224th Street and White Plains Road. Has a Negro population of about 2,000.

One Hundred Twentieth Precinct: Has a Negro population of 13,750 and takes in Stapleton, Fort Richmond and West Brighton, Staten Island.

One Hundred Twenty-third Precinct: Has a Negro population of 265 and takes in Pleasant Plains and Sandy Ground.

Sixtieth Precinct: From West 21st Street to West 36th Street; from Neptune to Surf Avenues, Brooklyn. Has a Negro population of 900.

Sixty-first Precinct: Sheepshead Bay Road to East 12th Street, Brooklyn. Has a Negro population of 3,000.

Sixty-second Precinct: From 17th Avenue to 18th Avenue and from 86th Street to Bath Avenue, Brooklyn. Has a Negro population of 13,000.

Seventy-eighth Precinct: Has a colored population of about 6,000 located from Bergen to Baltic Street and from Fourth Avenue to Nevin, and from Cumberland Street to Vandam Street, between Atlantic Avenue and Fulton Street.

The colored population consists of laborers, porters and relief recipients.

Eighty-fourth Precinct: Has a colored population of 10,500 and is located from Lawrence Street to Johnson Avenue to Jay Street to Willoughby Street, Brooklyn.

The colored population consists of porters, laborers and relief recipients.

Sixty-ninth Precinct: Has a colored population of 500 which reside from Hegeman Avenue to Lett Avenue on Rockaway Avenue, Brooklyn.

Seventy-first Precinct: Has a colored population of approximately 100, residing on East New York Avenue, Old Glove Road and Montgomery Avenue, Brooklyn.

Seventy-third Precinct: Has a colored population of 18,000 residing on Belmont Avenue, Rockaway to Snediker Avenue, Rockaway Avenue from Sutter Avenue to Livonia Avenue and Livonia Avenue, Chester to Snediker Avenue and Thatford Avenue, Osborne Street to Howard Street, Brooklyn.

Seventy-fifth Precinct: Has a colored population of 4,000 residing at Pitkin Avenue to Belmont Avenue, Joralemon Street to Ellen Street and Blake Avenue.

Seventy-seventh Precinct: Colored population of 60,000 residing from Fulton Street to St. Marks Avenue, New York Avenue to Ralph Avenue.

Seventy-ninth Precinct: Colored population of 65,000 located from Quincy Street south to north side of Fulton Street and Myrtle Avenue from Franklin to Stuyvesant Avenues.

Eightieth Precinct: Has a colored population of 20,000 located from Fulton Street to St. Marks Avenue and Franklin Avenue to Vanderbilt Avenue.

Eighty-first Precinct: Has a colored population of 40,250 located from Fulton Street to Macon Street and Patchen Avenue to Greene Avenue and Ralph Avenue, Brooklyn.

Eighty-eighth Precinct: Has a colored population of 30,000 located from Park Avenue to Fulton Street; engaged principally as factory workers, Navy Yard and WPA workers.

Eighty-fifth Precinct: Has a colored population of 4,200.

Ninetieth Precinct: Colored population of 4,800.

One Hundredth Precinct: Has a colored population of 4,000 residing from 70th Street to 85th Street, from the north side of Rockaway Beach Boulevard to the south side of Beach Channel Drive.

Ninety-five per cent of the colored population of the precinct are employed at various hotels, bath houses and private homes.

One Hundred First Precinct: Colored population of 2,000 residing in the vicinity of Red Fern Avenue and Butler Avenue, Nameohe Street to the City Line.

Eighty-five per cent of the colored population are employed at hotels, rooming houses, bath houses and private homes.

One Hundred Third Precinct: Colored population of 50,000 residing on Sutphin Boulevard and Liberty Avenue, east on Liberty Avenue to 175th Street, south on 175th Street to 114th Avenue, west on 114th Avenue to Sutphin Boulevard, north on Sutphin Boulevard to Liberty Avenue.

One Hundred Fourteenth Precinct: Colored population of 4,000 located between 94th Street and 114th Street, Northern Boulevard to Astoria Boulevard.

One Hundred Tenth Precinct: Negro population of about 13,500 residing in the northeast of the Corona territory bounded by Junction Avenue to 114th Street and Northern Boulevard to Worlds Fair Boulevard.

One Hundred Ninth Precinct: Has a colored population of 5,000 located west end of Flushing between Main Street and Flushing River and from 10th Street to Sanford Avenue.

Social and Economic Conditions Causing Unrest and Dissatisfaction

Employment

It is reported that the overwhelming majority of the Negroes in New York City are employed in unskilled labor or in domestic or other service positions. In the 1930's almost 70 per cent of the Negroes in New York City were on relief rolls and from February 1939 until February 1942 Negro employment on WPA rolls rose from 14.2 per cent to 17.6 per cent. This is said to be due not to any growth of employment on WPA rolls among Negroes but to be due to the fact that white workers enjoyed a priority in obtaining employment in private industries.

It has been estimated that 51 per cent of the jobs afforded by war industries are barred to Negroes as a matter of policy. As a result, about 85 per cent of the Negroes in New York City are reportedly employed in one of the following three occupation groups:

1. Domestic and personal service—52 per cent.
2. Manufacturing and mechanical—22 per cent.
3. Transportation and communication—11 per cent.

It is said that as a result of the lack of equal opportunities for employment in industries, the Negroes in this area suffer severely from economic insecurity. It is also alleged that in recent years Negroes have been displaced in private employment at twice the rate of white people and have been re-employed at half of that rate. The income of the poorer half of the Negro population in New York is said to reflect that the Negro earns about one-half the amount earned in one year by the average in the poorer half of the White population.

Housing

It is stated that the creation of a Negro district in New York has encouraged the development of a landlord monopoly which enable[s] leaseholders or owners to set rentals at the maximum which Negro tenants can meet rather than maintain a rental level met by tenants elsewhere under similar circumstances. It is said that the Negroes are allowed to rent only property which is immediately adjacent to other property occupied by Negroes and that about 85 per cent of the dwellings are more than 35 years old. As a result, a serious housing condition exists which materially affects thousands of Negro families. Zoning restrictions, lack of rent control, together with a tremendous increase in the Negro population of New York City have produced a scarcity of housing for Negroes and have forced them to occupy dwellings maintained in substandard condition.

It has been expressed in at least one daily newspaper in New York City that high rents, unsanitary living conditions and the shortage of residences are factors in the increase of crime conditions in Harlem. (NY Journal American) A magistrate in one of the courts in New York City who is familiar with the situation in Harlem has stated regarding the crowded housing conditions, that in many instances the rentals are such the wages of the tenants cannot meet the cost and it is consequently necessary that they engage roomers or boarders, as a result of which, i.e., the crowded and unsanitary conditions, morality is in many instances broken down and juvenile delinquency increased.

Educational Facilities

Although they are a part of New York City's public schools, Harlem's public schools are reported to be seriously handicapped by poor and inadequate equipment. It is alleged that certain discriminatory practices, existing as a result of zoning regulations, force Negroes into certain schools not of their choice.

In addition to the reported vicious neighborhood conditions affecting the younger Negro adversely, it is alleged that the vocational schools, to which the younger Negroes turn in great numbers, give them little or no encouragement or training. It is also said that vocational training is discouraged in many instances among the Negroes because of the limited employment opportunities for skilled Negro tradesmen.

On the other hand, one New York City magistrate has stated that although the educational facilities in Harlem are crowded, they are not out of proportion to other sections of the city.

Recreational Facilities

It is reported that the more heavily populated Negro sections of New York City are in many instances completely devoid of recreational facilities. These sections are usually inhabited by large families of small financial means and the areas are those having congested and poor housing conditions. In addition, those sections which do have recreational facilities are reportedly almost inaccessible to the Negroes. According to reliable reports, it is generally known that the recreational facilities in Harlem are not on a par with other sections of the city.

Delinquency and Crime

Coexistent with low incomes, substandard housing conditions and discriminatory employment practices, there is said to be a corresponding excessive rate of juvenile delinquency and adult crime. Juvenile delinquency in many instances seems to be confined to petty pilfering and offenses of like nature, while the adult criminal activity finds expression mainly in prostitution, narcotics and various forms of gambling.

Relative to this, an inspector of the New York Police Department has attributed juvenile delinquency and adult crime in Harlem to the crowded housing conditions and to the fact that in many instances mothers are employed outside of the Harlem district as domestics, with the result that children run free in the streets without proper supervision or the home atmosphere which is necessary to develop good citizenry.

Crime in Harlem

For a period of several months there have been reports received and considerable publicity noticed relative to the existence of an increased crime wave in the Harlem section of New York City. With regard to this crime wave, a confidential source who has had considerable experience in this area advised that it has the populace there aroused to such an extent that a majority of the Negro people are anxious that something be done about it. It is said that a wave of "muggings," robbery and even murder has so blighted this section that there has been a resulting loss in trade and business, especially among tourists and pleasure seekers who are said to supply considerable income to various groups in Harlem.

The underlying factors for this crime wave have been designated as being basically economic. It is reported that many of the crimes are perpetrated by youths between the ages of 17 and 23, many of whom are products of the depression and demoralization that accompanies the widespread unemployment and discrimination in employment which are said to be the misfortunes of the Negro people in the area. It has been further pointed out that the widespread juvenile delinquency is to a large extent the product of overcrowded conditions in housing and schools and the lack of sufficient recreational centers for children. Another factor mentioned by this source is that a large element of the people who migrated to New York City in recent years, did so because of the desire to find easier occupations and one in which money was more readily obtainable.

The same source of information has pointed out that a majority of the Negroes in this area are law-abiding and patriotic citizens. It is said that they understand that crime, regardless of the underlying causes for it, must be punished. In this respect, the majority are wholeheartedly in sympathy with the law enforcement agencies. It is reported that Negro-organized groups in Harlem such as churches and fraternal organizations have agitated for remedial measures to destroy the conditions that breed crime and that a few, though insufficient, steps have been taken in this direction.

Another source of information has pointed out that there are two schools of thought with regard to the crime situation in Harlem: one, which is fostered by the Amsterdam Star News, a Negro newspaper, attempts to reflect the sentiment of decent law-abiding people who are anxious to have something done about the crime situation. This newspaper is said to have run a series of articles aimed at crystallizing public sentiment into a campaign to clean up Harlem and rid it of the criminal element. On the other hand, it is said that the "People's Voice," a Negro newspaper, also published in Harlem, which is edited by Adam Clayton Powell, Jr., has completely given itself over to the Communist Party line of twisting and distorting facts in order to garner mass support and circulation. It has been pointed out that law enforcement agencies are hampered in their work by Communist groups who characterize the actions of the Police Department in enforcing law as attacks on the Negro people, especially when Negroes are arrested for the commission of crimes.

This source of information called attention to the "People's Voice," the "Daily Worker" and numerous Communist Party pamphlets which condemn other newspaper accounts of the crime situation in Harlem as a smear campaign. It is said that the Communists seize upon every instance to accuse the Police Department of brutality and frame-ups. In this connection, the same source pointed out that Communists have never called a meeting about the crime wave in Harlem but rather in effect justify it by blaming every Governmental agency and the "vicious system that breeds crime." Although it is true this informant stated, that economic factors are discussed at Communist Party meetings, they are discussed only for the purpose of attacking all constituted authorities and creating the impression that Communists are the only friends and champions of the Negroes.

As an example of this Party technique, this source of information referred to the riots in Harlem in March 1935 when, as a result of such riots, an unprecedented number of policemen were stationed in Harlem. He related that the Communists at that time called protest meetings against "the unwarranted presence of policemen in Harlem whose objective was not to protect property and maintain order but to intimidate the people."

Activities of Communist Groups or Organizations Influencing the Negroes

Negro Labor Victory Committee

The Negro Labor Victory Committee is exceedingly active in holding meetings and agitating among the Negroes in Harlem for the following program:

> "Demand effective use of human material both in industry and the armed forces and the wiping out of discrimination. Secure the rights of the Negro. The War Production Board should be compelled to place Negroes in the war industries. Abolition of Jim Crow pay.
>
> "Demand that the War Production Board be compelled to train one hundred thousand Negroes for war production by October, 1942, and finance them while in training.
>
> "Demand war orders for New York City and the creating of more war plants.
>
> "Demand that Negroes be placed on all war power commissions, joint labor and management groups to be set up to eliminate job and wage discrimination.
>
> "Demand that a national conference on discrimination be called as soon as possible.
>
> "Demand that the Federal Fair Employment Practices Committee be given power under Section 8802 to penalize firms that violate its decisions.
>
> "Demand that Federal action be taken to protect Negroes from police and mob violence.
>
> "Demand that President Roosevelt grant executive pardon to Odell Waller and the Scottsboro Boys now.
>
> "Demand that Negroes be appointed to all Government regulation bodies such as rationing boards, price control boards, etc.

"Demand full citizenship rights for the Negro everywhere. Immediate passage of the Pepper Anti-Poll Tax Bill. Abolition of the Jim Crow law.

"Demand that the Negroes be admitted in all branches of the Army and to all Naval training stations and schools."

The Negro Commission of the National Committee of the Communist Party was reported to be responsible for the organization of the Negro Labor Victory Committee with the objective in mind to counteract the inroads made among the Negro people by the March on Washington Movement, which organization will be treated hereinafter.

It is impossible to state the exact size or strength of the Negro Labor Victory Committee; however, it is known that it is supported by quite a number of international and local unions of the CIO and the AF of L which are reported to be Communist dominated.

People's Committee

At the end of 1942 a new Negro group was formed in New York City known as the People's Committee at the primary instigation of Adam Clayton Powell, Jr. The alleged purpose of Powell in forming the People's Committee was to coordinate all of the Negro organizations in fighting against discrimination and for the employment of Negroes in the New York area. The program of the organization has been referred to by the organizers as the "Harlem Charter." According to reports, this charter was drawn up by Ferdinand Smith, secretary of the National Maritime Union and alleged Communist, Walter White of the National Association for the Advancement of Colored People, Channing Tobias, prominent New York City Negro, and Max Yergan, President of the National Negro Congress and reported Communist Party member. At the first conference of this group held in January, 1943, a number of reported Communists are said to have taken an active part in the discussion, including Audley Moore, Benjamin Davis, Jr., Elizabeth Parker, Theodore Bassett, Charles Collins and Ferdinand Smith. One of the most active Negro organizations to support this group has been the Negro Labor Victory Committee, referred to hereinbefore. Reportedly the Communist Party has been anxious to use Powell to sponsor meetings which will carry out the Party's program, since he is able to command a good audience because of his position and popularity. It is further reported that at the meetings of this organization a large number of Communists take an active part. The exact size and influence of this organization have not been reported.

On June 7, 1943 at Madison Square Garden the People's Committee and the Negro Labor Victory Committee were co-sponsors of what was known as the "Negro Freedom Rally." It is said that this meeting was under Communist Party control and that Party functionaries were active in assisting in the arrangements for it. Among the people responsible for the staging of the meeting were Dorothy K. Funn of the Negro Labor Victory Committee, a reported Communist, Benjamin Davis, Jr., Max Yergan and Adam Clayton Powell, Jr.

A large crowd estimated at twenty thousand attended the meeting at which the following measures were urged: the passage of the Anti-Poll Tax Bill, the opening of a "second front now" and the elimination of "Jim Crow in the Armed Forces." It might be noted that urging a second front has recently resumed its place in the Communist Party line. The principal speakers at the meeting were Ferdinand Smith, Dr. Channing Tobias, Lester Granger, Max Yergan, Dr. Charlotte Hawkins Brown, Congressman Vito Marcantonio, Charles Collins, Michael Quill, Adam Clayton Powell, Jr., and Dorothy K. Funn. It is said that the general theme of the speeches dealt with race discrimination. Congressman Marcantonio spoke on the Anti-Poll Tax Bill and urged its passage.

A drama was presented at the meeting which was entitled "For This We Fight." This play, written by Langston Hughes, Negro poet and reported Communist, was described as impressive. It depicted alleged racial discrimination in the Armed Forces. The Negro artists, Paul Robeson and Duke Ellington, took part in the play. In this connection, Adam Clayton Powell, Jr., Reverend Thomas Harten and Ferdinand Smith were delegated to carry "the message of the people" to the President at an unknown date. This message reportedly contains a demand that alleged discrimination in the Armed Forces be abolished.

The "Daily Worker," which is generally recognized as the Communist daily news organ, under date of June 9, 1943 devoted considerable space to this meeting and pointed out the effectiveness and power in the demonstration of solidarity shown at the meeting. Robert Minor, National Committee member of the Communist Party pointed out that the meeting was "a discovery of strength" and eulogized the part of organized labor in the meeting.

The West Indies National Council

This organization was organized in June, 1940 by William [Wilfred] A. Domingo, Robert [Richard] B. Moore, Hope R. Stevens, Herman P. Osborne, and others, all of whom are Negroes and are said to be members of the Communist Party. The organization has its headquarters at 2007 Seventh Avenue, New York City.

According to information from a confidential source, this Council was decided upon by the Negro Commission of the Communist Party for the purpose of making Communist inroads among the West Indian Negroes, both in the United States and in the Caribbean Islands. One of the first efforts of the Council was to send Stevens to the Pan-American Conference held in Havana in 1940 to lobby for the self-determination or self-government of the Caribbean Islands.

The organization is said not to have been very successful and has recently been reported to have a membership of less than 100. Executive Board meetings are held weekly but mass meetings have not been held, with the exception of one shortly after the group was organized. The present activities of the West Indies National Council are reported to consist of agitating against racial discrimination and economic conditions in the Caribbean Islands. These activities are said to be carried out mainly through the writing of letters of protest to various United States and British officials.

In June of 1941 William A. Domingo, President of the West Indies National Council, went to Jamaica at the request of N. W. Manley, president of the People's National Party of Jamaica, with whom a close contact is maintained by the Council.

Domingo was to have assisted Manley in his activities in Jamaica, however, he was arrested by British authorities on his arrival there and has since been detained. Subsequent to this episode, a considerable amount of this organization's activity has centered around a campaign for the liberation of Domingo. It should be noted that the Communist Party has also demanded the liberation of Domingo.

The National Negro Congress

The National Headquarters of the National Negro Congress was moved on July 1, 1942, from Washington, D.C., to 290 Lenox Avenue, New York City. The President of the organization is Dr. Max Yergan; the Secretary, John P. Davis; and the Treasurer, Ferdinand Smith, Secretary of the National Maritime Union, CIO. In New York City there are two branches of the national organization, one known as the Manhattan Council and the other known as the Brooklyn Council.

The National Negro Congress has followed closely the policy or line of the Communist Party. In this connection, it has been ascertained that the National Negro Congress is used as a medium to recruit members for the Communist Party, the process being that a Negro becomes a member of the National Negro Congress where he is coached or schooled for a favorable attitude toward the Party, after which he is said to be easily persuaded to become a member of the Communist Party.

The very few public meetings sponsored by the organization have, as a whole, been poorly attended. A meeting held by this organization in May, 1942 was attended by approximately seventy persons although arrangements had been made to handle seven hundred. Usually the speakers at the meetings of this organization are representatives of other organizations which are Communist fronts and Hope R. Stevens, President of the Manhattan Council, is usually the presiding officer.

On April 10 and 11, 1943, this organization held an Eastern Seaboard Conference in New York City. The Communist Party was well represented, as were the various Communist Party front organizations interested in the Negro question. It is said that approximately fifteen hundred persons attended. Panels were held on the following subjects: manpower, "A People's Victory—A People's Peace," democratic rights and wartime living standards.

Council on African Affairs

The Council on African Affairs was organized in the spring of 1937. At the present time the organization is said to be merely a paper organization which when it sponsors meetings is supported by the Communist Party or other Communist fronts. The principal officers of the organization are Paul Robeson, Chairman; William J. Schiefflin, Vice Chairman; John Hammond, Treasurer; and Dr. Max Yergan, Executive Director. Its objective is said to be to make widely known the conditions and the needs of African peoples, the immediate importance of Africa in the world-wide "struggle to defeat Fascism," and to work for the improvement of African living conditions. It should also be stated that its objectives are conveniently enlarged in furtherance of the Communist Party line. In addition, the Council is stated to carry out a program of research activities from which arise publications, forums, discussion groups and public meetings.

Until recently the headquarters of the organization were located at 8 West 40th Street, New York City, where it occupied offices with a rental of $60 per month. At the present time its headquarters are located at 1123 Broadway, New York City.

During 1942 the organization held two public meetings at Manhattan Center, New York City, the average attendance being approximately 2,500 persons, equally divided between Negroes and white people. At both of the meetings two of the main speakers were Paul Robeson and Dr. Max Yergan, both of whom are said to be members of the Communist Party. In addition to the above, speakers have included such well-known figures as Joseph Curran, President of the National Maritime Union; Michael Quill, head of the Transport Workers Union; Adam Clayton Powell, Jr., New York City Councilman and co-publisher of the Negro newspaper "People's Voice;" and Pearl S. Buck.

The current issues taken up by this organization are racial discrimination, the freedom of India, and the opening of a second front. At the last meeting of the organization held on September 2, 1942, two resolutions were adopted, one calling for the opening of a second front, and the second, for the freedom of India. It was said that these resolutions were to have been sent to the President and the British Embassy.

Harlem Section of the Communist Party

The headquarters of the Harlem section of the Communist Party and the Young Communist League are located at 200 West 135th Street, New York City.

The Upper Harlem Section of the Communist Party has formed a number of new clubs in the Upper Harlem section in order to more adequately carry out the workings of the Communist Party in that section. The name, location and Chairman of each club are as follows:

Lincoln Douglas Club, 19th A.D., 315 Lenox Avenue, New York City
Lawrence "Larry" Washington, Chairman.

21st and 22nd A.D. Club, 702 St. Nicholas Avenue, New York City
Helen Samuels, Chairman.

John Brown Club, 13th A.D., 321 West 21st Street, New York City
Audley Moore, Chairman.

11th A.D. Club, 225 West 16th Street, New York City

Railroaders Club, 702 St. Nicholas Avenue, New York City
Charles Loman, Chairman.

Uptown Seamens Branch of the Communist Party, 200 West 135th Street, New York City
Huber Warner, Chairman.

At the present time, the activities of the Party among the Negroes are given particular stress with regard to the recruitment of Negro members. It is said that the Party considers the opportunity very favorable for mass recruiting during the present period of unrest among the Negroes. In this connection, it makes the appeal to the

Negroes that it is one of the leaders in the struggle for equal rights of Negroes. The widespread good will created as a result of Russia's role and position in the present war is also utilized to build the Party. It should be pointed out that reports have been received to the effect that the Party no longer thinks in terms of individual Party members here and there but rather in terms of hundreds and thousands and for this Party members have allegedly been mobilized.

The policy of the Party is further reflected in the allegation that it is attempting to build itself during the course of an existing "united front" as a necessary prerequisite for the fulfillment of its almost historical task—the liberation of the working class through the transformation of the great social upheavals and revolutionary movements that will arise out of the present war to a victory for Communism.

As a specific example of the Party's recruiting endeavors among the Negroes, it has been reported that at a street meeting the Party held in July of 1942 at 126th Street and Seventh Avenue, New York City, which was attended by approximately 200 people, the Arrangements Committee set up a table on the street to sell war bonds and stamps but at the same time to recruit members for the Party.

In addition to holding numerous protest rallies and meetings, the Harlem section of the Party has given active support to each meeting of the Negro Labor Victory Committee, previously referred to. At these meetings, in addition to various national problems such as demands for anti-discriminatory measures, the opening of a second front and the freedom of India have also been dovetailed into "local" problems.

At a recent mass meeting held by the Harlem section of the Communist Party and the Young Communist League, alleged police brutality was discussed and a demand for the release of several Negroes, who shortly before were arrested, was made. The technique used was to lay particular emphasis on the background and conditions of the Negroes arrested who had been accused of robbery and rape. The parents of these boys were brought before the audience to make an appeal for the freedom of their boys who they felt were innocent. Abner W. Berry, former Secretary of the Harlem section of the Communist Party referred to the arrest as a "frame-up" and viciously attacked the police, branding them as the creators of criminals. Benjamin Davis, Jr., Communist candidate for Congress and member of the editorial staff of the "Daily Worker," asserted that there are agents of Hitler and Fascists at home and that the winning of the war depends upon treating those who "frame" and attack Negroes as traitors and convict them of treason. He said that all those who attack Negroes should be shot. Characterizing the case wherein eight Negro boys were arrested for robbery and rape, he likened it to the Scottsboro case and said that the people of the State of New York and the nation should be aroused to expose the "frame-up."

It should be noted here that practically all of the protest meetings held by the Harlem section of the Communist Party are given wide publicity by the Negro newspaper, the "People's Voice," which is published by Adam Clayton Powell, Jr.

On June 25, 1943 a group of individuals, in the majority functionaries belonging to the State Committee of the Communist Party in New York State, met for the purpose of discussing the "race riot situation." This meeting, of course, took place just subsequent to the riots in Detroit. It is reported those present agreed upon staging mass demonstrations of both colored and white persons for the purpose of fostering "solidarity" and uniting the Negro and the labor movements. Leaflets were distributed throughout greater New York by the Party, which urged that steps be taken "to prevent Hitler's hand from striking in New York." A demonstration was tentatively planned for the City Hall Plaza in New York under the auspices of the Negro Labor Victory Committee and the Greater New York Industrial Union Council, CIO, as well as any "civic organizations" which could be rallied to the cause.

The Upper West Side Section of the Communist Party distributed a leaflet entitled "The Enemy Within," which briefly stated that every Negro in America must wonder whether his countrymen are making war against the Nazis or against the Jews and him. It rhetorically inquired concerning the individuals who "make Americans fight among themselves," and asked whether "Jews or Catholics will have to lock themselves in their homes to prevent a similar fate." The leaflet urged everyone to write and telegraph President Roosevelt concerning "this positive evidence of Fascism." The entire leaflet, of course, pertained to the Detroit riots and was circulated shortly after the occurrence of these riots. [*100-135-35-119*]

Concerning the reaction to the Detroit riots in the Harlem area the following observations have been made by a source of information in New York City who is well acquainted with this area. He has informed that the pictures printed in the June 23, 1943 issue of "PM" of incidents connected with the Detroit riots have created a feeling of resentment of considerable magnitude in this area. In this connection, another informant has advised of overhearing inhabitants of the Harlem area express their resentment and hate of white people after viewing these pictures. It was also pointed out at the time that Adam Clayton Powell, Jr., following the Detroit situation, expressed the opinion that New York City would see a phase of the Detroit riot in the way of a reprisal for the handling of the situation in Detroit. Powell was said to have organized an interracial committee to take steps to prevent such disturbances. The source of information has pointed out he believed Powell's action to be political and that Powell was endeavoring to catch the eye of the public. This source has also stated that the expressed beliefs of a possible riot by Powell caused more harm than good.

Pro-Japanese Activities Among the Negroes in This Area

Universal Negro Improvement Association

There are now in existence in New York City a number of units of the Universal Negro Improvement Association which have assumed different names. With practically no exception, leaders of these groups have been reported as having expressed extreme racial views, extreme anti-white feelings and strong distrust of the white race. In many instances they are said to have reflected pro-Japanese sympathies. It is said that these sympathies result from the feeling or desire to promote the supremacy of the dark race.

The number of Negroes belonging to the original Universal Negro Improvement Association is not known. However, over a period of time, approximately ten to fifteen years, a number of street speakers are said to have continued the preaching of the doctrine of Garveyism on street corners and in closed meetings in Harlem. The number of persons who have been noted listening to such speakers has been reported to be from twenty-five on up into the hundreds. There are evidences of extreme feeling on the part of the Negroes in Harlem toward the white people and although the preceding is not given as exemplifying the attitude of the general mass of people, it does tend to show some of the feelings which exist.

As a result of investigation and from a review of complaints submitted to the New York Field Division of the Federal Bureau of Investigation, it has been noted that in most instances the individuals alleged to have made pro-Japanese statements or who are stated to have sympathies for Japan were actually reported as followers of Marcus Garvey, the organizer of the Universal Negro Improvement Association.

With regard to the Universal Negro Improvement Association and the teachings of Garvey, it is said that **Robert Jordan,** who was recently arrested by the Federal Bureau of Investigation, is a follower and admirer of Garvey, while **Mimo De Guzman, Filipino organizer and propagandist** among Negroes for the Japanese and an organization known as the Pacific Movement of the Eastern World, was also a former speaker on the programs of the Universal Negro Improvement Association. **De Guzman was sentenced October 1, 1942, for a violation of the Postal Laws.** He had been arrested by the FBI and turned over to Postal authorities. **Vernal Williams, Negro attorney,** who supported and defended **Jordan** recently in Federal Court, is also a Marcus Garvey adherent. **Williams,** it should be stated, is known to be very anti-white and is reported to have volunteered to defend any street speaker who became involved with the law.

Arthur Reid, president of the African Patriotic League, a branch of the Universal Negro Improvement Association, has, until recently, openly expressed his anti-Semitic and extreme racial views. It was also pointed out that recently **Arthur Green, J. J. Thornhill and Carlos Cooks,** reported Garveyites and well-known street speakers and agitators in Harlem, were so radical in their statements and speeches that they were arrested by the New York City Police Department and prosecuted for the same.

Ethiopian Pacific Movement

This organization was exceedingly active in New York City from 1935 to 1937. It held its office at 200 West 135th Street. From 1937 to 1939 it was active spasmodically. In 1939 Robert Jordan, President of the organization, again became active and held street meetings throughout Harlem, preaching anti-Semitism and making statements opposing the white race. After December 7, 1941, in closed meetings at 113 Lenox Avenue, Jordan became radical and pro-Japanese and is known to have made statements that he would fight for Japan with every drop of his blood and that he would be ashamed to wear the United States uniform. **Jordan was arrested for sedition by the FBI and sentenced January 14, 1943, to 10 years in prison and fined $5000.**

The meetings usually held on Sunday evenings at 113 Lenox Avenue, New York, subsequent to the summer of 1941, were attended usually by 50 to 125 persons who have been described as more or less the unprivileged and uneducated. They are also said to have been largely made up of British West Indian Negroes.

Ethiopian World Federation

This organization is said to be national, if not international, in scope. Its headquarters and parent body are presently located in New York City and its executive offices are at 200 West 135th Street. It is said to have 28 locals in and out of continental United States; and in New York City, besides its parent body, there is a local in the Manhattan Borough, 290 Lenox Avenue, and one at 460 Jefferson Street in the Brooklyn Borough. The national officers of the organization are J. Finley Wilson, President, who is also National President of the Negro Elks, said to have a membership of over a half million Negroes; Wilfred E. Lewin, Executive Secretary; and William C. Husston (Attorney), Treasurer.

It is described as a charitable organization registered with the State Department and founded for the purpose of soliciting financial aid for refugees from Ethiopia and to promote good will among the American people. The strength of the organization is estimated to be approximately 1,000 paid members throughout all of its locals. However, meetings of various locals are said to be attended by a large number of people who are not active members of the organization.

The Ethiopian World Federation was originally founded by Dr. Malaku Bayen, onetime personal representative of Haile Selassie, who came to the United States with the purpose of organizing aid for Ethiopian refugees. Bayen is now deceased and Prince Lij Araya Abebe is said to have attempted to take his place among the Negroes in New York City. He is said to attend all functions of Local No. 26 and to have a considerable following among the members and sympathizers.

Although there is no indication generally that this organization is pro-Japanese in its tendencies, certain speakers who have addressed Local No. 26 in New York City at 290 Lenox Avenue have made pro-Japanese statements and have, in their conversations and speeches, made utterances that were extremely racial and anti-white.

There has recently been considerable dissension between Local No. 26 and the executive body of the Ethiopian World Federation. The Executive Secretary, Wilfred E. Lewin, has stated that the charter of Local No. 26 was revoked because of un-American statements made by some of the speakers before the group and several of its members. It is said further, that the local is attempting to gain control of the entire organization and install Prince Abebe as its leader. Prince Abebe presently denies obtaining funds from the organization but does admit the organization provides for his residence in New York City.

This organization has been pointed out to show the possible influence on the sympathies of the Negroes toward the people of a like race in the East, particularly Ethiopia and people of African descent. In this connection, Kingsley O. Mbadiwe, a member of the Royal Family of Nigeria, West Africa, has been a frequent speaker before this organization.

Moorish Science Temple

This organization of Moslem faith has several churches in various areas throughout the United States, one branch of which is known to be located at 640 Gates Avenue, Brooklyn, New York. Members of this organization have declined to enlist in the

Armed Forces, stating that they are Moors. It is also said that they are sympathetic toward Japan and it is known that in the past a prophet of the organization located in Brooklyn attempted to secure speakers from the Japanese Institute in New York City as late as 1941 to make addresses on circumstances in the East. As a further possible indication of sympathies toward Japan, speakers from the Japanese Institute actually spoke to the group prior to 1941.

Information has been received that the Moorish Science Temple has complained to Selective Service Headquarters in New York City that members of a Selective Service board had addressed their members as Negroes, taking offense at this because of their claims that they are Moors rather than Negroes.

It is pointed out that Mimo De Guzman, onetime associate of the Japanese organizer of Negroes, S. Takahashi, informed Agents of the Federal Bureau of Investigation at the time of his arrest by them in New York City on July 30, 1942, on a charge of violating the Selective Service Act, that the Moorish Science Temple Church was an organization influenced by the Japanese. He also said that this organization followed closely the pattern of the Universal Negro Improvement Association, the Ethiopian Pacific Movement, and the Pacific Movement of the Eastern World, which organizations were definitely propaganda organizations for the Japanese.

Miscellaneous Organizations

The Harlem Ashram

The Harlem Ashram, located at 2013 Fifth Avenue, New York City, is a cooperative enterprise operated by a religious group under the leadership of Reverend J. Holmes Smith who is employed by the Fellowship of Reconciliation, which organization, although not influencing or instructing the Harlem Ashram, sanctions it.

The activities of this group, which is interracial, are said to be patterned after those of Gandhi. They are non-violent in nature. They attempt to fight discrimination and segregation of Negroes by conducting protest campaigns. Recently, under the sponsorship of Reverend Smith, an interracial pilgrimage, on foot, was made to the Lincoln Memorial in Washington, D.C. It left New York City on August 26, 1942, and reached Washington September 9, 1942. The group composing the pilgrimage was small, varying from twelve to approximately twenty members who distributed circulars denouncing racial discrimination and carried posters condemning it. Along the way meetings were held and information was collected as to alleged instances of discrimination and segregation.

The organization maintains a study institute at 2013 Fifth Avenue, New York City, which is called an Ashram, the purpose of which is for rest, meditation, study and service.

The Interracial Club

This organization has its functions at 360 West 125th Street every Friday evening at 8:30 P.M. One Thomas L. Brown, white, is the President. The organization is apparently local with little following and is practically unknown by the general populace in New York City. The leanings of this group appear to be that of the Trotskyites, in that members of the group and their associates have been observed in the front of the organization's office selling the paper "Labor Action," the official organ of the *Workers Party* (Trotskyite).

The organization, as reported by a confidential source, is said to be "anti-everything" and opposed to all New Deal policies. Approximately 25 to 75 people generally attend its meetings. It is said to be an organization composed of men and women "regardless of race or color dedicated to participate in the struggle for the achievement of complete democratic rights." It advocates principally the fight for the Negroes' rights and increased employment for them. It is said that in the past on one occasion one Phillip Blake, an alien Negro, said to be in the United States on a student pass, spoke before the group and made un-American statements not only criticizing the Government but expressing sympathies for Japan.

March on Washington Movement

This organization was formed in 1941, under the leadership of A. Philip Randolph and has units in New York City and other large cities. The New York City division holds regular weekly meetings at the YMCA in Harlem which are attended by approximately 2,000 members. It constantly agitates for anti-discrimination and anti-segregation measures and for added and increased rights of Negroes.

National Association for the Advancement of Colored People

This organization has its national headquarters as well as local branches in this area. In New York City the organization is said to have a large membership and to receive contributions from both white and Negro people. The purpose of the organization is to uplift the downtrodden Negro and obtain better opportunities both in employment and social activities for them.

It is said that the weapon most effectively used by the organization is the propagandizing of every instance of discrimination on the part of white people against the Negroes. It is believed to be probably the most militant and powerful organization, besides being the most popular, among the masses of Negroes.

Recently an officer of the New York City Police Department informed that he noted in practically every instance of an arrest of a Negro by a white officer a representative of the organization, if present, would publicize the arrest and misrepresent the facts in order to make a racial issue of the arrest.

Other

There are numerous smaller organizations reported to exist among the Negroes in New York City and in this connection it is pointed out that it is a generally known matter that Negroes fraternize probably more than any other race of people. Organizations are said to constantly spring up which in many instances have the same purposes, the same officers, and often the same members. It is said that the Negro is generally jealous of his fellow man if any popularity has been received by him and it appears that everyone desires to hold office in his own particular organization. It is said that many times this leads to disunity and gives rise to a number of new organizations. This may be a contributing factor to the general dissatisfaction among the mass of Negroes. Although they have grievances, they are unable to remain organized long enough to accomplish the purpose they have in mind and consequently they are said to acquire a fatalist attitude and one of general dissatisfaction.

Individuals Who Agitate in Harlem

Reverend Adam Clayton Powell, Jr., New York City Councilman, pastor of the Abyssinian Baptist Church and editor of the Negro weekly, the "People's Voice," has been responsible for considerable agitation among the Negroes in the New York area in the past few years. Powell, as pastor of one of the largest Baptist churches in the United States, the membership of which is reported to be over 15,000, is said to have considerable influence among the Negroes in Harlem. He is well educated, makes a good appearance, and is said to be an eloquent speaker.

A few years ago Powell is said to have been the guiding influence in a movement on the part of Negroes in Harlem to picket various businesses there in an attempt to gain employment for Negroes in these establishments. He is said to have also led a similar movement against local utilities. Early in 1942 he sponsored and organized a publication, the "People's Voice", a Negro weekly paper which is said to have gained great popularity in this district among the greater mass of Negro people. The paper is strictly a Negro paper and every issue has displayed in an extreme degree instances of racial discrimination. Among the first issues it was noted that there was contained considerable comment on "Jim Crowism" in the Armed Forces. Usually contained in the paper are letters from subscribers citing instances of alleged discrimination on the part of white people against Negroes and other letters of individuals stating because of discrimination they would not enlist in the Armed Forces of the United States.

Powell is said to attempt to show indirectly that he is a champion of the Negro race. In this connection, it was confidentially reported that during the last mayoralty election in New York City Powell supported Mayor LaGuardia and the two worked in close contact. Subsequent to the election of Mayor LaGuardia there seems to have been a breach between the two inasmuch as Powell has taken every opportunity to criticize the City Government and the Police Department in his publication the "People's Voice". Powell writes as well as edits for this paper a column known as "On The Soap Box" in which he is very outspoken. He deals with both local and national political matters and continually agitates on behalf of his race through this medium.

Powell, to some extent, has been active in the March on Washington Movement and in the month of June, 1942, at the mass meeting of this organization in Madison Square Garden, he took the opportunity to announce his intention of running for Congress. This is said to have been looked on with disfavor by the prominent members of the March on Washington Movement in that they believed most of the work and effort on the part of Powell was for political reasons and in furtherance of his political aspirations. It is said that Powell's agitation among the Negroes is only in furtherance of his political desires. Powell is looked upon as exercising a great deal of influence in Harlem and recently a representative of the New York City Police Department in one of the thickly populated areas in the Harlem district expressed an opinion that Powell and his paper have had much to do with the present unrest in New York City among the Negro population. In this connection, it should be pointed out that Powell is stated to be a sympathizer of the Communist Party and to have supported many Communist front organizations. However, his actual membership in the Communist Party is not known.

Robert Jordan, until he was recently arrested by the Federal Bureau of Investigation, was President of the Ethiopian Pacific Movement. He has been a street speaker and agitator among the Negroes in Harlem for the past fifteen years. His full name is Robert Leonard Jordan. He is a British West Indian Negro who has not become a citizen of the United States and who made application for his first papers only last May (1942). He is stated to have informed that he was in central South America in 1914 in the Navigation Department of Great Britain and later served for the Japanese Steamship Company. He is alleged to have made the statement that while in Japan he found the Japanese to be very friendly to the Negroes and that he had the privilege of studying the customs of the Japanese and becoming a member of an outstanding society in Japan.

When he came to the United States he joined the Universal Negro Improvement Association and served as a faithful member after the deportation of Marcus Garvey, the founder of this organization. He claimed he noticed the Negroes of America were beginning to dissolve and for that reason he began to study conditions so that methods could be adopted to bring back proper racial spirit among them. In this connection, he felt that an organization should be begun among the Negroes that would enable them to affiliate themselves with other colored governments and organizations of the world. He was accordingly instrumental in organizing the Ethiopian Pacific Movement which has been in existence since 1935. As sponsor of such he held meetings on street corners and in halls in which his influence and following was varied over a period of years. It should be stated, however, that an investigation of Jordan has failed to reveal any foreign connections on the part of himself or his organization although he is known by the New York City Police Department as a racketeer and is believed to agitate among his fellow men only for financial gains.

The following is a list of individuals who are said to have been speakers on the streets of Harlem for the past several years together with their addresses and the organizations to which they belong:

William James, 169 West 133rd Street, New York City, Universal Negro Improvement Association.

James Kelly, 231 West 141st Street, New York City, Universal Negro Improvement Association.

Ros [Ras]. De Keller [Killer], alias Randolph Wilson, 59 East 128th Street, New York City, Universal Negro Improvement Association.

Carlos Cooks, 43 West 128th Street, New York City, Universal Negro Improvement Association.

Edgar Mortin, 54 West 131st Street, New York City, Universal Negro Improvement Association.

William Hendricks, alias Ros. De Murchrar, 54 West 131st Street, New York City, Universal Negro Improvement Association.

Ross Nassiber, 169 West 141st Street, New York City, Universal Negro Improvement Association.

Austin Carr, 100 West 132nd Street, New York City, Universal Negro Improvement Association.

Leroy Hudson, 169 West 133rd Street, New York City, Universal Negro Improvement Association.

Robert Harris, 128 West 127th Street, New York City, Workers Alliance.

Jack Gonzolis, 52 East 111th Street, New York City, Workers Alliance.

Charles J. Coleman, 43 West 131st Street, New York City, Ethiopian World Federation.

Larry Washington, 207 West 140th Street, New York City, Ethiopian World Federation.

Abner Green, 2087 Madison Avenue, New York City, Ethiopian World Federation.

John Reid, 254 West 135th Street, New York City, Branch of Universal Negro Improvement Association.

Jack Murray, 254 West 135th Street, New York City, Branch of Universal Negro Improvement Association.

Reggie Renaldo, 254 West 135th Street, New York City, Branch of Universal Negro Improvement Association.

Harry Fredericks—General.

As examples of what is said at meetings in which the above individuals speak from reports submitted by members of the New York City Police Department, the following are set out:

At a meeting held on July 9, 1941, on 125th Street, New York City, at 8:00 P.M., the principal speakers being Carlos Cooks, William Taylor and William Ferman, such statements as the following were made:

1. For every Negro lynched in the South there should be a white man lynched in the North.
2. Every white man seeking favor of a Negro woman should be beaten.
3. Every Negro should rightfully hate every white man for the injustices done to him.
4. No Negro should fight because this is a white man's war.

On July 31, 1941, at Lenox Avenue and 119th Street, among other speakers at a meeting was Robert Jordan who in his speech stressed the fact that Jews were the enemies of all Negroes and advocated that the Negroes side with Hitler.

On August 7, 1941, at 125th and 126th Streets, a meeting was held from 9:00 P.M. to 12:00 P.M., one of the principal speakers being Carlos Cooks. He is said to have particularly brought out his hate of the Jews and condemned all white people, even light-skinned Negroes.

On August 8, 1941, at Lenox Avenue and 127th Street, among other speakers was Randolph Wilson who openly confessed his hate of the President and of the Jews and made favorable remarks regarding Hitler.

On September 6, 1941, at 125th Street and Eighth Avenue, the principal speakers were Carlos Cooks, William Taylor, William Ferman, and an individual by the name of Ford. Ford in his speech is said to have made definite remarks against the Jews and went on to say that the white man kills his enemies, that is, Hitler and Mussolini are killing their enemies and the Negroes should organize and kill their enemies and that the white man is always the enemy of the Negroes.

In 1939 and 1940, Joe McWilliams, white, President of the Christian Mobilizers, was alleged to have had working agreements with Negro agitators in Harlem, as alleged proof of which they followed his program in agitating against the Jews and favored Fascist powers. It is known that McWilliams had a conference with Jordan in an attempt to gain his support and that of his organization, the Ethiopian Pacific Movement. In this connection, it is also pointed out that Joseph Hartery, white, has been a constant speaker and agitator before audiences at meetings of the Ethiopian Pacific Movement. He is said to have also roamed the streets of Harlem agitating among groups on street corners merely by conversation. Hartery admits being a member of the Christian Mobilizers and the Christian Front, as well as being an associate of Joe McWilliams.

Sufi Hammed, or Hammed Sufi, Negro, up until a year or so ago was one of the principal street speakers in Harlem. He is reported to have dressed similar to an Arab chief or prophet. He is said to have been very anti-white and to have followed the program and principles of Marcus Garvey in advocating the migration of Negroes to Liberia for the purpose of establishing a government there. In 1936 he is said to have been one of the leading agitators and supporters of a boycott of white merchants by Negroes for the employers' failure to hire Negroes in their establishments. He is known to the New York City Police Department to have been a petty racketeer, although he appeared to be well educated, a linguist, speaking several languages, and is stated to have been an interesting speaker who had a large following. It has been further reported that at the time of the Ethiopian-Italian war he travelled considerably in an effort to enlist men in the Ethiopian Army. Sufi is now deceased, having been killed in an airplane accident.

The New York City Police Department has reported that many of the persons referred to above, who are known speakers and agitators in Harlem, have not had permanent employment but have apparently derived their living from street speaking. The sincerity of these individuals is not known but it has been stated that their agitation is for personal gains. Their following was reportedly among those less informed individuals although at the same time considerable influence on their part was felt in creating dissatisfaction and anti-white feeling among the colored race. It is pointed out that attendances at these various street meetings have been reported to number from 25 to 400 and 500.

Possible Influence by Foreign Nationals

Yasuichi Hikida, a Japanese alien, recently repatriated to Japan, was formerly employed as translator in the Japanese Consulate in New York City. He is known to have been interested in Negro social and racial problems and to have had a wide acquaintance among Harlem Negroes for many years. For seventeen years prior to 1938 he was engaged as a cook in a residential home in Bedford Hills, New York. During this time he was known by his employers to be interested in Negro problems but they had no knowledge of his being actively engaged in Negro activities.

However, while employed as a domestic, he is said to have collected and stored in his quarters numerous books and pamphlets dealing with the Negro problem. A review of part of this material reflects that he translated several Negro publications into the Japanese language for distribution in Japan, and, further, that he lectured at various Negro schools and colleges and was a member and attended numerous conferences held by the National Association for the Advancement of Colored People. He is said to have been an admirer of Marcus Garvey.

The extent of Hikida's agitation is not known but a review of his speeches reflects that he attempted to create a kindred feeling between the dark races of the East and the West. He is reported by Japanese and other informants to have been a Japanese propagandist among the Negroes in the United States but inasmuch as he was repatriated and returned to Japan these allegations have not been conclusively borne out by investigation.

Kingsley O. Mbadiwe, son of Chief Mbadiwe of Nigeria, West Africa, and President of the International Club of New York City, has in the past year been apparently popular among the Negroes in the New York area. He has been in the United States for two years as a student and is presently attending New York University. He recently published a book entitled "The British and Axis Aims in Africa" which is an analysis of Africa's present struggle for existence. Mbadiwe has been a frequent speaker before one of the locals of the Ethiopian World Federation, mentioned previously, and advertises that he is available for lectures. His topics usually deal with the circumstances of the East and India's fight for independence. In this regard, it should be noted that a friend of Mbadiwe in a speech before the Ethiopian World Federation made a number of pro-Japanese statements. It is not known to what extent Mbadiwe has gone in his talks before groups, however, the fact that he continually is stated to refer to the African situation before the Negroes and has requested that Great Britain declare herself toward her colonies is said to have had considerable effect among the Negroes in this area. He is quoted, among other statements, as follows:

"After the last war nothing was done for Africa. Today we have taken up arms against the same force and we are determined at any cost to achieve victory but we want a definite declaration from Britain what our position in the new order will be if Britain wins."

Prince Lij Araya Abebe, nephew of Haile Selassie, presently resides in New York City and attends all social functions of the Ethiopian World Federation which is said to have been originally organized by a representative of Haile Selassie. Recently locals of the organization in New York City, Philadelphia and Chicago are said to have moved to make him president of the Federation. These particular units were stated by Wilfred Lewin, an officer of the national organization, to be very anti-white. Recently, while attending a dance sponsored by the Ethiopian World Federation, Prince Abebe and his wife were held in great reverence by those in attendance and he is said to be an inspiration to many in renewing their interest in Ethiopian affairs. More than 80,000 British West Indian Negroes are living in the New York area and they are believed to form a distinct national group within the Negro population of this city. They have migrated to the United States in the past thirty years and especially since World War I. During the worst years of the depression the West Indian Negro was affected considerably and he has not been able to orientate himself, as a consequence of which there is a large number which has been forced into the ranks of the unemployed. The decision to deprive foreign-born, non-citizens of WPA jobs is said to have thrown many thousands of them into unemployment. It is reported that only about 25 per cent of the West Indian Negroes have been naturalized.

According to persons interviewed in the Negro area of New York City, the West Indian Negroes are restless and dissatisfied as a group and are the first to agitate among themselves. It is also said that many organizations reported to be un-American in tendencies are largely made up of West Indian Negroes. This is particularly true in the Ethiopian Pacific Movement, the Ethiopian World Federation, and the Universal Negro Improvement Association.

Another reason given for the dissatisfaction among the West Indian Negroes is said to be that although they may secure better wages in the United States and better living conditions than in the British West Indies, there is allegedly more discrimination in the United States than in the homeland. It is pointed out that some of the leading and well-known agitators of the past and present have been British West Indian Negroes, namely Marcus Garvey, Robert Jordan and Carlos Cooks.

Influences of Publications

It is pointed out that Negro publications in the New York area have constantly featured in their papers every instance of racial discrimination and they continually carry articles severely criticizing the Negro in the South. They have constantly opposed the poll tax which exists in some States. There is reportedly an attitude of hate among the Negroes in New York City toward white Southerners. In this connection, a number of instances have been noted in which writers of Negro newspapers have criticized Southerners. As a result of inquiries made, it has been revealed that in colored areas both white and Negro people advise that instances of lynching and unfair treatment of the Negroes by Southerners as depicted in the Negro newspapers have caused more resentment and general feeling of unrest than any other known factor.

It has also been reported that prior to December, 1941, a large percentage of Negroes in this area had alleged sympathies for Eastern countries. It is said that Negro publications have followed closely Eastern affairs dating back prior to the last World War, especially as to those matters affecting colored races.

In this connection, "The Crisis" magazine, published by the National Association for the Advancement of Colored People and formerly edited by W. E. [B.] Du Bois, up until the year 1940 dealt considerably with this aspect. During this period, when Japan was criticized for her aggression on China, DuBois called attention to the United States Marines in Haiti and the English in India and asked why they did not withdraw also. He is said not to have favored the action of the Japanese but did favor Asia for the Asiatics. At the same time he commented on the program of Japan and speculated on the effect such would have on the outlook of white domination over the colored races.

As a result of inquiries, it appears over the period of time DuBois was editor of "The Crisis" magazine he probably enjoyed the greatest following as a journalist, lecturer and leader as any among the Negroes. He has always voiced his resentment as to the lack of Negro representation in Governmental and industrial fields. During that period he was considered radical by both white people and conservative Negroes. Today DuBois is a columnist on the "Amsterdam Star News" writing the column "As the Crow Flies". A review of several issues reflects he has stated his desire of the United States winning the war and his loyalty to the Government, at the same time, however, criticizing certain acts of discrimination against Negroes on the part of the democracies.

The "Amsterdam Star News", a principal Negro newspaper in this area, is said to be generally conservative although it features and headlines acts of discrimination. The "Pittsburgh Courier" also enjoys a large subscription figure in this area among the Negro people. The policy of this paper is to headline all acts of discrimination against the Negro. With regard to this newspaper, George Samuels Schuyler, a feature writer for the publication who is married to a Southern white woman and who has been said to have travelled extensively in Japan, is reported to be rabid on the subject of racial equality and has repeatedly attacked the Government for its alleged discrimination against Negroes. He is said to indicate in his writings certain pro-Japanese ideas which appear to be based on the fact that the Japanese have been the alleged victims of white racial discrimination which he also believes has victimized the Negro race. Schuyler at the present time is employed as Business Manager of "The Crisis".

The daily newspaper "PM", which is published by Marshall Field and other members of the white race, has continuously carried articles concerning racial discrimination in the United States. This has been noticeable since the origin of the publication, the "People's Voice", which has been referred to previously and which is printed on the press of "PM". It has carried feature articles, one of which consisted of some seven pages relative to discrimination against Negroes in the South. It has particularly criticized Governor Talmadge of Georgia and Governor Dixon of Alabama. It has commented much relative to the discrimination against Negroes in the United States Navy. It has also carried on a campaign relative to discriminatory advertisements in a number of white publications in New York City, particularly the "Daily News" and the "Journal American", relative to restrictions against Negroes and members of the Jewish race. Probably the strongest protest, however, on the part of this newspaper is that of the lack of employment for Negroes because of discrimination in national defense industries. This newspaper will be dealt with in another section of this study.

The "People's Voice", which has been referred to previously, is published by Adam Clayton Powell, Jr. It has been particularly rabid in its resentment of alleged discrimination, unfair practices, and segregation of Negroes on the part of white people. This newspaper has carried many notices, advertisements and the like relative to meetings of the Communist Party and Communist Party front organizations.

The "Daily Worker" has continuously agitated for the equality of the Negroes socially, economically and politically. Considerable stress has been placed on the alleged lack of opportunity for Negroes in employment, in industry and in military service. This paper has also been particularly interested in commenting on alleged discrimination in the United States Navy. It recently has carried on a campaign to have what it alleges to be the "Southern bourbons" investigated for their "Hitler-like tactics". The paper has given much space to the Negro question as a whole and, in particular, has commented on the lack of social equality of the Negroes in the Harlem area, emphasizing housing, educational and sanitary facilities.

In reference to the reported increase of crime in Harlem, the "Daily Worker" has taken sides with Negro publications and has attacked what they call the capitalist papers, that is, other white papers published in New York City, for their part in what they allege to be false reporting of the crime situation in Harlem. The "Daily Worker" has continuously denounced segregation of white and colored enlisted personnel and has demanded complete nondiscrimination and intermingling of white and colored people not only in the Armed Forces but socially, economically and politically, as has, of course, the Communist Party program.

In recent months local daily papers, that is, those generally recognized as published by white people in New York City, have featured articles on vice and crime in Harlem which, as referred to previously, have resulted in an outburst on the part of the Negroes and Negro press of protests against accusations contained therein. An attempt to refute these by stating that in certain parts of New York City inhabited solely by white people crime is more prevalent has been made in the Negro newspapers. They allege that white people are in many instances the cause of such crime in that they encroach upon the colored sections to further their practice of "thievery and graft" against the unsuspecting Negroes. This has resulted in certain groups in Harlem attempting to boycott daily papers, especially the "Daily News", the "World-Telegram" and the "New York Journal American". In this connection, it is believed timely to refer to a so-called feud between Westbrook Pegler and certain Negro newspapers, it being recalled that Pegler commented that several Negro newspapers are confusing and misleading in their statements. This has resulted in widespread accusations in certain Negro newspapers, as well as the Communist Party press, condemning the criticism of Pegler.

All the above-named newspapers are distributed on newsstands in Harlem and besides the Negro newspapers having a wide circulation, the newspapers "PM" and the "Daily Worker" are said to be widely circulated there and to be read by many people. In this connection, it is generally accepted by sources of information contacted that the constant display and publication of instances of alleged racial discrimination add to the resentment of the Negro already existing of the treatment afforded them by white people and it is further said that the tenor of the articles has a commanding effect on many of the Negroes.

International and Local Events Possibly Influencing Negroes

The following events and their surrounding circumstances are being set forth for consideration of their possible influence among the Negroes, especially with regard to Negro opinion and unrest. It should be stated that there are allegedly certain sympathies on the part of the Negroes in this country with colored foreign nations, more so than there are between white people of other nations. Many leaders among the Negroes and writers have criticized in the past what they term to be white imperialism in Asia and it is reported a frequent slogan heard among the Negroes is "Asia for the Asiatics and Africa for the Africans".

In 1934 Prince Lij Araya Abebe was rumored to have been affianced to Masako Kuroda, daughter of Viscount Kurod of Tokyo, Japan. This is stated to have created considerable comment and unrest internationally as it was thought that such a union would give Japan a foothold in Ethiopia. J. A. Rogers, noted Negro journalist, commented on this as being the joining of two of the oldest peoples of time. At this time there were numerous news dispatches alleging that Japan had been given Abyssinian land to grow cotton. In this connection, it is pointed out that Mimo De Guzman, Filipino organizer among the Negroes, who admitted to Agents of the Federal Bureau of Investigation that he worked for S. Takahashi in organizing Negroes, informed that this marriage was Japanese sponsored to obtain economic benefits from and gain prestige in Ethiopia. It was also reportedly believed that the union would show that the Japanese considered Negroes their equal and did not believe in discrimination against them.

With reference to the above, it is known that in New York City there are a small number of Japanese nationals married to Negresses. Some speculation has been made as to a fifth column move on the part of the Japanese in creating such marriages to build good will and sympathy among American Negroes. No notoriety or publicity has been given to such unions, and inquiries to date have failed to reflect any such move on the part of the Japanese. However, in 1934 Japanese officers were reported to be training Abyssinian troops for use in the Ethiopian-Italian war, and in 1935 the Ethiopians were reported to have received Japanese arms and Japanese nationals were said to have been enlisted in the Ethiopian Army.

In 1935 there were numerous meetings reportedly held in Harlem precincts which are alleged to have resulted in highly emotional racial feelings among the Negroes. These are said to have later resulted in riots in which a number of persons were killed and injured and millions of dollars worth of property was damaged. A report was made by a committee appointed by the Mayor of the city to look into the situation and, although said to be somewhat biased in that it favored the Negroes, it was said to have presented the facts truthfully, with the possible exception of its criticism of the police. It is noted that this report went into great length in criticizing the actions of police officers and recommended that a study be made of the arrests made by the Police Department.

It has been reported that in 1938 or 1939 Negro journalists were invited to make fellowship tours in Japan. In this connection, George Schuyler, previously referred to, was reported to have visited Japan and is noted to have written several articles pro-Japanese in their tenor subsequent to his return. It was also said that the Negro journalist, J. A. Rogers, travelled in Ethiopia during which time he was entertained by Japanese officers and at the time Rogers is alleged to have promised favorable publicity for the Japanese on his return to the United States.

In 1939 the Christian Mobilizers and the Christian Front were active in New York City under the leadership of Joe McWilliams. He and his associates were reported to have gained a following of Negro agitators in Harlem and during this time it was said there was a sudden rise in anti-Semitic street meetings in Harlem. The Jews were condemned and Axis powers lauded. At the same time there was organized the Harlem Labor Union, Inc., by Arthur Reed, Ira Kemp, Sufi Hammed and others. This was described as a racket used to "shake down" many merchants, Jews and otherwise in Harlem. It was alleged further that this was sponsored as a movement against discrimination but actually was only a racket on the part of Negro agitators.

Recently, when the Atlantic Charter was created, there was considerable comment among the Negro people and the Negro press that the President and Mr. Churchill in incorporating "the Four Freedoms" did not consider, or at least did not make public, their intention as to the future of colored nations and races.

And finally, the recent action of Britain with regard to India is said to have created considerable comment among Negroes and their reactions allegedly reflect a certain amount of unity with the other colored people of the world. However, it should not be overlooked that considerable comment, if not agitation, has been instituted by the Communist Party. It is said that many Negroes constantly comment on the fact that this is further evidence that British imperialism serves only to cast doubt upon the aims of the United Nations and leads to speculation as to the future of the dark races. The Negro public is said to view the action of Great Britain with considerable criticism and the instances of discrimination against Negroes in employment and the segregation of Negro soldiers, hunger riots in Jamaica, and the numerous restriction laws existing both in English colonies and in America have reportedly created considerable doubt on their part as to the future of Negroes after the end of the present war.

Apparent Grievances of Negroes Over a Period of Time Prior to 1941

A review of the Amsterdam Star News, the leading New York Negro newspaper, which has been made with regard to Negro grievances prior to December 1941, reflects the following trends. These are merely briefly set out and their justification has not been investigated:

1. The denial of equal employment and vocational training opportunities in national defense industries.
2. The denial of equal privileges for integration in all units of the Armed Forces.
3. Treatment of Negroes in Southern States including lynching, poll tax and "Jim Crow" customs.
4. Matters local to New York area.
   a. Alleged mistreatment of Negroes by New York City police.
   b. Discriminatory barriers against Negroes in public and quasi-public places such as hotels, restaurants and public carriers.
   c. The refusal to employ Negro mechanics and drivers on various bus lines.
   d. Alleged exorbitant charges on the part of white merchants and landlords in Harlem.
   e. General local economic, political and social conditions said to have caused the crime wave in Harlem.

Apparent Grievances of Negroes Subsequent to December 1941

With the reported increased effectiveness of the Fair Employment Practices Committee and the change in policy of the United States Armed Forces resulting in a greater integration of Negroes into the Services, there is somewhat less of a cry for these changes on the part of the Negro press. Although there has been some degree of correction in these two matters, there is still a great deal of discontent because of alleged discrimination in industry and in the Armed Forces. With these two exceptions, the protests and demands are not different since December 1941 than they were prior to that time.

There has been, however, some editorial comment relative to foreign-inspired agitation among the Negroes. In most instances this has been ridiculed and suggestions have been made that the real danger, so far as the Negroes are concerned, is not that they will become inclined to the pro-Axis point of view, but rather that discriminatory practices will ultimately make them feel they are not a part of the American war effort.

Sociological Aspects

A source of information has advised of making a study of existing conditions in Harlem and the following has been given as his opinion relative to the present unrest there.

This source has advised that the principal cause for the unrest and dissatisfaction is discrimination. He has explained his reason for making this statement by relating that as a result of discrimination the Negroes there are limited to an area far too small to accommodate the population which has resulted in crowded housing, unsanitary conditions and immorality. He has further stated with regard to the general lack of employment among Negroes that they are the last persons to be employed. As a result, it is necessary for many families to live together or for them to enlist roomers or boarders so that the rent may be met.

With reference to the above, the source of information has informed that at the present time there is but one housing project in process in this area which will by no means relieve the situation. This, of course, he explained, is part of the cause for the crowded conditions and when attempts are made to expand the area, restrictions prohibit the same.

Because of high rents, lack of good employment and the resulting low incomes, it has been explained, it is necessary for both husband and wife to obtain work which results in children running loose on the streets without proper supervision causing increased juvenile delinquency. As a result of the effect of racial discrimination and the ensuing condemnation of it by the grown people, children have grown up in such an atmosphere that they have lost faith in white people and distrust them, all of which makes it very difficult for people to aid them in their plight or to gain cooperation from them in planning for their needs, stated the informant. Such conditions are said to naturally result in a fruitful field for subversive and agitational groups to work in and accomplish their purposes.

A confidential informant who for many years was a member of the Communist Party and reached relatively important heights in that group has furnished a picture of the Negro situation in this area. This individual is a Negro and has lived for many years in this area. His remarks concerning this matter may be significant. His report is set out hereinafter:

"The American Negro fundamentally is patriotic and loyal. With the exception of a small minority that have accepted Communism as a way out of those conditions that are obnoxious it can be safely stated that the majority of the Negroes in the United States have a profound spiritual feeling of loyalty and devotion to American democratic ideals and principles and a sincere conviction that all their problems can and will be solved within the existing framework of the Declaration of Independence and the Constitution.

"However, there are certain conditions under which the Negro lives that tend to create grave dissatisfaction with the way democracy works. It is this dissatisfaction that Communists are using to spread among Negroes the seeds of lack of confidence in and disloyalty to American Democracy.

"Practically every Negro who speaks sincerely about the war feels that he has very little if anything to fight for. He feels that democracy does not work for him and that there is a sharp line of demarcation between what are the rights of Negroes and what are the rights of white people. The question is often heard 'Why should we fight for freedom for every race and nationality in the world when we ourselves are not free?'

"The basic cause of this growing conviction among Negroes may be found in a careful study of the record of our elected representatives in all branches of county, city, state and federal government. This study will reveal a gross indifference, lack of concern and in numerous instances open and brazen hostility in relation to the Negro problem. This is not true of all elected representatives of the people. There have been and there are many who have shown vision and foresight and understanding relating to the Negro problem and have sought to solve it but they are only a small minority. This minority have made some serious beginnings that attest to the efficacy and veracity of democracy.

"Let us examine impartially and without emotion the plight of the Negro in order that a clear and succinct picture can be drawn as a necessary prerequisite to an understanding of the problem and how it is being used by the enemies of our country in order to obtain their objectives.

"We are engaged in a great conflict for human freedom, the end of which will determine the course of history for many years to come. It is a life or death struggle for democracy. Yet the 12,000,000 or more Negroes in our country and the darker races of the world with the exception of China are not included in this program from the point of view of a clear definition of what their status is going to be now or after the war. The Atlantic Charter neither mentions nor infers that anything in its context or purpose affects these millions who love freedom and democracy as much as any other people.

"The sincerity of the Churchill government is seriously challenged because of its treatment of India. The arrest and imprisonment of India's leaders, shooting of patriots and the invoking of the old flogging law in reply to the request for independence has created grave doubts and hesitations in the minds of Negroes as to the sincerity of purpose of the leaders of the United Nations. The belief is widespread that India will move toward collaboration with Japan. The basis for this growing belief is lack of confidence in and deep rooted dislike of British rule evinced in the cooperation of the natives with Japanese in their conquest of Asia. All these developments are exploited by the pro-Japanese elements to crystallize sentiments among the Negroes for Japan and consequently the Axis. Likewise these developments are exploited by the Communists to win support for and membership in the Party by presenting the Party as the only sincere fighter for the liberation of the Negroes and the colonial peoples.

"Failure and reluctance to clarify the stand of our Government in particular and the United Nations in general as to our stand on the Negro and colonial questions does not help the situation but tends to create greater confusion and distrust.

"Let us link up the international situation with the one at home. We permitted racial lines to be drawn in our armed services. The Negroes are placed in separate units of the Army. There is practically no possibility for advancement in the Navy to say nothing of the Marines. We have sanctioned the creation of a Jim Crow section of our air force. All of this is a sort of capitulation to those prejudiced Americans who feel that the Negro must be kept separate from the white armed forces of our nation in conformity with the old established domestic policy Jim Crow. The sentiment among the majority of Negroes is for the integration of the Negro into every branch of the armed services with their white brothers in arms with the same rights and privileges. Their training and fighting together will create a better understanding, overcome distrust and lack of confidence and create the basis for a healthy and constructive relation upon which to build in the postwar period.

"The infamous Jim Crow law that exists in many states, the product of slavery and the bitterness that followed the Proclamation of Emancipation completely nullifies the Bill of Rights. It places the Negro in a position of inferiority. It denies him the very rights for which he is asked to die that other races may enjoy. Many soldiers on furlough speak of the insults, abuses, and disgusting treatment they receive at the hands of prejudiced white people in the South. Everywhere they go on the street cars, on the busses, in the public places and on the streets they are made to feel that regardless of their uniform they are still 'niggers' and have to stay in a 'nigger's' place. Such a state of affairs is not at all conducive to sound faith in the avowed aims of the democracies in the war. The Jim Crow law divides the American people through the drawing of artificial distinctions on the basis of color of skin, engenders and perpetuates prejudices that ought not to exist and therefore should be abolished. The Communists are constantly exploiting this law in order to rally the Negro under their banner.

"Moreover the poll tax is considered a law that tends to disfranchise millions of Negroes and poor white persons in the South and through it a minority of persons are able to perpetuate themselves in power. In recent months there has been a great demand among Negroes for the abolition of the poll tax as a necessary prerequisite to restoring the right to vote to millions of persons in the South who are now disfranchised because of their inability to pay the poll tax. The poll tax is considered the main obstacle to Negro representation in the government in those areas where they constitute the majority and a deterring influence in those sections where they hold the balance of power. The Communists are utilizing this to stir up the Negroes. They are linking up the demand for the abolition of the poll tax with the 'right of the Negro of the land' and the establishment of an autonomous Negro government in the Black Belt.

"Lynching of Negroes has been cause of bitterness and unrest among the Negroes for many years. Every effort by them to get Congress to pass the anti-lynch bill was in vain. The recent lynching of Negroes both of civilians and soldiers have added fuel to the fire which is as always being fanned by the Communists and other anti-American elements. The passage of the anti-lynch bill has been effectively blocked by the powerful block of Southern Congressmen. Depriving a Negro of life without the due process of law is considered a mockery of the Bill of Rights. The failure of the local governments and the Federal Government to protect the life and limb of Negroes accused of committing a crime; the failure to punish those that take the law into their hands shows a pronounced weakness of democracy and creates a danger. Objectively all this tends to give support and encouragement to the Axis on the one hand and material to be used by the Communists on the other, to rally the Negroes around their program by promising them that the Communist Program is the only way out.

"The complete integration of the Negro into every branch of the war effort finds as its main barrier racial discrimination. Millions of manpower hours are lost as a result of the policy of discrimination in the hiring of Negroes in those industries that manufacture the essentials for war. In New York the Negro constitutes 6.1% of the population; 25% are on relief and only 1% in defense industries or industries vital to defense according to statistics given by John A. Davis, Executive Secretary, State of New York Committee on Discrimination in Employment.

"According to Elmer Carter, member of the New York State War Council, 80% of the Negroes in New York are domestics. This is due primarily to the refusal of the heads of industry to give employment to Negroes in the skilled and semi-skilled jobs in industry. Thus the majority of Negroes are placed in the lowest pay categories. Young Negro boys and girls graduating from high school and college find very little opportunity to apply their talents and ability. Many leading Negroes feel that this situation can be remedied by the Government providing industrial training for Negroes, removing the barriers in industry and guaranteeing them the same rights and privileges to work in all industries. The result would be the full utilization of our country's manpower. The question of jobs for the Negro is one of the main slogans of the Communists because they know that this is a burning issue among the Negroes.

"The devastating effects of lack of employment in New York City, the small income of the Negro family, the fact that they pay 25% more rent than white people and live in inferior apartments and homes create a fertile field for agitation. The low income of the Negro makes it necessary for husband, wife and children to live in one kitchenette room and four and five families in one apartment. The effect of this condition is seen almost immediately. Prostitution and juvenile delinquency are born and reared in such surroundings. They grow to such enormous proportions that they crowd and choke those things that are essential to building good citizens. The Communists agitate for lower rents, right of the Negro to live in sections of the city other than Harlem, more schools because the present ones are overcrowded, better hospitalization because of its present inadequacy, more playgrounds, recreation centers and jobs in the higher pay brackets to provide more necessities of life for the Negro.

"The law enforcement agencies have sought to stamp out prostitution and robbery that is growing on a sweeping scale in Harlem but without success. Nearly every crime committed is the work of youngsters between the ages of 17 and 25. Most of them are the products of conditions, lack of employment, inability of parents to give them the things that others enjoy, lack of proper care and training in youth. In the effort of the law enforcement agencies to stamp out crime many grave injustices are committed such as beating persons when arrested and doing irreparable harm to innocent persons. This situation is further aggravated by the Daily News and the Journal who smear the whole community as a cesspool of crime. This has created considerable resentment among Negroes who feel that there is no attempt to understand the situation, the causes of it and the failure to give any remedial measures other than slander, shootings and arrests. Here again the Communists react to this situation, attack the city administration, urge the people to protest and fight against police brutality and to fight against discrimination and for jobs.

"The Communists are always alert and react quickly to each and every grievance of the Negroes and form some sort of committee to rally the people to struggle to eliminate the grievance. Their methods are devious. They form various front organizations making use of prominent persons to attain their objectives, the Daily Worker, the Negro papers and leaflets.

"Now to recapitulate. The Negro is a loyal, good American. His future is woven into the very fibre of America and cannot be separated without the destruction of the whole. It is primarily a problem of whether we are going to permit an alien group whose program is diametrically opposed in principle to our form of government and whose avowed purpose despite its professed patriotism is the overthrow of our Government to utilize the grievances of the Negroes in order to serve their ultimate objective.

"Farsighted, intelligent leadership is necessary. All these grievances can be eliminated if a sincere and constructive study is made to the end that a constructive program of giving full citizen rights to the Negro. Integration of the Negro into the armed forces, into the war industries, abolition of the poll tax, passage of the anti-lynch bill, abolition of the Jim Crow law, broad education on better race relations would take away the issues that are now being utilized by the Communists and other elements."

Another confidential source of information has submitted a report reflecting his opinion as to the causes for Negro unrest in Harlem. This individual, who has been a long-time resident of Harlem, is said to have a thorough understanding of the situation as it exists there. He has not been connected with any subversive organizations but on the contrary has been connected with several organizations, the purposes of which are of a very high standard. His remarks compared and contrasted in some instances with that of the preceding informant, may assist in presenting a solid exposition of the matter as a whole.

He attributes the teachings of Marcus Garvey and followers who are still active in New York as being one of the principal causes for unrest in that they have taken advantage of riots and other precarious conditions pertaining to the Negroes to spread the doctrine of the hate of all white people and the claim that they are responsible for the plight of the Negroes. Another important cause attributed by this informant to the present unrest is the lynching of Negroes and the failure of Congress to pass an anti-lynching bill. The general tenor of Negro newspapers is also blamed in that they continually bring to the attention of Negroes instances of discrimination whether there is basis for their remarks or not. Then, too, he states, there are discriminatory and segregating aspects of living conditions in Harlem. He says that the crowded conditions afford an excellent opportunity for landlords to overcharge their tenants or for merchants to ask higher prices from customers. This, of course, he says, is not alleviated by the large increase of Negroes coming into Harlem from different parts of the South.

He makes mention of the restriction of Negroes as a whole to certain types of employment which usually offer the lowest wages. In this connection, he has pointed out that although this condition is true, there are thousands in Harlem who "would not do an honest day's work or take a job if they were given the opportunity."

With regard to prices and charges for services and goods in Harlem, he has stated that rentals are far above those white people pay for similar apartments in other sections where the income level is approximately the same. He points out a recent survey made of Harlem's food markets and states that a comparison of prices which has been given shows that the average Negro housewife, who in many instances has not learned to read or make minor calculations, is taken advantage of by merchants. Relative to this, he has alleged that a large number of the markets are Jewish controlled and fruit and vegetable markets are controlled by Italians. He states that as a result of a few dishonest acts which have come to the attention of the Negroes in this area many Negroes have grown to hate the white race and the Jews in particular. He states that these things tend to create unrest, dissatisfaction, and racial hatred and present excellent material for "agitators and Communists."

In conclusion this confidential source of information has expressed himself in the following manner:

> "I would venture to say that every Negro in New York feels that President Roosevelt and his wife have done more to help them than anyone else since the time of President Lincoln. They really believe that God sent him to help free them from social and economic slavery. All the Negro women, and the girls also, actually worship Mrs. Roosevelt on account of her expression of sympathy towards them. They appreciate her visiting their civic functions, YWCA's, and speaking at several of their meetings. They are particularly gratified that Mrs. Bethune has been placed in a high position to take care of Negro youths, etc.
>
> "Of course, the depression hit the Negroes like everyone else, but if President Roosevelt and his Party did not create the WPA and other agencies during the depression, their plight would have been terrible. But now there is quite a lot of dissatisfaction among the ranks of the Negro because he claims that more attention is being paid to the whites in giving them jobs first and at the same time ignoring the Negroes. When the President's Executive Order No. 8802 (FEPC) was issued June 25, 1941, they felt that their problem of unemployment would be solved or at least greatly eased. Their cry now is that the President failed to do anything so as to force the big white employers from practicing discrimination

in the hiring of Negroes. The result is that as soon as a Negro is refused a job—whether he is qualified or not—he immediately raises the cry of discrimination; the agitators and newspapers keep them 'worked up'. Then the man in the streets who is looking for a job and those who wouldn't accept one put the blame on the shoulders of all white men. This gives more material for the ever-grinding race hatred machine, thereby creating additional unrest. But worst of all things, it [a]ffects the war program because the common saying among the Negroes in Harlem is 'Well, if I can't get a job when I need it I can't see why I should go and fight. What am I going to get out of it?' "

Anti-Semitism Among Negroes

It is believed significant at this time to add information received relative to alleged anti-Semitism among Negroes in this area. A source of information has advised there is anti-Negroism among the Jewish people in this area and anti-Semitism among the Negroes. He has made the statement that anti-Semitism among the Negroes in the United States is principally urban phenomena. He states that he believes the more overt and intense forms of anti-Jewish sentiment among the Negroes are to be found in certain rather definite areas of competition and conflict. These areas, it is stated, in the main form the face-to-face contacts by the Negro with the landlord, the merchant, the employer of domestic help, and to a lesser degree the professional man.

He has stated that in the congested areas of the Northern cities where the Negro housing problem has been and still is acute, there are certain residential restrictive covenants and what he terms "lily-white" agreements among property owners to keep Negroes segregated. On the other hand, the pressure of the steady stream of migrants, mainly Southern Negroes, is claimed to demand an expansion of the Negro neighborhood. In this connection, there is cited as an example the population density of Harlem which is said to be over 600 persons per acre in some sections, while for the Borough of Manhattan generally the population density is little more than 200 per acre.

In citing the Mayor's and Governor's Commission of New York Report, he has advised that rents are increased considerably whenever Negro tenants succeed white tenants in a given block. Moreover, he has stated that upon the arrival of Negro tenants, attention to needed repairs and other services expected of the landlords becomes indifferent.

The source of information continued stating that a landlord is still a landlord whether he be Negro, Greek, or Turk, however, he has said the belief is nevertheless widespread in the Harlem area that the large share of the exploiting landlords are Jewish.

Citing another instance of a possible cause for anti-Semitic feeling on the part of Negroes in this area, a source of information has referred to allegations that groceries and food centers in the Harlem area charge considerably more for given items than do those in other parts of New York City. Then, too, the quality of the products is often said to be inferior. Allegations of giving short weights or shortchanging people have also been made. The source of information then concluded with respect to this phase that although statistics do not exist as to the number of Jewish merchants in Harlem as compared with other nationalities in the same line of endeavor, the popular belief is that Jewish vendors are responsible for much of the alleged short dealings given the Negro there.

Another so-called custom in New York City has been cited by the source of information as a possible cause for anti-Semitic feelings. He referred to the "Bronx slave market" which he labelled indicative of the intention in the field of domestic labor which is a sore spot as far as Jewish-Negro relations are concerned. He has stated that the majority of the inhabitants of the Bronx Borough, New York, are Jewish. Keeping this in mind, he said that there are certain spots in this area where Negro domestic workers gathered each morning to be hired for daily work rates which are alleged to be as low as 15 cents per hour. Negro girls are said to stand on corners in all kinds of weather waiting to "sell" themselves to the housewives who are said to often bid for the cheapest price. It should be stated that this situation has been exposed by newspapers in New York and to some extent alleviated.

Another example of the situation which possibly causes anti-Semitic feelings among the Negroes is stated to be that involving professional people. The hospitals of Harlem are alleged to be a case in point. A source of information pointed out that Negro medical students are often barred or almost barred from many of the universities and that after graduation the medical student's plight is more serious inasmuch as it is difficult for him to find hospitals which will permit him to serve his internship or to join a particular staff. He reasons that accordingly the Negro doctor is frustrated when he encounters difficulty in securing a place on staffs of even the Negro hospitals. It is said that a number of Negro medical men have the point of view that the white doctors—especially the Jewish doctors—work together in a clique and effectively limit the Negro staff members almost to a point of exclusion even in segregated institutions like the Harlem Hospital.

No investigation has been conducted with regard to the foregoing and it is pointed out that the information set forth hereinbefore is merely the opinion of a source of information. However, it is believed that such a matter should be referred to in adding to the picture of the Negro in Harlem.

Preventive Measures

No definite attempt has been made to go into matters of local or statewide concern in this survey. For that reason it has not been definitely ascertained what steps have been taken to alleviate the situation among the Negroes as it exists in local New York City areas. However, the following observations are offered:

During the Fall of 1941 there were several instances of "mugging" in Central Park of white people and colored people alike by young colored youths. This led to the assignment of additional police protection in this area, which is near Harlem.

Recently Mr. Frank Crosswaith was appointed to the New York City Housing Board. Crosswaith is a well-known and respected Negro.

A number of houses or tenements in Harlem have been condemned and were boarded up until repairs were made by the landlords. At the present time there is a housing project in Harlem which it is contemplated will alleviate to some extent the crowded housing conditions.

It has also been reported that there is an increase, though slight, being made in the number of Negro schoolteachers appointed in New York City.

At the present time there is also a move on foot to have a committee appointed by the Mayor of New York City to make a survey of present conditions in Harlem.

Harlem Riots, August 1–2, 1943

At approximately 10:00 P.M. on August 1, 1943, a white police officer attempted to arrest a Negro woman for disorderly conduct at the Braddock Hotel in the Harlem area of New York City. Thereafter a negro soldier (described in the press as a military policeman) reportedly interfered with the officer, seizing his night stick and beating him to the floor. The police officer shot the negro soldier in the shoulder and both were removed to the hospital. Accordingly a crowd of approximately 300 Negro civilians and soldiers gathered and demonstrated. Shortly thereafter approximately 200 negro soldiers and sailors also demonstrated in front of the 28th Precinct Station in Harlem.

Within a short time groups of hoodlums and criminals began looting and pillaging stores and retail establishments, centering their interests on liquor stores. Innumerable glass windows were broken, people hurt and general damage caused. It has been estimated that approximately $5,000,000 in damage was caused by the rioters and the hoodlums. The area involved in this trouble included 110th Street on the South, 155th Street on the North and 6th, 7th and 8th Avenues, which run between these two boundaries. Five people were killed, 40 policemen were injured, including one seriously, and 465 males and 74 females were arrested.

The situation has been described by city authorities as having a spontaneous origin, and it was stated further that no indications whatsoever were reported that the trouble was caused by planned or organized movements. In addition no indications were reported of any white people taking part in the affair other than white police. Numerous rumors were begun, however, one of which became fairly prevalent according to a confidential source. This was to the effect that a negro soldier had been killed by a white policeman, and for that reason the rioting was begun. This rumor was without foundation, and on the contrary the negro soldier who was shot by the policeman at the Braddock Hotel received but a minor wound. The press also carried an indication that rumors and allegations were being spread of the Ku Klux Klan and outside hoodlums participating in the trouble. Concerning this no specific information, allegations or complaints were received either by the New York City Police Department or the Federal Bureau of Investigation. In fact the negro press namely, the "People's

Voice" carried such headlines as: "No Detroit in New York", and "Racial Element not Present". This paper also commended the police for their prompt and efficient action and stated that blame could not be placed on any group of individuals for the rioting.

Sporadic looting and clashes occurred throughout the day of August 2, 1943, but the situation became comparatively quiet on the night of that same day. A few minor incidents are said to have occurred during the early morning of August 3, 1943, but by later that morning the situation had quieted completely.

The peak of the trouble occurred during the early hours of the morning of August 2, 1943. Several radio addresses were made by the Mayor of New York City in an attempt to quiet the people and to urge them to return to their homes. Five thousand police and one thousand detectives were immediately assigned to the area for duty and the United States Army moved trucks into the area in an attempt to remove all Army personnel. By 9:15 A.M., August 2, 1943, the disturbances had subsided considerably.

The situation has been likened to the 1935 riots in the Harlem area when similar trouble occurred, arising, according to the reports, from the arrest of a negro youth by a police officer. Damage caused then is said to have been exceeded by the trouble of 1943.

According to confidential informants, members of the Communist Party first branded the affair as being the result of "Fascism, police brutality, race discrimination and 'Jim Crowism' ". At a meeting held by the Party, which included functionaries and activists, at Academy Hall in New York City on August 2, 1943, the decision was arrived at that the Party would take no action until the rioting and trouble were quelled. The Party did, however, evidence an extreme interest in the appointment of 1,000 negro auxili[a]ries whose duties were to accompany white police officers. In this connection allegations were received that the Communist Party through Ben Davis, Jr., who sat in on police conferences, had a voice in the appointing of the recruits. Max Yergan, President of the National Negro Congress, a Communist front organization, and Ferdinand Smith, reported Communist and Vice President of the National Maritime Union, were reported to have been active in assisting city officials and offering their advice. It might be noted that Yergan is also a reported Communist. The Daily Worker, in an article in its August 3, 1943, issue, made the following statement, "Not racial feeling, but resentment against high prices and discrimination motivated much of the violence against the stores, ..."

With regard to the meeting held by the Party at Academy Hall, it was reported that a Party functionary rose and spoke, saying that "they" were not race riots and the situation was not analogous to the Detroit riots. She also emphasized, "We (referring to the Communists) are not working independently as a Party, but are cooperating with the Mayor." She also stated, "Negro liberals and other negro leaders mobilized today to quiet the negro people. At the moment there is no job for us as an organized Party. There was no organized band of hoodlums. The riots were not planned although the city was wonderfully prepared for such a riot. Most of the shopkeepers are Jews. They are naturally incensed, and have the usual fears. There must be no splitting in our approach to this problem. The State Committee (of the Communist Party) wanted to do something but there isn't anything to do."

Philadelphia Field Division

Information has been received reflecting that individual instances of pro-German, pro-Japanese, and anti-Semitic agitation exist among the Negroes in this area. Reports have also been received that many Negroes have expressed pleasure over Japanese victories in the Pacific and in the Far East, considering it well that whites have suffered humiliation. However, no general pro-German or pro-Japanese sentiments are known to exist among the local Negroes. Additional information received reflects that following the attack on Pearl Harbor, efforts were made by Negroes including unidentified Haitians to create sentiment against the participation of Negroes in the war and against assistance to England.

At the present time, in Philadelphia, there is stated to be approximately two million people. Of this, the Negro population has variously been estimated from 250,000 to more than 300,000. The Negro population is said to have increased since the World War in and around Philadelphia, and particularly so in the past decade. The Negro population in the beginning of the 20th century was largely centered in South Philadelphia near 12th Street. During the time of the World War, West Philadelphia was built up as a residential section and a great many households, employing Negroes, moved to West Philadelphia. Accordingly it is stated Negro servants also moved to West Philadelphia occupying chiefly the area north of Market Street centering around Powelton Avenue. As the Negro population increased Negroes moved into North Philadelphia mostly west of Broad Street and centering around Ridge Avenue and a small group took up residence in the general vicinity of 10th Street and Fairmount Avenue. It is said that this latter group includes the worst of the criminal element and that it is a constant source of trouble to the police. The handling of narcotics and crimes of even a more heinous and serious type are committed in this area. Subsequent to the World War, especially during the depression years the influx of Negroes increased, partially due to rumors that jobs were to be had by Negroes in Philadelphia. Provisions are made under the Pennsylvania state law for relief and comparatively small sums are provided for so called "mother's relief." This is stated to provide a certain sum for the first child and additional payments for succeeding children. Consequently it became economically profitable for Southern Negroes to come to Philadelphia and it is alleged that many of them found it more simple to raise families than to find jobs. It is further stated that the newcomers from the South were not accepted socially by the Philadelphia Negroes and that they settled for the most part in North Philadelphia east of Broad Street in the general vicinity of Temple University. They are stated to be considered by local authorities as an undesirable element since they lack any sense of responsibility and stability and are a constant problem on the relief load. It is also alleged that they are trouble makers.

It is related that during the 1930's when the Negro population was estimated to be about 13½% of the total in Philadelphia, Negroes represented about 23½% of the relief load. At the present time Negro children are stated to constitute about 23% of the public school population, due, probably, to several causes: first, there are about 5,000 school children whose parents still reside in the South; second, the birth rate among Negroes is at least constant and third, the white population is decreasing in Philadelphia, both by percentage and by number due particularly to their moving from that city into the suburbs and due partly to the decreasing birth rate among the whites. Reportedly the school population percentage is also affected by the fact that many white parents have enrolled their children in private schools, rather than have them attend schools with Negroes. It is said that inter-racial violence is a regular thing and that school authorities during the recent past have found increasing numbers of deadly weapons such as guns, knives, and clubs in the possession of Negro school boys. It is further reported that up to and including the last term of school in Philadelphia, there were many Negro boys in high school who, because of size and appearance, were believed to be between 18 and 20 years, which is stated to be higher than the normal school age. It is said that some of these boys either do not know, or claim not to know their ages and have continued to go to school and to live on relief as dependent minors, rather than go to work. It is claimed that they present a great problem, not only because of their trouble with white boys, but because of the fear that they might molest high school girls in co-educational schools. In addition reports received indicate that there are several hundred cases of syphilis and several hundred cases of gonorrhea in the high schools, that 98% of these cases are Negroes and that most of the high school girls found to be pregnant are Negroes.

Information from this area is to the effect that there are very few individuals or groups of individuals among the Negroes who are looked upon by the majority as real leaders. It is said that there are many Negroes of prominence in the churches, in political life and in professions who have a certain following but that there is no agreement as to who are the outstanding leaders of the race in the Philadelphia Area. The explanation in this is said to lie in several causes. It is claimed that most of the leaders are considered by the Negroes and by the white people, familiar with the Negroes in Philadelphia, to be primarily interested in their own personal advancement with the consequences that most of them are not trusted by the people they claim to represent. It is also claimed that there are differences arising from sharp class distinction, rivalries and the like. These class distinctions are claimed to be based partly on differences in shades of color and particularly on social prominences as acquired by color, wealth, professional standing and family history. It is said that most of the people who purport to be the leaders and who are accepted as leaders by the white people, are comparatively conservative in sentiment and actually represent only the feelings of the middle class of the professional Negro group, and for that reason it appears doubtful whether many of them have close enough contact with the people they claim to represent to know what those people actually desire.

Sources of information in the colored race who have been interviewed, indicate that there is a strong sentiment of bitterness and resentment among the Negro people in the Philadelphia area as well as throughout the country. It is claimed that this feeling has now reached unprecedented intensity, that the Negroes' complaint, it is generally agreed upon, has centered primarily on, one, indignities and lack of opportunities in the Southern states where the bad conditions are aggravated and two, lack of opportunities and segregation in civil life, both with regard to everyday life and employment. It is said that Negroes in the North are not so personally concerned with such matters as poll tax as they are with matters which [a]ffect their own daily life, such as military service and jobs. However, one informant, who is in a position to observe men being inducted into the Army, has advised that the spirit of Negroes being inducted into the Army is good, and that they are patriotic.

There are a number of Negro newspapers published in Philadelphia most of which are published either daily or weekly. In addition, other newspapers, such as the Pittsburgh Courier, publish a Philadelphia edition. From material observed in Negro newspapers to date, it appears that these papers contain almost no news of national and international importance. News items deal largely with the doings of local Negro society and with general items concerning local Negroes such as fights, crimes of violence and arrest. Much space, however, is devoted to news items and editorial material, dealing with the Negro problems, such as segregation, jobs, military forces and the like. Almost always these items are said to be presented in such a manner as to incite feelings.

The Communist Party, the Young Communist League, and Communist front organizations have worked extensively among Negroes in the Philadelphia area for more than a decade; however, this work is reported to have slackened since the invasion of Russia; and the Communist following among the Negroes in this area has greatly decreased, probably due to the return of Negroes to work. It is reported that the Communist following was largely among the more ignorant group of Negroes who could not comprehend the entire Communist program, and among a few Negro intellectuals.

A confidential source of information, **a Negro who is exceedingly active in Negro civic affairs in the Philadelphia area,** has informed that during the past several months he has noted a decided change in the attitude of Negroes toward white people in this area. He said that this attitude is decidedly anti-white and in some respects can be considered anti-American, inasmuch as numerous Negroes in the area have been overheard by him to speak of the day "to come for the Negro." This source of information described the movement or change in attitude as working like an undercurrent which is definitely influenced and even inflamed by the Negro press and by well recognized Negro leaders, some of whom, he claimed, while at one time conservative, have become domineering and hateful as far as white people are concerned.

This source also advised that recently Negroes have been forming themselves into small groups and holding meetings in their homes, in taprooms and on corners of streets, at which times they have expressed an anti-white sentiment. He furnished no figures or specific information as to the size or number of these groups. He also pointed out that alleged incidents resulting in fights between whites and Negroes have become more frequent, that only a small percentage of these incidents have been investigated by the police and that a still smaller percentage have received notice in the public press. He stated, however, that the Communists as well as the North Philadelphia Civic League and other allied organizations have taken a great interest in these incidents.

This same informant has related of hearing the term "new Negro" used extensively by leaders, as well as by men in the street, and explained that this term refers to the younger and more militant Negro who is resisting alleged discrimination and segregation by action rather than by words. He, also, has informed that the term is used to differentiate the militant Negro from the conservative type. As an example of this, he referred to the recent visit of President Barclay of Liberia to Philadelphia. He related that one Negro leader, a friend of the chairman of the reception committee, was supposed to have been in attendance at the time President Barclay was honored with a dinner. However, this leader did not attend. The leader made the excuse that he would have to stay away because of his work, however, at the same time he remarked vehemently that he felt that President Barclay had missed an opportunity to speak for the Negro when he addressed Congress and, further, he felt President Barclay was nothing more than a "handkerchief-head Negro," which term is purportedly used to designate those Negroes who are not militant. The informant has further pointed out that at the time President Barclay visited the Sun Shipyard in Chester, Pennsylvania, he heard several Negroes who lined the streets speak of him as a "handkerchief-head."

In this connection, the same source of information has pointed to the lack of good leadership among the Negroes in the Philadelphia area, saying that there is too much jealousy between the common man and those who attempt to assume the leadership.

This informant, as well as numerous other white informants in a position to know situations as they exist in the various Negro residential areas, have informed that Philadelphia is extremely tense regarding racial matters, and all feel race riots are but a short time away. They have all commented on the increasing number of "muggings" and attacks upon white men and women by Negro youths. Along these lines, these informants have pointed to the State Civil Liberties Law, which, according to them, has tied the hands of the police and has made the solution of the problem much more difficult. They have referred to "laws without teeth" and expressed their alarm over the attitude of the Negro press and Negro speakers. They have also referred to the white-colored friction as involving white people who have come from southern states and who have not been in Philadelphia for many years. They have also stated that they know of groups of white boys who band together and patrol the streets with the inevitable result of trouble arising between themselves and Negroes. [*100-135-38 pa 68*]

Another source of information, a Negro who is **prominent as a lecturer and who is presently the manager of a large Negro housing development** in Philadelphia, has referred to what he termed the "new Negro" and his increasing alarm over the attitude of the present-day Negro toward the white people in the Philadelphia area. He advised that he feels the problem is becoming very serious and that most of the anti-white agitation is brought about by the Negro newspapers. In this connection, he cited an article in the "Pittsburgh Courier" by George Schuyler, who compared publicity given to the American aviators captured in Japan with Negro soldiers in the South who are allegedly brutally treated, complaining no mention was made of the latter in the newspapers.

Regarding pro-German activity in this area, one report has been received that an unidentified white man approached a source of information about holding meetings in the latter's home stating he would pay the informant for the same. This unidentified white individual is said to have displayed a good knowledge of the history of foreign nations, and to have spoken generally on behalf of Germany and against the Jews. No other specific data in this regard have been developed, however.

A Negro source of information, a politician in Philadelphia who is interested in recreational projects for Negro youth, supplied the following information concerning pro-Axis sympathies, as well as anti-Semitism, on the part of Negroes in the Philadelphia area:

In this regard the informant expressed the opinion that Jews in the United States are a minority as well as the Negroes, and that Negroes feel any organization, institution or individual who attacks the Jews is an enemy of the Negroes as well. He added, however, that he believes there is no love lost between Negroes and Jews, although from a propaganda standpoint it would be foolish to approach Negroes by condemning the Jewish minority in view of their likewise being a minority. He also pointed out that Negroes are well aware Hitler despises their race and that they would have no part to play in an economic or social order under Nazi domination.

The informant further advised that Negro leaders, especially the thinking ones, constantly point out to their followers and in the press the fact that the Negro in this country has more opportunity than in any other country in the world although at times they express their bitterness over racial discrimination.

Very few complaints have been received concerning pro-Italian or pro-Spanish activity among the Negroes. However, one complaint has been received to the effect that Italian taxicab drivers at Broad and South Streets have been overheard advising the Negroes not to register under the Selective Training and Service Act and telling them that the war is a white man's war caused by the Jews.

Pro-Japanese, Anti-White Groups

Twentieth Century School of Bible Research (*Philadelphia Branch of Triumph, the Church of the New Age*)

In 1933 the Twentieth Century School of Bible Research was established by Reverend Joseph S. Croom as an auxiliary to Triumph, the Church of the New Age, the headquarters of which are now in Brooklyn, New York. However, the two organizations reportedly have no financial connections at the present time. The Twentieth Century School of Bible Research was organized into three branches, namely: 1702 South Street, Philadelphia (Leon Humphrey, teacher); 1536 North Twelfth Street; and 21st Street and Columbia Avenue (McDowell Memorial Church). Croom, who is the leader of the organization, is known to have been a member of the old "Marcus Garvey Back to Africa Movement," now known as the Universal Negro Improvement Association. The doctrine put forth by this group is that there are two races of people, the Israelites and the Gentiles, the only true Israelites in America being Negroes. Croom denies, however, that the term "Negro" is a true name of a people or a race but claims it to be merely an appellation, and that his people should refuse to accept it. He preaches to his people that the present war is Armageddon in which all existing nations will be destroyed and then the Israelites (Negroes) as God's chosen children will rule. The Israelites, according to this belief, are not to take up the sword because the Bible has told them not to do so, rather they are to remain passive and permit the Gentiles to fight. It is also said that God has chosen Japan to destroy the existing nations, and that the Negroes also will be used as God's battle-ax to help in the destruction. Japan is alleged to have been chosen because the Japanese are historically the only people who have not had slaves, while America showed the Negroes no mercy when they were slaves.

Several witnesses have informed that Croom has taught this is a race war between the colored and white races, yet, that it is a white man's war and not that of the Negroes. Croom cannot see what the Negroes have to fight for.

Latest reports are that there are approximately one hundred fifty members of the organization, and the regular meetings are normally attended only by members with comparatively few visitors. The outdoor meetings, however, are said to be frequently attended by one hundred or more persons at a time. There are indications that Croom has connections with the Pacific Movement of the Eastern World and, also, had connections with the International Reassembly of the Church of Freedom League, Incorporated, in New Orleans prior to the arrest and conviction of Ethelbert Anslem Broaster. It is further reported that Croom has had in the past contact with prophet Frank S. Cherry of the Church of the Living God, which will be referred to hereinafter. It is also to be noted that Croom was an acting president of one of the Philadelphia chapters of the Universal Negro Improvement Association in 1930. A charter to this effect has been observed in the possession of Croom, although Croom claims no longer to have any connection with the organization. Investigation is of course being conducted and continued with reference to Croom and his organization.

Pacific Movement of the Eastern World

The Pacific Movement of the Eastern World had an active unit in the Philadelphia area beginning in 1934. It is supposed to have held meetings in the Salem Baptist Church at 12th Street and Bainbridge Street, Philadelphia. At the present time, informants have advised, the activities of the Pacific Movement of the Eastern World are believed to be confined to undercover movements—possibly with Reverend Croom's Twentieth Century School of Bible Research. Investigation in this regard is being continued.

Ethiopian World Federation

At the present time there are five locals of the Ethiopian World Federation which are as follows:

Local No. 2, 1221 North Tenth Street; Emmett Jones, President.

Local No. 4, 2015 South Street; Frank Knight, President.

Local No. 15, 1246 North Tenth Street; Caesar Moore, President.

Local No. 22, YMCA, Christian Street.

Local No. 27, 2214 Bolton Street; Colie Covington, President.

It is said that this organization grew out of what was known as the Rising Sun Club, formed in 1934 to raise money for the relief of Ethiopians. The club is said to have continued in existence for several years but made a "racket" of the original purpose and became corrupt with graft. In 1937 the Ethiopian World Federation was formed, absorbing the membership of the Rising Sun Club. According to a confidential informant, the purposes of the foregoing locals are to teach Amharic culture, to bring about a better fellowship between the international groups of black people of the world and to speak of Ethiopia as their country to which they can expatriate if the need arises.

Locals Nos. 2 and 15, mentioned above, broke from the others and incurred their dislike when they attempted to establish Lij Araya Abebe as representative of the crown of Ethiopia in America and, consequently, as head of the organization in this country. This took place at the 1941 convention in New York City. An attempt was also made to place Dr. J. W. Shirley of Local No. 2 as President of the national organization at the convention in 1941.

No indications have been received that the teachings of this organization are inimical to the best interests of the United States, and likewise no information has been received that the various locals have in any way become connected with other organizations, the doctrines of which are un-American. It is said that according to the doctrines of the Ethiopian World Federation the white man is not the friend of the black man; therefore, the latter should not believe in the former's philosophy, but rather in that of the darker races. It is said that beliefs are held by the members that in another five years a war will be waged between the lighter and the darker races of the earth, the latter to be the conqueror.

Universal Negro Improvement Association

At the present time this organization is said to have four divisions in the Philadelphia area, the locations and officers of which are as follows:

Offices at 1230 South Street.

Division 121, located at 2109 West Columbia Avenue; A. J. Joseph, President.

Division 337, located at 1522 Christian Street; S. B. Barbour, President.

Division 812, located at 610 South 16th Street; Herman C. Mitchell, President.

In 1942 the Philadelphia delegation at the national convention of the organization is said to have threatened to bolt because Stewart, the national President, could not account for $16,000 which he had collected. It has also been reported that Ethelbert

Anslem Broaster was scheduled to speak at an August, 1942, meeting of Division 121 of the organization under the sponsorship of the Twentieth Century School of Bible Research. Reportedly part of the former membership of this organization is presently in the Twentieth Century School of Bible Research, brought to that organization by Croom when he formed it. The organization is also said to have cooperated with the North Philadelphia Civic League at one time, although it withdrew when, after raising the question of returning to Africa, a difference of opinion arose.

Church of the Living God

A church by this name is located at 2132 Nicholas Street in Philadelphia and is headed by prophet Frank S. Cherry. It has a usual attendance of from forty to forty-five persons. They are said to observe the tenets of Judaism and members of the church are taught they are Hebrews, descendants of Abraham, Isaac and Jacob. They are also reportedly taught by Cherry that according to their religion they cannot fight outside the United States. It is alleged that some of the doctrines compare with some preached by Croom of the Twentieth Century School of Bible Research. Several conscientious objector cases under the Selective Training and Service Act of 1940 as amended have been developed on members of this sect. It should also be noted that confidential informants have stated that lately meetings of this organization are "crowded" with young Negroes—the "zoot suit" type.

The Church of the Living God, Pillar and Ground of Truth

This church is headed by one Bishop A. A. White with the main church at 43rd and Aspen Streets in Philadelphia and two branches, one located at Warnock and Poplar Streets, the other at 1712 South Street. The branches hold their meetings in private homes or in small halls, having an attendance numbering not more than twenty. The branch located at 1712 South Street is headed by a woman named Bishop Dora Evans, who has an assistant, Pastor Milton Threats, who is also an assistant of Reverend Croom. The meetings at this address are said to have pro-Japanese sentiments expressed at them. There are also two other organizations using the above-captioned name, which are said to have no connection, however, with those previously mentioned. One is at 18th and Federal Streets, and the other is at 13th and Webster Streets.

Bishop Ida Robinson

This individual operates the Mount Olive Church located at 2128 Oxford Street, Philadelphia. According to one source of information, this individual in her sermons, although not referring directly to the Japanese, infers as follows: "The wicked race is being destroyed and God is building a race that will obey. The present race and the present nations are so wicked that they are destroying themselves and the Lord is raising up a race that will obey. This is being done right now." Bishop Ida Robinson is said to have considerable funds at her disposal and has reportedly purchased radio time to speak to her followers. No indications have been received other than an opinion expressed by a source of information, set out above, that the followers of Bishop Robinson are unpatriotic. The organization has several branches and a considerable list of officers.

Moorish Science Temple of America

It is related that approximately nine years ago (1934) the first Moorish Science Temple was opened in Philadelphia, in the 1500 block of Lombard Street, South Philadelphia. It is reported that the organization now has the following temples:

Tenth Street above Callowhill.

604 North Seventh Street under the leadership of L. Dublin El.

1420 North 20th Street under the leadership of William Bradley El.

18th and Christian Streets under the leadership of Albert Smith Bey.

These units reportedly have about five hundred members.

The Temple located at 18th and Christian Streets is said to have a ritual identical with that of the Moorish Science Temples in Chicago and in Detroit. The Koran is used, and all the men wear red fezzes and the women wear long dresses and red or green turbans. An American flag and a Moorish flag hang on either side of the pulpit across which is written, "To Allah, the Father of the Universe." Nothing has been reported indicating that anything pro-Japanese in nature, either statements or activities, has been apparent at the meetings.

Temple No. 11, which is located at 18th and Christian Streets, is under the leadership of Noble Drew Ali, while the other three Temples are under the leadership of C. Kirkman Bey of Chicago, Illinois.

Reports of Pro-Japanese Sentiments

For over a period of a year and a half a number of complaints and reports have been received in this area of expressions and statements wherein a sentiment for the Japanese has been expressed. Inquiries have been conducted into each of these reports, and negative results have been encountered in all. The results are reflected in reports of ignorance, illiteracy, hallucinations or drunkenness on the part of the individuals expressing the statements or utterances.

Filipino Activities

According to a source of information, a Filipino who is in close contact with the activities of Filipinos in the Philadelphia area, there are approximately five hundred in the Philadelphia area, eighty or eighty-five of whom are reportedly married to Negroes. It is said that Filipinos who marry Negroes are treated as outcasts by the rest of the Filipino population and they do not mix with them or attend any of their social functions. This source of information stated that there is always a degree of friction between those who have married Negroes and those who have married members of their own group.

The same source has also advised that he has heard of no remarks made by Filipinos of a pro-Japanese nature. He stated, the Filipinos are essentially loyal to the United States, although on occasions some of them may make statements which may indicate their sympathies are not entirely with this country. He has not come in contact with any pro-Japanese propaganda being spread among his countrymen in the Philadelphia area.

Communist Party Activities

With respect to Communist Party activity and agitation among the Negroes in this area, it has been reported that the same has generally been carried out through direct approach, by meetings, both indoors and outdoors, through the use of literature, handbills and the like, and through the work of those front organizations whose activities are directed or influenced by the Communist Party.

Among the Communist Party front organizations and other organizations alleged to be influenced by the Communist Party line which have been active in this area are:

National Negro Congress

Tenants League of Philadelphia

Young People's Improvement Committee

Coordinating Housing Council

Citizens Committee for Food and Shelter

Community League for Civic Improvement

Housewives' League

West Philadelphia Defense and Rehabilitation Committee

North Philadelphia Civic Improvement Association

Community Council

The general program or Communist Party line as it relates to the Negroes in the Philadelphia area is said to be as follows:

1. The struggle for Negro rights must become part of the war service work.
2. The white supremacy movement in the South must be fought as these elements are traitorous.
3. The turnover of Negroes in plants and other places of employment is too great.
4. Bring forward our Negro people.
5. The branches (of the Party) should give additional attention to the Negroes.
6. In organizing, better forces (white) should be sent into the Negro field.

7. Branches should hold meetings around the question of the Negro and the war.
8. The Party is to continue the question of job surveys.
9. As part of the mass work of the Party, the Negro Youth Organization should become involved in war service work and a delegation should be organized on baseball.

During the year 1942 Communist Party membership in the area covered by this Field Division increased 39 per cent, and as of January 1, 1942 the Negro membership represented about 11½ per cent of the Party's registration. As of January 1, 1943 Negroes represented about 15½ per cent of the Party's registration (excluding members "on leave"). It is believed that Negroes represent actually about 13 per cent of the total population of Philadelphia at the present time, although the only precise statistics are those available as previously set out. While no accurate figures are known to be available at the present time on the strength of the Young Communist League in the Philadelphia area, a strong recruiting drive has been carried on by the organization during the past year, and it is thought that a very high percentage, probably nearly 75 per cent, of the new recruits have been Negroes.

An additional technique on the part of the Communist Party has been evidenced recently in the Philadelphia area, particularly with regard to fostering Negroes who have run afoul of the law. Recently a Negro, James Foster, age sixty-three, engaged in a gun battle with the police. Immediately the Party issued handbills to the effect that Negro and white citizens of the "30th Ward" should unite against "political terror" and "protest police shooting of Mr. Foster." The police in the 30th Ward were likened to the Gestapo.

On March 12, 1943 one Peter Clark, a Negro, was arrested by the police as an idle and disorderly person, when he was allegedly on his way to his draft board in an effort to enlist. He was sentenced to serve three months in prison. His case was taken up by the Communist Party, and he was represented by Phillip Dorfman, the leading Communist Party attorney in Philadelphia. An appeal brought about the release of Clark. Handbills were thereupon distributed by the Party, bearing Clark's photograph and reading: "Frame-up exposed! He was getting ready to serve in the United States Army, but a Jim Crow frame-up sent him to Holmesburg Prison! He didn't have a chance! Read the true facts in the April 11 issue of the Worker, America's leading anti-Hitler newspaper."

After Clark's release, arrangements were made for his induction into the Army, which was scheduled for May 8. The Party's activity was climaxed by giving Clark a place of honor on the speakers' platform at the Philadelphia May Day Rally at Town Hall in the City of Philadelphia on the night of May 1. He was introduced from the platform by Sam Adams Darcy, Secretary of Communist Party District No. 3, who said that Clark was not a member of the Party but that he, Darcy, hoped he would soon become one. At the same time Darcy and Thomas Nabried, Negro Communist Party organizer and Chairman of the City Committee, protested against police brutality in relation to Negroes, claiming the campaign against "mugging" publicized the crimes of violence as originating with Negroes, although this was incorrect.

National Association for the Advancement of Colored People

While this organization until recently was not active to any great extent, recently the organization initiated a membership drive and became active in obtaining jobs for Negroes in industry. It is said that the Communist Party has shown considerable interest in the organization in this area and has frequently been in contact with Theodore Spalding, local President, for information and news releases. No indications have been reported, however, that the Party exerts any degree of influence on the local chapter. The principal campaign of recent date on the part of this chapter is to obtain better positions for Negroes in the Philadelphia Transit Company.

Other Organizations

The Allied Organizations of North Philadelphia as a group was established with headquarters at 2064 Ridge Avenue, Philadelphia. The purpose of the group was to band together other unaffiliated organizations with the theory that unity is power. The North Philadelphia Civic League, the Universal Negro Improvement Association, the Workers' Alliance, the Tenants' League and the Youth Civic Committee made up this group. Later the North Philadelphia Civic League broke away. The organization disbanded in 1941 because of internal trouble.

The Institute on Minorities allegedly represents combined efforts of several organizations active in advancing social theories, and more particularly religious, civic, political, social, labor and interracial problems. It was sponsored during the period April 30–May 2, 1943 by the Youth Committee for Democracy and a number of prominent speakers, including James B. Carey, National Secretary of the Congress of Industrial Organizations, and Pearl S. Buck, writer, addressed the audience on matters involving the Negro people.

The Educational Equality League held a public meeting May 19, 1943, at the Allen A.M.E. Church, 19th and Bainbridge Streets, which was attended by approximately three hundred Negroes reportedly of the conservative type. The Attorney General of the United States, the Superintendent of Schools in Philadelphia and others addressed the meeting.

The Citizens' Committee of the Thirteenth Ward sponsored a meeting on April 29, 1943, at the Varick A.M.E. Zion Church at 19th and Catherine Streets. The main speaker was Adam Clayton Powell, Jr., New York City Councilman and preacher, who in the past has reportedly cooperated closely with Communists. He made a highly militant speech, ending his address, "It is better to die fighting for freedom than to live in slavery." Other prominent leaders in the Philadelphia area spoke.

The Committee for the Formation of a Mixed Regiment, made up of such organizations as the National Association for the Advancement of Colored People, has recently been organized in the Philadelphia area. It was reported that the Young Communist League of Philadelphia, however, was the motivating force behind the movement. A meeting was sponsored by it April 27, 1943, which was attended by approximately eighty persons, 25 per cent of whom were Negroes. Various speakers were introduced by James Morgan, a Negro member of the Young Communist League, who acted as chairman. The speakers, including Angelo Herndon, reported Communist, spoke against discrimination and segregation in the Armed Forces.

The North Philadelphia Citizens' League is reportedly sponsored by the North Philadelphia Civic League. It sponsored a meeting on June 13, 1943, at the McDowell Community Church, 21st and Columbia Avenue, Philadelphia, at which there were only approximately twenty persons present. Dr. John K. Rice, a Negro, was chairman, while Dr. John W. Shirley was one of the main speakers. He is said to have related instances involving discrimination against Negroes and referred to them in a highly colored manner, speaking in a militant way.

The Interracial Fellowship with headquarters at 1431 Brown Street, Philadelphia, was organized under the auspices of the Committee on Race Relations of the Society of Friends. It has supported a program of nonviolence, direct action as a means of breaking down barriers of discrimination and segregation.

The Emblem Club, an organization begun early in 1943, has in its ranks some of the outstanding Negro leaders in Philadelphia. It has sponsored meetings at which outstanding Negro leaders have agitated for the Negro cause, among whom have been A. Philip Randolph, leader of the March on Washington Movement, and Dr. Charles H. Wesley of Wilberforce University.

The March on Washington Movement, while it does not have an active unit in the Philadelphia area, is said to have been represented on several occasions by A. Philip Randolph, its leader, who has made several public speeches in the area. Various pamphlets and publications of the organization have been distributed in this area.

The Federation of Negro Women's Clubs has been organized in the Philadelphia area, consisting of approximately twenty clubs with about two hundred members. The purpose is to combine in a federated union the various clubs of Negro women for the purpose of advancement of Negroes, and, further, for the purpose of gaining greater political power.

The Pyramid Club, made up of Negro professional and businessmen, was organized for the purpose of establishing a social club to foster and develop and advance the social and economic well-being of the Negro citizens.

A Colored United Service Organization was opened during the latter part of March, 1943, at 510 South Broad Street. It is said that this has been the scene of considerable trouble, including fights between Negro members of the Armed Forces. According to a confidential source of information, a white policeman was unfortunately assigned there to maintain order, which assignment was resented by the sponsors and patrons of the organization. This officer was subjected to considerable abuse, whereupon a colored policeman was sent there for the purpose of keeping order. This action was also criticized. It is further alleged that there is a bitter feeling existing between

Negro members of different Armed Forces who appear there and, further, that liquor is too much in evidence. It should also be noted that several of the Negro leaders in Philadelphia objected to the establishment of the all Negro unit of the USO on the ground that it was segregation.

The North Philadelphia Civic League has been organized for several years and is led by its President, Dr. John K. Rice, a Negro dentist. The organization is said to have approximately one thousand members, although only fifty are active. Its original purpose was to work for the improvement of the neighborhood in North Philadelphia, and its early activity consisted mainly of a struggle to obtain jobs for Negroes in local stores whose patronage was almost entirely colored. Protest meetings, picketings and other mass activities were resorted to for the furtherance of their desire. It is alleged that there is some possible affiliation with Communist forces, inasmuch as the meetings, according to informants, are of a Communist type. At a meeting on May 25, 1943, the President of the organization brought up a petition given him by members of the Communist Party seeking the sponsorship of the League in the Communist Party's fight to obtain positions for Negroes as conductors with the Philadelphia Transit Company. While there were objections from the persons in attendance, Rice, the President, indicated he felt it would not be detrimental for the League to affiliate itself with a cause sponsored by the Communist Party. Numerous other meetings have been held by this organization at which, it is said, militant speeches were made, especially by Dr. Shirley and Dr. Rice.

Relations in Industrial Plants

There are being set out hereinafter certain instances of controversies and arguments arising over the question of Negro employment in national defense industries which appear to portray the situation as it exists in this area. It is noted that reports reflect that most of the agitational activities with regard to employment of Negroes in national defense industries are being carried on by individuals or groups who are not known at the present time to have any connection with the Communist Party, and by possible Communist Party front organizations.

An example of Communist Party maneuvering is reflected in an instance where the Communist Party made desperate efforts to place a Negress in a plant. It is reported that a Communist organizer in West Philadelphia told a Negress to call a Mrs. Anna Brown of the United Office and Professional Workers of America who would place her in the General Electric Company's plant. The following day the Negress communicated with an individual at Communist Party Headquarters and stated that she would start work on Monday if everything went well.

On the following Monday the woman is stated to have told the individual previously contacted at Communist Party headquarters that she had not been hired. She was then instructed to get in touch with the organizer for the United Electrical Radio and Machine Workers Union. Later, the Negress recontacted the individual in Communist Party headquarters and advised that she had been told that Negro girls were to be the next ones hired and the person she had spoken to had accused the Negroes of raising a rumpus and appearing to take over the office when they wanted to get a job.

The individual at Party headquarters advised the Negress to get in touch with a known Negro Communist who was to bring the matter up at a meeting that same evening. It was later reported that the union organizer became angry because the Negress and two other colored girls had gone over the union's head and took their troubles directly to the Fair Employment Practices Committee without seeing the organizer. Subsequently the Negress advised the individual at Communist Party headquarters that she had received a letter from James W. Ford, national Negro leader in the Communist Party concerning the matter. It is to be noted that this same person made application for a position at the Frankford Arsenal.

A complaint arose regarding the Frankford Arsenal in the Philadelphia area, regarding the handling of fourteen Negro girls employed by the Arsenal alleged to have been segregated after which they were discharged. The dispute is stated to have culminated on July 23, 1942. The girls are said to have been employed as shell inspectors and were discharged when the union protested their transfer to a box factory operated by the Arsenal located several miles away. The union, the United Federal Workers of America, CIO, stated that the action constituted segregation.

Concerning the aforementioned situation it has been reported that at the same time efforts were being made by the United Federal Workers of America, Arsenal Local 190, to organize the Frankford Arsenal. The Union made no substantial headway in its attempt and at the same time its organizers were under suspicion. One was stated to have been formerly employed at the Philadelphia Navy Yard, but had been investigated there and had been discharged because of Communist activities. Another, **Anne Wharton,** was unable to produce proof of citizenship and consequently had not been permitted to enter the yard. One Abraham Sturcaky Endler, secretary of the Local, is stated to have been investigated and discharged from the Arsenal in the month of July because of his Communist activities.

Information received concerning racial conditions at the Frankford Arsenal reflected in previous years it had employed five per cent Negroes as compared with the Negro population in Philadelphia, estimated to have been 13½ per cent of the entire population. At the present time, however, it is said the Arsenal employs 2,200 Negroes out of a total of 19,250 employees, corresponding with the percentage of Negroes in the population in that area. It is stated that most of them, however, are employed as laborers, doing heavy and unpleasant work for the most part. For several years, it is reported, there have been Negro apprentices at the Frankford Arsenal learning to do machine work. Some are employed as draftsmen, others as guards, and some as machinists at the present time. In addition, a great many Negro girls have been hired recently to do assembly work. These girls are mostly still considered apprentices. They are stated to be working together with white girls completely integrated and doing the same work. It has also been reported that recently the Arsenal has been visited by various representatives of Negro groups and that these have, according to a confidential source of information, expressed satisfaction in the manner in which the Negro problem is being handled at the Arsenal.

Another set of circumstances in connection with the Frankford Arsenal has been reported, reflecting that recently it was desired at that plant to employ a number of girls to be trained as sub-inspectors. The Civil Service register had been depleted and consequently the registration of mechanical apprentices totaling one hundred fifty persons was called for at that plant. Of the one hundred fifty, it was found that one hundred twenty-six were Negro girls. Some of them were employed as sub-inspectors. After a trial period a number of them were found to lack the capacity for sub-inspectors and rather than discharge them, they were transferred to a school to be taught the trade of box making. Seventeen girls were transferred in all, all being Negroes. According to the informant, this was purely a coincidence because the group from which they were originally chosen were practically all Negroes. It is stated that before they were put to work, learning box making, they were told that this was an opportunity for women to start woodworking trade. They were not told that they had failed to make the grade as inspectors and upon being asked questions, all appeared to be satisfied. While they were being trained, however, it was found that they were being allegedly "stirred by the National Association for the Advancement of Colored People."

The President of the local branch of the National Association for the Advancement of Colored People was called to the Arsenal and asked to observe the training school. He is stated to have been satisfied. Prior to this it is stated, however, that complaints had been made to Major Good by Reginald Johnson of the War Manpower Commission, Philadelphia Region War Production Board, who complained that discrimination, segregation and general mistreatment of the Negro race existed in the Arsenal.

During the course of the training, it was stated, the Negro girls, whose attitude was formerly good, seemed to lose interest and acted like martyrs, and are stated to have become inefficient. It was said that after six weeks of training it was found that the entire group was producing only fifty per cent of what was expected of them and that their attitudes were all bad, so all of them were discharged, but without prejudice.

The same source of information has referred instances of racial trouble involving the Electric Storage Battery Company in Philadelphia which maintains two plants there. One plant is stated to have employed Negroes for many years, at least since the first World War, although the average employment is said to have dropped somewhat during the years because of resignations. Recently the company is stated to have awarded, as is customary, gold watches to several 25-year employees, and one of these was a Negro. The company is said to be making efforts at the present time to increase the number of Negro employees, but does not expect to use them on production work, since the company is afraid that the public will not have confidence in its product if it becomes known that Negroes are used in its production. It has been stated that in 1937 the company opened a battery plant in Dallas, Texas, and made a poll of its dealers at that time, with the result that it became convinced that it could not hire Negroes to work in that plant on production work.

With reference to this company, it has been stated that additional Negroes have been hired at one of the plants, all of whom have been used for maintenance purposes. Separate accommodations for comfort and rest have been set up for them. The United Electrical Radio and Machine Workers Union, CIO, has organized both plants of this company and following the public endorsement by the Congress of Industrial Organizations of Negro employment in defense industries, the particular local of the plant also endorsed such employment. Yet, the local is said to have told the plant that trouble might occur if the white employees and the Negroes were permitted to use the same locker room, that it would avoid trouble if the employment of Negroes was not made so extensively. In May, 1943, it is alleged that difficulties were encountered by the management as regards Negro employment. It is said that in one department where Negroes had already been employed, arrangements were made to place additional Negroes there and to have them use the same locker facilities as the white employees. This is said to have resulted in a flare-up among the white employees and a short work stoppage in the department.

Information has been received to the effect that the regional representative of the Third Regional Labor Supply Committee of the War Production Board has been changed. The former representative, a Negro, served until the early part of 1942 when he is reported to have acted improperly on one occasion. This occasion is said to have arisen over a plant involved in hiring and employing about 30 per cent Negroes, which desired to employ additional help to raise the proportion of Negroes to one-third. The former representative is stated to have insisted that the percentage of Negroes be increased to one half of the total employed. The employer is said to have protested and the representative was transferred from the Philadelphia area. The replacement representative is stated to be an ideologist and is unduly aggressive in his manners and demands so that he has become disliked by many of the people with whom he comes into contact. At some plants, it is stated, where his demands have been refused, he has evidently given up. At other plants, however, where efforts are made to compromise with these demands, it is stated that this individual has become very insistent so that he has hurt his own cause.

Several other instances in this area have been reported, reflecting that the tension among employees has risen over the employment of Negroes in certain departments of manufacturing plants engaged in national defense work. In these instances, it appears that the companies are endeavoring to employ Negroes, however, the white employees do not desire to work with them. Active in at least one of these instances of trouble in agitating for more help for the Negro, is a Communist Party front organization, the National Negro Congress.

On May 26, 1942, it was announced that the Sun Shipbuilding and Dry Dock Company, Chester, Pennsylvania intended to employ 9,000 Negroes in the new north yard at Chester. It was stated that about 2,500 were to be employed at first, and others were to be trained and added. It was said that white supervisors were to be used at first but that Negro supervisors were to take over as soon as they had been trained and upgraded. With reference to this policy it was said that neither the company nor the Congress of Industrial Organizations had any objection to the employing of Negroes in the plant and that the C.I.O. had given its official sanction. It was also said that the company was desiring to employ Negroes who applied for positions because they needed the additional manpower.

It has been reported that subsequent to the announcement of the company's policy with regard to the new yard, various individuals, newspapers and organizations among the Negroes expressed different shades of opinion. It was said that the more conservative of them voiced approval since the new shipyard opened a new field for Negroes because it gives them additional opportunities. It was said that the more radical elements, including the Communist Press, however, complained bitterly over the new shipyard since they termed it another form of segregation.

In this connection, it has been reported that on the evening of June 12, 1942, the Communist Party held a meeting at Columbia Hall, 345 Cuspy Street, Chester, Pennsylvania, with the chairman, one W. Harry Heller, Communist Party organizer of Delaware County, Wilmington, Delaware, opening the meeting, in the name of the Communist Party and addressing those in attendance as "we of the Communist Party." Heller is stated, on behalf of the Communist Party, to have endorsed the employment of Negroes in the Sun Shipyard, but be berated the public relations director as a capitalist representing interests which gained huge profits at the expense of the working man and spoke vehemently against the segregation of Negroes in the new yard. Other speeches were made including the urging of a second front, the urging of protests against the action of the Attorney General in the Bridges case, the urging of protests against discrimination against Negroes and statements in support of the President in the war effort.

In the early part of 1943 a report was received concerning the activities of some of the Negro employees at the Sun Shipbuilding Company, particularly at the north yard in Chester, Pennsylvania. According to the source of information, many of the Negro employees in this particular yard, where there are approximately three thousand, live in Philadelphia and must necessarily return to that place by train leaving Chester at 3:14 p.m. It is alleged that they have been causing trouble on the train by their activities, such as mobilizing [monopolizing] seats by the windows and gambling.

It is to be noted that reports have also been received that Negro employees of this company and allegedly a great many Negro resident[s] of Chester, Pennsylvania, have been carrying knives, some of which have been made from broken hack saws. According to the source of information, the employees of the company do not require large blades for their work. Reports have been received in this area that there has been an unprecedented sale of long-bladed knives, particularly in the fall of 1942. These reports, however, were proved unfounded, inasmuch as the type of knife referred to (a switchblade) has not been obtainable for some time in view of its being on the priority list. It is reported, however, that an unprecedented demand for this type of knife has been noticed, although requests were not fulfilled because of the shortage. It is possible, according to the source of information, that the large number of requests received in recent months may result from the shortage of this type of knife, which predominantly is requested by Negroes, sailors, soldiers and shipyard workers. It is also alleged that workers need large pocketknives for their work at the Sun Shipbuilding Company.

An article appearing in the "Daily Worker" for May 25, 1942, written by Carl Reeve, Education Secretary of the Communist Party, Eastern Pennsylvania, concerns the alleged Jim Cro[w] condition in Coatesville and in the Lucind Steel Mill in Coatesville, Pennsylvania, where 1,500 Negroes are employed. A similar article appeared in the same issue of the "Daily Worker" relating to the practices of the Bethlehem Steel Mills at Steelton, Pennsylvania.

Report of the Pennsylvania State Temporary Commission

A temporary commission to study the conditions of the urban colored population was created by the State Legislature in 1939, and in January, 1943, a voluminous report with a brief summary and recommendations was made by this commission. In this connection, it is to be noted that the chairman of the commission was approached by a Communist Party functionary in the Philadelphia area with the request that he, the chairman, collaborate with the Party. This was refused by the chairman, who stated that although the Party preached interracial and personal tolerance, its members were extremely intolerant. Since the refusal on the part of the chairman to collaborate, the Party has not attempted to contact the chairman or the commission.

There follows digests of information appearing in the report of the commission, broken down into subsections:

Housing

The Negro population in the State is 99 per cent non-farming, and 85.1 per cent of the Negroes in the State are tenants. This is above the national average, since nationally 22.8 per cent of Negro-occupied dwellings were in 1940 owner-occupied, whereas in Pennsylvania only 14.9 per cent were owner-occupied.

Approximately three-fourths of all Negro-occupied dwellings were substandard. Negro housing, particularly in defense areas, is also more scarce than average, since, with the exception of Pittsburgh, there has been little provision for defense or war housing for Negroes.

The Commission recommends private and public subsidy for improved housing conditions and housing developments, enforcement of the housing sanitation laws, impartial application of policing and fire patrol measures in order to effect adequate decent housing for the lowest income groups.

Health

Negroes generally and those in Pennsylvania particularly are ill-fed, ill-clothed and ill-housed. As a consequence, the vitality of the Negro population is so low that it is far more susceptible to disease than the general population. The results are accentuated by ignorance, bad health habits and an unusually high use of home and patent remedies, and as a consequence Negro morbidity and mortality rates are disproportionately high.

Negro death rates in Pennsylvania exceed national Negro death rates and are even higher than those of Southern Negroes. Conditions have improved in the last thirty years, but even now Negro death rates are much higher than those of whites. In 1910, the death rate for Negroes in Pennsylvania was 1.55 times that of whites. In 1920, it was 1.56; in 1930, it was 1.53; and in 1940, it was 1.36.

A recommendation is made that additional financial assistance be given the Negro-staffed hospitals, but it is especially necessary to break down the restrictions and limitations presently in force against the admission of Negro patients to the other hospitals and the use of Negro physicians and nurses.

Recreation

A recommendation is made for closer cooperation between State support and private institutions and the creation of recreation facilities largely centering about the school system.

Crime and Delinquency

This section starts with the statement, "Negro delinquent and criminal rates range from two to nearly eight times their proportion in the general population. Taken per 100,000 population, the rate of law violation of Pennsylvania Negroes exceeds that of Negroes throughout the nation. . . . Racial discrimination in the administration of justice tends to promote law violation among Negroes. . . . Neither the number of arrests and the alleged reasons therefor, nor the number of convictions and severity thereof, nor yet the prison sentences afford racially a proportionately accurate picture of the volume of Negro crime and delinquency. . . . With the exception of crimes against the person or property of whites, law enforcement involving Negroes is often too lax. . . . In nearly every municipality in the State, 'official protection' in certain forms of vice is the most frequent and often the only 'political plum' given most Negro politicians. . . . As compared with mixed and all white neighborhoods, all Negro neighborhoods have an excessive number of taprooms, unsupervised poolrooms, bawdy houses, gambling places, 'bootleg liquor places,' and similar establishments, which either tend to promote law violations or are themselves illegal.

". . . In many instances, officers of the law have themselves been ruthless and illegal . . . without search warrants and often without sufficient evidence of suspicion or of provocation, policemen enter Negro homes, hotels and other Negro-occupied dwellings and make mass arrests.

". . . In the case of 'official protection,' the 'third degree, and 'cold storage,' the evidence seems to indicate that although both races suffer, Negro citizens suffer unequally therefrom. . . . The hatred and disrespect for the law resulting therefrom are always serious and enduring. They tend greatly to encourage recidivism."

The report points out that a great influx of Negroes from outside the State has further accentuated the crime wave. The white population increased 9 per cent from 1920 to 1930, while the Negro population increased 51.5 per cent in that period. In 1930, 33.9 per cent of the Negro population was born in the State as compared with 79 per cent of the white population; 65 per cent of the Negro population was born in other states, and 1 per cent was foreign born.

The migrants fell heir to established practices of discrimination, and in many cases gave occasion for the crystallization of discriminatory practice. They were crowded into substandard housing areas; frequently, moreover, they were transposed from the rural Southern area to an urban Eastern area and were poorly adjusted.

The conclusion is, therefore, that the high percentage of urban and nonfarm residents was conducive to a greater frequency of crime. Another aggravating circumstance is the fact that Negroes are employed in the more menial, poorer paying jobs and are far more subject to unemployment. This gives rise to a lack of self-respect and community respect which makes for additional law violation.

The conclusion is reached that the excessive crime rate is primarily due to a general social maladjustment and that "full social justice and citizenship, suitable employment, proper recreational facilities, better housing and related improvements will result in the eradication of excessive rates of Negro crime and delinquency."

Education

The percentage of Negroes between the ages of five and twenty attending school has been increasing steadily since 1900. Negro pupils, however, tend to withdraw from school at a rate exceeding that of the general population, particularly as the Negro pupils reach noncompulsory school age.

In 1940, of persons twenty-five years of age and over, there were seven times as many Negroes proportionately as native whites who had no schooling. More than one-fourth of the Negro population twenty-five years of age and over had less than a fourth grade education. About three times as many native whites as Negroes proportionately had completed high school, and about four times as many had completed college.

Except for the few educational institutions whose student bodies are exclusively colored, there are less than twenty Negroes teaching regular subjects in the secondary schools and institutions for higher learning in Pennsylvania.

Recommendation is made that an equitable number of qualified Negroes be placed on the faculties; that the public school curriculum be revised to include subjects such as Consumer Education, Public Welfare, and Public Administration, and Inter-Cultural Education. Adult education should be extended. Schools should institute a program to discover and treat predelinquents. The colleges and universities in the State have been too conventional and have followed and promoted prejudice by thought and action. "So far as Negroes and all Americans are concerned, education must teach and practice the Democracy for which we are fighting; otherwise, we may win the war, but lose the peace."

Employment

* * * * * * *

"Moreover, the Negro rate of unemployment has been far in excess of that of the general population of the State. However, in 1939, the Negro rate of employment began to improve, so that by March 30, 1940, the date on which the census was completed, 4.09 per cent of the total persons employed in the State were Negroes. However, Negroes were 5.19 per cent of the total labor force and 4.70 per cent of the total population.

". . . Negro males were only 3.44 per cent of the total male persons employed, whereas Negro women were 6.05 per cent of the total female persons employed. In 1940, Negroes were only 2.76 per cent of the total employees in the industrial concerns in the State. . . . Beginning October, 1940, the volume of Negro employment began to increase very rapidly. Today it compares very favorably with the general population.

"Prior to 1940, Negro women were employed in a highly disproportionate rate as compared with white women, and most of these were employed in domestic and personal service fields. Even with increased employment of Negroes, most of them are not employed in industry, and those who are employed are generally in unskilled and semiskilled fields.

"The War Production Training Program has been of some assistance, but although Negroes are 4.70 per cent of the total population, during the period from January 1, 1941, to June, 1942, only 1.49 per cent of the trainees registered in supplementary courses were Negroes. Only 1.1 per cent of the 1003 trainees interviewed during the period from July, 1940, to November, 1941, were engaged in the employment for which their respective defense training courses prepared them. There was little significant improvement until May, 1942; thereafter, there was much improvement."

The report quotes figures of the United States Employment Service covering the period from 1938 to July, 1942, showing that at no time did the Service succeed in placing as many as 10 per cent of the skilled Negro applicants, and even during the end of 1941 and early 1942, only 1.10 per cent of all Negroes placed were given skilled jobs.

During the past decade in many cases relief grants have been more profitable than wages. NYA and NPA workers numbered more than twice their ratio of the general population and have been on relief rolls in numbers approximately five times the ratio to the general population. For certain periods during the past decade, more than one half of the income of the State's Negro population was derived from public and private charity.

As a result of employment due to the war, grants of charity have been reduced, living costs have increased, and the income of the Negro population is still comparatively low, and the conclusion is reached that current earnings are not sufficient to enable the Negroes to raise their standard of living to that of the general population.

Pittsburgh Field Division

Various sources of information who come in contact with the Negroes in this area have advised they have no definite knowledge of foreign-inspired agitation existing among the Negroes in Pittsburgh, Pennsylvania. However, they have advised of agitation of a domestic nature prevalent among the Negroes already established for the purpose of bettering conditions of the Negro people in the United States.

Reports have been received to the effect that Negroes in this area are in the sense apathetic to the war as a result of political and economic factors and that the claim of injustice is further based upon alleged discrimination in private industry and in the Armed Forces.

The Negro newspaper, the "Pittsburgh Courier," a weekly publication, which has a circulation of approximately 200,000, is published at Pittsburgh, Pennsylvania. An examination of various issues of this newspaper since December, 1942, reflects many articles manifesting the present national agitation among the Negroes.

Numerous reports have been received relative to individual Negroes making statements which outwardly reflect a sympathy for the Axis powers. Investigations are being continued relative to such reports to determine the actual sympathies of the individuals involved. In none, however, has there been substantiating or corroborating information reflecting organized subversive activity.

Early in the Summer of 1942 an organization known as the Citizens Coordinating Committee was formed in the Pittsburgh, Pennsylvania, area. Its purpose was to seek "an adequate place in the war effort" for Negroes. It also concerns itself with the question of Negroes in the Armed Forces, in the government agencies, as well as Negro housing. It is made up reportedly of representatives of more than forty trade unions, civic and fraternal organizations, both Negro and white. On September 27, 1942, the organization held a mass meeting at the Soldiers and Sailors Memorial Hall in Pittsburgh. A Negro by the name of Samuel Parr presided at the meeting. Seated on the rostrum were Homer F. Brown, member of the Pennsylvania State Assembly; one M. Moff, Secretary of the Urban League in Pittsburgh; Fred Holmes, President of the National Negro Congress in Pittsburgh; B. F. Gibson, Secretary of the National Negro Congress; Judge Musmanno of Common Pleas Court, Allegheny County, Pennsylvania; Jacob Adler; a Dr. Greenwalder, Personnel Director of Kaufman's Department Store; and a Professor Watson of the University of Pittsburgh. Speeches at the meeting dealt with the right of Negroes to more adequate housing, better employment and alleged instances of discrimination and police brutality. The National Association of Manufacturers is also said to have been assailed by a speaker for not providing Negroes with adequate employment in defense industries. There were approximately 800 persons present at this meeting of whom 50 reportedly were white persons.

The organization has a membership of approximately 55 people representing such organizations as the YMCA, the National Association for the Advancement of Colored People, Governmental agencies, and fraternal and religious groups. It should be pointed out that activities on the part of members of the National Negro Congress have been apparent in this organization. The National Negro Congress is a Communist front organization. The organization has the following leaders: Ben Careathers, Chairman of the Communist Party in Pittsburgh; B. F. Gibson, secretary of the National Negro Congress in Pittsburgh; and Fred Holmes, President of the National Negro Congress there. It is further reported that Careathers controls the Committee entirely, the Executive Committee of which meets at Careathers' store, and that the organization follows the Communist Party line.

In this area there has been recently organized a group known as the Equal Rights Movement. The leading figure in this organization is also Ben Careathers. At a meeting held on November 2, 1942, at the Odd Fellows Hall at Washington, Pennsylvania, Careathers is reported to have made a speech in which he inferred that if the

United States does not give the Negro what he wants the Negro will cooperate with the Japanese. There were approximately 50 persons in attendance at the meeting.

There are several anti-white, if not pro-Japanese, groups active in the Pittsburgh area, including the African Moslem Welfare Society of America, the Moorish Science Temple and the Universal Negro Improvement Association.

The African Moslem Welfare Society was originally incorporated under the laws of Pennsylvania in 1928. It has had public meetings on an average of twice a week and it is reported that many private meetings are held in the homes of various members. According to informants, leaders of the organization use every available opportunity to make speeches in favor of the Japanese government and strike out viciously against the United States. It is further alleged that some of the leaders have been calling at homes in the colored section of Pittsburgh advising there is a kindred blood relationship between the Japanese and the Negroes. They also reportedly state the white man has fooled the colored people and cannot be trusted. In addition, there are indications of possible collusions and fraud on the part of organizers of the group. Among the various places where the organization has held meetings are 10½ Townsend Street, 115 Continental Street, Homewood, and the Winco Club, Homewood, all Pittsburgh. There are approximately 12 individuals who are active in speaking for this group, some of whom retain their American names while others bear Mohammedan or Moorish names. There are approximately 50 individuals whose identities are known who attend the meetings and take part in the activities of the organization. It is to be noted, however, there appears to be some dissension among the members, some claiming to be solely interested in the Moslem teachings, while others assume anti-American and anti-white stands. Numerous instances of pro-Japanese sentiment have been reported in connection with this group.

While various open meetings are held at one of the several addresses listed above, it is also known that private meetings are held in the homes of the more militant members. It is at these meetings that the more radical statements are made.

It has been ascertained recently that the Moslems in the Pittsburgh area operate in four distinct groups. Two of the groups operate under the charter granted to the African Welfare Society of America; the third meets at 115 Continental Street and is headed by James Jemel and Frank May, both Negroes, and the fourth, headed by Elijah Martin, holds meetings at the home of Martin or at the Winco Club in the Homewood district in Pittsburgh.

The Moslems meeting at 10½ Townsend Street, Pittsburgh, Pennsylvania, are led by Mohamad Jalajel, a naturalized Arab. There are also indications of a group of Moslems meeting in Braddock, Pennsylvania, allegedly under the leadership of Walter Bellenger. The group headed by Frank May meeting at 115 Continental Street on occasions has no more than nine members present. In this group there were indications of dissension over May's reported unpatriotic statements and in March 1943 the group reportedly disintegrated. However, in May 1943 an attempt was made to reorganize the particular group formerly under May and there were also indications that Jemel was looking toward reorganizing the group. May, however, at the time reappeared at the meeting. Investigations concerning this group and their un-American leanings are being continued.

There is active in the Pittsburgh area a temple of the organization known as the Moorish Science Temple of America which allegedly has approximately 200 members with a former membership of approximately 700. The leader of this group is one C. Johnson Bey, 311 Burrows Street, Apartment 1006. This group follows the dictates of Noble Drew Ali, leader in the national headquarters of this particular faction in Chicago, Illinois. The other faction, it will be recalled, is under the leadership of "Colonel" C. Kirkman Bey. Investigation to date has failed to reveal un-American or subversive activities in this particular temple. However, one member recently was arrested for failure to register. He claimed this was through negligence and subsequently registered and prosecution was declined. Another member has filed claim as a conscientious objector under the dictates of his Islamic beliefs.

There is a branch of the Universal Negro Improvement Association in the Pittsburgh area which meets at 2157 Center Avenue with a usual attendance of approximately 20 members. It is said that at least two members of this organization in Pittsburgh when they speak at its meetings utter anti-American remarks to the effect that the Government of the United States is a white man's government and not that of a Negro, and, further, that the Negro should follow the "government" of Marcus Garvey. Recent warning at a meeting held on June 6, 1943, by this group was made to the effect that the Federal Bureau of Investigation was "watching" the Universal Negro Improvement Association.

In the Braddock, Pennsylvania, area there is said to be another unit of this organization under the leadership of one James Smith, the meetings of which are said to have the attendance of approximately 12 persons. Investigation concerning this, as well as the foregoing unit, is being continued.

The National Association for the Advancement of Colored People in the Pittsburgh area is said to have three officers who are Communists—the Treasurer, the Secretary and the Sergeant-at-Arms. There are, of course, other branches in the surrounding area in Pennsylvania, covered by the Pittsburgh Field Division. In this connection, the Clairton, Pennsylvania, branch is said to have recently filed suit against a theater in that city for its attempt to exclude Negroes. Reportedly the organization had Negroes of light skins purchase tickets and gain admittance to the theater immediately after which Negroes of darker skin were refused admittance with the excuse that the theater was crowded and no seats were available. There are, according to the latest reports, approximately 1,700 members of the National Association for the Advancement of Colored People in the Pittsburgh area, a recent membership campaign resulting in 235 new members.

Perhaps the most active branch of the Communist Party in the Pittsburgh area is the "Hill Branch" headed by Ben Careathers, previously identified. It is located at 1800 Center Avenue and has affiliated itself with the Citizens Coordinating Committee of Pittsburgh. Its current activity with regard to the Negro situation is that of making an effort to obtain jobs for Negroes in public utilities in the Pittsburgh area. There are also indications that the Communist Party and this particular branch are endeavoring to infiltrate the Negro Elks organization in the Pittsburgh area. The organization, of course, assumes the general Communist Party line and more particularly has adopted a program of endeavoring to fight for the employment of Negro women in war industries, to organize anti–John L. Lewis groups, and to organize a drive to increase Negro voting power. The leading figure in all of the steps of this program is Ben Careathers.

Mention is to be made hereinafter of the "Pittsburgh Courier" and its organizational setup. It is to be recalled that the paper is published in Pittsburgh, Pennsylvania, and has a good size circulation in the area.

A recent incident occurred at Camp Shenango, Pennsylvania. It had its origin in a fight between a small number of Negro and white soldiers at a post exchange at the camp on June 11, 1943. A rock battle ensued and at approximately 9:45 P.M. of the same night military police declared the white and Negro areas at the camp to be segregated. In connection with this trouble, it is reported that a supply room of the 4th Battalion (Negro) of a regiment at Camp Shenango was broken into at 9:45 P.M. on June 11, 1943, and 11 of approximately 30 Garand rifles were extracted along with an unknown amount of the supply of ammunition. Later, on the same night, shooting broke out and one Negro soldier was killed, two seriously injured, while seven, believed to be both Negro and white, were hospitalized. There is no indication that the shooting resulted from the theft of the guns in the supply room of the 4th Battalion and reportedly the injuries inflicted were done by white military police. No indications were reported of any organized subversive activity in connection with the affair.

Providence Field Division

The Negro population in the State of Rhode Island as of 1940 was reported to be approximately 11,024, the majority of which were located in the Cities of Pawtucket, Cranston and Providence.

A source of information, a Negro, who is active in the program to better his own race, and who is stated to be conversant with the Negro situation throughout the State of Rhode Island, has advised he is unaware of any propagandizing attempt among the Negroes which might be attributed to pro-Axis or Communist sources. This source considers the Negroes of Rhode Island to be relatively conservative in thought and passive in outlook as a result of their economic situation which is considered better than that of other sections of the country. Several years ago, it is reported, Communists endeavored to organize a local chapter of the National Negro Congress but at the present time this organization is not active. The same source of information advised that Negroes in this area have shown little interest in Communist Party activity.

Only one Negro newspaper is published in this area, namely, the Providence Chronicle, which is said to be controlled by the Boston Chronicle, published in Boston, Massachusetts. This paper is considered conservative in its outlook and is stated to be edited by a Negro of very conservative views. Two other Negro newspapers have a comparatively large circulation in this area. They are the Afro-American, published in Baltimore, Maryland, and the Chicago Defender, published in Chicago, Illinois.

Unverified statements have reportedly been made by an unknown white man to the effect that the Negroes would be better off under Japanese domination. The person supplying this information, however, was unable to supply specific information concerning these statements.

With regard to Communist Party activity in this area, it has been reported that approximately three years ago a Communist Party leader contacted a prominent Negro professional man for his support in setting up a local Negro Communist organization. However, the efforts of this individual and other Communists among the Rhode Island Negroes are stated to have met with no success.

No instances other than the incident of the unidentified white man uttering pro-Japanese statements have been reported reflecting pro-Axis propaganda among the Negroes in this area. [*100-135-56*]

St. Louis Field Division

Information received concerning agitation among the Negroes in this area reflects that the Negroes are restless and are pressing demands for equal opportunities with white people in industry. The 1940 census credits St. Louis proper with 108,765 Negroes and 706,795 whites, or a percentage of 13.3 Negroes. Informants who have close connection with the Negro population in this area either advise they have heard of no un-American agitation among the Negroes or that there was no existing foreign-inspired agitation among the Negroes in that area.

Perhaps the most active Negro organization in the City of St. Louis is the March on Washington Movement unit. According to a statement made by its leader, T. D. McNeal, in the latter part of January 1943 there were more than 4,000 members in this unit. The officers of this group, besides the Chairman, are Layton Weston, Assistant Director; Nita Blackwell, Secretary; Jordan Chambers, Treasurer; Executive Board members: William Smith, N. A. Sweets, James E. Cook and Mrs. Thelma Grant.

Not only has this unit followed the policies laid down by the national organization but it has stressed considerably the obtaining of additional jobs for Negroes and advocating nonsegregation. There are also indications that the unit cooperates with the Fellowship of Reconciliation, especially in using the non-violent civil disobedience technique. It also devotes much of its effort toward instances of alleged discrimination against Negroes in the St. Louis area, making militant demands of employers, et cetera, for improvements. The organization claims to have obtained 8,000 jobs for Negroes during the year 1942. As an example of this activity in this regard the unit sponsored a mass picketing of the United States Cartridge Company in St. Louis on June 20, 1942. It has been stated a result of this action was an amicable settlement of the demands made for the retention of Negro employees as well as an increase in the percentage of the number of them employed at this plant. On August 14, 1942, this unit sponsored a mass meeting at which the principal speaker was A. Philip Randolph, leader of the national organization. The general demands of the organization as well as militant speeches were made at the meeting. More than 8,000 people were in attendance.

The most recent mass meeting held by the St. Louis unit of this organization was attended by approximately 2,500 Negroes at which time a dramatic sketch was presented entitled "Moses and Pharaoh." This sketch portrayed the Negro people as being in the same plight as were the Israelites who were refused freedom by the Pharaoh. Various speeches were made including the main address by A. Philip Randolph.

Besides sponsoring large meetings, this organization holds periodic meetings to discuss local matters as well as the future activity of the St. Louis unit. Much of the time at these meetings is devoted to discussions as to how to obtain additional employment for Negroes in defense industries and how to secure employment of Negroes in public utilities, especially in the telephone company.

While there have been reports that the organizations known as the Moorish Science Temple of America and the Pacific Movement of the Eastern World were at one time active in the St. Louis area, there are no indications at the present time of these groups carrying on their activities. With regard to the latter organization, it is to be recalled that St. Louis has been the home of David Daniel Erwin who was at one time the principal speaker and organizer for the national organization. Erwin was arrested for his activities in this connection but subsequently released. According to informants, this action, however, had a decided effect in quelling the activities of any followers that Erwin may have had in the St. Louis area *[65-40879-202]*

At the present time Erwin is still residing in St. Louis where he is operating a barbecue stand.

There are in addition to the above-named organizations two chapters comprised of approximately 30 members of the Universal Negro Improvement Association. The headquarters of this organization is located at 2732 Delmar Street, St. Louis. There are no indications that either of these two groups is engaged in activities inimical to the best interests of this country. The two groups grew out of a split of the original chapter in 1930, the primary disagreement being among the officers. At that time there were approximately 500 members.

The only connection these chapters are said to have with the national headquarters of the Universal Negro Improvement Association is through the subscription to the magazine "The New Negro World." There have been no indications received of any pro-Japanese sentiments on the part of any of the present members; however, inquiries are being continued in view of the character of the national organization.

The Communist Party has also been active among the Negro population in this area. However, the extent of Negro membership in the Party in and around St. Louis is not believed to be large and it cannot be said that the Party has near the influence among Negroes in this area as does the local unit of the March on Washington Movement which, it is to be noted, the Party has condemned as a promoter of activities which would affect the war effort and the Party has loudly called for investigations to end discrimination allegedly existing in the area as well as called for the establishment of a joint Negro and white fair employment committee.

It is reported that the chapter of the National Association for the Advancement of Colored People in the St. Louis area has about 4,000 members. Its leader is Sidney

Redmond who serves as President and the headquarters of the chapter are at the office of Redmond and Espy, 2103 Market Street, which is described as the clearing house for all complaints. In this area the chapter reportedly wages a militant fight for civic rights for Negroes.

The St. Louis Urban League has been described more as a social agency for Negroes. It is said to have headquarters at 3017 Delmar, St. Louis, Missouri. According to reports, it has been active in cooperating with the March on Washington Movement unit.

The following information has been received concerning the circulation and type of various Negro newspapers in the St. Louis area:

1. "The St. Louis American": 11 North Jefferson; N. A. Sweets, Managing Editor; circulation about 5,000.
2. "St. Louis Argua": 2314 Market Street; J. B. Mitchell, Publisher; circulation about 22,000; said to have a racial editorial policy.
3. "Evening Whirl": 213 North Jefferson; Baron Ben Thomas, Publisher; described as a tabloid scandal sheet; circulation about 8,000.
4. "World Tattler": 11 North Jefferson; Dewey J. Johnson, Publisher; circulation about 5,000; described as a tabloid scandal sheet.
5. "Pittsburgh (Pennsylvania) Courier": Nationally circulated with circulation of about 6,000 in St. Louis; Mrs. Inge, 11 North Jefferson, is St. Louis Circulation Manager; said to have a racial editorial policy.
6. "Chicago (Illinois) Defender": Nationally-circulated with circulation of about 5,000 in St. Louis; Mrs. Inge, 11 North Jefferson, is St. Louis circulation manager; said to have a racial editorial policy.
7. "New York Amsterdam News": Published New York, New York, weekly; M. Henderson, 3400 Easton Avenue, St. Louis, distributor.

Several rumors have been reported to the effect that Negroes should not enlist in the Armed Forces. It is stated that the argument used is that the Negroes are being discriminated against and that the Japanese would treat them differently. However, no information has been received tending to verify the prevalence of statements or literature to this effect.

In the vicinity of Cape Girardeau, Missouri, information has been received that a local chapter of the National Association for the Advancement of Colored People has been sponsoring meetings in the vicinity although no indications have been received reflecting that there is any subversive influence in this particular group. At a meeting held on June 19, 1942, there were no indications of subversive activities. A source of information in this area has advised that there has always been unrest in that vicinity but there are no indications that the unrest is inspired by any un-American force. Several years ago a representative of the Pacific Movement of the Eastern World reportedly attempted to organize the Negroes in this area; however, there has been no evidence of any such activities for the past five years.

In the vicinity of Charleston, Missouri, there is a large Negro population. Except for an uprising over labor conditions in the vicinity of Wyatt, Missouri, in May 1942, it is reported that very little trouble has been caused by or among the Negroes there.

In Mississippi County, Missouri, there are no indications of un-American or foreign-inspired activities among the Negroes there. It is reported, however, that the Negroes in this community appear to feel that they are being underpaid for their work in the cotton fields and on a few occasions have attempted to organize themselves for the purpose of bettering working conditions.

Following the lynching of Cleo Wright in January, 1942, it was reported that a large number of Negroes left the Sunset Addition, a Negro section in Sikeston, Missouri, allegedly through fear of physical harm. In this connection, it is reported that shortly after the lynching an unusually large amount of guns and ammunition ha[d] been sold to the Negroes in this area. On the other hand, it was reported that white people there were the actual purchasers of the large amounts of ammunition.

In and around the area of Poplar Bluff, Missouri, there have been indications of unrest and it is said several meetings have been held among Negroes since the lynching of Wright. The identity of the persons organizing the meetings is not known but in the opinion of a source of information in this area the meetings were sponsored principally as a result of the fear element of the Negroes rather than through influence of foreign and subversive elements.

Reports were received during the latter part of 1942 that Negroes in the area of St. Louis, as well as in other parts of Missouri, were purchasing large amounts of firearms and shipping them to the East. These allegations were checked on through sources of information and confidential informants with negative results. No indications were received of any planned action in this regard. Inquiries which were also made in Cape Girardeau, Sikeston, Charleston, Wyatt and Caruthersville, Missouri, met with the same negative results.

In the area of Klondike, which is said to have approximately 6,000 Negro citizens living in it, it is said that the relationship between white and Negro inhabitants has been comparatively peaceful although a confidential source has stated that the community is regarded as an ideal spot for the introduction of un-American ideas and isms. It is said that there is a chapter of the National Association for the Advancement of Colored People with approximately 35 members. The Universal Negro Improvement Association is said to have a unit there with approximately 85 members.

In Wellston, Missouri (a suburb of St. Louis), there are approximately 5,000 Negroes, with a chapter of the National Association for the Advancement of Colored People having a membership of approximately 65. It is said that [the] relationship between white and Negro inhabitants there is peaceful and there has been no appearance of friction or racial conflict.

The population of Negro citizens in the Festus, Missouri, area is said to reach approximately 700. There has been, according to reports, recent agitation in this area for the equalization of teachers' salaries for Negro and white employees. A representative of the March on Washington Movement is said to be the backer of a court trial on the teacher-pay issue. A recent incident involving striking white employees at the Pittsburgh Plate Glass Company who struck because of the employment of Negroes by this company has reportedly added to ill feelings. It is further alleged that some Negroes in this area dislike the superintendent of schools whom they blame for the low salaries of Negro teachers.

Reports have been received concerning the Lemay area wherein the community is said to be predominantly white. It is said that trouble exists in this area as a result of the proximity to Jefferson Barracks and the Negro soldiers in training there. Allegations have been spread that Negroes, presumably soldiers, have molested white families and as a result anti-Negro sentiment is at a high pitch. It is said that residents have threatened violent action if incidents recur and are arming themselves.

The Webster Groves area, a suburb of St. Louis, has an estimated Negro population of 2,000. No Negro-white disturbances have been reported in this area and it is alleged the relationship between Negro and white inhabitants is peaceful. There is a chapter of the National Association for the Advancement of Colored People there with approximately 50 members.

In the area of Kirkwood, a suburb of St. Louis, it is said that cooperation and good will exist between the Negro and white inhabitants, the former numbering approximately 400.

In the Mississippi County area it is said that the Negroes there who allegedly are largely uneducated are discontented and that they would be an easy prey for Communism or any un-American project.

Springfield Field Division

In this area there are well over 300,000 Negroes, the majority of whom are located in and around East St. Louis, Illinois. In that particular area it is reported that during the depression the Communist Party gained somewhat in its following among the Negroes but when conditions became better the Negro population was regarded as having forgotten the Communist ideas that had been preached to them.

A source of information in this area has advised that practically every Negro in the East St. Louis area who desires work has it and that this is the easiest and quickest way to keep the Negroes appeased. The same source of information has advised that there is some dissatisfaction among Negroes with regard to the Selective Service program and that they feel they are not being drafted into the Army fast enough. Another phase of dissatisfaction is reflected in the refusal of unions to recognize the Negroes' rights of seniority and their failure to help the Negroes advance in industry.

An organization known as the Citizens Defense and Urban League Committee is reported to have been active in East St. Louis, Illinois, during the latter part of 1941. However, at the present time there are no indications that the organization is active. This organization, stated to have been comprised of outstanding Negroes of East St. Louis, promoted anti-discrimination and anti-prejudice measures for the Negroes. It also called for the participation of the Negro in the affairs of "the Church and the State." The organization advised that the Negro was going to demand his right and lawful place in the defense program and that "he desired the privilege of making the bullets that he is expected to shoot."

In the Alton, Illinois, area, information has been received that the United Mine Workers and unions affiliated with the CIO are stirring up trouble among the Negroes in that city. A source of information has advised that the instant situation is alarming and that it would take little to start a riot. The opinion has been expressed that the situation has been caused by unions endeavoring to organize the Negroes and at the time telling the Negroes that they are being mistreated and that if they joined the unions and work collectively they would be able to demand and obtain their rights.

Published in East St. Louis is the publication called The Crusader. Articles have appeared in this publication concerning the Negro situation in East St. Louis to the effect that Negroes have had some difficulty in securing national defense work in the community and similar articles. No indications, however, have been reported of any subversive activity on the part of this newspaper.

Also in the City of Alton is a branch of the National Association for the Advancement of Colored People. This branch is stated to be ultra-conservative and its main interest is the betterment of the colored race. No reports of subversive activities on the part of this branch have been reported.

In December of 1941, it was reported that a Robert Washington was organizing Negroes in and around Pulaski, Illinois, and urging them to become members of the Moorish Science Temple of America. Washington is stated to have advised prospective members that when the Japanese conquer the United States the Negroes will not be molested and, further, that the instant war is one between races in which the colored race will finally be victorious. This organization, however, is reported not to have been successful as the organizer was only able to obtain seven members. He is stated to have abandoned his activity when threatened by the State's Attorney in that area with an indictment for obtaining money under false pretenses. Washington was a follower of the section headed by C. Kirkman Bey in Chicago, Illinois.

It is reported that the East St. Louis area branch of the Pacific Movement of the Eastern World known as Unit No. 3, was at one time established at 1507 Hoover Street, East St. Louis. However, recent information received reflects that this group is reportedly inactive at the present time. On September 15, 1942, books, records, correspondence and other material pertinent to the Pacific Movement of the Eastern World, Incorporated, were seized by the Federal Bureau of Investigation from members and officers and branch organizations in East St. Louis, Illinois, under search warrant authorized by the United States Attorney for the Southern District of Illinois. In the material received it was indicated that at least some of the officers were definitely pro-Japanese. The records reflected that there were approximately two hundred members of this organization according to its membership book. The testimony and material obtained was presented to an investigative Federal Grand Jury at East St. Louis, Illinois, September 22, 1942 to September 29, 1942. On January 27, 1943, indictments were returned in the Federal Court District for Southern Illinois against the national president of the organization, General Lee Butler; the national advisor, David

Erwin; and one "John Doe," a Japanese said to have helped organize the group. The indictments charged violations of the Sedition Statutes and the Selective Training and Service Act of 1940, as amended. On June 15, 1943, the organization was fined by the Federal District Court in an amount of $1,000, while General Lee Butler was sentenced to serve two years and David Erwin sentenced to serve four years. This act is said to have caused a halt in the activities of the members, as well as the organization and it is said that the organization is practically defunct at the present time.

[*65-40879*]

Several reports have been received reflecting considerable racial tension in the East St. Louis area. No indications were reported of any organized or subversive activity in connection with the reports. In addition several individual and unrelated instances have been complained of in the East St. Louis area indicating militancy on the part of individual Negroes in the East St. Louis area. In no instance, however, was there anything shown reflecting a subversive connection.

Further inquiries made with regard to the Negro situation in the southern part of Illinois fail to reflect active subversive organizations in that area.

Washington Field Division

Among the groups active in varying degrees in this area was the Allah Temple of Islam which has also been known as the "Moslem". This organization resembled in many respects the Moorish Science Temple of America and was also active in the Chicago area. In May, 1942, various leaders of the organization in Washington were apprehended for violations of the Selective Training and Service Act of 1940, as amended, inasmuch as they had informed their members, including Negroes, that they were Moslems and according to the tenets of their religion were not required to fight in any war or to register in compliance with the law. The group in Washington is said to have had at one time approximately forty active members. No indication, however, has been received of its being active since the arrest of its leaders in Washington, and four members for violations of the Selective Training and Service Act. The leaders in Washington who were taken into custody and sentenced to serve in prison were Gulan Bogans, also known as Elijah Mohammed and Elijah Poole, Nancy Beverly, secretary of the Washington Temple and David Jones, with aliases Brother Duvon and David X, also a leader in the Washington Temple. A total of four members of the Washington group were also convicted for a violation of the Selective Training and Service Act.

Aside from the activities of this particular group, no reports have been received of indications or instances of organized or pro-Japanese agitation among the Negroes in this area. There have been, however, examples of un-American statements made by individual Negroes in the area; such as the case of Harold Adolphus Gady, a prominent Negro, concerning whom investigation revealed that he repeatedly stated he hoped Japan and Germany would win the war and that he did not care to see the

United States victorious. No indications were received that Gady belonged to any organization or group promoting such doctrines.

Several complaints concerning individuals of this nature have been received. The investigation has been conducted relative to them but as yet no concrete information has been received reflecting they are engaged in any organized activity to promote pro-Japanese sentiments in this area. It should also be pointed out that no concrete information or evidence has been developed reflecting any pro-German, pro-Italian or pro-Japanese activities or organized propaganda among the Negroes in the City of Washington.

In this connection allegations were received that "Eleanor Clubs" were prevalent among Negro inhabitants in the District of Columbia and that these clubs were inspired by pro-Axis forces. Numerous inquiries into complaints and allegations that these clubs existed were made and in each instance negative results were obtained, it being found that idle gossip, unfounded rumors and misunderstanding were the basis for the allegations.

The Communist Party and the Young Communist League have been exceedingly active in incurring the favor of Negro citizens in Washington, exploiting their situation and attempting to obtain increased membership among them besides attempting to recruit Negro members. One of the foremost examples of Party activity in this regard has been the agitation for their employment in public utilities, such as the Capital Transit Company and the Telephone Company. The local Communist Party, of course, following the line of the national organization, has loudly decried the alleged instances of discrimination against segregation of Negroes. Social equality is also demanded, as well as mixed regiments of Negro and white personnel in the United States Army. The recent membership drive of the Communist Party had brought the total membership in the District of Columbia to over 625 members with a quota of new members of 175 having been exceeded in the recent recruiting campaign from February, 1943 to May, 1943. It is said that of the 175, a large number were Negro recruits. With regard to the Young Communist League, it is believed that the membership therein is well over fifty, and according to confidential informants the membership consists of at least half of Negro members. The Young Communist League has generally carried out the Communist Party line in its work in the Negro situation. As an example of the Party's appeal to Negro citizens of the District of Columbia, it is reported that a large meeting was held in February, 1942, at the National Press Club Auditorium, at which meeting approximately fifteen to twenty per cent of the auditorium were Negroes numbering 150 to 200.

In addition to its own organizational activities, the Communist Party in the City of Washington has been working, in fact, with several organizations which have been active in the past year and one-half in this area. Among them are the Committee on Jobs for Negroes in Public Utilities, the Council of United Negro Labor Leaders of Washington, the Washington Bookshop, the National Negro Congress and the Committee Against Jim Crow in Baseball. These organizations are still active. In addition there have been such organizations which have dealt specifically, at least in part, with the Negro situation in this area. Included among these were the Citizens Committee Against Police Brutality, a temporary organization headed by the National Negro

Congress, the American Peace Mobilization, the Washington Committee for Democratic Action and the National Federation for Constitutional Liberties. Another organization which is said to have distributed literature agitating for Negro rights is the Union for Democratic Action, 120 East 16th Street, New York City. This organization distributed a form in the area which is said to have also been used by the local office of the Elks Lodge (Negro) in Washington. It was entitled "Eliminate Discrimination in the Armed Forces," and made demands for the correction of the following conditions:

"1. Numerical restriction against Negroes in the Air Corps."

"2. Refusal of the Navy to grant commission to qualified Negroes."

With particular regard to the Committee on Jobs for Negroes in Public Utilities. Its particular aims center around the securing of employment for Negroes in public utilities in the Washington area, especially in the Capital Transit Company. Numerous meetings have been held by this organization at which reported Communist members and alleged pro-Communist sympathizers have spoken. It has imported speakers from out of the city and has cooperated with groups in other areas, which have sent delegates to Washington particularly interested in some phase of the Negro question. Doxey A. Wilkerson at one time acted as chairman of the Membership Committee of this organization. He is now a Communist Party organizer in the Baltimore area. The meetings sponsored by this organization, which are comprised of militant speeches, as a whole attract a large attendance. The committee meetings of this organization at times ha[ve] from fifty to seventy-five members attending, among whom are reportedly Negro Communist Party members and sympathizers. It is alleged that the Party closely guides the activities of this organization.

This organization devoted the entire week of May 2 through May 7, 1943, to agitation designed to compel the employment of Negro operators by the Capital Transit Company. It is said that several weeks of planning culminated in daily picket lines employed at important street intersections in the District of Columbia. The pickets were reportedly recruited from sympathetic affiliates of the Congress of Industrial Organizations. Petitions were circulated and tags sold in support of the organizations' activities, and it is alleged that approximately 50,000 leaflets were distributed to advertise the final day's activity, which included a parade and an open air rally.

During this week of demonstration, rumors were prevalent in the City of Washington indicating a possibility of racial violence. It appears that they grew in proportion as the week passed, and newspapers were flooded with inquiries on the matter. In tracing such rumors back to the original source, it was usually ascertained that some person had made the remark there would be a race riot "some day" in Washington and this remark had then been turned and twisted until the riot was "expected today" and finally that "we are having a race riot". It is possible that the demonstrations, in the form of picketing, merely having given impetus to these rumors. However, informants reported that leaders of the Committee on Jobs for Negroes in Public Utilities were most anxious to avoid any violences realizing that such would defeat their own purposes. It is also said that the Communist Party members interested in this organization had similar feelings.

On the night of May 7, 1943, the week's activities culminated in a parade beginning at Tenth Street and Vermont Avenue, N. W. and extended to Franklin Park in Washington, the scene of the open air rally. The leaders in the organization, as well as in the march of the parade, were Doxey Wilkerson, Richmond Bancroft, Calvin Cousins, Lewis Williams, Robert Robinson and others each of whom is an active Communist Party leader in the affairs of this organization in the District of Columbia. Those participating in the parade and in the mass meeting never exceeded 800 in number, and conducted themselves in an orderly fashion. The principal speakers were Vito Marcantonio, United States Congressman, and Charles A. Collins, Negro leader and a reported member of the Communist Party in New York City.

Following the week of agitation carried out by the Committee on Jobs for Negroes in Public Utilities, the committee became comparatively inactive reportedly as a result of the scheduled hearings of the Fair Employment Practices Committee on the Capital Transit Company issue having been postponed, and because of the reorganization of the latter named committee.

Mostly affiliated with the Committee on Jobs for Negroes in Public Utilities is the Council of United Negro Labor Leaders of Washington. This organization was formed in October, 1942, by representatives of affiliates of the AFL and the CIO, as well as representatives of independent labor groups in the District of Columbia. The purpose of the organization is to assist and agitate for the rights of Negro workers, and to cooperate with the aforementioned committee. There are indications of Communist influence in the group, especially through one Jewell Mazique, corresponding secretary of the organization, who was reportedly designated by the Party to work in the council. It should be noted that the organization has cooperated on numerous occasions with delegations specifically interested in a phase of the Negro situation which have come to Washington to discuss matters and make demands with Governmental representatives. It has also distributed circular letters urging the free action of the Fair Employment Practices Committee in agitating for its independence of action from the War Manpower Commission. In this connection it has supported and given assistance to delegations visiting Washington with regard to this particular matter. Recently, however, the organization has become inactive in view of the activities of the Committee on Jobs for Negroes in Public Utilities, and in view of its close cooperation with this organization.

An organization known as the Committee Against Jim Crow in Baseball was reportedly organized in the late Summer of 1942 in the District of Columbia. The purpose of this organization is said to be to work against alleged racial discrimination in organized baseball, and particularly to agitate for the employment of Negro players in the major leagues. From information received with regard to the activities of this group it was indicated that the agitation has been directly inspired by the Communist Party in this instance. A meeting was held in the Fall of 1942 by this organization in the Lincoln Congressional [Congregational?] Church at 11th and R Streets, N. W., Washington, D. C. It was reported that the only literature present at the meeting was a large quantity of Daily Worker newspapers. Among the persons in attendance was reported to be Martin Chancey, secretary of the Communist Party of the District of Columbia; Oscar Weatherford, in charge of circulation of the Daily Worker in the District of Columbia and Robert Hall, member of the Communist Party and active in various public functions. Among those who spoke at the meeting were reportedly William Taylor, sports editor of the Daily Worker and Jack Zukor, an alleged member of the Communist Party. It has been said that no definite program emerged from the meeting, although suggestions were considered to contact the president with regard to discrimination against Negroes in baseball and also to get a statement on the subject from Joe Louis.

An organization, national in scope, has its offices in the City of Washington, namely, the National Committee to Abolish the Poll Tax. This organization is led by its Executive President Silver Beitscher, and Virginia Durr, its executive secretary, both of whom are reported to have had Communist connections or affiliation in the past. This organization extends a national effort to seek the passage of an Anti-Poll Tax Bill, and has lobbied and propagandized to this effect. In addition, its offices at 10 Connecticut Avenue, S. W., Washington, D. C., have been the scene of meetings of several delegations sent to Washington late in the Fall of 1942 and in the Spring of 1943. These delegations had the purpose of not only agitating for the passage of an Anti-Poll Tax Bill, but also such matters as urging action by the Fair Employment Practices Committee and other matters akin. Such a delegation made up of members from Chicago, Detroit and New York, arrived in Washington during the period November 20 through 23, 1942. Concerning these delegations, it has been reported that a majority of them were believed to be Communist inspired.

The delegations were reportedly sponsored by such organizations as the National Negro Congress, a Communist Party front; the Negro Labor Victory Committee, New York City, a reported Communist front; the National Committee to Stop Lynching, New York City, an organization said to have Communist Party connections; the National Maritime Union, a Chicago Citizens Committee of One Thousand; the Committee on Jobs for Negroes in Public Utilities, Washington, D.C., and the Citizens Committee for War Jobs, Detroit, Michigan.

Among the colored persons interested in various capacities in the delegations were:

Benjamin Davis, New York City Communist Party functionary;

A. Clayton Powell, Jr., New York City minister and councilman with reported Communist Party affiliations;

A. Philip Randolph, National Director of the March on Washington Movement;

John P. Davis of the National Negro Congress who is said to have Communist Party affiliations;

George Murphy of the National Maritime Union, reported Communist;

Ferdinand Smith, reported Communist and Secretary of the National Maritime Union;

Saul Mills, President of the Greater New York Industrial Union Council, CIO, who is said to have Communist leanings.

To meet the various delegations, a group was chosen from the Committee on Jobs for Negroes in Public Utilities. On November 23, 1942, the delegations, composed of about sixty-five persons, visited the Senate gallery to listen to the proceedings there relative to the poll tax question. After the Anti-Poll Tax Bill was dealt with in the Senate all delegations were reported to have taken part in a conference sponsored by the National Committee to Abolish the Poll Tax where plans were made for the local delegations to return to their respective states and organize committees to maintain agitation for the repeal of poll tax statutes in various states and to work for the reintroduction of a bill similar to the recent one before Congress at the next session.

There is a branch of the National Negro Congress located in Washington where until recently the organization has maintained its national headquarters. In 1940 the Third Congress of the organization was held in Washington, where reportedly 1264 delegates assembled representing twenty-eight states. Of this number, 888 were said to be Negroes, while 376 were white people.

In the early months of 1943, the organization renewed its activities, and the Washington unit was revived and a program was adopted as follows:

1. Fight for democratic rights for all citizens for the passage of the Civil Rights Bill for the District of Columbia.
   A. Suffrage for the District of Columbia.
   B. Anti-Poll Tax Bill.
2. Adequate living conditions and just costs.
3. Legal Aid Bureau.
4. Organizational drive for organizational affiliates and individual memberships.

The national setup of this organization can be termed a Communist Party front organization. With regard to the local unit of this organization in Washington, it should be noted that a recent group of delegates sent to the Eastern Seaboard Conference of the National Organization held in New York City in April, 1943, were in the majority Communist Party members.

There also exists in the Washington area, a unit of the March on Washington Movement organized early in 1942. It has approximately twenty members and has engaged in little activity other than supporting meetings held in Washington at the instigation of the national group of the organization. It reportedly adheres to the same aims and purposes, as well as the same program of the National Organization. At the recent National Conference held in Chicago, June 30–July 4, 1943, the unit was represented by two delegates. It is alleged that the inactivity of this unit is due largely to the lack of initiative on the part of its leader Thurman Dodson.

The local unit in Washington of the March on Washington Movement supported a temporary group known as the Provisional Committee for the Organization of Colored Locomotive Firemen, which was organized at the behest of A. Philip Randolph, International President of the Brotherhood of Sleeping Car Porters, A. F. of L., and the national leader of the March on Washington Movement. On January 24, a mass meeting was held by this group in Washington at the Vermont Avenue Baptist Church, where numerous local and national labor leaders, a majority of them being Negroes, spoke. The main purpose of the meeting was to compel the scheduling of hearings by the Fair Employment Practices Committee in the railroad industry. Approximately 300 people attended the meeting, where there were also plans made to send delegates to various Governmental officials urging the establishment of hearings by the Fair Employment Practices Committee. The organization has been inactive except for holding an occasional conference meeting to take action by the Fair Employment Committee. With respect to the activities of this organization, it should be noted that there ha[ve] been indications of some Communist influence. It has been observed by informants that this is contrary to the general practice of Randolph, as well as the March on Washington Movement, especially as far as the national outlook of the organization is concerned.

On October 24, 1942, a luncheon was held by the League for Industrial Democracy at which time approximately 100 people were in attendance. A. Philip Randolph, national leader of the March on Washington Movement was the principal speaker. It was pointed out that the League for Industrial Democracy was formed in 1905 as an inter-collegiate Socialist Society. At present its headquarters are in New York City. Until recently there has been no chapter of the organization in Washington, D.C.

Randolph in his speech at the luncheon, reportedly stated that race prejudice was acquired through Colonialism and Imperialism, the countries of Britain, Belgium, France and Germany being the main offenders. He is said to have continued saying that in a world in which such an order exists it is only natural that the darker races seek power. Thus Japan seeks to establish a Monroe Doctrine for Asia for her Imperialistic desires; and the Chinese will turn upon their white benefactors who have through their financial and economical power drained their country of its natural resources leaving the populace in poverty. He referred to Ghandi Nehru of India as distrusting American Democracy inasmuch as the American Government is unwilling to solve its internal social problem involving the relationship of Negro and white citizens. He is also reported to have stated that China and India will be mistreated by the white and yellow imperialists until they are united internally and that the Negro likewise is weak because of lack of organization.

Randolph in his speech also referred to the organization of the March on Washington Movement. He is said to have stated that it was a consideration of the problem referred to previously that led to its organization. He reportedly related that both Mr. and Mrs. Roosevelt have tried to dissuade him from actually having a March on Washington. That he attributed the executive order of the President No. 8802 to his conferences with the President with regard to the March on Washington Movement. In this connection Randolph is reported to have assailed the War Manpower Commission and said that it is subject to whims of Southern Congressmen. Randolph is also said to have charged at the luncheon that the Government's action connected with the War Manpower Commission and other matters made it a carrier of discrimination against the Negroes.

There is located in Washington at 1538 New Jersey Avenue, N.W., an organization known as the Minorities' Work Shop, the broad general plan of which is to endeavor to further such aims as civil rights and the abolition of discrimination against minority groups. According to a confidential informant, the organization appears to be Socialist inspired and has had active support of Al Hamilton, Socialist leader in the Washington area. It has interested itself in local matters such as the employment of Negroes as bus and street car operators with the Capital Transit Company, and with such national issues as the passage of an Anti-Poll Tax Bill. There are indications that it has cooperated with the Urban League in Washington, and has made such plans as supporting or considering "incidents" helping Negroes or interracial groups that will endeavor to permit them to eat in restaurants and hotels normally restricted to white people.

No indications, however, have been received that it has actively engaged in promoting such "incidents." It is to be noted, however, that reports have been received that in January, 1943, a group of Negro students from Howard University allegedly attempted such action. The organization has, in the past, held regular meetings, the attendance of which is said to be comparatively small, yet at which discussions are generally held involving such subjects as discrimination against Negroes and segregation of them.

There is a Washington chapter of the National Association for the Advancement of Colored People in the District of Columbia. It recently has engaged in an extended drive for additional members. The exact size of the present group is not known, however, its campaign was for 10,000 new members. The local chapter's activities consist of generally those promoted by the national setup of the organization. They are as follows:

1. Agitation against reshowing of the motion picture "The Birth of a Nation," which resulted in its being banned from the screen by the Office of War Information.
2. Agitation with regard to alleged discrimination against Negroes in the armed services. In this connection, it should be noted that WILLIAM H. HASTIE resigned as Civilian Aide to the Secretary of War on January 31, 1943, because his recommendations with regard to the elimination of such discrimination were not followed by the War Department. It should also be noted that HASTIE was one of the speakers at the Victory Mass Meeting of the N.A.A.C.P. inaugurating the National Membership Drive in Washington, D.C., at which time he related the events leading up to his resignation from the War Department.
3. Elimination of the rules of the Office of Censorship which bar the news with regard to racial difficulties in the United States from transmission abroad.
4. Discrimination between Negroes and white people and segregation of the races in Red Cross Clubs for the armed services.
5. Cooperation with the Minorities' Work Shop in its campaign against alleged discrimination against Negroes by hotels and restaurants in the District of Columbia. The N.A.A.C.P. is reported to have agreed to press cases arising out of this matter in the courts.
6. Endeavoring to secure permission to question witnesses from the railroad unions with regard to the policies of such unions toward Negro workers, and cooperating in the agitation for the holding of hearings on alleged discrimination against Negroes by the F.E.P.C.
7. Cooperation with other organizations and delegations working for the support of the Fair Employment Practices Committee, including the visiting of Government officials and Congressmen.

Recently several incidents have occurred at the Union Station in Washington, D.C., where there appeared to be a degree of racial animosity. The following information is set forth as exemplifying the situation.

Through a confidential source it has been determined that on the night of June 22, 1943, a porter at the Union Station, Washington, D.C., jostled a sailor, whereupon an altercation resulted. The sailor involved struck the porter and, according to the informant, racial violence would have occurred had not prompt action been taken by the police and the Navy Shore Patrol. It was subsequently learned from the Metropolitan Police Department, Washington, D.C., that this incident occurred during the dispersement of a large number of sailors from the Union Station on leave. A number of these sailors were under the influence of liquor and as a result of the disturbance a number of arrests were made among the sailors involved. A subsequent contact with the confidential source mentioned hereinbefore indicates the situation at the Union Station is considered very tense. In the opinion of the informant, it is likely that racial violence might be expected to break out there in the immediate future.

In evaluating the statements made by this source, it is of interest to note that he is a Negro and has been employed in the Union Station for a number of months and has had an excellent opportunity to observe conditions existing there. On other matters he has been found to be reliable in his evaluation of existing circumstances, and on the last contact with him on June 24, 1943, he seemed sincerely concerned over the prospect of racial violence growing out of the feeling existing among the porters at Union Station and the people with whom they come in contact.

Another informant has voiced similar views to those set out above. Although he is not employed at the Union Station, he is in close contact with a number of people who are so employed, one of whom he considers a Negro of radical tendencies. The latter has frequently indicated to the informant the tense situation allegedly existing. This situation reportedly dates back to an incident that occurred approximately six months ago, at which time the Washington Terminal Police, who are not members of the Metropolitan Police Department, allegedly physically mistreated one of the porters. The reason for this incident was not known, but it is said that bad feeling has existed since that time among the porters. The informant in the latter regard voluntarily supplied his views concerning the outbreak of possible racial violence at the Union Station and was not prompted or urged to submit his opinions or observations along this line.

In the Washington area there are numerous Negro newspapers distributed, including the "Afro-American," the nation's capitol edition and the "Pittsburgh Courier." These newspapers are believed to have a fairly wide distribution among the Negro population in this City, thereby bringing to Washington the general type of news reporting and editorializing found in these publications.

In July, 1943, a confidential source stated that in his opinion the current racial situation in Washington is "tense." The informant stated he would estimate approximately 90 per cent of the Negro population in Washington felt that racial difficulty was imminent. The informant further advised that such discussion was common among this proportion of the Negro population and that most Negroes fearing such disorders believed that it was necessary for them to prepare themselves. The informant explained that this statement meant that they, the Negroes, should purchase guns and ammunition. According to the informant, he did not believe any of the Negroes desired to purchase knives or ice picks since in the event of racial disturbance the Negroes might expect guns used against them. The confidential source stated he had no knowledge of any Negro having purchased a gun or ammunition, but that approximately ten people with whom he had talked indicated a belief that the Negroes should prepare themselves in such a manner.

The informant said in the event it was desired to purchase guns, he believed the average Negro would resort to the pawnshops as a source for such weapons.

According to this informant, the places wherein trouble might be expected in the District of Columbia were principally the Union Terminal, the Greyhound Bus Terminal and the streetcar and bus lines of the city. He pointed out that these places were practically the only places where Negroes and whites were not segregated. He stated the most critical transportation line in the city in this connection was the Benning streetcar line.

As to the element in the Negro population which might be the source of trouble, this informant said that in his opinion it was made up of the young Negroes, principally those between sixteen and nineteen years of age, who have not yet been inducted into the Army. He stated that the attitude of these young Negroes was that they would take nothing from anyone and that unless they learned they could not persist in such an attitude, trouble would probably ensue. He stated the young Negro men now in the Army also had this same attitude and it was the common belief of the Negro population in Washington that if racial difficulties did not occur prior to the end of the war, such outbreaks might fully be expected with the return to civilian life of these young soldiers.

Another highly confidential source described the current racial situation in Washington as "tense." This informant said that there was a good deal of conversation among Negroes with regard to the possibility of racial violence. He indicated that conversation of this type among the Negro population in Washington was restricted principally to the lower type of Negro and the laboring Negro. He estimated the group who felt that racial difficulties might soon appear constituted approximately 30 per cent to 40 per cent of the Negro population.

This source also indicated there was some feeling among the Negroes that in view of the possibility of racial outbreak, the Negroes should prepare themselves. The informant added that he knew of no case where a Negro had purchased guns or ammunition, but he had heard the remark that no guns were available for purchase in Baltimore, Maryland. The informant also said that a Negro had told him he had tried to purchase a gun and ammunition in Alexandria, Virginia, without success. According to the informant, these statements indicated that some effort had been made to secure firearms.

As to the danger spots in Washington, this informant was of the opinion that they might be found along 6th and 7th Street, N. W., and along U Street and Florida Avenue, particularly around the pool halls and hangouts for the young Negroes of the City. He indicated the bus and streetcar lines were also danger spots. This source singled out as the most dangerous transportation line as a source of racial disturbances, the Benning streetcar line. He stated that this streetcar line served the heavily populated

Negro district of northeast Washington and that all streetcars on this line were usually so crowded that it was necessary to "force one's way in" and there to remain in close contact with other people. He stated it was usually necessary to permit several cars to pass before one would stop so that as a result a person boarding the streetcar would already "be mad." The informant also pointed out that the Capital Transit Company, which operates this line, apparently uses it for the training of new operators, for which reason the operators on this line were generally inexperienced. As a consequence, the informant stated, these operators were unable to handle the crowds found on this line and there was a lot of antagonism between the patrons and the operators. The informant continued that recently a white woman had been assigned to this line as a streetcar conductor and this had aroused a great deal of antagonism, since the Negroes living adjacent to this line were familiar with the program to require the Capital Transit Company to employ Negro streetcar and bus operators. According to the informant, the employment of a white woman on this line appeared to the Negroes as an action on the part of the company to show that they would employ anyone before employing the Negro. This informant also mentioned various incidents which had occurred on this streetcar line and which he believed might be built up towards racial violence inasmuch as, in his opinion, people using this line felt a flare-up might come at any time.

This same source stated in regard to the elements in the Negro population from which racial violence might be expected that it was his opinion it might be expected from the young group of Negroes, principally those who had no regular employment. He stated he had noted the average employed Negro was most anxious to avoid any type of racial conflict and advised it had been his observation that all organizations active in the City of Washington at this time were likewise bending every effort to prevent racial trouble. He stated that employers in the District, as well as all labor unions, actively endeavored to prevent any type of racial outbreak. However, the informant mentioned that in his opinion the Negro press played up racial incidents so much that as a result, Negroes generally were aroused to feelings of hate or else of fear, either of which might tend toward bringing about a racial incident.

Neither of the confidential sources believed there was presently any indication of open racial violence other than the undercurrent, as has been previously mentioned. Both believed that the overcrowding in Washington might result eventually in open violence. Both also believed that in the event violence took place, it would probably arise spontaneously from some small incident and would not be the result of any organized plan on the part of any particular group

III

SOUTHERN SECTION OF THE UNITED STATES

This section, for the purposes of this study, involves generally those areas south of the Mason-Dixon Line, including the States of Arkansas, Oklahoma and Texas as well as the State of New Mexico. In many places of this section of the country the Negro population equals, if not surpasses, the white population. The age-old question of race relationship in this area is, of course, historical and involves local customs, habits and modes of living which have been generally accepted throughout the United States for many years. This acceptance has been evidenced among both the Negro and white races.

While there has been in the past general acceptance of these customs and habits in the southern part of the United States on the part of Negroes, reports which have been received reflect a general change in attitude of Negroes in this area, as well as a new militancy on their part. This has been attributed in part to the new degree of complexity of economic life in the South, namely, the increased chances of employment in war industries located there, as well as the knowledge which has come from other parts of the United States that economic gains are to be had. In addition, there are stationed in the South in practically all areas Negro troops, a large number of which have come from northern cities where customs, restrictions, and habits generally prevalent in the South are not present.

Along with the reported change of attitude on the part of Negroes generally in that area have come demands and requests on their part. These have been made mainly for better and increased employment and for remuneration for work done which is equivalent to that received by white people in this area for the same type of work. There have also been general demands for better educational facilities and especially for more adequate transportation means. With regard to the latter it is particularly prevalent in those centers where the population has increased because of the location of war industries there. The segregation practices in this matter are said to have resulted in a scarcity of rapid and available transportation for Negroes. This scarcity, coupled with the reported change in attitude of Negroes in the South, is said to be the cause of numerous minor clashes and fights between Negroes and whites throughout the South.

With regard to the demand for placement in skilled and better-paying positions on the part of Negroes in a number of areas, this is said to have indirectly resulted in walkouts and strikes. In Mobile, Alabama, a shipyard company, after placing Negroes in skilled positions, experienced a general strike and trouble in the form of rioting.

Among other issues which have been taken up in several areas of this section by Negroes in voicing their demands have been the abolition of the poll tax and equal pay for Negro teachers. With regard to the latter, it should also be noted that demands have been made in several localities for educational accommodations which are equivalent in size and convenience to those afforded white people.

Another part of the picture of racial conditions and race relationship in this area has been the prevalency of unfounded rumors and gossip. Perhaps the foremost subject matter of these has been the alleged existence of "Eleanor Clubs." In connection with the alleged existence of these groups, allegations and complaints were received that they were inspired by pro-Axis forces as a means of promoting unrest and dissatisfaction in this section of the country. Numerous complaints and reports of the existence of these groups failed to indicate any substantial basis for them. Explanations have been offered and perhaps the most prominent among these was that once the rumor was launched, it was elaborated upon, especially by members of the white race. The explanation has also been offered that the scarcity of domestic workers resulting from the opportunity of both sexes of the Negro race to obtain employment in better-paying fields of work such as war industries and agricultural employment added impetus to the rumors. In no instance have inquiries into the alleged existence of "Eleanor Clubs" resulted in anything specific. It is to be noted that the reported reason for the establishment of these fictitious clubs was to demand better conditions for Negro domestics and to force white employers into a position of being in dire need of this type of assistance. The slogan allegedly adopted was: "A white woman in every kitchen by Christmas."

In this section of the country there have also been numerous reports and complaints of individual members of the Negro race expressing un-American sentiments. In checking into these allegations, in no instance was any indication found of organized or planned activity to influence Negroes in making these statements. The reported reasons for their utterances generally were that they were made as a result of ignorance or drunkenness or they were repeated with no apparent malice but rather expressed as dissatisfaction over a certain condition or practice.

Another force which has been pointed to as an influence among Negroes in this section by both Negro and white sources of information is the northern Negro press. It is said while there is no great circulation, issues are often passed from one hand to another and for this reason have a wider effect. It is claimed by these sources that the inflammatory and biased manner of reporting and editorializing found in these newspapers is agitational and conducive to unrest.

Among those matters which have been reported to be the cause for unrest, dissatisfaction or agitation on the part of Negroes individually and collectively in this area are the following:

Recent lynchings.

Labor difficulties and antagonism between white and Negro workers.

The stationing of northern Negro military personnel into this section.

The spreading of unfounded rumors of pending racial difficulties and trouble.

Fights and clashes between Negroes and whites in public places where segregation is observed.

The activities of the Communist Party in larger cities of the South.

There are set out hereinafter digests of information received by the various Field Divisions of the Federal Bureau of Investigation located in this section of the country.

Atlanta Field Division

Sources of information contacted in this area have not advised of any evidences of attempts by pro-German or pro-Japanese forces to create unrest and dissatisfaction among the Negroes in this area. However, considerable agitation on the part of Negro leaders in an effort to allegedly better positions of the Negro so that the Negro can contribute more to the war effort has been reported. It is further reported that the Negro press in this area, both those newspapers published there and those published elsewhere which are circulated in this area are stated to be causing considerable agitation through exaggerating and emphasizing any incidents alleged to be considered an affront to the Negro race. It is reported that in the City of Atlanta, Georgia several Negroes known to have Communist connections have created an organization known as the Atlanta Workers Council which meets at the headquarters of the National Urban League in Atlanta. This organization is said to be presently attempting to organize Negro domestic workers.

It is also reported that considerable discontent is apparently being caused by the editorials appearing in the Atlanta Daily World, a colored newspaper. Another widely circulated newspaper in this area is the Pittsburgh Courier. Other newspapers stated to have some circulation are the Baltimore Afro-American, The Richmond Afro-American, the Chicago Defender, the Louisville Defender, the Amsterdam News, The People's Voice, the latter two being published in New York City. With regard to the Atlanta Daily World, it is reported that Robert F. Hall, secretary of the Communist Party District 17, Birmingham, Alabama, writes editorials which are published in this newspaper.

A source of information located in Atlanta, Georgia, **who is the editor of a Negro publication there,** has been contacted with regard to the unrest and dissatisfaction among the Negroes which has been reported in this area. It should be noted, however, **that that newspaper of which this individual is editor reportedly prints editorials written by a functionary of the Communist Party.** This individual has advised that there has been and would continue to be considerable agitation on the part of the Negro leaders in an attempt to gain for the Negroes an opportunity to make a greater contribution to the war effort. He stated that the Negroes are actively trying to call a halt to discrimination against the Negroes in war industries and in the armed forces. He advised, however, in the form of an opinion, that he believes there is no attempt by pro-Axis individuals or organizations to create any agitation or disturbance among the Negroes in this area. He further expressed the opinion that any German or Japanese propaganda to the effect that the Negroes would be better off if the Axis won the present war would be promptly rejected by the Negroes, who know as well as anyone that the promises of the Axis are empty promises.

This source of information has further elaborated that Negroes realize that they do not enjoy the same opportunities and rights of citizenship that the white race enjoys and since they are being called on to make the same contributions to the war effort and are being called upon to "fight for liberty and democracy for the people in Europe and Asia", the Negro leaders naturally feel that if they are to fight for other people they themselves should be granted democracy at home. The same source has advised that he believes the leaders of the Negro minority are intelligent men and realize that although they do not enjoy the same rights and liberties that are enjoyed by the white race, and occupy a position inferior to that of the white race they realize that the Negroes in the United States are much better off than the Negroes in any other country and consequently, while publicly demanding liberties and opportunities, he believes there is no danger of their resorting to violence unless it is to gain such liberties or opportunities. He related further that he believes Negro leaders fully realize that in the event of any violence it would be the Negroes themselves who would suffer, and they realize that some of the liberty which they now enjoy would be taken from them.

This individual has further related that Negroes have one great right of which they are very proud and very jealous, and that is "the right to complain about the rights that we do not have". He has stated that he realizes that such a right could not exist under Axis control and that consequently, in the event that Axis countries distributed propaganda to the effect that the Negroes would be better off under Axis control, such propaganda would be rejected.

Another source of information, **a Negro, who is the manager of a Federal Housing Project in the vicinity of Atlanta, Georgia, has advised upon interview that over 1200 Negroes and families reside in the Project managed by him.** He has stated that he is well acquainted with the conditions of the Negroes in all stations of life. This source of information has advised that he has heard or seen nothing which would indicate that any foreign power is attempting to create agitation or disturbances among the Negro race. He has advised, however, that there is presently considerable discontent among the Negroes of Atlanta and in the whole South, not caused by foreign interference or propaganda, but rather by the increased pressure placed upon all groups and by the discrimination in existing conditions. He states that there has always been a certain amount of discontent among Negroes and that this discontent has been greatly intensified by publicity given the war effort.

This source of information has pointed out that Negroes as well as white people are called upon to bear war burdens, contribute to war relief, and to enlist in the armed forces. He stated that Negroes are being drafted in the Army along with the white people, and that, although Negroes are called on to make the same contributions to the war effort as the white people and are expected to share the responsibilities that come with citizenship, they are not allowed to enjoy the privileges of being citizens of the United States. This individual stated further that the Negroes are faced with sectionalism everywhere they turn, pointing out that Negroes are forced to use separate drinking fountains, and allowed to use only certain elevators, required to sit at the rear of public conveyances, and that, although they were subject to taxes for the purpose of maintaining the various governmental agencies, they are not allowed to exercise a vote so that they might have a voice in how their tax money is being spent. In his latter statement it is believed that this individual refers to the poll tax system of the South.

An official of the Commission for Inter-racial Cooperation which is located at 710 Standard Building at Atlanta, Georgia, organized for the purpose denoted in its title, a person who is in constant contact with all classes of the Negro race in this area, has advised that he has received no information nor seen any indication that un-American individuals or organizations are working among the Negroes attempting to stir up trouble and dissention among them. He has advised, however, that there is an alarming amount of increased dissatisfaction and agitation among the Negroes of the South, and expressed the opinion that this discontent is the direct result of the activities on the part of Negro leaders in the North as portrayed by the Negro press.

This source of information has advised that it has always been the policy of the Negro press to print news which would be of interest to the Negroes, and that the Negro press has always given headline space to alleged discrimination among the Negroes. He said, however, that since Pearl Harbor certain Negro leaders in the North, particularly those Negroes associated with the National Association for the Advancement of Colored People, have become "touchy", that each incident, which by the faintest touch of imagination could be considered an affront to the Negro race, was grossly exaggerated and played up in the Negro Press.

The source of information has stated that the more stable leaders among the Negroes in the South are very much concerned over the Negro affairs because they felt that the ever increasing demands of the National Association for the Advancement of Colored People on the Administration for increased economic and social liberties for the Negroes were ill-timed and if pressed too far could only result in a loss of some of the now existing rights for the Negroes. This source of information has also stated that he believes considerable discontent has been caused among the Negro people by certain ill-advised public statements on the part of the white people in prominent places.

Recently organized among the Negroes in the Atlanta territory is an organization known as The Atlanta Workers Council which was organized by William M. Brooks, Joseph A. Moreland, Jesse E. Matthews, William Y. Bell, and one Weaver, all Negroes. Information received reflects that Moreland, Brooks, and Matthews are all active members of the Negro section of the Communist Party in the area of Atlanta, and that they all pay monthly dues to the Communist Party. This organization holds meetings at the office of The National Urban League, located in the Herndon Building, Atlanta, Georgia. Recently this organization called a meeting on July 20, 1942, the purpose of which was to discuss steps to be taken to organize Negro domestics, cafeteria workers in the city of Atlanta. It is reported further that some time ago the organization held a meeting which was addressed by two white women whose names are unknown to the effect that although the Negro has made some progress in gaining greater economic and social liberties they would make no definite progress until they were accepted as social equals by white persons everywhere. One of the women is stated to have said that Negroes should "continue to demand your rights with increasing vigor while the country is in a state of war and cannot refuse your rights".

On September 21, 1942, the Atlanta Workers Council held a meeting in the offices of the National Urban League, Herndon Building, Atlanta, Georgia with Joseph A. Moreland as Chairman. The following individuals, the first five of whom are all said to be active members of the colored section of the Communist Party in Atlanta, were in attendance:

Rufus Johnson
Claudia Jenkins
Whitman Day
J. E. Matthews
William Brooks
William Y. Bell
______Weaver

The latter two individuals who are not known as active members of the Party are said to be closely associated and affiliated with Negro Communists in Atlanta. At this meeting it was decided that the Atlanta Workers Council would work in connection with the National Association for the Advancement of Colored People inasmuch as it was said there was no other Negro organization in Atlanta with which it could affiliate itself. It was also decided that every precaution should be taken by the Atlanta Workers Council to prevent anyone from having any suspicion that the organization might in any way be connected with the Communist Party. [*100-135-3-34*]

Several reports have been received in the Atlanta, Georgia, area relative to the alleged existence of "Eleanor Clubs". All attempts to verify these allegations have been met with negative results. Individuals attributed with making the allegations who have been interviewed, have been unable to furnish definite information and ultimately they have advised that they were merely quoting rumors received in various conversations with friends or acquaintances.

Sources of information contacted in and around Marietta, Georgia, with reference to possible foreign inspired unrest and dissatisfaction among the Negroes in this area have all advised that they have failed to see indications reflecting un-American activities among the Negroes, inspired by pro-Axis groups.

In the City of Rome, Georgia an incident recently took place which resulted in nation-wide publicity. Mrs. Roland Hayes, wife of the Negro concert singer, is stated to have visited a store in this city and sat down near the front of the store, desiring to be waited upon. One of the clerks is stated to have asked her to move to the rear in the colored section which she refused to do, whereupon the clerk is said to have advised her that he was sorry that she could not be waited on if she remained where she was, that is, in the white section. After some talk, Mrs. Hayes is stated to have refused to go to the rear of the store and thereupon she was asked to leave the store in order that there would be no trouble. She is stated to have refused to do so, immediately, upon being requested but eventually did leave the store and obtained her husband, Roland Hayes, who returned to the store with her. It is said that argument and discussion took place and subsequently the owner and manager of the store called the police department to settle the alleged riot. It is reported that after some rough handling which seemed to be necessary in view of the refusal on the part of Hayes' wife to leave, they were taken into the police department and incarcerated for a period of an hour or so, after which time Hayes was given permission to sign a bond.

It has also been reported in the area surrounding the city of Rome, Georgia, that there has been in the past few months a certain atmosphere or attitude of haughtiness or superiority among the Negroes.

Sources of information in the Columbus, Georgia area, who are Negroes and who are prominent in their territory have advised of hearing no indications of attempts to stir up racial trouble or unrest, or spreading any doctrine that the present war is a race war and that the Negro should not fight for the country in this area. They have advised that they believe Negroes in this area with the exception perhaps of the less educated ones, are loyal and are cooperating by buying Bonds and answering draft calls as they are made.

Sources of information in and around the Macon, Georgia area have advised that during the past year Negroes in this area have exhibited indications of unrest and dissatisfaction and upon occasion have assumed belligerent attitudes which indicated their dissatisfaction regarding their present social position. No information has been reported, however, reflecting any attempt by any foreign inspired organization or group to agitate the Negroes. A source of information in this area advises that he believes the present unrest among the Negroes in this area is due to the infiltration in the South of Negroes from the North.

Another reliable source advises that the Negroes in this area, as a whole, have been rather impudent and disrespectful of their employers and that their dissatisfaction is stated to be due mainly to "labor". This source also advises of a few individuals attempting to instill in the Negroes in this area dissatisfaction with their labor status and their transportation rights. One of the leaders is stated to have been asked to leave the city and thereupon did so.

In this area it is further reported that Macon citizens realizing the need for harmony with and among the Negroes, have created a committee known as Inter-racial Committee, composed of 12 Negroes, 12 members of the white race who are to meet together and discuss the problems of the Negroes in an attempt to work out sensisble plans.

In the vicinities of Albany and Americus, Georgia, sources of information contacted there advised of no indications of foreign inspired agitation among the Negroes in these areas.

Information was furnished in this area to the effect that Negroes in the vicinity of Covington, Georgia were purchasing as much ammunition as possible from the hardware stores in that city. Presumably the purpose behind making such a report was the fear that if this were true an uprising would take place between Negro and white citizens in the area. Numerous inquiries with hardware store operators, and sources of information in the area fail to indicate out of the ordinary transactions of this kind.

[*100-135-3*]

A small group which could be termed a "crackpot" organization was active to some degree in the vicinity of Atlanta, Georgia. This organization was known as the Afro-American National Infantry, headed by one Clarence William Harding who at the time was in the United States Army. Harding boasted of his associations with Japanese in Chicago prior to his enlistment and expressed decided pro-Japanese sympathies. His organization had a military air about it and the technique of Harding was to commission Negroes in the Afro-American National Infantry. He was successful in commissioning three in Atlanta. A party was held for the newly commissioned persons on December 11, 1942, at which time Harding made a highly inflammatory speech.

The extent and influence of Harding's organization are believed to have been most limited and in all probability the total membership of it did not exceed twenty. It is believed that Harding promoted his organization to enhance his own prestige or even possibly to swindle people. He claimed to have associated with a Japanese named Sayeto Inishia and one Unogi. (It is to be noted that these two names, as a remote possibility, may be actual Japanese names; however, their spelling appears more to be an approximation.)

Harding was arrested by military authorities for his activities and prosecuted by the Adjutant General's Office of the United States Army. His sentence, given by a military court, was five years, subject to review by higher authorities. The final disposition of his case was not reported in June 1943. Subsequent to his apprehension, it is reported that one of the members of Harding's organization burned his membership papers and stated he wanted nothing more to do with the Afro-American National Infantry. An informant in a position to evaluate this particular matter has stated that the organization would die a natural death. [*100-135-3-50*]

Another example of an unnecessarily circulated rumor was found in the City of Winder, Georgia, where it was reported that Negroes were attending secret meetings. Sources of information contacted in this city have advised that meetings were held by Negroes there but were open and held in a Negro schoolhouse. The meetings pertained to the discussion of crops, church and school affairs and many other innocent subject matters.

A small section of the Baha'is Interracial Sect is reported to have been recently organized in Atlanta, Georgia. The leader is said to be one Essie Robinson who has expressed the purpose of the organization to establish a new order through evolutionary processes in which there will be no extremely rich or extremely poor class of people. The purpose also involves a world tribunal. The leader in Atlanta, Essie Robinson, has stated that the Baha'is are members of the Mohammedan religion worshiping the faith of Baha Ullah. The group in Atlanta, according to reports received, is interracial in character. The exact size is not known although it is believed to be small. (It is to be noted that no information has been reported that this organization has engaged in subversive activities although the possibility is offered through its interracial aspect of its serving as an espionage system inasmuch as representatives from this country are sent to Latin-American countries to "spread the faith.") [*100-135-3-59*]

In the following communities in the State of Georgia inquiries have brought no information that subversive groups or individuals have been active among the Negro populations:

> Hapeville, Cordele, Montezuma, Leslie, Valdosta, Thomasville, Fort Valley and Wellston.

In the vicinity of Athens, Georgia, Negroes have reportedly become "somewhat unruly" and seemed to have a hostile attitude toward white people. A confidential source in this area has advised the only trouble he has noticed or experienced is that a few Negroes have refused to observe the segregation customs on public conveyances.

Birmingham Field Division

The information set out hereinafter has been obtained as a result of a survey made in the State of Alabama to determine if those forces responsible for the current unrest, dissatisfaction and agitation among the Negroes in that area are subversive. In this connection, the following description of the Negro in Alabama has been furnished by a Northerner who, for over a period of eighteen years, has been closely connected with the colored people, especially in and around Birmingham, Alabama. This source of information advises that the Southern Negro is an accumulation of many unusual characteristics, some understandable, while others are strange. The Negro, he advised, is believed generally in this area to be at times even below normal intellectually, while the average Negro is considered not to be susceptible to work and, generally speaking, is slow, lazy, happy, carefree and irresponsible. In further describing the Negroes in this area, he stated that they are to some extent methodical in nature, that they originally do things in a set way and thereafter follow the same procedure in future attempts. This will continue until he is told or shown how to change his methods. On the other hand, the source of information advised, there is a portion of the Negro make-up that makes him quick to take advantage of a situation. He stated that for that reason, in dealing with the Negroes, it is necessary that their status be considered and that they be handled accordingly. He stated that once Negroes are allowed a privilege, they expect that such treatment will be continued and for this and other reasons the South has maintained its color distinction, insisted on segregation, and has especially insisted that the racial situation there is not one to be handled by misinformed outsiders. This source of information further stated that the problem is one of slow evolution, requiring education as well as continued efforts along other lines so that the Negroes can be brought to a place where what now appears to be discrimination can be done away with.

This source of information further advised that Southern Negroes, as a group, are not mistreated and that those who realize their position and maintain their place in the social strata in which they exist, are well treated, well cared for and can generally rely on receiving proper treatment.

Various sources of information who have been contacted and who are in a position as to be in close contact with the Negroes in this area have expressed belief that a "situation" does exist in the State of Alabama with regard to Negroes and that the same is liable to be serious if further publicity is given to its alleged existence. Some have further expressed themselves, saying that Negroes generally have quieted down and that if white people would do likewise and the question were to receive less publicity, the "situation" would be alleviated to a great extent.

The following forces believed by sources contacted to be responsible for the unrest and dissatisfaction among the Negroes in this area are:

1. The visit to this section by those people who are prominent in public, political and social affairs and who have publicly addressed audiences in thickly popu-

lated colored areas or at their educational institutions. In this same category are placed those individuals labeled "misinformed" who have been active with regard to the situation as it exists in the South.

2. A large number of Negro soldiers, many of whom are from Northern areas, have been brought to the State of Alabama.
3. Several speeches have been made by prominent political and national leaders in the State of Alabama with regard to the Negro question there which have tended to cause further unrest in that they reportedly were made in a militant manner. In connection with this, a public statement was made by a State governmental official to the effect that he would not sign a contract with the United States Government because of a nondiscrimination clause included therein.
4. There has been a continuous clamor on the part of the Communist Party through its newspapers, members and front organizations, for equality, nondiscrimination, abolition of segregation, as well as continued agitation upon each killing, arrest or conviction of a Negro. It should be noted that the effect of such Party activity is not that additional Negro members are obtained, but that the light in which its agitation is placed serves as a disturbing influence on the Negro mind.
5. There are circulated in this area Negro newspapers which have continued efforts to obtain at least equality and nondiscrimination for the Negro. These are believed by sources of information contacted to be another agitational force.
6. There has been considerable activity in this area on the part of various labor unions in referring to their ability to better the Negroes' position which has been made with the reported motive of increasing membership.

Another phase of the Negro situation in the State of Alabama is reflected in the composition as regards white and Negro population in cities of more than ten thousand in that State. A table is being set out hereinafter to reflect the percentage of Negroes as compared with white people:

Composition of the Population for Cities of 10,000 to 100,000—1940

					PERCENTAGES		
Cities	**Total Population**	**White**	**White Foreign Born**	**Negro**	**White**	**Foreign Born White**	**Negro**
Anniston	25,523	17,611	102	7,910	68.6	0.4	31.0
Bessemer	22,826	9,545	180	13,280	41.0	0.4	58.2
Decatur	16,604	12,348	76	4,256	73.9	0.5	25.6
Dothan	17,194	9,737	49	7,457	56.3	0.3	43.4
Fairfield	11,703	4,835	156	6,868	40.0	1.3	58.7

Cities	Total Population	White	White Foreign Born	Negro	PERCENTAGES White	Foreign Born White	Negro
Florence	15,043	11,688	76	3,355	77.2	0.5	22.3
Gadsden	36,975	29,415	153	7,559	79.1	0.4	20.4
Huntsville	13,050	8,335	67	4,710	63.4	0.5	36.1
Mobile	78,720	49,606	1,472	29,046	61.1	1.9	36.9
Montgomery	78,084	43,547	592	34,535	55.0	0.8	44.2
Phenix City	15,351	10,340	20	5,011	67.2	0.1	32.6
Selma	19,834	8,875	94	10,958	44.3	0.5	55.2
Tuscaloosa	27,493	17,314	183	10,178	62.3	0.7	37.0

(The above info has been taken from reports issued by the Bureau of Census U.S. Department of Commerce)

Economics

With regard to those economic forces causing unrest among the Negroes in this area, it has been reported that in several of the larger areas, employment for the Negroes there has been increased. In the vicinity of Birmingham, Alabama, the coal mines there employ approximately 60 per cent Negroes, the ore mines approximate[ly] 50 per cent, while the steel mills have a 35 per cent Negro representation.

In and around the vicinity of Tuskegee, Alabama, sources of information there advise that Negroes are well employed in this area. In this connection, it should be pointed out that one of the largest Negro universities in the world is located there, as well as a United States Army Air Corps flying field.

The Negro housing situation has improved in several localities in that several Negro housing projects have been undertaken.

With regard to those preventive or alleviating measures which have been taken to bring about a degree of satisfaction, it has been pointed out that although certain colored training schools have been maintained since February, 1942, offering instructions to qualified students as welders and automobile mechanics and shippers, it has been reported that the Negroes have been neither enthusiastic for this training nor cognizant of the opportunities it offers. In this regard, a representative of the United States Employment Service has stated that especially in the area of Tuskegee, employment for skilled and unskilled Negroes has been found and on several occasions the Service has been able to supply other districts with workers where a labor shortage has occurred. However, it should be noted that it is reported besides a few skilled carpenters and bricklayers, by far the average Negro in this area is unskilled and domestic, thereby not meeting with the qualifications to be recommended for employment by the Employment Service.

For some time there has been considerable advocacy of equal political and social rights in this State. An example of this is pointed out in the desire and the demand on the part of Negroes to sit in the white sections of street cars and buses. Other demands for Negro places in juries have, of course, been made.

In at least two large areas, such as Bessemer and Mobile, Alabama, there exists a sullen resentment on the part of the Negroes to the line of demarcation which has existed there for many years. One source of information interviewed advises that as a result of his conversation with Negro ministers and politicians, the agitation among the Negroes is almost exclusively limited to political and economic forces and was not based upon race hatred or desire to mingle with the white people socially on the part of Negroes.

Another source of information has pointed out the age-old line of social demarcation in Alabama and in the South and advises that it is his opinion this has been the basis for a strong friendship between Negroes and white people existing until recently. With regard to this line of social demarcation, this informant advises that the same has been a matter of necessity, not only for the betterment of the Negro race, but for its protection in the South, inasmuch as when people attempt to cross this line there is immediately created a racial prejudice, enmity and hatred. With regard to this opinion, of course, it should be pointed out that it is based upon the convictions of one who has always resided in the South.

It is believed worthy of note, as an example of social conditions causing trouble, to set forth the conception of the situation in Mobile, Alabama supplied by the source of information who has lived, worked and talked among Negroes in this city for the past eight or nine years. He has advised that one of the main causes of the racial difficulty in the city of Mobile is the bus situation. There are not enough buses for the number of people who wish to use them with the result that the white and colored people are jammed together with no division between them. This source has pointed out that Negroes complain that the bus drivers, if the bus is anywhere near full, will not stop for them with the result they are forced to wait sometimes as long as two hours before one will stop. He has informed that almost every day there are arguments on buses between whites and Negroes.

This source has also referred to a large influx of illiterate Negroes in Mobile, Alabama and his impression that these Negroes seem to be boiling over for a fight. He has stated that if there is any racial riot in Mobile it will be caused by the low class of whites and the illiterate of Negroes, the better class of Negroes not desiring to cause any trouble. He has stated the more stable Negroes do not desire any trouble and are afraid of the more radical type. Among this latter type this source claims there is a real hatred for white people and a desire that the United States will be defeated so that they will be paid back for the trouble caused to the Negroes.

This source of information in Mobile, Alabama, has also referred to another problem which he believes to be a major source of dissension between white and colored people. He has pointed out that the Negroes believe they should be able to work in the shipyards and other defense industries on a basis of equality with the white people, and further that they have the requisite skill to be hired as a skilled laborer and not as a helper. The source of information has stated that numerous Negroes have told him of having been hired as welder helpers in the Alabama Drydock and Shipbuilding Corporation, Mobile, Alabama, and having worked there a number of years after they obtained the required skill to be classified as an expert welder, they are required however to remain as a helper while a white man who knows little about the trade is employed as a welder. The source of information further advised that the colored people cannot understand why they are not employed in the Gulf Shipbuilding Corporation, that they read in the papers frequently the corporation is badly in need of help, yet when they make applications for work with the Company they are told Negroes are not being hired.

This source of information in Mobile, Alabama has informed that despite the fact Negroes are not being employed as skilled workmen they are receiving more money than ever before as common laborers and they are now better off financially than ever before. As a result of this increased financial status, according to the source, Negroes have a growing sense of importance.

Another source of information, a Negro teacher at the Tuskegee Institute, Montgomery, Alabama, has supplied what in his belief are the major causes of Negro agitation, unrest and dissatisfaction:

1. Inequality in wages.
2. Desire for all rights of Negroes to be equal to those of Whites although not necessarily using the same facilities.
3. Rough treatment by white people administered to Negroes.

This source of information has elaborated stating Negroes do not demand the right to mix and mingle with white people socially although they believe they should have the same facilities for themselves as are made available to the white people, as regards riding on buses. He informed Negroes do not desire to ride with white people in their section of the bus, but do feel that those sections reserved for Negroes should be retained for them and not used for white people in crowded conditions.

This source of information, **the Negro teacher at Tuskegee Institute,** has cited another situation wherein he pointed out large numbers of Negroes in Montgomery, Alabama, owe large debts. This, he advised, results from the desire of Negroes to live as do white people and consequently they have endeavored to live much beyond their income.

A Negro source of information in **Montgomery, Alabama, who has military connections** has expressed the following:

There is no foreign or Communist inspired agitation in this area and there is no need for any. He stated the Negroes are a minority group discriminated against by white people. He stated that the antagonism on the part of Negroes in this area results from their unpleasant experiences and not from any concerted effort to agitate them.

He believed at the time there is a feeling of discouragement among the Negroes and that the tension becomes greater as Negroes become more educated. Among other things this source of information said as instances which give [rise?] to dissatisfaction are:

1. Public utterances by Southern white political leaders who present a narrow view.
2. The increased reading of Negro newspapers which exploit racial matters.
3. The increased unemployment of Negroes.
4. The Poll Tax situation and the problem of voting.
5. Cases involving discrimination against individual Negroes.
6. Efforts on the part of the Government to have the Negro returned from defense employment, paying 40¢ an hour, to farm work paying 50¢ a day.
7. Occurrences of discrimination in the everyday treatment and dealings of white people with Negroes.

Another source of information, a white person, who has been contacted, has expressed the opinion that the white people, not only in the North, but in the South as well, have created a large portion of the present racial situation through their taking advantage of the Negroes' position and consequently must accept the responsibility for the same. This source of information predicated his remarks with the statement that he had been born and raised in the South and did not believe in equality.

During the past several months there has been considerable agitation for anti-poll tax legislation. It is reported that many Southerners regard this as being directed to the South as a whole and the rights of the States to control their own elections. It is looked upon as a force causing the respect and deference of Negroes for the white race to disappear. It is pointed out that this is the Southern attitude. The promulgation of the anti-lynch bills in Congress have also been regarded as an affront. It should be pointed out at this time that considerable agitation and activity with regard to the promotion of an anti-poll tax and anti-lynch bill may be attributed to the Communist Party and its various front organizations. However, it is believed that many sincere and well-meaning individuals and organizations also support such moves.

Organizations

National Association for the Advancement of Colored People

A source of information has advised with regard to this organization and its existence in the South that although it has on the surface the appearance of a small following throughout the South, its influence through its teachings and publications reaches the average Southern Negro. It is reported that it is believed the membership of this organization throughout the State of Alabama is comparatively small.

A source of information, believed to be unbiased in his beliefs has pointed out that this organization serves as an agitational force in that he believes a majority of the beliefs and ideas of the organization have their origin in the North and are possibly fostered by Northern Negroes who are stated not to thoroughly understand the problems of the South in this regard. Further criticism of the organization is reflected in the observation that a large number of the sponsors of the National Association for the Advancement of Colored People are white people who are also not familiar with the problems involved and, for that reason, the organization is looked upon as a definite agitational medium.

Southern Negro Youth Congress

It should be stated to begin with that this organization is a Communist front. Its meetings are held usually in the colored Masonic Temple in Birmingham, Alabama. It has been reported with respect to this organization, which is, of course, very active in its agitation for and among the Negroes, that it is becoming known as a Communist front and its membership consequently declining. At one time it held meetings at Tuskegee Institute, Tuskegee, Alabama, when it received the support of the president of that University. However, upon his learning of the Communist influence and control of the organization he declined further to associate with it or members of the group or to allow them to meet at the University.

Communist Party

The Communist Party is, of course, extensively and extremely active in its agitation among the Negroes, using as an appeal the demand for equality, nondiscrimination and nonsegregating moves. This, of course, has been trumpeted through the Party's generally recognized official organ, the Daily Worker, and other publications. It is not believed, however, that its membership among the Negroes in this area is exceedingly large, although it is pointed out that its appeal and method in its contact with and for the Negroes are in their very nature agitational.

The guiding figure of the Communist Party in this area is Robert Hall, District 17 Secretary of the Communist Party. His position has been stated very clearly in a letter of his published in the August 23, 1942, issue of the Daily Worker where he states:

> "Yes, it is true, there is a great upsurge among the Negro people, a powerful, domestic popular upsurge, inspired by profound aspirations for the racial liberation. You cannot stay this movement with words. You cannot ex[o]rcise it with counsels of caution. You cannot smash it with terror, but you can win its support as a noble, courageous, and selfsacrificing ally if you come to it with a program for the defeat of the Axis, which includes elementary rights for the Negro people."

The effect of this statement is, of course, in harmony with the Communist Party line in regard to the Negro question in that it demands loudly further and more extensive rights be granted to the Negroes but at the same time desiring to maintain and inspire an all-out effort on the part of the Negroes in the war program.

Southern Conference for Human Welfare

This organization has been reported to have a small degree of Communist influence in it and has collaborated in various issues with other Communist Party front organizations. An example of its attitude toward the Negroes is reflected in a recent advertisement inserted by it in the August 16, 1942, issue of the Birmingham News, Age-Herald which demanded further rights for the Negroes.

Labor Unions

A source of information has volunteered the opinion that labor unions are perhaps of the most important phases in connection with any discussion of the racial conditions existing at the present time in the South. In this connection, the premise is laid down that the success of a union undoubtedly depends entirely upon the number of its members. In elaborating, it is stated that in view of the large number of Negroes employed in the various mines and mills in the vicinity of the Alabama industrial area, many union organizers and representatives are naturally attracted with the prospect of increasing membership through the securing of Negro members. They are stated to openly advocate better positions or better work for the Negro and insist in some instances upon their being placed in certain elevated positions.

It is further stated that during the meetings of labor unions no rules or regulations governing the seating of those in attendance exists, thus resulting in social intercourse between white and Negro people. It is further pointed out that the majority of the members of various unions address one another with the prefix of "Brother." It is concluded that the Negroes receiving this treatment, which is a different social feeling extended to them, naturally expect the same treatment at other times. ▬▬▬▬▬

▬▬▬▬▬▬▬▬▬▬▬▬▬▬▬▬▬▬▬▬▬▬▬▬▬▬▬▬▬▬

In this connection, an incident was reported involving Mary Southard, Communist Party member and secretary to Robert Hall, previously referred to, and her husband, Ordway (Spike) Southard, who appeared at one of the mines in the vicinity of Birmingham and openly mixed with Negro miners, distributing literature, shaking their hands and slapping them on the back and at the same time advising them of their equal rights and urging them to seek the same. As a result of their activities, a group of white miners dispersed the small gathering and "Spike" Southard was attacked and injured. This incident was immediately seized upon by the Communist Party and various sympathizers in and around Birmingham as an affront to the Negroes and those promulgating rights for them. It is reported confidentially that the reason for the visit by the Southards to the particular mine in question was prompted by their organizational activity in attempting to win over miners in that particular mine from the United Mine Workers, District 50, to the Mine, Mill and Smelter Workers Union of America. The rift between the two unions, of course, goes deeper in that since the disaffection of John L. Lewis to the C.I.O., certain Communist interests therein ha[ve] caused considerable fighting back and forth.

Another incident involving labor unions has been reported to the effect that beginning August 19, 1942, there were numerous "slowdowns" at the Central Foundry Company, Holt, Alabama, as a result of the union activities of both the A.F. of L. and the C.I.O. unions in struggling for bargaining rights at the plant. At the present time, the C.I.O. union claims a membership of 450 persons, all Negroes, while the A.F. of L. membership is reported to be composed of 350 persons, 95 per cent of whom are white. The remaining Negro workers at the plant are said to be the center of the struggle for control of the balance of voting power.

It is claimed there have been a series of walkouts by the Negroes of the union affiliated with the C.I.O. which were not concerned with wages, hours, or other employer-employee relations, but were purely jurisdictional in character. It is further claimed that no list of grievances has been presented to the company.

With employees divided along racial and union lines, it is said that the company has decreed that no white foreman in the plant may use force, or request a Negro workman to do anything which it appears he might refuse to do.

Blame is reported to be laid to Noell Beddow, Southern Director of the Congress of Industrial Organizations, Birmingham, Alabama, who is alleged to have been very active in soliciting the membership of Negroes of this company. It is further reported that a representative of the C.I.O. frequently conducts meetings at Castle Hill, Alabama, a Negro settlement, at which addresses are delivered by various organizers and local leaders. The leaders are said to be for the most part Negroes, including Sam Houston, Robert Magruder, Jr., Wesley Williams, Ed Hatton, and an individual whose last name is Burrows. These individuals are blamed by company officials for causing the various disturbances.

Newspapers

There are two local Negro newspapers in publication in the State of Alabama. One, the Weekly Review, has a circulation of approximately 9,000, while the other, the Birmingham World, has a still more local circulation. These newspapers seek the extension of rights among the Negroes and at times deplore the situation. At times, however, it is noted they have taken a nonpartisan point of view on the question in that on several occasions they have attacked the Negroes for their laxity in connection with health matters, moral standards and civic activities.

The circulation of the Pittsburgh Courier and the Chicago Defender is stated to be increasing in this area, while the Daily Worker, generally recognized as the Communist Party news organ, is believed to have but a small circulation, the exact extent, however, is not known.

The influence of these papers is considered by those sources of information interviewed as being largely responsible for the "situation" inasmuch as nearly all instances involving the Negro race are the subject of considerable comment.

Fair Employment Practices Committee

This committee held hearings in Birmingham June 18, 19 and 20, 1942. Allegations from a confidential source have been made that the line of questioning followed by committee members and their counsel, as well as "comments" made by them "established to its own satisfaction that there was racial discrimination in the South." It was further alleged that contradictory statements were made by members and no "frank statement to this committee of the peculiar Negro problem which has been the South's for generations" was made.

It was stated that the agents of the Fair Employment Practices Committee found the following to exist in this area:

"Refusal to hire skilled Negro workmen for jobs where they will have to work alongside white workmen.

"Refusal to pay skilled or semi-skilled Negro workmen the same rate paid white workmen on the same jobs.

"Refusal to give Negroes in-plant training along with white workers.

"Failure to 'up-grade' Negro workers on the same basis as white workers are 'up-graded.'

"Failure to hire Negroes in proportion to their total population in the community."

Certain cases of discrimination in industries in this area were considered. The industries involved were:

Vultee Aircraft, Nashville

Gulf Shipbuilding Corporation, Mobile

Alabama Drydock and Shipbuilding Company, Mobile

Honeycutt Construction Company, Birmingham

Bell Aircraft, Atlanta, Georgia

Delta Shipbuilding Corporation, New Orleans

McEvoy Shipbuilding Company, Savannah

(Associated Industries of Ala. Brown. Marx Bld. Birmingham, Ala).

With regard to the hearings of this committee, a confidential source of information has offered the opinion that the full import of the meeting was not understood by the majority of Negroes in that area and that it was a good thing they did not. This opinion is, of course, merely furnished in addition to those previously referred to in this matter to reflect Southern attitude.

Schools

Separate schools for the Negro race are maintained in this State and as a rule they are staffed by Negro teachers. In this connection, it is pointed out that Tuskegee Institute is one of the largest Negro universities in the world. No information has been received indicating that Negroes in this area have complained concerning the educational facilities available to them there.

The United States Army

The information set out under this caption as it pertains to the problems arising from the present war conditions is to the effect that many Negro soldiers have been stationed in this State. This is stated to present a problem inasmuch as the Negroes are a mixed group of Northern and Southern troops and the Northern Negroes, who have become use[d] to nondiscrimination and the lack of segregation prevalent in the North, have caused some degree of unrest.

Ku Klux Klan

Rumors have been received indicating the possible existence and reorganization of the Ku Klux Klan in this area. However, nothing definite has been developed to date reflecting its existence. Likewise, rumors which have been checked into thoroughly with regard to the existence of Eleanor Clubs in this State have been gone into thoroughly with, however, negative results.

Individuals

Two diametrically opposed schools of thought exist on the part of individuals in this State who have expressed themselves openly, if not vehemently, relative to the Negro situation. First are those radical individuals such as Robert F. Hall, secretary of District 17 of the Communist Party, U.S.A., his secretary, Mary Southard, and her husband, Ordway "Spike" Southard. On the other hand, there are those individuals prominent in State affairs and politics who have expressed themselves in what is alleged to be a bigoted manner.

Another type of individual who has been active with regard to the Negroes in this area is the type who is prominent in national, political and social matters who allegedly is unfamiliar with Southern conditions but who has made expressions concerning the extension of Negro rights and as a result is believed to incite, if not inflame, the members of the Negro race. (The politically prominent person referred to is stated by a source of Info. to be Mrs. Eleanor Roosevelt.)

General

Besides the activity of the Communist Party among the Negroes in this area, there is to be considered the activity of the Southern Negro Youth Congress, a Communist front organization. The meetings of this organization are generally held in the colored Masonic Temple in Birmingham, Alabama. Robert S. Hall, Communist Party secretary for District 17 of the Communist Party including the state of Alabama, and Mary Southard, an active member in the Birmingham area, are said to be frequently present at the meetings of the organization and are constantly engaged in its activity. It is reported, however, that it has become known to some members of the organization that the same is being infiltrated with Communists and for that reason the membership is consequently declining.

In the area around and in the city of Mobile, Alabama, inquiries made for indications of foreign inspired agitation or unrest among the Negroes there, have met with negative results. It is reported, however, that some remarks made by Negroes there reflect pro-Axis sentiment. However, upon inquiries being made, no definite information has been developed.

There is a local chapter of the National Association for the Advancement of Colored People in Mobile which is said to be active in agitating for the betterment of Negroes. A confidential source of information has stated that it is his belief that there are no Communist affiliations on the part of officers of this chapter.

In the area of Mobile, Alabama, it has been reported that union activities among the Negroes there have been a source of some unrest and discontent. It is reported that at the Alabama Drydock and Shipbuilding Company, located in Mobile, a Negro organizer, one Alfred Dickinson arranges for meetings of Negroes in groups of ten or fifteen every night, at which the Negroes discuss their problems. It has been reported that Dickinson regards these meetings as organizational measures against fights and dissension at the shipyard as well as education for new men in unionism and democracy.

Extensive inquiries have been made in the following areas for evidence of un-American activities among and on the part of Negroes and all have met with negative results:

> Xufaula, Cullman, Jackson County, Madison County, Evergreen, Washington County, Jackson, Grove Hill, Fulton, Talladega County, Greenesville, Marion, Selma, Notasulga and Opelika.

Various reports have been received, however, in these areas, reflecting a "different" attitude on the part of the Negroes there, indicating possible unrest and sullenness on their part.

In the vicinity of Tuskegee, unrest and agitation among the Negroes there is said to be attributable to discrimination against them. Furthermore, some blame is laid to politically prominent people who have visited Tuskegee Institute.

It is reported that in the area of Tuscaloosa, Alabama, that organizers of affiliated unions of the Congress of Industrial Organizations through their union activities use racial hatred as a wedge to get their point. No information has been reported or received reflecting possible un-American activities among the Negroes in this area.

It has been further reported that a large percentage of the ammunition sales made by hardware stores in this Tuscaloosa area were made to Negroes. It was said that the heaviest purchases made were of hollow point .22 calibre ammunition.

In this connection it has been additionally reported that much of the trouble in Tuscaloosa area and in nearby Holt, Alabama, has resulted from jurisdictional battles between A.F. of L. and C.I.O. unions. It is said that considerable dissension has been caused by reason of the A.F. of L. offering to take Negroes into the union but on the other hand C.I.O. union organizers have promised Negroes social equality if they will stay with the C.I.O. union involved. At the Central Foundry Company in Holt, Alabama, on September 7, 1942, the A.F. of L. Union represented at that plant announced that a picket line would be established at 2 a.m. on the morning of September 8, 1942, at the company. It was said that the officials of the Central Foundry Company were asked to suspend operations in order to avoid bloodshed. It was further alleged that it was heard of Negroes that they were going through the picket line if it were established, if they had to shoot their way through. Officials of the company first agreed to suspend operations then changed their minds. Shortly after 2 a.m. September 8, 1942, the white workers established a picket line and were fully armed, according to reports. The Negroes allegedly approached the picket line from the top of the hill and were also armed. The conflict is said to have been avoided when the company ceased operations temporarily. On the same date it was further reported that an unprecedented number of Negroes had made inquiries in that community regarding purchasing of firearms and that one gun shop alone, until the latter part of August had received on the average of fifteen inquiries a day relative to the purchase of firearms. It is said that the owner of one particular repair shop for firearms had deliberately quoted highly excessive rates in order to avoid having to repair the guns offered by Negroes.

[*100-135-5*]

Allegations were received in the month of November, 1942, to the effect that there were in existence in the State of Alabama, especially in and around Mobile, Alabama, organizations known as "Eleanor Clubs". Further allegation received was to the effect that such groups were foreign inspired and were organized at the instance of un-American forces. Numerous inquiries were made to determine whether such allegations had any foundation and sources of information who were interviewed and contacted relative to the matter and who are believed to be in an excellent position to know the situation among the Negro race in that area, have all advised without exception that they knew of no such clubs in actual existence. In this connection no one has ever been able to state in the inquiries made, that they knew of persons actually belonging to such clubs and no persons interviewed could give the sources of their information when they suspected that such clubs were in existence.

On the night of May 24, 1943, a group of Negro welders and burners, whose employment in this capacity had allegedly been sponsored by the Industrial Union of Marine and Shipbuilding Workers of America, C.I.O., because of a reported shortage of available white welders, commenced work at the Alabama Drydock and Shipbuilding Company. The following morning white employees, upon arrival at the yards for the first shift beginning at 7:00 o'clock learned of the employment of the Negroes as welders, and, apparently in resentment of this fact, attacked other Negro employees of the yards at approximately 10:00 o'clock on that morning. As a result of the riot which resulted, approximately twenty-five persons were injured, only two seriously, these being Negroes. Rumors immediately gained circulation that numerous persons had been killed, but these were apparently without foundation. The riot was quelled by local policemen and deputy sheriffs with the assistance of a detachment of soldiers from Brookley Field, Alabama. Sailors were immediately assigned to the guarding of the United States Navy property at the yards, and soldiers began to patrol the streets of Mobile.

Shortly after the riot, plant officials were reported to have urged that Negro workers remain away from the yards until further notice. Consequently, of the several thousand Negro workers believed to be employed at the yards, none appeared for work on the afternoon of the riot; however, at this time information was that all of the white employees had resumed work. Several Negroes were said to have returned to their jobs on the night of May 26, but it was reported that white welders and burners, upon learning of this on the morning of May 27, forced the Negroes to leave and they, themselves, left the yards. The result of this was that practically no work was done on May 27. War Manpower Commission officials estimated that about 6,000 out of 15,000 employees were absent from the yards on the latter day. The Negro employees, it was stated, were being prevented from returning to work by the fact that white persons were stopping them on the highways and warning the Negroes not to return.

On the morning of May 28, 1943, it was estimated that ninety-eight per cent of the welders and burners were absent from the yards, although on that night two Negro welders resumed work on the third shift. As of May 29, production was estimated to be fifty per cent of normal when approximately four hundred of the twenty-two hundred negroes employed had returned. The yards were completely idle on Sunday, May 30, but this was partially explained by the fact that Sunday production is normally extremely light. On May 31, it was estimated that about two thousand out of a total of twenty-two hundred negroes returned to work on the first shift, beginning at 7:00 o'clock in the morning. Practically all of the white employees were then at work but a few left shortly thereafter, pending alleged plans for segregation of the negroes.

With regard to union activities at the yard it was understood that both the American Federation of Labor and the CIO were represented at the plant, the latter as aforestated, by the Industrial Union of Marine and Shipbuilding Workers of America. The CIO union as above mentioned reportedly sponsored the hiring of the negro welders and burners when it appeared that sufficient white welders and burners were not available. This union was also alleged to have promised the negroes skilled positions with the company. At the time of the rioting no action was taken by the CIO union although plans for an early meeting were alleged to have been immediately formed; however, negro members of the American Federation of Labor union were said to have been ordered by their officers to remain away from the yards.

Information was also received that Paul Elmer Babcock, former President of the CIO union at subject company, had called meetings of this union on May 27 and 28, 1943, for the purpose of voting on a general work walkout. Babcock was alleged to have made the statement that the reason for the walkout at the lower yard on May 27, 1943, was the fact that workmen there had not been represented at union meetings.

Charles Hanson, Regional Organizer of the Industrial Union of Marine and Shipbuilding Workers of America, CIO, branded the meetings called by Babcock as unauthorized, and reportedly ejected Babcock from the union. Babcock was accused by Hanson of fomenting trouble at the Alabama Drydock and Shipbuilding Company by the use of inflammatory statements. Hanson and Babcock are said to have long been bitter enemies and the latter was generally suspected of attempting to regain control of the CIO union by taking advantage of the riot.

With further regard to Charles Hanson, it was learned that he made statements to the effect that the riot was instigated by Axis Agents whose identities were known to him. On May 29, 1943, Hanson was interviewed with regard to these charges by the United States Attorney and an Agent of the Federal Bureau of Investigation at Mobile, Alabama. At this time Hanson denied that he had ever charged that the riot was instigated by Axis agents, and explained in this regard that his only comment was a suggestion that enemy-inspired sabotage might have been the reason for the riot. However, Hanson could provide no basis for his suspicions, nor could he name any persons whom he suspected of being enemy agents. He did refer, however, to one Nern, an employee of the company, who, on the morning of the riot, allegedly stated that he would not work side by side with negroes and that he would see to it that none of the white welders worked with negro welders.

Hanson also claimed that on the morning of the riot two unidentified men ran from ship to ship urging the white employees not to tolerate the negro welders. Eventually Hanson expressed the opinion that the trouble was purely racial in character. He claimed that it might have been averted had the company informed the employees that the use of negroes as welders and burners was planned. According to Hanson, the union was ruined by reason of its sponsorship of the negro welders and burners.

The rumor was rife that the riot was incited by subversive elements at the Alabama Drydock and Shipbuilding Corporation and that the Federal Bureau of Investigation was conducting an investigation of this allegation. Further, it was rumored that this Bureau arrested some men for spreading baseless statements, one of which was that all of the white men employed by the company would be inducted into the Army and that white women, most of whom were reported to be married, would have to work side by side with the negro employees. It was alleged that the Industrial Union of Marine and Shipbuilding Workers of America, CIO, was largely responsible for the spreading of these rumors.

Charlotte Field Division

In this area rumors and complaints have been received to the effect that statements were circulating among the Negroes of the benefits which would be received as a result of an Axis victory in the present world conflict. However, the information reported has been nonspecific and attempts to verify the same are met with negative results. Definite information has been received that the Communist Party is active in agitating among and for the rights of the Negroes and, in some instances, attempting to show that Negroes are being mistreated by white people and that discrimination, lack of equal rights and "Jim Crowism" exist.

Reliable and prominent Negro sources of information interviewed are of the opinion that Negro publications in this area play no small part in causing discontent among the Negroes inasmuch as these publications play up the alleged mistreatment of the Southern Negroes by the white people of the South. In this connection, information has been received indicating that the Negroes do not believe they are receiving equal rights and have instituted a drive relative to this allegation which is allegedly being used as a stimulant to revive the Ku Klux Klan.

Active in some localities in this area are several chapters of the National Association for the Advancement of Colored People and the Civil Rights League.

Unverified statements to the effect that one of the pro-Axis powers would win the war in the near future have been reported and attempts to verify the statements as having been made have met with negative results. In one instance the person uttering the statement was intoxicated at the time and when sober could not recall anything said.

Several pro-Japanese utterances have been reported. However, attempts to obtain specific information relative to them have proved negative. With regard to the Communist Party, information has been received reflecting that there is general widespread Party activity with regard to agitating among the Negroes. It is said that this activity is carried on in all sections of North Carolina and South Carolina. It has further been reported that in several of the local chapters of the National Association for the Advancement of Colored People there appeared to be indications of Communist influence.

Typical of the activity of the Communist Party is that reported by a confidential informant who has advised that the argument of the Communist Party in this area in attempting to recruit new members among the Negroes is that as Hitler is persecuting the Jews in Europe, so America is persecuting the Negroes. It is stated Communist organizers gave as an example the allegation that the Marine Corps, Air Corps and Coast Guard of the United States did not allow Negroes in those services and, therefore, why should the Negro fight to save democracy when democracy is not doing anything to help the Negro. In this connection, it is reported that 530 different Negro homes in Winston-Salem, North Carolina, were visited in July of 1940 and Communist literature distributed in all of them.

Educational matters are also said to be dealt with by the Party to the effect that no pretense is made about providing equal educational facilities and opportunities for the Negro people and that the Negro schools had been systematically discriminated against for more than forty years in this area. Emphasis is also said to be laid on the allegation that Negro teachers receive less pay for the same work as that of white teachers which is in direct violation of Federal court interpretations of statutes.

The Communist Party leader in this area, Bart Hunter Logan, who is stated to operate from High Point, North Carolina, is reported as attempting to indoctrinate Negroes with Communism on every available occasion, telling them that they are being treated unfairly and are being discriminated against by white people.

The following Negro publications are distributed in this area: the Afro-American, the Pittsburgh Courier, the Chicago Defender, the Norfolk Journal and Guide, the Peoples Voice and the Charlotte Post. Articles appearing in several of these publications are devoted to discussions of racial equality on the part of the Negro.

A prominent Negro in Wilmington, North Carolina, who is connected with Tuskegee Institute and who resides in Wilmington, North Carolina, has advised that he has preached in many churches throughout the South and knows Negroes of all walks of life in this area. This source of information has advised that he believes any plan on the part of foreign powers to inspire unrest and dissatisfaction among the Negroes would fail. He advises that the Negro element in the South is patriotic as a result of the Negroes' conception of the Government in the United States that it is a creation made possible by the Negroes' own efforts inasmuch as they have produced a large amount of wealth in this country and have, in a sense, been pioneers in its development. This same source of information advises of rumors he has heard with regard to anti-American and Communist organizations working among the Negroes and that he has traced these rumors down on numerous occasions finding them to be false. He states he believes these rumors are in many instances started by disgruntled white people who are jealous over high wages being received by Negroes. He points out that formerly where Negroes earned ten or twelve dollars a week they are now able to support their own homes without their wives doing domestic work in white homes and are earning from sixty to seventy dollars a week. He further states that this condition has created a shortage of domestic workers in some areas and many white people have been of the opinion that Negroes "were up to something" as they would not do domestic work.

This source of information has advised that while an affiliate of the Congress of Industrial Organizations was attempting to obtain the bargaining rights at the North Carolina Shipbuilding Company, many Negroes came to him daily asking his advice as to the advisability of joining the organization. He advises that he in turn told them that it was within their own opinion as to whether the company would be more productive with the union or without it. In this regard, he states that the average Negro worker is torn between two opinions—one, if he does not join the union and the union is successful in creating a closed shop, he would then be thrown out of employment; on the other hand, if he does join the union and strife between labor and capital develops, then he is subject to being unemployed. He further points out that decisions reached by the Negroes will not, in his estimation, be influenced by any form of foreign agitation but rather as a result of their personal convictions.

Another Negro source of information believed to be closely connected with the Negro population of Wilmington, North Carolina, advises that in his opinion there is no foreign-inspired agitation among the Negroes in that section although there is considerable local feeling between the Negroes and the white people with reference to such things as inadequate transportation facilities, particularly as to bus transportation from their homes to their places of employment inasmuch as there was at one time an insufficient number of buses for white and Negro workers to ride to work separately. Another influencing factor in the unrest of the Negroes, he advises, is the lack of adequate housing facilities. He has advised, however, that Negroes in this area have been purchasing war bonds.

With reference to the union said to be attempting to organize the North Carolina Shipbuilding Company, it is believed that it is the Industrial Union of Marine and Shipbuilding Workers of America. It is said that among the organizers are two members of the Communist Party, namely, one B. O. Borah and one James Evans, Negro, stated to have been affiliated with the Longshoremen in North Carolina.

Active in and around Chapel Hill, North Carolina, is said to be one Sidney Rittenberg, stated to be closely associated with Bart Hunter Logan, leader of the Communist Party in North Carolina, who is stated to have been active in telling Negroes that they should be equal with the white people and have equal rights and that they should have equal union rights. This individual is also reported as having told Negroes in this area that they would be unemployed in a very short time if they did not join the union but on the other hand, if they did join, the company for which they worked could not dismiss them.

Information offered by persons who are in a position to understand and know the sympathies of Negroes in and around the area of Davidson, North Carolina have advised that they know of no foreign inspired activities or sympathies among the Negroes in this area. Complaints were received however, reflecting that some Negroes in domestic positions were indifferent toward their work and had assumed a different attitude than was shown in that area. A confidential source has also advised that the Negro selectees in this area are complying promptly with the Selective Training and Service Act.

On October 20, 1942, the Southern Conference on Race Relations was held at Durham, North Carolina. The meeting was attended and conducted by a group made up of seventy-five prominent Negroes in the South. Various panel groups dealt with such subjects as: civil rights, education, industry, service occupation, agriculture, social welfare and health. It is pointed out that the various aims promoted at this Conference are set out hereinafter in a separate section, in view of the fact that steps promulgated, in the program reflect a different attitude on the part of Negro leaders than has been generally assumed in the Negro press and by national leaders of this race.

It has been said that closely related to the activities of the Communist Party is the membership drive presently being made by labor unions in North and South Carolina for membership among the Negroes there. It is said further that in the bargaining with employers, union organizers have demanded equality of job rating for Negroes and whites as well as the promise that discrimination will not be countenanced by the company. It has been related that such a contract was obtained by the Aluminum Workers of America, CIO, at the Baden, North Carolina plant of the Aluminum Company of America. Sources of information who have been contacted have advised among other things that southern labor as a whole, that is white labor, is far from being sympathetic with such a program. In this connection it has been pointed out that recently there was a four hour "shut-down" at the Argon-Baldwin Company at Whitmire, South Carolina, because the company had sought to hire Negro laborers, thereby breaking away from the company tradition of employing white persons only.

Another situation which is alleged to be arising has been described by sources of information and confidential informants in the North and South Carolina area. It is said that the white population of these two states is deeply aware of the fact that Negroes in certain areas are numerically equal or greater and has therefore viewed the Negro activity in this area with great concern. It is alleged that one manifestation of this concern is the wide spread rumor regarding Negro activities and plans. Typical rumors are those dealing with the wholesale purchase of weapons ranging from guns to ice picks, by Negroes. Another rumor has it that when all of the white men have been drafted the Negroes will take over their homes and wives. And still another set of rumors state that when the Germans take over the United States there will be a more equal distribution of property. A recent rumor is that incidents between white persons and Negroes presently taking place throughout the South on public conveyances are engineered and planned in advance by Negro leaders in order that the question of segregation will be kept before the public.

A second, and what is alleged as a more serious manifestation of the concern of the white population over the present Negro unrest is a reported revival of an organization similar to the Ku Klux Klan. Recently a confidential source of information submitted a report on the organization known as the "Blue Shirts" which was described as indicative of such spirit. The report described an alleged situation in the State of South Carolina near two large military encampments: Camp Croft at Spartanburg, and Camp Jackson at Columbia. There is also in this area a large air base at Greenville and one in process of building at Greenwood. In this area incidents of violence reportedly are aggravating the tense situation. It was said that during the middle of July, 1942, there were reported beatings of Negroes by groups of whites in Anderson, Spartanburg, Due West, Ninety-Six, and Greenwood. It was further alleged that in Greenwood, from the first week in July to the 25th day of that month, there were several scattered attacks on the Negroes by armed whites, and further, on Saturday, July 25, 1942, several Negroes were beaten in a midtown section of Greenwood. The Negroes then were reportedly ordered not to appear on the streets of the city after nine o'clock. It is said that these orders did not come from city authorities but from a group of people who were allegedly terrorizing the Negro population.

In connection with such incidents reported to have taken place was further alleged that on Saturday, July 18, 1942, approximately five automobiles and a truckload of white men held a meeting of an hour's duration on a farm near the city of Greenwood. It was said that several of the group were recognized and identified by witnesses. The group was allegedly believed to be the same group said to have held a meeting at the Greenwood brick yard which called themselves "Blue Shirts." A confidential source of information further stated that through this period, that is in the month of July, 1942, even Negro women were being molested and beaten by groups of white men. Much resentment was said to have been expressed by the Negro population and Negroes allegedly began to secretly arm themselves for protection. A rumor was reportedly spread to the effect that approximately fifty families left the area because of this alleged terrorism during the period.

A group of white people alleged to have been connected with such goings-on were described by sources of information of a confidential informant as being composed of irresponsible people, most of whom were drinking at the time, although it was alleged that there were some leading citizens in groups known as the "Blue Shirts." It was further reported that responsible citizens in and around Greenwood were taking steps to control them. The opinion was given that outside agitation was largely responsible for the position.

One source of information has advised that from his personal inquiry it has been revealed that a number of white people were using the rumor that Negroes were not being drafted as fast as whites to cause dissatisfaction. Rumors concerning "Eleanor Clubs," this same source of information advised, all prove to be mythical. The political campaigns carried on in the State of South Carolina and Georgia were pointed to, by this source of information, as a possible foundation for a good number of the rumors and reports concerning dissatisfaction among the Negroes.

With further regard to the National Association for the Advancement of Colored People, more recent information reflects that it presently has active chapters in the cit[ies] of Asheville, Charlotte, Durham, Fayetteville, Rocky Mount, Statesville and Winston-Salem, North Carolina. The actual membership of each of these groups is probably in the neighborhood of one hundred fifty to two hundred persons in each unit; however, the active membership is probably one-fifth of this number. In the early part of 1943 the organization instituted a major membership drive in this state with the aim of recruiting one thousand new members.

Among the points in its program in this area are:

1. Abolition of discrimination in the armed forces.
2. Urging equality of pay for white and Negro teachers.
3. Attacking alleged discrimination in the employment of Negroes as policemen and firemen.
4. Urging anti-lynching bills and the abolition of discrimination in all courts.
5. Seeking the abolition of the poll tax and other forms of allegedly discriminatory regulations which take the franchise from the Negro.

No information has been reported, however, that the various branches of the National Association for the Advancement of Colored People in North Carolina or in the western district of South Carolina, which is covered by the Charlotte Field Division, have attempted to agitate the Negro population along the lines of social segregation. Rather, it is reported, they have devoted themselves solely to the question of racial discrimination.

In this connection, it is reported that the Communist Party line in this area appears to parallel closely that of the National Association for the Advancement of Colored People. Furthermore, it is said that the Party does not desire to create open friction or to encourage race riots and for that reason does not deliberately incite the Negroes along the lines of social segregation. The Party is anxious to increase its membership among Negroes in this area. While certain Negroes are reported to have definite Communist tendencies, no indications have been received that the Party has successfully infiltrated the various Negro groups and especially the National Association for the Advancement of Colored People. Along these lines, the legal advisor and Secretary of the Charlotte branch of the National Association for the Advancement of Colored People has advised that if the Communist Party is permitted to obtain a foothold in the organization, an excuse would be offered to opposition groups for an open and sustained attack on the organization there. [*100-135-9-46*]

On April 3, 1943 several hundred Negro soldiers stationed at Camp Butner near Durham, North Carolina, as well as a few Negroes in civilian life in that city, were involved in what might be described as a racial disturbance in the Hayti section of that city. Their actions were directed primarily against the white law enforcement officers. The incident is said to have arose over an argument between a white liquor control board officer and a Negro soldier in a liquor store in that city, after the Negro was accused of having more than one ration book. He reportedly resisted and ran out of the store, the officer following. The Negro soldier succeeded in getting away, while the officer was confronted by the other Negro soldiers and was chased to the porch of a home at Fayetteville and Elm Streets. When officers arrived, they found the liquor control board officer with two other officers and one Negro Military Policeman on the porch of the home. Several colored lieutenants were attempting to quiet the soldiers, who were causing a considerable commotion and were throwing missiles. One civilian Negro was close by urging the soldiers on. The Negro soldier[s] failed to heed the requests of their officers as well as those of the police officers. Finally Military Police arrived and scattered the majority of the soldiers and ordered them to return to the camp.

The personal and the property damages were of a minor nature in this incident. It appears that the general tense feeling between white and Negro citizens in this community was responsible for the affair. This tense feeling, according to sources of information, arose out of several minor incidents involving attempts by local law enforcement officers to enforce segregation ordinances with respect to public conveyances. Trouble was also experienced by police in quieting or arresting unruly Negro soldiers until military authorities arrived. It has also been pointed out that there have been a number of situations wherein insults and vulgar remarks were made by Negroes to white people. This has been said to be possibly indicative of the outburst of feeling connected with the instant situation.

Another major factor contributing to this incident has been described by a source of information in a position to understand the various problems. This source of information has pointed out that there are approximately eleven thousand Negro soldiers at Camp Butner, who go into the city of Durham where there is a lack of proper facilities to absorb their activities. This source has also pointed out that Negroes coming from northern and western communities have different outlooks from those of southern origin. These Negroes give the impression they feel that southern law enforcement officers are "out to get them." Consequently, they are said to build up a defensive attitude toward law enforcement authorities.

A prominent Negro in the city of Durham has informed that the primary causes are the injustices and inequalities inflicted upon the Negro people. At this time he decried the abuses of Negroes by the police. He expressed the opinion that these conditions will probably continue to exist. He expressly stated that he believed there was no subversive inspiration behind the attitudes of the Negroes in this area, but rather they result from an awareness of discrimination.

In connection with the above mentioned incident, two Negro civilians were charged with violation of the peace statutes in the community. One was not apprehended while the other, one **Thomas C. Allen**, was found guilty of inciting and participating in unlawful assembly and ordered to serve six months in jail and placed on probation for a period of five years. Military authorities took no disciplinary action against the Negro soldiers, inasmuch as they were not identified. The original Negro soldier who scuffled with the liquor control board officer was not punished inasmuch as, according to military authorites, no evidence was presented to show he took part in the disturbance himself. [*100-135-9-57*]

A recent program has been adopted by Negro doctors and some schoolteachers in the city of Winston-Salem, North Carolina who are members of the Negro Chamber of Commerce there. These people are attempting to use their influence to change the administration of the Kate Bitting Hospital there. The reforms which are desired by them are as follows:

1. A separate hospital from the management of the city hospital.
2. Colored nurses to supervise each floor.
3. Colored doctors on the medical staff.
4. Resident doctors.
5. Respect of the white nurses for Negro doctors. [*100-135-9-58*]

Dallas Field Division

Investigation conducted in the vicinity of Fort Worth, Texarkana, Marshall, Denton, Whitesborro, Gainesville, Greenville, Sherman, Bonham, Amarillo, Lubbock, Tyler, Wichita Falls and Dallas, Texas, fails to indicate that any foreign-inspired agitation exists among the Negroes.

Investigations and inquiries made in this area, have failed to reflect any foreign inspired unrest or dissatisfaction among the Negroes there. However, there is stated to be unrest in the area due to alleged unemployment, discrimination, and a lynching that took place in Texarkana, Texas, this year.

In the areas covered by the city of San Angelo, and Abilene, sources of information contacted there advised that they are receiving no information reflecting unrest or any indication of agitation, on the Negroes of any type.

In the vicinity of Fort Worth, Texas, sources of information contacted there, advised that there is no agitation among Negroes at the present time. It is reported that the Negroes in this area are, of course, interested in sponsoring efforts in obtaining equal rights for themselves as in any other part of the United States. However, it is said that Negroes here have in no way attempted to evade the Selective Service laws or have even suggested that the instant war is a race war.

In the city of Texarkana, and its environs it is reported by sources of information that there has been pronounced agitation among the Negroes in that community, but it was not believed to have its origin or inspiration from any foreign or outside sources, rather it is said that much of it is based on alleged discrimination in defense projects against Negroes. Another source of unrest and dissatisfaction is said to exist in the denial of Negro occupancy in the Government housing projects there. It is said that one

Virgil Goree, a Negro editor and newspaper commentator, has agitated considerably against the denial of Negro occupancy in these housing projects as well as the lynching of a Negro who attempted to rape a white woman near the Red River Ordnance Depot in the vicinity of Texarkana, Texas.

Another matter causing agitation and unrest both among white and Negro people there, was the attempted rape by a colored man of a four year old daughter of a white family. A few hours after the event, however, the officers apprehended the Negro and spirited him out of town. He is presently confined in an unknown jail out of Texarkana, Texas. It is said by police officers there, that these attempted rapings had brought about such agitation.

Another phase of the situation in Texarkana, Texas, is the agitation among white householders who are said to have not been able to hold their colored servants as a result of the opportunities for the Negroes to obtain employment at higher wages on defense projects.

The only Negro newspaper published in the Texarkana area is the "Informer" which is published by Virgil Goree, supposedly either in Beaumont or Houston, Texas, and copies of the paper are expressed to Texarkana for distribution. The circulation of the paper, which is weekly, is said to be about thirty thousand copies per issue.

In and around the City of Marshall, Texas, sources of information have advised that there has been no agitation in this vicinity nor has there been any information reflecting any effort whatsoever from any outside force to cause dissatisfaction among the local Negro population which is said to be very large.

In and around the area of Denton, Texas, where there is said to be around a thousand Negroes, it is reported that there is no dissension or dissatisfaction among the Negro and white people and their attitude towards the war situation seems to be very good. It is said that outside of the "general brawls" among Negroes, they are generally well behaved and there is no trouble. It is said that the younger Negroes are anxious to get into the army and for that reason, a large number of the Negro boys are now in the service. At least twenty-five per cent having volunteered.

In the area surrounding and including Whitesboro, Texas it is reported that the only difficulty there is that a large majority of Negroes called for induction into the Army are rejected because of their physical condition.

In the areas covered by the Cities of Sherman, Gainesville, Greenville, Bonham, Amarillo and Tyler, Texas, it is reported that no indications of unrest or dissatisfaction exists.

In the vicinity of Lubbock, where Negro soldiers are assigned to the Lubbock Air Base it is believed that northern Negroes are attempting to get southern Negroes more privileges. However, outside of one or two instances in which Negro soldiers became abusive while in an intoxicated condition, no other indications of trouble have been reported.

In and around Wichita Falls, Texas, it is said there is a Negro population of approximately 5,000 persons or about 1,500 families. There are twelve Negro churches headed by L. C. Young, President of the Ministerial Alliance. There are many organizations active there including the National Association for the Advancement of Colored People Chapter, a Masonic Lodge, and other social organizations.

Sources of information there advised, however, of no indication of attempts by any pressure groups to regiment Negro opinion.

In the area of Dallas, Texas, sources of information contacted there advised of no indication or reports of subversive groups working among the Negroes. The Dallas branch of the National Association for the Advancement of Colored People is said, however, to be Militantly advancing social, economic and political rights for Negroes in this area. No trouble is said to have been experienced by Selective Service Boards in this area, other than individuals who failed to leave a change of address with them. There seems to be no intentional attempt to evade the law. At one time it is said that a group of Jehovah Witnesses were active but since their leaving the area no trouble has been experienced in this regard. A young Negro minister has advised that he has no knowledge of subversive groups working among the Negroes in his congregation and that from his observations of the members, that such persons or groups would meet with small success as the Negro knows what sort of treatment he would be afforded by Germany or Japan.

In this area there are but three Negro newspapers, one is published in Houston, Texas, the "Dallas Express", another previously mentioned, "The Informer," and the "Fort Worth Mind," edited in Fort Worth, Texas. These newspapers, of course, are said to devote their entire space to Negro activities and the phases of Negro economic, social and political life.

Rumors were reported in May, 1943, that subversive propaganda was being circulated among Negroes in the Marshall, Texas area. According to the reports, the distribution was common talk and the literature allegedly distributed was rumored to be that a change of government might benefit the Negro race. The particular sources of these pamphlets were alleged to be Wylie and Bishop Colleges. Inquiries conducted into this matter failed to substantiate the rumors and allegations. It was ascertained that various papers, manuscripts and publications were, of course, shipped into Marshall, Texas, from northern cities, mainly from colored presses. None of the sources of information who are in a position to know the situation in Marshall had any knowledge of anonymous literature or pamphlets promiscuously distributed throughout the campuses of the colleges or among the student bodies as rumors had it. [*100-135-13-22*]

El Paso Field Division

It is stated no reports of attempted agitation among the Negro population in Albuquerque and Gallup, New Mexico, have been received. It is further reported the Negro population in Albuquerque, New Mexico, is approximately 3000 and that in Gallup, New Mexico, the population is approximately 200. The above figures include Negro laborers employed in the coal mines in that vicinity.

Colored sources of information in and around El Paso, who are in a position to know the Negro activities in this area, advise of no knowledge on their part that there is any foreign inspired agitation among the Negro race. Several, however, have condemned the Communist Party for its activities among Negroes in other states.

During June, 1942, there was reportedly some trouble with Negro soldiers stationed at the Roswell Air Base, Roswell, New Mexico. It is reported this trouble was traced to a Staff Sergeant who made a practice of gathering a group of colored soldiers about him during the evenings and made statements to the effect that this was not their war and that they should quit the army and follow him.

During the summer of 1942, the Southern Pacific Railroad transmitted approximately 10,000 workmen from the Southern States through El Paso to points West for work on the road. It was advised that approximately thirty-five per cent of the Negroes returned through El Paso, refusing to work and voicing various grievances against the railroad such as the employment being misrepresented and that the railroad was exploiting the Negroes. It was believed that approximately 95 out of every 100 of the 10,000 workmen were Negroes. It was the opinion of a confidential source of information that some of the Negroes merely wanted free rides to the Southwest because of their health and refused to work upon arrival, but the far greater percentages refused to work as a result of apparent grievances against the railroad which grievances had apparently been instilled in the minds of the Negroes by outside persons. It was said further that the complaints were made in exactly the same wording by all the complainants, and that the complaints had been proved unfounded. The word "exploit" was used in many of the complaints and it was believed by this source of information that the average Negro worker did not know the meaning of the word "exploit".

Confidential sources of information who have contacts among Negroes in this area have advised that no reports have been received by them relative to information of attempts made to organize any Negro group against the United States Government. A number of Negroes had been in the area for several months in transit. It has been reported that these Negroes were not the peaceful type as the local Negroes, and did not mix with those residing in the area. No reports, however, reflecting trouble caused by these individuals have been received.

Sources of information state that the Negroes in this area are good, Loyal Southern type Negroes and it is not believed that there are un-American tendencies among them. It has been noticed however that some Negroes have not been adhering to Jim Crow practices as in the past but it is believed this has no bearing on their loyalty.

Sources of information in Albuquerque, New Mexico, have informed that they have no knowledge of organized activity among the colored population there and have found no evidences of subversive elements.

On June 19, 1943 in the city of El Paso a situation arose which involved approximately 400 Negroes. The origin was an argument and a subsequent fight between a Negro soldier and a Negro civilian. The soldier is said to have attacked the Negro with a knife but in turn sustained knife wounds. The civilian reported the matter to the police and then returned unaccompanied to his place of employment and he was met by a large number of Negro soldiers who are said to have shouted, "There he is—let's get him!" The civilian had in his possession a revolver and fired several shots, one striking a Negro soldier, wounding him severely. Police were dispatched to the scene whereupon the Negro soldiers disarmed one of the policemen and were attempting to disarm another when members of the El Paso County Sheriff's Office arrived to assist in quelling the disturbance. Order was restored in approximately two hours.

A collateral incident is reported to have occurred at Fort Bliss, Texas, where allegedly erroneous reports were received that rioting between Negroes and whites had broken out in El Paso. A group of Negro soldiers there are related to have disarmed a Negro sentry and subsequently shot a white sentry. The Negro soldier who killed the white sentry is said to have been immediately shot and killed by another white sentry. Several fights thereupon occurred between Negro and white soldiers before order was restored and Negro soldiers stoned busses and other conveyances on the military reservations during the disorder. [*44-801-1*]

Houston Field Division

In this area various rumors, complaints, and alleged un-American statements reflecting dissatisfaction and unrest among the Negroes have been reported. Statements to the effect that although Negroes would be slaves if the Nazis were to conquer this country, they are slaves at the present time, therefore the people should remain passive to the war and not participate in it, and to the effect that the Axis does not want to fight the Negroes and that the Negroes will be properly taken care of after the war if they refrain from taking part in it on the side of the Allies, are typical of those instances of un-American feelings which have been reported. Other statements or rumors of statements have been reported reflecting favoritism on the part of the Negroes to the Japanese cause. No indications have been reported, however, reflecting any organized campaign or plan to cause unrest among the Negroes in this area, or to urge them to be dissatisfied with this country's form of government.

In the area covered by the City of Beaumont, Texas, it is stated tha[t] an organization known as the Pacific Movement of the Eastern World is growing active among the Negroes in this area. It should be noted that in other sections of the country it has been reported that this organization is pro-Japanese. No indications as yet in this area have been reported reflecting that there is a definite pro-Axis trend in the activities of the group in this area.

In and around Corpus Christi, Texas it is reported there is restlessness among the Negroes and especially the Negro soldier. The only organization, however, reported to be existing in and around this area is a branch of the National Association for the Advancement of Colored People. Reports have also been received reflecting that the Negroes are discriminated against, especially with regard to the failure to pay Negroes doing the same kind of work as white men are doing, equal wages. In this regard, a Negress whose husband is employed at the United States Naval Air Base, Corpus Christi, Texas, and too, is the mother of two children and supports four orphan children whose father is in an asylum, has been interviewed. This woman has advised that the Negroes are not asking for social equality, but are only asking for equality in employment. It was advised that she did not believe Negroes should be discriminated against because of their color, and that they should receive equal salaries to those of the white people. It was also stated that the Negroes necessarily must win this war for the United States and by doing so they want to share in the benefits and in the treatment of white persons. She also stated that Negroes should be allowed in the United States Navy or in the Air Corps and should not be kept to menial duties such as mess boys and kitchen workers. This woman also pointed out that her husband works next to white men at the Naval Base, doing the same kind of work, but that he does not get equal pay.

In the area of Fannin, Texas, several reports have been received reflecting that Negroes in this area have stated that the Axis does not want to fight the Negroes and that the Negroes will be properly taken care of after the war if they refrain from taking part in it on the side of the Allies. Further reports are to the effect that although the Negro in this area in certain instances has been heard to discuss Hitler's favoritism of the Negro and the fact that he did not want to join the Army or participate in the present conflict, the statements were merely conversation along with the subject of war, and none of the Negroes seemed particularly excited about the matter and many of them remarked that it was just another of Hitler's schemes to defeat the United States.

Circulated in Fannin, as well as Victoria, Texas, is the Negro newspaper, "The Black Dispatch," published in Oklahoma city. With regard to this paper it is reported that there are numerous articles so styled as to reflect the apparent purpose of keeping the reader "class conscious."

In the City of Houston, Texas, there is published the Negro newspaper, The Houston Defender. In the issue for the week of March 28, 1942 this paper ran an editorial in an attempt to suppress rumors among the Negro population and urging them to disbelieve rumors being circulated among the race calculated to incite race prejudice. However, remarks have been reported in this area to the effect that the persons making the statement did not favor American war effort but that of either Japan or Germany. No information, however, has been reported reflecting any organized propaganda or foreign-inspired activity among the Negroes in this area. It is also reported in this area that Jehovah's Witnesses are contacting Negroes, especially in Hortense, Brazoria, Fort Bond, and Matagorda Counties, Texas, reportedly telling them that they should join the Jehovah's Witnesses sect and seek escape from the Army, and also advocated that it is foolish and unnecessary to salute the American Flag. It has also been reported that an injunction has been granted in favor of the Jehovah's Witnesses sect against sheriffs of the various counties enjoining them from arresting the Jehovah's Witnesses in their activities. Further rumors have been reported reflecting pro-Axis activities on the part of Spanish or Mexican individuals with regard to influencing Negroes in this area against the war effort.

It has been reported that the Communist Party is also active among the Negroes in this area, although it was reported that the Party in this area still advocates abolishment of "Jim-Crowism" in national defense industries and the establishment of equal rights between the white and Negro races, nevertheless it is expending most of its efforts along organizational lines rather than agitating among the Negroes. However, on the night of May 27, 1942, Abner W. Berry, national Communist Party functionary of the Communist Party, and a Negro, spoke at a Communist Party meeting at a lodge hall located at 1018 Schwartz Street, Houston, Texas. At this meeting Berry is stated to have discussed Party lines in which he strongly advocated the Second Front, that these Negro people abandon any sympathies they might have for the Japanese people, that the Negroes arouse themselves from their present state of complacency, that race segregation and discrimination be abolished in the United States, and that the rights of labor be protected in every field. Berry is further reported to have stated that the Negro is even mistreated in a democracy, that he is not mistreated in Russia, and that after the present war there will be a world-wide revolution which will make it possible for Russia to seize control of all other governments and thereby establish a social order that will protect the rights and liberties of all races.

In the vicinity of Houston, Texas, for several months during the latter part of 1942, numerous reports were received concerning an organization that supposedly was formed by colored female servants and cooks. The organization was labeled variously as the Eleanor Club, the Daughters of Eleanor, and the Eleanor Roosevelt Club. The alleged slogan of the organization was "The white woman in the kitchen by Christmas". These reports were checked for v[e]rifying and specific information, however, in no instance was any definite indication received as to an actual existing organization with such a name. The basis for such inquiry, based on the reported information, was the allegation that clubs were foreign inspired. It appears that the organization or clubs were merely based on rumors which were apparently circulated by white people employing Negro servants. It further appeared that the employers jumped to the conclusion that their servants belonged to such clubs when they asked for increased pay or better working conditions.

In and around two respective areas of Huntsville and Fort Arthur, Texas, additional anti-American sentiment has been reported on the part of individual Negroes, although no information has been received reflecting any organized activity among them agitating for un-American sympathies.

In the vicinity of the city of Galveston, Texas, no indications have been noticed or reported reflecting any agitation among the Negroes there. This is said also to be the situation in La Port, Texas and the surrounding area.

In the vicinity of Angleton, Texas it was rumored that there were organizational activities of an un-American nature among the Negroes. However, sources of information and informants in that area have advised of their inability to find any basis for such a rumor.

In the Madisonville, Texas area, a non-specific complaint was received to the effect that seditious literature had been distributed by white people among the Negroes in that area. Local authorities, sources of information and inquiries of persons in a good position to know the Negro situation there fail to establish any basis for such an allegation. [*100-135-20*]

Beaumont, Texas, Riots

In the early morning of June 5, 1943, Curtis Thomas, a Negro ex-convict, attacked and beat a nineteen year old white girl, a telephone operator in Beaumont, Texas. This occurred while the white girl was proceeding to her home about 12:10 A.M. on June

5, 1943. After four hours, when Thomas had fallen to sleep, the girl was successful in getting away from him and running to her home where she advised her father of the incident. He immediately called the Police Department, and officers were dispatched to the residence of the white girl. After ascertaining details, the police officers, along with additional men from the Police Department, proceeded to the Armour Packing Company Building near the Southern Pacific on Laurel Street in Beaumont, where they came across Thomas asleep. Aroused, he jumped up and ran down a dead end street, whereupon the officers began firing at him, four shots taking effect. Thomas was removed to the Hotel Diu Hospital, where at approximately 10:00 P.M. on June 6, 1943 a mob of about one hundred fifty people congregated for the purpose of lynching Thomas. The Chief of Police and Captain of Detectives in Beaumont was successful in discouraging the mob.

On June 8, 1943 at 9:20 A.M. Thomas died after admitting attacking the white girl. Thomas had been removed from the hospital to the hospital ward of Jefferson County Jail on the afternoon preceding the appearance of the mob at the hospital.

At 3:00 P.M., June 15, 1943 an unknown Negro criminally assaulted a white woman, twenty-three years of age, the mother of three children, in the country approximately two miles from the city of Beaumont.

It is reported that at approximately 9:00 P.M. on June 15, 1943 a mob of about two thousand men and women gathered in front of the Beaumont Police Station seeking the Negro who attacked the white woman. Part of the mob went to the Jefferson County Jail, and not finding the Negro there, returned to the Beaumont City Jail where they milled around until about 12:00 midnight. After the crowd was convinced the Negro was not in the City Jail, it split up into two groups (it is to be noted that the white woman had viewed all of the Negroes in the Jails who had been previously arrested as suspects, as well as other Negroes, with negative results. This information was given to the mob before it left the Police Station).

The Captain of Detectives in Beaumont informed that four-fifths of the mob consisted of employees on the night shift at the Pennsylvania Shipyards in Beaumont. Another estimate given as to the crowd was that 50 per cent consisted of employees of the Pennsylvania Shipyards, 25 per cent were employees of the Lummus Company and approximately 25 per cent were from the Consolidated Steel Corporation, Shipbuilding Division, Orange, Texas.

It is reported that after the mob left the jail, one group proceeded to Forsythe Street (predominantly Negro street) where they broke windowpanes of all Negro establishment[s], as well as those of some establishments owned and operated by white people. Another portion proceeded to Gladys Street (predominantly a Negro section) where they took similar action against the Negro establishments and set fire to some seven or eight buildings. Most of the business establishments, according to local law enforcement authorities, were ransacked and great quantities of clothing, whisky, cigarettes and other property were taken.

Between forty and fifty persons, including both whites and Negroes, were shot, cut and beaten during the melee. The assistance of the Texas Defense Guard was requested, and local law enforcement agencies of the Beaumont, Texas area were endeavoring to keep the situation under control. At approximately 6:05 P.M., June 16, 1943 a state of emergency was declared in Beaumont and a curfew was ordered for that night at 8:30 P.M. The day shift, numbering 4,500 men and women, at the Pennsylvania Shipyards reported for work at 7:00 A.M. on June 16, 1943, but at 8:30 A.M. they left their work, as did day shift workers at the shipyards of the Consolidated Steel Corporation.

The police in Beaumont have advised of an unfounded rumor prevalent on the morning of June 16, 1943 that Negroes were then gathering as a mob for the purpose of proceeding to a section known as Multimax Village, a shipyard workers' section in Beaumont, to take action against the homes of white citizens there. This unfounded rumor is not believed to have been planned. By noon June 16, 1943, the situation was considered serious.

Rangers of the Department of Public Safety in Texas were dispatched to Beaumont as well as members of the Texas Highway Patrol. Tear gas was used to break up a gathering of approximately two hundred at Park and Forsythe Streets near the Negro district. From 6:05 P.M. on June 16, 1943, to 10:00 A.M. June 20, 1943, the city of Beaumont was under martial law under the direction of the State Guard.

Only two deaths were reported, one involving a white man after a beating reportedly administered him by Negroes, the other involving a Negro who died on June 19, 1943, from gun shot wounds received on the night of June 15, 1943. At 12:00 midnight, June 15, 1943, some fifty-two Negroes who had been rejected at an induction center in Houston were waiting at the bus station in Beaumont for transportation to Port Arthur. The mob beat some of these Negroes while others were successful in getting away. Nine of the Negro rejectees were beaten to the point of requiring hospitalization.

The Chief of Police in Beaumont, Texas, has stated that in all of his experience in witnessing the action of mobs, this particular mob was the most unscrupulous and vicious he had ever seen. He advised that they not only wanted to kill Negroes but also desired to loot and steal.

After martial law had been placed into effect, no other disturbances occurred. Subsequent to the riots, several hundred Negroes who had come to Beaumont from other places and states to work in defense plants reportedly moved away from Beaumont, and a number of the old Negro inhabitants in Beaumont, according to the Chief of Police, asked him if they should leave the city. They were promised all the protection that the police and officials of Beaumont could offer.

The following information has been supplied by local law enforcement officers to set forth several incidents occurring in the city of Beaumont between whites and Negroes which preceded the race riot of June 15, 1943, and which, according to the sources of information, appeared to be a climax of the incidents:

The Chief of Police has informed of considerable difficulty incurred in segregating whites and Negroes in busses of Beaumont, Texas. Defense plants in the area are also said to have had incidents of a similar nature occur. The Chief of Police of Beaumont has informed he understood there were at the time some two or three hundred ex-convicts working in the Pennsylvania Shipyards. He has also pointed out that there were a number of youths ranging from seventeen to twenty years of age in the mob taking part in the riot and stated that it appeared to him that these youths were endeavoring to do everything possible to create as much disturbance as they could.

While the situation resulted in work stoppages in the various war plants in the Beaumont area as well as injuries to person and property, no indications have been reported either to the local law enforcement authorities or to the Federal Bureau of Investigation that the trouble was promoted by individuals who might be sympathizers of the Axis powers. In this connection, the National Defense Section of the Department of Public Safety in Texas has informed that approximately three hundred individuals were taken into custody for various infractions of state, military and civil laws, who were interviewed by a military court of inquiry. At no time, according to this source, were any indications received that the action of the mob was promoted for subversive forces or was instigated by anyone sympathetic to the Axis powers. Fifty persons were charged in the city court or in the state court at Beaumont, Texas, with various infractions of the law, including misdemeanors such as loitering and drunkenness, as well as with theft, burglary, arson and receiving and concealing stolen property.

The situation in Beaumont was exploited to a considerable degree by the newspaper "PM" and the Communist news organ, the "Daily Worker," and was charged by these publications to be inspired by subversive or fifth column forces. It was compared to the Detroit Packard Motorcar Company strike, as well as to the Mobile, Alabama, shipyard trouble. Another newspaper reported that the Chief of Police of Beaumont confirmed the fact that there were rumors of fifth column activity in the situation at Beaumont and stated that a check was being made. In this connection, the Chief of Policc at Beaumont, Texas, has informed that absolutely no information relative to such rumors was received by him, and that he made absolutely no statements to the press that the race riot was prompted by un-American groups.

Sec. Ref. Rept. SA ████████████ 6-28-43 Houston Texas, Re Race Riots. Beaumont Texas June 15-43 Civil Rights & Domestic Violence

[100-135-20-18]

Huntington Field Division

Sources of information contacted in this area fail to reflect any agitation among the Negroes indicating that it is possibly foreign-inspired. Several prominent Negro individuals are stated to be urging strenuously for equal rights for the Negroes, as well as a local branch of the National Association for the Advancement of Colored People in the City of Huntington. Other than local agitation, however, there are no indications reported reflecting a widespread organized activity among the Negroes to demand extraordinary things for the particular area in question. One prominent pastor, a Negro in the City of Huntington, is reported to have made the statement that he would fight for equal rights for the Colored People until the time would come that the Negro would be allowed to go to the movies, swimming pools, recreational parks, and be allowed all the privileges which the white people now have. No indications, however, have been reported that this pastor is guided in his fight for equal rights for the Negro by any foreign group.

Most popular among the Negro newspaper circulated in this area is stated to be the "Pittsburgh Courier," although the Negro weekly, "The Tri-State News," published at Charleston, West Virginia, has some circulation. The reported policy of this latter newspaper is stated to be aggressively war-minded.

Sources of information in the Cities of Wheeling, Clarksburg, Morgantown, Fairmont, Martinsburg, Charleston, Bluefield, Beckley, Logan, Parkersburg, and Huntington have advised of sensing an indication of foreign inspired activity or un-American sentiment among the Negroes there.

At Bluefield in McDowell County, West Virginia, sources of information have advised that there is an attitude on the part of some Negroes that the present war is a "White man's war" and the Negroes will be better off if the Japanese powers win. It has been alleged that flags resembling the Japanese flag have been seen in several of the Negro residences.

In the area of Kimball, West Virginia, a Negro doctor, Dr. Joe E. Brown, reportedly sent to white inhabitants of the area copies of the "Pittsburgh Courier". It was said that a note was written at the top of each issue to the effect that "we are all ignorant about lots of things, read what your best and biggest white americans say who have no racial prejudice or hatred, I'll always follow them; read paper on next page."

In this same area it was reported that in August, 1943, a patriotic short was shown at the Kimball theatre, in which the American Flag was displayed and the National Anthem played. It was said that everyone stood and sang, with the exception of about 30 Negroes who remained seated and booed the flag. When the picture of President Roosevelt appeared on the screen, the Negroes reportedly hissed. [*100-135-21*]

Other areas of the State of West Virginia have been checked for evidences of subversive activity, including Gery, Welch, Keystone, Parkersburg, Clarksburg and Logan, and no indications have been received that there are any elements at work either agitating or exploiting the Negro population in these localities.

In the Oak Hill, West Virginia, area the President of the local chapter of the National Association for the Advancement of Colored People, one Jesse Groggins, who is the leader of approximately 100 members, is reported to have been in attendance at meetings of the Communist Party, Section 17, in the State of West Virginia, holding sessions at Beckley, West Virginia. Apparently through these reported connections on the [part] of Groggins, various State Communist Party functionaries in West Virginia have been invited to speak before the Oak Hill Chapter of the National Association for the Advancement of Colored People. Allegations have also been received that a speaker, a member of the Communist Party, has addressed the Triadelphia branch of the National Association for the Advancement of Colored People at Accoville. No indications have been received, however, that the Communist Party has any extensive influence in this chapter.

There are also indications reported in the Charleston area of Negroes being members of the Communist Party and carrying on the work of the Party there. On the other hand, no indications have been received of any pro-Axis agitation among the Negroes there.

An incident has been reported taking place in the Charleston area which is said to have incensed the Negro population in the area to some degree. This situation involved five white youths making frequent and seemingly uncalled for attacks upon Negroes in this area. All information received indicates that the fundamental cause for the trouble was a personal dislike of Negroes on the part of these white boys. One of these youths has explained that two of them were originally involved in a fight between themselves and two Negroes in November, 1942, and that thereafter, they decided to get even with the colored race by making these attacks. Two of the youths have been placed on three years probation for their activities, while the other three were not tried although indicted, inasmuch as they had been inducted into the United States Army. The immediate results of these attacks by the white youths were various Negroes arming themselves with guns and knives for a period of several days. [*100-135-21-11*]

Jackson Field Division

Among the organizations active among the Negroes in this Field Division are stated to be the Moorish Holy Temple of Science, the Jehovah's Witnesses sect, the Mississippi Council of Inter-racial Cooperation, Incorporated, the Southern Negro Youth Conference, a Communist Front organization, The Southern Conference for Human Welfare, alleged to have Communist conventions, the Southern Leadership Training School System, an organization known as the Negro Improvement in Social Science Work, a group possibly known as the Negro Order of the Eastern Star, along with several itinerant Evangelists who have sponsored meetings at Kemper and Leake Counties, and at Holly Springs, Mississippi.

The Moorish Holy Temple of Science, has for its purpose the establishment of the conception that Negroes are actually Moorish American who are entitled to full rights and privileges of any American without the slightest racial discrimination. The organization is also stated to claim that if Japan wins the war the Negro (that is the Moorish-American) race will be on equality with other races. The Temple No. 16 of this group is stated to have been organized in September, 1941, at Tchula near Belzoni, Mississippi. It is stated to have been active in the Yazoo, Humphreys and Desota Counties. Temple No. 16 is reported to have been formerly led by one Jim Barnes, who was recently confined to the state penitentiary, Mississippi, for the duration of the war and not longer than five years, under the provisions of the Mississippi Anti-Sedition Laws. Since prosecution of some of the members, however, it is stated not to be very active.

Unity of membership is stated to be maintained through cards of identification, lapel badges in a form of a silver star and crescent, and the letters "M.A.", and the word "Wallah" in silver on blue, and by the wearing of a ceremonial uniform consisting of a fez, robe, and girdle. The paraphernalia costs approximately $9.00, and the identification card $1.00 the joining fee is said to be $1.35, dues 75¢ a month. Books on the organization and its teachings are said to be sold for 75¢ each. At present the exact size and the extent of influence of this organization is not known.

Followers of the Jehovah's Witnesses sect have been active in this area. Several have been arrested, sentenced and convicted under the Mississippi Anti-Sedition Law, some of whom have been charged with teaching that those who died at Pearl Harbor died for no good cause, that the President has exceeded his authority in the causing of men to be drafted, that a great many lives would be lost in any offensive for no good cause or purpose, and that Hitler would rule this country, but would not have to come here in person to do so. Further reports have been received that members of the Jehovah's Witnesses sect have been teaching the lower class of white people in this area and the Negroes not to salute the flag.

With reference to the Mississippi Council of Inter-racial Cooperation, Incorporated, this organization has been alleged to be dominated by Communists and used as a "jumping off spot" to enter the campaign to eliminate all poll tax and to foster the Communist Organizational methods of putting Black against White. The organization maintains local offices in Jackson, Mississippi and it is indicated that the yearly dues are $2.00. The leader in Jackson is said to be the Secretary of the organization, Robert Paine Noblett, Jr., who makes periodic trips thru the states of Mississippi, Alabama, Louisiana, and Georgia. Noblett has been reported to have been in attendance at a meeting of the Young Communist League at Tuskegee, Alabama on April 19, 1941, however, no information has been received reflecting that he took part in the meeting. Noblett is said to receive $3600 a year in his job as Secretary and it is further reported that he has a $1400 expense budget.

The purpose of this organization is stated to be ". . . the responsibility . . . to see to it that Negroes are included as an integral part of every local civilian committee." Another purpose is said to be the attempt to create attitudes of justice, equity, and fair play for all people without regard to race or religion. The organization is said to sponsor local councils in approximately eleven areas in the Jackson Field Division. No information as yet has been reported reflecting radical tendencies on the part of this group.

Another organization active in this area is The Southern Negro Youth Conference which is reported to have Communist affiliation. The Southern Conference for Human Welfare is also stated to have a membership in this area.

The Southern Leadership Training School System, is an organization which claims to operate summer schools where its aims are taught, and to conduct controversies to counteract subversive propaganda among colored people. According to its president, W. H. Lewis, it has been stated, "As long as Negroes cannot be white men, it is a next possible opportunity to do all we can to keep foreign whites from encouraging diversion in race prejudice as the foreign white would give much less than they would have under the present system." The organization claims to have made 50,000 house calls in the year of 1941 and to have covered approximately 60,000 miles of such work and to have distributed 30,000 pieces of literature. The organization has fifteen workers in the states of Mississippi and Alabama who aid in the holding of periodic "schools" as well as revival-type meetings.

The Negro Improvement in Social Science Work is an organization stated to be formed to promote better relations and understanding between the whites and Negroes, to carry on social work among the Negroes, and to improve the morals of Negroes, to increase the income of the two founders of the organization who claim "through our present work, we can pound out the inherent danger that lies hidden in Communism and 'Red' propaganda".

The membership is stated to be restricted to the members of the Congregations of the two Minister-founders, Reverend R. L. Hickman, Hattiesburg, Mississippi, President of the group, and Reverend Timothy Windfield, Secretary, also of Hattiesburg, Mississippi.

It is rumored that a Negro Order of Eastern Star has been active in Union, Mississippi where it is reported to have held a meeting shortly before July 4, 1940.

Itinerant evangelists have also been brought to attention in this area, as well as followers of the Jehovah's Witnesses sect. One was taken into custody by local authorities for reported seditious statements in violation of the Mississippi State Anti-Sedition Law. This individual claims he was endeavoring to influence Negroes so that he could possibly get financial help and lodging.

Complaints have been received in this area to the effect that Union organizers are active in agitating among the Negroes, encouraging them to demand complete social equality and pointing out that if Negroes would organize a union among themselves they would get better pay and more responsible positions.

Several Negro newspapers which are circulated and read in this area are "The Jackson Advocate", Jackson, Mississippi; "The Mississippi Enterprise", Jackson, Mississippi; "The Weekly Recorder", Jackson, Mississippi; "The Missippi Educational Journal", negro edition, monthly publication, Jackson, Mississippi; "The Delta Leader", Greenville, Mississippi; and "The Southern Frontier"; and "The Mississippian", Greenville, Mississippi. Other non-local papers are stated to be the Pittsburgh Courier, The Louisiana Progress, and the Chicago Defender.

At one time active in Meridian, Mississippi, was a branch of the National Association for the Advancement of Colored People. At the present time, it is stated to be active in Vicksburg, Mississippi, where it is stated to have two or three thousand members including leaders among the colored people.

Two sources of information in this area who are in a position to understand and know the Negro situation there advise of no evidence of dissatisfaction among the Negroes. Both claim that current rumors of negro unrest are highly exaggerated. Both claim that high wages along with increased tension induced by the war effort has excited the Negro mind and given rise to rumors which gained momentum and force, but which in their origin are not worth all the attention being paid to them. One source, however, does advise that he believes certain rumors are falsely created by unscrupulous persons having their own selfish motives in using that propaganda to draw the Negroes to their cause. The same source has expressed the opinion that the National Association for the Advancement of Colored people has capitalized on the present world situation by perverting patriotic appeals which results in increased Negro unrest as a by-product, thus adding to the membership of the organization.

In the Delta Region of Mississippi new cotton picking prices have been set and a price will probably run as high as $3.50 per hundred weight. This is stated to have a beneficial effect on the negro attitude toward work in general.

Miscellaneous reports have been received from police authorities in the counties of Gulfport, Oktibbeha, Chickasaw, and in the cities of Biloxi, Lena, and Jackson, Mississippi, to the effect that Negroes have been holding meetings, secret in nature, although no substantiating information has been received. On the other hand it has been reported that at the Panther Burn Co. Plantation, Panther Burn, Mississippi, 310 Negro families on this 1200 acre plantation recently subscribed to $20,000 in War Bonds. Rumors have been reported, however, that in Greenwood, Mississippi, Negroes who gather in the colored section of Greenwood on Saturday night have been talking about Negroes being American the same as white folks, but they would be better off if the Japs win the war because they are colored.

As an example of how rumors will spread, and what effect they will have in intensifying a situation the following set of circumstances is given as a sidelight on the Negro situation in this area. It was reported that Negroes in the vicinity of Tupelo, Mississippi, were during the month of October, buying all available stock of pistol cartridges and long handled knives from stores in that city. This information was received from two different sources. Possibilities of race riots were reported.

Inquiries were instituted with regard to this report, and it was ascertained from the owner of one hardware store in that area that he had heard reports that there was to be a run on ammunition due to anticipated trouble between white people and the Negroes. For this reason, he said, he removed all pistol and rifle ammunition from the shelves. Since that time, he stated that he attempted to watch the request for shells but had noted nothing of unusual interest. Another manager of a hardware store advised that sales in his store to Negroes of ammunition had run in the past, about 75 per cent of the gross sales, and that this was not unusual. In his opinion the trouble could only arise as a result of action on the part of the foolish white persons. He said the supply of ammunition was exhausted and future sales were impossible. No indications, however, have been reported reflecting any contemplated riots or trouble. [*100-135-55*]

In February, 1943, reports were received that many Negroes in the Greenwood, Mississippi, area cashed their War Bonds which had been purchased largely through deductions from their pay. Rumors were said to have been prevalent that the War Bonds could not be cashed after the War; that the Bonds could not be cashed for ten years; that War Bonds were soon to be canceled; that the Government was going to take one half of everything, including War Bonds.

Inquiries were made to ascertain the origin of these rumors with negative results. Numerous Negroes who cashed their Bonds were interviewed, and none could furnish any information as to the source of the rumors.

Various people were interviewed who are in a position to understand the situation in this area. One explanation which was given is that Negroes had in mind cashing their Bonds at the time they first purchased them, inasmuch as a number of them had asked if they had a right to do so at the time they purchased the Bonds. One source of information advised Negroes were forced to buy Bonds by their landlords or their plantation owners, and the reason so many of them had cashed their Bonds at about the same time was because settlements were made with the majority of them in December; therefore, the 60-day period on all of them expired at approximately the same time and consequently, they cashed them as they had originally planned. Other unconfirmed allegations were received that merchants might possibly have been behind the situation, in that more goods and materials could be sold to Negroes if they had the cash.

Inquiries to date have failed to reveal the source of the rumors or any reasons, other than those set out previously, why Negroes would be cashing their War Bonds in such a manner.

Numerous allegations have been received that "Eleanor" Clubs exist in the Mississippi area, and inquiries based upon additional allegations that these clubs were inspired by pro-German or pro-Axis forces have failed to reveal any such clubs in existence in the State of Mississippi. Explanations have been given as to the basis for such allegations, and one which is more often supplied is that white people in losing Negro domestics to employers largely in National Defense industries who will pay higher wages have assisted in the spreading of these rumors, possibly believing their domestics did join such a ficticious club. *[100-163965-17]*

On March 18, 1943, a group of three Negroes in and around Greenville, Mississippi, met with a representative group of whites and citizens of that locality in order that they, the Negroes, might present their grievances to the white leaders. One Negro was the owner of a Negro newspaper in Greenville, the other a doctor, while the other was reportedly the editor of a paper in Memphis, Tennessee. The summation of the recommendation made by these three Negroes is as follows:

1. Better schools for Negro children, with adequate equipment and teachers better prepared for that profession.
2. Adopt a uniform wage scale in agriculture.
3. Grant justice in the courts.
4. Strict compliance with segregation laws in all forms of transportation to be observed equally by white and black.
5. Discontinue intermingling of races in liquor establishments.
6. Enlarge the number of hospitals and medical clinics for the health of Negro workers.
7. A uniform policy among the planters of the Delta as to wage scales, including land breaking, ditching, cornering costs, etc., with a county grievance committee.
8. More courteous treatment of Negroes in retail establishments.
9. A coordinating organization to work with the Delta Council in the promotion of good will and mutual understanding.

It was reported that the Delta Council endorsed additional steps to promote practical solutions, namely the need of more study of the Negro problem as well as expanding the formulated program. *[100-135-55-62]*

The following information is set forth to reflect a situation in the State of Mississippi which is said to be one of the causes for unrest among the Negro population there.

It is related that on Friday night, May 28, 1943, a group of Negro soldiers of the 364th Infantry, United States Army, stationed at Camp Van Dorn, Mississippi, started a disturbance at one of the post exchanges at the reservation. This group of soldiers came to Camp Van Dorn on Wednesday, May 26, 1943, from Phoenix, Arizona, it being alleged that they were moved from Phoenix as a result of racial disturbances there. The contingent is said to be a part of the former New York State National Guard, which has been mustered into the Army. A number of these Negro soldiers entered one of the post exchanges reserved for white soldiers and demanded that they be served. When service was refused, they are reported to have literally cleaned out the place, tearing up fixtures and causing other damage.

On Saturday evening, May 29, 1943, a group of Negroes belonging to this same regiment, numbering about 50 to 75, entered the town of Centerville, Mississippi, with the purpose of causing a disturbance there. Remarks to this effect were reportedly heard by several people as the Negroes passed them going into the town. The Negroes, after arriving in Centerville, were met by the City Marshal, along with four law enforcement officers armed with shotguns. The City Marshal is said to have advised that he dispersed the group and made them return to camp. According to reports, these soldiers did not have passes from the reservation but had left without permission. In this connection, unconfirmed allegations are to the effect that on Friday and Saturday nights, May 28 and 29, disturbances were caused frequently at the military reservation and sporadic gunfire was heard.

On Sunday afternoon, May 30, 1943, the City Marshal and County Sheriff of Wilkinson County, Mississippi, were patrolling the area surrounding Camp Van Dorn when they saw a Negro soldier beating a white Military Policeman. The Marshal is said to have hurried to the scene, and upon arriving there, the Military Policeman asked that he "shoot him" (referring to the negro). The City Marshal has related that at this point the Negro soldier left the white Military Policeman and started for the Sheriff of Wilkinson County. The Sheriff warned the Negro to halt, and when the Negro failed to heed his warning, the Sheriff shot and killed him. It is further related that there were several other Negro soldiers looking on at the fight who did not participate and after the shooting left the scene running. It is said that the Commanding Officer at Camp Van Dorn has stated there were no casualties inside the camp, and that the only individual killed was the Negro soldier shot by the Sheriff. Allegations have been received, however, that several in the camp have been killed. Citizens of Centerville, Mississippi, have asked that these Negro soldiers be moved. It was alleged in this connection that such a situation could lead very easily to a race riot.

In connection with the foregoing incident, it has been confidentially reported that Negro members of the above-mentioned regiment were composed equally of troops from the East, North and South, a number of whom were of a very rough and tough nature prior to their entering the Army. It is said that they have shown very little respect for their officers and in some instances lack of control by the officers has been evidenced. [*100-135-55-58*]

Knoxville Field Division

In this area several nonspecific complaints have been received to the effect that some Negroes in this area have made remarks that they are not interested in the present war as it is a race war, and that since the Japanese are also a colored race, they will be better off if Japan conquers the United States and frees them from the rule of the white man. It is noted that these complaints are so nonspecific in nature that all efforts to trace the source of the agitation have met with negative results. Another type of agitation existing in this area is for the abolishment of "Jim Crowism" in the armed forces and for the abolishment of poll taxes. It is believed that this agitation is directly traceable to the Southern Conference for Human Welfare, an alleged Communist front organization and the Southern Negro Youth Congress, a Communist front organization, both of which organizations have urged Negroes to prove their fitness for equality with the whites by joining the army and making good soldiers, by working hard and accepting responsibilities in factories and war effort projects.

The National Association for the Advancement of Colored People has renewed its activity in its branch in the Knoxville area. Until the latter part of March, 1943 the organization was not holding regular meetings. However, at that time a membership drive was instituted to increase the number of members from twelve hundred to two thousand. The branch reportedly has for its purpose the rendering of legal assistance to members who are not in a financial position to procure such aid and to overcome discrimination against Negroes in industry and in the armed forces. More recently, discussions have been undertaken by the branch in preparation for selecting a Negro candidate to run for the City Council in Knoxville.

There have been indications of activity on the part of a branch of the Universal Negro Improvement Association, the headquarters of which is in Cleveland, Ohio. It is said that the meetings are held in a secret manner at the members' homes. However, it is reported that the organization has a meeting hall on West Vine Avenue in Knoxville, and at the meetings held there the largest reported attendance was twenty-five members. There are additional indications that speakers brought before this unit have made remarks somewhat sympathetic to the Japanese nation. The last reported officers of this organization are Frank Jackson, President, Atticus Freeman, presiding officer, and the wife of Freeman, Secretary.

In the Chattanooga, Tennessee area there are said to be approximately seventy-five members of the Moorish Science Temple of America. These members belong to two different Temples, Nos. 16 and 30. According to sources of information, these groups teach and feel that the Japanese are their brothers in color, and they are allegedly sympathetic toward Germany at the present time, inasmuch as it is allied with Japan; however, they do not feel kindly toward the German people as a nation or a race. Meetings of Temple #16 are reported to have taken place in a building located at East Eighth Street and University Place in Chattanooga, while Temple #30 is said to have its regular meetings in a small building at the rear of 1709 Long Street. Informants in these groups have stated that in recent months since the beginning of 1943 no matters have been taken up at the meetings which pertain to the United States Government or to any foreign government.

There is also reported to be a branch of the National Association for the Advancement of Colored People in the Chattanooga area which is said to be active and which reportedly holds meetings of local interest only. No indications have been received of any un-American or subversive tendencies on the part of this branch.

Published in Knoxville, Tennessee is the "Knoxville Flash Light Herald," a weekly Negro newspaper. This paper is stated to report in general local news and social events of Negroes in Knoxville and the surrounding community. It is stated that headline stories feature Negro brawls and how Negroes are often beaten by the police department. This paper is also said to be strongly backing the public candidates in the local election. Other issues of this paper are said to contain excerpts urging Negroes to fight the "Southern Congress Block" in an attempt to cut down NYA appropriations and urging the people to support senators and congressmen who will favor housing projects, the NYA and any legislation which will be beneficial to the Negroes.

Another newspaper published by Negroes circulated in this area is the "East Tennessee News" which was formerly published in Knoxville, Tennessee until 1939 when the paper was moved to Atlanta and subsequently consolidated with the "Atlanta World," a Negro daily paper. This paper is said to still continue carrying Knoxville, Tennessee news regarding Negroes there. It of course carries many items and articles relative to national questions with regard to the colored race.

It is to be noted that from the inquiries made with respect to subversive or un-American forces exploiting Negroes in this area, no indications have been received other than those set out hereinbefore that such matters are responsible for any unrest or dissatisfaction among Negroes in this area. No incidents reflecting organized movements to cause race riots or trouble have been reported. However, investigation is being continued with respect to those organizations hereinbefore referred to in which it is said there is a certain degree of pro-Japanese sentiment.

Little Rock Field Division

Numerous complaints have been received in this area indicating unrest and dissatisfaction among the Negroes. Various rumors have also been reported to the effect that there was allegedly considerable activity among the Negroes in the form of organizing efforts on the part of unknown white people attempting to cause favor among the Negroes for pro-Axis governments and advocating the overthrow of the United States Government. Exhaustive investigation conducted relative to those complaints have disclosed no specific organizations or definite persons engaged in such activity. Sources of information interviewed in this regard advised of no knowledge as to foreign-inspired agitation among the Negroes in the state of Arkansas. Information has been received, however, reflecting efforts on the part of the Negroes in this area to obtain better working and social conditions, but that such efforts in no way could be construed as active disloyalty to the United States. Sources of information interviewed including a reputable colored attorney in the city of Little Rock advised that privileges are denied the Negroes in this area, and that some discrimination exists. It has further been reported that a certain amount of unrest and dissatisfaction was caused by the lynching of a Negro in Texarkana, Texas, for an alleged attack on a white girl. Another instance along this line stated to have aroused feelings among the Negroes is one in which a Negro soldier was killed by local police officers in the city of Little Rock, Arkansas. The opinion was expressed that the Negroes in this area felt that the killing was not justified.

Another source of information, a prominent colored attorney in the State of Arkansas, has advised of no knowledge of foreign-inspired agitation among the Negroes in the state of Arkansas and expressed his feelings that the Negroes were at heart loyal to the United States. He has advised that although he feels there are certain social problems existing which confronts both races in the future, there was no cause for concern as to the ultimate conduct of the Negroes.

Other complaints in the form of charges that union organizers in this area are causing unrest among the Negroes have been reported. Also instances of individuals allegedly spreading "Communistic ideas" among fellow laborers, mainly Negroes, have been reported. It is complained that individuals charged with this activity point out unfairness in the economic situation of the United States and claimed that in the future there will be a change to government ownership of all property.

In the state of Arkansas among the more prominent Negro newspapers are the "Arkansas State Press," published in Little Rock, the "Arkansas World," published in Little Rock, and the "Arkansas Survey Journal." In general these newspapers are stated to be in favor of the betterment of the Negro race and the acquisition of more rights and liberties. However, no information has been reported reflecting that these newspapers carry articles of a subversive nature.

In the Newport and surrounding area, various rumors have been reported reflecting such instances as Negroes buying an unusual amount of ammunition. However, these have been found to be without basis. No indications of agitation among the Negroes, foreign inspired or otherwise, has been reported. With regard to recent primary elections in the state of Arkansas, it is said that a number of colored people around the city of Newport wanted to vote and that the question of Negroes voting in the primaries have been widely discussed in the press, both white and Negro. It is said that the colored people in this area having read such articles, came to the conclusions themselves, that they would like to vote in the primaries if it were permissible. In this connection, it is said that the Negroes there had been informed by the local authorities that they were not eligible to vote in the Democratic primaries in Arkansas. Since that time it is said that they have promptly dismissed the matter from their minds.

It was reported that in the City of Augustus, Arkansas, an organization known as the "Order of The Black Dragon Society" had recently been organized by the more intelligent type of Negro with the creed that if Axis powers win the war every Negro will be given a piece of land, money and tools and will be independent. Investigation of this organization, of course, is continuing. It is reported that the organization if in existence, actually is in its infant stage. No other indication of subversive activity, unrest or dissatisfaction among the Negroes has been reported.

In the vicinity of Joiner, Arkansas, it is reported that there are many Negroes in the neighborhood working on several large plantations. It is reported that there has been no trouble among them. However, in the past several months, there has been a noticeable change in their attitude in that they have become impertinent, independent and have maintained a sulky and surly disposition. Sources of information contacted attribute this attitude to meetings which have been held there among the Negroes. With regard to the meetings, it has been reported that Negroes in automobiles bearing out of state licenses, have been attending them and conducting them.

In the area covering Wilson, Arkansas, Negro workers in this vicinity are said to be seemingly well satisfied and no indications have been reported of un-American activities among them.

In the vicinity of Bauxite, Arkansas, there is a mine of the Republic Mining and Manufacturing Company. Negro employees of the plant or mine are considered loyal Americans and doing extremely hard and tedious work. It is reported, however, that practically all have withdrawn money under the payroll savings plan sponsored by the War Savings Staff. The Negroes' alleged desire in this area to spend all of his money is believed to be the cause attributed to this. Several instances have occurred where Negroes would submit their resignation to the Company and thereafter withdraw their savings. After they would spend their money, they would return to the plant to work again. It is said that because of their ability in a certain type of work in the plant, the company necessarily reemploys them.

In the following areas where inquiries and contacts have been made with respect to possible subversive or un-American exploitation of the Negro population, nothing but negative results have been received. It is to be noted that unrelated instances of individual Negroes making anti-American or anti-white remarks have been reported. In none of these, however, has there been any indication of an organized attempt to agitate Negroes and stir antagonism among them against the white inhabitants or against the United States: Snow Lake, Stuttgart, Brinkley, Helena, West Helena, Marianna, Forrest City, Augusta, Cotton Plant, Parkin, McCrory, Wynne, Earl, Crawfordsville, Marion, West Memphis, Ninety-Six Corner, Osceola, Blytheville, Barfield, Armorel, Monticello and Hughes.

A report has been received from a highly confidential source with regard to the opinion of a Negro who has been studying the Negro situation in this area. It is said that in this individual's opinion sensationalism in the Negro press is perhaps the most subversive influence among the Negroes. It was the opinion of this informant that at the present time there is no collective plot of subversive action among the Negroes, although the propaganda directed toward them is racial, and although it is not subversive it serves the same purpose because it places the white man in a position of an enemy, so to speak. The source of information has pointed out further that among the many factors, the most evident regarding the cause for the unrest and dissatisfaction among the Negroes are:

1. A militant attitude of the Negro press.
2. The contact of Northern soldiers in the South.
3. The influence of labor unions.
4. The propaganda effect that Joe Louis has had on the Negro.
5. Basic sociological changes that have taken place.
6. A collective hatred of Southern law enforcement officers.
7. The recognition of the National Association for the Advancement of Colored People as having a bargaining right for the Negro. *[100-135-26]*

It has been reported with regard to the War Savings program in this area that although in several of the defense industries many Negroes signed pledges authorizing their respective companies to deduct a specified amount each pay period for the purchase of bonds, many have recently been withdrawing the amount withheld. No information, however, has been received reflecting the mass movement in this regard.

A prominent Negro attorney in the city of Little Rock has been interviewed with regard to agitation among the Negroes and he has advised that he is cognizant of a rumor that subversive elements are at work on the Negro population of Little Rock, but stated that such rumor was without factual foundation. He advised that the Negroes in this area realize and appreciate the fact that their hopes and aims can be best realized in the South and further stated that all Negroes so far as he knows are loyal to the United States. He further claimed that it would be a fallacy for any Negro to believe that the race would fare better under any other type of government. He advised of efforts being made to obtain advantages and privileges which previously have been denied Negroes in the past, but that if such privileges were obtained they would only strengthen the unity of the Negroes in this country for the United States. He admitted that Negroes are not as enthusiastic over the present war effort as they should be but he explained that in his opinion this is because of the lack of organization having for its purpose the education of Negroes as to their obligations to the United States and the privileges to be derived therefrom.

This Negro attorney has further advised that the individual efforts of Negroes to better their educational facilities, election privileges, and possibilities for employment in defense industry, should not be construed as evidences of disloyalty to the United States. He further stated that in the event white people should appear among the Negroes in an effort to suppress subversive propaganda, he believed such efforts would be frowned upon by the Negroes in this area.

In the vicinity of Varner, Arkansas, no organizational activity among the Negroes has reportedly been in existence since the fall of 1941 when, it is reported, alleged union activities caused unrest among Negroes there.

In and around Dumas, Arkansas, no indications have been received of subversive or un-American agitation among Negroes there and that the only trouble exists in the situation of Negroes leaving work on plantations for defense employment thus reportedly causing labor shortages in cotton picking time.

In the Winchester, Arkansas, area, alleged union racketeering activities are stated to have caused some discontent among Negroes there approximately two years ago, but at the present time no information has been reported reflecting unrest or dissatisfaction among Negroes there and no indications of any subversive activity.

Louisville Field Division

Various verbal reports and rumors have been circulated in and around the City of Louisville, Kentucky, to the effect that the Negroes would rather live under the rule of Germany and Japan. Other remarks reported, emanating from unidentified sources, are to the effect that the Negroes will be in a better economic and social position when Japan and the Negroes rule the world. No definite sources have been located, however, for such rumors, reports or alleged statements.

Remarks such as "This is a white man's war," and "The white men won't let the Negro have anything to do with this war," have also been reported. Inquiries fail to reflect organized propaganda or activity from outside sources.

In such areas as Owensboro, Bowling Green, London, Pikeville, Paducah, Covington, Harlan, Lexington and Ashland, no information has been received reflecting any foreign-inspired agitation or trouble among the Negroes residing there.

It is reported that as of approximately five years ago an alleged Japanese speaker appeared in Covington, Kentucky. No information, however, has been reported reflecting subsequent appearance of alleged Japanese speakers.

Active in Louisville and Paducah, Kentucky, is stated to be a group sponsoring a "Double V" program. In Paducah it was advised that the Double V Club is believed to have been formed to oppose rival Negro political factions. It is reported that apparently these clubs have for their foundation the campaign undertaken by the "Pittsburgh Courier," a Negro newspaper published in Pittsburgh, Pennsylvania, calling for the winning of democracy at home as well as winning the war for democracy. A meeting in Paducah was sponsored by the Paducah Double V Club on July 4, 1942, in the form of a picnic. A speaker was imported for the meeting, however, there was a small attendance and the speaker is said to have been very conservative in his remarks.

One source of information has advised that he believes Negro preachers in this area do more harm toward creating race prejudice among the Negroes and agitating them to fight for equality with the white man than do other sources. However, in this same area it has been reported that a number of colored people, who appeared to be more agitated at one time, have been active in collecting food and clothing supplies to send to Great Britain and were consequently proud and happy when they received letters of appreciation for their work.

Among the newspapers that receive a comparatively wide circulation in this area are "The Pittsburgh Courier" and the "Chicago Defender." Other newspapers published locally are the "Ashland Daily Independent," published in Ashland, "The Louisville Leader," published in Louisville, and the "Kentucky Reporter," published in Louisville.

During the fall and early winter of 1942 sources of information have reported a growth of a religious Negro organization called the Moorish Shrine Temple in the Louisville, Kentucky area. The activities of the members of the church are reported to have been long observed by the Negro people in Louisville, because the members are seen publicly in the streets wearing fezzes and turbans, and have occasionally been seen wearing ceremonial Mohammedan garments. The leader of the organization is reported to be Harriet DeMoss and is alleged to be pastor of the St. Mary's Church and Power Center of Applied Christianity located at 439 South 9th Street, Louisville. The organization is said to have been originally made up of approximately twenty members while now it is said to have an excess of thirty. The members of the organization are said to be known to the colored people as the "Boys". The organization is reportedly causing some dissention among certain elements of the Negro population in Louisville.

Confidential sources of information have also noted that there is an increased agitation among the Negro laboring element in Louisville for the rights of union workers. In connection with this sources of information have stated that secretary of the Communist Party for the State of Kentucky has often been observed in the heart of the Negro section distributing pamphlets among the colored people.

With respect to the areas of Harlan and Paducah, Kentucky, some information relative to agitation among them has been reported. Numerous rumors and complaints concerning individuals making pro-Japanese statements have been reported relative to these areas and the Lexington, Kentucky area as well. There have also been reports of alleged existence of Eleanor clubs however, no specific or v[e]rifying information has been received in this regard.

In the area of Glasgow, Kentucky, information relative to activities on the part of members of the Jehovah's Witnesses sect has been reported. Two members were arrested by local authorities and were sued for breach of peace, this was during the month of August, 1942. It has been reported that an agreement was reached over this incident, whereby Jehovah's Witnesses sect members agreed to leave the county providing the prosecution was dropped. The Rev. Alonzo Webb, in the city of Glasgow, has advised that he has heard rumors of agitation among the negro people to the effect that the Negroes were advised that they were the same color as the Japanese and in event of a Japanese victory, Negroes being of the same race, would be favored. He pointed out that he saw no reason for any apprehension over such a rumor, inasmuch as the thirty-one Negro Baptist churches under his direction had ministers who preached Americanism in their sermons.

In the vicinities of Lynch and Barbourville, Kentucky, unverified and nonspecific information has been received alleging that Negroes in these areas have made numerous pro-Japanese and anti-American statements. Various sources of information have been interviewed to obtain definite information relative to the possibility of Japanese propaganda being circulated in these areas; no specific information, however, was received.

In the area of Lexington, Kentucky, numerous inquiries have been made of individuals in a position to furnish good information for indications of possible un-American activities among and by Negroes in the area. No information, however, has been received indicating such conditions exist. *[100-135-28]*

A series of incidents indicative of a degree of tension between white and Negro people in the area of Lexington, Kentucky, is reported to have occurred during the early part of February, 1943. Nothing, however, has been reported which might reflect organized or subversive inspiration or agitation in the trouble.

The first incident occurred on February 5, 1943, when a white urban bus driver in Lexington, Kentucky, was stabbed by a Negro youth after an argument following the driver's instructions to move to the rear of the bus and not to block the door. The knife wielder was arrested and was said to have been drinking.

On the same date during the evening, another Lexington bus driver instructed two Negroes to discontinue their actions and to stop annoying passengers if they did not wish to be put off the bus. It is related that a fight ensued and the driver was beaten with his assailants' fists whereupon his money "changer" was taken and the Negroes escaped from the bus. During this same evening several Negroes are said to have beaten another bus driver with their fists after he had attempted to quiet them. The three Negroes involved were apprehended by local police while fleeing and were placed in jail on charges of assault. The ages of the three individuals ranged from seventeen to twenty-seven years. The statement has been made that from their actions it was believed they were under the influence of marijuana.

On February 10, 1943, it is related, a white woman and a Negro woman argued over a seat on a Greyhound bus en route to Lexington, Kentucky. It is stated that the white woman had been drinking. During the argument the Negro slashed the white woman and escaped.

On February 12, 1943, rumors were prevalent in Lexington that Negroes there were going to create trouble on local busses on the same night and also that the Dixieland, a colored night club, would burn down. The origin of the rumors was not determined by the local authorities nor were the identities of persons who might have been involved in the burning of the dance hall.

The Dixieland has been described as an amusement center which sponsors prominent colored bands and it is said that a few white people buy admissions to hear the orchestras and to witness the dancing. The white people remain in separate partitions and do not dance.

On the night of February 12, 1943, and early in the morning of February 13, 1943, a series of shots were fired into the crowd in attendance and a white college student was killed and Negro youths were wounded. Local authorities are quoted as having stated that no previous trouble or controversies had arisen at the dances. It is also said that witnesses could not agree as to the number of shots which had been fired and as to the direction from which they came.

Inquiries in Uniontown have failed to reveal any subversive activity among the Negroes in that area. However, allegations have been received of secret meetings held by members of the colored race in this area. Inquiries into these allegations have failed to substantiate them.

Memphis Field Division

Reports received in this area reflect that there have been many rumors to the effect that Negroes were heard to say that they would be better off "under Hitler" or "under the Japs." Another example of a rumor arising in this area is reflected in information received that there would be a Negro uprising in Memphis, Tennessee, on a "blackout night" scheduled for June 9, 1942. However, such an uprising failed to materialize.

During the early part of the month of September, 1942, it was reported in the Memphis area that rumors were being circulated to the effect that Negroes had set the night of September 29, 1942 for the time of a general uprising. Investigations were conducted to determine if such rumors had any foundation, or to disaffirm them. The results failed to prove that the Negroes in the community had any organization of a subversive or radical character. As a matter of fact, it was determined that the only group that could be determined which were active among Negroes were those controlled by the churches. The rumors continued to multiply and on September 29, 1942 a rumor began to the effect that an uprising was to begin on October 6, 1942. The rumor spread and on Monday, October 5, 1942, additional armed guards were brought to a defense project located in Memphis, which in turn added to the fears of the individuals residing in the community, both negro and white. Also at this same defense project employees were sent home at early hours, reportedly to avoid their risking being harmed should a riot occur. All of these incidents combined with the general desire of the public to gossip and spread rumor, caused the people of Memphis to become quite concerned over the situation. The local authorities are said not to have been able to find out whether the Negroes intended to riot or not, and for that reason were reluctant to issue any kind of a statement to the press denying the fact for fear that they would be wrong in their prediction. On October 5, 1942 the sporting goods houses and hardware store, etc. were sold completely out of ammunition and guns. On the night of October 6, according to the rumor when the Negroes were "To take over", the streets of Memphis at 7:00 p.m. were deserted except for a straggler here and there. No incident, of course, involving trouble took place. The statement was issued by several officials of the Memphis city government, as well as the Special Agent in Charge of the Memphis Field Division of the Federal Bureau of Investigation, to the effect that investigations had failed to discover any indication of organized disloyalty among the Negroes in the Memphis area. These statements had a satisfactory and quieting effect. Since that time no such rumors have been reported to be prevalent.

During the period September 8 to September 13, 1942, the Negro National Baptist Convention was held in Memphis, Tennessee, at the Ellis City Auditorium. Among the issues promoted at this convention were:

1. The abolishment of legal injustice against Negroes.
2. The stamping out of race discrimination.
3. Preventing of lynching, burning or torturing of Negroes.
4. The assurance to every citizen of color the common rights of American citizenship.

5. The compelling of equal accommodations in railroad travel irrespective of color when the same fare is paid.
6. The securing for Negro children an equal opportunity to public school education through a fair apportionment of public education fund.
7. The emancipation in fact, as well as in name, of a race of more than 13,000,000 American born citizens.

Numerous complaints have been received with regard to the Negro situation in this area although no definite information was furnished at the time. Attempts to verify such information resulted in the development of evidence that the rumors started from gossip and mounted until they were a definite threatening factor.

Another type of complaint has been received in that area by white employers of Negro unskilled help, some to the effect that the Negroes "began to feel and talk as if they were as good as a white person." Another type of complaint received has been to the effect that difficulty was being experienced in employing young Negro boys who, it was charged, had become dissatisfied with their work allegedly as a result of someone "talking" to them.

Still another type of complaint has been received from white citizens to the effect that Negroes "are getting more bold and seem to be forgetting their place more often." As an example of this, it was reported that an unidentified Negro woman approached a lunch counter where white customers ate to order food. Upon being told to move away, reports state that the colored woman made the remark, "The colored people will be able to sit where they want when Hitler comes over here." Such complaints, however, are reported to have been based upon rumor and gossip according to local law enforcement agencies in Jackson, Tennessee.

Allegations were received that subversive meetings were being held in and around Jackson, Tennessee. Inquiries in this regard reflect that a responsible Negro attorney in Jackson advised definitely that there has been no one making any speeches of a subversive or un-American nature before any colored organizations in that city.

On February 1, 1943 the State Legislature of Tennessee approved a bill repealing that State's fifty year old poll tax law, and at the same time approved a bill establishing a permanent registration system in the State of Tennessee. This action has been hailed widely by the press as a movement toward abolishing discrimination against Negroes.

A summation of information received concerning this matter in the area covered by the Memphis Field Division of the Federal Bureau of Investigation shows there have been numerous complaints received over a period of many months, the large majority of which were of a general and nonspecific nature. They were to the effect that groups of Negroes or individual Negroes allegedly made statements or conducted themselves in such a manner as to indicate they were subjected to agitation by outside influence. There were also received rumors of race riots and secret meetings, as well as indications of general dissatisfied and restless feelings on the part of Negroes. There were also allegations of unrest and fear reported among white residents of the area. In many of these complaints, it was apparent the sources attempted to present the information in such a fashion as to indicate any difficulty that might be experienced with members of the Negro race would result or did result from outside agitation among the Negro populace. Yet, it was almost obvious in many of the cases that the situations were the result of personal difficulties or were prompted by personal motives.

On the other hand, there is a substantial circulation of national Negro newspapers which lay considerable emphasis on the race question, treating with discrimination against the Negroes in war industries and discrimination against them in the armed forces. Yet, it has been reliably reported that there is a definite feeling of resentment among members of the Negro race in this area against police departments because of the alleged treatment to which Negroes have been subjected upon arrest. There are also reported instances where differences or trouble between white and Negro inhabitants arose from the application of "Jim Crow" laws in public conveyances.

There have been allegations that exploitation was being carried on among Negroes by labor unions affiliated with the CIO in this area. No definite evidence to this effect has been reported. However, it is to be noted that the two unions which have a majority of Negroes as members, namely, International Woodworkers of America, CIO, and the United Cannery, Agricultural, Packing and Allied Workers of America, CIO, exert organizational efforts in the direction of Negro members. This is also borne out by the fact that these unions have bargaining rights with employers who, by the nature of their business, employ large numbers of Negroes in comparison to the number of white people.

In the areas of the counties of Tipton, Gibson, Maury, Fayette, Obion, Lake, Henry Lauderdale, Hardeman, Haywood, Madison and Shelby inquiries made of leading citizens both white and colored for organized agitation attributable to the foreign inspired forces have met with negative results. Inquiries and investigation, which have been made in an effort to establish any foundation to complaints of foreign inspired activity at work, have resulted in no substantial or specific information. In many instances the original complaint has proved to be nothing more than a malicious rumor. In a few isolated cases where the original source of information was established, it was ascertained that these sources based their reports on conversations which they allegedly overheard. [*100-135-29-26*]

Miami Field Division

Extensive investigation in this area, especially with regard to the cities of Jacksonville and Tampa, Florida, has failed to develop any showing of unrest or dissatisfaction among Negroes in this area caused by pro-German, pro-Italian, pro-Japanese or pro-Communist forces; rather that unrest and dissatisfaction among the Negroes in this area is stated to result from social and economic causes. Several complaints have been received, however, to the effects that Negroes have made pro-Japanese statements.

Jacksonville, Florida

With regard to the City of Jacksonville, sources of information contacted there advise that the Negro situation there is solely a result of local conditions involving social and economic matters. A source of information, who has resided in Jacksonville for many years and who has seen many strange faces among the Negroes, indicating that thousand have migrated to Jacksonville from other places to obtain employment. He stated in many instances these Negroes are trouble makers. He has advised that he has not heard of either white or Negro organizations attempting to incite the Negroes to riot but that the local problem among the Negroes is becoming more acute daily since so many Negroes are in the Armed Forces that expect and assert their demands for the same privileges as are enjoyed by the white men in the Armed Forces. He advised that the Negroes openly state that they want no discrimination of any sort such as segregated toilets, drinking fountains, theater seating, et cetera. He has informed that never in the history of the South has the Negro been able to earn as much as he presently gets and that the economic phase in his life urges him to take or demand the same privileges as are afforded white people.

Another source of information, who has for many months been making a study of the Negro problem in and around this city, believes that unrest, dissatisfaction and trouble among the Negroes are a result of the influx of many northern Negro civilians and soldiers. He has compared the conditions during the first World War with those of the present, saying that so many northern Negroes who had been brought into the South, or who have migrated there, attempt to indoctrinate the southern Negroes with northern ideas. He has advised that Negro soldiers informed the southern Negroes that "We are all fighting for the same cause, and a white soldier is no better than a Negro soldier, and that all Negro soldiers should insist on having the rights and privileges which are accorded to white men in uniform." In this connection it is reported that the situation is well in hand, having come about through the cooperation of the local Police Department and United States Army officials who have placed tried and experienced Negro Military Police in the Negro section of Jacksonville while the Police Department has stationed in this section officers experienced in handling Negroes who know how to cope with any situation outside of a general riot that may develop.

A complaint has been received from a member of the Jacksonville Ministerial Alliance who has stated that an investigation of the vice and gambling among the Negroes in Jacksonville should be made. The opinion was expressed that police authorities are inactive as far as this situation is concerned and it was alleged that some of the members of the Police Department may be involved in the gambling situation in the Negro sections.

Other causes for unrest and dissatisfaction among the Negroes in this area are attributed to editorials appearing in New York, Philadelphia and Chicago newspapers, as well as in northern Negro publications. It is stated that it is being constantly brought to the attention of the Negroes in this area that they are discriminated against in hotels, trains, buses, street cars, public parks and theaters. It is further brought to their attention that they are allegedly not assigned to the same duties as white soldiers when in the Army and that Negro school teachers are allegedly paid lesser wages than those received by white school teachers.

Tampa, Florida

In this area, where it is reported some unrest exists among the Negroes, investigation which has been made fails to disclose any agitation among the Negroes caused by un-American organizations or groups or individuals. Sources of information interviewed advise that conditions are much better for the Negroes at the present time in this area inasmuch as they have their own Federal housing project, their own theater, a hospital and are presently being paid higher wages than in other years. It is stated that there is little unemployment among the Negroes, many of them being employed on defense projects.

In April, 1942, a near race riot occurred at the Tampa Shipbuilding Yards which was started under the following circumstances:

While the workers were in line passing through the gate, a white man stepped on the toes of a Negro and thereupon apologized. However, the Negro made some remarks whereupon the white man slapped the face of the Negro. Soon Negro people and white people engaged in a fight but were subsequently halted by the guards. Subsequently all employees were searched with the result that an ice pick, a knife and a revolver were found. Inquiries made of this incident failed to reflect agitation from the outside but rather that the instance could be regarded as a personal altercation between white and colored employees.

It should be reported that a series of assaults on white women were made by several colored youths late in the Spring of 1942. At the time, the Police Department in Tampa was assisted by leading colored citizens who are said to have been anxious to have the wrongdoers apprehended. On the whole, it is said that the Negroes from this city are law abiding and patriotic.

Information has been received that the influx of northern Negroes in this area, especially the Negro soldiers, has caused some trouble among the Negro inhabitants in that the southern Negro is told by the northern Negro that the present war is everyone's war and that colored soldiers accordingly should be entitled to the rights and privileges afforded the white soldiers. It should be noted that it is reported that Negro soldiers complained about not being given the same duties as the white soldiers. To this has been attributed the unrest that is being caused and created by the Negro soldiers.

In this area, it is alleged, some of the unrest among the Negroes can be attributed to northern publications which advocate the equality of Negroes. Linked with these publications as part of the cause for unrest are the actions and statements made by the northern Negroes in this area which are said to influence the southern Negro to such an extent that he becomes dissatisfied.

Those incidents or situations wherein trouble was caused involving the Negro are said not to be caused by agitation by either white or colored individuals or by foreign forces. Those incidents which do involve a Negro soldier now and then are said to have been caused by an intoxicated Negro soldier or by some civilian attempting to get a Negro soldier to brawl. [*Rept* S.A. ▬▬▬▬ *9-9-42 Miami, Fla 100-135-30*]

It was reported in January, 1943 that a "run" on the post office had been made by Negroes who desire to cash their war savings stamps. The rumor accompanying this "run" was that Negroes had heard the stamps would be valueless after January 18, 1943. Inquiries made into this matter to determine if subversive forces were responsible for the rumor met with negative results. However, opinions were furnished by sources of information in a position to know and understand the Negro population in the area that the situation was caused by lack of education on the part of the Negroes who attempted to or did cash in war stamps. In this connection, the source of information has pointed out that in late 1940 or early 1941 a similar "run" was made by Negroes, who withdrew their postal savings because of a rumor floating around through the colored section of the city that postal savings were not safe investments. Several individuals who cashed in their stamps expressed their reason for so doing to be that they needed the money for clothes and other material. In all, no logical or specific information was developed or reported that subversive forces were responsible for the "run."

It was reported in May, 1943 that Negroes attached to an Engineer Corps at the Army Air Corps base under construction at Cross City, Florida, upon arriving in the vicinity of that city attempted to associate with white residents, especially in bars and eating places theretofore restricted to white people. A number of these soldiers were northern Negroes. At first, although after some argument, the situation was allegedly clarified and a solution arrived at. However, subsequently, it appeared, some of the Negro soldiers insisted on entering public gathering places normally restricted to white people. It is further reported that on one occasion Negro soldiers chased a proprietor out of his place of business after he had allegedly advised them "niggers" were not permitted to come into his place of business. As a result, the white citizens of the city allegedly began arming themselves in preparation for additional advances by Negro soldiers. This matter was taken up by local as well as state and Army officials, and a program was set out. Allegations were also received that Negro Military Police armed with firearms which, according to Army officials, were unloaded had fired their guns within the city limits of Cross City and had been seen by at least twenty-five people to be shooting fish from the bridge near the town. No trouble has been reported from this area since this time.

The situation in Monticello, Madison, Greenville and Perry, Florida, has been reportedly quiet, and there are no indications of any un-American activity among the Negroes there.

On April 4, 1943, what resulted in a near race riot took place at Orlando, Florida. It is reported that a short time prior to that date three battalions of Negro troops had been moved in. A truckload of the Negro troops had been taken into the city on that date, which stopped in the middle of Church Street where the Negro soldiers got out and blocked the traffic. A white man attempting to drive his automobile through blew his horn and was approached by one of the Negroes, who cursed him and referred to his wife in a derogatory sense. The white man is said to have started a fight with the Negro soldiers, and immediately a near riot was begun by the Negro troops with Negro civilians who took the part of the white man. The incident was finally quieted by local officers and the Military Police, but not until at least one knife had been drawn and several Negro soldiers badly beaten.

On April 13, 1943 three thousand Bahaman Negroes were being brought into the Everglades area of Florida to do farm labor. They had been quartered in army tents at three Farm Security Administration labor camps in the Everglades area adjacent to and in close proximity to settlements of native Negro citizens. Sources of information have advised that there is a possibility of trouble between the Bahaman Negroes and the Florida Negroes, in view of a long-standing animosity between the two groups.

It was reported in June, 1943 that in the city of Tallahassee there were evidences of members of the Jehovah's Witnesses sect approaching Negroes, attempting to obtain their affiliations with the sect. No indications have been received, however, that these workers for the Jehovah's Witnesses sect have been attempting to develop racial antagonism or un-Americanism among the Negroes there.

On the night of June 24, 1943, a company consisting of Negro soldiers at Camp Blanding, Florida, staged a dance at the camp. Members of another Negro company, Company D, milled about the dance and staged something similar to a demonstration. When ordered away by Military Police, they became angered and resentful. Subsequently, members of Company D gained access to gun racks which had been left unlocked and secured fourteen rifles, as well as ammunition which had been left over from range practice and war games. They fired rounds of ammunition into the crowd at the dance, and as a result nine Negro girls, eight Negro soldiers and one white officer received wounds. The origin of this trouble was allegedly founded in ill feelings which existed between the company staging the dance and Company D. These ill feelings reportedly grew out of action taken by Military Police of the company which had staged the dance prior to the outburst of trouble. Five Negro soldiers were taken into custody for their activities in connection with the shooting. Blame was also placed on officers who permitted the gun racks to get unlocked and did not collect surplus ammunition.

In addition, inquiries have been made in other communities of Florida where it has been ascertained that, although some degree of unrest appears prevalent, no indications are apparent that subversive or un-American forces have been agitating or exploiting the Negro population. However, opinions have been offered that a considerable amount of trouble has been caused by out-of-state Negroes, mainly northern Negroes being sent to this state for military training or service. [*100-135-30*]

New Orleans Field Division

Considerable investigation and inquiries in the State of Louisiana fail to reveal any pro-Axis inspired agitation among the Negroes in that area. Rather, information received reflects that one of the sources of agitation appears to emanate from the Negro press which carries on a militant campaign for equal rights as well as those against social, economic and political discriminations. Generally the press supports the war effort as against that of the Axis, but at the same time exploits war conditions to gain objectives and at times appears to indulge in threat not to support unless conditions for the Negroes are changed.

Another source of agitation which causes unrest and dissatisfaction among the Negroes in this area is the Communist Party of Louisiana, which is composed chiefly of Negroes and is militant although comparatively small in size. It is stated to have a degree of influence in trade unions in that area and has infiltrated to some extent into most Negro organizations. The present Communist Party line, however, in this area, appears to place the war effort in the foreground rather than the demand for equal rights for the Negroes. This is as compared with the Negro press which appears to advance the two propositions equally.

There are a number of militant Negro organizations in this area which continually urge the granting of voting rights to the Negro and constantly cited alleged instances of unfairness to the Negro whether it be in the court of law, in industry, in the armed forces, or in the federal government. On the other hand, it is reported that there are no highly influential Negro leaders.

The State of Louisiana has no poll tax law and accordingly the Negroes in this area as well as others, have privileges to vote. On the other hand, however, Jim Crow laws or customs are in effect and at present are particularly protested to by the colored race. Business and trade unions and occupational advantages for the Negroes are at present said to be good in this area. Educational standards for the Negroes in the City of New Orleans are high, but are believed not to be entirely satisfactory in rural Louisiana.

Housing projects are regarded by sources of information as very helpful in quieting conditions. Assistance at the polls in elimination of Jim Crow Laws have also been suggested by sources of information, as certain measures to obtain cooperation of the Negro race in this area.

Negro Newspapers

Among the Negro newspapers distributed in this area, the general make up of which are said to be inflammatory of nature, are "The Pittsburgh Courier," (Louisiana Edition); "The Louisiana Weekly;" "The Sepia Socialite;" "The New Orleans Sentinel;" "The Alexandria Observer."

The Louisiana edition of "The Pittsburgh Courier," printed in Pittsburgh, Pennsylvania, has an approximate total circulation of 17,000 in the State of Louisiana, with approximately 7,000 being distributed in New Orleans. With regard to this newspaper, it has been reported by confidential sources of information, that the Negro population in this area has been greatly influenced by "The Pittsburgh Courier's" V-V Program which is in effect "Victory at Home First and Then Victory Abroad". It is also alleged with regard to this paper that the column contained in it written by George S. Schuyler, carries considerable weight with the Negroes not only in Louisiana, but throughout the country.

"The Louisiana Weekly" is published every Saturday by the Louisiana Weekly Publishing Company, Incorporated, 632 South Rampart Street, New Orleans, Louisiana. It is a member of the Associated Negro Press and is a member of the Negro Newspaper Publishers Association. It is also served by the International News Photo.

The following aims and purposes reflect the platform of this newspaper:

"1. To stimulate a desire on the part of all for education.
2. To create a sentiment for better homes.
3. To condemn sectional differences, and make for unity of thought and purpose.
4. To agitate for more playgrounds, and urge the necessity of constructive thought with regard to the training of our youth.
5. To minimize fun-loving, and seek to secure interest in worth while pursuit.
6. To bring about cohesion of business forces for the economic progress of our group."

This newspaper has a state wide coverage and approximate circulation of 10,000, 7,000 of which is in New Orleans. The city editor of this newspaper, Samuel Hoskins, has been reported to this Bureau as being a member of the Communist Party as well as the Communist Party Front organization, The Southern Negro Youth Congress. Otherwise the newspaper is considered to be semi-conservative.

"The Sepia Socialite" is said by sources of information to carry considerable news concerning Negro rights and has for some time been one of the leaders in the agitation for equal rights for the Negro, particularly in connection with ballots. The newspaper is stated to have a state wide circulation of approximately 3,000. It is said that it is not dominated by the Communist Party or by any foreign controlled organization, but that it represents itself to be liberal, and progressive in nature, and as such, is thought to be the most radical of the Negro newspapers in the State of Louisiana. A source of information has pointed out that although he does not believe "The Sepia Socialite" to be a subversive newspaper he believes that by watching its columns, the unrest and agitation among the Negroes can best be detected.

In this connection it is pointed out that the New Orleans Press Club which is stated to be intended as a pressure group, is headed by Leon Louis, connected with "The Sepia Socialite". This club is an unchartered organization consisting of approximately 12 colored newspapermen, with the stated purpose of the discussion of problems in the field of mutual interests, exchange of ideas and the sponsorship of programs to advance the interests of the colored population as a whole.

Recently "The Sepia Socialite" and the New Orleans Press Club circulated a form letter with reference to the fifth anniversary edition of "The Sepia Socialite". It was entitled "The Negro in Louisiana" and was mailed to those alleged to be most liberal in the State of Louisiana.

It is believed that this letter represents the policy of the newspaper and the feelings of its editorial staff and for that reason, portions of it are set hereinafter:

> "A definite, unhappy and perilous disquietude—as careful reading of this issue will disclose—smoulders in the Louisiana *Negroe's* bosom because he is discriminated against as a citizen, having not yet been able to enjoy the practical citizenship granted him by the constitution of this great and glorious America, for whose defense he so many times has given his blood and for which even now, in foreign fields, he is giving his life. . . .
>
> You know in your own conscience that our legislative body, though charitable at times, in a whimsical sort of way, has not given the Louisiana Negro his full measure of benefits, his just and lawful rights, his man-to-man Christian consideration as a tax-paying citizen.

* * * * *

> "You cannot ignore what is; you cannot long continue to impose the discriminating life of circumscription upon two-fifths of a government's people; you cannot long encircle the initiative of a whole race of people who live by the side of a people who have made a world record of achievement. You cannot kill hope with the imposition of fear; you cannot blind your own conscience to every American left for the idea of freedom and justice, whether he is black or white."

* * * * *

"The New Orleans Sentinel", which is also known as "The New Orleans Sentinel and The Informer", is published weekly in New Orleans, Louisiana. It is stated to have an approximate circulation of 1,000. A source of information has advised that the paper in its editorial and news policy is sound and reflects a healthy American position. Its principles are stated as follows:

"1. To inspire and develop self-respect and self-reliance, and to awaken pride of race in our people.
2. To seek to establish in the community a positive force with working toward the elimination of prejudice WITHIN and WITHOUT the race.
3. To defend the race against false leadership.
4. To foster the creation of wider job possibilities among Negroes for Negroes.
5. To strive to obtain for the Negro his full and unqualified right under the constitution of the United States."

"The Alexandria Observer" is published weekly at Alexandria, Louisiana, and is edited and managed by Georgia Johnson who is also secretary of the Alexandria

Unit of the National Association for the Advancement of Colored People. A source of information has described her as being an agitator although she is not believed to be influential.

The Communist Party of the State of Louisiana

It was reported in November of 1942, with regard to the activities of the Communist Party in connection with the Negro, out of thirteen units and out of the number of members not assigned to units, there are 74 Negroes and 26 white people who are members of the Party in this area. In addition, however, there are three farm units which are stated to be comprised almost totally of Negroes. In the concentration of Party members in the Transport Workers Union in this area, there are 11 Negroes. And in a unit composed of officials of the Transport Workers Union, there are one white man and three Negroes. At the Todd Shipyard there are seven Negro Communist Party members in the Union. In the United Office and Professional Workers of America there are four Communist Party members, all of whom are Negroes. In the New Orleans Chapter of the Southern Negro Youth Congress, there are eight Negro women who are Party members. Of the Party members in the Amalgamated Union of Cleaners and Dyers there have been stated to be approximately seven Negroes and no white people. In the International Longshoremen's Union it is reported that there are five Negro Party members and no white members; while another unit has all white Party members. In the units represented in the Andrew Jackson Neighborhood Club there are six white people and no Negroes, while a neighborhood branch of the Party has twelve Negro members and no white members; and of the members who are not in a unit there are two who are Negroes. (It should be noted that the Andrew Jackson Neighborhood Club is a Communist Front Organization in the City of New Orleans, Louisiana.)

The three farm units are reported to have a total of fifteen or twenty Negro members. Thus it is believed that although the membership of the Party itself is somewhat small, it is comprised in the greater part of Negro members.

Information received with regard to the chief propaganda presently being issued from the office of the Communist Party through its contacts in the trade unions is for a second front. However, it has recently taken up the case in which three Negro soldiers at Camp Claiborne, Louisiana attacked and raped a white girl on the government reservation there. The Party activity with regard to agitating among the Negroes on this case, has been extensive and considerable.

It is believed significant to note the comment made by a confidential informant of this Bureau regarding the Communist Party machinations and maneuvering among the Negroes as well as how the Negro question is viewed from within the Communist Party. The confidential informant, it should be stated, is a member of the Communist Party. In his remarks this informant states that the general trend among the Negro masses in New Orleans is that the present time is the natural and logical time to obtain economic and even social equality.

These needs and demands of course have been stressed by the speakers, that is, Communist Party speakers or sympathizers with the Communist Party, at all the Negro meetings attended by this informant in the past two years. The informant furnished the opinion that the average Negro seems determined to fight against what is termed "White Supremacy" and that the Communist Party is exploiting this to the fullest degree.

Informant has advised that numerous reports have been received in the Communist Party of a growing tendency toward the building of a Negro mass movement among the Negro farmers in Louisiana. In this connection, he states that the Negro needs to be convinced that his economic, political and social level must be equal to those of the white people, and that the fight for these things is going on through the trade union movement and through the church and fraternal group. He believes that this is largely due to the Communist Party's influence among the workers in various trade unions, white as well as Negro, and that it will continue to spread among the black and white at least until the war is won.

The confidential informant has offered a statement reflecting the Communist Party line which is set out as an example of the Communist Party attitude in a particular territory, in this instance, New Orleans and its environs:

> "There have been too many incidents, such as the sentencing of three Negro soldiers in Alexandria to hang for an alleged rape of a white woman, New Orleans police beating a Negro draftee, the Ku-Klux-Klan on the loose setting fire to Negroes, lynching, etc., for the government not to make an investigation to see if there is not something more to these attacks on the Negroes than appears on the surface.
>
> "The Negro people are rapidly becoming convinced by incidents such as these that if the Japanese propaganda that they are the champions of the darker races isn't true, then neither is the American propaganda that this is a peoples' war, a democratic war, true.
>
> "These alleged undemocratic practices against the Negro people are playing into the hands of the enemy. The Fascist agents are on their toes and will use these attacks against the Negro people to great advantage."

A source of information whose connections are chiefly with the colored press, has been interviewed with regard to his opinion as to the influence of the Communist Party among the Negroes. In this regard he stated he is doubtful that the Communist influence is great; he advised that in the first place, the Negroes are by nature deeply religious and for this reason, do not find Communism attractive. Secondly, they are fundamentally loyal to the United States, that they have no interest in Soviet Russia, and that it was not even possible to arouse enthusiasm among the Negroes for Ethiopia at the time it was attacked. Another reason stated, is that undoubtedly Negro organizations are frequently used

by the Communists as vehicles for propaganda favorable to the Negroes, but it is doubted that the same has brought about a feeling of loyalty to the Communist Party on the part of the Negroes. In this connection, this source of information advised that he is quite certain no foreign propaganda of any kind is presently influencing Negroes in the State of Louisiana. He said rather the largest sources of influence in the South are the churches, particularly the Baptist church and the Negro press and that these forces are carrying on a strong agitation for Negro rights and largely for the support of the Negroes.

Other Organizations Active Among the Negroes in the State of Louisiana

Southern Negro Youth Congress

The Southern Negro Youth Congress which has its main offices in the City of Birmingham, Alabama, is an organization under Communist domination. It was apparently organized along the lines of the American Youth Congress and its first conference was held in Richmond, Virginia, in February, 1937 and its fourth conference in New Orleans, Louisiana, in April, 1940. The most recent conference was held in April, 1942 at Tuskegee, Alabama. The aims of this organization are stated to be in establishing the "unity of Southern Negro youth collaborating with white Southern youth and the abolition of the restrictions which prevent Southern youths from fully serving the nation."

The Southern Negro Youth Congress carries on an extensive agitational program for the granting of Negro rights, the abolition of the poll tax and the abolition of segregation of and discrimination against the Negroes. With regard to its influence in New Orleans and the vicinity, it should be pointed out that the following people are members of the National Council of the Southern Negro Youth Congress and that all are reportedly known members of the Communist Party:

Mrs. Noelie Cunningham of Gretna, Louisiana, a member of the National Association for the Advancement of Colored People.

Samuel Hoskins, editor of the Louisiana Weekly.

Alvin Jones, graduate of Dillard University and formerly active in the American Students Union, a Communist Front organization.

Ernest Wright, who is listed as an officer of the Congress for the years 1942 and 1943, is a member of the Communist Party and a representative of the International Longshoremen's and Warehousemen's Union, in New Orleans.

Samuel Hoskins and Ernest Wright were among a group of six delegates of this Congress who called on various departments of the government in the month of May, 1942, to present the grievances of the Negroes.

With regard to the local activities of the Youth Congress in New Orleans, the

Communist Party has been dominating in them. This is clearly indicated by preparations made for a rally held on July 4, 1942, the stated purpose of which was "support of the war against Fascism and for democracy." The organization of this rally was discussed at the meeting of the State Committee of the Communist Party of New Orleans on May 17, 1942, at which meeting Noelie Cunningham and Elizabeth Field made reports on the proposed rally; planned preparations were made; several Communist meetings held subsequently; and a letter to various prominent persons concerning it was prepared by Elizabeth Field, white leader of Communist activities in New Orleans.

The National Association for the Advancement of Colored People

The New Orleans Branch of the National Association for the Advancement of Colored People has an office at 2506 La Salle Street, in that city. The president of this Branch is Bennett B. Roff. As is true of the national organization, the local branch has for its program the following:

"1. To do away with police brutality, discrimination, and Jim-Crowism.
2. To work for the best interest of our race.
3. To seek the right to vote through the court of the land.
4. To fight for equal pay for school teachers and any other persons or group in need of the same.
5. To seek more playgrounds and better schools.
6. To create employment for our boys and girls, men and women.
7. To cooperate with all progressive organizations, that are working unselfishly for freedom OF OUR PEOPLE."

In the spring of 1942 it was reported that the New Orleans branch had for its goal for the year of 1942, twenty thousand members. The theme in the drive for new members was stated to hinge around the "Issues of the present war struggle and the efforts of the Negro to win complete equality in the American way of life."

With regard to possible Communist influence in the New Orleans branch of the National Association for the Advancement of Colored People, it is to be noted that circulars and reports reflect Ernest J. Wright, a leading colored Communist of New Orleans, as having been active in the National Association for the Advancement of Colored People as a speaker. It has further been reported that Wright, together with Raymond Tillman and Samuel Hoskins, both known Communist Party members and negroes were delegates from the New Orleans Branch to the Los Angeles National Convention of the organization. In this connection it should also be stated that Noelie Cunningham, a Negress of Gretna, Louisiana, who was active in the National Association for the Advancement of Colored People is a regular Party worker.

Although there is Communist influence in this branch of the National Association for the Advancement of Colored People, sources of information have advised that it is not dominated by the Party, although it is entirely possible, if not probable, that the organization is used from time to time as a vehicle for propaganda issued by the Communist Party.

The Urban League

The Urban League in New Orleans, Louisiana, is affiliated with the National Urban League which is a body interested in the advancement and promotion of Negroes. Sources of information interviewed advised that it cannot be considered as a radical organization and that, nationally, the organization is conservative. The local organization exhibits a degree of interest in union affairs in this territory, reportedly because of its industrial secretary, Clarence A. Laws, who is reported to have originated the painter's union in New Orleans and to be extremely interested in such matters.

Concerning the type of agitation carried on by this organization in New Orleans and its vicinity, it is reported that the National Urban League has issued statements in effect to prove that one-third of the population of New Orleans is of the Negro race, that 41% of the men inducted into the United States Army from that city are Negroes, while less than 5% are engaged in defense industry. The League also complains that since Pearl Harbor, the colored population has been called on for more than its proper proportion of men to serve in the United States Army and that prior to Pearl Harbor, it objected to the fact that fewer than the proper proportion were being inducted. The Urban League in this area is also stated to have pointed out that there are many more rejections of colored selectees in Louisiana because of illiteracy than in any other state.

Peoples Defense League

The Peoples Defense League, located at 2718 LaSalle Street, New Orleans, Louisiana, is an organization, local in nature, which has for its purpose the specific aid and benefit and the advancement of the interests of Negroes in that area. The League is presently headed by Ernest J. Wright and alleged to have approximately one thousand members. It is stated to be radical; however, no indications have been received that it has foreign connections. Its present activities consist chiefly in the attempt to secure the right of the colored people to vote in the primary elections, to protest against the alleged beating of a mother of a colored draftee, and to protest that the trial of the three colored soldiers recently convicted on rape charges in a federal court at Alexandria, Louisiana, was unfair.

In a speech at a meeting of The Peoples Defense League on September 21, 1941, at Shakespeare Park, New Orleans, Ernest J. Wright outlined the program of the League, saying that the immediate task was to right for and win the right to vote as American citizens. He said that the white workers were their natural friends and wanted to cooperate with the Negroes when they became organized. That as soon as the Negroes obtained the ballot, politicians would be forced to recognize and respect them as citizens. He related that the Negroes were being taken into the armed forces and were being "Jim-Crowed," that it was no accident that the Negroes in the Army were being trained with only sticks and not guns and it seems someone might be afraid to give them guns for fear they may turn them the wrong way.

On January 27, 1942, the day of the Democratic primary election for the City of New Orleans, eight Negroes, all members of the Peoples Defense League, submitted a complaint to the New Orleans office of the Federal Bureau of Investigation with respect to the alleged discrimination against colored persons, who presented themselves to vote in the Democratic primary. Those presenting themselves in this matter included:

Ernest Bayard, President of the Pelican State Democratic Association of Louisiana

Ernest J. Wright

W. R. Sterling

Candy D. Sartor

Horace Nash

Walter Roy

Samuel Hoskins, who has been referred to previously

Jonnie Clay

The complaint was that two Negroes had been allowed to vote but the rest of them were refused the right, whereupon an examination of the poll book was made and Bayard noted his name had been scratched off and after it appeared the word colored. Bayard had consulted the registrar of voters and the chairman of the Democratic Committee of the New Orleans Parish who is alleged to have advised that the Negroes would not be permitted to vote in the particular primary election. Facts of the case were presented to the Criminal Division of the Department of Justice and advice was received that the matter was one of local concern and did not involve a Federal election ballot.

Universal Negro Improvement Association

This organization, which held meetings in the past at 2223 South Liberty Street, New Orleans, Louisiana, was headed by a Dr. Clifford Bonds, who was president of the organization locally. It is presently the subject of an investigation in connection with various Selective Service cases involving its members. One member, a Collin Reed, was arrested for failure to register under the Selective Training and Service Act. Reed claimed to be a subject of Great Britain but denied that he owed allegiance to any country except the Negro race. He stated that he did not register because the present is a white man's war, that he believed the Japanese are closer to the Negro race than is the white race, and that if Japan were to invade the United States, he would assist them.

The national headquarters of this organization is located at 222 East 40th Street, Cleveland, Ohio, and is headed by one James Stuart. At its meeting there is said there were approximately forty persons present, according to statement furnished by Collin Reed, referred to above.

Recent reports concerning this organization are that it has several members who have made strong pro-Japanese remarks. However, the organization has been reportedly inactive for several months as a result largely, according to informants, of fear on the part of members of the organization resulting from the arrest and the conviction of leaders of the International Reassemble Church of the Freedom League, Incorporated.

International Reassemble Church of the Freedom League, Incorporated National Organization of the Colored People: E. A. Broaster

Ethelberth Anslem Broaster, who has styled himself as the General Messenger of the International Reassemble Church of the Freedom League, Incorporated, was active in the New Orleans, Louisiana, area during the latter part of 1941 and 1942. During the summer of 1942 he spoke on each Sunday afternoon to Negroes in Shakespeare Park, New Orleans, Louisiana, in an attempt to organize a semi-religious group, apparently for the purpose of evading the Selective Service Law. He taught members that they are not of the Negro race but rather Hebrews and that they should not go into the United States Army to be sent on expeditionary warfare, inasmuch as their faith forbids it. Although this individual has denied any connection with pro-Japanese organizations, he has spoken before the Pacific Movement of the Eastern World in East St. Louis, Illinois, July 11 to 13, 1941. He is also said to have been acquainted with members of various pro-Japanese cults in Chicago. In all the speeches made by Broaster in New Orleans and other places on which information is available, at no time did he show any pro-Japanese sympathy or give any evidence that he was under any foreign domination. On the contrary, he is reportedly said to have told members of this congregation that the Japanese are not the salvation of the Negroes and that they, the Negroes, would be worse off under Japanese domination than they would under the domination of the white man. Broaster and approximately ten of his followers were arrested by the Federal Bureau of Investigation for urging non-compliance with the Selective Training and Service Act. All convicted received heavy sentences, and Broaster received fifteen years.

Interesting sidelights believed to have been connected with this case are reflected in information received by the New Orleans Field Division to the effect that Negroes were buying firearms for the purpose of protecting themselves in a "great and bloody race war to come." Relative to this Broaster has admitted, since his arrest, the advocacy of purchasing firearms, in claiming that it was only for the purpose of protecting the homes of individuals against thieves and other ordinary menaces. Another interesting sidelight was reflected in information received from the manager of the department of the New Orleans Police Department handling blood donations, Mr. J. M. Tolivar. Mr. Tolivar has advised that until the time of the arrest of Broaster, there had never been a day passed without ten or twelve Negroes contacting him in his office asking where permits were obtained for the carrying of firearms. However, since the arrest of Broaster, not one individual has questioned him concerning the matter. He pointed out that his offices are adjacent to the entrance to the police department building.

[*100-135-34-30*]

The organization which was led by Broaster had a membership of 250 known members in the New Orleans area, with a branch in Chicago, Illinois, consisting of approximately thirty members. [*100-135-34-30*]

Louisiana Association for Progress of Negro Citizens

This organization was begun in March, 1943, allegedly for the purpose of obtaining votes for Negroes. It was originally organized to oppose the chapter of the National Association for the Advancement of Colored People in New Orleans, and all of the members of the organization were also members of the National Association for the Advancement of Colored People. No large membership has been obtained for the organization, although it was chartered on March 31, 1943, with the following objectives:

To promote the improvement of social, moral, and economic conditions of Negroes.

To teach the rights and obligations of citizenship, as well as the duties and responsibilities thereof to Negroes.

To promote better understanding and relationship between Negro and white citizens.

To use all proper means in the attainment of these duties.

The following individuals are the responsible organizers, all being Negroes:

Ernest J. Wright

Spencer Elliston

John Harvey Netter

Reverend A. L. Davis, Jr.

With regard to these individuals, no information is available that they have any radical connections, although Wright and Netter are reported to have been former members of the Communist Party in Louisiana.

Individuals Agitating Against the Negroes in This Area

Sources of information who have been contacted in this area have expressed the opinion that there are no outstanding leaders among the Negroes in this area, and for this reason, although considerable dissatisfaction is felt by the Negroes in this area with regard to social and political conditions, it is not believed that there is sufficient strength to rally the colored population and to effect insurrection or resistance to authority.

Ernest J. Wright

Ernest J. Wright, stated to be a graduate of Xavier and Michigan Universities, appears to be the most aggressive and energetic agitator among the Negroes in the New Orleans area at the present time. Ernest J. Wright, a Negro, is not to be confused, however, with Ernest Wright, Communist Party member and leader in the International Longshoremen's and Warehousemen's Union, C. I. O.

Ernest J. Wright in September of 1940 was one of the leaders of a strike against the Louisiana Industrial Life Insurance Company. Raymond Tillman, a Communist, and William Dorsey were other leaders in this dispute. It appeared that the strike had been called among the collectors of the company. The result was that the company immediately discharged all and hired new ones who were frequently subjected to attack during the course of their collection duties. The unions involved were reported to be the Insurance Union and the Workers Alliance. During this period, Ernest J. Wright was arrested and charged with attempted assault with a dangerous weapon. He was sentenced to serve two months in the Orleans Parish Prison. Although no specific information has been received reflecting this individual's connection with the Communist Party, it has been reported that he is a civic worker in behalf of the interest of his race. He worked in connection with the Workers Alliance, a Communist front, while in existence, and then began to work closely with Negro Communist Party members. Other indications of at least sympathy with the Communist cause are reflected in Wright's connection with the Southern Negro Youth Congress and the plans of the Party to make him a candidate for the position of Secretary in the C. I. O. Industrial Union Council in New Orleans.

The Alexandria, Louisiana, Riot

In January, 1942, in Alexandria, Louisiana, two white Military Police attempted to arrest two Negroes who were outside the Rex Theater in that city because one of the Negroes had used an obscene word and the owner of the theater had requested the MP's to arrest the two Negroes soldiers. The two white Military Police were joined by two colored MP's who insisted the responsibility of the arrest was theirs. Fights ensued between white and colored Military Police. Soon the colored Military Police were joined by many Negroes from that part of town, while other white MP's, City and State police assisted the two white MP's. Subsequently the mob was dispersed and twenty-eight Negroes were injured, two seriously. It was reported that an investigation by Army authorities reflected no evidence of subversive activities having caused the incident. The incident can presumably be laid to matters of local concern.

It should be pointed out, however, that there are three major Army camps in close proximity to Alexandria. There are approximately sixteen thousand Negro troops, and recreational facilities are said to be inadequate. A confidential source of information during the months of June and July studied the extent of agitation and reported there appeared to be no organized subversive efforts to stir up racial trouble among Negro civilians and soldiers in that area, although the situation was then started with many elements involved. It was pointed out that the population was concentrated and that paydays were not staggered for the soldiers. This, of course, allowed many men to be in the city with money at one time.

Then, too, it was reported that social problems were involved. Northern Negro soldiers were not aware of the custom of segregation in public conveyances. It was also pointed out that the Southern Negro soldier is not as retiring and subservient as would be expected, possibly due to the change occurring from better income in the Army than he previously had under the Southern economic system.

Some cause for the situation was laid to a certain amount of alleged bigotry on the part of white civilians and in some of the influential places of the State. On the other hand, it was said that the Negro newspaper, "The Pittsburgh Courier," which is widely distributed among and discussed by Negro soldiers, constantly reported incidents of discrimination against Negroes which, although probably a sincere medium of expression, resulted with impact upon uneducated or partly-educated Negroes who do not delve into all elements of the particular article involved.

The Alexandria Rape Case

It should be noted, preliminary to a discussion of this case, that one of the chief causes for complaint on the part of Negroes, as pointed out by the Negro press, is the alleged inequality of that race before the law; that is, discrimination against the Negro in the enforcement of law. In this area, practically all issues of Negro newspapers reflect items bearing on this topic or touching on alleged instances of police brutality. An example appears in the issue of "The Louisiana Weekly" dated at New Orleans, Saturday, September 5, 1942, which carries a large headline, "Police Brutality Victim Dies in Cell," and under a Ponchatoula, Louisiana, date line of September 3, 1942, the article refers to the alleged three days' "grilling" of a 17-year-old Negro boy administered in the jail of that town by police officers who, in turn, are said to have described the event as a suicide. This is said to be but one example of the type of stories commonly appearing in these newspapers.

At the present time, what appears to be the most serious bit of agitation in the State of Louisiana is centered around a case involving three Negro soldiers who received a death sentence in the Federal Court at Alexandria, Louisiana, for raping a white girl. Briefly, the facts of this case, which was investigated by the Federal Bureau of Investigation, are as follows:

> Hattie Rose Mason, a white girl, came to Alexandria, Louisiana, from Ripley, Ohio, in about April of 1941, approximately two weeks after her fiance, George Raymond Schuler, a private, Company D, 307th Medical Battalion, had arrived at Camp Claiborne, Louisiana, following his induction into the Army. She obtained a position in the Service Club cafeteria and stayed at the guest house at Camp Claiborne. After work, on the night of May 9, 1942, she and Schuler went for a walk near what is known as the service road. At about 2:00 a.m., after they had fallen asleep, they were awakened by three Negro sol-

diers, driving an Army jeep, one soldier being armed with a rifle and another with a 45 automatic. The three Negro soldiers placed both the victim and Schuler in the jeep, drove to the point where Schuler was returned to camp, put him out, and then continued on with Miss Mason. She was finally taken to an open field at which time she was criminally attacked by the three Negroes. Schuler identified one of the Negroes, while Miss Mason identified another by his voice. The identity of the third was subsequently determined.

Richard P. Adams, the last one to be identified, in a statement to a Special Agent of the Federal Bureau of Investigation, confessed being in the company of the other two, John Walter Bordenave and Lawrence Mitchell, and claimed that Mitchell and Bordenave assaulted the victim but denied that he did. Bordenave signed a confession to the effect that the three had attacked the white woman. Mitchell subsequently confessed having assaulted the victim.

The trial of the three Negroes began July 27, 1942, in the United States District Court at Alexandria, Louisiana, and on July 30, 1942, the jury returned a verdict of guilty. On August 10, 1942, the United States District Judge, Ben C. Dawkins, pronounced the death sentence for all three of the attackers.

The case was tried on the basis that Mitchell committed the act of rape and the two other Negroes were accessories before the fact, and as such, under the law, they became principals and were guilty in the same degree as the individual charged with the commission of the act.

Local newspapers, including "The Alexandria Observer," "The Louisiana Weekly," "The Sepia Socialite," "The New Orleans Sentinel," and "The New Orleans News Digest," carried articles condemning the sentencing and likening it to the Scottsboro case. Other articles have taken up the cry of protest against the sentences imposed and have published articles concerning it which appear to be designed to inflame the feelings of the Negroes against the courts. Such headlines as the following are typical:

"Alexandria Soldiers Make Plea to People for Fighting Chance"

"C.I.O. Council Protests Alexandria Soldiers' Death Sentence as Blow to Morale of Thirteen Million Negroes"

Other articles were to the effect that the treatment of Negroes was comparable to that given by the Gestapo; and Joseph Rose, port agent of the National Maritime Union in New Orleans, who is said to be a Communist, is quoted as having demanded of the President, the Attorney General, the Governor and Judge Dawkins, an investigation of the case.

The Communist Party has taken an active part, if not the lead, in all of the agitation, and reports received from confidential informants reflect that the case is discussed daily by officials of the Party in that area. Raymond Tillman, Negro member of the Communist Party and Secretary of the Transport Workers Union Local #206, New Orleans, Louisiana, is reported to have written letters to Congressman Vito Marcantonio, Chairman of the International Labor Defense, to John P. Davis of the National Negro Congress, to Benjamin Davis of the Daily Worker, and to Edward

Strong of the National Negro Youth Congress, asking all to use their influence and for their organizations to take up the case giving both legal and financial support. A confidential informant has advised relative to the feeling of the Communist Party members in this area that he and other members of the Party fear the case may have a serious repercussion against the war effort by alienating the Negroes. No explanation, however, was given as to why the great amount of agitation was carried on by the Communist Party.

Typical of the attitude of Party members with regard to the case is that of Harold Bolton, Secretary of the Communist Party in New Orleans. At a meeting of branch organizers, he spoke concerning the case and the activity with regard to it, stating it was assuming tremendous proportions and that although they have been able to get a great deal of action on it, there was still more to be done. He stated that petitions asking for a new trial should be circulated and everything done to exert mass pressure. (It should be pointed out that prior to the sentence, the attorneys for the Negroes in the case filed notices of appeal.) He further said that this was the only way to save the soldiers "to beat Hitler"; that they recognized these attacks not as against the Negro people alone, but as the whole working class in an effort on the part of "the appeasers and defeatists" to disunite the workers, both white and black.

Other Incidents

On November 1, 1942, a disturbance involving soldiers, sailors and civilians, as well as military and civilian police, occurred in the area surrounding 328 South Rampart Street in New Orleans. On the arrival of police at the scene, they found two soldiers fighting and when they attempted to arrest them a large number of soldiers interfered as a result of which one of the persons who was fighting escaped. A riot call was turned in and additional civilian and military police were sent to the scene, whereupon all of the Negro soldiers in the vicinity were arrested. The Negroes questioned the authority of the civilian police to arrest them and several fights broke out. During the time of the affray, remarks were reportedly made such as, "We are soldiers, you can't do this;" "This is a white man's war not ours;" "We want equal rights." Only one Negro civilian was said to have taken an active part in the affray, but he was not arrested. The riot was subsequently quelled when seventy-eight soldiers were finally arrested. No subversive or organized activity was apparent in the incident.

On January 3, 1943, shortly after midnight several Negro Military Police had difficulty getting a drunken Negro soldier into an Army truck to return him to Harding Field from New Orleans. It is related that while the Military Police were endeavoring to get him into the truck, civilian police arrived and upon their noticing the military police were unable to cope with the situation, they arrested all of the Negro soldiers and took them to the Baton Rouge Police Station where they were subsequently released to white Military Police. On returning to Harding Field, the Negro soldiers went to their company headquarters, overpowered the guard on duty and took approximately thirty-two rifles and a quantity of ammunition. Thereafter they began to mill around the outside of the building. They were finally persuaded to give up their rifles and all were placed in the guardhouse. The incident, which is reported to have had its origin at the Ever Ready Cafe in New Orleans, is reported to have involved no civilians.

On January 10, 1943, another brawl is said to have occurred in the City of New Orleans, which is alleged to have resulted in resentment on the part of Negroes being arrested by white Military Police and Civilian Police. The exact details of this incident have not been reported, although a confidential informant has expressed the opinion that possibly the Negro press could be blamed for part of this and other incidents involving Negro soldiers, in view of the attitude the press assumed that Negroes were discriminated against and the shooting, beating and cursing of white people by the Negroes was a common occurrence. This informant also expressed the opinion that many of the fights among Negroes in the area have been a result of jealousy on the part of Southern Negroes of Northern Negroes, whose financial status is better and who have more ability to gain the attentions of Negro women in the area.

On the evening of May 10, 1943, a near riot reportedly took place among Negroes in the area of Cravier and South Rampart Streets in New Orleans. It is related that a white Military Policeman arrested a drunken Negro soldier in this area whereupon several other Negro soldiers attempted to assist the soldier arrested. A passing civilian policeman did assist the Military Policeman, and after the two Negro soldiers were knocked down the drunken Negro was taken to the Police Station. It is said that approximately fifteen minutes after the Negro soldier had been taken to the jail, approximately fifteen Negro soldiers assembled and endeavored to take the arrested man from the jail by force. All were arrested and turned over to the Military Police after numerous precinct and detective cars had answered the call. Two city police were slightly injured.

On May 12, 1943, rioting took place at Lake Charles, Louisiana, which is related to have arisen out of an argument between a Negro and a white Military Policeman who took issues over the authority in the arrest of a Negro soldier. Shortly after the incite, five Negro Military Police began halting automobiles in the Negro district near Railroad Avenue and Boulevard Street, according to the reports, and dragging white occupants from the automobiles, inflicting injuries on them and damaging their vehicles. They were reportedly joined by Negro soldiers attached to a Negro unit, No. 925, the Air Base Security Battalion near Lake Charles, as well as Negro civilians. Thereafter rioting is said to have been principally in halting automobiles and injuring white persons, as well as throwing missiles through store windows. The number of people engaged has been estimated at from 150 to 175 Negro soldiers and approximately 150 Negro civilians. The rioting is reported to have halted by the use of tear gas and pistol shots. Several injuries were sustained to Negro soldiers, some of them serious and an estimate of approximately $500.00 has been given as the property damage. Approximately 150 Negro civilians were arrested by local authorities and seventeen "ring leaders" in the military personnel were held.

On June 1, 1943, it is reported that a disturbance arose between Negro soldiers and white Military Police in Leesville, Louisiana. It is related that seven Negro soldiers were causing a disturbance while in a drunken condition. Louisiana State Troopers and white Military Police were reportedly summoned and when the Negro soldiers refused to obey the warning of the Military Police to leave the particular area in which they were, a Military Police attempted to arrest the Negroes whereupon a fight ensued. Several white civilians are said to have entered on the scene and one of the white civilians allegedly shot and killed a Negro soldier. Five of the Negro soldiers were arrested and charged by State Troopers with inciting to riot. One is said to have escaped. No evidence has been developed showing any subversive or organized movement was responsible for the incident.

Rumors of Riots in New Orleans, May 1, 1943

For some time prior to May 1, 1943, rumors and allegations with no substantiating information were received that there would be trouble between Negroes and whites in the New Orleans area. In no instance were any specific data furnished. Thereafter rumors became more specific, namely, that on May 1 certain of the Negro population in New Orleans would stage a demonstration to demand civil equality. These grew in proportions until alleged remarks were received that Negroes were to get "even" with the white inhabitants on May 1, 1943. Hearsay information was such that a race riot would take place, and further that Negro violence of great proportions would occur on May 1. In this connection, it is related that approximately five or six days before May 1, 1943, the New Orleans Police Department became alarmed over the Negroes' remarks and cancelled leave for police officers over the week end of May 1. Numerous incidents were also reported of pamphlets to be distributed and other activity engaged in to incite Negroes in the area. These mounted in proportions to the extent that the rumors included supposed incidents of numbers of white and Negro citizens being killed in riots in different sections of the city. Approximately three days before the supposed riot was to take place on May 1, the full impact of the rumors is related to have reached the Negro people and, according to informants, it was the intention of all Negroes with whom they had talked to stay at home on May 1 and to remain off public conveyances and out of public places. It is said that a great amount of fear was evidenced among the Negro population.

On April 29, 1943, Ernest J. Wright, who was described as a prominent member of the Communist Party and a present militant Negro leader, visited the Offices of the Federal Bureau of Investigation in New Orleans at which time he emphatically stated no organizations of Negroes in New Orleans had in mind any civil disobedience program or any rioting. He stated that he was going to ask a number of Negro saloon keepers to close their place of business on May 1, believing that this action would relieve the ordinary congestion of Negroes. Wright was referred to the Police Department in view of the lack of jurisdiction of the Federal Bureau of Investigation in the matter which was local in nature.

In no instance could any of the persons who visited the Offices of the Federal Bureau of Investigation offer any information as to the origin or source of the rumors. In this connection various Negro citizens who visited the Offices advised they had overheard white people state if they, the Negroes, started anything the thing to do was to kill all of them. It was alleged that this was common talk in New Orleans at the time.

The rumors began to subside on the morning of May 1, 1943, when people began circulating in the streets. By the end of that day, people were finally quiet and the only incident reported was a fist fight between a Negro citizen and a bus driver.

The foregoing has been sought to reflect a situation in which rumors and wild statements amount to such a degree that considerable unrest, fear and agitation are caused among both white and Negro citizens. No reason for their circulation has been given other than the spread of gossip and unfounded statements.

It was reported that on March 12, 1943, a white citizen of New Orleans had been in an automobile accident which involved one of the Negro citizens there. The Negro was allegedly in fault but the white man, however, told the Negro to forget about the incident and go on his way. It is said that some unidentified Negro women living in the neighborhood became angry about the accident and told the white man, "You ain't no good, the Japanese are going to get you." The white man called the local Offices of the Federal Bureau of Investigation to report this matter and to point out the reference made to the Japanese by the unidentified Negro women.

There were reported in the latter part of May, 1943, statistics reflecting the number of screens which are used for the purpose of dividing white and Negro people in the streetcars and buses in the City of New Orleans removed and thrown out of the cars unlawfully. These statistics pertain to the past three and one-half years and according to a source of information are indicative of the growing general state of unrest among the Negroes in the New Orleans area. These statistics reflect that in 1940, 300 screens had been removed unlawfully. In 1941, 455 were removed and in 1942, 841 were jerked from their places. For the months of January, February and March, 1943, 330 screens had been so handled, thus showing a decided increase for a proportionate three months. [*New Orleans City Police Dept.*]

"Jim Crowism"

Segregation

It is said that almost all of the Cities in Louisiana have the customary Southern laws with regard to the segregating Negroes, although the City of New Orleans has none and Negro settlements are to be found in all sections of the City. In this regard, a source of information who has worked among the Negroes for many years has advised that with regard to the segregation of Negroes into certain residential sections there is no dissatisfaction felt by them. They are stated to be, however, keenly sensitive as regarding segregation on the public conveyances. In the State of Louisiana, it is believed that this is not a matter of law but of custom. Negroes are, of course, barred from restaurants and theaters and other places of amusement open to white people. The same source of information advises, however, that although other forms of segregation exist and although Negroes are afforded the same convenience in the way of transportation that white people are, the Negroes feel most keenly segregation on public conveyances.

Use of Ballot

There are no poll taxes or educational requirements existing as restrictions in voting in the State of Louisiana. The term "poll tax" is, however, commonly applied by Negro agitators in this area to acts of public officials. An example of this is cited in the condemnation of the verdict of the all white jury in the Alexandria rape case, which jury was referred to frequently in the Negro and Communist press as a "poll tax" jury. Apparently the term has thus been corrupted to refer to any official act deemed by the Negroes to be discriminatory.

Although there is no poll tax or other voting restrictions in this State, a source of information has informed that he believes local customs are such that often Negroes are prevented from exercising their right of franchise. He recalled an instance where a Negress, the wife of a sexton of his church, had presented herself to the registrar of votes on nine different occasions and each time had been put off or told to come back some other time. From this the source of information concluded that timid Negroes were probably discriminated against in some cases by what he termed officious persons in the registrar's office.

Customs

In Louisiana it is said that Negroes are never referred to by titles such as "Mr." or "Miss" although they are generally required to address the white people by those titles. In this connection, the Negro press has carried on a strenuous observation of this alleged type of discrimination and has linked it with, as it has all other types of discrimination, the argument that if Negroes are to fight in the Army they should be afforded the same courtesies as the white man.

Trade Union Activities

Among the more prominent trade unions so far as the Negro is concerned in this area, is the General Longshore Workers Local #1419 of the International Longshoremen's Association, A.F. of L. This local has a total membership of more than two thousand workers and is said to have worked to raise conditions to a higher standard for its members. Its president, J. Harvey Netter, has been opposed by the Communists in New Orleans, apparently because of the attitude of the cabinet of the union which denounced Communism as those radical elements of labor that tend to hamper the war effort.

Another more prominent union is the International Longshoremen's and Warehousemen's Union of America; C.I.O., Local #207, New Orleans, Louisiana. The president of this local is Willie Dorsey, a Negro Communist. Still another union is the Transport Workers Union of America, Local #216, of New Orleans. This local has three Negro officers who are also members of the Communist Party, and a white man who is the organizer is also a Party member. Among the rank and file, eleven Negro members of the union are also members of the Communist Party. It is stated that while the number of Party members in the unions is small, the Communist Party is reported to exercise a considerable degree of influence in the affairs of the union.

Education

The State of Louisiana, especially the City of New Orleans, is said to afford fairly good educational opportunities to the Negroes. There is a Catholic university for Negroes in New Orleans, St. Xavier, and another university, Dillard, which is conducted by the Methodist and Congregational churches.

With regard to the question of Negro education, one of the major issues said to cause unrest and dissatisfaction among the Negroes has been the Negro press' treatment of the question of salaries for Negro teachers. With regard to the "salary fight," it appears that the Louisiana Colored Teachers Association, first organized in 1900, had as one of its major objectives to the obtaining of equal salaries for white and colored teachers of equal qualifications. It is said that in the school year 1936–1937 public education of a white pupil cost over $62.000 while that of a Negro pupil was over $30.00. The average white teacher had a pupil load of thirty-five and received an annual salary per pupil of $47.77 while the average colored teacher had a pupil load of fifty-five with an annual salary per pupil of only $31.78. It is reported that at the time Negroes represented over twenty-four per cent of the teacher personnel while receiving only nineteen per cent of the pay roll. Recently, with regard to this situation, a decree was filed in the United States District Court by Judge Wayne G. Borah permanently enjoining the Board of Education in Orleans Parish from discriminating against Negro teachers in the payment of salaries. The decree states that the act of the Board in carrying out such a practice, which act has been in existence for many years, of paying Negro teachers smaller salaries was a violation of the equal protection clause of the 14th Amendment.

In connection with the salary dispute, the newspaper, "The Sepia Socialite", for September 5, 1942, pointed out that an agreement had been reached that during the ensuing school year Negro teachers would be paid half the difference between Negro and white teachers' salaries and beginning the following year they would be paid on an equal basis. The newspaper criticized the agreement editorially, stating that while the victory was far reaching in effect, it was certain that a more complete victory could have been obtained, that is, "equalization now". However, the other Negro newspapers appeared to have supported the action and from the comments generally it seemed apparent that a satisfactory conclusion had been reached.

Preventive Measures

With regard to those measures which may have been taken to prevent or alleviate situations or incidents causing unrest or dissatisfaction among the Negroes, the opinions have been furnished by sources of information that little anything has been done by local or State authorities. An example that has been cited is that of certain discriminations against Negroes when they appear to register for voting. It has been informed that a letter of protest was sent to the Governor of Louisiana complaining of such discriminatory practices. However, the same failed to arouse any action. In this connection, a source of information had advised that he knows of no campaign, program or proposed plan on the part of local or State authorities instituted in an attempt to curb the rising spirit of unrest and sense of injustice among the Negroes.

This source of information has advised that one remedial preventive measure has been the erection of several housing projects in Louisiana. He claimed that these projects have done wonders in building up the morale of the Negro people and making them feel that they are citizens and enjoying the abundance commonly referred to as the heritage of American citizens. With regard to education, this source of information has said that so far as its standards are concerned in the City of New Orleans, it is not equal to those of the white people although it had improved sufficiently to meet the demand of the colored people and they are quite satisfied at the present time.

A source of information, a white man, who has lived and worked among Negroes for many years in the State of Louisiana in the capacity of a missionary, has suggested two means of alleviating the racial tension presently existing. They are:

1. Through the leadership of white newspapers the removal of Jim Crow regulations on public conveyances.
2. By assisting and encouraging colored people to register and vote and participate as citizens in the operation of the Government.

He advised that while these are but two things and they would not go all the way toward removing what he termed was racial discrimination, he felt sure the suggestions if carried out would serve to bring about the highest cooperation during the war years.

As to the possibilities of an insurrection or a revolt, this source of information stated that he felt sure that there is not the leadership among the Negroes at the present time that will ever bring about a determined attempt to overthrow existing conditions but at the same time he felt that there may be a general lack of cooperation and possibly even some harm to industry. He added that he considered such steps to be almost certainly carried out if India is at all successful in its campaign presently being conducted against England.

With regard to the latter statement made by the above-mentioned source of information, another source of information, a Negro who has been active in newspaper work, thinks that there is no leadership at the present time to bring about a general uprising among the Negroes.

General Observations

There have been numerous reports and complaints made to the New Orleans Field Division of the Federal Bureau of Investigation over militant anti-white statements allegedly made by Negroes, as well as remarks reportedly indicating pro-Axis sympathies. An example of such remarks is, "When the Japs get over here and take over we'll put a stop to all of this." (This statement was made by a Negro who was drunk at a time when he was ordered to move to the rear of the bus. The Negro was subsequently fined for being drunk and disorderly.) Inquiries have been made into these complaints and allegations with negative results, as far as determining any organized subversive or un-American movement among Negroes in the area. In practically every instance, the remark was made as a result of ignorance, anger or drunkenness. Sources of information have reported, however, that there has manifested an increasing attitude of sullenness and insolence on the part of Negroes in the New Orleans area, particularly in the cities of New Orleans, Alexandria, Baton Rouge and Lake Charles, Louisiana. It is alleged that the attitude largely follows the lead set forth by various Negro newspapers such as "The Pittsburgh Courier," "Chicago Defender," "New Orleans Sentinel" and "The Informer," "The Louisiana Weekly" and "The Sepia Socialite." Allegations have also been made that the Peoples Defense League, headed by Ernest J. Wright, is extremely militant in its demands for Negroes and their rights.

Norfolk Field Division

Information has been received, although unverified, of various rumors in this area, to the effect that the Negroes would be "better off" if the United States were to be defeated in the present war and that the white race would be treated by its conquerors as the Negroes have been treated by the white race. Other remarks have been made such as, "wait til the Japs get here." Sources of information concerning these statements have indicated that incidents of pro-Japanese remarks have resulted from spontaneous anger on the part of Negroes rather than any deliberation on their part. To date, no substantiating information has been received reflecting pro-Japanese sentiments in this area on an organized basis.

Another type of rumor reported was to the effect that on a particular night scheduled for a "black out" under the direction of civilian defense authorities in this area, Negroes equipped with guns, ice picks and knives would cause a race riot. However, no such uprising did materialize and no definite indications have been reported reflecting that these rumors were backed by pro-Axis propaganda. A confidential source of information has advised, however, that it was possible that an organized protective force in the state of Virginia, and individuals connected with the civilian defense set up in that territory might possibly be active in spreading this rumor and others concerning racial conditions.

In the Newport News, Virginia area Addison C. Gayle, a Negro citizen and former Communist leader, during the latter part of 1941, instigated meetings for an organization named "True Democratic League." At these meetings Gayle extolled the Communist Party and advocated Negroes joining with it. Another Negro, one Isaiah Jones, also a leader of the true Democratic League is reported to have professed Communist Party principles and stated that he joined forces with Gayle to promote Communist Candidates. At the present time, however, these meetings are not being held and there is no indication that the True Democratic League is still in existence.

The organization demanded such things as:

1. That at least two Negro policemen be assigned to patrol those sections in which the Negro people are in the majority.
2. That Negro clerks be employed in all department stores in Newport News, including the Woolworth Five & Ten Cent Store.
3. That at least one Negro representative be appointed to appear on the local school board.
4. That the Negro people, constituting one-third of the population should and must be given their rights to jobs in all other branches of their local government.

Sources of information contacted in the Newport News area, who are in a position to know circumstances among the Negro population there, advised of receiving many rumors, all of which were unfounded. It is stated, however, that the Negroes in this area, as a result of a considerably increased income, had assumed an independent attitude which in effect is said to tend to irritate white people there.

In and around the area of Williamsburg, Virginia, information received reflects that the Negroes in this area have been very mild and it is stated that there is no reason to suspect that there is any subversive group at work among them.

In the vicinity of Hampton, Virginia, rumors have been received, all of which have indications of no foundation. Their threatening natures culminated in nothing. Such a rumor as to the effect that Negroes had purchased all the ice picks in local stores. Contacts made with the various stores selling such ice picks, resulted in information to the effect that no more than the ordinary quantity of ice picks had been sold.

Rumors received in the area of Phoebus, Virginia, have been ascertained to be without foundation and sources of information receiving complaints of contemplated trouble with regard to the Negro situation, have advised they tended to discount all such complaints when they were received.

An incident which happened in the month of August, 1942, in the City of Norfolk, is said to be indicative of the attitude of some white people with regard to the Negro, which in turn, tends to cause strained relations. It is said that a Negro minister while riding on a street car in the City of Norfolk was standing near the front of the car because he could not get to the back due to the crowded condition. A white man sitting near the front is said to have cursed the Negro preacher for standing in the front of the car and the minister was in turn very much embarrassed. The source of information has reported this incident to be an example of how unrest and riots are caused. He stated that the use of profane language was for a specific purpose—to cause trouble and to promote ill-feeling between the races around Norfolk.

It is said that such instances as set out above are common in the City of Norfolk and they are believed to be caused by the fact that the transportation facilities are taxed to a maximum, and at the same time the Company attempts to enforce the "Jim Crow" law. Another cause is said to be the mixing of both colored and white people from the North with those in the South, the result of the increased defense activity there.

[*100-135-53*]

It has been ascertained that there are several branches of the Universal Negro Improvement Association in the Norfolk area which are:

Norfolk Division, 962 Goochland Avenue, Norfolk, L. L. Booth, President.

Newport News Division, 639 24th Street, Newport News, Frank Bartlett, President.

Berkeley Division, 1734 Wilson Road, Norfolk, S. L. Ashley, President.

Oakwood Division, R. F. D. No. 1, Box 301, Norfolk, Robert Lamb, President.

The extent of membership in this area has not been ascertained. However, informants have advised of receiving no indications of pro-Japanese activity or sentiment on the part of this organization in this area.

While no active unit of the March on Washington Movement has been established in the Norfolk area, it is reported, however, A. Philip Randolph, national leader of the organization, spoke at the Hampton Institute recently in an endeavor to establish the program of the organization among the Negro students at this college.

Numerous complaints have been received in this area indicating that so-called "Eleanor Clubs" were in operation; however, investigation based on allegations that these clubs were Axis inspired failed to reflect their existence.

In regard to the Jehovah's Witnesses sect, it is to be noted that numerous complaints have been received alleging members of the sect have been associating with Negroes and have been attempting to indoctrinate some of their beliefs among the Negro people.

The National Association for the Advancement of Colored People has a number of chapters located within this area, namely, at Norfolk and Newport News, and in several of the other larger cities in the tidewater Virginia area. According to a confidential source of information, the chapter in Norfolk has reportedly suffered from poor leadership and had an antagonistic position in the eyes of the white citizens in the area. It has been active in championing the cause of racial improvement, although it is reported there is considerable friction in the ranks of the local chapter as a result of varying social philosophies. It is said to have a membership in Norfolk of approximately

2,000 representative of the cross-section of the Negro population. Its current program has been aimed at improving the treatment of Negroes on public conveyances, the increasing of salaries of Negro teachers and the bettering of their working conditions, and attempting to have Negroes police appointed as well as secure better treatment of Negroes by the Police Department. No reports have been received to indicate that the groups in Norfolk and the surrounding area have any connections with the Communist Party.

There is located in this area the Virginia Peninsula Teachers Union of the A.F. of L. comprised of the majority of the teachers on the faculty of Hampton Institute. It is said that one Richard Kidd is President of the local as well as a branch leader of the Communist Party in the Peninsula area. The Central Labor Union delegate of this local is said to have been in the past in contact with Alice Burke, State Secretary of the Communist Party in Virginia.

The Hampton Institute at Hampton, Virginia, one of the oldest Negro colleges in the United States is said to be the center of numerous conferences and meetings of various movements particularly interested in the Negro population of this country. Its faculty is composed of both Negro and white professors and its administrative staff contains both white and Negro personnel. On the campus actual race equality is practiced and both the United States Army and United States Navy maintain training schools for enlisted men at this place. There is a chapter of the National Association for the Advancement of Colored People as well as a local of the Virginia Peninsula Teachers Union located at this school.

The chief source of news for the Negro population in this area is the "Norfolk Journal and Guide" put out by the publishing company of that name. The editor and owner is P. B. Young who is associated with members of his family in the publication of the organ. Its entire staff is composed of well-educated members of the Negro race, most of whom are graduates of Harvard University. The paper is regarded as editorially conservative but it is said to be tempered with front-page spreads of headlines and news stories labelled as biased, dealing largely with alleged mistreatment of Negroes by police authorities in the area and the traditional "Jim Crow laws" in force on Southern transportation systems.

Inquiries and investigations based on reports and allegations of foreign-inspired activity among the Negroes in this area have failed to indicate any substantiating information. No evidence of any pro-German, pro-Japanese or pro-Fascist activities among the Negroes in the Norfolk area has been developed. However, there is believed to exist considerable tension between the Negro and white inhabitants of the area. As an example, a riot of some proportions occurred on the evening of May 21, 1943, in Suffolk which arose out of an argument between several Negroes and two white men. It is reported that one Willie Roney, Negro taxi operator, and another Negro, one Leland Britt, drove into a service station operated by one E. M. Moulds, white, located at the intersection of East Washington Street and White Marsh Road. The manner in which the Negroes drove into the station was described by the son of the service station operator as rapid and reckless and subsequently reprimanded the Negroes for their manner. The son was thereupon attacked by both Negroes. The father, coming to the assistance of his son, was also attacked, whereupon he returned to the station, obtained a pistol and shot Roney in the leg. The police were immediately summoned and Moulds was placed under arrest.

Soon after this incident, 250 or 300 Negroes reportedly gathered around the service station and the owner's residence nearby. The police dispersed the crowd immediately thereafter. Large groups of Negroes are said to have gathered at a place some distance away where several white people were attacked and fights resulted. Thereupon a group of white people, estimated at approximately 200, also gathered together. Subsequently several shots were fired and missiles were thrown. Tear gas was used by law enforcement authorities, numbering 128, dispersed the crowd. Several companies of the Virginia Protective Force were ordered mobilized for possible assistance if necessary. It is to be noted that during this fracas a Negro dance attended by approximately 1,000 Negroes was in progress in the Negro section. This dance ended about 2:30 A.M. on May 22, 1943, with no disorder or trouble.

The Chief of Police at Suffolk has informed he saw no excuse on the part of the Negroes in starting the trouble, especially after the filling station owner had been arrested for the shooting of the Negro taxicab operator. No opinion could be given by sources of information as to why Negroes took the government of the city into their own hands in total disregard of the law nor why white people were subsequently attacked by them. No indications of any organized effort on the part of the Negroes were visible and no information indicating any subversive tendencies was received by local law enforcement authorities. It is said that most of the Negroes participating in the disturbances were young hoodlums and taxicab drivers.

Oklahoma City Field Division

In 1940 the Negro population for the State of Oklahoma was set at 168,849, comprising 7.2 per cent of the State's total population. No definite information has been reported reflecting foreign-inspired agitation or activity among the Negroes in this area.

Perhaps the most outstanding force among the Negroes in this area is Roscoe Dunjee, Negro editor of the Negro newspaper "The Black Dispatch" which is published in Oklahoma City, Oklahoma. He is recognized as one of the foremost leaders of Negroes in the area. With regard to "The Black Dispatch," it is published by a company bearing that name. It is a member of the Associated Negro Press and is said to have the largest circulation of any Negro newspaper in the area. A review of its articles and editorials reflects that they strongly parallel Communist Party policies and tenets. It is outspoken in its demands for the abolition of discrimination and segregation and the granting of equal rights for the Negro. It is said by confidential informants that Allan Shaw, State Secretary of the Communist Party in Oklahoma, frequently confers with Dunjee and, furthermore, Dunjee's newspaper office does considerable printing for the Communist Party in that area. For over the past year "The Black Dispatch" has been outspoken in regard to practically all incidents in the country in which Negro troops are involved and in all cases, particularly in the South, where Negroes are brought to trial.

With regard to Roscoe Dunjee, sources of information advise that although Negroes of the vicinity have a great amount of respect for him, many of the more educated are reportedly afraid of Dunjee's stand in several matters. Dunjee is said to favor interracial marriages, free associations between Negroes and whites, and the placing of all blood donated in the Red Cross Blood Bank program in the same banks. He is further said to have bragged on various occasions of his associations with white people in Eastern and Northern Sections.

Dunjee is State President of the Oklahoma National Association for the Advancement of Colored People. He is also Vice President of the Southern Conference for the Advancement of Colored People. He is said to attempt to align its policies in the State of Oklahoma with those of the Communist Party. In an editorial in the October 10, 1942, issue of the "Black Dispatch" he commented, "We shall have to report that we personally do have Communistic leaning. . . . We do have Communistic leaning when it comes to the Communistic theory of the international state and the questions of racial equality. . . . Communism believes in racial equality and so does this writer." Several sources of information, including a Negro minister in Oklahoma City, have advised in their opinion "Black Dispatch" is responsible for much of the local strife between the white and Negro citizens in the State of Oklahoma. These sources have pointed to the inflammatory nature of the publication which appears calculated to keep Negroes upset and uncertain and leads to trouble. The Negro source of information, who has seen many years of service in his pulpit, has attributed the confusion among members of his race to the activities and attitudes of Dunjee [*redacted*] [*100-20076*]

It has been further reported that Dunjee employed recently in his office Ina Wood, a Communist Party member and a defendant in a case in the State Court of Oklahoma involving criminal syndicalism.

Dunjee recently made a tour of all the branches of the National Association for the Advancement of Colored People in the State of Oklahoma. It was hoped by the Party that through their influence with Dunjee, an opening wedge could be worked into the organizational setup in Oklahoma of the National Association for the Advancement of Colored People in an effort to obtain additional members and to convert Negroes to the doctrines of Communism.

With regard to the National Association for the Advancement of Colored People in Oklahoma, a recent campaign for membership recruiting has been in progress which had some degree of success. Among the prominent leaders in this State are Roscoe Dunjee, a Dr. Williamson of Idabel, Dr. Bullock of Chickasha, and Dr. Berry and Amos Hall of Tulsa, Oklahoma. With regard to the last named individual, it is said that while he is not a member of the Communist Party he is sympathetic to a degree with much of the Party's line.

As regards some of the work of the National Association for the Advancement of

Colored People, especially the elimination of racial discrimination, it is said that the organization coordinates its activities with the Communist Party in certain areas of the State. It is also said to place prov[o]cateurs on busses in Oklahoma City at the suggestion of the Communist Party. The plan allegedly works as follows: One Negro will occupy one seat just behind the section marker in the bus and another Negro, instead of occupying the seat immediately next to him, will occupy the seat across the aisle, thereby allegedly precluding a white person from sitting. After a white person complains to the bus driver of this situation, the bus driver in turn will request the Negroes to sit together so that two white persons may sit together. Both Negroes, however, will refuse, thereupon subjecting themselves to possible eviction from the bus by the white people.

Recent Communist Party activity which has been reported is that it has been increasing its infiltration of the Negro population by virtue of its encouragement of Negroes to fight for social equality. In the opinion of an informant, however, the race discrimination element has been stressed so heavily by the Communist Party in an attempt to obtain new members it has backfired on the Party. It is said this can be explained by virtue of the Party delving deeply into its plans for racial equality to foment the Negro population and incite it against white domination. It is alleged that this has been carried on to such an extent that Negroes become bitter and thus take the matter into their own hands immediately. The exact size of Negro membership in the Communist Party in this area has not been reported: however, it is known that Robert Wood, a leading white Communist organizer in Oklahoma presently residing in Tulsa, was recently invited to address a meeting of approximately 900 members in the First Baptist Church in Tulsa. It is said that Party leaders were elated over this opportunity to reach the Negro population with their doctrines.

In Tulsa, Oklahoma, there is published the "Tulsa Eagle," a Negro newspaper, which until recently, is said to have devoted its space to accurate reporting of the news, but since the beginning of 1943 it began playing up clashes between the races and protesting racial discrimination allegedly present in defense plants in and around Tulsa.

An informant in a position to know and study the Negro situation in the Oklahoma City area advises that she knows of no foreign agitation among the Negroes in that area and that the colored people in general are in favor of the war effort. With respect to the Negro leaders of that State, she has advised that these individuals are anxious to obtain as much equality and as many rights as possible.

With respect to trouble among members of the Armed Forces, it has been reported that at one time there existed some trouble between Negro troops and white officers at the Will Rogers' Air Base. An informant in a position to study the situation has attributed the trouble to local conditions and not to any organized effort. Recently it has been reported that no trouble exists among the soldiers at this Army reservation in view of a change in policy relative to colored troops.

Reports have been received to the effect that there have been clashes between Negro and white employees of the Douglas Aircraft Assembly Plant in Oklahoma City. It is said that scarcely a day passes without trouble between one or more Negro and white laborers there. Examples of such clashes were given, one of which reflected that in an argument over a parking space between a Negro and a white employee knives were drawn and a fight ensued. There were no indications of anyone being seriously hurt. Another example cited was one in which there was reported a fight between Negro and white people while they were entering the gate of the plant. One white man who was fought by several Negroes was said to have been handled roughly and his pocketbook stolen.

Reports have also been received concerning this plant to the effect that Negro employees were recently discovered leaving their work after they had signed the pay roll in the morning and returning in the afternoon in time to "sign out." No confirmation of this report, however, has been received.

A recent meeting involving a mixed group of Negro and white Baptist preachers was reported in this area in which a program embracing both white and Negro churches was drawn up. This meeting was described as one which was entirely pleasant and was thought to bring about added cooperation between white and Negro people in the area.

On February 7, 1943, a near riot took place on East 2nd Street in Oklahoma City in which a white military police lieutenant was struck with a whiskey bottle thrown by an unknown Negro. Later it was ascertained that one Frank Wheeler refused to cease brawling in a Negro restaurant in Oklahoma City when so requested by a Negro police officer. The trouble grew in serious proportions when military police arrived on the scene and were met by a large crowd of civilians who gathered to lend encouragement to Wheeler and other Negro soldiers. It is reported that the military police had trouble prevailing upon the Negro soldiers to obey orders and they had considerable difficulty in placing Wheeler under arrest and removing him to the police station. The entire situation has been described as simply a case wherein the mob went to the aid of the accused and opposed law and order.

There have been in the recent past several reports indicating a pro-Japanese sentiment among Negroes. In no case has any identity been supplied of those responsible for exhibiting the sympathies. There are also indications of an element among the Negro population which follows the Communist Party line of encouraging complete racial equality. Other elements are said to consist of those Negroes who with mental reservation of ultimately placing members of their race on a higher plane conduct themselves in loyal, patriotic and conservative fashion. In the over-all Negro population it is said that there is a tenseness on its part. This tenseness is also said to be reflected among members of the white population as well.

Richmond Field Division

Reports have been received reflecting unverified information that a few Negroes have pro-Japanese tendencies. However, no information has as yet been received substantiating these reports. Rumors have also been received to the effect that a group known as "The New Light" or "The New Light Church" has pro-Japanese tendencies, although no verifying information has as yet been received. In addition, some activity has been reported on the part of the Jehovah's Witnesses sect among the Negroes in distributing literature in an effort to influence them not to aid in the war effort and to fight against being inducted into the Armed Forces. Also indications have been received reflecting a change in attitude of the Negroes in this area, and in this connection there is said to be a rumor being spread among the Negroes that they are an oppressed race. Investigation, of course, is being conducted to identify the sources of pro-Japanese sentiment and source of rumors thereof.

A prominent Negro source of information in this area has advised that he is of the opinion that there are no subversive organizations among the Negroes there. He advised, however, that at this time the Negroes in and around Richmond, Virginia, were somewhat receptive to Communism, but that the enthusiasm had completely died out and for this reason he does not believe the Communist Party has any influence among the Negroes in this area. This source of information advised that he is of the opinion that Negroes are strongly advocating racial equality, and that one cannot condemn the Negroes too strongly in this belief inasmuch as Negroes are dying in the war the same as white men. He has further remarked, however, that he does not think that racial equality should come about overnight and was sure that it would not, stating that he could not and would not believe the Negro situation in this area is anything to be perturbed about.

There are several organizations active in the area of the State of Virginia covered by the Richmond Field Division. They are being set out hereinafter along with certain identifying information.

A colony of approximately 50 Negroes known as the National Home of the Moorish Science Temple of America is located approximately seven miles from Prince George, Virginia. These Negroes have an excellent reputation in the neighborhood, are registered for selective service, and make little effort to mix with other Negroes in the vicinity. No indication has been received that they have been subjected to pro-Japanese influence. The group publishes a monthly magazine and receives money orders from national headquarters in Chicago as well as smaller amounts of money from other temples throughout the country.

At one time there was an active chapter of the Universal Negro Improvement Association, having been revived in Richmond in 1941. It subsequently became inactive inasmuch as its membership dropped from 17 to 4.

Numerous rumors regarding the existence of "Eleanor Clubs" have been reported from all sections of the State of Virginia. Extensive investigation based on allegations that these clubs were Axis inspired have failed to disclose any evidence of their existence. The opinion has been expressed that these rumors of the existence of these clubs can be largely attributed to white people who have found difficulty in retaining their domestic servants as a result of better opportunities offered by various defense jobs.

Several reports have been received of the activity of members of the Jehovah's Witnesses sect among the Negroes. Allegations have been received that organizers or operatives of this sect urged Negroes to evade the Selective Training and Service Act. These allegations have not been substantiated. It is to be noted, however, that various members of this sect have been sentenced to prison terms for their failure to comply with Selective Service orders. It should also be noted that at a regional convention held in Richmond in September 1942 there was a reported attendance of approximately 2,500 persons, many of whom were Negroes.

A few reports have been received that the Ku Klux Klan might be revived in the State of Virginia; however, there is nothing to indicate that such a revival has taken place. The opinion has been offered in this connection that the State organization known as the Virginia Protective Force which holds regular meetings and which is prepared to become active in case of any racial outbreaks and its auxiliary force known as the Minutemen have served to lessen the fears of racial disturbances and hence there is no great demand for any undercover organizations such as the Ku Klux Klan.

Foremost among the Negro organizations in the State of Virginia is the National Association for the Advancement of Colored People which has been active in agitating against racial discrimination and segregation. Among the particular matters in which it has interested itself in the past year have been the Odell Waller conviction and subsequent execution, the formation of a segregated ration board, and the alleged discrepancies in the price of food charged consumers in Negro districts. The organization is under the leadership of Dr. James M. Tinsley, President of the Richmond branch as well as the State Conference of the National Association for the Advancement of Colored People. Dr. Tinsley has been active in seeking school facilities for Negroes throughout the State and in securing higher salaries for Negro school teachers.

The March on Washington Movement has been active in the City of Richmond and it is known that the City sent a delegate to the National Conference of the organization held in Chicago June 30–July 4, 1943. It is also to be noted E. Pauline Meyers, now National Executive Secretary of the organization, was formerly active in the Phyllis Wheatley branch of the Y.W.C.A. in Richmond.

The Southern Conference on Race Relations was organized in 1942 by several leading Negro educators in the South including two from the Richmond, Virginia area. It formulated a program of action for the betterment of the Negro race at a conference held in Durham, North Carolina, on October 20, 1942, which was attended by 75 Negro leaders. Its program includes a gradual improvement in the Negro's position rather than to demand the ultimate objective of complete equality immediately.

There is a branch of the National Urban League in the Richmond area, the chief function of which is to serve as a kind of an employment agency for Negroes. Its leader, however, Wiley Hall, is said to be affiliated to some degree with the Communist movement.

An organization formed in February 1941 known as the Southern Electoral Reform League is said to have several Negroes with alleged Communist leanings as members.

With regard to the Communist Party in Virginia, it is under the leadership of Alice Burke who has been active in agitating among Negroes by condemning the laws prevalent in the State of Virginia regarding segregation. The Party in this State has also called for social equality for Negroes and white people. One of its other chief aims is to abolish the poll tax. Of the 158 members of the Party in February 1943, 51 were Negroes.

There have been several local organizations in Richmond such as the East End Civic League, the Democracy Defense League for Negro Youth, and the Committee for Constitutional Rights. These organizations have as a whole agitated over local matters pertaining to the Negroes in the City of Richmond. In the last-named organization there is said to be actual Communist Party influence. In this connection, there was formerly active with a membership of approximately 20 a local branch in Richmond of the Communist front organization, the National Negro Congress. This chapter, however, ceased activity in the latter part of 1941.

In addition there have been several national organizations at work in the Richmond area with regard to the Negro situation. These are the Workers Defense League, the National Committee to Abolish the Poll Tax, and the International Labor Defense. The Workers Defense League was active in the Odell Waller case which involved a Negro charged with murder of a landlord who owned a tenant farm. This case caused nationwide interest especially among the more liberal, known Communist groups, namely the Socialist Party, the Workers Defense League which was active in defending the case, and a group known as the Labor Defense Congress, which organization is believed to have some influence in it of the Revolutionary Workers League.

A Negro, one Richard Harrison Allen of Richmond, Virginia, is President of the local of the United Cannery, Agricultural Packing and Allied Workers of America, CIO. He is said to have Communist connections and to have been in contact with Alice Burke. It has been further reported that the activities of the Southern Negro Youth Congress are conducted through the local of this union in Richmond. It is to be pointed out that the Southern Negro Youth Congress is a Communist front.

On January 1, 1943, a new organization was formed in the Richmond area when approximately 800 Negroes met at the Fifth Street Baptist Church in Richmond. The name adopted was the Richmond Civic Council and the purpose was to foster, protect and advance the rights of Negroes as well as to serve as a clearing house of information relative to such matters. The Negro pastor of the First Baptist Church, Dr. W. L. Ransome, was elected as the first President of this organization. It is reported that 90 per cent of the people attending the meeting were women and it was noted by a confidential source that several leading figures of the organization have connections with the Communist Party. The organization has confined its activities as a whole to local matters, mainly alleged instances of discrimination against Negroes.

It has been recently reported by a confidential informant that a union known as the Domestic Workers Union, CIO, has attempted to organize Negro domestics in the Richmond area and has distributed literature and pamphlets to this end. No reports have been received as to the success of this union; however, it is known they distributed leaflets showing the advantages to be gained, including increase of salaries and better working conditions, by affiliating with the organization.

On April 3, 1943, the 66th Emancipation Celebration was held in Tappahannock, Virginia, in which approximately 2,000 persons took part. There were church services attended by a few, while the remainder celebrated more boisterously. Liquor stores were closed in the city and the white inhabitants remained away from the activities. The mayor of the city made the welcoming address in which he stressed the necessity of cooperating with the war effort. He is said to have been well received as well as the assistant director of the Office of Civilian Defense in Virginia, who, according to an informant, contributed much to the work of Negroes in that area in the war effort through his speech.

The newspaper which enjoys the largest distribution in this area is the "Richmond

Afro-American" which is an edition published by the Afro-American Newspaper Company in Baltimore, Maryland. It follows the general setup and policy of the other editions of the "Afro-American." The extent of its distribution is not known; however, it is said to have the widest of any of the Negro newspapers.

In all localities of the State covered by this Field Division there have been reports of un-Americanism on the part of individual Negroes. Investigations and inquiries conducted into these reports have failed to reveal any organized movement and, rather, have reflected that there are isolated instances involving either ignorance, a misunderstanding or actual dissatisfaction. In May 1943, however, there were indications of rumors spreading throughout the Richmond area that racial trouble, if not riots, might occur. The rumors, however, failed to materialize. In this connection, it is to be pointed out that the March on Washington Movement has decided to use Richmond, Virginia, as one of the places where it will test its non-violent direct action program. It is possible that this contemplated move by the organization may give rise to additional rumors. All inquiries for indications of subversive activities on the part of Negroes in the State have met with negative results and it has been found generally that unrest or dissatisfaction that prevails is based upon alleged instances of discrimination and segregation.

San Antonio Field Division

Agitation among the Negroes in and around San Antonio, Texas is stated to be caused mainly by the Communist Party in that area. It is reported that here the method of operation is to agitate not only among the civilians but among the military personnel in that area. Informants contacted advised that they have not seen or heard of Japanese propaganda in this area. It has been stated that the most dangerous agitational medium in this area is the Negro press, including such newspapers as the "Free American", the "Chicago Defender", and the "Pittsburgh Courier."

Sources of information in this area who are in a position to know conditions existing among the Negro population, not only in the San Antonio area but in the State of Texas, have expressed opinions to the effect that blame for Negro unrest and dissatisfaction can be laid to both Negro and white elements. They have advised that there are Negroes who are more deeply concerned over the race problem than over the war and would rather give their money to help promote protest rallies than to buy War Bonds. It was further pointed out that there are many white people who are so bent on discrimination against the Negroes that they would rather risk the chance of a Japanese invasion or become slaves of Hitler than to allow Negro soldiers to be trained in the community where they reside. It has been further pointed out that lynchings, especially the two which have taken place recently in the State of Texas, have resulted somewhat in lowering the morale of Negroes. With regard to the general situation, it was stated that the trouble, unrest and dissatisfaction among Negroes is a matter of social and economic readjustment rather than any part of a well-defined pattern on the part of foreign propagandists or agents.

A confidential source of information has advised that Negro-white relations in San Antonio, in his opinion, are unsatisfactory at the present time. He has pointed out that the unrest on the part of Negroes could be attributed largely to news articles appearing in nationally known Negro newspapers, such as the "Pittsburgh Courier", the "Chicago Defender", and the "Afro-American." It has been pointed out, however, by another source of information that the Negroes in the San Antonio area are loyal and are solidly behind the war effort, although they may feel dissatisfied because of alleged discrimination against them.

There is published in San Antonio a Negro newspaper known as the "San Antonio Register" in the issues of which there is shown a continuing concern over instances of alleged discrimination against Negroes. The instances usually reported by this newspaper deal mostly with incidents of racial friction in busses, stores and other public places. The general policy of the paper, however, appears to be strongly pro-American, space being given liberally to all matters concerning the successful conclusion of the war.

The Chairman of the Communist Party City Committee in San Antonio is reported to be one John Inman, a Negro who was appointed by the present State Secretary. He is stated to be in charge of collecting dues from the Negro members. Recently a pamphlet has been distributed by the Communist Party in this area entitled "Negro Rights Must Be Granted Now Communists Declare;" however, there has been no wholesale distribution.

In the area of Austin, Texas it was reported that a considerable number of Negro troops have been quartered there and there have been evidences of trouble occurring in the Negro section of Austin between white and colored soldiers, mainly because there are no recreational facilities available for Negroes in the area and, further, white soldiers are entering the Negro area and making themselves undesirable.

Formed recently in Austin, Texas was the Wartime Emergency Conference of the Negro People of Texas, which stresses the removal of discrimination against Negroes through giving them the right to vote and racial equality. Among the Conference officers is stated to be a well-known Communist in Austin, Texas, one Mason Smith.

It is also reported that an instructor at the Sam Houston College in Houston, Texas, one **Ora Herman Elliott**, is stated to be extremely rabid in his demands for racial equality among the Negroes.

Published in Austin is "The Informer," a Negro newspaper which is stated to be read by most Negroes in that city, however, the "Pittsburgh Courier" and the "Chicago Defender" are stated to be also circulated there. This newspaper is stated to contain information grossly distorted and that on every occasion it emphasizes racial inequality and the poll tax question. An opinion has been expressed concerning this newspaper that it has a potent influence among the Negroes in Austin and that if it was so desired, the paper could be used to good advantage by Axis agents for the purpose of stirring up trouble among the Negroes.

In this territory, demands and statements made by Negroes are to the effect that they should have more relief and that they would obtain equal rights with the white people when the Japs or the Nazis came to the United States. No information, however, has been received that there is any organized effort behind these statements.

It is stated that of the present population of Austin which is 108,000, approximately 14.3 per cent are Negroes. This, however, is stated to be an unofficial record.

There has been active in the City of Austin an organization known as the Interracial Group, which meets at the YMCA in this city. It is said to be dominated by Communist influences and made up of students, principally from the University of Texas and from Tillotson and San Houston Negro colleges in Austin. There are indications that it has cooperated to some degree with members of the Young Communist League. The general program of this group involves dealing with interracial understanding. The group comprises approximately twenty people, usually half Negroes and half white members.

With regard to Waco, Texas and surrounding counties, informants contacted there have advised that they have received no reports reflecting any agitation among the Negroes residing there. This area includes a Negro population of approximately 31,000 Negroes.

In Freestone County, Texas it is stated that there are approximately 10,000 Negroes residing there. Informants advised that practically all the Negroes are loyal to the United States and have caused very little trouble. Some indications are reported, however, that members of the Jehovah's Witnesses sect are active among the Negroes, and it is stated that there has been some agitation for the betterment of laboring conditions of the Negroes.

It is also alleged that many of the younger Negroes upon being examined for induction into the United States Army are found to have syphilis, and that these Negroes do not want to take treatment because they feel if they do, they will be inducted into the United States Army. A drive recently was made to force them to take treatment, and orders have been issued that any Negro who is found to have syphilis and who refuses to take the treatment will be forced to either receive treatment or go to jail.

In this territory it has been noted that approximately four hundred Negroes have paid their poll taxes during the past year, which is considered a decided increase in view of no presidential election being held.

In Robertson County, Texas it is stated that there are approximately 6,000 Negroes residing there among whom, however, it is reported no agitation exists. The only recent racial trouble reported there is stated to have been caused by a fight between a Negro and a white man and not by any organized agitation.

It is stated that there are approximately 18,000 Negroes in McLennan County, Texas, 12,000 of whom reside in the City of Waco. In the county as a whole it is stated that there has been no agitation among the Negroes and that they seem very well satisfied with conditions existing there. Published in Waco, Texas is the "Waco Messenger", a weekly publication which is stated to be one hundred per cent American.

In Falls County, Texas it is reported that there are approximately 10,000 Negroes residing there, most of whom are employed as common laborers on the farms and in the cotton fields. It is reported that there are as many Negro students in Marlin, Falls County, Texas as there are white students. A few rumors have been received concerning agitation among the Negroes there for better living conditions, higher wages and more voice in the Government. It is the opinion of the Sheriff of that county that the Jehovah's Witnesses sect, who are somewhat active, might possibly be responsible for the agitation that exists in view of their teaching equality of the races. A number of Italians reside in Falls County who treat the Negroes as equal to the white people, which action is stated to cause some trouble.

In and around Laredo, Texas there is but a very small population of Negroes classified as Mexican Negroes in view of their intermarriage with Mexicans. No trouble or agitation among the Negroes is reported in this area.

In and around the City of Brownsville, Cameron County, Texas there are approximately 200 Negroes scattered throughout the county. It is reported that these Negroes are stated to be law-abiding and peaceful and nothing has been reported to indicate existence of agitation there.

In the City of Marligen, Texas there are approximately 150 Negro soldiers stationed at the Army Gunnery School, and in the city and vicinity there are approximately 350 Negro residents. No information has been reported reflecting any indication of agitation among the Negroes there.

In Raymondville, Willacy County, Texas there is only a transient Negro population consisting of approximately 100 persons who work in the cotton fields during the appropriate season. No information has been received from this area reflecting any agitation among the Negroes there.

In Rio Grande City, Starr County, Texas it has been ascertained that there are only two Negroes living there and no agitation or trouble in this area has been reported.

In the area of Seguin, Texas, there have occurred several disturbances among the Negro troops stationed there during the first part of June, 1943. There have been numerous fights between members of two companies of Negro soldiers bivouacking in the area. It is said that the companies were engaged in war games when they were in competition with one another, out of which grew somewhat of an antagonistic feeling amongst the individuals. It is said, also, the disturbances arose when the participants were drunk, one in particular occurring at the Municipal Auditorium in Austin at a dance given for the Negro companies. The local Negro girls are said to have refused to dance with Negro soldiers. It is said that the entire number of incidents involved merely discipline among the soldiers themselves, and no outside influences were indicated as being partially or totally responsible for the trouble.

Savannah Field Division

In this area there have been many reports of Negroes expressing their dissatisfaction with treatment being afforded them and claiming that Japan or Germany would treat them better. The majority of the statements refer to Japan, however. Other remarks and rumors reported are to the effect that white people will some day be working for Negroes. Inquiries, of course, are being continued to determine the sources of such statements as well as the reasons for their utterances. To date, however, no information has been reported reflecting that foreign propaganda or Japanese or German inspired agitation are the sources for such remarks.

An example of an allegedly misguided attitude on the part of white people in the State of Georgia, which is said to have an effect of sponsoring rumors and furthering racial distrusts, has been reported in the set of circumstances surrounding the issuance of a memorandum by the Commander of the Georgia State Guard. This memorandum is said to have concerned the possibility of white and colored agents working among Negroes to spread propaganda and try to defeat the war effort. The nature of this bulletin or memorandum is said to have been revealed and spread among the Negroes. In turn the Negroes are said to have understood the memorandum as reflecting the Georgia State Guard was organized to subdue the Negroes and anticipated race riots. In this connection, it is said one Negro asked a white family to allow him and his family to have shelter in the white family's residence when "the fighting started".

A confidential source of information, a Negro business and professional man, located in Augusta, Georgia, has been contacted with regard to his opinion relative to foreign-inspired agitation among the Negroes in this area. This source of information stated he believes the Negroes are behind the war effort and that they believe at the present time they owe to the American democratic form of government everything they possess. This source of information said that he has had no information relative to un-American sentiment among the Negroes there. He continued, citing the incident of Roland Hayes, a Negro singer in the City of Rome, Georgia. He stated he felt this incident was unfair to the Negro race and further, the alleged mistreatment of the police when making an arrest was another sore point.

Another source of information in the Augusta, Georgia, area, has advised he believes there is no subversive propaganda in the form of literature being distributed among the Negroes in the area. This source of information did, however, cite the possibility of the spreading of rumors, lies and propaganda by word of mouth.

In the vicinity of Charleston, South Carolina, additional complaints and rumors have been received reflecting unrest and agitation among the Negroes in this area, however, inquiries of reliable and prominent individuals here fail to reflect evidences of subversive elements or tending to organize Negroes into states of unrest and dissatisfaction. In connection with this, a reliable source of information, a Negro, has advised that although he is cognizant of considerable unrest among the Negroes in this area, he had not heard of any organizations being formed by them.

In the City of Sumter, South Carolina, it has been reported that Negroes employed in the Brooklyn Cooperage Company and the Williams Furniture Company have in great numbers asked to be relieved of the pledge to purchase War Bonds with 10 per cent of their wages. Upon being asked the reason for such withdrawal, many replied that "they needed money," with no other explanation. At one of the plants, approximately a thousand Negro employees had pledged to purchase War Bonds and very few withdrawals for such had been made until the month of August, 1942. Since that time more than 200 employees requested to withdraw their pledges. Several individuals who withdrew their money pledged for War Bonds advised they needed the money for specific purposes such as the payment of debts. One, however, upon being asked his reason for withdrawing his pledge, in an impertinent manner advised "that he heard that the Japs were not mad at the Negroes because they didn't do anything" and that if the Japs won the war the colored race would control. He further stated that if the Negroes would help the Japs, when the war was over everything would be equal. This individual, however, could not advise as to the source of such information.

In the City of Sumter, Negroes were also reportedly buying firearms, most of whom give the impression that they do not intend to hunt with them. The demand for guns and ammunition is stated to have begun around August 1, 1942.

In the cities of Blythewood, Columbia, Holly Hill, Edisto Island, Hopkins, Summerville and Beaufort, South Carolina, and in the city of Denton, Georgia, there have been reported various complaints either to the effect that Negroes are in favor of Japan winning the war or to the effect that their manner has become very insolent and arrogant.

Among the Negro newspapers available to the Negro population in this area are "The Chicago Defender," "Pittsburgh Courier," "The Southern Frontier," published in Atlanta, Georgia, "The Lighthouse and Informer," published in Columbia, South Carolina. These newspapers are stated to be primarily concerned with securing equal rights. In instances they urge support of the war effort on the part of Negroes but in editorials claim that the Government which requires the Negroes to pay taxes and which conscripts Negroes to fight in its war "owes him democracy's privileges as well as its duties." It is claimed that repetition of this theme and elaboration thereof by the uneducated appears to be the substance of much of the reported propaganda in this area.

In various other areas of the State of Georgia and Southern Carolina rumors have been reported of possible future trouble inspired among the Negroes by un-American sources, but investigations instituted and inquiries made relative to the specific information have met with negative results.

Complaints have also been received to the effect that there is a new type of arrogance on the part of Negroes in this area reflecting independence of aid or employment from white people. In the City of Sumter, South Carolina, Negroes are reportedly seeking to have redeemed war stamps and bonds they have purchased or demanding a return of the 10 per cent accumulation they have pledged. No information in this regard, however, has been reported reflecting any subversive activity in the background. In at least two cities of this area it has also been reported that Negroes are purchasing firearms and ammunition in unusual quantities.

In the City of Savannah, Georgia, it is stated, Negroes are expressing themselves to the effect that they would be better situated if Japan were to win the war and govern the United States. Similar statements are also reported to have been indicating an apparent lack of patriotism on the part of Negroes with whom one source of information has contact. This source of information, who has much contact with the Negroes in this area, as well as being in their favor, also advises that many have only an interest in earning as much money as they possibly can during the emergency.

Another source of information in the area of Savannah, Georgia, a colored man, advises that in his opinion statements made by Negroes in this area to the effect that their condition would be improved by Japanese were only a matter of repetition of ignorant words occasioned by anger over slights and of unthinking Negroes endeavoring to attract attention.

In and around the City of Savannah it is also reported that among colored soldiers there is circulated literature of a possible seditious nature through colored divisions of the United Service Organizations and the Soldiers Social Service in Savannah. Typical of this type of literature reported is stated to be a copy of "Calling America" in which appears an article particularly referred to, "We're Another," by Lewis Gannett, a paragraph of which points out unchanged instances of segregation and the likeness of Negroes to the Jews in "Hitler's Germany."

In and around the City of Augusta, Georgia, there have been numerous instances reported wherein Negroes are alleged to have made statements favoring domination by pro-Axis nations; furthermore, rumors have been reported that meetings have been held in this area wherein propaganda tending to cause unrest and dissatisfaction is disseminated.

In the City of Clarksville, Georgia, sources of information contacted there advised that Negroes seemed to be influenced and that the same is possibly being caused by outside interference. One occasion that has been cited in which a Negro woman, arrested on a liquor charge, while en route to jail, stated "White folks have been treating the Negroes like dogs long enough, and when the Japs take this place, the colored folks will tell the White folks what to do."

In the vicinity of Gainesville, Georgia, it is reported that a representative of the Jehovah's Witnesses sect lives among the Negroes and distributes literature.

It has been reported that in the City of La Grange, Georgia, members of the Jehovah's Witnesses sect also are active among the Negroes distributing propaganda regarding discrimination against them and attempting to show that Negroes are not equally treated in the United States Army.

Inquiries made at Jefferson, Clayton, Hiwassee, Blairsville, Dahlonega, and Cleveland, Georgia, in an attempt to ascertain any indications of possible pro-Axis activity among the Negroes have met with negative results.

In the City of Toccoa, Georgia, it is reported that Negroes here are receiving many outside Negro newspapers, one particularly printed in Pittsburgh, Pennsylvania, which are stated to be of a radical nature. In this area it is also stated that the Negroes are discontented with the present times, and that this discontent is believed to be a direct result of the newspapers which are being circulated in this territory. [*100-135-3*]

On November 5, 1942, six Negroes distributed circulars at the gates of the MacEvoy Shipbuilding Corporation, Savannah, Georgia, of a union affiliated with the Congress of Industrial Organizations which circulars pertained to union organizational activities. This corporation is said to have a contract calling for a closed shop with bargaining rights granted to an AFL affiliate. Five of the six Negroes were chased from the premises by white men, thought possibly to be leaders of the AFL affiliate and employed at the MacEvoy Shipbuilding Corporation. One of the Negroes, one Elijah Jackson, however, refused to leave stating, "I have a job to do and I'm going to do it," whereupon he was struck over the head with an iron pipe. Allegations were received that Jackson was struck by a president of an affiliate of the AFL.

While Jackson was reportedly lying on the roadside outside of the gate of the corporation at about 6:30 p.m., Negroes were leaving their jobs at quitting time and were coming out of the plant. Thereupon they formed a mob outside of the gate and proposals were made by members of the mob to beat up all of the white workers coming from the yard, five of whom apparently were beaten severely. It might be noted that the Negroes are said to have first refused to permit management to see that Jackson received proper medical attention. All indications which have been reported point to the fact that the trouble originated with union strife, and arguments over bargaining rights.

On November 9, 1942, an organizer for the affiliate of the CIO stated that his union had plans to organize the shipyard workers in Savannah and that this procedure was perfectly legitimate and in the exercise of organizational rights. On the other hand it has been reported that the MacEvoy Shipyards in Savannah had a bargaining contract with the AFL affiliate, which was allegedly regarded by the company employees as entirely satisfactory. It has further been reported that all workers at the yard were members of the AFL affiliate. According to reported remarks of the Safety Superintendent of the South Eastern Shipbuilding Company, the activity engaged in by the two different unions was of a serious nature and that it hindered production.

With regard to the plans of the organizers of the CIO affiliate, it has been alleged that prior to the time of the trouble a meeting was held at 114 Drayton Street, Savannah, Georgia, which is the address of the CIO headquarters there. It is said that at this meeting a national organizer, as well as Elijah Jackson and another partially unidentified individual took part. It is said that work among Negroes and Negro organizations was discussed at this meeting, as well as the recruiting of Negro members. It is alleged that the following was stated: "Build up white committees and do not let colored recruiting run away. It is necessary to have the whites go along with the colored in order to break down discrimination here and not to build up colored locals."

The foregoing has been cited as a reported example of how union organizational activities have caused racial misunderstanding in the Savannah area.

Throughout the Savannah Field Division, which covers the Eastern part of Georgia and the South Eastern part of South Carolina, numerous reports of alleged subversive meetings, statements and activities have been reported involving Negro inhabitants of the area. Inquiries into these reports and allegations have, in their entirety, met with negative results and it has been ascertained that the complaints, allegations and rumors were based on either misunderstanding or idle gossip. With regard to the allegations of expressions of un-American sentiments by Negroes, inquiries have developed that these were founded either through misunderstanding or it has been learned that the Negro inhabitants allegedly responsible for the remarks made them as a result of ignorance, anger or drunkenness. In no instance has there been found any organized activity or propaganda urging Negroes to make such utterances.

In this connection, a prominent Negro in the Savannah, Georgia area, who is the State President of the National Association for the Advancement of Colored People, has expressed the following observations. He has advised that he believes there is a loyalty on the part of the American Negro toward the United States at the present time, although it is without enthusiasm, which lack of enthusiasm he feels is caused by unequal distribution of justice in living conditions, law courts and labor. He has stated that the Negro in the Savannah area has encountered considerable difficulty in obtaining skilled employment in various war industries because of the unwillingness of local AFL unions to permit them to join. On the other hand, he has stated that the Congress of Industrial Organizations has welcomed Negroes into the various unions and for that reason is in greater favor with Negroes. He has said that Negroes have been more independent since the war started because of the fact that a great many Northern Negroes have come into the South with the United States Army and have told Southern Negroes that conditions in the North are better for them. He has further attributed this feeling to the intense publicity given to what he termed "principles of democracy" by newspapers and radios, the result being that Negroes are beginning to feel they should be entitled to better conditions.

As a matter to be considered with relation to the remarks made by the Negro source of information set forth above, the following information is set forth concerning the conditions at Camp Stewart and Hinesville, Georgia.

At Camp Stewart, which is a United States Army training base about forty-two miles from Savannah, there are approximately 40,000 troops, 15,000 of which are Negroes. A tension between the white and colored troops has existed for several months having commenced when northern Negro troops were assigned to Camp Stewart. One particular group of Negro soldiers who had previously been stationed in Michigan near the Canadian border was transferred to Camp Stewart about four and one-half months ago. This group is reported to have been allowed considerable freedom in Michigan.

Camp Stewart is located adjacent to Hinesville, Georgia, which is a small community of less than 1,000 people. There are no recreational facilities whatsoever for Negro soldiers in Hinesville and comparatively few recreational facilities for white soldiers. The Negro soldiers are not allowed in any of the stores in Hinesville and it is stated that they cannot even buy coca colas or obtain a drink of water in that town. To aggravate the situation the Negro soldiers have attempted to make dates with white girls in Hinesville which, of course, in this section is absolutely forbidden by local custom.

There is no apparent subversive influence present, but the northern Negro soldiers have reportedly had almost continuous trouble with the white military police and have continually agitated for racial equality. They think that they should be allowed the use of the white officers club and the white USO in spite of the fact that there are colored officers clubs and a colored USO at Camp Stewart.

There have been a number of incidents which could possibly have resulted in serious trouble and riots at the camp and in the immediate vicinity thereof. For instance, three Negro lieutenants went into the white theater in Hinesville on one occasion. The manager of the theater notified the Provost Marshal at the camp and in order not to cause any immediate trouble the Provost Marshal instructed the manager of the theater to allow the Negroes to remain, but to obtain their names and furnish them to the Provost Marshal.

More recently it was discovered that a number of rifles were missing from various supply rooms at Camp Stewart. Following this discovery a rumor spread through the Negro troops that a white military policeman had raped and killed a Negro girl in the vicinity of the camp. This rumor, as far as is known, was entirely false, but on the following night a number of Negro soldiers were observed by their commanding officer with rifles after dark when all rifles should have been turned in. The authorities were notified and immediately sent a number of military police into the Negro section. The military police were fired upon by Negro soldiers, one group of military police being forced to abandon the truck in which they were riding and seek refuge in a ditch. The Negro soldiers continued to fire at the military police resulting in the death of one military policeman, who was trying to make his way back to the main part of the camp, and the wounding of three other military policemen.

It was after dark when the shooting occurred and most of the shots fired by the Negro soldiers went wild or the casualties might have been much greater. It has been variously estimated that from 500 to 5,000 rounds were fired by the Negro soldiers although only two rounds were fired by the military police. An Army Board of Inquiry is understood to still be investigating this outbreak.

Another recent report is to the effect that eight to ten colored soldiers were seen climbing the camp fence headed towards Hinesville armed with rifles. The military police were not able to apprehend or identify these soldiers, but no disturbance was reported as a result of their alleged armed departure from camp.

The white residents of Hinesville are said to be armed and prepared to meet any violence. The opinion has been expressed that because of the tension at the camp it is possible that there may be further trouble. [*X44-805*]

IV

WESTERN SECTION OF THE UNITED STATES

The States which are included in this section are Arizona, Nevada, Utah, Colorado, Idaho, Wyoming, North and South Dakota, Nebraska, Minnesota, Iowa, Kansas, and the northern part of Missouri.

In this section the Negro population is comparatively small and in the main the Negro people in these areas are employed in agricultural and common labor pursuits. No indications have been received of foreign-inspired forces working among the Negro inhabitants of this section other than the activity of the Communist Party.

Indications have been received that a degree of unrest, as well as tension, has resulted in this section from the presence of Negro soldiers and the lack of facilities in some cities to provide them recreation. The consequence is said to be the Negro soldiers patronizing white establishments where they are not always cordially received by either the patrons or the management. A number of clashes and skirmishes have occurred between both Negro and white soldiers and white civilians in various parts of the section.

The most frequently expressed grievance which has been reported in these areas by Negroes individually and collectively as well as by Negro newspapers published therein has been the reported resentment against discrimination in employment. However, it is reported that the proportion of Negroes employed in defense industries in the State of Nebraska is larger than the proportion of the Negro population to the white population in the State. In some areas there are also reported indications of grievances over improper and unsanitary living conditions.

Incorporated hereinafter are digests of those Field Divisions located in this section of the country which contain information received with respect to racial conditions and race relationship.

Butte Field Division

Geographical survey of negro activities in the State of Idaho reflects no evidence that negroes or others are agitating or spreading subversive propaganda among the negro element. The largest congregation of negroes in the State are located in the vicinity of Boise, Pocatello and Twin Falls, Idaho.

A general intelligence survey of the Negro activities in the State of Montana reflects no evidence that Negroes or others are agitating or spreading subversive propaganda among the Negro element. It is reported the largest congregations of Negroes in the State of Montana are located in the areas surrounding Butte, Anaconda, Helena, Great Falls and Billings.

Although there have been a number of complaints and reports to the effect that un-American statements have been made by Negroes in this area investigation and inquiries fail to reveal any organized attempts to create disunity.

An incident occurred in the month of November, 1942 in the area of Butte, Montana, relative to the employment at the behest of Federal authorities of 37 negro soldiers in the Butte mines of the Anaconda Copper Mining Company. White members of the International Union of Mine, Mill and Smelter Workers of America (CIO) called two protest meetings, one held on November 23, 1942 and the other held November 25, 1942. Brigadier General Frank J. McSherry of the War Manpower Commission addressed the meeting. General McSherry explained the situation as to why soldiers were designated to work in the mines. He stated that when the acute shortage of copper was noted, it was also found that there was a shortage of miners and, faced with this shortage, government authorities felt that there were many miners in the armed forces who could be serving their country far better by getting out copper ore. He explained that the United States Army agreed to furlough soldiers serving in the country who had volunteered to work in the mines. Pursuant to the agreement, it was reported that 4,000 soldiers volunteered, among which were some colored soldiers. Under a quota, one thousand white soldier miners had been sent to Butte, yet only 37 negro miners were allocated there. In other areas where negro soldiers were sent to help in mining ore, it was said that little difficulty had been experienced.

It was assured at the meeting of the miners that the 37 negro soldier miners at the time at the Butte, Montana area would be removed within approximately 60 to 90 days. However, it is reported that a number of union members, miners got up at the meeting and expressed themselves vehemently, in many instances against the continued employment of negro soldiers in the mines.

Denver Field Division

It is reported the colored population in the state of Colorado is centered largely in the City of Denver. No reports of foreign inspired agitation have been received, but it is reported there is presently a great deal of national agitation fomented in part by the Communist Party. Two local colored newspapers, the "Denver Star" and the "Colorado Statesman", allegedly assist the Communist Party in this regard.

The following organizations are active among the colored population at Denver, Colorado:

The National Association for the Advancement of Colored People

National Negro Congress

Hispanic American Confederation of Colorado

East Denver Citizens Committee

The colored voting population was recently listed at five thousand by the "Colorado Statesman", a Negro newspaper in the Denver area. All colored organizations in the area, and activities of such, are therefore centered in the City of Denver. Further inquiries however, have been made in cities throughout the area covered by this field division. Generally speaking, no reports have been received reflecting the presence of any Axis-inspired propaganda in this area tending towards disunity. However, this is not to say that racial agitation is not present. On the contrary, it is reported that from the content of colored newspapers circulated in this area, racial consciousness is very pronounced and much is made in every item in the news affecting the Negro population either individually or as a group.

There are two Negro newspapers in the City of Denver, one is known as the "Colorado Statesman," published by E. V. Dorsey, weekly on Fridays and is devoted almost exclusively to racial matters. It is believed that as a rule, the Statesman treats racial matters more tolerantly than other Negro newspapers. However, every item of indicated discrimination is featured in the paper. It is a personal venture of the publisher and is not known to be financed from other than legitimate sources. There has been a report to the effect that the Communist Party in the area recently entered into preliminary negotiations to take the paper over as a Party organ, but nothing has been reported as yet, to indicate that this has occurred. Dorsey is reported to associate at times with known Communists but however, no direct information has been received reflecting that he is a member of the Party.

The "Denver Star" is another Negro newspaper published in Denver by George G. Ross, Negro attorney. It is published weekly. Ross is said to be rabid on the subject of racialism but is not regarded as a radical on any one issue. The paper is believed to have a difficult time existing inasmuch as much of the material published consists of reprints from New York papers, and the same item may appear in several successive issues, indicating that the editor has had insufficient time to obtain new material. It however, makes an issue of every incident affecting Negroes.

There is a branch of The National Association for the Advancement of Colored People in the City of Denver. No indications have been reported reflecting any subversive activities on the part of this organization nor any connections with the Communist Party. It is mainly concerned with the elevation of the Negro economically and culturally in this area, and whenever recognition comes to a member of the Negro race it is widely exploited by the organization, in the area.

There is a Negro Y.M.C.A. known as the Glenarm Y.M.C.A. located in Denver. There are also Negro churches which confine themselves to religious activities and are not used for propaganda purposes.

The Communist Party in this area is said to have a long range program of recruiting Negroes and in May of 1942 the Angelo Herndon Branch was organized under the leadership of W. R. Tollard. It is sponsored by Branch Four of the Communist Party which is made up not only of Negroes, but of other nationalities and races. It is said that the membership of this organization is not large and is estimated at approximately twenty-five. It meets at the homes of members and is permitted to use the Party address in Denver on its publications such as leaflets and other matter. The Branch publishes a mimeographed sheet known as the "Beacon", which is published at irregular intervals and clamors for employment in war industries for Negroes and full racial equality. The Negro leaders in the Communist Party are Lloyd Davis, Lillian Worthan, and W. R. Tollard.

In the fall of 1941 an attempt was made to organize a branch of the National Negro Congress in Denver. The National Negro Congress is a well-known Communist front organization. However, the attempt failed after several meetings. Following the failure of the branch of the National Negro Congress, William L. Patterson of Chicago, Illinois, is said to have attempted to stimulate some interest in Denver in what he chose to call the "Stop Hitler Committee". A Lieutenant Earl W. Mann was said to be an influential Negro politician and presently working for the War Department in Denver, sponsored the organization. A few meetings were held. Again due to the lack of interest and attendance, this organization was unable to get under way and finally in about February of 1942, it was announced that the project had been abandoned.

Confidential sources of information have advised that subsequently the "East Denver Citizens Committee" was formed and that there was no question but [t]hat the Communist Party was behind the organization. Its secretary is Lloyd Davis, a Negro Communist. At the present time it is reported that the "East Denver Citizens Committee" is undoubtedly the strongest Negro Organization in this area.

In the state of Wyoming, there are approximately one thousand Negroes, more than half of which number reside in Cheyenne. It is reported that there are no present indications of subversive forces at work among the Negro race in this state although it is alleged that some five or six years ago, the Communist Party made unsuccessful efforts to interest Negroes in becoming members. As regards the Japanese in this area, it is reported they have in no way attempted to cause unrest among the Negroes and have been very humble and law-abiding. [*100-135-14*]

Investigation and inquiries made in the area of Pueblo, Colorado have disclosed no indications of successful Communist or Japanese activity among Negroes there. The National Association for the Advancement of Colored People has a chapter there which is said to be opposed to Communism, contrary to some local chapters of this organization in which there is reported Communist infiltration.

In this same area, during July of 1942 the editor of the Western Ideal, a Negro newspaper, received a package of pro-Japanese propaganda material. The same was immediately burned and not used. This same newspaper has also been approached by the Daily Worker, the Communist Party organ published in New York City, however its overtures were not heeded.

At the Colorado Fuel and Iron Company, Pueblo, Negro employees are said to have recently exhibited an attitude of arrogance in some instances, which has heretofore been unknown. Membership in a labor union and sympathy with Communist principles were alleged to be the causes for such an attitude. [*100-135-14*]

On January 10, 1943, A. Philip Randolph, national leader of the March on Washington Movement, spoke in Denver under the sponsorship of the local branch of the National Association for the Advancement of Colored People and George Ross, Editor of the Negro newspaper, the Denver Star. In his speech, Randolph demanded full racial equality for the Negro, and he is said to have delivered it in a fiery manner. Following his appearance in Denver, a movement was apparently instituted to organize a unit of the March on Washington Movement. Subsequent information received from confidential informants was that the Negro members lost much of their original enthusiasm and interest they had in the March on Washington Movement.

[*100-135-14-6&7*]

Des Moines Field Division

Negroes constitute seven per cent of Iowa's total population. There are over 16,000 Negroes in Iowa, who are concentrated largely in Des Moines.

Investigation and inquiries which have been made indicate no evidences of foreign-inspired activities, although there are numerous instances reported on the part of the Communist Party wherein Party functionaries have attempted to obtain the favor of local Negro leaders. No indications have been received, however, which show that the Communist Party has any control or influence in the local Negro groups.

The National Association for the Advancement of Colored People has a small but strong chapter of reportedly reputable members in this area. There is also a local organization in Des Moines known as the Des Moines Negro Youth Forum which has attracted some publicity and popularity. No reports have been received to the effect that there is outside control or influence in the group.

A few complaints have been received that in several isolated instances Negroes have made anti-American utterances. One instance involved two young Negro high school girls who expressed pro-Axis sentiments. When questioned by their teachers about the matter, they were vague in their answers. The incident occurred in the classroom when Mark Twain's "Tom Sawyer" was being read. It has been reported that the home life of the two girls is highly satisfactory.

There are two weekly Negro newspapers which are published in this area: the "Iowa Bystander" and the "Iowa Observer". The former is published by James B. Morris, Negro attorney, whose editorial policy is for the advancement of the colored race by the obtaining of better employment and additional rights. According to the publisher's own statement, he is opposed to any belief that such advancement can be obtained under Axis domination.

The "Iowa Observer" is published by Charles P. Howard, Sr. who urges the granting of equal rights to Negroes but at the same time aims for the support of the United States government and opposes ideals inimical to its best interests.

[*100-135-15*]

Kansas City Field Division

A survey made in this area fails to reflect organized Communist Party or pro-Axis activity among the Negroes. Activities or agitation among the Negroes which has been reported is said to be caused by unrelated individuals or organizations. At one time it is reported, a Japanese individual is said to have assisted a Dr. A. Porter Davis, a Negro physician and politician in Kansas City, Kansas to form the Pacific Movement of the Eastern World in this city. The organization, however, is stated not to have subscribed to foreign influence or rule by the parent organization in St. Louis, Missouri. At the present time it is stated to be inactive, although until recently it is stated to have a membership of approximately 25 with Dr. Davis at its head. It is believed by sources of information to be a political faction. Dr. Davis is also said to be instrumental in forming the Citizens Advisory Council, a Negro organization, to campaign for defense jobs, Kansas City. At one time this Council promoted a march on the North American Aviation, Inc. Plant which however was stated to be frustrated by the action of other members of the Council.

A total of thirteen Negro members of the Moorish Science Temple of America in Kansas City, a part of the National Organization said to be subjected to Japanese influence, have been arrested for a violation of the Selective Training and Service Act. No information, however, has been reported reflecting any Japanese influence locally. Investigation of this branch is continuing.

It is stated that among the Communist Party Front Organizations active among the Negroes in this area at one time or another were the Human Rights Club, the American Peace Mobilization, the Stratosphereans, the Negro Civic and Economic Forum. With regard to the activity of the Communist Party in this area, it is stated to be limited for the major part to activities centered in greater Kansas City which included Kansas City, Missouri and Kansas City, Kansas. Its activity is calling for equal rights of the Negro, the abolition of "Jim Crow-ism" and increased employment for the Negro in national defense industries. Any other activity is said to be only occasional in the form of attendance by isolated Negroes at Communist Party meetings.

With regard to the Communist activities among the Negroes in this area, a typical example has been reported of Communist machinations with regard to Negroes, at a Communist meeting held September 6, 1942 at 404 West 39th Street, Kansas City, Missouri. Roger Bird, a well known Communist, introduced the principal speaker, Ralph Shaw, who was believed to come from St. Louis, Missouri. Shaw is an organizer for the Communist Party in St. Louis and for a union affiliated with the C.I.O., namely, the United Electrical, Radio and Machine Workers of America. When refreshments were served at the meeting, the Negro guests who were in attendance were served first.

Recently Roger Bird and John Jacob Karson, Communist Party functionaries in the Kansas City, Missouri area, enlisted in the United States Army and Communist Party activities have been under the direction of Helen Hester and her women associates. Negro support is one of the organizational policies fostered by Hester, and Negro women are being cultivated for prospective membership in the Communist Party.

[*100-135-24*]

Also active in this area is a branch of the National Association for the Advancement of Colored People, which is active in promoting the cause of the Negro race for more favorable legislation concerning personal equality and for better conditions both economically and socially. No information has been reported, however, reflecting that this branch is either connected with the Communist Party or subject to foreign control, inspiration or domination. It was announced in March, 1943 that the local branch of this organization in Kansas City had a membership of over one thousand persons. At that time it was instituting a membership recruiting campaign to add an additional one thousand members.

A report has been received from a confidential informant of a closed branch meeting of the Communist Party held at party headquarters in Kansas City which, although attended by only two Negroes, dealt considerably with the activities of the Party relative to Negroes. One of the leading functionaries at the meeting instructed the two Negroes present that the Negroes in the Kansas City area should demand equal rights and privileges with those of white persons, and they should go to public places where service was at the time denied the Negroes and demand service. In the event service was refused, the Negroes were then instructed to passively resist refusal, after which they were to solicit the assistance of their friends to go to this same public place and again demand service. They were further instructed to repeat this activity over and over again.

[*100-135-24-17*]

Subsequent reports concerning the Party's activities in relation to the Negroes are to the effect that it is particularly anxious to recruit Negroes. Meetings have been held in the homes of Negroes in the area, and the white Party activists have been devoting time in the Negro residential area of Kansas City. An alleged selling point to obtain Negro membership is in the form of promises made to prospective recruits that a movement will be initiated to obtain the admittance of Negroes in one of the principal theaters in Kansas City. This, plus other similar privileges, will be possible, according to Party members if Negroes become members of the Communist Party, which will assist them in obtaining their rights and privileges.

In March, 1943 a report was received of a Negress, an operator of a beauty parlor in Lebanon, Missouri, remarking in a discussion of the war that Japanese agents had visited the territory in which she lived and had endeavored to induce them to commit acts of sabotage and revolt. This Negress is said to have further related that her "group" was waiting to evaluate the treatment given them by white people before arriving at a decision. Inquiries made into this report developed the fact that this Negress was a habitual drunkard and very low mentally as well as being most unreliable. When questioned concerning her statement, she denied having ever made the remarks attributed to her and blamed the report on her "enemies". It is to be noted that no additional reports have been received concerning similar remarks in this area or any subversive forces at work.

On June 22, 1943, just subsequent to the quieting of the disturbances in Detroit, the Kansas City, Missouri Police Department was informed of an unidentified Negro distributing anti-racial handbills in a Negro residential section in Kansas City, which district is comprised of the more well-to-do Negroes, the majority of whom own their own homes and are employed. The handbill was approximately 5″ by 5″, on a very poor grade of paper with poor printing. The text of the handbill was that Negroes should strike from their defense employment and not aid in the war effort, yet not commit acts of violence. It referred, also, to the Detroit riots of June 20–22, 1943. The first reports of this distribution were made by Negro residents of the area who strongly resented its distribution and text. Many expressed their personal desire to be permitted to "take care" of the individuals who were responsible. Negro detectives assigned to the Kansas City Police Department, who bear an excellent reputation among other members of their race, ascertained that the general Negro population in the Kansas City area is patriotic and loyal. It was ascertained that they reacted in a very definite manner against the propaganda contained in the handbill. The "Kansas City Call" and its editor were very bitter in their denouncing the unknown individuals responsible for the printing and distribution of the handbills.

In connection with making inquiries concerning the distribution of this pamphlet by the Kansas City Police Department, it was ascertained that a racial feeling does not exist in Kansas City to the extent of damaging the war effort, although there is a certain dissatisfied feeling as a result of discrimination and inequality of work in some of the war plants and industries in the area. It was pointed out that there is a new militancy among the younger generation of Negroes, while the older generation is more stable and is peaceably inclined. No indications were received of extended Communist influence, although it was ascertained that considerable agitating was done by the Party. It was the general belief, further, that the Communist Party was in no way responsible for the distribution of the aforementioned pamphlet. To date no indications have been received as to the individual or individuals responsible for the distribution of the pamphlet.

In this area are two Negro newspapers, one, "The Plain Dealer", published in Kansas City, Kansas, which is a more conservative type newspaper, while the "Kansas City Call", published in Kansas City, Missouri, is stated to be more agitational and sensational in nature. The latter newspaper is reported to have at various times printed Communist Party articles which were furnished it in New York City.

Omaha Field Division

In 1941 an estimate was made that there were 12,364 Negroes in the area of Omaha, Nebraska, 40 per cent of whom are home owners, 45 per cent of whom are tenants, while 15 per cent live with their relatives. In the entire State of Nebraska it was said there were approximately 14,000 Negroes at that time. There are two Negro newspapers in the area. One is the "Omaha Guide," the other the "Omaha Star." As to the former it is said that the majority of the paper is devoted to press releases of the National Association for the Advancement of Colored People and advertisements. The latter is said to militantly seek added rights for Negroes as well as the abolition of discrimination and segregation.

Sources of information in walks of life wherein a good knowledge of the Negro population can be obtained, a number of them being Negroes, have advised of noticing no evidences of pro-Axis activity or propaganda work in the State of Nebraska. There have been, however, numerous reports of Communist Party activity among Negroes especially centering in the packing industry in the area. It is said that approximately 20 Negroes are members of the Communist Party in the Omaha area. A number of these Negro members are also members of the Packing Workers Organizing Committee.

With regard to the Negro membership in the Party in this area an informant has advised that recently national officers of the Party expressed disappointment at the relatively small Party membership in Nebraska. This informant has stated the national officers believed that too much attention has been paid in the past to the enlistment of support of Negroes and as a result at social gatherings and business meetings often Negro members outnumber white members and accordingly a number of white people have dropped out of the Party. Allegedly to correct this situation it has been worked out that the North Side Branch of the Communist Party in Omaha which is composed of practically all Negroes will have separate social functions and separate business meetings on most occasions. Under this arrangement it was thought that Negroes who are members will in no way outnumber white people who attend the meetings and it is felt more white people will attend the social functions of the Party. In this regard, it has been pointed out that Negroes themselves have felt that something must be wrong with the Party because so few white people have appeared at the meetings.

In March 1943 a local committee was formed calling itself the Fair Employment Practice Committee. There were said to be some 80 members of the Committee who nominated an acting committee composed of some 18 Negro members representing such organizations as the National Association for the Advancement of Colored People, the Urban League, the Negro Ministerial Alliance and the two Negro newspapers published in Omaha. The purpose of the organization was "to obtain a broadly representative and democratic community approach to the problem of discrimination in war industries because of race, creed, color, or racial origin. . . ."

The National Association for the Advancement of Colored People has been active in this area carrying out the general line of other chapters in other areas, namely, the urging of abolition of racial discrimination and segregation. In this connection, the "Omaha Guide," it will be recalled, publishes the releases of this organization and it has pursued a militant attitude in their regard.

It has been reported that in the Cudahy Packing Plant in Omaha there are some eight or nine Japanese employees. Sources of information have advised that they have observed no fraternization between these Japanese and Negroes and no complaints have been made with regard to any of their activities.

Several confidential informants have advised that the most recent attitude they have noticed among the Negro population is that the present time is opportune for the bettering of the economic status of Negroes, particularly in view of the shortage of labor. These informants have expressed their opinion they believed the Negroes in the

State of Nebraska as a whole receive on a comparative basis good treatment from their fellow white citizens and that those grievances which do exist are mainly against discrimination practiced against Negroes in employment. However, it is reported that the proportion of Negroes employed in defense industries in this area is slightly larger than the proportion of the Negro population to the white population in the State.

Phoenix Field Division

Information received concerning the Negro situation in this area fails to disclose any substantial amount of agitation among the Negroes in the State of Arizona. Informants contacted in this matter advise that the Negroes there had formerly resented exclusion from the Navy and defense work, but that inasmuch as the situation had been to some extent corrected, there is no substantial agitation at the present time. One source of information was a well-known and respected professional man closely associated with the colored people in and around Phoenix, Arizona, and he advised that he has not heard of anything indicating that organized propaganda is being disseminated among the colored people in the State of Arizona. From time to time, he has stated, he had heard individual complaints from colored people concerning the manner in which they are discriminated against by employers in defense work. He added that he personally feels that these complaints are fully justified by the fact that he does not consider them subversive in any way but rather expressive of a well-founded grievance.

Informants advised as a whole the colored people in that area are entirely loyal to the United States and that they will not be influenced by foreign inspired agitation, particularly that of the Japanese for whom they have a decided dislike. Isolationist instances have been reported, however, to the effect that Negroes here and there have made statements that this is a white man's war and that the colored people should not join the Army.

A Negro newspaper in Phoenix, Arizona, known as the "Sun" is stated to be a small and conservatively operated paper not printing anything of a controversial nature.

On the night of November 26, 1942, a riot took place at 17th and Washington Streets, Phoenix, Arizona, as the aftermath of an attempt of a colored military policeman to arrest a negro soldier. Before the riot was quelled more than 100 military and civilian police officers converged on the scene and 28 square blocks were barred to the public while police hunted for soldiers who were believed to be still armed and at large. A colored civilian and a colored soldier were killed in the riot and twelve negro persons were injured. According to reports the riot apparently had its inception in a dispute between a colored soldier and a colored girl. It is said that the soldier struck the girl on the head with a bottle and a negro military policeman attempted to arrest him. However, the soldier reportedly charged the military policeman and refused to heed commands to halt. The Negro military policeman drew his gun and fired and an uproar followed and city officers were subsequently called. After a short time the disturbance was quelled and the soldiers were ordered to board buses back to their camps. They were lined up on Washington Street and the first 150 soldiers had boarded a bus when a "jeep" filled with colored military police arrived at the scene closely followed by a car full of soldiers. A shot was fired but it was not determined who fired the same. Soldiers in the car behind the "jeep" were reportedly heavily armed and started firing. The other soldiers fled but were subsequently rounded up and jailed for questioning. On November 28, 1942, almost 200 Negroes had been arrested and questioned regarding the riot. The "Arizona Republic Newspaper" for November 27, 1942, had stated in part, "As the battle was at its height, the city was suddenly filled with a whiff of 'race riot' rumors, but reporters on the scene and all the officers involved emphasized that the whole riot was strictly a Negro soldier affair. The only white persons injured reached the scene long after the trouble started and were all military policemen who were asked to help the colored military police."

Confidential sources of information interviewed relative to this situation all advised that the riot or affair was strictly between colored soldiers from Papago Park and colored military police from the State Fair Grounds in Phoenix, Arizona. It was thought that trouble had been brewing for some time because there was a great deal of jealousy between the units. Formerly the Papago Park soldiers reportedly had had their own military police battalion but when the regular colored military police battalion was moved into this vicinity to supervise the activities of the Negro soldiers, the military police organization at Papago Park was disbanded. As a result, it was said that a great deal of friction resulted between the two units. [*100-135-39*]

In connection with the above-set-out incident in which sources of information have advised there was no indication of any agitation attributable to any subversive forces, it has been reported that shortly after the incident the Communist Party of Arizona issued a mimeographed leaflet concerning the cause of the riot. The text of the leaflet pointed out that a Negro soldier and a civilian were killed, while twelve other persons were wounded on November 26, 1942, and that the real culprit behind the scenes of the affair was racial discrimination. The leaflet also stated that the problem was deeper than local discrimination and that a direct and contributing cause was segregation of Negroes in the Armed Forces and southern army officers alleged to have no understanding of the Negro people. [*Ser 13 of 100-135-39 Sub 13*]

St. Paul Field Division

From information reported, as well as from inquiries and investigations made, no evidence has been developed that there is foreign inspired or pro-Axis agitation among the Negroes in this area other than the maneuverings of the Communist Party to exploit the Negro inhabitants of this area. With regard to the Communist Party, however, it is said that there are but a few Negroes involved in its activities, and an opinion has been expressed that the Negroes in the State of Minnesota for the most part are employed. A large number of them are said to own their own homes and for this reason are not susceptible to Communist Party propaganda. A few instances of pro-Japanese sentiments have been reported, although in none of these have indications been received that organized activity is responsible for them. Rather, indications point to the fact that they were expressed because of ignorance or drunkenness.

There are reports of considerable unrest among the Negroes in the twin city area based primarily on dissatisfaction arising from alleged instances of discrimination. It has been pointed out that while there is a considerable number of Negroes being hired by the Twin City Ordnance Plant at New Brighton, Minnesota, and although the International Harvester Company and the D. W. Onan Manufacturing Company have employed a proportionate number of Negroes, other plants in the twin cities are said to have an inclination toward discrimination against Negroes.

A number of instances have been reported where in the Socialist Workers Party, a Trotskyite group, has sought to curry the favor of Negroes in this area through agitating in their behalf. It is reported, however, but a few Negroes are sympathetic or affiliated with this group. This is true, also, with the Communist Party and the Young Communist League, the latter having at one time forty-two Negroes in its membership in this area but subsequently losing a considerable number of Negro members.

There is published in this area the "Minneapolis Spokesman," which is a Negro newspaper. This newspaper follows generally the type of news reporting and editorial policy usually found in other Negro newspapers throughout the country. It is outspoken in its resentment as to discrimination and the denial of equal rights of Negroes. It has but a local circulation, although it publicizes the activities of leading national Negro organizations and leaders.

A Negro newspaper editor has been interviewed in this area with regard to Communist activities among Negroes. He has advised that there are perhaps no more than fifteen Negro Communist Party members in the St. Paul area. He advised, however, that in the past Negroes associated themselves with the Communist Party because the Party offered them a chance to exercise vocal power where previously they had none. In his opinion, at the present time Negroes have gained considerable vocal power and no longer need such a vehicle as the Communist Party to put forth their ideas and as a result they have little to do with Communism. With regard to his own paper, he advised that Trotskyites and the Communists saw to it that he received copies of their respective publications, "The Militant" and the "Daily Worker." Furthermore, both factions are said to drop into his office in an attempt to influence him and the Negroes through his papers.

With respect to possible Japanese influence or activities among the Negroes in this area, the same Negro newspaper editor advised that at one time in the past he had received a publication called the "Japanese-American Review," but with the outbreak of hostilities in December, 1941, between this country and Japan he received no more copies of the publication.

It has been reported that another source of agitation among the Negroes in this area is the "Midwest Labor" which is the official organ of the Minnesota State Industrial Union Council, CIO. It is said that the Negro is played up in this paper and many articles deal with alleged instances of discrimination. It is reported that this publication is edited by Ray Munson, who is said to be a Communist Party organizer, and its manager is Sam K. Davis, who is also reported to be a Communist Party member and is known to have sent several checks to the Communist Party District Headquarters in Minneapolis, Minnesota. Irene Paul, who is reported to be the feature columnist of this newspaper, is also reported to be a Communist. With regard to the "Midwest Labor," it is said that the publication follows the Communist Party line.

[*100-135-44*]

Salt Lake City Field Division

A survey concerning the Negro problem in the States of Utah and Nevada fails to reflect foreign inspired agitation or dissemination or propaganda tending to create racial disunity. The following organizations are stated to be active in the State of Utah: National Association for the Advancement of Colored People; five churches; two Masonic Lodges; one Order of the Eastern Star, one Elks Lodge and a woman's auxiliary; one Odd Fellows Lodge; three Negro social clubs; and three A. F. of L. affiliated labor groups. Formerly two branches of the National Negro Congress, a Communist front organization, were active in Salt Lake City and in Ogden, Utah. The organizer of these branches is reported to have been D. N. Oliver, a Negro attorney in Salt Lake City who is alleged to be Communistically inclined. Approximately 100 Negroes were affiliated with the organization while it was active.

Census statistics for the State of Utah indicated a population of 1,200 Negroes, making a percentage of approximately 0.2 of the entire population. The more popular Negro newspapers and publications in this area are stated to be the Kansas City Call, the Chicago Defender, the Pittsburgh Courier, and the Crisis.

In the State of Nevada there has recently been an influx of approximately 2,000 Negroes into Las Vegas, Nevada as a result of increased employment at the Basic Magnesium, Incorporated plant located there. Approximately 1,100 male Negroes are employed as common laborers. During the past two months in Las Vegas it is stated that two minor race riots occurred, which were immediately quelled by the Police Department in Las Vegas without serious difficulties. Housing and sanitary conditions among the Negroes residing in Las Vegas are said to be extremely poor, while it is reported that there are no recreational facilities whatsoever. It is also stated that there are insufficient accommodations in the line of food service and residences.

It is reported that the personnel problem at the Basic Magnesium, Incorporated plant is stated to be somewhat serious and conditions are reported as becoming acute with regard to the Negro problem. It is stated that a Reverend C. C. Cox in Las Vegas, Nevada, has been instrumental in creating serious agitation among the Negroes in an effort to arouse them in an attempt to obtain what he considers their rights.

In the City of Reno, Nevada, it is reported that no information has been received of propaganda issued in an attempt to create dissemination or unrest among the Negroes. It is said that the Negroes in and around Reno are of the transient type. Here

Negroes are said to subscribe to newspapers originating in Pittsburgh and Kansas City.

Active among the Negroes in this area is the Negro Political Science Group. No indications have been reported that this organization has attempted to issue propaganda or literature attempting to create racial disunity. In this regard it is reported that the white people in and around Reno have aided the Negroes considerably in an attempt to better their conditions and have assisted in erecting a Negro church. [*100-135-45*]

It has been reported that during recent months the City of Ogden, Utah has been the scene of a number of skirmishes between the local police department and Negro soldiers. This trouble has occurred in the vicinity of 25th Street where there are approximately three blocks of hotels and bars reportedly frequented by Negroes and the lower class of white people. The incidents are said to have been the result of Negro soldiers who have arrived in this city having no recreational facilities, and, consequently, it is said that when they patronize white establishments, they are not always cordially received by either the patrons or the management. No indications have been reported of any subversive forces causing any of these situations involving racial trouble. A source of information has stated, however, that he believes the cause to be a result of the City of Ogden not being equipped to handle the large number of Negroes which the United States Army has stationed nearby, Ogden having a small colored population. It has also been pointed out by this source of information that a number of Negroes have migrated to this area to work for private contractors. These people also demand places of recreation and places to live. They have generally added to the congestion.

Sioux Falls Field Division

In the area covered by the Sioux Falls Field Division, which includes the Dakotas, approximately 675 Negroes reside. A large percentage of the Negroes reside in rural communities and are engaged in farming.

Inquiries made and sources of information contacted fail to reflect un-American activity or agitation among the Negroes in this area. One instance, however, has been reported in the form of nonspecific information to the effect that an unknown and unidentified white man spoke to the brother-in-law of the leader among the colored race in Sioux Falls, South Dakota, advising that he could see no reason why the Negroes should participate in the war efforts of the country in view of the fact that he, the unknown white man, was at a loss to understand any benefits the Negroes would receive from their efforts to help the white race in the present war. The source of information advised that his brother-in-law angrily terminated the conversation with the unknown white individual and because of his anger could not furnish specific information.

There are no Negro newspaper[s] published in the States of North and South

Dakota but there are circulated there Negro papers published in Eastern cities such as Pittsburgh, Chicago and New York.

Active in Sioux Falls is the Twentieth Century Club which is operated by a Negro named James Lee and is frequented by Negro porters and waitresses employed on pullman cars in the vicinity. A source of information has advised with respect to this club that he has never heard any reports of possible agitation among his race there.

V

PACIFIC COAST SECTION OF THE UNITED STATES

This section, for the purpose of this study, includes the States of Washington, Oregon and California.

Prior to the advent of the national defense and war effort, the Negro population in these three States was comparatively small. However, with the war demand for labor, especially in the shipyards located on the West Coast, large numbers of Negroes have migrated there from other sections of the country. In this connection, some manufacturing concerns have imported Negro personnel.

As a result of the increased Negro population, this section of the United States is believed to be comparable on a smaller scale to the Northern section of this country. Similar shortages in living accommodations are reported to exist, as well as in opportunities and places for recreation and amusement.

A number of clashes and fights between Negroes and whites, both civilians and military personnel, have occurred in this area. In this connection, there are a large number of mixed military and naval personnel in the area, all of which has added to the congestion already augmented by the civilians who have recently migrated to this section for war work. It is believed that this was one of the factors in the "Zoot Suit" situation in Los Angeles, California, which reached a climax in early June 1943. Although this primarily involved Mexican-Americans and white servicemen, it is reported that a number of Negroes figured in the affair. The trouble which has occurred, including the "Zoot Suit" situation, has not reflected any planned or organized activity responsible for its occurrence. However, it is indicative of unrest and tension.

Prior to December 7, 1941, a large number of Japanese, both foreign born and American born, resided in this section of the country. However, no indications of recent Japanese or pro-Japanese exploitation of the Negro inhabitants of this area have been evidenced. Likewise, no reports have been received of anti-white and pro-Japanese groups or cults having existed in this area within recent years.

By far the most active group or organization which attempts to influence the Negro population in this area is the Communist Party which, according to reports, is exceedingly active in attempting to obtain Negro recruits and to allegedly advance the cause of Negroes.

Perhaps the most outstanding economic and social grievances which have been expressed in this section of the country by Negroes individually and collectively have been alleged discrimination against them in industry and the lack of adequate housing and recreational facilities. With further regard to industry, it is reported that the practice of establishing segregated union locals for Negroes, especially in the shipyards, in this area has resulted in unrest and dissatisfaction. This practice has been the subject of widespread criticism by Negro groups and organizations and by the Negro press. The criticism has not merely been confined to the West Coast area, but rather has been made throughout the country. The Communist Party, it is to be noted, has been particularly interested in this matter and has devoted much time and activity to it.

There follow digests of information received by the Field Divisions of the Federal Bureau of Investigation located in this West Coast section of the United States.

Los Angeles Field Division

In this area it is reported that the majority of agitation among the Negroes by outside sources is that of the Communist Party. In its agitation the Party lays emphasis on alleged discrimination, segregation, and social inequality, at the same time, promising to remedy these "evils". At the present time, the recruiting of Negro individuals for party membership, is one of the main concentration points. It is reported that approximately fifty-four Negroes registered as Communist Party members in Los Angeles County, as of March 16, 1942. As further reflecting the Communist Party interests in activity among the Negroes, it is reported that Pettis Perry, a Negro, has established a Communist Party Branch Office in the Negro district in Los Angeles, California. It is further reported that the Young Communist League plans to open a social center located in the Negro section in Los Angeles with Lou Rosser, Negro Communist Party member, as suggested director. As of further indication of Communist Party activity among the Negroes in this area, it is reported that Pettis Perry, referred to previously, taught a course in the Los Angeles Workers School entitled "The Negro Question". Through the media of party literature and party sponsored meetings, constant appeals are made to the Negroes as well as many instances of segregation, discrimination, and violation of Negro rights. Among the leaflets and literature distributed among the colored section are: "The Communist Party of the United States of America", by Earl Browder; "The Communist Manifesto", by Karl Marx and Frederick Engels; "Thaddeus Stevens, Militant Democrat and Fighter for Negro Rights", by Elizabeth Lawson; "Negroes and the National War Effort", and an address by Frederick Douglass; "The Negroes' Stake in This War", by Pettis Perry.

During the period July 14, to July 19, 1942, the National Association for the Advancement of Colored People, held its 33rd annual conference at the 2nd Baptist Church, 2412 Griffith Avenue, Los Angeles, California. The theme of this conference was the "Fight Against Segregation" and "Discrimination and the Demand for Equal Rights". Militant speeches are stated to have been made pointing out these matters. Several instances of Communist Party activity at this conference have been reported, especially with respect to the local branch in Los Angeles of the National Association for the Advancement of Colored People.

In various issues of the Communist West Coast newspaper, the People's World, from June 11 to July 15, 1942 there appeared approximately sixty-four articles dealing exclusively with the Negro question and its various stages including "Jim Crowism", discrimination, segregation and social inequality. A very lengthy coverage in the form of many articles was had of the conference of the National Association for the Advancement of Colored People and all People's World readers were urged to follow the writers coverage of the section where, it was stated, a vast section of negro-Americans would shape the policies for the most effective participation in the struggle "for the defeat of Hitlerism".

The three leading Negro newspapers in the Los Angeles area are the "California Eagle," whose editor is Charlotta Bass, the "Los Angeles Sentinel," editor, Leon H. Washington, Jr., and the "Neighborhood News," editor, M. Erwing, all of which are described as subscribing to the flamboyant type of news reporting and each of which makes much to do about the reporting of incidents of discrimination against Negroes and social inequality of the Negroes. With regard to Mrs. Charlotta Bass, it is reported that the "People's World" has complimented her on various occasions, even going so far as to reprint an article from her editorial column in their own editorial column. It is further noted that in the columns of the "California Eagle," in the issue of July 9, 1942, a three column article describes the Festus Coleman case, in which the Communist Party has interested itself and as a result of its interests, has set up a Festus Coleman Defense Committee, the membership of which has several Communists. It was ascertained in December, 1942 that Charlotta Bass sought aid of Pettis Perry and Carl Winter, Communist Party functionaries, to help her in the management of the "California Eagle." Carl Winter, who is Los Angeles Secretary of the Communist Party, stated with respect to this request that the Party expected the "California Eagle" to play a role in its behalf in the future and, further, that Charlotta Bass would not last many years longer, and the Party should see that an individual favorable to it obtained control of the paper. It has been further reported that the Communist Party through its organizers has sold and distributed copies of the "California Eagle," and on March 11, 1943 Carl Winter reportedly visited Charlotta Bass at her office, allegedly for the purpose of discussing the placement of a Party member in the business office of the "California Eagle." It is said that they succeeded in putting a Negro, Robert S. Robinson, in the office of this newspaper as circulation manager. It is to be noted that Robinson joined the Communist Party in 1937 under the name of Bob Roberts and became a member of the professional section.

It was also reported in April, 1943 that Party functionaries discussed the possibility of taking over the operation of the "California Eagle," and was apparently ready to invest two or three thousand dollars in order to get control of it. It was said that the Party did not desire a staff which would impede the then present editorial policy of Charlotta Bass of fighting discrimination and social inequality but did desire one which would carry out her policy more effectively than was the case at the time.

The other Negro newspapers in Los Angeles, the "Los Angeles Sentinel," the "Los Angeles Tribune," and the "Neighborhood News," have not recently shown Communist tendencies in their articles, although in 1942 the "Los Angeles Sentinel," published by Leon H. Washington, Jr., is said to have carried editorials and articles favorable to the cause of the Communist Party and, further, to have carried an advertisement by the Party asking people to attend the summer session of the Workers' School. The "Sentinel" and the "Tribune" are said to continue an attack on businessmen and war industries for the purpose of having Negroes in these concerns employed in the same capacity as white people.

With regard to the recruiting campaign of the Communist Party among the Negro population in the Los Angeles area during the period February 12, 1943 through May 2, 1943, it is reported that one hundred fifteen Negroes were recruited. It is said that the quota had originally been set at sixty, and consequently, Party officials were elated over the fact that they had achieved one hundred ninety-two per cent of the total.

As a means of furthering its agitational program among the Negroes, it is reported that Party officials have recently concerned themselves with the Boilermakers' International Union, AF of L, operating in the shipyards in the Los Angeles harbor. This organization will not accept Negroes in the full membership of the union, but rather has set up an auxiliary union for Negroes. This auxiliary has been attacked by the Party as discriminatory.

It was reported in April, 1943 that racial trouble appeared imminent in several industrial plants in the Los Angeles area, particularly in the California Shipbuilding Corporation, the Western Pipe and Steel Company and the Bethlehem Shipbuilding Corporation. Negroes at the first two named plants were reportedly showing up for work with guns and liquor concealed in their clothing. It has been stated that a part of the difficulty appears to be that the Negroes insist that they be allowed to join regular unions rather than auxiliary unions. It was also said that there have been indications of a movement to establish an independent Negro union, possibly to be called the "Jim Crow Union." This action in turn was allegedly objected to by the regular unions. Instances have been cited wherein quarrels took place between white and Negro employees at time clocks and pay windows. A source of information has alleged that much of the agitation could be attributed to the Communist Party.

With reference to possible Japanese agitation among the American Negroes in this area, a source contacted advised of no definitely known Japanese inspired agitation. A Negro source of information in this area, has advised that in this opinion the Japanese and Negroes have never mixed, the Japanese placing a definite barrier between the two groups. It is advised that the Japanese are looked upon by the Negroes here as being snobbish and aloof.

Another source, who is Japanese, whose reliability is believed to be good, has advised that he has heard of no attempt made by the Japanese to influence the Negroes in this area.

A Negro who has been interviewed and who is stated to have lived among the Japanese for many years has advised of his association with Japanese-American citizens for the past thirteen years and of his being approached at one time to become a Buddhist priest. This source of information has advised that the Negroes and Japanese have never been friendly in the City of Los Angeles, the Japanese appearing to be prejudiced to them as a race. On rare occasions, he stated that he has heard Japanese make casual remarks to him to the effect that Negroes were being ill treated as a minority group. On the other hand, he has stated that he does not in any way feel that the Japanese have attempted to influence the Negroes in this area, either politically or otherwise.

Several Japanese-American citizens and Japanese aliens have been interviewed and these individuals have advised of no activity to their knowledge of attempt being made to influence Negroes by Japanese. One has advised that there was a distinct color line drawn by the Japanese against the Negroes. Several have recalled instances where the Japanese and Negroes were mingled in connection with YMCA work and that attempts had been made to bring Japanese and Negroes closer together in this work. However, he has stated that these attempts were not successful because of the reluctance of the Japanese YMCA officials and members to cooperate with the Negroes. Another source, a Negro, has advised of an incident coming to his attention of a Japanese individual marrying a Negress, and after the marriage having a life among the Negroes in Los Angeles, apparently being looked down upon by the Japanese colony because of his marriage.

Several Negro sources of information have advised that they have no knowledge of any Japanese influence among the Negroes in this area. They have also advised that the two races did not mingle closely in business, citing as an example, attempts by Japanese pedlars to sell their wares in a Negro community but being refused patronage by the Negro population in the particular area involved. Another source has advised that the Japanese have always adopted a very snobbish attitude toward the Negroes and have never mingled with them socially. This source has stated that the average Negro had no affection for the Japanese in Los Angeles and territory surrounding. He blamed the unrest and the situation of dissatisfaction largely on labor unions, stating that he realized the Government was gradually improving conditions among the Negroes, and were constantly giving them more opportunities to serve the United States. It was the further opinion of this individual that any attempt by the Japanese to create agitation among the American Negroes would meet with little response, and he felt that if such a movement was begun he would undoubtedly know about it.

Mexican Youth Gangs ("Zoot Suiters")

In view of the allegations which have been received as well as the number of references made in the press that there has been social intercourse between Negro youths and youths of Mexican-American nationality in the Los Angeles area, there is incorporated hereinafter information relative to trouble and fights between servicemen and, particularly, Mexican-American youths in this area during the latter part of May, 1943, and the first week of June, 1943. There is also incorporated certain background information which has been reported as bearing some weight on the situation.

At the outset it is to be noted that numerous charges and allegations, mainly from Communist forces, have been made that the fifth column or the Sinarquista (alleged to be Fascist and subversive by the accusers) were responsible for much of the trouble. There were also allegations that police brutalities in the past, as well as at the time of the trouble, had a part in the picture. However, in no instance has any specific evidence or substantiating information been offered or received to this effect.

The pertinent information as it has been reported is incorporated herein.

The fad of wearing zoot suits by the Mexican and Negro youths in the Los Angeles area has developed during the past two years. They have congregated in pool halls, dance halls, drug stores, theaters and other meeting places, and have organized into groups or gangs. That the Mexican youths have created a serious problem in the Los Angeles area from a social and rehabilitation standpoint is, of course, well recognized, and during the course of the inquiries on the part of the police and various committees in Los Angeles it has been brought out that the police facilities have not been sufficient to cope with the problem. Numerous crimes of physical violence, robbery, and even murder have been attributed to these Mexicans, although no specific information as to the extent of these crimes has been received.

These early troubles with the Mexican youths and Mexican youth groups did not involve servicemen, and their occurrences were not sufficiently frequent to merit national publicity. An exception, however, was the so-called "Sleepy Lagoon Murder Case," which will be referred to briefly hereafter.

Reference is made to a committee which was appointed in January 1943, by the Juvenile Court in Los Angeles. This committee made various recommendations to be used in an effort to stamp out what was termed the "Gang war menace." It was suggested that gang members over eighteen years of age be prosecuted for contributing to the delinquency of minors in the gangs; that a county junior forestry camp be established to rehabilitate delinquent boys of thirteen and fourteen years of age; that truancy details be established by the Los Angeles Police Department and by school districts to enforce school attendance, and that training schools be established with sufficient equipment and leadership to train and place these young people in proper occupations. This committee found that there were approximately thirty gangs of youths of Latin-American descent with seven hundred and fifty boys under eighteen years of age as members of the gangs.

In August, 1942, a fight and riot occurred at a Mexican dance hall in which one individual was killed, while others were seriously cut and injured. In October, 1942, twenty-two Mexican youths were arrested and implicated in the riot, and on January 12, 1943, seventeen of the original twenty-two were convicted of felony charges ranging from assault to murder. The convictions of these seventeen defendants have been appealed and the appeal is pending.

Reference is here made to the fact that shortly after the apprehension of the twenty-two youths implicated in the murder, a Communist front organization was created known as the Citizens Committee for the Defense of Mexican-American Youth. This Committee will be referred to more fully later.

In 1942 there reportedly took place isolated attacks by various gangs upon soldiers and sailors. Many of these were ordinary incidents provoked by arguments between members of the Armed Forces and the "zoot suiters." The activities of these gangs continued to increase, although little national publicity resulted. However, in May of 1943 the activities of these gangs became so widespread and violent that the national press began to cover the matter. During the week ending May 25, 1943, three bands of Mexican youths attacked, beat up and stripped four people in the metropolitan area of Los Angeles. These four were civilians. Two had parked their automobile for a few minutes and were soon surrounded by eight Mexicans who attacked them when they got out of the car and cut them with razors. Another, a 16-year-old boy, was attacked by twenty to twenty-five youths, while another, aged 17, was suddenly attacked by a group who inflicted deep cuts on his back with razors.

During May other cases were reported of wives of Navy men being robbed and raped by "zoot suiters" and there were also reports of alleged unprovoked attacks by these "zoot suiters" on lone servicemen. Two servicemen were in hospitals near death, and several others were hospitalized as a result of the attacks.

Early in June, 1943, groups of servicemen got together and retaliated with attacks on groups of "zoot suiters" wherever they found them. The press immediately took up the matter and for six days carried it in the headlines. It was alleged that during these six days in early June, 112 individuals were hospitalized, 150 others had been hurt, and 114 had been arrested. Of the 112 treated at hospitals, 94 were civilians while 18 were servicemen. On June 8, 1943, following some attacks made on sailors by Mexican youths, servicemen in the Los Angeles area organized in large groups to search for Mexican youth gangs. Numerous individual and gang fights occurred which were, however, quickly suppressed by local authorities and the Shore Patrol. The practice followed by the servicemen was to attack the "zoot suiters" with weighted ropes or clubs and to beat the "zoot suiters" and tear their clothes off.

A confidential source has advised of remarks made by members of these gangs who reportedly feel that the servicemen are persecuting them because they are Mexicans and because they are wearing zoot suits. They admit that there are criminal elements among them, but claim that there are also criminal elements among all groups. They feel justified in repelling the attacks made upon them by the servicemen and appear to have the intention of continually resisting these attacks.

It is noted further that the Communist press and individuals who have interested themselves in this problem who have been found to possess "radical" connections, have always linked the Mexicans and Negroes together in discussing this situation, and it is observed further that in almost all instances, the riots were referred to as "race riots." Attention is called here to a report which has recently been prepared by a Communist front organization known as the Los Angeles Committee for American Unity. This report was submitted to a Citizens Committee which was appointed by Governor Earl Warren to inquire into the zoot suit situation. This report alleges that the riots are not the result of a crime wave of the zoot suit gangsters, and states that the number and severity of the crimes committe[d] have been grossly exaggerated and that proof is lacking that the crimes charged to this group were actually committed by them. This Committee further stated that the press was responsible for attaching a criminal character to the wearer of a zoot suit, and further, they charge that the police have discriminated against Mexican-American youth and are extending their discrimination to other minority groups, particularly the Negroes. This report also pointed out that attacks had been made upon Mexican-American youths even though they wore no zoot suits, and similarly, attacks were made in two instances on Negroes who were not wearing zoot suits.

The following reports have been received concerning the Selective Service status of members of these gangs. It is said there are approximately 45,000 Mexican children of school age in Los Angeles, and during the past year 1,400 have been arrested for various offenses. The zoot suit group ranges in age from 16 to 20. He stated that at least 60 per cent of these persons are between the ages of 16 and 18, and of the remaining 40 per cent nearly all have been rejected by the Army at the time of induction or have been discharged after induction. All of the individuals arrested by the Los Angeles Police Department over the age of 18 are checked out under the Selective Service.

Newspaper items have indicated that the reason is because of criminal records against these persons. Contact was had with the medical officer in charge of the largest local induction station, and it was his opinion that Mexicans do not show a higher rate of rejections than other nationalities; most of the rejections among this class being the result of poor health standards or low mental conditions. He pointed out the prevalence of tuberculosis among this group, together with a rather high percentage of poor education, both being the result of their low standard of living. He does not believe that there is any higher percentage of rejections because of criminal records among the Mexicans than in any other nationality group. He pointed out that at the time of induction many times an inductee is rejected if it is shown he has a single conviction of a heinous crime such as rape, sodomy, arson, narcotics or any crime pertaining to sex perversion. He stated anyone who appears to be an habitual criminal would be rejected at the induction station.

It has been confidentially reported that it was pointed out to the Mayor of Los Angeles and a committee accompanying the Mayor by an Army official that most of these Mexican youths are not fit material for the Army because of physical disabilities or criminal records, and he felt this matter is a local social problem and not one to be shoved off on the Army.

It has been further reported the majority of the Mexican youths between 18 and 20 not now in the Army have been rejected either by the induction station or by the Army after induction, or have been classed 4-F by their local board, this classification being for physical, mental or moral reasons. He pointed out that recently local draft boards have adopted a much more liberal attitude towards the classification of these Mexican youths and have been ordering a larger portion of them to report for induction; that even though they are so ordered, many of them are not acceptable to the Army.

There were no indications reported that an unusually large percentage of 4-F classifications or rejections are being given to Mexican youths because of prior criminal records.

Previous reference was made to the fact that the Citizens Committee for the Defense of Mexican-American Youth was created by the Communist Party in the Los Angeles area shortly after the apprehension of the twenty-two youths involved in the "Sleepy Lagoon Murder Case." The Los Angeles reports on this Committee indicate quite definitely that it is a Communist front. It was organized following a conference of known Communist leaders in the Los Angeles area including Carl Winter, Executive Secretary of the Communist Party, U.S.A., for Los Angeles County, LaRue McCormick, a Communist Party member, who was a candidate for

State Senator on the Communist Party ticket, and Josephina Fierro Bright, who is also a Communist. This organization had for its ostensible purpose the raising of funds for the defense of the twenty-two Mexican youths originally arrested. This organization engaged in extensive activities which, in addition to organizing a defense of these Mexican youths, also served to gain for the Communist Party a large Mexican following. At the time the Citizens Committee was organized, LaRue McCormick was a candidate for public office on the Communist Party ticket, and it was hoped by the Communist Party that the activities of the Citizens Committee would serve to bring a large number of Mexican votes for her candidacy and that through this means it would be possible to recruit new Communist Party members from the Mexican minority.

The activities of the Citizens Committee consisted principally of distributing literature, holding public meetings and sponsoring radio addresses charging that the defendants had not obtained a fair trial and that the police had used force in handling the defendants. The public meetings stressed the minority's question and made the issue a racial one and followed the organizational and propaganda methods frequently employed by the Communist Party in similar causes such as the cases involving the Scottsboro Boys, Angelo Herndon, Harry Bridges and Earl Browder.

The Los Angeles Committee for American Unity was formed on June 11, 1943, in Los Angeles for the specific purpose of bringing influence to bear upon the Mexican problem recently made acute by gang warfare. It has been set up with the view of its being a permanent anti-discrimination committee. Many of the individuals active in this committee are also members of the Citizens Committee for the Defense of Mexican-American Youth.

The Los Angeles Office has advised that the organizational meeting of this group was held in Los Angeles on June 11, 1943, and the purpose of the Committee, as expressed by Carey McWilliams, West Coast attorney, who played an active role in the committee previously referred to, was to create a public committee not dominated by Government control so as to bring the basic Mexican problem out before the public. The initiative at this opening meeting was taken by Clore Warne, an attorney who has long been affiliated with Communist Party activities on the West Coast.

At this meeting, mention was made of an agreement made with the local Mexican Consul to exchange affidavits supporting charges made by the "zoot suit boys" against the servicemen and private citizens. It was also mentioned that Philip M. Connelly of the State CIO was also present at this meeting.

A highly confidential source has made available a copy of a ten-page, typewritten report dated June 11, 1943, prepared on behalf of the subject organization. It was contemplated that this report would be filed with Robert W. Kenny for consideration by the committee appointed by Governor Earl Warren to investigate the "zoot suit" disturbances. This report appears to have been executed by Harry Braverman, who in September 1939 was a member of the Communist Party.

There follows an excerpt of this report reflecting the points emphasized by the committee and the conclusions which it feels should be reached by the Governor's committee:

"This communication is addressed to you for presentation to and consideration by the Committee appointed by Governor Earl Warren to consider and report on the riots and disorder recently occurring and presently existing in Los Angeles County. It is submitted on behalf of the Los Angeles Committee for American Unity, a local voluntary group representative of the community including the two racial groups directly the victims of such rioting. Our Committee has investigated in part and considered the causes of the current outbreaks and the occurrences of the past few days and is continuing its work. We feel that there are certain fundamental underlying reasons for the mob violence which occurred and which your report should reflect. Likewise, there are certain facts which your Committee should find to have been immediately provocative of and causes for the outbreaks, rioting, and disorder which occurred."

The report then charged that the number and severity of the crimes said to have been committed by the "zoot suit" gangsters were grossly exaggerated, and proof in many instances was lacking that they actually committed the crimes. It condemns the press as being responsible for the public's willingness to attach a criminal character to the wearing of a "zoot suit." It charges that police discrimination existed.

This same report then sets out what is believed by the committee to be the conclusions which should be reached by the Governor's committee:

1. The riots resulted from the conduct of the press and police—not from any actual or fictitious crime wave among gangsters wearing "zoot suits."
2. The civil and military police failed entirely to take necessary action.
3. The press not only laid the basis for the riots, but caused them to continue.
4. High military and naval officers and high civil authorities were dilatory in their duties.
5. The outbreaks were not sporadic, but well organized with specific objectives and plan.
6. The definite indication of possible fifth column activity back of these disturbances requires the fullest investigation.
7. Great damage already has been done to the war effort and general morale, particularly among minority groups.
8. The Axis have been given [a] new weapon against Unity of United Nations. The Good Neighbor Policy has been struck a severe blow. The position of the United States in relation to colored people throughout the world has been prejudiced.
9. The fight against discrimination throughout the land has been seriously damaged. It is necessary to redouble efforts to eliminate racial discrimination and move in [the] direction of American unity.

The report concluded with a request for open public hearings in order that the individuals and groups responsible might be ferreted out. A Grand Jury investigation was requested so that indictments could be presented against those responsible, and a

Federal investigation was believed essential, according to the report, in view of the national and international complications.

Portland Field Division

In the City of Portland, according to the 1940 census, there resided approximately 2,500 Negroes, and information received from various informants and prominent Negroes in that area fails to disclose un-American or subversive elements other than the Communist Party working among them. The Negroes in that area are striving to obviate racial discrimination through their membership in local branches of the National Association for the Advancement of Colored People. Sources of information contacted in that area advise that no inroads were made among the Negro population by the Japanese.

With regard to the Communist Party in that area, it is reported that subtle attempts have been made to obtain Negro members but that information received reflects that the Negroes exhibit a disapproval of the Communist Party.

The Communist Party activity among Negroes in this area has reportedly not resulted in so much the obtaining of added membership from the ranks of the Negroes, but rather has been devoted to pointing out alleged instances of discrimination and segregation and demanding the abolition of alleged instances of the denial of equal rights to Negroes.

Indications have been reported that Negroes in this area feel some discrimination but as a whole are loyal to the United States. A source of information, who is a Negro attorney and president of an active Negro organization in Portland, Oregon, has pointed out that discrimination against the Negro in such a form as refusal to employ them in the national defense industry gives rise to a potentiality of unrest and trouble among the Negroes.

It has been said by a source of information, a Negro minister, in his opinion the only connections the Negroes in this area have had with members of the Japanese race have been in Japanese hotels where Negroes are said to have been permitted to sleep, at the same time being disallowed in white hotels. Since the declaration of war on Japan, however, Negroes are said to have taken over the hotels formerly operated by the Japanese in this area and are now operating them.

Recently, approximately 1,200 Negroes have come into the Portland area from the East to obtain employment in defense industries. This, of course, has led to some labor disputes and several union locals have been charged with flagrant discrimination. This is said to be discouraging and damaging to the morale of Negroes in this area. It is said that because of their inability to obtain admittance into some of the local unions, Negroes at times are called to military duty and are required to offer their lives in their country's service. It has been expressed by at least one Negro source of information that this gives the impression to Negroes that they do not have anything for which to fight. It has been charged, too, in this connection, that representatives of industry in the

Portland area have gone to the East and allegedly made false promises, luring Negroes away from their homes with promises of high wages. When the Negroes then arrived at the West Coast, it is said that they have had to accept unskilled employment and consequently lower wages. This situation is said to be the result of the inability of the other representatives to "claim them as skilled laborers."

On November 1, 1942, there was held in Portland, Oregon, an open forum sponsored by the National Association for the Advancement of Colored People. Roy Wilkins, Assistant Secretary of this organization and Editor of "The Crisis" magazine, its newspaper, gave an address which was entitled "The Negro and Democracy." A mixed group of approximately 250 persons were in attendance, half of which were colored. Wilkins is said to have pointed out that the Negro is the largest minority in this country and that because of his coloring, matters have been complicated. It is said that a Negro is easily visible because of his characteristics and for that reason stands out when he allegedly oversteps the social barriers placed against him. Wilkins then said there are direct consequences. Then it is said that the war has entered the picture and attention has been focused on the Negro. He is now working as a typist or as a clerk in a drugstore, which work previous to the war did not exist.

In his speech Wilkins then dealt with the Kaiser Shipbuilding Yards situation as it involved Negroes and attacked Thomas Ray, leader of the Boilermakers Union in that area. In this connection, the following is quoted from his speech which is believed to be significant in showing the attitude of many Negroes in this country, not only in the Portland area but elsewhere:

> "Tommy Ray has said that they cannot let the colored man work with the white. Everything that he is doing in this line is damaging the war effort. Who can say that the colored man is not skillful and cannot work with machines? The sense to this is given by a war correspondent in Africa. This correspondent said that in a renovated warehouse in Africa they are turning out ammunition. Who is turning out this ammunition? Native Africans three weeks out of the brush are making shells and bullets. Why, then, are our boys here who are graduates of schools told that they cannot run them? If you cannot get a job this influences your attitude toward the war. This creates a rage and frustration of the treatment of Negroes in the Armed Forces. All of our people, black or white, have been affected by the Selective Service. It does not matter whether a mother is black or white if her boy is in the Army. Every mother, father and relative should want every person to have those rights which they are entitled to as American citizens. For the Negro boys, what do we have? In some sections of the country the Negro is not a soldier in uniform, but is only another man. In some sections of your own cities right here in Oregon if he walks into a restaurant and asks for a cup of coffee he is refused because they do not serve colored people. This happens in Spokane, Seattle and Portland. This is helping the Axis. Also in the Army their activities have been restricted. One bright spot in the Army is being an officer. The Army has a private white regiment and a private colored regiment. Joe Louis joined the Army. Joe Louis found himself in with the white troops, but some

Army officer called attention to the fact and dragged Louis out of the line and put him with the colored boys."

In connection with the labor union activities at the Kaiser Shipbuilding Yards in Portland, it is to be recalled that a separate union was established under the direction of Thomas Ray, head of Local No. 72 of the International Brotherhood of Boilermakers, Ironworkers, Shipbuilders, Welders and Helpers of America, A. F. of L., for Negro membership. This action was made the national issue by the Communist press and was attacked by Negro newspapers as well as "PM". In Portland, however, the Communist Party issued instructions that the Negro question, especially in connection with the Kaiser Shipyards, should not be "tampered with." These instructions were issued, according to informants, in view of the jurisdictional labor dispute between the American Federation of Labor and the Congress of Industrial Organizations. It was suggested that an overall broad policy was not desired with respect to the Negro question since the Communist Party in this area desired to wait for the decision in the jurisdictional dispute, the feeling being that CIO unions would not tolerate separate or "Jim Crow" locals for Negroes. The jurisdictional dispute arose out of the contract between the A. F. of L. and the Kaiser Shipbuilding Yards for bargaining rights. The CIO attempted to obtain through the National Labor Relations Board the right to also engage in organizational activities at this company. The Party did not direct activities toward this situation but it has attacked the system of establishing separate local unions for Negroes. Inasmuch as the dispute between A. F. of L. and the CIO has not as yet been decided, it was suggested that the Party will continue to follow this procedure.

While the Communist Party could not agitate over the separate locals directly, a group of what was reported to be 200 Negroes under the leadership of Paradis Santiago Rodriquez formed what was known as the Negro Shipyard Workers Victory Council. Rodriquez was subsequently elected President. It is to be noted he, along with the Vice President, Walter Carrington, is reported to have connections with the Communist Party. The purpose of the group was to organize Negroes to fight for equal rights for membership in the Boilermakers Union.

There have been recent reports of considerable unrest among the Negroes in the Portland area, especially those who have come from the East to work in the various shipyards there. Clashes in the various housing developments and residential quarters of workers have been occurring not only between white and Negroes but among the Negroes themselves. It has been pointed out that gambling and drinking occur in these quarters, both of which are barred by company regulations. A confidential and reliable source of information has pointed out that unless gambling is curbed at the shipyards serious racial disturbances among the workers will break out.

San Diego Field Division

Inquiries made in this area for agitation, unrest or dissatisfaction caused by pro-Axis activity among the Negroes have met with negative results. However, the San Diego County Communist Party has for many years endeavored to interest San Diego Negroes in joining the Communist Party. It has continually agitated against discrimination against the Negro, "Jim Crowism", alleged denial of equal rights, and other matters concerning the Negro, through the Peoples World, generally considered the Communist Press on the West Coast. The Communist Party has also endeavored to infiltrate Negro groups at the National Association for the Advancement of Colored People and the Allied Organizations Committee. However, these attempts are said to have met with practically no success.

Outside of church and religious organizations, the National Association for the Advancement of Colored People is the largest and most important group in San Diego representing the Negro people. As part of the Communist program of infiltrating this organization, **Robert R. Warren** and his wife, **Vera,** joined the organization. It should be stated that the **Warrens,** particularly **Vera Warren,** are prominent leaders in the San Diego Communist Party and are of the white race. At the time, the San Diego Party contained only two or three Negro members. Most of the propaganda work—infiltration is handled by white members.

As an example of Communists maneuvers relative to Negroes, and especially to the National Association for the Advancement of Colored People, leaders of the National Association for the Advancement of Colored People were persuaded to call a meeting of its members at the house of the pastor of one of the negro churches which would be addressed by some of their white friends on subjects of "vital importance" to the colored people. The meeting was arranged for May 1, 1941. The carefully laid plans of the Party, were reportedly frustrated inasmuch as some of the alert members of the National Association for the Advancement of Colored People are said to have ascertained the identity of the individuals wishing to address this group. Several days before the date set for the meeting a group of the organization prevented the meeting and when **Pettis Perry,** active Negro Communist in the Los Angeles, California area, arrived at the meeting place, he found but one individual present who was the pastor. He is said to have assured him in no uncertain terms that there would be no meeting there that night, that the Negro people were fully well able to decide for themselves what action they should take in matters affecting them. He is reported to have said that they needed no aid from people who felt that secret meetings were the way to solve problems of the Negro people. The **Warrens** who had accompanied **Pettis Perry** protested, but to no avail and the group of Party members and sympathizers departed.

At the present time the Communist Party is said to be exerting every effort to organize and recruit the Negro population. In addition to the "discrimination" propaganda being indulged in as a means of recruiting, the Party is and has been for some time championing the cause of a Negro, one **Festus Coleman** who was sentenced to 65 years in San Quentin Penitentiary on charges of rape and robbery. The Communist

Party is said to have resorted to its usual tactics in maintaining that **Coleman** was "railroaded" for a crime that he did not commit.

In November of 1941 a meeting was called by Robert Warren; Reverend W. L. Harris who is said to have Communist connections and who is pastor of the Calvary Baptist Church, 1901 Julian Avenue, San Diego, California; Guy T. Nunn, a field representative of the Minority Groups Unit, Labor Division of the Office of Production Management; C. D. Jolly, head of the San Diego Branch of the National Association for the Advancement of Colored People; and Rebecca Kraft, President of the Women's Civic League in San Diego, at Mrs. Kraft's home. Nunn is said to have explained the procedure in fighting racial discrimination and a movement was started to institute a procedure whereby anti-discrimination measures could be taken. Jolly and Mrs. Kraft took charge of the movement while the Communist representatives were left in the background. This is another example of how the Communists attempted to gain control in Negro movements but failed in this particular area.

Allied Organizations Committee

In the Fall of 1941, an organization known as the Allied Organizations Committee was formed and many prominent Negroes in that area were obtained as sponsors. However, among them were several individuals said to have radical connections. The organization continued having meetings and dealt with matters affecting the Negroes, especially discrimination. At one meeting of the organization, on January 9, 1942, Reverend Harris, referred to previously, brought up the matter of the **Festus Coleman** case and suggested a mass meeting. However, he did not gain favor and the procedure used by the National Association for the Advancement of Colored People in defending Negroes in trouble was adopted. Again Reverend Harris attempted to bring up the matter of having Paul Robeson sing in San Diego. However, the motion was defeated by the conservative element. Subsequent meetings of this organization were held with various prominent individuals speaking at them. Certain cases of alleged discrimination were taken up in what was said to have been an orderly, businesslike manner.

The Allied Organizations Committee had for its purposes the following:

1. "That we fight for and support the unity of America and her allies in the Armed Forces of the nation."
2. "That we condemn the policy of discrimination against Negroes in the Armed Forces and Negroes in industry, as well as discrimination against all other oppressed minorities and that we brand those who practice or advocate these policies as allies of Hitler, and the common enemy of the people."
3. "That we support President Roosevelt and the National Administration in any action that may be taken to destroy Hitler and the Axis forces."

The attendance of the meetings of this organization varies from approximately 50 to 100 individuals, most of whom are Negroes. There have been indications of Communist influence at the meetings and on occasions Communists have addressed the meetings. Reverend Charles Hampton, who is chairman of the organization, has attempted to steer the meetings away from radicalism. However, on occasions he has had little support from those in attendance.

Individuals Agitating Among the Negroes in This Area

On November 9, 1941, one Floyd C. Covington, Executive Secretary of the Los Angeles branch of the Urban League, spoke in San Diego. His subject was "The Vicious Circle", the topic of which was to the effect that there are circumstances under which industry has refused employment to the Negroes because they are untrained and the schools refuse to train Negroes because the plants will not employ them.

Among the prominent Communists who have been agitating among the Negroes in this area are Robert E. Warren, Henry Richardson, Gray Bemis, Josephine Wood, Ed Ruby, Teresa Vidal and William Becker.

Reverend W. L. Harris, who is pastor of the Calvary Baptist Church, 1901 Julian Avenue, San Diego, California, a Negro, is very active among the Negroes in this area. He is described as a forceful person and a fighter and as a result having considerable influence among his listeners. Harris is reported by a confidential informant to be very close to the Communist Party, if not a member of it.

Pettis Perry, Chairman of the Los Angeles County Communist Party, is reported to have been active to a considerable degree in the San Diego area in promulgating Communist Party principles and agitating for and among the Negroes there. In June, 1942, he spoke at a "Victory Rally" at the Negro Elks Hall in San Diego. At the meeting he reportedly asked Negroes in attendance to join the Communist Party, pointing out to them that Hearst, Dies, Fish, Wheeler, and others, were enemies of all the people. He is stated to have said that the Negro people must utilize the offices the Government has already set out to guard against discrimination and that they cannot battle against discrimination by themselves, but need the help of progressive organizations and labor unions. He added that demonstrations or carrying banners to the effect that "we want jobs" and other such activities are fruitless and breed discrimination. He is said to have stated that these were a backward approach to the solution of the problem. He is also reported as having stated that the Negroes have the most to lose if the present war is lost, along with other minorities, pointing out that they could expect very little if they were subjected to the rule of a dictator.

In June 1941 a Negro, one John K. Larremore, was arrested by the San Diego Police Department. When he was arrested he had in his possession a manuscript of some 144 pages entitled "Ebony in Bronze". The general theme of this manuscript was that there should be an Alliance of Japanese and Negroes for the purpose of wiping out the Caucasian race and establishing a black republic in the southern part of the United States. Larremore, who was later prosecuted in Federal Court as a result of an investigation conducted by the Federal Bureau of Investigation, advised that the manuscript he had in his possession when he was originally arrested was written by

him in 1932. It is interesting to know that **Larremore** also had in his possession a membership card in the International Labor Defense, a Communist front and organized unit. It is further noted that **Vera Warren,** the wife of **Robert R. Warren,** both of whom are well-known San Diego Communist Party members, **appeared as a defense witness at Larremore's** hearing before the United States Commissioner. At the time, she stated that she was a member of the National Association for the Advancement of Colored People.

Claude Jolly, who is an outstanding Negro in San Diego and Secretary of the National Association for the Advancement of Colored People, has said that **Vera Warren** first came to his attention in the Spring of 1941 when she attended an open meeting of the National Association for the Advancement of Colored People and took out a membership and paid a year's dues in advance. Jolly is reported to have advised with the exception of **Mrs. Warren** he was positive there were no other Communist Party members in the National Association for the Advancement of Colored People.

Pro-Axis Agitation

Considerable inquiry has been made in this area both by the Federal Bureau of Investigation and by the San Diego Police Department for indications relative to pro-Japanese activities among Negroes. No concrete evidence or verifying information has been received. *[100-135-47-1]*

San Francisco Field Division

In the area covered by this Field Division there are approximately 31,000 Negroes: Alameda County 12,335; San Francisco and County 6,000; Berkeley, California 3,400; and Oakland, California 8,400. The most active organization in this area is the National Association for the Advancement of Colored People. At one time a branch of the Communist front organization, the National Negro Congress, existed in San Francisco; however, since the German invasion of Russia this organization is stated to have ceased its activities there.

Sources of information report that some attempt by the Japanese in this area has been made to propagandize among the Negroes, and scattered instances are reported of Japanese distributing mimeographed pamphlets in an attempt to obtain the sympathy of the Negroes for Japan. However, sources of information contacted, voice the opinion that any anti-American inclinations by Negroes in that area are the outgrowth of discrimination against them and the inequality of rights rather than any sympathetic attachment to the Axis powers. It is reported that Negroes in this area are resentful of discrimination in the national defense industries and in branches of the armed forces.

They advise, however, that since the Government has taken a "more liberal" attitude toward the Negro and access to employment in better paying jobs has been afforded, the Negroes in this area have been more satisfied.

One source of information has advised that he knows of numerous instances of dissatisfied Negroes most of them young men who had been rejected by various branches of the armed forces, and that some talk has been heard among the Negroes that the United States Government does not appreciate the efforts of the Negroes in the war program. With respect to this situation this source of information advised that some of the reports received concerning disloyal Negroes by the Government were concerning those who were somewhat outspoken in their condemnation of the lack of equality and opportunity.

There have been indications reported of some literature and propaganda distributed among the Negroes in this area. It has been reported that a mimeographed sheet of paper containing an appeal to the Negro by the Japanese and concerning the Negroes' mistreatment in the United States was circulated shortly after December 7, 1941. No concrete information concerning this, however, has been reported.

Another source of information has advised of hearing a shortwave broadcast emanating from Tokyo which concerned the lynching of a Negro in a southern state and cited it as an example of democracy for the Negro under the "white man's rule". Another story circulated, although not verified, was to the effect that a troop transport being fired upon by Japanese was found to contain Negroes, and thereupon the Japanese ceased their firing and took the Negroes aboard their ship.

A confidential source of information has advised of receiving information to the effect that the Japanese attempted to gain favor among the Negroes through fraternization and increased friendliness with the Negroes. There has been, however, a wide gap made in this policy through the evacuation of the Japanese from the West Coast area according to this informant.

Another type of Japanese propaganda reported is to the effect that the Negro in this country in spite of his liberation, is little better off than before.

Other sources of information contacted with regard to pro-Japanese or pro-Axis sympathies with respect to Negroes in this area advise that they have received no information indicating the Japanese had made any inroad upon the Negroes' thinking. To substantiate this belief it was cited that there appeared to be little business contact between the Negroes and Japanese. Another source has advised that he believes the Negroes are loyal to the United States although disgusted or dissatisfied because of their economic conditions, and that the Negro as a whole, felt antagonized toward the Japanese for their supercilious attitude and underhanded tactics.

Another source in this area, who minimizes Japanese effect upon the Negroes, states that it is his impression that Negroes are anxious to stop Japanese aggression, because they realize that if the Japanese ever obtain control of this country the Negroes would be forced to live under conditions worse than slavery. This source has also informed that he believes some Negroes might be inclined to be sympathetic towards the pro-Axis powers, but he did not believe them intelligent enough to commit espionage and he did not believe any of them had enough nerve to commit acts of sabotage. He advises of hearing statements made by Negroes to the effect that "the United States underestimated the Japanese. The United States better get going or Japan will win." These statements he did not construe as being disloyal but characterized them as being observations or statements of opinion.

The Communist Party in this area, in actively agitating among and for the Negroes, has taken up from time to time the cases of Negroes who for various reasons have allegedly been discriminated against. Following the nationwide agitation over the Scottsboro case and that of Angelo Herndon, formerly active in the California Communist Party, the Party transferred its attention to the case of **Festus Coleman,** a local Negro who is presently serving a sentence for rape in the California State Penitentiary at San Quentin. Because of the unsavory nature of this case, the Party then transferred its attention to **Audrey Cole,** agitating that he be allowed a position on the San Francisco Civil Service list. More recently the Party has taken up the cause of one **Charles Sullivan,** a Negro machinist who was refused membership in a union.

It is likewise noted that the Western Worker, the onetime official organ of the Communist Party in the West, and the Peoples World, successor thereto, have consistently over the last ten years, devoted considerable space to the Negro problem. The basis for such agitation is obviously to gain the support of the Negro population for the Communist cause and to bolster the ranks of the Party with Negro members.

It is likewise noted that the Communist Party schools in this area, especially in Alameda and San Francisco, California, offer a course of instruction including the topic "The Negro Question." The Communist Party is reported to have kept complete figures of the number of Negroes recruited during the last year, and to date approximately twenty-five per cent of the new members have been Negroes, this figure being for the San Francisco County and the East Bay area.

In March 1943, according to reports received from confidential informants, functionaries of the Party were concerned over Negro members inasmuch as they had not been evidencing an interest in Party problems except in so far as they concerned the Negroes themselves directly. Rudie Lambert, the labor director of the Communist Party in this area, is said to have remarked that the Party had a problem in keeping new members (Negroes) interested. He further advised that only eighty-nine of the three hundred Negro recruits obtained in 1942 had registered for the year 1943. At the time, he reportedly emphasized that the Party should not forget the weaknesses of Negroes in organizational work and too much could not be expected of them. Along these lines, it is further reported that a known Communist Party member stated during this time that the main problem in dealing with Negroes, as far as the Party was concerned, was that Negroes are afraid of terrorism and are therefore backward in taking an active part in Party problems. [*100-135-48-15*]

The Communist Party has, during the past several months, interested itself in agitating over "Jim Crow" local trade unions in the San Francisco area. (It is to be noted that the Negro employment in shipyards where such locals exist is as follows: 1600 Negroes, including Malayans, employed in the East Bay Shipyards; 2500 Negroes in San Francisco and Marin County Shipyards.) However, the Party has met with certain obstacles in the San Francisco area inasmuch as these "Jim Crow" locals were already established. Therefore, the policy with regard to those locals already established was that Negroes should be urged to join them to maintain their jobs and thereafter use their membership as a level to get into union work. At no time, however, was the Party to be satisfied in the establishment of additional "Jim Crow" locals.

This situation was clarified by **Steve Nelson**, national committee member of the Communist Party in the San Francisco area, who differentiated between the situation in the Los Angeles, California area where the "Jim Crow" locals had not as yet been formed there. According to informants, it was perfectly all right for the Party to fight against the formation of them. With regard to the Oakland and San Francisco, California area, it was pointed out, according to informants, that the "Jim Crow" locals had already been formed and that either the Party had to take an extreme leftist position or urge that the comrades go into the auxiliaries and work. Moreover since there were about 15,000 Negroes in the shipyards and 7000 of them members of the International Brotherhood of Boilermakers, Ironworkers, Shipbuilders, Welders and Helpers of America, AFL, it would be impractical for the Party to assume an extreme leftist position. [*100-135-48-16*]

In the San Francisco Bay area, as well as in San Francisco and the surrounding communities, there are well over 200 Negro Communist Party members (registered). These members are from an approximate total population of 70,000 Negroes in the area. A recruiting drive resulted in the addition of eighteen new Negro recruits during the month of March, 1943, and it appears that the Party is concentrating on signing up new Negro recruits. This reportedly applies to the Young Communist League as well. Included in its activities in this area are local matters such as securing the rights for Negroes to bowl in bowling alleys ordinarily restricted to white people. It, of course, follows the general Communist Party line and in this connection has been active in agitating for mixed Negro and white regiments in the armed forces.

The Communist Party in the San Francisco area has exhibited considerable interest in the Shipyard Workers Committee Against Discrimination. This organization was formed in 1942 and has been under the recognized leadership of one Roy Thompson. The purpose of the organization is to combat "Jim Crow" local labor unions. Recently Thompson appeared to direct his activities at breaking up these local unions and in turn setting up a separate Negro union. Thompson has been criticized by Communist Party leaders in the area, although he is sympathetic with the Party he is not a member of it, for his actions in this matter their claim being that Thompson does not know what he is doing and has not been fully integrated into the Party to the extent that he can understand and dictate Party policies. According to the latest reports, this committee has approximately 160 members, both white and Negroes, who represent the various Bay area shipyards. The committee is said to have furnished the Communist Party in the area with twenty Negro recruits. More recent information which has been reported reflects that the Party contemplates deposing Thompson in view of what they term his "nationalistic attitude."

In May, 1943, the Communist Party organized a group known as the Negro Victory Committee in this area. It functions as an overall committee handling matters of policy relative to matters of discrimination. According to the functionaries of the Party in the San Francisco area, the Party had good possibilities in using the committee to deal with all classes of Negroes. It was planned that the committee will deal with issues affecting the whole Negro community. This committee is to serve in addition to the Shipyard Workers Committee Against Discrimination. [*100-135-48-19*]

With reference to the crime situation it is reported that the same among the Negroes appears to be on the increase in Oakland, California. It is stated that crime is the problem confronting this Police Department and not that of un-American activities. The opinion has been expressed that many Negroes have been amazed at the apparent ease of obtaining employment in the shipyards. Many are stated to have criminal records. Many come from Texas, Florida, Alabama and other southern states, and it is stated that for the first time they have an increase of rights and are thus impressed by the liberal attitude shown towards them. For this reason it is stated some are attempting to capitalize relative to this treatment and are continually overstepping the bonds of law and order.

In the East San Francisco East Bay area which includes Berkeley, Oakland and Alameda, Negro organizations are said to be highly disorganized and appear to operate within themselves too much. It is said that there is no central institution to which Negroes can express their feelings and no particular organization can offer a good leadership. It has been pointed out that this is one reason for the dissension and disorganization evident among the Negro people in this area. In this connection, it has been stated that at times outsiders move into the Negro community and have attempted to take steps to remedy the undesirable situation. However, these individuals are said to have been soon taken into certain cliques and their responsibilities to the Negro community were soon forgotten.

In this area it is reported that Negroes are generally accepted in practically all defense industries and the average income has increased approximately two or three times. However, it is said that the employment situation is not altogether satisfactory and that there are several sore spots in the employer-employee relationship and also in the Negro membership in trade unions. It is said that Negroes, although taken into various unions, do not always enjoy the advantages and benefits of the union to the extent the white man does although they pay the same fees. In this connection, it has also been pointed out that it is believed Negroes are not being promoted from unclassified work to better positions with higher pay as readily as they should be.

With reference to possible pro-Japanese sympathies in this area, a confidential Negro source of information has further advised that he has seen indications of Negroes being somewhat sympathetic to the problems of the Japanese with regard to their evacuation and in some instances appreciated their plight, yet by no means could anyone say that the Negroes desired a complete Japanese victory. This source of information has pointed out that Japanese merchants and landlords have given Negroes good business deals on household goods and the rental of homes. He has advised that he has heard no expression attributable to a Negro wherein a complete Japanese victory was wished for, but he has heard some say that the Japanese were just as fair to Negroes as they were to white people.

Another source of information, a Negro, has reiterated that he believes the Negro loyalty to the United States is unimpeachable and that there is no foreign-inspired group or individual attempting to agitate among the Negroes in this area. This individual has expressed his opinion that any discontent among the Negroes can be attributed to the shortsightedness of the white people in their discriminatory attitude displayed against the Negro or in the absence of discrimination in the conciliatory attitude displayed by them toward the Negro.

On November 29, 1942, the San Francisco branch of the National Association for the Advancement of Colored People held its annual election of officers. A confidential source of information in attendance at this meeting has stated that the Communists were successful in their attempt to gain control of this National Association for the Advancement of Colored People chapter by placing their members and sympathizers in controlling positions, and by concentrating enough Party members on the Board of Directors to further insure such control. It was alleged that the president, one Berlinda Davidson, although not known to be a Party member, has apparently cast her lot with the Communist Party to insure her reelection to the presidency of the chapter. It was said that this was obvious for some time inasmuch as her action before the election was reflected in her taking work away from committees and handling it entirely by her own selected group, which reportedly consists of three individuals who are all considered to be Party members.

Another method of exploitation among the Negroes on the part of the Communist Party is reported in a new method which is said by the confidential sources of information to be a means of attracting the attention of the Negro people. The method reportedly consists of holding cocktail parties in homes of various Communists, to which Negroes are invited.

Another confidential source of information has advised that until the past year, San Francisco had had a low colored population. As the result, the Negroes were poorly organized and a front organization of the Communist Party found San Francisco difficult to secure Negro support. It was alleged, however, that the war has changed this with the influx of many Negroes from the South, which is said to have practically doubled the Negro population in the San Francisco Bay area. Considerable more activity is expected to be expanded by the Communists among the Negroes.

In the area of Berkeley, California, as well as Oakland, California, sources of information advise there is one thing which creates disunity of Negroes and whites at the present time. It is said that this is the critical situation existing in housing facilities. There are reportedly four or five thousand Negroes employed in the Kaiser shipyards, and nearby Richmond shipyards; yet until the latter part of November, it was alleged, there was not a Negro family living in the defense housing project built to house such employees. This fault was blamed on the arrangement providing a policy to permit only essential workers to live in these project units, designated by the employers as essential workers. In this connection it was further alleged that Negroes are discriminated against by the employers and few advance to essential positions, and consequently are not granted housing units. It is said the employer discriminates against the colored man by refusing to promote him to a better position such as a "leaderman", as he assumes that the white man will not work under a Negro foreman, and therefore does not promote the deserving and meritorious Negro employees.

In the area covered by Oakland, California, information has been received relative to the five or six hundred Negro employees of the Moore Dry Dock Company, a shipbuilding concern in the City of Oakland. It is said that in the past there have been alleged incidents of discrimination that were handled satisfactorily on an individual basis, but recently two discrimination committees sprang up among the company employees. One is led by a Vernon McCalla, a Negro employed there, a member of the Ship Fitters Local No. 9, described as the Negro branch of the Boilermakers Union. McCalla is said to have organized the Miscellaneous Workers Limited, Incorporated. He claims it to be a non-profit organization started by the State with no membership dues although donations are accepted by it.

McCalla is reported to have stated that this discrimination committee was begun in the absence of a chapter of the National Urban League: That its purpose is to "go to bat for Negroes, contact unions, shipyards and so on, to get Negroes jobs and to defend them against discrimination."

Another organization is said to have cropped up in the Moore Dry Dock Company, which is known as the Shipyard Workers Committee Against Discrimination. It is said that the president of this Committee is Roy Thompson, another Negro employee alleged formerly to have been active in the plant on behalf of the Bay Area Committee Against Discrimination. It is further alleged that Thompson has severed his connections with the latter organization and has set up a new organization of his own within the plant. With respect to Thompson, it is reported that he is a known Communist Party member.

In connection with the reported shortage of housing for Negroes in this area, it is said that the recent action of the Santa Fe Improvement Club led by Albert Anaclerio, an Italian gardener living in Berkeley, California, has not improved matters. This individual is described as the leading spokesman at a meeting held for the purpose of organizing property owners toward the exclusion of Negroes from living in, and owning properties in a large area of Southwest Berkeley, California. It was said that the exclusion was to be done by means of inserting covenants in the leasehold contracts.

A confidential source of information has cited this action along with a lack of public housing and job restriction among Negroes as having an effect on the morale and mental attitude of the Negroes. It was alleged with the housing situation being acute as it is, along with the influx of Negro war workers who are already living in shacks, tents, or garages for the lack of homes and with the added situation of white property owners denying Negroes the right to live where he wishes to, provides arguments for Fascists "or other subversive forces", whose purpose may be to break up the unity of the American forces. [*100-135-48*]

On the nights of December 24, 25, 26 and 27, 1942, there were several clashes between Negro sailors and white sailors and Marines in Vallejo, California. It was estimated that there were approximately four hundred men involved. Sources of information have advised that from all indications, it was a racial controversy, and not merely a fight between sailors and Marines, inasmuch as the white sailors paired with the white Marines. There were no casualties, although several men were slightly wounded. Military Police and civilian police eventually quelled the riot.

On December 31, 1942, the mayor of the City of Vallejo met with military officials, governmental representatives, and local governmental representatives, as well as law-enforcement authorities and other clients, to make plans for the prevention of a recurrence of such rioting. It was reported that the consensus of opinion of those civilians present, that the rioting was caused by too many service men being placed in a small town unable to provide recreational facilities. It was said no one present offered any suggestion that the rioting was the result of subversive inspired activity or influence. [*100-135-48-13*]

It is believed worthy of note to incorporate immediately hereinafter observations made by a confidential informant, a Negro minister in the San Francisco area, concerning Negroes in the armed forces. This informant has observed in Negroes in the armed forces with whom he has come in contact a low morale at the present time. He has pointed out that a lot of them feel if it is necessary for them to die or be wounded in the war, they may as well obtain such injuries fighting for their rights on American soil. He added that Negroes in the Navy believe white sailors resent their becoming seamen, and not confined to service positions as heretofore. He has also expressed the opinion that there is need for a Negro chaplain at the Vallejo Naval Base, as well as several of the Army camps located in the San Francisco, California, area.

[*San Francisco* ▬▬▬▬▬]

Another informant, a Negro has confirmed the above information and has, in addition, given the following explanation. He stated that Negro youths living in the South are very poor, have no opportunity, are usually downtrodden and are subsequently willing to go to most any length to escape the alleged persecution and discrimination to which they are subjected. In many cases, this informant stated, Southern Negro youths are unable to leave this section of the country because of the lack of funds. The escape, according to the informant, is enlistment in the Navy or in the Army. As a result, the informant advised, there is a larger percentage of Southern Negroes in the Navy than Northern Negroes. Many of the Negro sailors from the South, who have been in the Navy for several years, have visited other ports of the world where they allegedly received kinder treatment and have become accustomed to being considered equal to the white sailors. For these reasons, the informant has stated Negroes have decided to stand up and fight for their rights at home and have a "chip on their shoulder" because of the feeling of discrimination. This informant has further stated that the Negro soldiers in the riot at Vallejo, California, were largely Southern Negroes who he believed had this feeling. It is further stated that in conversation with many of the Negroes, they have all asserted if conditions are not improved they will fight again.

The informant has further corroborated saying there is an increasing feeling of bitterness among Negro enlisted personnel. For that reason he feared more race riots will occur in the future. He asserted he felt he expressed the sentiment of Negroes in the armed forces when he stated they would not tolerate mistreatment when released from active duty, and practically all of them are unanimous in saying that if they are mistreated they will take things in their own hands.

[*San Francisco* ▬▬▬▬▬ *100-135-48-15*]

Seattle Field Division

The Negroes in the City of Seattle, Washington, are divided chiefly into two classes, the higher and better educated class and the lower class stated to consist of unskilled laborers, gamblers and tavernkeepers. They are stated to number approximately 4,000. The opinion of different sources of information with respect to these Negroes is that they believe in social equality but at the same time urge education and self-betterment in that they feel that some of the rights and opportunities demanded will come easier only if they are prepared from an educational standpoint. As a whole they are stated to be behind the country's war effort and have not complained of treatment by the Army and Navy.

Another source of information advises that Negroes feel that the war is the greatest thing that ever happened from their standpoint because of increased employment opportunities. This source has stated that Negroes feel in this area that they would fare and live badly under Hitler's rule and domination because of the way he has treated the Jews. Negroes are stated not to trust the Japanese to any great extent because of their treatment of the Chinese.

With regard to Japanese agitation among the Negroes in this area it has been reported that there are indications of a certain amount of race feeling as a result of the war. Statements have been reported to the effect that the Japanese now represent the colored race and that they are fighting for the colored people. It is reported by a source of information that those uttering such remarks were of a lower type of Negro. It has further been reported that statements have been made by Negroes to the effect that Japanese landlords in Seattle were the only ones who had ever given Negro tenants fair treatment. Several colored individuals have been reported as having pro-Japanese sentiments.

Negroes in this area generally are stated not to trust Germans for at least one reason, namely the treatment of Jesse Owens, Negro athlete, at Olympic games in Berlin. One individual, pro-German in sympathy, is stated to have made the remark, "Hitler and Germany have treated the colored people very well, in fact much better than the Government of the United States did, and the colored people should be in favor of Germany."

At the present time the Communist Party, although continually attempting to recruit Negroes as members, is regarded as not making much progress, either because the organizers are not competent or because those recruited soon drop out of the Party because they are lazy intellectually. The agitation at the present time seems to be under the direction of one Ostervold Carl Brooks, a Negro in Seattle, Washington. Brooks is described as a fanatical Communist. The type of agitational activity centers around instances of "Jim Crowism" in treatment of the Negroes.

It has also been reported that during the Spring term of the Workers School in Seattle a course was offered on the "Negro People" and basic Marxism education with regard to the subject.

With reference to Communist Party activity among the Negroes, it has been recently reported that at the election of representatives, who were to attend the National

Convention of the National Association for the Advancement of Colored People, Communist representatives were defeated by a narrow margin. It was reported that the Progressive Colored Youth organization was active in its support of the Communist nominees. An officer in the local branch of the National Association for the Advancement of Colored People has stated that he frankly feared the results of the next election in that branch because the aforementioned group could easily pack the meeting and control the ballots.

The only Negro newspaper published in the State of Washington is the Northwest Enterprise which is operated by a Negro, one S. A. Robinson. Mr. Robinson is stated to be a high type of person. This newspaper is regarded as a legitimate publication, and while it attacks discrimination, the same is done in a manner that does not give offense.

The Washington New Dealer sponsored by the Washington Commonwealth Foundation, an alleged Washington Communist front organization, is also stated to have some distribution among the Negro population. The Pittsburgh Courier, a Negro newspaper published in Pittsburgh, Pennsylvania is also said to be widely read among the Negroes in this area.

With further regard to possible Japanese influence causing unrest and dissatisfaction among the Negro people in this area, the opinion was furnished by one source of information that most Negroes in this area feel the only reason the Japanese associate with the colored people was that they were able to get their money much easier than any other race. Another source of information, a Negro, has advised that he is a tenant in a home owned by a Japanese landlord. This source of information has also traveled in the Orient and has dealt considerably with Japanese. In his opinion he believes that the average American Negro is behind the American war effort. He realizes that if the Japanese win the war he would be far worse off than under American control. In this connection, another source of information has advised that a large majority of the Negroes realize that Japanese have always considered themselves much better than the Negroes and that if Japan were to win the war the Negroes would no doubt be made slaves.

A general evaluation of the Negro situation in the Northwest leads to conclusion that the Negro people there are entirely loyal to the United States. The general belief is that in a large measure racial bigotry and discrimination will disappear if they prove their loyalty, industry and devotion to the United States, especially at the present time. It has been stated that the Japanese in this country have at times treated Negroes when in contact with them more fairly than white people in many respects. It is said they have provided in certain areas reasonable rentals, equal use of hotels, stores and the like. It is, of course, true that the establishments operated by Japanese are usually of the poorer class. It is further true, however, that the Negroes have reportedly never mingled with the Japanese socially and are believed not to have particularly trusted them. The Japanese have indicated a pride in their alleged racial superiority and have not been able to avoid disclosure of this.

The leaders and better educated Negroes are said to have realized that attempts are being made by subversive groups to take advantage of incidents to convince Negroes that they can achieve equality only through cooperation with the particular group. Local leaders in the sole northwest Negro publication, the Northwest Enterprise, are said to have in the past constantly warned their people against being used by others for purely subversive ends. A number of Negroes, while loyal to the United States, are fighting the battle against racial discrimination vigorously and are said to be ready to use all means at hand to force the accomplishment of political and of economic equality for Negroes.

Attempts have been made continuously over a period of years to recruit Communist Party members from the ranks of the Negroes in Seattle and an effort was made to create a Negro unit. It is said that the Communists themselves believe that the Negroes react more favorably in this community to the recruiting efforts for an all-Negro organization. It is said that the membership of these units fluctuate to a tremendous degree. According to a former member, the Negroes are recruited by promises of betterment but normally lose interest and drop out after several meetings.

The Washington New Dealer, the official publication of the Washington Commonwealth Federation, which has without disguise followed the Communist Party line and publicized the Communist Party program, is making a strong play for Negro support by being extremely active in the fight against alleged discriminations shown to Negroes and by giving primary credit to Communist front organizations for every success in this fight.

With further regard to Communist activity, it is reported that **Joe Harris, business agent** of the Marine Cooks and Stewards Union who is said to have Communist Party connections, is in a position to cause harm and does have the power to indoctrinate Negroes who are members of the union. This individual, however, is said to be ignorant and has no influence on the larger part of the Negro community.

At one time **Revels Cayton,** Negro Communist Party Member, presently in a functionary position in the Los Angeles Communist Party setup, was an organizer in the Northwest. It is reported that his primary interest in the Communist Party seemed to be the entry it afforded into white society and he is trusted only by Negroes who hold a similar ambition.

An organization which is reported to be entirely free of any subversive influence and is sincere in its effort is the Seattle Branch of the National Urban League which has long been active in its attempt to aid the Negroes in solving the problems of racial discrimination in economic, social and political fields. Its leader is Bernard E. Squires who is secretary of the organization. He is said to be a well-educated, militant, but honest Negro leader.

In the vicinity of Bellingham, Washington, sources of information have reported no indication has come to their attention of any exploitation by subversive forces among the Negroes, or information reflecting that Negroes are actively engaged in propaganda work among members of their race.

In the vicinity of Everett, Washington, no reports have been received reflecting that there is any foreign-inspired trouble among the Negroes in this area. It is said however, that a few of the Negroes in this area are considered somewhat radical inasmuch as their views on social equality and discrimination are militant. A confidential source of information, a Negro has advised of not hearing of any Japanese or Communist Party activities in spreading propaganda among the Negroes in this area. He advised that he was friendly with some Japanese in Everett prior to their exclusion, yet he never heard any mention a need for a different type of government for the Negroes.

At Aberdeen, Washington, reports received concerning the Negroes in this area failed to reflect any subversive activities among them.

At Olympia, Washington sources of information there advise of no indication coming to their attention of the activities of subversive groups or individuals among the Negro race.

In and around the vicinity of Vancouver, Washington, until the Fall of 1942 there were possibly only about 25 Negroes, however, at that time, 150 Negroes were reportedly transported into this area by the Kaiser Shipbuilding Company, from the East. It is related that a few of these Negroes caused trouble in the local shipbuilding union, because of their being refused membership in the Union. It was alleged that many of these Negroes were below average in intelligence and in many instances caused the company to pay transportation of some of the workers back to New York as they were unable to pass physical tests.

It was reported that in connection with the alleged trouble with Negro workers at the Kaiser Shipbuilding Company, one **Marion Hill,** a Negro, was the leader of the first group of Negroes which came to Vancouver. **Hill** reportedly merely came to Vancouver to "lick the Union Deal". It is reported that Negroes in the Company have been accepted into labor unions, although none of them were accepted into any trade unions. It should be pointed out that the situation at the Kaiser Shipbuilding Yard in Vancouver has been given considerable publicity in the press especially the newspaper "P.M." and the "Daily Worker". *[100-135-51]*

The following information is set forth to demonstrate the maneuvers of the Communist Party with regard to Negroes. Late in the Fall of 1942 **Ostervald Carl Brooks,** Negro Communist Party member, along with **Eugene Moszee,** reported Negro member of the Young Communist League, appeared at the Olympic Hotel Grill in Seattle, Washington, with three colored sailors demanding that all receive service in the eating place. According to an informant, these individuals were not given immediate service as a result of the extreme shortage of help; thereupon **Brooks** and **Moszee** raised considerable disturbance in the grill, claiming that they were being discriminated against because of their color. The management of the hotel was called upon and the matter was settled, the colored sailors being offered service and given a glass of beer or milk as they desired, however **Brooks** and **Moszee** were not given service.

According to an informant who was present at the time the demonstration was arranged, the same was sponsored by the Young Communist League. He expressed the opinion that the colored sailors who accompanied **Brooks** and **Moszee** were unaware of what they were getting into. The version of the colored sailors was also to this effect and in fact they advised they thought the individuals whom they accompanied to the Olympic Hotel were members of the National Association for the Advancement of Colored People and were attempting to break down discrimination against Negroes in that area. They stated that **Brooks** and **Moszee** gave the impression they were going to "break it up", referring to the alleged discrimination against Negroes.

Later another informant was contacted by **Eugene Moszee** who identified himself as a member of the Young Communist League. **Moszee** reportedly stated that his organization had sent a number of its members to the Olympic Hotel Grill and after service was refused **Moszee** and the rest of the party requested that they see the manager. **Moszee** then admitted that a riot almost ensued. He also admitted to the informant that the Young Communist League had been responsible for the previously mentioned incident.

The National Association for the Advancement of Colored People has a chapter in Seattle with approximately 2,500 members. There are also branches of the organization in Bellingham, Everett, Walla Walla, Yakima, Tacoma and Spokane, Washington. It is reported by confidential informants that the Communist Party has not been successful in infiltrating the organization in the Seattle area.

There is also a unit of the Urban League in Seattle which has similar aims to those of the National Association for the Advancement of Colored People, those of advancing and promoting the interests of the Negro people in that area. Recently this organization, along with the chapter of the National Association for the Advancement of Colored People, conducted a survey to determine how many skilled Negro workers were qualified and available to serve in war industries in the Seattle area. The results are said to have shown that between sixty-five and seventy Negroes had training as welders, yet the rules of the local union of the International Brotherhood of Boilermakers, Ironworkers, Shipbuilders, Welders and Helpers of America, AFL, has kept these men in the status of a common laborer and has prevented them from earning a livelihood in the occupation in which they had been trained. This information has been supplied by a confidential informant who has also advised that this union, as well as other unions, has been a great source of irritation to the leaders of these two Negro groups.

There was recently formed in Seattle an organization known as the Council for Minority Rights. It is alleged that **Eugene Dennett**, reported Communist, was one of the motivating forces in the establishment of this group. It is said to have among its officers six who are sympathetic to the Communist Party. It is said to have approximately eighty-five interested members, of whom there are ten who are reported to be members of the Communist Party. The purpose of the group is to oppose discrimination against particular Negroes and Jews in the Seattle area. It is said that the Council recently devoted itself primarily to a study of discrimination against Negroes in the national defense industries in the Seattle area. In March, 1943, it was reported that the more conservative members of the Council were resigning rapidly.

[100-135-51-11]

Another organization was recently formed in the early part of May, 1943, in the Seattle area which is known as the Federated Defense Club, the purpose of which allegedly is to fight racial discrimination and to gain recognition for Negroes in defense plants in the area. It is said to have Communist influence in it through **Ostervold Carl Brooks**, member of the Negro committee of the Communist Party. He is said to have been one of the organizers of the group. One of the other organizers, **Reverend Benjamin Davis**, a Negro minister in the area who is described as very militant in his speeches, is said to be close to **Brooks**. The plans for the club include the establishment of separate units in all defense plants where Negroes are employed. In this connection Brooks is said to have expressed himself that the club is merely a step toward bringing Negro people within the reach of the Communist Party.

In March, 1943, an incident took place at a housing project in the City of Seattle known as the Holly Park Housing Project. It had its origin in the circulation of a petition by a white citizens group known as the Greater Empire Way Community Club. The petition was circulated because of alleged indiscretion committed by Negroes residing in the project, such as indecent exposures. The petition was circulated, and one who engaged in the circulating was an air raid warden. The Communist Party and its various forces in the Seattle area immediately seized upon this act and made an issue of it. Considerable publicity was given to the matter and Negro protests were made largely, according to the informant, at the behest of the Communist Party. The people responsible for the petition were described as Fascists, members of the Ku-Klux Klan and in various other manners. A Board of Hearing met to decide on charges against the individual who was an air raid warden and who circulated the petition. The air raid warden was charged with conduct unfitting in his position. The conclusion reached was that there was no evidence to substantiate this claim.

With further regard to the Communist Party in the Seattle area, the following statistics have been reported. It was reported that approximately fifty-five Negro members have been recruited from February, 1943, to May, 1943. On May 2, 1943, the Northwestern District of the Communist Party held a "war convention" which was attended by approximately 300 delegates. Of these, it is said there were only fifteen Negroes in attendance. Relative to the Young Communist League, it was reported that the Dorie Miller branch of that organization held a meeting on June 22, 1943, at which time, according to informants, contradicting opinions were expressed by the members in that a United Nations meeting would not gain an improvement to the position of the Negroes in the United States. At that time a prominent Negro member is said to have stated that the Dorie Miller branch, together with other Communist branches, planned a city-wide demonstration in the Seattle area in the near future which would make the city thoroughly conscious of the problem of discrimination.

VI

AREAS OUTSIDE CONTINENTAL UNITED STATES

This section is devoted to the territories of Alaska, Hawaii, and Puerto Rico. These areas have been grouped together solely for the sake of convenience and not to reflect a connection by virtue of conditions existing therein.

It is believed that the digests set out hereinafter are explanatory in themselves as regards racial conditions and race relationship in the three areas.

Honolulu Field Division

In the Territory of the Hawaiian Islands the civilian Negro population is estimated at approximately eleven hundred, of which approximately seven hundred fifty are defense workers, who are stated to have arrived within the past year and who are presently residing at the Naval Cantonment, Pearl Harbor. Historically, there is a slight Negro strain in the racial classification "part Hawaiian," and also in the Portuguese. However, these strains are stated to have been entirely assimilated into the numerically larger Hawaiian and Portuguese races. Other colored individuals have come to the Hawaiian Islands in scattered instances, but in most cases have been regarded as Hawaiian or Portuguese and have lost or discarded their identity as Negroes. In fact, it is reported, there is no native Negro population as such.

It is reported that no Negro publications, societies, or organizations of any kind exist in the islands. The only exception, as far as organizing any type of a colored society is concerned, was the unsuccessful attempt in 1941 to establish in Honolulu a branch of the National Association for the Advancement of Colored People. It is stated that the organizers at the time held themselves out as being interested not only in the cause of the Negro, but in the progress of all racial groups other than the Caucasians. In February of 1941, an individual by the name of **Williams,** a Negro, who attempted the organizational activity of this branch, is stated to have publicized the fact that he intended to establish a branch in Honolulu and a few organizational meetings were held. At the few meetings which were held, there were some fifty persons or less in attendance who are stated to have displayed comparatively little interest in the activity of the group. The organizations, however, is stated to have never gone beyond the organizational stage and a branch was never established.

With regard to the status of the American Negroes who have settled in the islands, it is reported that the same type of alleged prejudice exists among the white persons there as exists on the mainland. For the most part the Negroes are reported to have mingled with the Hawaiian and Portuguese and to a lesser extent with the Koreans and Chinese. No instance has been reported, however, reflecting instances where Negroes have married or even associated to any extent with the Japanese.

In Honolulu, it is said the few Negroes that are there are not known as such, and it is said no attention is paid to their racial identity. It has further been stated that the greater number of Negroes in that territory are either service men or defense workers who seem for the most part to keep their own company and to mingle only to a very small extent with the permanent residents in Hawaii.

At the Naval Cantonment, Pearl Harbor, which is stated to house some forty-five hundred defense workers, who have been brought to the islands within the past year to work on naval construction projects, of those seven hundred fifty are said to be colored. It has been confidentially reported that there has been considerable difficulty in maintaining a satisfactory situation in the cantonment by reason of the occasional clashes of personalities to each other.

It is reported that the general behavior of these colored workers has been very satisfactory and in many instances superior to that of the white workers, and that they have tried to conscientiously obey the rules of the cantonment. It is said that some of the white workers are of a low type and some are definitely trouble-makers and quick to indicate racial prejudice. Living quarters are said to be separated from those of the white workers, and the difficulties which have been encountered are in the mess halls where the workers are obliged to mix without regard to color.

Sources of information in this area advise of no knowledge whatever of any subversive activity among the Negroes presently residing in the Territory of Hawaii, and that there has not been the slightest occasion to believe that the Negroes residing there would be inclined to listen to subversive or un-patriotic statements. A recent report received from a confidential source, however, reflects indications of Japanese-Negro collaboration, especially on the Island of Oahu. The majority of Negroes involved are said to represent Negro soldiers and seamen. This collaboration has also consisted of social intercourse among the two peoples, as well as interracial discussion groups which allegedly deal with minority problems.

It was further reported that a Negro war worker at the Navy Yard in Pearl Harbor is engaged in organizing a Negro Elks Lodge in Honolulu, his goal being to enroll a thousand Negro war workers and servicemen. It is said that once the lodge is established, it is planned to extend the privilege of joining to people of other racial minorities, including Americans of Japanese ancestry. In this connection, the reported organizer is alleged to have said he was approached by a real estate broker (allegedly a representative of large interests in Honolulu) and offered the sum of $10,000 if he would agree to drop his plans for organizing a lodge. This offer was allegedly refused with the statement that Negroes are in Hawaii to stay.

The source of this information relative to Japanese-Negro collaboration has advised of receiving information that should the organization of this Negro Elks Lodge materialize, it will undoubtedly be a prelude to a strongly organized Negro influence in Hawaiian affairs. This same source has further pointed out in view of the enthusiasm being manifested in the present Japanese-Negro collaboration, it is possible a coalition of these two peoples will be the ultimate result. In this connection, it has been further alleged by the same source that although there has been no definite evidence of any subversive activity in connection with the present collaboration on the Island of Oahu, letters written by Japanese to their friends in Honolulu indicate enthusiasm among them in their collaboration with Negroes and allegedly a growing Negro influence in their way of thinking. *[100-135-19-13]*

Juneau, Alaska

No evidences of foreign inspired agitation among the Negroes in the territory of Alaska have been received. The total Negro population in this area excluding Negro Army troops is estimated at around 200 persons. Selective Service records indicate that the majority of the Negroes are over 45 years of age.

Likewise no reports have been received reflecting racial agitation among the Negroes in this area of a local nature. No Negro newspapers or other publications dealing with the Negro race are published in this area and it is reported that no societies, clubs, lodges, schools or other organizations where Negroes are known to exist. Furthermore, no information has been received reflecting that Negroes in Alaska are Communistically inclined or are disloyal to the United States. *[100-135-23]*

San Juan Field Division

In this area considerable information has been received reflecting that the Communist Party and its members are agitating among the colored people for "equality between whites and blacks." At the annual assembly of the Party held in Caguas, Puerto Rico, in June of 1942, a motion was made and seconded that in the future delegates to the conventions of the Communist Party should not be classified as white or Negro but merely as Communist. At the meeting a Communist leader was also reported to have urged that the Communist Party in Puerto Rico make an issue of the racial question.

Further reports with respect to Communist Party agitation reflect that the leaders of the Party insist that discrimination is rampant against the colored people in Puerto Rico. A confidential source of information has advised with respect to such allegation that he has never noticed any sharp discrimination against the Negroes and that the Communists never alleged specific instances of discrimination but seem to be trying to make the most of it and build it up for the sake of acquiring new members among the Negroes.

A Negro source of information has advised that he believes there is very little discrimination against the Negroes in Puerto Rico. In this connection, he stated that an enterprising Negro who was willing to study and work hard can obtain practically any position he wants. He stated that the only group in Puerto Rico which has made an issue of alleged discrimination against the Negroes is the Communist Party which is always "using some trick or another to gain new members among the workers."

No indications have as yet been reported of any racial trouble or other foreign-inspired agitation among the Negroes in this area. [*100-135-49*]

VII

CONCLUSION

As evidenced from the foregoing details and as apparent in the appendix of this survey, there are and there have been subversive forces at work among the American Negroes causing unrest and dissatisfaction. The most outstanding force, as evidenced from the information received by this Bureau, is the Communist Party.

The Communist Party, it should be pointed out, at the present time ostensibly is extremely interested in accomplishing all possible to further the war effort. However, as a means of furthering its revolutionary program, the Party fosters an agitational program allegedly for the advancement of the Negro race in this country. In this program, demands are made for the abolition of discrimination, segregation and such political matters as the poll tax. Social equality, social intercourse and generally the granting of equal rights for Negroes are urged. At the same time, it is to be noted that from information received concerning Party activities involving Negroes obvious attempts by the Party are made to utilize and to exploit Negro inhabitants of this country as well as conditions which affect them directly. While the number of Communist Party members of the Negro race is comparatively small (numbering approximately 10,000 out of an approximate total membership of 75,000), the effect of the Party's program, as it is applied through its own apparatus as well as by the use of a disguised and "boring-from-within" technique, is farther reaching than might be indicated from the total Negro membership.

While apparent efforts and activities on the part of the Party seemingly indicate it is a champion of the advancement of the Negro race, there have been several incidents and situations reported in which the sincerity of the Party in its program in this matter is reflected upon adversely. With respect to these incidents and situations, as well as other ramifications of Communist Party activity concerning Negroes and racial conditions, the section entitled "Communist Party and Negroes" in the appendix of this survey should be referred to.

There have also been active among the Negro inhabitants in a number of areas in the United States organizations and pseudo leaders having apparent pro-Japanese sympathies. Since the declaration of war frequent complaints and numerous reports of pro-Japanese sympathies and of Japanese attempts to disrupt the national security of the United States by undermining the morale and loyalty of the American Negro have been reported to this Bureau. Many of these complaints, allegations and reports have been baseless although it has been demonstrated the Japanese Government has endeavored to implant ideas and attitudes in the minds of the colored people as well as to call attention to racial prejudice and restrictions to further its propaganda that the present war is a race war. The extent of success in this activity cannot be gauged solely by the amount of membership reached in pro-Japanese Negro organizations which are described in the appendix under the title "Japanese Influence and Activity Among the

American Negroes." It is believed that the influence obtained by individual members generally among the Negro population must be considered.

Through footholds of various sizes obtained in the following organizations, it is believed a means of implanting pro-Japanese ideas and attitudes, as well as anti-white sentiments, in the minds of the colored people who were members of the groups was found: Universal Negro Improvement Association, Development of Our Own, Pacific Movement of the Eastern World, Peace Movement of Ethiopia, Ethiopian Pacific Movement, Moorish Science Temple of America, Colored American National Organization also known as Washington Park Forum and Brotherhood of Liberty for the Black People of America, Allah Temple of Islam, African Moslem Welfare Society of America, Addeynue Allahe Universal Arabic Association, International Reassemble Church of Freedom League, Inc., and a number of other smaller units.

Reference is also made to numerous reports and complaints made to the Federal Bureau of Investigation in practically all areas of expressions and utterances on the part of individual Negroes reflecting, on the surface, either an anti-white or pro-Japanese sympathy. Inquiries have been made into each and it has been found in many instances that allegations of un-American sentiments on the part of individual Negroes were based either on unfounded rumors or on the misinterpretation of actions or statements. It might be noted opinions have been offered by sources of information that many of the complaints along these lines were a result of construing discontent on the part of colored people because of their economic and social conditions as un-Americanism or lack of interest in the war effort. Militant demands by Negroes for a higher economic or social position have been regarded at times in some sections of the country as being inspired by anti-American sentiments. Yet, a number of inquiries have resulted in ascertaining such sentiments were expressed by Negroes as a result of ignorance or drunkenness.

Many of the utterances which have been accredited to individual Negroes have reflected an anti-white attitude. There have been reported feelings that the present war is one that is racial and for this reason Negroes should align themselves with the Japanese. However, sources of information have offered explanations for such attitudes, the opinion being presented that Negroes are presently growing increasingly militant in their demands for equality and opportunity since it is felt by them the war period offers an excellent foothold. It is believed in regard to this that the program and the activities of the March on Washington Movement, which is described fully in the appendix, should be referred to. Furthermore, the utterances of Negro leaders in public, while not definitely reflecting an anti-white attitude, have evidenced a militancy which at times has included urging that Negroes, if necessary, die in their attempt to have their demands met.

Sources of information in practically all parts of the country, especially in the southern section of the United States, have alluded to the changed attitude on the part of Negroes as evidenced by their statements and activities. Various reasons have been offered, among which are the increased tempo of living during the present wartime, the migration of both Negroes and whites to already heavily populated areas resulting in an overcrowding, the alleged instances of discrimination and the denial of rights, the influence of the Negro press, the influence of Negro leaders and organizations, the cognizance of better employment opportunities in other sections of the country, and the circulation of baseless rumors and malicious or wholly unnecessary gossip.

Although there are numerous reports of changed attitudes, aggressiveness or militancy, sources of information, on the other hand, in all areas have advised Negroes in general are fundamentally loyal to the United States and desire to participate and assist in the war effort. At times, however, it is explained the Negroes' interests and their attempts to further them are met by some factions with an antagonism based on the belief that "Negroes must be kept in their places." The alleged lack of opportunity for Negroes in some sections has also been pointed to as a reason for some of the strong sentiments of bitterness and resentment.

Various opinions have been expressed by sources of information as to how Negroes and their leadership when confronted by alleged instances of frustration of their desires should conduct themselves. One source of information with an aggressive outlook has advised there has been and will continue to be considerable agitation on the part of Negro leaders in an attempt to gain opportunities and what is due their race. This source has further stated that Negroes do not have the same opportunities and rights of citizenship the white race enjoys, and since they are called on to make the same or similar contributions to the war effort at home and abroad, Negro leaders naturally feel if they are to fight "for other people," they themselves should be granted "democracy at home." [redacted]

[redacted] *[100-135-3]*

Other sources, who are colored with what is believed to be a less aggressive outlook, have pointed to economic and social discrimination as causes for Negro unrest and discontent. However, they have pointed to militancy and alleged bias on the part of Negro leaders and the Negro press as contributing factors to discontent on the part of the Negro population.

While general reports have been received that Negroes are fundamentally loyal, it is believed pertinent to refer to those arrests and convictions of members and leaders of what have been termed "crackpot," anti-white, pro-Japanese organizations. The section in the appendix of this survey dealing with "Japanese Influence and Activity Among the American Negroes" reflects numerous arrests, indictments and convictions of these persons for violations of the Selective Training and Service Act of 1940, as amended, and the Sedition Statutes of the United States.

Although there have been isolated reports of expressions pro-German in nature attributed to individual Negroes, no reports or data have been received by this Bureau reflecting any organized German-inspired or planned activity to exploit the Negro race of the United States.

The section appearing in the appendix entitled "The Negro and National Socialism" reflects, however, that the German Government has had certain offices interested in national socialist propaganda among the American Negroes, and in 1939 a conference was held relative to this problem to consider the practical application and to crystallize ideas. It was decided at the conference that all propaganda addressed to the American Negro would be based on the primary premise that he is the subject of suppression and discrimination in the United States. Another approach has been pointed out which was contemplated to take the following trend:

> "You in your (American) propaganda are accusing us of subjugating peoples—but you in 1863 were freed but we know that you are the subject of prejudice and suppression, industrially and economically. The right of the ballot is voided, justice in the courts is questioned, and lynching is practiced."

Yet, an extensive survey of agitation among the Negroes in this country has not revealed any pattern that can be identified with German planning and resourcefulness along this line. The known German organizations in this country which have exhibited favoritism for the present regime in Germany have made little attempt to appeal to racial emotions of the population other than individuals of German descent and origin. No definite instances have been noted wherein German organizations in this country have attempted to propagandize or utilize the Negroes. The German-American Bund at no time attempted to effect cooperation with Negro groups. It is believed apparent that the Germans would be in an anomalous position should they appeal to the American Negro and identify this appeal with Germany. This is particularly evident in view of the attitude of national socialism toward inferior races which has been expressed in the past, and the doubt that Germany "would stoop" to abandon its own theory of racial supremacy sold to the German people merely for the purpose of agitating among the Negroes and thereby strengthening opposition.

It is believed the only possibility of agitating would be through the use of agent provocateurs, that is, the encouraging of agitation among the Negroes by persons actually sympathetic with the German regime but ignoring the theory of national socialism. The appeal would undoubtedly have to take the line adopted by reformists or, for that matter, the Communists, the former appealing to the human side of the question and the latter expounding racial equality and the cause of common people. It might be stated, further, that none of the agents of the German Government who have been arested in this country are known to have assumed such a technique.

The matter of pro-Italian forces conducting a planned or organized agitational or exploitation program among Negroes in this country has not come to light in any of the investigations or inquiries made by this Bureau since the origin of the national defense program.

Another phase of organizational activity among the colored race throughout the country is that engaged in by numerous unaffiliated or independent Negro groups or organizations. These have, as a whole, the advancement of the colored race for their purpose, although they vary in their degree of aggressiveness and militancy. Some of these groups, both national and local, have been pointed to as furthering unrest and dissatisfaction in that they allegedly adopt an inflammatory program such as constantly bringing to the attention of Negroes in a biased manner alleged instances of discrimination, segregation and alleged denial of rights of Negroes.

Perhaps the oldest of the unaffiliated Negro groups is the National Association for the Advancement of Colored People. This organization originally had as its purpose the uplifting of colored men and women in the United States and obtaining justice for them. It has also been active in defending Negroes in the need of legal assistance. Recent programs adopted by this organization, both nationally and locally, have included abolishing segregation in both civil and military life. With regard to local chapters of this organization, a number of them, as described in the body of this survey, reportedly are Communist influenced.

Another organization which is classified herein as independent and unaffiliated as far as its national body is concerned is known as the March on Washington Movement. This more recently organized group, headed by A. Philip Randolph, Negro labor leader, has on numerous occasions threatened to march on the City of Washington to demonstrate its sentiments unless certain demands are met by the United States Government. The organization's program, which provides for only Negro members, also adopts what is termed "non-violent direct action." This activity involves the use of methods without introducing violence to break down what are commonly referred to as "Jim Crow" practices, as well as local segregation and restriction customs. During 1942 the organization held several meetings throughout the East and Middle West which were attended by crowds involving a majority of Negroes which varied in size from 8,000 to 18,000.

The organization still publicly maintains its position that it will march on the City of Washington unless its demands are met. In various cities where it is active the organization devotes its program largely to local economic and social factors as they pertain to the local Negro inhabitants.

In the matter of Negro leadership throughout the country, a number of opinions have been expressed, both by Negro and white sources of information, that it is weak and not capable of acting in the best interests of its race. It is said further that many Negro leaders are the cause of much unrest and discontent and that their demands and accompanying accusations relative to alleged discrimination against Negroes and the denial of equal rights to them are, of course, effective and influential. It has been pointed out that Negro leaders subject to this criticism, rather than being selfish and unscrupulous, should have as their primary objective the advancement of their race. The practice of exploiting and enlarging beyond each alleged incident which acts to the detriment of Negroes by some Negro leaders is cited as an influential factor in stirring up unrest and discontent rather than promoting the best interests of their race.

It is also related actual confusion in some areas exists as to whom the leaders of the Negro population in the particular area are. The reason for this, it is said, is that some Negro leaders are considered both by members of their own race and by white people to be primarily interested in their own personal gain or advancement. Then, too, it is said that in some areas there is confusion within the Negro population as a result of class discrimination and rivalries which are allegedly based on differences of shades of skin or social background as reportedly acquired by shades of color or on the differences of wealth, professional standing and even family history.

Another aspect with regard to some Negro leadership has been pointed to which, it is said, involves Negro leaders oftentimes being too conservative in sentiment and as a result only representing the field of the middle or upper class of Negroes. It is said for this reason some Negro leaders are doubted to have close enough contact with other members of their race whom they claim to represent so as to actually know what these people desire or need. Recently, it might be pointed out, attacks have been made by more aggressive Negro leaders on others whom they term "handkerchief heads" or "Uncle Toms" (meaning the objects of their criticism are too conservative). Those who have expressed their criticism are said to have referred to themselves as the "new Negro."

That which has been reported as one of the outstanding agitational as well as influential forces among the Negro race is the Negro press. It will be recalled from the foregoing digests that complaints have been received from both Negro and white sources that the Negro press devotes itself to the sensational, if not inflammatory type of news reporting and editorial writing, especially where the subject matter concerns Negroes. The majority of these newspapers reportedly devote much space to alleged instances of discrimination against Negroes and violations of their rights along with sensational matters such as crime. While the reports and complaints, as well as opinions, which have been supplied concerning the Negro press were not meant to include all Negro newspapers, they nevertheless pointed to the larger Negro newspapers. In connection with this particular matter, the section devoted to "The Negro Press" appearing in the appendix should be referred to.

What have also been reported as important factors in a number of racial controversies and clashes and an influence in race relationship are the antagonism and feelings existing between white and Negro laborers in various areas. Closely related to this are said to be the reception and treatment given Negro workers by various labor unions. In both the northern and southern sections of the United States there have been strikes and walkouts in industrial concerns which were based upon the distaste or dislike of white workers to work unsegregated from Negroes. Several strikes have occurred which are related to have been caused by the up-grading or the placing of Negroes into skilled positions where they come in contact with white workers of an equal standing.

It should be noted, in this connection, that Negro workers have also been involved in several disputes which have resulted in their refusal to work because, as it was claimed, they were discriminated against by not being placed in better-paying jobs or classified as skilled employees although allegedly qualified. Another reason reported to have been adopted by Negro workers was that they were refused entrance to training programs operated by various industries.

With regard to labor unions, it will be recalled that a number of digests incorporated hereinbefore reflect that the policy of certain unions of segregating Negro members into separate locals has been the basis for considerable criticism and contention. On the other hand, it has been reported that some unions which have as a national policy opposed discrimination against and segregation of Negroes have experienced opposition on the part of their members to working or associating with Negro workers. Recently, in a large manufacturing plant in Detroit, approximately 25,000 white workers struck because reportedly two Negroes had been up-graded and placed into skilled positions in one of the plant's departments.

It has been further reported that there has been a degree of exploitation or utilization of Negroes and racial conditions by labor unions to obtain bargaining powers already held at a particular industrial plant by another union. It is also reported that this activity has been engaged in to obtain additional membership in a particular union or to take from the reach of "opposing" unions prospective members. The theme said to be used in this activity is that increased employment in certain industries should be granted to Negroes or that alleged discrimination or segregation be done away with. Charges and allegations have also been received that union organizers are demanding these things solely for the purpose of increasing the number of dues-paying members by offering an attractive programs to Negroes and thereafter using their increased membership as a wedge to obtaining further bargaining powers. At the same time, it should be pointed out several instances have been reported wherein representatives of a particular union demanded that Negro workers be segregated from white workers, claiming their white members would not work alongside the Negroes or use the same recreational or comfort facilities.

It has been noted throughout the various digests appearing in this section Negro churches and their leaders have participated actively in seeking additional rights for their race. It will be recalled that economic and political matters as they affect the colored race have been dealt with on a widespread scale. While these matters were, prior to the origin of this war, in all probability dealt with to some degree, it appears that a trend has been established in which Negro churches, as well as their leaders, have branched out into other fields rather than strictly to confine themselves to religious activities. This is believed to be an important consideration in respect to racial conditions and race relationship in light of the historically deep religious feeling of Negroes and their close adherence to their various churches. Although reports are received of a new militancy or aggressiveness expressed by Negro church leaders, at the same time in practically all sections of the country indications are received that various Negro churches are the centers for plans and programs to better racial conditions and race relationship.

With all of the foregoing organizational forces and factors which are important in this matter, there must also be considered the current tempo of living in this country for all races which has been increased by the national defense program and the war effort. Not only has everyday life been increased in tempo, but it has become more complex and this has been experienced in areas which are already crowded by large populations. To these areas have come people from other sections of the country, large numbers of whom probably have never before experienced urban life. This migration, which results primarily from the increased demand by war industries for more labor, has brought about an increased congestion in the already heavily populated areas and has created a tension and new complexity in race relationship heretofore nonexistent in many areas. Shortages of everyday facilities and conveniences have also been caused and ordinary habits and tastes for amusement and entertainment already affected by the war program are further frustrated by the unavailability of regular recreational and amusement facilities. Necessities such as housing and transportation in most areas where war production is engaged in have become seriously inadequate. In those areas wherein segregation is applied to housing and public transportation, a shortage and overcrowding are pointed to as highly influential factors in the unrest and discontent of Negroes. Consequently, demands are made either for increased facilities and service or for the elimination of restrictions or for both. In other areas where segregation is not generally customary in either housing or in public transportation, the lack of availability or the curtailment of service, whether based on lack of equipment or material or the shortage of personnel, has been pointed to as discrimination against Negroes, especially when the situation affects Negro neighborhoods.

Collateral to but involving the transportation issue have been the heated campaigns in some municipalities for the employment of Negroes as streetcar and bus operators and conductors. This has been exploited by such forces as the Negro press and the Communist Party and in some areas it is said to be the cause of considerable unrest, especially when it is brought to the attention of Negro residents who are reportedly affected by curtailed or inadequate transportation service. Furthermore, transportation facilities are said to be the source in many areas of fights, clashes and altercations between Negroes and whites. These have occurred in many sections of the country and have not been confined to areas where segregation or restriction practices relative to Negroes are prevalent.

An additional factor to be considered in the migration of people from other areas into industrial sections is that the new inhabitants have brought with them the same sentiments and feelings which they had in areas wherein they previously resided and where entirely different customs and habits prevail and a completely different population make-up exists. There has also been reported an increase of juvenile delinquency as well as evidences of hoodlumism, especially in the larger cities of the country. This has been particularly apparent in such cities as Detroit and in the Harlem section of New York City where recent rioting and trouble in both places involved juvenile delinquents and hoodlums.

In the new areas there is available increased income for the new arrivals which logically provides an added want and desire for both the ordinary necessities and nonnecessities. In a number of places where this situation is in existence and where segregation is usually practiced only with regard to a few ways of living, Negroes, as a natural result, have sought out places normally the habitat of white people. This has led to increased tension which, as it did in Detroit with added contributing factors, provided fuel for riots. In those places where segregation and other restrictions normally affect Negroes a decided resentment or discontent is said to have been aroused.

Another aspect of the opportunity for increased income and better employment for Negroes in industrial areas has been reportedly the resulting discontent in areas where these are unavailable to the inhabitants. The cognizance of Negroes in these latter areas that there are chances for better economic gains in other areas has been pointed to by sources of information as a cause or perhaps a justification of unrest.

As it has been indicated throughout the first section of this survey, there have been certain economic, social and political factors existing throughout the country which are designated as being at least partially responsible for current dissatisfaction and unrest among Negroes in many areas. Although many of these factors have been dwelt upon for a considerable period of time by leaders and organizations interested in the advancement of the Negro race, more recently the attitude and program of these leaders and groups have become increasingly aggressive. Demands for immediate, if not revolutionary, changes in certain phases of everyday life have been made. Yet generally no overall program has been presented. There are, on the other hand, a number of individuals as well as groups interested in racial conditions which promulgate seemingly a more temperate and over-all program concerning race relationship and cooperation. It is believed by these latter individuals and groups that a program of education extended over a period of time must be given to the white and Negro races in the United States. They do not advocate that a long-established custom or habit be done away with immediately, nor is the abolition of segregation or certain restrictions urged as an immediate step. What is reported to be actually the focal point of objections is the discrimination as it is claimed to exist in various social and economic phases.

Outlined hereinafter are the more widespread and more frequently reported problems involving social, economic and political aspects which are alleged to be responsible, at least partially, for discontent on the part of members of the Negro race.

I. Discrimination and the attitude of promoting discrimination as it affects equal rights of Negroes.
   A. In war production industries.
   B. In labor unions.
   C. In the Armed Forces.
   D. In civilian life involving—
      1. Lack of more remunerative employment.
      2. Unequal returns for equal efforts to those extended by other races.

II. Lack of educational facilities.
   A. Inadequate facilities and lower pay for Negro teachers.
   B. No uniform or widespread training for skilled trades.

III. Low standards of living as a result of—
   A. Crowded areas.
   B. Lack of healthful and ample housing facilities.
   C. Inadequate medical treatment and health care.
   D. Lack of ample recreational facilities and places of amusement.

IV. Lynching and alleged brutality afforded Negro criminal suspects.

V. Poll tax as an alleged means of denying suffrage to Negroes.

VI. The controversial matters of racial segregation and restrictions.

VII. Inherent or acquired indolence or lack of aggressiveness alleged to exist among some individual Negroes.

SECTION 2

Appendix

(SECRET)

Federal Bureau of Investigation
United States Department of Justice
J. Edgar Hoover, Director

OUTLINE

SECTION II (APPENDIX) SURVEY OF RACIAL CONDITIONS IN THE UNITED STATES August 15, 1943

I

THE NEGRO PRESS

One of the most effective and important forces attracting the attention of the colored race and swaying their opinion is the Negro press. This has been borne out in the opinions and information which have been supplied by those interviewed in connection with the various surveys, as well as by confidential informants. As of 1940 there were listed one hundred and fifty-five Negro newspapers in the United States which had a total circulation of 1,276,600.

[*Ref. for figures: The Negro Handbook, page 201; orig. source Bureau Census*]

Sources of information have volunteered the opinion that the Negro press is a strong provocator of discontent among Negroes. It is claimed that its general tone is not at all, in many instances, informative or helpful to its own race. It is said that more space is devoted to alleged instances of discrimination or mistreatment of Negroes than there is to matters which are educational or helpful. The claim is that the sensational is foremost while true reportorial material is sidetracked.

Recently, a Negro writer, who is connected with an organization with a membership reportedly composed of individuals leaning towards liberalism, criticized the Negro press and described it as being detrimental to the present cause of the Negro race. It was said that many Negro newspapers attacked prejudicial interests to the Negro race in such a manner as to place the Negro press in a prejudiced position. The news writing in the Negro press was described as portraying the Negro at his worst, as well as publishing news of the white community in such a light which shows it at its worst. It was the opinion that a distorted and dishonest picture of this country and of the progress and opinion of the Negro in it was painted.

Concerning this situation in which the Negro press has allegedly placed itself, this same writer has pointed out that no white community would tolerate, as its own, sensational hate-making newspapers. It was the further opinion that the Negro community cannot afford to tolerate them any more than can the white community.

[*"A Negro Warns the Negro Press" by Warren Brown, PhD. Jan. '43 Readers Digest*]

Appearing in one of the national Negro newspapers was an article by an individual whose past connections are said to reflect his radical leanings, if not close affiliations with the Communist Party. This article attacked the foregoing opinion of the Negro press, first, by bringing the personal into his side of the argument and condemning the afore-mentioned writer. He said that the writer erred when he claimed that the Negro press "plays up the colored man at his worst." The individual writing for the newspaper said that the Negro press is "forced to leave this for the enlightening white press which features every colored person's arrest on the front page and every subsequent acquittal on the back." No further defense or counterattack was made in the newspaper article. [*Wash. Afro. American Pg. 1, 1-3-43, A. Clayton Powell, Jr.*]

The Negro publishing company, the Afro-American Company, Baltimore, Maryland, which publishes the Afro-American newspapers, also attacked this opinion of the Negro press in an advertisement appearing on page 10 of the Washington Post, Washington, D.C., under date of January 17, 1943. The newspaper publishing company answers the afore-mentioned article. First it attacks the author of the article criticizing the Negro press and then answers the seven points said to have been made in the original criticism.

With respect to the assertion that Negro leaders are irresponsible and live upon agitation, the point is made in the advertisement that there are many Negro leaders in whom thousands of colored people have complete confidence. Frederick Douglass, Mary Church Terrell, Kelly Miller, and W. E. B. Du Bois are some of the famous colored people referred to in the advertisement, apparently as an example of Negro leaders.

Another point in the article of criticism which the advertisement claims was made was that the campaign to embitter colored people began with the Communists. The advertisement attempts to answer this by saying the American Communist Party was organized in 1919 while the National Association for the Advancement of Colored People began fighting for Negro rights in 1910. No further answer was made to this point.

With respect to the allegation in the criticism that most Negro newspapers are "colored first and American second," the advertisement answers by bringing into play the "personal," saying that the writer should "take his Ph.D. into 99 per cent of the essential activities of American life and discover which is valued more highly, color or American citizenship."

In the article the point was made that the Negro press uses every possible instance to breed ill will between the races and to portray the Negro and white people at their worst. As an answer to this, it was stated in the advertisement that newspapers cannot continuously publish stories for which there is no basis in fact. Also it was said that if Negroes were to receive the same treatment as all other Americans the Negro press would soon disappear and that it exists and expands is the best proof that it is indispensable.

To the charge that Negro newspapers defend Negro criminals and print too many crime stories with headlines, the statement is made that what the Negro press defends is the right of the accused to a fair trial and, when guilty, his right to have competent attorneys point out to court mitigating circumstances. The advertisement elaborated: "Justice frequently goes awry, through ignorance or poverty of the accused and through prejudice or indifference of the police and courts."

With respect to the charge that Negro newspapers print too many crime stories, it was said in the advertisement that the Afro-American Company's survey of six leading Negro newspapers for the week of January 11 to 17, 1943, showed less than five per cent of the news dealing with "police courts." The advertisement also stated that newspapers print what their readers demand and that they "fold up quickly when they lose the common touch."

With respect to the point made in the article criticizing the Negro press, that the Negro press should be in worthier hands, the "personal" is brought into play again in the statement that if the writer "thinks he could do a better job, no field is open wider than the profession of journalism."

With respect to the allegation that the Negro press "twisted mistreatment of Negro troops in England" out of proportion, it was countered by allegations in the advertisement that the publications Time and Nation had articles which were not censored while the Afro-American correspondents' articles had been censored. The Nation's story was reprinted in the general Afro-American of January 9, 1943. No statement was made with regard to the facts.

The advertisement continues making allegations against the writer of the article and hints that although it does not say that the writer is a tool of intolerant and bigoted groups with respect to the Negroes, he serves their purpose.

[*Wash. Post pg. 10, 1-17-43*]

There follows hereinafter information relative to those Negro newspapers which have the largest circulations in this country. It should be noted that in the previous digests of information received in each Field Division there appears general information concerning those newspapers which have been alleged to be sources of unrest or discontent among the Negro race in the area in question.

The Afro-American

The Negro newspaper, the Afro-American, is said to have been organized in 1891 and throughout the period of its existence, it is stated to have been controlled by the same family. Its editions are believed to be the most widely read of all newspapers. The material contained therein is devoted exclusively to items of interest to the Negro race in the Mid-Atlantic and in the Southern section of this country. The officers of this organization are:

Carl J. Murphy, President

B. Arnett Murphy, Vice-President

George B. Murphy, Secretary

John H. Murphy, Jr., Treasurer

Howard H. Murphy, Assistant Secretary

The Board of Directors consists of the above-listed officers with the exception of the Assistant Secretary. All of the officers except Howard H. Murphy are brothers.

The Baltimore Afro-American, the edition published for Baltimore and its vicinity, is put on the newsstands biweekly and the four other papers controlled by the Afro-American Company are published weekly. These papers are the Philadelphia Afro-American, the Washington Afro-American, the Richmond Afro-American, and the New Jersey Afro-American. Distribution is said to be principally through newsstands in the various cities where editions are published and in other large and small towns throughout the South, in addition to which the company has approximately 2,500 mail subscribers. The weekly circulation figures total approximately 135,000 copies. The company is said to have about 165 employees, 105 of which have headquarters in Baltimore.

The organization publishing the various Afro-American papers is said to have had as of December 31, 1941, a tangible net worth of $14,076.07. Its total current liability was slightly over $20,000. The organization is a Maryland corporation, chartered August 7, 1907. The corporation was formed to continue a business established in 1891 by John H. Murphy, Sr., father of the present officers.

There have been several indications received reflecting Communist connections on the part of the newspaper and individuals connected with it. As examples the following information is set out:

With further reference to the officers in this organization, it should be pointed out that George B. Murphy, Jr., former secretary of the paper, has recently been appointed National Administrative Secretary of the National Negro Congress, a Communist influenced organization.

In the June 2, 1942, edition of the Afro-American, the column entitled "Big Parade" by Ralph Matthews contains a section captioned "Persecuting the Communists." Therein an opinion is expressed by the writer that there was a connection between the pardoning of Earl Browder and the ordering of Harry Bridges' deportation by the Attorney General. It is said that this connection is readily apparent inasmuch as the former action was democratic and wholly justified although opposed by "Fascist elements" in the person of large industrialists, while the order to deport Bridges was an effort to placate the industrialists. This editorial then pointed out those matters in the Communist Party line which allegedly would benefit the Negro race and stated that it would be "a tragedy if any group, . . . clamoring for these things, should be silenced on a technicality. . . ."

In the month of August it was reported that William Taylor, Chairman of the Communist Party for the State of Maryland, considered one Mrs. Smith of the Afro-American to be an excellent person to handle all advertisements which the Communist Party might submit from time to time to the Afro-American.

In the September 19, 1942, issue of the Afro-American a message from the Communist Party and the Young Communist League, as was given by William Taylor to Mrs. Smith, previously referred to, was set out extending "heartiest birthday greetings to the Afro-American on its 50th Anniversary. . . ."

The issue of the Afro-American for September 26, 1942, carried an announcement as furnished by Dorothy Rose Blumberg, wife of Dr. Albert E. Blumberg, Secretary of the Communist Party of Maryland and the District of Columbia, describing a radio program relative to "the second front" sponsored by the Communist Party.

It was reported that an article written by Dorothy Blumberg, referred to previously, relative to the demand that Negroes be used as bus drivers on a specified route of the Baltimore Transit Company was to have been printed in the paper on November 6, 1942. It is said that Mrs. Blumberg explained to the city editor of the newspaper that the Young Communist League was sponsoring a campaign to force the Chesapeake and Potomac Telephone Company to use Negroes as operators, while the Communist Party was backing the Transit Company issue. It is further reported that the city editor expressed great satisfaction with the progress in both campaigns at that time, as well as appreciation for the efforts of the Communist Party. It was said at that time the city editor made it clear that in the future the Afro-American newspaper would be glad to print any other information concerning these or related programs which the Communist Party might sponsor.

Issues of the Baltimore Afro-American, which, it is said contain practically the same articles and editorials as do the other editions of the Afro-American, have been reviewed for a period covering November 1, 1941, to September 15, 1942. Typical topics will be set out hereinafter as taken from a chronological review, all of which have been paraphrased but in effect give the meaning of the article in general or the idea or purpose behind the particular editorial:

> The War and Navy Departments, alleged segregation and discriminatory policy in them denounced.
>
> The alleged deplorable conditions in army camps and the alleged inability of colored soldiers to advance dealt with.
>
> The alleged mistreatment of colored stenographers in the War Department and alleged Jim Crow stenographic pools labeled a form of sabotage.
>
> United States army camp conditions made colored soldiers prefer jail or desertion.
>
> Southern white officers the worst enemies colored soldiers face.
>
> Alleged statements that the American and British governments have made a secret agreement not to hire colored Americans in construction and maintenance work at the Government's leased island bases.
>
> Denunciation of a Baltimore Navy "E" firm for alleged failure to employ colored workers in alleged defiance of presidential order.
>
> Colored people urged to pray for a long war so all race hate and evil can be destroyed.
>
> Allegations that the Army would rather keep the colored people in place than win the war.
>
> Suggestion that Jews rise up and resist defiance of "Americanism" which caused the Detroit riot.
>
> Suggestion that lynchings and other unbearable conditions will be imposed on colored soldiers when they leave the United States.
>
> Suggestion that rioting between colored soldiers and civilians may be expected soon in that the morale of the colored soldier is being crushed.
>
> Allegation that "Florida Democracy" makes soldiers wonder what they are fighting for and that they consider the various racial conditions worse than Japanese rule.
>
> Allegations to the effect that some of the Army's methods are comparable to those of Hitler.
>
> Industrialists who will not hire Negroes crippling the war effort and guilty of treason through disloyalty and of sedition through revolt against the orders of the President.

During this same period, the articles in this newspaper continued stressing segregation, job discrimination, police brutality, mounting race unrest, and mistreatment of colored soldiers and merchant seamen. It was stated that the South "prefers lynchings to orderly processes in courts." It was said, "We have to fight segregation before we can get to Hitler." Again it was said, "Only a traitor will say we are satisfied"; and again, "Time is ripe to test whether the Constitution is a charter of freedom or a diarrhea of words." It was headlined, "War and Work in Mississippi Called 'Worse than Slavery.' " It was said, "Axis power is not our greatest enemy"; and again that, "every argument for tyranny and oppression for colored people has been evoked against foreigners, especially Irish, Catholics and Jews." It denounced persecution of the Communists, stating that deporting Bridges was to quiet the "howl" caused by freeing Earl Browder. It is again alleged that colored soldiers in Georgia would prefer "a bunk in Hell." It has commended the Communist Party policies and its fight favoring the Negro.

The September 19, 1942, issue carried a reprint of an article by Victor Bernstein which appeared in PM and which is entitled, "Deep South Fights, But Not For 4 Freedoms." This article presents the conclusions arrived at by Bernstein concerning racial conditions in the South. The article in effect is very critical of the South's treatment of the Negroes as well as of the customs and practices in that area.

The September 19, 1942, issue also carried an article entitled, "NAACP President Lauds AFRO's Battle," in which the president of the city and state branches of this organization at Richmond, Virginia, is quoted as follows: "Colored Americans . . . cannot feel that they are fighting for democracy until they are permitted to enjoy some of it. . . . Uncle Toms and those who would sell our rights for personal gain are themselves denied their own rights just as are all others of us. Such persons are a menace to the race and should be exposed at every possible opportunity."

Following are titles of articles appearing in various issues of this paper during the fall of 1942:

9-19-42 "Bethlehem Refuses Skilled Job to Employee of 16 Years."

9-19-42 "Colored Librarian to Replace White, but Still No Training."

9-19-42 "Minister Beaten Because He Touched White Woman."

9-19-42 "Phone Company Still Mum on Job Policy—Officials Playing 'Confidence' Game, Jiving Both Races."

9-19-42 "Are Major League Clubs Fooling Fans on Admitting Colored Players in 1943."

9-22-42 "Soldiers Meet Color Bar in London—Can't Enter Certain Bars or Dance Halls, AFRO Writer Reports—U.S. Military Chiefs Blamed for British Action; Officials 'Have No Comments.' "

10-6-42 "The Suckers Did Not Get the Jobs—3,000 Colored Laborers Recruited for Work in California. Left Stranded While Government Sends for Mexicans."

10-10-42 "Speak Out Mr. Roosevelt—Your Inconsistent War Department Kowtows to Camp Lee Jim Crow and Asks England to Permit a Color Bar Abroad."

10-10-42 "Jones Prefers Jail to Jim Crow Army."

10-13-42 "Professional Rank Closed to Us—Navy."

10-13-42 "Speak Out Mr. Roosevelt: Tell the Minority Groups What They are Fighting for; Define Democracy as it Applies to Them."

10-13-42 "Some Nasty Situations Colored Actors Must Face Touring Democratic America."

10-17-42 "Racial Bias Keeps Baltimore Man Out of CAA Pilot Course."

10-24-42 "Transit Company Jobs for 'Master Race' Only." (This article contained the following statement: " 'No present plans for changing this policy' is the answer of the Baltimore Transit Company to the request of the Communist Party of Baltimore that colored bus drivers be hired. . . . to eliminate discrimination and aid in the war effort.")

10-24-42 "War Called Blessing for Dark Races."

11-21-42 "Hitler's Allies." (There is a swastika beside this caption and the article denounced Montgomery Ward for its alleged refusal to use colored persons in other than menial jobs. Subheadings in this article are: "Jobs for Members of 'Master' Race" and "Plans to Cling to Fascist Policy.")

11-28-42 "Labor Surprised at Color Prejudice Among U.S. Troops; General MacArthur Advised that U.S. Army Disunity is Menance to the War Activity 'Down Under.' "

12-1-42 "Youth Won't Fight to Save Segregation and Injustice."

12-1-42 "N.Y. Man Balks on Jim Crow Draft Call" (This article refers to and explains the Winfred Lynn Selective Service case which is set forth in the section contained herein devoted to the March on Washington Movement.)

12-12-42 "Communists Make Issue of Phoenix Riot; Demand Reforms."

12-19-42 "Lay Racial Strife to Dixie Whites at Dix."

The October 6, 1942, issue of the newspaper carried a reprint of a letter allegedly received by the paper from a white sergeant at Camp Lee, Virginia. It bears the caption, "A White Sergeant Sends a Letter From His Pal in Far-Off Georgia, U.S.A." The letter is purportedly from a Negro private. Among the statements contained in this letter are: ". . . I am almost living in 'hell.' It appears to me that I have been marooned in a place far set from the democratic country called America. . . . The transportation . . . is more than words can describe . . . the white get on first and if there is room left maybe you can get a ride. . . . Truthfully, I can see that we are in for a long war unless things are changed. In fact, as things get worse and worse, I feel myself changing more and more. I feel less a part of it all."

The December 29, 1942, issue carried an article by Leon W. Taylor of the American Negro Press. He stated in commenting on the efforts of the Japanese to reach colored Americans through propaganda: "There are millions of colored Americans, unswerving in loyalty and devotion to the country of their birth, whom foreign propaganda can never touch. But among those whom a sectional way of life has blighted with the course of stagnation, Japanese propaganda has found its mark. Behind their proverbial grin, a world of emotions lie hidden. Within the very souls of these lower classes burn the smouldering embers of revenge upon the perpetrators of brutalities which have besmirched the fact of American civilization."

The January 2, 1943, issue contains an article captioned, "Army's Segregation Pattern Climaxed at Tuskegee Air School." This article begins, "Race segregation is being practiced at the Army . . . Flying School here, despite its bad effect on the morale of colored students who are being trained for combat duty with the Army Air Forces. The intolerant and patronizing attitude of some Southern white officers who are in command is said to be particularly irksome. . . ."

The January 5, 1943, issue carries a cartoon under the caption, "Booker T. Never Thought it Would Happen Here," which depicts the Army Flying School at Tuskegee Institute with two spiked Army boots with the inscription, "Army Jim Crow" on them, squarely astride the runway.

In the January 5, 1943, issue in the column entitled, "The Big Parade," by Ralph Matthews, a section is devoted to the principal events in 1942 relative to the Negro race. Matthews states in part: ". . . and later we trudged together over the bloody streets of Alexandria, Louisiana, where Dixie cops had mowed down black boys who wanted a taste of the four freedoms for themselves right here at home. . . . You recall also when we travelled . . . to Rome, Georgia, to hear Roland Hayes relate how he had been clubbed and beaten by his fellow white citizens because he had failed to stay in his place. And then again we went hand in hand down into the black jaws of a coal mine in Birmingham to get eyewitness accounts of the murder of a laborer by a thewy deputy which sent 500 comrades out on a protest strike. That was a sorely ugly day when the white faces of gun-toting crackers were besmirched with glares blacker than the ebony skins of the indignant, frustrated miners. . . ."

The January 9, 1943, issue in an article entitled, "Court Won't Pass on Quotas," also refers to the Winfred Lynn Selective Service case. Lynn is quoted as saying, "I was willing to go to jail rather than to fight where there is discrimination." This same issue carries a reprint from the magazine, "The Nation," entitled, "Davis Report on Troops in England Misleading." This article begins, "The colored Brigadier General, Benjamin O. Davis, was recently sent to investigate reports of trouble between colored and white American troops stationed in the British Isles. After an inspection that lasted only a few days, he issued a statement to the effect that the situation had been greatly exaggerated, that generally the boys were getting along fine together . . . so far as the Army was concerned, there was no problem—'White and colored troops are treated as equal, having exactly the same rights and privileges.' It is hard to reconcile General Davis' report with my own observations during my recent two months' stay in England or with what colored soldiers told me. . . ." The above article was written by one Joseph Julian.

The January 23, 1943, issue carries the column of Reverend Baxter L. Matthews of Baltimore, Maryland, and is given the heading, "I Predict for 1943." It is stated therein: "The war will not end in 1943. That's my prediction and my hope. It will be most unfortunate for the colored people were it to end. It should continue until the two races are better acquainted and every human being has value as a person. The white race does not know us, our ability to think, to achieve, to accomplish under similar circumstances. . . ."

In the January 26, 1943, issue, the Afro-American in an editorial entitled, "OWI's Two Million Pamphlets," refers to a pamphlet put out by this agency entitled, "Negroes and the War." The paper states in this connection: "It appears to be directed to the colored people to show them how much better off we are under Uncle Sam than under Hitler. But 100,000,000 propaganda pamphlets cannot undo the great harm that Congress heaps up by filibustering against poll tax repeal and anti-lynching bills. And McNutt's collaboration with the railroads in sabotaging the FEPC renders ineffective anything OWI can print."

In the January 30, 1943, issue an article written by Edgar G. Brown entitled, "The Washington Scene," in commenting on the resignation of Judge William H. Hastie, Negro civilian aide to the Secretary of War, states, "What can their boys expect on the home front menu, Bill, old friend, besides killings, humiliation, discrimination, jim crow and other signs of Dixie's gestapo and 'verboten' at every turn? Truman Gibson, Louis Lautier, in fact, the whole race advisers unit should be liquidated. These bluffers and 'buffers' should cut loose from the Government pay roll, end the pussyfooting and join the 'agitators' in a commando raid to blast out the Ku Kluxers in Washington. . . ."

The February 16, 1943, issue has an article entitled, "NAACP Hits Use of Colored Troops for Snow Removal." This article states: "Why were colored troops brought 60 miles from Fort Lewis to clean snow in downtown Seattle, Washington, while none of the white soldiers at near-by Fort Lawton were detailed for this work? The NAACP this week asked Secretary of War Stimson. Is it the purpose of the War Department to use colored troops drawing pay of $50 a month to relieve municipalities of the legitimate expenses for carrying on the regular services of these cities? These men could not protest. They are in the Army and had to obey orders."

The February 20, 1943, issue has an article captioned, "British, Trinidad Folks Resent American Inspired Jim Crow." Here the paper has reprinted parts of an article appearing in the Daily Worker, Communist news organ, concerning conditions of Negro troops stationed in Trinidad. A quotation from this article is set forth: "But it seems that a group of officers, Southerners, most of them, have gone out of their way, not only to make life difficult for the colored troops here, but to shut off all contact between these troops and the British population. There have been cases here where colored troops are worked all week long without respite. Pay has been held up for colored troops and passes refused. Regulations have been passed preventing colored and white troops from leaving the camps on the same night. And most shocking of all . . . is the fact that American officers have actually come to British homes forewarning them about the colored troops, spreading all sorts of positively nasty stuff about rape tendencies and disease among colored troops."

The March 6, 1943, issue has an article entitled, "Building Alcan Highway Had its Hardships; Returning Soldiers Say Prejudice Made the Job Tougher." Quotations are then set forth apparently taken from unknown Negro soldiers. Such quotations are: "We worked every day and never knew when Sunday came. Not only was there no association between colored and white line troops, but some white officers in the colored units went out of their way to make it as unpleasant for us as possible; At one point along the road . . . white Canadian girls met our train and wanted to distribute knick-knacks to the soldiers. White officers, many of them Southerners, patrolled the platform with drawn revolvers and refused the men permission to leave the train or speak to the girls. We were treated more like convicts than members of the United States Army. We were put to work building barracks for a contingent of white soldiers who had not even left the States, while we were still forced to live in tents. Sometimes if the boys built too many fires along the project in order to keep warm, officers would order all fires to be put out. Some of our men are reported to have lost their ears and other members of their bodies in the bitter cold. . . ."

The March 13, 1943, issue commented on the reversal of the first conviction of George Sylvester Viereck under the caption, "The Viereck Case and Us." It was stated: "If Viereck deserves to be free then all Japanese now being held in concentration camps simply because they are members of an alien race and are considered potential enemies deserve to be free. If Viereck deserves to be free, then all members of the Islam Cult, convicted of alleged seditious activities because they passively refused to fight for the preservation of white supremacy, deserve to be free. If Viereck deserves to be free, then every black boy convicted because he refused to register and serve in the American armed forces because they discriminated against him and denied him all full rights as a citizen, deserves to be free. . . . The jails of the South are crammed today with black men, some guilty and others innocent, who were convicted by prosecutors whose language was both prejudicial and offensive and appealed to the emotions of all white juries wherever the defendant came in conflict with a white accuser. . . ."

The March 20, 1943, issue carries an article entitled, "Army Wants Only 1 Colored Doctor in 64." Therein it is stated that only 153 of the 9,900 doctors accepted by the Army during 1943 will be colored. It is further stated, ". . . the Army is continuing its pattern of racial segregation and confining colored doctors to colored station hospitals or colored wards or with colored regiments in the field."

The March 23, 1943, issue has an editorial with the caption, "1400 Guinea Pigs at Fort Benning." This editorial denounces a statement by the War Department that sulfathiazole tablets had been given to 1400 Negro troops at Fort Benning, Georgia, over a period of five months. There is listed each reason advanced by the War Department for this practice and each was in turn described as utterly without merit. The drug itself is criticized as unsafe for human use. The editorial concludes, "We cannot agree with the Fort Benning doctors that a high V.D. rate justifies their taking chances with the lives of 1400 of our soldiers. . . . If there are to be any more mass guinea pig tests in the Army, the parents back home would prefer that the bright young doctors use somebody else."

In this same issue a cartoon is carried bearing the caption, "Just a Guinea Pig," which depicts one of these animals on the side of which is written "1400 colored soldiers." Being inserted into the flesh of this guinea pig is a syringe on which is written "U.S. Army Sulfa-Drug Experiment."

The March 23, 1943, issue also carries an article entitled, "Red Cross Defender Blames High Colored Officer for Blood J. C." In the article following this headline a charge is made that Brigadier General B. O. Davis, colored, sanctioned the institution of separate facilities for taking blood of both colored and white persons under the Red Cross plan. This alleged action of General Davis is denounced by the paper which states there can be no justification whatever for separating blood plasma.

It should be noted that the newspaper during the winter of 1942 and 1943 on several occasions carried not only articles but advertisements pertaining to the Communist Party and the Young Communist League. Beginning January 19, 1943, each issue of the Afro-American carried mention of the fact that Earl Browder, General Secretary of the Communist Party, would be the principal speaker at the Lincoln-Douglas victory rally held February 12, 1943, at the Lyric Theater, Baltimore, Maryland. On February 16, 1943, the paper carried an account of Browder's speech.

Amsterdam Star News and People's Voice, New York City

The only two Negro newspapers with a circulation of more than 25,000 in New York City are the Amsterdam Star News and the People's Voice. These two newspapers are opposed to one another's policies and it is said there is considerable rivalry as far as obtaining wider circulation is concerned.

The Amsterdam Star News is described as a well-established newspaper, having been formed in 1909. It is presently located at 2271 Seventh Avenue, New York City, and it is reported that it has a circulation of approximately 29,000. This newspaper is described as a comparatively conservative publication and has on several occasions openly expressed itself against Communism. In this regard, the newspaper has opposed the Communist Party line relative to the Harlem Section of New York, especially the crime wave there. The Amsterdam Star News has expressed itself editorially in a manner which is said to be descriptive of the law-abiding people in Harlem. It ran a series of articles aimed at crystallizing public sentiment and a campaign to clean up Harlem and to rid it of the criminal element. The Communist Party line with regard to the crime wave in Harlem gave itself to the twisting and distorting of facts in order to garner mass support. Communist groups are said to attack the police enforcement and attempt to characterize the actions of the Police Department in enforcing law as attacks on the Negro people. This is so especially when Negroes are arrested for the commission of crimes.

The People's Voice, which is edited by Adam Clayton Powell, Jr., a Negro New York City Councilman and preacher, has been described by sources of information as a very helpful transmission belt for the Communist Party. It is said that its editorial and reportorial policy is definitely pro-Communist. In this connection, Adam Clayton Powell, the editor and publisher, has been affiliated on many occasions with pro-Communist individuals, groups and organizations. At one time it was rumored that the paper was being published by the publishers of the newspaper PM, a New York

City daily, however, no supporting information has been received in this respect. An examination of the paper over a period of time reflects that it contains articles of an inflammatory nature which have been described by sources of information thoroughly familiar with the Communist Party line as being in direct support of the same. In the month of August 1942, publication was suspended, as stated by Adam Clayton Powell, temporarily because of differences with certain people over the editorial policy of the paper.

With regard to the crime wave in Harlem, which was described as being rampant during the summer months of 1942, it is said to have completely given itself over to the Communist Party line with respect to this situation. It condemned other newspaper accounts of the crime situation in Harlem as a "smear campaign" against the inhabitants of that section of New York City. To further bear out the charges of Communist connections on the part of the People's Voice, there has been reported recently information reflecting that Max Yergan has contributed money to the paper and his name is now carried in the publication block of the paper. Estimates on the sum invested by Yergan have varied from $3,000 or $4,000 to $75,000.

With regard to Yergan, considerable information has been received reflecting that he is close to the Communist Party, if not an actual Party member. He is a leader in such Communist front organizations or reportedly Communist influenced groups as the National Negro Congress and the Council on African Affairs. It is said that the reason for obtaining support from Yergan was laid to the withdrawal of the financial support by Marshall Field, publisher of PM and the Chicago Sun. This necessitated "seeking new money." In this connection, it was reported that one of the editors of the People's Voice expressed sharp disagreement with the publishers in their step in taking in Max Yergan. He is said to have felt that adopting a partisan policy had cut down on the circulation of the paper. He believed that the paper, had it continued its non-partisan policy, would have become one of the most successful Negro newspapers in the Eastern States and would have built up a large circulation.

The Black Dispatch

The Black Dispatch, which is published by the Black Dispatch Publishing Company, Roscoe Dunjee, Editor, is said to have been organized in 1941. The exact circulation figures for this paper are not known, however, it is published every Wednesday. The guiding and controlling light is reported to be Roscoe Dunjee. With regard to Dunjee, it has been reported that although he is not believed to be an actual member of the Communist Party, he is said to be sympathetic with the Communist cause to such an extent that he has allowed his name to be used by many Communist front organizations and is said to have used his talent as a speaker in appearing at meetings of these groups. In this regard, it is said that Allen Shaw, State Secretary of the Communist Party in the State of Oklahoma, frequently confers with Dunjee, and that it is believed that the newspaper office of Dunjee does a considerable amount of printing for the Communist Party in the State of Oklahoma.

Dunjee is said to be classed as the strongest Negro leader in the State of Oklahoma, both from the point of his leadership of other Negroes and in his actual political power. It is said that although many of the Negroes in the State of Oklahoma have a great deal of respect for Dunjee, most of those who are termed as having more than average intelligence are afraid of Dunjee's stand on a good many matters. Dunjee is said to favor interracial marriage, free association between Negroes and white people, and he is said to have been heard to boast of his associations with white people on various occasions.

At the present time he is said to be State President of the Oklahoma Chapter of the National Association for the Advancement of Colored People.

For some time the Black Dispatch has been outspoken against practically all incidents in the country in which Negro troops are involved and in all cases, particularly, in the South where Negroes are brought to trial. There are being set out hereinafter digests of articles and editorials as obtained from various issues of the publication which are believed to be inflammatory in nature and which are thought to be a reflection of the general tone of this newspaper.

In the June 20, 1942, issue, an article related of an alleged assault on a Negro soldier in the Oklahoma City Bus Terminal. The article contained the following sentence: "Uncle Sam's Army uniform did not prevent these three Negro soldiers from feeling the sting of American race prejudice."

In the same issue, another article, page 4, contained the following excerpt: "Should Negro troops lose their strength, temper and morale, having to fight white ruffians in the South?"

In the July 11, 1942, issue, an article styled "The Lily-White Parade" contained a protest against the use of all white soldiers in military parades, stating that there was nothing "in this fight" which could stir the soul and spirit of black mothers, nothing to indicate that the Government under local citizens knew that black boys as well as white boys on Independence Day were making the supreme sacrifice for a nation that "Jim Crows" them even in a parade line.

In the August 29, 1942, issue of the Black Dispatch there is an article written by Albert White in which White says, "Lincoln faced the same issue which now faces Roosevelt. Lincoln had to free the Negro to save America. Roosevelt must protect the Negro to save American and Western civilization. . . ."

In the Black Dispatch issue of September 5, 1942, an article on the front page deals with the trial of four Communists in the State Court of Oklahoma and there are listed the names of prominent Negroes who have protested the convictions in these cases commonly known as the Oklahoma Criminal Syndicalism cases.

[*100-20076-21*]

An editorial in the October 10, 1942, issue was written by Roscoe Dunjee and two columns were devoted to the position of Communists in the United States. Extracts from this editorial are "We shall have to report that we personally do have Communistic leaning:" "We do have Communistic leaning when it comes to the Communistic theory of the international state and the questions of racial equality:" "Communism believes in social equality and so does this writer."

More recently, headlines from some of the leading American newspapers were placed together in an article in the Black Dispatch in such a way that approximately twenty of them appeared all dealing with "mugging" attacks on white people by Negroes in Harlem. This display was handled in such a manner that the impression was left white newspapers were causing a "crime smear" against the Negro population of Harlem. The insinuation was made that these news accounts concerning Negroes were untrue.

On March 28, 1942, Roscoe Dunjee spoke at a meeting at the First Unitarian Church, 13th Street and Dewey Avenue, Oklahoma City, which affair was sponsored by the Frederick Elliott Forum. Dunjee's topic was "Post-War Peace Aims of the American Negro." The meeting was attended by approximately 100 persons, predominantly white, including men of the Armed Forces. In his speech, according to an informant, Dunjee gave as his idealism the friendly understanding by black and white of the interlocking relationship which exists between them. The early part of his speech is said to have been devoted to an attack on the imperialistic form of government in England and the United States and France, stating it had caused a decrease of population from 7,500,000 Negroes in French Africa to 2,000,000 in ten years and has also caused higher taxes and a burden on the people. He then stated that Churchill had given a foul interpretation to the Third Section of the Atlantic Charter by excluding India and Africa. He is said to have then emphasized the strength of the colored races at the present time and stated the thirteen million Negroes in the United States represented the strongest minority in this country and, further, they are opposed to any union with England as long as that country adheres to its colonial policy.

Dunjee is said to have continued, remarking that for 2,000 years one-fifth of the world's population, the white race, had held the colored in submission, but now the colored people have learned to use mechanical weapons as evidenced at Corregidor. He is then said to have stated the only reason he could think of why the black race has remained friendly to the white was because they considered themselves next in kin to the white man.

With regard to the Beveridge and Delano Plans of State Socialism or Social Security, Dunjee is said to have remarked these plans are merely imperialistic methods to compete with Communism. He stated as a representative of the black race he was opposed to rushing into a plan of state socialism and stated further no such plan could be understood until the book "The Soviet Power" by the Dean of Canterbury was first read. (It should be noted that this book has been highly touted by the Communist Party.) Then he remarked that Russia really "must have something there" that the man would die like lice and fleas for their form of government.

Dunjee then reportedly quoted the definitions of democracy given by Booker T. Washington and Abraham Lincoln and then proceeded to give his own idea of democracy, stating this was not in existence today. He indicated that his belief in democracy is that there should be equal influence in the government by each individual, rich, poor, colored, white, alike. According to Dunjee, this latter democracy could not exist where there is segregation inasmuch as segregation implies superiority of one group over another. [*100-20076-35*]

Chicago Defender

The Chicago Defender began as a private enterprise by Robert S. Abbott, said to have been one of the leading Negroes of his day. He died in 1940 and left his estate, including the Robert S. Abbott Company, in the form of a trust. At the present time James B. Cashin, Negro attorney, is Chairman of the Board of Trustees. Cashin is reported to be one of the wealthiest Negroes in the United States and bears an excellent reputation. The newspaper is said to have a circulation of approximately [8]3,500.

John Sengstacke, nephew of Robert S. Abbott, is presently the active manager of the publication. Metz T. P. Lochard is the Secretary-Treasurer. He is said to have been with the publication for approximately twenty-five years, having worked his way from the position of an office boy to that of Secretary-Treasurer. Lucius Harper is the Editorial Manager and is said to be in a large part responsible for the policy of the Chicago Defender.

Considerable information has been reported concerning Metz Lochard and Lucius Harper to the effect that these individuals have been present at meetings of the Communist Party, District #8, Chicago, Illinois, and at several meetings held since July, 1942 both Harper and Lochard have been seated on the speaker's platform and have made addresses at such meetings. With regard to Harper, it has been stated he takes advantage of every opportunity to appear at Communist Party affairs and that his political party work has always been for the Communist Party. A review of the editorials appearing in the Chicago Defender reflects that the publication is strongly behind the war effort and that it is most active in calling for a "second front." A review of the issues of the paper reflects that a considerable number of news items dealing with alleged discrimination against Negroes and alleged acts of brutality where they are concerned appear in its issues. It militantly sets forth such matters. In this connection, it should be pointed out that Metz Lochard has been in frequent contact with William L. Patterson, Negro Communist Party functionary in the Chicago area and it is reported that Patterson has influenced some of the editorial policies of the paper. It is reported, with regard to one specific editorial matter, Patterson told Lochard that he should emphasize the matter in the newspaper.

There are being incorporated hereinafter short digests of articles appearing in this newspaper since January 1, 1942, which are believed to portray those types of articles making an appeal to, or creating one among, the Negroes reading the newspaper.

In its April 4, 1942, issue, page 13, it was stated with regard to the slaying of Negro soldiers in Little Rock, Arkansas, that the same "brings just one more incident that proves that in the South the uniform of the United States has no respect if the wearer is a Negro."

In the April 11, 1942, issue, it was stated on page 14, "While President Roosevelt has not seen fit to have a Negro in his Cabinet and Cordell Hull, Secretary of State, has not appointed a Negro to function in the State Department, we can still, as Americans, have some concern about matters that are strictly confidential. . . ."

In its July 18, 1942, issue, page 9, it was stated, "While blood donations gathered by the Red Cross (Boston) are being accepted by White and Negroes alike and shipped without labeling as to source, the Army through its Surgeon General, Major General McGhee, persists in its insistence that the blood be separated."

An article appearing in the August 8, 1942, issue, page 1, refers to a Negro military policeman shot by local police July 20, 1942, in Beaumont, Texas, because he refused "to acquiesce to the humiliation of a Jim Crow motor bus."

In its September 19, 1942, issue, on page 12, an article stated, "When the Navy Department Press Relations representative, Lieutenant Allen, could give no satisfactory answers concerning the WAVES, the AKA, non-partisan lobby through its representative, Thomasina Walker Johnson, immediately addressed a letter to the President, calling upon him to end the farce of organizing at taxpayers' expense a battalion of women to train as naval officers and excluding Negro women."

In its October 10, 1942, issue, page 7, it was said that at Madison, Wisconsin, "racial discrimination flared up in this city at the beginning of the school year at the University of Wisconsin and prevented the return of several of the Negro students because they were unable to obtain housing facilities in the capital city."

In the October 17, 1942, issue, page 1, there were related the plans for the erection of a dormitory in Washington, D.C., at the Union Station plaza. It was said the plans were abandoned and new plans substituted calling for the erection of two dormitories, one for white girls, the other for Negro girls. It was further stated in this regard, "In the original plans white and colored girls were supposed to use the same facilities in one reception dormitory, but Southern Congressmen controlling the expenditures under the Langnam Act disapproved of this and fought the proposal every time it came up."

Again in this issue, page 5, an article referred to Los Angeles, stating, "Lowering a barrier that has long been accepted as unsurmountable, the Los Angeles Street Railway Company sprung a surprise on the whole city last Wednesday by opening jobs for colored women and girls as conductorettes."

Special attention is directed to the September 26, 1942, issue of this newspaper which was called the Victory Edition of the Chicago Defender. It contained five sections, two of which in magazine form contained statements and articles by many prominent people in the country. Among these, however, there appeared writings by several individuals with either known or reported Communist affiliations:

Max Yergan, writing on India, referred to the need of granting India freedom from English domination and likened the situation there to the treatment of Negroes in this country. He stated, among other things,

> "Negro people are vitally concerning in what happens in India. They are concerned first because, more than any other section of the American people, they

appreciate, understand and feel the humiliating experiences to which the Indians have been subjected for so many years. The cup from which the Indian masses have drunk is also pressed to the lips of Negro Americans and its bitter taste lingers. By discrimination in terms of caste, race or color, the Negro people know the sting of the lash which India's millions have felt.

* * * * *

"Finally, freedom for India, that greatest of colonial areas, will mark the beginning of the end of the India colonial system. . . ."

William L. Patterson, member of the National Committee of the Communist Party and Communist functionary in the Chicago area, wrote on the subject "A Negro Looks at Russia." In this article the Soviet Union was eulogized and its attitude toward racial and minority discrimination was set forth.

John P. Davis, former Executive Secretary of the National Negro Congress, entitled his article "Beware the Hate Vendors." Davis has been reported to be a member of the Communist Party. In his article he attacked individuals in the South and who were termed Southern poll tax Congressmen. He urged:

> "We Negro people must intensify our efforts to unite around a common program for full participation of our people in the war effort unhampered by discrimination and segregation. We must find a way to bring our Negro organizations together in joint or paralleled action on this program."

An article was also written for this edition by *A. Philip Randolph* who has in the past openly opposed Communism. Under the title, "Freedom on Two Fronts" Randolph referred to the fight of Negroes for democracy both in Europe and in this country. He referred to the Indian situation, condemned the British Government for its treatment of the Indian people and stated that the United Nations "may lose the war because of their dangerous culture and mind-set against equality, freedom and independence of the darker races." He then referred to the contemplated social, political and economic program of civil disobedience to be entered into by the March on Washington Movement of which he is the leader. He ended his article by saying, "And the Negro and Indian people are not fighting for freedom now for themselves alone, but for moral and spiritual salvation of America and England, if not of western civilization."

It should be pointed out with respect to this special edition of the Chicago Defender that William L. Patterson was in contact with editorial officials of the Chicago Defender and afforded his assistance in obtaining articles from individuals who have been reported to have Communist connections.

[*100-122319-18 9-26-42 issue Chicago Defender*]

Michigan Chronicle

The Michigan Chronicle, published in Detroit, Michigan, by the Michigan Chronicle Publishing Company, is said to have approximately a circulation of 16,000. According to a confidential source of information the paper is actually printed on the press of the Chicago publication known as the Chicago Defender and, further, it is said that the Chronicle is owned by the same company controlling the Chicago Defender. It is alleged that on Monday of each week a messenger from the Michigan Chronicle travels to Chicago carrying the news for that week for publication. On Wednesday night the papers are reportedly sent to Detroit from Chicago and are available for distribution on each Thursday. It is a standard-sized paper published weekly consisting of generally about 25 pages divided into two sections—the first section containing largely local news and the editorial page, and the second section covering generally matters of national and international character and features a religious page, legal notices, a sports section and the society page. Those articles concerned with other than local events usually carry a by-line of the Associated Negro Press.

Louis Emmanual Martin, a Negro, serves in a full-time capacity as Editor of the Michigan Chronicle. He is said to be a graduate of the Journalism School of the University of Michigan in 1934 and was active during his student days in the National Student League, a Communist front group, out of which was formed the American Student Union. Confidential informants have advised that an examination of Martin's editorials over a period of years has revealed nothing in opposition to the current Communist Party line. In this connection, it is also reported that Martin, while believing sincerely in Communism, has not joined the Communist Party because of his fear that the newspaper might suffer a bad reputation. It might be noted that Martin was observed at the State Convention of the Communist Party in Michigan held in March 1943.

The wife of Martin, Gertrude Scott Martin, writes a column entitled "Book Notes" for the paper and in the October 10, 1942, issue she criticized Herbert Agar's book "A Time for Greatness" for calling Russia a totalitarian country.

The sports editor is Russell J. Cowans, while the following Negroes are authors of various columns: John Wood ("I Cover the Town"); Larry Chism ("Swinging with Nite-Lifers"); and Alfonso Cato ("The Bowlers Hall of Fame"). Theodore T. Jones, the Negro author of "I'd Rather Be Right" column, does not contribute regularly to the Chronicle. He is said to have at one time been an official of the Detroit chapter of the National Negro Congress, a Communist front. William L. Sherril, Negro author of the regular column "We, the Negro" is said to be an international organizer for the Universal Negro Improvement Association. He is said to have been at one time active in the affairs of the Civil Rights Federation, a Communist front group in Detroit. Reverend Horace A. White, Negro, is the author of the column entitled "The Facts in Our News." He has been the director of the Detroit unit of the March on Washington Movement. In addition, he has sponsored such Communist front organizations as the National Negro Congress and the National Free Browder Congress.

Louise Blackman, a Negro reporter for the Michigan Chronicle, is said to have been a member of the Communist Party at one time by a confidential informant and this membership was held with the knowledge and the consent of Martin.

An examination of the articles, features and photographs printed in this newspaper reflects that much has been devoted to discussions of the part played by Negroes in the war effort, at the same time attacking alleged discrimination and segregation in industry and in the Armed Forces as concerns Negroes. Its columns widely herald new organizations, conferences or other events, the purpose of which is to eliminate discrimination against Negroes. Individual instances of alleged mistreatment of Negroes in the South are discussed fully and are generally introduced by sensational headlines. In no instances have Negroes of pro-Japanese sentiments been defended by the newspaper, rather they are termed "crackpots" who hold no prestige in the Negro communities.

The Michigan Chronicle has followed the policy of publicizing to the fullest extent the activities of local organizations, several of which have been reported to be Communist inspired or infiltrated and have as their objectives elimination of discrimination against and segregation of Negroes. Among the organizations in the Detroit area are the Citizens Committee for Jobs in War Industries, the National Negro Congress, the Communist Party, the Civil Rights Federation, the Detroit chapter of the National Association for the Advancement of Colored People, as well as the Detroit unit of the March on Washington Movement and the Afro-American Benevolent Improvement Association. Local instances of alleged discrimination are given prominent attention and those in which some form of violence has been displayed are attributed often to the activities of the Ku Klux Klan. Scandal, shootings, murders, divorces, lawsuits, family trouble have all been given front-page attention.

It has been stated hereinbefore that editorials and articles in this paper have been in accord with the current line of the Communist Party. An editorial appeared in the October 10, 1942, issue entitled "No Explanation Necessary." This editorial was an attack on Congressman Dies and "red baiting." The January 23, 1943, issue carried an article which set out that James W. Ford, Negro, and Roy Hudson, both National Committee members of the Communist Party would speak at the V. I. Lenin Memorial Meeting scheduled for January 28, 1943, in Detroit, Michigan.

It should be noted that a confidential informant has advised of remarks made by James W. Ford on February 7, 1943, at the Fort Wayne Hotel in Detroit concerning the Michigan Chronicle. At the time, Ford delivered a speech entitled "The Negro and Racial Unity." During this address, Ford, according to the informant stated the Michigan Chronicle was a newspaper which truly represented the colored people. He added that a short time previous he had a conversation with the editor of the Michigan Chronicle, who at the time was in the audience. Ford reportedly stated that at the time of his conversation with Martin he was told that he, Martin, wrote no editorials or invaded no issues which did not take the same side as the Communist Party, as to trade unionism, the poll tax question, Westbrook Pegler, the Dies Committee and other matters.

A confidential source of information, who is a Negro **in a prominent professional capacity in the City of Detroit,** has stated with regard to the Michigan Chronicle that he has been reading the editorials of Martin in that paper for several months and that they have caused him growing concern. Mentioning that he was in

Birmingham, Alabama, during riots which took place just subsequent to World War No. 1, he advised in his opinion Martin was inciting a condition which, if Martin's editorials were to continue, would lead to similar race riots in the Detroit area during or immediately after the war. *[100-122319-27]*

The Pittsburgh Courier

The Pittsburgh Courier, published in Pittsburgh, Pennsylvania, was incorporated in Pennsylvania in 1910. Its editions are printed at 2628 Center Avenue, Pittsburgh, Pennsylvania. It has twelve weekly editions going to different parts of the country. In early 1942 its circulation is said to have been approximately 141,525. Its policy with regard to publishing many different editions is said to be based on the purpose of procuring a large number of subscribers and a large amount of advertisements within the area where the particular edition is mailed. It is said that the large number of subscribers and the large number of advertisements of the newspaper is based upon the fact that the edition going, for instance, to Chicago carries more news pertaining to that area than would the edition printed for the Pittsburgh area which in turn does not carry Chicago news. Following are those editions published by the Pittsburgh Courier along with the number of subscribers to each and the dates of mailing of each:

Edition	**Subscribers**	**Date of Mailing**
Chicago	288	Thursday
Detroit	1,276	Wednesday
Florida	12,410	Tuesday
Local	284	Thursday
Louisiana	3,655	Tuesday
Midwest	3,842	Wednesday
National	38,774	Monday, Tuesday, Wednesday
New York Seaboard	2,060	Wednesday
Ohio State	8,348	Wednesday
Pacific Coast	4,159	Tuesday
Philadelphia	579	Wednesday
Washington, D.C.	4,086	Wednesday

The following individuals are the officers of the organization:

Ira F. Lewis, President and General Manager

Daisy E. Lampkin, Vice President

Jessie M. Vann, Treasurer

Chester L. Washington, Secretary and Assistant Business Manager

Editorial Staff

P. L. Prattis, Executive Editor

William G. Nunn, Managing Editor

James M. Reid, News Editor

Wendell Smith, City Editor

Julia B. Jones, Women's Editor

George S. Schuyler, Associate Editor

Bessie M. Holloway, Assistant Women's Editor

W. B. Bayless, Circulation Manager

Earl V. Hord, Advertising Manager

The paper sponsored what is termed the "Double V" program in which it has urged the formation of groups of Negroes throughout the country to fight for two victories, one at home in the United States, a victory to be won over discrimination and Fascist elements, the other abroad against enemies of the United States.

There will be incorporated hereinafter short digests of articles and editorials appearing in the various editions of the Pittsburgh Courier which are believed to show the type of appeal the newspaper makes to Negroes or has among Negroes.

An article appeared in the December 6, 1941, issue in which anti-Japanese sentiments were expressed by J. A. Rogers who concluded his article with the statement, "Of course, the facts I have stated above are for rational, humane folks and not for those fanatics who see in Japan some sort of racial deliverer."

The December 20, 1941, issue contains numerous editorials and columns written in a pro-American, anti-Japanese vein. The general editorial uses the theme "The Negro Marches with America for Victory." The articles were written by columnists such as J. A. Rogers, M. S. Stewart, Joseph D. Bibb and A. Philip Randolph.

In the December 27, 1941, issue J. A. Rogers made comments to the effect that he had noticed expressions sympathetic to Japan made by writers and correspondents in the Negro press. He then condemns them for such expressions.

In the January 10, 1942, issue, George S. Schuyler in his column "The World Today" commented on the fall of Manila and stated, "The United States has been defeated! It has been defeated by a foe it despised because of his color. . . ."

In the same issue, Schuyler, in a column entitled "Views and Reviews," writes in the vein that the Negro could not possibly be worse off under Japanese victory.

In the January 31, 1942, issue, Schuyler in his column "Views and Reviews" states, ". . . No matter what a large portion of the Negroes may think in private about

Japanese aggression and the magnificent British retreats, they are *PUBLICLY* behind this Government 100 per cent."

In the February 7, 1942, issue, the "Double V" slogan, "Victory at home; victory abroad," appears for the first time. The "Double V" symbol appearing in the upper left-hand corner of the front page. In this issue, however, no explanation appears as to the meaning of this symbol and slogan. In the February 14, 1942, issue this program was explained in an editorial across the front page. The explanation is that the Negro has two victories to fight for, one at home in the United States, a victory to be won over discrimination and Fascist elements, the other abroad against the enemies of the United States.

In the March 28, 1942, issue Ira F. Lewis, President of the paper, writing instead of Schuyler in "The World Today" column, states, "The Japanese now are enemies of the United States and are necessarily enemies of all Negro Americans. But between the Japanese and the Chinese, the Negroes much prefer the Japanese. The Chinese are the worst 'Uncle Toms' and stooges the white man has ever had. . . . In this country, as soon as he gets a chop suey place which is anything like decent, the first thing he does is put up a color bar."

In this same issue of the Pittsburgh Courier Schuyler devotes his "Views and Reviews" column to an expression of his admiration of the Japanese "for their cleanliness, their courtesy, their ingenuity, and their efficiency." In this particular column, although he devotes it to admiration of Japanese culture, Schuyler at no time made any anti-Japanese remarks.

An editorial in the May 2, 1942, issue of the Pittsburgh Courier was entitled "Hysteria Over Negroes" and discusses the alleged concern in Washington over low Negro morale as well as the remedy (apparently to be attributed to Washington) by extending Jim Crowism and suppression of Negro newspapers. It is stated such an attitude will only serve to further depress Negro morale and goes on to state, "All this should be clear to the most obtuse minds in the capital but it seems not to be, if one is to judge by the increasing queries as to whether this or that Negro editor, publisher or columnist is or is not in the pay of Axis Powers, and veiled threats of 'cracking down' on Negro newspapers for recounting factual occurrences and preaching the gospel of democracy."

In the May 16, 1942, issue there appears an article anti-Japanese in flavor written by P. L. Prattis, editor, wherein the theme is that compared with Hirohito and the Japanese he prefers white southerners.

The August 29, 1942, issue contains an editorial which can be described as pro-Indian and anti-British in which the theme is that John Bull wants the little black man of India to fight for him while the little black man is still kept in chains.

The issue of September 5, 1942, carries an article entitled "Japanese Freeing All Colored War Captives" in which it is stated the Japanese High Command at that time was endeavoring to convince the native population in the Far East that Japan is not fighting with imperialistic aims but for the liberation of Asia from the yoke of white domination and had ordered the freeing of Asiatics and other colored prisoners of war captured during the fighting against the British. The article continues, stating that Subhas Chandra Bose, ex-president of the Indian National Congress, who reportedly escaped from India in 1941, was allegedly in Berlin organizing a "Free India Army" to help the Japanese upon their invasion of India. The article further stated reliable news had reached London that the Japanese established a joint Japanese-Burmese government headed by the nationalist leader in Burma, Dr. Ba Maw. The article bore a date line of London, September 3, 1942, and was designated as having been written by "our London correspondent."

Since October 1942 the Pittsburgh Courier has conducted what it terms a poll of Negro opinion. Following are examples of questions asked:

October 10, 1942—"Do you believe that India should contend for her rights and her liberty now?"

October 24, 1942—"Do you believe that the Negro should soft-pedal his demands for complete freedom and citizenship and await the development of the educational processes?"

October 31, 1942—"Do you believe that the Negro has a standard of living in this country today worth fighting and dying for?"

November 7, 1942—"Do you believe conditions would be better for the Negro if the Japanese controlled this country?"

November 14, 1942—"Do you believe the A.F. of L. offers more to the American Negro than the CIO?"

November 28, 1942—"Do you believe Jews in Germany are treated better than Negroes in America?"

December 5, 1942—"Do you think the interests of colored Americans are related to the problems of the colored people throughout the world?"

December 19, 1942—"Have you been convinced that the statements which our national leaders have made about freedom and equality for all peoples include the American Negro?"

December 26, 1942—"If the Negro's white friends in the South refuse to renounce segregation—should the Negro remain loyal to these friends?"

January 2, 1943—"Do you believe there is more segregation and discrimination now than there was before the war started?"

January 23, 1943—"Do you approve of the Crusade which the Negro press is conducting for full integration of the race into the life of America?"

February 13, 1943—"Do you believe the United States Army Air Force has been fair to Negroes in the training of fliers?"

February 20, 1943—"Do you believe the Negro should fight against segregation even when it is the accepted pattern of the community?"

March 13, 1943—"Do you believe our Government has done what it should to furnish China with materials of war?"

The October 17, 1942, issue contained an editorial entitled "Gesture to China" which intimates the giving up of extraterritorial rights by the United States and Great

Britain in Asia is a fraud inasmuch as they are nonexistent because of Japanese occupation.

In the November 7, 1942, issue an editorial entitled "Why Morale Is Low" lists the various grievances of the Negroes and concludes, "At present he (the Negro) cannot be enthusiastic or even satisfied about his lot and it is high time to let those in authority know why."

In the January 2, 1943, issue, Schuyler, in his "Views and Reviews" column states, ". . . The war is being waged to destroy the Axis Powers who are challenging the domains in world affairs of Anglo-American-Dutch allies and their associates. That is perfectly all right with me because I prefer Allied to Axis rule, and so do almost all other Americans. I do not expect to see the Africans and Asiatics untethered and permitted to work out their own destiny in their own way after the Axis has been defeated. I don't expect to see jim crowism and color discrimination ended when the United States inevitably comes to rule the world. I may be disappointed, and hope that I am, but I don't think that I will."

In the January 16, 1943, issue, Horace R. Cayton's weekly column is concluded as follows: "It is easy to blame the Negro press but the truth of the matter is that you cannot promise freedom to people all over the world and not expect Negroes in the United States to demand that same freedom. That there will be conflict, violence, and bloodshed no one can doubt. That, however, is the price which the world must pay to achieve political freedom and a new world order, and which America—black and white America—must pay to achieve it within our own country."

In the February 20, 1943, issue, George Schuyler, in his "World Today" column, refers to the statement, "I have no country" which was reportedly made by Robert Moses, New York City Selective Service violator who was sentenced to three years' imprisonment. Schuyler states in his column, "What Moses said, many Negroes could be thinking and it is up to American white people to make them think otherwise. Jailing them will not change their minds but democracy, fair play, citizenship rights, and equality of opportunity will. . . ."

In the February 20, 1943, issue, J. A. Rogers, in his column "Roger Says," makes these statements: "I am not half so scared about the Hitlers, Mussolinis, and Tojos thousands of miles across the seas as I am of the Hitlers, Mussolinis, and Tojos right here at home . . . and as for what Hitler has said about Negroes I could quote you worse and in far greater volume from the Congressional Record."

George S. Schuyler's "Views and Reviews" in the March 13, 1943, issue states: "Whatever may be the outcome of the war for democracy abroad, it has certainly been lost at home so far as colored Americans are concerned. . . . Indeed, we are farther away because the pattern of segregation was not so widespread nor was it sanctioned or promoted by the National Government as it is today. . . . Those now controlling the country have indicated beyond a doubt that the only future they envision for the colored folk is a segregated one." [*100-31159-90*]

II

PROGRAMS CONCERNING RACE RELATIONS

Incorporated hereinafter are the results of various conferences which have been held in different parts of the country beginning in October, 1942. The purpose of these conferences was primarily to formulate a program to make demands and to present claims, all pertaining to race relations. It will be noted from a review of these conferences that the programs vary in militancy and in conservatism. The most conservative of these programs was promulgated at the Southern Conference on Race Relations which was held in Durham, North Carolina, on October 22, 1942. There, in formulating a program, Southern Negro leaders were described as choosing to "hedgehop" from one position for the Negro to the next most favorable position, rather than "soaring majestically" and oftentimes "tragically" from a current position of the Negro race in America to what was alleged the "desideratum of racial integration in the American body politics." No attempt is being made to compare or contrast these various programs which are being set out hereinafter in view of their application to different sections of the country. However, it is believed worthy of note that a different degree of conservatism appears in each.

Southern Conference on Race Relations

Durham, North Carolina—October 22, 1942

On October 20, 1942, there was held at North Carolina College for Negroes at Durham, North Carolina, a Southern Conference on Race Relations. The purposes of the Conference, which was made up of 75 leaders of the negro race in the southern states, were:

1. To find a common denominator for the use of liberal whites and Negroes in the South in their efforts to bring about a better relationship between the races.
2. To write a new charter of race relations which would be fraternal and scientific in preference to being fraternal and traditional.
3. This charter, or findings, is not to be used as a frame of reference but as a beginning point from which would flow patterns of biracial living in the South during this war and in the period immediately following its cessation.
4. This charter will not be an appeal for tolerance or a demand for rights, or even a statement of racial aspiration. It will be an attempt to formulate a racial basis

for biracial living in the South in the framework of coming world concepts of human relations, and with realistic regard for the social and racial tradition of the region.

5. Negroes in the southern region are willing and anxious to work and fight for a United Nations' victory and to help build a more democratic world in the post-war period.

An Appraisal of the Conference

It is reported that the Southern Conference on Race Relations was organized and directed principally by Dr. Gordon B. Hancock, head of the School of Sociology at Virginia Union University, Richmond, Virginia; Dr. Charles S. Johnson, Director of the School of Social Sciences, Fisk University, Nashville, Tennessee; Dr. Plummer B. Young, Sr., Editor of the Journal and Guide, Norfolk, Virginia; and Dr. Luther P. Jackson, head of the Department of History, Virginia State College, Ettrick, Virginia. The Conference was attended by 75 leaders of the South, including presidents of colleges, business and insurance executives, several Urban League executives, representatives of the Southern Negro Youth Congress, a reported Communist front organization, and social and civic leaders.

It was said that the Conference was not a body representing the more than 8,000,000 Negroes of the South but rather it was specifically a representative group of a cross section of the leaders of such Negroes. It was described as a meeting unique in its kind, although not a secession from the Negroes of the North and their leaders. It was a proposal for a technique which could be used in American race relations and which would be better suited to the interests of the whole country.

In a summary of the ideas presented by those who attended it was shown that all of them would "welcome opportunities to cooperate in planning and initiating constructive interracial programs which would insure the continuously improved status of the Negro and which would lead ultimately to complete democratic participation."

The guiding principle has been summarized as follows: "We reserve the right, however, to continue to press for improvements in our status as a minority group in all important areas of American life—occupational, educational, civic, etc.—in so far as such pressure will not MATERIALLY HINDER THEIR UNITED WAR EFFORT."

The 75 leaders were divided into study groups, to compile findings and recommendations of action in the following fields: (1) civil rights, (2) education, (3) industry, (4) agriculture, (5) social welfare and health, (6) employment in service occupations.

The approach of the Conference to the Negro question has been described as that of the sociologist, rather than the civil and political approach recommended by Negro leaders in the North. The program of the Conference has been further described as one differing from the plan of action of the Northern Negro leaders.

General Consideration

1. ". . . The signatories to these articles do not approve of the principle of the compulsory physical segregation of racial, or class, or religious groups in any

part of America, but in view of the prevailing sentiment of the white population of the region at this time, regard it as necessary to seek a first basis for mutual development within the framework of the region's traditional policy."

2. A distinction is made between segregation and discrimination. The first is regarded as a social policy which, while not generally acceptable, is yet theoretically capable of yielding equitable group values and opportunities. The second is untenable and unjust both in principle and practice, and, in the opinions of this group, should and can be actively opposed, now, in all its forms. . . ."
3. "It is the opinion of this group that the strategic objectives of the Negro minority of this region are not indiscriminate social intermingling, but full equity of citizenship status."
4. ". . . Historical circumstances and traditional practices in the region have contributed to the cultural retardation of a large proportion of the region's Negro population, and that this retardation itself makes difficult any re-conceptualizing of Negro status in terms of this larger citizenship. It is the considered opinion of this group that this situation can be met more wisely by the concerted effort to wipe out the cultural differentials through accelerated educational and economic opportunities and facilities, than by permitting the retardation itself to delay or limit these opportunities and facilities."
5. "Inasmuch as the large proportions of Negroes in the population of some States of the South occasions concern about political control, and provokes measures of repression and unethical evasions of the fundamental law, this group favors, in the interest of both races, the wider geographical distribution of the Negro population.
6. "The nation . . . has assumed a moral as well as military responsibility for a new order of human relations. . . . It cannot sustain this role, or in fact, save itself without revision of those concepts and cessation of those practices that are sharply inconsistent with the democracy that it espouses. Already the anomaly of the Negro minority has proved an embarrassment to the efforts of the government to take a clear cut position in relation to India and China. . . ."

Propositions Formulated

1. "The institution of general education and qualifications . . . can make possible the extension of suffrage without racial discrimination and eliminate both the Negroes and the whites who are not yet qualified for the sound exercise of the franchise."
2. "The same educational qualifications as a primary basis for the selection of jurors can improve the quality of jury service at the same time that it avoids the unconstitutionality of racial exclusions from such service."
3. "The poll tax . . . should be abolished in both state and Federal elections. . . ."

4. "It is essential that qualified Negro voters have an opportunity to express their choice in the election of local officials. . . ."
5. "Civil rights include personal security against abuses of police power by white officers of the law. Their duty is the maintenance of order and the apprehension of violators of the law, and not the enforcement of their personal interpretations of racial etiquette, or the personal punishment of offenders or suspected offenders without court trials. Corrections of this practice can, in part, be achieved by raising the educational requirements for police officers, special training for them in police methods, institution of civil service regulations, and the privileges of appeal of any citizen to a board of control over these representatives of the law. . . . A contribution can be made by Negroes themselves to the control of lawless elements in their own group by investing qualified Negroes with police power."
6. "In public carriers and terminals where segregation of the races is made mandatory by law as well as by established custom, it is the duty of Negro and white citizens to insist that these provisions be equal in kind and quality, and in character of maintenance, and adjusted to the racial proportions to be served. . . ."

Education

1. "Basic to improvement in Negro education is better schools, . . . the minimum requirement now is (a) equalization of salaries of white and Negro teachers on the basis of equal preparation; (b) a long range school building program for Negro schools designed to overcome the present racial disparity in physical facilities within a period of five to ten years; (c) reconstruction of the tax base for school financing; (d) revision of the school program in terms of the social setting, vocational needs and marginal cultural characteristics of the Negro children; and (e) extension of the school year for all Negro children to at least 180 days."
2. Professional training should be made available equally for white and negro eligible students in terms defined by the Supreme Court.
3. "Where it is established that States cannot sustain the added cost of equalization, Federal funds should be made available to overcome the differentials."
4. "It is the belief of this group that the special problems of Negro education make demands for intelligent and sympathetic representation of these problems on county and city school boards by qualified persons, preferably and wherever possible, Negroes."
5. "Further, the education of Negro youth can be measurably aided by the use of Negro enforcement officers of the truancy and compulsory education laws."

Industry

1. "The only tenable basis of economical survival and development for Negroes is inclusion in unskilled, semi-skilled, and skilled branches of work in the indus-

tries of the region to the extent that they are equally capable, and to the limit of their population proportions. Circumstances will vary so as to make impossible and impracticable any exact numerical balance, but the principle as enunciated by the President's Fair Employment Practices Committee is regarded by this group as sound."

2. "There should be the same pay for the same work when the work is of equal quality."
3. "It is the duty of Negro and white citizens to insist upon provisions for the industrial training of Negroes in a measure equal at least to that of whites in quality and kind."
4. "Negro workers should seek collective security through membership in labor organizations . . . ," whether it be in labor unions of white workers or unions consisting wholly of Negro workers.
5. "Negro representation on regional organizations concerned with the welfare of workers is advocated."
6. "The South's economic and cultural development can be accelerated by increasing the purchasing power and skills of Negro workers."

Service Occupations

Realism indicates that Negroes will be employed is greatest proportions for yet a long space in service occupations. There are great possibilities in making of these fields the scientifically guided areas in which, with a rise in the standard of living generally, rewards within them are not as unsatisfactory as they are now. . . ."

Agriculture

1. ". . . provide for more security for tenants and share-croppers by requirement of written contracts, longer lease terms, higher wages or at least a more equitable distribution of the cash returns from the joint production!"
2. "Discouragement of the system of tenancy and aid to farm ownership by Negroes, without discrimination in price or location, are advocated."
3. "There should be more Federal assistance to Negro farmers and more equitable handling of these funds when available by local agents of the Federal government. . . ."
4. "The following deficits are recorded as unjustified and uneconomic and correctable now: (a) Federal funds for Negro land-grant colleges; (b) experiment and other research provisions in the Negro land-grant schools; (c) Negro agricultural agents."
5. "For appropriate representation and mutual benefits, we advocate the appointment of qualified Negroes to governmental planning and policy-making bodies concerned with the farmer, and membership in farm organizations and economic cooperatives."

Social Welfare and Health

1. "We believe that the more acute problems like Negro health and family and personal disorganization are a reflection of deficiencies in economic opportunity, but that social and health services for Negroes will continue to be necessary in considerable amounts even with the improvement of their economic status. . . . Reasonable health measures would include the following: (a) . . . a proportion of the facilities in all public hospitals be available for Negro patients; (b) that Negro doctors be either included on the staff for services to Negro patients, according to their special qualifications, or permitted as practitioners the same privilege and courtesy as other practitioners in the public hospitals; (c) that Negro public health nurses and social workers be more extensively used. . . ."
2. "There are qualified Negro physicians, social workers, and educators in certain areas who can serve with benefit to the general community as members of state, county and city health boards and welfare councils. . . ."
3. "The present high adult mortality and morbidity and infant mortality among Negroes of low income presents the demand for increased numbers of free clinics as a measure of general community health. . . ."
4. "We advocate the extension of slum clearance and erection of low-cost housing as a general as well as special group advantage. The Federal government has set an excellent precedent here with results that offer much promise for the future."
5. "There is no justification for the exclusion of Negroes from public parks and playgrounds without provision for separate comparable facilities. Separate playgrounds can be viewed, under the circumstances, in the same light as separate public schools; but there seems no social necessity for separate parks or the exclusion of Negroes from any public park."

On December 15, 1942, a charter on race relations was released and signed by the following individuals: Gordon B. Hancock, Benjamin E. Mays, Ernest Delpit, Rufus E. Clement, Horace Mann Bond, James E. Jackson, William M. Cooper, P. B. Young, and Charles S. Johnson. It was issued in the form of a printed booklet entitled "A Basis for Interracial Cooperation and Development in the South." The program set forth therein compared very closely with that previously incorporated, according to reports received.

The People's Committee Meeting

December 7, 1942—New York City

This organization held a large meeting at the Golden Gate Ball Room in the Harlem section of New York City on December 7, 1942. The guiding figure of this organization is Adam Clayton Powell, Jr., Negro preacher and Councilman in New York City who has in the past cooperated closely with Communists and Communist front organizations. The program as formulated by this meeting is being incorporated hereinafter as a possible contrast to that program promulgated by the Southern Conference on Race Relations held in Durham, North Carolina, in October, 1942.

The following people are officers of this Committee: Adam Clayton Powell, Jr., Chairman; Channing Tobias, Vice Chairman; Joseph Ford, Secretary; G. Chinn, Treasurer; and the Sponsoring Committee is composed of the following: Charles Collins, Chairman of the Negro Labor Victory Committee; Walter White, Executive Secretary of the National Association for the Advancement of Colored People; Mabel Stauper, Negro graduate nurse; Charles Keller of the New York State Conference of Negro Youth; George Murphy, formerly an executive officer in the National Negro Congress; Dr. George Cameron of the Manhattan Central Medical Society; Reverend Eldridge of the Baptist Ministers Conference; Reverend Sweeney, President of the Interdenominational Ministers Conference; and representatives of the Brooklyn and New York branches of the Urban League and the March on Washington Movement.

Prior to giving the platform or program of the People's Committee meeting, Powell spoke on the achievements gained for the Negro race during the year 1942, at which time he enumerated various benefits and advantages received by Negroes, either individually or as a group, as an example of which he referred to the activities of the Fair Employment Practices Committee.

While a majority of the points in the platform which is incorporated hereinafter deal largely with local matters in New York City, it can be stated that they are typical of the more militant demands for Negroes made by such forces as the Communist Party; the National Negro Congress, a Communist front group; the March on Washington Movement; the Negro Labor Victory Committee; and local New York Communist-influenced organizations, as well as other pro-Communist Negro groups in such larger cities as Detroit and Chicago. The platform set forth at this meeting is as follows:

Health

1. The use of competent men and women of the Medical Service in all city institutions.
2. To work for a low cost hospitalization plan.
3. To demand complete clinic facilities in Negro areas.
4. To fight for the abolition of segregated blood bank and other discriminatory processes of the Red Cross.

Social Service

1. Increase relief for Negro clients due to artificially high cost of living.
2. The establishment of a full recreational program using all city buildings and park facilities on a full-time basis.
3. The establishment of daytime nurseries for the parents of children engaged in war work.
4. Education of the metropolitan press so that Negro life will be reported without bias.

Education

1. More Negroes appointed to the faculties and clerical staff of the College of New York.
2. The appointment of a Negro to:
   (a) Board of Education
   (b) Board of Higher Education
   (c) Region of the State of New York
   (d) Supervisory position in elementary and secondary school

Consumer

1. Establishment of a Harlem public market.
2. Appointment of Negroes as market inspectors.
3. To urge enforcement of OPA orders.
4. To work a strong consumer movement.

War

1. End discrimination and segregation in the armed forces.
2. The immediate investigation and prosecution of all individuals who have murdered or brutalized the Negro soldiers.
3. The full use of all recreational facilities by Negro troops.
4. The passage of a Kilgore-Tolan-Pepper bill for the establishment of a central planning organization.
5. The winning of the war and the peace with full democracy for all black, brown, yellow and white people of the world. [*100-109061-3*]

National Negro Council

January, 1943

The following ten-point program of the National Negro Council was publicly set forth in January, 1943. While there are points in it involving directly the District of Columbia, it will be noted that there are certain national issues incorporated.

1. A civil rights law for the District of Columbia.
2. Federal antilynching law.
3. Anti-poll tax and anti-registration legislation.
4. Enforcement of the Thirteenth, Fourteenth and Fifteenth Amendments of the U.S. Constitution, cutting down Southern representation in Congress in proportion to disfranchisement. Abolishing all Jim-Crow in trains, buses and street cars as a war measure and forever by executive order of the President.
5. Denial of the Federal Government's benefits to labor unions that continue the practice of race discriminations—cancellation of government contracts with industries that deny employment to colored workers.
6. Congressional authorization of a Fair Employment Practices Commission, as a Federal agency with necessary powers similar to the Interstate Commerce Commission and National Labor Relations Board. A colored member of U.S. Civil Service Commission.
7. Reduction of all non-essential Federal personnel and appropriations for Federal departments, especially those violating non-discrimination laws. Appointment of colored persons on all OPA Price and Rationing Boards in all sections of the country.
8. Appointment of colored lawyers on the U.S. Supreme Court and Federal District Courts in the U.S., as well as the Virgin Islands.
9. Equal Federal educational funds for Southern States regardless of race. Social Security benefits, old-age pensions and unemployment insurance for domestics, farm laborers and ministers.
10. A $100,000 fund to carry on this campaign in Washington by the National Negro Council.

III

UNAFFILIATED OR INDEPENDENT NEGRO ORGANIZATIONS

There are three organizations active in the United States composed largely of members of the Negro race, which are believed to have considerable influence in their field. Their primary purpose is the advancement of their race in this country. These organizations are classified for the purpose of this study as unaffiliated or independent, and no information has been received that, on a national basis, they are dominated or influenced by any subversive group or organization. They are:

National Association For The Advancement of Colored People

National Urban League

March on Washington Movement

Identifying information concerning each of these groups is incorporated hereinafter.

At the same time it is to be pointed out that there cannot be overlooked those smaller groups and organizations, local in scope, which have the same fundamental purpose and which have been described previously in the main body of this study.

National Association For The Advancement of Colored People

The National Association For The Advancement of Colored People was organized in February, 1909, the hundredth anniversary of the birth of Abraham Lincoln and the year following the notorious race riot in Springfield, Illinois. It was incorporated in May, 1911, under the laws of the State of New York. The original organizers of this association were Oswald Garrison Villard, Jane Addams, Lillian Wald, John Dewey, Rabbi Stephen Wise and Samuel Bowles.

The headquarters of the National Association For The Advancement of Colored People is located at 69 Fifth Avenue, New York City and the national officers, which include both white and colored persons, are as follows:

Arthur B. Spingarn, President

Dr. Louis T. Wright, Chairman of the Board

Hon. Charles E. Toney, Acting Chairman of the Board

Vice-Presidents

Mary McLeod Bethune

Nannie H. Burroughs

Godfrey Lowell Cabot
Hon. Arthur Capper
Dr. Walter Gray Crump
Bishop John A. Gregg
Rev. John Haynes Holmes
Manley O. Hudson
Hon. Ira W. Jayne
Hon. Caroline O'Day
Rev. A. Clayton Powell
Oswald Garrison Villard
William Allen White
Mary White Ovington, Treasurer

Executive Officers

Walter White, Secretary
Roy Wilkins, Assistant Secretary and Editor, "The Crisis"
Thurgood Marshall, Special Counsel
Daisy E. Lampkin, Field Secretary
Ella J. Baker, Assistant Field Secretary
E. Frederic Morrow, Assistant Field Secretary
Randall L. Tyus, Assistant Field Secretary
Charlotte B. Crump, Publicity and Promotion
Madison S. Jones, Jr., Youth Director
Frank D. Reeves, Administrative Assistant, Washington Bureau
Richetta G. Randolph, Clerk of the Conference

"The Crisis" is the official publication of the National Association For The Advancement of Colored People and is issued monthly. The subscription price of this magazine is $1.50 per year.

This association claims to have 43,000 members and various local chapters throughout the United States. The membership fee is $1. a year, half of which is forwarded to the National Headquarters in New York City and the other half is retained for the support of the local organization.

Arthur B. Spingarn, President of the organization, is a wealthy white man. He is reported to donate large sums to the activities of the National Association For The Advancement of Colored People. The association is stated to be financed by private subscriptions and contributions from various foundations. The Notorious Garland Fund, a supporter of many radical organizations, is alleged to have contributed $8,082. to the National Association For The Advancement of Colored People in 1935.

[*100-135-45; 61-3176*]

In 1912, the National Association For The Advancement of Colored People summed up the purposes of its organization in the following words:

> "The NAACP seeks to uplift the colored man and woman of this country by securing to them the full enjoyment of their rights as citizens. Justice in all courts and equality of opportunity everywhere. It favors and aims to aid every kind of education among them save that which teaches special privilege or prerogative class or caste. It recognizes the national character of the Negro problem and not sectionalism. It believes in the upholding of the Constitution of the United States and its administration in the spirit of Abraham Lincoln. It upholds the doctrine of 'all men up and no man down.' It abhors Negro crime but still more the conditions which breed crime and most of all the crimes committed in the mockery of the law. It believes that the scientific truths of the Negro problem must be available before the country can see its way clear to righting existing wrongs. It has no other belief than the best way to upli[f]t the colored man is the best way to aid the white man to peace and social content; it has no other desire than exact justice, and no other motive than humanity."

The specific contemporary purposes of the National Association For The Advancement of Colored People are reported to be as follows:

1. The end of lynching
2. The ending of disfranchisement
3. The abolition of injustice in legal procedure based solely upon color or race.
4. Equitable distribution of funds for public education.
5. Abolition of segregation and discrimination, insult and humiliation based upon race or color.
6. Equality of opportunity to work in all fields with equal pay for equal work.
7. Abolition of discrimination against Negroes in the right of collective bargaining through membership in organized labor unions.
8. The ending of peonage and the debt slavery of southern sharecroppers and tenant farmers.
9. Abolition of segregation in the Army and Navy.

In order to accomplish its ends, the National Association For The Advancement of Colored People has organized a lecture bureau, a bureau of legal assistance, a bureau of information, and a bureau of publicity and research.

Walter White, the Secretary of the National Association For The Advancement of Colored People, appears to be the most active executive of this organization and has been connected with them since 1918. He was born in Atlanta, Georgia, on July 1, 1893. He received an A. B. Degree from Atlanta University in 1916 and was awarded a L.L.D. Degree by Howard University in 1939. White is reported to be an author and was in France in 1927 and 1928 engaged in creative writing in prose as a fellow of the John Simon Guggenheim Memorial Foundation. White was appointed by President Roosevelt as a member of the Advisory Council for the Government of the Virgin Islands which position he resigned in 1935. He is a member of the American Committee on Economic Policy; Board of Visitors, New York Training School for Boys, and a member of the Governor's Commission on the Constitutional Convention, New York in 1938.

A. Philip Randolph, a reported Socialist and President of the International Brotherhood of Sleeping Car Porters, A. F. of L., is a member of the Board of Directors of the National Association For the Advancement of Colored People and was awarded the Spingarn Medal by the National Association For the Advancement of Colored People for achieving the greatest improvement for the Negro race in 1942. Randolph organized the March on Washington Committee in 1942, which resulted in President Roosevelt issuing Executive Order 8802, which provided for the establishment of the Fair Employment Practice[s] Committee. This executive order directed that the Negro race be given fair employment representation in the war industries and provided for the correction of various Negro grievances. Previous to the issuance of this executive order the March on Washington Committee threatened to march 100,000 Negroes on Washington, D.C. from all parts of the country to protest against Negro discrimination in the war effort.

Information has been received from reliable sources that the Communist Party, from time to time, has attempted to infiltrate the National Association For The Advancement of Colored People. Information has been likewise received that the Communist Party has been successful to a limited extent in this regard and that the responsible leadership of the National Association For The Advancement of Colored People has spurned various overtures on the part of the Communist Party leaders who promised that the plight of the colored race in the United States would be improved by the activity of the Communist Party. However, certain individual members and local chapters of the National Association For The Advancement of Colored People are reported to be radical and possibly friendly to the Communist Party.

In several local chapters of this organization it is said that there is some degree of Communist influence or control. In this regard, it has been reported that any Communist control or influence in the National Association For The Advancement of Colored People would only exist in local chapters. In the Atlanta, Georgia, chapter there is reportedly cooperating with the group there a Communist Party front organization. In the Detroit area several officers of the branch located there are said to be either members of the Communist Party or closely affiliated with it. In the Los Angeles branch Communist Party activity is reportedly in existence therein. It is said that in the New Orleans chapter members have either Communist Party connections or membership. Other areas in which there is reportedly Communist influence in local chapters are: Buffalo, Charlotte, Cleveland, Oklahoma City, Pittsburgh, San Diego, Seattle, Washington, D.C.

A confidential source in August, 1941, advised that one Leroy Willkins, Editor of the official organ of the National Association For The Advancement of Colored People, is strongly suspected of being a member of the Communist Party and is known to write material which could be construed as Communist. [*61-7563-222; 40-6760*]

Walter White, in 1931, expressed contempt for the Communist Party as a result of the Communist Party interfering with the National Association For The Advancement of Colored People in assisting the Negro defendants in the celebrated Scottsboro case. The interference of the Communist Party in this situation led to the withdrawal of the National Association For The Advancement of Colored People from the Scottsboro case. [94-1-27323]

A. Philip Randolph likewise disclaimed the Communist Party in 1940 when he resigned as National President of the National Negro Congress and attributed his resignation to the fact that he no longer could serve an organization which was dominated by the Communist Party. [61-6728-57]

The thirty-third annual convention of the National Association For The Advancement of Colored People was held in Los Angeles, California, July 14–19, 1942, at which time one hundred voting delegates participated. The slogan of this convention was "Victory is vital to minorities." Wendell Willkie was the chief guest speaker and President Roosevelt wired the convention, stating that the Administration "will accept its responsibility to the Negro people". This convention passed twenty-eight resolutions including a statement of support of the war against the Axis. The only resolution presented by the Resolutions Committee which failed passage was a proposal calling for action to mobilize pressure for the opening of a second front against the Axis in Western Europe. A. Philip Randolph condemned this last mentioned resolution as being a "Communist maneuver" within the association. He accused the Communists of being "agents of Russia" and stated that the second front was being advocated by Communists merely as a move to save Russia.

Charlotta A. Bass, a Negress, Editor of the California Eagle, the leading Los Angeles Negro weekly, is reported to have addressed the convention of the National Association For The Advancement of Colored People and to have closely adhered to the Communist Party line during the course of her speech including a demand for the immediate opening of a second front in Europe and a scathing attack on A. Philip Randolph. [61-3176]

Recently the National Association For The Advancement of Colored People has reportedly been working in cooperation with the March on Washington Movement in furnishing assistance to the organizational activities of the latter group. The wide area coverage of the Association is said to be a benefit to the movement. This appears to be a new type of activity and militancy for the organization in that formerly, it is reported, the Association confined its work to legal assistance to members of the colored race, lobbying, and conducting lecture and propaganda tours.

During the early part of June, 1943 the emergency conference on "The Status of the Negro in the War for Freedom" was held by the National Association For The Advancement of Colored People in Detroit, Michigan. The conference extended from June 8 through June 10, 1943. A large mass meeting was held at the Olympia Stadium with the principal speaker[s] being R. J. Thomas, president of the United Automobile, Aircraft & Agricultural Implement Workers of America, Philip Murray, president of the Congress of the Industrial Organizations and former Judge William H. Hastie, who also received the 28th award, Spingarn Medal which is offered to the Negro attaining the outstanding achievement of the year.

The conference is said to have been conducted on the basis of discussions led by people of national reputation who spoke briefly. They are said to have been followed by questions and answers so that a full participation between delegates could be had.

The key note address was made by Walter White, executive secretary of the organization who is said to have summarized the complaints and demands of the American Negroes. It is said that the business sessions dealt with the armed services, the right to work for victory, the treatment of the Negro in the press, radio and the motion picture, the securing of democracy at home and the church as a force for democratic rights.

The discussion leaders included former Judge William H. Hastie, and Earl B. Dickerson, former members of the Fair Employment Practice[s] Committee; George S. Schuyler of the Pittsburgh Courier; Albert Deutsch, columnist of the newspaper PM; Thurgood Marshall, special coun[se]l of the National Association For The Advancement of Colored People; Dr. Channing H. Tobias, of the National Council of the YMCA; as well as other representatives from the newspaper, government and labor fields.

It is said that there were 550 delegates from 150 cities in the United States who participated in the conference. [*Issue of "Pittsburgh Courier" 6-12-43*]

National Urban League

It has been reported that the National Urban League is an organization composed of whites and Negroes dedicated ostensibly to the promotion of the interests of the colored race in regard to better working and living conditions, education, race relationship, and health.

As of August 12, 1942, the national headquarters of the organization was located at 1333 Broadway, New York City, and one Lester B. Granger was Executive Secretary. It has been reported that said organization publishes a magazine called "The Opportunity," a journal of Negro life, and with regard to this publication, it has been alleged that "the tone of this publication is Communistic." The individual making this allegation gave the following quotation from the June, 1942 issue of said publication as the basis of his statement that same was Communistic in tone: "Added to the indefensible and shameless segregation and discrimination in the armed forces and widespread and cruel exclusion of Negroes from defense industry. . . ."

The Urban League has affiliates and branches throughout the country. The names of the affiliated organizations are not being set out along with the various cities wherein they exist. There are in the following cities affiliated or branch organizations of the National Urban League:

Akron, Ohio
Albany, New York
Anderson, Indiana
Asbury Park, New Jersey

Atlanta, Georgia
Baltimore, Maryland
Boston, Massachusetts
Brooklyn, New York
Buffalo, New York
Canton, Ohio
Chicago, Illinois
Cleveland, Ohio
Columbus, Ohio
Detroit, Michigan
Englewood, New Jersey
Fort Wayne, Indiana
Greenville, South Carolina
Kansas City, Missouri
Lincoln, Nebraska
Little Rock, Arkansas
Los Angeles, California
Louisville, Kentucky
Massillon, Ohio
Memphis, Tennessee
Milwaukee, Wisconsin
Minneapolis, Minnesota
New Orleans, Louisiana
New York, New York
Newark, New Jersey
Omaha, Nebraska
Omaha, Nebraska
Philadelphia, Pennsylvania
Pittsburgh, Pennsylvania
Providence, Rhode Island
Richmond, Virginia
St. Louis, Missouri
St. Paul, Minnesota
Seattle, Washington
Springfield, Illinois
Springfield, Massachusetts

Tampa, Florida
Toledo, Ohio
Warren, Ohio
Washington, D.C.
Waterbury, Connecticut
White Plains, New York

With regard to two of the branches of the National Urban League, it has been reported that allegations have been made that persons affiliated with the Atlanta and Chicago Urban Leagues have Communist sympathies or affiliations.

In the Atlanta Urban League it has been alleged that certain officers of the branch are either members of the Communist Party or sympathetic with its principles. In the Chicago branch it has been alleged that certain persons who were alleged to be sympathetic with Communist philosophy had penetrated in an effort to utilize it as a medium for the promotion of their doctrines among the Negro people. It was also alleged that unidentified officers of the Chicago branch had records of cooperation and association with Communism.

The organization is reportedly looked upon in most sections of the country as a conservative organization with the purpose of assisting Negroes in a particular area to obtain employment or better employment conditions as well as other economic or social improvements. In at least two areas, namely St. Paul and Milwaukee, the organization has been likened to a "Negro Chamber of Commerce."

Re: March on Washington Movement

Origin

The present March on Washington Movement has as its origin a reportedly anti-Communist group of Negroes who separated themselves from the National Negro Congress, a reported Communist front organization, in April, 1940. During the latter part of 1940 it has been reported this group of Negroes met with A. Philip Randolph, the head of the Brotherhood of Sleeping Car Porters, and decided to plan an organization for an actual march on the City of Washington, D.C. The march, it is reported, was contemplated to be carried out during the spring of 1941.

The original purposes of the organization are reportedly as follows:

1. Presentation in the American way the grievances of the Negro people to the President of the United States and Congress.
2. Inclusion of the Negro in the eight-point Atlantic Charter.
3. Stop the exploitation of the grievances of the Negro by Communists and other subversive element[s].

It has been confidentially reported that at its inception the Communist Party was very critical of the March on Washington Movement; however, it is stated that it later changed its policy from negative criticism to one of boring from within in an attempt to control and direct the policy of the organization through a Party faction.

The actual March on Washington, as originally planned by the organization, was abandoned by A. Philip Randolph upon receipt by him of a letter from the President requesting delay of such action until the matter could be studied and recommendations made. When the march was called off, it is alleged that Communists who had "wormed" their way into the organization were "furious." It has been reported that an attempt was made by Communist Party members in the organization to enlist support to oust Randolph and proceed with the march. The move, however, was unsuccessful. Information received reflects that thousands of Negroes agreed with A. Philip Randolph and denounced members of the Communist Party, branding them as insincere.

Subsequent to the acceptance of the President's request for a delay of any action, an executive order was issued to end discrimination in employment in defense industries. During the interim between the President's request and the issuance of the executive order, the officers and executive members of the organization are reported to have "purged" the movements of Communists and Communist sympathizers within the organization.

Aims and Purposes

The following accusations and demands constitute important factors in the program of this organization. These have been elaborated on by alleged examples in a press release issued by the organization for use after the holding of the National Conference of this organization in Chicago, June 30 through July 4, 1943.

The following accusations and allegations are made:

1. "NEGROES ARE DISCRIMINATED AGAINST IN THE VERY ARMED FORCES WHICH SUMMON THEM TO SHED THEIR BLOOD FOR THEIR COUNTRY.
2. NEGROES ARE DENIED EQUAL OPPORTUNITY IN BOTH PUBLIC AND PRIVATE EMPLOYMENT.
3. NEGROES ARE DENIED THE RIGHT TO VOTE IN MOST OF THE SOUTHERN STATES.
4. NEGROES ARE DENIED EQUAL EDUCATION OPPORTUNITY.
5. NEGROES ARE CARICATURED AND SLANDERED IN THE PRESS AND ON THE STAGE, SCREEN AND RADIO.
6. NEGROES ARE DENIED PARTICIPATION IN THE POLICY FORMING ADMINISTRATION OF THE GOVERNMENT.

7. NEGROES ARE FORCED TO LIVE IN RESTRICTED RESIDENTIAL AREAS AND SEGREGATED HOUSING PROJECTS.
8. NEGROES ARE JIM-CROWED IN TRAINS, BUSES, THEATRES, HOTELS, RESTAURANTS AND OTHER PUBLIC PLACES: AND THROUGHOUT THE SOUTH FORCED INTO JIM-CROW SCHOOLS, LIBRARIES, HOSPITALS AND OTHER INSTITUTIONS SUPPORTED BY TAXES PAID BY ALL OF THE PEOPLE.
9. NEGROES ARE LYNCHED AND MURDERED BY MOBS AND COWARDLY NIGHT-RAIDER BANDS."

The following demands were made by the organization:

"I. "WE DEMAND A DEMOCRATIC ARMY. We call upon the President to enforce Section 4 A of the 1940 Draft Act which reads:

> 'In the selection and training of men under this act and in the interpretation and execution of the provisions of this act, there shall be no discrimination against any person on account of race or color.'

II. WE DEMAND EQUAL ACCESS TO EMPLOYMENT OPPORTUNITIES. This means a Fair Employment Practice[s] Committee which has power to enforce decisions based on its findings and no discrimination in training opportunities, placement, wages, promotions and membership in trade unions.

III. WE DEMAND AN END TO DISFRANCHISEMENT IN THE SOUTH. The enactment of a federal anti-poll tax law, abolition of the white primaries and other registration device that limits a free suffrage and enforcement of the 14th and 15th amendments to the constitution will guarantee the right to vote to all men.

IV. WE DEMAND EQUAL ACCESS TO EDUCATIONAL OPPORTUNITIES. This means equal facilities for the Negro child, equal pay for the Negro teacher and equal access to public, tax-supported institutions of learning for the Negro student.

V. WE DEMAND AN END TO CARICATURE AND SLANDER IN THE NEWSPAPERS, ON THE SCREEN, STAGE AND RADIO. The suppression of the story of the contributions of the Negro to America and the world must cease.

VI. WE DEMAND NEGRO AND MINORITY GROUP REPRESENTATION ON ALL ADMINISTRATIVE AGENCIES SO THAT THESE GROUPS MAY BE ABLE TO DETERMINE POLICIES FOR ALL OF THE PEOPLE.

VII. WE DEMAND AN END TO RESIDENTIAL GHETTOS AND 'RESTRICTIVE COVENANTS.'

VIII. WE DEMAND ABROGATION OF EVERY LAW WHICH

MAKES A DISTINCTION IN TREATMENT BETWEEN CITIZENS BASED ON RELIGION, CREED, COLOR OR NATIONAL ORIGIN.

IX. WE DEMAND A FEDERAL ANTI-LYNCH LAW AND THE PROTECTION OF THE LIVES AND PROPERTY OF ALL CITIZENS."

Organization

The headquarters of the March on Washington Movement are located in the Hotel Theresa, 2084-7th Avenue, New York City. There are branches of the organization active in varying degrees located in the following cities:

Pittsburgh, Pennsylvania
Chattanooga, Tennessee
Flint, Michigan
Meridian, Mississippi
Tampa, Florida
Jacksonville, Florida
Richmond, Virginia
New York, New York
Cleveland, Ohio
Cincinnati, Ohio
Denver, Colorado
Detroit, Michigan
New Orleans, Louisiana
Knoxville, Tennessee
Atlanta, Georgia
Washington, D.C.
Birmingham, Alabama
Mobile, Alabama
Nashville, Tennessee
Salt Lake City, Utah
Newark, New Jersey
Buffalo, New York
West Medford, Massachusetts
Chicago, Illinois

Los Angeles, California

Saint Louis, Missouri

Memphis, Tennessee

Miami, Florida

Oklahoma City, Oklahoma

With regard to the formation of these branches, information has been received that the organizational work is done by Benjamin McLaurin and A. Philip Randolph, both executives in the International Brotherhood of Sleeping Car Porters, A.F. of L. The organizational work is performed while these individuals tour the country in their work for the union, Randolph being the President and McLaurin the National Field Organizer. It is said that the transportation and expenses of their travel are provided for by the union.

In June, 1943, the temporary national offices were established in Chicago, Illinois for the purposes of the organizational activities connected with the National Conference held there in the period June 30 through July 4, 1943.

Officers

The following individuals and their respective capacities represent the officers and members of the National Committee of the organization:

A. Philip Randolph, Director

E. Pauline Myers, Executive Secretary

B. F. McLaurin, Secretary

Aldrich Turner, Treasurer

Dr. Lawrence Ervin, Eastern Regional Director

Dr. Charles Wesley Burton, Mid-Western Regional Director

Harold A. Stevens, Legal Counsel

Dean William Stuart Nelson, Chairman, National Advisory Committee on Mass Action and Strategy

Neil Scott, Public Relations

National Committee

J. A. Burns, Meridian, Mississippi

Thurman T. Dodson, Washington

Miss Layle Lane, New York City

Rev. M. C. Strachen, Tampa, Florida
C. L. Dellums, Oakland, California
Mrs. Senora Lawson, Richmond, Virginia
T. D. McNeal, St. Louis, Missouri

Activities

National Conference at Detroit, Michigan, September 26–27, 1942

Some 66 delegates were present at the conference in Detroit, Michigan from the states of Illinois, Michigan, Missouri, Florida, Louisiana and New York. An added purpose of the conference was to decide policy to be placed before the contemplated convention, nation-wide in character, of this organization to be held in Chicago, Illinois in May, 1943. Besides the adoption of a constitution, a Committee on Resolutions submitted for the National Policy Conference some 36 resolutions. The resolutions will be set out briefly as follows:

1. A resolution endorsing the fight of the United Nations to wipe out the Axis menace.
2. Endorsement of the policy of a mixed army on the grounds that it is a negation of democracy to segregate soldiers.
3. A resolution to call upon the President to in turn call upon Churchill to give independence and freedom to India and to release National leaders.
4. A resolution that President Roosevelt call upon Prime Minister Churchill to grant democratic status with broad suffrage rights to the peoples of the West Indian Islands.
5. Endorsement of the Trade Union Movement and a call upon the A.F. of L. and C.I.O. to abolish discrimination, segregation, Jim-Crow and the color bar in all forms in various affiliated unions.
6. A call for the representation of the Negro people of America on the committee appointed by the President to sit at the peace table at the end of the war.
7. Condemnation of the Sun Shipbuilding Project establishing a separate shipyard for the Negroes as a policy of freezing "the pattern of racial segregation in industry."
8. Endorsement of the Fair Employment Practice[s] Committee in a demand that it be restored to its original status of independence and be supplied with ample funds.
9. The adoption of a program to fight to abolish discrimination, segregation and Jim-Crow before the war ends and a condemnation of all "Negro Appeasers who count for closing ranks and forgetting our grievances."
10. Endorsement of the Pepper Anti-Poll Tax Bill.
11. A call to Congressmen, Senators and President Roosevelt to support "a Federal anti-lynching bill."

12. A demand for the revision of the Atlantic Charter to include the darker races and that the President of the United States take steps to see to it that the Negro people of America become a beneficiary of the Four Freedoms.
13. A resolution opposing any cooperation with the Communist Party or Communist front organization, at the same time stating that the same is not an expression of opposition to Russia in her fight against Hitler.
14. Condemnation of anti-Semitism and anti-Catholicism as undemocratic, unsound and a dangerous form of religious bigotry.'
15. A resolution that the March on Washington Movement be non-sectarian in character.
16. A resolution recommending that the National March on Washington Movement collaborate with sound democratic, liberal and labor groups which are not under Communist control.
17. The resolution that no member of the March on Washington Movement may commit the organization to any political party or candidate although members individually may engage in politics.
18. Condemnation of pro-Japanese, pro-German or pro-Italian activities among Negroes and a call upon Negroes everywhere to repudiate all such activities.
19. A condemnation of "the White Primary" and a call for its abolition.
20. A condemnation of the policy "of the President in refusing to meet with Negro leaders" and a call upon all Negroes together with white liberals to join in sending telegrams and letters to the President demanding that he meet with a committee of Negro leaders selected by the March on Washington Movement for the purpose of discussing the problems of the Negro people.
21. Endorsement of the staging of giant public protest meetings.
22. Endorsement of "mass action including marches on city halls, city councils, defense plants, public utility works, picketing" and the establishment of a pressure campaign.
23. A resolution to approve the holding of a national conference of the Negro people of America for the purpose of expressing the desires of the people and to take action on the question of when Negroes should march on Washington to win their rights from the Government.
24. Recommendation to the National Conference that it declare its approval of the March on Washington of Negroes from all over America for the purpose of "pressing home to the President, the American people, the Congress, that Negroes want their full democratic rights now, during the war."
25. A resolution opposing the acceptance by the March on Washington Movement of any donations from any people except Negroes.
26. A resolution that the organization go on record setting forth as its goal economic equality, political equality, social equality and racial equality for ultimate attainment; as an immediate goal the abolition of discrimination and segregation.

27. A demand that the Government prepare a booklet for white American and foreign soldiers showing the contributions of Negroes to America and pointing out that Negroes are not in America by sufferance, thus that more respect be shown to the Negroes.
28. A resolution that the organization go on record as approving the idea of organizing millions of Negro people for the purpose of exercising pressure upon the Government leaders in the interests of securing equality, freedom and justice.
29. Endorsement of a program to raise a million dollars to provide for monthly broadcasts by Negro leaders to America and the world setting forth the cause of Negroes for equality and freedom and democracy.
30. Endorsement of Negroes entering public places and places of amusement that are acceptable to any other citizen in States where civil rights and laws protect them; also a recommendation that this practice be continued so as to bring the question of Negro rights before the American people, thereby warning them of the fact that Negroes will not remain quiet so long as they are holding the status of second-class citizens.
31. The resolution to boycott "anti-Negro movies".
32. A condemnation of all the Amos and Andy radio scripts and a resolution urging that Negroes and others send telegrams and letters to the National Broadcasting Company expressing their condemnation of the act.
33. An endorsement of the "Bloc system" or city square type of organization for the March on Washington Movement.
34. A resolution to go on record as welcoming youth into the March on Washington Movement.
35. Resolution to give representation [to] women and youths on the executive board of the March on Washington Movement.
36. Resolution that the National Director of the March on Washington Movement, A. Philip Randolph, will be in power and will have the power to appoint officers provided for in the proposed national constitution of the March on Washington Movement to serve until the meeting of the national conference, at which time their successors will be elected by the national body.

All of the foregoing resolutions were adopted by the National Policy Conference.

Attention is directed to resolution No. 13 which placed the national organization on record as being opposed to Communism and the Communist Party. It is recalled that as early as 1940, A. Philip Randolph broke with the National Negro Congress because of the Communist control and influence in it. This resolution, however, should not be taken as all-inclusive, as it has been said by confidential informants, since it is reported that various local units of the organization have Communist influence in them. Although the Communist Party has attacked the March on Washington Movement at times, it is claimed by confidential sources that attempts have been and will be made to obtain control in local units. In this connection, the Chicago and Detroit local units are said to have members who are either sympathizers or members of the Party.

The cooperation between this organization and the National Association for the Advancement of Colored People should not be overlooked. The latter organization is said to have extensive coverage and, of course, such will provide fertile organizational fields for the March on Washington Movement. Such will also add to the field of activities of the National Association for the Advancement of Colored People in that it appears that this organization has confined its activities to legal assistance, lobbying, and general lecture and propaganda tours by officials. It is a new type of militancy.

"Non-Violent Good Will Direct Action"

Late in 1942, the organization discussed undertaking a special type of activity as a means of accomplishing some of its aims. At first, these discussions centered around the technique of Mohandas Gandhi, Indian leader, that of civil disobedience, the purpose being to bring about a change of attitude and action toward the Negro population in this country by disobeying or disregarding "Jim Crow", segregation or restriction laws, measures or customs. In these discussions, as well as the consideration of this particular type of technique, it was reported that the Fellowship of Reconciliation, through various members of that organization, played an important part. It is to be noted that this organization is a militant pacifist group whose activities not only are devoted to strict and utter pacifism but to such matters as the promotion of conscientious objection to war, inter-racial matters, a negotiated peace and related subjects.

The technique of Gandhi was changed to some extent in the contemplated action which was given the form of "non-violent civil disobedience". Subsequently, the terminology given to this action was "non-violent good will direct action", and with regard to this, the organization in early 1943 issued a digest of its study, portions of which are incorporated hereinafter as an explanation of the technique. In the publication of the findings, the fundamental form of the March on Washington Movement was discussed, and it was pointed out that different parts of the country were ready for different kinds of action (with regard to the obtaining of equal rights for Negroes). Certain conditions were referred to as existing in such cities as Richmond, Virginia; Chicago, Illinois; and New York City. These conditions were pointed out as necessitating a change. It was noted in the manuscript that the program to bring about the change should first include conferences between people's representatives and civil authorities who are to be approached "in the spirit of good will". If the conference should fail then, it is pointed out, public opinion must necessarily be mobilized. The use of petitions, letters, mass meetings of protest and other means are suggested. If this form of action fails to bring about a change in the repugnant condition, then more drastic action is in line (here in the manuscript solutions such as boycotting public conveyances and walking; acquiring by purchase separate conveyances for Negroes, are condemned.) The more drastic action, or what is termed "the real solution" was set forth as "non-violent direct action".

The manuscript states "Americans are familiar with several forms of direct action, for example, picketing, the strike, the boycott, and mass migration but riots might result if direct action is taken without non-violence and good will, for which the March on Washington Movement stands. There is a double aim in non-violent direct action, first, to help opponents into a change of heart with reference to the injustice and, second, to change the system under which we suffer. If, after reasonable effort, opponents refuse to change, we are nevertheless morally obligated to refuse to cooperate further in the evil system, but in any case violence should not be resorted to and a strong effort should be made to appeal to the better side of the opponent as well as to the public sympathy."

The findings indicated that training for this type of technique or action must necessarily be given so that non-violence and good will may be instilled in those participating. In this regard the pamphlet has suggested "While training is going on, the agitation by means of ordinary methods should be kept up. In this way, the spirit of the resistors will be kept aflame, the public further awakened, and new recruits added. As the campaign gathers momentum and the public is more favorable it is to be expected that more and more white allies will be won over but well in advance of the campaign, at least a few of the leaders should have taken a substantial training course in non-violent direct action in a suitable center. They will then be ready to take up the job of training the local non-violent resistors in weekend institutes, in which some *resource* leaders from outside may be used to advantage."

The manuscript of the findings digest stated in conclusion, "The kind of action that refuses to give in and yet will not inflict injury requires courage superior to, rather than inferior to, that which is necessary for physical combat. . . . There is almost no limit to the resources for social change in the many forms which non-violent direct action may take, according to the circumstances."

A. Philip Randolph, national leader, in defense of this technique and in distinguishing it from what he termed "non-cooperation" as advocated by Gandhi in India, stated that the objective in India is to effect a transition of governmental power from the hands of the British "Imperialists" into the hands of the Indian people, and that such activity [a]mounts to a breaking down of British civil government. As distinguished from this, Randolph stated that the March on Washington Movement does not seek to bring about a transition of government, rather the modification of "behavior pattern" by process of reconditioning. He added that the organization will not call on Negroes in the armed forces or in the defense industries to disobey commands or to stop work at any time in carrying out this technique. He stated that these groups would not come within the category of Negroes who would be called upon. These statements by Randolph are believed to have been made in defense of the organization which was criticized by not only the Communist Party but by such newspapers as PM and the negro publication The Pittsburgh Courier, the latter publication condemning the March on Washington Movement in its May 8, 1943 issue by stating that the organization has stirred indignation and unrest and lacks constructive administrative leadership. It also condemned the leadership by saying that it is evidenced by irresponsible talk about "suicidal civil disobedience and mass marches which never materialize."

[*100-95014-368*]

Prior to the National Conference of the organization, held in Chicago, a meeting of the planning committee took place in Washington, D.C. on May 22, 1943, at which time a discussion took place of this particular type of action. The following information portrays that which occurred at this meeting:

Dean William Nelson of the School of Religion at Howard University, Washington, D.C., is reported as having acted as the chairman of the meeting while Reverend J. Holmes Smith, white, who is connected with the Fellowship of Reconciliation and who has been affiliated with the March on Washington Movement to make a study of non-violent civil disobedience, made a report to the meeting. Smith is said to have read a set of principles upon which the program of civil disobedience was to be based and stated that such a program was the logical outgrowth of the resolutions passed at the Detroit conference held early in the Fall of 1942 by the March on Washington Movement. The resolutions referred to are related to be as follows:

1. Organize the mass of the Negro people.
2. Press home the fact that Negroes want their rights *now*.
3. Discipline the mass in order to wage an effective demonstration.
4. March on government establishments and defense plants all over the country.
5. Push the Negro's demand for admission to all public places.

Smith is said to have continued, describing "non-violent direct action" as drastic and as being entirely non-violent direct action, which is taken against an evil law and in which all of the better points of other "Protestant action" are used and both courageously organized and fearlessly executed. A confidential source has advised that Smith digressed slightly when questioned closely as to the value of such by Thurman Dodson, leader of the Washington unit of the March on Washington Movement, who indicated that he would not approve of deliberate disobedience to an established law. Smith is reported to have replied that M[o]handas Gandhi once indicated that if the All-India Congress decided to dispense with this type of action as a weapon, he as an individual alone would have to continue.

Smith is reported to have elaborated on the statement of principles, mentioning the following steps to be taken in the application of this type of a program:

1. Negotiation.
2. Self-examination and self-discipline.
3. The pursuit of this program appeals to the better nature of an opponent.
4. The program must be based upon a devotion to truth, with no exaggeration and must derive confidence and respect.
5. Great courage is necessary to carry through the program.

It is related that it was also brought out in the meeting that the advanced stages of the program of non-violent direct action include picketing, boycotting, and mass demonstrations, all of which must be conducted in an orderly fashion and no resistance shown toward anyone seeking to molest individual participants. Smith is said to have stated that the non-violent direct action movement never recedes from justice, although from time to time it may revise its views of what constitutes justice. He is further said to have remarked that members must have an inspired, spiritual outlook and this must lead them to destroy the oppressive system, rather than to destroy the individual.

At this point in the meeting, **Vincent Baker**, a member of the organization in Harlem known as Modern Trend, a group alleged to have some Trotskyite influence in it, asked for a differentiation between good and bad laws, inasmuch as non-violent direct action presupposes the cause, intent and effect of any law under consideration. It is reported that a discussion was then held with regard to the nature of good and bad laws as defined for the purpose of such a program.

At the meeting recommendations were reportedly made as to the areas in which demonstrations of the non-violent direct action program would be held. It is said that such action or demonstrations should be held in Washington, D.C., Richmond, Virginia, or in the State of New Jersey, or in perhaps all areas. A confidential informant has advised that New York City was eliminated inasmuch as the Negroes in that city now enjoy so many of the advantages that a campaign of this nature might not attract a large following. It is reported that Detroit was also eliminated because of the preponderance of Southern people in its population. Richmond is said to have been particularly selected inasmuch as it was believed that this city would afford an opening of the gates to such a movement in the South. Washington, D.C., was reportedly chosen because of its large Negro population and its status as the capital of the nation. According to the informant, it was felt that the Negroes in New Jersey would also properly respond to such a program.

The confidential informant reporting on this matter advised that at this point of the meeting **Bayard Rustin**, a member of the Fellowship of Reconciliation, related a story illustrative of this program of action in order to dramatize the application of non-violent direct action. **Rustin** is said to have told of his experiences in Knoxville, Tennessee, where he purposely sat in the white section of a public bus and was ejected and beaten by policemen. According to the story reported, **Rustin** was taken to the police court where he was again struck by policemen. At no time did **Rustin** make any effort to oppose the physical violence to which he was allegedly subjected. **Rustin** reportedly stated that after he discussed what had happened with the District Attorney he was released.

Indications have been reported, however, that varying conceptions of this activity are had by different national officers of the organization. In this connection, a confidential informant has reported on an Executive Committee Meeting, held April 12, 1943 at the headquarters of the March on Washington Movement in Chicago, at 4304 South Parkway, where ten persons were present, and the presiding officer was E. Pauline Myers, National Executive Secretary of the organization.

In her remarks the Executive Secretary stated that the Fellowship of Reconciliation had been taking an active interest in the March on Washington Movement, and that it was at the time rapidly becoming closely affiliated with the organization. She indicated that on a recent tour her traveling expenses had been paid by the Fellowship of Reconciliation. She then referred to actual "marches" by local units in furtherance of the non-violent good will action program. She said that they were going to march with the technique of non-violence in view, but if necessary to obtain their demands, they were going to fight. She added that the first groups which would march on any particular place would be peaceful, and in the event they were attacked they would not retaliate in any manner. She continued that there would be follow-up groups, and where units had been met with violence from discriminating sources the follow-up units would, if necessary, fight. [*Cgo F.D.-71 100-94014-249 pg. 7*]

The most recent decisions with regard to this type of activity were arrived at at the National Conference of the organization held in Chicago, June 30 to July 4, 1943. The non-violent good will action committee at the conference submitted a five point resolution recommending a program of non-violent direct action in fields of employment, civil and constitutional rights, "Jim-Crowism" and voting. It was decided to experiment with this technique in the cities of New York, Washington, Richmond, Chicago and Los Angeles. It was further recommended that the March on Washington Movement establish an institute to teach this technique, as well as appointing a paid national director to act in this field.

Later at a closed meeting at the conference held on July 3, 1943, the following resolutions were adopted by the delegates:

1. That the actual march on the City of Washington be used as one of the techniques of the non-violent direct action good will program.
2. That local marches on city and state government buildings be held by local chapters as soon as plans can be made which are to be used to train and condition marchers for the "National March Demonstration" in Washington.
3. That the time of the National March be determined by the National Executive Committee.

Meetings Preliminary to National Conference

A regional conference was held by leaders of the March on Washington Movement at the Y.M.C.A., 1816 12th Street, N.W., Washington, D.C., on May 1, 1943. According to a confidential source of information, this was a regional conference of representatives of the Washington, D.C., and Richmond, Virginia, units of the March on Washington Movement with national officers of the organization. It is reported that the program for the National Convention of the organization, held in Chicago, Illinois, from June 30 to July 4, 1943, was discussed at length along with the proposed panel discussions at the convention.

Among the panels which were said at the time to be contemplated for the National Convention were those concerning the Fair Employment Practices Committee and the question of "Clash of Color Here and Abroad." It is reported that an individual by the name of Epstein, who is alleged to have served as an attorney for the Committee at one time, was being considered to lead the first-named panel discussion. With respect to the latter, it was contemplated that this panel would be headed by Dr. Rayford Logan, and it was reportedly suggested that among the contributors to this panel should be Kingsley O. Mbadiwe, a native of West Africa, and Dr. Allen [Alain] Locke.

According to the source of information, the key people scheduled to participate in the National Convention were A. Philip Randolph, leader of the instant organization;

Reverend A. J. Muste of the Fellowship of Reconciliation; Dr. Rayford Logan; Max Yergan, a reported Communist Party member and president of the National Negro Congress, a Communist front organization; Dr. Channing Tobias of the instant organization; Henry Johnson of the United Mine Workers; James Farmer of the Fellowship of Reconciliation; and a Dr. Charles Wesley who was reportedly to speak on the question of race imperialism.

It has been further reported that at the National Convention the question of the campaign of non-violent civil disobedience was to be discussed. In this connection it was further reported that A. J. Muste would make a report on the subject. It was said at that time this program was being studied for the March on Washington Movement by Dr. J. Holmes Smith, said to be a paid employee of the Fellowship of Reconciliation whose duty is to study the principles and philosophy of Gandhi.

It should be pointed out that Dr. J. Holmes Smith in September, 1942, was the leader of an inter-racial pilgrimage to protest discrimination against Negroes made from New York City to Washington, D.C. With respect to Dr. Smith's participation, the observation has been made by an informant in this matter that although Dr. Smith is a white man and Randolph's policy has been to restrict his movement entirely to Negroes, it is, nevertheless, consistent with Randolph's policy to secure the assistance of white people even though they cannot become members of the Movement.

It is said that E. Pauline Myers, Executive Secretary of the March on Washington Movement, announced at the meeting that J. Holmes Smith, who had formerly worked with Mahatma Gandhi in India, would make a report on May 22 with regard to his recommendations on the civil disobedience campaign. In this connection, Natalie Moorman is said to have spoken at the regional conference on the role of youth in the March on Washington Movement. She is related to have discussed a recent picketing of the Little Palace Restaurant, 14th and U Streets, N.W., which had previously served only white customers, and stated that the activity had been a complete success and the pickets, who were students from Howard University, were successful in forcing the restaurant to serve Negroes.

According to the source of information in this matter, approximately twelve to fifteen people took part in the meeting, most of whom were from the City of Washington. A. Philip Randolph was not present. However, among those in attendance who were identified are the following: Horace Sheffield of the United Automobile, Aircraft and Agricultural Implement Workers of America, C.I.O.; Horace and Roscoe Mitchell of Richmond, Virginia; F. B. McLaurin, a national officer of the March on Washington Movement; and E. Pauline Myers, Executive Secretary of the organization. It is said that among local Washington people attending the meeting were Lillian Speight, Lynwood Cundiff, Elizabeth Craig, Alexander Ronier, P. C. Speight, George Briscoe, Mazie Sandle, Natalie Moorman and Thurmon Dodson.

On June 20, 1943, a meeting was held at the Woodlawn Methodist Church in Chicago, at which Randolph was the principal speaker. He dwelt on the alleged treatment received by Negroes in the armed forces, saying that he had received numerous letters from Negro youths in the Army wanting to know if something could not be done. He referred to alleged mistreatment in various branches of the armed forces, and followed up by making in substance the following statements:

"The only thing that is wrong with this country is that it is being run by a lot of bourgeois politicians. The only way we can defeat them whether they are Democrats, Republicans, Socialists or Communists, is to form a solid block of our own. It can be done because we have shown it can be done in our organization. These bourgeois politicians are violating the law every day and nothing is done about it because in the Selective Service law it says, 'Every American citizen, no matter what his race, creed or color, will be given equal rights in the United States Army, Navy, Coast Guard and Marines.' Instead, our boys are being segregated in some branches of the armed forces, and in other branches they are permitted to enjoy the privileges of the white boys.

"Our enemy is now the Germans, Italians and Japanese. After this war they will enjoy the same privileges as the Americans and will even be allowed to become American citizens, while the Negro who is the real American will be segregated and pushed around unless we act and act now. Now is our chance to be put on an equal basis with the white men and have an equal right to rule." ▬ ▬ [*100-95014-364*]

On June 23, 1943, A. Philip Randolph called an emergency meeting of Negroes at the Metropolitan Community Church in Chicago, Illinois, the purpose of which was to discuss the race riots in Detroit. From 700 to 2,000 Negroes were reportedly present. At this meeting a resolution was adopted to be sent telegraphically to the President, and delivered personally to Governor Green of Illinois and Mayor Edward Kelly of Chicago. This resolution contained the following steps:

1. That Negroes and white people have no riot in Chicago.
2. That Detroit riot be condemned as a disgrace to the country.
3. That a special grand jury be appointed to investigate the riot.
4. That Negroes be appointed to the grand jury.
5. That plant managers of national defense industries recognize rights of Negro workers.
6. That Detroit Police Department be investigated for their weakness in failing to prevent the riot and for killing the majority of Negroes while protecting white rioters.
7. That a fund be set up to reimburse those persons who suffered personal losses through no fault of their own.
8. That the Governor of Michigan be commended for his speedy action but condemned for failure to name Negroes to the Fact Finding Committee.
9. That President Roosevelt give a comprehensive statement to the people on race relations.
10. That Mayor Kelly appoint a racial group committee to study social problems in Chicago.
11. That race riots be condemned.

It was announced at the meeting that subsequent meetings would be held on June 24 and June 29, 1943. It was reportedly contemplated that the latter of these meetings would deal with policy and strategy of the organization and that it would be attended by Norman Thomas, Frank Crosswaith, Dean William Stuart Nelson, and all section leaders of the March on Washington Movement.

Another meeting was held by the subject organization on June 25, 1943, at 305 North Leavitt Street, Chicago, Illinois, at which Charles W. Burton, E. Pauline Myers, A. Philip Randolph, and James Farmer, Negro national officer of the Fellowship of Reconciliation, were speakers. Farmer, at the meeting, urged that Negroes everywhere adopt the non-violent civil disobedience program as an independent movement to secure additional rights for Negroes. He stated that members of the Fellowship of Reconciliation would attend the National Conference of the March on Washington Movement.

A. Philip Randolph reportedly instructed that the Non-Violent Direct Action Committee of the March on Washington Movement hold meetings in abeyance pending the decision of the National Conference as to what is the best way to proceed under this program. E. Pauline Myers in turn is said to have announced that Winfred Lynn, or his brother, Conrad Lynn, would be a featured guest at the conference.

National Conference, June 30–July 4, 1943

The March on Washington Movement held its opening meeting at the Metropolitan Community Church in Chicago on June 30, 1943, at 8:30 P.M. It was attended by approximately 500 persons. A. Philip Randolph, National Leader of this organization, presided, and he is related to have said that the March on Washington Movement was founded to express condemnation of those Governmental policies which permit racial discrimination and segregation. He is said to have announced that the Convention would consider the development of what he described as a powerful nonpartisan political bloc to bring pressure on Congress for the enactment of the anti-poll tax and anti-lynching bills. This political bloc, according to Randolph, will ask that Negroes be given "first-class citizenship status."

Randolph is reported to have also stated the President would be requested to form a national race commission for the purpose of achieving a Congressional investigation of race riots.

Dr. Lawrence Ervin, who is the Eastern Regional Director of the organization, also spoke at the opening meeting and stated "the Negro must fight for his rights" and "who in hell is going to tell the Negro how he should go about getting his rights."

At 12:00 noon, July 1, 1943, a business session of the Convention was held and in attendance were approximately 110 people. The Credentials Committee at this meeting made various reports. The Convention's program was outlined and permanent national committees previously appointed by the Executive Board of this organization were announced.

An afternoon session was held on July 1 which was attended by approximately 370 delegates and members of the public. A discussion on "The Outlook And Future of the Fair Employment Practice[s] Committee" was engaged in by Earl B. Dickerson and Milton P. Webster, both of Chicago, who were former members of this Committee, and Harold Stevens and Thurman Dodson, delegates to the Convention from Washington, D.C. A dispute arose between the Protestants and Catholics when Dodson is said to have attacked the President for appointing Monsignor Haas as head of the Fair Employment Practice[s] Committee on the ground that Monsignor Haas was not suitable because of his training as a Catholic priest. Stevens, a Washington delegate, led the dispute against Dodson.

There were two resolutions adopted at the afternoon meeting on July 1, one condemning the action of Monsignor Haas for his decision in the Alabama Dry Dock and Shipbuilding Corporation case in Mobile, Alabama, which permitted Negroes to work on only four of the ways in the shipyards. This action was labeled as discrimination against Negroes. The second resolution was an appeal to have Dickerson and Webster reappointed to the new committee of the Fair Employment Practice[s] Committee.

It is said that both of the resolutions were sent to the President by telegram. In this connection, Randolph is reported to have read a resolution in the form of a telegram to the minority and majority leaders of both Houses of Congress, to the Vice President, and to Congressmen Fish of New York in which an appeal was made that legislation be passed to create a "Commission on Race in America." It is allegedly desired that this commission rule on all racial questions arising in the United States. The last resolution was unanimously adopted.

The March on Washington Movement held a meeting on "Jim Crowism in America" at 9:00 P.M., July 1, 1943, in the Metropolitan Community Church, Chicago, Illinois. Approximately 600 persons were in attendance, including 25 white people. Reverend Archibald J. Carey, Jr., Pastor, Woodlawn A.M.E. Church, Chicago, presided and introduced the following speakers, all of whom are Negroes: Layle Lane, March on Washington Movement Secretary, New York City; Carl Hansberry, President, National Negro Progress Association and wealthy Chicago real estate owner; Cordelia Green Johnson, President, Beauty Culturists League of America, Jersey City, New Jersey; Hank Johnson, United Mine Workers Union representative, New York City; Bayard Rustin, Fellowship of Reconciliation, New York City, and Dr. George Edward Haynes, Federal Council of Churches in America.

All of the speakers criticized the alleged discrimination against and segregation of the Negro in labor and in the Army. Reverend Carey stated that Negroes should not go to Burma to save freedom if they can't get freedom in Birmingham. He asserted that the cause of the riot in Detroit is to be found in the heart of the Negro who is oppressed. Layle Lane suggested that Negroes can secure political, social and economic freedom by use of the purchasing power and the right to vote found in the total Negro population. Hansberry advised Negroes to take advantage of all legal means to secure freedom from racial discrimination, and Cordelia Johnson suggested that Negroes take advantage of all opportunities to join inter-racial groups. She also quoted a colored friend who had stated that she would rather shoot her son than see him in the uniform of the United States Army, but continued by stating that she had tried to dissuade her friend from this course of action. Johnson stated, "Why should he (referring to the Detroit Negro) fight for freedom when his own citizens were being shot by policemen who were sent to protect him." She also advocated legislation to abolish

"Jim Crowism" and placed the responsibility for the existence of "Jim Crowism" in the Army and in labor on the Federal Government. Bayard Rustin urged members of the March on Washington Movement to follow a direct action non-violence program to secure Negroes' rights at the present time. He stated that freedom would not come from the use of laws, but will come from the application of the non-violence technique. He asserted that violence would be suicidal and freedom would not come by the use of force.

Voluntary contributions were solicited from those in attendance at the meeting, and the booklet, "Jim Crow in Uniform—War's Greatest Scandal" was sold. Copies of "Labor Action", a Trotzkyite newspaper, were distributed.

On July 2, 1943, a meeting was held from 10:00 A.M. until 1:15 P.M., the purpose of which was to present the program of the March on Washington Non-Violence Direct Action Good Will Committee. Only delegates were permitted to attend this meeting, and members of the press were excluded upon the instructions of A. Philip Randolph, National Director. Several members of the Socialist press, however, whose names are presently unknown, were permitted to attend. Dr. William Edward Nelson, Chairman of the Non-Violence Direct Action Good Will Committee, and Dean of the School of Religion, Howard University, Washington, D.C. presided. The following persons who are members of this committee addressed the delegates: Miss Rita Baham, Chairman of the Chicago Local Non-Violence Committee and member of the Committee on Racial Equality; Dr. J. Holmes Smith, former missionary to India from New York City and operator of the Harlem Work Shop; Reverend James Farmer, Resident Secretary of the Fellowship of Reconciliation, Chicago, Illinois; Bayard Rustin, Field Representative, Fellowship of Reconciliation, New York City; Mrs. Melba Wilson, Fellowship of Reconciliation representative, Columbus, Ohio, and E. Pauline Myers, National Executive Secretary of the March on Washington Movement.

The speakers stressed the importance of not responding to violence on the part of white agitators and policemen, and a direct action non-violence program was suggested whereby Negroes would be educated by a March on Washington Movement school for teaching the non-violence technique. This technique, it was stated, would consist of approaching white proprietors of restaurants, bus companies and theaters to secure service for Negroes as well as whites. The program as outlined by speakers Rustin, Baham, Smith and Myers stressed the fact that Negroes should passively resist until service is given. No alternative action was decided upon in the event the services are denied.

The Non-Violence Direct Action Committee submitted a five-point resolution which, according to confidential informants, will probably be adopted in its entirety. This resolution recommends that the program of non-violence direct action take effect in the fields of employment, civil and constitutional rights, "Jim Crowism" and voting. It was decided upon by the committee during the morning session of July 2, 1943, to experiment with the non-violence technique in the cities of New York, Washington, Richmond, Chicago and Los Angeles. It was also recommended that the March on Washington Movement establish an institute to teach the non-violence technique with headquarters to be located in New York City. In addition, it was advocated [that] a paid National Director of the March on Washington Movement be appointed.

At the afternoon session, which began at 2:00 P.M. on July 2, 1943, the discussion was devoted to the problem of "The Negro in Peace and Postwar Planning—Africa, the Caribbean and the United States." The speakers at this session were: Dr. Lawrence Reddick, a March on Washington Movement delegate from New York City who is connected with the New York City Library; Dr. Eric Williams, Professor of Social and Political Sciences, Howard University, and Dr. Louis Wirth (white) Professor of Sociology at the University of Chicago.

On the evening of July 2, 1943, the organization held a "Town Hall" meeting which was attended by approximately 650 Negroes and 20 white persons. Colden Brown, President of the New York local of this organization as well as Chairman of the national committee dealing with the Winfred Lynn Selective Service case, presided at the meeting which dealt mainly with the subject "Jim Crow in Uniform—The War's Greatest Scandal". Penny postal cards were distributed at the beginning of the session to be addressed to the President urging that he reschedule the railroad hearings of the Fair Employment Practice[s] Committee and reappoint Earl B. Dickerson to that Committee. The recipients of these cards were urged to write their own messages concerning these two matters.

The following individuals spoke at the meeting: Vincent Baker, Negro, National Director of the Modern Trend Progressive Youth Group; James Farmer, Negro, Secretary of the Fellowship of Reconciliation; Roscoe Mitchell, Negro, Richmond, Virginia, delegate at the Conference; David Grant, Negro, St. Louis, Missouri, delegate at the Conference; Norman Thomas, Chairman of the Socialist Party; Ira Reed, Negro, head of the Department of Sociology, Georgia University; and Edgar G. Brown, Negro, representative of the National Negro Council.

Colden Brown, as Chairman, announced at the outset that the National Conference of the March on Washington Movement proposed to lift "the lid from the foul Jim Crow situation" which exists in the United States. He alleged that the problem originated from the Federal Government itself and stated that it is a sad commentary that all groups can serve in the country's war effort except the Negroes. He further alleged that 90 per cent of the Negro troops in the United States are in labor battalions rather than in combat units and urged segregation in the United States Army be eliminated.

With regard to the Winfred Lynn Selective Service case, Brown stated the March on Washington Movement plans to carry it to the United States Supreme Court and warned if the Supreme Court fails to rule in favor of Lynn, then the Negro has no recourse to the courts of the United States. He added if the Supreme Court ruled in favor of Winfred Lynn, then the "Jim Crow policy of the War Department" will have to be changed. He stated that July 4 means nothing to the Negro soldier; that to him hymns and prayers are fraud and deception, for revolting hypocrisy and barbarism are rampant.

Vincent Baker at the July 2 evening session remarked that Negroes are told not to be emotional over riots, yet if Negroes are to be indignant over the slaughter of Americans in Japanese internment camps, then surely they are entitled to become indignant over the slaughter of Negroes in American camps. He then stated that Hitler and Goebbels could not have done a more effective job of breaking up American unity than

"Stimson and Knox" and alleged that everywhere American troops have gone the prejudice of "Jim Crowism" has followed it.

James Farmer of the Fellowship of Reconciliation informed that "Jim Crowism" exists throughout the United States and the world at large, and alleged the United States Army is under the hand of reactionaries in the South. He urged segregation be abolished for unity in order that true unity can be based on equality and justice. He then stated that Winfred Lynn is not breaking the law, rather upholding it in opposing segregation in the United States Army. He urged all Negroes to protest through demonstration and letters and telegrams to their Congressmen.

David Grant avowed the riots in Detroit were caused by segregation inaugurated by industrialists and urged agitation, exploitation and the expose of existing conditions by Negroes to cure "evils of Jim Crowism."

Norman Thomas in his speech urged the abolition of "Jim Crowism" in America and stated also that no Negro or white man can hope to have freedom without doing away with the war system and conscription under it. He urged Negroes not only to fight "Jim Crowism" but to fight against the whole system which permits conscription to exist.

In connection with the evening meeting of July 2, 1943, it was ascertained by a confidential informant that the Non-Violence Direct Action Committee of the March on Washington Movement would stage a demonstration composed of Negroes and white persons at the Walnut Room of the Hotel Bismarck in Chicago during the dinner hour on July 5, 1943. It was alleged that the March on Washington Movement would observe the outcome of this demonstration to determine the course of further activity on their part. James Farmer, previously referred to, was reportedly scheduled to make the initial demand for service at the hotel which would be followed by demands for service by other demonstrators.

On July 3, 1943, from 3:00 P.M. to 9:00 P.M., a closed meeting was held at the Metropolitan Community Church in Chicago. This was a meeting of the Non-Violence Direct Action Committee of the March on Washington Movement, and the purpose of it was to present the recommendations on future activity in this particular field. There it was recommended that plans for an actual march on the City of Washington be made at the present time and a date be set for this march. It was further recommended that local chapters institute marches immediately upon their delegates' return from the National Conference to be directed at State and municipal buildings. William Stuart Nelson, Dean of Religion at Howard University and Chairman of the Non-Violence Direct Action Committee of the instant organization, introduced a resolution which was adopted by the delegates:

1. That the actual march on Washington be used as one of the techniques of the non-violence, direct action, good will program;
2. That local marches on city and state government buildings be held by local chapters as soon as plans can be made which are to be used to train and condition marchers for the "national march demonstration" in Washington; and
3. That the time of the national march be determined by the National Executive Committee.

This resolution was adopted unanimously. In this connection, it is reported that A. Philip Randolph, the national leader, in a private conversation, advised if a crisis comes as a result of local demonstrations, then the actual march on the City of Washington will be called and those persons participating in it will remain in Washington until a bill is passed creating a "racial commission". The contemplated purposes of the "racial commission" are:

1. To outlaw "Jim Crowism" in the Army.
2. To investigate all racial questions in the Army and elsewhere.

On July 3, 1943, the delegates at the National Conference numbering 104 elected a new National Executive Committee composed of 26 persons and divided the United States into 7 geographical districts. They provided for three members in each district to hold membership in the Executive Committee and for five members at large from New York City. A quorum of the Executive Committee was set at five persons, which body has been given the power to meet at any time and to issue the "call" for a national march. It was voted 103 to 2 to exclude white persons from membership in the organization. Randolph, who apparently accounted for the extra vote, was in favor of permitting Socialists to become members. Layle Lane, National Executive Committee member, favored permitting white persons to become members inasmuch as the March on Washington Movement has accepted contributions from them. It is to be noted in this connection that representatives of the Socialist Party's newspaper "The Call" and "The Militant" which is generally recognized as the official publication of the Socialist Workers Party, a Trotzkyite group, were permitted to attend the closed session.

The members of the subcommittee interested in the Winfred Lynn Selective Service case, referred to previously, issued recommendations at the closed meeting of July 3, 1943, that each local unit of the March on Washington Movement obtain additional cases of this character. They further recommended that Negroes be approached prior to their induction into the Army for the purpose of acquainting them with "the law" so that after they are inducted they can institute legal action against the War Department. According to a confidential informant, there was some discussion as to whether the Negroes approached should institute legal action before induction took place, although nothing definite was settled in this regard.

Among the other resolutions passed at the closed meeting of July 3 was that Communists be excluded from the membership of the organization. An additional resolution was that $12,000 must be raised to finance the organization by the local units through staging rallies, concerts and dances. Another resolution, which was adopted by a vote of 104 to 1, urged assistance in winning the war and purchasing war bonds. In this connection, Layle Lane opposed the resolution on the ground that the war is "capitalistic" and requested that her vote be recorded.

On the morning of July 4, 1943, a morning prayer was given for the National Conference at the Negro Soldier's Monument in Chicago. This was followed at 2:00 P.M. by a parade from the Metropolitan Community Church in Chicago to the Du Sable High School where the final mass meeting of the Conference was held. Approximately 50 persons participated in what was called the "freedom parade".

At 3:45 P.M., July 4, 1943, the final meeting of the National Conference was held at the Du Sable High School in Chicago. In attendance were approximately 2,200 Negroes. The Chairman of the meeting was Dr. Charles Wesley Burton, Negro, President of the Chicago unit. He announced that the March on Washington Movement had decided to maintain the idea of marching on the City of Washington as the strategy to get rid of "Jim Crowism". He advised, however, this would be used only as a last resort. Burton also announced that the March on Washington Movement would prepare to discipline its members for the national march by instituting local marches upon various cities and State capitals in the United States. He welcomed an investigation by the Federal Bureau of Investigation, stating that that Bureau stood for justice.

The following individuals also addressed the meeting: Dr. William Stuart Nelson, who has been referred to previously and who was appointed to direct the "action program" of the March on Washington Movement; Dr. E. Stanley Jones, white, a missionary to India, who was described as an aide of Mohandas Gandhi; A. Philip Randolph; Dr. James Horace, Negro, preacher of the Monumental Baptist Church; and Reverend T. B. Chapman, Shilo Baptist Church, Engelwood, Illinois.

In his speech, Dr. James Horace stated, "The Church must come to grips with the race measure, the Church has upheld segregation and it is time it started confessing its sins. The Church has preached dogma and not brotherhood. It is a sin for a Negro to go to the Solomon Islands to fight for democracy that he doesn't have at home. I want the FBI to communicate that to the President."

Dr. E. Stanley Jones addressed the audience on the subject of non-violent solutions to the race program. He described the non-violent action program of Mohandas Gandhi and stated it was a principle of "we won't hate you, but we won't obey you". He recommended the organization to institute such a technique.

A. Philip Randolph in his speech stated the present war is one of imperialism and of white people's supremacy. He claimed the cause for freedom is in full retreat and the Allies may win but democracy will lose. He stated the Negro is not free and never has been free because of the inequalities which have existed in America. He compared the liberation of Negroes to that of other enslaved peoples. He pointed out alleged instances of segregation of the Negro in the social, economic and political fields in the United States.

In his speech Randolph advocated the members of the local units of the March on Washington Movement contact public utilities through sending committees to seek employment for Negroes with the public utilities. He further advocated if employment is not obtained, the local units conduct picketing, institute marches, and stage demonstrations. He added that demands would be made by the March on Washington Movement of President Roosevelt to gain employment for Negroes in all branches of the United States Government. He stated the March on Washington Movement proposes a united Negro political bloc, mass picketing of public utilities and marches on city halls and State capitals. He called upon the Negro soldiers to vote in support of anti-lynching and anti-poll tax laws as well as similar measures.

Randolph also remarked in his speech that the March on Washington Movement will demand an answer from the Republican and Democratic Parties on the question of racial discrimination. He also said the organization proposes to purge labor unions of discrimination by similar means. He severely criticized Monsignor Francis Haas, head of the Fair Employment Practice[s] Committee, for his decision in the Mobile, Alabama, shipyards case, terming it another example of race segregation.

It was claimed by Randolph in his remarks that the Federal Government was entirely responsible for the race problem existing in America at the present time, and it would only do what was right when forced to by measures proposed by the March on Washington Movement. He added that Congress will be called upon to enforce that section of the Fourteenth Amendment which provides that individual States discriminating against races be cut down proportionately in their representation in Congress.

On July 5, 1943, the National Executive Committee of the March on Washington Movement met in the Metropolitan Community Church in Chicago where subcommittees were appointed. William Stuart Nelson of Howard University, Washington, D.C., was re-appointed Chairman of the Non-Violence Good Will Direct Action Committee, and Thurman Dodson, a Washington, D.C., attorney, was named Chairman of the committee to work with the Fair Employment Practice[s] Committee.

A new group was set up at this meeting to make plans for a conference to be held next year in New York City to discuss post war planning for "free Negroes and darker peoples". At this proposed conference it is planned to draw up "a manifesto of four freedoms to apply to Chinese, Indian peoples and Negroes" for presentation to the United Nations Peace Conference following the war.

Charles W. Burton announced that a series of institutes are planned to teach non-violent, good will direct action, the first one to be held at Howard University. He also asserted that transportation and public utility companies of Chicago and elsewhere would be asked to hire Negroes equally and that if these requests are met with refusals, mass demonstrations will be employed.

The Winfred Lynn Selective Service Case

On October 28, 1942, a Negro, Winfred William Lynn admitted he had failed to report to his local Selective Service board No. 261, Jamaica, Long Island, New York, for induction into the United States Army after he had been placed in a 1-A classification. The date on which he was supposed to report was September 18, 1942. Lynn stated he had had no intention of reporting for induction, nor would he report in the future, saying that although he was not a conscientious objector and had no beliefs to keep him from fighting, he would refuse to enter the armed forces because he felt that there was racial discrimination against Negroes in the United States Army. He said he did not believe there should be segregation of black or white, and that that was the reason for his refusal to be inducted.

Upon his arrest, Winfred Lynn was represented by his brother, Conrad Lynn, an attorney, who presented a brief to the United States Attorney for the Eastern District of New York in the form of a memorandum which he, Conrad Lynn, said portrayed the exact position of his client and brother. An analysis of this memorandum sets forth the facts of Winfred Lynn's case and points out that the local board with which he had registered selected Winfred Lynn's name as "one of a quota for Negroes" after receiving a "notice of call" from the State Director of the Selective Service System indicating that a certain number of Negroes were wanted for induction on September 18, 1942 and a certain number of whites. Conrad Lynn, in his brief on behalf of his brother, stated:

1. The Selective Training and Service Act of 1940, as amended, forbids "discrimination by race".
2. That it provides no instructions for separate quotas of Negroes and general quotas for all other racial groups.
3. Volunteering is provided for by any person "regardless of race or color."
4. Taking the foregoing reasoning as a whole, it is plain that Congress did not intend to countenance race discrimination in selecting men for service."

The resume continues:

1. Segregation is discrimination. (Various cases are cited pro and con.)
2. Health and economy are the sole factors to be considered in the classification of Selective Service inductees.
3. The method of using quotas unlawfully interferes with the liberty of the person, and although the Selective Service statute provides for equal protection, its operation can be attacked if it is in violation of due process.
4. A "race quota" violates the "spirit of conscription" and the preamble of the Act states that a fair and just system is provided for.

On December 19, 1942, Winfred Lynn was inducted into the United States Army, and on January 4, 1943, a petition for a writ of habeas corpus was presented to the Federal District Court for the Eastern District of New York in this case. The judge of this court stated that Winfred Lynn through his attorney had failed to prove his induction was pursuant to an induction quota stipulating separate groups of Negroes and whites, and therefore, no question of racial discrimination in his induction could be raised. It was said that inasmuch as Lynn had reported for induction on December 19, 1942 alone and not in an induction group he had been accepted not as part of any "quota" group but had been inducted separately without regard to his race, color or creed. No ruling was given as to the "quota" system.

It should be noted that Arthur Garfield Hays of the American Civil Liberties Union was an associate counsel and presented the brief in this case.

In the meantime, on November 11, 1942, Conrad Lynn spoke relative to his brother's case at a meeting of the New York City unit of the March on Washington Movement. At this meeting he urged that the March on Washington Movement go on record as opposed to the quota system.

On February 24, 1943, at a subsequent meeting held by the New York unit of the March on Washington Movement, Ashley Totten, an officer of the organization and National Secretary of the Brotherhood of Sleeping Car Porters, A.F. of L., spoke. (Totten at the time was chairman of local Selective Service Board No. 55, 307 Lenox Avenue, New York City). Totten at the meeting requested the organization to support Winfred Lynn in his effort to obtain a writ of habeas corpus to bring him from the Army before the United States Court of Appeals in Brooklyn, New York, in March,

1943. He added that the participation of the March on Washington Movement in this case would serve as a rallying point for a nationwide struggle against alleged racial discrimination in the armed forces. Totten further requested that a representative be sent to a national conference contemplated for March 5, 1943 at the New York office of the Brotherhood of Sleeping Car Porters, A.F. of L., at which time it was also contemplated that a National Committee for the Defense and Support of Winfred Lynn was to have been formed.

On March 31, 1943, a committee consisting of A. Philip Randolph, Benjamin McLaurin, E. Pauline Myers, and Layle Lane was appointed to conduct negotiations with various organizations to enlist their support in the Winfred Lynn case. A mass meeting was scheduled for April 22, 1943, at which the Lynn case was contemplated to be one of the main issues. Endorsements were reportedly received from the American Civil Liberties Union, the Workers Defense League, and the Brooklyn and Long Island branches of the National Association for the Advancement of Colored People. At the time it was reported that the National Office of the National Association for the Advancement of Colored People had not officially endorsed this case, and further, the participation of the branches did not in any way express the views of the national body.

A mass meeting on the Winfred Lynn case was held April 22, 1943 at the Golden Gate Ballroom, Lenox Avenue and 142nd Street, New York City. Approximately 750 people were present, including A. Philip Randolph, Arthur Garfield Hays, members of the Brooklyn and Long Island branches of the National Association for the Advancement of Colored People, and a member of the Workers Defense League, all of whom served as speakers. Randolph in his speech stated that "this" is a revolutionary period, and therefore he and his organization must use revolutionary methods to accomplish their objective. He referred to national and international affairs and to matters affecting the Negro population. At this time the Winfred Lynn case was discussed.

It is also to be noted that the sale of a pamphlet entitled, "The War's Greatest Scandal! The Story of Jim Crow in Uniform", was promoted. This pamphlet will be referred to hereinafter. It incidentally refers to the Winfred Lynn case.

It is to be recalled that at the July 2, 1943 evening session of the National Conference, which was attended by approximately 650 Negroes, Colden Brown, president of the New York unit and chairman of the committee dealing with the Winfred Lynn case, spoke relative to this case, saying that the March on Washington Movement plans to carry it to the United States Supreme Court, and further, if the Supreme Court fails to rule favorably in the case then the Negro has no recourse to the courts of the United States. He added that if the Supreme Court ruled favorably, then the "Jim Crow policy of the War Department" will have to be changed.

Later, at a closed meeting on July 3, 1943, the subcommittee interested in the Winfred Lynn Selective Service case issued recommendations that each local unit of the organization obtain additional cases of this character. It was recommended that Negroes be approached prior to their induction into the Army for the purpose of acquainting them with "the law" so that after they are inducted they can institute legal action against the War Department.

It is to be noted that the March on Washington Movement has distributed mimeographed copies of a reprint of the magazine "The Nation", dated February 20, 1943, which sets out detailed information concerning the Lynn case. In addition to setting out the facts concerning this case, the reprint states that it is the beginning of a case which has received almost no publicity but which is the only legal test case that has yet been made of the "Jim Crow" practices by which the military authorities are violating the spirit, if not the letter, of the basic law under which the present army is being selected and trained. It further states that while the case has received little publicity in the newspapers, it is known of in various places including not only the North but in the South. [*100-95014-279*]

"The War's Greatest Scandal! The Story of Jim Crow in Uniform"

The March on Washington Movement published during the latter part of 1942 a pamphlet entitled as above. This pamphlet has been given wide distribution and it is hoped by the organization that one million copies of it will be distributed. A confidential source has reported that Layle Lane, an executive of the New York local, secured 100 of these pamphlets which, she said, would be mailed to soldiers in the armed forces. This action, it is reported, was not looked upon favorably by other members of the organization.

It is confidentially reported that at a meeting of the March on Washington Movement, held on June 2, 1943, at 180 West 135th Street, New York City, one Private McAllister, who was said to have been on leave from the Tuskegee Air Base at Tuskegee, Alabama, was introduced to the meeting, and he is reported to have stated he would tell his comrades of the good work that the March on Washington Movement is doing for them.

At this meeting Layle Lane, of the New York unit, reportedly proposed that Private McAllister take several pamphlets of "The War's Greatest Scandal! The Story of Jim Crow in Uniform" back to his post and distribute them among his friends. This proposal was bitterly assailed by several members who stated Private McAllister would become involved with the military authorities if he were to distribute literature of this nature to his follow soldiers. Layle Lane, in turn, contended, according to the reports, she had been sending the pamphlets through the mail to soldiers in various camps throughout the country and would continue to do so, so as to publicize "Jim Crow in Uniform". It is said that the final decision was to give one pamphlet to the soldier to carry back to his post for exhibition among his friends.

It has also been reported that a copy of the pamphlet was forwarded to an enlisted man in the New York area bearing the return address Layle Lane, 226 West 150th Street, New York City.

The pamphlet itself was written by Dwight Macdonald of the Workers Defense League, with the notation that the research was done by Nancy Macdonald. At the outset paragraphs in the form of news releases showing alleged mistreatment of negro soldiers in various areas are set forth. The comment is made thereafter:

> "These things have happened in an Army supposed to be fighting for democracy. They could be multiplied a hundredfold. It is mere good luck that this undeclared war against part of our own armed forces has not broken out into large-scale rioting, bloodshed and lynching. The pattern is always the same: brutal and humiliating treatment of Negroes wearing the uniform of their country, and complete failure of the Army authorities to protect those wearing that uniform. A fantastic situation in an Army supposedly dedicated to wiping out Nazi racialism. And yet how can we expect anything else when we see those in command of this Army and Navy adopting as their official policy this very doctrine of Hitler?"

The next section is entitled " 'Master Race' Vs. 'White Supremacy' ". This section points out the various personnel needs of branches of the armed forces and then decries the alleged discrimination, segregation and mistreatment in the armed forces.

The next two sections deal with the Winfred Lynn case and thereafter incidents of heroism on the part of Negro members of the armed forces in past wars fought by this country are set forth.

There is then a section entitled, "Segregation is Discrimination" which states:

> "Every one of the half million Negroes now serving in the armed forces is doing so on a jimcrow basis. Every regiment, every ship, every battery, every flying squadron and medical staff and jeep company is either all white or all colored. The most ingenious planning, the most complicated and voluminous quantities of paper-work, the tireless efforts of thousands of officers are devoted to the great task of keeping apart the two races. The instant he puts on the uniform of his country, the Negro becomes a deadly plague carrier, to be quarantined, isolated at all costs from his white comrades in arms.
>
> "The military authorities, like the Supreme Court, deny that segregation is in itself discrimination. Actually, however, the record of the armed forces to date in this war is the strongest possible proof that discrimination is inextricably bound up with segregation. The Negro civilian in jimcrow states finds that, even if he is willing to accept segregation, he does not in actuality—whatever legal theories the Supreme Court may spin about it—get equal educational, housing and transportation facilities. And the Negro soldier or sailor also discovers, and even more dramatically, that even if he accepts segregation, he gets anything but equal treatment. The medieval Jew knew that ghetto-segregation was discrimination; the modern Jew in Nazi Germany knows that Nuremburg-law-segregation is discrimination; and the American Negro soldier knows that jimcrow-segregation is discrimination—whatever the Supreme Court or the Secretary of War says about it. Again, let us have a look at the record."

The next four sections deal with alleged discrimination in the United States Army, United States Navy, United States Army Air Corps and the Red Cross (particularly with regard to segregated blood banks).

The following points are then made in the pamphlet:

"Those are the facts, and it is not a pretty picture. What can be done about it? There are three important factors:

"(1) The colored people of America have come a long ways since the last war; they are no longer willing to be pushed around as an inferior race.

"(2) The Roosevelt Administration has backed up the jimcrow policies of the military authorities as much as it has dared; nothing can be hoped for from Washington without a much tougher fight than the Negroes and other friends of democracy have put up so far.

"(3) This great issue must be faced; it cannot longer be evaded and compromised as our political leaders are trying to do. Either you advance towards real democracy, and the Negro with you; or you go backward to racialism and fascism."

The next three sections entitled "The Negro is the March"; "The Roosevelt Record—Words Vs. Deeds"; and "The Issue Must Be Faced—Now!" refer in order to:

1. The advance in the rights for Negroes since World War Number One, especially with regard to service in the armed forces;
2. An attack on the administration in which it refers to its formula as "Democracy in Words, Jimcrow in Deeds"; and
3. The need for changing the present policies in the armed forces.

With regard to the last point, the pamphlet says that intelligent American Negroes are thinking in the terms expressed in a dialogue which the pamphlet attributes to a Negro teacher and a student:

"Student: I hope Hitler wins this war.

Teacher: How can you make such a statement?

Student: Because I am convinced that is the only thing that will teach these white people some sense—their knowing what it means to be oppressed.

Teacher: But don't you realize that conditions would be even worse under Hitler?

Student: They can't possibly be any worse than they are for Negroes in the South right now. The Army jimcrows us. The Navy lets us serve only as messmen. The Red Cross segregates our blood. Employers and labor unions shut us out. Lynchings continue. We are disenfranchised, jimcrowed, spat upon. What more could Hitler do than that?"

The pamphlet ends:

"Jimcrow in uniform must go! Every colored person in America, every real friend of democracy in America must take up the fight and refuse to be satisfied with anything less than the smashing of racial barriers throughout the entire armed forces. Jimcrow in uniform must go!"

On the back cover page the March on Washington Movement, its aims and purposes and its activities are set forth in question and answer fashion.

Mass Meetings

New York City Mass Meeting, June 16, 1942, Madison Square Garden

On June 16, 1942, this organization sponsored a meeting held at Madison Square Garden, New York City, which was attended by an estimated crowd of 17,000. The following individuals spoke at this meeting: Dr. Lawrence Mace Ervin, Chairman; Dr. Mary McLeod Bethune, Director of Negro Youth Division of N.Y.A.; Reverend A. Clayton Powell, Jr., member of the New York City Council; Reverend John La Farge, Associate Editor of America; Dr. Channing H. Tobias, Director of Negro Division of YMCA; Mr. Frank R. Crosswaith, Chairman, Negro Labor Committee; Mr. Walter White, Executive Secretary, N.A.A.C.P.; Reverend W. O. Carrington, President, AME Zion Ministers Alliance of New York City and vicinity; Mr. Lester B. Granger, Executive Director, National Urban League; Dr. C. Clay Maxwell, Sr., Pastor, Mount Olivet Baptist Church; Mr. Arthur Reid, organizer, 100 25th Street Job Campaign; and Mr. A. Philip Randolph.

It was reported that the majority of the speakers stressed Negro loyalty to the United States and the determination for "all out effort" to win the war. The determination, however, was expressed to continue the resistance for the "same rights and liberties" accorded to "other citizens of this country", not only during the war but subsequent to it. The speakers also stressed that while democracies might be able to win the war without the Negro, they cannot win peace unless there is "complete equality of opportunity and privileges for all races".

It was further reported that the most effective propaganda of the entire program were a series of short plays depicting a refusal of the Army, the Navy, Labor Unions and hospitals to accept services of the Negro in the same capacity as white persons.

It was announced at the meeting that the organization was to be continued until the demands of Negroes were granted. It was also announced that a committee would soon call on the President of the United States to make its requests for equality of opportunity and privileges. The attitude of the Communist Party with regard to the March on Washington Movement was clearly expressed in an article appearing on page four of the Communist Party organ, "The Daily Worker" for June 18, 1942. This article was written by Ben Davis, Jr., Secretary Treasurer of "The Daily Worker" and member of the Communist Party. The article states that the meeting of the March on Washington Movement in Madison Square Garden, June 16, 1942, "recorded a new high point in the militancy and aggressiveness of the Negro people for their just demands of equal integration into the war effort and complete citizenship in the United States."

The article continued, praising the "deep anti-Fascist feelings of the Negro people" shown at the meeting, the loyalty and devotion of the Negro people to their country, and condemning the discriminations existing against them.

With regard to the organization itself, however, the article stated, ". . . The meeting further revealed that Norman Thomas Socialists, Trotzkyites, Lovestoneites and other malignantly defeatist elements are seeking to exploit the just grievances of the Negro people to turn them against the Negro's own best interests. These nondescript, unpatriotic elements—who insult the honor of the Negro people by trying to incite them to disloyalty to their country and to their own interests—have a heavy influence in the so-called March-on-Washington Movement, which conducted the rally."

The article termed A. Philip Randolph "a Socialist who has never repudiated the unpatriotic opposition of his 'party' to the country's war and who has never revealed this 'party's' danger to Negro rights."

The article praised such speakers as Dr. Channing Tobias, Director of the colored division of the National Y.M.C.A., Councilman A. Clayton Powell, Jr., and Mrs. Mary McLeod Bethune. The article continued, terming a twenty-minute sketch, "The Watchword is Forward", presented at the meeting, as insidious poison of the Trotzkyites, Norman Thomasites and Lovestoneites. The article stated that the tone of the sketch was that the main enemy of the Negro people is the National Government rather than "Hitler and the Fifth Column defeatists, the Norman Thomases, Coughlins, and poll taxers, . . ."

A copy of the playlet, "The Watchword is Forward", by Dick Cambell, is being incorporated herein as reflecting possible seditious activity and utterances on the part of this organization and/or its members. (A copy of this playlet was furnished the Criminal Division of the Department under date of July 22, 1942, requesting an opinion as to whether the composition and presentation of it constitute a violation within the Sedition Statutes. By memorandum dated July 31, 1942, Assistant Attorney General Wendell Berge requested that investigation of the March on Washington Movement be continued as well as a coverage to be made of the presentation of this playlet at subsequent meetings of the organization.) The copy of the script is set out as follows:

"Negro Draftee: Good Evening.
Draft Official: Good Evening. Have a seat. Mrs. Jones, what's the physical on Charles Williams, 1A-628?

Clerk presents card to official.

Draft Official: Williams, you've been judged physically fit by the examiners, so it looks like you'll be inducted soon. I'd advise you to get your affairs all straightened out and hold yourself in readiness for the call.
Draftee: Uh, huh.
Official: Aren't you proud of the opportunity to serve your country?
Draftee: I . . . guess so.

Official: What do you mean, guess so? You've got to make up your mind, Williams. Don't you know whether you want to go to camp or not.

Draftee: Yes Sir.

Official: Well?

Draftee: All right, I'll tell you. If what I've been hearing about how negro soldiers are treated in some of the camps is true, the answer is No! *I don't want to go!* Mister, What the Hell have I got to fight for? Don't hand me that 'Make the world safe for democracy' crap. We fought for *that* in the last war. And what did it get the black man? I ought to let *you* answer that just to see how much you can lie.

Official: How dare you talk to me like that.

Draftee: You ain't heard nothing yet, Mister. I'm gonna get this off my chest *before* you send me to Texas 'cause I may find them crackers down there worse than Hitler, Mussolini and the Japs put together. What about all them Negro soldiers killed by crackers and white M.P.'s in Army camps all over the country? What about them towns in Louisiana where a black soldier's face is an invitation to a riot? That Khaki uniform on a black man down there makes them crackers hate you all the more. Listen, Mister, get this straight. I ain't afraid to fight nobody, see? If I got to go to this man's Army I'll go. I'll take on Hitler, Mussolini and the Japs put together, see? But the same damn thing goes for them dirty crackers in Georgia. I don't like them no better'n I do Hitler. And if you send me down there, anything might happen. I just want you to know that in front, see?

Official: Williams, you're talking like a traitor. That sort of attitude will lead you straight into trouble.

Draftee: What kind of attitude do you expect, Mister. Do you know nearly half of the white people in this country hate Negroes worse than Hitler hates Jews. Do you know Negroes are still being dragged through the streets of Sikeston, Mo. and burned at the stake? Do you know that slavery still exists in Georgia? That's what I said, Slavery! Do you know that the Klu Klux Klan in Detroit is strong enough to tell the Government to keep Negroes out of the Federal houses that were built especially *for* Negroes, and named after a Negro woman, Sojourner Truth? What kind of attitude do you expect, Mister.

Official: Williams, this is not a war of sectionalism. This is not a war of *Black* against *White.* This is a total war. A world war of Democracy against *Fascism* and *Naziism.* Can't you understand that.

Draftee: Yeah, I can understand that. I can understand a lot of things. And there's some things I can't understand. Maybe *you* can

> tell me why Negroes were barred from Australia 'til the Japs started dropping bombs there. Maybe you can tell me why the British never thought about India's independence 'til a few weeks ago. And even now they can't make up their minds. Telling India you will get it after the war. That's a hot one. Seems to me America told Negroes the same thing before the last war. You'll get it after the war. I want it now. And by God I'll get it. Go ahead. Sign me out. I ain't none of them conscientious objectors. I'm ready to fight. But I ain't waitin' 'til I get to Australia to do it. I'm starting at Union Station and going straight through Georgia. And so Ladies and Gentlemen I'll be leaving for camp in a few days. Pretty soon I'll be some where fighting, fighting for freedom they say. Well there's one last word I want to leave with you folks I'm leaving behind. While I'm taking care of them Hitlers across the water, you take care of the Hitlers back here, Join that 'March on Washington Movement'."

On June 26, 1942, the March on Washington Movement sponsored a meeting at the Coliseum, Chicago, Illinois. It has been reported that approximately 8,260 persons were in attendance. The admission is stated to have been free. It is reported that there were no threats or indications of any violence.

The meeting is reported to have been first addressed by Charles Wesley Burton, who has been identified as the permanent Chairman of the Chicago Division of the March on Washington Movement. He is stated to have immediately made the comment that he knew there were FBI Agents present in the throng and that he welcomed their presence and in fact wished that the Attorney General himself could have been there.

Other speakers at the meeting were: David Grant, Attorney, St. Louis, Missouri; Mrs. Annie Baxter, Colored Woman's Club; J. Albert Wilkins, President of the Cook County Bar Association; Walter White, Executive President, National Association for the Advancement of Colored People; Milton P. Webster, President's Committee on Fair Employment Practices; A. Philip Randolph, National Leader, March on Washington Movement; Reverend Archibald J. Carey, Jr., Chicago, Illinois.

It was reported that Milton P. Webster, of the President's Committee on Fair Employment Practices, criticized various Senators and Congressmen from southern states for their backing of the Poll Tax. He is stated to have reminded the audience that these Senators and Congressmen would not be in their present offices if it were not for the restrictions caused by such a tax.

The general tenor of the speeches made at the meeting was reported to have been in protest of the alleged discrimination against members of the Negro race in the armed forces and in defense industries. Demands were again made, as are made by the organization itself, for full social, economic and political equality for the Negro race. It should be stated that there were no indications at the meeting that an actual march on the City of Washington would take place.

It has been reported that the Communist Party in Chicago supported the Unit of the March on Washington Movement, located there in an attempt to gain leadership of it. As an example of this, it has been reported that Communist Party members and sympathizers were ordered to spread information concerning the meeting in order to obtain a large attendance. It was also reported that Morris Childs, Chairman of District 8 of the Communist Party, extended money for the down payment of the Coliseum rental. It has also been advised that Sam Lissitz, an organizer for the International Longshoremen's and Warehousemen's Union, spoke at a meeting of unit chairmen and section organizers of the Chicago Division of the March on Washington Movement held on June 22, 1942, at the Abraham Lincoln Center, 700 East Oakwood Boulevard, Chicago, Illinois, saying that activity of the Party in the organization would present an opportunity to obtain new members.

On July 2, 1942, a letter was addressed to Mr. Percy M. Gash, Manager of the St. Louis Municipal Auditorium, by the St. Louis Unit of the March on Washington Movement, requesting the use of the Auditorium for that organization on August 14, 1942. The letter stated that the purpose of the meeting would be the protest against discrimination against Negroes in defense industries, the armed forces and Governmental agencies.

Listed as officers of this unit are:

T. D. McNeal, Chairman

Leyton Weston, Assistant Chairman

Mrs. David M. Grant, Secretary

Attorney George L. Vaughn, Speakers Committee

Attorney David M. Grant, Complaint Committee

Columbus S. Ewing, Organizing Committee

Richard A. Jackson, Publicity Committee

Jordan Chambers, Treasurer

Harold Ross, Chairman, Finance Committee

Prior to its sponsorship of the mass meeting held at the Convention Hall of the Municipal Auditorium in St. Louis, Missouri, on August 14, 1942, several meetings were held by this unit. On July 15, 1942, a meeting was held with reference to discrimination against the Negroes as well as segregation of them, especially at the United States Cartridge Company in St. Louis, Missouri. Again on July 22, 1942, a meeting was held at which time preparation for the mass meeting on August 14, 1942, was dealt with. On August 5, 1942, further discussion with reference to the plans for the mass meeting at St. Louis, Missouri, on August 14, 1942, was held. Again, on August 12, 1942, a meeting was held at which further plans were discussed relative to the mass meeting and a financial report was read to the effect that $940.00 was on hand.

On several days prior to the mass meeting held August 14, 1942, handbills were distributed on the street by this organization, bearing the heading in large print, "WAKE UP NEGROES", and requesting 25,000 Negroes to storm the Municipal Auditorium on the night of August 14, 1942, for the purposes of demanding jobs and protesting against: "Jim Crow St. Louis labor unions in war plants"; "lynching at Sikeston and Texarkana"; "mobbing and shooting our boys in Uncle Sam's uniform"; "violation of President Roosevelt's Order #8802"; "Jim Crow policy of the Navy, Army and U.S. Marines"; and "insult of the Red Cross in segregating Negro blood".

On the night of August 14, 1942, there was held at the Municipal Auditorium, Convention Hall, St. Louis, Missouri, a large meeting sponsored by the St. Louis Unit of the March on Washington Movement, in attendance at which were approximately 9,000 Negroes. It is reported that the group was orderly and no trouble or riots in connection with the meeting were reported.

Charles Wesley Burton, Chairman of the Chicago Unit and attorney, was the first speaker. He outlined the purpose of the Axis doctrines as well as the democratic doctrines of the United States.

Burton is reported to have stated that Japan favored a war between the white and darker races, as the Japanese well know that the darker race outnumber the white about four or five to one. He also mentioned that the Negroes will make the supreme sacrifice if the same rights are granted to them as to others.

The second speaker was a Negro woman, Mrs. Sallie Parham, whose speech was entitled "Message from St. Louis Women". She is stated to have outlined the colored woman's place in the March on Washington Movement, stressing the abolition of racial groups in defense industries and stated that colored women must fight and in carrying on this fight would necessarily have to be in the picket line.

The third speaker was David M. Grant, an attorney in St. Louis, who spoke on "St. Louis Negroes and the War Effort". In his speech he outlined the Negro grievances in the St. Louis area, mentioning segregation of the Negroes at the ball park, 10-cent stores and theaters. He went on to cite abuses in local war plants, stating that none of the Negroes were engaged in production. He further stated that one plant, the name of which he did not mention, did not have a single Negro employed; that this plant was ripe for a march; and that it would have a march in the very near future.

The next speaker was Walter White, Executive Secretary for the National Association for the Advancement of Colored People. In his speech he gave an advisory talk, listing grievances and explaining that there must be a unified action on the part of Negroes in obtaining their objective. He referred to alleged practices of discrimination and denial of equal rights of Negroes in the South.

The fifth speaker on the program was Milton P. Webster, whose topic was "Fair Employment Practice, What it Means". Webster was identified as being a member of the Fair Employment Practices Committee and First International Vice President of the Brotherhood of Sleeping Car Porters. He outlined discrimination practiced against the Negroes since Civil War days, stating that these discriminatory practices are more evident during this war period. In speaking of discrimination, he cited several cases of such and what the Fair Employment Practices Committee was doing in their regard. Webster was reported to have intimated that his Committee was powerful in so far as it was directly under the supervision of the President and that the President had a wide latitude, especially during war time.

The next feature on the program was a playlet entitled "The Watchword is Forward", which portrayed the scene of a Negro youth appearing before a draft board official relative to his induction into the Army. The script of this playlet has been set out hereinbefore.

Subsequent to the presentation of the playlet was an address made by A. Philip Randolph, National Director of the March on Washington Movement, who outlined the purposes of the organization, saying that it was the belief of the March on Washington Movement that Negroes needed an all-Negro movement, the same as Jews have the Zionist movement and the Catholics have an all Catholic movement and Labor, a movement of which only workers are members; and, further, that an all-Negro movement does not imply that there should not be a movement of mixed groups any more than a Zionist movement means that there should not be a movement composed of Jews and Gentiles. He is stated to have further remarked that the purpose of the March on Washington Movement was to definitely stress and emphasize that the main and basic responsibility for effecting the solution of the Negro problem rests upon the Negroes themselves; that the Negro should supply the money and pay the price, make the sacrifices, and endure the suffering to break down the barriers to a realization of full citizenship rights in America; and that the March on Washington Movement believed in racial equality and proposes to fight for it.

In his talk, Randolph dealt with prior meetings in New York City and in Chicago of the March on Washington Movement and how the March on Washington Movement in 1941 was responsible for obtaining from the President his order establishing the Fair Employment Practices Committee.

He advised that several of the newspapers had stated that the March on Washington Movement was abandoned, which was entirely incorrect; that it had only been postponed; and that a march on the City of Washington would take place unless grievances were corrected. He also referred to the following cablegram which was to be sent to Mahatma Gandhi in India:

> "The March on Washington Movement represents the Negro people of America. They owe the struggle of India for independence. Your cause is just and win you must. The Negro people believe that the denial of independence to the people of India is inconsistent with a fight of a United Nation for a free world."

In this connection, a resolution suggesting that this cablegram be sent was directed to the audience and the same was adopted and passed. [*100-95014-11*]

Local Units

As has been pointed out previously under the section involving the organization of the March on Washington Movement, there are a number of local units. The amount of activities of the local units vary considerably. Perhaps the most active is the New York unit, followed closely by the St. Louis unit, thereafter coming the Chicago unit. A small degree of activity is engaged in by the Detroit and Washington local units;

however, in these interest previously evidenced in the organization has seemingly been lost, although delegates were sent by these units to the National Conference.

The more active units fight alleged instances of discrimination as well as segregation; however, the issues generally involved are local in nature and have included such matters as obtaining increased employment of Negroes in defense industry, opposing "Jim Crow" and segregation conditions and attempting to break down employment rules in public utilities, especially in various telephone companies. In this regard, the St. Louis unit claims to have obtained more than 8,000 jobs for Negroes in that area, allegedly adding to the income of the Negro population there in the amount of over one million dollars. Similar action is said to have been taken by the Chicago unit where also actual use of the non-violent good will action technique has been put into effect.

As regards the New York unit, it is to be noted that this unit also serves as a "testing ground" for policies of the national organization either actually in effect or contemplated for future enactment.

Varying estimates have been made as to the strength of the local units, although it is said that the St. Louis unit has approximately 4,000 members, the Chicago unit anywhere from 2,500 to 7,000 members, and the Washington unit approximately 20 members. No accurate figure has been reported as to the total membership of this organization although it is known that 270 delegates representing a large number of cities attended the National Conference.

The influence of the organization, however, can be seen in referring to the various mass meetings held by this organization wherein the attendance varied from 8,000 to 15,000. No accurate estimate can be made as to how many Negroes this organization can influence, although it is said Randolph has made the statement that he hoped 20,000 Negroes could be obtained for a march on the City of Washington.

With regard to Communist Party influence in the various local units, it has been reported that there were in the past evidences of Communist infiltration into the Washington, Detroit and Chicago units; however, no indications have been received that control was ever obtained by Communist forces. In this connection it is to be recalled that the National Conference as well as national leaders have opposed any cooperation with Communist-controlled groups or organizations.

It is also to be noted that there have been indications of cooperation by the local units with local chapters of the National Association for the Advancement of Colored People. This has been evidenced particularly in the action taken by the New York local unit of the March on Washington Movement with regard to the Winfred Lynn Selective Service case. Therein it is recalled the Brooklyn and Long Island chapters of the National Association for the Advancement of Colored People have supplied their support.

Reception of Organization by Other Forces

It has been pointed out hereinbefore that the Pittsburgh Courier, perhaps the largest Negro newspaper in the United States, has attacked the March on Washington

Movement, and more specifically, its National Director, A. Philip Randolph. In addition, the organization has been subjected to numerous accusations and tongue lashings by the Communist Party.

Typical of these is an article written by James W. Ford, National Committee Member of the Communist Party, who wrote in the July 23, 1943 issue of the Communist news organ, The Daily Worker. This article was entitled, "Randolph Policy Aids Enemies of Negro-White Unity Fight". It appeared on page 8. It should be stated in this connection that while the Communist Party has militantly and blatantly called for social equality, added rights, abolition of discrimination and segregation, and other matters of interest to the Negro, it has also attempted to coordinate that part of its line urging all-out effort in the war program with its maneuverings and machinations among the Negroes. It should also be kept in mind that the national organization of the March on Washington Movement has opposed and has kept out influence of Communist forces within its branches.

In his article, Ford alleges that the movement for Negro rights has reached an extraordinary degree of development in the trade unions and states that "big results have been scored among win-the-war forces generally for the betterment of the position of colored citizens in American life." Ford then works into a condemnation of Randolph, the National Director of the organization, and a statement attributed to him by the New York Times in which Randolph referred to the barring of whites from the organization to avoid Communist infiltration. Ford claims that Randolph by his statement concludes that of all white people in the United States, only white Communists fight for Negro rights, and that he is irritated by the unquestionable fact that there are many Negroes in the Party. He then states that the Communists would seem silly sectarians if they held any such designs as wishing that non-Communists be kept out of the fight for the rights of Negroes. He then states that Randolph is not helping to win the war, nor is he interested in conducting a genuine struggle to win Negro rights.

Ford also takes to account the March on Washington Movement National Conference, which he alleges placed the blame for the position of the Negro people and the anti-Negro riots at the door of the present Administration. He claims further that Randolph is playing on narrow racial interests and endeavoring to get the Negro people to oppose the war and strike at the President. Randolph is then likened with John L. Lewis. Thereafter, Randolph is condemned for his attitude toward the Soviet Union. Throughout the article Ford eulogizes the activity of the Communist Party with regard to Negroes.

As early as June, 1942, the two Trotzkyite factions, the Workers Party and the Socialist Workers Party, expressed their opinions through their representative publications "Labor Action" and "The Militant". Comments in these two organs I believe worthy of note and are accordingly incorporated hereafter.

As reflecting the attitude of the Workers Party, a Trotzkyite group of Communists, the official publication of this Party, the "Labor Action", in its June 8, 1942 issue, carries an article styled, "March on Washington Movement Stirs Again". The article is written by one Ria Stone.

The article traces the activities of A. Philip Randolph in arousing the "hopes of Negro masses" by proposing a march on Washington in the Spring of 1941. It states that the march was planned as a movement to put pressure on the Roosevelt administration, "which was then moving toward a war abroad, while forms of Hitlerism existed at home." The article advises that the march was postponed because "Roosevelt, after conferences with Randolph, and in the face of a mass Negro march, issued an executive order against discrimination in the war industries."

The article continues stating that nearly a year has passed since the executive order of the President regarding Negroes, but that "on all sides it is admitted that Jim Crow is still boss in the war industries". The article accuses the setting up of the Naval Unit for Negroes as a "Jim Crow" measure, and states that Negroes who aspired to be sailors are employees in shipyards at low military pay instead of the usual civilian rates. The article attempts to point out other alleged discriminations.

The article criticizes the March on Washington Movement leaders, stating that there is a reluctance on their part to arouse "real mass pressure", and that they are curbing such. The article states, "they curb the natural inclinations of the masses because they, as leaders, are afraid that mass action will go 'beyond bounds'." The article further states that the Negro people find little satisfaction in the orders of the "Administration" to cease discrimination. It calls the orders "face-saving devices" for the Administration and states that "the masses know this".

The article contends that "today the Negro masses want a March on Washington", but Randolph "since Pearl Harbor, is even more reluctant than before to call for a March on Washington."

The article demands "the Negroes must march on Washington to prove to Government officials and to employers all over the country the mass strength which lies behind their demands!" In addition, the article insists, "they must march on Jim Crow plants to prove to each employer the Negro workers will no longer stand by passively and suffer want and privation while jobs are available!"

It is stated that the Workers Party supports the March on Washington proposal, in that "class conscious workers understand that through the initiative and mass actions of Negro workers in conflict with their political and economic oppressors, Negro workers will develop their class consciousness."

The article concludes stating that, "the March on Washington Movement can really become a mass movement if the Negro masses insist on making it their movement. . . ."

Appearing in the June 27, 1942 issue of the publication, "The Militant", which is the official organ of the Socialist Workers Party, a Trotzkyite organization, is an article styled "The Stalinists Betray the Negro Struggle". This article is by Albert Parker.

This article attacks the Communist Party in its attitude toward the Negro situation at the present time and the attitude expressed in the "Daily Worker" on June 12, 1942, in an article by Benjamin Davis, Jr., which attacked the March on Washington Movement.

The article advises that prior to the meeting of the March on Washington Movement in New York City on June 16, 1942, the "Stalinists" attacked the March on Washington Movement and its National Leader, A. Philip Randolph, stating that there is an attempt "to exploit the just demands of the Negro. . . ."

The article continues, stating that "the Stalinists" recognized the impression made by the March on Washington Movement on the Negro people in New York City, and as a consequence "the Stalinists" desired to counteract this impression by holding another Negro meeting on June 28, 1942, under the auspices of the Negro Labor Victory Committee "which includes non-Stalinist elements but is dominated by the Communist Party."

The article then quotes a statement made by Randolph with respect to the meeting "dominated by the Communist Party":

> " 'This is a typical Communist-front movement that has been roping people in. It wants the Negro to forget all his grievances and to make it appear Negroes are not concerned with discrimination in the army and navy and the war industries. It is definitely in opposition to the March-on-Washington movement.' "

The article then advises of Randolph's "policy". It states that without the backing of the Negro masses "Randolph does not amount to two cents and he knows it." It advises that without the support of the Negroes Randolph would not be permitted "into even the back door of the White House." The article claims that it is not Randolph's support of the war alone which attracts the Negro people but that to keep the mass support he wants, Randolph has to speak "the language of militancy." The article continues that it is Randolph's illusion that by speaking militantly he can secure a number of concessions from the Administration and thus maintain his leadership with the Negro movement. The article accuses Randolph of being afraid to lead a fundamental struggle against the capitalist class.

The above article explains "The Stalinist policy." It states "their line on the Negro question as on everything else is determined by the Stalin bureaucracy in Moscow, which is concerned only with protecting its own interests. Sometimes these interests seem to coincide with those of the Negro and white workers in the United States, sometimes they clearly do not; but that does not concern the Stalin bureaucracy or its stooges in this country. In this you can find the explanation for the Daily Worker's attack on a movement which despite the defects of its leadership expresses the aspirations of the Negro people."

IV

THE NEGRO AND NATIONAL SOCIALISM

In viewing foreign-inspired agitation among the American Negro population, it is believed pertinent to set forth the possibilities of German and National Socialistic propaganda compiled to bring about disaffection in this particular minority group. In approaching this problem it is believed significant at the outset to examine the official German attitude toward the colored race. Consequently some of the most pertinent sources and happenings are being briefly reviewed.

Attitude Toward the Negro in Germany

It should first be noted that Germany is comprised of a homogeneous population. There are few, if any, real minorities existing within the territorial boundaries of Germany. Negroes of any origin are extremely rare in Germany and the attitude of the State and the people is not at all favorable to any alien people residing in the community, particularly when there is a difference in color. The question of intermixture between Germans and the Negro race dates back to the time when Germany as a nation maintained the semblance of a colonial empire. The intermixture of German colonists so freely with negro women in Africa caused bitter debate in the German Reichstag in 1912. Germany's attitude toward Negroes in their colonies in Africa prior to the first World War was never one of consideration and humaneness. It was largely a question of exploitation of natural resources available to further develop the colonial empire then possessed by Germany.

The occupation of the Ruhr and other border sections by French colonial troops after the World War did not serve to increase the favoritism of Germany and its people toward the colored race. This fact has been used as a propaganda argument by Adolf Hitler on many occasions in showing the unfairness of the Versailles Treaty and the depravity of the Allies in subjecting Germany to a disgraceful armistice.

In point of time the attitude toward the Negro is next seen in the book entitled "Mein Kampf". This book is replete with references to the racial policy upon which National Socialism is based. It is this racial policy which was placed in effect at the time Hitler became Chancellor of the Third Reich on January 30, 1933. The majority of the rantings in "Mein Kampf" are leveled at the Jew, however, the Negro is not completely overlooked nor is any race overlooked. All races with the exception of the Aryans are considered inferior. In his chapter on "People and Race," Hitler endeavors to impress his readers by arguments against intermixture of any kind between races, basing this theory upon the natural law that all animals mate with their own species. This is followed by argument after argument that the Aryan race has been the fountainhead of all culture and advancement in the history of the world and that the diluting of the Aryan race with alien blood has caused the demise of all prominent civilizations. As an example of the attitude expressed in this chapter as applied to the Negro race, it is stated that history "shows with alarming plainness that every mingling of Aryan blood with inferior races results in the end of the sustainers of civilization. North America, whose population consists overwhelmingly of Germanic elements which have mingled very little with inferior colored peoples, can show a very different sort of humanity and culture from Central and South America in which the predominantly Latin settlers mingled, sometimes on a large scale, with the aborigines." Further, "mingling of blood, with the decline in racial level that is caused, is the sole reason for the dying-out of old cultures; for men are destroyed not by lost wars, but by losing that stamina inherent in pure blood alone."

In the chapter entitled "World Concept and Party," Hitler devotes much time to the alleged faulty premises of Marxism as compared with what he terms the fundamental law of nature with reference to racial elements. He rejects the racial equality theories of Marxism and proletarianism, pointing out that the populist world concept realizes the racial inferior or superior merit with their variations and feels the necessity of assisting the victory of the better and stronger and demanding the subordination of the worse and weaker. He then contends that this concept acknowledges the aristocratic basic idea of nature and concludes by stating that an ethical idea cannot be permitted to exist if this idea represents a threat to racial life of the sustainers of a higher ethics. He then states "in a bastardized and negroid world any concept of the humanely beautiful and noble as well as any image of a idealized future for our part of humanity would be lost forever. Human culture and civilization on this continent are inseparable from the existence of the Aryan."

In his chapter on "The State," Hitler again reveals himself as a hater of all races except the Aryan. In this chapter he castigates the churches and their activities in Germany for failing in their attempt to improve future inhabitants of that country by working among them yet trying to find recompense in the blessings of the church among Hottentots and Zulus. While our European peoples, praise God, are falling into the condition of physical and moral outcasts, the pious missionary travels to Central Africa and sets up Negro missions so that our 'higher culture' may turn healthy, if primitive and low-grade, human beings into a corrupt brood of bastards even there.

"It would accord far better with the spirit of this world's noblest Man if, instead of annoying the Negroes with missions that are neither desired nor understood, our two Christian Churches would teach Europe, kindly but seriously, that in the case of not wholly sound parents, it is a work more pleasing to God to take pity upon a healthy little poor orphan, giving him father and mother, than to bring into the world a sickly child of ones own, which would only cause suffering and misery to itself and the rest of the world." In this same chapter Hitler also advances the theory that "creative achievements can occur only when ability and knowledge are mated." He then illustrates by stating:

> "From time to time the illustrated powers show the German bourgeois how a Negro has for the first time become a lawyer, a teacher, perhaps even a minister or a heroic tenor somewhere or other. The feeble-minded bourgeoisie takes notice

of such a miracle of animal-training with admiring astonishment, and is full of respect for this marvelous result of modern education; in the meanwhile the Jew is very shrewd about constructing from it a new proof that the theory of the equality of man, which he is forcing down the peoples' throats, is sound. It never dawns on the degenerate middle-class world that this is truly a sin against all reason—that it is criminal madness to train a born half-ape until one believes one has made a lawyer of him, while millions of members of the highest of civilized races must remain in a position altogether unworthy of them; that it is a sin against the will of the Eternal Creator to let hundreds and hundreds of thousands of his most gifted creatures decay in the modern proletarian bog while Hottentots and Zulus are being gentled for intellectual professions. For animal-training it is, just as with the poodle, and not 'scholastic' education. The same care and pains spent upon intelligent races would equip every individual for similar achievements a thousand times more quickly."

The above quotations from "Mein Kampf" are only a few that could be cited to show the true attitude of Adolf Hitler and National Socialism toward the Negro. This attitude is exemplified by its contempt toward a race which is considered inferior and only to be used for exploitation by the "Herrenvolk"—the master race. An analysis of the various expressions set forth above permits only one conclusion, that is, from the National Socialist standpoint the Negro is placed in the same category with the Jew. A view of the persecution to which the Jew has been subjected in Germany can only permit one conclusion, that is, in the event of the success of National Socialism as a world concept, the Negroes' economic state in America would be lost. He would not be permitted to engage in the professions, lynching in its most reprehensible form would probably be prevalent and all of those steps which Germany considers necessary to restrict the growth and development of a so-called inferior race would be practiced. The Negro would not be permitted his own newspapers, his own church, his own societies, or his own way of life.

Germany today has two separate and distinct lines of propaganda with reference to the Negro, the first as applied in Germany, and the second as applied to the Negro as a minority in the United States. Under this subheading the attitude in Germany will be treated. In this regard attention is directed to an article entitled "The Nazi Plan for Negroes," by Hans Habe, German refugee writer, published in March, 1941. This article states in part:

"In recent weeks the German press has devoted more and more attention to American Negroes; the three or four latest issues of Der Sturmer, Hitler's anti-Semitic sheet, have been directed entirely against the Negroes. Julius Streicher, its editor, is the Fuehrer's own intimate friend, an 'old militant,' and the only Party leader who may 'Thou' Hitler. Streicher declares: 'The emancipation of the Jews and the liberation of the black slaves are two crimes of civilization committed by the plutocrats in the last few centuries."

Habe also states in this article that Negroes are isolated from white prisoners in German prison camps. Barbed wire is placed around Negro barracks and no white man can converse with them. Although the conditions of the white prisoners were miserable enough, those of the Negro were described as much worse, and food rations were a starvation diet and those who became ill were not provided for.

Under date of May 18, 1942, an article entitled "Roosevelt Interned Women and Children," by Heinz Cramer, former New York Deutsche Nachrichten Buro representative, appeared in the Schlesische Zeitung, Breslau, Germany. This article was written entirely for home consumption with a view to inspiring hate on the part of the Germans for the treatment given Germans in the United States in the beginning of the war in December, 1941. Conditions were described as inadequate and insanitary and other complaints were made about the treatment of Germans by the American authorities. The article states, in part, "In order to round out the picture of degrading treatment which was documented by a thousand summary individual reports let us only note that they (the Americans) did not even spare the Germans on Ellis Island from being guarded by Negroes. In other internment camps Germans were even locked up with Negroes. . . ."

As a further indication of the propaganda being distributed within Germany and bearing on this subject, it will be noted that on September 28, at 4:00 p.m., Eastern Standard Time, a broadcast was made in German to the German people by the Frankfurt Radio Station which stated, in part, "The wife of the United States President appears to enjoy playing the role of protectoress of Negroes in the United States," adding "according to Time (Time Magazine) Negroes in the southern part of the United States are forming 'Eleanor Clubs.' Negro girls form 'Daughters of Eleanor.' " Further excerpts include, "The Negroes are said to be grateful for Mrs. Roosevelt's participation in Negro meetings and the fact that she allows herself to be photographed with them. She even reviews parades of Negro soldiers.

"Mrs. Roosevelt is a good business woman and the fact that she has 'discovered' means nothing but business. This farce is a large scale attempt to gain as much black cannon fodder for Roosevelt's war as possible."

Information has been secured from an individual who was formerly affiliated with the monitoring service maintained by the German propaganda radio in Berlin, Germany, that news broadcasts from the United States were translated literally and made available to the Analization Section of the Foreign Office, Saarlandstrasse, Berlin, Germany. Experts on all subjects and linguists possessing social and political background then reviewed this material. Selections and excerpts thought of possible value for use in the German propaganda scheme were digested therefrom. The monitoring service was only one of the mediums through which material was obtained, since various American publications after a reasonable lapse of time became available for analization and excerpting. From past experiences it is known that attention is given to any item of news that could in any way be used to influence a minority such as the American Negro. Selections are also taken from this material for use in the propaganda scheme within Germany. This same individual points out that while in Germany he saw numerous posters in which the Negro served as a medium of propaganda for home consumption and mentioned two posters specifically, one containing a photograph of a Negro lynching in the United States which bore the caption, "This is How Democracy Works." The other poster specifically mentioned contained the photograph of Mrs. Roosevelt shaking hands with Marian Anderson and bore the caption, "This is Mrs.

Roosevelt Handshaking with a Negress to Counteract Their (the Americans) Well-Known Atrocities." These posters reportedly received wide distribution in Germany.

Another factor that left an engraved impression upon the American Negro is the treatment of Jesse Owens at the time he was a member of the American Olympic team in 1936 and won a number of medals at the Olympic games in Germany. A majority of the winning contestants were afforded the opportunity of meeting the Chancellor of the Third Reich, Adolf Hitler, however, he outwardly avoided shaking hands with Jesse Owens. One source prominent in Negro activities in America states that this action was one of the main factors absolutely alienating the intelligent American Negro from any favoritism toward National Socialism.

The attitude toward the Negro is not an isolated one since a reading of "Mein Kampf" and other quasi expressions of the German attitude on the racial policy will show this feeling also exists toward the Japanese, the Mongolians, the Jew, and, in fact, all races not Aryan.

It is believed that the racial policy of National Socialism, the statements of its leaders, the prosecution of minorities, and the ruthlessness of Germany's social and economic policies absolutely preclude Germany from effective proselyting among the Negroes in this country.

Trends of National Socialist Propaganda Among the American Negro

It is believed of primary interest to set forth the fact that Germany has considered the problem of using the American Negro population as a potential group for agitation in America. The German government does have existing certain offices which have interested themselves in this problem although the exact extent to which plans have been put into effect are not known. It has been determined through a confidential source that this problem would logically fall within the jurisdiction of the Aussenpolitisches Amt der NSDAP (Foreign Policy Office of the National Socialist German Workers Party), headed by Reichsleiter Alfred Rosenberg. Rosenberg bears this title as a Nazi Party official, but as a state officer bears the title of Reichsminister of Russia. He is the interpreter of Hitler's ideas on National Socialist ideology and Hitler allegedly considers that his theories along this line most closely coincide with his own. Rosenberg is considered as "the appointed one of the Fuehrer for education and schooling of the National Socialist German Workers Party," and this statement reportedly appears upon the letterhead used by him. Various departments are set up under the Foreign Policy Office of the Nazi Party and according to the informant the Negro problem would fall under the Scientific Bureau headed by Walter Malletke. Dr. Draeger, Director of the Bureau of Interstate Cultural Relations in the Foreign Policy Office of the Nazi Party could be considered a helper of Malletke in a problem of this nature and Malletke would probably remain in the background. The Scientific Bureau headed by Malletke maintains a special training school for the purpose of instructing individuals who are academically superior to learn the dialect of the country to which they are to be assigned in the future. This training school is to supply individuals to take the place of those who in the past had served the Party abroad. Rosenberg is the head of all of these activities and holds a position extremely enviable in the Nazi Party. He has wide authority which permits him to call upon the Foreign Organization of the Nazi Party or the Foreign Office of the German government for whatever assistance he deems necessary. For administrative purposes there are various commissions existent in the high authority of the Party in Germany and the German Government which is 100 per cent party controlled. Men on these commissions represent the interest of the Party or agency with reference to the problem at hand, and the system be compared to interlocking directorates. The informant advises that in July, 1939 a conference of what is known as Rosenberg's Commission met in Berlin, Germany, and considered the problem "The Practical Exploitation of National Conditions Concerning Existing Friction on the American Continent." This commission was made up of the informant, Dr. Albrecht Haushofer as a representative of the Geopolitical Institute, Munich, Germany, and Walter Malletke, mentioned hereinbefore. In addition, Dr. Draeger, mentioned above, and Dr. Karl Boemer, a specialist on conditions in the United States and one or two others were present. Dr. Karl Boemer at the time was the Director of the Press Bureau in the Foreign Policy Office of the Nazi Party and also lectured on various subjects in the University of Berlin. He is considered as a man of high calibre by the informant and one purely conversant with the practical aspects of propaganda.

It will be recalled that Dr. Boemer, shortly prior to the invasion of Russia by Germany, betrayed Hitler's intention of a military advance to the East. He was tried before the People's Court in Berlin and was only saved from the firing squad by the intercession of Dr. Paul Joseph Goebbels, Minister of Propaganda. He was eventually released, although having previously been convicted of treason, upon the condition that he would go to the front as a common soldier. He was wounded at Krakov, Russia, and reportedly died at a Hospital in Cracow during the latter part of August, 1942.

The conference mentioned above was to consider the practical application of propaganda to the American Negro and according to the informant is believed to be the first consideration given this particular problem by those interested. Its real objective was to effect a crystallization of ideas and along this line the results of the discussion were described by the informant as follows. All propaganda addressed to the American Negro would be based on the primary premise that they were the subject of suppression and discrimination in America. The general theory behind the approach utilizing these conditions admits this type of propaganda is wholly destructive, consequently some constructive propaganda in the nature of promises was not only desirable but necessary. This crystallized into two parts, first, offering the Negro for his very own a country located in South America. This was considered particularly clever since it did not interfere to a large extent with the ideas of the American white population and secondly would not entail the transportation of the Negro over too great a distance. Part two of the plan was to offer the American Negro certain northern states in the United States which could be considered a promise of higher living conditions and was thought to be the most readily accessible answer to the problem due to the short distance of transportation and the fact that it is generally conceded that northern states are much more highly industrialized than the southern states which now are occupied by the Negroes. It was understood that Dr. Boemer would handle the propaganda to the colored people, emphasizing suppression and discrimination. The first wave of approach would be passive resistance to cooperation with the white population and secondly urging an armed uprising with the assistance of Germany through the supplying of money, arms, and leaders. In addition to the propaganda it was considered desirable to train agents to work among the Negroes. This part of the program would fall within the jurisdiction of Walter Malletke's training schools mentioned hereinbefore. Dr. Draeger, Director of the Bureau for Interstate Cultural Relations would also have a prominent part in the program. In analyzing the cultural side of the appeal to the American Negro, Malletke would be further assisted by Hans Scheidt, Director of the Foreign Political Training Bureau of the Nazi Party, a subdirectorate of the Foreign Policy Office. Dr. Albrecht Haushofer of the Geopolitical Institute and son of General Karl Haushofer who is considered the father of German Geopolitics today would have the job of conducting a large portion of the research in Germany incident to this program. His approach would be largely scientific. As an example, the development of language similarities and differences, political similarities and differences, economic similarities and differences affecting the American Negro might quite well also involve the comparison between the condition of the American Negro and that of the Negro in Liberia or other areas inhabited by colored races. Malletke, through his established agents, would forward the information to the Geopolitical Institute for consideration and analysis and this in turn would be passed on to the young men being trained by Malletke who were expected to go into the field at a later time. At this conference, which was held two months prior to the invasion of Poland in September 1939, mention was made of Father Divine and a discussion was had as to possible methods of using him and his immense following for the benefit of Germany. There was no reference in any way inferring that Father Divine had been approached, or was the subject of approach, but he was merely used as an example of the type of appeal that necessarily would have to be made to the Negro in America. It would have fallen within the prerogatives of Dr. Draeger as the Director of the Bureau for Interstate Cultural Relations to analyze the religion expounded by Father Divine and adapt it to German use. The general conclusion along this line was that the appeal to the American Negro would have to be conditioned to his mentality and practically applied to insure the greatest of dividends. Dr. Albrecht Haushofer brought up various issues in which he was particularly interested and would attempt to analyze and adapt to any program ultimately put into effect. In this regard Haushofer was interested in information as to the number of Negroes in police forces, military services and local, state and national government. He was also interested in the number of Negro students and the number of Negro professional and businessmen. Upon the compilation of this information Haushofer would have supervised the necessary research in the compilation of points to be used to propagandize among the Negroes.

The fact that the above conference actually transpired in Berlin in July, 1939 is indicative of the thoroughness of German planning to the end of exploiting minorities in all countries. As was pointed out in the beginning there is no indication apparent that the initial discussion described above resulted in any definitely executed plan as applied to agitation among the Negroes in America and as will be seen hereinafter no instance has occurred that would counter this conclusion. From another source who was affiliated at one time with the monitoring service maintained by the German Propaganda Ministry, it has been pointed out that the German approach to the Negro problem in the United States takes the following trend: "You in your (American) propaganda are accusing us of subjugating peoples—but you in 1863 were freed, but we know that you are the subject of prejudice and suppression, industrially and economically. The right of the ballot is voided. Justice in the courts is questioned and lynching is practiced." This trend is obviously an appeal to the Negro that although he is told by the white Americans that he is free, in reality he is still the subject of discrimination and injustice.

An extensive survey of agitation among the Negroes has not revealed any pattern that can be identified with German planning and resourcefulness along this line. Isolated instances have occurred where individual Negroes have commented that the Negro race "would get somewhere" if Hitler and the Japanese win this war. Inquiries, however, fail to reveal that these statements are foreign inspired in any way. They are generally made by disgruntled individuals whose intelligence has in no way presented them with the opportunity of viewing the true attitude of the Germans toward so-called "inferior races." Those Negroes who can be considered leaders of their race in no instance have brought forth any evidences whatsoever of activity that can be traced to German sources. The known German organizations in this country which have exhibited favoritism for the present regime in Germany have made little attempt to appeal to any racial sections of the population other than the German and no definite instances have been reported wherein German organizations have attempted to propagandize or utilize the Negroes as such. The German-American Bund at no time attempted to effect cooperation with Negro organizations. In fact, the lecturers and speakers who have appeared before various units of this organization over a period of years were almost without exception of German background. There are several instances where an Indian lecturer was advertised by individuals active in the Bund and by the Bund itself in that particular area, but this lecturer himself had apparently adopted the racial theory of National Socialism since he ranted openly against the Jews.

It can be readily seen from what has been set forth hereinbefore that the Germans are in an anomalous position should they appeal to the American Negro and identify this appeal with Germany. The only possibility of agitation would be through the use of agent prov[o]cateurs, that is, the encouraging of agitation among the Negroes by persons actually sympathetic with the German regime, but ignoring the theory of National Socialism. The appeal would have to take the line adopted by reformists or, for that matter, Communists. The former appealing to the humane side of the question, suppression and discrimination, and the latter expounding the usual mouthings of racial equality and the cause of the common people. It is doubtful that Germany would stoop to abandoning its own theory of racial supremacy which has been sold lock, stock and barrel for a period of years to the German people merely for the purpose of agitating among the Negroes in this manner and thereby strengthening the opposition.

One should not be prone to identify anti-Semitism among the Negroes with foreign inspired propaganda. It is generally conceded, particularly in industrial areas, that reports recur from time to time of a strong feeling of anti-Semitism on the part of the Negro population. Although not entirely based on fact this feeling is probably traceable to the landlord-tenant relationship and the merchant-consumer relationship always prevalent in a section of the population which largely lives from hand to mouth. Added to this, the sharp practices of certain small loan agencies and the rigid collection policies of some businesses and a condition is existent that must have some value of exhaust. The normal trend is for the victim of these conditions to single out some particular type of merchant and heap all the criticism thereon. This problem could be very well alleviated by a more sensible landlord-tenant relationship and more elasticity in the subjection of the American Negro to economic pressure. There is no indication that where these rumors of anti-Semitism have occurred that they have originated with foreign sources. It is apparent that the conditions current in the community itself were far more responsible for the rumors than any alien-inspired ideology that incidentally possesses the same attitude on anti-Semitism.

In conclusion it can be seen that Germany has either not attempted agitation among the Negroes or has utterly failed in any plan that she might have adopted. In viewing agitation among the Negroes there is a striking absence of any German-inspired movement as distinguished from the infiltration that has been attempted by the Japanese and the Communist elements. Those reports that have been received where Negroes have allegedly expressed a favoritism for National Socialist Germany have been without exception unsubstantiated. The above treatment of this subject, coupled with the fact that German agents qualified to engage in agitation among the Negroes cannot now enter the United States, leaves only one view at this time, that is, in analyzing Negro agitation one must look to other than the Germans for its origin.

V

JAPANESE INFLUENCE AND ACTIVITY AMONG THE AMERICAN NEGROES

Since the declaration of war there have been frequent complaints and numerous rumors of a pro-Japanese sympathy existing among the colored people and of Japanese attempts to disrupt the internal security of the United States by attacks upon the morale and loyalty of the American negro. Many of these complaints and rumors have been baseless but it has been clearly demonstrated that the Japanese government has endeavored to implant pro-Japanese ideas and attitudes in the minds of the colored people and to call attention to racial prejudices and restrictions to further their propaganda that this war is a race war for the purpose of creating disunity within this country to diminish or destroy its military strength.

Much of the Japanese inspired agitation has been traced to organizations promoted by persons believed to be connected with the Japanese government or in contact with individual Japanese. However, to present a perspective of Japanese influence and activity among the American negroes so that the dissemination of Japanese inspired propaganda and its effect upon negro organizations and views may be properly evaluated, it is well to first briefly summarize similar activities of the Japanese in Asia, the islands of the South Pacific and among colored races in other parts of the world.

A resume of Japanese influence upon the American negroes or other minority groups in the United States and elsewhere should, at the outset, point out that the Japanese are highly nationalistic and race conscious as evidenced by their belief in the myths of their divine origin and the conclusion that the Japanese are therefore, "The master race". They propose, as such, to lead the people of the East in a "Greater East-Asia Co-prosperity Sphere" under the banner of "Asia for Asiatics". Through this scheme Japan would break Caucasian economic and political control and reduce the white people to a subordinate race or class and thus lead in liberating the dark-skinned element of the world population.

Japan has not failed to capitalize on the superior economic position of the white races in the Far East and their leadership of "non-white" races elsewhere in their attempt to assume the position of the "savior" of the colored, i.e., "non-white", races throughout the world, when obviously seeking to substitute their dominance for that of the Caucasian under the guise of liberating colored people as well as "Asiatics". Their schemes of political liberation emphasized the economic inequality of the native races throughout the East Pacific and their domination by European countries. These aims have been accepted by certain nationalistic movements in the East without regard to the fact that such meant only a change of leadership as exemplified by the formation of Japanese controlled puppet governments rather than an improvement of economic and social conditions. The same political liberation schemes and particularly the inequality theme were readily translated to appeal to a certain type of American negro because of previous agitation designed to raise their standards of living. These were adopted in varying forms and in different degrees by certain negro movements within the United States. [*MID 100-135-X1 DNI 100-135-63*]

That Japan was endeavoring to assume the position as champion of the "non-white" races was manifested soon after the Russian defeat by the Japanese in 1904–05. At this time, the Mohammedans as well as some other colored races expressed their pleasure over the defeat of the Russians, a white race, by the Japanese, a "colored" race, the term colored again being used in the sense of non-white. This may have laid the foundation for a propaganda campaign designed to make Japan appear as the "protector of Islam" in order to gain sympathy and prestige among the Eastern and South Eastern Asiatic populations. In 1935 Mitsuru Toyama, the head of the Black Dragon Society (Kokuryu Kai) was said to have financed the training of four Japanese students who were dispatched to Arabia and Egypt to prepare themselves to act as propagandists in Mohammedan countries. To justify their interest in Islamism, a small group of Mohammedans was located and brought to Japan. For them and a small number of Japanese Islamites, Mosques were constructed and ceremoniously opened at Kobe in 1935 and at Tokyo in 1938. The Koran and other Moslem holy books were thereafter printed in Japan to prove the enthusiasm of the Japanese government and people for Islam. This apparent championship of an African people, that is, the adherents of Islamism, a religion indigenous to Africa, may be one reason why certain negro groups, who call themselves Moslems or followers of Allah and identify themselves as part of a large "colored race" which apparently includes the Japanese and all races other than white, exhibit a sympathy toward Japan. However, no positive evidence has been developed to accurately prove negro, pseudo-Moslem groups expressing similar beliefs which may have been obtained from Japanese sources.

[*"Ten years of Japanese Burrowing in the Netherlands East Indies," Netherlands Info. Bur.*]

Japan's interest in the negroes in the United States began a number of years ago. In April of 1919, when en route to the Peace Conference at Versailles, a Japanese Diplomat engaged an American negro of intelligence and standing in conversation. The diplomat referred to this negro as "one of us", and made many inquiries about racial differences existing in the United States, pointing out that he could not understand how colored citizens of the United States could remain loyal in the face of conditions existing here. He was also concerned as to what the Japanese influence on American citizens of color would be in a crisis, and indicated that Japan considered the use of racial prejudice in furthering any plans they may have against the United States. This same negro pointed out that Japanese sailors ashore from Japanese ships in the Monrovia, Liberia harbor expressed similar thoughts relative to the loyalty of Negroes to the United States. This Japanese delegate to the Peace Conference was of the opinion that in the event of another war, Mexico would not ally itself with the United States, explaining his conclusion by stating that Mexicans are of mixed blood, reddish-brown in color, and for the most part anti-Nordic in sentiment. He was equally confident that in the event of such a war, American negroes by the thousands would cross into Mexico and join forces on the other side. He was also of the opinion that the American negroes would welcome an opportunity to rebel in the event of a race war.

[*100-135-X*]

The proceedings of the Preliminary Peace Conference reflected that on February 13, 1919, Baron Makino, who was one of the Japanese delegates in attendance at the Peace Conference submitted to the Commission of the League of Nations an amendment to the Covenant embodying principles of racial equality.

> "The equality of nations being a basic principle of the League of Nations, the High Contracting Parties agree to accord, as soon as possible, to all alien nationals of States Members of the League equal and just treatment in every respect, making no distinction, either in law or in fact, on account of their race or nationality."

At the Plenary Session of April 28, 1919, Baron Makino explained the grounds for the amendment proposed by the Japanese delegate to the Commission with a view to secure recognition in the Covenant for the equality of all nations and their subjects, and held the amendment out as an example of the Japanese readiness to contribute their utmost to any and every attempt to found and secure an enduring peace of the world. He also stated that "If just and equal treatment is denied to certain nationals, it would have the significance of a certain reflection on their quality and status. Their faith in the justice and righteousness which are to be the guiding spirit of the future international intercourse between the Members of the League may be shaken, ..."

Baron Makino concluded by pointing out the regret of the Japanese government and people at the failure of the Commission to approve their just demand for laying down a principle aiming at the adjustment of this long-standing grievance.

[*"My Diary at the Conf. of Paris" by David Hunter Miller; Vol. XX pages 104 et seq.*]

The fact that the Japanese have long considered the use of negro organizations and negro leaders as a means of creating unrest and racial dissension within the United States has been reflected by the interest of certain Japanese residents of the United States in the negro problem.

Yasuichi Hikida, an alien Japanese who entered the United States on April 14, 1920, and who was employed by the Japanese Consulate at New York City as a translator from April through November, 1941, was apprehended as an alien enemy on January 13, 1942. He did not at this time claim diplomatic status but was subsequently removed to Hot Springs, Virginia, in accordance with the program of interning various Japanese diplomats and was repatriated as a diplomat with the Japanese diplomatic group. Prior to his open employment with the Japanese Consulate, Hikida worked as a cook, guide and interpreter, but even during this period, he was actively interested in negroes and had written several articles concerning them, one bearing a title similar to "The Yellow Man Looks at The Black Man."

It was learned that Hikida, prior to his employment by the Japanese Consulate, gave the impression that he was a spokesman for the Japanese government. At this time he had no visible means of support, but was in funds as he reputedly bought a life membership in the organization known as "The National Association for the Advancement of Colored People". In this connection, it is observed that Hikida was said to have translated an article, "Fire In Flint", written by Walter White, secretary of the National Association for the Advancement of Colored People, into the Japanese language. He also claimed membership in this group in an official questionnaire. [*40-22241-1*]

On Hikida's apprehension it was determined that he possessed a large quantity of literature concerning the negroes in the United States, supporting a previous statement that Hikida had been in charge of Japanese propaganda among the negroes for four or five years and had formerly been employed by the Japanese Consulate to spread propaganda among the negroes. One of his associates, Tateki Iriye, an employee of the Japanese Institute in New York City, indicated that Hikida, a frequent visitor at the Institute, wrote articles under the name of Yonezo Hirayama. A document, interesting in view of Hikida's association with both the Japanese Consulate and the Japanese Institute, was found among the records of the Japanese Association at 1819 Broadway, New York City. This paper, captioned "Interracial Understanding Between the Japanese and American Negroes" did not bear the name of the author but referred to letters of Hikida and a translation prepared by Hirayama which, together with its style, strongly indicated that it was written by Hikida. This outline claimed that the white people of the United States are anti-Japanese while the negro is sympathetic to them. It also pointed out that the American negroes were deeply interested in the Japanese nation during the Russo-Japanese war. When Japan proposed racial equality principles at the Peace Conference after the World War, many negroes of America were said to have decorated their homes with pictures of the Japanese Baron Makino. The negroes were said to have protested vigorously against the Japanese Exclusion Act and during the Manchukuo and Shanghai incidents of 1921 and 1922, the Negro Press was assertedly pro-Japanese. [*Japanese inspired agitation among Am. Negroes NY lett 10-19-42*]

The writer of this outline also suggested that the negro be given an opportunity for first hand observation in Japan and Manchukuo to afford them a knowledge of Japan to be thereafter disseminated to the negro population through syndicated articles. In this connection he stated that the opinions of the American negroes who have visited Japan are overwhelmingly favorable to Japan and pointed out that Dr. R. R. Moton, when head of the Tuskegee Institute, visited Japan as did Dr. Eugene Dibble, also of Tuskegee. Others visiting Japan were said to be James Weldon Johnson, deceased, who attended the Kyoto Pacific Conference; Dr. W. E. B. DuBois, who visited Japan in 1936 and 1937; Dr. and Mrs. Charles H. Thompson of Howard University, who attended an educational conference in Japan in 1937 and Dr. Benjamin Mays, who is apparently connected with the Negro Y.M.C.A.

This outline alleged that Japanese literature on the Sino-Japanese conflict had been sent to an unidentified professor at a negro university in the south who requested additional copies for class discussion. This statement was followed by the paragraph: "It is the general opinion of intellectual negroes in the United States that the negro's concern of Japan is not small. In this world of white arrogance against the oppression of colored races in Africa and in America it is natural that the negro should hope that Japan will not be crumbled. As long as Japan is able to face squarely the Western Powers, there is hope for the negroes." Among other recommendations was the suggestion that a Negro press agent be sent to Japan, Manchukuo, and China to connect the Domei News Agency with the Associated Negro Press; to establish a Negro Problem Research Center in Japan, and to employ negroes to aid in the dissemination of information concerning Japanese culture and civilization to American audiences. He also suggested the establishment of a Japanese-Negro Interracial Committee in the United States and the publication of English language text books on Japanese history written from a racial angle. In conclusion the writer urged Japan to pay special attention to a sympathetic American negro audience eager to learn something about Japanese culture and civilization as by "fate of color they are sympathetic toward Japan and her leadership in Asia." [*Ibid*]

In the fall of 1939 the Japanese Foreign Office held a meeting for the determination of policy in the investigation of Communism and other trends and activities in the United States. The document reporting the conclusions pointed out Japan's desire to know the extent of certain influences, including negro, on public sentiment and in public affairs and discussed the appropriation of funds and plans agreed upon for the investigation of these influences and activities. Vice Consul Inag[a]ki, then in attendance, was designated to take charge of the project and instructed to make his headquarters at San Francisco, California. He was to be assisted by a Consul and a secretary at New York and secretaries at Los Angeles and San Francisco, California, Chicago, Illinois, and Vancouver, Canada. This "special information net" was to expand to South America and proceed independently of the intelligence agencies of the Japanese army and navy. An appropriation of $51,210 was made to finance this project for 1940. It was also indicated that substantially similar appropriations had been made in 1938 for the same purpose.

It was learned from official Japanese quarters that in June, 1941, the Japanese government again considered the use of propaganda among the negroes as a scheme to disrupt the internal security of the United States and requested its officials in this country to advise them immediately as to the feasibility of training and utilizing negroes for their ends and possible methods of contacting leaders and agitators among the negroes in both left and right wings. That they intended to spend money to subvert the colored people in the United States was expressed in their desire to know what expense would be incurred in carrying out these directions.

[*Intercept Tokyo to Jap Embassy Wash. 6-11-41-100-135-5[23?]*]

That Japan has sought to capitalize upon the legitimate grievances of the negro and endeavored to curry their favor by alleging racial affinity, that is, asserting both are "dark races" as opposed to the white race, is reflected by the action of the Japanese Ambassador at Buenos Aires, Argentina, Tomii, who, when reporting to the Japanese Minister of Foreign Affairs on August 6, 1942, on conditions in North Africa, discussed the status of the negro worker in the United States, and stated in connection therewith that riots in Detroit over housing facilities for negro workers were effective propaganda material for both Germans and Japanese. On May 15, 1942, grasping that situation, the Manchukuo foreign radio broadcast that the "so-called Democracy of Anglo-America is a history of racial prosecution and exploitation" and had subsequently "frequently broadcast advice to the colored people".

This contact of the Ministry of Foreign Affairs at Tokyo also advised his principal that the colored people within the United States are "complete isolationists" and have "no connection with regions abroad as the majority were born in the United States". He continued by pointing out a number of jobs which he claimed were not available to colored workers and further, asserted that certain labor unions will not grant charters to negro unions.

It is interesting to note this Argentine contact commented that "Germany, the originator of Mein Kampf, has not addressed the colored people publicly but Japan has been very active and has carried on propaganda work among the colored people." He also stated Japan has used the racial issues which have been employed in Asia and thinks these should be effective among the colored people of the United States.

[*Radio Intercept 4296; 65-33586-589;*
Ambas Tomii, Buenos Aires to Jap Foreign Ministry 100-135-41-4]

Other experiences have shown that the Japanese give attention to any items, however minute, that can be used to attract, or which tend to influence minority groups such as the American negroes.

Even Japanese fiction has manifested their interest in utilizing negroes against the United States as illustrated by a book entitled "Michibeisen Miraiki" (Forecast of Future American Japanese War) written by Lieutenant Commander Kyosuke Fukunaga and prefaced by Admiral Kanji Kato, both of the Imperial Japanese Navy, published as a supplement to the Japanese magazine "Hinode" on November 28, 1933. This story concerns a fictitious battle between the American and Japanese Navies in which the Japanese emerge victorious. One incident relates that a negro mess boy, won over by the Japanese, procured information as to the time United States warships would pass through the Panama Canal after the commencement of hostilities between the United States and Japan. This negro mess boy leaves the fleet at Havana after planting a time bomb which resulted in the fictitious destruction of the Battleship Oklahoma while it was passing through the Canal lock. [*100-147158*]

The Japanese racial propaganda, that is, propaganda directed against white economic and political leadership, was attractive to certain classes of unscrupulous and pseudo-intellectual negro leaders who found the more ignorant class of colored people receptive to any scheme or philosophy which offered to relieve their economic condition and real or imagined discriminations practiced against them. The organizations proposing colored domination of the United States found many followers among the credulous as did those which provided mystic rituals and theatrical trappings such as the so-called negro "Moslem" groups. These appear to have a tenuous relation to the Japanese Moslem overtures but only an abstract connection with the Japanese government or Japanese aims. Few of these organizations had Japanese affiliations or contacts of any consequence even with them as individuals. These societies appear to be chiefly devices used by racketeering negroes to solicit funds and to enhance their position with their followers. Some of these so-called leaders, preying on the ignorance of the type of negro attracted to them, apparently assumed fictitious connections with Japan and used the seeds planted by Japanese propagandists to suggest that the authority of the Japanese government was behind them to lend credence to their contention that they were leaders in a "race war" in which the Japanese were the champions of oppressed negroes in the United States and of "colored" people the world over.

Several negro organizations which had no direct connection with Japan, and are not definitely known to have received subsidies or money from Japanese organizations or individuals, have seized upon the *Japanese "'race war" theories, furthering the propaganda efforts of the Japanese government without cost to it and leaving its imprint on negro thinking.* This is illustrated by these organizations *placing a program of social amelioration before the war effort* and *undermining the confidence of the colored in the sincerity of the proclaimed war aims.* This type of organization also identified the negro with not only Japanese but other peoples such as Moslems and British East Indians. The arguments of these groups center upon the "Why fight the white man's war?" formula, stir up old hates, fears and prejudices and thereby, perhaps unconsciously, work for Japan's ends.

It may be seen by reference to the *highly nationalistic and race conscious attitude of the Japanese* that they place themselves in an anomalous position in propagandizing the alleged racial suppression and discrimination against the negro in the United States and in ethnologically identifying Japanese with the negro. This stand is incompatible with Japanese racial theories for their conception of racial superiority long antedates Nazi race theories. Their conviction that they are superior to all other people goes back to the myth that they are descendants of the Sun Goddess who sent the Emperor Jimmu to Japan in about 660 B.C. to found "the master race"—the "Sons of Heaven", although they are, as a race, of a mixed and uncertain origin. Within Japan, in addition to the traditional subservience to authority and practices which not only include class distinctions having their origin in the not distant Japanese feudal order, discrimination along racial lines exists as exemplified by the contempt in which are held residents of the Okinawa Prefecture because of their Malayan characteristics and the Ainu, the aborigine of Japan again because of racial distinctions. It may also be noted that there has been little intermarriage between the Japanese and persons of other races either in Japan or the United States. In Hawaii, where interracial marriages are common, the marriage of a Japanese to a person of another race would result in social ostracism. It follows that these practices would thus prevent effective proselyting among intelligent negroes.

It would therefore seem that any scheme advocated by the Japanese proposing resettlement of the Negroes would fare better. Further, an "Africa for Africans" campaign would be in line with their widespread "Asia for Asiatics" propaganda and give them a sort of geopolitical basis for the dissemination of propaganda among the negroes. This line of propaganda has recurred among negroes from time to time since World War I and was present in Japanese inspired or infiltrated organizations such as the Pacific Movement of the Eastern World which endeavored to indoctrinate the negroes with the belief that since the Japanese are a colored race, the negroes would achieve their victory should the Japanese win the war.

The fountainhead from which stem most of the crack-pot negro organizations seeking escape from social and economic restrictions is the Universal Negro Improvement Association founded by Marcus Garvey, a West Indian negro who sought to be the Messiah of the millions of colored people in this country. His announced intention to take possession of Africa and establish a government with himself, of course, as president found many followers willing to pay for shares in his "Black Star Line" which was to transport his people to Liberia but resulted in his conviction for mail fraud in 1922 [1923] and subsequent deportation.

It appears that the financial success of Garvey led a number of the more ambitious and less scrupulous members of the Universal Negro Improvement Association to emulate him as a prophet by striving to create their own organizations, adopting the technique of Garvey and superimposing any other trends or theories that may appear currently popular.

The ingenuity and effectiveness of the presentation of the philosophies, if they may be called that, of the newer movements are far below the standards of the parent group. This, as well as familiar earmarks of rackets, leads to the conclusion that the promoters were active in the associations more for personal monetary gain and less because of the commitment to a cause. Yet they provided the means of implanting pro-Japanese ideas and attitudes in the minds of the colored people.

The "Back-to-Africa" slogan and the curious ethnology of Garvey admirably fitted into the Japanese racial propaganda pattern. The Japanese co-prosperity theme, "Asia for Asiatics", was easily transposed to "Africa for Africans" and was not incompatible with the negro schemes of resettlement based on the teachings of Garvey. It also served the Japanese in identifying themselves as kindred negroid people under the oppression of the white race. This was apparently acceptable to negro leaders who were in need of some act, program or connection to enhance their prestige and distinguish their organization from others of similar aim and expression, and provided the Japanese with a vehicle for an attack upon the loyalty of the American negro.

The infiltration of pro-Japanese ideology into negro organizations previously concerned with improving the social and economic welfare of their members as well as the converting of an essentially anti-white attitude into a pro-Japanese sympathy is best illustrated in the promotion of these organizations themselves. The series of groups influenced by Naka Nakane alien Japanese are the only groups of this type in which a direct contact with Japanese forces was traced. They are described hereinafter.

Development of Our Own

The use of existing negro organizations as a front by the Japanese was first observed in the investigation of Naka Nakane who appears in Japanese agitation among the American negroes as the promoter of the "Development of Our Own", also known as "The Onward Movement of America" and the "Ethiopian Intelligence Sons and Daughters of Science", and other groups. This alien Japanese came to the attention of the Federal Bureau of Investigation in 1933 following the report that he originated what was then termed a secret organization for colored people, the Development of Our Own, by representing himself as Satakata Takahashi, a Major in the Japanese army and a representative of the Kokuryu Kai, the Black Dragon Society, in the United States. He was alleged to have been associated at this time, with other Japanese, one of whom was Chosuke Ohki, and a British Indian, M. A. Kahn. Nakane, born in Tokyo, Japan, emigrated to Victoria, British Columbia, in about 1903 and while living in Canada married Annie Craddock, said to be an English woman and became a Canadian citizen. On June 2, 1922, he moved to Tacoma, Washington, and lived there until 1926 when he disappeared because of financial difficulties. He claimed that his occupation was "special doctoring, a kind of religion in which he acted as a preacher", having received instruction in that field at an institution similar to a seminary in Japan thereafter becoming a Shinto priest. It is noted with reference to his statement that he engaged in "special doctoring" that the doctrines of Shinto include faith healing. Nakane related that he was preaching his own doctrines among the colored people in Detroit, Michigan, where he appeared in 1933. It was learned that he visited numerous negro churches in Detroit, representing himself to be Major Satakata Takahashi, and through acquaintances developed in these churches, formed the movement, Development of Our Own, advocating the joining together of the "Dark Races" of the world and in cooperation with Japan, to overthrow white supremacy. There is no indication he was spreading the Shinto faith or was interested in the establishment of a Shinto shrine or temple.

His efforts resulted in the incorporation of the Development of Our Own at Lansing, Michigan, on October 5, 1933. It was termed, in the articles of incorporation, a patriotic, independent and loyal brotherhood, proposing "through organization, education and cooperation and otherwise to advance the interests of the members along the lines of cultural, intellectual, social, industrial and commercial activities as deemed necessary by the organization." It was to be financed by initiation fees, dues and assessments and to be a non-profit organization. An amendment was filed on January 30, 1934, listing the officers. This was followed by another on June 8 of the same year again reflecting changes in the identities of these officers.

Nakane was said to have promised assistance, arms, money and supplies to negroes in a war against the white race and further, stated that Japanese agents were covering the entire United States in the interests of this organization, working in conjunction with the United Negro Improvement Association. This latter organization is probably the Universal Negro Improvement Association. Nakane and his wife, Pearl Sherrod Takahashi, a negress, both claimed to have been in contact with the Japanese Consul at Chicago and with various other Japanese organizations and government officials.

It has been reported that Mrs. Takahashi, accompanied by six or seven other negroes, contacted Dr. I. Tashiro, a Japanese dentist at Chicago, in 1938 as delegates of the Development of Our Own to arrange an audience with the Japanese Consul for the expressed purpose of making a contribution to the Japanese war effort. These delegates again called on Dr. Tashiro in 1939 and he was of the impression that on each occasion these delegates contributed in excess of $300 to the Japanese government or one of its agencies. *[65-30721-74]*

Nakane was deported to Japan on April 20, 1934, by the United States Immigration and Naturalization Service, but on August 29 of the same year, he reappeared at Vancouver, Canada, possessing about $2,000 although he was without funds when deported four months earlier and without a visible source of income. He resided at Vancouver, Windsor and Toronto, Canada, directing the policies of the organization through his wife, Pearl Sherrod Takahashi. As a result of marital difficulties, Nakane removed his wife from the group and appointed Reverend Cash C. Bates, a negro, as the executive officer which action was fought in the circuit court of Wayne County, Michigan. Of interest in these proceedings was the statement that Mrs. Takahashi married a Japanese alien, that is, Nakane, who represented an idea or plan to ultimately undermine the system of American government; that Mrs. Takahashi was spreading propaganda since the deportation of her husband to the effect that the American Government was depriving the colored people of their rights and that they should claim allegiance with the Japanese government and its principles so that the Japanese government could ultimately give the Negroes their full support.

Nakane illegally reentered the United States at Buffalo, New York, on January 11, 1939, using the identification of another Canadian Japanese, Hisazi Kubo, presumably because of the strife occurring within the organization. He reorganized the negroes remaining loyal to him into another association of similar type known as the Onward Movement of America which was, in fact, identical with the Development of Our Own except for the absence of Mrs. Takahashi. This organization was incorporated in the State of Michigan on January 30, 1939, for the same purposes as the original group. Nakane did not appear as one of the incorporators but his associate, Cash C. Bates, did. This group continued to operate the Producers and Consumers Market, a cooperative incorporated by Nakane as an adjunct to the Development of Our Own.

Nakane was arrested on June 22, 1939, for illegally entering the United States and the attempted bribery of an immigration inspector. He was convicted of this offense in the Federal Court at Detroit, Michigan, on September 28, 1939, and was sentenced to a term of three years imprisonment and a $4,500 fine. Nakane was transferred from the Federal Penitentiary at Leavenworth, Kansas, to the medical center for Federal Prisoners as a mental case and was released therefrom on February 27, 1942. He was immediately apprehended as a dangerous enemy alien and was interned as such on April 2, 1942. *[65-562-43]* *[65-562-96-106]*

The organization reputedly recruited members throughout the United States dispatching field organizers as far south as Louisiana and Alabama, and claimed that within six months of the initial meeting obtained 60,000 members in the State of Michigan. At its height, this group was reported to have had 20,000 members at St. Louis, 6,000 at Kansas City and smaller numbers in other towns. These claims were apparently greatly exaggerated as Nakane in 1934, only claimed approximately 3,000 members in the Development of Our Own. *[65-562-43 & 82]*

He asserted that because of his success in organizing among the colored people of the United States, he was granted an interview with Ryobei Uchida, president of the Kokuryu Kai, in which an agreement was reached wherein he was to be the representative of the Kokuryu Kai in the United States as both he and Uchida were interested in effecting the same end, namely, the unification of all "dark races". Nakane denied, however, that he was an official of the Kokuryu Kai; that the Kokuryu Kai was connected with the Japanese government or that he had any purpose other than to help raise the living standards of the colored people. There is nothing to substantiate or even indicate any connection between the Development of Our Own and this Japanese terroristic group except Nakane's unsubstantiated claim that he is the representative of the Black Dragon Society. There exists the possibility that Nakane may have claimed membership in the Black Dragon Society in the same manner and for the same purpose that he adopted the Japanese military title of Major, that is, to impress his negro followers. [*65-562-43*]

The conviction of Nakane on September 28, 1939, seems to have stripped the Onward Movement of America of its leadership and the organization has gradually died out although Cash C. Bates remains the nominal head of the group in Detroit. It may be pointed out that the Development of Our Own was incorporated in the State of Illinois on October 1, 1936, as a non-profit organization but was dissolved in that state on October 27, 1939, for failure to file required annual reports to the Secretary of that state. It also appears that the names of at least some of the incorporators were fictitious or fraudulently used. [*100-135-16-58*]

Bates stated that the Onward Movement of America has at the present time no more than 170 members in all of its five units. It is also known that the group still meets at Gary, Indiana, under the leadership of Central G. Pope and is active at Chicago, Illinois.

Bates recently indicated that Nakane taught that the Japanese would lead the negroes as the leader of all "dark races" and bring about their "liberation", but claims these teachings have been discontinued since Nakane's removal from the group.

[*65-562-43*]

Pacific Movement of the Eastern World

This is another negro organization founded through the efforts of Naka Nakane who injected pro-Japanese sympathies into a scheme of social amelioration patterned after that of the Universal Negro Improvement Association. He began his organizational efforts which resulted in this Movement among members of the Universal Negro Improvement Association who had already shown they were receptive to any scheme promising relief from their economic ills. Nakane approached and obtained the assistance of a Filipino, Policarpio Manansala, commonly known as Mimo De Guzman, after a meeting of negroes at Chicago in 1931 and probably after having learned that De Guzman had been attending meetings of the Universal Negro Improvement Association with Elsie De Mena, a West Indian negress reputedly national organizer of the group.

Manansala, or De Guzman as he will be called, advised that De Mena introduced him to the theories of Marcus Garvey, founder of the Universal Negro Improvement Association, and enlisted his services, introducing him thereafter as a Japanese, Dr. Ashima Takis, before negro audiences in Chicago, Illinois, Cincinnati and Columbus, Ohio, to impress these audiences with the idea that the Universal Negro Improvement Association was sponsored and encouraged by the Japanese government.

[*100-124410-50*]

Nakane, who represented himself to De Guzman as Major Satakata Takahashi, Imperial Japanese Army, solicited his services to organize colored people into groups which would follow his principles and accept speeches of a pro-Japanese tenor. The ostensible purpose of this organization was to establish a government for negroes in Africa, provide means for them to return to that continent and alleviate their racial grievances, but was in reality designed as a propaganda front to stir up racial prejudices and resistance to the war program under the guise of liberation and impair the loyalty of Americans of the negro race. The resettlement scheme was apparently adopted from the doctrines of the Universal Negro Improvement Association, an organization active in proposing the resettlement of negroes in Africa and anti-discrimination measures in the United States.

De Guzman averred in a signed statement that Nakane represented that he, a Japanese official, had been sent to the United States by the Japanese government to organize the colored people explaining that the Japanese Baron Tanaka prepared a memorial outlining the policy of the Black Dragon Society in Japan which proposed, among other things, the unification of all the "dark people" of the world by organization and promulgating a policy of "Asia for Asiatics" wherein Japan would assist "dark people" to organize themselves and form their own government. De Guzman stated that Nakane claimed to be affiliated not only with the Black Dragon Society but the Japanese Consulate at San Francisco, California. Nakane informed him there were Japanese situated in various communities in the United States working among the negroes as it was then a good time to organize "because the people of the United States were unsuspecting and would laugh at such propaganda but, in fact, the time was not far off when Japan would take action". De Guzman admitted that after his discussion with Nakane he agreed to pursue his plan to organize the colored people in what subsequently became known as the Pacific Movement of the Eastern World, a name said to have been suggested by Madam Mittie Maud Lena Gordon, president of the Peace Movement to Ethiopia, with whom De Guzman previously became acquainted at Chicago and who was an officer of the branch of the Pacific Movement of the Eastern World organized there by De Guzman. The name of this branch was subsequently changed to the Peace Movement of Ethiopia. Nakane was said to have paid De Guzman and a Chinese, Moy Liang, who was said to have died in 1938, each $100 to initiate the Movement.

De Guzman made a number of pro-Japanese speeches at meetings of the Universal Negro Improvement Association posing as a Japanese and assuming the names of Dr. Ashima Takis, Lima Takada, Dr. A. Koo and Conrado De Leon. He appeared at Indiana Harbor, Indiana, representing himself as Japanese in 1932, and was arrested because of the inflammatory nature of his speeches but was not prosecuted.

He claimed to have been successful in securing a membership of 20,000 persons in Chicago after working among the negroes there for about two years. He then disagreed with Nakane, according to his statement, because he did not follow Nakane's instructions when speaking before his audiences, and subsequently endeavored to organize for his own benefit a similar group at Pittsburgh, Pennsylvania. There he promoted a chapter of the Pacific Movement of the Eastern World with one E. C. Baker, a negro, and met Leonard Robert Jordan who sought his assistance in founding the

Ethiopian Pacific Movement at New York City. He continued his organizational efforts at St. Louis and Kansas City, Missouri, Cincinnati, Ohio, Philadelphia, Pennsylvania and New York City. In 1938 he met and obtained the assistance of a negro, Walter Lee Peoples, now deceased, who introduced him to Universal Negro Improvement Association audiences at St. Louis as a Japanese. After establishing a large membership, Peoples incorporated the group but failed to include De Guzman as an officer. After this rebuff, De Guzman proceeded to Kansas City where his efforts were not productive. He stated that he engaged in similar activity at Cincinnati but was exposed as a Filipino rather than a Japanese by a negro and a Japanese whom he believed was previously associated with Nakane. *[65-40879-224]*

De Guzman states that after leaving Pittsburgh, he went to Philadelphia and with the assistance of a colored preacher, organized a similar group which may have subsequently become a branch of the Development of Our Own.

There was issued by the Corporation Department of the State of Illinois a certificate of incorporation which sets out that the "Pacific Movement" was incorporated in Cook County, Illinois, on December 7, 1932, as a non-profit religious, civil and educational organization with the purpose of promoting the welfare of citizens. These incorporation papers vested the management of the "Pacific Movement" in a board of three directors, namely Ashima Takis, President General, Chicago; Samuel Nichola, Robbins, Illinois, and J. L. Logan, Chicago. The organization was ordered dissolved on June 4, 1937, by the Secretary of the State for failure to file annual reports. It is observed that Ashima Takis was the alias used by Mimo De Guzman at this time, and that the date of organization is identical to that of the Peace Movement of Ethiopia. *[65-40879-253]*

The corporate records of the State of Missouri reflect that the Pacific Movement of the Eastern World was incorporated by Peoples on October 2, 1933, as a non-profit organization to, among other purposes, encourage the return of those people who have no opportunity for development in the United States to the land of their fathers. *[65-40879-215]*

The by-laws of this organization also provided for a military unit to have charge of the organization of their military forces. It was learned that uniformed guards presumably representing the "military forces" have been in attendance at meetings to deny entrance to unauthorized persons. The organization conferred military titles on members of the unit and they drilled with wooden guns prior to the declaration of hostilities. *[65-40879-224]*

A similar charter was also obtained in Pennsylvania on August 30, 1935, to permit operation of the society in that state, and the Pittsburgh unit of the Pacific Movement of the Eastern World was organized under its authority.

Reverend A. L. Hill, who was made state president of the Pacific Movement of the Eastern World in Mississippi by Walter Peoples in 1933, endeavored to incorporate the Movement in Mississippi but was refused permission in view of its presumed foreign origin. It is interesting to note in this connection that Hill deleted the phrases "Asia for Asiatics" and "Africa for Africans at home and abroad" from the motto of the Movement distributed in Mississippi. *[65-40879-207]*

A charter issued by the Secretary of State of Kansas on December 27, 1933, lists

697 members in Kansas City. This branch was also said to have been organized by a Filipino, undoubtedly Mimo De Guzman, posing as a Japanese. It is said that Dr. A. Porter Davis, a negro physician, president of the association and one of its incorporators, sought political office and used the organization to solicit political support which resulted in a rapidly diminishing interest. The organization was said to have reached its peak in 1936–37 with about 5,000 members but interest soon died out and the membership dwindled to about 20 in 1938 and ceased to exist in that city soon thereafter.

The group purchased, in 1936, a two-story building at 1129 Grandview Street, Kansas City. To save their interests, Davis and five others formed "Redemption Club" and paid the balance due on this property, entering into contract whereby the Pacific Movement of the Eastern World could redeem the building at any time it chose. Dr. Davis denied there were pro-Japanese influences within the organization stating its purpose was primarily to effect the resettlement of American negroes in Africa. He did admit, however, that Dr. K. Furuichi, a Japanese, addressed one meeting, but could not recall if Furuichi uttered pro-Japanese statements.

It is reported that Dr. Davis was elected president of the Kansas City branch of the National Association for the Advancement of Colored People on December 20, 1942, to succeed R. B. Brown. [*100-135-24-13*]

David B. Erwin, the national president of this organization after the death of Peoples and subsequently national adviser, is said to have made statements at East St. Louis, Illinois, to the effect that no person who was a member of his organization will be required to fight for the United States because they have a means of making each member of draft age a licensed preacher and thereby exempt from serving in the armed forces, offering the status of minister in the pseudo-religious adjunct of the Movement for a fee. Erwin denied making this statement but admitted he had the power to ordain anyone as a minister in the "Triumph, The Church of the New Age", and also that he planned to merge units of the Pacific Movement of the Eastern World and this church as the members of the Movement were also members of the church. It may also be pointed out that Erwin was once associated with Marcus Garvey. [*65-40879-248*]

Leaders of various units including General Lee Butler, president of the organization succeeding Erwin, have asserted that the lives and property of members of the organization will not be seized or molested by the Japanese when they invade this country as they have signs and banners familiar to the Japanese and that members qualified to give these signs or display these banners will not be subjected to any discomfort by invading Japanese. Erwin is also reported to have stated in a speech at one of their meetings that the Japanese would soon invade and conquer the United States, and thereafter the organization would attain all of its objectives. He is alleged to have said, following the attack on Pearl Harbor, that he would not mind dying if he could take twenty or twenty-five white people to death with him. This same leader informed his members that if it became necessary for them to fight the Japanese they should recall that the Japanese have plenty of food and clothing and would accord excellent treatment to the negroes. He is also said to have advised prospective negro soldiers to surrender to the Japanese. Searches of the hall of the instant organization at East St. Louis, Illinois, disclosed six wooden guns and a similar number of billy clubs.

Searches of the residences of officers and members of the organization at East St. Louis disclosed firearms and ammunition, and investigation revealed that leaders of the group in East St. Louis were making an effort to obtain ammunition.

The searches also disclosed a Japanese travel pamphlet and a newspaper entitled "Pacific Topics" published by the organization at Chicago naming A. Takis, presumably Mimo De Guzman, as editor. The newspaper contained pro-Japanese articles and the statement that the Pacific Movement was born out of the rejoicing over the victory of Japan over Russia as it was regarded as a victory of the East over the West.

[*65-40879-224 & 202*]

Along the same line, it is noted that there was found in the files of Madam Mittie Maud Lena Gordon, leader of the Peace Movement to Ethiopia at Chicago, a membership card of William Green Gordon in the Pacific Movement of the Eastern World signed by "Sato Kata Takahaski, President General, Kito, Japan" which indicates at least a pretended affiliation with Japan if not an actual sponsorship by a representative of that government. It has been established that Takahashi is an alias of Naka Nakane. [*100-124410-55*]

Leaders of the Pacific Movement of the Eastern World claimed branches in all countries of the world and throughout the United States but Erwin stated, in September, 1942, that there were only three units of the organization then active—Boynton, Oklahoma; St. Louis, Missouri, and East St. Louis, Illinois. It was also learned that Erwin urged members to migrate to South America where a colony was to be established and operated under Japanese control and solicited the sum of $10 from each member who expressed his desire to make the trip. It is interesting to note that in connection with the oriental names appearing in the minutes of the meetings as officers of the international body of the organization were apparently truthfully explained by Erwin as having been copied from the signs of business establishments in El Centro, California, as the names Okamura, Sukiyaki and Buena Comida are translated as Okamura (a proper name), Japanese meal, and a good dish and were probably taken from the sign of a Japanese restaurant.

While Erwin was in the southwest, he promoted units of this organization in Arizona, ostensibly as benefit societies. These were not successful because of limited membership and alleged misappropriation of funds. The Yuma unit was disbanded in about 1936 and those at Phoenix and Gila Bend in about 1940. The Movement was also active at Newark, New Jersey from about 1934 to 1937 and was reported to have been organized by a "Dr. Katasha" or "Takahashi", probably Mimo De Guzman. Reuben Thomas, alias Reuben Israel, head of the "House of Israel", a negro group advocating evasion of the Selective Service Act, was said to have been an ardent follower of the Pacific Movement of the Eastern World, then the Pacific Movement, and a co-organizer with De Guzman. [*65-40879-247; 140-135-32-14*]

In 1940 a Japanese and a number of negroes from East St. Louis were said to have organized units of this organization at Bardwell and Blandville, Kentucky. These units were not successful and went out of existence upon the commencement of hostilities.

The records of the Secretary of State of Oklahoma disclosed that the Pacific Movement of the Eastern World was incorporated in that state on October 6, 1939.

The charter was delivered to David D. Erwin who then gave his address as Okmulgee, Oklahoma. Erwin, Reverend F. R. Baker, W. H. Clement and Fred Brown were named as directors and Erwin, on September 16, 1939, certified it to be a church society. Branches were established at Tulsa, Boynton, Okmulgee and Sapulpa, Oklahoma, by J. W. Isom in about 1934. After the death of Isom in 1938 meetings were conducted in a desultory manner and the organization ceased to exist in Oklahoma. *[65-40879-282]*

William S. Washington, a negro war veteran, promoted a unit at Omaha, Nebraska, which was active in 1935 and 1936 but of little consequence. It died out prior to Washington's departure from that city in 1938 and was apparently not reestablished. *[65-40879-269]*

Mimo De Guzman was arrested on July 30, 1942, at New York City for a violation of the Selective Training and Service Act of 1940. He was removed to St. Louis, Missouri, where an indictment had been outstanding against him since June 20, 1942, for a violation of the Postal Laws arising out of a forged money order. He entered a plea of nolo contendere to the charges contained in this indictment and was sentenced on October 1, 1942, to a term of three years on each count of the indictment, such sentence to run concurrently.

This matter was presented to an investigative Federal Grand Jury at East St. Louis, Illinois, on September 22, 1942, and a similar Grand Jury inquiry was held at Pittsburgh, Pennsylvania, on September 17, 1942. The testimony pertaining to this investigation was also heard by a Federal Grand Jury at St. Louis, Missouri, on July 22 and 23, 1942. No indictments were returned as the object in presenting this testimony to these Grand Juries was exploratory to determine the extent of the organization in that area. A Grand Jury investigation was also made at Oxford, Mississippi, on September 21 and 22, 1942. These facts were presented to a similar investigative Federal Grand Jury at Kansas City, Missouri, on November 2, 1942. *[65-40879-224, 234, 248]*

The Department of Justice authorized the United States Attorney at East St. Louis, Illinois, to institute prosecutive action against David D. Erwin, General Lee Butler and the corporation. Thereafter the November term of the Federal Grand Jury was ordered to reconvene at East St. Louis to consider this case and on January 27, 1943, this Grand Jury returned an indictment charging the organization, General Lee Butler, and the national president, David D. Erwin, the national adviser and one John Doe, a Japanese, with conspiracy to cause insubordination, disloyalty, mutiny and refusal of duty in the military and naval forces of the United States in violation of Section 34, Title 50, U.S. Code. A second count of the indictment charges these persons with conspiracy to hinder compliance with the Selective Training and Service Act of 1940 by offering the status of minister in the "Triumph, The Church of the New Age" to all members of the Movement who paid the required fees. *[65-40879]*

Butler and Erwin entered pleas of not guilty when arraigned before the Federal Court on February 2, 1943. Both were remanded to the custody of the United States Marshal in default of bond, set at $5,000 each.

Peace Movement of Ethiopia

The Peace Movement of Ethiopia owes its origin to the same circumstances as the Pacific Movement of the Eastern World and the Ethiopian Pacific Movement and embraces substantially the same schemes, an anti-white attitude and pro-Japanese sympathies superimposed on a plan for the resettlement of negroes in Africa modeled upon the program of the Universal Negro Improvement Association. It will be recalled that a Filipino, known as Mimo De Guzman, mentioned in connection with the Pacific Movement of the Eastern World and other negro organizations attended meetings of the Universal Negro Improvement Association at New York City in 1931, and there met Elsie De Mena, a West Indian negress. De Guzman related that she provided him with a book on the theories of Marcus Garvey, the founder of that organization, and informed him she was the national organizer traveling throughout the United States promoting units of the association. She enlisted his services by offering to defray his expenses if he would agree to pos[e] as a Japanese, Dr. Ashima Takis, with whom she claimed to have been previously acquainted. [*100-124410-55*]

This woman thereafter introduced him as a Japanese before negro audiences at Dayton, Toledo, Cleveland, Columbus and Cincinnati, Ohio, Indianapolis, Indiana, and Chicago, Illinois. He stated that he was then unable to speak sufficient English to address a group and merely sat on the platform to impress the audiences with the idea that the Universal Negro Improvement Association was sponsored by Japan.

Madam Mittie Maud Lena Gordon said that she joined the Universal Negro Improvement Association in 1923 or 1924 and had invested money in the bonds of the association shortly before Garvey was convicted for mail fraud. She was a member of the "division" which met at 3333 South State Street, Chicago, but claimed she was not active in the Association; yet at the same time she admitted attending the so-called international conference of the Universal Negro Improvement Association at Kingston, Jamaica, in August, 1929. She said she became disgusted with the conduct of the leaders and convinced there would be no real gains made by the organization. Because of this conviction she claimed she no longer took an active part in the organization; yet she admitted she had met with others to keep alive what she termed the legitimate objectives of the Universal Negro Improvement Association. This was the first indication of the formation of a new organization by Madam Gordon.

[*100-124410-115-18*]

Madam Gordon related that she heard of one Takis, a Japanese major, and Liang, a Chinese, appearing before meetings of the Universal Negro Improvement Association in Chicago making speeches to the effect that they would assist colored people to return to Africa. She advised Takis announced that he was financed by the Japanese Consul at Chicago and shortly thereafter that he approached her with the proposition that he was promoting the Pacific Movement of the Eastern World and desired her assistance which she claims to have declined. However, Madam Gordon subsequently attended a meeting at Indiana Harbor, Indiana, and there apparently fully agreed with the statements of De Guzman, then known to her as Takis, as she asked and received his permission to circularize a petition among his listeners calling for the repatriation of negroes to Africa. She said several thousand persons signed her petition and she and others interested in the movement thus developing opened headquarters in Chicago subsequently moving to 3333 South State Street, the previous address of the Chicago division of the Universal Negro Improvement Association. She refused to give the petition and its signatures to De Guzman upon his demand principally because she feared that he was rapidly becoming a leader in her Movement which was then known as the Pacific Movement of the Eastern World, a name said to have been suggested to her by Liang, and on December 7, 1932, De Guzman refused to allow her to enter one of the meetings. She and her followers evicted him, and on the same day, assembled and organized the Peace Movement of Ethiopia for the expressed purpose of repatriating negroes to Ethiopia. Madam Gordon claimed she broke with De Guzman because of her feeling that he was not sincerely interested in assisting the colored people but was defrauding them of their money rather than over the question of leadership. She did not mention her quarrel with Elsie De Mena, the organizer of the Universal Negro Improvement Association shortly prior to her disagreement with De Guzman. It therefore appears that through personal disagreements of Madam Gordon the Chicago division of the Universal Negro Improvement Association successively became the Pacific Movement of the Eastern World and the Peace Movement of Ethiopia. The close relationship of these associations is further exemplified by Madam Gordon's terming the Pacific Movement of the Eastern World as her organization and her possession of a membership card in the Pacific Movement of the Eastern World issued to William Green Gordon, her husband, and signed by "Sato Kata Takahashi, President General, Kito, Japan". [*100-124410-18*]

In pursuance of their announced plan to repatriate negroes to Africa, Madam Gordon, in imitation of the efforts of the Universal Negro Improvement Association to resettle in Liberia, directed a letter to President Edward Barclay of Liberia on October 20, 1938, proposing the immigration of American negroes to that country. This was followed by the dispatching of delegates to confer with Liberian authorities on the premise that the United States government would provide passage and subsequent subsistence for the migrants. David J. Logan, an officer of the Movement, and Joseph Rockmore, now deceased, arrived in Liberia on December 5, 1938, as representatives of the organization which subsequently resulted in an accounting action being brought against Madam Gordon by several members of the Movement to determine the disposition of funds collected by the organization. Following these discussions with the Liberian government, Madam Gordon stated that she and many of her members indicated their desire to obtain Liberian citizenship and forwarded a list bearing their names to Liberia. Thereafter she informed those who had so expressed their willingness to return to Liberia that they were Liberian citizens. Claiming she was subsequently advised by the President of Liberia that it was neutral, she publicly advised her members on the premise that as citizens of Liberia, a neutral country, they need not respond to the Selective Training and Service Act of 1940. [*100-124410-16*]

After the return of their delegation from Africa, Madam Gordon continued to claim that the Liberian Government favored the immigration of negroes sponsored by this movement but failed to advise them that Liberian officials did not look with favor on mass migration but would only consent to a select immigration of negroes skilled in some trade and financially able to find themselves in a new country. [*100-124410-55*]

The Peace Movement of Ethiopia ostensibly embraced Mohammed[ism] but the members did not adopt "Moslem" names, a characteristic of other negro pseudo-Islamitic cults as the Moorish Science Temple and the Allah Temple of Islam, or prepare a "Koran". Madam Gordon related that she and her members talked at their rallies of worshiping Allah, their God, and Mohammed, his prophet. There was no indication of a sincere or thoughtful effort to learn and follow the precepts of that religion but rather the mere use of Mohammedan terms as a device to further distinguish the negro from the white races. This is expressed in one of the objects of the constitution of the Peace Movement of Ethiopia, "We believe in the God of our forefathers, the history, language and Islam religion", and by their speeches urging the negroes not to follow the "white man's religion". Yet, at the same time, the by-laws claim the organization is built "on a Biblical standpoint" and refers to the scriptures to illustrate this contention. [*100-124410-7 & 18*]

The constitution of this organization, prepared in 1941, describes the movement as a "social, charitable and expansive society" having as its aims the "return to our motherland, to our true name, to our own language and to our own true religion" and concludes with the statement that each of the members is "wholly devoted to my country, Africa". Of interest in other stated objects are the expressions of belief in the slogan "Africa for Africans", and negro national rights and the "nationalistic principles of Marcus Garvey", who, it is recalled was the founder of the Universal Negro Improvement Association. This printed document urges the repatriation of negroes to Africa because of the discrimination and prejudice against the negroes and the lack of opportunity for them in the United States. It also alleges that Senator Bilbo of Mississippi presented on their behalf a "repatriation bill" before Congress on April 24, 1939. [*100-124410-7*]

David James Logan, one of the delegates dispatched to Liberia, observed upon his return in January, 1939, that Liberia maintained an army. This observation apparently prompted Madam Gordon to institute military training within the organization, forming, as stated in the constitution, a "detective" corps presumably meaning and also referred to as a "protective corps." It is stated therein that a military department was established to protect the principles of the organization. The Movement conferred military titles and a few members drilled with wooden guns, carrying a Liberian flag. Its duties seemed to be limited to maintaining order at meetings, acting as ushers and promoting the sale of the movement's literature. [*100-124410-7 & 18*]

Madam Gordon was arrested upon a complaint filed before the United States Commissioner at Chicago on August 2, 1941, charging her with counseling negro registrants to evade the provisions of the Selective Training and Service Act of 1940. This complaint was based specifically on her counseling Johnnie Lee Johnson not to execute his Selective Service questionnaire. The matter was presented to a Federal Grand Jury at Chicago on August 21, 1941, and a no bill was returned on August 27, 1941. The case against her was then dismissed by the Commissioner upon her assurance that she would not further interfere with the Selective Service Act and instruct the members of her Movement to comply with the provisions of this Act. She made no statements in keeping with her promise but on the contrary, and under the impression that she would or could not be prosecuted, became bolder and more antagonistic toward the United States as well as distinctly pro-Japanese in her speeches, instructions and remarks, such becoming more virulent after Pearl Harbor.

[*100-124410-4*]

Madam Gordon and other leaders of this group admitted telling the members they are not American citizens notwithstanding their birth in the United States or the Amendments to the Constitution relating specifically to the citizenship of persons of the negro race. Several members, in executing their Selective Service questionnaires, followed her declarations to that effect and made notations as "African citizen, not United States citizen" in response to the inquiry as to their citizenship. Other members refused to execute questionnaires upon Madam Gordon's instructions that they were not citizens of the United States. She appeared before a Local Board at Chicago in connection with the registration of Johnnie Lee Johnson, and, among other things, stated that if she had been able to contact all the registrants prior to registration, she would have advised them not to register. She continued by stating that as it was too late for this course of action, she held meetings three nights each week at 4451 South State Street, where registrants were instructed to refuse to fill out their questionnaires. Members who had completed their questionnaires were told to file Form 47 for conscientious objectors. She mentioned that she had given assistance to some thirty men in helping them fill out conscientious objector forms but later retracted that statement. Attempting to prove that her members were not citizens of the United States, Madam Gordon procured a history book setting forth the "Dred Scott" decision of Chief Justice Taney of the Supreme Court in 1920 to the effect that negroes whose ancestors were brought to the United States as slaves could not be citizens of this country.

Following the declaration of war, the leaders and speakers of the Peace Movement of Ethiopia made frequent and numerous speeches of a seditious nature showing a strong Japanese sympathy as exemplified by statements quoted hereinafter.

At a meeting on May 31, 1942, at the Boulevard Hall in Chicago Madam Gordon addressed an audience of approximately four hundred persons consisting of members of this association stating among other things "that on December 7, 1941, one billion black people struck for freedom . . . that the Japanese were going to redeem the negroes from the white men in this country"; "that the spoils of the United States would be equally divided between Hitler and the Japanese."

Under similar circumstances Madam Gordon addressed a similar audience stating "that it is impossible for America and Britain to win this war." On August 2, 1942, at the same place and before the same group she publicly stated that "the members of this organization are not citizens of the United States . . . they are citizens of Liberia and they have no flag except the flag of Liberia," "that because they have no flag they owe no allegiance to the United States; that when Japan bombed Pearl Harbor they wrought vengeance against the United States for the injustices that were visited upon her"; "that you," referring to the members of her organization, "should not fight for the United States because there is nothing worth fighting for here." At subsequent dates Madam Gordon made similar public statements before audiences composed of members of this organization.

David Jones Logan, who bears the title of Executive Chaplain and who was a member of the Executive Council of the Peace Movement of Ethiopia, Seon Emanuel Jones, president of the main local branch of the group, Local #1, and a member of the Executive Council, and William Green Gordon, the husband of Madam Gordon, who bears the honorary title of "Father Gordon" attended executive council meetings of the Peace Movement of Ethiopia and formulated the policies of the group and carried on its activities. Each of them occupied positions on the speakers platform and addressed assembled audiences on many occasions and were present when Madam Gordon made the statements attributed to her.

Jones addressed members of the Peace Movement of Ethiopia at Boulevard Hall on August 21, 1942. An excerpt from his speech "and now is the time for the negroes to act because if they wait until after the war they will be back in slavery again, but if they act wisely they will free themselves now and they will be free and it won't be very long" reflects the context of this and other speeches made by him. In subsequent public utterances, Seon Jones expressed his belief that the Japanese would win the war and that negroes should not register for the draft or fight for the United States as they would then be fighting for something they did not have. He also pointed out that the negroes should not fight the Japanese as the Japanese are not fighting them and further that the negroes should do their fighting here as the white man is their enemy.

David J. Logan, among other things, is said to have stated before a meeting on September 6, 1942, "that the members of this organization did not have to register for the draft because they were Liberians and as such did not owe any allegiance to the United States." A Japanese connection or at least a pro-Japanese sympathy on the part of the leaders of this organization was indicated by the attendance of orientals at a meeting of the organization on June 21, 1942.

Madam Gordon introduced a Mr. Shaack to her audience on September 13, 1942, who stated in his address that the present war was a racial war between the white and colored people and in the same speech related that a Japanese Prince married an Ethopian Princess for the purpose of creating good will among the negroes. Shaack also spoke of the friendliness of the Japanese to the natives of Liberia.

Madam Gordon advised in a statement that the Peace Movement of Ethiopia continually advocated the affinity of all black groups and that it was her belief that the black race and the Japanese race were one and the same. A four-page handwritten letter was found among the effects of Madam Gordon, addressed "To His Highness General Sadao Araki, Esq., War Office, Tokio, Japan." This letter, briefly, petitioned that in the event of war between the United States and Japan the members of the Movement be advised as to their conduct as they are not enemies of the Japanese and were hopeful of uniting the dark races of the world. It also asked for a truce between them and the "dark skinned people of the eastern world." It concluded with the statement that they will not fight against "our dark skinned brothers of the eastern world" and expressed their desire to enter into a secret alliance with the Japanese government. A notebook of the same source contained the names: Dr. Doera Ariyoki, Commerce

Department, Japanese Colonial Affairs, Tokyo, Japan; Captain Sunao Ota; Japanese "Council," Addis Ababa Ethiopia; Japanese "Council" S. Ognichi. There was also found a copy of a two-page typewritten letter addressed to the "Honorable Kenji Nakauchi, Chicago, Illinois," over the typewritten signature of Madam Gordon as President of the Peace Movement of Ethiopia, seeking his cooperation and advice. Nakauchi was Japanese Consul General at Chicago during 1934 and 1935. A receipt for a registered article was also located among these effects which indicated that Madam Gordon forwarded such to the former Japanese Ambassador, Hirosi Saito. The contents of this letter or article are not known. [*100-124410-63*]

The leaders of the Peace Movement of Ethiopia endeavored to branch out in other cities and states. Their efforts resulted in the formation of a branch at East Chicago, Indiana, under the leadership of Harry Collins. The speeches made before this branch were similar in content to those made at Chicago but emphasized their scheme for resettlement in Africa. Collins denied that the purpose of the organization was subversive, contending that the organization aimed to provide a haven for the colored people. The secretary of this branch indicated that there were about 400 members at East Chicago and Collins furnished a list purporting to be the entire membership of the Peace Movement of Ethiopia in the United States. This list contained approximately 4,100 names.

Tommie Thomas, a negro, endeavored to organize a local near Grady, Arkansas, in the fall of 1940 but the attempt failed through dissension between the members.

William Ashley Fergerson, Platka, Florida, corresponded with Madam Gordon from time to time and was designated as organizer for that state. It appears that in the early part of 1936, he read of this organization in the Pittsburgh Courier, a negro newspaper, and thereafter inquired of Madam Gordon concerning the Movement. She subsequently designated him as leader of the Peace Movement of Ethiopia for the State of Florida and urged him to solicit members. From time to time she instructed him concerning the conduct of the group. Fergerson spoke in colored churches and in the homes of colored people in and about Platka, Florida, frequently reading letters from her to his audiences. Fergerson had approximately one hundred names listed in a book purported to be the roster of the Movement in Florida. However, many of the persons named had no knowledge of the Movement and it appears that Fergerson actually contacted only a few but recorded the names of many negroes known to him. The organization was not very active or effectively led in Florida.

In 1937, a Mrs. C. J. Allen of Chicago, Illinois, appeared in Mississippi as the national organizer of the Peace Movement of Ethiopia. She enlisted the services of Thomas H. Bonner, at Mathersville, Mississippi, and with his assistance set up a local chapter. Bonner subsequently organized other locals terming them Locals #10 and #11, and acted as the leader of both. He claims that there were, in November, 1942, three hundred members in that state. Bonner received instructions from time to time from Madam Gordon but insisted the Movement in Mississippi only advocated the return of negroes to Africa. Celia J. Allen also contacted George C. Green at Long, Mississippi, in 1936 or 1937 as organizer in the State of Mississippi, and with him promoted what was termed Local #9 at Long, Mississippi. This was not received with enthusiasm, had no regular meeting place, but did obtain the names of two hundred persons as members. Of these, only about fifteen were said to be present at meetings.

The Peace Movement of Ethiopia was also active in Jersey City, New Jersey, from 1935 to 1937 meeting at the Fraternal Hall, 49 Kearny Avenue. Leonard Robert Jordan and "Dr. Takis," that is Mimo De Guzman, appeared before the meetings. Takis apparently organized the group subsequently turning over the leadership to local negroes. Reuben Thomas, also known as T. Thomas, may also have been affiliated with this organization.

Earnest Sevier Cox, a White man interested in negro affairs, particularly organizations advocating resettlement of negroes, was an unofficial representative of the Peace Movement of Ethiopia in Virginia. Cox, who resides in Richmond, did not organize any branches of the group and claims he was only interested in the Movement because of its resettlement aims.

On September 19, 1942, complains were filed before the United States Commissioner at Chicago charging Madam Mittie Maud Lena Gordon with violation of Sections 33 and 34, Title 50, United States Code, and William Green Gordon, David James Logan, and Seon Emanuel Jones with a violation of Section 34, Title 50, United States Code. They were apprehended and arraigned on September 21, 1942. All were ordered held and on the following day Madam Gordon posted a bond in the sum of $10,000. The other defendants were remanded to the custody of the United States Marshal in lieu of bonds of $5,000 each. The facts in this case were presented to a Federal Grand Jury sitting in Chicago, Illinois, considering seditious activities in the Northern District of Illinois. This Grand Jury returned an indictment on October 23, 1942, charging Madam Gordon, in eight counts, with violating the above-mentioned sections of the United States Code; that is, with wilfully making certain oral statements with the intent to cause insubordination, disloyalty, mutiny and refusal of duty in the military and naval forces of the United States, and wilfully to obstruct the recruitment and enlistment in the service of the United States to the injury of the service and of the United States. On the same date this Grand Jury returned an indictment against each of the defendants including Madam Gordon with a violation of Section 34, Title 50, United States Code, that is to say with conspiring to violate Section 33 as set forth above. They were ordered held by the United States District Judge on October 28, 1942, and were brought to trial on January 25, 1943. Madam Gordon, Seon Emanuel Jones, and William Green Gordon were found guilty of the charges named in the indictment against them on February 15, 1943. Madam Gordon and Jones were sentenced to terms of two years each and were placed on probation for three years, the probation period to commence at the expiration of their prison terms. William Green Gordon was also placed on probation for three years but no other sentence was imposed upon him. David James Logan, who was indicted jointly with the other persons named for conspiracy to commit sedition was found not guilty.

The defendants' attorney, Lloyd T. Bailey, on February 16, 1943, requested a stay of execution pending an appeal which was granted for forty days during which period a bill of exceptions will be filed. Madam Gordon posted bond in the sum of $5,000 and Seon Jones $2,500 for their release.

A number of the members of the Peace Movement of Ethiopia became delinquent under the provisions of the Selective Service Act by reason of their failure to execute a questionnaire or report for induction and for other reasons. These persons were afforded an opportunity to comply with the provisions of the Act and subsequently many removed their delinquencies. Some complied upon apprehension and others only after indictments were returned against them resulting in the dismissal of the charges filed. These persons were: Granville Kirkendall, Johnnie Lee Johnson, Eddie Davis, Alexander Lyle, Samuel Brown, Lonnie Warnegy Sims, Ernest Charles, Sylvester Washington, Willie Dixon, Jesse Carpenter, Dan Tillman, and William Jerry McLendon, all of Chicago. Leo Weatherspoon, Indiana Harbor, Indiana, became delinquent but subsequently removed his delinquency and was inducted into the armed forces.

Edmund Holiday, Secretary General of the organization was sentenced to a term of three years for a violation of the Selective Service Act on March 5, 1942, and Elijah Ross received a similar sentence on July 19, 1942. [*100-124410-103*]

On April 6, 1943, Otey was rearrested after he had failed to appear before the Federal district on April 1, 1943. He was brought before court where his sentence was stayed and he was placed on probation for two years.

Clevis DePugh, formerly a national organizer for the Peace Movement of Ethiopia violated the Selective Training and Service Act in the spring of 1943. He reportedly had departed from Chicago after the arrest of Madam Gordon and other leaders of the organization. On June 11, 1943, he was apprehended by agents of the FBI and placed in custody of the United States Marshal to await trial.

Ethiopian Pacific Movement

Reference has been made to this organization in discussing the activities of the Pacific Movement of the Eastern World and the Peace Movement of Ethiopia. The Ethiopian Pacific Movement was closely connected in its inception with these groups and their ostensible purposes were identical, that is, the resettlement of American negroes in Africa as suggested by the "redemption of Africa" scheme proposed by the Universal Negro Improvement Association, the alleviation of racial grievances, and the elimination of racial discrimination and segregation. This movement also owes its origin to the same pro-Japanese influences asserted through Naka Nakane, an alien Japanese, and his proselyte, Mimo De Guzman, a Filipino, and like the other groups, was founded and expanded among the followers of the Universal Negro Improvement Association by former members who were apparently willing to capitalize upon the legitimate racial grievances of the colored people for their own financial benefit. It differed from them, however, in that it did not have a religious bias or flavor comparable to the pseudo-Islamism of the Pacific Movement of the Eastern World and the Moorish Science Temple of America.

Mimo De Guzman, who was involved in the organization of the Pacific Movement of the Eastern World and the Peace Movement of Ethiopia, held himself out as a

Japanese propaganda agent engaged in promoting the Pacific Movement of the Eastern World on behalf of the Japanese for almost two years prior to his meeting Leonard Robert Jordan in 1935. De Guzman related that he associated with this negro, whom he knew as Robert O. Jordan, for almost six months and assisted him in establishing a group which subsequently became the Ethiopian Pacific Movement at New York City, utilizing the principles as well as a name suggested by the Pacific Movement of the Eastern World. De Guzman admitted receiving money from Naka Nakane which was presumably from funds of the Japanese government, for his services in connection with the establishment of the Pacific Movement of the Eastern World. He denied that he received Japanese financial assistance to promote the Ethiopian Pacific Movement, insisting that he aided in the organization of this movement solely for his own financial benefit and was not then employed by the Japanese government or any Japanese national. During this period, De Guzman assumed the name of Dr. Takis, posing as a Japanese and pretending to have influential Japanese contacts. It was noted in connection with this pretended connection that Jordan stated, when publicly addressing his audiences, he promoted the movement with the assistance of Dr. Takis, a Japanese. However, Jordan subsequently disagreed with De Guzman and according to De Guzman's statement brought several Japanese who were members of a Japanese organization, presumably the Japan Institute at New York City, to a meeting where they exposed him as a Filipino and thus terminated his connection with the Ethiopian Pacific Movement. De Guzman could not furnish any information which would indicate the extent of Jordan's contact with these Japanese or substantiate their affiliation with the Japan Institute. He also could not state whether or not Jordan was employed by the Japanese to disseminate their propaganda but related that during the time when he was employed by Nakane, the Japanese were anxious to engage persons who could work among the negroes and it was, therefore, his opinion that Jordan may have been contacted by Japanese and was in their employ. In discussing the possibility that Jordan was employed by the Japanese, De Guzman said that Jordan urged him to join the Ethiopian Pacific Movement in the fall of 1941, assuring him that he was about to get financial aid from the Japanese, and, therefore, both would be able to make money through the organization. Jordan was said to have exhibited letters which he claimed were from Japanese. De Guzman observed that one of the signatures appeared to be a Japanese name and further, another letter was on the stationery of the Japanese Consulate at New York City. [*100-56894-129*]

De Guzman also pointed out that prior to the formation of the Ethiopian Pacific Movement he and Jordan were active workers and speakers in the Universal Negro Improvement Association and had become associated through their membership in that group.

Jordan continued with the Ethiopian Pacific Movement after his differences with De Guzman and was named as one of its officers prior to its first annual meeting as a corporation according to the records of the County Clerk which also reflect that the Ethiopian Pacific Movement was incorporated in New York County on September 18, 1935. Its principal offices were to be located in New York City and its officers were to include not less than five nor more than twenty persons. The expressed purposes of the group were to create a better understanding between races, nations, and classes of people; to foster a desire for universal peace; to promote disarmament and to stimulate the intellectual advancement of the members and friendship among them as well as between other Pacific Movements. It was noted that Leonard Robert Jordan, as Robert O. Jordan, appeared first in the list of officers named in the incorporation papers.

Weekly Sunday evening meetings of the Ethiopian Pacific Movement were held, usually at 113 Lenox Avenue, New York City, under the guidance of Jordan with about one hundred to one hundred fifty persons, chiefly colored, in attendance. Leonard Robert Jordan always appeared as one of the principal speakers and was frequently followed by James Thornhill, Lester Holness, Ralph Green Best and Joseph Hartrey. These speakers continually expressed a distinct pro-Axis sympathy and disparaged American institutions and service in the armed forces of this country. Jordan made statements such as "Those that have the interest of the black man at heart should make every effort to give Japan every protection that he can. Japan is not interested in Japan alone. She is interested in the one hundred fifty million dark races of the world. She will liberate the dark races so that the black people can rule black people and have their own country." His attempts at persuasion were accompanied by threats voiced as follows: "I am trying to prepare you for the coming of the new order. Everybody who did not hear of the new order when we have one will be beheaded. So you had better get your name down on the books as members of this organization." [*100-56894-21*]

Interspersed in his address were statements such as "The black man would be a sucker to join the United States Navy." Jordan also made commendatory remarks about Hitler and Mussolini, usually in connection with the statement that he had the Axis powers behind him. [*100-56894-120*]

Jordan often claimed connections with the Japanese and in an address on January 25, 1942, stated he served for three years as a second officer in the Japanese Navy. He also claimed that he had been a Japanese agent since 1922, the date he finished his training with them. He openly boasted that he was a fifth columnist and urged every negro to be a fifth columnist. In another address, he stated he would never fight under the American flag and would give his life under General Tojo if necessary because Japan was going to form a government in Africa which the negroes could rule under Japan.

Jordan on other occasions stated that he had been a second engineer in the Japanese Marine service but upon his apprehension, stated only that he had been employed on a Japanese merchant vessel as chief quartermaster. It is interesting to note that he could not recall the true name of the ship, stating it was the "S.S. Maru." The word "Maru" is customarily used in the names of Japanese merchant ships and does not signify any particular vessel.

Lester Holness made numerous statements following the pattern set by Leonard Robert Jordan of which an example is: "Japan is doing a great piece of work. The fulfillment of her plans will be the emancipation of the black people."

Ralph Green Best, in an address before the Ethiopian Pacific Movement, made statements in a similar vein such as "I am on the side of Japan to win this war, I shall not be any more liberation except this and the almighty and eternal God through the working of the Japanese government, the great Nipponese, the rising sun is going to chop the whole link right down and will not stop fighting until they bring liberation to every black man, woman and children the world over." Best claimed that he was the spiritual adviser of the group and had been ordained as a minister in the New York Colored National Spiritualist Organization.

Joseph Hartrey was a regular Sunday night speaker of this organization from November, 1941, to June 7, 1942, declaiming on racial discrimination and expressing his opinion that a Japanese victory would be of great assistance in establishing a free Africa for colored people all over the world. He stated that Jordan knew of his pro-Axis sympathies and had, therefore, invited him to take part in his program. In a speech made before the assembled members of the Ethiopian Pacific Movement on February 8, 1941 [1942], Hartrey stated that the United States had been beaten at Pearl Harbor and that the Allies had "ganged up on Japan and are trying to put the blame upon Japan that she ganged up on this country." He also attacked the Jews as being responsible for racial discrimination practiced against the negro and their generally low economic condition.

Hartrey, a white man, was born in the United States and was employed for several years as a laborer by the Work Projects Administration, and had received relief for a number of years. He related that he had been a street speaker beginning with the "Scottsboro CAse." Hartrey was associated with the Christian Front organization in 1938 and 1939 as a speaker. In June, 1939, he started speaking in behalf of Joseph McWilliams and his Christian Mobilizers. Hartrey was active with this organization until the fall of 1940 and was chairman of the Board of Speakers as well as a member of the Executive Council, receiving a small salary for his services.

James Thornhill, a former member of the Universal Negro Improvement Association and of the Citizens League for Fair Play, became acquainted with Jordan in the early 1920's when both were members of the Universal Negro Improvement Association. He began as a speaker in the Ethiopian Pacific Movement at Jordan's request and at the same time also addressed meetings of the African Nationalist Pioneering Movement in New York City. It is interesting to note that Thornhill held meetings of the African Nationalist Pioneering Movement in the hall used by the Ethiopian Pacific Movement after its meetings were discontinued in August, 1942. [*100-56894-153*]

All of the leaders mentioned except Hartrey were West Indian negroes. Thornhill was born in the Virgin Islands; Holness and Jordan at Jamaica, British West Indies, and Best in Barbados, British West Indies.

It was determined that Leonard Robert Jordan endeavored to make contacts with Japanese organizations. Jordan accompanied by Dr. Thomas F. Cathcart, called at the Japan Institute in June, 1941, bearing a letter of introduction from Kyuya Abiko, Executive Secretary of the Japanese Association. Jordan claimed that he visited the Japan Institute merely for the purpose of obtaining magazines and other sources of Japanese history. He also admitted visiting the Japanese Christian Society at 1819 Broadway, New York City. It is also interesting to note that Jordan claimed to be able to speak some Japanese.

Jordan stated in addresses before the meetings of this organization that the Ethiopian Pacific Movement was recognized by both the German and Japanese governments and that if every man in the audience were not so stupid each could have $100 if they would cooperate with him in his work. Jordan stated that he and Holness were members of the Japanese Black Dragon Society and demonstrated signs with his hands which were supposed to represent membership in that Society. As a further indication of his strong pro-Japanese sympathy, Jordan is said to have made a speech to the effect that the Japanese and the negroes are radically similar. [*100-56894-4*]

Jordan mentioned in connection with his pro-Japanese activities that he would have received $20,000 for the establishment of a weekly newspaper to be used for the dissemination of Japanese propaganda in this country if the attack on Pearl Harbor had not occurred. [*100-56894-153*]

Jordan was acquainted with a Japanese, Byron Kikuchi, who advised that Jordan visited many Japanese and tried to display his influence and standing among them to members of his own race by inviting Japanese to attend meetings of his group, as far back as 1935 and 1936. Kikuchi stated that Jordan urged these Japanese to speak on racial discrimination but the Japanese subsequently reached the conclusion that Jordan was using them to further his own private ends and he was thereafter unsuccessful in obtaining persons of that race as speakers. [*100-56894-217*]

It is observed that Jordan and Holness were arrested on February 18, 1942, upon a charge of conspiracy to violate the Alien Registration Act. They were released upon their own recognizance and were thereafter arrested by the Immigration authorities and charged with not possessing an unexpired Immigration Visa. On March 4, 1942, an information was filed against Jordan in three counts charging him with violation of the Alien Registration Act in that he failed to file a change of address with the proper government authority. He was found guilty in the United States District Court of the Southern District of New York and was sentenced on March 11, 1942, to ten days on each count, to be served consecutively. During Jordan's confinement in the Federal Detention Home in New York City, meetings of the Ethiopian Pacific Movement were regularly held with Thornhill appearing as a speaker. Jordan resumed speaking after his discharge from jail on April 12, 1942. He claimed that he was arrested on a "silly charge" and was prevented from showing in court the real reason for his arrest because the Judge and the United States Attorney were afraid of what he might have to say. This statement met with great applause from his members and Jordan concluded with the statement that he knew those with whom he would "get even when he took over in Africa." [*100-56894-92*]

An indictment was returned by a Federal Grand Jury for the Southern District of New York at New York City on September 14, 1942, against Leonard Robert Jordan, Ralph Green Best, Lester Holness, James Thornhill and Joseph Hartrey for sedition. All of them entered pleas of not guilty upon their arraignment on September 14, 1942. Joseph Hartrey, who was charged in this indictment with conspiracy to commit sedition, changed his plea to guilty on September 25, 1942. On September 30, 1942, a Federal Grand Jury returned a second indictment against Jordan, Best, Holness and Thornhill charging them with sedition (Title 50, Section 33, United States Code) in that on or about the fifth of July, 1942, at a meeting of the Ethiopian Pacific Movement, Incorporated, held at 113 Lenox Avenue, New York City, these defendants, when the United States was at war, did unlawfully, wilfully and knowingly cause and attempt to cause insubordination, disloyalty, mutiny and refusal of duty in the military and naval forces of the United States; that the said defendants stated to a person wearing the uniform and distinctive insignia of a member of the United States Army and to others, in substance, that negro soldiers should not fight for the United States against Japan and the other Axis Powers with which the United States was at war. On December 14, 1942, the prosecution of these persons began in the Federal Court of New York. There were three negroes on the jury, two men and a woman, the latter being chosen forewomen, which returned a verdict of guilty against all defendants on both indictments recommending leniency for Best on both charges. [*100-56894-217*]

These persons and Hartrey appeared before the Court on January 14, 1943, and received the following sentences:

Leonard Robert Jordan—10 years and $5,000 fine on each of the two indictments, sentences to run concurrently.

James Thornhill—8 years on each of the two indictments, to run concurrently.

Lester Holness—7 years on each of the two indictments, to run concurrently.

Ralph Green Best—4 years on each of the two indictments, to run concurrently.

Joseph Hartrey—6 years on the conspiracy indictment.

Moorish Science Temple of America, Incorporated

This organization came to attention in 1931 when J. T. Bey, a negro barber at Reading, Pennsylvania, asserted he was the 'Supreme Grand Governor' of the Moorish Science Temple and explained that the cult was organized in 1913 at Newark, New Jersey, by Noble Drew Ali who headed the American organization from 1913 until his death in 1929. According to Bey, the organization then had temples in seventeen different cities throughout the United States including Cleveland, Milwaukee, Chicago, Baltimore, Richmond and Norfolk, and was part of a world-wide organization. However, he could not state the location of the international headquarters or name even one other country where the organization may have existed. Bey related that the temples discontinued public meetings in 1933 and adopted the policy of carrying on the work of the organization as individuals. He said it was not really inactive but had merely ceased public operations to enable it to conduct its work in secret. He claimed the organization had 3,200 enrolled members with national headquarters at 3603 Indiana Avenue, Chicago, Illinois, at the time it changed its policy in 1933.

The Moorish Science Temple has as its bible a pamphlet which they term "The Holy Koran of the Moorish Science Temple of America". This book names Noble Drew Ali reputedly a North Carolina negro named Timothy Drew, as the "last prophet in these days" who was "divinely prepared by Allah to redeem man from their sinful ways". Marcus Garvey, who is remembered as the founder of the Universal Negro Improvement Association, a movement proposing the resettlement of Africa by American negroes is described in this pamphlet as the "divinely prepared forerunner who was to prepare the earth to meet the coming prophet bringing the divine creed of

Islam, Noble Drew Ali". The Koran appears to have been put together during the life of Marcus Garvey and contains a curious mixture of Christianity and Islamism weaving Mohammedan terms into Christian precepts and biblical stories.

The "Koran" describes what it terms the divine origin of the Asiatic nations, names the United States as the Asiatic nation of North America, and asserts that the Egyptians were the progenitors of the Japanese and Chinese and describes similar sources of origin of other people concluding with the statement that all are Moslems. It also contains the statement that "according to all true and divine records of the human race there is no negro, black or colored race attached to the human family because all the inhabitants of Africa were and are of the human race". This curious ethnology concludes with the expression that, through slavery, "the nationality of the Moors was taken away from them in 1774 and the word negro, black or colored was given to the Asiatics of America who were of Moorish descent".

An examination of the "Koran" disclosed that much of it was abstracted word for word from "The Aquarian Gospel of Jesus the Christ" by Levi H. Dowling, published by E. S. Dowling for the Aquarian Commonwealth, Chicago, Illinois, which is described as "the philosophic and practical basis of the religion of the Aquarian Age". Mohammedan terms, such as "Allah" for "God", were substituted for the Christian names and material like the "Koran Questions for Moorish Children" and "Laws for Moorish Americans" were added.

The organization also utilizes well known Christian hymns with the verses changed usually by substitution of "Allah" for "God" and "Islam" for "Lord".

Following the theories expressed in "The Koran" Bey explained the organization proposed to recover the "Birthright of the Moors" which he alleged was taken from them in 1774 by persons whom he could not name or describe, and thus enable them to again be known as Moors and govern their own country, Morocco. As descendants of the Moors, the negro members of this temple claimed to adhere to the Mohammedan faith and to pay homage to Allah and Mecca. It was learned that the Moorish Science Temple at this early date seemed to favor a revolution of some sort and sought to promote equality of all races.

It may be seen that this embodied a scheme of resettlement similar to that of the Universal Negro Improvement Association and other negro organizations such as the Pacific Movement of the Eastern World which were pro-Japanese in sympathy. It was reported that on several occasions in the summer of 1939, members of the Japanese Chamber of Commerce spoke at meetings held by the Hartford, Connecticut Chapter of this organization and, therefore, the possibility existed that the Japanese government might be disseminating propaganda through the organization.

Frederick Turner El, a resident of Brooklyn, New York, who claimed to be head of the Eastern Division of the organization established this branch, Number 35, of the Moorish Science Temple at Hartford, Connecticut, in 1936 for the express purpose of "uplifting the lot of the poor negro in the United States". El claimed at this time there were 8,000,000 members throughout the United States, an unsubstantiated and grossly exaggerated claim.

Turner, as "Tamad Frederick Turner El, Grand Sheik and National Counsellor of Brooklyn" also organized a Branch at Bridgeport, Connecticut, on November 21,

1941, under the direction of Jacob E. Holmes. It then claimed 100 members, now dwindled to less than 20 because of the prevalent opinion among colored people of Bridgeport that it is a subversive organization. Turner claimed it "patriotic and non-subversive" and that it proposed to engender self-respect among his people through teaching them of their Moorish descent and nationality.

Temple Number 45 at Louisville, Kentucky, organized in 1938, has about 106 "adept" and "regular" members under the leadership of Arthur Slaton Bey, "Grand Sheik", and Goldie Mae Porter El, "Assistant Grand Sheikess". In their regular Sunday meetings they have identified the negroes with the Japanese, Chinese, Mexican and other dark races and as members of the "Asiatic Nation". The speakers also made statements to the effect that the Japanese were laying down their lives for their brothers, the negroes, and that soon the people of color will become the rulers of the world. Goldie Mae Porter stated that President Roosevelt went to the Moors for guidance, referring to the Casablanca Conference and that this country is now ruled by a Sultan, C. Kirkman Bey, "who tells Roosevelt what to do". They have also addressed audiences to the effect that President Roosevelt will be the last European in that office and that after the fall of Europeans, the country will be ruled by C. Kirkman Bey.

It was reported on December 24, 1941, that Robert Washington, an organizer for the temple, made statements at Mound City, Illinois, to the effect "that when the Japanese take over this country those who are members of his organization will not be molested" and further that colored people are not negroes but Asiatics.

Rubin Payne, who had in his possession a certificate which referred to him as 'Rubin Payne El Sheik', certifying him to be a Moor, issued by the Moorish Science Temple of America at Chicago, was organizing in Yazoo and Humphreys Counties, Mississippi, and apparently established locals at Belzoni and Mileston, Mississippi. It was reported that the group was there teaching that negroes who joined the organization would not be required to register under the Selective Training and Service Act, and if they had registered, would not be required to report for induction as the organization would get them out of any trouble caused by their failure to comply with this Act. These men claimed that membership tickets, sold for $1.25, would keep the holders out of the United States Army and insure them of good treatment when the Japanese invaded the United States. Payne also advised that a burial policy, valued at $60.00 was included as one of the benefits of membership. Barnes, who was subsequently joined by Payne, solicited members for this organization at the prompting of J. Shelby, Chicago, to whom he forwarded the membership fees collected.

Rubin Payne and Jim Barnes were tried in the Circuit Court of Holmes County, Mississippi, and Barnes was sentenced to five years imprisonment and Payne to two years, neither sentence to exceed the duration of the war, for violation of Chapter 178 of the Mississippi Laws of 1942 making it a criminal offense to teach any belief that advocates the overthrow by violence of the present form of Government. The conviction of these men terminated the activities of this organization in that vicinity and has made the colored people there reluctant to pay dues to, or attend meetings of similar organizations.

Members of the organization have expressed the belief that they are in possession of signs and signals and passwords which will preclude harm from Japanese or German troops when they invade the United States. It is observed that the members of the Pacific Movement of the Eastern World were similarly taught signs purportedly for their protection in the event of invasion. It also appears that there is a military unit within the organization termed the "Brothers of the Military Department", another indication of similarity between this organization and the Pacific Movement of the Eastern World. It is noted in the "Moorish Voice" that this group provides entertainment at their meetings.

It was learned that the head of the organization is known as "Colonel" C. Kirkman Bey, Supreme Grand Advisor and Moderator, who maintains the national headquarters at 1104 Sedgwick Avenue, Chicago, Illinois. The headquarters of the organization publishes a mimeographed pamphlet known as the "Moorish Voice" which appears to be issued monthly and is sold for 10¢. It seems to be concerned with the social activities of the various branches and the sale of devices and trappings of the organization.

Investigation has disclosed that the Moorish Temple of Science of America was incorporated under the "Not For Profit Act" of the state of Illinois on November 29, 1926. A certificate was filed with the state of Illinois on May 21, 1928, changing the name to the Moorish Science Temple of America. The organization was incorporated in the state of Indiana on March 17, 1930, for the expressed purpose of teaching the Koran, to establish the Mohammedan faith in America and to conform to that faith by annexing the names of Ali, El and Bey. It was also incorporated in the state of New York with the principal office at 44 Jefferson Avenue, Brooklyn and attempted to domesticate in the state of Virginia but was there refused permission on the ground that the state constitution prohibits the incorporation of a religious denomination previously incorporated under the laws of another state.

The Moorish Science Temple of America also maintains a colony near Prince George, Virginia, known as the National Home of the Moorish Science Temple of America. The local leader, F. Nelson Bey, claims over one million members in the organization and has indicated that these members support the colony which in turn prints the "Moorish Voice" and manufactures various devices for the use of the organization. It appears that the inhabitants of the home come from various branches of the Moorish Science Temple, utilizing it as a refuge.

Investigation and an examination of copies of the Moorish Voice have disclosed that there are or have been branches of this organization in a number of cities. These were designated as Temples and given a number. In some cities there were two or more Temples with different numbers and other Temples had branches in more than one town. These Temples, listed in order of their numbers, are as follows:

Temple	Location	Leader
Temple #1	Chicago, Illinois	T. Rhodes El
Temple #2	Charleston, W. Va.	H. White Bey
Temple #3	Milwaukee, Wisconsin	B. Johnson Bey
Temple #4	Detroit, Michigan	W. Allison El

Temple	Location	Leader
Temple #5	Columbus, Ohio	D. Busby Bey
Temple #6	Richmond, Va.	Mosley El
Temple #7	Cleveland, Ohio	M. Fuller Bey
Temple #8	Pine Bluff, Ark.	A. Brown El
Temple #9	Chicago, Illinois	Sister M. Dove El
Temple #10	Newark, New Jersey	William Edward Moore El
Temple #11	Philadelphia, Pa.	L. Dublin El
Temple #12	Youngstown, Ohio	P. Edison El
Temple #13	Baltimore, Maryland	H. Graham Bey
Temple #14	Akron, Ohio	W. Owens Bey
Temple #15	Columbus, Indiana	C. Frasier Bey
Temple #15	Indianapolis, Ind.	C. Frasier Bey, or T. Beckwith Bey
Temple #16	Chattanooga, Tenn.	Sister Irene Williams Bey
Temple #17	South Bend, Ind.	J. Jones Bey
Temple #18	Fostoria, Ohio	McGaughy El
Temple #18	Toledo, Ohio	J. Donald El
Temple #19	Flint, Michigan	J. Nelson Bey
Temple #20	Pontiac, Michigan	T. Rhodes Bey
Temple #21	Brooklyn, New York	Frederick Turner El
Temple #22	Indiana Harbor, Ind.	I. Cook Bey
Temple #22	Gary, Indiana	C. Wells El, or C. Barker Bey
Temple #22	East Chicago, Ind.	N. Smith El
Temple #23	Brooklyn, New York	Sister Z. Abel Bey
Temple #24	Atlanta, Georgia	Sister P. Beyshauret Bey
Temple #25	Detroit, Michigan	W. Davis El
Temple #26	Steubenville, Ohio	Sister G. Butler El
Temple #27	New York, New York	D. Carrington Bey
Temple #28	Glassboro, New Jersey	D. Smith Bey
Temple #29	Cairo, Illinois	B. Griffin Bey
Temple #30	Chattanooga, Tenn.	Sister H. Neal Bey
Temple #31	Boston, Mass.	
Temple #32	Springfield, Mass.	N. Taylor Bey
Temple #33	Philadelphia, Pa.	W. Bradley El
Temple #34	New York, New York	J. Cortin El

Temple	Location	Leader
Temple #35	Hartford, Conn.	Countryman Bey
Temple #36	Benton Harbor, Mich.	A. Wise Bey
Temple #37	Harvey, Illinois	C. Brakins El
Temple #38	Cincinnati, Ohio	H. Hampton Bey
Temple #39		
Temple #40	Philadelphia, Pa.	S. Smith Bey
Temple #41	New York City	W. Price Bey
Temple #42	Anderson, Ind.	Will Townsend El
Temple #43	Mt. Clemens, Mich.	W. Washington El
Temple #44	Saginaw, Mich.	
Temple #45	Louisville, Ky.	Arthur Slaton Bey
Temple #46	Kansas City, Kan.	Sister Bessie Burton Bey
Temple #46	Kansas City, Kan.	Sister Maryann Walker Bey
Temple #47	Atchison, Kansas	William Bey
Temple #48	Trenton, N.J.	
Temple #	Bridgeport, Conn.	Jacob E. Holmes

The records of the 12th annual Convention held at 218–220 West Oak Street, Chicago, Illinois, from September 15 to 20, 1939, are said to have listed what were termed the 'Grand Governors' of several states. These are:

Illinois	S. Lovett Bey
Indiana	I. Blakely Bey
Ohio	A. Bryant Bey
Michigan	F. Nelson Bey

The letterhead of the New Haven Division of the Moorish Science Temple reflects that F. Turner El is "Executive Councilor and Moderator of the Eastern District", 340 Hancock Street, Brooklyn, New York, and that R. Scott Bey is the National Chairman. Harold Peters Bey, 707 Grand Avenue, New Haven, Connecticut, is named "Grand Deputy Councilor of the Eastern District."

The organization has recently been somewhat active in Detroit, Michigan, where it has been reported the organization has taught that Japan will overthrow the United States; that after the United States and Japan go to war, the colored people will not be attacked providing they surrender to Japan; that America should arm the negro and then the negro should surrender to the Japanese and that it is necessary for the Negroes to establish a front in the United States. It has been reported that Naka Nakane, who will be recalled as the promoter of the Development of Our Own in Detroit, was at one time active in the Moorish Science Temple of America under the name of Satakata Takahashi, a major in the Japanese army, and a representative of the so-called Japanese Black Dragon Society.

A negro known as Father Mohammed Bey founded a unit of this organization at Kansas City, Kansas, which was said to have broken away from the national association in about 1935. The organization was at one time very active and in 1936 or 1937 had approximately 500 members. The membership subsequently dwindled, possibly because of the death of Mohammed Bey. This organization differed from the National Moorish Science Temple chiefly in that it prohibited male members from shaving and required them to wear red fezzes at all times. There were also other requirements as to dress, particularly of the women. Thirteen members of this cult were arrested on July 24, 1942, for violations of the Selective Training and Service Act of 1940. Seven of them, Winifred Boyd Bey, Jr., Winifred Boyd Bey, Sr., Roy Lee Boyd Bey, Otha McGee Bey, Paul Jackson El, Lenzie David Bey and John Hunter El, were convicted in the United States District Court at Kansas City and were each sentenced on January 19, 1943, to terms of four years and to pay a fine of $1,000. The remaining persons arrested were released on October 24, 1942, by order of the Attorney General.

Claudius O. Watson, a negro janitor employed by the Walt Manufacturing Company, Springfield, Massachusetts, admitted placing hardened pieces of metal on a milling machine, knowing that this action would ruin a cutter as well as hinder the importance of the production. He denied an intent to impede war production but stated the negro race would be better off if Japan won the war. He formed this conclusion on the premise that the basis for the war is discrimination between white and colored races. He said he would not serve in the United States Army because of the racial segregation of the troops. He admitted membership in the Moorish Science Temple in this area and is alleged to have been strongly influenced by its teachings.

Colored American National Organization, aka, Washington Park Forum, and The Brotherhood of Liberty for the Black People of America

The Colored American National Organization was known by several names, the Washington Park Forum, the Afro-American National Organization and the Brotherhood of Liberty for the Black People of America, and appeared to be an offshoot of the Pacific Movement of the Eastern World or at least influenced by the Japanese racial propaganda emanating from the same sources. It was founded by Charles Newby and Stokely Delmar Hart in 1939 ostensibly for the purpose of promoting the welfare and better economic conditions of the negroes. Newby, the president of the organization prior to August 10, 1942, is an ex-convict who served a term of one to ten years for grand larceny in the State Reformatory at Pontiac, Illinois, in 1920, and another term of one year and one day in the Federal Penitentiary at Leavenworth, Kansas, for a violation of the National Motor Vehicle Theft Act. He is a soapbox haranguer who has posed as an evangelist concerned with negro welfare, and a former associate of Mimo De Guzman, a Filipino instrumental in the formation of other negro organizations of similar stripe, the Ethiopian Pacific Movement and the Pacific Movement of the Eastern World.

Newby and Hart claimed to be furthering the principles of Marcus Garvey, a negro organizer who advocated the resettlement of colored people in Africa through his Universal Negro Improvement Association. The speakers for the Colored American National Organization demanded that all negroes join a negro movement and demanded that if they did not join their movement, they must join Madam Gordon's movement, that is, Pacific Movement of the Eastern World [Peace Movement of Ethiopia], or the Universal Negro Improvement Association. [*100-129633-244*]

Stokley Delmar Hart among others addressed a large number of persons assembled at a meeting of the Colored American National Organization held at a public forum in Washington Park, Chicago, among whom were persons available and eligible for recruitment and enlistment in the military and naval forces of the United States as well as others who were liable for military and naval service under the Selective Training and Service Act of 1940. On May 22, 1942, Hart made an address containing in substance, the statement that anybody who joins the army or navy is a damn fool. A negro should not support this country's war effort—there is a common bond between the Japanese and the negroes because both are members of the 'colored race' and that he, Hart, would not fight for the United States because he would rather go to the penitentiary than go to the army and that the Japanese will liberate the negro from the white man's yoke. On another occasion Hart, in a speech, referred to Tojo, the Premier of Japan, as the savior of the American negroes and continued by stating that when the Japanese invade this country the people belonging to this organization will assist the Japanese and those not members would be killed when the Japanese arrive. At still another meeting Hart spoke to an audience and stated among other things, that his "prayers to Tojo were answered by the bombing of Pearl Harbor"; that "the negroes only interest in this war is to see a Japanese victory", and that "the negroes freedom depends on a Japanese victory." Hart made numerous other speeches in which he identified the Japanese as a "colored race" and kindred people of the American negroes.

Charles Newby, the president of the organization, addressed a large audience consisting of members of the organization and other persons stating among other things that "colored men should not join the United States Army . . . Colored men should not register for the draft and colored men should do all in their power to hinder our war effort."

On July 16, 1942, Newby, speaking from the Forum in Washington Park said in substance, that the "negroes would fare better under the Japanese than they have under the white people"; that "the only good white man was a dead white man"; that "the more white people killed in this war, the better chances the colored men will have to come out on top"; that it was "to the negroes advantage to fight with the Japanese in this war"; and that "those negroes who would not fight with the Japanese should have their heads cut off". On another occasion he made the statement that Hitler and Tojo are the 'light of the world' for the negroes and that the negroes of America need not worry if Hitler and Tojo win the war.

The leaders from time to time expressed their belief in a Japanese victory and that the American negroes would assist the Japanese in achieving such a victory, declaring they had connections with Japan and were in a position to inform the Japanese army upon its arrival in the United States which negroes were uncooperative with their movement and thereby unfriendly to Japan.

The organization first held its meetings in a public forum in Washington Park which had been, in the past, the scene of many discussions usually of a political nature. After the organization had secured sufficient members, it held meetings at Bacon's Casino in Chicago where motion picture films were exhibited. Some of these pictures included scenes of Japan and others were advertised to depict scenes of the bombing of Pearl Harbor. Frederic Harold Robb, who styled himself Hammurabi Robb, made comments to the audiences concerning the films. He described himself as an "African lecturer and world traveler" who did research work in connection with the history of the black man and his contribution to civilization throughout the world.

Newby continued as president of the organization until August 10, 1943, when he was evicted from a meeting then in progress. At this time The Brotherhood of Liberty for the Black People of America was founded as a successor to the Colored American National Organization. Hart was elected president and James Graves, vice president. At this meeting Robb commented in connection with the pictures he was exhibiting "that Japan is one of the 'dark races' and it is time for the 'dark races' to take over the world"; that "the United States does not have a chance in this war" and that "Tojo would rule this country and it would be better for all of us negroes." At a subsequent meeting Robb continued in the same vein by asserting "negroes owe no allegiance to the American flag because it was not the black man's flag," and that they "should learn the color of the Japanese flag if they were to go on living." He also stated that the negroes were going to deal with the white men here on the home front and in order to take over this role, they would have to learn how to handle a gun, drill and exercise.

The meetings of the Colored American National Organization were also said to have been addressed by Robert Chino, a member of the War Resisters League who was convicted of a violation of the Selective Training and Service Act of 1940.

The facts in this case were presented to the Federal Grand Jury sitting at Chicago, Illinois, on October 23, 1942. An indictment was returned against Stokely Delmar Hart charging him in ten counts with violation of Section 33, Title 50, United States Code, by wilfully making certain oral statements with intent to cause insubordination, disloyalty, mutiny and refusal of duty in the military and naval forces of the United States and to obstruct the recruiting and enlistment service of the United States. On the same date a similar indictment was returned against Charles Newby charging him in eight counts with a violation of the same law. These two persons together with

Frederic Harold Robb, James Graves and Mrs. Annette Goree were charged with conspiracy to violate the sedition laws. These facts were resubmitted to a Federal Grand Jury at Chicago on December 7, 1942. This Grand Jury returned on December 18, 1942, a true bill similar to the original indictment. Their trial was set for January 14, 1943, but has since been continued to March 8, 1943. [*100-129633-47*]

On April 14, 1943, Newby was sentenced to three years' imprisonment while later, on July 11, 1943, Hart was found guilty and was sentenced to three years in the custody of the Attorney General.

Allah Temple of Islam, aka, The Moslems

This organization professes to follow the Mohammedan religion and is in many respects similar to the Moorish Science Temple of America. It has been particularly active in Washington, D.C., and Chicago, Illinois. The leaders of the organization at Washington were apprehended in May, 1942, for violations of the Selective Training and Service Act of 1940 as they had informed their members, American negroes, that they were Moslems and according to the tenets of their religion, were not required to fight in any war or to register in compliance with the Selective Training and Service Act. A number of the members of this organization were taken into custody for failure to register under this Act. The leaders of the organization at Chicago, Illinois, were taken into custody on September 20, 1942, for conspiracy to commit sedition and also for violation of the Selective Training and Service Act. Seventy members of the organization were also apprehended at this time because they had not properly registered for Selective Service.

Thirty-one of thirty-eight negroes who were indicted for Selective Service violations in connection with this matter entered pleas of guilty and thirty of them were sentenced to three years each. One, Emanuel Mohammed, with aliases, the son of Elijah Mohammed who w[as] indicted for sedition, was sentenced to five years upon his plea of guilty. Six of these negroes pleaded not guilty and were held for trial. Seven were released when it was determined they had complied with the provisions of the Selective Service Act. The remaining twenty-five of the negroes apprehended were indicted for violations of the Selective Training and Service Act and were arraigned on October 22, 1942. At this time, eighteen entered pleas of guilty and each of them was sentenced to three years in custody of the Attorney General. The seven who entered pleas of not guilty were found guilty after trial and each of them was sentenced to identical terms.

A Federal Grand Jury sitting at Chicago returned an indictment on October 23, 1942, against Elijah Mohammed in eight counts charging sedition. An indictment was also returned at this time against Mohammed, Lynn Karriem and Pauline Bahar, as well as Sultan Mohammed of Milwaukee, Wisconsin, and David Jones of Washington, D.C., charging them with conspiracy to commit sedition. The trials of these persons as well as a Selective Service case against Karriem were postponed until April 5, 1943. Voluminous records and correspondence were seized at the Temple of Islam and at the homes of the leaders upon their arrest. These were examined but failed to disclose any indication of Japanese activity within the organization since 1933 or 1934. Among the records seized were minutes of meetings held during the period from 1933 to 1934. These minutes referred to a speech made in the latter part of 1933 wherein Elijah Mohammed stated that the Japanese had sent a teacher to the black people and that the Japanese were brothers and friends of the American negroes.

The records of subsequent meetings did not indicate that any Japanese attended meetings of the organization or had been active within it. Further no correspondence was located which would indicate any connection between the leaders of this group of colored people and the Japanese government or any Japanese person.

It was reported that various leaders of the Japanese people in Chicago believe the government was justified in arresting the leaders of this cult. These Japanese were said to have stated that there had been no Japanese active within the organization in recent years and if there had been any Japanese active in the organization, he must have returned to Japan long ago. [*100-6582*]

On April 23, 1943, Lynn Karriem was sentenced to five years' imprisonment for a violation of the Selective Training and Service Act.

African Moslem Welfare Society of America

The African Moslem Welfare Society presents three of the characteristics common to pro-Japanese negro organizations: the adoption of the Mohammedan religion; the identification of Japanese and the negroes as kindred colored people, and the resettlement of American negroes in negro colonies.

It was organized at Pittsburgh, Pennsylvania, in 1927 and incorporated under the laws of Pennsylvania, filing its name as required by the Pennsylvania Fictitious Name Act on January 5, 1928. The purposes of the organization as stated in these proceedings were, among others, to unite the Moslem people and eradicate racial differences due to their color and nationality and bring them in closer association with each other. The records of this society provided for the establishment of branches and indicated that such existed in Cleveland, Ohio, New York City, New York, and Detroit, Michigan. Murad Jemel, Elias Mohammed, Helena Klale, Joseph Taisr and Siedetha Gama all of Pittsburgh subscribed to the incorporation petition which was prepared by Joseph I. Winslow, a Pittsburgh attorney.

Jemel was president of the organization at its inception although one Majid, who is said to have later returned to his home in Sudan, Egypt, was reported to have been responsible for its organization. Two years after its incorporation, Elijah Martin assumed control of the society and subsequently permitted it to cease functioning. In about 1938, Ishmel Moore, alias Abraham Moore, together with Frank May, Albert Stewart and Joseph Taisr obtained possession of the original charter and again activated the group. It has since been meeting at a hall at 115 Continental Street, Pittsburgh, frequently used by other negro groups. This action split the organization in two groups, the other being headed by Martin who reputedly conducts meetings at his home and a school in Islamic.

The members professed to sincerely follow the Mohammedan religion and although American negroes, professed to be Mohammedans. However, it has been reported that Moore was born in Arabia and others were born in the West Indies. Members have worn fezzes and long robes at meetings and speakers have read from the Koran, the Mohammedan equivalent of the bible. The organization also had in its possession Egyptian, Turkish and Moroccan flags.

The society was said to have conducted itself as a religious organization until approximately nine months ago when several of the persons connected with it exhibited pro-Japanese sympathies as illustrated by the statement of Mohammed Zayn "when you belong to this organization you are in touch with a foreign government of your mothers' land and our ancestors". Zayn explained that the government he referred to was that of the Japanese with the further statement that "they are a dark race and are fighting our cause". Another member, Frank May, stated at a meeting that "the negroes should not fight for the United States. The United States is gone. The Japs and Turks will deliver us". Jemel is also said to have stated in private conversation that his mission is working for the Japanese government and further that Majid was sent to the United States to organize the colored people for the Japanese government. He is also alleged to have said before a meeting of this group that "all of us who have found ourselves state we are for the United States Government, but if the Japs take us prisoners we will come back as soldiers . . . Japan counts on the negroes to help them" and "the Japs won't harm us".

This organization is unusual in that it claims affiliations with Turkey or at least Turkish persons. Frank May stated at a meeting on December 6, 1942, that he was required to report on the organization's affairs to Winslow, the attorney previously mentioned, who desired that they select sixteen representatives to meet with a Turkish representative at Washington, D.C. May also stated at this time that the Japanese and Turks will deliver them.

There appears to be considerable internal dissension within this organization as several of the members have accused others of making seditious statements and have warned the members to not talk freely or make pro-Japanese remarks. It appears that they were aware of the prosecution of the leaders of pro-Japanese negro organizations at Chicago at this time inasmuch as they criticized the Government's action in entertaining prosecution.

Addeynue Allahe Universal Arabic Association

This organization teaches that its members, American negroes, are of Arabic descent and have for years been living under "slave" names. It is their belief that American names given them by slavers who brought their ancestors to America, must be changed by the adoption of the African names of their forefathers. This premise varies only a little from the reasons given for the adoption of the surnames Bey and El by the adherents of the Moorish Science Temple of America, which this organization strongly resembles. The members also profess to follow the Mohammedan religion, term themselves Moslem, and express the belief that they are not really negroes.

[*100-135-7-9*]

Mohammed Ez Al Deen, the head of the organization, has conducted classes of the association's school at 473 Central Avenue, Rochester, New York, speaking in favor of Japan and exhibiting bitterness against the white race. Mobarrak Hasson, a teacher at the school, has made similar expressions such as his hope that Japan will win the war and that the white race will be conquered. Hasson has indicated that the purpose of the organization is to locate all of the "Hamitic Arabs" in the United States and teach them their history. In this connection, it may be stated that the society is reported to be actively engaged in teaching the Arabic language and history.

[*100-135-7-7 & 12*]

The group is said to have originated at Buffalo, New York, in about 1938 and now is estimated to have about 200 members in Buffalo and 75 in Rochester, New York.

All of the members of the organization eligible under the Selective Training and Service Act of 1940 are said to have registered as conscientious objectors. Troy Vaughn, who assumed the name of Arrefa Rukabun, directed a letter to his Selective Service Board stating that he could not take an active part in military service; that he was of the Mohammedan faith; that the majority of the Mohammedans are Japanese and that as the Japanese are of the "dark race" he regarded and respected them as his people. Others have claimed exemption on the ground that they are unable to eat food other than that prepared by members of their own faith and thus could not eat the food served in the army. [*100-135-7-9*]

International Reassemble of the Church of Freedom League, Incorporated

Ethelberth Anslem Broaster, a West Indian negro born at Belize, British Honduras, has resided in the United States for more than twenty years. He is registered under the provisions of the Alien Registration Act of 1940 but has not taken out citizenship papers. He preached in Philadelphia from 1934 to 1937 and in the latter year promoted the International Reassemble of the Church of Freedom League, Incorporated, at New Orleans, Louisiana, which now has a membership of 257 including 243 men.

Broaster taught that the American negroes are the direct descendants of Abraham, Isaac and Jacob and are the true members of the Hebrew race. He insisted that it is against the beliefs of his organization for any of its members to engage in "expeditionary warfare", but claims none of them are conscientious objectors.

There is no indication of any direct Japanese contact with this organization but investigation has disclosed that Broaster, who terms himself as 'General Messenger' of this society, appeared before meetings of the Pacific Movement of the Eastern World at East St. Louis, Illinois, the Allah Temple of Islam, the Universal Negro Improvement Association, and the Colored American National Organization in July, 1941. He urged members of the Pacific Movement of the Eastern World who were interested in avoiding military service to see him privately or communicate with him through his New Orleans office. He also advocated that colored people should buy guns for their protection at home and which would prove helpful in carrying out some of the plans set out in "God's Plan".

Broaster also filled frequent lecture engagements before religious, fraternal and civic groups in New Orleans and the activities of his League were well publicized by New Orleans negro newspapers. Frank Alonzo Carlton, a member of the Communist Party indicated that the Communists were greatly perturbed over the activities of Broaster and feel that he is a paid Japanese agent. There is no indication that Broaster has engaged in any pro-Japanese activities other than his association with groups of pro-Japanese sympathy and his interference with the Selective Training and Service Act of 1940, which may not be construed as a definite illustration of Japanese activity or sympathy.

In July, 1941, Broaster promoted a unit of his league at Chicago, Illinois with Vernon B. Williams, Jr., as secretary and leader of the unit. Investigation is being conducted at this time relative to possible violations of the Selective Service Act by Williams and Chicago members. He is reported to have advised members of the League, who have previously been instructed not to report for induction, to fulfill their obligation under the Selective Service Act and to report for induction. He also has made the statement that "any members blood being shed on foreign soil will be required of the President of this country".

In connection with Broaster's instructions to obtain guns, it is interesting to note that at the time of the arrest of members of this League at New Orleans the majority of them were in possession of firearms. The New Orleans Police Department substantiated the purchase of firearms by negroes, possibly in preparation of a coming race war, by stating that eight to ten negroes sought permission each day to carry concealed weapons.

Broaster was sentenced to serve a total of fifteen years in a Federal Penitentiary by Federal Judge Caillouet in the United States District Court for the Eastern District of Louisiana on February 3, 1943, upon his conviction for conspiracy to violate the Selective Service Act and aiding and advising members of the League to evade service, the latter offense being in six counts. He was first sentenced to ten years imprisonment and placed on probation for five years, but upon his protest against the probationary term, Judge Caillouet changed the sentence to a total of fifteen years. Thirteen other officers and members of the League were convicted and sentenced at the same time. Roynell Lawson was sentenced to a term of one year and one day on each of the seven counts named in an indictment against him, such sentences to run consecutively. Other members received suspended sentences and were placed on probation for five years each. At the same time three members of the League were sentenced to terms varying from three to nine months for failure to report for induction, the sentences to run consecutively with those imposed upon members who were convicted for conspiracy.

The sentence imposed upon Broaster is one of the heaviest ever given under the Selective Training and Service Act of 1940. Sentences totaling twenty-two years and seven days in the Federal Penitentiary, 291 months and one day in suspended sentences, and sixty years probation were imposed against the officers and directors of the League for conspiracy and for aiding and advising members of the League to evade the provisions of the Selective Service Act. In addition four of the defendants were sentenced to serve a total of eighteen months in a Federal Penitentiary for failure to report for induction, the sentences to run consecutively with those previously imposed upon the members for conspiracy. One defendant was convicted of all seven counts of the indictment but sentence was not imposed as the Judge believed him to be feeble minded.

Miscellaneous Organizations

A number of organizations composed of colored people and colored persons as individuals have been reported to be pro-Japanese in attitude and sympathy or at least interfering with the internal security of the country by causing racial unrest and racial disturbances. It appears that the anti-white attitude of these persons and organizations, ostensibly developed by racial discriminations, has brought about expressions of sympathy for the Japanese on the premise that a Japanese victory will 'liberate' the negroes, a kindred colored people. Some of these groups exist in name only, some are very limited in membership and influence and others, which at first seem to be distinct groups, merely represent a succession of different names used by loosely organized societies with much internal friction. Some of these groups are the Ahamadiya Religious Movement at Baltimore which is reported to practice rituals similar to those of the Moorish Science Temple of America and may be a part, or at least an off-shoot of that organization; the Afro-American Benevolent Improvement Association and the March Toward Liberty of the Black Man in America at Detroit, Michigan; Environment at East St. Louis, Illinois; the Liberian American League at Chicago and the National Congress of Afro American People and its affiliate, the Afro-American National Infantry at Atlanta, Georgia. These groups are presently under investigation.

VI

THE COMMUNIST PARTY AND NEGROES

The Communist Party's activities among the Negroes in this country and in Negro organizations is another phase of the united front policy of the Party. To understand the aims of the Party in such work, the directives and resolutions of the Communist International must necessarily be referred to, so that all aspects may be brought to the surface. It is believed that the fundamental premise in the Communist Party theory of its work among the Negroes is the resolution with regard to the colonial question and "oppressed nationalities" as set forth at various times in resolutions or directives of the various World Congresses' and Executive Committees' meetings of the Third (Communist) International.

Along with information relative to the Party's activities among and allegedly for the Negroes in this country there will be set out in this subdivision directives and resolutions not only of the Communist Party in this country but of its international affiliate, the Third (Communist) International, or the Comintern.

The Second Congress of the Communist International set forth twenty-one points which were adopted as the rules or conditions for the various Communist Parties throughout the world to join the Communist International. Attention is drawn to Point #21 which stated, "Those members of the Party who reject the conditions and the theses of the Third International are liable to be excluded from the Party."

Point #8 stated with regard to this matter:

> "In the colonial question and that of the oppressed nationalities there is a necessary and especially distinct and clear line of conduct of the Parties of countries where the bourgeoisie possesses such colonies or oppresses other nationalities. Every party desirous of belonging to the Third International should be bound to denounce without any reserve all the methods of 'its own' Imperialists in the colonies, supporting not only in words but practically a movement of liberation in the colonies. It should demand the expulsion of its own Imperialists from such colonies and oppressed nationalities, and carry on a systematic agitation in its own army against every kind of oppression of the colonial population". (Theses and Statutes of the Third (Communist) International, pp. 27–32—adopted by the Second Congress 7/17–8/7/1920)

To list completely and extensively all directives and resolutions is not deemed necessary, however, those important and pertinent parts thereof will be set forth as taken from the policy making directives and resolutions which have been issued and adopted since 1920.

The colonial question was again dealt with at the Sixth World Congress of the Communist International held in 1928. It involved the subject of the revolutionary movement in the "colonies". As part of the thesis on this subject the Negro question in the United States was dealt with. Pertinent parts as reflecting the Party's policy with respect to the Negroes in the United States will be set out hereinafter:

> "In connection with the Colonial question, the Sixth Congress draws the close attention of the Communist Parties to the Negro question. The position of the Negroes varies in different countries and accordingly requires concrete investigation and analysis. . . ."

Among the countries dealt with were:

> "The United States and some South American countries, in which the compact Negro masses constitute a minority in relation to the white population".

The Communist International felt that:

> ". . . the Growth of the Negro proletariat is the most important phenomenon of recent years. At the same time there arises in the Negro quarters—the Negro ghetto—a petty bourgeoisie, from which is derived a stratem of intellectuals and a thin stratem of bourgeoisie, the latter acting as the agent of imperialism."

The section of the thesis concerning the Negro question continues:

> "One of the most important tasks of the Communist Party consists in the struggle for a complete and real equality of the Negroes, for the abolition of all kinds of racial, social and political inequalities. It is the duty of the Communist Party to carry on the most energetic struggle against any exhibition of white chauvinism, to organize active resistance against lynching, to strengthen its work among Negro, proletarians, to draw into its ranks the most conscious element of the Negro workers, to fight for the acceptance of Negro workers in all organizations of white workers, and especially in trade unions (which does not include, if necessary, their organization into separate trade unions), to organize the masses of peasants and agricultural workers in the South, to carry on work among the Negro petty bourgeoisie tendencies such as "Garveyism" and to carry on a struggle against the influence of such tendencies in the working class and peasantry. In those regions of the South in which compact Negro masses are living, it is essential to put forward the slogan of the "Right of Self-Determination for Negroes". A radical transformation of the agrarian structure of the Southern States is one of the basic tasks of the revolution. Negro Communists must explain to non-Negro workers and peasants that only their close union with the white proletariat and joint struggle with them against the American bourgeoisie can lead to their liberation from barbarous exploitation and that only the victorious proletarian revolution will completely and permanently solve the agrarian and national questions of the Southern United States in the interests of the overwhelming majority of the Negro population of the country."

It can be thus seen that the Third (Communist) International regarded the Negro population in the United States and the manner in which it is to be dealt with as part of the revolutionary work to be done in various colonies. The colonial sections of the world have been referred to in explaining sections of the thesis on the colonial question as "an unquenchable blazing furnace of the revolutionary mass movement". It has been said further in this regard that:

"The revolutionary emancipatory movements of the colonies and semi-colonies more and more rally around the banner of the Soviet Union, convincing themselves by bitter experience that there is no salvation for them except through alliance with the revolutionary proletariat, and through the victory of the world proletarian revolution over world imperialism."

It was said further that:

"In this struggle every conflict between two imperialistic states and war of the imperialists against the U.S.S.R. must be utilized in colonies for the mobilization of the masses and for drawing them into a decisive struggle against imperialism for national emancipation and for the victory of the workers and the peasants."

[Ref: pp. 56 & 57, pp. 1–9, of Booklet entitled "The Revolutionary Movement in the Colonies" as containing a thesis adopted by Sixth World Congress of Third (Communist) International 1928 published by Workers Library Pub. Co. 35 E. 125th St. NYC]

In 1929, when the Sixth Convention of the Communist Party of the United States of America was held, a letter was directed by the Executive Committee of the Communist International to the Convention and several criticisms and suggestions were made with reference to Party work in America. One of the criticisms dealt with the Party's work among the Negroes in this country. It was stated:

". . . it has as yet done little to shift its base from the immigrants to the native Americans employed in the basic industries. It has done still less in relation to the millions of the Negro proletariat."

With reference to suggestions from the Executive Committee of the Communist International it was stated that:

"Your principal conditions are now essential in order that the Party may definitely enter the path leading to its transformation into a mass Communist Party, four conditions, the decisive significance of which neither the majority, which is responsible for the leadership nor the minority have understood."

Among the conditions listed was:

"(3) Freeing the Party from its immigrant narrowness and seclusion and making the American workers its wide basis, paying due attention to work among the Negro."

Among the decisions of the Central Committee of the Communist Party of the United States of America on the address of the Communist International which were made on Saturday, May 18, 1929, it was stated in #5 of the decision:

> "The Central Committee instructs the Secretariat to proceed immediately, in agreement with the Executive Committee of the Communist International, to take all measures necessary to put into application the decisions and to realize the objectives of the Comintern as expressed in the Address."

In apparent answer to the criticisms and suggestions, there was among the decisions of the Central Committee of the Communist Party of the United States of America the following decision (#5):

> "The Central Committee approves all decisions of the Secretariat of the same date, excepting in ordering immediate publication in the entire Party press of the Address of the ECCI to the American Party membership and instructs the Secretariat to put these decisions into effect immediately."

Early in 1929, an address containing instructions was made by the Executive Committee of the Communist International "To All Members of the Communist Party of the United States". Regarding the Negro situation, instructions were additionally issued to the Communist Party of the United States that it:

> ". . . must widen its agitational and organizational work in the big plants, in the main branches of industry and *among the Negroes*, and must secure for the Party an independent leading role in the industrial struggles of the working class that are developed, organizing in the process of the struggle the unorganized workers".
>
> [*Ref. pp. 44, 45, 46, 21, 22 of pamphlet "On the Road to Bolshevization" published and printed in U.S., 1st edition August 1, 1929, by Workers Library Publishers, Inc., New York City.*]

In 1930 at the Seventh National Convention of the Communist Party of the United States of America the Negro question was again dealt with and a resolution with regard to work by the Party among the Negro masses was adopted. The pertinent part of this resolution (#26) will be set out in view of its character and in view of its indication of the struggle by the Communist Party to overthrow the Government of the United States by force and violence:

> "The building and the work of the party cannot be effective without a serious change in its attitude and practices in regard to the work among the Negro masses and the transformation of passivity and underestimation to active defense and leadership of the struggles of the Negro masses. The Party must be made to express in energetic action, its consciousness that revolutionary struggle of the American workers for power is impossible without revolutionary unity of the Negro and white proletariat. To achieve this unity and to win for Communist

leadership also the masses of Negro workers, the Party must root out all traces of a formal approach to Negro work. The Party program for Negro work must become a living guide for the widest activity among the Negro and white masses and participation in the struggles of the Negro masses.

"The influence of white chauvinism is still felt in the Party and has recently manifested itself in St. Louis (opposition in the fraction to a correct Bolshevik line on Negro work); Detroit (opportunist reluctance in fraction to struggle against white chauvinism); Chicago, (Lithuanian fraction). In many instances there has been opportunist failure to expose such manifestations. Also, wrong, however, is the tendency, displayed by some Negro comrades (which they have since corrected more or less completely) to surrender to the propaganda of the Negro bourgeoisie and petty bourgeois intellectuals of race-hatred directed against all whites without distinction of class."

(It is noted in the foregoing paragraph that in the machinations of the Party itself there appeared to have been racial differences).

"Protest against the special oppression to which Negroes are subjected, must take the form of intensive political campaigns, and mass organizations to fight against lynching . . . the Party must carry on an uncompromising political struggle against all discriminatory laws, such as laws legalizing disfranchisement, segregation, laws against intermarriage, etc."

Resolution #27 also dealt with the Negroes in the United States, especially in connection with the "slogan of self-determination":

"The Party must organize a most intensive struggle around the demand of social and political equality for Negroes, which is still the main demand of our Party in its work among Negroes. At the same time the Party must openly and unreservedly fight for the right of Negroes for national self-determination in the South, where Negroes comprise a majority of the population. Self-determination for the Negro masses is the logical continuation and highest expression of the struggle for equal rights (social equality). As the Negro liberation movement develops, it will, in the territories and states with the majority of Negro population, take more and more the form of a struggle against the rule of the white bourgeoisie, for self-determination. Therefore, in its every day struggles for the concrete issues of social equality, against lynching, against all race discriminatory laws, the Party must systematically advance the demand for the right of the Negroes for self-determination. The demand must be popularized among the working masses of the whole country to win these workers for the support of the struggle of Negroes."

Another resolution (#28) dealt with the method, plan of attack, and technique in working among the Negroes:

"Special propaganda must be carried on among the Negro masses on the question of imperialist war, making full use of the victimization of the Negro masses both in the colonies and in the United States by the imperialist war makers who only plunge the Negro masses deeper into slavery.

"Unless our Negro program is concretized and energetically pushed, the work of our Party in winning the majority of the working class will be fruitless in the North as well as in the South."

The Party's proposed tactics in the South were set out in a subsequent resolution (#29):

"The industrialization of the South, the proletarianization of new masses under conditions of the most intense exploitation, turns the South into an ever more important battle field of the class struggle in America. This field becomes doubly important because Negro oppression here reaches its most violent and extreme forms, with its widest ramifications embracing both industry and agriculture. Southern white ruling class terrorism, directed against both white and Negro workers, assumes particularly vicious forms against the Negroes . . . the Communist International has correctly pointed out that the Negro masses in the rural districts of the South are not 'reserved of capitalist reaction' as conceived by Lovestone and Pepper, but potential allies of the revolutionary proletariat.

"Our Party cannot function in the increasingly frequent mass battles of the workers of the South without being rooted in the working class there. The problem of Communist leadership . . . therefore, is the problem of building our Party in the South, of building it in those struggles and of putting into living practice a truly Bolshevik line in regard to the Negro question.

". . . not less than half of the personnel of the leading functionaries in the South shall be Negro workers. Systematic preparation of this campaign shall insure the best possible use of these forces. . . ."

With further reference to the South, it was resolved at the Seventh National Convention of the Communist Party that:

"Our struggle for the defense of the Soviet Union and against the imperialist war danger must take on more of a popular character since the Southern bourgeoisie and the petty bourgeoisie are the most vicious and ardent supporters of patriotism, militarism and imperialism. Socialist construction in the Soviet Union must be contrasted with the terrible conditions of the Southern masses. . . ."

[Ref. pp. 24, 25, 26, 27, 54–63, pamphlet entitled "Theses and Resolutions of Seventh Nat. Convention of Communist Party of U.S.A." by Central Committee Plenum—Mar. 31 to April 4, 1930, published by Workers Library Publ. Inc. NYC]

Perhaps the most important directive to the Communist Party of the United States issued by the Communist International with regard to the instant matter was set forth in a resolution adopted by the Executive Committee of the Third (Communist) International in October, 1930. It is believed that the policy set down in this resolution with regard to the Party's handling of the Negro question in this country is still in effect and evidences of its being followed are constantly being reported. The resolution appeared not only in the official organ of the Communist International, "The Communist International", which was published bimonthly by Workers Library Publishers, Inc., 35 East 125th Street, New York City (pages 65–74, February, 1931 issue), but also in the official organ of the Communist Party, "The Communist" for February 1931 (pages 153–167).

There are being set out hereinafter excerpts from this resolution which is the underlying theory of the program of the Communist Party in its activities among the Negroes in the United States:

1. "The Communist Party of the United States has already acted openly and energetically against Negro oppression, and has thereby won increasing sympathy among the Negro population. . . .

"In the interest of the utmost clarity of ideas on this question, the Negro question in the United States must be viewed from the standpoint of its peculiarity, namely as the question of an oppressed nation, which is in a peculiar and extraordinarily distressing situation of a national oppression, not only in view of the prominent racial distinction, (marked difference in the color of skin, etc.), but above all because of considerable social antagonism (remnants of slavery) . . . furthermore, it is necessary to face clearly the inevitable distinction between the position of the Negro in the South and in the North, owing to the fact that at least three-fourths of the entire Negro population of the United States (12,000,000) live in compact masses in the South, most of them being peasants and agricultural laborers in a state of semi-serfdom, federaled in the "Black Belt" and constituting the majority of the population, whereas the Negroes in the Northern states, are for the most part industrial workers of the lowest categories who have recently come to the various industrial centers from the South (having often even fled from there).

"The struggle of the Communists for equal rights of the Negroes, applies to all Negroes, in the North as well as in the South. The struggle for this slogan embraces all or almost all of the important special interests of the Negroes in the North, but not in the South, where the main Communist slogan must be: The Right of Self-Determination of the Negroes in the Black Belt. . . .

I. "The Struggle for the Equal Rights of the Negroes

2. "The basis for the demand of equality of the Negroes is provided by the special yoke to which the Negroes of the United States are subjected by the ruling classes . . . this is partly due to the historical past of the American Negroes as imported slaves, but is much more due to the still existing slavery of the American Negro which is immediately apparent, for example, in comparing their situation even with the situation of the Chinese and Japanese workers in the West of the United States, or with the lot of the Filipinos (Malay race) who are under the colonial repression.

". . . all through the South, the Negroes are not only deprived of all rights, and subjected to the arbitrary will of the white exploiters, but they are also socially ostracized, that is, they are treated in general, not as human beings, but as cattle . . . everywhere the American bourgeoisie surrounds the Negroes with an atmosphere of social ostracism.

"The 100 per cent Yankee arrogance divides the American population into a series of castes, among which the Negroes constitute, so to speak, the caste of 'Untouchables', who are in a still lower category than the lowest categories of human society, the immigrant laborers, the yellow immigrants, and the Indians. . . . Negroes have to live in special segregated ghettoes (and, of course, have to pay extremely high rent). . . marriage between Negroes and whites is prohibited . . . as wage earners, the Negroes are forced to perform the lowest and most difficult work; . . . many American Federation of Labor trade unions do not admit Negro workers. . . .

". . . the origin of all this is not difficult to find: This Yankee arrogance towards the Negroes stinks of the disgusting atmosphere of the old slave market. . . .

3. "The demand for equal rights in our sense of the word, means not only demanding the same rights for the Negroes as the whites have in the United States at the present time, but also demanding that the Negroes should be granted all rights and other advantages which we demand for the corresponding oppressed classes of whites, (workers and other toilers) . . . this is to be obtained by constant struggle by the white and black workers for effective legal protection for the Negroes in all fields, as well as actual enforcement of their equality and combating of every expansion of Negrophobia. . . .

"The struggle for the equal rights of the Negroes does not in any way exclude recognition and support for the Negroes' rights to their own special schools, government organs, etc., wherever the Negro masses put forward such national demands of their own accord . . . the broad masses of the Negro population in the big industrial centers of the North are, however, making no efforts whatsoever to maintain and cultivate a national aloofness, they are, on the contrary, working for assimilation. This effort of the Negro masses can do much in the future to facilitate the progressive forces of amalgamating the whites and Negroes into one nation, and it is under no circumstances the tasks of the Communists to give support to the bourgeois nationalism in its fight with the progressive assimilation tendencies of the Negro working masses.

4. ". . . the struggle for equal right for the Negroes is, in fact, one of the most important parts of the proletarian class struggle of the United States. . . .

* * * * *

"The increasing unity of the various working class elements provokes constant attempts on the part of the American bourgeoisie to play one group against another, particularly the white workers against the black, and the black workers against the immigrant workers, and vice versa, and thus to promote the divisions within the working-class, which contribute to the bolstering up of the American capitalist rule. The Party must carry on a ruthless struggle against all these attempts of the bourgeoisie and do everything to strengthen the bond of class solidarity of the working-class upon a lasting basis.

"In the struggle for equal rights for the Negroes, however, it is the duty of the white workers to march at the head of this struggle . . . they, the white workers, must boldly jump at the throat of the 100 per cent bandits who strike a Negro in the face. This struggle will be the test of the real international solidarity of the American white workers.

"It is the special duty of the revolutionary Negro workers to carry on tireless activity among the Negro working masses to free them of their distrust of the white proletariat and draw them into the common front of the revolutionary class struggle against bourgeoisie. . . .

"Furthermore, the Communist Party must resist all tendencies within its own ranks to ignore the Negro question as a national question in the United States, not only in the South but also in the North. It is advisable for the Communist Party in the North to abstain from the establishment of any special Negro organization, and in place of it to bring the black and white workers together in common organizations of struggle and joint action. . . .

II. "The Struggle for the Right of Self-Determination of the Negroes in the Black Belt

5. "It is not correct to consider the Negro zone in the South as a colony of the United States . . . on the one hand, the Black Belt is not in itself, either economically or politically such a united whole as to warrant its being called a special colony of the United States, but on the other hand this zone is not, either economically or politically, such an integral part of the whole United States as any other part of the country. . . .

6. "Owing to the peculiar situation in the Black Belt (the fact that the majority of the resident Negro population are farmers and agricultural laborers and that the capitalist economic system as well as political class rule there is not only of a special kind, but to a great extent still has pre-capitalist and semi-colonial features), the right of self-determination of the Negroes as the main slogan of the Communist Party in the Black Belt is appropriate. This, however, does not in any way mean that the struggle for equal rights of the Negroes in the Black Belt is less necessary o[r] less well founded than it is in the North. . . .

"The slogan of the right of self-determination occupies the central place in the liberation struggle of the Negro population in the Black Belt against the yoke of American imperialism. But this slogan, as we see it, must be carried out only in connection with two other basic demands. . . .

(a) "*Confiscation of the land and property of the white landowners and capitalists for the benefit of the Negro farmer.* . . without this revolutionary measure, without the agrarian revolution, the right of self-determination of the Negro population would be only a Utopia, or, at best, would remain only on paper without changing in any way the actual enslavement.

(b) "*Establishment of the state unity of the Black Belt*. . . if the right of self-determination of the Negroes is to be put into force, it is necessary wherever possible to bring together into one governmental unit all districts of the South where the majority of the settled population consists of Negroes. Within the limits of this state there will of course remain a fairly significant white minority which must submit to the right of self-determination of the Negro majority . . . every plan regarding the establishment of the Negro state with an exclusively Negro population in America (and, of course, still more exporting it to Africa) is nothing but an unreal and reactionary caricature of the fulfillment of the right of self-determination of the Negroes. . . .

(c) "*Right of self-determination*. This means complete and unlimited right of the Negro majority to exercise governmental authority in the entire territory of the Black Belt as well as to decide upon the relations between their territory and other nations, particularly the United States . . . first of all, true right to self-determination means that the Negro majority and not the white minority in the entire territory of the administratively united Black Belt exercises the right of administrating governmental, legislative, and judicial authority . . . therefore, the overthrow of this class rule in the Black Belt is unconditionally necessary in the struggle for the Negroes' right to self-determination. This, however, means at the same time the overthrow of the yoke of American Imperialism in the Black Belt on which the forces of the white bourgeoisie depend. . . .

7. ". . . even if the situation does not yet warrant the raising of the question of uprising, one should not limit oneself at present, to propaganda for the demands: 'Right to Self-Determination', but should organize mass actions such as demonstration[s], strikes, tax boycott movements, etc.

". . . it goes without saying that the Communists in the Black Belt will, and must try to win over all working elements of the Negroes, that is, the majority of the population, to their side and to convince them not only that they must win the right of self-determination, but also that they must make use of this right in accordance with the Communist program. . . .

8. ". . . . Complete right to self-determination includes also the right to governmental separation, but does not necessarily imply that the Negro population should make use of this right under all circumstances, that is, that it must actually separate or attempt to separate the Black Belt from the existing governmental federation with the United States. . . .

". . . . If the proletariat has come into power in the United States, the Communist Negroes will not come out for but against separation of the Negro Republic from Federation with the United States. But the right of the Negroes to governmental separation will be unconditionally realized by the Communist Party, it will unconditionally give the Negro population of the Black Belt freedom of choice even on this question. Only when the proletariat has come into power in the United States the Communists will carry on propaganda among the working masses of the Negro population against separation, in order to convince them that it is much better and in the interest of the Negro nation for the Black Belt to be a free republic, where the Negro majority has complete right of self-determination but remains governmentally federated with the great proletarian republic of the United States. . . .

". . . . At the present time, however, the situation in the national struggle in the South is not such as to win mass support of the working Negroes for this separatist struggle; and it is not the task of the Communists to call upon them to separate, without taking into consideration the existing situation of the desires of the Negro masses.

". . . . In this sharpening of the situation in the South, Negro separatism will presumably increase, and the question of the independence of the Black Belt will become the question of the day. Then the Communist Party must also face this question and, if the circumstances seem favorable, must stand up with all strength and courage for the struggle to win independence and for the establishment of a Negro republic in the Black Belt.

9. "The general relation of the Communists to separatist tendencies among the Negroes, described above, cannot mean that the Communists associate themselves at present, or generally speaking, during capitalism, indiscriminately and without criticism with all the separatist currents of the various bourgeois or petty bourgeois Negro group. . . .

". . . . The question of power is decided not only through the demand of separation, but just as much through the demand of the right to decide the separation question and self-determination in general. . . .

". . . . One cannot deny that it is just possible for the Negro population of the Black Belt to win the right to self-determination during capitalism; but it is perfectly clear and indubitable that this is possible only through successful revolutionary struggle for power against the American bourgeoisie, through wresting the Negroes' right to self-determination from the American imperialism. . . .

10. "The slogan for the right of self-determination and the other fundamental slogans of the Negro question in the Black Belt does not exclude but rather pre-supposes an energetic development of the struggle for concrete partial demands linked up with the daily needs and afflictions of wide masses of working Negroes. . . . Communists must above all remember this:

(a) "The direct aims and partial demands around which a partial struggle develops are to be linked up in the course of the struggle with the revolutionary fundamental slogans brought up by the question of power, in a popular manner corresponding to the mood of the masses. . . . .

(b) ". . . Every kind of national oppression which arouses the indignation of the Negro masses can be used as a suitable point of departure for the development of partial struggles, during which the abolition of such oppressions, as well as their prevention through revolutionary struggle against the ruling exploiting dictatorship must be demanded.

(c) "Everything should be done to bring wide masses of Negroes into these partial struggles. This is important—and not to carry the various partial demands to such an ultra-radical point that the mass of working Negroes are no longer able to recognize them as their own. . . .

(d) ". . . . Negro Communists must clearly dissociate themselves from all bourgeois currents in the Negro movement, must indefatigably oppose the spread of the influence of the bourgeois groups on the working Negroes. In dealing with them they must apply the Communist tactic laid down by the 6th C. I. (Communist International) Congress with regard to the Colonial Question, in order to guarantee the hegemony of the Negro proletariat in the national liberation movement of the Negro population, and to coordinate wide masses of the Negro peasantry in a steady fighting alliance with the proletariat.

(3) "One must work with the utmost energy for the establishment and consolidation of Communist Party organizations and revolutionary trade unions in the South. . . .

11. "It is particularly incumbent on Negro Communists to criticize consistently the half-heartedness and hesitation of the petty bourgeois national-revolutionary Negro leaders in the liberation struggle of the Black Belt, exposing them before the masses . . . their constant call to the Negro masses must be: *Revolutionary struggle against the ruling white bourgeoisie, through a fighting alliance with the revolutionary white proletariat.* . . . But it is also clear that 'only a victorious proletarian revolution will finally decide the agrarian question and the national question in the South of the United States, in the interest of the predominating mass of the Negro population of the country' (Colonial Theses of the Sixth World Congress).

12. "The struggle regarding the Negro question in the North must be linked up with the liberation struggle of the South, in order to endow the Negro movement throughout the United States with the necessary effective strength. . . . The Communist Party of the United States must bring into play its entire revolutionary energy in order to mobilize the widest possible masses of the white and black proletariat of the United States, not by words, but by deeds, for real effective support of the struggle for the liberation of the Negroes. . . . The more American imperialism fastens its yoke on the millions-strong Negro masses, the more must the Communist Party develop the mass struggle for Negro emancipation, and the better use it must make of all conflicts which arise out of the national differences, [as] an incentive for revolutionary mass action against the bourgeoisie. This is as much in the direct interest of the proletarian revolution in America . . . whether the rebellion of the Negroes is to be the outcome of a general revolutionary situation in the United States, whether it is to originate in the whirlpool of decisive fights for power by the working class, for proletarian dictatorship, or whether on the contrary the Negro rebellion will be the prelude of gigantic struggles for power by the American proletariat, cannot be foretold now. But in either contingency, it is essential for the Communist Party to make an energetic beginning now at the present moment with the organization of joint mass struggles of white and black workers against Negro oppression. This alone will enable us to get rid of the bourgeois white chauvinism, which is polluting the ranks of the white workers of

America, to overcome the distress of the Negro masses caused by the inhuman barbarous Negro slave traffic still carried on by the American bourgeoisie—inasmuch as it is directed even against all white workers—and to win over to our side these millions of Negroes as active fellow-fighters in the struggle for the overthrow of bourgeois power throughout America."

[Ref. p 65 thru 74 of the Communist International for February, 1931]

As positive indication that the directives of the October 1930 Resolution on the Negro question by the Executive Committee of the Communist International are still being followed, it has been reported that any course taught by Pettis Perry, Negro Communist Party functionary in Los Angeles, California, in the Los Angeles Workers School deals with the Negro question. In the outline of this course on Page 10 there is contained Lesson 4 which is entitled "The Negro Question as a National Question: The Struggle for the Right of Self-Determination for the Black Belt". In this lesson there is discussed the characteristics of the "Black Belt" and the right of self-determination in direct harmony with the directives laid down in the above-mentioned resolution of the Executive Committee of the Communist International. Furthermore, at the end of this lesson there is set forth suggested reading. Article No. 3 as stated on page 14 where Lesson 4 ends is the "Resolution of the Communist International, October 1930", its source being designated as "The Communist", February 1931. Additional suggested reading which in turn refers to the Resolution of the Communist International is said to be in Harry Haywood's article entitled "The Theoretical Defenders of White Chauvinism in the Labor Movement" as appearing in "The Communist", June 1931. In his article Haywood, who, of course, has been a Communist Party member, makes reference to the program of the Communist International on "the Negro Question". Haywood states with regard to this:

"The correctness of the program of the Communist International on the Negro Question is conclusively proven in the present crisis by the response of the Negro masses to the slogans of the Party, and by their increasing participation together with the white workers in joint struggles against the capitalist offensive."

The article then goes on to deal with an attack made on the Resolution of the Communist International by one Will Herberg in the publication "The Revolutionary Age" which was the official organ of the "Lovestoneites".

[100-135-27-2, p. 6 ("The Communist" June 1931)]

In a draft resolution for the Eighth Convention of the Communist Party of the United States of America, 1934, a section was devoted to "The Role of the Negro Reformist". It was stated:

"Among the Negro masses, the Negro reformists are being revealed more and more as the chief social support of imperialist reaction, ([N]. A. A. C. P., White, Pickens, DuBois etc.) They have supported the Roosevelt New Deal as a "New Deal" for the Negroes. They carried through treacherous actions in

> connection with the Scottsboro Campaign and sabotaged the mass movement of the Negroes against the Scottsboro verdict.
>
> "Because of the radicalization of the Negro masses the ever growing readiness of the Negroes to struggle, the revolutionary energy developed among the Negro masses, and the growing unity of the white and Negro workers, there are cropping up all kinds of petty-bourgeois nationalist movement[s]. . . ."

With further reference to the Negro, it was stated in the rough draft resolution with regard to Party work:

> "It must expose chauvinist propaganda, and spread the ideas of solidarity and unity of Negro and white, of native and foreign born, and proletarian internationalism, fighting for equal rights for Negro and foreign born, for the right of self-determination of the Negro people and the black race. . . ."

The draft resolution for the Eighth Convention of the Communist Party, United States of America contained a section with reference to "Struggle for Negro Rights and Self-Determination". It was stated:

> ". . . . The Party must recruit Negroes into the Party in revolutionary mass organizations, and promote Negro padres. . . . The Party must build the L. S. N. R. (League of Struggles for Negro Rights) as the mass organization around the Party program on the Negro question, organize a struggle of the Negro tenant Farmers and sharecroppers in the South.
>
> "The strengthening of our Party among the Negro proletariat, the winning of a strong proletarian base for leadership in the liberation movement, as a whole, becomes a condition for the further extension of our work among the Negro masses.
>
> "The situation among the Negroes brings to the fore as an urgent task, the preparation and organization of national rebellion of the Negro people as an integral part of the tasks of the preparation of the working class for the struggle for power. . . ."
>
> [*Ref. 13th Plenum of E.C.C.I. also draft resolution Eighth Convention Communist Party, USA, pub. by Workers Library Publishers, 58-13th St. NYC, March 1934*]

In 1935, James W. Ford, one of the foremost Negro Communist Party leaders who is extremely and importantly active in work among the Negroes, stated:

> "There is no question about the outcome of our united front activities among Negro organizations, providing the Communists and the advanced Negro workers and intellectuals undertake their work seriously."

With reference to church organization, he states:

> "The church represents a fertile field for work as an institution that has a solid contact with the Negro masses, forming a social as well as a religious center. Long

before there were social clubs, meeting halls or fraternal halls the church served their purposes. Marriages, baptisms, funerals, dramas, amusement, religion, all the features of Negro social activities were bound up in the church."

[*Ref. article entitled "The United Front in the Field of Negro Work" by James W. Ford, appearing Feb. 1935 issue Communist*]

At the Ninth Convention of the Communist Party, in 1936, a resolution based on the report of Earl Browder, General Secretary of the Communist Party, was passed concerning "The Struggle Against Reaction, Fascism, and War". With reference to the Negroes, it was stated in this resolution:

"The central task in promoting the unity of action of the Negro people remains the policy of bringing about a United Negro Peoples Front as initiated by the Negro Congress. The success of this movement demands more intensive mass mobilization for daily struggles against Negro discrimination (in unions, jobs, relief, education, etc.), against lynching and for equal rights. The main practical tasks are to build a Negro Congress, to promote the organizations of the Negro workers in the unions, to improve our work in the South and develop the Negro leading personnel."

[*Ref. pamphlet entitled "Resolution 9th Convention of the CP, p. 25 published 1936 by Workers Library Publishers.*]

Speaking before the Tenth National Convention of the Communist Party of the United States of America on May 28, 1938, at Carnegie Hall, New York City, Earl Browder, General Secretary of the Party, dealt with "The Negro Liberation Movement":

". . . . For many years we labored, giving our utmost cooperation for the most advanced Negroes in their efforts to arouse a new liberation movement among them, giving our energies to winning the white workers and democratic masses to alliance with the Negroes to fight for that equal citizenship so vital to white and black alike.

"At our ninth convention, we could note hopefully the foundation, a few months before of the National Negro Congress which assumed the task of gathering together such a liberation movement. Today, at our tenth convention, we can declare that the National Negro Congress is beginning to realize its task in a serious way. . . . It has formulated the demands of the Negro people in such clear but restrained form as to win the attention and respect of the broadest masses of the population.

"We must continue to give the National Negro Congress our heartiest support. We should help it to solve its organizational problems, of linking up closely together in practical cooperation all the multitude of organizations of the Negroes pressing evermore stubbornly among the general labor and democratic organizations the full recognition of the Negro and his problems as the condition for the advance of all.

"Recruitment of Negroes into our Party, and their training for leadership, have made some advances in the past two years, but we can by no means be satisfied with what we have accomplished. Constant attention to this question is necessary, constant self critical examination of our work, let the outstanding contribution to our Party of Comrade James Ford, be a constant reminder to everyone of us of the great resources waiting for our Party among the Negro masses. We have been called "The Negro Party" by our enemies in the South; we repeat again that we claim this title as a badge of honor but let us deserve it by serious recruitment of Negro members."

[*Rept to 10th Nat'l Convention CP of the USA on behalf of Central Committee by Earl Browder, Gen'l Secty, p. 72 & 73, pub. by Workers Library Publishers, NYC*]

In 1938, the Negro Commission of the National Committee of the Communist Party reasoned purportedly with regard to the Negroes in this country:

* * * * *

"Clearly the interests of the Negro people lies in the continuation and strengthening of this alliance (The alliance of Negroes and whites). It is for this reason that we must emphatically reject all ideas which tend to weaken this unity, all ideas which contend that the fight for Negro rights, i.e., for our full participation in American democracy, is something separate and apart from the sight of the whole American people for the preservation and extension of democratic freedom. This is why the fiction of Fascist Japan, as the champion of the darker races against a presumably solid white world, based as it is on the false conception of race against race, is so dangerous to the interests of our people. The supporters of this theory would direct our justified hatred of the white ruling class oppressors into channels of hatred of all whites; that is, they would separate us from our true allies and thus weaken our fight. Such doctrines can only play into the hands of our bitterest enemies.

". . . the tremendous cultural advances made by the liberated multi-colored nationality in the U.S.S.R. shatters the chauvinist theory of the 'inherent inferiority' of the darker people.

"Of a population of 175,000,000 people in the Soviet Union, more than one-fourth are dark skinned people. These peoples are today sharing the general prosperity and cultural advance that has been achieved under Socialism.

* * * * *

"The example of the Soviet Union in its abolition of race hatred, its successful solution of the question of national minorities through full equality in fraternity of people, points clearly the path which the Negro people and other oppressed peoples must follow in a successful struggle for their liberties. The main lesson of the Soviet Union for her people is the necessity of united action with other victims of Capitalism against the common enemy. In this country, it means the unity of

Negro and white toilers and all progressive forces in the democratic front against the Fascist-minded bankers of Wall Street, for jobs, security, democracy, and peace."

[*Pamphlet "Is Japan the Champion of the Colored Races?"; "The Negroes' Stake in Democracy." Issued by Negro Commission, Nat. Comm of the CP USA pub. Workers Lib. Pub. Inc., NYC, 8-1938*]

In the election platform of the Communist Party for 1940, one plank dealt with the Negro race in this country:

* * * * *

"3. Guarantee the Negro people complete equality, equal rights to jobs, equal pay for equal work, the full right to organize, serve on juries and hold public office. Pass the anti-lynching bill, demand the just penalty for lynchers. Enforce the 13th, 14th and 15th amendments to the United States Constitution.

* * * * *

The above platform plank has been taken from a pamphlet entitled "Election platform of the Communist Party", published by the Workers Library Publishers, August 1940, New York City, and which bore the pictures of Earl Browder who ran for president, and James Ford who ran for vice-president. It should be noted in this same pamphlet there were contained resolutions that demand to the effect that the war in 1940 was an imperialist war and that all steps should be taken to see that America did not aid or engage in the war.

With regard to the "Negro People and the New World Situation", James W. Ford (Negro), member of the National Committee of the Communist Party and three times Communist Party candidate for Vice-President of the United States in August, 1941 stated:

"This situation demands and places before us the following tasks for the immediate future:

"1. To work for greater collaboration between the Negro peoples' movement and the organized labor movement, because the fate of our country and that of the Negro people lies in the progressive organized labor movement that has the opportunity and ability to organize all the toilers for the defense of the best interests of our country and to help annihilate Fascism at home and abroad, and also for the defense of the special interests of the Negro people . . . the Negro people must work towards the fullest cooperation with the labor movement. The trade unions have a splendid chance to take bold, organized steps to abolish discrimination in industry and in the trade unions against Negroes.

"2. The threat of Fascism requires that the Negroes work to influence the foreign policy of the government, to the end that its action corresponds with the spoken words of Roosevelt of 'All possible aid' to the U.S.S.R., to encourage and support the President's policy of 'All possible aid to the Soviet Union' in order to defeat Hitler Fascism . . . the Negro people must fight against the unjust political persecution of Earl Browder.

"3. To work to unite all the forces and organizations of the Negro people. . . .

"4. We must work among the people in such a way as to achieve cooperation with all sincere and progressive people; we must avoid the danger of sectarianism, and find the way to all those elements in this changing International situation, who are inclined to go along in this struggle against Fascism reaction and to join with us and with the Progressive forces.

"5. We must fight against discrimination in the armed forces for the right of the Negroes to bear arms in defense of democracy on the basis of equality.

"6. The Communist Party must increase its efforts on behalf of the Negro people and win Negroes for the Communist Party. The reports of this National Committee meeting have been shown that in many sections in the district substantial gains have been made in recruiting Negroes, especially Negro industrial workers, into our Party in that great campaign in behalf of the freedom of Comrade Earl Browder, and I think the possibilities today are still greater for winning Negroes into the Communist Party.

* * * * *

"However, in this new period we must begin to develop more intensive ideological work among the Negroes, explaining to them the struggle against Fascism, explaining the policies of the Soviet Union, explaining Socialism and Communism.

"7. . . . our greatest attention should be given to winning the Negro proletariat into the trade unions and into the Communist Party.

"8. At the same time we must give great attention to the problems of the Negro middle class and intellectual elements, who bear in great measures the great cultural aspirations of the Negro people, and who play an important role in the struggle of the Negro people for democracy and for defense of the democratic institutions of our country.

"The attack on the Soviet Union opens up the possibility for the unity of forces on a world scale to wipe Fascism from the face of the earth, and develop a path of freedom and democracy for people throughout the world."

It is pointed out that James W. Ford in furthering the Communist Party Line prior to the German invasion of Russia protested strongly against such things as lend-lease aid to England, the Selective Service system, and urging non-interventionism on the part of the United States in the world conflict.

[*Ref. "The Negro People and the New World Situation", a pamphlet by James W. Ford publ. by Workers Library Publishers, Aug. 1941, NYC.*]

The 1942 Communist Party platform carried the following plank:

* * * * *

"Winning the war demands the fullest integration of all sections of the American people in the common war effort. This must be achieved by enforcing the Federal and New York State Constitutional guarantees and ending every form of discrimination—of the Negro people, and the Jewish people—the loyal foreign born people of our State, those naturalized and those not yet citizens.
[*Ref. Daily Worker, 8-30-42, p. 4. "Abridged Text of NY Communist Platform"—1942*]

* * * * *

In the Spring of 1943 the Communist Party devoted considerable effort to the distribution throughout the country where active Party units are located and likewise where heavier Negro populations were centered, of a pamphlet written by Benjamin Davis, Jr., Negro member of the National Committee of the Communist Party and writer for the Communist Daily Worker, entitled "The Negro People and the Communist Party." This pamphlet, which was published by the Workers Library, Publishers, in March 1943, has been distributed, according to reports, on a wide basis.

In view of such wide distribution it can be considered as being looked upon in a favorable light by the Communist Party, especially in its organizational and recruiting activities among Negroes. In effect it is an invitation for Negroes to join the Communist Party and purportedly an explanation of the Communist Party. It is introduced by a portion of the biography of the writer, particularly that period in which he became a member of the Communist Party. Thereafter in a section entitled "The Negro Stake in Victory," the writer sets forth how poorly the Negro population of this country would fare under Nazi or Japanese domination, as well as how unfruitful are the attempts of other political groups in this country to obtain added rights for Negroes. An eulogy to Russia is set forth, saying that it is the greatest champion for freedom and equality for all peoples, and it is stated that Russia's participation in the present war was one of the decisive factors in determining the character of the war as one for survival of national liberation. Thereafter in the pamphlet is a section entitled "The Soviet Union and the War" in which an additional eulogy is given to the Soviet Union as well as the necessity of close relations between Russia and the United States.

In the next section, which is entitled "Victory Will Help Smash Jim Crow," the theme is taken that through the successful prosecution of the war additional rights will be obtained for Negroes, yet in this prosecution there must be a constant fight for the abolition of discrimination and segregation. (This theme is to be distinguished from that taken by Negro organizations and groups which put forth the program that winning the war and winning added "equal rights" for Negroes are on a par.) Certain statements in this section are believed to be significant in that not only do they set forth the ostensible Communist Party line but they are familiar to those used in the directive of the Communist International of October, 1930, which has been set forth previously in this section:

"The urgency of military necessity requires that all treatment of the Negro people and the *Colonial people* [a]s 'inferior' and 'second class' human beings be promptly ended. . . . *The right to self determination* for India, for the Colonial peoples of Africa, the West Indies, Asia, Puerto Rico, and Latin America must be recognized in order to mobilize these peoples for a peoples' victory and a peoples' peace.

"In order to speed the tempo of ending Jim Crow it must be fought for actively by labor and the people. Total mobilization for winning the war can spell the death knell of the disgraceful Jim-Crow system.

"The Communist Party, equipped with the scientific teachings of Marx, Engels, Lenin and Stalin, is the only Party that has placed the elimination of all 'race supremacy' practices and theories as a pre-condition for swift victory.

* * * * *

"*The struggle for Negro rights* was always a matter of justice and the enforcement of the Constitution. Now this fight must be pursued relentlessly as a military necessity—as a matter of achieving victory at the earliest moment and at the least cost.

* * * * *

"We Communists fight against the Jim-Crow system as a part of the national effort to speed production and to speed all-out offensive—especially the opening of the second front against Hitler on the European Continent. . . ." (The reference to the "opening of the second front" brought in connection with the theme of this pamphlet is not the first instance this demand of the Party has been put forth in connection with its exploitation of the Negro population in this country. This has been done in numerous articles appearing in Communist publications and it is to be recalled that the charge, unsubstantiated by corroborative information, was made by Communists subsequent to the Detroit riots in June, 1943, when it was stated by Communist functionaries in Detroit that the riots had been prompted by fifth column forces as a hindrance to the war effort "on the eve of an invasion" of the mainland of Europe.)

A recent publicized statement of Earl Browder was given space in the Daily Worker, Communist news organ, for July 14, 1943. This statement, with regard to the Negro situation, was made in answer to the hypothetical question: "Does the Communist Party ever undertake to stir up racial and group antagonisms . . . ?" Browder, in his answer, is quoted as follows:

"No, that charge is a falsehood, complete and unconditional. There are no more relentless enemies of racial antagonism.

"Communists stir up racial antagonism by demanding equal rights for all, thereby provoking riots by those who would deny equal rights, then I can only say that the Communists stand upon the U.S. constitution in this respect, while our critics stand upon evasion or flouting of the Constitution. The Communists openly fight against anti-Semitism, anti-Negroism in the U.S. as evidence of Hitlerism which must be completely destroyed. If the question infers the old charge that Communists incite strike movements, that is absolutely the opposite of the truth in this wartime in which the Communists are restraining all strike action or trends among the workers. No matter how justified they might be in peace time, as for labor struggle in general, that is not a special issue of the Communists. The Communists work for the most complete national unity for the war, for unity among the United Nations, for victory and for the post-war reconstruction of the world, for the elimination of all artificial divisions among mankind—in short for the practical realization of the brotherhood of men."

[July 14, 1943 issue "Daily Worker"]

Instances of Exploitation

From time to time information has been received from confidential sources which reflects the Party's maneuvering among and exploitation of members of the Negro population in this country. These actions appear to controvert that which appears on the surface to be fostering the advancement of Negroes in this country by the Communist Party.

A digression should be made momentarily to information which has been received concerning the general broad program of the Communist Party in the United States in which all of the propositions point to a calculation of strengthening in the long run the world position of the Communist Party. Numerous examples have been quoted in which Party leaders in various districts of the Party are working day by day with the rank and file members of the Party and actively preaching revolution and preparing for revolutionary activity when the opportunity presents itself. *[Memo AG Apr. 1943]*

Along these lines a confidential informant who has been a Communist Party member and who is believed to be schooled in its technique, has commented as follows: The consensus of opinion among Party members is that no trouble will result from their efforts until after the war when Negro labor and employees hired during this war will be replaced by men returning from the armed forces. The Communist Party believes that after the war is over there will be at least a short period of unemployment, after which men returning from the armed forces will replace the newly trained workers, including Negroes, who will then be forced out on to a waiting list. Discontent will be the result. It is then that the Communist Party will be able to spread further seeds of discontent.

The foregoing reasoning was offered by this confidential source as an explanation for the Party's interest in supporting the Negro population along with the war effort by decrying alleged abuses or discrimination against Negroes and supporting social intercourse and the abolition of the suppression of races.

Another confidential informant, a Negro who was for many years a member of the Communist Party and reached important heights in this group, has made the following comments:

"However, there are certain conditions under which the Negro lives that tend to create grave dissatisfaction with the way democracy works. It is this dissatisfaction that Communists are using to spread among Negroes the seeds of lack of confidence in and disloyalty to American democracy."

(Referring to "Jim-Crow" laws): "The Communists are constantly exploiting this law in order to rally the Negro under their banner."

(Referring to the poll tax): "The Communists are utilizing this to stir up the Negroes. They are linking up the demand for the abolition of the poll tax with the 'right of the Negro of the land' and the establishment of an autonomous Negro government in the black belt."

"The recent lynchings of Negroes . . . have added fuel to the fire which is always being fanned by the Communists and other anti-American elements."

(Referring to crime in Harlem and its publication in white newspapers): "Here again the Communists react to this situation, attack the city administration, urge the people to protest and fight against police brutality and to fight against discrimination and for jobs."

"Communists are always alert and react quickly to each and every grievance of the Negroes and form some sort of committee to rally the people to struggle to eliminate the grievance. Their methods are devious. They form various front organizations, making use of prominent persons to attain their objectives, the Daily Worker, the Negro papers, and leaflets."

As a practical example of the foregoing, information has been received from two areas, namely, Detroit and Washington, wherein known Communists have sent Negroes, properly qualified, to various industrial places to seek employment with the intent that, jobs being denied these Negroes, the Party, through its various forces, would publicize the matter as discrimination. It is also known that Communist Party members have offered to "drum up" alleged cases of discrimination against Negro workers for the Fair Employment Practices Committee.

An additional example of the Party's machinations involving the Negro question is incorporated in the following information wherein it will be seen that the Party's participation in labor union matters was turned into an incident allegedly involving the racial question.

During the period of August 1 to August 5, 1942, a series of conferences were held in Room 514, Masonic Temple Building, Birmingham, Alabama. In attendance at these conferences were Robert F. Hall, Communist Party Chairman for District 17; John P. Davis, colored, a representative of the National Negro Congress, Washington, D.C.; Louis Burnham, colored, Executive Secretary of the Southern Negro Youth Congress; Mary Southard, Executive Secretary of the Young Communist League for District 17; Anne Mayfield, colored, Communist Party member; Mike Ross, a representative of the International Union of Mine, Mill and Smelter Workers of America,

CIO; and Bernard Borah, Southern Director of the National Council of Gas, Coke and Chemical Workers of America, CIO.

At the meeting held on August 1, 1942, Hall advised those in attendance that recently Ordway "Spike" Southard (white), husband of Mary Southard, had been attacked by a group of approximately 15 individuals while selling copies of the Daily Worker at a steel plant in Birmingham. Southard was injured severely. At the time, he was accompanied by Dorothy Burnham, colored, a Communist Party member, and an unknown white girl, also a Party member.

The issue of the Daily Worker sold by Southard carried a story about a racket being perpetrated upon the United Mine, Mill and Smelter Workers by John L. Lewis and those individuals in that union who favored Lewis' policies. It was stated that the information contained in the Daily Worker was furnished to the Party by one Mayfield, whom Hall described as a member of the Communist Party and a member of the United Mine, Mill and Smelter Workers.

During this meeting on August 1, 1942, Hall attacked Governor Dixon of Alabama and a Birmingham attorney, one Horace Wilkinson who is stated to be the controlling factor of the organization known as the League for White Supremacy and the Ku Klux Klan. Hall also brought up an incident wherein a brick was thrown into a house close to the residence of Ethel Goodman, a colored Communist, and that he believed this was an attempt to wreck her home.

Hall stated that the Communist Party should make every effort to publicize these attacks upon its members as attacks upon labor and the Negro race. He stated that he had flown to New York City on July 30, 1942, to take up the matter with members of the National Committee of the Party and that he talked it over with Robert Minor who expressed the opinion that since the rights of the Negroes were involved, it would be better for the Party to proceed through the Southern Negro Youth Congress.

At the meeting on August 1 Hall dictated the following telegram to Malcolm McLean, Chairman of the Fair Employment Practice[s] Committee, a similar one being forwarded to the Director:

> "This is to advise you that myself, Mike Ross, International Representative of our union, and several officers of our local unions have been threatened with violence and some physically assaulted because of activity of our organization in carrying through policies of President's Committee on Fair Employment Practice[s]. Ross and I have received threatening anonymous communications. We believe federal agencies should investigate and Government should prosecute those interfering with enforcement of federal war measures."

This telegram, it was noted, was signed by Alton Lawrence, Regional Coordinator of the United Mine, Mill and Smelter Workers, Birmingham, Alabama.

On August 2, 1942, another meeting was held at the same place, which is the office of the Southern Negro Youth Congress, and all persons attending the previous meeting attended this meeting. At this meeting, those present discussed possible ways of circulating material among "reactionaries," leaving no trace of Communist activity behind such material. Discussions at the meeting centered on alleged attacks and instances of discrimination against Negroes in Georgia, Mississippi, Tennessee and Virginia. Another letter was prepared then at the direction of Hall, denouncing the Governor of Alabama, which was forwarded to the President. Mention was also made in this letter to Horace Wilkinson, the Ku Klux Klan and generally the practice of discrimination against and segregation of Negroes in the South. This letter was signed by five [*sic*] individuals representing various unions in Alabama. They are:

Noel R. Beddow, CIO Regional Director, President Alabama CIO Council, Southern Director United States Steelworkers of America.

Bernard Borah, Southern Director National Council of Gas, Coke and Chemical Workers.

Van D. Jones, Executive Board Member, International Union of Mine, Mill and Smelter Workers.

Alton Lawrence, Coordinator of Organization, International Union of Mine, Mill and Smelter Workers.

Frank Allen, International Representative, International Union of Mine, Mill and Smelter Workers.

Leo Kendrick, Secretary, Red Ore Council, International Union of Mine, Mill and Smelter Workers.

During the meeting on August 2, 1942, Alton Lawrence advised that he had just contacted Ben Davis, Jr., Staff Member of the Daily Worker, New York City, in an attempt to have Davis come to Birmingham. Lawrence advised that Davis informed him that since he, Davis, is a known Communist, he would not be effective in operating with the Southern Negro Youth Congress.

After the meeting on August 2, 1942, Hall instructed Louis Burnham, colored, Communist Party member, to go to Tuskegee, Alabama, to see Dr. Patterson, President of Tuskegee Institute, to enlist his aid against Governor Dixon of Alabama. At the time, Hall instructed Burnham that he was to attempt to go by bus, telling him that the bus would in all probability be overloaded and that he probably could not get a seat, pointing out that in the event there was no space available on the bus, it would give him an opportunity to state that the bus companies were discriminating against Negroes.

On August 3, 1942, a meeting was held at the Office of the Southern Negro Youth Congress which was attended by Louis Burnham, Dorothy Burnham, John P. Davis and Mable Temple, all colored and all believed to be Party members. At the meeting Burnham stated that the Party had done more for the Negro race than any other political party, that it gives active support to the Southern Negro Youth Congress and that it always aids Negroes in a controversy over their rights. He stated that all Negroes should support the Party and that members of the Southern Negro Youth Congress were given the same training and instructions as given to members of the Young Communist League, and that as soon as they were ready, those who were thought worthy were taken into the Party. At the time, Burnham also stated that seven Southern Negro Youth Congress members would attend the Southwide Conference of the Communist Party at Birmingham on August 23, 1942. In this connection, he stated that the Southern Negro Youth Congress, when dealing with the general public, dealt under the name of Southern Negro Youth Congress, but in closed and secret meetings it was the Communist Party. He stated that the policies and activities of the Congress were decided upon and directed by the Communist Party.

On August 4, 1942, a meeting was held at the office of the Southern Negro Youth Congress, attended by Robert F. Hall, Louis E. Burnham, John P. Davis, Bernard Borah, Alton Lawrence and Mike Ross. Hall advised that a committee had been formed which was to proceed immediately to Washington to see various executives in the Government and protest to them of alleged violence and discrimination against Negroes and labor in the South. The following individuals were members of the committee, it being noted that Joseph Curran was contacted by telephone and his acceptance of membership received:

John P. Davis, colored, Representative of the National Negro Congress.

William Y. Bell, colored, Representative of the National Urban League.

Forrester B. Washington, colored, Professor at Atlanta University, Atlanta.

Joseph Curran, President, National Maritime Union.

Alton Lawrence, colored, Coordinator of Organization, International Union of Mine, Mill and Smelter Workers, Birmingham, Alabama.

Bernard Borah, Southern Director of the National Council of Gas, Coke and Chemical Workers, CIO, Chattanooga, Tennessee.

During the meeting on August 4, 1942, Burnham stated that he had contacted Dr. Patterson, President of Tuskegee Institute, and that Patterson stated he could not afford to serve on any "bi-racial" committee because of his position, however, that he was in accord with the purpose of the committee and sent a contribution of $10.00 for the committee. Burnham also reported that he had attempted to purchase a bus ticket to visit Dr. Patterson but that there was no space left on the bus. Hall in turn stated that this was a clear case of discrimination "against the Negroes" and should also be taken up by the committee in Washington.

Immediately after the meeting on August 4, 1942, Davis is reported to have left Birmingham by plane for New York City where he was to discuss the matters to be brought up in Washington by the committee with Earl Browder and James W. Ford. It was also stated that Davis was to receive suggestions which Browder saw fit to submit.

At the meeting on August 4, 1942, Hall also said that there would be a meeting of CIO officials on August 8, 1942, and that the committee after its return from Washington would make a report on its accomplishments to the meeting of union officials. He stated that Mike Ross would be present at these meetings and would report to him and that he, Hall, in turn would relate the information to the Party in New York City. [redacted]

It is interesting to note that in the August 16, 1942, issue of The Worker, the Communist Party Sunday organ, an entire page (page 2) was devoted to "The Threat Against Unity in the South," an article by Earl Browder, and the "Conspiracy in the South" by Sender Garlin. In the middle of the page appeared a reprint of a letter directed to the President and signed by those individuals listed above and contains practically all the paragraphs dictated at the meeting on August 1, 1942.

Also on page 2 of the August 16, 1942, issue of The Worker appeared statements issued by the United Automobile Workers of America, CIO, the Greater New York Industrial Union Council, CIO, the National Negro Congress and the National Federation for Constitutional Liberties (the latter two being Communist Party front organizations and the two unions penetrated with Communists) which attacked certain discriminatory practices in the South. [*The Worker, Aug. 16, 1942, p. 2*]

In view of the appearance of the letter to the President in this issue of The Worker, it is possible that this page resulted from the conferences previously referred to.

An article appeared on page 3 of the Daily Worker for August 17, 1942, bearing the headlines "Lewis Linked to 'White Supremacy' Plot." In this article it was charged that John L. Lewis and "his District 50 agents are active collaborators in the current copperhead conspiracy in the South. . . ." The article stated that Lewis' agents were responsible for a series of instances wherein Negroes were either physically attacked or discriminated against. The article also stated that members of the United Mine, Mill and Smelter Workers Union of America, CIO, were attempting to overcome these practices. [*Daily Worker, 8-17-42, p. 3*]

It should be noted here that one Carl Frederick Geiser, President of Local 1227, United Electrical, Radio and Machine Workers of America, CIO, Long Island City, New York, reportedly advised he had received a letter dated August 10, 1942, from the Greater New York Industrial Union Council, New York City, signed by Joseph Curran, President, and Saul Mills, Secretary, directed to all CIO affiliates. He allegedly stated that the letter was a call to prevent destruction of the unity of white and Negro Americans behind the Nation's war effort and that it advised of a conspiracy in the South aimed at undermining the war effort through incitement to race hatred and open violation of the anti-discrimination policy of the Government. He reportedly stated that the letter advised that the campaign included beating of CIO organizers and terrorization of white and Negro workers in the South. The letter is stated to have requested the sending of telegrams to various officials in the Government including the President and to the Department of Justice. He is said to have also advised of a memorandum being attached to the letter which had been prepared by CIO representatives and other "progressive forces" in the South, citing specific instances occurring there.

With reference to the letter prepared by the CIO Industrial Union Council which Geiser referred to, it is recalled that Joseph Curran was reportedly a representative of the committee formed by the Communist Party in Birmingham on August 4, 1942. It is also recalled that Robert Hall advised after the meeting on August 4, 1942, that the committee would report on its accomplishments to a meeting of CIO union officials on August 8, 1942, and that the results of this meeting would be furnished by Hall to the Communist Party in New York.

There has been obtained a mimeographed release in the form of a memorandum entitled "Threats to National Unity in the South—A Statement of the Southern Delegation—Washington, D.C.—August 6 (1942)". This memorandum refers to an alleged conspiracy in the South in "organizing open opposition against the war policies of the Government of the United States." It is said that the reason for the conspiracy is for "maintaining white supremacy." The memorandum then refers to Horace C. Wilkinson, Birmingham, Alabama, and a speech made before the Kiwanis Club of Bessemer, Alabama, on July 22, 1942; a statement issued by Governor Dixon of Alabama on July 23, 1942, relative to known discrimination clauses in war production contracts; and to several Southern newspapers said to have championed Governor Dixon's statement. Other broad statements, allegations and recommendations are made in this memorandum.

The above memorandum was circulated by the Greater New York Industrial Union Council, CIO.

It has been further reported with regard to this mimeographed statement, or memorandum, that the material contained therein is believed to have been prepared on August 3, 1942, at a meeting attended by Robert Hall, John P. Davis, Louis Burnham, Mary Southard, Mike Ross, Bernard Borah, Van Jones and Alton Lawrence, the latter four being affiliated with various unions of the CIO in the South. It is said that Robert Hall and Louis Burnham, both Communist Party members, dictated the majority of the statement.

While the Communist Party decries social segregation of Negroes as well as racial chauvinism, several instances have been reported wherein the Communist Party has set up separate units or branches for Negroes. The general explanation for this has been that this action is convenient for organizational purposes as well as for the attendance of members at Party meetings. It is known that such separate branches or units are established in New York, San Francisco, Los Angeles, Chicago, and Indianapolis. In this connection information has been reported that in Omaha, Nebraska, a separate branch composed of Negroes was established on the North Side of that City at which there will be separate social functions and business meetings held for Negroes. The reason for this action, according to a confidential informant, was that previously Negro members often outnumbered white members and as a result a number of white people had dropped out of the Party. It was felt, according to the informant, by functionaries of the Party that, by doing this, more white people would attend the social functions of the Party. In this regard, it was also pointed out that the Negroes themselves felt something must be wrong with the Party because so few white people appeared at the meetings.

In February, 1943, at a meeting of functionaries of the Communist Party for the States of Illinois and Indiana, Phil Bart, organizational secretary of that district, mentioned a Negro Communist Center in Chicago, Illinois, and reportedly pointed out the success which the Party had with the Negro situation in that city. He is said to have remarked: "Our most fertile field of recruiting at present is the Negro—we are recruiting more Negroes than white." He suggested, according to the informant, that the one Negro Center could be used as the foundation for smaller Negro groups in the city. He said that the Party should take these people and train them, and use them in community work, and mentioned specifically they might be influential in housing projects and fighting for the rights of Negro workers.

The informant advised that Bart continued, saying that the leader of this group should be made a "public figure;" even though all members could not be known publicly because of the possibility of persecution the chairman of the group could afford to be well known. Bart stated: "We will have to show we are not building a Jim-Crow party." He thought that such a group might have two or three representatives trained in Income Tax matters by a Party attorney, in order that they could help other members fill out their income tax returns. In this way, he said the people would feel that the Party was answering a real need.

During this discussion the idea of establishing a Negro center for Indianapolis, Indiana, was discussed. It was suggested that one Sam Ferguson was to be contacted for financial aid for the group. It should be noted that Ferguson is one of the most influential people of the Indianapolis Negro section. It was planned that a group of Negroes in the Party in Indianapolis would be called together for a meeting on February 4, 1943, to make plans for the opening of the Negro center in Indianapolis. The Negro Center as suggested for Indianapolis, according to information received, was formally opened at 1208 North Senate Avenue in that city.

The Communist Party, it has been observed previously in this section, has and is continuing to exert considerable effort toward obtaining Negro recruits. It will be recalled that in the various digests of the Field Divisions a degree of success has been obtained by the Party in recruiting added Negro membership, varying, of course, in different communities. The general approach in obtaining membership from Negro ranks is that the Party is the only political group advocating true democracy and the granting of equal social rights to Negroes. Information has been received, however, which reflects that there possibly is a lack of sincerity on the part of the Communist Party in its activity of recruiting Negro members. Information is to the effect that in February, 1943, Ned Sparks, Secretary of the Communist Party for the State of Wisconsin, after ascertaining that what he termed were "rank and file" Negroes had been recruited into the Party, became angry with another Party member who had done the recruiting. At the time, Sparks is said to have stated that the Communist Party desired not quantity but only quality in its Negro recruiting. He is said to have ordered that only outstanding Negroes be recruited, saying that the ordinary Negroes were not an asset to the Party because they would not work. He also reportedly pointed out that they were active as members but for a short time and thereafter drop their membership. It is to be noted that these remarks by Sparks, according to the informant, were directed to Katherine Hartmann, an organizer for the International Fur and Leather Workers Union of the United States and Canada, CIO, and an active Communist Party member. [*100-135-31-12*]

As an example of an attitude exhibited by functionaries of the Party, the following information is set forth to show how Negroes are regarded as Party workers. In March 1943 confidential informants reported that functionaries of the Party in the San Francisco area were concerned over Negro members inasmuch as they had not been evidencing an interest in Party problems except in so far as they concerned Negroes themselves. Rudie Lambert, labor director of the Party in that area, is said to have remarked that the Party had a problem in keeping new Negro members interested and that the Party should not forget the weaknesses of Negroes in organizational work since too much could not be expected of them. Along these lines, it was further reported that a known Communist member stated the main problem in dealing with Negroes, as far as the Party is concerned, is that Negroes are afraid of terrorism and are, therefore, backward in taking an active part in Party problems. [*100-135-48-15*]

It has been reported that the Communist Party in the San Francisco area has exhibited in the past considerable interest in an organization formed by Negroes known as the Shipyard Workers Committee Against Discrimination. This organization was formed in 1942 and was brought under the recognized leadership of one Roy Thompson, a Negro. The purpose of the organization is to combat "Jim Crow" local labor unions, particularly those of the International Brotherhood of Boilermakers, Ironworkers, Shipbuilders, Welders and Helpers of America, AFL. In recent months Thompson is said to have directed his activities at attempting to break up these segregated union locals and in turn setting up a separate Negro union. Thompson was thereupon criticized by the Communist Party leaders in the area for his action in this matter, their claim being that Thompson does not know what he is doing and has not been fully integrated into the Party to the extent that he can understand and dictate Party policies. (It is to be noted that Thompson has been reported to be a member of the Party.) The Committee is said to have over 160 members, both white and Negro, who represent the various Bay area shipyards and has furnished approximately 20 Negro recruits for the Communist Party in the past several months. It is believed that Thompson's actions opposed the Party's plan of infiltrating the "Jim Crow" union locals with the view of thereafter obtaining control of them and the Party for this reason, opposed Thompson's tactics. It has been reported also that the Communist Party in the San Francisco area contemplated deposing Thompson in view of what they termed his "nationalistic attitude." (It might be stated here that Thompson is stated to have been militantly opposed to the white leadership of the union having the bargaining rights in this area for shipyard workers.) [*100-135-48-19*]

During recent months, particularly on the West Coast and involving specifically the Los Angeles, San Francisco and Oakland, California areas, the Communist Party has varied its approach to opposing the establishment of separate labor union locals for Negroes. In the Los Angeles area, led by Pettis Perry, Negro Party functionary, the Party has militantly fought the establishment of the "Jim Crow" locals. However, in the San Francisco area, where such locals had been already established, observations were made by Steve Nelson, National Committee member of the Communist Party and leader in the San Francisco area, that this situation presented itself with respect to the shipyards there. It was pointed out by Nelson, according to an informant, that the "Jim Crow" locals had already been formed and that the Party either had to take an extreme leftist position (possibly to call strikes or to take other such militant action) or to urge that the "comrades" go into the auxiliaries (or "Jim Crow" locals) and work. It was further stated, according to the informant, that since there were approximately 15,000 Negroes in the shipyards and 7,000 of them were members of the International Brotherhood of Boilermakers, Ironworkers, Shipbuilders, Welders and Helpers of America, AFL, it would be impractical for the Party to assume "an extreme leftist position."

The Communist Party has interested itself in segregation of Negroes not only in labor fields but also in public places. In this connection, the following information has been received with regard to the maneuvers of the Party in the Seattle, Washington, area:

Ostervald Carl Brooks, Negro Communist Party member along with Eugene Moszee, reported Negro member of the Young Communist League, appeared at the Olympic Hotel Grill in Seattle, Washington, with three colored sailors demanding that all receive service in the eating place. According to an informant, these individuals were not given immediate service as a result of the extreme shortage of help; thereupon Brooks and Moszee raised considerable disturbance in the grill, claiming that they were being discriminated against because of their color. The management of the the hotel was called upon and the matter was settled, the colored sailors being offered service and given a glass of beer or milk as they desired; however Brooks and Moszee were not given service.

According to an informant who was present at the time the demonstration was arranged, the same being sponsored by the Young Communist League. He expressed the opinion that the colored sailors who accompanied Brooks and Moszee were unaware of what they were getting into. The version of the colored sailors was also to this effect and in fact they advised they thought the individuals whom they accompanied to the Olympic Hotel were members of the National Association for the Advancement of Colored People and were attempting to break down discrimination against Negroes in that area. They stated that Brooks and Moszee gave the impression they were going to "break it up" referring to the alleged discrimination against Negroes.

Later another informant was contacted by Eugene Moszee who identified himself as a member of the Young Communist League. Moszee reportedly stated that his organization had sent a number of its members to the Olympic Hotel Grill and after service was refused Moszee and the rest of the party requested that they see the manager. Moszee then admitted that a riot almost ensued. He also admitted to the informant that the Young Communist League had been responsible for the previously mentioned incident.

Negro Membership in Communist Party

The exact figure representing Negro membership in the Communist Party has not been reported. However, the National Committee of the Communist Party in June 1943 made available information showing the comparative figures between the composition of the registered total membership and the composition of new members obtained as a result of the national recruiting drive that extended from the beginning of February 1943 through April 1943. The figures it released reflect that 10 per cent of the registered membership were Negroes and 27 per cent of the total new recruits were negroes. Using these percentages in connection with the figures of membership in the Party previously reported, along with the figure of new recruits, it is believed that a fairly accurate figure of Negro membership in the Party can be obtained.

As of May 1, 1943, the Party is reported to have recruited 14,998 members since the beginning of February, 1943. A recent announcement in the Daily Worker stated that the aim of the Party was to recruit between 25,000 and 30,000 additional members in 1943 for the purpose of bringing the total membership figure up to 100,000. Using these two figures brings the result of a membership at the beginning of February 1943 of between 60,000 and 65,000. This figure varies slightly from a figure arrived at from the registration of members at the end of 1942 which totaled slightly over 59,000. However, the figure 59,000 was exclusive of sympathizers, fellow travellers and members in trade unions and other groups whose affiliation with the Party has remained secret.

Therefore, 27 per cent of 14,998, the recruitment total, would bring a total of Negroes recruited by the Party during the period February through April 1943 to a figure slightly over 4,000. Taking 10 per cent of a registered total of Party members of 60,000 at the beginning of 1943 would result in approximately 6,000 Negro members. This figure plus the 4,000 referred to above would total in the neighborhood of 10,000 Negro members of the Communist Party at the present time. This figure compared with the total Party membership (approximately 75,000) represents about 13.3 per cent Negro membership in the Communist Party. This figure, of course, is in excess of the per cent of Negro population in the United States to the entire population.

It might be noted that it has been determined in several Party districts throughout the country the number of Negro recruits in the recent recruiting campaign total well over 50 per cent of all recruits in the particular districts.

[*100-3-364; Monthly Intelligence Surveys for June and July 1943*]

VII

COMMUNIST PARTY FRONT ORGANIZATIONS AND NEGROES

During the period of the existence of the Communist Party in this country, and concerning its activities with regard to the Negroes, there have been coexistent at various times three organizations formed by or at the instigation of the Party to carry out its program in respect to the Negro race. They are, in their respective chronological order, the American Negro Labor Congress, the League of Struggle for Negro Rights, and the National Negro Congress. The first two are out of existence. Each organization was formed to replace the other, as the result of some failure or malfunction of the preceding organization.

The most recent Communist Party front organized for work among Negroes is the Negro Labor Victory Committee, which was formed in the month of May, 1942 to combat and destroy the popular appeal of the March on Washington Movement.

All four of these organizations are described hereinafter. In reviewing this material it should be kept in mind that there are numerous other Communist Party fronts which have been established by the Party for other purposes. However, there appears almost universally at least one point in their respective programs which deals directly or indirectly with the Negro situation. That these organizations are agitational in effect cannot be overlooked, although a particular group is not solely devoted to this matter. As an example, a Communist front group may clamor for the end of the poll tax system or demand that Negroes be given increased employment in defense industries, yet it may have been formed originally through demands of non-interventionism or isolationism. Numerous front organizations have fought for regiments in the United States Army which are formed of mixed races and at the same time urged the opening of a "second front" in Europe. Yet the group was organized for the fundamental purpose of aiding "political prisoners."

It is believed that the following statement issued by the National Committee of the Communist Party should be set forth herein to show the "blue print" which the Party follows in forming Communist Party front organizations as a part of its United Front program:

> "The Communist Party is obliged to penetrate all existing working class organizations and to form other open organizations to reach the masses, using these organizations as tools or auxiliaries of the Communist Party."

American Negro Labor Congress

This organization is stated to have been founded in October 1928 just subsequent to the Fourth National Convention of the Workers (Communist) Party of America in August 1925. In this connection, it is said that in the "Report of the Central Executive Committee" of the Party under the subheading "Negro Work" it was reported "a Negro Comrade was sent to the Fifth Congress (of the Communist Internationale) after which the Central Executive Committee authorized him to stay for training. It is believed that the Negro Comrade referred to here was Lovett Fort-Whiteman. Shortly after Fort-Whiteman's return to America, according to records with the Department of State, the American Negro Labor Congress, a Communist enterprise, was founded in which Fort-Whiteman was to become the outstanding figure.

Under date of June 3, 1925, in the publication known as the Negro Champion, Volume 1, Number 1, wherein on page 1 it is stated that this publication is the organ of the National Committee for organizing the American Negro Labor Congress, the call to the American Negro Labor Congress is set out. Following are statements taken from this call:

> "The American Negro Labor Congress will consider such problems as the payment of equal wages for equal work, regardless of race and sex."
>
> "The American Negro Labor Congress will fight for the abolition of Industrial discrimination in factories, mills, mines, on the railroads, and in all places where labor is employed."
>
> "The American Negro Labor Congress proposes to stir the working masses to take some organized action against the unjust conditions of residential segregation imposed upon the Negro in our larger cities, . . ."
>
> ". . . the American Negro Labor Congress proposes to make plans for the waging of war against policy of the officialdom of the trade unions which bar Negroes from membership, . . ."
>
> ". . . the American Negro Labor Congress shall propose that the seat of action be changed to the masses themselves and shall endeavor to stimulate and promote the organization of interracial committees throughout the nation with the aim of bringing about a better feeling between white and black workers."
>
> "The American Negro Labor Congress shall demand the abolition of Jim Crowism, not only in the Southern States but throughout the nation."
>
> "The American Negro Labor Congress shall bring to bear the full force of its organized strength against any measures on the part of any section of the nation to curtail the right of the ballot of any section of the working class."

In this same publication it was stated that the Congress was to be composed of delegates from the various independent Negro labor unions and from mixed unions from unorganized factory groups of Negro workers, of representatives of Negro agricultural workers, and of individual advocates, both Negro and white, who are well-known for their championship of the cause of the Negro.

The call was signed by:

William Bryant, Business Manager of the Asphalt Workers Union, Milwaukee, Wisconsin

Edward L. Doty, organizer of Negro Plumbers, Chicago, Illinois

H. V. Phillips, organizer of Negro Working-Class Youth, Chicago, Illinois

Elizabeth Griffin, President of the Chicago Negro Women's Household League

Everett Greene, Chicago Correspondent of the Afro-American, Baltimore, Maryland

William Scarville, Pittsburgh American

Charles Henry, representative of the unorganized Negro Steel Workers, Chicago

Otto Hall, Waiters and Cooks Association, Chicago

Louis Hunter, Longshoremens Protection and Benevolent Union, New Orleans, Louisiana

Otto Huiswood, African Blood Brotherhood, New York City

Lovett Fort-Whiteman, organizer of the Congress

Arron Davis, Neighborhood Protective Association, Toomsuba, Mississippi

John Owens, organizer of the Negro Agricultural Workers, Ripley, California

Rosina Davis, Secretary of the Chicago Negro Women's Household League

E. A. Lynch, paternal delegate from the West Africa Seaman's Union, Liverpool

Jack Edwards, representative of the Negro Pullman Car Workers, Chicago

Sahir Karimji, fraternal delegate from Natal Agricultural Workers, South Africa.

With reference to the above-named Otto Huiswood of the African Blood Brotherhood, it was reported that this individual was active as a member of the Soviet Red Army at one time.

As a matter of background information, it is reported that Trotsky in 1923, at the time he was an official of the Third (Communist) International, in a letter to an American Negro Communist named Mackay published in the Moscow "Izvestia" of February 15, 1923, stated under the subheading "The Training of the Black Agitators Is the Most Important Revolutionary Problem of the Moment":

> ". . . one of the most important methods of struggle against this capitalistic corruption of mind is to wake up the human dignity and revolutionary protests among the black slaves of America and capital. This work can be best carried on by the devoted and politically educated Negro Revolutionists. Naturally the work must not assume the character of 'black chauvinism' but must be carried on in a spirit of solidarity among all laborers regardless of the color of their skin. I am at a loss to say what are the most expedient organization forms for the movement among the American Negroes, because I am not familiar with the concrete conditions and possibilities. But the organization formed will be found as soon as sufficient will for action is displayed."

It is believed that Trotsky referred to an organization comparable to the American Negro Labor Congress.

The first convention of the Congress is said to have taken place in Chicago during the week beginning October 25, 1925.

With reference to the first congress it is reported that in the August 27, 1925, issue of the International Press Correspondent (reportedly a former official Bolshevik organ) there is an article on the then approaching Congress by Lovett Fort-Whiteman opening with the following paragraph:

> "The American Negro Labor Congress will take place in Chicago beginning on October 25, 1925, and lasting about a week. It will be made up of delegates coming from the various Negro labor unions throughout the country, from organizations of Negro agricultural workers and representatives from unorganized industries. The fundamental aim in calling the American Negro Labor Congress is to establish in the life of the American Negro labor working class an organization which may serve as a medium through which the American Communist Party may reach and influence the Negro working class, and at the same time may constitute something of a recruiting ground for the Party."

It is stated more significantly in the "Report of the Central Executive Committee (of the Workers (Communist) Party of America) on Past Activities" submitted to the Fourth National Convention of the Party in August 1925. Under the subheading "Negro Work" it is said, "In accord with the instructions of the Communist Internationale, most of our work has been carried on in connection with the American Negro Labor Congress."

It has been reported that the first public announcement of the Congress appears to have been made in the Daily Worker of April 14, 1925. Therein is listed a provisional organizational committee headed by Lovett Fort-Whiteman. In this connection it should be noted that in July 1925 the first issue of the Negro Champion, the organ of the Congress, appeared with Fort-Whiteman as editor.

It has been further stated with regard to the Convention that only 40 delegates attended instead of the 500 as had been forecast. It is said that William Green, President of the American Federation of Labor, appeared to have been largely responsible for the so-called failure of the Congress. He is stated to have remarked to the Convention:

> "It will not be held to benefit the Negro, but to instill into the lives of that race a most pernicious doctrine—race hatred." *[61-4960-9]*

Failure

The extent and influence of this organization at the time of its existence is not known. However, it is believed that although its membership may not have been large, the effect created by its agitation through meetings or publications was felt in at least a few areas. The organization failed and the reasons for its failure have been pointed out by James W. Ford, Negro, National Committee member of the Communist Party. He has stated with regard to its weaknesses and shortcomings:

> ". . . the A.N.L.C. (American Negro Labor Congress) was too narrow in its approach. For the period of its existence it was almost completely isolated from the basic masses of the Negro People; this shortcoming was carried over into the League of Struggle for Negro Rights. The class contents of the program of the A.N.L.C., which was essentially correct, was, however, not carefully adapted to the feeling and moods of the Negro People. The Local Councils were too rigid instead of uniting broad masses of the Negro People through their organization: the councils were built on a basis of individual membership composed in almost all cases of those people and individuals who were dissatisfied with the existing organization and were breaking away from them completely . . ."
>
> "I recall particularly the strict and unyielding attitude taken by the leaders of the American Negro Labor Congress toward religion. This attitude prevented the Congress from becoming a mass influence among church people. At an A.N.L.C. meeting in Chicago, 1926, composed of a large number of religious people, a leader of the organization in the course of his remarks said, 'To hell with religion; damn the church' . . . .
>
> "Despite its shortcomings, the A.N.L.C. served as a useful purpose. The last convention of the American Negro Labor Congress was held at St. Louis in November, 1930, where, by unanimous decision, the name was changed to the League of Struggle for Negro Rights. There was a change in program also; the program called for the destruction of the plantation system in the South, for confiscation without compensation of the land of the big landlords, and declared for the complete right of self determination for the Negro people in the black belt of the South. Such a program prevented the development of a broad movement; the masses did not understand this full program; furthermore, the L.S.N.R. followed the same sectarian methods of work as the A.N.L.C. It did not base its activities sufficiently on immediate, daily needs of the people. Naturally, this narrowed down the L.S.N.R."

In comparing the National Negro Congress with the above-named organization, Ford stated:

> "It is precisely on this point that the National Negro Congress has made a great step forward to the advantage of the United Front and joint action of different organizations.
>
> "What actually happened was the following: Branches of individual members of the L.S.N.R. (League of Struggle for Negro Rights) became, invariably, as in the A.N.L.C., small sectarian groups, and, as such, remained isolated and even were unable to hold these people who were willing to break away from other organizations. These branches could have attraction for unorganized Negro People but contrary to opinions held by many, the Negro People are an organized people, that is, they are members of churches, lodges, fraternal organizations, etc."
>
> [*"The Negro & the Democratic Front" by James W. Ford, pa 81, 82, 83, 84*]

Character

In the decision of the Honorable Francis Biddle, Attorney General, on May 28, 1942, in the matter of Harry Bridges, the Attorney General identified the American Negro Labor Congress as a front organization of the Communist Party.

It is reported that out of the American Negro Labor Congress grew the League of Struggle for Negro Rights at the St. Louis Convention of the American Negro Labor Congress held in 1930. The American Negro Labor Congress was then abolished and its most recent successor, the Communist front organization presently in existence, is the National Negro Congress.

[Dies Comm. Rept. Vol II pa 6988 testimony William Odell Nowell]

League of Struggle For Negro Rights

Origin

At the last convention of the American Negro Labor Congress held in St. Louis in November of 1930, by unanimous decision, the name was changed to the League of Struggle for Negro Rights. There was a change in program also. The program called for the destruction of the plantation system in the South, for confiscation without compensation of the land of the big landlords and declared for the complete right of self determination for the Negro people in the Black Belt of the South. (It should be pointed out that it was in October of 1930 when the resolution with regard to the Negro situation in the United States was issued by the Executive Committee of the Communist International. In this resolution it is recalled that such a program was called for as was that of the League of Struggle for Negro Rights.)

The League of Struggle for Negro Rights was reported by a confidential informant of the Federal Bureau of Investigation, who was at one time in the Communist Party, to have been based on the program of the Communist International relative to the Negro question in the United States. It is recalled that the resolution regarding this matter made in October, 1930, by the Communist International has been set out hereinbefore. The essence of the resolution, it is further recalled, was the fight for equal rights to be extended to Negroes with the simultaneous effort to foment a revolutionary overthrow of the landowners in the "Black Belt," or as it was commonly called, the "Cotton Belt", and the subsequent establishment of an autonomous Negro government there.

The membership of the League of Struggle for Negro Rights is said to have never been more than several thousand members on a national basis. These members are claimed to have been mostly Communist Party members or sympathizers.

[Rept [redacted] 5-13-42 61-6728-236]

James W. Ford, Negro Communist and member of the National Committee of the Party, in criticizing the League of Struggle for Negro Rights, stated that the program of this organization prevented the development of a broad movement, and that the masses did not understand its full program. He stated further that the League of Struggle for Negro Rights fell into the same sectarian methods of work as the American Negro Labor Congress, that it did not base its activities sufficiently on immediate daily needs of the people.

Ford did, however, commend that practical part of the program of the League which was the "Bill of Negro Rights", which aimed to develop a movement to enforce the enactment of legislation for Negro rights and the suppression of lynching.

Speaking of the organizational weaknesses of the League of Struggle for Negro Rights, Ford claimed that they were identical with those of the American Negro Labor Congress. He stated that calling for affiliation on the basis of the complete program, the League of Struggle for Negro Rights tended to make existing organizations suspicious. He stated that the by-laws provided for the leadership of struggle for the League of Struggle for Negro Rights' program of immediate and general demands, but many organizations could not be drawn into the United Front struggle on the basis of the full program of the league.

National Council

The following were officers and National Council members of this organization. Asterisks preceding various names reflect either the individual's known or reported affiliation with the Communist Party:

*Langston Hughes, President
*James W. Ford)
Mrs. Jessica Henderson)
*William L. Patterson) Vice-Presidents
*Robert Minor)
*Benjamin Davis, Jr.)
Hose Hart)
*Richard B. Moore, General Secretary
Herman MacKawain, Assistant Secretary
Esther Anderson, Financial Secretary
Bernice Da Costa, Recording Secretary
Dr. Reuben S. Young, Treasurer
*Louise Thompson, Director of Education and Culture
Harold Williams, Director of Defense Activities
Charles Alexander, Director of Bureau—International Relations
*Leonard Patterson, Director of Young People's Activities
Williana Burroughs, Director of Activities Among Women
*Eugene Gordon)
Maude White) Liberator Staff

Tom Truesdale, Director of Research

Steve Kingston
Henry Shepard
*Harry Haywood
Dr. Arnold Donawa
James Moore
Rabbi Ben Goldstein
George Maddox
Mrs. Mary Craik Speed
Bonita Williams
Hanou Chan
*James Allen
*Cyril Briggs
*William Fitzgerald

New York

Eleanor Henderson, Agricultural Workers Union
*Joseph Brodsky, International Workers Order
*Clarence Hathaway, Daily Worker
Myra Page, Writer
*William Z. Foster, Trade Union Unity League
*Robert Dunn, Labor Research Association
*Irving Potash, Needle Trades
*Henry Shepard, Trade Union Unity Council of Greater New York
*Louis Weinstock, American Federation of Labor
Joseph Moore, Mechanics' Association of Harlem
*B. D. Amis, Communist Party
*Israel Amter, National Committee Unemployed Councils
Peter Uffre, Tobacco Workers of Harlem
*William Dunne, Trade Union Unity League
Gladys Stoner, National Student Committee on Negro Student Problems
*Ben Goldstein, National Committee for Defense of Political Prisoners
*Earl Browder, Communist Party
Ruth Ruben, National Student League
Samuel Patterson, Caribbean Union
Steve Kingston, L.S.N.R.
*Harry Haywood, Communist Party
*Bill Lawrence, International Labor Defense
*Leonard Patterson, Young Communist League
*Louis Coleman, International Labor Defense
*J. Adler, International Workers Order
James Toney, L.S.N.R.

*Gil Green, Young Communist League
William Burdell, L.S.N.R.

Southern Section

Al Murphy, Sharecroppers Union, Alabama
*Mrs. Mary Craik Speed, Montgomery, Alabama
Rev. J. A. Morten, Angelo Herndon Defense, Alabama
*Jane Speed, International Labor Defense, Birmingham, Alabama
*Angelo Herndon, Fulton Tower Prison, Georgia
Mrs. Ada Wright, Scottsboro Mother, Chattanooga, Tennessee
Mrs. Janie Patterson, Scottsboro Mother, Chattanooga, Tennessee
Attorney Pierson, Durham, North Carolina
*Anna Williams, Communist Party, Charlotte, North Carolina
*Bernard Ades, International Labor Defense, Baltimore, Maryland
Gough McDaniels, High School Teacher, Baltimore, Maryland
*Robert Hall, National Farmers' Action Committee, Washington, D.C.
Macey, New Orleans Railroad Workers, New Orleans, Louisiana
Manny Jackson, Savannah Longshoreman, Savannah, Georgia

Chicago

*Herbert Newton, Communist Party
*Claude Lightfoot, L.S.N.R.

Pennsylvania

Dr. Patterson, Physician, Pittsburgh, Pennsylvania
*Tom Meyerscoff, National Miners Union, Pittsburgh, Pennsylvania
Henry Wickman, Marine Workers Industrial Union, Pittsburgh, Pennsylvania
*Ben Careathers, Communist Party, Pittsburgh, Pennsylvania

Detroit

Joe Billups, L.S.N.R.

Minnesota

Alfred Tiala, National Secretary, United Farmers League, Minneapolis, Minnesota

New England

Mrs. Cravath Simpson, Federation Women's Clubs, Boston, Massachusetts
*Ann Burlak, National Textile Union

California

*Tom Mooney, San Quentin, California
Lauren Miller, Journalist, Los Angeles, California
Matt Crawford, San Francisco National Scottsboro Action Committee

Buffalo

*Manning Johnson, Communist Party

Missouri

*A. W. Berry, Communist Party, Kansas City, Missouri
Carrie Smith, Nut Pickers Union, St. Louis, Missouri

Cleveland

Arthur Murphy, Steel and Metal Workers Industrial Union

Radical Activities

In a booklet entitled "Proceedings of the First Pacific Coast Congress Against War on Fascism", dated at San Francisco, California, April 27–28, 1935, the League of Struggle for Negro Rights was listed as having representatives in attendance at this Congress. This Congress is stated to have been Communist inspired.

It has been reported that on August 2, 1933, a mock trial of a police officer who was alleged to have shot a Negro, one **James Porter,** was held at the Communist Hall, 3040 South Antonine Street, Detroit, Michigan. The mock trial was held under the sponsorship of the League of Struggle for Negro Rights.

James W. Ford was the first Vice President of the League of Struggle for Negro Rights at which time Langston Hughes, prominent poet and author and reported Communist, was President. Ford, of course, has been a Communist for many years and is presently a member of the National Committee of the Communist Party.

At a mass meeting held on May 25, 1934, attended by 8,000 Civil Works Administration Workers, in protest against the proposed demobilization of the CWA, there was in attendance Dan Young of the League of Struggle for Negro Rights. The meeting is said to have been dominated by left-wing and Communist elements. Young is said to have addressed the meeting.

It was reported in March, 1932, that one of the addresses to be used for the receipt of literature from the International Trade Union Committee of Negro Workers in Hamburg, Germany, was that of the League of Struggle for Negro Rights, Room 506, 50 East 13th Street, New York City. It should be stated that James William Ford, National Committee member of the Communist Party, was the editor responsible for the policy and publication of the magazine "The Negro Worker" and was also at the time functioning as Chairman of the International Trade Union Committee of Negro Workers. The "Southern Worker" was reported to have been also distributing the publication "The Negro Worker" at that time. The "Southern Worker" was issued by the Communist Party weekly.

Communist Affiliations

Appearing in the September 1, 1932, issue of the "Liberator," which is the official organ of the League of Struggle for Negro Rights, was a map of eleven southern States. On this map were shaded various areas which were referred to as the "Black Belt." It was stated that the " 'Black Belt' which runs through eleven southern States includes not only the one hundred and ninety-five counties with over 50% Negroes, but also the two hundred and two counties with from 35% to 50% Negroes. These three hundred and ninety-seven counties form a continuous area in which the Negroes are over 50% of the total population." Under this map it was stated, "The Communist Party and the League of Struggle for Negro Rights demand the right of the Negroes of the 'Black Belt' to rule over this territory, including any white minority residing there, and even to separate this territory from the United States if they so desire."

The map referring to the "Black Belt" and the above statement are, of course, in direct harmony with the resolution passed by the Executive Committee of the Communist International concerning the Negro question in the United States in October of 1930 which has hereinbefore been referred to. *[61-7563-72X17]*

Referring to the League of Struggle for Negro Rights, in the report of the Central Committee to the Eighth Convention of the Communist Party held in Cleveland, Ohio, April 2–8, 1934, it was stated:

"A broad and all-inclusive organizational form for the Negro liberation struggle is the League of Struggle for Negro Rights. This should embrace, in its activities, all of the basic economic organizations of Negro and white workers standing on the program of Negro liberation, and further, unite with them all other sections of the Negro population drawn towards this struggle, especially those large sections of the petty-bourgeoisie, intellectuals, professionals, who can and must be won in the national liberation cause. The L.S.N.R. must, in the first place, be an active federation of existing mass organizations; and secondly, it must directly organize its own membership branches composed of its most active forces and all supporters otherwise unorganized. The present beginnings of the L.S.N.R. and its paper, the 'Liberator,' which with only a little attention have already shown mass vitality, must be energetically taken up and spread throughout the country." *["Communism in the U.S." by Earl Browder, pa 49]*

With regard to the League of Struggle for Negro Rights, the following information has been supplied by a confidential informant who was a former member of the Communist Party and who was a National Council member of the League of Struggle for Negro Rights:

> "The League of Struggle for Negro Rights" was based on the program of the Communist International on the 'Negro question' (October 1930). The essence of the program was the fight for 'Equal rights for Negroes generally with the simultaneous effort to foment a revolutionary overthrow of the landowners in the 'Black Belt', or as it was commonly called, the old 'Cotton Belt', in the establishment of an autonomous Negro government in the 'Black Belt'.
>
> "The Revolutionary overthrow of the white landlords in the 'Black Belt' is to be accomplished by organizing white and Negro farmers and workers to fight against lynching, the poll tax, right to sell their own crops, Jim Crowism, and the right to ownership of the land. In the course of the development of this struggle involved in the above-mentioned issue, the following slogans were raised: 1. Confiscation of the land and property of the white landowners and capitalists. 2. Unite the 'Black Belt' into an autonomous state or government with the right of this Black Republic to secede from the rest of the United States. 3. The right of this newly formed government to determine its own form of government."

This same informant has advised that the League of Struggle for Negro Rights was abolished and its publication the "Liberator" suspended because the Party considered the organization a duplication of the Communist Party and the "Liberator" a replica of the Daily Worker. The membership of the League of Struggle for Negro Rights was never more than several thousand members nationally. These were mostly Party members and sympathizers.

It is further advised that in December of 1934 at a meeting of the Central Committee of the Communist Party of the U.S.A., held in the Finn Hall on 126th Street near Fifth Avenue, New York City, the abolition of the League of Struggle for Negro Rights was approved and the recommendation made to build a broad united front organization embracing all the existing organizations among Negroes

In November 1933 there were published and circulated by the National Council of the League of Struggle for Negro Rights several drafts which definitely presented the aims and purposes and objectives of this organization. Included in the draft of the program of the League of Struggle for Negro Rights were the following:

* * * * *

> "We proclaim before the whole world that the American Negroes are a nation—a nation striving to manhood but whose growth is violently retarded and which is viciously oppressed by American Imperialism. . . .

* * * * *

"Today nine and one-half million Negroes still live in the prison of the South, stifled by oppression, cut off from even a breath of freedom. . . .

* * * * *

"The League of Struggle for Negro Rights therefore demands the confiscation without compensation of the land of the big landlords and capitalists in the South and its distribution among the Negroes and white small farmers and sharecroppers.

"These plantations are concentrated in what is known as the 'Black Belt'—that continuous territory stretching from the eastern shore of Maryland to the southeastern corner of Virginia, cutting a strip through North Carolina and comprising practically the whole state of South Carolina passing through central Georgia and southern Alabama, engulfing Mississippi and the delta regions of Louisiana and Arkansas, including the southwestern tip of Tennessee, and driving a wedge into Texas.

* * * * *

"The League of Struggle for Negro Rights stands for the complete right of self determination for the Negro people in the 'Black Belt' with full right for the toiling white minority.

* * * * *

"The Soviet Union offers the shining example of the correctness of this program. There, nations and races, who, under the old Czarist regime, suffered oppression equal to that of the Negroes of the United States, are now under the New Soviet Government of the workers and farmers, enjoying complete freedom, equality and the rights of self determination: There the workers and farmers of the varied nationalities have united in fraternal and harmonious union in the work of building up a Socialist society."

At the same time an immediate program was set forth by the League of Struggle for Negro Rights; it was as follows:

"1. Against Jim Crowism, and discrimination in all forms, and in every field, on jobs, in professions, public places, trains, boats, busses, all institutions, places of residence, etc.

"2. A relentless fight to wipe out all forms of forced labor, chain gangs, forced work on roads and public work for payment of taxes, and all other hangovers from chattel slavery.

"3. A constant daily fight for ordinary human and civil rights for Negroes in all parts of the country, for the actual enforcement of their rights as human beings.

"4. A determined fight against the whole system of social segregation in which Negroes are set apart from the rest of the population as a despised and outlawed people.

"5. A ruthless combating of all ideas of 'White Supremacy' and 'Superiority' fostered by the white rulers to justify their enslavement of Negro people."

[*61-7563-2-3 "Equality, Land & Freedom: A Program for Negro Liberation" pub for L.S.N.R. by Workers Library Publishers, Nov 1933*]

National Negro Congress

Origin

The National Negro Congress is said to have been formed after its suggestion at a meeting of leading Negro Communist Party members, among whom are said to have been James W. Ford, Harry Haywood, Otto Hall, Louise Thompson, William Patterson, James Fitzgerald, Richard B. Moore, Audley Moore, Cyril Briggs, Edward Strong, Maude White, and Ben Davis. The suggestion was based on the failure of the Communist Party to build the League of Struggle for Negro Rights and its predecessor organization, the American Negro Labor Congress, into effective Communist transmission belts among Negroes.

In the summer of 1934 the abolition of the League of Struggle for Negro Rights was approved and the recommendation to build a broad united organization embracing all existing organizations among Negroes was made. The Political Buro is said to have sent instructions to all Party districts to begin work on the Congress immediately by grouping together "liberals" and Communist sympathizers in forming professional committees for local conferences to lay the foundation for the National Negro Congress.

It is said that every effort was made by the Party to make the first Congress a success and every leading Negro Communist and many white Communists were instructed to go to the Congress as delegates in order that the Congress would pursue the Party line and would not be captured by certain Negro leaders. It is further reported that the most capable Communists were placed on all Congress committees and given key positions in discussion groups to guarantee control. This, of course, is typical in the Party moves to infiltrate or form a Party front organization.

Present at the Congress were such outstanding known or reported Communists as:

Henry Johnson, Chicago National Organizer of the International Workers Order

John P. Davis, subsequently National Secretary of the National Negro Congress

Columbus Alston, President of the Young Peoples Protective League, New York City

Rosa Raiside, New York Organizer for the Domestic Workers Union

Neva Ryan, Chicago Organizer of the Domestic Workers Union

Thyra Edwards, Chicago Social Worker

Richard B. Moore, New York Organizer for the International Labor Defense

Dr. Arnold Donawa, New York

B. D. Amis, former District Organizer of the Communist Party in Cleveland, Ohio

Merrill Work, New York

Marty Richardson, Jacksonville, Florida

Layton Weston, St. Louis, Missouri, President of the Dining Car Cooks and Waiters Union, A.F.L.

Abner W. Berry, Communist Party

Arthur Huff Fanset, Philadelphia, Pennsylvania

Edward Strong, Vice President, American Youth Congress

James W. Ford, Communist Party

Max Yergan, Secretary, International Committee on African Affairs

Al Jackson, Montgomery, Alabama

Harry Haywood, Communist Party Section Organizer, Chicago, Illinois

Louise Thompson, New York, National Organizer of the International Workers Order

Benjamin J. Davis, Jr., Communist Party, New York; Legal Staff of the International Labor Defense

Angelo Herndon, New York

Manning Johnson, New York

Maude White, Cleveland, Ohio

Audley Moore, New York

The Congress was held in February 1936 at the Eighth Illinois Armory in Chicago, Illinois. It was attended by some 912 delegates and it is said there were several thousand people present at the opening sessions.

The certificate of incorporation of the National Negro Congress (No. 22570) filed in the District of Columbia reflects that the National Negro Congress was incorporated on April 30, 1934, and that the terms of the organization were perpetual. The business and the objects of the corporation were listed as follows:

1. To suppress the spread of the Doctrines of Communism among Negroes.
2. To investigate and present in proper form to the right and proper Governmental agencies, the economic, social and political needs of the Negroes, with a view to their enhancement.
3. To foster a movement having as its ultimate aid, a periodic meeting in convention of Negro representatives from all the States, elected by Negroes, so that the problems affecting the Negroes generally may be discussed and means of their solution determined upon.

4. To promote the welfare of all Negroes.

A National Conference was held early in 1935 at Howard University, Washington, D.C., under the auspices of the Joint Committee on National Recovery. Out of this conference at Howard University, there arose plans for the organization of the National Negro Congress as it exists today. Shortly thereafter, the Joint Committee on National Recovery became inactive with the exception of John F. Davis. In October, 1935, this individual wrote an article published in pamphlet form, entitled, "Lets us Build a National Negro Congress". This pamphlet was reportedly distributed throughout the Country and urged all sympathetic organizations to meet together and form sponsoring committees for the new National Negro Congress to be held in Chicago, Illinois, February 14, 1936.

In the latter part of 1935, a call was issued for a National Negro Congress to meet in Chicago, Illinois, on February 14 to 16, 1936. This call was:

> "To all Negroes, native and foreign born. To all Negro organizations, churches, labor unions, farm and sharecroppers' organizations. To all fraternal, civic, professional and political groups. To all organizations and persons of whatever race, who are willing to fight for economic and social justice for Negroes."

The purpose of the Congress is said not to have been to usurp the work of existing organizations, but rather to seek to accomplish unity of action of existing organizations.

James W. Ford, prominent Negro Communist, addressing the November, 1935 Plenum of the Central Committee of the Communist Party, declared that the National Negro Congress

> "promises to be one of the broadest movements ever organized among the Negroes in this country.
>
> "The Congress should be a broad Congress for Negro rights.
>
> "The Communist Party endorses the National Negro Congress. We support any sincere movement that will unify the Negro people for their daily needs and demands. It is under these conditions that we are supporting the building up of this National Negro Congress. It is based upon a minimum program which we agree with."

"These are some of the minimum demands of the program around which we can develop and built up a broad united front movement. Let us help build the National Negro Congress. It doesn't intend to destroy nor replace other Negro organizations. Every Party member, every Negro comrade, must now begin to throw every bit of energy he can into building local sponsoring committees in communities helping to raise funds."

The following are the points which the Congress planned to accomplish as outlined by John P. Davis in the call and pamphlet:

> "1. The organization of the protest of Negro organizations against civic, social and economic injustices heaped on the Negro and a heightening of that protest.

"2. United Front of Negro and white organizations around a basic minimum program of Negro rights.

"3. Holding on a nation-wide scale, as never before accomplished, public opinion, both Negro and white, against these injustices.

"4. A reaction as a result of the first three items listed above among federal, state and local governments which will result in the improvement of the conditions of Negro people in this country, and finally,

"5. A reaction as a result of the first three items listed above in the trade union field which will result in fairer treatment of Negro workers by trade unions."

To further show the interest of the Communist Party in the National Negro Congress, the following is quoted from page 35 of "People's Front", written by Earl Browder, General Secretary of the Communist Party at the time. It was published by the International Publishers in 1938. "Significant progress has been made in building a United Front of struggle for Negroes' liberation. The National Negro Congress, which met in Chicago in February, 1936, and established a permanent organization, found the correct road—the Negro people have learned to expect and demand of the Communists, the greatest sensitivity of their problem."

Aims and Purposes

The First Congress made the following seven demands:

1. The right of Negroes to jobs at decent living wages and for the right to join all trade unions. For the right to equal wages and equal labor conditions with other workers. For the organization of Negro workers with their fellow white workers into democratically controlled trade unions.
2. Relief and security for every needy Negro family; for genuine social and unemployment insurance without discrimination.
3. Aid to the Negro farm population, to ease the burden of debts and taxation; for the fight of farmers, tenants and sharecroppers to organize and bargain collectively.
4. For a fight against lynching, mob violence and police brutality; for enactment of a federal anti-lynching law; for the right to vote, serve on juries and enjoy complete civil liberty.
5. The right of Negro youth to equal opportunity in education and in the economic life of the community.
6. For complete equality for Negro women; for their right, along with all women, to equal pay for equal work; for their right to suitable environment for themselves and their children—an environment which demands adequate housing, good schools and recreational facilities; for their right to organize as consumers.

7. To oppose war and fascism, the attempted subjugation of Negro people in Ethiopia, the oppression of colonial nations throughout the world, for the independence of Ethiopia."

Second National Negro Congress

The Second National Negro Congress was held in Philadelphia, Pennsylvania, on October 15, 16, and 17, 1937. The Congress is claimed to have represented more than 500,000 members organized in trade unions, churches, civic, political and fraternal groups.

This Congress was addressed by such prominent Communists or near-Communists as:

James W. Ford

Clarence Hathaway

Dr. Harry F. Ward

Louise Thompson

William L. Patterson

The following is a list of discussions entered into at this Congress in Philadelphia:

"1. The right of Negroes to jobs at decent wages and the right to join on an equal basis all trade unions; the right to equal wages and equal labor conditions with other workers; the organization of Negro workers with their fellow white workers into democratically controlled trade unions.

"2. Relief and security for every needy Negro family; and genuine social and unemployment insurance without discrimination.

"3. Aid to the Negro farm population, to ease the burden of debts and taxation; the right of farmers, tenants and sharecroppers to organize and bargain collectively.

"4. A fight against lynching, mob violence and police brutality; for the right to vote, serve on juries and enjoy complete civil liberty; and for enactment of a federal anti-lynching law.

"5. The question of the Scottsboro Boys as a special demand, by bringing forward its full social and political significance.

"6. The right of Negro youth to equal opportunity in education and in the economic life of the community.

"7. For complete equality for Negro women; for their right, along with all women, to equal pay for equal work; for their right to a suitable environment for themselves and their children—an environment which demands adequate housing, good schools, and recreational facilities; for their right to organize as consumers.

"8. The struggle for economic, political, social and cultural equality of the Negro people; the necessity of joining with all the progressive forces in the land to defeat in a common front the forces of fascism and war breeding."

Third National Negro Congress

The Third National Negro Congress was held in Washington, D.C. in the Labor Department Auditorium on April 26, 27, and 28, 1940. This Congress was attended by 1,264 delegates. It approved the following major resolutions:

1. To accept unanimously and enthusiastically the offer of John L. Lewis to establish a working agreement with Labor's Non-Partisan League.
2. To condemn this imperialist war and the policies of the Roosevelt Administration which lead toward war and to cooperate with the progressive and labor forces in working for peace.
3. To demand the immediate dissolution of the Dies Committee as a great threat to our fundamental rights.
4. To press for immediate passage of the Anti-Lynching Bill.

A split occurred between the Communist and Non-Communist forces within the Third National Negro Congress. A Philip Randolph, who had been its President up to that time, refused to be a candidate for the presidency. On May 5, 1940, he issued a statement that the Congress was

"deliberately packed with Communists and C.I.O. members who were either Communists or sympathizers with Communists."

He added that most of the contributions to the Congress came from C.I.O. unions and said that John P. Davis of Washington, D.C., the Secretary of the Congress, had said during an Executive Committee meeting in New York,

"That the Communist Party contributed $100 a month to the Congress."

Randolph declared that the Communist Party, instead of trying to refute charges of the Dies Committee that it was a transmission belt for Communist propaganda,

"has brilliantly succeeded in giving the charge every appearance of truth and validity."

In his stead Max Yergan was the unopposed nominee for President of the Congress. He is a lecturer at the City College of New York and Treasurer of the International Committee on African Affairs. During his speech to the Congress he defended the Soviet Union and attacked President Roosevelt's foreign policy. It is interesting to note that James W. Ford was elected to the Executive Committee at this Congress.

The principal address was made by John L. Lewis.

John P. Davis, Secretary of the National Negro Congress, in outlining the peace program, followed the identical program of the Communist Party when he declared:

> "The position which our Congress should take on the question of war should be to oppose loans, credits, arms or any other aid direct or indirect to either side of the belligerents. We speak out firmly against aid to Nazi Germany but we speak out equal firmness against aid to imperialist Britain and imperialist France."

He said he believed that:

> "The American Negro people will refuse to follow American imperialism in an attack upon the Soviet Union, will refuse to fall victim to anti-Soviet adventures, will refuse to join American or world imperialism in an attack against the Soviet people."

A second Congress was held in 1937 in Philadelphia, and the third was held in Washington, D.C., in April, 1940, at which time a split occurred between the Communist and non-Communist forces. A. Philip Randolph, negro labor leader, resigned and later formed the March on Washington Movement, a militant, anti-Communist negro organization.

Officers

The only reported change in the officers of the National Negro Congress is to the effect that Ferdinand Smith, Secretary of the National Maritime Union, C.I.O. and a reported Communist, in May of 1942, was made National Treasurer of the Congress. Henry Johnson, one of the former Vice Presidents, was removed as an officer and member of the organization. It was also announced that George B. Murphy was made Administrative Secretary. With regard to Henry Johnson, it is said that he was expelled from the National Negro Congress because of his actions as "an agent of John L. Lewis", thus rendering him as "inimical to the best interests of the National Negro Congress, the Negro people, labor and national unity". *[61-6728-235 ▬ 6-8-42]*

The following individuals are reported to be the present officers of this organization:

Max Yergan, President

Reverend William H. Jernigan, Washington, D.C., Vice President

Mrs. Fay Allen, Los Angeles, California, Vice President

Reverend Owen Whitfield, Missouri, Vice President

Reverend Charles A. Lewis, Philadelphia, Pennsylvania, Vice President
Dr. Robert A. Simmons, Massachusetts, Vice President
John P. Davis, Washington, D.C., National Secretary
George B. Murphy, Jr., New York City, Administrative Secretary
Ferdinand C. Smith, New York City, National Treasurer
Julius A. Bostick, Atlanta, Georgia, Financial Secretary
Louis Burnham, New York City, National Youth Secretary

[61-6728-235- ▇▇▇ 6-8-42]

Organization

The National Negro Congress is being reorganized on a regional, or district, and local council basis. A region or district is composed of several states, with a vice-president in charge. There are to be also state organizations. These are made up of city bodies or local councils within the state. The local council is the basic form of organization. The local sponsoring committees, which initiate the movement for the National Negro Congress, automatically become local councils. These councils are to be federated bodies of already existing organizations which affiliate to the council on the basis of a part or the whole of the program adopted at Chicago.

Branches

The organization is said to have branches in the following states:

Alabama (Birmingham)
Connecticut (South Norwalk, Hartford)
Illinois (Chicago)
California (Los Angeles)
Washington, D.C.
Indiana (Gary, South Bend)
Massachusetts (Boston)
Missouri (St. Louis)
New York (Manhattan, Brooklyn)
South Carolina (Greenville)
Virginia (Suffolk, Richmond, Roanoke)
Maryland (Baltimore)
Michigan (Detroit)
New Jersey (Orange)
Ohio (Akron)
Pennsylvania (Philadelphia, Pittsburgh)

Rhode Island (Providence)

Texas (Waco) *[61-6728-235 ███ pa 3 6-8-42]*

Headquarters

Recently the headquarters of the National Negro Congress was moved from Washington, D.C., to 290 Lenox Avenue, New York City. It was stated, however, that the Congress would maintain a Washington Bureau with John P. Davis, National Secretary in charge, while George B. Murphy, Jr., Administrative Secretary, would be in charge of the New York City office. *[D.W. 61-8-42 pa 3]*

Officers

The history of the Congress reflects that since its inception it has been under the leadership, for the most part, of two men: James W. Ford, Negro candidate of the Communist Party for Vice President of the United States in 1934, 1936 and 1940, and John P. Davis, who although he has not been proven to be a member of the Communist Party has been definitely identified with that Party for the past five years.

Max Yergan, who became the President of the National Negro Congress, has been likewise identified with the Communist Party for the past five years. Scarcely an issue of the Daily appears which fails to reflect the name and accomplishments of Yergan, who is a Negro.

An article appearing on pages 546–547 of the periodical, "The Communist", June, 1940, attributes the following statement to John P. Davis, a leader of the Negro Congress:

> "I have visited the Soviet Union. I have talked with the Soviet people. I have witnessed their accomplishments and achievements. I know of their ideals and aspirations. I have witnessed the real and genuine rights of its freedom. I have witnessed their many nations and peoples, business and work in amity, collaboration and peace. I know of their deep friendship and aid to all oppressed peoples and on the basis of that experience and knowledge, which is shared by thousands of people, I firmly believe that the American Negro people will refuse to fall victim to anti-Soviet ventures. Will refuse to join American or World Imperialists in any attack against the Soviet people. . . ."

As further indication of the cooperation and infiltration of the Communist Party in connection with the National Negro Congress, it was noted in an article appearing in the October 30, 1940, issue of the Daily Worker that:

> "In a panel section of the Convention devoted to a discussion of political parties, Mother Ella Reeve Bloor Ohmbolt, Communist candidate for Congress from Pennsylvania, Second District, spoke, advancing her Party's Program to aid the economic status of both Negroes and whites and abolish the poll tax in the South."

Accomplishments

The principal work of the National Negro Congress, in addition to being a part of the United Front for the Communist Party, has been its campaign on behalf of the Scottsboro Boys, organizing Negro workers in the Congress for Industrial Organizations and its campaigns on behalf of Anti-Lynching and Anti-Jim Crow legislation.

Radical Activities and Connections

The following statements have been issued by James W. Ford concerning the interest of the Communist Party in the National Negro Congress:

> "In all of these issues, the role of the National Negro Congress becomes of utmost importance for us. The Congress does not receive sufficient support from us. It is still weak organizationally. It needs to be built and it is up to the Communists to do their share in helping to build it."
>
> "We Communists were never doubtful about the significance or the outcome of the National Negro Congress. We were not deterred by the charges of 'Communist domination.' We were guided by what we knew of the desire of the Negro masses for united action."
>
> "The Communists have played a big part in this development as well as in the struggle for unity of the Negro people and the white masses. Our Party as a whole has helped to organize the Negro people and has gained wide support for their struggles. There has been a better understanding on the part of Negro Communists of how to work among the Negro masses, bringing to them Communist methods of struggle, and creating faith among them in the ability of the Communist Party to break down the barriers of prejudice. . . ."
>
> "Today the tactic of the united front bringing together large masses of Negroes. . . ."
>
> "The National Negro Congress (First Congress) recorded progress made by Communists and many delegates who supported our program, in the increasing work we are carrying on in the various organizations of the Negro people. Our modest successes are, however, just beginnings. We must now undertake to profit from our experience, mistakes, shortcomings and successes, by showing what changes are necessary in our methods of work to build the National Negro Congress."
>
> "It is necessary for the Party membership, particularly the Negro members, to see the need and possibility of strengthening our influence in the existing Negro organizations, by joining them where possible and becoming useful members. We can today unite the Negro people on the basis of their day-to-day needs, and for the preservation of democratic rights in such a way that the greatest number of people will be brought together in common struggle."

"We do not contrapose immediate issues to the revolutionary objectives; we are concerned daily, hourly, with the miserable life of the whole of the Negro people, as a part of the larger struggle for socialism."

"As a duly elected member of the Executive Committee (of the National Negro Congress) at the 'recent Congress at Philadelphia, in the name of the Communist Party, I pledge one thousand Negro Communists to become members of the National Negro Congress during its drive. Our Communists must become the most active and enthusiastic workers in the National Negro Congress. We must see that the best of these comrades are utilized for work in the National Negro Congress."

"We Communists must organize all our forces to render great assistance to the National Negro Congress in carrying out its program. If we develop systematic work we shall be able to fulfill very soon the task of developing a broad People's Front among the Negro people in the United States against Fascism and war and for the liberation of the Negro people."

"Great united front organizations such as the National Negro Congress . . . will be an important sector of the Democratic Front."

James W. Ford has further characterized the National Negro Congress as:

"A broadening of the People's Front in America. The Congress is built upon the organizational idea of a federation of Negro organizations which, in effect, is the Negro People's Front."

A. W. Berry, one of the leaders of the National Negro Congress, has in the past been a member of the Central Committee of the Communist Party and an Upper Harlem Section Organizer of the Communist Party.

Edward Strong, an executive of the National Negro Congress, has been reported to be a high functionary in the Young Communist League.

The National Negro Congress is affiliated with the American Council on Soviet Relations. This latter group is regarded as the

"most intellectual Red setup in America."

The National Negro Congress was one of the organizations sponsoring the American Peace Mobilization at Turner's Arena in Washington, D.C., on September 13, 1940. John P. Davis, Chairman of the National Negro Congress, was chairman of the meeting in Washington, D.C., and introduced such well-known radicals as

Vito Marcantonio

Fred Keller, former member of the Abraham Lincoln Brigade in Spain

Dr. Max Yergan, now President of the National Negro Congress, has identified himself with the Communist Party for at least the last five years. An examination of the issue of the Daily Worker would indicate that it constitutes itself as being his advance press agent. There appeared in the Daily Worker for July 26, 1938, a statement to the following effect:

> "Dr. Max Yergan is not only an expert on African affairs but is also close to the throbbing pulse of the American Negro. As Executive Vice President of the National Negro Congress he participates in the shaping of policies that affect the lives of millions of Negroes."

William Z. Foster, writing in "The Communist" for November, 1936, under an article styled "The Crisis in the Socialist Party," declared, in part:

> "The Party's role was also one of significant importance in the organization of the great united front National Negro Congress in Chicago, February, 1936, of 1,817 delegates representing 1,200,000 members organized in trade unions, churches, youth groups and so forth. In all these united front movements the Communist Party is an official participant."

The Communist Party of California issued the following statement concerning Communist work in the National Negro Congress:

> "The Communist Party has given full support to the program of the National Negro Congress, both nationally and in California. Communist Party members in California worked very actively for the achievement of this United Negro People's Front."

A. Philip Randolph, President of the Brotherhood of Sleeping Car Porters, resigned in April, 1940, as President of the National Negro Congress on the grounds that it is controlled by Communists. Speaking before the Fifteenth Anniversary of the Brotherhood of Sleeping Car Porters in Harlem, New York, on September 17, 1940, Randolph declared:

> ". . . we reject the Communist program as a solution of the problems of the Negro because it is the negation of democracy. We condemn all Communist-Front and transmission belt organizations as a peril to the constructive and sound program of the Negro people since they seek only to serve the cause of the Communist Party, which is only concerned about the success to the foreign policy of Soviet Russia."

It was reported in April of 1941 that the combined forces of the National Negro Congress and the Maryland Youth Congress would carry on a drive to win jobs for 7,000 Negro Workers in the "Jim-Crow" Plant of the Glenn L. Martin Aircraft Company and the Bethlehem Steel Company. [*DW 4-21-42*]

Prior to the repudiation of the Non-aggression Pact between Germany and Russia, Doctor Max Yergan, President of the National Negro Congress, issued the following statement on May 24, 1941, in connection with the organization campaign to secure employment of Negroes in various National Defense Industries, ". . . it would be a mistake and it would do serious harm to the Negro People, if they demand jobs in exchange for support of war-making plans and of War itself, so this War holds no good for the Negro but will usher in destruction of his Democratic Right and further denial of the meager Civil Liberty he enjoys already.

"The Negro people must insist on jobs while at the same time opposing this imperialistic war and our independent interests. It is a war which cannot possibly serve to save Democracy or to liberate the people, for it is an instrument of oppression of the people the world over."

On July 4, 1941, subsequent to the German invasion of Russia, the National Negro Congress issued a significant policy statement calling on the Negro people "to give their fullest support to the cause of a genuine struggle against Hitlerism both at home and abroad. . . . this is the only way to secure manhood rights for the Negro people and to truly defend American Democracy." The statement continues:

"The slightest possibility of successful conquest by the Forces of Hitler of the vast territory and resources of the Soviet Union is a cause for alarm to all American people, but especially the Negro people for whom the world domination of Hitlerism would mean disaster for all their hopes for Democratic Rights".

The statement concluded: "The pledge of our Government for full aid to the Soviet Union in the brave fight against Hitlerism, will find welcome response from the Negro people."

"This is true not only because of the grave military disadvantage to which our country would be put by the defeat of the Soviet Union, but, equally because of the genuine admiration which the Negro people have for the land where race discrimination has been abolished."

". . . . It is now the clear task of every section of the Negro people to give their fullest support to the cause of a genuinely Democratic struggle against Hitlerism, both at home and abroad. This is the only way to secure Manhood Rights for the Negro people and to truly defend American democracy."

It was reported in November, 1941 that the Manhattan Council of the National Negro Congress demonstrated in front of the R. H. Macy Department Store, Herald Square, New York City. The demonstration is said to have been a failure inasmuch as it was planned to have approximately 5,000 persons present, however, actually there were approximately 25 persons in the demonstration. The purpose of the demonstration is said to have been to negotiate with the Macy Department Store to employ Negro personnel.

More currently, the National Negro Congress has been carrying on a campaign against the policy of the Army and Navy in refusing to accept donations of Negro blood, for "blood banks", which are stored to provide transfusions for men in battle. The Congress has alleged that this attitude of the Army and Navy is another demonstration of its Jim-Crow practices. In addition, there has been a demand on the part of the National Negro Congress, as well as related groups, for Negro Employment in National Defense Industry. Charges have been made, also, that there has been discrimination against the Negro race in employment in these industries. It has been additionally reported with respect to this program that the Communist Party and the Communist Front organization, the International Workers' Order participated in it. It is stated that this way Communist Doctrines may be presented to the Negro Race.

The following excerpt is taken from a pamphlet advertising a meeting of a unit of the National Negro Congress held March 2, 1942, at the New York Public Library, 9 West 124th St., New York City. "America has been at War for nearly three months! Sufficient time has elapsed and sufficient events have occurred for us again to "take stock" . . . examine the situation . . . and see where the Negro people stand in relation to the War. . . ."

It is reported in May, 1942 a meeting was held by the Manhattan Council of the National Negro Congress at which many of the speakers spoke against alleged discrimination against the Negro and called for mixed regiments of white and black soldiers. The question involving the people of India and Africa was dealt with by various speakers and it was urged that they be properly armed to guarantee the defeat of the Axis. Hope Stevens, who presided at the meeting, is said to have expressed their disappointment that only 70 persons were in attendance after arrangements had been made for 700.

In June 1942 the National Negro Congress issued an appeal styled "This is Our War—Wipe Out Discrimination—Let Negroes Fight Equally". It stated that "Negro Americans, especially, want to defeat Hitler, because Nazi slavery threatens our onward march to full freedom. The security of America and the defeat of Hitler make it imperative to open a western front in Europe now". In the appeal there were also demands that alleged discrimination against Negroes in war industries, in the Armed forces, and in civilian life be abolished and that the Negro people be integrated into all phases of the war effort. Along with the appeal were the following instructions:

1. Do everything you can to win the war.
2. Urge the removal of all discriminatory bars from the war effort.
3. Expose the disrupters of war unity.
4. Promote unity among Negroes for victory and full citizenship.

The above-set-out "appeal" is, of course, in direct harmony with the Communist Party line in that it urges full participation by Negroes in the war effort but on the other hand, in effect, agitates them. It is the reported theory that the Communist Party and its front organizations desire to attract the Negroes by such appeals and statements, but at the same time keep them within the bounds of the war effort.

[*DW 6-8-42 pa 3*]

The Daily Worker on March 15, 1943, announced that at a session of the National Executive Board of the National Negro Congress it was decided that a series of three regional "Victory Conferences on the Problems of the War and the Negro People" would be held in three areas; the Eastern Seaboard, the Middle West and the Pacific Coast. It was further stated that the conferences would be designed to bring together official representatives of organization among the Negro people as well as among progressive white Americans to consider and to act upon the basic problems of the negro as they relate to the war. It was decided that the conferences, the first of which would be held on the Eastern Seaboard, April 10 and 11, 1943, would be based primarily upon three vital issues before the negro people, namely,

1. Manpower (FEPC, Negro women in industry, the organized labor movement).

2. The Poll Tax (a united campaign to abolish the Poll Tax in the 78th session of the Congress).
3. Democratization of the stage, screen and radio (a national campaign for an accurate interpretation of the life and culture of the Negro people).

It was said further that in addition to the above questions, there would be such matters as the armed forces, "The Fascist Defensive on the Home Front", and the problem of strengthening civilian morale (rationing, price control, child care, high cost of living) to consider.

Accordingly, a "call" was issued by Max Yergan, president of the National Negro Congress, to bring together official delegates from the Northeastern states and the Eastern Seaboard who represented the leading organizations concerned with the problems of the Negro people.

On April 10 and 11, 1943, the conference was held with an estimated attendance of 1500. The main speakers were Max Yergan; Thelma Dale, executive secretary of the National Negro Congress; Edmonia Grant, member of the National Council, Y.W.C.A.; James B. Carey, Secretary-Treasurer, Congress of Industrial Organizations, and Vito Marcantonio, U.S. Congressman and president of the International Labor Defense, a Communist Party front organization.

Among the people taking a prominent part in the conference were the following individuals who are reported to be Communist Party members:

Ferdinand Smith, Secretary, National Maritime Union

Edward E. Strong, National Executive Secretary, National Negro Congress

Hope R. Stevens, Legislative representative of the National Negro Congress

James W. Ford, member of the National Committee, Communist Party

Ben Davis, Jr., member, National Committee, Communist Party

Dorothy Funn, of the Negro Labor Victory Committee

Audley Moore, Communist Party functionary, New York City

Doxey A. Wilkerson, Howard University

Charles Collins, Executive Secretary Negro Victory Committee

George Marshall of the National Federation for Constitutional Liberties

Clifford McAvory, Legislative Representative of the Greater N.Y., CIO, Industrial Union Council

The following panels were held at the conference "Manpower Panel", "A People's Victory—A People's Peace Panel", "Democratic Rights Panel", Wartime Living Standards Panel."

Writing in the Worker, James W. Ford, previously referred to as a member of the National Committee of the Communist Party, had this to say about the conference:

"The Conference was timely because of urgent problems connected with effective prosecution of the war and sentiments among the Negro people for unity. It will be a big step forward towards national unification behind the President, providing immediate measures are taken, first, by government and labor to break down barriers that still operate against the fullest mobilization of Negro citizens for the war; and secondly, providing broader organizational unity is established among the Negro people behind the central political and military issue that faces the nation, namely, the immediate opening of a second military front in Europe against Hitler. In this connection a great responsibility rests upon the shoulders of Negro leaders.

"Despite significant and outstanding advances which have been made in placing large numbers of Negro workers into war industries through the elimination of discriminatory bars, and by the fact that hundreds of thousands of Negro soldiers are sharing the burdens of our armed forces, it is stupid to fail to see that there still operates a conspiracy of Negro-baiting and discrimination. The Fair Employment Practice Commission which was set up to force employers to hire Negro citizens, men and women, was abandoned through a conspiracy of poll-tax Congressmen, defeatists and appeasers.

"Labor and the Negro people face new and greater common problems. A reactionary group of defeatists and appeasers headed by poll tax Congressmen and Martin Dies of the Dies Committee, is out to hamstring both labor and the Negro people. The initiators of the anti-labor Hobbs bill, the Johnson bill, opponents of a law to abolish the poll tax are Negro baiters, labor baiters and anti-Semites. Ties between the Negro people and labor must be made stronger. The fight to break down discrimination against Negroes in industry is a central task of labor. The trade unions must fight more aggressively for the re-establishment of the FEPC. They must stand in the forefront of this fight, so that the President's Executive Order 8802 against discrimination will not become a dead letter law.

"The regional Eastern conference of the National Negro Congress outlined a campaign for securing one million signatures in favor of re-establishment of the FEPC. Labor's participation in the conference is a pledge of support and assistance to this campaign. . . .

"Red-baiting and anti-Soviet activities in our country were linked with the poll taxers and appeasers in Congress. By his sterling example Congressman Marcantonio delivered a stinging rebuke at all of those who are thus hindering the struggle for rights of all citizens, black and white. At the present moment in the war when certain forces are trying to do everything possible to strain the relations between the Soviet Union and our own country, it behooves every loyal American to understand the meaning and full danger of red-baiting and Soviet-baiting to success in the war against Nazi Germany. This was the fundamental and contribution to the conference of Congressman Marcantonio, himself a democratic American and friend of the Negro people.

"The Conference brought together a broad representation of labor and of organizations of the Negro people. It demonstrated that the Negro people desire unity and are seeking the closest alliance with labor. . . .

". . . . The chief responsibility for failure to gain Negro rights and unity for the war effort will be at the door of all those who oppose unity and lag behind the spirit of fight now prevailing among broad masses. . . ."

A midwest conference of the National Negro Congress was held at the Masonic Temple, 275 East Ferry Street, Detroit, Michigan, on May 29 and 30, 1943. The conference was called to consider the problems of the war and the Negro people. The number of delegates and observers in attendance was said to be approximately three hundred on each day.

Pat Toohey, Michigan State Secretary of the Communist Party, and Jack Raskin, reportedly a known Communist Party member and Executive Secretary, Civil Rights Federation of Michigan, were in attendance during the conference. Raskin conducted a panel discussion on "Democratic Rights."

The following individuals were reported to have addressed the conference at some time during the two day session, either to the conference as a body or to the panel groups:

C. Lebron Simmons—President of the Detroit Council, National Negro Congress, reported Communist

Edward E. Strong—Secretary of the National Negro Congress, reported Communist

A. Clayton Powell, Jr.—Editor, "People's Voice"

Shelton Tappes—Sponsor, Michigan Free Browder Congress, reported Communist

G. James Flemming—Fair Employment Practices Committee

Ray Campbell—Of Local 633, International Brotherhood of Teamsters, Helpers, Chauffeurs, and Warehousemen, AF of L

Arthur Bowman—Chairman, Negro Youth Council for Victory and Democracy

Mrs. Rosa L. Cragg—Michigan Division, Office of Civilian Defense

Jack Raskin—Executive Secretary, Civil Rights Federation of Michigan, reported Communist

William L. Patterson—Of the Abraham Lincoln School, Chicago, Illinois, National Committee member of the Communist Party

Clayborne George—Attorney, representing the Cleveland branch of the National Association for the Advancement of Colored People

Gloster Current—Executive Secretary, Detroit Chapter, National Association for the Advancement of Colored People, reported Communist

I. P. Flory—Mine, Mill and Smelter Workers Union, C.I.O., Chicago, Illinois

The theme of the conference was to end discrimination in the armed forces and against Negro women in war plants. The resolutions adopted consisted of a six page statement which called for:

1. The opening of a second front.
2. Endorsement of the Marcantonio Anti-Poll Tax Bill.
3. Enforcement of the rationing laws.
4. End of discrimination.

5. Hiring of Negro women in all war plants.
6. For the Department of Justice to enforce the anti-lynching laws.
7. For all the Negroes to support the Administration's plan to fight the Axis until unconditional surrender.
8. The endorsement of the formation of an active Executive Committee for the midwest branch of the National Negro Congress.
9. A request that a full-time paid executive secretary be appointed to carry on the program of the conference.

There was distributed at the conference the following literature:

1. A sixteen-page booklet published by the National Federation for Constitutional Liberties, entitled "Poll Tax Repeal—A Priority for Victory."
2. A flyer which announced a freedom rally to be held Sunday, May 30, at Scott Methodist Church, 609 East Kirby, Detroit.
3. A publication of the National Negro Congress, entitled, "Congress Vue," which announced a Negro Freedom Rally at Madison Square Garden on June 7, 1943.
4. An announcement of the Negro Youth Council for Victory and Democracy to be held in Detroit on June 12–13, 1943.
5. A printed folder of the National Council of American-Soviet Friendship, Incorporated, soliciting financial contributions.
6. A printed flyer from the Detroit chapter of the American Council on Soviet Relations, which cautioned the readers to beware of those who seek to show distrust and suspicion of the Soviet Union, because "these people are doing Hitler's work."

Re: Negro Labor Victory Committee

Background

On the weekend of June 27 and 28, 1942, there were held two separate meetings, one the Trade Union and the Negro Peoples Victory Conference at the Fraternal Club House, 110 West 48th Street, New York City, on June 27, 1942, and the other the Negro Labor Victory Committee Meeting held at the Golden Gate Ballroom, Harlem, New York City, on June 28, 1942. It has been reported that these two meetings were part of the same program.

As a matter of background information concerning these two meetings, it has been confidentially reported that they were planned by the Negro Commission of the National Committee of the Communist Party, USA. The reason for this, it has been stated, was arrived at during a meeting held sometime in the middle of May, 1942, by the Negro Commission of the Party, at which time James Ford, member of the National Committee of the Party, is reported to have stressed the need of counteracting the influence of and the interest in the March on Washington Movement. It was reported that the Movement was deemed anti-Party in character and was considered a danger to the "united front policy" of the Party.

It was reported further that the Communist Party believed that danger existed of the Negro Movement falling under the leadership of the Socialist Party as allegedly represented by A. Philip Randolph. It has been further reported that it was decided at the meeting that a form of negative criticism of the March on Washington Movement was not enough and that simultaneously with the criticism by the Party of the Movement there should be set up an organization with the policy of the Party in contradistinction to the purely "Nationalist Movement" led by A. Philip Randolph.

It has been reported that Benjamin Davis, Jr., was assigned by the Party to write an article for the "Daily Worker" criticizing the March on Washington Movement. It should be noted at this time that an article concerning the March on Washington Movement appeared in the June 18, 1942, issue of the "Daily Worker" and was written by Ben Davis, Jr., who is Secretary-Treasurer of the "Daily Worker" and reported to be a member of the Communist Party.

The article referred to the meeting of the March on Washington Movement on June 16, 1942, in Madison Square Garden, New York City, and advised that the meeting "recorded a new high point in the militancy and aggressiveness of the Negro people for their just demands of equal integration into the war effort and complete citizenship in the United States."

With regard to the organization itself, however, the article stated:

> . . . The meeting revealed further that Norman Thomas Socialists, Trotskyites, Lovestoneites and other malignantly defeatist elements are seeking to exploit the just grievances of the Negro people to turn them against the nation, spread disunity, and ultimately to use these grievances against the Negro's own best interests. These nondescript, unpatriotic elements—who insult the honor of the Negro people by trying to incite them to disloyalty to their country and to their own interests—have a heavy influence in the so-called March on Washington Movement, which conducted the rally."

Prior to the above-mentioned article, an article appearing in the June 14, 1942, issue of the "Daily Worker," styled "Call Parley to Increase Negro Role in War," announced the Trade Union and Peoples Victory Conference. The article stated that the Conference was sponsored by the "People's Voice," a Negro weekly paper published in New York City, the National Conference of Negro Youth, and the Negro Labor Victory Committee.

In the above-mentioned article a "call" to the Conference was set out. The substance of this "call" was that for a victory of the United Nations in 1942 to become a reality "a WESTERN FRONT MUST BE OPENED," and that a failure to strike quickly might mean the danger of "a Hitler Victory." The "call" continued, pointing out that such a victory would impose "upon us all their false ideas of 'racial superiority'." It stated that the Negro people were anxious to make their contributions to the war effort and that they should be given an opportunity. The "call" concluded by demanding a "full and complete integration of the Negro people into all war activities . . ." *[100-115471-2]*

The Trade Union and Peoples Victory Conference

The Trade Union and Negro Peoples Victory Conference was held June 27, 1942, from 10:00 A.M. until 6:30 P.M., at the Fraternal Club House, 110 West 48th Street, New York City.

It has been reported that the meeting was attended by 350 delegates and 75 observers, representing eleven international unions affiliated with the American Federation of Labor, and seventy-five local unions and seventy-nine international unions affiliated with the Congress of Industrial Organizations. It was further reported that 45 of the delegates represented religious, fraternal, political and civic groups.

The "keynote address" was given by Ferdinand Smith, Secretary of the National Maritime Union and reported member of the Communist Party. Smith has been confidentially reported to have been selected by the National Committee of the Party to organize the Party's work among the Negro people. [*D.W. 6-28-42*]

In his "keynote speech" Smith is reported to have stated that the Negroes "are denied real participation in this struggle for freedom." He is reported to have said that "they are Jim Crowed in the armed services," and he is reported to have attacked "appeaser groups" who, he stated, are attempting to divide the Negro people.

The second session of the Conference was opened by Harry Reich. Reich is stated to have been a member of the Communist Party since 1933. He is also reported to have been an organizer of the Food Workers Industrial Union, an organization reportedly built by the Communist Party which was affiliated with the Trade Union Unity League.

The main speaker at the second session of the Conference was Congressman Vito Marcantonio. In his speech he is reported to have announced that he was introducing a bill for punishment of discriminatory employers.

Among the other speakers listed were John A. Davis, Executive Secretary of Governor Lehman's Committee on Discrimination, and Elmer Carter, Member of the New York State War Council.

A twelve-point program was adopted at the Conference calling for such measures as the training of 100,000 Negroes for war production, a demand that a National Conference on Discrimination be called, a demand for full citizenship rights for Negroes, and a program to rid the Army and Navy of Jim Crowism.

Fourteen resolutions were passed at this Conference, the majority of which pertained to the promotion of the adoption of anti-discrimination measures. However, certain political resolutions were adopted, including independence for Puerto Rico, the ending of foreign domination of foreign countries by the United States, the granting of political amnesty for political prisoners in the West Indies and Puerto Rico, and urging that the Civilian Conservation Corps and the National Youth Administration be extended.

Negro Labor Victory Committee "Unity for Victory" Rally

On Sunday, June 28, 1942, at the Golden Gate Ballroom, 142nd Street and Lennox Avenue, New York City, the Negro Labor Victory Committee sponsored a "Unity for Victory" Rally. This meeting is reported to have been attended by approximately 6,000 persons, 4,000 of whom were seated and 2,000 of whom were reported to have stood on the outside.

The main speaker at the Rally was the Honorable Paul V. McNutt, Chairman of the War Manpower Commission. Other speakers were Congressman Vito Marcantonio; Reverend A. Clayton Powell, New York City Councilman; Ferdinand Smith of the National Maritime Union; Winifred Norman, Chairman of the National Conference of Negro Youths; and Eddie Tolan, former Olympic track star.

A twelve-point program was adopted at this meeting, the substance of which called for the extending of anti-discrimination measures and the ending of Jim Crow practices.

The Chairman of the meeting was stated to be Charles Collins, an organizer of the Hotel and Club Employees Union, Local No. 6, American Federation of Labor. Collins is reported confidentially to be a member of the Communist Party and one whom the Party is building up in the trade union field.

The following individuals are reported to have been active in the organizational activities connected with the meeting and are stated to be members of the Communist Party:

George Brown—International Vice President of the Hotel and Restaurant Employees International Alliance and Bartenders International League of America, AFL.

James Alston—Business Agent and organizer of Local 623 of the Amalgamated Meat Cutters and Butcher Workman of North America, AFL.

Arthur Garvin—Organizer for the Hotel Front Service Employees Union, Local 144, AFL.

Sabina Martinez—Organizer for the Cleaners and Dyers Union, Local 328, CIO. *[100-115471-2]*

As reflecting the attitude of the Communist Party toward the "week and conference" of the Negro Labor Victory Committee, June 27 and 28, 1942, an editorial appeared in the "Daily Worker" of June 30, 1942. The editorial stated that the conference "was a tremendous expression of the Negro people's patriotic desire for their country's victory over Hitler," and that at the same time "it was a powerful demonstration, demanding the full rights of the Negro people. . . ." It commented favorably on the speeches of the Honorable Paul V. McNutt, Congressman Vito Marcantonio and Councilman A. Clayton Powell, Jr.

The editorial continued, advising that "The Negro people showed their desire for unity behind win-the-war candidates in November, when thunderous acclaim greeted Councilman Powell's request that Harlem vote for Marcantonio."

The editorial concluded demanding that "An immediate program and action by our national government against every single discriminatory practice . . . is urgently necessary."

Activities

On July 1[5], 1942, at the Renaissance Casino, 138th Street and 7th Avenue, New York City, the Committee held a meeting in conjunction with the National Conference of Negro Youth, described as a Communist Party instructed and sponsored organization. It was stated that the meeting was part of a campaign the Party organized on a nationwide scale around the "Odell Waller execution," the purpose of which is said to be the abolition of the poll tax and lynching. At the same time, it has been stated, the meeting was part of the movement to counteract the effect of the March on Washington Movement. [*100-115471-12*]

The meeting was also attended by representatives of Local 65, Fur Workers Union, CIO, and the National Negro Congress. The Confidential Informant has described the meeting as being composed of a series of speeches made by individuals who posed as "first time speakers" but whose Party "jargon and manner" indicated that they were not beginners. The meeting was said to have been attended by approximately 100 persons. The outward purpose of the meeting was to protest against the lynching of one Willie Vinson, a Texarkana, Texas, Negro. [*100-115471-15*]

On July 15, 1942, it was also ascertained that the Committee prepared and sponsored a petition in cooperation with Local 91, United Furniture Workers of America, CIO, 186 Romson Street, Brooklyn, New York, directed to Mr. Donald Nelson, Chairman, War Production Board, urging the utilization of the skill of the workers and the facilities of the Spring Products Corporation, Long Island, New York, through the allocation of war contracts to that company. The petition further stated that 400 Negro workers were employed at this company and that they faced loss of their jobs because war contracts had not been allocated to this plant. [*100-115471-11*]

It has been reported that the Committee, in connection with the Young Communist League, on July 17, 1942, called a meeting which was held but a half of a block away from the meeting place of the March on Washington Movement. Circulars were stated to have been distributed near the meeting place of the March on Washington Movement in order to confuse the people and to attract them to the Communist-inspired meeting away from the March on Washington Movement meeting. [*100-115471*]

On July 24, 1942, the Committee sponsored a meeting held at the Uptown Fur Center, 2132 7th Avenue, New York City, the purpose of which was to draw up an action program "for getting Citizens Rights for the Negro in America today." At the meeting a report was given by Ewart Guinier, a reported Communist concerning a conference had with the Attorney General wherein alleged facts were presented concerning recent lynchings and injustices committed against the Negro people. Guinier stated that he urged the Attorney General to ask the President to issue a proclamation for Negro rights. At the meeting a resolution was passed to bring pressure to bear on the Attorney General and President Roosevelt for the issuance of the proclamation. Several members of the Communist Party spoke and it was decided to hold a mass rally in Brooklyn on August 8, 1942.

The Committee voted to support the March on Washington parade and mass meeting held on July 25, 1942, in New York City. It was decided that instead of getting out their own petitions, members would use the petitions of the March on Washington Movement.

A committee, consisting of Ferdinand Smith, Solomon Harper, Sabina Martinez, Ewart Guinier and George Murphy, was appointed to visit local Congressmen in an attempt to obtain their signatures for a petition urging members of the House of Representatives to support the Geyer Anti-Poll Tax Bill. It should be pointed out that all members of the committee had been reported to be either Communist Party members or closely affiliated with the Party. [*100-115471*]

On July 27, 1942, the Daily Worker announced that a letter had been forwarded by the Committee to Admiral Emory S. Land, Chairman of the War Shipping Administration, where it was demanded that a Negro sea captain, one Hugh Mulzac, be "used immediately as a ranking officer" in the interest of "defeating the Axis."

The letter is stated to have also pointed out the maritime industry "is still protecting its prejudice at the cost of transportation for victory. This is near treason, especially when we need to use every shipping resource to transport men and materials . . ." [*DW 7-27-42*]

On August 12, 1942, the Negro Labor Victory Committee held a meeting at the Harlem Workers Club, 125th Street near Lenox Avenue, New York City, attended by approximately 40 persons. A report and discussion were centered around efforts to obtain the passage of the Geyer Anti-Poll Tax Bill. The report pertained to the results obtained by the delegation stated to have visited Congressman Gavigan to obtain his support in the passage of the Geyer Anti-Poll Tax Bill. It was stated that the delegation was assured that Congressman Gavigan would do all within his power to see that the bill was brought to the floor of the House.

The delegation is reported to have consisted of Ewart J. Guinier, Secretary of the Negro Labor Victory Committee; Charles Collins, organizer of the Hotel, Restaurant and Club Employees, AFL, Local No. 6; George B. Murphy, the Administrative Secretary, National Negro Congress; Elinor Kahn, National Federation for Constitutional Liberties; and James Allen, head of the New York State National Association for the Advancement of Colored People. It was reported further that all of these individuals are Communist Party members except James Allen. [*100-115471*]

On August 31, 1942, the Negro Labor Victory Committee sponsored a meeting which was attended by approximately 2,000 people at the Golden Gate Ballroom, Harlem, New York City. The meeting is said to have been endorsed by the State,

County and Municipal Workers of America; Local No. 65 of the Wholesale and Warehouse Union, CIO; the United Electrical, Radio and Machine Workers of America; Local No. 125, Fur Floor Boys and Shipping Clerks; Joint Board of the Fur Dressers and Dyers Union, CIO; and the United Shoe Workers of America.

The meeting was presided over by Charles Collins, organizer for Local No. 6 of the Hotel and Club Employees Union, AFL, a reported Negro Communist from Trinidad, British West Indies. The following individuals are stated to have spoken:

Lyndon Henry, Manager of Local No. 88 of the Fancy Fur Dyers.

James Lustig, organizer, District No. 5, United Electrical, Radio and Machine Workers of America, CIO.

Thomas Jasper, Executive Secretary of the Negro Labor Victory Committee.

Canada Lee, former boxer and actor in the play "Native Son."

Reverend Adam Clayton Powell, New York City Councilman and Pastor of the Abyssinian Baptist Church.

Louis Wainstock, Secretary, District Council No. 9, Painters Union, AFL.

All of the speakers referred generally to discrimination against the Negroes and exhorted the listeners to do something about it. It was stated that they were particularly vitriolic in their denunciation of the Police Department of New York City, the Governor of Alabama, the Governor of Georgia, the Daily News, the World Telegram and the Journal-America, branding all either as Hitler agents or agencies. It is stated that numerous examples of what particular unions are doing to provide jobs for Negroes were cited. The crime wave in Harlem was attributed to the economic conditions of the Negro which were asserted to be deplorable. All are said to have been vehement in their demand for the opening of a "second front" immediately as a solution of all the problems of the people. Resolutions were stated to have been made for the independence of India and the opening of a "second front."

The National Maritime Union is said to have provided a delegation of Negro seamen who served on ships which were torpedoed. These individuals in turn served as a color guard, it is reported.

The meeting was described as evidencing a marked lack of enthusiasm except when Adam Clayton Powell spoke. Powell, in his speech, is stated to have praised the fight of the Russians, stressed the need for unity to create a "new world where there will not be any rich or any poor people—a people's world based on justice and equity."

[*100-115471-23*] ████████

On November 15, 1942, at the Golden Gate Ballroom the Negro Labor Victory Committee sponsored a "Peoples Rally and Drama on the Four Freedoms," in attendance at which were said to have been approximately 1,000 persons. The chairman of the meeting was Earl Robinson who made introductory remarks, explaining the purpose of the meeting as being to dramatize the "Four Freedoms" and to make them a living reality. Juan Antonio Corretjer, Secretary of the Puerto Rican Nationalist Party, spoke on the Puerto Rican situation and attributed starvation in that country to the United States Government. He charged the American policy with regard to Puerto

Rico as being imperialistic and said that the Puerto Rican Nationalist Party aims to set up a democratic republic in Puerto Rico.

Barbara Watson, described as the daughter of Municipal Court Judge Watson, New York City, is reported to have spoken on Africa and expressed the aspirations of Africans for freedom.

An individual by the name of Lui Liang-Mo spoke on China and condemned American isolationism prior to December 7, 1941.

Kumar Goshal is said to have spoken on the Indian situation, in effect condemning Great Britain, and said that the Indians do not want a dominion status, rather they want a government of their own.

Congressman Vito Marcantonio spoke on the Puerto Rican situation and urged lend-lease aid to the Puerto Rican Government. At the same time he denounced the filibustering in the Senate on the poll tax bill.

Charles Collins, a reported Communist, who made the collection appeal, spoke against lynching, "Jim Crow," and urged the application of the Four Freedoms to all countries. *[100-115471-31]*

On January 22, 1943, members of the Negro Labor Victory Committee who had been designated as delegates formed a delegation which visited several officials in Washington to protest over the curtailment of activities of the Fair Employment Practice Committee. The delegation was composed of approximately 20 people and was led by A. J. Isserman representing the National Federation for Constitutional Liberties, a Communist front. It is said that the delegation advised representatives of the Fair Employment Practices Committee that they wanted to support the Committee but that they desired to see it returned to an autonomous status rather than to have it controlled by "appeasers." After visiting the various Governmental representatives, the delegation reportedly went to the local offices of the National Federation for Constitutional Liberties at which time they selected four individuals who were allegedly to fulfill an appointment at the White House on the same day. The individuals selected were William Bassett, A. J. Isserman, Moran Weston and Zera Dupont. *[100-115471-36]*

On February 16, 1943, members of the Negro Labor Victory Committee reportedly had an appointment with the Honorable Paul V. McNutt at which time it presented the following proposals:

A. That the railroad hearings of the Fair Employment Practices Committee should be rescheduled at once.

B. That the Fair Employment Practices Committee function as an independent Governmental agency responsible to the President.

C. That the Committee be granted an adequate budget.

D. That the Committee be given power to apply penalties for violations of the President's Executive Order.

E. That the Committee be comprised of representatives of labor minorities and industry functioning on a voluntary basis.

F. That Mr. McNutt issue a stern warning to contractual agencies to cease their discrimination practices against Negro workers who leave their nonessential jobs for war work in compliance with the "work or fight" order.

On June 7, 1943, at Madison Square Garden, New York City, the "Negro Freedom Rally" was held under the auspices of the Negro Labor Victory Committee, the Brooklyn Committee and the Peoples Committee. Approximately 20,000 individuals are said to have attended this function with several thousands remaining on the outside.

Confidential informants have advised that considerable Communist Party control and influence have existed behind the scenes of this meeting and that Party functionaries have been active in assisting in the arrangements for the affair. Among the people who are said to have been responsible for staging this meeting are Dorothy K. Funn of the Negro Labor Victory Committee, a reported Communist; Ferdinand Smith, Secretary of the National Maritime Union and reported Communist; Benjamin Davis, Jr., National Committee member of the Communist Party; Max Yergan, reported Communist and leader of the Council on African Affairs; and Adam Clayton Powell, Jr., New York City Councilman and minister who is said to have numerous connections with the Communist Party and Communist Party front groups. All of the foregoing individuals are Negroes.

A large crowd estimated at 20,000 attended the meeting at which the following measures were urged: the passage of the anti-poll tax bill, the opening of a "second front now" and the elimination of "Jim Crow in the Armed Forces." It might be noted that urging for a second front has recently resumed its place in the Communist Party line. The principal speakers at the meeting were Ferdinand Smith, Dr. Channing Tobias, Lester Granger, Max Yergan, Dr. Charlotte Hawkins Brown, Congressman Vito Marcantonio, Charles Collins, Michael Quill, Adam Clayton Powell, Jr., and Dorothy K. Funn. It is said that the general theme of the speeches dealt with race discrimination. Congressman Marcantonio spoke on the anti-poll tax bill and urged its passage.

A drama was presented at the meeting which was entitled "For This We Fight." This play, written by Langston Hughes, Negro poet and a reported Communist, was described as impressive. It depicted alleged racial discrimination in the Armed Forces. The Negro artists Paul Robeson and Duke Ellington took part in the play. In this connection, Adam Clayton Powell, Jr., Reverend Thomas Harten and Ferdinand Smith were delegated to carry "the message of the people" to the President at an unknown date. This message reportedly contains a demand that alleged discrimination in the Armed Forces be abolished.

The "Daily Worker," the Communist Party news organ, under date of June 9, 1943, devotes considerable space to this meeting and points out the effectiveness and power in the demonstration shown at the meeting. Robert Minor, National Committee member of the Communist Party points out that this meeting was "a discovery of strength" and eulogizes the part of organized labor in the meeting.

Officers

The following individuals, according to a public release of this organization, are the officers of it:

Co-Chairmen: Ferdinand C. Smith, National Secretary, National Maritime Union; George E. Brown

Vice Presidents: Roger Straughn; Amelia Lockhart, Ladies Auxiliary Local 370, Dining Car Employees Union

Executive Secretary: Charles A. Collins

Administrative Secretary: Dorothy K. Funn, Teachers Union

Treasurer: Arthur Garvin

Organizational Secretary: Thomas Jasper, Assistant Manager, Fur Floor Union

Finance Committee: James Alston, Meat Cutters Union, AFL; Thomas Astwood; Amy White

ADDENDUM

FBI DOCUMENTS

22 June 1942 Letter from J. Edgar Hoover, director, FBI, to Special Agents in Charge

27 August 1942 Internal memorandum from FBI Security Division section chief J. K. Mumford to Security Division head D. M. Ladd

27 August 1942 Letter from J. Edgar Hoover to Special Agent in Charge, New York, N.Y.

17 September 1942 Internal memorandum from Supervisor J. K. Mumford to D. M. Ladd

3 October 1942 Internal memorandum from J. Edgar Hoover to Special Agents in Charge

October 1942 Bureau Bulletin No. 108, Series 1942, Section (G): Procedure for reporting all matters under FOREIGN-INSPIRED AGITATION AMONG THE AMERICAN NEGROES—INTERNAL SECURITY

5 August 1943 Letter from J. Edgar Hoover to Special Agents in Charge

13 September 1943 Letter from J. Edgar Hoover to Special Agent in Charge, New York, N.Y.

14 September 1943 Internal memorandum for J. Edgar Hoover from Security Division head D. M. Ladd

June 22, 1942

STRICTLY CONFIDENTIAL

SAC	ALBANY	HUNTINGTON	PHILADELPHIA
	ATLANTA	INDIANAPOLIS	PHOENIX
	BALTIMORE	JACKSON	PITTSBURGH
	BIRMINGHAM	JUNEAU	PORTLAND
	BOSTON	KANSAS CITY	PROVIDENCE
	BUFFALO	KNOXVILLE	RICHMOND
	BUTTE	LITTLE ROCK	ST. LOUIS
	CHARLOTTE	LOS ANGELES	ST. PAUL
	CHICAGO	LOUISVILLE	SALT LAKE CITY
	CINCINNATI	MEMPHIS	SAN ANTONIO
	CLEVELAND	MIAMI	SAN DIEGO
	DALLAS	MILWAUKEE	SAN FRANCISCO
	DENVER	NEWARK	SAN JUAN
	DES MOINES	NEW HAVEN	SAVANNAH
	DETROIT	NEW ORLEANS	SEATTLE
	EL PASO	NEW YORK	SIOUX FALLS
	GRAND RAPIDS	NORFOLK	SPRINGFIELD
	HONOLULU	OKLAHOMA CITY	WASHINGTON, D. C.
	HOUSTON	OMAHA	QUANTICO

RE: FOREIGN-INSPIRED AGITATION
AMONG THE AMERICAN NEGROES;
INTERNAL SECURITY.

Dear Sir:

Since the declaration of war by the United States against the Axis powers, the Bureau has received complaints and information from all sections of the country that it is believed the Axis Powers have endeavored to create racial agitation among American negroes which would cause disunity and would serve as a powerful weapon for adverse propaganda.

A great deal of this racial agitation has been traced back to organizations which were originally set up by representatives believed to be connected with the Japanese government or individuals with Japanese contacts.

It is believed that agitation has been incited among the American negroes by telling them that the present war is a "race war" and that they should not fight against the Japanese, who are also of the colored race. The negroes have also been told by propagandists that they should not register under the provisions of the Selective Service Act and that after Japan wins this war, the negroes will be permitted to set up their own government in Africa.

Numerous reports have also been received from all sections of the country that indicate part of the agitation among the American negroes may be traced back to the Communist Party. Activity in this field of the Party and Communist Party front organizations is reflected in agitating for the employment of negroes in defense industries and Government agencies. Other agitation is for the abolishment of "Jim Crowism" in the armed forces. Further activity of the Party is carried on in economic and political fields by calling for such measures as the abolishment of poll taxes.

It is also noted that certain influential and prominent negroes with apparently no present subversive affiliations have been conducting similar campaigns of agitation to those related above. Local groups have also been reported as conducting comparable programs.

It is desired that a survey be conducted immediately in your territory as well as a review of your files to ascertain the extent of agitation among the negroes which may be the outgrowth of any effort on the part of the Axis powers or the Communist Party. As noted previously groups and individuals with apparently no present subversive affiliations are also conducting similar programs of agitation. The Bureau is nevertheless interested and the same should be reported in the survey and subsequent investigative reports.

It is also believed that an examination of the colored newspapers or publications will describe the true feelings of many of the colored communities. You are directed to subscribe to copies of any negro publications which appear to be pro-Axis or pro-Communist in nature, in order that a close scrutiny of the same may be maintained.

In the event any individual or organization is discovered disseminating propaganda to the American negroes which tends to create unrest or dissatisfaction in the American form of Government, it is desired that individual cases be opened and that these cases be vigorously followed for possible prosecution under the Sedition statutes, Selective Service Act, Registration Act or Voorhis Act.

With respect to the material developed it is desired that the same be reported as "FOREIGN-INSPIRED AGITATION AMONG THE AMERICAN NEGROES IN THE ______________ DIVISION." The character of these reports should be "INTERNAL SECURITY." Each Field Office should consider itself as the Office of Origin. The activities of the various groups or individuals must be reported in separate and distinct sections of the report.

It is desired that each Field Office make full use of the negro informants within their respective territories and that efforts be made to develop reliable negro informants in order that the Bureau may receive all pertinent information in this regard.

It is, of course, necessary to use the usual care in protecting the identities of confidential informants, inasmuch as you are expected to furnish copies of the reports to the appropriate Offices of Military and Naval Intelligence.

It is not contemplated that instructions contained herein are to be interpreted that the American negroes are a subversive group. The purposes of this survey and investigation are solely to make it possible for the Bureau to keep currently abreast with such agitation and to be cognizant of the identities of groups and individuals responsible for the same.

It is desired that the results of this survey be made available to the Bureau not later than thirty days after the receipt of this letter. A supplemental report must be submitted on the twentieth day of each month thereafter.

Very truly yours,
John Edgar Hoover
Director

August 27, 1942

MEMORANDUM FOR
MR. LADD
RE: AGITATION AMONG THE NEGROES,
INTERNAL SECURITY.

There are attached hereto letters concerning the captioned matter which are being directed to the Birmingham, Chicago, Detroit, Miami, New Orleans and New York Field Divisions. The purpose of these letters is to instruct the above-named Offices to conduct additional surveys in their Field Divisions to ascertain information reflecting the reasons or causes of unrest and agitation among the Negroes in those areas.

It is believed that the Field Divisions chosen are representative of areas in which there exists considerable agitation and unrest among the Negroes. With respect to the Chicago, Detroit and New York Field Divisions, they have been instructed to center particular attention to the situation in those three cities.

Not only is it requested of the Field in this instance to obtain information concerning those individuals and/or organizations agitating or causing unrest among the Negroes, but the Field has also been instructed to obtain data pertaining to economic, social or political circumstances in the area involved which possibly add to the unrest or dissatisfaction.

As you will note, the Field has been asked to ascertain through highly discreet inquiries what preventive steps have been taken within the area in question to alleviate or to cope with this situation.

As you will further note, the Field is instructed to report the results of the surveys in a logical and orderly fashion, giving appropriate titles for the different sections.

It is recommended that these letters be forwarded to the Field to aid in the study to be made by the Bureau of the Negro situation.

Respectfully,
J. K. Mumford

August 27, 1942

PERSONAL AND CONFIDENTIAL

Special Agent in Charge
New York, New York

RE: AGITATION AMONG NEGROES
IN NEW YORK FIELD DIVISION,
INTERNAL SECURITY.

Dear Sir:

It is my desire that you immediately institute a comprehensive survey within your Field Division with particular regard to the City of New York to ascertain all reasons, or causes, for unrest and agitation among the Negroes in that area. This survey is to be regarded as a separate project from that requested of you in my letter dated June 22, 1942, entitled "Foreign-Inspired Agitation Among the American Negroes, Internal Security."

I wish to point out to you that I have chosen New York City, among other cities, as a representative city where there exists considerable agitation and unrest among the Negroes. Additional surveys are being made by the following Field Divisions: Birmingham, Chicago, Detroit, Miami, New Orleans. It is pointed out to you that the results of your survey are to be used in the preparation of a study by the Bureau of the situation.

It is expected that you not only include in your survey information concerning those individuals and/or organizations agitating or causing unrest among the Negroes, but data pertaining to economic, social or political circumstances which possibly add to the unrest or dissatisfaction among the Negroes in this area.

In this connection, I want you to ascertain through highly discreet inquiries what preventative steps are being taken within the area in question to alleviate or to cope with such situation. I must insist upon the utmost discretion in this particular phase of your survey so that absolutely no impression may be given or inference taken that the Bureau is inquiring into matters of local concern.

All evidence of foreign-inspired agitation must, of course, be given your most careful attention. Furthermore, all information reflecting that individuals or organizations for their own personal gain or popularity are agitating for or among the Negroes must be given like attention.

I desire that the results of your survey be submitted to the Bureau within ten days of the date of this letter. It is expected, of course, that all information obtained by you will be set out in the most logical and orderly fashion in which there will be given appropriate titles for different sections. It is my desire that separate sections of your report be devoted to organizations; to individuals; to economic, social or political conditions; and to preventive measures taken in the locality involved. With regard to information concerning activity of individuals and organizations, the same must be appropriately separated so as to reflect the amount and type of agitation caused or carried on by pro-German, pro-Italian, pro-Japanese and pro-Communist forces.

I want this survey assigned to at least one experienced Agent in your Office who is entirely familiar with local conditions as they exist in this matter. I expect that you will afford this project your most expeditious attention and careful supervision. I cannot overemphasize the highly important nature of it.

Very truly yours,

John Edgar Hoover
Director

September 17, 1942

MEMORANDUM FOR
MR. LADD
RE: AGITATION AMONG AMERICAN NEGROES

There are attached hereto digests of surveys conducted by the Field with regard to the captioned matter. There are as yet lacking surveys from the Charlotte, Cleveland, New York, San Diego and Sioux Falls Field Divisions. The information submitted to the Bureau by the Field, as you will recall, has been in compliance with Bureau instructions contained in its letter of June 22, 1942, directed to all Special Agents in Charge. The information consists of data set forth as a result of a review of the files in the Field concerning un-American activities among and by the Negroes along with data obtained as a result of investigation and opinions concerning the Negro situation received from interviews with prominent people in the particular area who are looked upon as authorities on the subject. It is believed that the material as reflected in the accompanying digests gives a preliminary picture of the unrest and dissatisfaction on the part of Negroes and those individuals, organizations and other forces responsible for the same.

There is being set out hereinafter a summarization of the material as submitted by the Field, which will be set forth in related order:

Reports and Complaints of Unrest, Dissatisfaction and Un-Americanism Among the Negroes

In a great majority of the Field offices numerous complaints and rumors have been reported by the public of unrest and dissatisfaction among the colored people alleged to be caused by foreign-inspired agitation and un-Americanism on the part of Negroes more often reported and reflected in statements and utterances, but at the same time, in isolated instances, reflected in the activities of a few Negroes.

Many utterances stated to have been made by Negroes, which have been reported throughout the country, reflect pro-Japanese sentiments or the attitude that the present war is a racial war, and for that reason Negroes should align themselves with other colored races such as the Japanese. It is pointed out that very few reports reflect pro-German activity or statements on the part of Negroes, although in certain instances there have been alleged statements received to the effect that Hitler or Germany as the case may be, would be helpful and kindly toward the Negroes should the United States be conquered by Germany.

Numerous reports have been received especially by the Southern Field offices to the effect that Negroes are arrogant, dissatisfied, or are changed in their formerly respectful attitude. Accompanying these reports are complaints or statements to the effect that this change in the attitude of the Negro is possibly a result of un-American activity among them.

Another type of complaint or report which has been received is to the effect that Negroes are discriminated against and are not given equal rights to those of white people. Instances of alleged discrimination existing in defense industries, Governmental agencies and in the Armed Forces have been reported with the accompanying opinions that the same are responsible for the situation of unrest among the Negroes in the United States.

In at least two Field offices in the South rumors have been reported that during an ensuing "black out" designated by the Civilian Defense setup, a riot between colored people and white people would take place and, more specifically, that Negroes were preparing to "rise up against the whites." In each of these instances, no riot demonstration or fight have occurred, and the origin of the rumor has not been determined, although extensive inquiries and investigation have been made. In the vicinity of Norfolk, Virginia, an area in which one of these rumors was spread, the origin was attributed to Civilian Defense authorities by Governor Darden of Virginia. No specific accusations, however, were made.

It is pointed out that in practically every instance of reported un-Americanism among the Negroes, no specific or identifying information is submitted. Innumerable inquiries have been instituted in an attempt to verify the reports with negative results. In some instances where the individual who was allegedly engaged in the un-American activity or who allegedly made the un-American statement, it was ascertained that either the statement was made at a time when the speaker or doer was intoxicated or when the same was said or done as a result of ignorance or dissatisfaction. Also, attempts made to identify possible pro-Axis activity as a cause or influencing factor have been met with failure to obtain something tangible other than those organizations presently under investigation for pro-Japanese activity.

Agitational Forces at Work Among the Negroes

Un-American Organizations and Groups

Generally those un-American forces which have been reported as being active among the Negroes since the beginning of the war are pro-Japanese organizations, very few and isolated pro-German individuals and the Communist Party and its various machinations.

Following are those organizations, which in at least some of the areas where they are active, are said to be pro-Japanese:

1. The Moorish Science Temple of America.
2. The Moslem, Islamic or Mohammedan Sects.
3. The Development of Our Own.
4. The Peace Movement of Ethiopia.
5. The Universal Negro Improvement Association.
6. The Ethiopian Pacific Movement.

Investigations of the foregoing are being continued; and, with reference to some of the organizations, Federal Grand Juries are sitting and individual leaders of some of the organizations have already been incarcerated as a result of violations on their part of the Sedition and related Statutes. With reference to the Moorish Science Temple of America and the Moslem, Islamic or Mohammedan Sects, organizations and groups which reportedly promote non-participation in the war, individual members have been arrested to some extent for violations of the Selective Service and Training Act.

More widespread than any other un-American activity among the Negroes appears to be that of the Communist Party, which has been active in every Field Division with few exceptions. This activity, agitational in effect, has been entered into on the part of the Communist Party by Party members or sympathizers and Party front organizations, both of which distribute literature and sponsor meetings agitational in effect, and the Communist Party press, including the "Daily Worker" in the East and the "People's World" in the West. With reference to the Communist Party press, aligned with it in several instances are Negro newspapers. However, it is pointed out that these Negro newspapers, with Communist connections in some form or other, are located in various areas throughout the country. These colored newspapers which have been definitely determined to have Communist influence in them in practically every instance have but a local circulation.

Indications have also been reported reflecting activity, especially in the South, by members of the Jehovah Witnesses Sect among the Negroes. It is pointed out that this sect advocates non-participation in the war and in some areas has been reported to be un-American.

Independent Groups

Existing in the United States are a group of Negro organizations of nationwide scope which are independent of nature, but all of which have a decided influence among the Negroes. In local areas, some of the organizations have been reported to be Communist infiltrated.

The most prominent of these organizations, the one which has perhaps the largest membership and area coverage, is the National Association for the Advancement of Colored People. This organization was organized early in 1900 with the purpose of seeking the advancement of rights and opportunities for members of the Negro race. The national character of this organization is reported to be free of any Communist connections. However, in various local branches, there have been indicated instances of Communist infiltration. Those areas reported wherein branches are said to be definitely infiltrated by the Communist Party are the Detroit and Los Angeles field divisions. In one area a Negro source of information expressed the opinion that the National Association for the Advancement of Colored People has capitalized on the present world situation by perverting patriotic appeals resulting in increased Negro unrest; however, at the same time adding to the membership of the organization. In other areas, however, the organization is said to be a benefit for the Negro race.

[██████████████████ *Miss. See Jackson, Miss., Digest*]

It should be noted at this time that reports have been received reflecting that Negroes who had pledged a certain percentage of their wages for the purchase of war bonds have been withdrawing the reserved amounts, offering no explanation in most instances. Information received in this regard, too, fails to reflect any widespread activity of this sort in the two known areas and the only explanations received are to the effect that the money was needed for other purposes. [*Savannah and Little Rock areas*]

The Negro organization known as the Urban League, or Urban League of America, is reported to have several branches throughout the country and to be active in those areas in obtaining employment and better conditions for the Negroes. This organization, however, is reported as conservative in its activities and has not been reported to have subversive connections.

An organization of more recent origin, known as the March on Washington Movement, has been active in the cities of New York, Chicago, St. Louis, Detroit, Cincinnati and Washington in demanding increased employment in defense industries and Governmental agencies, the abolishment of "Jim Crowism" in the Armed Forces, and the discontinuance of alleged discriminatory practices. This organization is headed by A. Philip Randolph, head of the Pullman Car Porters Union, who is said to have a considerable following. The March on Washington Movement has sponsored meetings in New York, Chicago and St. Louis, which have been attended by many thousands of people in each instance. It should be noted that information has been received that the organization plans a meeting in Detroit in the latter part of September to formulate definite plans for a march on the City of Washington. The organization is, of course, being closely followed.

Prominent Personages in Political, Governmental and Private Life

Considerable information has been received from all sections of the country to the effect that the activities and utterances of individuals who are prominent in political,

Governmental or civilian fields are responsible for much of the unrest and dissatisfaction existing among the Negroes. Charges are made, especially in the South, that the acceptance by prominent individuals of Negroes on an equal social basis have caused demands to be made by the Negroes, especially in this area, for privileges never before accorded them. On the other hand, information has been received reflecting that individuals opposed to the granting of social equality to the Negroes are making an issue of the racial question which is alleged to further unrest and dissatisfaction. This is said to be especially true in southern States such as Georgia and Alabama. Opinions have been expressed both by colored and white people to this effect.

It should be pointed out that two instances have been reported wherein allegations have been made that representatives of the Government through their activities have caused unrest among Negroes in two areas. In the Philadelphia area, a representative of a national defense agency demanded an increase in the percentage of Negro employees when the particular company already had 33 per cent of its employees Negroes. In another area in the South, allegations have been received to the effect that representatives of the Fair Employment Practice Committee, there to hold hearings, had also caused unrest among some of the Negroes.

Labor Unions

Much of the unrest and dissatisfaction on the part of the Negroes, especially in industrial centers, has been attributed to the activities of labor unions, both affiliates of the Congress of Industrial Organizations and the American Federation of Labor. Two diametrically opposed types of activity among the Negroes on the part of labor unions have been reported. One type of activity reported is to the effect that labor unions and consequently union organizers have been militantly demanding increased employment in industry for the Negro and the abolishment of segregation and discrimination. Some charges and allegations have been made to the effect that union organizers are demanding these things solely as a basis of obtaining increased membership in unions, winning over the members of one union to the other union, or using their demands as a wedge to obtain further bargaining rights from manufacturers.

On the other hand, it has been reported in many instances that labor unions, through their representatives, have been demanding segregation of Negro workers from white workers, claiming that the white workers will not work alongside of Negroes and use the same facilities afforded to Negro workers. Several strikes have been reported which are based on dislike and distaste on the part of white workers in working with Negroes. In this connection, several instances have been reported wherein employers are at a loss to know what to do inasmuch as they are bound by the Fair Employment Practice Order, if they have contracts with the Government, and yet are faced with the refusal on the part of white employees to have Negroes work along with them.

Prominent Negroes (Local and National Figures)

In numerous areas complaints and reports have been received to the effect that prominent Negro personages active there are the cause for unrest and dissatisfaction. It is said that their demands and accusations with reference to discrimination and lack of equal rights among the Negroes are, of course, effective among the Negroes and are a source of much trouble. In this connection, both Negro and white sources of information state they believe that rumors of discrimination and unequal rights are caused by unscrupulous or unthinking colored leaders in furtherance of their own selfish motives by using this approach to attract or bind Negroes to their own cause. Other reports have been received to the effect that some Negro leaders are perverting the patriotic appeal for political or financial purposes. [*See Jackson, Newark & Philadelphia Summaries*]

In this same connection, it is reported that in such an area as Philadelphia, where there is a considerable number of Negroes, confusion exists as to who the actual leaders of the Negro race are. The reason for this is said to be that the leaders are considered both by Negroes and white people to be primarily interested in their own personal advancement. Furthermore, it is said that there are differences arising from within the Negro population from sharp class distinctions, rivalries and the like. It is said that class distinctions are based partly on differences in shades of color, social background as sometimes is acquired by shades of color, wealth, professional standing and even family history.

With further reference to Negro leaders, it is said that many are conservative in sentiment and actually represent only the feelings of the middle or upper class of Negroes and, for that reason, it is doubtful whether many of them have close enough contact with the people they claim to represent to know what those people actually desire and need.

The Negro Press

It appears that one of the outstanding agitational forces among the Negroes is the Negro press. Complaints have been received both from Negro and white sources of information to the effect that the Negro press devotes itself to the more sensational, if not inflammatory, type of news with regard to Negroes and in proportion gives little consideration to the war effort. In this connection, the larger of Negro newspapers devote much space to alleged instances of discrimination against Negroes and violations of their rights along with reportedly sensational matters such as crime.

Perhaps the most widespread circulation of Negro newspapers is that of the Pittsburgh Courier, published in Pittsburgh, Pennsylvania, which, although it is said to have but approximately a two hundred thousand circulation, is read and reread by non-subscribers and non-buyers. This newspaper is said to be typical of the sensational and inflammatory type. This publication originated the "Double V" slogan and the idea of forming "Double V" clubs. The "Double V" program stands for victory not only in the war to preserve democracy for the United States but for victory in obtaining democracy for the Negroes in the United States. In several areas "Double V" clubs have been formed with considerable following.

Closely paralleling the type of news reporting appearing in the Pittsburgh Courier is that in the Chicago Defender published in Chicago, Illinois, the Afro-American published in Baltimore, Maryland, and in branch offices throughout the East, the Black Dispatch edited by Roscoe Dunjee, alleged agitator, in Oklahoma City, Oklahoma, and numerous publications of a local nature throughout the country.

Economic, Social and Political Situation of the Negro

The economic, social and political situation among the colored race in the United States is also reported to be largely responsible for the present unrest and dissatisfaction existing among the Negroes. In this connection, numerous reports of segregation and denial of equal rights have been received throughout the United States. There are being listed hereinafter the more widespread problems affecting this field to which blame is laid for the unrest among the Negroes:

1. Discrimination against Negroes in industry.
2. Infiltration of Southern Negroes of the North.
3. Lack of better-paying employment.
4. Crowded areas and lack of healthful and ample housing.
5. Lack of educational and recreational facilities.
6. Widespread disease among Negroes, including venereal diseases.
7. Lack of uniform opportunity in defense employment (defense projects too centralized in certain instances).
8. Unequal pay for equal work done to that of white people.
9. Attitude of white people in certain sections regarding the granting of equal rights.
10. Increase of crime among Negroes.

Recently, two widely publicized lynchings of Negroes in Missouri and Texas have been seized upon mainly by the Communist Party and also by Negro organizations with reportedly no un-American connections along with the Negro newspapers. In several sections of the mid-West and the Southwest, reports have been received reflecting these lynchings have caused considerable unrest. *[Missouri, Arkansas, Texas]*

Loyalty of the Negro

Both Negro and white sources of information who have been interviewed in representative areas advise that the Negro in general is loyal to the United States but that there does exist among the Negroes a strong sentiment of bitterness and resentment among the Negro people. It is said that this feeling has reach[ed] an unprecedented intensity. The primary complaint said to be existing among the Negroes is to the effect that a lack of opportunities exist.

Two types of Negro sources of information have been interviewed who have different approaches to the situation. One type of Negro interviewed, who is prominent in the area in which he resides among the Negro people, has a militant attitude with regard to the demands of the Negro for better conditions. This type advises that there has been and will continue to be considerable agitation on the part of Negro leaders in an attempt to gain opportunities for the Negroes. This type further states that Negroes do not have the same opportunities and rights of citizenship that the white race enjoys and since they are being called on to make the same contributions to the war effort at home and abroad, Negro leaders naturally feel that if they are to fight "for other people" they themselves should be granted democracy at home. It is said that the Negro is increasing his efforts to be of assistance to the gaining momentum of the national defense program, yet in instances his attempts will be met by some factions with the rising tide of antagonism "that Negroes must be kept in their place."

The other type of Negro source of information claims that current rumors of Negro unrest are exaggerated. They advise that high wages, along with increased tension induced by the war effort, has excited the Negro mind and given rise to rumors which have gained momentum and force but which in their origin are not worth all the attention that is being paid to them. It is further stated that it is believed in certain instances rumors are falsely created in an attempt by unscrupulous colored leaders to obtain self-advancement.

Conclusions which may be drawn from the foregoing with reference to the causes for Negro unrest or dissatisfaction reflect that although many complaints, reports and rumors have been received to the effect that un-American sentiments and activities exist among the Negroes, the apparent forces responsible for this situation are entirely national in scope.

Respectfully,

J. K. Mumford

October 3, 1942

SAC	ALBANY	HUNTINGTON	PHILADELPHIA
	ATLANTA	INDIANAPOLIS	PHOENIX
	BALTIMORE	JACKSON	PITTSBURGH
	BIRMINGHAM	JUNEAU	PORTLAND
	BOSTON	KANSAS CITY	PROVIDENCE
	BUFFALO	KNOXVILLE	RICHMOND
	BUTTE	LITTLE ROCK	ST. LOUIS
	CHARLOTTE	LOS ANGELES	ST. PAUL
	CHICAGO	LOUISVILLE	SALT LAKE CITY
	CINCINNATI	MEMPHIS	SAN ANTONIO
	CLEVELAND	MIAMI	SAN DIEGO
	DALLAS	MILWAUKEE	SAN FRANCISCO
	DENVER	NEWARK	SAN JUAN

DES MOINES	NEW HAVEN	SAVANNAH
DETROIT	NEW ORLEANS	SEATTLE
EL PASO	NEW YORK	SIOUX FALLS
GRAND RAPIDS	NORFOLK	SPRINGFIELD
HONOLULU	OKLAHOMA CITY	WASHINGTON, D. C.
HOUSTON	OMAHA	QUANTICO

RE: FOREIGN-INSPIRED AGITATION
AMONG THE AMERICAN NEGROES;
INTERNAL SECURITY.

Dear Sir:

I want to bring to your attention again the instructions contained in Bureau letter dated June 22, 1942, with reference to the captioned matter, wherein it was stated, "In the event any individual or organization is discovered disseminating propaganda to the American Negroes which tends to create unrest or dissatisfaction in the American form of government, it is desired that individual cases be opened and that these cases be vigorously followed for possible prosecution under the Sedition Statutes, Selective Service Act, Registration Act or Voorhis Act." There have been noticed in various reports submitted in compliance with the above letter many instances wherein information is set forth which would justify the opening of separate cases. However, there is no mention made that separate investigations are being instituted in those instances.

It has further been noted, in reviewing reports submitted by the Field in this matter, references are made to Negro publications published within a particular Field Division although no accompanying indication is given that these publications are being scrutinized carefully for pro-Axis or pro-Communist inclinations. The reference Bureau letter contains specific instructions in this regard.

The important nature of the survey being made by the Field concerning the captioned matter cannot be over-emphasized and I am holding you strictly responsible for handling it in a logical, careful and exhaustive manner.

I also want to impress on you the necessity for submitting reports in this survey expeditiously and the incumbency upon you to advise the Bureau immediately upon receipt of information concerning serious instances of racial trouble occurring within your Field Division. You, of course, must not lose sight of the necessity for using the utmost of discretion in making inquiries relative to this matter so that the Bureau will not under any circumstances be regarded as interfering with or involving itself in matters outside of its jurisdiction.

Yours truly,

John Edgar Hoover
Director

October 1942

Bureau Bulletin No. 108, Series 1942

Section (G) FOREIGN-INSPIRED AGITATION AMONG THE AMERICAN NEGROES; INTERNAL SECURITY-X—The following procedure is being set out for the handling of all matters previously submitted to the Bureau under the above entitled caption:

A. The Bureau should be promptly advised by letter, teletype, or telephone—depending upon the importance of the situation—of all—

(1) racial disturbances or potential racial outbreaks which may have an effect upon the national security;

(2) Communist-inspired racial agitation;

(3) information regarding outbreaks or impending strikes in the labor field which involve racial agitation;

(4) all racial disturbances which may receive national notoriety;

(5) Communist exploitation of racial matters involving civil rights cases. The necessary inquiries should be made through reliable and established sources.

No active investigation should be conducted without Bureau authorization.

B. The general Communist infiltration among the Negro race, as well as the Communist activity among the Negroes in each field division should be briefly summarized and reported in the general Communist Party reports.

C. A report entitled "Communist Party—Negro Question" should be submitted when matters of evidentiary value are obtained indicating the activity of the Communist Party among the Negro race which is in furtherance of its program of self-determination for the Negro, or other tactics of the Communist Party; that is, in violation of a Federal law under the jurisdiction of this Bureau. In each of these instances the report should be written in such a way so that it may be furnished to the Department for its consideration.

It should be pointed out that the above-outlined procedure is not meant to de-emphasize in any way the significance of full and complete coverage of all racial matters by this Bureau. As you are aware, the Communist Party has re-emphasized its Marxist-Leninist theory of self-determination for the Negro race which is one of its more revolutionary tactics. The incumbency still will remain with each field office to maintain adequate coverage through reliable and established sources so that the Bureau will be promptly advised of all potential racial outbreaks or racial disturbances coming within the scope of the above-outlined procedure.

August 5, 1943

PERSONAL ATTENTION

SAC, New York

RE: INFORMANT COVERAGE OF RACIAL CONDITIONS
IN THE NEW YORK FIELD DIVISION

Dear Sir:

You are undoubtedly aware of the current widespread racial unrest in the country. In connection with this situation, I desire to be furnished with the extent of informant coverage through which accurate and immediate information can be obtained and which will reflect the true conditions existing in those Field Divisions wherein the most trouble exists.

In view of the reported unrest and tense race relationship in your Field Division as evidenced by information you have supplied, you are instructed to immediately make a survey of the informant coverage in this matter. It is expected that the following information will be included in this survey:

I. Confidential Informant Coverage—

A. List names, addresses and symbol designations of informants as well as their race.

B. Describe the type of information made available by each.

C. List place of outside employment of each informant.

D. Enumerate and describe organizations to which each informant belongs.

II. Coverage Through Sources of Information and Contacts—

A. Supply information desired under I.

III. Coverage by Technical Sources—

A. Enumerate and describe each and show type and extent of information obtained.

IV. Average Coverage—

A. Show extent of coverage of colored areas and colored neighborhoods by all sources.

B. Show coverage of focal points of possible racial trouble.

V. Coverage of Organizations Involving Negro Question—

A. Tabulate organizations and show extent of coverage.

VI. Conclusion—

A. Furnish estimate of total coverage of situation.

I expect that you will give this matter your immediate and careful attention. You are requested to supply this survey to the Bureau not later than three days after the date of receipt of this letter.

Very truly yours,

John Edgar Hoover
Director

September 13, 1943

PERSONAL ATTENTION

SAC, New York

RE: INFORMANT COVERAGE OF RACIAL CONDITIONS IN THE NEW YORK FIELD DIVISION

Dear Sir:

Reference is made to your letter of August 10, 1943, concerning the informant coverage of racial conditions in the New York Field Division. It is noted you have advised an adequate coverage is maintained as to racial conditions in the area covered by your Field Division.

You are advised that you are being held strictly responsible for the development and maintenance of an adequate informant coverage to insure the immediate availability of all pertinent information concerning racial conditions as well as all underlying factors connected therewith. It is also your responsibility to see that the Bureau is advised along these lines at all times.

It is further noted that you have advised the [redacted] and various representatives of it are cooperative in furnishing reliable information concerning Negro activities. While such cooperation as this is desired at all time, it is pointed out that your informant coverage of racial conditions should be developed to such an extent where reliance on other agencies or law enforcement bodies to report pertinent information in this matter is reduced to a minimum and where you will have available a clear independent picture of racial conditions in the area covered by you at all times.

It is desired that you afford this matter your personal attention and close supervision. These observations should be taken into consideration along with the Bureau's instructions in its letter to all Special Agents in Charge dated August 10, 1943, entitled "Coverage of Racial Conditions."

Very truly yours,

John Edgar Hoover

September 14, 1943

MEMORANDUM FOR THE DIRECTOR

RE: INFORMANT COVERAGE OF RACIAL CONDITIONS

There is attached a summarization of surveys prepared by some thirty-nine Field Divisions reflecting the character of informant coverage each has with respect to racial conditions. These surveys were made pursuant to your request that the areas wherein the most racial tension prevails be checked into to determine the extent of the informant coverage. The Field Offices involved are those which according to the information furnished by them have at least a degree of racial tension existing in the areas covered by them. They are set forth alphabetically.

Briefly, what appears to be the most outstanding oversight and that which is most widespread is the failure of the Field Offices to extend their informant coverage to the point where all underlying factors which are of influence in racial conditions and interracial relations will be reported on. Generally, the Field Offices involved appear to have covered extensively organizational and un-American activities as they affect racial conditions.

To have a clear and complete picture as to the causes and contributing factors in racial unrest, pertinent information as to all forces must necessarily be made available. Accordingly letters have been directed to those Field Divisions where necessary, pointing out the necessity of the development and maintenance of an informant coverage which supplies not only data relative to organizational and un-American activities, but as to all factors involved. It has been pointed out further to the Field that many of the factors have a political, social, or economic aspect and obviously direct inquiries and investigation cannot be made with respect to them and pertinent information must necessarily come from reliable informants and sources.

In addition, besides those instances wherein additional coverage would appear in order, it has been noted that a number of Field Divisions have indicated reliance on the cooperation of local law enforcement agencies or the Offices of Military and Naval Intelligence in this matter. With respect to such reliance, it has been pointed out in the letters which have been directed to the Field that it should be reduced to a minimum by the development of an adequate informant coverage so that a clear, independent picture of racial matters will be available at all times. At the same time it has been pointed out that to reduce reliance on the cooperation of these sources in no way means cooperation and good relationship are not desired at all times.

Attached is the summarization of the informant coverage in the Field Offices which have been requested to submit a survey. The coverage of each is briefly described and comments are made thereupon based not only on the character of the coverage but upon the conclusion arrived at by each Field Office with respect to its informant coverage of racial conditions. As it will be noted, letters have been directed to those Offices setting forth the Bureau's observations and instructions.

Respectfully,
D. M. Ladd

[Handwritten] *It is well we made this survey for it has uncovered some glaringly weak spots. See that immediate corrective measures are taken. H[oover].*
Some offices look very bad—they should be carefully followed—EAT[Edward A. Tamm]

Re: Informant Coverage of Racial Conditions

Albany Field Division

This Office has informed that the Negro population is in the larger cities covered by it is a minor percentage of the total and it believes the coverage of racial conditions adequate so as to properly evaluate racial conditions. However, it does not appear there are any confidential informants in the City of Albany to report pertinent information in this matter. A number of sources of information, the majority being Negroes, are maintained, however, in this City.

Comment: With the exception of Albany, the coverage appears to be adequate. A letter has been directed to the Albany Office pointing out the lack of confidential informants in Albany and advising that it is the personal responsibility of the Special Agent in Charge to see that informant coverage in this matter is adequate.

Atlanta Field Division

This Office at the present time in the larger areas covered by it which it points to as being the focal points of racial unrest maintains ten confidential informants, seven of whom are Negroes. In these same areas it also maintains twenty Negro sources of information and contacts and sixteen white persons in the same category. In the smaller cities, the Office has advised, good contacts are maintained and if racial disturbances take place in these cities, the Office will be immediately notified. With respect to the larger cities, the Office has advised it believes its informant coverage is adequate.

Comment: This Office appears to stress that it will be fully advised as to racial disturbances occurring in the area covered by it but does not appear to consider being currently informed as to all matters which affect racial conditions or which might lead to racial disturbances. The Office has also pointed out that cooperation with local law enforcement authorities will provide additional information in case of disturbances.

A letter has been directed to this Office in which it is instructed to develop its informant coverage to the point where it will be currently advised as to all matters affecting interracial relations in the area covered by it by its own informant coverage. The Office has also been instructed to see to it that its reliance on local law enforcement agencies is reduced to a minimum. It has also been pointed out to the Office that frequent contact must be made with its reliable sources and contacts so as to insure their cognizance of the Office's desire to be currently informed as to all matters concerning racial conditions.

Baltimore Field Division

This Office has pointed to the Baltimore areas as being that in which racial trouble will most likely occur. It has a total of ████████ confidential Negro informants in this area and in other sections of the States of Maryland and Delaware. In addition, the Office is undertaking the development of additional coverage and has instituted a program of developing Negro informants from the entire area covered by the Field Division. The Office has also ten Negro sources of information and seven white sources of information who supply information relative to racial conditions.

Comment: The Baltimore Office has confidential informants in this matter in the Delaware area, although it is undertaking a program to develop more in the State of Delaware. A letter has been directed to this Office instructing that concentrated effort be made to develop additional informant coverage and pointing out that this coverage should be of such calibre that the Bureau will be kept currently informed in all matters pertinent to racial conditions.

Birmingham Field Division

In the State of Alabama there are two general types of areas, one, industrial, and the other, agricultural. This Office has pointed out that with regard to the latter areas informant coverage is maintained chiefly through police departments and sheriffs in view of the scattered nature of the population. The observation has been made that informants are not necessary or practical in agricultural sections.

With regard to the industrial areas, the Birmingham Office has pointed out that to obtain an adequate coverage on an area basis it has been necessary only to obtain a coverage with respect to the Cities of Mobile and Birmingham. In Birmingham there are confidential informants and sources of information and contacts. In Mobile there are confidential informants and sources of information and contacts. Throughout the entire State the Office has pointed out there are confidential national defense plant informants as well as American Legion contacts in posts.

This Office has also pointed out that racial disturbances can be expected from certain specific causes and sources, mainly labor union activities, including company union relationships and inter-union conflict; the Communist Party and the Southern Negro Youth Congress, a Communist front; presence of Negro troops from the North; and miscellaneous matters such as segregational practices in transportation and employment, as well as crimes committed by Negroes against white people. With regard to these, the Office feels it has adequate coverage, with the exception of the Communist Party, which, however, is being developed. It is pointed out also that a close relationship exists between the Birmingham Office and each military establishment in the area covered by it.

Comment: Throughout the survey the Office refers to incidents and occurrences affecting racial conditions. However, with the exception of the three above-mentioned major factors tó be considered, it is apparent the Office does not stress a coverage of all underlying forces as they affect interracial conditions. The Office has also referred to its close cooperation and contact with law enforcement agencies and military authorities.

A letter has been directed to the Birmingham Office in which it is pointed out that the Office should have its informant coverage extend to matters which are not of an organizational or subversive nature. It has also been pointed out to the Office that reliance on other Governmental agencies and local law enforcement authorities should, if at all feasible, be reduced to a minimum in this matter.

Boston Field Division

This Office has a considerable number of informants which, it advises, furnishes general information concerning the Negro situation. informants and sources of information are maintained in the Boston area where there are approximately 22,000 Negroes. In New Bedford there are 2,000 Negroes informants are maintained, while in the Springfield area there are approximately 3,500 Negroes informants are currently maintained. The Boston Office has stated that a careful survey of racial conditions has indicated there have been no incidents of any type arising from racial difficulties and no trouble is anticipated by well-informed sources. There are no focal points of possible trouble except areas in the City of Boston where the Negro population is most dense. These areas are presently covered by informants.

Comment: The Boston Office has concluded that in the area covered by it there are no indications of racial problems or race rivalry and the only indications of possible difficulties have resulted from activities of the Communist Party operating particularly through the ranks of the National Association for the Advancement of Colored People and the National Negro Congress, the latter being a Communist front. It considers its informant coverage adequate. In this connection, it is believed, however, that attention has not been centered on matters of a social, economic or political nature although un-American groups and organizations have been covered fully. A letter has been directed to the Boston Office advising that an adequate informant coverage must be maintained with respect to all aspects of racial conditions in the areas covered by it.

Buffalo Field Division

This Office has pointed out that the colored population of Buffalo is approximately 38,000 at the present time and is the largest Negro population in any area covered by that Office. It is stated, however, that Rochester, Niagara Falls and Elmira have a racial problem although racial groups in this area are comparatively small. It states in its conclusion with respect to its informant coverage that any impending disturbances or crises will be reported to the Office and, furthermore, the Buffalo Police Department has been very cooperative with respect to this matter.

In the City of Buffalo there are confidential informants and sources of information and contacts who are considered as the coverage in this City. In Rochester there is one confidential informant and no sources or contacts, and in Elmira there are confidential informants and contacts.

Comment: This Office appears to stress the cooperation of the police departments, especially in Buffalo, as a part of its informant coverage. In addition, while stating it will undoubtedly be advised of impending trouble, it does not refer to being advised of the various factors which might lead to racial trouble. While there are numerous sources of information and contacts in the Buffalo area, there are ▬▬▬▬ confidential informants. It is believed that additional confidential informant coverage should be developed, especially in view of the industrial nature of the City of Buffalo and the undoubtedly large number of persons from other sections migrating into this area.

A letter has been directed to this Office pointing out the foregoing observations and instructing that additional confidential informant coverage be developed, especially in the Buffalo area. In the Bureau's letter it has also been observed there are certain factors which the Office must be kept advised of in connection with racial conditions. It was pointed out further that reliance on local law enforcement agencies in this matter must be reduced to a minimum.

Charlotte Field Division

This Office has informed that efforts are being made to develop a larger confidential informant coverage of such organizations as the National Association for the Advancement of Colored People and the Communist Party. With respect to general informant coverage, however, the Charlotte Office has pointed out that it has received a steady stream of information from a variety of sources. Furthermore, the Negro question is of considerable interest among the residents of both North and South Carolina and most of the white citizens and a number of Negro leaders are watching the problem closely and are constantly reporting incidents which have come to their attention to this Office. It is pointed out by the Charlotte Office an effort to deliberately increase the informant coverage in this Field would not appreciably increase the extent or quality.

With respect to its confidential informant coverage, the Charlotte Office maintains ▬▬▬▬ scattered throughout both North and South Carolina. It also has throughout the area covered by ▬▬▬▬ sources of information and contacts.

With respect to two areas, namely, Durham and Monroe, it has been pointed out by the Charlotte Office that the problem is primarily one for military authorities in that Negro troops have been stationed almost constantly at nearby reservations. Miniature race riots have occurred in these two areas involving white and Negro personnel. The Office has stated in view of this situation no particular effort has been made to extend the coverage to these two cities.

Comment: It is believed that this Office should develop informants in the Durham and Monroe areas so that the Bureau will not have to depend upon the cooperation of other agencies. There should be an additional development of informants in the Statesville and Winston-Salem areas where there is considerable industrial activity.

In connection with its informant coverage, this Office has stressed organizational and un-American activity. While this, of course, is important, there are also other factors which must be considered and a letter has been directed to the Charlotte Field

Division pointing this out as well as the foregoing observations under "Comment." It has also been pointed out to the Charlotte Office that there should be a minimum of reliance on other agencies and local law enforcement agencies in this matter.

Chicago Field Division

This Office estimates the Negro population within its Field Division between 350,000 to 400,000 Negroes. For this amount of Negro population this Office has confidential informants and sources of information. The Office states in its conclusions that it was believed it has sufficient coverage of the racial situation at the present time.

Comment: This Office appears to stress the cooperation of the Police Department as a part of its informant coverage which reduces the reliance on confidential informants to a minimum. It is believed that this Office has placed considerable stress upon coverage of the subversive activities among the Negroes and there has been a tendency to overlook other matters of either social, economic or political aspects which have an influence in racial conditions.

A letter has been directed to this Office pointing out the foregoing observations and instructing that an adequate informant coverage be developed and maintained in this Field.

Cincinnati Field Division

This Office estimates its Negro population in the City of Cincinnati as 55,000 Negroes. As to informant coverage, the Office designated informants and sources of information. At Columbus, Ohio, the Office furnished confidential informants and sources of information and estimated the Negro population at 60,000. At Dayton, Ohio, where the Negro population is estimated at 25,000, this Office informants sources of information. In the City of Steubenville and Springfield, Ohio, this Office confidential informants and sources of information.

This Office notes its inadequate coverage at Columbus, Dayton and Springfield, Ohio, and advises that steps are presently being taken to correct this situation.

Comment: While this Office has a large number of sources of information, it is believed that frequent contact should be made with those who are reliable so as to insure their cognizance of the Bureau's desire to be fully and promptly informed as to all pertinent information relating to racial conditions and all factors involved. Also, this Office, while stressing its coverage of organizational or un-American activities does not refer to its coverage of all underlying factors involved in racial conditions.

A letter has been directed to this Office incorporating the foregoing observations and setting forth instructions that its efforts to develop additional coverage be concentrated so as to insure the immediate availability of all pertinent information.

Cleveland Field Division

There are a number of large cities with a corresponding large Negro population in the area covered by this Office. In Cleveland, where there are approximately 85,000 colored inhabitants, this Office [redacted] confidential informants and [redacted] sources of information. In Akron, Ohio, where there are over 13,000 Negroes, there [redacted] confidential informants [redacted] sources of information. In Toledo, where there are nearly 15,000 Negroes, there [redacted] confidential informants and [redacted] sources of information. In Youngstown, where there are over 17,000 colored inhabitants, there are [redacted] confidential informant [redacted] sources of information. The Cleveland Office has informed that additional coverage is being secured in the Cities of Canton, Massillon, Lima and Mansfield in view of the increased Negro populations in the areas during the past three years. This Field Division appears to stress the coverage of Negro organizations and un-American groups and does not appear to have an adequate coverage of local matters affecting interracial relations other than plant informants and sources of information who supply information concerning labor issues.

Comment: It is believed that additional confidential informants should be developed in this area, especially to supply data concerning all fundamental factors which have a definite bearing on racial conditions. A letter has been directed to the Cleveland Office pointing this out and instructing that immediate attention should be given to the informant coverage of racial conditions in the area covered by it.

Dallas Field Division

This Field Division has pointed out that its total coverage of racial conditions in the territory covered by it furnishes a representative picture. It has stated, however, that continuous efforts are being made to effect a more complete coverage in view of the general racial unrest. The following is a breakdown as to the various cities in this Field Division and the type of informant coverage: Abilene [redacted] sources of information; Amarillo, [redacted] confidential informant, [redacted] Dallas, [redacted] confidential informants [redacted] sources of information; Fort Worth [redacted] confidential informant, [redacted] sources of information; Lubbock [redacted] sources of information; Sherman and Texarkana [redacted] sources of information; Tyler [redacted] confidential informant, [redacted] sources of information; and, Wichita Falls [redacted] confidential informants [redacted] sources of information.

Comment: This Office has advised that it is developing additional informants in practically all of the areas where a large Negro population exists. Throughout its survey it has indicated that it relies considerably on the cooperation of law enforcement authorities. It has also indicated that its main interest is receiving information concerning racial disturbances, indicating that its informant coverage is centered around this rather than maintained for a general and complete picture of racial conditions and the factors involved. A letter has been directed to the Dallas Office pointing this out and, further, advising that prompt attention be given to the development of additional informants as indicated in this Field Division's survey letter.

Detroit Field Division

The Detroit Field Division has ████████████████ informants. ██. In addition, there are ████████ confidential informants supplying information concerning agitation among the Negroes. The Detroit Office also has ██ This Office has also pointed out that it has ████████████ informants who are also in a position to furnish information concerning racial conditions. ██

With respect to the coverage, Special Agent in Charge Bugas has stated he realizes the racial situation is critical and that he is continuing to improve coverage in this matter. He has also stated that the current extent of coverage assisted in the Office's handling of the Detroit riots.

Comment: This Office has a large number of sources of information, ██████████████ informants and contacts who, it points out, furnished information concerning racial conditions in Detroit. However, it appears that the confidential informants are confined more to furnishing information with respect to subversive groups as they affect racial conditions in the City of Detroit.

A letter has been directed to the Detroit Office pointing out that there are additional factors to be considered in this matter and that present confidential informants should be instructed to keep this in mind and that the development of additional informants be made with this idea. Furthermore, the Detroit Office has been advised it should frequently contact its various sources, ██████████████ informants and contacts so as to keep them constantly alert for pertinent information relative to the Negro situation and racial conditions generally in the Detroit Field Division.

El Paso Field Division

This Office advises that there have been no racial disturbances within its division and further, there is but a small Negro population in the area covered by it. The Office also advises that there are no strong Negro organizations, except churches, within its territory and that its Negro population is mainly in the City of El Paso. Other coverage within its territory is the reliance placed upon local law enforcement officers.

Comment: It is believed that this Office's confidential informant coverage in the

City of El Paso is adequate; however, informants should be developed within its Western Texas territory and other cities where Negro troops are stationed.

A letter has been directed to this Office pointing out the foregoing observation and instructions so as to insure this Office's alertness for the matters of interest relative to racial conditions.

Huntington Field Division

This Office has ▇▇▇▇▇▇ confidential informants and is in the process of developing ▇▇▇▇ additional. It also has ▇▇▇▇▇▇ confidential informants who supply information relative to conditions. Also, it has numerous sources of information and contacts who, the Office states, supply information relative to this matter. Throughout the State the Office has approximately ▇▇▇▇▇▇▇▇▇▇ sources of information and ▇▇▇▇▇▇ sources of information who are regarded as part of the Office's informant coverage of racial conditions. The Office has pointed out it believes its coverage to be adequate with the exception of the focal points of possible racial trouble, with particular reference to Charleston and Montgomery, West Virginia.

Comment: The Huntington Office has been directed a letter instructing that immediate attention be given to the development of proper coverage of those focal points of possible racial trouble designated in its letter which supplied a survey of informant coverage. In addition, it has been pointed out that frequent contact must be maintained with the Office's sources of information to insure their alertness for matters of interest to the Bureau. The Bureau's letter has also pointed out the personal obligation of the Special Agent in Charge to see that the Bureau is currently and promptly advised as to all pertinent matters affecting racial conditions and interracial relations within the area covered by the Huntington Field Division.

Houston Field Division

In this Field Division there are five large cities in addition to Houston where there are racial problems. This Office has ▇▇▇ confidential informants who are acquainted with and are in a position to furnish information regarding conditions and activities among the Negroes in the Houston Field Division. ▇▇▇▇▇▇▇▇▇▇▇▇▇▇▇▇▇▇▇▇▇▇▇▇▇▇▇▇▇▇▇▇▇▇▇▇▇▇▇. The Office also has a number of sources of information who have not been designated as confidential national defense informants in view of their not furnishing information regularly. They have been used at regular intervals as contacts whereby certain specific information could be obtained regarding Negro activities. ▇▇

The foregoing cities are the focal points of possible racial trouble. The Houston Office has informed that further efforts are being made to obtain additional coverage in Corpus Christi, Port Arthur and Baytown, Texas, and deems that the coverage it has to be sufficient in other places. In its estimation the Office has also advised that through contact with local law enforcement officials that Office will be apprised of any developments tending to cause any racial disturbances.

Comment: This Office appears to rely to some extent on contact with law enforcement authorities and tends to stress un-American organizations but is inclined to overlook other factors which are influential in racial conditions. Outside of Houston, with but one exception, the City of Beaumont, there are no confidential informants.

A letter has been directed to Houston pointing out these matters as well as its duty to be fully advised of all pertinent aspects of interracial relations in the area covered by it. It has also been pointed out that frequent contact should be had with all informants, sources of information and contacts to insure being properly advised in this matter.

Indianapolis Field Division

The areas in which the largest Negro populations exist in the territory covered by this Field Division are Gary, East Chicago, Hammond, Evansville, Terre Haute, Fort Wayne and Indianapolis. In these particular localities the following number of confidential informants and sources of information and contacts are maintained:

Gary ▬▬ confidential informants and ▬▬ sources of information and contacts.

Fort Wayne ▬▬ confidential informant and ▬▬ sources and contacts.

East Chicago ▬▬ confidential informants and ▬▬ sources and contacts.

Hammond ▬▬ confidential informants.

Terre Haute ▬▬ confidential informants and ▬▬ sources and contacts.

Indianapolis ▬▬ confidential informants and ▬▬ sources of information.

In other areas, which include smaller communities and small Negro populations, there are maintained ▬▬ confidential informants and ▬▬ sources and contacts. With respect to the confidential informants, the majority of them are ▬▬ informants.

Comment: While this Office appears to have a large number of confidential informants as well as sources of information and contacts, it is believed that considerable stress has been placed upon coverage of organizational and subversive activities among the Negroes while there has been a tendency to overlook other matters with social, economic or political aspects which have an influence in racial conditions. No indication has been given as to the frequency in contacting sources of information for pertinent information nor has any indication been given that sources of information and contacts voluntarily remain alert for information which is pertinent to racial conditions in this area. There is also an indication that the Indianapolis Office has placed reliance on law enforcement agencies in the State of Indiana in this matter. While this is, of course, desirable, the informant coverage should be such that information can be obtained on pertinent matters without this reliance. In its conclusion the Office has advised that Lake County, Indiana, which includes the areas of East Chicago, Gary, Hammond and Whiting, is probably the most dangerous of any other section in the State. The Office has pointed out it has more good paid confidential informants in that County than in any other section. The Office believes that its informant coverage at the present time is sufficient.

A letter has been directed to this Office pointing out the foregoing observations under the "Comment" and instructing frequent contact should be made with sources of information and contacts so as to insure their alertness for matters of interest relative to racial conditions and their promptly reporting them to the Indianapolis Office.

Jackson Field Division

This Field Division has [redacted] sources of information and [redacted] sources who have been supplying, at various intervals, information concerning racial conditions in the area covered by this Field Division. The Office has pointed out that inasmuch as the sources of information were not reporting regularly and recontacts with them developed that none had obtained information indicating subversive elements exploiting the Negro population they have not been classified as confidential informants. It has also been pointed out by this Field Division that, with regard to rural areas, the provost marshal and other military authorities stationed in various camps in the area covered by the Office have been furnishing information concerning racial matters. Furthermore, the Mississippi Auxiliary Patrol informs the Jackson Field Division regularly on racial matters. The conclusions arrived at by the Office that the coverage of racial conditions in Mississippi is adequate for the Office to be kept advised of present activities affecting racial conditions as well as in the effort pointing to organizational activities among the Negroes.

Comment: It is believed that although there is a large number of sources of information, both Negro and white, maintained by this Field Division, frequent contact should be had with them so as to keep them alert for information in which the Bureau is interested, as well as cognizant of the Bureau's desire to be informed as to all factors influencing racial conditions. Accordingly, a letter has been directed to the Jackson Office instructing that frequent contact be maintained with reliable sources and contacts with the purpose in mind. In addition, it is noted that the Office, while being alert for indications of subversive activities as well as organized agitation, does not stress the point that its informant coverage furnishes the Jackson Office with a current picture of racial conditions as they are influenced by social, economic, and political factors. This has also been pointed out in the letter to the Special Agent in Charge at Jackson with the advice that the Bureau must naturally be informed of these factors to have available a complete picture of racial conditions in all areas.

Kansas City Field Division

This Office maintains in the Kansas City area █████ informants and █████ informants. In this same area it has █████ sources of information. Throughout the entire area covered by it it maintains █████ sources of information and contacts and █████ same category.

This Office has advised it believes its informant coverage with the utilization of police contact is sufficient to keep this Office advised generally concerning racial conditions. However, it has stated a concerted effort will be made to develop additional informants capable of furnishing more specific data concerning racial conditions.

Comment: This Office has advised that an appreciable amount of information relative to racial conditions has been obtained from contacts with police officials and that these sources have been relied upon inasmuch as they have consistently furnished information to the Kansas City Office. The Office has further advised that in view of the lack of investigative jurisdiction on the part of the Bureau in matters concerning interracial relations not affected by subversive activities, intensified efforts have not been made to develop informants specifically on this question.

A letter has been directed to this Office pointing out that its informant coverage in this matter must be extended to the point where there is a minimum of reliance on local law enforcement agencies. It has also been pointed out that from its informant coverage the Office must necessarily obtain a complete picture of racial conditions and that information concerning matters of a political, economic or social nature must obviously come from the informant coverage and not from investigation or direct inquiries.

Knoxville Field Division

This Office advises that the focal points in which racial disturbance might occur are at Knoxville and Chattanooga, Tennessee, in which there is a total of approximately 50,000 Negroes. It is to be noted that this Office believes that informant coverage is adequate; however, it was noted that it has █████ confidential informant and █████ sources of information.

Comment: It is believed that informant coverage in the Knoxville Field Division is not entirely adequate and further that this Office has failed to consider all underlying factors which have an influence in racial conditions.

Accordingly a letter has been transmitted to this Office setting out the foregoing observations and instructing that immediate steps be taken to remedy this situation and advising that frequent contact be made with reliable sources and informants to insure the immediate availability of all pertinent information in this matter.

Little Rock Field Division

This Office advised that the Negro population within its Field Division is domiciled principally in nine of the seventy-five counties of Arkansas. In this connection, it is to be noted that in 1930 the Negro population in the State of Arkansas was 488,000. As to informant coverage, this Office has developed ████ confidential informants as well as a large number of sources and contacts. However, it was noted that this Office does not refer to fundamental factors as it does with regard to organizational activities as causes for racial unrest and disturbances.

Comment: Accordingly a letter has been transmitted to this Office pointing out the above observations and instructing that an adequate informant coverage be maintained so that the Bureau will be advised of all forces which possibly are causes of racial unrest and disturbances.

Los Angeles Field Division

This Office advised the only focus points of racial unrest or disturbance within its territory from the City of Los Angeles where there are approximately 63,000 Negroes. For coverage of this situation this Office furnished ████ confidential informants and ████ sources of information and, further, is maintaining ████ sources of information. This Office has taken into consideration not only the organizational and subversive activities as a cause of racial unrest, but also factors relating to such matters as transportation, housing, employment, et cetera.

Comment: This Office appears to have an adequate coverage. A letter has been directed to this Office advising that frequent contact be made with its reliable informants to insure their cognizance of the Bureau's desire to be currently and fully advised of racial conditions and factors related thereto.

Louisville Field Division

This Office has advised that the focal points of racial unrest within its territory are at Louisville and Paducah, Kentucky. In this connection, it is to be noted that in Louisville this Office has ████ confidential informants, and in Paducah ████ confidential informants. No sources of information are available in the Paducah area. The total informant coverage for the area covered by this Office is ████ confidential informants, ████ This Office advises of ████ sources of information for coverage of racial conditions being available.

Comment: The Louisville Office, while stressing the importance of organizational activity among the Negroes in the area covered by it, overlooks entirely other underlying factors which are, of course, definitely influential. Furthermore, it has evidenced reliance upon the police departments and Military Intelligence Service for current information.

This Office requested advice from the Bureau as to whether its further efforts in the development of confidential informants should be confined to informants who had information of organized racial disturbance or whether the future informant coverage should be of such a nature as to provide not only this information, but information of any racial disturbance even though not influenced by organizational forces. In this connection, this Office has been advised by letter that its informant coverage should not only be directed as to organizational or subversive activity, but to include all factors which are pertinent to racial conditions and interracial relations.

Memphis Field Division

This Office supplied █████ confidential informants for the City of Memphis which has a total population of 171,000. It is to be noted that of this population 121,000 are reported to be Negroes. At Nashville, Tennessee, where the population is reported to be 120,000, the number 47,000 represents Negroes. This Office has no confidential informants at Nashville. The Office further advised that at Millington, Tennessee, it was expected that 1,200 Negro sailors would be stationed. In this connection it is to be noted that no informant coverage has been developed to handle this situation.

Comment: This Office does not appear to have adequate confidential informant coverage for the amount of Negro population within its Field Division. This Office apparently fails to consider all underlying conditions and stresses, in the main, organizational activity.

A letter has been directed to this Office pointing out the foregoing observations and instructing that immediate steps be taken to remedy this situation.

Miami Field Division

Within the Miami Field Division it is to be noted there are approximately 500,000 Negroes throughout the area covered by it. The Miami Office has █████ confidential informants for coverage of the racial conditions within its Field Division. It is to be noted that in Miami there are █████ confidential informants; in Tampa █████ confidential informant; in Jacksonville █████ confidential informants; and Palatka █████ confidential informant. The above-mentioned cities were noted as the focal points at which racial disturbances might occur. It is also to be noted that this Office has throughout the State █████ sources of information █████ █████ This Office advised it believes its informant coverage adequate to supply information concerning any concentrated effort or drive to cause a substantial racial upheaval within the State of Florida. This Office stated further efforts were being made to develop more confidential informants.

This Office appears to stress foreign or organizational inspired agitation in developing its informant coverage but does not refer to other factors which must be taken into consideration in this matter.

Comment: A letter has been directed to this Office pointing out that it should vigorously pursue its efforts to develop an adequate informant coverage and that this should be of such a character that the Bureau will be insured of current and full information covering racial conditions and factors affecting them.

Newark Field Division

This Office has advised that in Newark, New Jersey, where the Negro population numbers 50,000, it has ████ confidential informants and ████ sources of information. At Atlantic City, New Jersey, where the Negro population numbers 16,000, this Office has no confidential informants; at Camden, New Jersey, where the Negro population is 13,000, this Office has ████ confidential informants; at Jersey City, New Jersey, where the Negro population is 14,000, this Office has ████ confidential informants; and at Paterson, New Jersey, where the Negro population is 6,000, this Office has ████ confidential informant.

This Office advised that it believed it would be advised of any unusual activities or racial tension of sizable proportions which might develop among the Negroes within the Newark area or with focal points of possible racial trouble. However, this Office noted that more confidential informants will be developed in various Negro organizations as well as informants and sources of information generally.

Comment: This Office, while stressing the importance of organizational and subversive activity among the Negroes in the area covered by it, overlooks entirely other factors which are, of course, definitely influential in racial conditions. Furthermore, this Office points out that Atlantic City, Camden, Jersey City, Trenton and Paterson are the focal points in which racial disturbance might occur. It is believed that more confidential informants within these areas should be developed.

Accordingly, a letter has been directed to this Office pointing out the foregoing observations and instructing them that it is incumbent upon that Office to insure enough coverage to be advised of other factors as well as organizational and subversive activities which might cause racial disturbances.

New Haven Field Division

This Office advises the focal points of possible future racial disturbances as Bridgeport, Fairfield, Hartford and New London, Connecticut. In Bridgeport, the Office lists ████ confidential informants ████ In Fairfield ████ confidential informants are listed; Hartford, ████ confidential informants; New Haven ████ confidential informants; and in New London ████ confidential informants.

Comment: A review of this informant coverage reflects that the coverage is apparently adequate. However, it was noted that considerable reliance has been placed upon plant informants and upon local law enforcement agencies.

The foregoing observations and suggestions have been incorporated in a letter to this Office instructing that its dependency on local law enforcement agencies for information in this matter be limited.

New Orleans Field Division

This Office maintains ▇▇▇▇ confidential informants for the purpose of receiving information concerning racial conditions. ▇▇▇▇▇▇▇▇▇▇▇▇▇▇▇▇ In addition, the Office has the following number of sources of information and contacts: ▇▇▇▇▇▇▇▇▇▇▇▇▇▇▇▇▇▇▇▇▇▇▇▇▇▇▇▇ The confidential informants are all centered in and around New Orleans. In addition, there are ▇▇▇▇ sources and contacts in this area. The Office has pointed out that a sufficient informant coverage is presently in effect to supply the Office's need, although it is continuing to widen and increase not only the quantity but the quality of informants as a result of the ever-present possibility of an outbreak between races. The Office has pointed out that the New Orleans Police Department, as well as other local law enforcement agencies throughout the State, reports directly to the New Orleans Office information relative to racial conditions. It is further advised a sufficient coverage exists whereby the New Orleans Office will learn of the activities of any agitating or radical group as well as any planned movement with respect to interracial relations.

Comment: This Office, while recognizing subversive and organizational activities with respect to racial conditions, does not indicate its informant coverage reports upon all underlying factors which are influential in racial conditions. Accordingly, a letter has been directed to this Office pointing out this observation. The Office has been further advised that its informant coverage should be developed to the point where a minimum of reliance on other agencies and law enforcement bodies is reduced to a minimum. It has also been instructed to concentrate on its development of additional informant coverage, both from a standpoint of quality and quantity.

New York Field Division

This Office has ▇▇▇▇ confidential informants who are maintained for information concerning racial conditions. ▇▇▇

In addition, the New York Office has ▇▇▇▇▇▇▇▇ sources of information and ▇▇▇▇ sources of information who supply information concerning the racial situation in the New York area. All of the sources of information and contacts ▇▇▇ ▇▇▇▇▇▇▇▇▇▇ There are ▇▇▇▇▇▇ and ▇▇▇▇▇▇▇▇▇▇▇▇

The Office has pointed out that the Police Department, New York City, has been very cooperative in furnishing information relative to racial conditions. The New York Office has advised it believes its informant coverage is adequate with respect to racial conditions.

Comment: A letter has been directed to this Office pointing out that it is the personal responsibility of the Special Agent in Charge to see that an informant coverage is developed and maintained by the New York Office in this matter so that there will be insured the immediate availability of all pertinent information with respect to general racial conditions as well as all underlying factors which must necessarily be considered. It has also been pointed out that the informant coverage should be developed to the point where reliance on other agencies and law enforcement bodies will be reduced to a minimum.

Norfolk Field Division

This Office has ▬▬ confidential informants located in the Norfolk, Newport News and Portsmouth areas. In addition, there are ▬▬ confidential ▬▬ informants ▬▬▬▬▬▬▬▬ Located in these three cities, as well as in the Suffolk area, there are a total of ▬▬ sources of information and contacts. ▬▬▬▬▬▬▬▬ The Office advises it would be informed as to any uprising or any agitation fomented by a subversive organization. It has advised additionally that it is continuing its efforts to develop more confidential informants and sources of information to insure being informed in advance of any subversive-inspired action among the Negro inhabitants.

Comment: This Office, it is noted, refers solely to subversive activities among the Negroes and fails to mention other underlying factors which contribute to racial unrest. Accordingly, a letter has been forwarded to this Office instructing that its informant coverage should be developed to the point where the Office will not only be informed of possible subversive-inspired activities tending towards riots or trouble, but also as to all underlying factors which tend to create racial unrest in the area covered by it. The Office has also been advised it should continue its efforts to develop additional informant coverage.

Oklahoma City Field Division

This Office has ▬▬ informants ▬▬▬▬▬▬▬▬ Of the ▬▬ sources of information retained by this Office ▬▬▬▬▬▬▬▬

Comment: From a review of the informant coverage by this Office, it is believed there are not enough Negro confidential informants in Tulsa, where there are between 15,000 and 18,000 Negroes. It is also thought that there is a considerable reliance on the sources of information who, while valuable in many respects, cannot always be counted upon to report independently pertinent matters coming to their attention. There is also an indication of reliance on the Police Department as well as on cooperation with G-2 and ONI. A letter has been directed to this Office pointing out the foregoing observations and advising that the Office's informant coverage should be such as to insure being promptly and fully advised of pertinent information.

Philadelphia Field Division

This Office maintains ▬ confidential informants with respect to the coverage of racial conditions ▬ It also maintains ▬ sources of information and contacts and ▬ This Office has in the past furnished considerable pertinent information with respect to racial conditions as received from its coverage which has included not only organizational and subversive activities but social, economic and political factors. Outside of the Philadelphia area the Office maintains ▬ sources of information.

Comment: A letter has been directed to this Office instructing that frequent contact be maintained with its reliable sources and contacts to insure their cognizance of the Bureau's desire to be informed of all matters which are pertinent to racial conditions and interracial relations. In addition, it has been pointed out to them that while it is entirely satisfactory to have the full cooperation of the Police Department in Philadelphia, the Office's coverage should be developed to the point where any reliance on law enforcement agencies will be reduced to a minimum. It has also been pointed out that the Office should insure the availability of information concerning racial conditions in areas outside of the City of Philadelphia as well as in that City.

Pittsburgh Field Division

This Office maintains ▬ informants and ▬ informants who report information concerning racial conditions. ▬ In addition, in the City of Pittsburgh and immediate surrounding territory there are ▬ sources of information and contacts and ▬ sources of this character. Of these sources of information and contacts, both Negro and white, the Pittsburgh Office has indicated ▬

The Office has advised that the most critical points of racial unrest in the area covered by it are covered by informant coverage which constantly keeps the Office advised as to day by day developments. It has also advised that continuous contact is made with sources of information and contacts and it is making an effort to develop a number of sources of information into confidential informants. It has also advised that Office's contact and relationship with members of law enforcement bodies afford an excellent and immediate coverage of any incidents which might occur.

Comment: While this Office shows an adequate informant coverage of organizational and subversive activity, it fails to set forth the fact that it is receiving information concerning other underlying factors from its informant coverage which are important from the standpoint of racial conditions. In addition, it indicates considerable reliance on the police department and other law enforcement agencies.

A letter has been directed to the Pittsburgh Office wherein these observations are pointed out and instructions have been given that reliance upon law enforcement agencies for information along these lines should be reduced to a minimum by the development of an adequate informant coverage in this matter.

Portland Field Division

This Field Division considers its informant coverage of racial conditions in the area covered by it sufficient. It has advised that there have been no racial outbreaks although close attention is being paid to any such activities. The Field Division has ████████ confidential informants in the City of Portland, along with ████ sources and ████ sources of information. Outside the City of Portland, in such areas as Vanport City, Burns, and Vancouver, coverage of racial conditions is had through a few sources of information but mainly through the cooperation of local law enforcement authority. It might be noted that the Negro population in these areas is not as great as it is in Portland, with the exception of Vanport City, where there has been a large influx of Negroes seeking work in the shipyards. In Vanport City there are maintained ████ contacts who are aware of the Bureau's interest and it is indicated that the Portland Office has received good cooperation from these contacts.

Comment: It has been stated that this Office considers its informant coverage of racial conditions in the area covered by it to be adequate. However, with respect to its coverage in the Vanport City area, it is noted that information is obtained through contacts there, all of whom are connected with local law enforcement agencies. A letter has been directed to this Office pointing out that there should be less reliance on local law enforcement authorities and that it is believed additional confidential informant coverage should be developed to reduce this reliance to a minimum.

Richmond Field Division

This Office maintains ████ confidential informants ████████ ████ Spread throughout the State of Virginia there are ████████ sources of information and contacts ████████

In its conclusion as to its informant coverage the Office advises that a growth in the development of Negro organizations as well as their activities is indicative of the fact that racial trouble of any consequence will arise out of an organized movement initiated or sponsored by one of the several organizations existing in the area covered by this Field Division. It has advised that expeditious attention is being given to obtaining additional confidential informants, contacts and sources of information in this matter. It points out also that contacts with law enforcement agencies afford accurate information relative to racial conditions.

Comment: This Office has developed a good informant ████████████ ██ ████████████ He has been supplying considerable and good information. The Office relies a great deal on his information concerning Negro organizations.

The Office does not indicate that its informant coverage extends to factors other than organizational and subversive activities among the Negroes. Accordingly, a letter has been directed to this Office pointing this out. It has further been instructed to maintain frequent contact with its reliable sources of information and contacts and to concentrate on the development of additional informants. The Office has been instructed that it is its duty to develop an informant coverage which will insure the availability of all pertinent information concerning racial conditions in the area covered by it and, further, that its reliance on local law enforcement officers and other agencies for information along these lines must be reduced to a minimum.

St. Louis Field Division

In the area covered by this Field Division there is a large Negro population, especially centered in the St. Louis, Missouri, area. The St. Louis Office, as its informant coverage of racial conditions, maintains at the present ████ confidential informants ████████████ and ████ sources of information and contacts ████ of whom are affiliated with either law enforcement agencies or the Office of Military Intelligence.

In its conclusion, with respect to its informant coverage, the Office has advised it will be immediately notified prior to the outbreak of any premeditated racial trouble. It points out that the St. Louis Police Department is vitally interested in racial conditions in St. Louis and they are undoubtedly alert for developments along these lines and will immediately notify the St. Louis Office of any plan of action. The Office has also advised that efforts are being continued to develop additional sources of information and confidential informants among the Negro element and among Negro organizations.

Comment: While this Office has advised it is endeavoring to develop additional informant coverage of racial conditions, it is believed that such coverage at the present time is inadequate in view of the large number of Negro inhabitants in the area covered by it and inasmuch as there are a number of national defense plants located in this Field Division. It is noted further that the Office stresses reliance on the St. Louis Police Department. It is further noted that the Office apparently is not concerned with receiving information from its informants on matters affecting racial conditions other than those which are organizational or subversive. A letter has been directed to this Office making the foregoing observations and instructing the Special Agent in Charge that it is his personal responsibility to see that an informant coverage in this matter is developed to the point where he is insured of the immediate availability of information, not only concerning organizational or subversive activity, but data relative to fundamental factors and causes which might be influential in interracial relations in this area.

San Francisco Field Division

This Office maintains ▬▬ confidential informants who reside in and around the Bay area. It has also available ▬▬ sources of information and contacts, all of whom are Negro and all of whom have been supplying information relative to racial conditions.

The Office has advised that efforts for a complete informant coverage have been made and will be continued until the coverage is felt to be entirely adequate. The Office further advised it realizes racial trouble will not necessarily spring from an organized segment, yet with its present coverage of organizational and subversive activity and with the development of additional informants, it will be insured of the availability of information concerning advanced manifestation of racial trouble.

Comment: There are presently about 66,000 Negroes in the Bay area who are centered mainly in three areas, in San Francisco, in Oakland and in Berkeley. The present informant coverage is spread rather evenly throughout these three areas and covers rather fully organizational and subversive activities. It is believed, however, that additional attention should be given to forces other than these which must necessarily be considered in this matter. Accordingly, a letter has been directed to the San Francisco Office pointing this out and requesting that the Office give its close attention to the development of additional informant coverage as outlined in its letter setting forth the extent of its informant coverage.

Savannah Field Division

This Office has a large number of confidential informants, sources of information and contacts throughout the area covered by it, especially in the larger cities. As an example, it has ▬▬ confidential informants and ▬▬ confidential informants who supply information relative to racial conditions. In addition, it has ▬▬ sources of information and contacts and ▬▬ informants in these categories. The Savannah Office has advised, with respect to its informant coverage, that it is confident any pending racial tension which may develop in the area covered by it will be promptly reported. It has also advised that extensive investigation which has been conducted by it has failed to develop any evidence concerning subversive activity or activity of outside persons propagandizing or agitating relative to racial matters.

Comment: A letter has been directed to this Office pointing out that there are, of course, conditions and factors which might lead to possible racial trouble or outbreaks and that it must necessarily be in a position to be advised currently of such matters. These observations have been made in view of the failure of the Savannah Office to mention that it is being currently advised along these lines. It has been further pointed out that in view of the large number of sources of information and contacts the reliable ones should be contacted frequently to insure cognizance on their part of the Bureau's interests in being advised of factors whether political, social or economic or organizational and subversive which might tend to cause racial upheavals.

Seattle Field Division

This Office has █████ confidential informants █████ of whom are located in the Seattle area █████ Tacoma and █████ Vancouver. There are also available to the Seattle Office █████ sources of information and contacts who are able to supply information concerning racial conditions. With respect to its informant coverage, the Seattle Office has advised that it is believed adequate in so far as it concerns the only organized sources of racial agitation, the Communist Party and the Young Communist League. The Office has stated that racial disorders may arise spontaneously without planned activity and it is not possible to develop an informant coverage which will forewarn the Office of such disorders. It concludes that the coverage by sources of information and confidential informants is presently adequate so that the Office may ascertain the facts of any such occurrences within a very short time.

This Office has also pointed out that in contacts made by Agents with representatives of various defense plants in the area, they have, in many instances, been asked for advice as to how the Negro problem may be the best handled or for information as to the method of handling it in other parts of the country. The Agents have uniformly advised that the Bureau cannot make recommendations along these lines. Special Agent in Charge Fletcher has, however, stated he would appreciate receiving any suggestions along these lines which might be of benefit to the plant officials. With respect to this particular matter a letter has been directed to the Seattle Office pointing out that of course the Bureau has no jurisdiction in such matters inasmuch as they are primarily concerned with local factors; furthermore, varying circumstances and forces responsible for strained racial conditions make it impossible to apply any general program or plan which may have been adopted in other places to the Seattle area. This has also been pointed out along with the instructions that obviously no recommendations can be made. It has been suggested, however, to the Seattle Office, that in such contacts with defense plant officials in the future should the question arise they may wish to refer the officials to the local police department in view of its duty to handle the situations or occurrences which might arise out of strained racial conditions.

Comment: It is believed that the Seattle Office overlooks the desire of the Bureau to be informed currently of all factors which affect racial conditions and which might cause tension or strained feelings. Consequently a letter has been directed to that Office setting forth this desire and pointing out that it is the duty, through an adequate reliable informant coverage of racial conditions, of the Special Agent in Charge to be currently advised along these lines. It has been pointed out that of course an informant coverage cannot be such that the Bureau will be forewarned of every spontaneous outbreak between races, yet there should be the immediate availability of information concerning factors which currently exist and which may possibly give rise to racial disturbances. It is pointed out that the informant coverage of the Seattle Office must be adequate along these lines as well as sufficient to inform the Office of organized or subversive activities.

Springfield Field Division

This Office has advised that in the absence of any evidence that organizations are actively stirring up racial strife, it feels that the present informant coverage is adequate and satisfactory. The Office has further pointed out that should additional information be received that any organization becomes active or that the causes of racial strife are other than the result of economic, political and social forces, it will take immediate steps to obtain additional informant coverage. The Office maintains confidential informants in Cairo, East Saint Louis, Kankakee, and Peoria, and has sources of information in these cities as well as Canton, Decatur, Galesburg and Urbana. The total number of confidential informants reporting on matters concerning racial conditions is ████ while the Office has ████ sources of information in this matter.

Comment: This Office, while stressing the importance of organizational and subversive activity among the Negroes in the area covered by it, overlooks entirely other factors which are of course definitely influential in racial conditions. Furthermore, it is evidenced reliance on the police departments and Military Intelligence Service for current information.

A letter has been directed to this Office pointing out the need for additional informant coverage so that it will be currently advised of all aspects of racial conditions within the area covered by it. It has also been pointed out that there are other factors besides organizational or subversive activity, information concerning which must necessarily be available to have a complete picture of racial conditions.

ABBREVIATIONS

ACLU	American Civil Liberties Union
AFL	American Federation of Labor
AG	Attorney General
APR	A. Philip Randolph
ATI	Allah Temple of Islam, *aka* Nation of Islam
BI	Bureau of Investigation, U.S. Department of Justice
CANO	Colored American National Organization, *aka* Washington Park Forum
CIO	Committee for Industrial Organization/Congress of Industrial Organizations
CORE	Congress of Racial Equality
DOJ	Department of Justice
EAB	Ethelbert Anselm Broaster
EPM	Ethiopian Pacific Movement
FBI	Federal Bureau of Investigation, U.S. Department of Justice
FDR	Franklin D. Roosevelt
FEPC	Fair Employment Practices Commission, U.S. Office of Emergency Management
FR	Fellowship of Reconciliation
INS	Immigration and Naturalization Service, U.S. Department of Justice
IRCFL	International Reassemble Church of the Freedom League
HUAC	House Committee on Un-American Activities
JEH	J. Edgar Hoover
LRJ	Leonard Robert Jordan
MG	Mittie Maud Lena Gordon
MID	Military Intelligence Division, U.S. War Department
MOWM	March on Washington Movement
MSTA	Moorish Science Temple of America
NAACP	National Association for the Advancement of Colored People
NLVC	Negro Labor Victory Committee
NNC	National Negro Congress
OFF	Office of Facts and Figures, U.S. Office of War Information

ONI	Office of Naval Intelligence, U.S. Department of the Navy
OPM	Office of Production Management, U.S. Office of Emergency Management
OWI	Office of War Information, U.S. Office of Emergency Management
PME	Peace Movement of Ethiopia
PMEW	Pacific Movement of the Eastern World, Inc.
STFU	Southern Tenant Farmers Union
UAW	United Automobile Workers of America
UNIA	Universal Negro Improvement Association
WMC	War Manpower Commission, U.S. Department of Emergency Management

CHRONOLOGY OF EVENTS

13 May 1924 Attorney General (AG) Harlan F. Stone orders that the activities of the Bureau of Investigation (BI) "be limited strictly to investigations of violations of law." Intelligence efforts of the Department of Justice (DOJ) are also curtailed by the order.

10 Dec. 1924 J. Edgar Hoover (JEH), head of the Bureau's General Intelligence Division, is promoted from acting director to the position of director of the entire BI.

July–Aug. 1928 The Sixth Congress of the Communist International convenes in Moscow. It inaugurates the so-called third period, characterized by militant class struggle ("class against class"). The congress also enunciates the Communist Party's new line on the race question in the United States, characterizing the African American as an oppressed nation entitled to the right of self-determination.

19 Jan. 1931 JEH expresses his opposition to Congressman Hamilton Fish's proposal to expand the BI's responsibility beyond criminal investigation by granting it power to investigate "Communist and revolutionary activity." He contends that it would require the BI to resume "undercover" activities and that it would be necessary for the BI "to secure a foothold in Communistic inner circles" and "to keep fully informed as to changing policies and secret propaganda on the part of Communists."

25 Mar. 1931 Nine black youths are arrested for allegedly raping two white women riding a freight train near Paint Rock, Alabama. They are hastily tried and convicted; all except one of the youths are sentenced to death. Dubbed the Scottsboro Boys, the case of the nine becomes an international *cause celebre* throughout the 1930s after the Communist-led International Labor Defense mounts a massive political campaign for their liberation and takes over their legal defense. Partly as a result of its leadership of the Scottsboro defense campaign, African American support for the Communist Party increases.

18 Sept. 1931 Japan launches its military occupation of Manchuria.

Nov. 1932 Franklin D. Roosevelt (FDR) is elected president.

7 Dec. 1932 The Pacific Movement of the Eastern World (PMEW) is incorporated in Illinois. The incorporation papers list a board of three directors, including the prime mover in the organization, Ashima Takis, *aka* Mimo De Guzman, president general. The organization becomes the main source for promotion of pro-Japanese sympathies among African Americans during the thirties. It originated following a meeting in Chicago of members of Marcus Garvey's Universal Negro Improvement Association (UNIA), at which Naka Nakane—a Japanese alien representing himself as a major in the Japanese army and a representative of the so-called Black Dragon Society (*Kokuryu Kai*) as well as a Shinto priest—met and recruited Mimo De Guzman—a Filipino UNIA follower, *aka* Ashima Takis.

7 Dec. 1932 Mittie Maud Lena Gordon (MG), leader of the Chicago UNIA, intervenes and reorganizes the PMEW, renaming her wing of the movement the Peace Movement of Ethiopia (PME). The main objective of the PME is repatriation to Africa.

30 Jan. 1933 Adolf Hitler becomes chancellor of Germany.

4 Mar. 1933 FDR is sworn in as America's thirty-second president.

16 June 1933 The National Industrial Recovery Act is signed into law by the president. Among other things, it guarantees to the labor movement the right to organize and bargain collectively, leading to a rapid upsurge of industrial organizing and a renewed spirit of unionism among workers. It also creates the National Recovery Administration to supervise the preparation of codes of fair competition in each industry and to provide for a program of public works.

16 Sept. 1933 The Office of Naval Intelligence (ONI) forwards to JEH a copy of an intelligence report by the officer-in-charge of the Navy Recruiting Station, Kansas City, Mo., relative to the visit and activities of a "Japanese organizer" who is reported to be "organizing among the negroes an Anti-White Race Movement." According to the original report, "The Japanese organizer is said to have promised Japanese assistance in arms, cash, and supplies, in a war against the white race."

18 Sept. 1933 JEH writes to the Military Intelligence Division (MID) to report that the FBI was taking no action to investigate a report submitted to the Bureau's Kansas City field office regarding "a Japanese man who was going around the country organizing negroes with the purpose that they would not support this country in future wars."

26 Sept. 1933 The ONI furnishes JEH with a subsequent report on the "Japanese organizer" active in organizing blacks at Kansas City, Mo.

27 Sept. 1933 Another ONI report is forwarded to JEH; it encloses a photostatic copy of the certificate of membership setting out the objects and creed of the PMEW.

Sept. 1933 Harold L. Ickes, director of the Public Works Administration established under the National Industrial Recovery Act, issues a general order prohibiting "discrimination on the basis of color or religion in employment for public works" and drafts a nondiscrimination clause for all public works contracts.

2 Oct. 1933 A branch of the PMEW is incorporated in the state of Missouri by Walter Lee Peoples, a leader of the St. Louis UNIA; he is recruited by Mimo De Guzman, to "encourage the return of those people who have no opportunity for development in the United States to the land of their fathers."

5 Oct. 1933 The Development of Our Own is incorporated in the state of Michigan. Described in its articles of incorporation as "a patriotic, independent and loyal brotherhood," it results from the promotion efforts of Naka Nakane. Support is garnered among the black community in Detroit where Nakane first preaches his doctrine of racial solidarity.

26 Oct. 1933 The ONI furnishes JEH with a report from a "reliable source" in Chicago regarding Japanese activities among blacks. According to the report, "A movement is under way for the amalgamation of the Moorish Americans with the UNIA which is being instigated by members of the Moorish Americans who are members of the Pacific Movement, Inc., and to then merge the Negro group with Pacific Movements. The Moorish Americans . . . are reported to be a fearless and militant group."

2 Nov. 1933 MID forwards to JEH two more reports received by it in connection with Japanese activities among African Americans in greater Kansas City.

3 Nov. 1933 JEH writes to the director of the ONI, informing him that the FBI "is now conducting an investigation" of the reported activities of Japanese propagandists and "any further information you can furnish will be appreciated."

10 Nov. 1933 Robert F. Kelley, chief of the division of Eastern European Affairs, Department of State, transmits to JEH "as of possible interest" an extract from an article in the 20 Sept. 1933 issue of the *Daily Worker* by A. W. Berry regarding alleged propaganda activities among African Americans in Kansas City by a Japanese organizer.

21 Nov. 1933 The director of the ONI again supplies JEH with copies of reports lately received from the commandant of the Ninth Naval District, Great Lakes, Ill., and the Navy Recruiting Officer, Kansas City, Mo., regarding Japanese activities among black organizations.

28 Nov. 1933 *Michibeisen Miraiki* ("Forecast of Future American-Japanese War") is published as a supplement to the Japanese magazine *Hinode*. The fictional story includes an incident involving a "Negro mess boy," who gives information to the Japanese about U.S. military strategy, and later plants a bomb that destroys an American warship.

2 Dec. 1933 Naka Nakane, *aka* Satohata Takahashi, is arrested in Detroit and charged with illegal entry into the U.S.

8 Dec. 1933 The ONI forwards another confidential report received from the Navy Recruiting Officer, Kansas City, Mo., regarding Japanese activities among blacks.

11 Dec. 1933 The *Washington Evening Star* reports that a Japanese named "Takahashi" has been arrested at Detroit, Mich., on the charge of having illegally entered the U.S.

19 Dec. 1933 The MID forwards to JEH copies of a letter from the village president of the village of Madison, Madison County, Ill., and from the unit instructor, 340th Field Artillery, U.S. National Guard, Wichita, Kan., concerning Japanese activities among African Americans in the middle west.

27 Dec. 1933 A charter issued by the State of Kansas for establishment of the PMEW lists 697 members in its Kansas City branch. The moving force behind the organization is Mimo De Guzman who poses as a Japanese man. Dr. A. Porter Davis, a black physician, is listed as president and one of its incorporators (Davis would later be elected president of the Kansas City branch of the NAACP on 20 Dec. 1942).

28 Dec. 1933 JEH receives a copy from MID of a report submitted by the unit instructor of the 340th Field Artillery, Wichita, Kan., regarding the activities of the PMEW.

1933 Rev. A. L. Hill is made Mississippi state president of the PMEW by Walter Lee Peoples. However, the organization is refused permission to incorporate in Mississippi because of belief that is of foreign origin.

1933 3,200 members are reported to be enrolled with the national headquarters of the Moorish Science Temple of America (MSTA), but it soon discontinues public meetings and begins to work secretly.

10 Apr. 1934 The National Negro Congress (NNC) is incorporated in the District of Columbia. It supersedes the former League of Struggle for Negro Rights, one of a succession of Communist Party front organizations active in the African-American community. The NNC is established in an attempt to develop a broader organization among blacks.

18 Apr. 1934 Five warrants are issued against Walter Lee Peoples and David Erwin, both leaders of the PMEW, charging them with fraud. Charges are dropped on 24 July 1934.

20 Apr. 1934 Naka Nakane is deported from the U.S. to Japan by the Immigration and Naturalization Service (INS). However, he reappears at Vancouver, Canada, on 29 Aug. 1934. He soon moves to Toronto and Windsor, Ontario, directing from there the activities of the Development of Our Own organization through his wife, Pearl Sherrod Takahashi. As a result of marital difficulties, however, Nakane removes his African-American wife and appoints Rev. Cash C. Bates as chief executive officer of the organization.

10 May 1934 FDR requests JEH to investigate "the activity of the Nazi movement in this country," specifically William Dudley Pelley and his Silver Shirts of America. A limited intelligence investigation is carried out in conjunction with the Secret Service and INS.

16 May 1934 JEH sends to MID director Brig. Gen. Alfred T. Smith a copy of a letter received from C. D. Wilson of Crosno, Mo., referring to "the organization by certain Japanese and negroes [negro] persons into a secret society called the 'Original Afro Pacific Organization.' "

28 June 1934 JEH sends MID a copy of a letter reporting on the activities of one *Adachi Kinnosuki* among the African Americans in Pittsburgh. He informs the director of MID that "No action is being taken by this Division in connection with the activities of this individual."

June–July 1934 Blacks in Harlem launch an aggressive mass picketing campaign against white store owners along Harlem's 125th Street. The campaign is spearheaded by "The Citizens League for Fair Play," a coalition of 62 Harlem organizations that represents the first "united front" of the New York black community. After six weeks Blumstein's, the target store of the campaign, capitulates and agrees to hire 15 black saleswomen.

July 1934 The Southern Tenant Farmers Union (STFU) is formed in Arkansas to protest treatment of sharecroppers.

28 Aug. 1934 JEH provides the MID with a copy of a letter received from Frederick D. Stark of St. Louis, Mo., reporting on the organization of a secret society created by certain Japanese and African Americans.

19–20 Mar. 1935 A 16-year-old black youth, Lino Rivera, is arrested for stealing a ten-cent knife from an S. H. Kress store in Harlem. A riot erupts after false rumors circulate that the boy was beaten to death by police. Roving bands sweep through Harlem's streets, destroying the property of white merchants and assaulting white store owners who try to defend their property. Four men are killed, two of them as the result of police firing into a crowd during the riot. Economic ills are blamed as the basic cause of the conflagration, the first major riot to occur in Harlem.

22 Apr. 1935 JEH shares with MID a memorandum prepared by FBI special agent R. H. Emory, setting forth information concerning the "alleged efforts of certain Japanese to organize the negroes in this country." JEH informs MID: "Please be advised that no further action is being taken by the Bureau in this matter, and these data are submitted for your information."

May 1935 "The National Conference on the Economic Crisis and the Negro" meets at Howard University, Washington, D.C., sponsored by the Joint Committee on National Recovery.

June 1935 The name of the *Bureau of Investigation* is officially changed to the *Federal Bureau of Investigation* (FBI).

3 July 1935 The National Association for the Advancement of Colored People (NAACP) charges that workers in the South are intimidated into accepting a lower wage scale than is provided for in codes established through the National Recovery Act.

July–Aug. 1935 The Seventh Congress of the Communist International convenes in Moscow. The triumph of fascism forces the Communist International to change its disastrous "class against class" line, thereby paving the way for the development of the successful Popular Front strategy.

30 Aug. 1935 A charter is issued by the State of Pennsylvania for operation of the PMEW, and a unit is organized in Pittsburgh.

3 Sept. 1935 Fascist Italy invades Ethiopia. The conflict brings about widespread feeling of racial solidarity among African Americans as well as outpouring of support for Ethiopia.

18 Sept. 1935 The Ethiopian Pacific Movement (EPM) is incorporated in New York County. It is led by Leonard Robert Jordan (LRJ), a Jamaican, who, prior to the creation of the EPM, had been active in the UNIA. Through his association with the UNIA, he became acquainted with Mimo De Guzman, who introduced him to the teachings of the PMEW.

4–5 Oct. 1935 Angry blacks attack Italian-American street vendors in Harlem and at PS 178 in Brooklyn to protest the Italo-Ethiopian conflict. Mayor LaGuardia asks for police protection of Harlem storekeepers against threats of violence. Black leaders call for a national boycott of Italian American businesses.

15 Nov. 1935 The Committee for Industrial Organization (CIO) is founded, inaugurating the nationwide organizing drive for industrial unionism. Nominally an adjunct of the American Federation of Labor (AFL), after June 1936 the CIO ceases to have any meaningful ties with it.

Nov. 1935 James W. Ford, leading black communist, addresses the central committee of the Communist Party. He discusses the objectives of the newly formed NNC and states that the Communist Party "endorses the National Negro Congress."

1935 A unit of the PMEW becomes active in Omaha, Neb., under the leadership of African-American war veteran William S. Washington.

1935 Father Mohammed Bey, founder of a unit of the MSTA in Kansas City, Kan., breaks away from the national organization with a large following, reportedly numbering as many as 500 members.

ca. 1934–35 The Universal Temple of Tranquility is founded in Harlem by Eugene Brown, *aka* Sufi Abdul Hamid, *aka* "the Black Hitler."

6 Jan. 1936 Secretary of War George H. Dern advises AG Homer Cummings that there is "definite indication" of foreign espionage in the U.S. and that in a national emergency "some organizations . . . would probably attempt to cripple our war effort through sabotage." Dern urges that the DOJ establish "a counterespionage service among civilians to prevent foreign espionage in the U.S. and to collect information so that in case of an emergency any persons intending to cripple our war effort by means of espionage or sabotage may be taken into custody."

14–16 Feb. 1936 A. Philip Randolph (APR), leader of the Brotherhood of Sleeping Car Porters, AFL, is elected president of the NNC. The opening sessions are attended by 912 delegates and several thousand additional people. The congress announces seven demands, including the right of blacks to equal wages, union membership, equal opportunities, equality of black women, and its opposition to war, fascism, and Italian imperialism in Ethiopia. The congress draws the struggle of blacks into close alliance with the struggle of industrial unionism under the leadership of the CIO.

Feb.–Mar. 1936 A Goodyear strike paralyzes Akron, Ohio, helping to set the pace for the rapid development and expansion of industrial unions and helping the rise of the CIO.

5 May 1936 Italian forces occupy the Ethiopian capital of Addis Ababa. Ethiopia is formally annexed to Italy and along with Eritrea and Italian Somaliland becomes part of Italian East Africa.

19 May 1936 An estimated 400 African-American sympathizers of Ethiopia erupt in rioting in Harlem, following a mass meeting to protest the Italian occupation of Ethiopia. Two Italian stores are looted.

14 July 1936 Fresh outbreaks of street violence erupt in Harlem.

17 July 1936 General Francisco Franco leads a revolt in Morocco against the Spanish Republican government, thus setting off the Spanish Civil War. African Americans enlist in the Abraham Lincoln Brigade to fight on behalf of the Spanish Republican Government.

24 Aug. 1936 JEH meets with FDR to discuss subversive activities in the U.S., "particularly Fascism and Communism." The meeting deals almost exclusively with Communist activities, particularly with the alleged Communist control of the West Coast International Longshoremen's Union headed by Harry Bridges, Communist attempts to gain control of the United Mine Workers Union headed by John L. Lewis, and the "strong Communist leanings" of the Newspaper Guild. JEH claims that "there is at the present time no governmental organization which is getting any so-called 'general intelligence information.' " He recommends to the president that since the FBI's legal authorization would not allow it to investigate any intelligence matters unless referred by the State Department, a formal request by the State Department could initiate the required investigation.

25 Aug. 1936 FDR meets at the White House with Secretary of State Cordell Hull and JEH to discuss the president's concern "relative to Communist activities in this country, as well as Fascist activities." FDR informs Hull that he would like to have a "survey" made of both subjects, since these movements were "international in scope." Hull agrees and requests JEH to make the necessary investigations. Under the agreement, the FBI is required to coordinate its investigative activities with both the State Department and the agencies of military and naval intelligence.

10 Sept. 1936 JEH meets with AG Cummings to discuss "the radical situation" and informs him of the request made by the secretary of state "to have investigation made of the subversive activities in this country, including communism and fascism." Cummings approves of the request and directs JEH to proceed as well as to coordinate information obtained with the directors of the MID and the ONI as well as the State Department.

1 Oct. 1936 The Development of Our Own is incorporated in the State of Illinois.

3 Nov. 1936 FDR is reelected president.

30 Dec. 1936 Workers at General Motors' Fisher body plant in Flint, Mich., launch a historic sit-down strike. The struggle involves other plants and continues for six weeks, leading over the next six months to widespread and successful labor efforts by the CIO to organize workers in the automobile and steel industries on the basis of collective bargaining, which had not previously been allowed.

1936 The Kansas City branch of the PMEW purchases a two-story building in Kansas City.

20 Jan. 1937 FDR is inaugurated for a second term.

11 Feb. 1937 General Motors, America's largest corporation, negotiates an end to the Flint strike by recognizing the United Auto Workers of America (UAW). It marks a major triumph for organized labor. Sit-down strikes by Detroit's non-unionized, semiskilled workers proliferate.

Feb. 1937 The Southern Negro Youth Congress holds its inaugural meeting.

4 June 1937 The PMEW is dissolved by the State of Illinois for failing to file required annual reports.

7 July 1937 Japan launches a series of military campaigns in China but without declaring war. The fighting spreads rapidly, leading to Japan's seizure of Peiping and Tientsin.

25 Aug. 1937 The Ethiopian World Federation is formed in New York by Dr. Malaku Bayen, personal representative to the U.S. of the Ethiopian emperor and the Ethiopian government in exile. It seeks to coordinate existing Ethiopian relief efforts by combining several smaller groups and by dissolving older groups, such as United Aid for Ethiopia, which had come under Communist Party influence.

15–17 Oct. 1937 The second meeting of the NNC is held in Philadelphia. It claims to represent a membership of more than 500,000. The meeting discusses the Scottsboro Boys case, the need for equality of wages and of opportunity, the right of farmers, tenants, and sharecroppers to bargain collectively, opposition to lynching, and opposition to fascism and war.

1937 Mrs. C. J. Allen of Chicago, Ill., visits Mississippi as the national organizer for the PME and sets up a local chapter.

1937 The Ethiopian World Federation is formed in Philadelphia and absorbs the membership of the Rising Sun Club, a group of African-American nationalists.

1937 The CIO launches a southern organizing drive ("Operation Dixie").

16 Feb. 1938 The Nazis' coup in Austria leads American newspapers to call for security to be tightened by the government against activities of the German-American Bund in the U.S.

10 May 1938 The House Rules Committee of the U.S. House of Representatives headed by the conservative Texas Democrat Rep. Martin Dies launches an investigation of foreign "isms," establishing a Special Committee to Investigate Un-American Activities that would be succeeded in 1947 by the House Committee on Un-American Activities (HUAC).

12 May 1938 The FBI announces that it has completed a 12-volume report on Nazi espionage activities.

20 June 1938 The government indicts 18 American Nazis for participating in what is described as "the greatest peacetime spy ring in history."

Sept. 1938 JEH informs the House Appropriations Committee that the FBI has begun compiling information on the "press and groups engaged in . . . subversive activities, in espionage activities, or any activities that are possibly detrimental to the internal security of the United States."

20 Oct. 1938 AG Cummings submits to the president a joint FBI-ONI-MID plan for the organization of domestic intelligence. The plan calls for the FBI to be the "exclusive governmental agency" to investigate cases of espionage, counterespionage, and sabotage. Cummings recommends that the plan "be handled in strictest confidence." Cummings also attaches a memorandum prepared by JEH noting that the FBI had secretly established a General Intelligence Section that collected information dealing with subversion and intelligence matters. Following receipt of the report, the president instructs the director of the budget to increase the sums requested by the three agencies for counterespionage. Meanwhile, Cummings is designated by the president to serve as chairman of a cabinet committee to study the "so-called espionage situation."

20 Oct. 1938 The PME writes to Liberian President Edward Barclay to propose the emigration of African Americans to Liberia.

2 Nov. 1938 FDR informs JEH that the plan to develop a special counterespionage drive and expand the structure of intelligence work has been approved. The president grants the FBI $150,000 in additional discretionary funds to expand its domestic intelligence operations.

14–18 Nov. 1938 The CIO is established as an autonomous organization, entirely separate from the AFL, at a national convention in Pittsburgh.

5 Dec. 1938 David J. Logan and Joseph Rockmore arrive in Liberia as representatives of the PME.

1938 Pearl Sherrod Takahashi, Nakane's former wife, along with six other African Americans, contacts Dr. I. Tashiro, a Japanese dentist in Chicago, to arrange a meeting with the Japanese consul and to make a donation to the Japanese war effort. Tashiro reports that they donated more than $300.00.

1938 The Conference for Human Welfare, an umbrella organization for Communist united front groups in the south, meets in Alabama.

1938 The Addeynue Allahe Universal Arabic Association is incorporated and established in Buffalo, N.Y. Members of the organization register themselves as conscientious objectors to war.

1938 The membership of the Kansas City branch of the PMEW dwindles to around twenty and soon becomes defunct.

1938 Ishmael Moore, *aka* Abraham Moore, reactivates the African Moslem Welfare Society.

1938 MSTA temple no. 45 is organized in Louisville, Ken.

9 Jan. 1939 Approximately 1,200 sharecroppers in southeast Missouri stage a roadside demonstration by camping along U.S. 60 and U.S. 61. Missouri state police, county sheriffs, and deputized citizens order the demonstrators to leave their campsites. Many demonstrators are forcibly removed.

11 Jan. 1939 Naka Nakane illegally reenters the U.S. at Buffalo, N.Y. He reorganizes the followers remaining loyal to him into a new association known as the Onward Movement of America.

12 Jan. 1939 The president asks Congress for $552,000,000 for the national defense program. He more and more openly expresses sympathies for the European democracies.

30 Jan. 1939 The Onward Movement of America is incorporated in the state of Michigan. The FBI reports that it is identical to The Development of Our Own, except for the absence of Nakane's former wife, Pearl Sherrod Takahashi. The new organization continues to operate the Producers and Consumers Market, which was an adjunct to the former body.

Jan. 1939 David Logan returns to the U.S. from Liberia.

3 Feb. 1939 Newly appointed AG Frank Murphy announces the establishment within the Criminal Division of the DOJ of a special Civil Liberties Unit (later renamed the Civil Liberties Section and subsequently raised to the status of the Civil Rights Division). Its aim is to supervise the enforcement of federal constitutional rights. It results in the expansion of the FBI's criminal jurisdiction to include investigation of alleged civil rights violations, thus making the FBI the investigative arm of the federal government's civil rights program.

7 Feb. 1939 At JEH's behest, Joseph Keenan, assistant to the AG, sends a circular letter to the civilian investigative agencies of the U.S. government informing them that the FBI has "undertaken activities to investigate matters relating to espionage and *subversive* activities."

13 Mar. 1939 Under Secretary of State Sumner Welles reminds the AG of the president's desire to have fascist, communist, and communist-front organizations investigated. The DOJ selects the German-American Bund, the Communist Party, and the American League for Peace and Democracy as initial targets of investigation.

16 Mar. 1939 JEH informs the AG that the FBI is devoting increasing resources to the investigation of espionage, counterespionage, and sabotage matters but says nothing about subversive activities. He states that other government agencies are trying to "usurp" the FBI's jurisdiction, but reiterates that the ONI and MID have agreed that the FBI should serve as the government's clearing house for domestic intelligence.

24 Apr. 1939 Senator Theodore Bilbo of Mississippi introduces the Greater Liberia Repatriation Bill before congress.

20 June 1939 JEH announces that 700 cases of espionage were investigated by the FBI during 1938, whereas in the previous five years only 35 cases were reported.

22 June 1939 Nakane is arrested for illegally entering the U.S. and for attempting to bribe an immigration inspector.

26 June 1939 FDR issues a directive establishing guidelines governing intelligence operations. It dissolves the domestic intelligence coordinating committee made up of various governmental agencies and concentrates all "espionage, counterespionage, and sabotage matters" in the FBI, ONI, and MID. The directive grants the FBI exclusive authority to coordinate domestic intelligence.

17 July 1939 JEH makes the "growing problem" of espionage the chief topic for a two-week meeting of special agents in charge of FBI field divisions.

23 Aug. 1939 The Nazi-Soviet nonaggression pact is signed at Moscow. Regarded in the west as a demonstration of Russian perfidy, it brings to a sudden end the Popular Front strategy of the Communist parties.

1 Sept. 1939 German forces invade Poland, leading to the start of World War II.

2 Sept. 1939 JEH instructs all FBI field divisions to review their files in order to secure information regarding individuals deemed disloyal or potentially disloyal to the U.S.

5 Sept. 1939 The U.S. proclaims its neutrality in the European war. Intensive investigative efforts carried out by the DOJ following the outbreak of war results in prosecution of several Communist-front organizations for failure to register as foreign agents.

7 Sept. 1939 AG Murphy asks the American public to report suspected incidents of sabotage and espionage as well as other disloyal activities to the FBI, at the same time that he cautions against turning the campaign against spies into a "witch hunt." The ACLU criticizes Murphy's statement as not only indiscreet but also an incitement to the witch hunt that it claimed to decry.

8 Sept. 1939 The president declares a state of limited national emergency.

9 Sept. 1939 FDR augments his directive of June 26 with a declaration instructing "the Federal Bureau of Investigation of the Department of Justice to take charge of investigative work in matters relating to espionage, sabotage, and violations of neutrality regulations," and instructing all law enforcement officers in the U.S. "promptly to turn over to the nearest representative of the Federal Bureau of Investigation any information obtained by them relating to espionage, counterespionage, sabotage, subversive activities and violations of the neutrality laws." The President's request paves the way for close cooperation between the FBI and local law enforcement agencies.

11 Sept. 1939 INS district offices are instructed to report immediately to the FBI any information "relating to espionage, counterespionage, sabotage, subversive activities or violation of the neutrality laws" obtained in the handling of any alien applying for naturalization.

15–20 Sept. 1939 The twelfth annual convention of the MSTA is held in Chicago.

25 Sept. 1939 JEH tells graduates of the National Police Academy that "forces alien to American peace and democracy are seeking to burrow deep into our social order" and that "these exponents of foreign isms have no moral right to bite the hand that feeds them."

28 Sept. 1939 Naka Nakane is convicted in federal court in Detroit on the charge of illegal entry into the U.S. and sentenced to three years imprisonment and a $4,500 fine. He is later transferred as a mental case from the federal penitentiary at Leavenworth, Kansas, to the medical center for federal prisoners at Springfield, Mo. Following his conviction, the

Onward Movement of America becomes defunct, though Rev. Cash C. Bates would remain the nominal leader of the organization in Detroit.

6 Oct. 1939 A branch of the PMEW is incorporated in the State of Oklahoma. One of the leaders, David D. Erwin, certifies on 16 Sept. that it is a church organization.

10 Oct. 1939 Speaking at the annual convention of the International Association of Police Chiefs, JEH declares that "it is the unfortunate plight of America, in this period of chaos in world affairs, to become the jousting ground for the subversive forces which work against our best interest, even our national existence" and warns that "these may go beyond the ordinary espionage activities and into the realms of sabotage and the fomenting of outbreaks and riots."

24 Oct. 1939 JEH announces that the FBI is receiving complaints of espionage, sabotage, and neutrality violations at the rate of 214 daily.

27 Oct. 1939 The State of Illinois dissolves the Development of Our Own for its failure to file required annual reports.

Oct. 1939 Charles Newby and Stokely Delmar Hart form the Colored American National Organization (CANO) *aka* Washington Park Forum, Afro-American National Organization, and Brotherhood of Liberty for the Black People of America, in Chicago.

Oct. 1939 The DOJ considers plans for establishing a special subunit within the Civil Liberties Unit to deal with espionage, propaganda, and similar matters. The plan is finally implemented in Apr. 1940.

25 Nov. 1939 The FBI begins compiling a "custodial detention list" of individuals with "strong" Nazi and Communist tendencies who could be considered a "menace to the public peace and safety" in the event of war. Preparation of the list is undertaken by the FBI without consulting the AG or gaining his approval. Retroactive approval would not be provided until June 1940.

30 Nov. 1939 The FBI forwards to the White House a copy of a report obtained from a confidential source, *Japanese Propaganda in the U.S., 1939*. Prepared by Allen Zoll, an advertising executive and private public relations consultant for the Chinese government, the report includes a one-page description of "Japanese Propaganda Among the Negro People."

1939 A temporary commission is created by the Pennsylvania State Legislature to study the conditions of the urban black population of Pennsylvania.

3–5 Jan. 1940 JEH informs the House Appropriations Committee that the demands on the FBI in 1939 were the heaviest in fifteen years, with the number of espionage investigations reaching a total of 1,651. He also apprises the committee that the Bureau's General Intelligence Division was reactivated in 1939 following the president's directive increasing the FBI's investigative authority. The latter statement stirs a national uproar.

6 Feb. 1940 Without benefit of a search warrant FBI agents raid the New York headquarters of the Veterans of the Abraham Lincoln Brigade; they also arrest ten activists in Detroit and two others in Milwaukee who, more than three years earlier, had recruited Abraham Lincoln Brigade volunteers to fight on behalf of the Spanish Republican government.

15–16 Feb. 1940 AG Jackson, who played no part in the decision to prosecute the Spanish Loyalist recruiters, moves to have the cases against them dismissed. The federal district court complies the following day.

1 Mar. 1940 *Native Son* by Richard Wright is published by Harper and Brothers. The publication marks a major literary event: the book sells 215,000 copies within three weeks.

18 Mar. 1940 AG Jackson forbids wiretapping by the FBI.

5 Apr. 1940 The ACLU releases a study of various federal and state prosecutions. It finds that there is some basis for the accusation that federal and state authorities are using criminal statutes for "ulterior political purposes." It lays the blame "at the door of the President" and his order authorizing the FBI to conduct investigations of "subversive activities."

9 Apr. 1940 Germany invades Norway by air and sea.

26–28 Apr. 1940 The third annual meeting of the NNC is held in Washington, D.C., attended by 1,264 delegates. A major split takes place between Communist and non-Communist members. APR refuses to offer himself as a candidate for the presidency of the organization. He resigns when the convention passes a resolution of non-intervention in the European war. A group of non-Communist black members withdraws and later forms the nucleus of supporters around APR and the March on Washington Movement (MOWM).

5 May 1940 APR declares that the NNC was "deliberately packed with Communists and CIO members who were either Communists or sympathizers with Communists." He also reveals that the Communist Party is subsidizing the activities of the NNC.

10–12 May 1940 Germany invades the Netherlands, Belgium, and Luxembourg.

17–21 May 1940 German mechanized divisions launch an invasion of northern France.

21 May 1940 The U.S. Supreme Court imposes restrictions on wiretapping. FDR establishes internal security exceptions, however. He maintains that "the Supreme Court never intended any dictum . . . to apply to grave matters involving the defense of the nation." On this basis, he issues a secret wiretapping directive to the AG, authorizing FBI agents "to secure information by listening devices directed to the conversation or other communications of persons suspected of subversive activities against the Government of the U.S., including suspected spies." The AG does not maintain any record of approval of FBI wiretapping requests, however, thus opening the way for unbridled use of wiretaps by the FBI.

28 May 1940 A British expeditionary force of some 250,000 men, along with 140,000 French troops, is rescued from the beaches of Dunkirk. British losses total 30,000. Significant loss of war materials during the withdrawal causes Britain to appeal to the U.S. for war supplies.

May 1940 The Committee on Participation of Negroes in the National Defense Program is organized under the aegis of the *Pittsburgh Courier.* Headed by Dr. Rayford W. Logan of Howard University, it attempts to press for equal participation of African Americans in civilian and military aspects of the defense program.

5 June 1940 A secret presidential directive delimiting respective spheres of U.S. intelligence operations gives the FBI primary responsibility for intelligence within the western hemisphere, except for the Panama Canal Zone. JEH is given responsibility not only for coordinating intelligence gathered by all federal intelligence agencies, but also for preventing enemy spying and acts of sabotage in the U.S. and the entire western hemisphere.

12 June 1940 The president asks his secretary, Gen. Edwin Watson, to write to JEH, "thanking him for all the reports on investigations he has made, and tell him I appreciate the fine work he is doing."

13–18 June 1940 Paris is evacuated and France falls to the invading German army.

21 June 1940 The FBI creates a Special Intelligence Service for the purpose of collecting economic, political, industrial, and financial information concerning the countries of Latin America.

28 June 1940 The Alien Registration Act ("Smith Act") is adopted by Congress. It is an omnibus statute constituting America's first peacetime federal sedition law since the Sedition Act of 1798. It is aimed directly at aliens and seeks to prohibit "subversive activities." It marks the start of a series of laws enacted by Congress during 1940 designed to combat internal threats to national security.

June 1940 In an article entitled "Stamping Out the Spies," JEH declares that "We must not stoop to un-American methods, no matter how great the provocation or how patriotic the aim."

6 July 1940 JEH praises local law-enforcement officers for their cooperation in the nationwide program to guard against "fifth column" activity.

22 July 1940 An indictment is issued against David D. Erwin by the State of Illinois for "committing conspiracy" in Pulaski county.

23 July 1940 JEH delivers an ominous warning against "fifth columnists" and pledges that the FBI urgently desires to cooperate with local police authorities. He accuses the communists of undertaking a "smear" campaign against the FBI and denounces their "parrot-like followers in classrooms, in pulpits, in the press and in high places of government." He declares that "fascism and Nazism did not come into being until the wickedly winding way was paved by communism."

July–Aug. 1940 Germany launches an aerial bombing offensive against British cities, airfields, and vital industries.

5 Aug. 1940 In a message to a two day federal–state conference on law enforcement problems and national defense, FDR calls on congress and state legislatures to enact additional laws dealing with "subversive activities, seditious acts and those things which might slow up or break down our common defense program."

6 Aug. 1940 As part of its investigation of "fifth column" suspects, the FBI places all field divisions on a 24-hour schedule.

27 Aug. 1940 The INS central office in Washington, D.C., sends out a circular letter to all INS district offices, instructing them "to coordinate alien registration with naturalization work." Every alien applicant for naturalization is now required to register under the Alien Registration Act of 1940.

20 Sept. 1940 The FBI receives a report "to the effect that a Japanese in Washington, D.C., has been going around addressing a group of colored people in homes and at other places." According to the report, "In these addresses his [the Japanese man's] major promise is that if the colored people will help the Japanese out, the Japanese will take care of the colored people."

23 Sept. 1940 JEH tells an American Legion conference that a "fifth column of destruction" is on the march in America. He calls upon the Legion to work with FBI investigators in combating "the scheming peddlers of foreign 'isms' " and asks its members' aid in keeping the FBI informed of suspicious activities. He asserts that foreign powers have been sending agents to America to carry on a campaign to recruit as allies "the disloyal and malcontent."

Sept. 1940 FDR signs a conscription bill that contains a racial nondiscrimination clause. However, when a delegation of black leaders meets with him, the president refuses to make any major concessions to end discrimination in defense industries.

7 Oct. 1940 Germany intensifies its bombing of London.

7 Oct. 1940 The State of Illinois, believing that David D. Erwin has fled to St. Louis, Mo., requests that the State of Missouri arrest him and return him to Illinois.

9 Oct. 1940 The White House announces a policy of proportional representation in the army, with more black commissioned officers. However, the statement declares that, except for three regiments, all present and future black units will have white officers. The War Department also announces that "the policy of the War Department is not to intermingle colored and white enlisted personnel in the same regimental organization." This is regarded as a national insult by African Americans; the black press expresses the overwhelming indignation of the black community.

10 Oct. 1940 JEH forwards to the DOJ copies of two Sept. issues of the *Chicago Defender*, along with the complaint of a citizen in Savannah, Ga., who maintains that the papers contained propaganda that "might possibly hinder the Government in securing registrations from negroes who come within the draft age," and JEH asks for an assessment as to whether they violate any federal statute.

16 Oct. 1940 JEH notifies the special agent in charge of the FBI's Washington, D.C., field office of the report that the Bureau received regarding the activities of a Japanese agitator active in the black community in Washington, D.C. The special agent is instructed to "conduct the necessary investigation to determine the identity of this individual and see if he is violating the [Alien] Registration Act."

16 Oct. 1940 Congress passes the Selective Training and Service Act, providing for registration of all men between 21 and 36 years of age and for training of 1,200,000 troops and 800,000 reserves. After one month, 16,400,000 men are registered.

17 Oct. 1940 Speaking on the fifteenth anniversary of the Brotherhood of Sleeping Car Porters, APR declares his objection to communist ideology as a solution to the problems of the African American.

17 Oct. 1940 The Registration of Certain Organizations Act ("Voorhis Act") is passed by Congress. It requires that all foreign-controlled organizations and groups advocating the overthrow of government by force register with the DOJ.

25 Oct. 1940 Members of the Committee on Participation of Negroes in the National Defense Program meet with FDR.

25 Oct. 1940 One week before national elections, three African Americans are appointed to high posts by the military: Judge William H. Hastie is appointed a civilian aide to the secretary of war; Colonel Campbell Johnson is made a special aide to the director of the draft; and Benjamin O. Davis, Sr., the only black colonel in the regular army, is made the first black brigadier general in the U.S. Army.

27 Oct. 1940 FDR is presented with a seven-point program calling for equal treatment for African Americans in all branches of the armed forces by a delegation made up of Walter White (NAACP executive secretary), T. Arnold Hill, and APR.

5 Nov. 1940 FDR is reelected president for an unprecedented third term.

7 Nov. 1940 The DOJ informs JEH that the issues of the *Chicago Defender* previously submitted by him do not violate any federal statute.

16 Dec. 1940 JEH reports that the FBI is checking on 16,000 reports of "fifth column" activity. From the data collected, the FBI had assembled a custodial detention index of 6,000 names ("a list of persons whose activities were considered so dangerous as to justify consideration of their detention in the event of a national emergency"). Meanwhile, the furor generated by the FBI's arrest of recruiters for the loyalist cause in the Spanish Civil War leads to a demand for a congressional investigation of the FBI by the highly respected Senator George Norris of Nebraska.

29 Dec. 1940 FDR delivers his "Arsenal of Democracy" speech, pledging additional American aid to Great Britain.

1940 There is a run on the Post Office at Tampa, Fl., when African Americans withdraw their postal savings in response to a rumor that postal savings are no longer safe investments.

8 Jan. 1941 The Office of Production Management (OPM) is established to coordinate defense activities.

25 Jan. 1941 APR meets with former NNC members who sided with him and split from the organization in Apr. 1940. He also writes an article for the *Pittsburgh Courier* that points to the failure of various committees and groups to achieve any positive result against defense discrimination. He proposes that 10,000 Negroes march on Washington, D.C., with the slogan: "We loyal Negro-American citizens demand the right to work and fight for our country."

26 Jan. 1941 The NAACP sponsors mass meetings in 24 states to protest discrimination against blacks in the national defense program.

31 Jan. 1941 The Chicago office of the MID reports that the publisher of the *Chicago Defender*, John Sengstacke, was encouraging blacks to become conscientious objectors to protest against the Army's racial segregation policies.

8 Feb. 1941 The MID office in Rhode Island complains that the *Courier* and the *Providence Chronicle* are agitating the issue of racial discrimination.

8 Feb. 1941 In a speech before members of the EPM in New York, Joseph Hartrey, a white pro-Nazi sympathizer, attacks Jews as responsible for racial discrimination and economic privation suffered by blacks.

Feb. 1941 The Southern Electoral Reform League is formed in Richmond, Va.

1–3 Mar. 1941 JEH transmits to Assistant AG Wendell Berge copies of investigative reports regarding alleged subversive activities of Naka Nakane and PMEW to consider for possible prosecution.

3 Mar. 1941 The FBI Washington, D.C., field office opens a broadly based investigation of the NAACP, after receiving a request from the navy to investigate protests against racial discrimination by "fifteen colored mess attendants." Through the use of an informant, the FBI attempts to determine the NAACP's "connections with the communist party and other communist controlled organizations."

19 Mar. 1941 Assistant AG Berge informs JEH that the activities of Naka Nakane and the PMEW do not appear to constitute a violation of any federal criminal statutes and that the criminal division of the DOJ "does not desire any additional investigation of this matter at the present time."

Mar. 1941 Activities of the "Moslem Cult" come to the attention of the FBI's Washington, D.C., field office. It learns that the group advocates "absolute non-participation in armed conflicts in defense of the U.S."

Mar. 1941 Hans Habe, a German refugee, publishes an article, "The Nazi Plan for Negroes."

1 Apr. 1941 JEH declares that it is "highly important that the Federal Bureau of Investigation be unhampered in its authority to conduct investigations into situations involving potential danger to the Government of the U.S.," particularly as this pertains to "the obvious menace and danger to the internal security of this Nation presented by the present activities of foreign agents in labor union fields."

11 Apr. 1941 Sidney Hillman, co-director of the OPM, urges defense contractors to eliminate discriminatory hiring practices.

12 Apr. 1941 APR announces that "plans for an all-out march of ten thousand Negroes on Washington are in the making and a call will be issued in the next few weeks."

25 Apr. 1941 The OPM discloses that more than 3,000 telegrams and long-distance telephone calls protesting discrimination against African Americans in national defense activities were received during the first few weeks of a drive sponsored by the Alpha Kappa Alpha sorority. A spokesman of the OPM describes the sorority's campaign as "one of the most dramatic and forceful demonstrations of mass unity encountered in recent years."

Apr. 1941 The NNC, along with the Maryland Youth Congress, announces it is undertaking a drive to gain employment for 7,000 African Americans in the "Jim Crow" plants of the Glenn L. Martin Aircraft Co. and the Bethlehem Steel Co.

Apr. 1941 The NAACP issues a press release urging that the 17,000 black workers employed by the Ford Motor Co. in Detroit not permit themselves to be used as strikebreakers against the UAW strike to organize the company. Ford capitulates on 11 Apr., after only 11 days.

1 May 1941 The MOWM formally calls for blacks to prepare to march on Washington, D.C. Support for the movement spreads rapidly throughout the African-American community.

2 May 1941 The body of Private Felix Hall is found hanging from a tree at Fort Benning, Ga., arms and legs bound. The NAACP *Bulletin* charges that at Fort Benning "concentration camp tactics are allegedly being used against colored soldiers, and torture and killings take place at the pleasure of the military police."

2 May 1941 Secretary of the Navy Frank Knox declares that to introduce a change in the navy's policy by admitting African Americans, other than in the messmen's branch, would "provoke discord and demoralization" and would lower the efficiency of the navy.

15 May 1941 The FBI, MID, and ONI present a joint memorandum to the president, outlining their respective intelligence operations undertaken in conformity with the secret presidential directive of 26 June 1939.

16 May 1941 The army sends an MID officer to interview *Afro-American* publisher Carl Murphy regarding the newspaper's publication of the army's classification test. The officer takes the opportunity to question Murphy regarding his views on "certain political factions and alleged subversive organizations, which were reputed to have communistic leanings."

24 May 1941 Max Yergan, president of the NNC, issues a statement suggesting that campaigns to secure jobs for African Americans in the defense industries "would do serious harm to the Negro people."

31 May 1941 The FBI erroneously informs the White House that the NNC plans to lead a mass demonstration in Washington, D.C. against "alleged 'Jim Crow' practices" and that the demonstration is scheduled to take place on June 1.

5 June 1941 An MID officer at Camp Claiborne, La., complains that articles in the *Courier* by executive editor P. L. Prattis describing conditions for black soldiers at the camp are "radical" and inaccurate and likely to cause problems among black troops. He recommends that the FBI investigate Prattis.

10 June 1941 First Lady Eleanor Roosevelt writes to APR, chairman of the MOWM, telling him that he would be "making a very grave mistake at the present to allow this march [on Washington] to take place."

15 June 1941 The president orders the OPM to end the "nationwide discrimination against Negroes in defense industries, at a time when the nation is combating the increasing threat of totalitarianism."

18 June 1941 The president and cabinet officials meet at the White House with leaders of the MOWM. Mayor LaGuardia of New York is appointed by the president to head a committee charged with evolving an acceptable plan to facilitate the "full utilization of our productive manpower."

19 June 1941 The FBI furnishes the White House with a memorandum concerning APR, pointing out that "the Communist Party has expressed a very real interest in the proposed undertaking" of the MOWM and speculating that the Communist Party "will endeavor to convert the March into a Communist demonstration."

21–22 June 1941 Germany invades the Soviet Union across a broad, 2,000-mile frontier. The Communist Party immediately reverses its previous political direction, promulgating the "People's Program" that calls for full and unlimited collaboration of the Western Allies and the Soviet Union in a "people's war" against Germany. The party's reversal and embrace of a pro-war policy places it in direct conflict with the leaders of the MOWM.

24 June 1941 Mayor LaGuardia confers with members of the MOWM in New York regarding the text of a proposed presidential order.

25 June 1941 FDR issues executive order 8802 that states "there shall be no discrimination in the employment of workers in defense industries or government because of race, creed, color, or national origin" and orders employers and labor organizations to "provide for the full and equitable participation of all workers in defense industries." The order establishes the president's Committee on Fair Employment Practices (FEPC).

28 June 1941 APR announces that he is "postponing" the march on Washington, following the president's issuance of executive order 8802. The Youth Division of the MOWM protests APR's decision.

June 1941 Leonard Robert Jordan (LRJ) and Thomas F. Cathcart visit the Japan Institute in New York with a letter of introduction from Kyuya Abiko, executive secretary of the Japanese Association.

June 1941 The Japanese government reportedly considers propagandizing African Americans as a method of disrupting internal security in the U.S. It requests that its representatives in the U.S. report on the feasibility of employing black agents.

June 1941 John K. Larremore is arrested by the San Diego Police Department. He had in his possession a 144-page manuscript, "Ebony in Bronze," which advocated an alliance between the Japanese and African Americans. He claims that he wrote the manuscript in 1932. He would later be prosecuted in federal court as a result of an FBI investigation.

June 1941 The War Department requests that the FBI undertake an investigation of the *Courier*. Initially, the special agent in charge of the Bureau's Pittsburgh field office ignores the request from FBI headquarters dated 24 July. JEH again writes to the agent on 4 Oct. to remind him that MID is "particularly interested in this case." The agent finally replies on 21 Oct.

3 July 1941 At a meeting of the EPM in New York, LRJ argues that because Jews are the enemies of blacks, all blacks must side with Hitler.

4 July 1941 The NNC, following Germany's invasion of the USSR, issues a statement urging blacks to pledge strong support for the war effort.

9 July 1941 Carlos Cooks, William Taylor, and William Ferman, EPM speakers in New York, urge that for every African American lynched in the south, a white should be lynched in the north, that every white man romantically interested in a black woman should be beaten, that every African American should hate every white man for injustices perpetrated on black people, and that no black man should fight in a white man's war.

11 July 1941 The MID furnishes JEH with a copy of a black agent's report that contains the assertion that "Japanese and Communist press agents are releasing news in all available negro publications and in some cases, Communists or Communist sympathizers are employed on the editorial staffs of these papers." In addition, the agent claims that he had been asked by a Japanese newspaper editor to write news releases for the black press. The report also labels five African-American journalists as communists or communist sympathizers or radicals. The agent characterizes the series of articles on army camp conditions published in the *Courier* in June as "sensational." He states that the articles "caused a great deal of dissatisfaction among the colored soldiers and their families at home." The report concludes that "the source of this subversive activity [should] be investigated at the earliest possible moment."

11–13 July 1941 Ethelbert Anselm Broaster (EAB), the General Messenger of the New Orleans-based International Reassemble Church of the Freedom League (IRCFL), speaks before the PMEW in East St. Louis, Ill.

17 July 1941 FDR names two blacks as members of the FEPC, Alderman Earl B. Dickerson of Chicago and Milton P. Webster, vice president of the Brotherhood of Sleeping Car Porters.

2 Aug. 1941 MG is arrested on a complaint filed before the federal grand jury in Chicago, charging that she counseled black registrants to evade the Selective Training and Service Act.

6 Aug. 1941 Sergeant E. L. Hargraves, a white military policeman, and Private Ned Turman, an African-American soldier stationed at Fort Bragg, N.C., are shot to death in a gun battle between white and black soldiers on a crowded bus going from Fayetteville, N.C., to the camp. Several black soldiers are wounded in the altercation.

7–8 Aug. 1941 At a meeting in New York of the EPM, it is reported that Carlos Cooks expressed his hatred for Jews, whites, and light-skinned blacks. Randolph Wilson reportedly spoke about his hatred for Jews and expressed his support for Hitler.

14 Aug. 1941 The Atlantic Charter, consisting of a joint declaration of American and British peace aims, is signed by President FDR and British Prime Minister Winston S. Churchill. Among other things, it calls for fair labor standards and freedom from fear and want for the peoples of the world.

14 Aug. 1941 Sergeant Owen Russell, tried for the shooting of Private Ned Turman on Aug. 6, is acquitted by a general army court-martial.

17 Aug. 1941 43 black soldiers from the 97th Engineer Battalion go AWOL and return to their former station in Michigan, following weeks of violent attacks by local whites in Prescott, Ark.

21–27 Aug. 1941 The case against MG is presented to a federal grand jury in Chicago. A "no bill" is returned, whereupon the U.S. commissioner dismisses the case against her after she gives the court her assurance that she would no longer instruct members of the PME not to comply with the Selective Training and Service Act.

26 Aug. 1941 After serving for more than a year and a half as solicitor general, Francis E. Biddle is named attorney general. JEH wonders if his liberal reputation will make him "soft" on Communists. Meanwhile, Biddle is supported by a number of blacks as "a friend of the colored people of America." Biddle serves as AG throughout the remainder of World War II.

Aug. 1941 The FBI requests that its Oklahoma City field office investigate "Communist Party domination" of the NAACP. The investigation also forms part of the FBI's development of "Nationalistic Tendency Charts."

6 Sept. 1941 At a meeting in New York of the EPM, Carlos Cooks, William Taylor, William Ferman, and an individual by the name of Ford speak. Ford reportedly makes anti-Semitic remarks and urges blacks to kill their enemies.

6 Sept. 1941 Biddle is confirmed by the senate and officially sworn in as attorney general.

13 Sept. 1941 The FBI's Washington, D.C., field office calls the attention of JEH to a report on the subject of Nazi propaganda entitled "Pro-Axis Propaganda in Harlem," published in the *Hour* magazine of 23 Aug. 1941. Described as a "confidential bulletin," the *Hour* is edited by Albert E. Kahn.

18 Sept. 1941 JEH forwards a transcript of the *Hour* exposé to E. J. Connelley, assistant director of the FBI New York office, for his investigative attention. Connelley is instructed to open individual cases on the three subjects mentioned in the article, namely, Arthur Reid, Robert Jordan, and "Ras de Killer."

19 Sept. 1941 The FBI Oklahoma City field office reports that "there is a strong tendency of the NAACP to steer clear of Communistic activities. Nevertheless, there is a strong movement on the part of the Communists to attempt to dominate this group through an infiltration of Communistic doctrines. Consequently, the activities of the NAACP will be closely observed and scrutinized in the future."

20 Sept. 1941 In Los Angeles, the FEPC holds its first hearing into discrimination against African Americans in defense industries.

20 Sept. 1941 Articles begin appearing in the black press on the mistreatment of African Americans in the South and against blacks and Jews in the army and navy.

21 Sept. 1941 At a meeting of the Peoples' Defense League, the leader, Ernest J. Wright, states that the league's immediate task is to fight for the right to vote. He also speaks on the subject of cooperating with white workers and working to end discrimination in the armed forces.

24 Sept. 1941 Under Secretary of War Robert P. Patterson, after receiving complaints concerning publication of anti-discrimination articles in the *Courier*, *Afro-American*, and *Amsterdam News*, protests to the director of civilian defense that black newspapers are agitating for "social gains which have not been attained in the country as a whole and using the Army as a means of promoting such gains among the civilian population. . . . Such activities . . . materially impede the War Department in its present desire to build promptly and efficiently an Army capable of defending the nation in the existing crisis and organized so that it will fit into the accepted social order of this country."

9 Oct. 1941 AG Biddle, at his first press conference, announces that he backs wiretapping by the FBI.

11 Oct. 1941 Ralph Matthews, a columnist for the *Baltimore Afro-American*, criticizes the U.S. and England for enriching themselves by exploiting people, "especially the darker races." He contrasts this with Russia, which, he claims, has tried to "perfect a way of life for her own people which will spread out the good things of life to the greatest number instead of to a chosen few."

Oct.–Nov. 1941 Controversy erupts when the American Red Cross announces that it will refuse to accept the blood of African Americans in the collection and preservation of blood plasma that is to be used in transfusions for wounded soldiers.

6 Nov. 1941 U.S. extends lend-lease credit of one billion dollars to the Soviet Union.

19 Nov. 1941 Following the *Hour's* exposé of Nazi propaganda in Harlem, the FBI conducts a review of its internal security files on the subject of pro-Axis organizations and propagandists among blacks. It forwards a summary of the resulting information, which is negligible, to its New York field office, along with the request that the latter make contact with "sources" in Harlem in an effort to determine "whether in fact they [organizations cited in the published report] are being used for the distribution of pro-Axis propaganda." JEH directs that "This investigation should be in the nature of a preliminary inquiry for the initial purpose of determining whether these groups are in fact subversive in the sense that they are under foreign control."

29 Nov. 1941 After investigating the *Courier* at the request of the MID, JEH notifies the War Department that no evidence was found to indicate that the newspaper was engaged "in questionable activities with reference to the national defense program."

Nov. 1941 JEH meets with Walter White at the suggestion of the AG to discuss two civil rights cases in Texas as well as "Nazi, Communist, and Fascist agitators." The meeting opens a channel between the FBI and the NAACP. JEH tells White: "I feel it is important that reputable Negro organizations be diligently alert to keep Nazism, Communism, and Fascism from attaching themselves to Negro movements." He gives White the home telephone number of every FBI special agent in charge and asks him to have NAACP branches pass on any information about subversive activities to FBI field offices.

4 Dec. 1941 The ONI's Counter Subversion Section produces a 26-page report, "Japanese Intelligence and Propaganda in the United States during 1941"; it includes a section on coverage of "Relations with the Negroes."

7 Dec. 1941 Japan launches a devastating surprise sea and air attack on the U.S. naval base at Pearl Harbor in Hawaii. The surprise attack, which thrusts the U.S. into World War II, leaves 19 warships, including 6 battleships, sunk or disabled, and kills 2,403 soldiers, sailors, and civilians. The attack reflects a major intelligence failure on the part of the FBI, forcing JEH to take steps to deflect blame away from the Bureau and direct it toward other branches of the intelligence establishment. The Pearl Harbor disaster represents one of the most difficult moments in JEH's entire career, almost costing him his job.

8 Dec. 1941 Congress declares a state of war with Japan.

9 Dec. 1941 JEH writes to the FBI New York field office requesting to be advised as to the exact status of its investigation of pro-Axis propaganda among blacks, particularly as it relates to the activities of Arthur Reid, LRJ, and "Ras de Killer."

11 Dec. 1941 Germany and Italy declare war on the U.S.

12 Dec. 1941 JEH sends a memo to FDR that blames the lack of preparedness before the attack on Pearl Harbor on the failure of ONI officers as well as the military authorities in Hawaii. The joint congressional commission investigating the attack would refute the basis of JEH's charge as misleading and inaccurate, motivated as it was both by the need to deflect criticism away from the Bureau and by the desire to blame rivals within the intelligence establishment for the intelligence fiasco involved in the Pearl Habor catastrophe.

15 Dec. 1941 Congress appropriates 10 billion dollars for war mobilization and for lend-lease aid to Allies.

16–17 Dec. 1941 In a speech dedicating the Thomas Jefferson Room in the Library of Congress annex, AG Biddle cites the Bill of Rights as a war issue. The following day he rules that the consent of the DOJ is needed for prosecution of seditious speech.

18 Dec. 1941 The FBI's New York field office opens investigation of EPM.

21 Dec. 1941 AG Biddle warns against abridgement of free speech as a result of war hysteria.

24 Dec. 1941 Robert Washington, an organizer for the MSTA, speaking at Mound City, Ill., is reported to have stated that "when the Japanese take over this country those who are members of [his] organization will not be molested." He is also reported to be organizing blacks in and around Pulaski, Ill., to join the MSTA.

ca. 29 Dec. 1941 The *Washington Times-Herald* publishes a story by John O'Donnell placing the blame for Pearl Harbor "directly in Hoover's lap," since, according to the author, "Army and Navy intelligence are not primarily responsible for the detection of enemy civilians operating as Fifth Columnists." The report goes on to state that the official inquiry into the disaster will "provide the ammunition for an all-out drive to oust Hoover from his seat of tremendous power." JEH responds by immediately denouncing the story, claiming that "jurisdiction over Hawaiian matters was vested principally in the naval authorities and not in the FBI." Meanwhile, an anonymous memo begins circulating through the government, calling upon the presidential commission looking into responsibility for the disaster to assess "the adequacy of the FBI, the agency directed by the President and supposed by the public and Congress to deal with the fifth column in our territory."

29 Dec. 1941 FDR orders his press secretary Stephen Early to call and inform JEH that he still has the president's confidence. The call relieves JEH's anxiety regarding his job.

30 Dec. 1941 FBI Assistant Director P. E. Foxworth transmits to JEH a series of reports by the New York field office, dated 18, 23, 27, and 29 Dec. 1941, providing the results of investigations into the pro-Axis propaganda activities of LRJ and his "Ethiopian Pacifist League, Inc." Among its findings, Foxworth reports that LRJ is sometimes referred to as the "Black Hitler" of Harlem.

Dec. 1941 The Fellowship of Reconciliation (FR) refuses to participate in the American war effort and supports those who have suffered from U.S. participation in the war.

Dec. 1941 Herbert S. Boulin, a black FBI agent and former member of the DOJ's "radical squad" in the twenties, befriends LRJ and testifies subsequently at the latter's sedition trial.

6 Jan. 1942 In his annual State of the Union message, the president describes America's gigantic war mobilization. He calls for Americans to guard against "divisions among ourselves," and to be vigilant against "racial discrimination in any of its ugly forms."

10 Jan. 1942 At a conference of black leaders called by Judge William Hastie, civilian aide to the secretary of war, to consider the problems that face "Negro citizens in a world at war" as well as the wartime role of blacks, a poll is taken on whether African Americans fully support the war effort. The black leaders present agree 36–5, with 15 abstentions, that the black community is not "whole-heartedly, unselfishly, all-out in support of the present war effort." The vote produces a nationwide controversy.

11 Jan. 1942 A major riot occurs in Alexandria, La., between black soldiers and military and civilian policemen. It began when two white military policemen (MPs), responding to the request of the owner of a theater, attempted to arrest two black men outside the theater for using an obscene word. Two black military police arrive on the scene and argue that the arrest is their responsibility. The two groups of military policemen begin fighting and are joined by additional white military police, city and state police, and black residents. 28 African-American soldiers are shot, 3 of them seriously. 3,000 black soldiers are placed under arrest by white MPs as well as city and state policemen.

13 Jan. 1942 JEH informs the New York field division that "it appears that a successful prosecution under the Sedition Act might be had against subject [Robert] Jordan and possibly others," in accordance with new guidelines contained in Bureau Bulletin No. 72,

Second Series, 1941, dated 31 Dec. 1941. JEH declares: "It is the Bureau's desire that this case receive immediate and vigorous attention. . . . Particular attention should be given to any connection between Japanese and negroes and what influence, if any, the Japanese Institute of New York City has over the Ethiopian Pacifist League [*sic*], Inc."

13 Jan. 1942 Yasuichi Hikida, employed by the Japanese consulate in New York City as a translator during the period Apr. through Nov. 1941 is apprehended as a Japanese alien. He is subsequently removed to Hot Springs, Virginia, where Japanese diplomats are interned. Prior to employment by the Japanese consulate, Hikida bought a life membership in the NAACP and translated into Japanese an article, "Fire in the Flint," by Walter White, NAACP secretary. At the time of his apprehension, a large quantity of literature concerning blacks is found in his possession, leading officials to believe that Hikida was the person placed in charge of Japanese propaganda among blacks. Hikida is also suspected to have been the author of a document entitled "Interracial Understanding Between the Japanese and American Negroes" found among the records seized from the Japanese Association in New York.

15 Jan. 1942 JEH authorizes the New York FBI office to institute microphone surveillance of the EPM. It was discontinued on 17 Feb. 1942, however, after being considered unproductive.

17 Jan. 1942 The *Pittsburgh Courier* moves to counter charges of disloyalty: "The Japanese, Germans, Italians and their Axis stooges know that it is futile to seek spies, saboteurs or Fifth Columnists among American Negroes. . . . Every attempt in that direction has been a miserable failure."

20–21 Jan. 1942 JEH instructs the FBI's New York field office that Bureau authority is granted to present the EPM case to the U.S. attorney for prosecution for sedition. A memorandum is prepared for AG Biddle setting forth the information collected by the FBI on the EPM, on the basis of which the Bureau's authorization for presentation of the case was granted.

21 Jan. 1942 Under heavy pressure from the black community, the American Red Cross changes its policy of refusing blood from blacks. It now welcomes black donors, but it maintains that their blood must be segregated "so that those receiving transfusions may be given plasma from blood of their own race."

21 Jan. 1942 Arresa Rukabun, *aka* Troy Vaughn, a member of the Addeynue Allahe Universal Arabic Association, Inc., writes a letter to his draft board stating that he cannot serve in the armed forces because of his Muslim faith and his identification with the Japanese as a "Dark race."

25 Jan. 1942 The first lynching of an African American after America enters World War II occurs at Sikeston, Mo., when Cleo Wright, suspected of assaulting a white woman, is removed by a white mob from jail and dragged through the streets behind an automobile before he is set on fire and burned to death. Wright had been wounded by policemen while allegedly resisting arrest. A large number of African Americans leave Sikeston for fear of physical harm. The murder of Wright, for which no indictment was returned, incenses blacks nationwide, resulting in adoption by the NAACP of the slogan "Remember Pearl Harbor . . . and Sikeston, Mo."

27 Jan. 1942 An FBI agent visits *Atlanta Daily World* columnist Cliff MacKay ("The Globe Trotter") and inquires whether the newspaper has received any Japanese news releases or if the Communist Party has tried to influence the newspaper editorially. MacKay denies that either has occurred. The visit is the first recorded instance of the FBI visiting a black newspaper during World War II.

27 Jan. 1942 Eight African American members of the Peoples Defense League submit a complaint to the FBI's New Orleans office alleging racial discrimination against black voters who attempted to vote in the Democratic primary. The FBI presents the case to the Criminal Division of the DOJ, which finds the matter to be of only "local concern" because the complaint did not involve a federal election ballot.

29 Jan. 1942 In a confidential memorandum to the president following a series of meetings with blacks and whites concerning the country's racial situation, AG Biddle concludes: "There is widespread discontent among Negroes, . . . Politically, I think the administration is losing the support of the Negro population."

30 Jan. 1942 JEH asks Assistant AG Berge to make a determination as to whether the *Baltimore Afro-American* violated any federal statutes in publishing in its issue of 20 Dec. 1941 an article containing the responses of blacks in Richmond, Va., to the question as to what Japan's attitude toward blacks would be if Japan won the war. One of the interviewees (a printer) asserted, "The colored races as a whole would benefit, . . . This would be the first step in the darker races' coming back into their own."

31 Jan. 1942 JEH is notified that the U.S. district attorney in New York has conferred with AG Biddle with regard to prosecution of the EPM but that he was informed by the AG that no prosecution should be instituted at this time. The U.S. district attorney nonetheless remains interested in arranging for a grand jury hearing of the facts in the case.

Jan. 1942 The *Crisis*, official organ of the NAACP, in an editorial entitled "Now Is the Time Not to be Silent," declares that it would neither endorse nor return to the "Close Ranks" policy it had adopted during World War I under pressure by the U.S. government. The editorial concludes, "If all the people are called to gird and sacrifice for freedom, and the armies to march for freedom, then it must be for freedom for everyone, everywhere, not merely for those under the Hitler heel."

Jan. 1942 The Office of Facts and Figures (OFF), created in July 1941 as part of the Office of Civilian Defense, issues the first in a series of reports entitled "Negro Attitudes Toward the War."

3 Feb. 1942 Edwin R. Embree of the Rosenwald Fund urges the president to create a commission of experts on race relations to advise him on steps that the government ought to take to improve conditions for blacks. FDR will answer on 16 Mar. that "we must start winning the war . . . before we do much general planning for the future."

5 Feb. 1942 Assistant AG Berge informs JEH that the article complained about in the *Baltimore Afro-American* was within the law, since the answers of the three black interviewees were "mere expressions of individual opinion as to the possible course of future events" and did not constitute "false statements," which would have made them subject to federal statutes. However, Berge urges JEH to investigate the "character and pertinent activities" of the *Afro-American's* editors to ascertain whether a link exists between them and "hostile or subversive sources." The request sets in motion an extensive FBI investigation of the *Afro-American* that lasts for the duration of World War II.

7 Feb. 1942 The "Double V" slogan, signifying "Victory at home; victory abroad," makes its first appearance in the *Pittsburgh Courier*. The idea for the campaign was suggested by

James G. Thompson, a 26-year-old cafeteria worker at the Cessna Aircraft Corp., in Wichita, Kan., in a letter to the *Courier* in Jan. ("Should I Sacrifice to Live 'Half American'?"), in which he argued that "if this V sign means [victory] to those now engaged in this great conflict, then let we colored Americans adopt the double V for a double victory. The first V for victory over our enemies from without, the second V for victory over our enemies from within." The appeal of the Double V campaign spreads rapidly, capturing imaginations and leading to the development of an extraordinary ideological cohesiveness within the black community.

9 Feb. 1942 JEH and the directors of MID and ONI sign a revised delimitation agreement covering "respective responsibilities of Military and Naval Intelligence and the Federal Bureau of Investigation under various conditions." The revised agreement is approved by the president. It gives to the FBI a monopoly in domestic intelligence by limiting the domestic surveillance interest of MID and allowing the FBI to conduct all investigations "involving civilians in the U.S.," while at the same time keeping MID and ONI informed of "important developments . . . including the names of individuals definitely known to be connected with subversive activities."

10 Feb. 1942 AG Biddle orders the DOJ's Criminal Division to investigate the lynching of Cleo Wright in Sikeston, Mo.

14 Feb. 1942 The *Baltimore Afro-American* publishes a report that is critical of the FBI beneath the headline "FBI Budget $29,000,000 but Won't Employ You." Readers are informed that "J. Edgar Hoover's organization excludes colored clerks and agents as vigorously as the lily-white Navy."

14 Feb. 1942 An ultimatum made jointly by the management, the union, and war production officials ends a sit-down strike by white workers in the Chrysler Highland Park plant in Chicago that was called after blacks were placed in skilled jobs in the plant.

16 Feb. 1942 The FBI informs the White House that detained German nationals have reportedly expressed the view that "the only way to defeat America is through internal disruption," with the "Negro situation" providing "a likely menace to the U.S."

16 Feb. 1942 FBI Assistant Director Foxworth York notifies JEH that the U.S. district attorney in New York has advised him, in connection with the EPM case, that his office is "definitely interested in this case and believes elements of sedition violation exist but no arrest or indictments will be authorized in absence of departmental authorization for reason of policy on racial angles." Foxworth reports that "it is apparently the desire of the U.S. attorney to preclude any possibility of criticism of the DOJ on [the ground of] racial discrimination which has been played up considerably by colored element in this area."

17 Feb. 1942 The Fraternal Council of Negro Churches calls upon the president to end discrimination in defense industries and the armed forces. It is decided by one of the president's advisers that "it would be very bad to give encouragement beyond the point where actual results can be accomplished."

18 Feb. 1942 LRJ and Lester Holness, leaders of the EPM, are apprehended by FBI agents and New York city police and charged with conspiracy to violate the Alien Registration Act. The two men are released but are immediately re-arrested by INS authorities on charges of not possessing valid immigrant visas.

18 Feb. 1942 The U.S. House of Representatives passes an appropriation bill that includes an amendment earmarking $300,000 of the FBI's funds for an investigation of Japanese activities on the West Coast. Several representatives declare that AG Biddle has failed to stop "the potential alien threat" and that the DOJ was derelict in its duty of "wiping out the alien menace."

18 Feb. 1942 AG Biddle, in testimony before a subcommittee of the House Judiciary Committee, urges passage of legislation to permit the army, navy, and FBI to tap telephone lines in order to combat sabotage and espionage. The pending bill would permit army and navy intelligence and the FBI to tap telephones with the permission of the AG.

19 Feb. 1942 The president signs executive order 9066, authorizing the War Department to exclude anyone from anywhere in the U.S. without trial or hearing. The order sets the stage for the mass roundup, removal, and detention of some 120,000 Japanese-American citizens.

19 Feb. 1942 JEH formally requests AG Biddle to advise him "whether you desire to authorize prosecution of Jordan at this time for violation of the Sedition Acts." He also writes to inform the DOJ's Criminal Division that he has made available to the AG "information as to some of the statements made by Jordan, together with facts pertaining to the arrest of Holness and Jordan and the admissions made by them, with a request to be advised whether he will authorize prosecution of Jordan for violation of the Sedition Acts."

22 Feb. 1942 James Stewart, president of the UNIA, speaks in Cincinnati, Ohio, where he, *inter alia*, declares "We will remember Missouri and then Pearl Harbor," and "To hell with Pearl Harbor."

23 Feb. 1942 A lone Japanese submarine surfaces off the California coast near Santa Barbara and launches a 15-minute attack on an oil refinery; no injuries and little damage results, but the incident creates a national sensation in the press.

27 Feb. 1942 Naka Nakane is released from the medical center for federal prisoners at Springfield, Mo., where he had been transferred as a mental case from the federal penitentiary at Leavenworth, Kan. Prior to his release, a presidential warrant was issued for his arrest. He is immediately apprehended and detained in the custody of the INS until 2 Apr., following which he is interned as a dangerous alien enemy, as recommended by the Enemy Alien Hearing Board.

28 Feb. 1942 A riot occurs when 65 black families attempt to move into the Sojourner Truth Housing Project in Detroit and are resisted by white residents and "anti-Negro agitators" who stone the first two families arriving with truckloads of their furnishings. Nearly 100 people are arrested. The project was designated exclusively for blacks after political pressure was exerted by the Michigan Communist Party and the Civil Rights Federation, but the Federal Housing Administration responded to the protest from the white community surrounding the project by changing regulations to make the housing exclusively white.

Feb. 1942 Harry Carpenter, a black truck driver, is arrested in Philadelphia on a charge of treason, for allegedly saying to a black soldier: "You are crazy, wearing that uniform! This is a white man's war." At his trial in March, Assistant U.S. Attorney Walter A. Gay, Jr., tells the court that AG Biddle, after a thorough investigation of the case, did not believe that the prosecution was justified. Carpenter is exonerated.

Feb. 1942 The FBI's first monthly "General Intelligence Survey in the United States" asserts that "it has been ascertained that the [Communist] Party is definitely intensifying its original drive to recruit new members from among the negro race."

Feb. 1942 The federal government begins extensive investigations of African-American morale in order to find out how to improve it. The project is undertaken by the OFF and its successor, the Office of War Information.

1 Mar. 1942 Dr. Channing Tobias, the sole black member of the National Committee on Selective Service, speaking at a conference sponsored by the National Urban League, denounces racial discrimination in the army and navy and in industry. The conference adopts resolutions pledging full support to the war and against "the equally dangerous enemy within—racial and class bigotry, prejudice, discrimination and segregation."

2 Mar. 1942 AG Biddle declares that the FBI has "run down an abortive 'fifth column' in America" without resorting to the "Gestapo's persecution and official brutality." He asserts that all enemy aliens whose records indicated disloyalty had been swiftly interned, while others remain under surveillance.

4 Mar. 1942 LRJ is found guilty in U.S. District Court of the Southern District of New York on three counts charging him with violating the Alien Registration Act by failing to file a change of address with the proper government authority. He is sentenced on 11 Mar. 1942 to ten days on each count, to be served consecutively.

5 Mar. 1942 PME Secretary General Edmund Holiday is sentenced to a term of three years for violating the Selective Training and Service Act.

5 Mar. 1942 The Bureau of Employment Security publishes a report that reveals that, in the period from Sept. 1941–Feb. 1942, more than half of the available employment opportunities in all categories nationwide were closed to African Americans.

6 Mar. 1942 JEH teletypes request to New York field office requesting to be advised immediately as to the "exact statements upon which prosecutive action might be based" against LRJ and other leaders of the EPM.

9–11 Mar. 1942 The AG presses the DOJ to undertake a grand jury investigation to determine whether the civil rights of blacks in Detroit were violated when black families were prevented from moving into the Sojourner Truth Housing Project, a federal government–supported project of the Detroit Housing Commission.

11 Mar. 1942 The FBI informs its Chicago field office that AG Biddle has approved implementation of "technical surveillance" of the NNC.

11 Mar. 1942 Immigrant inspector in charge of temporary detention quarters in Kansas City, Mo., writes to Kansas City INS director, informing him that George L. Mansfield, janitor at the detention quarters, had reported on this date that "he (Mansfield) and his wife had been advised that four Japanese persons were going to various homes in the vicinity of 8th and Oakland, Kansas City, Kan., talking to the colored people about the war and wanting them to become active in trying to overthrow the government of the U.S., saying that all colored people should stick together in the matter."

12 Mar. 1942 Kansas City, Mo., INS office informs the local FBI field office regarding "certain alleged subversive activities among the colored people of this city."

14 Mar. 1942 The *Pittsburgh Courier* reacts editorially to a visit from FBI agents, declaring: "This sort of thing is an obvious effort to cow the Negro press into soft-peddling its criticism and ending its forthright exposure of the outrageous discrimination to which Negroes have been subjected."

17 Mar. 1942 Rep. Hale Boggs of Louisiana blasts the AG's "benign policy . . . toward treasonable publications" and states that such "filth" should be suppressed.

19 Mar. 1942 The president signs executive order 9102, establishing the War Relocation Authority, with Milton Eisenhower as its first director.

20 Mar. 1942 OFF Assistant Director Archibald MacLeish meets in Washington, D.C., with 50 black leaders to discuss ways of improving black morale. He is informed by the delegates, who are ministers, businessmen, educators, and labor leaders, that African Americans are cool to the war effort because of continued segregation. He is also told that there could be no "national unity" and "high morale" among blacks unless they were granted their rights.

20 Mar. 1942 FDR receives a confidential memorandum from his secretary, Stephen Early, reporting on a conversation with JEH regarding the president's request for the DOJ to vigorously pursue indictments against seditionists. According to Early, JEH claims that both he and his agents have been "blocked by the AG time and time again in case after case." JEH suggests that before the FBI "would be permitted to act in these cases" it will be necessary for the president to talk with AG Biddle.

20 Mar. 1942 During a cabinet meeting FDR strongly presses AG Biddle for prompt action to bring an end to seditious utterances and publications. As a result, Biddle relents in his outspoken advocacy of civil liberties, abandoning his refusal to move against seditionists.

23 Mar. 1942 Assistant AG James H. Rowe, Jr., writes a three-page memorandum to AG Biddle recommending that the DOJ could improve its image immediately by moving quickly and publicly against radical seditionists. "The hard, down to rock, fact is that we are at war and the entire Department of Justice is not equipped to fight a war. . . . We had better get moving fast and set up some machinery that can *move fast*," Rowe writes.

24 Mar. 1942 The first civilian exclusion order against Japanese Americans is issued by the army. By the end of Oct. 1942, 108 exclusion orders are issued. All Japanese Americans living in Military Area No. 1, comprising the western portion of California, Oregon, Washington, and part of Arizona; and the California portion of Military Area No. 2, consisting of the rest of the four states, are rounded up and incarcerated in concentration camps spread throughout California, Arizona, Idaho, Utah, Wyoming, Colorado, and Arkansas.

25 Mar. 1942 Bureau Bulletin No. 24 instructs FBI field offices to hold in abeyance all prosecutions charging subjects with sedition. FBI field offices are advised that they would have to have the prior authority of the Bureau, which, in turn, would need to have the authority of the AG and the DOJ before proceeding.

25 Mar. 1942 AG Biddle holds a press conference to announce that sedition charges would soon be filed. He explains that the DOJ has moved slowly because he believed that "we would get stronger cases—and we have." He states that in the future, seditious utterances will be considered the equivalent of seditious acts. He is also forced to give up his opposition to the forced removal of Japanese Americans.

27 Mar. 1942 *Atlanta Daily World* columnist Cliff MacKay publishes a column in the *Birmingham World* accusing JEH of having no black FBI agents and refusing to appoint blacks.

27 Mar.–4 Apr. 1942 The DOJ launches a crackdown against leading Nazi sympathizers, arresting the organizers of the Fascist Crusader White Shirts, the Friends of Progress Movement for National Socialism, and the leaders of the pro-German Silver Shirts of America.

Mar. 1942 A near race riot takes place at the Tampa shipbuilding yards when a fight breaks out between white and black workers. It is eventually broken up by security guards.

3 Apr. 1942 The FBI's St. Louis, Mo., field office produces a report on the activities of the PMEW, a copy of which is provided to the DOJ's Criminal Division.

3 Apr. 1942 Two black soldiers and a white military policeman are killed in a 15 minute riot at Fort Dix, N.J. Five other soldiers are wounded. Racial friction was reported to have been smoldering for several months between black soldiers and white military policemen from the South.

4 Apr. 1942 The FBI's Birmingham, Ala., field office transmits to JEH a copy of Cliff MacKay's column that appeared in the *Birmingham World* issue of 27 Mar. 1942.

4 Apr. 1942 JEH submits a further memorandum to AG Biddle regarding prosecution of the EPM, advising him that "the activities of this movement relative to the inciting of the negroes against the U.S. has [*sic*] not waned." The memorandum ends: "Will you please advise me relative to your desire for further investigation concerning the activities of this movement."

4 Apr. 1942 Packard Motor Car Co. in Detroit warns white workers objecting to the hiring of two African-American skilled workers that they would be dismissed if they refuse to work with them.

7 Apr. 1942 The navy announces that it has relaxed its previous policy of recruiting Negroes as messmen only and would now enlist black volunteers in the Navy Reserves, Coast Guard, and Marines, for "general service."

10 Apr. 1942 JEH writes to the editor of the *Birmingham World*, Emory O. Jackson, complaining that publication of Cliff MacKay's column criticizing the FBI was "grossly" inaccurate and "a slander in my opinion upon the many loyal, patriotic Negro members of this Bureau." Jackson publishes JEH's letter in the *World*; he also asks for an opportunity to meet JEH in Washington, D.C.

12 Apr. 1942 LRJ is released from jail in New York, after which he resumes speaking publicly.

13 Apr. 1942 The FBI informs the White House that the Communist Party has instructed all its sections to reprint a *Daily Worker* editorial reporting the shooting incident at Fort Dix that resulted in the killing of one white and two black soldiers and that they are to stress the "Jim Crow angle."

15 Apr. 1942 The MID's Evaluation Section produces a 23-page report, "Japanese Racial Agitation Among American Negroes." The report also includes a "Japanese-Negro Organization Contact Chart" and a "Japanese-Negro Leadership Contact Chart."

17 Apr. 1942 The FBI informs the White House that the Communist Party is planning to intensify its organizational drive among African Americans, by telling them that the party is their only hope of equality, and claiming credit for eliminating racial discrimination in defense plants and in the navy.

22 Apr. 1942 The MID provides the FBI with a copy of its report, "Japanese Racial Agitation Among American Negroes."

23 Apr. 1942 *Birmingham World* editor Emory O. Jackson visits the FBI in Washington, D.C. He meets with Louis B. Nichols, the FBI official in charge of public relations, who advises him that "certain subversive forces were seeking to use the Negro press to stir up disunity." Nichols explains to Jackson that "one of their principal lines of attack was to the effect that the FBI and Mr. Hoover particularly had racial prejudices; that unfortunately a lot of reputable and outstanding Negro editors had fallen for this line; that obviously this was what happened to Mr. Cliff MacKay. . . ." Jackson responds by admitting that the MacKay column ought not have been published. He states also that "he feels now as at no other time we must all stick together." Jackson goes on to report that two nights previously he had attended "a meeting of the 'Islams'" in Washington, D.C., at which "they said that God is dead, that the white men ought to be dead, that only Allah would give the colored people a place in the world."

28 Apr. 1942 JEH informs the director of the ONI that the activities of the EPM in New York are presently being investigated by the FBI.

28 Apr. 1942 Westbrook Pegler, a white syndicated columnist, severely criticizes the black press, calling it sensational and inflammatory. The attack generates a storm of protest from the black press.

29 Apr. 1942 The FBI's Little Rock, Ark., field office produces a report on the PMEW, a copy of which is provided to the DOJ's Criminal Division.

Apr. 1942 Black families are finally able to move into the Sojourner Truth Housing Project in Detroit.

Apr. 1942 The MOWM formulates plans for a series of mass rallies to demonstrate the movement's strength and continuing dissatisfaction with discrimination in America.

Apr. 1942 Jonathan Daniels, assistant director in charge of civilian mobilization at the Office of Civilian Defense, proposes to his superiors the creation of a "Division of American Unity," but the idea is turned down because the question of black morale is regarded as "too hot a potato."

Apr. 1942 First Lady Eleanor Roosevelt attends the Southern Negro Youth Congress conference at Tuskegee, Ala. Her attendance fans rumors throughout the South regarding the organization of "Eleanor Clubs" among black domestics.

6 May 1942 JEH transmits to the DOJ copies of additional FBI reports regarding the PMEW and its leaders. He inquires once again about possible prosecution for sedition.

8 May 1942 A DOJ examination of the black press concludes that "the Negro press is not disloyal or subversive." It also takes the view that "there is no problem with the Negro press such as we [have] had with other newspapers and mediums."

14 May 1942 Assistant AG Berge informs JEH that FBI reports concerning activities of the PMEW have been reviewed but that "the conclusion reached [is] that the facts do not as yet warrant prosecution of the group and its members for violation of any Federal statute." Berge recommends that the FBI get evidence that would warrant prosecution of General Lee Butler for violating the Selective Training and Service Act, and gain evidence that will indicate violations of the sedition statutes.

14 May 1942 A DOJ memorandum discloses that thirty or forty different departments or agencies are presently investigating the problem of discrimination against blacks nationwide.

15 May 1942 In one of its broadcasts, the Manchuko foreign radio declares that the "so-called Democracy of Anglo-America is a history of racial prosecution and exploitation."

18–20 May 1942 A federal grand jury called at the request of AG Biddle begins hearing testimony on the lynching of Cleo Wright at Sikeston, Mo. It is the first federal grand jury ever called to investigate a lynching.

19 May 1942 The OFF's Extensive Survey Division releases a study of black attitudes toward the war.

22 May 1942 Stokely Delmar Hart, addressing a meeting of the CANO in Washington Park in Chicago, discusses the relationship between African Americans and Japan and dismisses the idea of loyalty to the U.S. war effort.

22 May 1942 The OFF's Bureau of Intelligence produces a report on the black press based on an examination of the five largest black newspapers for the period 18 Apr.–16 May. It concludes that the "basic concern" expressed in the articles and editorials published was discrimination against blacks and that this was hurting black morale.

22 May 1942 The question of black morale is discussed at a cabinet meeting as part of a general discussion of the racial situation which, according to AG Biddle, "everybody seemed to think was rather acute." The president recommends that Biddle and Postmaster General Frank Walker meet and talk with some black editors "to see what could be done about preventing their subversive language."

26 May 1942 The Sun Shipbuilding and Dry Dock Co., Chester, Pa., announces that it will employ 9,000 black workers for its new north yard and that black supervisors will take over the positions of white supervisors as they are trained. Various radical organizations, including the Communist Party, complain that this arrangement constitutes segregation.

27 May 1942 In a speech before a Communist Party meeting in Houston, Tex., Abner W. Berry, a Communist Party functionary, argues that blacks should abandon any feelings of sympathy for the Japanese.

27 May 1942 In a speech at La Salle College in Philadelphia, AG Biddle declares that the U.S. must grant African Americans equality of opportunity, if it is to keep faith with democratic ideals. He asserts that there is a point beyond which "compromise becomes intolerable."

27 May 1942 The OFF's Bureau of Intelligence produces a report, "Negroes in a Democracy at War," which concludes that "Negroes in the United States have only partially identified their own interests with those of the nation."

29 May 1942 FDR issues executive order 9176, transferring registration of "foreign propagandists" from the secretary of state to the AG.

30 May 1942 Under Secretary of State Sumner Wells tells a Decoration Day audience at Arlington National Cemetery that discrimination based on race, color, or creed "must be abolished." He declares that the age of imperialism has ended and that the "principle of the Atlantic Charter must be guaranteed to the world as whole—on all oceans and in all continents."

30 May 1942 JEH submits to Assistant AG Berge ten issues of the *Baltimore Afro-American* deemed by him to be potentially seditious.

30 May 1942 Cleveland *Call and Post* publisher William O. Walker reveals that a Texan black newspaper publisher had written to him that "the FBI has frightened all of the Negro editors in the southland." Walker suggests that "the papers in the northern and more liberal states are going to have to assist those in the South to resist intimidation."

30 May 1942 The NAACP's Walter White summons black newspaper editors to an emergency conference in Washington, D.C., to present his concern of a government crackdown. "It is my conviction," White informs the editors in his letter of invitation, "that the possibility of some sort of pressure on Negro papers within the near future is far from beyond the range of possibility."

31 May 1942 MG speaks before a meeting of the PME at Boulevard Hall in Chicago, attended by approximately 400 members. She praises the Japanese for their role in the war.

May 1942 An "uprising" by black workers reportedly takes place in the vicinity of Wyatt, Mo., in a dispute over labor conditions.

May 1942 Gulan Bogans, *aka* Elijah Mohammed, and other leaders of the Allah Temple of Islam (ATI) in Washington, D.C., are apprehended and charged with violating the Selective Training and Service Act by informing their members that, as Muslims, they are not required to register or fight in the armed forces.

May 1942 The black commission of the national committee of the Communist Party decides to form an organization in order to counter the influence of the MOWM.

1 June 1942 The navy yields to pressure and announces that African Americans will again be accepted for regular combat service, with the provision that all black enlistments are to terminate six months after the war is over.

3–6 June 1942 At the Battle of Midway, the U.S. navy scores a tremendous victory against the Japanese navy, turning the tide of the Pacific War.

10 June 1942 Lawrence W. C. Smith, chief of the Special War Policies Unit, War Division, DOJ, sends a memorandum to the FBI that provides information relative to pro-Japanese propaganda being disseminated among African Americans.

10 June 1942 Black troops in the Army Day parade in Savannah, Ga., are forced to march at the end of the parade behind garbage trucks.

12 June 1942 JEH reports to the White House on the growth of the MOWM, noting that the Communist Party in Washington, D.C., was giving the movement "their full and complete cooperation."

12 June 1942 J. K. Mumford, a section chief of the FBI's Intelligence Division, submits a draft of the letter to be sent to all special agents in charge of FBI field divisions, requesting that "a survey be made to ascertain the extent of agitation among the American negroes in the U.S."

12 June 1942 The Office of Strategic Services (forerunner of the Central Intelligence Agency set up in 1947) is established by military order.

13 June 1942 A federal grand jury at Little Rock, Ark., exonerates white policeman A. C. J. Hay in the killing of Sergeant Thomas B. Foster, stationed at Camp Robinson. The shooting was reported to have occurred during a fight that ensued when Private Foster protested against the whipping of another black soldier by a white civilian policeman while a military policeman looked on.

15 June 1942 JEH urges Assistant AG Berge to approve the prosecution of individuals connected with the EPM in New York. The memorandum also seeks Berge's advice "for the purpose of deciding whether or not the aliens connected [with the EPM] may be apprehended for custodial detention for creating unrest among the negro element in New York City."

16 June 1942 The MOWM holds the first in a series of mass meetings. An estimated 18,000–19,000 people pack the rally at Madison Square Garden in New York. The speakers pledge black support for the war effort and describe plans to try to meet with the president to press for equality. Adam Clayton Powell, Jr., announces at the rally that he will run for Congress.

18–20 June 1942 The FEPC holds hearings in Birmingham, Ala. It finds evidence of discrimination in employment practices at several companies producing war materials.

19 June 1942 The NAACP holds a meeting near Cape Girardeau, Mo. FBI agents monitor the meeting but report that no "subversive activities" took place.

20 June 1942 The MOWM pickets the U.S. Cartridge Co. in St. Louis, Mo. The protest succeeds in settling demands for the retention of black employees and an increase in the percentage of blacks employed at the plant.

20 June 1942 Mimo De Guzman is indicted in St. Louis, Mo., for violating postal laws by forging a money order. De Guzman pleads *nolo contendere* to the charges.

20 June 1942 The navy discharges four white employees charged with responsibility for staging a wildcat strike at the Hudson Naval Ordinance Arsenal following the hiring of 11 African Americans. Officers of the UAW support the navy's decision and settle the strike without the dismissal of any of the black workers.

22 June 1942 JEH instructs special agents in charge of the FBI's 56 field divisions to conduct a survey "immediately in your territory as well as review of your files to ascertain the extent of agitation among the negroes which may be the outgrowth of any effort on the part of the Axis powers or the Communist Party."

22 June 1942 The Special Services Division of the Office of War Information (OWI) produces a memorandum entitled "Is the Negro Press Pro-Axis?"

24 June 1942 Sylvester R. Meyers of the Civil Rights Section of the DOJ submits a memorandum in which he sets forth the view that "Japanese elements are attempting to incite riots" in St. Louis, Mo.; he observes that the PMEW is using the Sikeston lynching as one of its main talking points.

24 June 1942 Assistant AG Berge declines JEH's request to indict the *Baltimore Afro-American* for sedition.

26 June 1942 JEH provides the White House with a supplemental memorandum regarding the MOWM. He reports that he has been "closely following the activities of the MOWM as well as other groups for indications of possible race riots or demonstrations."

26 June 1942 The MOWM holds a rally at the Coliseum in Chicago. In his address, Charles Wesley Burton, chairman of the Chicago division of the MOWM, states that he is aware that FBI agents are present.

ca. 26 June 1942 *Chicago Defender* publisher John Sengstacke meets with AG Biddle in Washington, D.C. At the outset of the meeting, Biddle informs Sengstacke that black newspapers are doing a disservice to the war effort and warns that if they do not change their tone he is "going to shut them all up" for being seditious. Sengstacke responds, "You have the power to close us down, so if you want to close us, go ahead and attempt it!" A compromise is eventually reached between the two men, with Biddle announcing that the DOJ will not indict any black publisher for sedition, while Sengstacke promises to cooperate with the war effort in exchange for being granted more access to high government officials, many of whom had refused interviews with black reporters and not allowed them into press conferences.

27 June 1942 The Trade Union and Negro People's Victory Conference, the Communist Party's rival organization to the MOWM, holds a meeting at the Fraternal Club House in New York City attended by 350 delegates and 75 observers representing unions and political and civic groups. 14 resolutions are adopted at the conference, several of which demand an end to discrimination in defense industries and the armed forces. One measure adopted at the conference calls for the training of 100,000 African Americans for the defense industries.

27 June 1942 Louis Martin, in an editorial in the *Michigan Chronicle*, suggests that the KKK and their "fifth column allies" were responsible for the racial conflict in Detroit at the Sojourner Truth Housing Project and the staging of wildcat strikes, a number of which had occurred at the Dodge, Packard, and Hudson defense plants. The Communist Party also argues that the strikes were instigated by the KKK.

28 June 1942 The Negro Labor Victory Committee (NLVC), a Communist-front organization, holds a "Unity for Victory" rally at the Golden Gate Ballroom in Harlem attended by approximately 6,000 people. The meeting adopts a 12-point program calling for the extension of anti-discrimination measures and the abolition of Jim Crow.

30 June 1942 Mimo De Guzman is arrested by FBI agents in New York on a charge of violating the Selective Training and Service Act.

30 June 1942 For fiscal year 1941–42, it is reported that the FBI and DOJ handled more than 300,000 national security complaints, including complaints of treason, espionage, sabotage, and sedition.

June 1942 The NNC issues an appeal entitled "This Is Our War—Wipe Out Discrimination—Let Negroes Fight Equally."

June 1942 The Congress of Racial Equality (CORE) is formed in Chicago by a group of blacks and whites committed to direct nonviolent action. It undertakes its first major effort with a sit-in strike against discrimination at a Chicago restaurant.

June 1942 The FBI and the Post Office propose that action be taken against a number of black newspapers, but AG Biddle refuses to approve any indictment for sedition. Meanwhile, both the FBI and the Post Office continue their investigations of the black press.

1 July 1942 An FBI agent once more visits *Atlanta World* columnist Cliff MacKay who responds in the *Birmingham World* with a column on 10 July 1942 entitled "Now Just Who Is Subversive?"

2 July 1942 Odell Waller, a black sharecropper of Gretna, Va., convicted in July 1940 for the shooting death of his former white landlord, is finally executed after five stays of execution. The case is the most celebrated criminal case of 1942, attracting widespread national interest, with many persons believing Waller's statement that he shot the landlord in self-defense and out of fear for his own life.

2 July 1942 In a report, "Racial Conflict in the South," the MID acknowledges that "a combination of factors is creating a situation in the South which may result in disorder or bloodshed." It reports also on the prevalence of white fears of "racial uprisings."

6 July 1942 JEH instructs the special agent in charge of the FBI's Baltimore field division to continue to send in material from the *Baltimore Afro-American* that might be considered potentially seditious.

7–18 July 1942 JEH sends Assistant AG Berge four issues of the *Oklahoma City Black Dispatch*, requesting that they be evaluated for violation of wartime statutes. JEH specifically calls attention to articles that complain of black soldiers riding for 24 hours on trains without food and being fed in Oklahoma City in "dirty, filthy, Jim Crow" kitchens in the rear of white restaurants. He also mentions an editorial that recommends that all men should be equal instead of only one race being granted "special dispensation to inherit happiness."

11 July 1942 Roland Hayes, internationally famous black tenor, is beaten by three white policemen in Rome, Ga., where he lived with his family, after a brief argument that had ensued between his wife and a shoestore clerk.

11 July 1942 A black soldier, Private Jesse Smith, is shot to death at Flagstaff, Ariz., in a riot between white civilian policemen and eight black soldiers when the latter insist upon being served in a white-owned restaurant. The coroner's jury exonerates the white officer who killed Smith. Five of the eight Negro soldiers are charged with "unlawfully committing a riot." Convicted in Jan. 1943, they are sentenced to hard labor for from one to four years each. Three will later be exonerated.

13 July 1942 Willie Vinson is lynched in Texarkana, Tex. Accused of attempting to rape a white woman, Vinson was severely wounded during his arrest. Abducted from a hospital bed, he is dragged behind a car to the outskirts of town and hanged from a cotton gin winch.

13 July 1942 Assistant AG Berge notifies JEH that the case of the PMEW and its leaders will be presented to a grand jury at St. Louis, Mo., on 21 July. He declares that "there is an apparent tie-up between the Sikeston lynching of Cleo Wright, and the reported Japanese activity among the Negro population. It is for this reason that the Department desires to submit this matter to the same grand jury."

14 July 1942 AG Biddle formally approves a grand jury investigation of the activities of "Japanese agents with Negroes," citing alleged correlation between pro-Japanese propaganda and the Sikeston lynching.

14–19 July 1942 The NAACP holds its 33rd annual conference in Los Angeles. APR is awarded the Spingarn Medal as the Outstanding Negro of 1941.

15 July 1942 Assistant AG Berge instructs JEH to furnish U.S. District Attorney Harry C. Blanton at St. Louis, Mo., with "complete copies of the investigative reports of the Federal Bureau of Investigation in relation to this matter and the Sikeston lynching case."

15 July 1942 The NLVC, along with Local 91 of the United Furniture Workers of America, CIO, sponsors a petition addressed to Donald Nelson, chairman of the War Production Board. The petition demands that war contracts be allocated to the Spring Products Corp. plant on Long Island in order to maintain the employment of 400 black workers there.

15 July 1942 The NLVC and the National Conference of Negro Youth hold a meeting in New York City in order to protest the execution of Odell Waller and speak out against lynching and the poll tax. The FBI reports that the meeting is also intended to counter the influence of the MOWM.

16 July 1942 In a speech in Washington Park in Chicago, Stokely Delmar Hart is reported to advocate that blacks not join the U.S. army and that they instead fight for the Japanese.

19 July 1942 The NAACP, at the conclusion of its annual convention, declares that it is behind the war "in which racial minorities have a great stake," but demands "all the rights accorded to our white fellow citizens" and the right "to die for our country without segregation or discrimination in the armed forces." Other resolutions are passed denouncing the poll tax, the Dies Committee, the policy of the Red Cross toward blood segregation, and evacuation of aliens "solely on the basis of color" (a reference to the evacuation of Japanese from the West Coast).

19 July 1942 Elijah Ross, a member of the PME in Chicago, is sentenced in Chicago to a term of three years for a violation of the Selective Service and Training Act.

19 July 1942 The Communist Party in Buffalo, N.Y., holds a "Conference for full use of Negro labor Power to produce for Victory."

20 July 1942 The Atlanta Workers Council meets to discuss plans to organize black domestic and cafeteria workers.

21 July 1942 28 white right-wing extremists are indicted by a Washington, D.C., grand jury for violating the Espionage Act and the Smith Act.

22–23 July 1942 A federal grand jury in St. Louis, Mo., hears testimony pertaining to the activities of the PMEW.

23 July 1942 The Frankford Arsenal near Philadelphia discharges 14 black women after their union, the Federal Workers of America, CIO, protests the arsenal's transfer of the women to a box factory several miles away. The union protests that the action constitutes segregation.

24 July 1942 13 members of the faction of the MSTA led by Father Mohammed Bey are arrested in Kansas City, Kan., and charged with violating the Selective Training and Service Act.

24 July 1942 The NLVC sponsors a meeting in New York City at which a resolution is adopted demanding that FDR and AG Biddle issue a "proclamation for Negro rights." At the meeting, Ewart Guinier states that he met with the AG and urged him to request that FDR issue such a proclamation.

25 July 1942 Several blacks are beaten in a midtown section of Greenwood, N.C. A group of whites is said to have ordered blacks not to appear on the streets of Greenwood after 9:00 P.M.

25 July 1942 Assistant AG Berge replies that none of the *Black Dispatch* issues submitted earlier by JEH violate the Espionage Act.

25 July 1942 The MOWM holds a parade and mass meeting in New York City. The FBI reports that the NLVC voted to support the parade and meeting.

27 July 1942 The trial of three black soldiers accused of raping a young white woman on 9 May 1942 in Alexandria, La., begins in the U.S. District Court. The jury returns a verdict of guilty.

27 July 1942 The FBI Los Angeles field office reports on the proceedings of the NAACP national conference in Los Angeles. The report forms part of a continuing investigation "to follow the activities of the NAACP and determine further the advancement the Communist group has made into that organization." Reports on the NAACP are filed by field offices in Richmond, Va., Springfield, Mass., Chicago, Ill., Boston, Mass., Indianapolis, Ind., Savannah, Ga., and Louisville, Ken.

30 July 1942 The federal grand jury in St. Louis, Mo., issues a special report that concludes that the lynching of Cleo Wright, though "a shameful outrage against the rights which all Americans hold dear," does not constitute "any federal offense." In the wake of the grand jury report, the case is closed.

30 July 1942 Mimo De Guzman is removed from New York to St. Louis, Mo., where he was indicted on 20 June 1942 for forgery of a postal money order.

30 July 1942 The FEPC is transferred from the War Production Board and placed under jurisdiction of the War Manpower Commission (WMC), headed by Paul V. McNutt. The action precipitates a storm of protest from black leaders and liberal whites.

July 1942 Beatings of blacks by groups of whites are reported in various areas around Spartanburg and Greenwood, N.C. It is reported the "blue shirts," a racist organization similar to the KKK, may be responsible for the beatings. Throughout the month black women are also beaten and arrested by whites. A rumor spreads that 50 black families have left the area during the month.

1 Aug. 1942 Following the FEPC's hearings in Birmingham, Ala., Governors Dixon of Alabama and Talmadge of Georgia issue a joint statement declaring that the federal government is attempting to break down the segregation laws of the South and that they will brook no interference with the South's system of separating the races.

3 Aug. 1942 The ONI provides the FBI with a confidential report entitled "Subversive Activities Among the Negroes."

6 Aug. 1942 The Japanese ambassador to Buenos Aires informs Japan's minister of foreign affairs that the conflict in Detroit over housing facilities for black workers represents potential propaganda material for Japan and Germany.

6 Aug. 1942 FDR's secretary informs APR by letter that "extreme pressure" precludes the president's meeting with a committee of black leaders.

9 Aug. 1942 Rev. Richard A. G. Foster speaks at Varick Memorial Zion Church in New Haven, Conn., against the prevailing system of segregation and job discrimination.

10 Aug. 1942 In Alexandria, La., U.S. District Judge Ben C. Dawkins sentences to death three black soldiers accused of raping a white woman.

10 Aug. 1942 Private Charles J. Reco, a black soldier, is clubbed and shot by two city policemen in Beaumont, Tex., after the policemen order Reco off a bus for occupying a seat in the white section. No action is taken by military authorities against the perpetrators.

10 Aug. 1942 Charles Newby, president of the CANO since 1939, is evicted from a meeting of the organization. The organization is superseded by the Brotherhood of Liberty for the Black People of America. Stokely Delmar Hart is elected president, with James Graves as vice president.

12 Aug. 1942 The NLVC holds a meeting in New York attended by approximately 40 people. The campaign to pass the anti-poll tax bill is discussed.

14 Aug. 1942 A giant MOWM rally is held in St. Louis, Mo., attended by more than 8,000 people. Officials of the organization refer to "fascistic activity" in the American South, citing repression on military bases. APR advocates the idea that blacks need to have an all-black movement, just as Jews have their Zionist movement. A resolution in support of Indian independence is adopted and forwarded to Gandhi.

15 Aug. 1942 A riot takes place at a black-owned nightclub in Indianapolis after two white policemen arrest a prostitute outside. Between 100 and 200 black men are involved in the fighting, in which the two policemen are severely beaten.

15 Aug. 1942 A grand jury sitting at Jefferson Country, Tex., absolves four white policemen of criminal responsibility in connection with the fatal shooting of Private Charles J. Reco. The exoneration follows a federal investigation ordered by AG Biddle.

20 Aug. 1942 The Metropolitan Detroit Council for Fair Employment Practices holds a meeting to discuss discrimination against black women at the Ford bomber plant. Participants also discuss what role the UAW local should take in the situation. The Ford plant is picketed later that day, when approximately 800 people march on gate no. 2.

20 Aug. 1942 The FBI's Chicago field office advises the U.S. District Attorney that prosecution at the present time of persons connected with the PMEW, CANO, and ATI would interfere with pending investigations "to the point where it might be definitely ascertained what the Japanese influence was in these organizations."

21 Aug. 1942 Seon Jones addresses members of the PME at a meeting at Boulevard Hall in Chicago, calling upon African Americans to act in order to "free themselves" before the war ends.

21 Aug. 1942 The MID notifies the FBI of a joint walk planned from New York to Washington, D.C., by an interracial group of whites and blacks as a protest against segregation and discrimination.

23 Aug. 1942 The Afro-American Benevolent Employment Association holds a meeting in Detroit attended by approximately 200 people. An FBI source describes the purpose of this meeting as that of "stirring Negroes into racial resentment."

23 Aug. 1942 The *Daily Worker* publishes a letter from Robert Hall, district 17 secretary of the Communist Party, urging that Communists support the black protest movement and encouraging blacks to support the war effort.

24 Aug. 1942 Assistant AG Berge informs JEH that the evidence of Japanese agents operating among African Americans presented before the grand jury sitting at St. Louis, Mo., necessitates further investigation by the grand jury process in federal court districts in Arizona, Illinois, Indiana, Kansas, Michigan, New York, Ohio, Oklahoma, Pennsylvania, and Mississippi, and that the various U.S. attorneys in these states are being instructed to institute grand jury investigations. JEH is instructed to forward to each of the attorneys a complete set of FBI investigative reports regarding the PMEW.

26 Aug. 1942 A group of 12 to 20 members of the Harlem Ashram leaves New York on foot for the Lincoln Memorial, Washington, D.C., on an interracial pilgrimage to protest against racial discrimination. The group arrives in Washington, D.C., on 9 Sept. 1942, led by Dr. J. Holmes Smith of the FR.

27 Aug. 1942 The FBI's internal security division submits the draft of a follow-up letter to be sent to FBI field divisions in Birmingham, Chicago, Detroit, Miami, New Orleans, and New York ("areas in which there exists considerable agitation and unrest among the Negroes"). It requests additional surveys be conducted "to ascertain information reflecting the reasons or causes of unrest and agitation among the Negroes in those areas." It also emphasizes the collection of data pertaining to "economic, social or political circumstances in the area involved which possibly add to the unrest or dissatisfaction." The draft letter also asks "what preventive steps have been taken within the area in question to alleviate or to cope with" the state of racial unrest.

27 Aug. 1942 E. H. Winterrowd of the FBI's internal security division meets with representatives of the MID and the ONI, seeking "information concerning trouble with the Negro situation arising in those areas under [their] investigative jurisdiction" as well as "information concerning possible radical or subversive influences in surrounding territories of the areas in which trouble occurred and its relation to that trouble."

28 Aug. 1942 The grand lodge of the Elks at its annual convention votes to petition FDR to put an end to the "intolerable conditions based upon white supremacy."

29 Aug. 1942 OWI Director Elmer Davis praises four Southern newspapermen, one of them the editor of the *Norfolk Journal and Guide*, P. B. Young, Sr., for investigating and exposing false rumors of impending racial disturbances in their respective areas.

31 Aug. 1942 The NLVC sponsors a meeting in New York attended by approximately 2,000 people, most of whom are union representatives. Adam Clayton Powell, Jr., speaks on racial discrimination, the opening of a "second front," and economic conditions in Harlem.

Aug. 1942 A large number of black employees of the Brooklyn Cooperage Co. and the Williams Furniture Co., in Sumter, S.C., who had pledged to purchase war bonds with 10% of their salary, begin withdrawing their pledge.

Aug. 1942 Members of the UNIA and the PMEW hold a joint meeting in East St. Louis, Ill.

Aug. 1942 At a showing of a patriotic film in Kimball, W. Va., it is reported that about 30 blacks boo the American flag when it is shown and also hiss when FDR is shown.

Aug. 1942 The Briggs Manufacturing plant in Detroit is approached by several groups demanding that the company employ black women.

1 Sept. 1942 A complaint is filed and warrant for arrest is issued charging Sultan Mohammed and four other members of the ATI in Milwaukee with violation of the Selective Service Act. All five individuals are indicted by federal grand jury on 16 Sept.

1 Sept. 1942 The FBI requests that the Special War Policies Unit of the DOJ furnish it with "results of any survey or study made by your Research and Analysis Unit" relating to agitation among African Americans, "especially with regard to Negro newspapers."

2 Sept. 1942 The Council on African Affairs holds a rally in New York City at which resolutions calling for the opening of a second front and for the freedom of India are adopted and sent to the president and the British embassy in Washington, D.C.

4 Sept. 1942 JEH informs the White House that the MOWM, which "has come into prominence recently through its sponsorship of mass meetings protesting discrimination against the Negroes," has revived its plan to promote a march in Washington, D.C.

6 Sept. 1942 David J. Logan, in a speech before a meeting of the PME, tells members that they need not register for the draft because they are in fact Liberians and are not loyal to the U.S.

8–13 Sept. 1942 The National Baptist Convention meets in Memphis, Tenn. Racial discrimination and the securing of civil rights are among some of the main topics discussed at the convention.

11 Sept. 1942 FBI Assistant Director Edward A. Tamm advises Assistant Director D. M. Ladd that, on the advice of the solicitor general, the DOJ has decided to recommend prosecution of the leaders of the ATI, CANO, and PME.

13 Sept. 1942 A "Mr. Shaack" speaks before a meeting of the PME in East St. Louis. He tells the audience that the war is in fact a racial war; he also maintains that a Japanese prince married an Ethiopian princess in order to develop goodwill among blacks.

14 Sept. 1942 A federal grand jury for the Southern District of New York returns indictments against LRJ, Ralph Green Best, Lester Holness, James Thornhill, and Joseph Hartrey for sedition (50 USCS § 33 and 18 USCS § 2388). When they are arraigned, all plead not guilty. Although the New York field office of the FBI participated in the grand jury hearings, the U.S. Attorney fails to advise it of the indictment. The first that the office hears of the indictment is through the New York newspapers.

14 Sept. 1942 FBI Assistant Director Foxworth of the New York field office telephones FBI headquarters in Washington, D.C., to inform it that U.S. District Attorney Mathias F. Correa has issued a press release to the newspapers regarding the indictment of LRJ et al. for sedition. Foxworth reports that he has been informed by a newspaper reporter that "there is no mention of the FBI in the entire story." The seditious conspiracy of Jordan and other EPM members is characterized in the press release as "a fantastic dream of a coalition between Africa and Japan in an Axis-dominated world."

15 Sept. 1942 The grand lodge of the Fraternal Order of Vulcan holds a meeting in Youngstown, Ohio, at which the subject of discrimination against blacks is discussed.

15 Sept. 1942 The FBI seizes books, records, correspondence, and other materials from the PMEW in East St. Louis, under a search warrant authorized by the U.S. district attorney for the Southern District of Illinois. General Lee Butler and Finis Williams, members of the PMEW, are also arrested.

15 Sept. 1942 The military's First Service Command headquarters, Intelligence Division, as part of its coverage of "Negro Activities in New England," produces a special report entitled "The Negro Press."

17 Sept. 1942 A federal grand jury hears testimony regarding the activities of the PMEW in Pittsburgh.

19 Sept. 1942 Complaints are filed before the U.S. commissioner in Chicago charging MG with violating 50 USCS §§33 and 34, and William Green Gordon, David James Logan, and Seon Emanuel Jones with violating 50 USCS §34 (section 33 of the Espionage Act covered seditious or disloyal acts or words in time of war, while section 34 related to conspiracy to violate section 33).

20 Sept. 1942 FBI agents in Chicago arrest some 80 members of ATI, CANO, and PME, in what is the only mass arrest of suspected seditionists during World War II. A considerable amount of correspondence and other records is seized by agents. Some of those arrested are charged with sedition and conspiracy to commit sedition by encouraging sympathy with Japan, while others are charged with evasion of the draft by failing to register under the Selective Training and Service Act. Among those arrested are Elijah Mohammed.

20 Sept. 1942 70 members of the ATI in Chicago are indicted for selective service violations. 31 members enter guilty pleas and 30 of them are sentenced to three years each. One member, Emanuel Mohammed, son of Elijah Mohammed, is indicted for sedition, pleads guilty, and is sentenced to five years. Six members who plead not guilty are held for trial. Seven are released when it is determined that they had complied with the law. The remaining 25 members are arraigned on 22 Oct. 1942.

21 Sept. 1942 MG, William Green Gordon, David James Logan, and Seon Emanuel Jones are apprehended and arraigned in Chicago. MG posts a bond of $10,000, but the others remain in custody of the U.S. marshal.

21 Sept. 1942 The Atlanta Workers Council decides to work jointly with the NAACP.

21–22 Sept. 1942 A federal grand jury in Oxford, Miss., hears testimony regarding the activities of the PMEW.

22–29 Sept. 1942 Testimony and materials obtained by the FBI in its search of the East St. Louis branch of the PMEW are presented to a grand jury in East St. Louis.

23–24 Sept. 1942 A race riot erupts at Lincoln High School in Detroit. Three white students and several black students are arrested.

25 Sept. 1942 Joseph Hartrey, charged with conspiracy to commit sedition in connection with the EPM in New York, changes his plea from not guilty to guilty.

26–27 Sept. 1942 The MOWM convenes a national conference in Detroit and 66 delegates attend from Michigan, Illinois, Missouri, Florida, Louisiana, and New York. A constitution is adopted and the organization's principles are formulated. A decision as to whether to march on Washington, D.C., is postponed until the MOWM national convention that is scheduled for May 1943. Meanwhile, Walter White of the NAACP and Lester Granger of the National Urban League end their participation.

27 Sept. 1942 Indictments are returned in the U.S. District Court for Southern Illinois against General Lee Butler, national president of the PMEW, David Erwin, national advisor, and "John Doe," alleged to be the Japanese organizer in the group, for violations of the sedition statutes and the Selective Service and Training Act.

27 Sept. 1942 The Citizens Coordinating Committee of Pittsburgh, Pa., formed during the early summer in order to address discrimination in the armed forces, government, and housing, holds a mass meeting at the Soldiers and Sailors Memorial Hall. It is attended by approximately 800 people, half of whom are white. Instances of discrimination and police brutality are discussed, as well as the rights of blacks to better housing and employment. One speaker protests against the National Association of Manufacturers for not providing enough employment for black workers in defense industries. The organization is made up of more than 40 trade unions and black and white civic and fraternal organizations.

30 Sept. 1942 A federal grand jury returns a second indictment against LRJ, Ralph Green Best, Lester Holness, and James Thornhill, charging them with sedition under 50 USCS §33. They are accused of telling a soldier that black soldiers should not fight for the U.S. against Japan.

Sept. 1942 *People's Voice* reports that approximately 115 black soldiers are threatening a mass desertion in Boise, Idaho, in response to mistreatment.

Sept. 1942 Rumors circulate in early Sept. in the Memphis area that blacks are planning a "general uprising" on the night of 29 Sept. When the rumors are not fulfilled, a new rumor spreads that an uprising is to take place on 6 Oct.

Sept. 1942 The National Progressive Negroes of America is incorporated in the state of Wisconsin. The organization's promoter, Moses Joseph Albany, is alleged to have been one-time head of the PMEW in Kansas City, Mo.

3 Oct. 1942 JEH notifies special agents in charge of FBI field divisions that some of their preliminary surveys regarding agitation among African Americans "would justify the opening of separate cases" of prosecution; he complains, however, that no mention was made in their reports that "separate investigations are being instituted in those instances." He reminds them that "the important nature of the survey being made . . . cannot be overemphasized."

3 Oct. 1942 The CIO establishes a national committee aimed at abolishing racial segregation within its constituent unions. The decision follows a report made by an investigating committee.

5 Oct. 1942 Armed guards are brought into a defense project in Memphis, Tenn., and employees are sent home early in anticipation of the rumored black uprising.

6 Oct. 1942 The date passes without incident in Memphis. The FBI investigates and finds no evidence of "organized disloyalty among the Negroes in the Memphis area."

6 Oct. 1942 The MID produces a report on the activities of the "Negro Pacific Movement," covering the period 17 Aug.–14 Sept. 1942.

12 Oct. 1942 In Quitman, Miss., Charlie Lang and Ernest Green, both 14-year-old boys, accused of attempted rape of a 13-year-old white girl, are taken from jail and hanged from a river bridge. The FBI assists in the investigation, but no arrests are made.

12 Oct. 1942 A Conference to End Discrimination is held in New Haven, Conn.

15 Oct. 1942 Mimo De Guzman is incarcerated in Sandstone, Minn., federal prison, after being sentenced to a term of three years' imprisonment for counterfeiting and passing U.S. postal money orders.

17 Oct. 1942 A third lynching within a week takes place in Mississippi. Howard Wash, sentenced to life imprisonment for the murder of his employer, Clint Welborn, a white dairyman, is taken from jail and hanged from a bridge about 30 miles from the place where the two 14-year-old boys were hanged.

20–22 Oct. 1942 The Southern Conference on Race Relations, composed of 75 southern black leaders, opens at North Carolina College for Negroes in Durham, N.C. Proposals are discussed and adopted on education, racial discrimination, industry, agriculture, health, and social welfare.

21 Oct. 1942 27 priests of the Clergy Conference on Negro Welfare appeal to FDR and to Secretaries Knox and Stimson of the army and navy to investigate discrimination in the armed forces. They specifically protest against discriminatory practices at Camp Stewart, Ga.

22 Oct. 1942 25 of the 70 members of the ATI arrested in Chicago are indicted and arraigned. 18 plead guilty and are sentenced to three years. Seven who plead not guilty are found guilty and receive the same sentence.

22 Oct. 1942 The board of trustees of Princeton University vote against the admission of Negroes to its undergraduate school.

23 Oct. 1942 A federal grand jury in Chicago returns an indictment charging MG with eight counts of sedition. It also charges MG, William Gordon, Seon Jones, and David Logan with conspiracy to commit sedition. All plead not guilty. The same grand jury returns an indictment against Elijah Mohammed, Lynn Karriem, Pauline Bahar, Sultan Mohammed, and David Jones, charging them with eight counts of sedition. Similar charges are also returned against CANO's Stokely Delmar Hart and Charles Newby, who are charged with ten and eight counts, respectively, of violating 50 USCS §33 for obstructing recruitment and enlistment.

23 Oct. 1942 The Afro-American Benevolent Employment Association holds a meeting in Detroit. The principal speaker, Leonard D. Smith, discusses the "alleged injustices and inequalities said to have been forced on the Negroes."

24 Oct. 1942 Six of the 13 breakaway MSTA members led by Father Mohammed Bey that were arrested on 24 July are released by order of the AG.

24 Oct. 1942 At a luncheon of the League for Industrial Democracy, APR criticizes the WMC for being "subject to the whims" of southern congressmen.

26 Oct. 1942 EAB and Bertrand Simmons, secretary of the IRCFL, are arrested by the FBI in New Orleans. During the summer, EAB spoke every Sunday afternoon at Shakespeare peare Park, for the purpose of organizing what the FBI describes as a "semi-religious group, apparently for the purpose of evading the Selective Service Law."

28 Oct. 1942 Winfred William Lynn admits that he failed to report to the local selective service board in Jamaica, Long Island, for induction into the army. He bases his refusal to enlist on the presence of racial segregation in the army. His case becomes one of the celebrated conscientious objector cases of World War II.

28 Oct. 1942 MG, William Green Gordon, David James Logan, and Seon Emanuel Jones are ordered held by the U.S. District Court in Chicago. MG pleads not guilty.

Oct. 1942 Walkouts and work slowdowns "caused by the racial animosity" occur at the foundry of the Ford Motor Car Co. in Detroit. Equal numbers of black and white workers are employed at the foundry.

Oct. 1942 Detroit police report that the number of permits for blacks to purchase firearms has tripled in the past year.

Oct. 1942 A Council of United Negro Labor Leaders is formed in Washington, D.C., made up of representatives of affiliates of the AFL, CIO, and independent labor organizations.

1 Nov. 1942 A disturbance occurs in New Orleans involving black and white soldiers as well as military and civilian police. 78 soldiers are arrested.

1 Nov. 1942 Dr. Edwin R. Embree, president of the Rosenwald Fund, advises African Americans, in a special issue of *Survey Graphic*, to keep moving out of the South. "There is no decent life for you in the Southern rurals as far as the mind of man can see," he declares. "You will have a hard time in the North and West, but at least you will once in a while be treated as human beings."

1 Nov. 1942 Roy Wilkins of the NAACP speaks in Portland, Ore., on discrimination at the Kaiser Shipbuilding yards and in the boilermakers' union at the yards. Throughout the fall of 1942 there is a large influx of blacks into Seattle in search of work at the Kaiser Shipbuilding Co. The local shipbuilding union refuses to grant them membership.

2 Nov. 1942 Ben Careathers, a leading figure in the Equal Rights Movement in Washington, Pa., declares that blacks will ally themselves with the Japanese if "the United States does not give the Negro what he wants."

2 Nov. 1942 A federal grand jury in Kansas City, Mo., begins an investigation of the PMEW.

5 Nov. 1942 Six blacks affiliated with a CIO local distribute circulars at the gates to the MacEvoy Shipbuilding Corp. in Savannah, Ga. Five of the men are chased from the premises by white employees. The one person who remained, Elijah Jackson, is struck in the head with an iron pipe, allegedly by the president of the competing AFL affiliate that had contractual bargaining rights with the company. Black employees, who found Jackson outside upon leaving work, fight with white employees, severely beating five.

5 Nov. 1942 Assistant AG Berge requests that JEH conduct an investigation of the Development of Our Own organization "to ascertain the background and extent of the subversive activities of the members of this organization" in Indianapolis, Chicago, and other places where meetings are held. Berge also requests that the organization's meetings be attended "by someone who can report and testify to the actual statements made." In addition, information is requested as to the whereabouts of Naka Nakane ("the purported Japanese organizer of the movement") and his former wife.

9 Nov. 1942 FBI Assistant Director D. M. Ladd informs JEH that the *Afro-American* published in its 7 Nov. issue an interview with AG Biddle, in which the latter defended the progress made during the past year in erasing "racial inequality," while also describing the duties and activities of the Civil Rights Section of the DOJ.

9 Nov. 1942 The Evaluation Branch of the MID produces a 23-page report, "The Negro Problem and Its Factors."

10 Nov. 1942 The military's First Service Command headquarters issues a report, "The Negro Press—Labor and the Negro."

11 Nov. 1942 Approximately 200 white workers at the Bethlehem Steel Co. shipyard in Baltimore, Md., walk off their jobs in protest against the placing of two African-American men in the company's training school for welders. The workers return to work the next day, but bitter feelings develop when the international president of the Union of Marine and Shipbuilding Workers, CIO, orders five white union leaders expelled.

14 Nov. 1942 A riot involving hundreds of Negro soldiers and white civilian officers and citizens erupts in Florence, S.C.

23 Nov. 1942 Delegations from a number of political organizations supporting the anti–poll tax bill visit the senate gallery to hear the debate on the legislation; afterward, the delegates, numbering about 65, take part in a conference convened by the National Committee to Abolish the Poll Tax.

23–25 Nov. 1942 White workers at the Butte, Mont., mines of the Anaconda Copper Mining Co. and members of the International Union of Mine, Mill and Smelter Workers of America, CIO, meet to protest the employment of 37 African-American soldiers as required by federal authorities. Brig. Gen. Frank J. McSherry of the WMC addresses the meetings. He gives assurance that the 37 soldiers would be removed in 60–90 days.

24 Nov. 1942 According to a surveillance report, Frank Hart, an active member of the PMEW in East St. Louis and head of the UNIA East St. Louis chapter, announced that there would occur a "big blow off," in which rifles, pistols, and bullets stored for this purpose would be used "in assistance of Japan."

26 Nov. 1942 A riot takes place in Phoenix, Ariz., after an African-American military policeman attempts to arrest a black soldier. (The soldier had allegedly struck a black girl in the head with a bottle.) About 100 military and civilian police officers are required to put an end to the fighting. The Communist Party in Arizona issues a leaflet attributing the riot to racial discrimination, in particular segregation in the armed forces. The leaflet asserts that a black soldier and civilian were killed and twelve other people wounded in the fighting.

27 Nov. 1942 The FEPC announces that it will hold a series of hearings in five key cities, with the first hearing in Detroit in Feb. 1943.

27 Nov. 1942 Private David Woods is shot and killed in the foyer of a Fort Dix, N.J., movie theater by a white military policeman, Private James Greggs. Greggs will later be convicted of manslaughter and sentenced to ten years at hard labor.

28 Nov. 1942 Approximately 200 African Americans are arrested and questioned about the riot that took place in Phoenix, Ariz., on 26 Nov.

Nov. 1942 A two-hour work stoppage is staged on army tank production at the Ford Island Park plant in Michigan, after a black worker's pay was docked for time spent talking with officials of his union regarding a fight that had taken place between two black employees and a white employee.

Nov. 1942 A Negro Cultural Foundation is established at the University of Wisconsin, Madison, headed by Argyle Stoute.

1 Dec. 1942 A sealed indictment against LRJ, Joseph Hartrey, Lester Holness, James Thornhill, and Ralph Green Best, is opened. All plead not guilty to charges that they violated 50 USCS §33.

6 Dec. 1942 Frank May, speaking before a meeting of the African Moslem Welfare Society, states that the organization intends to send 16 representatives to meet with a Turkish representative in Washington, D.C.

7 Dec. 1942 Facts are submitted to a federal grand jury in Chicago investigating CANO leaders and members Stokely Delmar Hart, Charles Newby, Frederick Harold Robb, James Graves, and Annette Goree for conspiracy to violate the sedition laws.

7 Dec. 1942 The People's Committee, led by Adam Clayton Powell, Jr., holds a meeting in Harlem, to present its platform on health, social services, education, and the war.

8 Dec. 1942 Max Yergan, speaking at a meeting at Walker Hall, in Milwaukee, Wis., advocates greater democracy for African Americans as well as for China, India, and Africa, and warns his audience against the potential of fascism in the U.S. About 150 people, most of them black, attended.

9 Dec. 1942 An unidentified Japanese individual reportedly speaks before a black audience at the Holy Ghost Church in New Haven, Conn., advocating ties between the Japanese and African Americans.

14 Dec. 1942 The trial of LRJ et al. begins in federal court in New York.

15 Dec. 1942 The Southern Conference on Race Relations releases a charter entitled "A Basis for Interracial Cooperation and Development in the South."

15 Dec. 1942 EAB and 21 members of the IRCFL are indicted. 17 are charged with violating the Selective Training and Service Act and three with failure to report for induction.

18 Dec. 1942 Stokely Delmar Hart and Charles Newby of the CANO are indicted for conspiracy to violate the sedition laws by a federal grand jury in Chicago.

22 Dec. 1942 EAB et al. are arraigned in federal district court for obstructing the draft, in violation of 50 USCS § 31. They all plead not guilty.

24 Dec. 1942 Detroit NAACP Executive Secretary Gloster B. Current meets with Pat Toohey, secretary of district 7 of the Michigan State Communist Party, to discuss the prospect of "cohabitation" of blacks and whites at dormitories at the Willow Run plant of the Ford Motor Co. Toohey relates to Current the concerns that union leaders have expressed with the notion of "mixed" living conditions.

24–27 Dec. 1942 Several confrontations take place between black soldiers and southern white sailors and marines at Vallejo, Calif. Approximately 400 men are involved before they are stopped by military and civilian police. There are no fatalities, but several men are wounded.

30 Dec. 1942 The MOWM announces that it proposes to employ Gandhian civil disobedience tactics as a means of accomplishing its aim of protesting Jim Crow laws and measures.

In the discussion leading up to the announcement, the FR plays an important part. A digest of the group's deliberations, released in early 1943, renames the technique of Gandhian civil disobedience "non-violent good will direct action."

30 Dec. 1942 The jury in the sedition trial of LRJ et al. finds all the defendants guilty.

Dec. 1942 Elijah Mohammed is sentenced in Washington, D.C., to a prison term of one to five years on a charge of violating the Selective Training and Service Act.

Dec. 1942 The FBI reports that the New Orleans branch of the NAACP is seeking to achieve a local membership of 20,000 for 1942.

1942 During the summer, 35% of the black workers who make up 95% of 10,000 workmen employed on the Southern Pacific Railroad refuse to work and file complaints that they are being exploited. A local FBI agent suggests that their complaints are unfounded, particularly since "the average Negro worker did not know the meaning of the word exploit."

1942 Rubin Payne and Jim Barnes, members of the MSTA, are tried and sentenced to five years for violating chapter 178 of the Mississippi laws of 1942, under which it is a crime to advocate the violent overthrow of the government.

1942 The Committee against Jim Crow in Baseball is formed in Washington, D.C., during the late summer.

5 Jan. 1943 After two years of futile efforts to get the U.S. armed forces to eliminate racial discrimination, William H. Hastie resigns as civilian aide to the secretary of war. The immediate cause of his resignation is attributed to the air corps' decision in Dec. 1942 to set up a Jim Crow officers' training camp, a step backward relative to previous army practice regarding officer training.

11 Jan. 1943 WMC head Paul V. McNutt orders the FEPC to postpone its scheduled public hearings on railroad employment discrimination.

11 Jan. 1943 After a white foreman at the Hudson plant in Detroit attempts to have a "Negro loafing on the job return to work," he is attacked by the worker and another nearby black employee. A white plant protection official, after failing to break up the fight, shoots the black workers in their legs.

12 Jan. 1943 George Clarence Myers, a 19-year-old black janitor at the Chrysler plant in Detroit, is indicted for sabotage for writing "obscene and unpatriotic statements" on "patriotic posters" on display in the plant.

13 Jan. 1943 The FBI arrests Reuben Israel and six members of the House of Israel in New Jersey for violating the Selective Training and Service Act.

14 Jan. 1943 LRJ, Lester Holness, Ralph Green Best, James Thornhill, and Joseph Hartrey are sentenced. Jordan is sentenced to ten years in prison and fined $5,000. James Thornhill is sentenced to two eight-year terms to run concurrently. Lester Holness receives seven years on each of the two indictments, to run concurrently. Ralph Green Best is given four years on each of the two indictments, to run concurrently. Joseph Hartrey is sentenced to six years on the conspiracy indictment.

15 Jan. 1943 A delegation of blacks from Detroit meets with Paul V. McNutt to protest the cancellation of hearings by the FEPC. The delegation includes Ferdinand Smith, secretary of the National Maritime Union and a Communist Party member.

19 Jan. 1943 Seven of the 13 members of the MSTA breakaway faction arrested on 24 July 1942 are convicted and sentenced in the U.S. District Court in Kansas City. Each receives terms of four years imprisonment and is fined $1,000.

19 Jan. 1943 APR heads a 20-odd-member delegation that attempts to meet with Paul V. McNutt to protest the cancellation of FEPC hearings. McNutt stipulates that he will meet with only four members of the group, including APR. The group refuses to meet on this basis and the meeting is thereupon canceled.

21 Jan. 1943 Laurenza Robinson, Alfred Joseph Harrison, and five other defendants in the trial of EAB et al. change their pleas from not guilty to guilty to the indictment charging them with violation of 50 USCS §31 for obstructing the draft.

22 Jan. 1943 About 20 delegates representing the NLVC visit officials in Washington, D.C., to protest the curtailment of the FEPC's activities. Afterward, the delegation meets with the local office of the National Federation for Constitutional Liberties, where they select William Bassett, A. J. Isserman, Moran Weston, and Zera Dupont to meet with officials at the White House.

24 Jan. 1943 The Provisional Committee for the Organization of Colored Locomotive Firemen, an organization established by the Washington, D.C., unit of the MOWM, holds a mass meeting to try to "compel" the FEPC to schedule hearings on the railroad industry.

25 Jan. 1943 The trial of MG and other leaders of the PME begins in Chicago.

25 Jan. 1943 The trial of EAB et al. begins in New Orleans.

25 Jan. 1943 The NLVC and People's Committee of Greater New York hold a meeting at Harlem's Abyssinian Baptist Church to demand that the FEPC be given autonomous status and that railroad hearings by the FEPC be resumed immediately.

27 Jan. 1943 AG Biddle announces that a federal grand jury sitting in East St. Louis has returned a two-count indictment against the PMEW; General Lee Butler, national president; David D. Erwin, national advisor; and "John Doe, a Japanese," charging them with conspiracy to violate the sedition statute (50 USCS §34) by causing insubordination, disloyalty, mutiny, and refusal of duty in the military and naval forces of the U.S. and with conspiracy to obstruct compliance with the selective service laws. Commenting on the indictment, Biddle asserts that "attempts by Japanese agents to infiltrate Negro groups have been indignantly repudiated by responsible leaders of our Negro citizens throughout the country."

28 Jan. 1943 EAB and 13 other defendants are found guilty on all seven counts of their indictment.

Jan. 1943 Near riots result when an Ohio movie theater operator refuses to admit African Americans to afternoon and evening performances. The FBI reports that the action may have been "instigated" by students and faculty at Wilberforce University and Antioch College.

Jan. 1943 A small, organized group of black students from Howard University attempts to be served in restaurants and hotels that discriminate against blacks in Washington, D.C.

Jan. 1943 A temporary commission created by the Pennsylvania state legislature to study conditions among the state's urban black population produces its report and recommendations. The report discusses housing, health, recreation, crime and delinquency, education, and employment.

Jan. 1943 The People's Committee, under the leadership of Adam Clayton Powell, Jr., holds its first conference in New York City.

Jan. 1943 There is a run on the post office in Tampa, Fl., after a number of African Americans seek to cash in their war savings stamps. A rumor spreads that the stamps would lose their value after 18 Jan. A similar situation existed in late 1940 and again in early 1941, when African Americas withdrew their postal savings in response to a rumor that they were not safe investments.

Jan. 1943 A committee appointed by the Los Angeles Juvenile Court reports that there are approximately 30 gangs of Latino youths in Los Angeles, comprising 750 boys under 18.

Jan. 1943 The NNC adopts a ten-point program that includes demands for civil rights in the District of Columbia and passage of a federal anti-lynching law and anti-poll tax legislation. The program also calls for abolition of Jim Crow in the armed forces, permanent establishment of the FEPC, and an end to racial discrimination.

1 Feb. 1943 The Tennessee state legislature approves a bill repealing Tennessee's 50-year-old poll tax law and a bill establishing a permanent registration system.

2 Feb. 1943 General Lee Butler and David Erwin enter pleas of not guilty when they are arraigned in the U.S. District Court for the Eastern District of Illinois. They are remanded to the custody of the U.S. marshal in default of $5,000 bond each.

3 Feb. 1943 EAB is sentenced in the U.S. District Court in the Eastern District of Louisiana to serve 15 years for violating the Selective Training and Service Act and aiding members to evade military service. 13 officers and members of the IRCFL receive suspended sentences and are placed on five years' probation. Three members receive sentences of three to nine months on charges of failure to report for induction.

5 Feb. 1943 A black youth stabs a white bus driver in Lexington, Ken., following an argument over the driver's demand that he move to the rear of the bus.

7 Feb. 1943 A near riot takes place in Oklahoma City when a white military police lieutenant is hit in the head with a bottle thrown by an "unknown Negro." African-American soldiers inside a black restaurant also resist military police who attempt to apprehend Frank Wheeler when he "refused to cease brawling" at the restaurant.

9 Feb. 1943 Moses Joseph Albany of the National Progressive Negroes of America, Inc., is arrested by Milwaukee police on a vagrancy charge. On the same date, Meshack Jones, vice-president of the organization, is arrested for bigamy.

10 Feb. 1943 A black woman slashes a white woman and escapes after arguing with the woman over a seat on a Greyhound bus destined for Lexington, Ken.

11 Feb. 1943 Indicted members of the House of Israel plead guilty in the U.S. District Court of the District of New Jersey charging them with violating the Selective Training and Service Act by failing to register. They are sentenced to three years imprisonment.

11 Feb. 1943 The OWI's Special Services Division produces a memorandum that describes the rapid proliferation of "Rumors on Minority Groups" during Dec. 1942.

12 Feb. 1943 Rumors circulate in Lexington, Ken., that blacks are going to "create trouble" on local buses and that the Dixieland, a black nightclub, will be burned down.

12 Feb. 1943 AG Biddle, in a speech in Philadelphia, declares, "The Negro press throughout the country, although they very properly protest, and passionately, against the wrongs done to members of their race, are loyal to their government and are all out for the war."

12–13 Feb. 1943 Shots are fired into the crowd at the Dixieland nightclub in Lexington, Ken. A white college student is killed and several black youths are wounded.

15 Feb. 1943 MG, Seon Emanuel Jones, and William Green Gorden are found guilty of conspiracy to commit sedition. MG and Jones are sentenced to terms of two years in prison and three years' probation. William Green Gordon is sentenced to three years' probation. David Logan is found not guilty.

16 Feb. 1943 Moses Joseph Albany is sentenced to 90 days and is ordered to leave Milwaukee after he is released. The National Progressive Negroes of America, Inc., is disbanded.

16 Feb. 1943 Members of the NLVC meet with WMC head Paul V. McNutt. They present him with proposals to revive the FEPC and strengthen its mandate and autonomy.

19 Feb. 1943 Reuben Israel pleads guilty in the U.S. District Court for the District of New Jersey to charges of violating the Selective Training and Service Act by failing to register. He is sentenced to four years in prison.

Feb. 1943 Blacks in Greenwood, Miss., attempt to cash in their war bonds. Rumors circulate that the war bonds are not going to be paid in full when they mature.

6 Mar. 1943 Marines armed with submachine guns are called out in Vallejo, Calif., to disperse a riotous crowd of 350 black and white servicemen as well as some civilians. It is the third such incident in less than three months.

8 Mar. 1943 The trial of CANO members Stokely Delmar Hart, Charles Newby, Frederick Harold Robb, James Graves, and Annette Goree begins.

18 Mar. 1943 White employees in the gear division of the Packard plant in Detroit stop work to protest the hiring of four black women as machine operators.

18 Mar. 1943 180 black workers walk off the job at the Chrysler Highland Park plant in Chicago.

18 Mar. 1943 After black employees are hired at the Aluminum Co. of America in Detroit, some white employees walk out. During the afternoon, some 400 black workers congregate in one part of the plant and refuse to work.

18 Mar. 1943 Three blacks meet with a group of white representatives in Greenville, Miss., to present demands for better educational facilities, equal distribution of justice, and an end to discrimination and segregation.

19 Mar. 1943 Workers walk out of the Wilson Foundry and Machine Co. in Detroit because of the "racial issue."

20 Mar. 1943 Private Haif G. Williams is fatally shot in Hampton, Ark., by a white deputy sheriff following an altercation between the black soldier and a white truck driver.

23 Mar. 1943 Black workers strike at the Chrysler Lynch Road plant in Detroit to protest the hiring of black women to mop floors. The women contend that the buckets are too heavy. The strike is resolved two days later.

24–26 Mar. 1943 After a fight at Lincoln High School in Ferndale, Mich., a group of white "hoodlums" institute a reign of terror among black residents of the Eight-Mile Road community.

26 Mar. 1943 The FR convenes an Institute on Race Relations and Non-Violent Solutions at the Metropolitan Baptist Church in Boston. 151 people attend.

26 Mar. 1943 200 white workers walk out of the Vickers plant in Michigan, after two blacks workers are hired. Later, additional white workers quit and demand segregation of blacks and whites as well as segregated rest rooms.

26 Mar. 1943 Richard Oliver is found guilty in the U.S. District Court for the District of New Jersey on one count of violating the Selective Training and Service Act for failing to register and is sentenced to a term of three years in prison.

28 Mar. 1943 32 of 64 employees of the all-black "chip pulling" and janitorial departments of the Plymouth Motor Co. in Detroit stop work to protest a government freeze on jobs.

31 Mar. 1943 Charles Hill, Forrest Sheffield, and Gloster Current visit the FBI office in Detroit to urge that the bureau undertake an investigation of "alleged subversive forces causing anti-Negro demonstrations" in Detroit-area defense plants.

31 Mar. 1943 The Louisiana Association for Progress of Negro Citizens is chartered. The FBI reports that it is established for "the purpose of obtaining votes for Negroes."

Mar. 1943 The Greater Empire Way Community Club, a white citizens' group in Seattle, circulates a petition regarding an "alleged indiscretion committed by Negroes" at the Holly Park Housing Project. The Communist Party protests the circulation of the petition and a board of hearing charges an air-raid warden with circulation of the petition and with conduct unfit for his position.

3 Apr. 1943 A racial disturbance occurs at Camp Butner, near Durham, N.C., when several hundred black soldiers and civilians clash with white officers and police after a black soldier resists a white liquor control board officer.

4 Apr. 1943 A near race riot takes place in Orlando, Fl., when a white man starts a fight with a truckload of African-American soldiers that had stopped and was blocking traffic. Local police officers and military police bring the fighting to a halt. Several black soldiers are badly beaten.

5 Apr. 1943 A "Klan-inspired mob" of 100 whites riots in the Central Avenue section of Detroit's west side, smashing the windows in seven homes of black residents.

6–7 Apr. 1943 A riot takes place between black and white students in Flint, Mich. The conflict stems from a fight between blacks and whites at Lowell Junior High School in Flint two days earlier. An estimated 1,000 students are involved in the latest bout of fighting.

8 Apr. 1943 Glen Wagner, a white foreman at the Ford River Rouge plant, dies as a result of a fractured skull. Earlier, Paul Jackson hit Wagner after Wagner called him a "nigger." Jackson is indicted for manslaughter.

10–11 Apr. 1943 The NNC holds the first in a series of three "Victory Conferences on the Problems of the War and the Negro People."

11 Apr. 1943 The NAACP, joined by the Interracial Committee of the UAW, sponsors an anti-discrimination parade and rally in Detroit. Participants include representatives of the Socialist Party, Workers Party, NNC, unions, and black churches. A resolution entitled "The Cadillac Charter" is presented; it advocates the ending of discrimination, segregation of army housing, the poll tax, and lynching.

12 Apr. 1943 JEH forwards to Assistant AG Berge the 13 March issue of the *People's Voice*, which is alleged to contain articles that contribute to "the breach and extreme feeling between white and colored races." The legality of a cartoon, depicting a black soldier with heavy chains around his wrists symbolizing the frustration of blacks in fighting the war, is also questioned.

12 Apr. 1943 More than 100 black workers stay away from work for a day as part of a dispute with management over seniority rights at the Packard plant in Detroit.

16 Apr. 1943 The Total War Employment Committee sponsors a mass meeting at the Enon Baptist Church in Baltimore, Md. 17,000 people are present, all of them black except for seven or eight whites. Adam Clayton Powell, Jr., is one of the featured speakers at the meeting.

18 Apr. 1943 Charles Newby of the CANO is sentenced to three years in prison.

23 Apr. 1943 Lynn Karriem of the ATI is sentenced to five years in prison for violating the Selective Training and Service Act.

23 Apr. 1943 The Intelligence Division of the army's First Service Command headquarters produces a 22-page report, "Recent Trends in Negro Leadership."

27 Apr. 1943 The Boston branch of the NAACP sponsors a mass meeting at the People's Baptist Church attended by 200 blacks. Julian B. Steele, president of the Boston branch, urges attendees to participate in a membership drive so that the NAACP can protest segregation at Old Orchard Park, a Boston housing project.

27 Apr. 1943 The Committee for the Formation of a Mixed Regiment, composed of organizations including the NAACP and the Young Communist League, holds a meeting in Philadelphia attended by about 80 people, 25% of whom are black. James Morgan, an African-American member of the Young Communist League, and Angelo Herndon, speak against racial discrimination in the armed forces.

29 Apr. 1943 Ernest J. Wright visits the FBI office in New Orleans and informs agents that rumors circulating of an impending race riot on 1 May are false. The FBI, finding the matter to be "local in nature," refers Wright to the police department.

30 Apr. 1943 Assistant AG Berge informs JEH that the editorial cartoon in the *People's Voice* does not violate the Espionage Act. At the same time, he requests any additional information that the FBI can supply on the *People's Voice* for use in the study of the black press that the DOJ's Special War Policies Unit was preparing.

30 Apr.–2 May 1943 The Youth Committee for Democracy sponsors an "Institute on Minorities" in Philadelphia. James Carey, national secretary of the CIO, and writer Pearl S. Buck, speak on racial issues.

Apr. 1943 Black students from the University of Wisconsin, Madison, clash with white navy men assigned to the Naval Radio Training School in Madison.

Apr. 1943 The Communist Party winds up an intensive three-month national recruiting drive. The figures that it releases show that 27% of the total number of new recruits are African Americans, even though only 10% of the registered party membership is made up of black members. In some districts, well over 50% of all recruits are black.

1 May 1943 Rumors persist in New Orleans that a race riot will take place on this date, but the date passes without incident.

2–7 May 1943 The Committee on Jobs for Negroes in Public Utilities stages an organized protest against the Capital Transit Co. in Washington, D.C., demanding that it hire black operators. There are daily lines of pickets recruited from affiliates of the CIO. It is rumored throughout the week that there will be "racial violence" in Washington, D.C. The week of demonstrations ends with a parade through the city and a rally in Franklin Park.

3 May 1943 JEH writes to Assistant AG Berge, requesting that the *Pittsburgh Courier* be indicted for sedition.

8 May 1943 The *Pittsburgh Courier* condemns the MOWM for stirring up indignation and unrest among blacks, while also accusing it of lacking "constructive administrative leadership." It condemns the group's leadership for encouraging irresponsible talk about "suicidal civil disobedience and mass marches which never materialize."

15 May 1943 Following the hiring on the previous day of the first black toolmaker at the Hudson Naval Arsenal, Michigan, all the white employees walk out of the toolroom. The strike continues into the second shift, when 600 white workers walk off the job. The next day the strikers return and work with the black employee.

19 May 1943 The Educational Equality League holds a public meeting in Philadelphia, attended by 300 African Americans "reportedly of the conservative type." AG Biddle is among the speakers at the meeting.

21 May 1943 A riot takes place during the evening in Suffolk, Va., when the operator of a service station shoots a black taxi driver who allegedly got out of his taxi and began attacking the operator's son after the latter had criticized the driver for driving into the station recklessly. The police arrest the owner, after which groups of blacks and whites begin fighting. Shots are fired and "missiles" thrown during the fighting. Police authorities use tear gas to disperse the crowd.

22 May 1943 The MOWM holds a planning meeting in Washington, D.C., at which Rev. J. Holmes Smith presents a report on a program of civil disobedience. There is also discussion regarding the list of cities in which demonstrations are proposed to be held.

24–25 May 1943 A group of black welders and burners are promoted by the Alabama Drydock and Shipbuilding Co. The following morning, at a change of shifts at 10:00 A.M., a mob of white workers attacks the black workers. 25 people are injured in the disturbance. The fighting is eventually stopped by local police and soldiers from Brookley Field, Ala. Sailors are assigned to guard the navy property at the yards and soldiers are sent to patrol the streets of Mobile, Ala. Production is slowed for the next few days while blacks and some whites absent themselves from work. Agreement is reached setting aside a segregated shipway—and subsequently others—in which black workers are permitted to advance to as highly skilled positions as are available within a given segregated way.

25 May 1943 The North Philadelphia Civic League holds a meeting at which its president, Dr. John K. Rice, a black dentist, introduces a petition that seeks to gain positions for blacks as conductors with the Philadelphia Transit Co.

25 May 1943 Three bands of Mexican youths reportedly attack and strip four white male civilians in Los Angeles, after surrounding them while they are parking their car.

26–27 May 1943 Reporters for black newspapers are permitted for the first time to enter the White House as well as the House of Representatives' press gallery to cover the official visit of Liberian President Edwin Barclay.

27 May 1943 Stokely Delmar Hart is found guilty on charges of violating the sedition statutes.

27 May 1943 The U.S. District Attorney in Chicago advises that he is considering dismissal of the indictment of sedition against Elijah Mohammed and presents the facts to the department for an opinion.

27 May 1943 FDR signs executive order 9346 reconstituting the FEPC.

28 May 1943 A group of African-American soldiers of the 364th Infantry stationed at Camp Van Dorn, near Centerville, Miss., enter a post exchange reserved for white soldiers and demand service. When they are refused, the soldiers are said to have "literally cleaned out the place." The group had arrived at Camp Van Dorn on 26 May 1943 from Arizona.

29–30 May 1943 The NNC holds a Midwest conference in Detroit, attended by some 300 delegates and other representatives. The theme of the conference is racial discrimination in the armed forces and discrimination against black women in the war plants. Several resolutions are adopted expressing support for the opening of a second front, the anti–poll tax bill, the ending of discrimination, enforcement of anti-lynching laws, and support for the war effort. Adam Clayton Powell, Jr., Jack Raskin, Gloster Current, and others speak at the conference.

29 May 1943 Private William Walker Smith is killed by a white sheriff and another black soldier is wounded during a series of disturbances at Camp Van Dorn, Miss. Shortly after the disturbances, the nearby town of Centerville is declared a "restricted area."

30 May 1943 The county sheriff of Wilkinson County, Miss., shoots and kills an African-American soldier who was beating a white military policeman. Although the sheriff reports that the only person killed was the black soldier whom he had shot, there are allegations that several more black soldiers were also killed.

May 1943 Statistics are published showing that in 1940 a total of 300 screens used to segregate blacks and whites on buses in the New Orleans area were removed unlawfully. The number increased in 1941 to 455 screens and during 1942 to 841. For the three months Jan.–Mar. 1943, 330 screens were removed.

May 1943 The FBI reports the circulation of "subversive propaganda" among African Americans in Marshall, Tex. The literature allegedly distributed is rumored to assert that "a change of government might benefit the Negro race."

May 1943 Frank May attempts to reorganize the African Moslem Welfare Society in Pittsburgh.

May 1943 African-American soldiers attached to an engineer corps at the Army Air Corps base under construction at Cross City, Fl., attempt to associate with white residents and enter establishments that discriminate against blacks. The soldiers, many of whom are from the North, are received by the residents with hostility. The white residents allegedly begin to arm themselves in anticipation of the arrival of additional black soldiers.

May 1943 White workers engage in a work stoppage at a plant operated by the Electric Storage Battery Co. in Philadelphia, when management arranges for black employees to use the same locker facilities as whites.

May 1943 The Southern Negro Youth Congress lobbies the U.S. Employment Service in an effort to obtain jobs for African Americans.

May 1943 The Federated Defense Club is formed in the Seattle area to protest racial discrimination in defense industries. The club plans to establish units in every defense plant where blacks are employed. Ostervold Carl Brooks is one of the club's organizers.

May 1943 Rumors are reported that a major racial conflict is imminent in Richmond, Va.

May 1943 The Communist Party organizes a Negro Victory Committee in the San Francisco area in order to address the problem of racial discrimination.

1 June 1943 At Leesville, La., a white civilian shoots and kills an African-American soldier during a fight between black soldiers and military police after seven allegedly intoxicated black soldiers refuse to obey military police order. Five African-American soldiers are arrested and charged by state police with inciting a riot.

2 June 1943 At a meeting of the MOWM in New York, members debate distributing to an African-American private on leave from the Tuskegee air base copies of *The War's Greatest Scandal! The Story of Jim Crow in Uniform* by Nancy and Dwight Macdonald. It is decided that one copy will be provided to him.

3 June 1943 White employees of the aircraft division of the Packard Motor Car Co. plant in Detroit employing more than 20,000 persons walk out after three African-American workers are assigned to skilled jobs in the plant. (The black workers were earlier removed after they had been upgraded in May 1943, which was followed by a walk-out by white workers.) The striking white workers return to work on 7 June; one foreman and 26 white workers are discharged by the War Labor Board for their actions. UAW president R. J. Thomas publicly blames the KKK for instigating the strikes.

3–8 June 1943 For six days white sailors and army servicemen stationed in Los Angeles organize and pursue Mexican youths ("zoot-suiters") with weighted ropes and clubs and proceed to cut their clothes off after apprehending them. 112 people are hospitalized, 150 others are hurt, and 114 are arrested. The Los Angeles city council officially bans the wearing of zoot suits. A ten-page report on the Los Angeles rioting reveals that in two instances blacks who were not dressed in zoot suits were attacked by white servicemen. Other so-called zoot-suit clashes are reported in Philadelphia, Pittsburgh, Baltimore, and other cities, though not on the scale seen in Los Angeles.

5 June 1943 A Conference on Racial Problems is held at City Hall in Chicago. The meeting is arranged by Fullerton Fuller of the Chicago Industrial Union Council, CIO, and Communist Party leaders. Representatives of many organizations, including the NAACP and Urban League, speak at the conference.

5–8 June 1943 Curtis Thomas, a black ex-convict, allegedly attacks a 19-year-old white woman in Beaumont, Tex. After the woman returns home and reports the incident, police find Thomas and shoot him, as he allegedly attempts to flee. Thomas is taken to the Hotel Diu hospital the following day. A mob assembles outside the hotel but it is dispersed by police. Thomas dies on 8 June, after allegedly admitting to attacking the girl.

7 June 1943 The People's Committee and the Brooklyn committee of the NLVC cosponsor a "Negro Freedom Rally" at Madison Square Garden. The event receives considerable support from the Communist party and the trade union movement. An estimated 20,000 attend the rally, at which resolutions are passed urging passage of the anti–poll tax bill, the opening of a second front, and eliminating discrimination in the armed forces. Adam Clayton Powell, Jr., Rev. Thomas Harten, and Ferdinand Smith are delegated to transmit the "message of the people" to the president. The rally devotes particular attention to the plight of the 369th infantry at Camp Stuart, Ga. The issue of discrimination in the armed forces is also the subject of a special skit presented at the rally. The final portion of the program consists of a series of dramatic skits, entitled "For This We Fight," written by Langston Hughes.

7 June 1943 Three shop stewards at the Acme Backing Co. in Brooklyn, N.Y., strike in protest at the promotion of a black worker. Two of the three shop stewards are subsequently expelled from the Coke and Chemical Workers Union, CIO.

8–10 June 1943 The NAACP holds an emergency conference in Detroit., "The Status of the Negro in the War for Freedom." The conference includes a large mass meeting at Olympia Stadium, where UAW president R. J. Thomas is the principal speaker. 550 delegates representing 150 cities attend the conference.

9 June 1943 In a clash between black soldiers and white military police at Camp Stewart, Ga., one military policeman is shot and killed and four are seriously wounded. The clash is precipitated by a rumor that a white military policeman struck the visiting wife of an African-American soldier.

11 June 1943 Clevis DePugh, formerly a national organizer for the PME, is apprehended by FBI agents and placed in the custody of the U.S. marshal to await trial for violating the Selective Training and Service Act.

11 June 1943 Shooting breaks out at Camp Shenango, Pa., leaving one African-American soldier dead, two injured, and seven black and white soldiers hospitalized. A supply room of the Negro 4th Battalion was earlier broken into and 11 Garand rifles and ammunition were stolen that evening, but the military insists that the shootings are not related to the theft of these guns.

11 June 1943 Stokely Delmar Hart is sentenced to three years imprisonment.

11 June 1943 The Los Angeles Committee for American Unity is formed for the purpose of addressing the "Mexican problem" in Los Angeles. Many of the committee's members are also members of the Citizens Committee for the Defense of Mexican-American Youth. An organizational meeting of the Los Angeles Committee is held at which a proposal is discussed with the Mexican consul to exchange affidavits supporting the charges of the "zoot suit boys" against their attackers.

12 June 1943 The FR organizes a conference in Indianapolis, at which James Farmer discusses nonviolent forms of protest and Bayard Rustin explains the "action project," under which blacks and whites would together seek service in restaurants that discriminate. The meeting is held under the auspices of the Indianapolis Institute on Race Relations.

12 June 1943 Assistant AG Berge declines to grant JEH's request that the *Pittsburgh Courier* be indicted for sedition.

13 June 1943 A riot takes place at Eastwood Park in east Detroit, when approximately 70 white teenage "hoodlums" enter the park and evict all African Americans present. The police intervene and stop the riot.

13 June 1943 North Philadelphia Citizen's League holds a meeting at the McDowell Community Church in Philadelphia. The FBI reports that the chairman of the organization, Dr. John W. Shirley, speaks "in a militant way" about racial discrimination.

13 June 1943 15 soldiers are jailed and two are shot in the aftermath of a clash between members of the Camp Shelby, Miss., baseball team and white state highway patrolmen.

15 June 1943 After an African American allegedly assaults a 23-year-old white woman about two miles away, a white mob assembles at the police station in Beaumont, Tex., made up largely of employees from the Pennsylvania Shipyards, the Lummus Co., and the Consolidated Steel Corp. The mob proceeds to smash the windows of black-owned establishments and loot property. At midnight, a mob descends upon 52 blacks waiting for a bus to Port Arthur. Approximately 40 to 50 people, both white and black, are shot or beaten—or both—during the rioting.

15 June 1943 The U.S. District Court for the Eastern District of Illinois finds the PMEW, General Lee Butler, David E. Erwin, and John Doe guilty on two counts of violating 50 USCS §33, and the Selective Training and Service Act of 1940. Butler is sentenced to two years on each count to run concurrently in the custody of the AG. Erwin is sentenced to four years on each count to run concurrently in the custody of the AG. The organization is fined $500. At the same time, the U.S. District Court for Southern Illinois sentences Butler to two years in jail and David Erwin to four years. The court also fines the PMEW $1,000.

16–20 June 1943 A state of emergency is declared in Beaumont, Tex. Two deaths are reported from the rioting that erupted on 15 June.

16 June 1943 A riot breaks out between black workers and company guards at the Sun Shipbuilding and Drydock Co. in Chester, Pa., which employs only African-American workers. Four workers are wounded from shots fired by guards.

19 June 1943 In El Paso, Tex., African-American soldiers are shot by a white civilian. The white civilian had earlier attacked a black soldier with a knife. When a large number of black soldiers return later to the scene, the civilian fires several shots at them. The incident involves approximately 400 soldiers. The sheriff's department stops the disturbance when black soldiers attempt to disarm police who had been dispatched to the scene.

20–22 June 1943 An altercation between blacks and whites at the Belle Isle amusement park on the Detroit River triggers the start of the worst race riot in America during World War II. The fighting and rioting quickly spread to black sections of Detroit, where several stores are looted. Whites pull blacks from cars and buses and beat them throughout the day of 21 June. FBI agents are witnesses to these events but refrain from intervening. Several Detroit plants are forced to operate at less than capacity as a result of the disturbances, with 60% of black workers failing to report for work at the Ford Motor Car Co.

21 June 1943 Michigan Governor Kelley requests that federal troops be dispatched to Detroit and that they be placed under state control. The president declares a state of martial law in effect in Detroit at 10:20 P.M. A total of 2,500 federal troops are sent into the area.

21 June 1943 280 black soldiers, members of the 543rd Quartermaster's Negro Battalion at Fort Custer, Mich., break into the Quartermaster's warehouse and take 178 rifles and ammunition, which they load into several army trucks. The soldiers proceed toward Detroit, but they are stopped by an armed sentry. Ten of the soldiers are taken into custody by commanding officers and later charged with mutiny.

21 June 1943 The Committee for Jobs in War Industries holds an emergency meeting at the Lucy Thurman YWCA in Detroit. 200 people attend. Harper Poulson of the Young Communist League declares that the riots are the result of work by the KKK and a "fifth column."

22 June 1943 The rioting in Detroit is finally brought under control at 3:00 A.M.

22 June 1943 At a meeting of Communist Party section organizers in Detroit, Patrick Toohey calls upon the U.S. AG to investigate the riots using information supplied by Communist Party members; he insists that affidavits showing the parties responsible for the riots can be obtained and turned over to a grand jury.

22 June 1943 When a large number of sailors on leave arrive at Union Station in Washington, D.C., a porter gets into a fight with one of the sailors. Arrests are made and the FBI informant reporting the incident claims that "racial violence might be expected to break out there in the immediate future."

22 June 1943 30 black workers walk out of the Dravo Corp. yards at Wilmington, Del., demanding higher wages. The strike is not authorized by the union. The supervisor of construction work expresses his fear of the possibility of a race riot.

22 June 1943 The Dorie Miller branch of the Young Communist League holds a meeting in Seattle at which a citywide demonstration against racial discrimination is planned.

22 June 1943 A black male is reported to have distributed "anti-racial handbills" in a black residential neighborhood in Kansas City, Mo., calling upon black employees of defense industries to strike.

23 June 1943 The final tally of casualties during the Detroit riot is put at 34 persons killed, 25 of them black. Approximately 700 people were injured and 650 hospitalized. Approximately 900 people are arrested; of the 54 given 90-day jail sentences, 22 are white and 32 are black.

23 June 1943 The Communist Party holds a meeting in Indianapolis at which the Detroit race riots are discussed. Party officials assert that the KKK, Father Coughlin, Henry Ford, and Gerald L. K. Smith are responsible for the riots. Additionally, they argue that the riots are part of a "national conspiracy against the war effort."

23 June 1943 53 people, 15 of whom are black, are arrested for rioting in Hamtrack, Mich. The police question those arrested for "evidence of subversive inspiration," but "with negative results."

23 June 1943 APR calls an emergency meeting of African Americans at the Metropolitan Community Church in Chicago, to discuss the Detroit race riots. A large number attend. A resolution demanding that federal and local officials take steps to prevent further violence is sent to the president as well as the governor of Illinois and Chicago Mayor Edward Kelly.

24 June 1943 The FBI's New York field office advises that publication of photographs from the Detroit riots in the 23 June issue of the newspaper *PM* "has caused considerable resentment on the part of the Negro populace" in Harlem and that a confidential informant "has been requested to be on the alert and to report any indications of possible disturbance in this area."

24 June 1943 A shooting takes place at Camp Blanding, Fl., when members of a black company, ordered away from a dance being held by another company, return with rifles and begin shooting inside the dance hall. Nine black women, eight black soldiers, and one white officer are wounded. Five black soldiers are taken into custody for involvement in the shooting.

24 June 1943 Secretary of War Stimson observes that the cause of racial tension in the country is "the deliberate effort . . . on the part of certain radical leaders of the colored race to use the war for obtaining . . . race equality and interracial marriages."

25 June 1943 Detroit Mayor Edward Jeffries appoints an interracial committee to study the "general problem in Detroit." The committee includes representatives of local civic organizations and unions.

25 June 1943 The MOWM holds a public meeting in Chicago on the subject of the Detroit race riots. James Farmer, national officer of the FR, speaks and advocates a civil disobedience program.

29 June 1943 JEH supplies AG Biddle with an extensive report on the Detroit race riots.

29 June 1943 FDR appoints Jonathan Daniels as White House coordinator of information on racial tensions.

29 June 1943 A rally is held by the National Urban League in Milwaukee to discuss the Detroit riots.

30 June–1 July 1943 During the evening of 30 June and early morning of 1 July, a riot breaks out near Hallen and Main Streets in New London, Conn., between black members of the U.S. Maritime Training School at Fort Trumbull, in New London, and white enlisted navy men stationed at the State Pier, in New London. The conflict begins with rock throwing between the men. After the police break up the fighting, 30 African Americans are identified and held for investigation.

30 June–4 July 1943 The "We Are Americans, Too" national conference of the MOWM opens at the Metropolitan Community Church in Chicago, attended by approximately 500 persons. APR states that the president will be asked to form a "national race commission" so that there will be a congressional investigation of the race riots in Detroit. At an evening session on 1 July, a "direct action non-violence" program is advocated by Bayard Rustin of the FR and discussed. The conference adopts a resolution barring communists from membership in the MOWM.

30 June 1943 The FBI reports that national security investigations for the 1942–43 fiscal year have reached a total of 390,805.

30 June 1943 The OWI's Bureau of Special Services produces a special survey, "Opinion in Detroit Thirty-Six Hours After the Race Riots."

June 1943 Several conflicts break out between African-American and Italian-American high school students in Newark, N.J., resulting in fatal shootings of a black boy and an Italian youth.

June 1943 CORE establishes itself as a national organization.

June 1943 An FBI informant attending the NAACP national convention in South Carolina reports on his conversations with NAACP counsel Thurgood Marshall. The informant states that he believes Marshall is "a loyal American" who "would not permit anything radical to be done."

June 1943 Republicans and southern Democrats in Congress vote to eliminate the OWI's Domestic Branch, following publication, in mid-1942, of an illustrated 72-page booklet, *Negroes in the War*. Two and a half million copies are distributed. It seeks to show the progress that blacks have made since 1933 as well as the role that they are playing in helping to win the war. Southern politicians decry the pamphlet as subversive, while blacks reject its rosy and optimistic message.

June–Aug. 1943 The police in Clairton, Duquesne, and Homestead, Ill., carry out arrests of so-called senators, black laborers brought in from Washington, D.C., to work at the United States Steel Corp. It is alleged that the "senators" are responsible for "creating disturbances."

1 July 1943 At an afternoon meeting of the MOWM national convention in Chicago, a resolution is adopted calling for legislation to be introduced to create a "Commission on Race in America" that would "rule" on all racial matters.

1 July 1943 A new FEPC is constituted by presidential order. Its first cases involve three military contractors, the Capital Trust Co. of Washington, D.C., a group of railroads, and several war industries in Detroit.

1 July 1943 JEH again inquires from Assistant AG Berge regarding the legality of material in the *People's Voice*. This time the material pertains to a letter published in the 29 May issue of the newspaper and written by a black army corporal in Africa, in which the author complains about discrimination against black personnel, giving specific examples, and calls for a government investigation.

2 July 1943 A MOWM committee proposes that the movement should experiment with the nonviolence technique in major metropolitan cities (New York, Washington, D.C., Richmond, Chicago, and Los Angeles).

3 July 1943 JEH supplies the White House with the first in a series of reports on the proceedings of the MOWM national convention in Chicago.

4 July 1943 In a speech before the MOWM convention, APR urges local units to seek employment of African Americans with public utilities and to stage demonstrations in the event they are refused. He also severely criticizes Monsignor Francis Haas, newly appointed FEPC chairman, for his decision on the Alabama Dry Dock and Shipbuilding Corp. case in Mobile, Ala., which restricts blacks to working in only four of the shipways at the yards.

5 July 1943 In retaliation for the imprisonment of some of their companions, a group of black soldiers leave Camp McCain in Miss. at night and fire on the homes of white residents living in Duck Hill. 13 of the soldiers are later tried and sentenced to from 10 to 15 years at hard labor by army court martial.

6 July 1943 AG Biddle, after a review of the operation of the FBI's Custodial Detention program, orders that JEH discontinue using the classification. He also orders that the program be discontinued.

8 July 1943 A rumor circulates that blacks nationwide are planning an action to protest segregation and will attempt on this date to gain admission to restaurants, theaters, and other places that discriminate against them.

10 July 1943 Private Otis Gardner is killed by a white guard at Fort Bliss, Tex., allegedly as he attempts to leave the camp to go to El Paso, where a race riot was said to be in progress.

10 July 1943 A fight breaks out between white and black employees in the plant cafeteria at the Bethlehem Fairfield Shipyards in Maryland. Several white and black workers are arrested and fined.

11 July 1943 Private Norman Taylor is killed and several other black soldiers are wounded in a racial clash between soldiers at Camp Shenango, Pa.

12 July 1943 Assistant AG Berge once more declines JEH's request that the *People's Voice* be prosecuted.

12 July 1943 The MID's Evaluation Branch produces a ten-page report, "The Communist Party and the Negro Problem."

19 July 1943 85 black workers at the Campbell, Wyant and Cannon plant at Muskegon, Mich., a foundry manufacturing war material, stage a walk-out, refusing to work under a white steward.

24 July 1943 *The Nation*, in an article entitled "Washington Gestapo," claims that "J. Edgar Hoover, who has steadfastly refused to include Negroes among his 4,800 special agents, has a long record of hostility to Negroes."

25 July 1943 Vice-president Henry A. Wallace, speaking in Detroit before a crowd estimated at 20,000, states that the U.S. cannot fight to crush Nazi brutality abroad "while condoning race riots at home."

26 July 1943 A group of riveters at the Bethlehem Steel shipyards at Sparrows Point, Md., walk off their jobs to protest the newly established training school that includes black workers. The majority of the workers return to work on 29 July. Seven men are suspended and eventually discharged. During the protest, several thousand black and white workers mass in the plant's yard.

27 July 1943 White women working at the Timken Gear and Axle Co. in Detroit strike to protest their having to use the same toilet facilities as black women. All but four of the white women return to work after the management refuses to make any changes.

July 1943 Chaplain Luther M. Fuller of the People's Baptist Church, Chelsea, Mass., is tried by an army reclassification board on charges that he made regarding army brutality against blacks.

July 1943 Secretary of the Navy Knox approves a proposal to use black women in Jim Crow units, but the proposal included no provisions "for Negroes to become officers in the WAVES."

July 1943 Strikes by black longshoremen take place in Memphis and St. Louis after the Mississippi Barge Line Co. refuses to meet demands for a 40-hour work week.

July 1943 An FBI source in Washington, D.C., describes the "current racial situation" in the nation's capital as "tense." According to the informant, the source of any conflict will originate with young African Americans between the ages of 16 and 19 who have not been inducted into the army.

July 1943 African-American soldiers stage a strike at an ordnance plant near Flora, Miss. The soldiers are responding to the beating of a black soldier and the "abuse" of several black soldiers' wives by Jackson, Miss., police.

1–3 Aug. 1943 Rioting erupts when a white police officer attempts to arrest a black women for disorderly conduct at the Braddock Hotel in Harlem. A black soldier intervenes during the arrest. The officer shoots the soldier, whereupon approximately 300 black civilians and soldiers stage a protest at the scene, while another 200 people march to the 28th Precinct station in Harlem to protest. Shortly afterward, rioting breaks out and lasts through the early morning of 3 Aug. Five people are killed, 40 policemen are injured, and 465 men and 74 women are arrested.

2 Aug. 1943 The mayor of New York urges in several radio addresses that people return to their homes. 5,000 police and 1,000 detectives are assigned to the riot area.

2 Aug. 1943 Communist Party leaders meet at Academy Hall in New York City and decide that the party will not take any action in connection with the Harlem riot until the actual conflagration is quelled.

14 Aug. 1943 JEH circumvents AG Biddle's order banning the Custodial Detention program by simply renaming it. Special agents in charge of FBI field divisions are advised that thenceforth the "character of investigations of individuals (other than alien enemies) who may be dangerous or potentially dangerous to the public safety or internal security of the United States shall be 'Security Matter' and not 'Custodial Detention.' "

25 Aug. 1943 The OWI's Bureau of Special Services, Division of Research, produces a report, "Opinions About Inter-Racial Tension."

26 Aug. 1943 Private Otis Gardner of the 394th Artillery is shot to death by a white sentry in a racial clash at Fort Bliss, Tex. At the same time, Private Paul V. Brown, white, is critically wounded by a black soldier.

30 Aug. 1943 The ONI produces a report, "Topical Study Memorandum on the Negro Press."

4 Sept. 1943 The War Department informs the NAACP that racially mixed units in the army would be "inadvisable." The statement is in response to a request from African Americans and some whites that a racially mixed army unit be formed with volunteers.

10 Sept. 1943 The FBI internal security division presents JEH with its *Survey of Racial Conditions in the United States.* It calls JEH's attention to the report's conclusion regarding "the economic, social and political causes for the present racial unrest."

12 Sept. 1943 The Provisional Committee for the Organization of Colored Locomotive Firemen meets at Vermont Avenue Baptist Church, in Washington, D.C. APR addresses the meeting and calls for blacks to organize throughout the country on a political basis, with local, state and national candidates running for office. He also calls for a western hemisphere conference to formulate black participation in any postwar peace conference and the convening of a world conference of "darker-skinned peoples" at the conclusion of the war, in order to formulate a program through which nonwhite peoples of the world could gain a voice in the postwar era.

13 Sept. 1943 The ONI produces a report, "Topical Study Memorandum re Japanese-Negro Collaboration."

15 Sept. 1943 The FEPC holds public hearings on railroad discrimination.

24 Sept. 1943 JEH submits copies of *Survey of Racial Conditions in the United States* to the DOJ, the White House, and MID and ONI directors.

27 Sept. 1943 The FBI's internal security division produces a 308-page monograph, *Japanism and Japanese in the United States.* It includes a chapter entitled "Japanese Influences and Activity among American Negroes."

11 Oct. 1943 JEH sends Assistant AG Tom C. Clark a column from the 19 June 1943 issue of the *Chicago Defender* criticizing the treatment of black soldiers in U.S. army camps. The author of the article concluded: "Mainly, their bitterness adds up to 'I just as soon die fightin' for democracy right here in Georgia, as go all the way to Africa or Australia. Kill a cracker in Mississippi or in Germany, what's the difference!' " JEH points out that the column refers to a gun battle between black and white soldiers at two Georgia camps. He asks if such material does not violate the Espionage Act.

12 Oct. 1943 AG Biddle writes to JEH requesting a copy of the *Survey of Racial Conditions in the United States*. Section 1 is eventually returned by the DOJ to Hoover in October 1944, without notification or explanation. A year later, Section 2 is returned after Biddle is appointed by President Harry S. Truman as a member of the Nuremberg war crimes tribunal.

SELECT BIBLIOGRAPHY

REFERENCE WORKS

Blackstock, Paul W., and Frank L. Schaf. *Intelligence, Espionage, Counterespionage, and Covert Operations: A Guide to Information Services.* Detroit: Gale Research, 1978.

Davis, Thadious M., and Trudier Harris, eds. *Afro-American Fiction Writers After 1955. Dictionary of Literary Biography.* Vol. 33. Detroit: Gale Research, 1984.

Guzman, Jessie Parkhurst, ed. *Negro Year Book: A Review of Events Affecting Negro Life, 1941–46.* Tuskegee Institute, Ala.: Negro Year Book Publishing Co., 1947.

Haines, Gerald K., and David A. Langbart. *Unlocking the Files of the FBI: A Guide to Its Records and Classification System.* Wilmington, Del.: Scholarly Resources, 1993.

Harris, Trudier, ed. *Afro-American Writers, 1940–1955. Dictionary of Literary Biography.* Vol. 76. Detroit: Gale Research, 1988.

Murray, Florence, comp. *The Negro Handbook: A Manual of Current Facts, Statistics and General Information Concerning Negroes in the United States.* Vols. 1–4. New York: Wendell Malliet and Co./Current Reference Publications, 1942–1949.

Niiya, Brian, ed. *Japanese American History: An A-to-Z Reference from 1868 to the Present.* New York: Facts on File, 1993.

Theoharis, Athan G. *The FBI: An Annotated Bibliography and Research Guide.* New York: Garland Publishing, 1994.

Yust, Walter, ed. *10 Eventful Years; A Record of Events of the Years Preceding, Including and Following World War II, 1937 through 1946.* Chicago: Encyclopedia Britannica, 1947.

GOVERNMENT PUBLICATIONS

Comptroller General, General Accounting Office. *FBI Domestic Intelligence Operations: An Uncertain Future.* GAO no. GGD-78-10. November 9, 1977.

U.S. Department of Commerce. *Negro Newspapers and Periodicals in the United States: 1940.* Negro Statistical Bulletin no. 1. Washington, D.C., 1941.

———. *Negro Newspapers and Periodicals in the United States: 1943.* Negro Statistical Bulletin no. 1. Washington, D.C., 1944.

U.S. Department of Justice. *Guidelines for Domestic Security Investigations.* Washington, D.C.: Department of Justice, 1976.

———. Office of Congressional and Public Affairs, Research Unit. *Conducting Research in FBI Records.* Washington, D.C.: Federal Bureau of Investigation, 1988.

U.S. House of Representatives. Government Information and Individual Rights Subcommittee. *Hearings: FBI Compliance with the Freedom of Information Act.* 95th Congress, 2d session. Washington, D.C.: U.S. Government Printing Office, 1984.

U.S. House of Representatives. Committee on the Judiciary. Subcommittee on Civil and Constitutional Rights. *Hearings: FBI Counterintelligence Programs.* Serial 55. 93d Congress, 2d session. Washington, D.C.: U.S. Government Printing Office, 1974.

U.S. House of Representatives. Committee on Rules. *Hearings. Attorney General A. Mitchell Palmer on Charges Made Against Department of Justice by Louis F. Post and Others.* 65th Congress, 2d session. 3 parts. Washington, D.C.: Government Printing Office, 1920.

U.S. House of Representatives. Select Committee on Intelligence. *Hearings: U.S. Intelligence Agencies and Activities: Domestic Intelligence Programs.* 94th Congress, 1st session. Washington, D.C.: U.S. Government Printing Office, 1975.

———. *U.S. Intelligence Agencies and Activities.* Pts. 1–6. 94th Congress, 1st and 2d sessions. Washington, D.C.: U.S. Government Printing Office, 1975–76.

U.S. Senate. *Investigation Activities of the Department of Justice, Letter from the Attorney General, Transmitting in Response to a Senate Resolution of October 17, 1919, a Report on the Activities of the Bureau of Investigation of the Department of Justice against Persons Advising Anarchy, Sedition, and the Forcible Overthrow of the Government.* 66th Congress, 1st session. Document no. 153. Washington, D.C.: U.S. Government Printing Office, 1919.

U.S. Senate. Select Committee to Study Governmental Operations with Respect to Intelligence Activities. *Hearings on Intelligence Activities, Senate Resolution 21, Vol. 6, Federal Bureau of Investigation*, 94th Congress, 1st session. Washington, D.C.: U.S. Government Printing Office, 1975.

———. *Intelligence Activities and the Rights of Americans. Final Report of the Select Committee to Study Governmental Operations with Respect to Intelligence Activities*, Book II, 94th Congress, 2d session. Washington, D.C.: U.S. Government Printing Office, 1976.

———. *Supplementary Detailed Staff Reports on Intelligence Activities and the Rights of Americans. Final Report of the Select Committee to Study Governmental Operations with Respect to Intelligence Activities*, Book III, 94th Congress, 2d session. Washington, D.C.: U.S. Government Printing Office, 1976.

———. *Final Report. Supplemental Reports on Intelligence Activities. Final Report of the Select Committee to Study Governmental Operations with Respect to Intelligence Activities*, Book VI, 94th Congress, 2d session. Washington, D.C.: U.S. Government Printing Office, 1976.

U.S. Senate. Select Committee to Study Undercover Activities of Components of the Department of Justice. *Senate Report no. 682*, 97th Congress, 2d session. Washington, D.C.: U.S. Government Printing Office, 1982.

MICROFILM PUBLICATIONS

COINTELPRO: The Counterintelligence Program of the FBI. Wilmington, Del.: Scholarly Resources, 1978.

Department of Justice Investigative Files. Edited by Mark Naison. Frederick, Md.: University Publications of America, 1989.

FBI File on A. Philip Randolph. Wilmington, Del.: Scholarly Resources, 1990.

FBI File on the House Committee on Un-American Activities (HUAC). Wilmington, Del.: Scholarly Resources, 1986.

FBI File on the National Negro Congress. Wilmington, Del.: Scholarly Resources, 1986.

FBI Files on the NAACP. Wilmington, Del.: Scholarly Resources, 1990.

Investigative Case Files of the Bureau of Investigation, 1908–1922. Washington, D.C.: National Archives, 1983.

J. Edgar Hoover: New York Times *Articles between May 18, 1924 and May 4, 1972.* Sanford, N.C.: Microfilming Corporation of America, 1980.

Malcolm X: FBI Surveillance File. Wilmington, Del.: Scholarly Resources, 1978.

Marcus Garvey: FBI Investigation File. Wilmington, Del.: Scholarly Resources, 1979.

The Martin Luther King, Jr., FBI File. Edited by David J. Garrow. Frederick, Md.: University Publications of America, 1983.

Official and Confidential Files of FBI Director J. Edgar Hoover. Wilmington, Del.: Scholarly Resources, 1988.

FEDERAL BUREAU OF INVESTIGATION (FBI) INVESTIGATIVE FILES

	Sedition
14–1187	Ethiopian Pacific Movement, Inc.
	Selective Service Act
25–33007	Allah Temple of Islam
25–86808	Moorish Science Temple of America
	Treason
61–4960	American Negro Labor Congress
61–6728	NAACP
61–6728	League of Struggle for Negro Rights
61–6728	National Negro Congress
61–7563	Moorish Science Temple of America/C. Kirkman Bey
	Espionage
65–562	Development of Our Own/Naka Nakane
65–4306	Black Dragon Society
65–4370	Japanese Espionage Activities
65–25889	Moorish Science Temple of America
65–30721	Development of Our Own/Chicago/Detroit
65–40879	Pacific Movement of the Eastern World among Negroes/General Lee Butler
	Domestic Security
100–3	CPUSA Membership
100–135	Foreign-Inspired Agitation Among American Negroes
100–6582	Allah Temple of Islam
100–20076	*The Black Dispatch*
100–31159	*The Pittsburgh Courier*
100–56894	Ethiopian Pacific Movement/Robert Jordan
100–88143	Universal Negro Improvement Association
100–95014	March on Washington Movement
100–109061	People's Committee (New York)
100–115471	Negro Labor Victory Committee
100–122319	*The Chicago Defender*
100–122319	*Michigan Chronicle*
100–124410	Peace Movement of Ethiopia
100–129623	Colored American National Organization/Washington Park Forum/Brotherhood of Liberty for the Black People of America
100–161936	Addeynue Allahe Universal Arabic Association

100–163965	Negro Domestics, loss of
100–211520	Racial Controversies in Defense Plants
100–236342	Black Dragon Society
100–247094	Addeyune Allahe Universal Arabic Association, Inc.

FEDERAL BUREAU OF INVESTIGATION CONFIDENTIAL MONOGRAPHS

Survey of Racial Conditions in the United States (August 1942)

Japanism and Japanese in the United States (October 1943)

The Communist Party and the Negro, 1919–1952 (February 1952)

The Communist Party and the Negro, 1953–1956 (October 1956)

FEDERAL BUREAU OF INVESTIGATION REPORTS

Franklin D. Roosevelt Library, Hyde Park, New York, Franklin D. Roosevelt Papers, Official File 10B, FBI Reports, No. 2420.

MILITARY INTELLIGENCE DIVISION (MID) REPORTS

The Communist Party and The Negro Problem, Supplement #7 (July 12, 1943)

Current Activities of The Communist Party in regard to The Negro Problem, Supplement #9 (April 3, 1944)

Ahamadujya Religious Movement (August 21, 1942)

Council on African Affairs (September 12, 1942)

Interracial Club (August 13, 1942)

Moorish Science Temple of America (Moorish Holy Temple of Science) (February 26, 1943)

Ethiopian Pacific Movement (December 17, 1942)

Ethiopian Pacific Movement (January 19, 1942)

Japanese Racial Agitation Among American Negroes (April 15, 1942)

March on Washington Movement (March 18, 1943)

Moslem Japanese and Negro Activities in Eastern United States (August 26, 1942)

Negro Activities Series (November 10, 1942)

The Negro in the Area of the Western Defense Command (July 10, 1943)

Negro Newspaper Survey (September 17, 1943)

Negro Pacific Movement (October 6, 1942)

The Negro Press, Negro Activities in New England Series 7 (September 15, 1942)

The Negro Press: Labor and the Negro, Negro Activities Series 11 (November 10, 1942)

The Negro Problem and Its Factors (November 9, 1942)

Negro Situation in the United States (July 13, 1942)

Pittsburgh Courier: Summary of Information (December 30, 1942)

Proposed Mutiny of Negro Troops (August 30, 1944)

Racial Agitation (August 27, 1942)

Racial Conflict in the South (July 2, 1942)

Recent Trends in Negro Leadership (April 23, 1942)

Report on Activities of the Negro Pacific Movement (October 6, 1942)

Survey of Negro Publications (August 16, 1943)

Survey Report, Negro Situation, Representative Cities (August 30, 1943)

OFFICE OF NAVAL INTELLIGENCE (ONI) REPORTS

Japanese Intelligence and Propaganda in the United States during 1941 (December 4, 1941)

Topical Study Memorandum on Japanese-Negro Collaboration (September 13, 1943)

Topical Study Memorandum on Negro Agitation in the Ninth Naval District, Report no. 4, "Evidences of Racial Tension in the Ninth Naval District" (February 28, 1944)

Topical Study Memorandum on the Negro Press (August 1943)

U.S. OFFICE OF WAR INFORMATION (Office of Emergency Management) BUREAU OF INTELLIGENCE REPORTS

Negroes in a Democracy at War (Survey of Intelligence Materials, no. 25, May 27, 1942)

Opinions about Inter-Racial Tension (Division of Research, Report no. C12, August 25, 1943)

Opinions in Detroit Thirty-Six Hours After the Race Riots (Bureau of Special Services, Surveys Division, Special Memorandum no. 64, June 30, 1943)

Rumors on Minority Groups, December 1942 (Special Services Division, Memorandum no. 39, February 11, 1943)

SPECIAL WAR POLICIES UNIT (War Division, DEPARTMENT OF JUSTICE) REPORTS

Memorandum Re: Negro Press (ca. October 17, 1942; October 26, 1942; ca. November 20, 1942; December 21, 1942; February 17, 1943; February 25, 1943; March 18, 1943)

BOOKS AND MONOGRAPHS

Anderson, Jervis. *A. Philip Randolph: A Biographical Portrait.* Berkeley: University of California Press, 1973, 1986.

Asher, Robert, and Charles Stephenson, eds. *Labor Divided: Race and Ethnicity in United States Labor Struggles, 1835–1960.* Albany: State University of New York Press, 1990.

Baldwin, James. *Notes of a Native Son.* Boston: Beacon Press, 1955.

Bartley, Numan V. *The Rise of Massive Resistance: Race and Politics in the South during the 1950's.* Baton Rouge: Louisiana State University Press, 1969.

Belknap, Michael R. *Cold War Political Justice: The Smith Act, the Communist Party, and American Civil Liberties.* Westport, Conn.: Greenwood Press, 1977.

Bernstein, Irving. *Turbulent Years: A History of the American Worker, 1933–1941.* Boston: Houghton Mifflin, 1969.

Biddle, Francis. *In Brief Authority.* Garden City, N.Y.: Doubleday, 1962.

Blackstock, Nelson. *COINTELPRO: The FBI's Secret War on Political Freedom.* 3d ed. New York: Pathfinder Books, 1988.

Blantz, Thomas E. *A Priest in Public Service: Francis J. Haas and the New Deal.* Notre Dame: University of Notre Dame Press, 1982.

Blum, John Morton. *V Was for Victory: Politics and American Culture During World War II.* New York: Harcourt Brace Jovanovich, 1976.

Broderick, Francis L. *W. E. B. Du Bois: Negro Leader in a Time of Crisis.* Stanford: Stanford University Press, 1959.

Brody, David. *Workers in Industrial America: Essays on the Twentieth Century Struggle.* 2d ed. New York: Oxford University Press, 1993.

Browder, Earl. *Victory—and After.* New York: International Publishers, 1942.

Brown, Earl. *Why Race Riots? Lessons from Detroit.* New York: Public Affairs Committee, 1944.

Brown, Earl, and George R. Leighton. *The Negro and the War.* New York: Public Affairs Committee, 1942.

Buchanan, A. Russell. *Black Americans in World War II.* Santa Barbara, Calif.: Clio Books, 1977.

Buni, Andrew. *Robert L. Vann of the Pittsburgh* Courier. Pittsburgh: University of Pittsburgh Press, 1974.

Cantor, Louis. *A Prologue to the Protest Movement: The Missouri Sharecropper Roadside Demonstration of 1939.* Durham, N.C.: Duke University Press, 1969.

Capeci, Dominic J., Jr. *The Harlem Riot of 1943.* Philadelphia: Temple University Press, 1977.

———. Race Relations in Wartime Detroit: The Sojourner Truth Housing Controversy of 1942. Philadelphia: Temple University Press, 1984.

Capeci, Dominic J., Jr., and Martha Wilkerson. *Layered Violence: The Detroit Rioters of 1943.* Jackson, Miss.: University Press of Mississippi, 1991.

Carr, Robert K. *Federal Protection of Civil Rights: Quest for a Sword.* Ithaca, N.Y.: Cornell University Press, 1947.

Carroll, Peter N. *The Odyssey of the Abraham Lincoln Brigade: Americans in the Spanish Civil War.* Stanford: Stanford University Press, 1994.

Carson, Clayborne. *Malcolm X: The FBI File.* New York: Carroll & Graf, 1991.

Cayton, Horace, and George S. Mitchell. *Black Workers and the New Unions.* Chapel Hill, N.C.: University of North Carolina Press, 1939.

Churchill, Ward, and Jim Vander Wall, eds. *The COINTELPRO Papers: Documents from the FBI's Secret Wars Against Domestic Dissent.* Boston: South End Press, 1990.

Cochran, Bert. *Labor and Communism: The Conflict that Shaped American Unions.* Princeton, N.J.: Princeton University Press, 1977.

Color: The Unfinished Business of Democracy. Special Issue in "Calling America" Series. *Survey Graphic,* 31, no. 1 (November 1942): 453–542.

Couto, Richard A. *Lifting the Veil: A Political History of Struggles for Emancipation.* Knoxville: University of Tennessee Press, 1993.

Dalfiume, Richard M. *Desegregation of the U.S. Armed Forces: Fighting on Two Fronts, 1939–1953.* Columbia: University of Missouri Press, 1969.

Donner, Frank J. *The Age of Surveillance: The Aims and Methods of America's Political Intelligence System.* New York: Alfred A. Knopf, 1980.

Du Bois, W. E. B. *Black Reconstruction in America: An Essay Toward a History of the Part Which Black Folk Played in the Attempt to Reconstruct Democracy in America, 1860–1880*. New York: Harcourt, Brace, 1935.

Durr, Robert. *The Negro Press: Its Character, Development and Function*. Jackson, Miss.: Mississippi Division, Southern Regional Council, 1947.

Elliff, John T. *The Reform of FBI Intelligence Operations*. Princeton, N. J.: Princeton University Press, 1979.

Ellison, Ralph. *Shadow and Act*. New York: Random House, 1964.

Fine, Sidney. *Frank Murphy: The Washington Years*. Ann Arbor: University of Michigan Press, 1984.

Finkle, Lee. *Forum for Protest: The Black Press During World War II*. Rutherford, N.J.: Fairleigh Dickinson University Press, 1975.

Foner, Philip S., and Ronald L. Lewis, eds. *The Black Worker from the Founding of the CIO to the AFL-CIO Merger, 1936–1955*. Vol. VII of *The Black Worker: A Documentary History from Colonial Times to the Present*. Philadelphia: Temple University Press, 1983.

Foster, William Z. *History of the Communist Party of the United States*. New York: International Publishers, 1952.

Freidel, Frank B. *F.D.R. and the South*. Baton Rouge: Louisiana State University Press, 1965.

Friedly, Michael, and David Gallen. *Martin Luther King, Jr.: The FBI File*. New York: Carroll & Graf, 1993.

Gabler, Neal. *Winchell: Gossip, Power and the Culture of Celebrity*. New York: Alfred A. Knopf, 1994.

Garfinkel, Herbert. *When Negroes March: The March on Washington Movement in the Organizational Politics for FEPC*. New York: Free Press, 1959.

Garrow, David J. *The FBI and Martin Luther King, Jr.: From "Solo" to Memphis*. New York: W. W. Norton, 1981.

Gentry, Curt. *J. Edgar Hoover: The Man and the Secrets*. New York: W. W. Norton, 1991.

Glaberman, Martin. *Wartime Strikes: The Struggle Against the No-Strike Pledge in the UAW During World War II*. Detroit: Bewick Editions, 1980.

Goldfield, Michael. *The Decline of Organized Labor in the United States*. Chicago: University of Chicago Press, 1989.

Goldstein, Robert. *Political Repression in Modern America*. Cambridge, Mass.: Schenkman, 1978.

Griffith, Barbara. *The Crisis of American Labor: Operation Dixie and the Defeat of the CIO*. Philadelphia: Temple University Press, 1988.

Griffler, Keith P. *What Price Alliance? Black Radicals Confront White Labor, 1918–1938*. New York: Garland Publishing, 1994.

Halperin, Morton H., et al. *The Lawless States: The Crimes of the U.S. Intelligence Agencies*. New York: Penguin Books, 1976.

Harris, Joseph E. *African-American Reactions to War in Ethiopia, 1936–1941*. Baton Rouge: Louisiana State University Press, 1994.

Harris, Robert, Nyota Harris, and Grandassa Harris, eds. *Carlos Cooks and Black Nationalism from Garvey to Malcolm*. Dover, Mass.: Majority Press, 1992.

Honey, Michael K. *Southern Labor and Black Civil Rights: Organizing Memphis Workers.* Urbana: University of Illinois Press, 1993.

Horne, Gerald. *Black & Red: W. E. B. Du Bois and the Afro-American Response to the Cold War 1944–1963.* Albany: State University of New York Press, 1986.

———. *Black Liberation/Red Scare: Ben Davis and the Communist Party.* Newark: University of Delaware Press, 1994.

Howe, Irving, and Lewis Coser. *The American Communist Party: A Critical History, 1919–1957.* Boston: Beacon Press, 1957.

Hughes, Langston. *Selected Poems.* New York: Alfred A. Knopf, 1959.

Isserman, Maurice. *Which Side Were You On? The American Communist Party During the Second World War.* Urbana: University of Illinois Press, 1982.

Jackson, Walter A. *Gunnar Myrdal and America's Conscience: Social Engineering and Racial Liberalism, 1938–1987.* Chapel Hill: University of North Carolina Press, 1990.

Janken, Kenneth Robert. *Rayford W. Logan and the Dilemma of the African-American Intellectual.* Amherst: University of Massachusetts Press, 1993.

Johanningsmeier, Edward P. *Forging American Communism: The Life of William Z. Foster.* Princeton: Princeton University Press, 1994.

Johnson, Charles S. *To Stem This Tide: A Survey of Racial Tension Areas in the United States.* Boston: Pilgrim Press, 1943.

Johnson, Loch K. *A Season of Inquiry: The Senate Intelligence Investigation.* Lexington: University Press of Kentucky, 1985.

Keller, William W. *The Liberals and J. Edgar Hoover: Rise and Fall of a Domestic Intelligence State.* Princeton: Princeton University Press, 1989.

Kelley, Robin D. G. *Hammer and Hoe: Alabama Communists During the Great Depression.* Chapel Hill: University of North Carolina Press, 1990.

Kinnamon, Kenneth, and Michel Fabre, eds. *Conversations with Richard Wright.* Jackson: University Press of Mississippi, 1993.

Kirby, John B. *Black Americans in the Roosevelt Era.* Knoxville: University of Tennessee Press, 1980.

Klehr, Harvey. *The Heyday of American Communism: The Depression Decade.* New York: Basic Books, 1984.

Klehr, Harvey, and John Earl Haynes. *The American Communist Movement: Storming Heaven Itself.* Boston: Twayne, 1992.

Kovel, Joel. *Red Hunting in the Promised Land: Anticommunism and the Making of America.* New York: Basic Books, 1994.

Latham, Earl. *The Communist Controversy in Washington: From the New Deal to McCarthy.* Cambridge, Mass.: Harvard University Press, 1966.

Lee, Alfred McClung, and Norman Daymond Humphrey. *Race Riot.* New York: Dryden Press, 1943.

Lee, Ulysses. *The Employment of Negro Troops. United States Army in World War II. Special Studies.* Washington, D.C.: Office of the Chief of Military History, United States Army, 1966.

Leeming, David. *James Baldwin: A Biography.* New York: Alfred A. Knopf, 1994.

Lewis, Earl. *In Their Own Interests: Race, Class, and Power in Twentieth-Century Norfolk, Virginia.* Berkeley: University of California Press, 1991.

Lichtenstein, Nelson. *Labor's War at Home: The CIO in World War II.* New York: Cambridge University Press, 1982.

Logan, Rayford W., ed. *What the Negro Wants.* Chapel Hill: University of North Carolina Press, 1944.

Lowenthal, Max. *The Federal Bureau of Investigation.* New York: Sloane Associates, 1950.

Lynch, Hollis R. *Black American Radicals and the Liberation of Africa: The Council on African Affairs, 1937–1955.* Ithaca, N.Y.: Africana Studies and Research Center, Cornell University, 1978.

Macdonald, Nancy, and Dwight Macdonald. *The War's Greatest Scandal! The Story of Jim Crow in Uniform.* New York: March on Washington Movement, 1942.

McCoy, Donald R., and Richard T. Ruetten. *Quest and Response: Minority Rights and the Truman Administration.* Lawrence: University Press of Kansas, 1973.

McMillen, Neil R. *Dark Journey: Black Mississippians in the Age of Jim Crow.* Urbana: University of Illinois Press, 1990.

McWilliams, Carey. *Brothers Under the Skin.* Boston: Little, Brown, 1943.

Malcolm X. *The Autobiography of Malcolm X.* New York: Grove Press, 1965.

Marable, Manning. *W. E. B. Du Bois: Black Radical Democrat.* Boston: Twayne, 1986.

Mazon, Mauricio. *The Zoot-Suit Riots: The Psychology of Symbolic Annihilation.* Austin: University of Texas Press, 1984.

Meier, August, and Elliott Rudwick. *Black Detroit and the Rise of the UAW.* New York: Oxford University Press, 1979.

———. *CORE: A Study in the Civil Rights Movement, 1942–1968.* New York: Oxford University Press, 1973.

Moore, Jesse Thomas, Jr. *A Search for Equality: The National Urban League, 1910–1961.* University Park: Pennsylvania State University Press, 1981.

Morgan, Richard E. *Domestic Intelligence: Monitoring Dissent in America.* Austin: University of Texas Press, 1980.

Murray, Robert K. *Red Scare: A Study in National Hysteria, 1919–1920.* Minneapolis: University of Minnesota Press, 1955.

Myrdal, Gunnar. *An American Dilemma.* 2 vol. New York: Harper & Row, 1944.

Naison, Mark. *Communists in Harlem During the Depression.* Evergreen ed. New York: Grove Press, 1984.

Northrup, Herbert R. *Organized Labor and the Negro.* New York: Harper and Brothers, 1944.

Odum, Howard W. *Race and Rumors of Race: Challenge to American Crisis.* Chapel Hill: University of North Carolina Press, 1943.

O'Reilly, Kenneth. *Black Americans: The FBI Files.* Edited by David Gallen. New York: Carroll & Graf, 1994.

———. *Hoover and the Un-Americans: The FBI, HUAC, and the Red Menace.* Philadelphia: Temple University Press, 1983.

———. *"Racial Matters": The FBI's Secret File on Black America, 1960–1972.* New York: Free Press, 1989.

Ottley, Roi. *'New World A-coming': Inside Black America.* Boston: Houghton Mifflin, 1943.

Pfeffer, Paula F. *A. Philip Randolph: Pioneer of the Civil Rights Movement.* Baton Rouge: Louisiana State University Press, 1990.

Polenberg, Richard. *War and Society: The United States, 1941–1945*. Philadelphia: Lippincott, 1972.

Powell, Adam Clayton, Jr. *Marching Blacks*. New York: Dial Press, 1945.

Powers, Richard Gid. *G-Men: Hoover's FBI in American Popular Culture*. Carbondale, Ill.: Southern Illinois University Press, 1983.

———. *Secrecy and Power: The Life of J. Edgar Hoover*. New York: Free Press, 1987.

Rampersad, Arnold. *The Art and Imagination of W. E. B. Du Bois*. New York: Schocken Books, 1976, 1990.

Rampersad, Arnold, and David Roessel, eds. *The Collected Poems of Langston Hughes*. New York: Alfred A. Knopf, 1994.

Record, Wilson. *The Negro and the Communist Party*. Chapel Hill: University of North Carolina Press, 1951.

Reddick, L. D., ed. *The Negro in the North During Wartime*. Special issue of *The Journal of Educational Sociology*, vol. 17, no. 5 (1944): 257–319.

Rose, Arnold M. *The Negro's Morale: Group Identification and Protest*. Minneapolis: University of Minnesota Press, 1949.

Rosengarten, Theodore. *All God's Dangers: The Life of Nate Shaw*. New York: Vintage Books, 1974.

Ross, Caroline, and Ken Lawrence. *J. Edgar Hoover's Detention Plan: The Politics of Repression in the United States, 1939–1976*. Jackson, Miss.: American Friends Service Committee, 1978.

Ross, Malcolm. *All Manner of Men*. New York: Reynal & Hitchcock, 1948.

Rowan, Carl Thomas. *Dream Makers, Dream Breakers: The World of Justice Thurgood Marshall*. Boston: Little, Brown, 1993.

Ruchames, Louis. *Race, Jobs, and Politics: The Story of FEPC*. New York: Columbia University Press, 1953.

Schlesinger, Arthur M. *The Age of Roosevelt. Vol. 2: The Politics of Upheaval*. Boston: Houghton Mifflin, 1960.

Schuyler, George S. *Ethiopian Stories*. Compiled and edited by Robert A. Hill. Boston: Northeastern University Press, 1994.

Scott, William R. *The Sons of Sheba's Race: African-Americans and the Italo-Ethiopian War, 1935–1941*. Bloomington: Indiana University Press, 1993.

Shapiro, Herbert. *White Violence and Black Response: From Reconstruction to Montgomery*. Amherst: University of Massachusetts Press, 1988.

Shogan, Robert, and Tom Craig. *The Detroit Race Riot: A Study in Violence*. Philadelphia: Chilton Books, 1964.

Silberman, Charles E. *Crisis in Black and White*. New York: Random House, 1964.

Sitkoff, Harvard. *A New Deal for Blacks: The Emergence of Civil Rights as a National Issue. Vol I: The Depression Decade*. New York: Oxford University Press, 1978.

Sorrentino, Frank M. *Ideological Warfare: The FBI's Path Toward Power*. Port Washington, N.Y.: Associated Faculty Press, 1985.

Sosna, Morton. *In Search of the Silent South: Southern Liberals and the Race Issue*. New York: Columbia University Press, 1977.

Sternsher, Bernard, ed. *The Negro in Depression and War: Prelude to Revolution, 1930–1945.* Chicago: Quadrangle Books, 1969.

Strickland, William. *Malcolm X: Make It Plain.* New York: Viking, 1994.

Sullivan, William C. *The Bureau: My Thirty Years in Hoover's FBI.* New York: W. W. Norton, 1979.

Summers, Anthony. *Official and Confidential: The Secret Life of J. Edgar Hoover.* New York: Pocket Books, 1994.

Sundquist, Eric J. *Contexts for Ralph Ellison's* Invisible Man. Boston: Bedford Books, 1995.

Theoharis, Athan. *Spying on Americans: Political Surveillance from Hoover to the Huston Plan.* Philadelphia: Temple University Press, 1978.

Theoharis, Athan, ed. *From the Secret Files of J. Edgar Hoover.* Chicago: Ivan R. Dee, 1991.

Theoharis, Athan, and John Stuart Cox. *The Boss: J. Edgar Hoover and the Great American Inquisition.* Philadelphia: Temple University Press, 1988.

Thorne, Christopher. *Allies of a Kind: The United States, Britain, and the War Against Japan, 1941–1945.* London: Hamish Hamilton, 1978.

———. *The Issue of War: States, Societies, and the Far Eastern Conflict of 1941–1945.* London: Hamish Hamilton, 1985.

Trotter, Joe William, Jr., ed. *The Great Migration in Historical Perspective: New Dimensions of Race, Class, and Gender.* Bloomington: Indiana University Press, 1991.

Turner, William W. *Hoover's FBI: The Men and the Myth.* Los Angeles: Sherbourne Press, 1970.

Tushnet, Mark V. *Making Civil Rights Law: Thurgood Marshall and the Supreme Court, 1936–1961.* New York: Oxford University Press, 1994.

Ungar, Sanford J. *FBI.* Boston: Little, Brown, 1975.

Ware, Gilbert. *William Hastie: Grace Under Pressure.* New York: Oxford University Press, 1984.

Washburn, Patrick S. *A Question of Sedition: The Federal Government's Investigation of the Black Press During World War II.* New York: Oxford University Press, 1986.

Watters, Pat, and Stephen Gillers, eds. *Investigating the FBI.* Garden City, N.Y.: Doubleday, 1973.

Watts, Jerry Gafio. *Heroism and the Black Intellectual: Ralph Ellison, Politics, and the Afro-American Intellectual Life.* Chapel Hill, N.C.: University of North Carolina Press, 1994.

Wedlock, Lunnabelle. *The Reaction of Negro Publications and Organizations to German Anti-Semitism.* Howard University Studies in the Social Sciences, 3, no. 2. Washington, D.C.: Graduate School, Howard University, 1942.

Weiss, Nancy J. *Farewell to the Party of Lincoln: Black Politics in the Age of FDR* (Princeton: Princeton University Press, 1983.

White, Walter. *A Man Called White: The Autobiography of Walter White.* New York: Viking Press, 1948.

———. *How Far the Promised Land?* New York: Viking Press, 1955.

Whitehead, Don. *The FBI Story.* New York: Random House, 1956.

Wilson, Joseph F. *Tearing Down the Color Bar: A Documentary History of the Brotherhood of Sleeping Car Porters.* New York: Columbia University Press, 1990.

Wise, David. *The American Police State: The Government against the People.* New York: Random House, 1976.

Wolseley, Roland E. *The Black Press, U.S.A.* Ames: Iowa State University Press, 1971.

Wright, Richard. *Early Works*. New York: Library of America, 1991.

Wynn, Neil A. *The Afro-American and The Second World War*. New York: Holmes & Meier, 1975.

Yinger, J. Milton. *A Minority Group in American Society*. New York: McGraw-Hill, 1965.

Zangrando, Robert L. *The NAACP Crusade Against Lynching, 1909–1950*. Philadelphia: Temple University Press, 1980.

Zieger, Robert H. *John L. Lewis: Labor Leader*. Boston: Twayne, 1988.

Zieger, Robert H., ed. *Organized Labor in the Twentieth-Century South*. Knoxville: University of Tennessee Press, 1991.

ESSAYS AND PAPERS

Anderson, James D. "Black Liberalism at the Crossroads: The Role of the *Crisis*, 1934–1953." *Crisis*, 87, no. 9 (1980): 339–46.

Anderson, Jervis. "A. Philip Randolph, 1889–1979." *Labor's Heritage*, 4, no. 3 (1992): 22–33.

Arnesen, Eric. "The African-American Working Class in the Jim Crow Era." *International Labor and Working-Class History*, no. 41 (Spring 1992): 58–75.

Bailey, Beth, and David Farber. "The 'Double V' Campaign in World War II Hawaii: African Americans, Racial Ideology, and Federal Power." *Journal of Social History*, 26, no. 4 (Summer 1993): 817–43.

Baldwin, James. "Me and My House." *Harper's Magazine*, 211 (November 1955): 54–61. Reprinted as "Notes of a Native Son," pp. 85–114 in *Notes of a Native Son*. Boston: Beacon Press, 1955.

Belknap, Michael R. "The Mechanics of Repression: J. Edgar Hoover, the Bureau of Investigation, and the Radicals, 1917–1925." *Crime and Social Justice*, 7 (Spring–Summer 1977): 49–58.

Bell, W. Y., Jr. "The Negro Warrior's Home Front." *Phylon*, 5 (Third Quarter 1944): 271–78.

Blackwood, George D. "The Sit-Down Strike in the Thirties." *South Atlantic Quarterly*, 55, no. 4 (1956): 438–48.

Bond, Horace Mann. "Should the Negro Care Who Wins the War?" *Annals of the American Academy of Political Science and Social Science*, 223 (September 1942): 81–84.

Brown, Earl. "The Truth About the Detroit Riot." *Harper's Magazine*, 187, no. 1122 (November 1943): 487–98.

Burran, James A. "Urban Racial Violence in the South during World War II: A Comparative Overview," pp. 167–77. In Walter J. Fraser, Jr., and Winfred B. Moore, Jr., *From the Old South to the New: Essays on the Transitional South*. Westport, Conn.: Greenwood Press, 1981.

Capeci, Dominic J., Jr. "The Lynching of Cleo Wright: Federal Protection of Constitutional Rights During World War II." *Journal of American History*, 72, no. 4 (March 1986): 859–87.

Capeci, Dominic J., Jr., and Martha Wilkerson. "The Detroit Rioters of 1943: A Reinterpretation." *Michigan Historical Review*, 16, no. 1 (Spring 1990): 49–72.

Catledge, Turner. "Behind Our Menacing Race Problem." *New York Times Magazine*, (August 8, 1943): 7, 15.

Cayton, Horace R. "Fighting for White Folks?" *Nation* (September 26, 1942): 267–70.

———. "The Negro's Challenge." *Nation*, 157, no. 1 (July 3, 1943): 10–12.

Chibnall, Steve. "Whistle and Zoot: The Changing Meaning of a Suit of Clothes." *History Workshop Journal*, no. 20 (Autumn 1985): 56–81.

Clark, Kenneth B. "Morale of the Negro on the Home Front: World Wars I and II." *Journal of Negro Education*, 12, no. 3 (Summer 1943): 417–28.

Clark, Kenneth B., and James Barker. "The Zoot Effect in Personality: A Race Riot Participant." *Journal of Abnormal and Social Psychology*, 40, no. 2 (April 1945): 143–48.

Cosgrove, Stuart. "The Zoot-Suit and Style Warfare." *History Workshop Journal*, no. 18 (Autumn 1984): 77–91.

Critchlow, Donald T. "Communist Unions and Racism: A Comparative Study of the Response of the United Electrical Workers and the National Maritime Union to the Black Question During World War II." *Labor History*, 17, no. 2 (1976): 230–44.

Current, Gloster B. "Walter White and the Fight for Freedom." *Crisis*, 76, no. 3 (1969): 113–19, 134–35.

Dalfiume, Richard M. "The 'Forgotten Years' of the Negro Revolution." *Journal of American History*, 55, no. 1 (1968): 90–106.

Daniel, Pete. "Going among Strangers: Southern Reactions to World War II." *Journal of American History*, 77, no. 3 (December 1990): 113–32.

David, Martin. "Investigating the FBI." *Policy Review*, 18 (Fall 1981): 113–32.

Davis, Ralph N. "The Negro Newspapers and the War." *Sociology and Social Research*, 27, no. 5 (May–June 1943): 373–80.

Dudley, J. Wayne. " 'Hate' Organizations of the 1940s: The Columbians, Inc." *Phylon*, 42, no. 3 (Fall 1981): 262–74.

Dyson, Lowell K. "The Southern Tenant Farmers Union and Depression Politics." *Political Science Quarterly*, 88, no. 2 (1973): 230–52.

Elliff, John T. "Aspects of Federal Civil Rights Enforcement: The Justice Department and the FBI, 1939–1964." *Perspectives in American History*, 5 (1971): 605–73.

Ellis, Mark. "Federal Surveillance of Black Americans During the First World War." *Immigrants and Minorities*, 12, no. 1 (1993): 1–20.

Ellison, Ralph. "The Way It Is." *New Masses*, 45 (October 20, 1942): 9–11.

Ellison, Ralph. Editorial comment. *Negro Quarterly*, 1 (Winter 1943): 295–302.

Eversole, Theodore W. "Benjamin J. Davis, Jr. (1903–1964): From Republican Atlanta Lawyer to Harlem Communist Councilman." *Journal of the Afro-American Historical and Genealogical Society*, 8, no. 1 (1987): 27–33.

Finkle, Lee. "The Conservative Aims of Militant Rhetoric: Black Protest During World War II." *Journal of American History*, 60, no. 3 (December 1973): 692–713.

Ford, Nick Aaron. "What Negroes Are Fighting For." *Vital Speeches of the Day*, 9, no. 8 (February 1943): 240–42.

Franklin, John Hope. "Their War and Mine." *Journal of American History,* 77 (September 1990): 576–79.

Frazier, E. Franklin. "Ethnic and Minority Groups in Wartime, with Special Reference to the Negro." *American Journal of Sociology,* 48, no. 3 (November 1942): 369–77.

Fregoso, R. L. "The Representation of Cultural-Identity in Zoot Suit." *Theory and Society,* 22, no. 5 (October 1993): 659–74.

Gerstle, Gary. "Working-Class Racism: Broaden the Focus." *International Labor and Working-Class History,* no. 44 (Fall 1993): 33–40.

Gilfoyle, Timothy J. "The Moral Origins of Political Surveillance: The Preventive Society in New York City, 1867–1918." *American Quarterly,* 38, no. 4 (Fall 1986): 637–52.

Gill, Glenda E. "Careerist and Casualty: The Rise and Fall of Canada Lee." *Freedomways,* 21, no. 1 (1981): 15–27.

Goldfield, Michael. "The Decline of the Communist Party and the Black Question in the U.S.: Harry Haywood's *Black Bolshevik.*" *Review of Radical Political Economy,* 12, no. 1 (1980): 44–63.

———. "Race and the CIO: The Possibilities for Racial Egalitarianism During the 1930s and 1940s." *International Labor and Working-Class History,* no. 44 (Fall 1993): 1–32.

Graves, John Temple. "The Southern Negro and the War Crisis." *Virginia Quarterly Review,* 18, no. 4 (Autumn 1942): 500–17.

Hachey, Thomas E. "The Wages of War: A British Commentary on Life in Detroit in July, 1943." *Michigan History,* 59, no. 4 (Winter 1975): 227–38.

———. "Walter White and the American Negro Soldier in World War II: A Diplomatic Dilemma for Britain." *Phylon,* 39, no. 3 (1978): 241–49.

Harris, William H. "A. Philip Randolph as a Charismatic Leader, 1925–1941." *Journal of Negro History,* 64, no. 4 (1979): 301–15.

Hill, Robert A. " 'The Foremost Radical Among His Race': Marcus Garvey and the Black Scare, 1918–1921." *Prologue: Journal of the National Archives,* 16, no. 4 (Winter 1984): 215–31.

———. "Racial and Radical: Cyril V. Briggs, *The Crusader Magazine,* and the African Blood Brotherhood, 1918–1922." Introduction to *The Crusader Magazine.* New York: Garland Publishing, 1987.

Hill, Robert A., Michael W. Fitzgerald, and Michael Furmanovsky. "The Comintern and American Blacks, 1919–1943," pp. 841–54 in *The Marcus Garvey and Universal Negro Improvement Association Papers,* edited by Robert A. Hill. Vol. 5. Los Angeles: University of California Press, 1986.

Himes, Chester B. "Zoot Riots Are Race Riots." *Crisis,* 50 (July 1943): 200–201, 222.

Honey, Michael. "Labour Leadership and Civil Rights in the South: A Case Study of the CIO in Memphis, 1935–1955." *Studies in History and Politics,* 5 (1986): 97–120.

———. "Operation Dixie: Labor and Civil Rights in the Postwar South." *Mississippi Quarterly,* 45, no. 4 (1992): 439–52.

———. "The Popular Front in the American South: The View from Memphis." *International Labor and Working-Class History,* no. 30 (1986): 44–58.

Horwitz, Gerry. "Benjamin Davis, Jr., and the American Communist Party: A Study in Race and Politics." *UCLA Historical Journal,* no. 4 (1983): 92–107.

Johnson, Guion Griffis. "The Impact of the War Upon the Negro." *Journal of Negro Education,* 10 (July 1941): 596–611.

Keeran, Roger R. "Everything for Victory: Communist Influence in the Auto Industry During World War II." *Science and Society*, 43, no. 1 (1979): 1–28.

Kelley, Robin D. G. "The Riddle of the Zoot: Malcolm Little and Black Cultural Politics During World War II," pp. 155–82, in *Malcolm X: In Our Own Image*. Edited by Joe Wood. New York: St. Martin's Press, 1992.

———. " 'This Ain't Ethiopia, But It'll Do'," pp. 5–57 in Danny Duncan Collum, ed., *African Americans in the Spanish Civil War: "This Ain't Ethiopia, But It'll Do."* New York: G. K. Hall, 1992.

———. " 'We Are Not What We Seem': Rethinking Black Working-Class Opposition in the Jim Crow South." *Journal of American History*, 80, no. 1 (June 1993): 75–112.

Kellogg, Peter J. "Civil Rights Consciousness in the 1940s." *Historian*, 42, no. 1 (November 1979): 18–41.

Kilson, Martin. "Politics and Identity among Black Intellectuals." *Dissent*, 28, no. 3 (1981): 339–49.

Klehr, Harvey, and William Thompson. "Self-Determination in the Black Belt: Origins of a Communist Policy." *Labor History*, 30, no. 3 (1989): 354–66.

Koppes, Clayton R., and Gregory D. Black. "Blacks, Loyalty, and Motion-Picture Propaganda in World War II." *Journal of American History*, 73, no. 2 (September 1986): 383–406.

Kornweibel, Theodore, Jr. "Apathy and Dissent: Black America's Negative Responses to World War I." *South Atlantic Quarterly*, 80 (Summer 1981): 322–38.

———. "Black on Black: The FBI's First Negro Informants and Agents and the Investigation of Black Radicalism During the Red Scare." *Criminal Justice History*, 8 (1987): 121–36.

Korstad, Robert. "The Possibilities for Racial Egalitarianism: Context Matters." *International Labor and Working-Class History*, no. 44 (Fall 1993): 41–44.

Korstad, Robert, and Nelson Lichtenstein. "Opportunities Found and Lost: Labor, Radicals, and the Early Civil Rights Movement." *Journal of American History*, 75, no. 3 (December 1988): 786–811.

Langlois, Janet L. "The Belle Isle Bridge Incident: Legend Dialectic and Semiotic System in the 1943 Detroit Race Riots." Journal of American Folklore, 96 (1983): 183–99.

Lee, Alfred McClung. "Subversive Individuals of Minority Status." *Annals of the American Academy of Political Science and Social Science*, 223 (September 1942): 162–72

Lichtenstein, Nelson. "Another Time, Another Place: Blacks, Radicals and Rank and File Militancy in Auto in the 30s and 40s." *Radical America*, 6, nos. 1–2 (1982): 131–37.

Lively, Adam. "Continuity and Radicalism in American Black Nationalist Thought, 1914–1929." *Journal of American Studies*, 18, no. 2 (1984): 207–35.

Locke, Alain. "The Unfinished Business of Democracy." *Survey Graphic*, 31, no. 11 (November 1942): 455–59.

Lott, Eric. "Double V, Double-Time: Bebop's Politics of Style." *Callaloo*, 11, no. 3 (Summer 1988): 597–605.

Lynch, Hollis R. "Pan-African Responses in the United States to British Colonial Rule in Africa in the 1940s," pp. 57–86 in *The Transfer of Power in Africa: Decolonization, 1940–1960*. Edited by Prosser Gifford and Wm. Roger Louis. New Haven: Yale University Press, 1982.

McCoy, Donald R. "Towards Equality: Blacks in the United States During the Second World War," pp. 135–53 in *Minorities in History*. Edited by A.C. Hepburn. London: Edward Arnold, 1978.

McCoy, Donald R., and Richard T. Ruetten. "The Civil Rights Movement, 1940–1954." *Midwest Quarterly*, 11, no. 1 (1969): 11–34.

McGuire, Phillip. "Judge Hastie, World War II, and Army Racism." Journal of Negro History, 62, no. 4 (1977): 351–62.

McKnight, Gerald D. "A Harvest of Hate: The FBI's War Against Black Youth—Domestic Intelligence in Memphis, Tennessee." *South Atlantic Quarterly*, 86, no. 1 (Winter 1987): 1–21.

Martin, Charles H. "The International Labor Defense and Black America." *Labor History*, 26, no. 2 (1985): 165–94.

Martin, Louis. "Fifth Column Among Negroes." *Opportunity* (December 1942): 358–60.

Meier, August, and Elliot Rudwick. "Communist Unions and the Black Community: The Case of the Transport Workers Union, 1934–1944." *Labor History*, 23, no. 2 (Spring 1982): 165–97.

———. "How CORE Began." *Social Science Quarterly*, 49, no. 4 (1969): 789–99.

Modell, John, Marc Goulden, and Sigurdur Magnusson. "World War II in the Lives of Black Americans: Some Findings and an Interpretation." *Journal of American History*, 76, no. 3 (December 1989): 838–48.

Muraskin, William. "The Harlem Boycott of 1934: Black Nationalism and the Rise of Labor-Union Consciousness." *Labor History*, 13, no. 3 (Summer 1972): 361–73.

Murray, Florence. "The Negro and Civil Liberties During World War II." *Social Forces*, 24, no. 2 (December 1945): 211–16.

Naison, Mark. "Richard Wright and the Communist Party." *Radical America*, 13, no. 1 (1979): 60–63.

Nelson, Bruce. "Organized Labor and the Struggle for Black Equality in Mobile during World War II." *Journal of American History*, 80, no. 3 (December 1993): 952–89.

Nelson, Daniel. "Origins of the Sit-Down Era: Worker Militancy and Innovation in the Rubber Industry, 1934–38." *Labor History*, 23, no. 2 (1982): 198–225.

Olson, James S. "Organized Black Leadership and Industrial Unionism: The Racial Response, 1936–1945." *Labor History*, 10, no. 3 (Summer 1969): 457–86.

O'Reilly, Kenneth. "A New Deal for the FBI: The Roosevelt Administration, Crime Control, and National Security." *Journal of American History*, 69, no. 3 (December 1982): 638–58.

———. "The Roosevelt Administration and Legislative-Executive Conflict: The FBI vs. the Dies Committee." *Congress and the Presidency*, 10, no. 1 (Spring 1983): 79–93.

Park, Robert E. "Racial Ideologies," pp. 165–184 in *American Society in Wartime*, edited by William Fielding Ogburn. Chicago: University of Chicago Press, 1943.

Patton, Randall L. "The CIO and the Search for a Silent South." *Maryland Historian*, 19, no. 2 (1988): 1–14.

Powell, Adam Clayton, Jr. "Is This a 'White Man's War'?" *Common Sense*, 11, no. 4 (April 1942): 111–13.

Randolph, A. Philip. "Pro-Japanese Activities among Negroes." *Black Worker*, 7, no. 209 (September 1942): 4.

Rosen, Sumner M. "The CIO Era, 1935–55," pp. 188–208 in *The Negro and the American Labor Movement*, edited by Julius Jacobson. Garden City, N.Y.: Anchor/Doubleday, 1968.

Ryon, Roderick M. "An Ambiguous Legacy: Baltimore Blacks and the CIO, 1936–1941." *Journal of Negro History*, 65, no. 1 (1980): 18–33.

Sancton, Thomas. "The Race Riots." *New Republic* (July 5, 1943): 8–13.

Sitkoff, Harvard. "The Detroit Race Riot of 1943." *Michigan History*, 53, no. 3 (Fall 1969): 183–206.

———. "Racial Militancy and Interracial Violence in the Second World War." *Journal of American History*, 58, no. 3 (December 1971): 661–81.

Stevenson, Marshall F., Jr. "Challenging the Roadblocks to Equality: Race Relations and Civil Rights in the CIO, 1935–1955." Working Paper (WP-006), Center for Labor Research, Ohio State University, 1992.

Swan, Alex L. "The Harlem and Detroit Race Riots of 1943: A Comparative Analysis." *Berkeley Journal of Sociology*, 16 (1971–72): 75–93.

Theoharis, Athan G. "Dissent and the State: Unleashing the FBI, 1917–1985." *History Teacher*, 24, no. 1 (November 1990): 41–52.

———. "The Escalation of the Loyalty Program," pp. 242–68. In *Politics and Policies of the Truman Administration*. Edited by Barton J. Bernstein. Chicago: Quadrangle Books, 1970.

———. "The FBI and Dissent in the United States," pp. 86–110, in *Dissent and the State*, edited by C. E. S. Franks. Toronto: Oxford University Press, 1989.

Tolbert, Emory J. "Federal Surveillance of Marcus Garvey and the UNIA." *Journal of Ethnic Studies*, 14, no. 4 (Winter 1987): 25–45.

Tyler, Bruce M. "Black Jive and White Repression." *Journal of Ethnic Studies*, 16, no. 4 (Winter 1989): 31–66.

Washburn, Patrick S. "J. Edgar Hoover and the Black Press in World War II." *Journalism History*, 13, no. 1 (Spring 1986): 26–33.

———. "The Pittsburgh *Courier* and Black Workers in 1942." *Western Journal of Black Studies*, 10, no. 3 (Fall 1986): 109–18.

———. "The Pittsburgh *Courier's* Double V Campaign in 1942." *American Journalism*, 3, no. 2 (1986): 73–86.

Williams, David. "The Bureau of Investigation and Its Critics, 1919–1921: The Origins of Federal Political Surveillance." *Journal of American History*, 68, no. 3 (December 1981): 560-79.

———. "'They Never Stopped Watching Us': FBI Political Surveillance, 1924–1936." *UCLA Historical Journal*, no. 2 (1981): 5–28.

Williams, Robin, Jr. "Social Change and Social Conflict: Race Relations in the United States, 1944–1964." *Sociological Inquiry*, 35, no. 1 (Winter 1965): 8–25.

Wirth, Louis. "Morale and Minority Groups." *American Journal of Sociology*, 47, no. 3 (November 1941): 415–33.

Wright, Richard. "How 'Bigger' Was Born," pp. 851–81 in Richard Wright, *Early Works*. New York: Library of America, 1991.

Wynn, Neil A. "Black Attitudes Toward Participation in the American War Effort." *Afro-American Studies*, 3 (1972): 13–19.

———. "The Impact of the Second World War on the American Negro." *Journal of Contemporary History*, 6 (May 1971): 42–53.

Zeitzer, Glen. "The Fellowship of Reconciliation on the Eve of the Second World War: A Peace Organization Prepares." *Peace and Change*, 3, nos. 2/3 (1975): 46–51.

Zieger, Robert H. "The Union Comes to Covington: Virginia Paperworkers Organize, 1933–1952." *Proceedings of the American Philosophical Society*, 126, no. 1 (1982): 51–89.

THESES/DISSERTATIONS

Bailer, Lloyd H. "Negro Labor in the Automobile Industry." University of Michigan, 1943.

Barton, Betty Lynn. "The Fellowship of Reconciliation: Pacifism, Labor, and Social Welfare, 1915–1960." Florida State University, 1974.

Boles, Frank Joseph. "A History of Local 212 UAW-CIO, 1937–1949: The Briggs Manufacturing Company, Detroit, Michigan." University of Michigan, 1990.

Brunn, Paul Dennis. "Black Workers and Social Movements of the 1930s in St. Louis." Washington University, 1975.

Burran, James A. "Racial Violence in the South during World War II." University of Tennessee, Knoxville, 1977.

Buseel, Michael Robert. "Hard Travelling: Powers Hapgood, Harvey Swados, Bayard Rustin and the Fate of Independent Radicalism in Twentieth Century America." Cornell University, 1993.

Glen, John Matthew. "On the Cutting Edge: A History of the Highlander Folk School, 1932–1962." Vanderbilt University, 1985.

Griffler, Keith P. "The Black Radical Intellectual and the Black Worker: The Emergence of a Program for Black Labor, 1918–1938." Ohio State University, 1993.

Gunther, Lenworth Alburn, III. "Flamin' Tongue: The Rise of Adam Clayton Powell, Jr., 1908–1941." Columbia University, 1985.

Halpern, Eric Brian. "'Black and White United and Fight': Race and Labor in Meatpacking, 1904–1948." University of Pennsylvania, 1989.

Hamilton, Donna Cooper. "The National Urban League During the Depression, 1930–1939: The Quest for Jobs for Black Workers." Columbia University, 1982.

Honey, Michael Keith. "Labor and Civil Rights in the South: The Industrial Labor Movement and Black Workers in Memphis, 1929–1945." Northern Illinois University, 1987.

Kearney, Reginald. "Afro-American Views of Japanese, 1900–1945." Kent State University, 1991.

Kim, Sam Gon. "Black Americans' Commitment to Communism: A Case Study Based on Fiction and Autobiographies by Black Americans." University of Kansas, 1986.

Korstad, Robert Rodgers. "Daybreak of Freedom: Tobacco Workers and the CIO, Winston-Salem, North Carolina, 1943–1950." University of North Carolina at Chapel Hill, 1987.

Lawrence, Charles Radford. "Negro Organizations in Crisis: Depression, New Deal, World War II." Columbia University, 1953.

Leonard, Kevin Allen. "Years of Hope, Days of Fear: The Impact of World War II on Race Relations in Los Angeles (California)." University of California, Davis, 1992.

Linsin, Christopher Edward. "Not By Words, But By Deeds: Communists and African Americans During the Depression Era." Florida Atlantic University, 1993.

O'Brien, Kevin J. "*Dennis v. U.S.*: The Cold War, the Communist Conspiracy, and the FBI." Cornell University, 1979.

O'Reilly, Kenneth. "The Bureau and the Committee: A Study of J. Edgar Hoover's FBI, the House Committee on Un-American Activities, and the Communist Issue," Marquette University, 1981.

Ottanelli, Michele Fraser. " 'What the Hell Is These Reds Anyways?': The Americanization of the Communist Party of the United States, 1930–1945." Syracuse University, 1987.

Prickett, James R. "Communists and the Communist Party Issue in the American Labor Movement, 1920–1950." University of California, Los Angeles, 1975.

Rosenberg, Roger Elliot. "Guardian of the Fortress: A Biography of Earl Russell Browder, U.S. Communist Party General-Secretary from 1930–1944." University of California, Santa Barbara, 1982.

Ryan, James Gilbert. "Earl Browder and American Communism at High Tide, 1934–1945." University of Notre Dame, 1981.

Sanford, Delacy Wendell, Jr. "Congressional Investigation of Black Communism, 1919–1967." State University of New York at Stony Brook, 1973.

Seabrook, John Howard. "Black and White Unite: The Career of Frank R. Crosswaith." Rutgers The State University of New Jersey, 1980.

Skotnes, Andor D. "The Black Freedom Movement and the Workers' Movement in Baltimore, 1930–1939." Rutgers The State University of New Jersey, 1991.

Streater, John Baxter, Jr. "The National Negro Congress, 1936–1947." University of Cincinnati, 1981.

Thomas, Richard. "From Peasant to Proletarian: The Formation and Organization of the Black Industrial Working Class in Detroit, 1915–1945." University of Michigan, 1976.

Williams, David J. " 'Without Understanding': The FBI and Political Surveillance, 1908–1941." University of New Hampshire, 1981.

INDEX

The present index records all instances of proper names and place names as well as references to pertinent subjects made within the body of the text. The original FBI report included separate rudimentary indexes divided broadly into personal and organizational names. The present index was prepared from scratch using an electronic concordance generator and indexing system. Indexed entries include not only proper names of individuals but also organizational entities and institutions as discussed in a large historical work such as this. The index of subject matter reflects the basic scope and purpose of the FBI report and ancillary FBI documents in determining the most pertinent references and topics to include.